12/6
L.
12.95

The Great Quotations

BOOKS BY GEORGE SELDES

You Can't Print That

Can These Things Be?

World Panorama

The Vatican: Yesterday—Today—Tomorrow

Iron, Blood and Profit

Sawdust Caesar

Freedom of the Press

Lords of the Press

You Can't Do That

The Catholic Crisis

Witch Hunt

The Facts Are . . .

Facts and Fascism

1000 Americans

The People Don't Know

Tell the Truth and Run

the GReat Quotations

compiled by George Seldes

with an introduction by J. Donald Adams

THE CITADEL PRESS : SECAUCUS, NEW JERSEY

Published by Citadel Press
A division of Lyle Stuart Inc.
120 Enterprise Avenue
Secaucus, N.J. 07094
In Canada by Musson Book Company
A division of General Publishing Co. Limited
Don Mills, Ontario

Queries regarding rights and permissions should be
addressed to: Lyle Stuart Inc.
120 Enterprise Avenue, Secaucus, N.J. 07094

Manufactured in the United States of America

Type set by The Polyglot Press

Library of Congress Catalog Card No. 58-10231

ISBN 0-8065-0817-5

5   4   3

PATRONS

In another day, many outstanding works were produced through the intervention and support of patrons of the arts.

In a sense, this gracious custom has been revived in order to publish *The Great Quotations*.

To these twentieth century "patrons of the arts" who saw the worth and need for an anthology of the truly great quotations, this book is dedicated:

George Abrahms
Steve Allen
Ellis Arnoff
Benjamin H. Ashman
Marvin Bank
J. J. Bassi
Professor and Mrs. H. C. Benedict
Mrs. Naomi A. Benson
Samuel Berke
Wiley O. Bolton
Monwell Boyfrank
John P. Burke
Irving Caesar
Ira D. Cardiff
Howard H. Carwile
Howard Chynoweth
Julian Claman
William O. Dapping
Alice A. DeLamar
Albert Ellis
Meyer Field
Harvey Furgatch
Ira Gershwin
Jean A. Gnagy
Jack D. Gordon

Oscar Hammerstein
Otto Harbach
E. Y. Harburg
Charles Havlicek
Harold and Marjorie Johnson
Judith R. Jones
Samuel Kipnis
Karen Kissin
Corliss Lamont
Michael Leffert
Lester and Helen Lewis
Alex Lewyt
A. L. Loomis
Louis M. Lyons (for the Lauterbach Fund)
Ben Mankin
Edwin L. Neirlle
Walter M. Nelson
Arthur J. Neumark
Mrs. Linus Pauling
Clorinda Pizzati
Mrs. I. Rabinowitz
Walt Raschick
Karl Robbins
William C. Rohn
Mason Rose
Morris Rosenblum
Harrison Roth
Edwin Milburn Sabin
Ben Sackheim
Sam Salz
M. Lincoln Schuster
Gilbert Seldes
Samuel Silverman
Nathan Sobel
Edward Sroczyk
Louis E. Stern
Cora E. Striegel
Lyle Stuart
Earl L. Vance
Martin Werner
Herbert Faulkner West

DEDICATION

To Lyle Stuart and Irving Caesar, who risked their judgment (and their money) as publishers.

To Helen Larkin Seldes, who helped in the compilation from 1952 to 1959.

To Nannine Joseph, my literary agent, who can never be repaid for her efforts.

To Eileen Brand and William Rodgers, who struggled with the manuscript and the proofsheets.

To The Polyglot Press for the conscientious craftsmanship and extraordinary interest that it has lavished on this project.

To Dr. Milton Kissin (for many reasons).

To the many patrons who made publication possible—especially to Steve Allen; Attorney Louis E. Stern and lyric writer Ira Gershwin (each of whom induced many others to subscribe); and to Ira D. Cardiff (whose *What Great Men Think of Religion* is quoted in extenso).

—George Seldes

INTRODUCTION

By J. Donald Adams

It took courage and conviction to come forward at this date with a new dictionary of quotations. Mr. Seldes has those qualities, and I think he is to be congratulated, not only for his possession of them, but on the book they have enabled him to produce. One might suppose that, in a field already occupied by several well-known and useful compilations, there would be scant need for another; but Mr. Seldes has proved otherwise.

The oldest and most famous of such dictionaries is, of course, Bartlett's *Familiar Quotations*, first published in 1855, and now in its fifteenth edition. It was completely revised as recently as 1980. Burton Stevenson's *Home Book of Quotations*, another leader in the field, first appeared in 1934; its ninth revised edition came out in 1967. These two were followed in 1941 by the *Oxford Dictionary of Quotations*, of which a third, revised edition was published in 1979. In 1942 appeared H. L. Mencken's *A New Dictionary of Quotations*.

Each of these had its reasons for being, and each its individual merits. I don't propose to discuss their several qualities in detail, but rather to explain why I think there was a need for what Mr. Seldes has done. His book does not displace these others, but it does supplement them in what seems to me an effective and even necessary fashion. I would go so far as to say that, no matter what your attachment may be to one of its predecessors, Mr. Seldes' *The Great Quotations* demands a place beside it.

As he has explained in his Foreword, Mr. Seldes was moved to compile this book because he had become convinced that earlier dictionaries of quotation had fallen short in their representation of the ideas which have moved mankind—for better or for worse. He felt that they contained too large a proportion of safe sentiments, and I think this objection is substantiated by the contents of his book. The objection applies less markedly, perhaps, to Mencken's dictionary, but that, in turn, is open to the criticism that it is a highly personal compilation, shot through with its editor's many prejudices.

There are several reasons why I like *The Great Quotations*. I like, for one thing, Mr. Seldes' recognition of the revolutionary character of much that was said by our founding fathers, and his annoyance with the tendency of his predecessors to choose only their more hackneyed utterances. I think that rightly he has undertaken to remedy their insufficient attention to the pronouncements of men like Marx and Hitler and Stalin, which, while destructive in their end effect, are nevertheless significant and sometimes illuminating in the history of human thought. He has succeeded, too, in revealing the scantiness with which the wide-ranging reflections of some seminal minds have previously been represented. Finally, he has brought his book more up to date than any of the others by his more generous inclusion of contemporary thinkers.

To accomplish these ends, there is much that he has intentionally sacrificed, but it must be granted that he has explained his reasons for these omissions. His dictionary is not the place to go for liberal quotation from the poets, particularly when they rhapsodize about the beauties of nature; for nourishment of that kind, you had best stick to Bartlett, Stevenson, and Oxford. In a dictionary which emphasizes revolutionary concepts, he has omitted the sayings of Jesus, but as he observes regarding his by-passing of both the Bible and Shakespeare, theirs is a body of wisdom readily obtainable elsewhere.

I think that from browsing in this book readers can obtain a vivid sense of what the conflict of ideas has meant in man's history. It is well that we should have that sense, since at this moment we are living through a bitter and as yet unresolved contest for the possession of men's minds. Therein, of course, lies the essence of the cold war—a conflict in which the ultimate triumph, I am convinced, lies not with the use of bombs and missiles, but through the manipulation of man's emotions and the appeal which can be made to his reasoning faculties. It is upon such grounds as these that the ultimate fate of mankind will be decided. Any book which helps to clarify the issues upon which the world is now split demands our earnest attention.

In assembling this collection of man's best thinking about the problems upon the solution of which his very survival depends, Mr. Seldes has provided us with a source-book of great value.

J. D. A.

CONTENTS

	Page
Introduction	ix
Foreword	1
Editorial Notes: Sources	9
Some "Dangerous" Quotations	12
Uses and Misuses of Quotations	15
Uses and Misuses of Lincoln Quotations	18
They Never Said It	23
Who Said It First?	25
Confirmations and Correspondence	26
Quotations	35
Index	767

FOREWORD

In the dozen, the score or the hundred volumes in many languages under the classification "quotations" in large and small libraries, there is none consisting entirely and exclusively of what for titular purposes I have called "great," by which I mean to include important, significant, notable (and even noble) quotations, dealing with the important, significant, notable (and even noble) ideas which are (or should be) of interest to modern man.

I first collected short paragraphs for chapter epigraphs a quarter of a century ago, and continued, for my own use and pleasure, without plan or purpose, until 1952, when I began preparing the manuscript for this book.

In the *Saturday Review* of November 22, 1958, Dr. Mortimer J. Adler, who had been assisted by a large research staff for eight years, answered the questions, What is an idea? and What are the great ideas? Dr. Adler reported that his group considered 700 possible candidates, and "determined that the irreducible minimum numbered 102"; and that there have been no additions of comparable magnitude in the last six years.

The list of the 102 great ideas begins with Angel, Animal, Aristocracy, Art and Astronomy. Under *D* we have Definition, Democracy, Dialectic and Duty, but not Dissent, nor Dictatorship, although both subjects are probably included under Religion or Government, the latter undoubtedly under Oligarchy. The modern Isms of political life—Communism, Socialism, Naziism, Fascism, even Republicanism and Liberalism—are not named separately, but Tyranny and Democracy certainly take care of them all.

Liberty, Justice, Labor, Life and Death, Love, Man, Opinion, Philosophy, Progress, Religion, Science, Truth, War and Peace, Wealth, Will, Wisdom and World are among the greatest of the 102 great ideas. According to Dr. Adler some great ideas—God, State, Man, Knowledge, and Wealth— involve as many as forty or fifty different topics. Since I do not find Rebel nor Radical I presume they come under Government or Politics; and no doubt Agnosticism and Atheism and Non-Conformity are among the topics covered by the word Religion.

The index of this volume shows that it contains quotations, a few to a hundred or more, of almost all of the 102 Adlerian ideas. And many more, including those suggested by Aldous Huxley, who, in returning his proof-sheets with corrections, wrote:

> "It might be interesting to have a short section in your book devoted to what may be called negative quotations—utterances of pure nonsense, Pollyanna uplift, anti-intelligence and anti-liberty—all drawn from the speeches or writings of the eminent. E.g., passages in praise of the executioner as the main pillar of civilized society from Joseph de Maistre's "Soirée de St. Petersbourg." Passages from Louis Veuillot's "Parfums de Rome," holding up the pre-1870 papal government as the best in the world. Passages on infant damnation from St. Augustine and from the Calvinists. Passages on Jesus as a salesman from Bruce Barton. And so forth. A few pages of these would constitute a stimulating Chamber of Horrors . . ."

I have included many quotations which are anti-libertarian, anti-intellectual, anti-humanitarian, etc., judging them only by their own importance, or the importance of their authors; and I am grateful to Mr. Huxley for his suggestions.

✲ ✲ ✲

In the available popular household and familiar, standard and conventional books of quotations, which for almost a century have served writers and orators, preachers and politicians, school boys and scholars, there are in addition to hundreds of really great quotations, a hundred thousand commonplace, sweet, hackneyed, stereotyped quotations, most of them maxims, epigrams, aphorisms, wise saws and folk sayings, a great number devoted to nature, the sky, the clouds, the sea, flowers and birds, and dogs; the homely virtues; and all the sentimentalities of the centuries, especially those expressed in rhyme, which pass for "poetry."

But when I began collecting them there was not one quotation from John Stuart Mill's essay "On Liberty" in the most familiar of the popular volumes; in fact, there was no mention of John Stuart Mill at all!

I also needed Milton's famous "Give me the liberty to know, to utter, and to argue freely according to conscience, above all liberties" from the

"Areopagitica." Could I trust my memory for the exact wording, the correct punctuation? Obviously not. I found fifteen and one-half pages of Milton in my volume. All the schoolboy literary lights were aglow, beginning with "Of Man's first disobedience" from Book I of "Paradise Lost" to the concluding "They also serve who only stand and wait" from "On His Blindness." I found the well-remembered "autumnal leaves that strow the brooks at Vallombrosa," the sweet breath of morn, the gems of heaven, the starry train; and spicy nut brown ale, and "Laughter holding both her sides," and "meadows trim, with daisies pied / shallow brooks, and rivers wide"; every delight of the glorious natural world is explored, and there is even a reference to the mountain nymph, sweet Liberty. But of Milton's prose there was only one page, half of which had six quotations from the "Areopagitica," but not my "Give me the liberty to know, to utter, and to argue freely according to conscience, above all liberties."

Not only Milton, but Shelley and Byron and Lowell, and even Browning and Tennyson and Coleridge and Wordsworth, and also many minor Longfellows, were neither ivory tower nor flowery landscape dwellers— they were concerned with their times, concerned with life and liberty and the freedom of the individual and of his world. Because these quotations are available elsewhere there is no mention whatever of their concern with cooling showers for thirsting flowers, or their ecstasy at first beholding a rainbow in the sky, or the breathtaking joy of a field of yellow daffodils, apostrophes to Spring, to Autumn, to all the months and seasons, and all the varieties of flowers and trees, and the joys of the woods and the sky and the fields and the garden. The most beautiful poetry in the world may and may not contain great ideas, or any ideas at all, and still be great poetry.

I have omitted "Hail to thee, blithe spirit! / Bird thou never wert." And I have included a score of rebellious libertarian verses by the same author. I have generally omitted references to the beauties of nature. This book is devoted largely to the nature of man himself.

Two sections, quotations from the Old and New Testament of the Bible and from Shakespeare, were omitted because they are completely included everywhere.

Although I have not tried to find any evidence of wilful censorship in the compilations of the conventional books, I began to suspect, year after year, that the unconscious censor who dominated not only the Victorian era, but the major part of the history of writing and publishing, did not miss the volumes which, from time to time, I needed for my work.

[3]

In 1938 I was asked by a new publisher to produce a small volume on the status of the Bill of Rights in our time. It was to deal with censorship and suppression, with intolerance, intimidation, lawless enforcers of the law, the 100% patriots, and the dangers from individuals and organizations which secretly and sometimes openly declared their admiration for Mussolini, if not Hitler.

The American Civil Liberties Union gave me an enormous amount of material, and a good bibliography on freedom, democracy, liberty, human rights, the dignity of man.

It was then that I realized, with considerable shock, that most of the great words on these subjects do not appear in the conventional compilations of quotations. Authors, statesmen, preachers, rulers, and ordinary men risen to great occasion, who have conceived ideas and uttered and written words known to all lovers of liberty, are unknown to the compilers of the familiar, household, conventional books; and where they are known and mentioned, as for examples, John Adams and Thomas Jefferson, and even Abraham Lincoln, there are omissions which are the more impressive because of the inclusion of so many trivialities.

John Adams told the Mohammedan peoples that the United States was not a nation founded on the Christian religion; Jefferson wrote Adams that he was a Christian but hated the perversions of the moral and ethical religion of Jesus Christ which began with Paul in its earliest days, and were continued by the commentators into Jefferson's time.

Yet, if both Jefferson and Adams had been small calibre Presidents like William McKinley and Warren ("Normalcy") Harding—men with neither brilliance nor depth or any importance—it would be impossible to dismiss them because of the fact that they were among the fathers of a nation founded on libertarian principles. It so happens that both expressed great thoughts. Adams is worth something to us—something more than two paragraphs from letters to his wife; and Jefferson, surely more than one page, chiefly parts of his First Inaugural Address. Of course, Jefferson in his time was denounced and vilified. He was called a menace, an atheist, and a Jacobin, which is to say a contemporary "red" or enemy of order and property. Can it be possible that those stale historically humorous accusations find a validity in some Tory mind today?

 ✧   ✧   ✧

All great ideas are controversial. Or have been controversial at one ime. The safe cowardice of omitting controversial subjects seems to have animated several editors, past and present, of some of the most imposing and popular volumes of quotations. They seem to have lived in the world of the moralities of Queen Victoria and the customs and conventions of Mrs. Grundy. To me at least their compilations seem unconsciously censored.

If we are to omit ideas considered most controversial, we have only a fraction of a book. We omit the subjects popularly considered most controversial: politics and religion. Even today Christianity is considered not only controversial by a majority of the inhabitants of this earth, but inferior to their own faiths, although no longer fought with fire and sword. Politics, during the past hundred years, has been married to economics, the presiding high priest being the man known long before Nietzsche as the modern Anti-Christ. Karl Marx's ideas, truly tried or not, perverted perhaps, perhaps already refuted, have been accepted or forced upon a sixth of the earth's surface and at least a third of the earth's population and, whether they are brilliantly written, or dull and boring, they cannot be dismissed in half a page and a footnote or two; and to ignore Marx's dead and living disciples or treat them shabbily because we are coldly at war with them, may reasonably be called censorship or suppression.

My suspicion became a conviction when, following the revelation under Mill and Milton, I continued to study the M section: Marx, Machiavelli, Mussolini. . . .

Was the choice of M fortuitous? I turned to the pages of patriots and rebels, the popular and the unpopular, the conventionally accepted heroes, the saints and the sinners: Edmund Burke, George Washington, Adam Smith, Henry Thoreau, Henry George, Patrick Henry, philosophers, poets, economists, writers, Americans, English, and faraway foreigners, ancient and modern. . . .

❀　❀　❀

A great soldier may never have said anything worth repeating, a man may become the father of his country but not the parent of an important phrase, but what shall we say of George Washington, with five small quotations, a total of 18 half-column lines, when in historic fact a good hundred and more Washingtonian quotations are in use today—not only in the Fourth of July oratory of loud politicians but in the learned writings of historians and sober speeches of statesmen, at home and abroad?

General Washington thought highly of Tom Paine, who helped pre serve the morale of an army which numbered fewer men than its deserters but Paine apparently is still a controversial figure in his adopted country frequently subjected to censorship and silence. His treatment in many an thologies is mean. Even Patrick Henry and Sam Adams and other patriots of their time seem to have frightened later day compilers. They have found "nice" quotations from "Walden," but omit the more vital ones from "The Duty of Civil Disobedience." Some phrases Burke used in pleading for conciliation with America, some of his reflections on the French Revolution are no more brilliant, or important, or quotable (in my opinion) than those he expressed in his "Vindication of Natural Society." The reader may judge from the pages which follow.

Henry George is frequently omitted or grudgingly mentioned. "Prog ress and Poverty" has not changed the world; the doctrine of the Single Tax was not spread with fire and torture. Nevertheless, disciples and principles are still alive.

Bernard Shaw's encounter with Henry George is an excellent illustra tion. We know that there are books which have changed the world, books which have influenced the life of many individuals—there are even books which are devoted to these circumstances. Can it be possible that a page or two, a few quotations from a book, can do the same? Shaw in his later years wrote that this had happened to him. At a second-hand shop in Charing Cross Road he picked up "Progress and Poverty," was so impressed that he bought it; and it changed his life. It was an experience in truth.

Among Henry George's living disciples—and quoters—is Nehru of India.

The poet who wrote "To a Skylark" also wrote the "Song to the Men of England." Shelley was an iconoclast, a fighter against the commonplace and against corruption. He was the singer of man's emancipation. These are subjects with which this volume concerns itself.

Wendell Phillips, the American, and Wolfgang von Goethe, the German apostle of human liberty, are largely represented here. Adam Smith's "Wealth of Nations" is worth more than a footnote; he is quoted for several pages.

❖   ❖   ❖

If there are important omissions they are not intentional. Every living person mentioned was asked not only to correct proofsheets, but to sug gest great quotations, his or her own, and those of notable (or notorious)

ersons, of all times and countries, which they had not found in the con-
entional books. The first replies, from Einstein and Bernard Shaw, ap-
ear in the text, that of Aldous Huxley above. Scores of writers, statesmen,
oliticians, have replied. Six members of the Supreme Court thought this
ork worthwhile—they themselves or their law clerks sent in corrections
nd suggestions. I hope the few who did not return my proofsheets will no
omplain of either errors or omissions.

Thanks to Francis Brown, editor of the New York Times Book Review,
appealed via an Author's Query to perhaps more than a million readers,
mong them reviewers and critics who habitually complain of errors and
missions, for assistance. A hundred persons wrote me, but not one re
iewer or critic.

*   *   *

Many readers will question my choice of quotations, their "greatness
r importance, or significance. With them I cannot argue. But, I want to
epeat, the omissions are due neither to censorship nor suppression. To para-
hrase a famous editor, what the good Lord lets happen I am not afraid to
rint.

This book can never be complete. I hope readers will send additions
nd suggestions, and that there will be a demand for other editions, edited
erhaps by other hands, and that the book will change, and will grow, in
mportance, if not in weight.

Jefferson dedicated his University of Virginia to "the illimitable free-
lom of the human mind," as good a guide as any for a compiler; and to
hose who would "follow truth wherever it may lead." This too I have tried
o do.

George Seldes

Iartland-4-Corners, Vermont

EDITORIAL NOTES: SOURCES

The majority of quotations in this volume are actually quotations; by which I mean that someone—Plato, perhaps, or Francis Bacon, or a contemporary writer—picked a phrase, or a line, or a paragraph or a page for his own use. Thousands of quotations have been used by authors as epigraphs for their chapters. Many newspapers make quotations a regular feature—the New York *Times,* with its daily, Sunday and monthly quotation departments, uses thousands each year.

In some instances, my collection of clipped and copied quotations from a certain book or essay became so large that I returned to the original source. "On Liberty," by John Stuart Mill, is a good example. This is, I think, the greatest writing on the subject; and it is always being quoted. Nevertheless, there was no mention of Mill and there were no quotations from any of his works in the first eleven editions of Bartlett; and then, in the twelfth, a few lines were taken from an address on being made rector of a university; and, finally, only a few paragraphs, but less than a page. I therefore arranged my score of cards and made additions.

Thoreau's "Civil Disobedience" is another example. And Burke's "Vindication of Natural Society," a third. Adam Smith's "Wealth of Nations" gives statesmen and economists of all schools, Marxists and anti-Marxists, monopolists and laissez-faire advocates, social scientists and others, phrase and paragraph ammunition for their views today. He is a living supplier of ideas, and not a buried footnote in Bartlett. And there are others; scores, perhaps hundreds of others. These writings contain quotations which are used—at least by the intelligent minority. They come under the rubric "great." All of them are important and vital, or very much alive today, appearing in books and plays and newspapers and speeches, and sometimes in the concessionary culture hours of radio and television. I have, therefore, reread these authors.

[9]

When Plato quotes Protagoras ("Man is the measure of all things.") this is the only source we have.

Under Socrates I have placed the quotations attributed in the "Apology"; although I am aware that great Greek authorities do not do so. Whether or not these are the words of Socrates, or of Plato himself, is less important than the words themselves.

Aristotle (in "Nicomachean Ethics") quotes Agathon ("Even God cannot change the past."). This likewise cannot be authenticated or confirmed. And Hobbes quotes Aristotle (in "Leviathan").

In order to clarify his own position, Tolstoy's letter to the Single Tax League of Australia quotes Rousseau on the man who first fenced in land and called it his.

Jefferson, on the other hand, quoted Hume ("It is belied by all history and experience that the people are the origin of all just power.") in order to refute him.

Chief Justice Hughes in a great decision (Near v. Minnesota) quotes Blackstone, but does not give chapter and page. Justice Douglas in his "Almanac of Liberty" quotes a score of persons; and, where I had no previous source for them, I have credited this excellent book.

Although Lincoln may be the most quoted American of all time, I believe that John Stuart Mill is the writer most quoted by other writers.

Karl Marx in "Das Kapital" quotes Mill ("Principles of Political Economy"): "It is questionable if all the mechanical inventions yet made have lightened the day's toil of any human being."

Bertrand Russell in "Portraits from Memory" quotes Mill: "It is the common error of Socialists to overlook the natural indolence of mankind."

And Adlai Stevenson in "Call to Greatness" quotes the well-known statement, "That which seems the height of absurdity in one generation often becomes the height of wisdom in the next."

Marx, incidentally, was a voluminous quoter of paragraphs he approved and paragraphs to be attacked. He approved of Benjamin Franklin's, "Trade in general being nothing else but the exchange of labor for labor, the value of all things is most justly measured by labor."

Thousands of frequently used quotations require simple confirmation or considerable research. An example of the latter is one attributed to Washington or Adams or another Founding Father, and frequently given as: "The United States is not a Christian nation."

I myself was not able to find the exact wording. My thanks are due

Miss Virginia Close of the reference department of the Baker Library at Dartmouth College, who, within a few days, was able to produce eighteen or twenty volumes with references, of which two or three gave the complete document from which the frequently wrongly attributed and usually incorrect quotation was taken. (It will be found under John Adams.)

An example of the difficulties of tracing and correcting a quotation is given in Editor & Publisher of January 7, 1950; at the time the Scripps-Howard newspaper chain added the New York *Sun* to its *World-Telegram.*

Where did the quotation, "Give Light and the People Will Find Their Own Way," which appears in the left ear of the latter newspaper (and in all Scripps-Howard papers except the Memphis *Commercial-Appeal*) come from? And a very similar quotation inscribed above the entrance of the main building of Compton College in California?

The phrase, with the added source "Dante," was used by Carl McGee in his Albuquerque *Tribune* column, "Turning on the Light." When Roy Howard bought the *Tribune,* he put the quotation on other papers, omitting Dante.

Compton College faculty assigned a distinguished colleague, C. Kinzek, says Editor & Publisher, who, with the aid of Dr. H. B. Austin, emeritus professor of the University of Southern California, came up with the following passage from Purgatory XXII 67-69: "Thou didst as one who passing through the night bears a light behind, that profits not himself but makes those who follow wise." Dr. Kinzek "decided this could be chopped down" to "Give Light (in darkness unselfishly) to have the people become wise to find the right way." Carl McGee may have read Dante, or more likely a translation, and being a newspaper editor, took as much liberty as he would with a cub reporter's copy. He, however, did give light—he published the great Teapot Dome scandal. Unfortunately other editors using the same misquotation did not.

EDITORIAL NOTES: SOME "DANGEROUS" QUOTATIONS

An illustration of the brilliant use of quotations appeared in the New York *World-Telegram*, under a two-column headline, on its front page of March 24, 1938, with the subhead: "Patriot . . . Labels Famous Quotations Dangerous." The news story deals with a dispute over Americanism between Richard S. Childs, president of the City Club of New York, and a member, name not disclosed, who opposed his views. In his final letter to his opponent, Mr. Childs stated his "doctrine," concluding:

"If there be any among us who would wish to dissolve this Union or to change its republican form let them stand undisturbed as monuments to the safety with which error of opinion may be tolerated where reason is left free to combat it. This country, with its institutions, belongs to the people who inhabit it. . . . If by mere force of numbers a majority should deprive a minority of any clearly written constitutional right, it might, in a moral point of view, justify revolution. . . . This, I say is sound Americanism."

Mr. X indignantly replied:

"Your interpretation or distortion of constitutional rights is such as to almost make it appear ridiculous. . . . Your entire argument is so unsound and so dangerous to the best interests of the United States and of the State of New York that perhaps it would be best if you were disassociated from it. . . ."

Whereupon Mr. Childs crushed his opponent by pointing out that the first sentence was from Jefferson's 1801 inaugural address; the second, part of Lincoln's 1861 inaugural address; and the concluding sentence, from Governor (and later, Chief Justice) Hughes' 1920 statement on the ouster of New York Socialist assemblymen.

In retelling this episode on its editorial page, the *Gazette & Daily* of York, Pennsylvania (October 21, 1955), pointed out that the Jefferson,

[12]

Lincoln and Hughes statements "are not given in most of the popular books of quotations which are in every library, in every school in the United States. They are not in Bartlett. . . . Hughes himself is not known to Bartlett. But what is worse, Jefferson and Lincoln are censored whenever they speak or write ideas which are being quoted today in Congress, in the press, in speeches and in books—quotations known to the American people, but omitted by the standard books of quotations because, apparently, of their 'controversial,' perhaps their 'liberal' or libertarian nature."

The editorial discusses notable American patriots and Founding Fathers, Jefferson, Paine, Joel Barlow, John Adams, and Washington; also President Grant's message to Congress, 1875, which suggests "the taxation of all property equally, whether church or corporations," and concludes:

"But it is not religious or church items whose suppression is the most flagrant—actually, the greatest quotations of the greatest men of all time dealing with liberty and democracy are censored, or wilfully omitted, in Bartlett—so much so, in fact, that it is possible to produce a volume equal to Bartlett—up to 1600 pages—giving none but the greatest quotations of all time, not one of which is in Bartlett."

(This was actually my first intention; but in instances where one or two or three great quotations do appear in the familiar, popular, and household volumes, I have included them along with the scores I have collected, so that the author would be quoted completely.)

During one of our recurrent witch-hunts, some years ago, America's leading historian, Charles A. Beard, wrote: "You need only reflect that one of the best ways to get yourself a reputation as a dangerous citizen these days is to go about repeating the very phrases which our founding fathers used in the great struggle for independence."

More recently, well proving this statement, one of the popular polls took several paragraphs from the Bill of Rights and asked sundry citizens what they thought of them. Several were so frightened by the "radical" ideas that they refused to go on record, and the majority of those who did declared them dangerous, un-American, even "red."

Another instance occurred during the Senate Judiciary Committee hearings on a new sedition law. Appearing for Americans for Democratic Action, attorney Joseph Rauh quoted Jefferson: "I hold it that a little rebellion, now and then, is a good thing."

Senator A. V. Watkins (R., Utah) "was almost bowled over," said the *Gazette & Daily* (May 23, 1956): "He 'exclaimed,' the Associated

Press reported, that he didn't believe it." When Mr. Rauh gave his source (Letter to Madison, 1787) Watkins retorted: "If Mr. Jefferson were here and advocated such a thing, I would move that he be prosecuted."

But the most amazing and frightening instance of the suppression of great quotations, and the common attitude towards the very principles upon which the United States was founded, was brought to the attention of the American people by no less a person than the Chief Justice himself. At a time when some California state employees refused to permit quotations from the Bill of Rights to be posted, on the ground that these were controversial, Earl Warren declared:

"It is straws in the wind like this which cause some thoughtful people to ask the question whether ratification of the Bill of Rights could be obtained today if we were faced squarely with the issue."

EDITORIAL NOTES: USES AND MISUSES OF QUOTATIONS

Quotations are used—and misused—everywhere, and in many ways. Thick volumes no doubt could be written on this subject.

True quotations have been used to forward every cause and movement throughout history, crusades to Jerusalem, to Utopia, to the 1000-year Nazi Reich, to totalitarian conformist dictatorship and philosophical anarchistic freedom from law and restraint. False quotations also abound.

Almost every newspaper has a quotation somewhere, as a slogan, a policy, a credo. Mussolini, for example, placed in the right and left ears of the *Giornale Socialista* (long before he betrayed Socialism for money) these two quotations:

La rivoluzione e un' idea che ha trovato delle baionette: Napoleone. (Revolution is an idea which has found bayonets.)
Chi ha del ferro had del pane: Blanqui. (Who has steel has bread.)

This was a rare instance of Mussolini giving others credit. In his score of years as a fascist leader, Mussolini came up with the most brilliant quotations (which duly appeared in the newspaper and magazine press throughout the world, and in many books) all of them stolen from other authors. A laudatory article in Hearst's Cosmopolitan magazine believes Mussolini the originator of Machiavelli's dictum on Fortune being a woman, who must be beaten, and in the Chicago *Tribune* he is the originator of the maxim, "Live dangerously," for which neither gives credit to Nietzsche. He appropriated dozens of paragraphs of Georges Sorel. He rewrote the majority of the Marx and Engels ten points at the conclusion of the Communist Manifesto as a program for reactionary Fascism. He never hesitated to steal and to falsify.

No less august and Olympian an organ than The *Times* of London accused the Duce of misquotation. In an address to the Senate, Mussolini

[15]

said his policy was to "do the maximum of good to a friend and the maximum of evil to an enemy," adding, "this formula is not by a fascist squadrist, it is by Socrates."

But it is not by Socrates, declared The *Times*. It appears in Plato as the idea of Polemarcos, the violent and bragging demagogue whom Socrates despised and silenced.

In 1912, one of the most important battles of the presidential campaign in the United States centered on the use of a quotation. Candidate Woodrow Wilson had said, in an address to the New York Press Club:

"Do we conceive social betterment to be in the pitiless use of irresistible power? Or do we conceive it to rise out of the irresistible might of a body of free men?

"Has justice ever grown in the soil of absolute power? Has not justice always come from the press of the heart and spirit of men who resist power?

"Liberty has never come from government. Liberty has always come from the subjects of government. The history of liberty is the history of resistance.

"The history of liberty is a history of the limitation of governmental power, not the increase of it."

Mr. Wilson's opponent, Theodore Roosevelt, evidently ignorant of Jefferson's statements, of which the last two paragraphs are no more than a paraphrase, picked them up out of context, and accused Wilson of being a dangerous radical, an anarchist. The TR press heralded these charges throughout the nation; nor was Wilson's explanation able to counteract the blast. (Wilson, as did Lincoln in 1860, won because the opposition divided; there were three parties in each instance instead of two; both great men were minority presidents.)

The use and misuse of quotations in the religious field is not uncommon. Both the Rev. Dr. William A. ("Billy") Sunday and the Rev. Father Charles E. Coughlin appropriated and falsified quotations, the former from a source he denounced as atheist, the latter from a source immediately exposed as being the anti-Semitic Nazi minister of propaganda.

When evangelist Sunday addressed the Civil War veterans in Beaver Falls, May 26, 1912, a local newspaper quoted the best paragraphs and said editorially this eloquence was "tipped with the fire of God." But all of these quotations, as a New York *Times* reporter found later, are parts of the Memorial Day 1882 address of Robert G. Ingersoll (which appears in the Dresden edition of the Ingersoll "Complete Works.")

Sunday, accusing Ingersoll of Atheism, illustrated his indictment with numerous false quotations. One begins with the words, "I would rather be the humblest peasant that ever lived . . . at peace with the world" than be "the greatest Christian that ever lived."

This is corrupted from one of Ingersoll's most eloquent passages which says he "would rather have been a French peasant and worn wooden shoes . . . than to have been that imperial impersonation of force and murder known as Napoleon the Great."

Among Coughlin's numerous misuses of quotations was a paragraph of an encyclical of Pope Pius XI, which he turned against Detroit automobile strikers, when, in fact, it dealt with the duties of employers. This misquotation was exposed by the Rev. Father Raymond C. Clancy on November 15, 1939, and published in the New York *Times* the next morning. But Coughlin's most daring achievement was to use as his own a complete speech by Dr. Goebbels, both men being dedicated to the spread of anti-Semitism.

EDITORIAL NOTES: USES AND MISUSES
OF LINCOLN QUOTATIONS

Everyone quotes Lincoln. Speeches and publications from the liberal-left to the extreme-left repeat endlessly Lincoln's views on the people having "the right to rise up and shake off the existing government," the "revolutionary right" to change it. But the conservative also quotes the same author.

The Republican Party and the National Association of Manufacturers send out editorials, cartoons, quotations, on Lincoln's birthday, all fitted to their own policies. For examples, The Norwalk (Conn.) *Hour,* which uses material from both sources, but does not identify it as propaganda, published (February 12, 1949) an excellent drawing above the quotation, "the government ought not to interfere" in all that the people can do for themselves. And David Lawrence in his U.S. News, omitting the lines about labor being prior to capital, reprints the Lincoln quotation that "Property is desirable; it is a positive good in the world."

President Franklin D. Roosevelt reprinted and framed the Lincoln quotation about "all the attacks that are made upon me" and sent one to Churchill. Eisenhower's quotation (February 11, 1959) appeared next day on the front page of the *Times* under a two-column headline: "President Quotes Lincoln Speech. . . ."

The Freethinker, published by the Freethinkers of America, placed above its title a Lincoln quotation which concludes: "I belonged to no Church." The Friends Intelligencer, published by the Quakers, devoted a quarter of a page to Lincoln quotations on the right of labor, and the general welfare. "Whenever there is a conflict between human rights and property rights, human right must prevail," appears as an epigraph in a dozen books. Almost every liberal-labor daily, weekly and monthly publication in America at some time publishes Lincoln quotations for May Day or Labor Day issues.

In his propaganda sheet, "America in Danger. Christ or Chaos!" C. B. Iudson of Omaha, who in 1938 appeared on Hitler's Welt-Dienst approved ist and later was one of the defendants in the U. S. alleged sedition cases, quoted Lincoln on his masthead: "To keep silent when we should protest, nakes cowards of men."

In April, 1920, the *Popolo d'Italia,* edited by Benito Mussolini, published a (false) Lincoln quotation urging the unification of Italy and predicting Rome would be the capital of a United States of Europe.

And more recently (February 12, 1956) the N. Y. *Herald Tribune* carried a headline saying: "South's Segregationists Take to Quoting Lincoln," under which a correspondent says that "whether or not these Lincoln utterances are taken out of context of his writings and lifework, the act remains that as a propaganda instrument they are a major phenomenon in the agitation going on throughout the Deep South today." Through the use of certain quotations, "Lincoln has been transformed into a hero of the anti-Negro, anti-integrationist South."

In a history of false quotations, one of the largest chapters would be devoted to Lincoln.

Republicans, Democrats, liberals, labor and big business have sought to gain converts to their views by quoting the Bible or great persons whose words are valued by the public. The conservatives make use of Hamilton, the liberals of Jefferson, all of whose writings and speeches are well authenticated; but Lincoln dates from another age, he was always a controversial character, he made impromptu speeches, of which only hearsay reports are known, and he was misquoted even in his lifetime.

There are authentic statements by Lincoln endorsing the right of labor to form unions and to go out on strike; there is the paragraph from his inaugural address placing labor ahead of capital, and there is a declaration which reads as if it came out of *Das Kapital,* saying labor should receive the good things it produces. For Labor Day, 1943, I collected these quotations and included this one:

"All that serves labor serves the nation. All that harms labor is treason to America. No line can be drawn between these two. If any man tells you he loves America and hates Labor, he is a liar. If any man tells you he trusts America and fears Labor, he is a fool. There is no America without Labor, and to fleece one is to rob the other."

Looking for my source, after this very Lincolnesque Lincoln quotation was published, all I could find was a clipping from "The Country Parson"

sent me by the Rev. Mr. Don West of Lula, Georgia, who could n
enlighten me. Nor could Editor B. Alsterlund of American Notes & Querie
an excellent publication, which also asked its readers for information. Th
Railroad Trainman, which had reprinted the quotation, traced it back t
the Railway Carmen's Journal of February, 1936. Carl Sandburg wrot
that, if anyone could prove that Lincoln was the author, he would "com
to Cleveland during a blizzard and roll two peanuts around the bron
statue of honest old Tom Johnson."

Dr. Louis A. Warren, director of the Lincoln National Life Foundatio
wrote he was "very certain that Abraham Lincoln was very sympatheti
with labor and its ideals," but he was "positive that he never made a stat
ment" such as the one submitted. Paul Angle, librarian at the Illinois Stat
Historical Library, wrote it could not be found anywhere—"It is my opinio
'hat the quotation is apocryphal."

On February 13, 1954, the Associated Press report (headlined, "'
Lincoln Hoax' Charged to G.O.P." in the N. Y *Times*) finally nailed
Lincoln falsehood which the Republican Party and numerous conservative
reactionary, wealthy and anti-labor organizations had been using for year
a series of quotations beginning:

You cannot bring about prosperity by discouraging thrift.
You cannot strengthen the weak by weakening the strong.
You cannot help the wage earner by pulling down the wage payer.
You cannot further the brotherhood of man by encouraging clas
hatred.
You cannot help the poor by destroying the rich.

The quoter was Postmaster General Summerfield. The man wh
charged it was "one of a series of recent Republican fakes and hoaxes" wa
the Democratic National Committee chairman, Stephen A. Mitchell. Th
hoax had been traced by Roy Basler, (Abraham Lincoln Quarterly, De
cember, 1949) to a 1942 leaflet distributed by the Committee for Consti
tutional Government, one of whose leaders was Edward A. Rumely, wh
had served time as a German agent.

A false Lincoln quotation is chiseled into the stone entrance of th
New York *Daily News* skyscraper in New York: "God must have loved th
common people; He made so many of them." Captain Joseph Patterson
owner of the paper, had been a radical Socialist at Yale, he still had
troublesome conscience, and dedicated his newspaper, which had the larg

est circulation in America, to the "masses," to whom he also fed the most reactionary and frequently irresponsible and outrageous editorials.

James Morgan in "Our Presidents" wrote, without any evidence to back him, that Lincoln had said in a dream, "The Lord prefers common-looking people. That is the reason he makes so many of them." Captain Patterson did not even quote apocrypha correctly.

A deeply religious statement, a reply attributed to Lincoln on being given a Bible, was declared false by Herndon, but still appears regularly in Sunday school publications.

Two pages of false Lincoln quotations appear in the Congressional Record of August 31, 1950; they are from an article by A. A. Woldman, and were inserted by Representative Stephen Young of Ohio. Along with several items reproduced above, Woldman gives the "vicious anti-Catholic diatribe which bigots like to repeat," also known as the "Lincoln warning," and containing these lines:

"I see a very dark cloud on our horizon. That dark cloud is coming from Rome. It is filled with tears of blood . . . spreading ruin and desolation. . . . After it is over . . . Popery with its Jesuits and merciless Inquisition will have been forever swept away from our country. . . ."

It is true, Woldman points out, that Lincoln once defended Charles Chiniquy, a recusant Catholic priest, who later claimed that the President confided anti-Catholic feelings to him, and made the foregoing (false) statement.

The letter of condolence which Lincoln is alleged to have written Mrs. Bixby has been called "the most sublime letter ever penned by the hand of man," but many years ago Sherman Day Wakefield, author of "How Lincoln Became President," sent me the result of his research into the fate of the five soldier sons of Mrs. Bixby and the various facsimiles of the Bixby letter, with his conclusion that a great fraud had been committed.

In 1950, Macmillan published the long-awaited 395-page compendium of Lincoln quotations, "The Lincoln Encyclopedia." However, in a criticism (Saturday Review, March 11, 1950) Mr. Basler points out that even this work reveals "a few forgeries, spurious stories, and highly dubious sayings quoted cheek-by-jowl with Lincoln's authentic words."

The most notorious of the widely used and still current but false quotations, which Basler and others have frequently but apparently unsuccessfully nailed, is the following:

I see in the near future a crisis that unnerves me, and causes me to tremble for the safety of my country. As a result of war, corporations have been enthroned and an era of corruption in high places will follow, and the money power of the country will endeavor to prolong its reign by working upon the prejudices of the people until all the wealth is aggregated in a few hands and the republic destroyed.

As Reinhard H. Luthin, author of "The First Lincoln Campaign," points out (Saturday Review, February 14, 1959) this is a fraud, first used during the Greenback agitation for "paper" money as a panacea against "Wall Street" monopoly, during the 1880's.

Luthin concludes: "Students of Lincoln and those desiring to read about him merely for pleasure long have been confounded by misinformation that is either based on false quotations allegedly from the Emancipator's lips or pen or by deliberately forged letters. The road to Lincoln learning, unfortunately, is strewn with published frauds and forgeries."

And Woldman declares that "the list of Lincoln 'quotations' grows larger from year to year."

EDITORIAL NOTES: THEY NEVER SAID IT

On the other hand, there are many famous, sometimes brilliant, and very often great quotations attributed to notable persons, which, though false or incorrect, are usually improvements by anonymous re-quoters.

For example, every American schoolboy is certain that Charles Pinckney defied Talleyrand's bribe-seeking agents with the words "Millions for defense but not one cent for tribute." Mr. Pinckney made no such remark. What he did say, according to Stefan Lorant ("The Presidency") is: "No, no, not a penny." "Millions for defense" appears as one of the toasts honoring James Marshall (Philadelphia, June 18, 1798).

The Duke of Wellington did not say, "The battle of Waterloo was won on the playing fields of Eton," a statement which every British schoolboy and every enthusiast for sports at educational institutions has quoted for more than a century.

The seventh Duke of Wellington several years ago offered a reward for the historic facts about this saying. The best reply came from the headmaster of Eton itself: Robert Birley found in Montalembert's *De L'Avenir Politique de l'Angleterre* (1885) that the first Duke of Wellington, on a visit to the class rooms, not the playing fields of Eton, said: "It is here that the battle of Waterloo was won."

One of the most important quotations of all time, its greatness due largely to its supposed authorship—Voltaire—appeared for many years over the letter-to-the-editor department of the New York *Herald Tribune,* also topping the editorial department of David Lawrence's U. S. News, and many other publications:

"I disapprove of what you say, but I will defend to the death your right to say it."

The quotation came into use shortly after 1906, when the British biog-

[23]

rapher, E(velyn) Beatrice Hall, writing under the pen name "S. G. Tallentyre," published "The Friends of Voltaire." Half a century later it is still in use, despite repeated denials and explanations.

Miss Hall herself wrote in 1935: "I have not a copy of my book 'The Friends of Voltaire' by me, but I believe I did use in it the phrase . . . as a description of Voltaire's attitude to Helvetius's book 'On the Mind' (De l'Esprit)—and more widely, to the freedom of expression in general. I do not think, and I did not intend to imply, that Voltaire used these words verbatim, and should be surprised if they are found in any of his works. They are rather a paraphrase of Voltaire's words in the Essay on Tolerance —"Think for yourselves and let others enjoy the privilege to do so too."

The New York *Times* on September 1, 1935, published the above letter. It has been repeated or mentioned in Time (August 24, 1936), the editorial page of the *Times* (November 10, 1944), The American Mercury (April, 1946), the Saturday Review (August 2, 1947) and scores of other places; but it still makes its rounds, because a good misquotation (like a bad lie) never grows old.

EDITORIAL NOTES: WHO SAID IT FIRST?

Among the anonymous quotations I find this one most appropriate to his heading: "If it is the truth, what does it matter who said it?"

In discussing the priority of Francis Bacon, Henry W. Thoreau, and Franklin D. Roosevelt to the phrase "nothing to fear but fear," J. Donald Adams, contributing editor of the New York *Times* Book Review, wrote (January 11, 1948):

The fundamental truths are all men's property. Whether or not we live by them, we all know them, with a deep instinctiveness. In the realm of human conduct, particularly, I do not suppose it is possible for any man, however acute or profound his mental processes may be, to say anything bearing the stamp of universal truth that many other men, in equivalent words, have not said before him. Back of each of us there are those many thousands of years of race experience.

"Eternal vigilance is the price of liberty," and its variations, are great quotations, whether the credit is given to Jefferson, Patrick Henry, or John Curran or Wendell Phillips. "Peace with honor" is credited to a dozen personalities, including Disraeli.

On the other hand, a phrase such as "A new order" becomes significant only because of its authorship and the circumstances under which it is born. There is no doubt that Hitler made much of this point among his many promises; but historically it is Woodrow Wilson's, according to Ray Stannard Baker's "Wilson and World Settlement," (1923).

Likewise, the phrase, "the iron curtain," becomes important when related to Churchill in his Fulton, Missouri, speech, vis-à-vis Goebbels, or von Krosyg or other Nazi leaders.

In 1937, I heard Pasionaria in Valencia, Spain, say, "It is better to die on one's feet than live on one's knees," and on June 19, 1941, President Roosevelt, receiving a degree from Oxford University, sent Viscount Halifax a letter in which he wrote: "We . . . would rather die on our feet than live on our knees,'" which became a headline in the next morning's newspapers.

Mr. Adams's point is well documented.

EDITORIAL NOTES: CONFIRMATIONS AND CORRESPONDENCE

When there was a question of authenticity, date or source, I wrote to all living persons and with few exceptions they replied. The objections sent by two or three are published in full. Following are references or extracts from the correspondence:

Dr. Alfred Adler. "They undoubtedly are my father's," wrote Dr Alexandra Adler. However, she suggested sending the quotations to Drs Heinz and Rowena Ansbacher (Journal of Individual Psychology and University of Vermont), who corrected them and added several; for which am grateful.

Richard Aldington wrote: "You are quite right about Bartlett, but then most reference books, especially encyclopaedias and histories, have a propaganda slant."

Sir Norman Angell was gracious enough to recall my writings on war and the munitions makers; he suggested eliminating one quotation as redundant and sent a substitute; also a correction of the date of birth as given in all reference books: "It is, alas, 1872 not four."

David Ben-Gurion, prime minister of Israel. The first and third quotations were confirmed by his secretary, Schlomo Argov, but the date and exact source of the second could not be found, although it is authentic.

Sir Isaiah Berlin. Professor Berlin found that a quotation (from a most reputable magazine) "is the precise opposite of what I believe." He had written the paragraph to describe views he was attacking. I have eliminated this quotation and replaced it with several from Professor Berlin's inaugural lecture at Oxford, "Two Concepts of Liberty."

Edward L. Bernays. In addition to correcting his proof, Mr. Bernays kindly suggested that quotations from the works of his uncle, Sigmund Freud, be sent to Dr. Ernst L. Freud, whose address he sent.

Francis Biddle was one of the few persons who answered my request for suggestions; he sent an excellent quotation from the poet Allen Tate.

Justice Hugo L. Black was one of the first persons to whom I wrote (in 1956). All the quotations were found correct—Justice Black supplied the exact sources for several.

Justice William J. Brennan, Jr., found a news magazine item a "rather garbled condensation" and sent the original Georgetown University lecture; also the entire opinion in *Roth* v. *U. S.*, from which I made corrections.

Albert Camus, about to leave Paris, asked his publisher, Gallimard, to write "en son nom, pour vous remercier de votre lettre et de votre interêt et pour vous dire que vos citations sont exactes."

Stuart Chase thought *The Great Quotations* "a colossal and fascinating project," and was one of several who assisted in many ways. With the aid of Mrs. Chase, he collected pages of important quotations from several persons.

Henry Steele Commager related his experience in looking for and not finding John Stuart Mill in Bartlett and elsewhere.

John Cowles, the publisher, suggested it be noted that his quotations were twenty years old, and that "there has been a great improvement in newspapers' editorial standards in the intervening two decades. Today only a small fraction of our newspapers let outside pressures influence their news columns. Almost all of our dailies now try to keep their news columns objective."

Nelson Antrim Crawford agreed with Mr. Cowles: "Newspapers are much readier than they were to give the public the facts." He sent numerous suggestions.

Daniel DeLeon. I am greatly indebted to Eric Hass, editor of *Weekly People*, official organ of the Socialist Labor Party, for sending me a hundred quotations from the works of "one of history's greatest champions of freedom."

Justice William O. Douglas. In 1956, Miss Edith Allen, his secretary, and in 1959, Mr. Charles A. Miller, his law clerk, did considerable research in checking, correcting and confirming numerous quotations.

Max Eastman was especially helpful, not only in correcting his proofsheets but in suggesting great liberal quotations.

Mary Baker Eddy. Permission to quote and corrections were sent by Mrs. Verna A. Hayter, corresponding secretary of the Trustees Under the Will of Mary Baker Eddy.

Albert Einstein was the second person I wrote to—the first was Shaw. Professor Einstein's 1954 letter is in the text. He carefully numbered all quotations, and on a separate sheet himself typed out corrections and suggestions. He probably spent more time on his proofsheets than any other person to whom I wrote.

T. S. Eliot's reply was similar to others in one respect: "While I recognize the quotations as being by myself—or at least I recognize the idea, for I cannot remember the exact wording which, I presume, is correct—I cannot place them."

Bergen Evans asked to be put down for a copy of the book.

Justice Felix Frankfurter. I am grateful to Richard N. Goodwin, law clerk, for an extraordinary amount of work in making the dissents and opinions perfect. Every Supreme Court Justice or his law clerk replied to my request for confirmation and corrections.

William Randoph Hearst. The reference room of the New York *Journal-American* sent all the missing information. Mr. W. R. Hearst, Jr., also sent a volume of the writings of his father.

Professor William Ernest Hocking's letters were so brilliant and interesting that I have added a quotation from one of them.

Eric Hoffer wrote: "I am a longshoreman on the docks of San Francisco. I have never had a look at Bartlett."

Herbert Hoover. I am indebted to Miss Loretta F. Camp for several important items, including her report on the "chicken in every pot" and other sayings attributed to the President. I also sent Miss Camp two quotations frequently published, including the actual newspaper clippings (San Francisco *Daily News*, August 13, 1931), the report by Benjamin Marsh, head of the People's Lobby, (also, American Freeman, February 27, 1932). Mr. Hoover was reported saying, when Secretary of Commerce, "The ambition of my life is to crush out Soviet Russia." Miss Camp declared the attributions false, and added: "But why treasure all these second and third-hand infamies?"

J. Edgar Hoover wrote: "I appreciate your courtesy in giving me an opportunity to confirm them."

Langston Hughes, as did a score of others, wrote he was "happy to be included in your book."

Aldous Huxley. His brilliant suggestion of including "negative quotations," or some of the most anti-intellectual and outrageous quotations, as a separate section arrived too late, as many were already in type alphabetically; but others from the books suggested by Mr. Huxley may be added in following editions.

Sir Julian Huxley corrected each quotation and sent an extract from his "Religion Without Revelation."

Robert G. Ingersoll. I am thankful to Mr. Joseph Lewis, of The Freethinkers of America, for confirming the Ingersoll quotations, including those whose exact source is not given.

Dr. Carl G. Jung. Mrs. A. Jaffé, secretary, writes: "I have to tell you in the name of Dr. Jung that the quotation you chose is not only twenty-six years old! but also not characteristic of his Oeuvre." The purpose of this volume is not to present a resumé of a man's thinking, views, or change of views. Since the quotations are not challenged, I include them; but I shall add several from more modern writings suggested by Mrs. Jaffé.

Miss Helen Keller sent her confirmation of the quotation I used, via her attorney, Mrs. Nella B. Henney.

Rockwell Kent wrote: "Reading your letter, I was promptly struck by the importance of the work you are preparing and reminded of the inadequacy of Bartlett and Stevenson to be of service to dissenters."

John L. Lewis. My thanks to Rex Lauck, editor, United Mine Workers Journal, and biographer of Mr. Lewis, for much assistance. The quotation, "You can't dig coal with bayonets," could not be placed. It was a slogan, probably originated by Mr. Lewis.

Charles A. Madison. Several quotations in this volume are credited to Mr. Madison's "American Labor Leaders" and "Critics and Crusaders."

André Malraux. In addition to corrections, M. Malraux wrote on the proofsheet "Supprimer propos . . . par un journalist," referring to a New Yorker attribution.

Jacques Maritain did not approve of the translation, "The people must have a religion." He changed it to, "There must be a religion for the people."

W. Somerset Maugham wrote: "The quotations are quite correct. I hope you have success with the book."

George Meany, president, AFL-CIO, replied regarding a famous quotation of Sam Gompers, and sent the text of an address, to correct one of his.

Lewis Mumford wrote: "What a job you've undertaken!" Being in the midst of a book himself, he, as did some other writers, asked his wife to do the research I requested.

Jawaharlal Nehru. Private Secretary C.R.S. . . . (surname undecipher able) wrote: "The Prime Minister desires me to inform you that the quota tions attributed to him . . . appear to be correct as they are. But they are naturally taken away from their context."

Thomas Paine. The secretary and head of the Thomas Paine Founda tion, Joseph Lewis, corrected the three galleys, confirmed those Paine quotations of which the exact source is not given.

Dr. Theodore Reik in his letter included a quotation from a talk to his circle of students by Freud.

Mrs. Eleanor Roosevelt corrected a carbon copy of the manuscrip in 1955, and proofsheets in 1959. The only important change was a mis quotation by Time, which she rewrote.

Franklin D. Roosevelt. I am indebted to Judge Samuel Rosenman, to whom my literary agent, Miss Nannine Joseph, sent all the FDR proofs, for confirming them in 1955.

Bertrand Russell. Lord Russell wrote: "I am glad to know that you are doing such a book as you mention and I like your selection of quota- tions from me, which I return herewith with one or two trivial proof cor- rections. Would you like to add, 'Philosophy is a stage in intellectual devel- opment and is not compatible with mental maturity,' from the essay called 'Philosophy's Ulterior Motives' in *Unpopular Essays?*"

George Sarton. May Sarton wrote: "What a splendid idea yours is, and how delighted I am that you are using those fine passages of my father's in it." Miss Sarton suggested quotations from Simone Weil, "that amazing French philosopher."

Albert Schweitzer. From Lambarene, in Gabon, Clara Urquhart wrote: "Dr. Schweitzer has asked me to write and thank you for his letter and to tell you that he regrets his inability to comply with the request contained therein. If you could see the pressure under which he works, you would understand. He sends his greetings."

G. Bernard Shaw. Mr. Shaw's answer to my request, in 1937, for con- firmation of a quotation, was written on one of his famous postcards which gives his cable address as "Socialist-London." The disputed quotation and the reply are in the text.

André Siegfried, shortly before his death, wrote: ". . . j'approuve le choix qui me parait fort judicieux. Je vous remercie donc infiniment d'avoir inclu ces lignes signées de moi dans votre publication. Ma santé mal- heureusement n'est pas bonne et m'empêche de vous offrir une collaboration plus étroite. . . ."

Upton Sinclair. I owe him a double debt. His "Cry for Justice" is a source for scores of great quotations. So are his own books. Those I did not have he sent me with pages indicated; and letters with many suggestions, all useful.

The Rt. Hon. John Strachey, M. P. In the 1930's when John Strachey was held on Ellis Island by the U. S. Government, Louis Bromfield, William Rose Benét and I were sent by the American Civil Liberties Union to confer with him. Strachey later became a cabinet member in the Labour Party government of Britain. He writes: "How very nice to hear from you again. The quotations are all O.K. I am honoured to think that you are using them."

Arthur Hays Sulzberger. The quotations used were sent me by Mr Sulzberger. They were substituted for quotations which could not be confirmed and which did not sound correct. Mr. Sulzberger kindly corrected the proofsheet of his predecessor as editor and publisher of the New York *Times,* Adolph S. Ochs, and wished the book good luck.

Arnold Toynbee wrote "They seem all right," on his proofs.

Henry A. Wallace in 1956 corrected the manuscript. He could not find the quotation I got from one of his Department of Agriculture yearbooks, but wanted it included. His long letter discusses the Century of the Common Man.

Chief Justice Earl Warren. I am indebted to the clerk of the Supreme Court of the United States, James R. Browning, for a painstaking job of comparing every quotation with the originals, and making numerous (but minor) corrections.

In addition I received confirmations (and frequently an expression of interest and approval) from the following persons or their secretaries or law clerks:

Thurman Arnold, Alan Barth, Bernard Berenson, Judge Curtis Bok, Judge George H. Boldt, Congressman Chester Bowles, Van Wyck Brooks, John Mason Brown, Justice Tom Clark, Taoiseach Eamon de Valera of Ireland, Professor Eric F. Goldman, President Griswold of Yale, Judge Learned Hand, John Hersey, Paul G. Hoffman, Dr. Robert M. Hutchins, Dr. Horace M. Kallen, George F. Kennan, Arthur Koestler, Alfred M. Landon, Max Lerner, Joseph Lewis, Lester Markel, General George C. Marshall, Dr. Karl Menninger.

The Great Quotations

THE GREAT QUOTATIONS

Abd-el-Raham
(912-961)
Caliph of Córdoba

I have now reigned above fifty years in victory and peace, beloved by my subjects, dreaded by my enemies, and respected by my allies. Riches and honors, power and pleasure, have waited on my call, nor does any earthly blessing appear to be wanting for my felicity. In this situation, I have diligently numbered the days of pure and genuine happiness which have fallen to my lot: they amount to fourteen. O man, place not thy confidence in this present world!

Abu'l-Ala-Al-Ma'arri
(973-1057)
Syrian poet

The world holds two classes of men—intelligent men without religion, and religious men without intelligence.

Lord Acton (John E. E. Dalberg)
(1834-1902)
English historian, statesman

Liberty, next to religion, has been the motive of good deeds and the common pretext of crime, from the sowing of the seed at Athens, two thousand four hundred and sixty years ago, until the ripened harvest was gathered by men of our race.
The History of Freedom in Antiquity,
1877.

In every age its (liberty's) progress has been beset by its natural enemies, by ignorance and superstition, by lust of conquest and by love of ease, by the strong man's craving for power, and the poor man's craving for food. *Ibid.*

At all times sincere friends of freedom have been rare, and its triumphs have been due to minorities, that have prevailed by associating themselves with auxiliaries whose objects often differed from their own; and this association, which is always dangerous, has been sometimes disastrous, by giving to opponents just grounds of opposition, and by kindling dispute over the spoils in the hour of success. *Ibid.*

By liberty I mean the assurance that every man shall be protected in doing what he believes his duty against the influence of authority and majorities, custom and opinion. *Ibid.*

The most certain test by which we judge whether a country is really free is the amount of security enjoyed by minorities. *Ibid.*

[35]

Their (the Athenians') history furnishes the classic example of the peril of Democracy under conditions singularly favourable. . . . They were the most religious of the Greeks. They venerated the Constitution which had given them prosperity, and equality, and freedom . . . They tolerated considerable variety of opinion and great licence of speech . . . They became the only people of antiquity that grew great by democratic institutions. But the possession of unlimited power, which corrodes the conscience, hardens the heart, and confounds the understanding of monarchs, exercised its demoralizing influence on the illustrious democracy of Athens. *Ibid.*

It is bad to be oppressed by a minority, but it is worse to be oppressed by a majority. For there is a reserve of latent power in the masses which, if it is called into play, the minority can seldom resist. But from the absolute will of an entire people there is no appeal, no redemption, no refuge but treason. *Ibid.*

Liberty and good government do not exclude each other; and there are excellent reasons why they should go together. Liberty is not a means to a higher political end. It is itself the highest political end. *Ibid.*

Increase of freedom in the State may sometimes promote mediocrity, and give vitality to prejudice; it may even retard useful legislation, diminish the capacity for war, and restrict the boundaries of Empire . . . A generous spirit prefers that his country should be poor, and weak, and of no account, but free, rather than powerful, prosperous, and enslaved. *Ibid.*

The great question is to discover, not what governments prescribe, but what they ought to prescribe; for no prescription is valid against the conscience of mankind. *Ibid.*

Before God, there is neither Greek nor barbarian, neither rich nor poor, and the slave is as good as his master, for by birth all men are free; they are citizens of the universal commonwealth which embraces all the world, brethren of one family, and children of God. *Ibid.*

I cannot accept your canon that we are to judge Pope and King unlike other men, with a favourable presumption that they did no wrong. If there is any presumption it is the other way, against the holders of power, increasing as the power increases. *Letter to Mandell (later, Bishop) Creighton, April 5, 1887. Historical Essays and Studies, 1907.*

Historic responsibility has to make up for the want of legal responsibility. Power tends to corrupt, and absolute power corrupts absolutely. *Ibid.*

Great men are almost always bad men, even when they exercise influence and not authority, still more when you superadd the tendency or the certainty of corruption by authority. *Ibid.*

There is no worse heresy than that the office sanctifies the holder of it. That is the point at which the negation of Catholicism and the negation of Liberalism meet and keep high festival, and the end learns to justify the means. *Ibid.*

Advice to Persons About to Write History —Dont'. *Ibid. Postscript.*

A Historian has to fight against temptations special to his mode of life, temptations from Country, Class, Church, College, Party, Authority of talents, solicitation of friends. *Ibid.*

Murder may be done by legal means, by plausible and profitable war, by calumny, as well as by dose or dagger. *Ibid.*

We are forced, in equity, to share the government with the working class . . . If there is a free contract, in open market, between capital and labour, it cannot be right that one of the two contracting parties should have the making of the laws, the management of the conditions, the keeping of the peace, the administration of justice, the distribution of taxes, the control of expenditure, in its own hands exclusively. It is unjust that all these securities, all these advantages, should be on the same side . . . Before this argument the ancient dogma, that power attends on property, broke down. Justice required that property should—not abdicate, but—share its political supremacy.
Letter to Mary Gladstone, April 24, 1881.

There is no error so monstrous that it fails to find defenders among the ablest men. Imagine a congress of eminent celebrities, such as More, Bacon, Grotius, Pascal, Cromwell, Bossuet, Montesquieu, Jefferson, Napoleon, Pitt, etc. The result would be an Encyclopaedia of Error. They would assert Slavery, Socialism, Persecution, Divine Right, military despotism, the reign of force, the supremacy of the executive over the legislation and justice, purchase in the magistracy, the abolition of credit, the limitation of laws to nineteen years, etc.
Ibid.

The danger is not that a particular class is unfit to govern. Every class is unfit to govern. *Ibid.*

The law of liberty tends to abolish the reign of race over race, of faith over faith, of class over class. It is not the realisation of a political ideal: it is the discharge of a moral obligation. *Ibid.*

Almost all that has been done for the good of the people has been done since the right lost the monopoly of power, since rights of property were discovered to be not unlimited. *Ibid.*

The man who prefers his country before any other duty shows the same spirit as the man who surrenders every right to the state. They both deny that right is superior to authority.
Nationality. The Home and Foreign Review, July, 1862. Reprinted in Essays on Freedom and Power.

A State which is incompetent to satisfy different races condemns itself; a State which does not include them is destitute of the chief basis of self-government. The theory of nationality, therefore, is a retrograde step in history. *Ibid.*

Whenever a single definite object is made the supreme end of the State, be it the advantage of a class, the safety or the power of the country, the greatest happiness of the greatest number, or the support of any speculative idea, the State becomes for the time inevitably absolute. *Ibid.*

Liberty alone demands for its realisation the limitation of the public authority, for liberty is the only object which benefits all alike, and provokes no sincere opposition. *Ibid.*

Patriotism is in political life what faith is in religion, and it stands to the domestic feelings and to homesickness as faith to fanaticism and to superstition. *Ibid.*

Two forces which are the worst enemies of civil freedom are the absolute monarchy and the revolution. *Ibid.*

[37]

History is not a web woven with innocent hands. Among all the causes which degrade and demoralize men, power is the most constant and the most active.

Essays on Freedom and Power, xlvii.

I am not thinking of those shining precepts which are the registered property of every school; that is to say—learn as much by writing as by reading; be not content with the best book; seek sidelights from the others; have no favourites; keep men and things apart; guard against the prestige of great names; see that your judgments are your own; and do not shrink from disagreement; no trusting without testing; be more severe to ideas than to actions; do not overlook the strength of the bad cause or the weakness of the good; never be surprised by the crumbling of an idol or the disclosure of a skeleton; judge talent at its best and character at its worst; suspect power more than vice, and study problems in preference to periods.

Inaugural lecture on The Study of History, Cambridge, June 11, 1895.

But the weight of opinion is against me when I exhort you never to debase the moral currency or to lower the standard of rectitude, but to try others by the final maxim that governs your own lives, and to suffer no man and no cause to escape the undying penalty which history has the power to inflict on wrong.   *Ibid.*

Praise is the shipwreck of historians.
                                     Ibid.

It is they (men of science) who hold the secret of the mysterious property of the mind by which error ministers to truth, and truth slowly but irrevocably prevails. Theirs is the logic of discovery, the demonstration of the advance of knowledge and the development of ideas, which, as the earthly wants and the passions of men remain almost unchanged, are the charter of progress and the vital spark in history.   *Ibid.*

A man who started in life . . . a sincere Catholic and a sincere Liberal; who therefore renounced everything in Catholicism which was not compatible with Liberty and everything in Politics that was not compatible with Catholicity.

                          (*on himself.*)

The immediate purpose with which Italians and Germans effected the great change in the European constitution was unity, not liberty. They constructed, not securities, but forces. Machiavelli's hour had come.

The History of Freedom and Other Essays, Introduction to Il Principe.

The sentiment on which (papal) infallibility was founded could not be reached by argument, the weapon of human reason, but resided in conclusions transcending evidence, and was the inaccessible postulate rather than a demonstrable consequence of a system of religious faith.

Ibid., The Vatican Council.

To proclaim the Pope infallible was their compendious security against hostile States and Churches, against human liberty and authority, against disintegrating tolerance and rationalizing science, against error and sin.   *Ibid.*

The influence which religious motives formerly possessed is now in a great measure exercised by political opinion.

Ibid., Political Thoughts on the Church.

Abigail (Smith) Adams
(1744-1818)
American writer, wife of John Adams

I long to hear that you have declared an independency. And in the new code of laws which I suppose it will be necessary for you to make, I desire you would remember the ladies, and be more generous and favorable to them than your ancestors . . . If particular care and attention is not paid to the ladies, we are determined to foment a rebellion and will not hold ourselves bound by any laws in which we have no voice or representation.
Letter to John Adams, 1774.

I am more and more convinced that man is a dangerous creature; and that power, whether vested in many or a few, is ever grasping, and like the grave, cries "Give, give!"   *Ibid., November 27, 1775.*

Brooks Adams
(1848-1927)
American historian

Thought is one of the manifestations of human energy, and among the earlier and simpler phases of thought, two stand conspicuous—Fear and Greed. Fear, which, by stimulating the imagination, creates a belief in an invisible world, and ultimately develops a priesthood; and Greed, which dissipates energy in war and trade.
The Law of Civilization and Decay.

When surplus energy has accumulated in such bulk as to preponderate over productive energy, it becomes the controlling social force. Thenceforward, capital is autocratic, and energy vents itself through those organisms best fitted to give expression to the power of capital. In the last state of consolidation, the economic, and, perhaps, the scientific intellect is propagated, while the imagination fades, and the emotional, the martial, the artistic types of manhood decay.   *Ibid.*

Law is merely the expression of the will of the strongest for the time being, and therefore laws have no fixity, but shift from generation to generation.   *Ibid.*

The power of the priesthood lies in the submission to a creed. In their onslaughts on rebellion they have exhausted human torments; nor, in their lust for earthly dominion, have they felt remorse, but rather joy, when slaying Christ's enemies and their own.
The Emancipation of Massachusetts.

The horrors of the Inquisition, the Massacre of St. Bartholomew, the atrocities of Laud, the abominations of the Scotch Kirk, the persecution of the Quakers had one object—the enslavement of the mind.
     Ibid.

Democracy is an infinite mass of conflicting minds and conflicting interests . . . which loses in collective intellectual energy in proportion to the perfection of its expansion.
The Degradation of the Democratic Dogma.

I had rather starve and rot and keep the privilege of speaking the truth as I see it, than of holding all the offices that capital has to give from the presidency down.
     Ibid.

Francis Adams
(1862-1893)
Irish-American writer

Take, then, your paltry Christ,
Your gentleman God.

We want the carpenter's son,
With his saw and hod.
*Quoted by Upton Sinclair, The Cry for
Justice.*

Franklin Pierce Adams ("F.P.A.")
(1881-1960)
American author

Then here's to the City of Boston:
The town of the cries and the groans,
Where the Cabots can't see the
Kabotschniks,
And the Lowells won't speak to the
Cohns.
*A parody on John Bossidy's verse
which ends, "And the Cabots speak
only to God," which was a 1910 par-
ody on an 1880 Harvard verse.*

Christmas is over. Uncork your ambition!
Back to the battle! Come on, competition!
Down with all sentiment, can scrupulosity!
For the Other 364 Days.

Money is all that is worth all your labors;
Crowd your competitors, nix on your
neighbors! *Ibid.*

Frenzy yourself into sickness and dizziness—
Christmas is over and Business is Business.
Ibid.

There are plenty of good five-cent cigars
in the country. The trouble is they cost a
quarter. What the country really needs is a
good five-cent nickel.
*A reply to a Ken Hubbard ("Abe Mar-
tin") quotation, q.v., usually attributed
to Vice-President Marshall.*

Henry Brooks Adams
(1838-1918)
American historian

The American mind had less respect for
money than the European or Asiatic mind

. . . It shunned, distrusted, disliked, the
dangerous attractions of ideals, and stood
alone in history for its ignorance of the past.
The Education of Henry Adams.

Seneca closed the vast circle of his knowledge by learning that a friend in power was
a friend lost. *Ibid.*

Those who seek education in the paths
of duty are always deceived by the illusion
that power in the hands of friends is an
advantage to them . . . Power is poison. Its
effect on Presidents has always been tragic,
chiefly as an almost insane excitement at
first, and a worse reaction afterward; but
also because no mind is so well balanced as
to bear the strain of seizing unlimited force
without habit or knowledge of it; and finding it disputed with him by hungry packs
of wolves and hounds whose lives depend
on snatching the carrion. *Ibid.*

The effect of unlimited power on limited
minds is worth noting in Presidents because
it must represent the same process in society, and the power of self-control must
have limit somewhere in face of the control
of the infinite. *Ibid.*

Modern politics is, at bottom, a struggle
not of men but of forces. The men become
every year more and more creatures of
force, massed about central powerhouses.
The conflict is no longer between the men,
but between the motors that drive the men,
and the men tend to succumb to their own
motive forces. *Ibid.*

Double standards are inspiration to men
of letters, but they are apt to be fatal to
politicians. *Ibid.*

No honest historian can take part with
—or against—the forces he has to study. To
him even the extinction of the human race

should be merely a fact to be grouped with other vital statistics.   *Ibid.*

The usual conspiracy of silence inevitable to all thought which demands new thought-machinery.   *Ibid.*

To the highest attractive energy, man gave the name of divine, and for its control he invented the science called Religion, a word which meant, and still means, the cultivation of occult forces whether in detail or mass.   *Ibid.*

Hunger, whether for food or for the infinite, sets in motion multiplicity and infinity of thought, and the sure hope of gaining a share of infinite power in eternal life would lift most minds to effort.   *Ibid.*

The world is made up of a few immense forces, each with an organization that corresponds with its strength. The church stands first; and at the outset we must assume that the church will not and cannot accept any science of history, because science, by its definition, must exclude the idea of a personal and active providence. The state stands next; and the hostility of the state would be assured toward any system of science that might not strengthen its arm. Property is growing more and more timid and looks with extreme jealousy on any new idea that may weaken vested rights. Labor is growing more and more self-confident and looks with contempt on all theories that do not support its own. Yet we cannot conceive of a science of history that would not, directly or indirectly, affect all these vast social forces.
Presidential address, American Historical Association, 1894, written as a letter, from Mexico; quoted in The Practical Cogitator.

The present evils of the world—its huge armaments, its vast accumulations of capital, its advancing materialism, and declining arts.   *Ibid.*

If, finally, science should prove that society must at a given time revert to the church and recover its old foundation of absolute faith in a personal providence and a revealed religion, it commits suicide.
             Ibid.

The press is the hired agent of a monied system, and set up for no other purpose than to tell lies where the interests are involved. One can trust nobody and nothing.
The Letters of Henry Adams.

Some day science may have the existence of mankind in its power, and the human race commit suicide by blowing up the world.   *Letter, 1862.*

The devil is strong in me . . . Rebellion is in the blood, somehow or other. I can't go on without a fight.
The Great Secession Winter of 1860-1861 and Other Essays, Sagamore, 1958.

We may some day catch an abstract truth by the tail, and then we shall have our religion and our immortality.
Henry Adams: The Middle Years, by Ernest Samuels, Belknap-Harvard, 1958.

J. Donald Adams
(1891-1968)
American editor, writer

Nothing, surely is more alive than a word. ✓

The fundamental truths are all men's property. Whether or not we live by them, we all know them, with a deep instinctiveness.
N. Y. Times Book Review, January 11, 1948.

In the realm of human conduct, particularly, I do not suppose it is possible for any man, however acute or profound his mental processes may be, to say anything bearing the stamp of universal truth, that many other men, in equivalent words, have not said before him. Back of each of us there are those many thousands of years of race experience.   *Ibid.*

John Adams

(1735-1826)
2nd President of the United States

Numberless have been the systems of iniquity contrived by the great for the gratification of this passion in themselves; but in none of them were they ever more successful than in the invention and establishment of the canon and the feudal law.
Dissertation on the Canon and the Feudal Law, 1765.

By the former of these (canon law), the most refined, sublime, extensive, and astonishing constitution of policy that ever was conceived by the mind of man was framed by the Romish clergy for the aggrandizement of their own order.   *Ibid.*

They even persuaded mankind to believe, faithfully and undoubtingly, that God Almighty had entrusted them with the keys of heaven, whose gates they might open and close at pleasure; with a power of dispensation over all the rules and obligations of morality; with authority to license all sorts of sins and crimes; with a power of deposing princes and absolving subjects from allegiance; with a power of procuring or withholding the rain of heaven and the beams of the sun; with the management of earthquakes, pestilence, and famine; nay, with the mysterious, awful, incomprehensible power of creating out of bread and wine the flesh and blood of God himself.

All these opinions they were enabled t spread and rivet among the people by re ducing their minds to a state of sordi ignorance and staring timidity, and by in fusing into them a religious horror o letters and knowledge. Thus was huma nature chained fast for ages in a cruel shameful, and deplorable servitude to hin and his subordinate tyrants, who, it wa foretold, would exalt himself above all tha was called God and that was worshipped
Ibid.

They (the Puritans) saw clearly that o all the nonsense and delusion which hac ever passed through the mind of man, non had ever been more extravagant than th notions of absolutions, indelible characters uninterrupted successions, and the rest o those fantastical ideas, derived from the canon law, which had thrown such a glar of mystery, sanctity, reverence, and righ reverend eminence and holiness around the idea of a priest as no mortal could deserve and as always must, from the constitutior of human nature, be dangerous to society For this reason they demolished the whole system of diocesan episcopacy, and, derid ing, as all reasonable and impartial mer must do, the ridiculous fancies of sanctified effluvia from episcopal fingers, they estab lished sacerdotal ordination on the founda tion of the Bible and common sense. *Ibid.*

Liberty cannot be preserved without a general knowledge among the people.
Ibid.

The preservation of the means of knowl edge among the lowest ranks is of more importance to the public than all the prop erty of all the rich men in the country.
Ibid.

But none of the means of information are more sacred, or have been cherished with more tenderness and care by the settlers of

America, than the press. Care has been taken that the art of printing should be encouraged, and that it should be easy and cheap and safe for any person to communicate his thoughts to the public. And you, Messieurs printers, whatever the tyrants of the earth may say of your paper, have done important service to your country by your readiness and freedom in publishing the speculations of the curious. The stale, impudent insinuations of slander and sedition with which the gormandizers of power have endeavored to discredit your paper are so much the more to your honor; for the jaws of power are always opened to devour, and her arm is always stretched out, if possible, to destroy the freedom of thinking, speaking, and writing.   *Ibid.*

Be not intimidated, therefore, by any terrors, from publishing with the utmost freedom whatever can be warranted by the laws of your country; nor suffer yourselves to be wheedled out of your liberty by any pretenses of politeness, delicacy, or decency. These, as they are often used, are but three different names for hypocrisy, chicanery, and cowardice.   *Ibid.*

Let us dare to read, think, speak and write.   *Ibid.*

Set before us the conduct of our own British ancestors, who defended for us the inherent rights of mankind against foreign and domestic tyrants and usurpers, against arbitrary kings and cruel priests; in short against the gates of earth and hell. *Ibid.*

Let the pulpit resound with the doctrines and sentiments of religious liberty. Let us hear the dangers of thralldom to our consciences from ignorance, extreme poverty, and dependence; in short, from civil and political slavery. Let us see delineated before us the true map of man. Let us hear

the dignity of his nature, and the noble rank he holds among the works of God —that consenting to slavery is a sacrilegious breach of trust, as offensive in the sight of God as it is derogatory from our own honor or interest or happiness—and that God Almighty has promulgated from heaven liberty, peace, and goodwill to man! *Ibid.*

My country has in its wisdom contrived for me the most insignificant office that ever the invention of man contrived or his imagination conceived.
Letter, as vice-president, 1789.

The Hebrews have done more to civilize men than any other nation. If I were an atheist, and believed in blind eternal fate, I should still believe that fate had ordained the Jews to be the most essential instrument for civilizing the nations.
Letter to F. A. Van der Kamp, February 16, 1809.

Indeed, Mr. Jefferson, what could be invented to debase the ancient Christianism, which Greeks, Romans, Hebrews and Christian factions, above all the Catholics, have not fraudulently imposed upon the public? Miracles after miracles have rolled down in torrents, wave succeeding wave in the Catholic church, from the Council of Nice, and long before, to this day.
To Jefferson, December 3, 1813.

There is but one element of government, and that is THE PEOPLE. From this element spring all governments. "For a nation to be free, it is only necessary that she wills it." For a nation to be slave, it is only necessary that she wills it.
To John Taylor, 1814.

If the Christian religion, as I understand it, or as you understand it, should maintain its ground, as I believe it will, yet Platonic, Pythagoric, Hindoo, and cabalistical Chris-

tianity, which is Catholic Christianity, and which has prevailed for 1500 years, has received a mortal wound, of which the monster must finally die. Yet so strong is his constitution, that he may endure for centuries before he expires.
To Jefferson, July 16, 1814.

If there is ever an amelioration of the condition of mankind, philosophers, theologians, legislators, politicians and moralists will find that the regulation of the press is the most difficult, dangerous and important problem they have to resolve. Mankind cannot now be governed without it, nor at present with it.
Letter to James Lord, February 11, 1815.

The question before the human race is, whether the God of nature shall govern the world by his own laws, or whether priests and kings shall rule it by fictitious miracles? *To Jefferson, June 20, 1815.*

You ask, how has it happened that all Europe has acted on the principle, "that Power was Right" . . . Power always sincerely, conscientiously, *de très bon foi*, believes itself right. . . . Power must never be trusted without a check.
To Jefferson, February 2, 1816.

I do not like the late resurrection of the Jesuits. . . . If ever any congregation of men could merit eternal perdition on earth, and in hell, according to these historians, though, like Pascal, true Catholics, it is this company of Loyolas.
Letter to Jefferson, May 5, 1816. Official edition, Writings of Thomas Jefferson, Vol. VI, p. 604.

My History of the Jesuits is not elegantly written, but is supported by unquestionable authorities, is very particular and very horrible. Their restoration is indeed "a step

toward darkness," cruelty, perfidy, despotism, death and—! I wish we were out of danger of bigotry and Jesuitism.
To Jefferson, August 9, 1816.

Conclude not from all this that I have renounced the Christian religion . . . Far from it. I see every page something to recommend Christianity in its purity, and something to discredit its corruptions . . . The ten commandments and the sermon on the mount contain my religion.
To Jefferson, November 4, 1816.

My History of the Jesuits is in four volumes . . . This society has been a greater calamity to mankind than the French Revolution, or Napoleon's despotism or ideology. It has obstructed progress of reformation and the improvement of the human mind in society much longer and more fatally.
Ibid.

As I understand the Christian religion, it was, and is, a revelation. But how has it happened that millions of fables, tales, legends, have been blended with both Jewish and Christian revelation that have made them the most bloody religion that ever existed?
Letter to F. A. Van der Kamp, December 27, 1816.

The Revolution was effected before the war commenced. The Revolution was in the hearts and minds of the people . . . This *radical change in the principles, opinions, sentiments, and affections of the people was the real American Revolution.*
To Hezekiah Niles, February 13, 1818.

When people talk of the freedom of writing, speaking or thinking I cannot choose but laugh. No such thing ever existed. No such thing now exists; but I hope it will exist. But it must be hundreds of years after you and I shall write and speak no more. *To Jefferson, July 15, 1818.*

I wish your nation may be admitted to all the privileges of citizens in every country of the world. This country has done much. I wish it may do more; and annul every narrow idea in religion, government and commerce. Let the wits joke; the philosophers sneer; what then? It has pleased the Providence of the "first cause", the universal cause, that Abraham should give religion, not only to Hebrews, but to Christians and Mohemetans, the greatest part of the civilized world.

Letter to Mordecai M. Noah, July 31, 1818.

Abuse of words has been the great instrument of sophistry and chicanery, of party, faction, and division of society.

To J. H. Tiffany, March 31, 1819.

I would define liberty to be a power to do as we would be done by. The definition of liberty to be the power of doing whatever the law permits, meaning the civil laws, does not seem satisfactory. *Ibid.*

Can a free government possibly exist with the Roman Catholic religion?
To Jefferson, May 19, 1821.

The moment the idea is admitted into society that property is not as sacred as the laws of God, and there is not a force of law and public justice to protect it, anarchy and tyranny commence.

Letter, quoted in Fortune, February, 1951.

In every society where property exists there will ever be a struggle between rich and poor. Mixed in one assembly, equal laws can never be expected; they will either be made by the members to plunder the few who are rich, or by the influence to fleece the many who are poor.

*Quoted by Senator Estes Kefauver, with the remark: "A remarkable antici-*pation of the basic presumption of Marxism."

The proposition that the people are the best keepers of their own liberties is not true. They are the worst conceivable, they are no keepers at all; they can neither judge, act, think, or will, as a political body.

Defence of the Constitution. (Quoted by W. E. Woodward in his Tom Paine: America's Godfather.)

Liberty, according to my metaphysics . . . is a self-determining power in an intellectual agent. It implies thought and choice and power. *Letter to John Taylor.*

I almost shudder at the thought of alluding to the most fatal example of the abuses of grief which the history of mankind has preserved—the Cross. Consider what calamities that engine of grief has produced!

On the Abuses of Grief. Letter to Jefferson, in Jefferson's Works, Vol. VII, p. 35.

As the government of the United States of America is not in any sense founded on the Christian Religion,—as it has itself no character of enmity against the law, religion or tranquility of Musselmen, . . .

Article 11, Treaty of Peace and Friendship between The United States and the Bey and Subjects of Tripoli of Barbary. Treaties and Other International Acts of the United States of America. Edited by Hunter Miller. Vol. 2. 1776-1818. U.S. Government Printing Office, Washington, D.C., 1931; p. 365.*

---

* Now be it known, That I, John Adams, President of the United States of America, having seen and considered the said treaty do, by and within the consent of the Senate, accept, ratify and confirm the same, and every clause and article thereof.

Ibid., p. 383.

What havoc has been made of books through every century of the Christian era? Where are fifty gospels, condemned as spurious by the bull of Pope Gelasius? Where are the forty wagon-loads of Hebrew manuscripts burned in France, by order of another pope, because suspected of heresy? Remember the *index expurgatorius,* the inquisition, the stake, the axe, the halter, and the guillotine.

Letter to John Taylor, The Life and Works of John Adams, Boston, 1851, v. 6, p. 479.

Shall we have recourse to the art of printing? But this has not destroyed property or aristocracy or corporations or paper wealth in England or America, or diminished the influence of either; on the contrary, it has multiplied aristocracy and diminished democracy. *Ibid., p. 510.*

Admit that the press transferred the pontificate of Rome to Henry VIII—Admit that the press demolished in some sort the feudal system, and set the serfs and villins free; admit that the press demolished the monasteries, nunneries, and religious houses; into whose hands did all these alienated baronies, monasteries, and religious houses and lands fall? Into the hands of the democracy? Into the hands of serfs and villins? Serfs and villins were the only real democracy in those times. No. They fell into the hands of other aristocrats . . .

Ibid.

The priesthood have, in all ancient nations, nearly monopolized learning . . . And ever since the Reformation, when or where has existed a Protestant or dissenting sect who would tolerate A FREE INQUIRY? The blackest billingsgate, the most ungentlemanly insolence, the most yahooish brutality, is patiently endured, countenanced, propagated, and applauded. But touch a solemn truth in collision with a dogma of a sect, though capable of the clearest proof, and you will soon find you have disturbed a nest, and the hornets will swarm about your eyes and hand, and fly into your face and eyes. *Ibid., p. 517.*

John Quincy Adams
(1767-1848)
6th President of the United States

Let us not be unmindful that liberty is power, that the nation blessed with the largest portion of liberty must in proportion to its numbers be the most powerful nation upon earth.

Our Constitution professedly rests upon the good sense and attachment of the people. This basis, weak as it may appear, has not yet been found to fail.

Always vote for a principle, though you vote alone, and you may cherish the sweet reflection that your vote is never lost.

America, in the assembly of nations, has uniformly spoken among them the language of equal liberty, equal justice, and equal rights. *1821.*

Samuel Adams
(1722-1803)
American revolutionary leader

I believe that no people ever yet groaned under the heavy yoke of slavery but when they deserved it.

Article published in 1771.

The truth is, all might be free if they valued freedom, and defended it as they ought. *Ibid.*

The liberties of our country, the freedom of our civil constitution, are worth defending at all hazards; and it is our duty to defend them against all attacks. We have received them as a fair inheritance from our worthy ancestors: they purchased them for us with toil and danger and expense of treasure and blood, and transmitted them to us with care and diligence. It will bring an everlasting mark of infamy on the present generation, enlightened as it is, if we should suffer them to be wrested from us by violence without a struggle, or be cheated out of them by the artifices of false and designing men. *Ibid.*

Among the natural rights of the colonists are these: first, a right to *life*; secondly, to *liberty*; thirdly to *property*; together with the right to support and defend them in the best manner they can. Those are evident branches of, rather than deductions from, the duty of self-preservation, commonly called the first law of nature.

The Rights of the Colonists, 1772.

In regard to religion, mutual toleration in the different professions thereof is what all good and candid minds in all ages have ever practiced, and both by precept and example inculcated on mankind. . . . The only sects which he (Locke) thinks ought to be and which by all wise laws are excluded from such toleration are those who teach doctrines subversive of the civil government under which they live. The Roman Catholics or Papists are excluded by reason of such doctrines as these: that princes excommunicated may be deposed, and those they call heretics may be destroyed without mercy; besides their recognizing the pope in so absolute a manner, in subversion of government, by introducing as far as possible into the states under whose protection they enjoy life, liberty, and property that solecism in politics, *Imperium in imperio,* leading directly to the worst anarchy and confusion, civil discord, war and bloodshed. *Ibid.*

What has commonly been called rebellion has more often been nothing but a manly and glorious struggle in opposition to the *lawless power of rebellious* kings and princes.

If ye love wealth better than liberty, the tranquillity of servitude better than the animating contest of freedom, go home from us in peace. We ask not your counsels or arms. Crouch down and lick the hands which feed you. May your chains set lightly upon you, and may posterity forget that ye were our countrymen. *1776.*

Driven from every corner of the earth, Freedom of Thought and The Right of Private Judgment in matters of conscience direct their course to this happy country as their last asylum.

Speech, Philadelphia, August 1, 1776.

Our contest is not only whether we ourselves shall be free, but whether there shall be left to mankind an asylum on earth for civil and religious liberty.

T. S. Adams
(b. 1873)
American writer

In the last six centuries the laboring population has risen from a condition of serfdom to a state of political freedom. In this struggle for economic equality the victories have been won by the wage-earners themselves. Where they did not pursue their interest, they lost their interest. When they forgot to demand their full reward, they failed to receive their full reward. . . Their weapons were the strike and the trade union.

Labor Problems. Macmillan, 1905.

Jane Addams
(1860-1935)
American social worker

Civilization is a method of living, an attitude of equal respect for all men.
Address, Honolulu, 1933.

Joseph Addison
(1672-1719)
English essayist, poet

A day, an hour, of virtuous liberty
Is worth a whole eternity in bondage.
Cato.

Liberty or death. *Ibid.*

It must be so,—Plato, thou reason'st well!—
Else whence this pleasing hope, this fond desire,
This longing after immortality? *Ibid.*

Red with uncommon wrath, to blast the man
Who owes his greatness to his country's ruin? *Ibid.*

Justice discards party, friendship, and kindred, and is therefore represented as blind. *The Spectator.*

But in all despotic governments, though a particular prince may favour arts and letters, there is a natural degeneracy of mankind. *Ibid.*

An honest private man often grows cruel and abandoned when converted into an absolute prince. Give a man power of doing what he pleases with impunity, you extinguish his fear, and consequently overturn in him one of the great pillars of morality. *Ibid.*

There is no greater sign of a general decay of virtue in a nation, than a want of zeal in its inhabitants for the good of their country. *Freeholder.*

Konrad Adenauer
(1876-1967)
Chancellor of Germany

The good Lord set definite limits on man's wisdom, but set no limits on his stupidity—and that's just not fair!
The Churchman, January 15, 1957.

Alfred Adler *
(1870-1937)
Father of individual psychology

The feeling of inferiority rules the mental life and can be clearly recognized as the sense of incompleteness and unfulfillment, and in the uninterrupted struggle both of individuals and of humanity.
Social Interest.

There is a Law that man should love his neighbor as himself. In a few hundred years it should be as natural to mankind as breathing or the upright gait; but if he does not learn it he must perish. *Ibid.*

The only worthwhile achievements of man are those which are socially useful.

We must interpret a bad temper as a sign of inferiority.

To be human means to feel inferior.
The Individual Psychology of Alfred Adler, edited by Prof. Heinz L. Ansbacher and Rowena R. Ansbacher. Sinn des Lebens, 1933.

---

* This section was read by Drs. Heinz and Rowena Ansbacher, who supplied missing sources and stated all quotations "true to Adler's thinking."

To be a human being means to possess a feeling of inferiority which constantly presses towards its own conquest. The paths to victory are as different in a thousand ways as the chosen goals of perfection. The greater the feeling of inferiority that has been experienced, the more powerful is the urge to conquest and the more violent the emotional agitation. *Ibid.*

All failures—neurotics, psychotics, criminals, drunkards, problem children, suicides, perverts, and prostitutes—are failures because they are lacking in social interest.
What Life Should Mean to You, 1931.

Life (and all psychological expressions as part of life) moves ever toward overcoming, toward perfection, toward superiority, toward success. You cannot train or condition a living being for defeat.
International Journal of Individual Psychology, Vol. 1, No. 1, 1935.

What an individual thinks or feels as success (as an acceptable goal) is unique with him. In our experience we have found that each individual has a different meaning of, and attitude toward, what constitutes success. Therefore, a human being cannot be typified or classified. *Ibid.*

The truth is often a terrible weapon of aggression. It is possible to lie, and even to murder, with the truth.
Problems of Neurosis, 1929.

The common people seem always to have been on the track to social interest, and every intellectual and every religious uprising has been directed against the striving for power; the logic of the communal life of man has always asserted itself. But all this has always ended again in the thirst for dominance. All social legislation of the past, the teaching of Christ, and the tablets of Moses have fallen, again and again, into

the hands of power-craving social classes and groups. *Bolshevismus, 1918.*

The rule of Bolshevism is based on the possession of power. Thus its fate is sealed. While this party and its friends see ultimate goals which are the same as ours, the intoxication of power has seduced them. . . . Fair becomes foul, foul becomes fair!
Ibid.

It is easier to fight for principles than to live up to them.

The tests for one's behavior pattern: relationship to society, relationship to one's work, relationship to sex.

Interview with G. S., N. Y. World, 1926.

Mortimer J. Adler
(b. 1902)
American educator

(1) Emancipation from the arbitrary rule of other men.
The Idea of Freedom, Doubleday, 1958, pp. 380-1.*

(2) Emancipation from compulsory toil by which mankind satisfies its economic wants, together with emancipation from degrading poverty, long hours of labor, and economic insecurity. *Ibid.*

(3) Emancipation of human labor from economic servitude and exploitation, i.e., from organizations of production in which the conditions of work are determined by a master class who own the means of production, and in which the fruits of work are alienated from workers to the benefit of masters. *Ibid.*

---

* A summary of views in common held by Comte, Bakunin, Marx and Engels; "Comte's theory does not include . . . economic emancipation."

(4) *Complete* emancipation from the state or political community as that has so far existed in the history of mankind, i.e., from the essential features of all past and present societies. *Ibid.*

Victor Adler
(1852-1918)
Austrian labor leader

The last anti-Semite will die only with the last Jew.
Address, Social-Democratic Congress, Vienna, 1898.

Aeschylus
(525-456 B.C.)
Greek dramatist

A state that is prosperous always honors the gods.

The force of necessity is irresistible.
Prometheus Vinctus.

Aesop
(620-560 B.C.)
Greek fabulist

Better die once for all than live in continual terror.°

Those who voluntarily put power into the hands of a tyrant or an enemy, must not wonder if it be at last turned against themselves.

Aga Khan III
(1877-1957)
Mohammedan leader

There is a great deal of truth in Andrew Carnegie's remark: "The man who dies rich,

---

° Cf. Ibarruri (La Pasionaria).

dies disgraced." I should add: The man who lives rich, lives disgraced.
The Memoirs of Aga Khan: World Enough and Time.

(Jean) Louis (Rodolphe) Agassiz
(1807-1873)
Swiss naturalist and teacher in America

I cannot afford to waste my time making money.°

The time has come when scientific truth must cease to be the property of the few —when it must be woven into the common life of the world.

Agathon
(447?-401 B.C.)
Athenian tragic poet

Even God cannot change the past.
Attributed by Aristotle, Nicomachean Ethics, vi.

Henry D. Aiken
(b. 1912)
Professor of philosophy, Harvard

The ideology called "dialectical materialism", regardless of the propriety of its title, has taken hold of the imaginations of men as perhaps no doctrine has been able to do since the time of Christ.
The Age of Ideology.

ben Joseph Akiba
(c. 50-132)
Jewish rabbi and martyr

The paper burns, but the words fly away.
Last words, at the stake, when the Torah was also burned.

° Refusing an offer for a course of lectures.

(Amos) Bronson Alcott
(1799-1888)
American teacher, philosopher

Millions of minds are in a state of slavery. How shall they escape? Rebel, think of yourself, let others grumble. Dare to be singular—let others sleep.

Alcuin (Flaccus Albinus Alcuinus)
(735-804)
English scholar

Vox *populi, vox dei.* (The voice of the people is the voice of God.)
To Charlemagne.

Men can be attracted but not forced to the faith. You may drive people to baptism, you won't move them one step further to religion.

Richard Aldington
(1892-1962)
English poet, novelist, critic

Patriotism is a lively sense of collective responsibility. Nationalism is a silly cock crowing on his own dunghill.
The Colonel's Daughter.

Alfonso X (Alfonso the Wise)
(1226-1284)
King of Castile

Had I been present at the creation of the world I would have proposed some improvements.

A tyrant doth signify a cruel lord, who, by force or by craft, or by treachery, hath obtained power over any realm or country; and such men be of such nature, that when once they have grown strong in the land, they love rather to work their own profit, though it be to the harm of the land, than the common profit of all, for they always live in an ill fear of losing it.
Las Siete Partidas.

They (tyrants) use their power against the people in three manners. The first is, that they strive that those under their mastery be ever ignorant and timorous, because, when they be such, they may not be bold to rise against them, nor to resist their wills; and the second is, that their victims be not kindly and united among themselves, in such wise that they trust not one another. . . . ; and the third way is, that they strive to make them poor, and to put them upon great undertakings, which they can never finish, whereby they may have so much harm that it may never come into their hearts to devise anything against their ruler.
Ibid.

Alighieri
See Dante Alighieri

Ethan Allen
(1737-1789)
American officer in Revolutionary War

Reason the Only Oracle of Man.
Title of pamphlet, first freethought publication in America.

I have generally been denominated a Deist, the reality of which I never disputed, being conscious I am no Christian, except mere infant baptism makes me one; and as to being a Deist, I know not strictly speaking, whether I am one or not.
Reason the Only Oracle of Man; preface, first edition, Bennington, Vt., 1784; Scholars' Facsimiles & Reprints, N.Y.C., 1940.

For mankind to hate truth as it may bring their evil deeds to light and punishment, is very easy and common; but to hate truth as truth, or God as God, which is the same as to hate goodness for its own sake, unconnected with any other consequences, is impossible even to a (premised) diabolical nature itself. *Ibid., p. 31.*

There is not any thing, which has contributed so much to delude mankind in religious matters, as mistaken apprehensions concerning supernatural inspiration or revelation; not considering, that all true religion originates from reason, and can not otherwise be understood, but by the exercise and improvement of it. *Ibid., p. 200.*

In those parts of the world where learning and science has prevailed, miracles have ceased; but in those parts of it as are barbarous and ignorant, miracles are still in vogue. *Ibid., p. 265.*

That tradition has had a powerful influence on the human mind is universally admitted, even by those who are governed by it in the articles of discipline of their faith; for though they are blind with respect to their own superstition, yet they can perceive and despise it in others. Protestants very readily discern and expose the weak side of Popery, and papists are as ready and acute in discovering the errors of heretics. *Ibid., p. 337.*

The Roman Catholics, to avail the evils of imperfection, fallibility and imposture of man, have set up the Pope to be infallible; this is their security against being misguided in their faith, and by ascribing holiness to him, secure themselves from imposture; a deception, which is incompatible with holiness. So that in matters of faith, they have nothing more to do, but to believe as their church believes. *Ibid., p. 454.*

Witchcraft and Priestcraft, were introduced into this world together, in its non-

age; and has gone on, hand in hand together, until about half a century past, when witchcraft began to be discredited . . . This discovery has depreciated Priestcraft, on the scale of at least fifty per cent per annum . . . *Ibid., p. 456.*

Such of mankind, as break the fetters of their education . . . exalt reason to its just supremacy, and vindicate truth and the ways of God's providence to men; are sure to be stamped with the epithet of irreligious, infidel, prophane, and the like.

Ibid., p. 468.

Virtue and vice are the only things in this world, which, with our souls, are capable of surviving death. *Ibid., p. 473.*

Ever since I arrived at the state of manhood and acquainted myself with the general history of mankind, I have felt a sincere passion for liberty. The history of nations doomed to perpetual slavery, in consequence of yielding up to tyrants their natural-born liberties, I read with a sort of philosophical horror; so that the first systematical and bloody attempt, at Lexington, to enslave America, thoroughly electrified my mind, and fully determined me to take part with my country.

Quoted in the Beards' Basic History.

(To his physician, who said, "General, I fear the angels are waiting for you"): Waiting, are they? Waiting, are they? Well, goddam 'em, let 'em wait!

Quoted, Saturday Review, April 5, 1958.

Fred Allen
(1894-1956)
American humorist

Advertising is 85% confusion and 15% commission.

Treadmill to Oblivion.

John Peter Altgeld
(1847-1902)
Governor of Illinois

All of our greatness was born of liberty, even our commercialism was rocked in the cradle of democracy, and we cannot strangle the mother without destroying her children.

The laboring people found the prisons always open to receive them, but the courts of justice were practically closed to them.

None of the defendants could be at all connected with the case. Wholesale bribery and intimidation of witnesses were resorted to. The defendants were not proved guilty of the crime charged under the indictment.
Governor's pardon for Fielden, Neebe and Schwab, three of the "Chicago Anarchists," June 26, 1883.

Those fellows did not have a fair trial and I did what I thought was right.
(referring to the Anarchists.)

All great reforms, great movements, come from the bottom and not the top. . . Wherever there is a wrong, point it out to all the world, and you can trust the people to fight it.
Quoted by Madison, Critics and Crusaders.

We can not for a moment admit that by simply applying an unpopular or obloquious name to men, whether that name be anarchist, or socialist, capitalist or vagabond, republican or democrat, an officer can be justified in depriving men of rights guaranteed by the fundamental law, and can break up their meeting, can club, search and imprison them, not for what they have done, but for what he, in his wisdom, or his prejudice, or his caprice, fears they might do.
If this principle were once admitted, there is no limit to its application. While it is sought to apply it to one class today, it could be applied to any other class tomorrow, and a precedent made in one case would be sure to be cited and acted on in another, and a political party, for the time being in power, could prevent its opponents from meeting and put them in jail.
To the chief of police, Chicago, November 14, 1891; in Live Questions, 1899.

Freedom of thought and freedom of speech in our great institutions of learning are absolutely necessary for the preservation of our country. The moment that either is restricted, liberty begins to wither and die and the career of a nation after that time is downwards.
To George H. Shipley, September 25, 1897.

Amalric
(13th century)
French theologian, philosopher

Kill them all. God will easily recognize His own.
To Simon de Montfort, at the massacre at Béziers, 1209.

St. Ambrose
(340?-397)
Bishop of Milan

How far, O rich, do you extend your senseless avarice? Do you intend to be the sole inhabitants of the earth? Why do you drive out the fellow sharers of nature, and claim it all for yourselves? The earth was made for all, rich and poor, in common. Why do you rich claim it as your exclusive right?

Property hath no rights. The earth is the Lord's, and we are his offspring. The pagans hold earth as property. They do blaspheme God.

A wise man, though he be a slave, is at liberty, and from this it follows that, though a fool rule, he is in slavery.
Letters, quoted by Mortimer Adler, The Idea of Freedom, p. 253.

There is nothing evil save that which perverts the mind and shackles the conscience.
Hexaem, 1, 31.

American Anthropological Association

(1) Race involves the inheritance of similar physical variations by large groups of mankind, but its psychological and cultural connotations, if they exist, have not been ascertained by science.
(2) The terms "Aryan" and "Semitic" have no racial significance whatsoever. They simply denote linguistic families.
(3) Anthropology provides no scientific basis for discrimination against any people on the ground of racial inferiority, religious affiliation, or linguistic heritage.
Resolution unanimously adopted, December, 1938.

American Civil Liberties Union

Liberty is always unfinished business.
Title, annual report, 1955-6.

American Federation of Labor

Whereas, a struggle is going on in all the nations of the civilized world between the oppressed and oppressors of all countries, a struggle between the capitalist and the laborer, which grows in intensity from year to year, and will work disastrous results to the toiling millions if they are not combined for mutual protection and benefit
Preamble, Constitution.*

Whether you work by the piece, Or work by the day—
Decreasing the hours, Increases the pay
AFL song.

American Legion

For God and Country, we associate ourselves together for the following purposes: To uphold and defend the Constitution of the United States of America; to maintain law and order; to foster and perpetuate a one hundred per cent Americanism**; to preserve the memories and incidents of our associations in the Great War; to inculcate a sense of individual obligation to the community, state and nation; to combat the autocracy of both the classes and the masses; to make right the master of might; to promote peace and good will on earth; to safeguard and transmit to posterity the principles of justice, freedom and democracy; to consecrate and sanctify our comradeship by our devotion to mutual helpfulness.
Preamble to its Constitution.

---

* Dropped from AFL-CIO unity constitution, 1955.
** See G. B. Shaw, letter to George Seldes.

Henri Frédéric Amiel
(1821-1881)
Swiss poet, philosopher

Man defends himself as much as he can against truth, as a child does against a medicine, as the man of the Platonic cave does against the light. He does not willingly follow his path, he has to be dragged along backward. This natural liking for the false has several causes: the inheritance of prejudices, which produces an unconscious habit, a slavery; the predominance of the imagination over the reason, which affects the understanding; the predominance of the passions over the conscience, which depraves the heart; the predominance of the will over the intelligence, which vitiates the character. A lively, disinterested, persistent liking for truth is extraordinarily rare. Action and faith enslave thought, both of them in order not to be troubled or inconvenienced by reflection, criticism and doubt.
The Private Journal of Henri Frédéric Amiel, translated by Van Wyck and Charles Van Wyck Brooks.

The are of achieving the true is very little practiced, it is not even known, because there is no personal humility or even love of the true. We desire, as a matter of course, the kind of knowledge that strengthens our hand or tongue and serves our vanity or our desire for power; but the criticism of ourselves, of our prejudices and inclinations, is antipathetic to us. *Ibid.*

The great artist is the simplifier.
Ibid., November 25, 1861.

They (Americans) must win gold, predominance, power; crush rivals, subdue nature. They have their hearts set on the means and never . . . think of the end . . . They are eager, restless, positive, because they are superficial. To what end all this stir, noise, greed, struggle? *Journal.*

Self-interest is but the survival of the animal in us. Humanity only begins for man with self-surrender. *Ibid.*

Truth above all, even when it upsets and overwhelms us! *Ibid.*

In order to see Christianity, one must forget almost all the Christians. *Ibid.*

Philosophy means the complete liberty of the mind, and therefore independence of all social, political, or religious prejudice. . . . It loves one thing only—truth. If it disturbs the ready-made opinions of the Church or the State—of the historical medium—in which the philosopher happens to have been born, so much the worse, but there is no help for it. *Ibid.*

Philosophy means, first, doubt; and afterwards the consciousness of what knowledge means, the consciousness of uncertainty and of ignorance, the consciousness of limit, shade, degree, possibility. The ordinary man doubts nothing and suspects nothing.
Ibid.

Emancipation from error is the condition of real knowledge. *Ibid.*

Knowledge, love, power,—there is the complete life. *Ibid., April 7, 1851.*

An error is the more dangerous in proportion to the degree of truth which it contains. *Ibid., December 26, 1852.*

What governs men is the fear of truth.
Ibid., March 1, 1869.

The efficacy of religion lies precisely in what is not rational, philosophic, nor eternal; its efficacy lies in the unforeseen, the miraculous, the extraordinary. Thus religion attracts more devotion according as it demands more faith—that is to say, as it becomes more incredible to the profane mind.

Ibid., June 5, 1870.

The philosopher aspires to explain away all mysteries, to dissolve them into light. Mystery on the other hand is demanded and pursued by the religious instinct; mystery constitutes the essence of worship.

Ibid.

Without faith a man can do nothing. But faith can stifle all science.

Ibid., February 7, 1872.

Marcellinus Ammianus
(4th Century, A.D.)

Roman historian

The language of truth is unadorned and always simple.

Cleveland Amory
(b. 1917)

American writer

I will omit but I will not distort.
N. Y. Times, October 22, 1955: "the cornerstone of the Ghost Writers' Declaration of Principles."

Anacharsis
(c. 600 B.C.)

Scythian philosopher

Written laws are like spiders' webs, and will like them only entangle and hold the poor and weak, while the rich and powerful will easily break through them.

To Solon.

The market is the place set apart where men may deceive each other.

Quoted by Diogenes Laertius.

Maxwell Anderson
(1888-1959)

American dramatist

What Price Glory?   Play title, 1924.

If two stand shoulder to shoulder against
    the gods,
Happy together, the gods themselves are
    helpless
Against them while they stand so.

Elizabeth the Queen.

When a government takes over a people's economic life it becomes absolute, and when it has become absolute it destroys the arts, the minds, the liberties and the meaning of the people it governs.

The Guaranteed Life.

Sherwood Anderson
(1876-1941)

American writer

As soon as a man here, in America, shows some talent as a writer, they pounce down on him. They want to buy his talent.
They usually do too, I'll tell you that.
So they offer him money, position, security.
All he has to do, you see, is to corrupt slightly everything he does.
They want to make a clever man of him, a cunning twister of words and ideas, spoiling his own tools, going crooked, you see, selling the people out.

Speech, National Committee for the Defense of Political Prisoners, 1932, following Harlan, Ky., arrest of Theodore Dreiser.

The disease we all have and that we

have to fight against all our lives is, of course, the disease of self.

I am pretty sure that writing may be a way of life in itself. It can be that, because it continually forces us away from self toward others. Let any man, or woman, look too much upon his own life, and everything becomes a mess. I think the whole glory of writing lies in the fact that it forces us out of ourselves and into the lives of others. In the end the real writer becomes a lover.
Letters of Sherwood Anderson, edited by Howard Mumford Jones.

To me there is no answer for the terrible confusion of life. I want to try to sympathize and to understand a little of the twisted and maimed life that industrialism has brought on us . . . There is something terrible to me in the thought of the art of writing being bent and twisted to serve the ends of propaganda.
Letter to Upton Sinclair, Money Writes, p. 119.

Everyone in the world is Christ and they are all crucified.   *Winesburg, Ohio.*

Leonid Andreyev
(1871-1919)
Russian writer

What do I want? To free the earth, to free mankind.   *Savva.*

Man—the man of today—is wise. He has come to his senses. He is ripe for liberty. But the past eats away his soul like a canker. It imprisons him within the iron circle of things already accomplished.
Ibid.

I want to do away with everything behind man, so that there is nothing to see when he looks back. I want to take him by the scruff of his neck and turn his face toward the future!   *Ibid.*

Sir Norman Angell
(1872-1967)
English writer

Generally speaking, it would be true to say that no one believes that war pays and nearly every one believes that policies which lead inevitably to war do pay. Every nation sincerely desires peace; and all nations pursue courses which if persisted in, must make peace impossible.
The Great Illusion, 1933.

The demonstration that war, however victorious, spells ruin, has results alike disastrous and incalculable (especially to capitalists who are supposed to carry an especial load of guilt for war), produces a political and social chaos whose end no man can see—all this is too plain, too inescapable, not to make the desire to avoid it a genuine one. The explanation is that popular thought does not grasp the relation between policies which seem on the surface legitimate or advantageous, and the final effect as a cause of war and chaos.   *Ibid.*

The vested interests—if we explain the situation by their influence—can only get the public to act as they wish by manipulating public opinion, by playing either upon the public's indifference, confusions, prejudices, pugnacities or fears. And the only way in which the power of the interests can be undermined and their maneuvers defeated is by bringing home to the public the danger of its indifference, the absurdity of its prejudices or the hollowness of its fears; by showing that it is indifferent to danger where real danger exists; frightened by dangers which are non-existent.   *Ibid.*

The modern conquerer cannot "take" any spoils.   *Ibid.*

[57]

The capitalist can only make a whole people go to war—want war, clamor for war as, again and again, we have seen whole peoples doing—by capturing the popular will. The only prophylactic against that situation is to make the public aware of the way in which it is being misled.   *Ibid.*

In arguing that capitalism as such is not the cause of war, I must not be taken as arguing that capitalists do not often believe in war, believe that they and their country benefit from it.   *Ibid.*

The theory that the "international financier" has some special interest in war defies nearly all the facts.   *Ibid.*

War, more ancient than any history, is the outcome of passions, follies, fallacies, misconceptions, and defective political institutions common to the great mass of men. They are not incurable misconceptions, not incurable follies. But they may well become so if we persist in assuming that they don't exist; that we need not trouble ourselves about them because war is due to a little clique of evil "interests". So long as we take the line that "the people" (i.e., we ourselves) are innocent of error, then we might hang every war profiteer in existence, and find, on the morrow, human society as helplessly as ever in the grip of some new folly, stimulated by a new group interested in exploiting it.   *Ibid.*

We know now without any possibility of doubt that the outcome of war in the modern world is unpayable debts, repudiations, ruined investments, the utter disorganization of finance, the collapse of the money system, the disappearance of the greater part of foreign trade, and, usually, on top of it, revolution from below.
Peace, November, 1933.

The root problem is very simply stated: if there were no sovereign independent states, if the states of the civilized world were organized in some sort of federalism, as the states of the American Union, for instance, are organized, there would be no international war as we know it . . . The main obstacle is nationalism.   *Ibid.*

It is part of the moral tragedy with which we are dealing that words like "democracy," "freedom," "rights," "justice," which have so often inspired heroism and have led men to give their lives for things which make life worth while, can also become a trap, the means of destroying the very things men desire to uphold.
Freedom and Union Magazine; Gazette & Daily, January 6, 1959; Sunday Times, London, April 13, 1956.

Democracy and our Western civilization will always be in danger until we liberals face the fact we tend to ignore, namely, that "the People" are not exempt from the Christian doctrine of original sin, from the "natural" tendency of men to obey anti-social, sadistic impulses, unless restrained by a culture which makes them sufficiently aware of the nature of the emotion to which they yield.   *Ibid.*

The greatest service we can do the Common Man is to abolish him.
The Steep Places, Harper's, 1947.

Annunzio
See d'Annunzio

Anonymous and Multiple Authorship

The best things, when perverted, become the very worst: So Printing, which in itself is no small Advantage to Mankind, when it is Abus'd may be of most Fatal Consequences.   *Anonymous pamphlet, 1712.*

The right of a newspaper to attract and hold readers is restricted by nothing but consideration of public welfare . . .

Freedom of the press is to be guarded as a vital right of mankind. . . .

Freedom from all obligations except that of fidelity to the public interest is vital.

Partisanship, in editorial comment which knowingly departs from the truth, does violence to the best spirit of American journalism; in the news columns it is subversive of a fundamental principle of the profession.

Canons of Journalism, 1923; the chief author was H. J. Wright, founder of the New York Globe.

The United Voice of all His Majesty's *free* and *loyal* Subjects in America—Liberty and Property, and no Stamps.

Motto of several colonial newspapers, quoted by Emery & Smith.

Life is a God-damned, stinking, treacherous game, and nine hundred and ninety-nine men out of every thousand are bastards.

Newspaper editor, quoted by Theodore Dreiser, A Book About Myself.

Kommt der Krieg ins Land
Gibt Luegen wie Sand.
Quoted by Arthur Ponsonby, Falsehood in Wartime.

The modern newspaper is half ads and the other half lies between the ads.

Journalism has two patron saints: Ananias and Nell Gwynn.

However little some may think of common newspapers, to a wise man they appear the ark of God for the safety of the people.

Pennsylvania Gazette, January 7, 1768.

A newspaper is a private enterprise, owing nothing to the public.

Wall Street Journal, January 20, 1925.

Civil liberties are always safe as long as their exercise doesn't bother anyone.

N. Y. Times editorial, January 3, 1941.

The sanctity of the institution of marriage and the home shall be upheld. Pictures shall not infer that low forms of sex relations are the accepted or common thing.

Motion Picture Code, March 31, 1930.

Miscegenation is forbidden.   *Ibid.*

It (alcoholic beverages) sloweth age, it strengtheneth youth, it helpeth digestion, it abandoneth melancholie, it relisheth the heart, it lighteneth the mind, it quickeneth the spirits, it keepeth and preserveth the head from whirling, the eyes from dazzling, the tongue from lisping, the mouth from snaffling, the teeth from chattering, and the throat from rattling; it keepeth the stomach from wambling, the heart from swelling, the hands from shivering, the sinews from shrinking, the veins from crumbling, the bones from aching, and the marrow from soaking.

Thirteenth century.

We, the undersigned, recognizing the evils of drunkenness and resolved to check its alarming increase, with consequent poverty, misery and crime among our people, hereby solemnly pledge ourselves that we will not get drunk more than four times a year, viz., Fourth of July, Muster Day, Christmas Day, and Sheep-Sheering.

Massachusetts temperance societies, 1820.

It may be thought strange and unbeseeming to our sex to show ourselves by way of petition to this Honourable Assembly. But matters being rightly considered

. . . it will be found a duty commended and required.

(1) Because Christ hath purchased us at as dear a rate as he hath done men, and therefore requireth like obedience for the same mercy as men.

Petition for redress of grievances, 1641; Parliamentary History, Vol. II., p. 1673; quoted in British Freewomen, 1894.

(2) Because in the free enjoying of Christ in His own laws, and a flourishing estate of the Church and Commonwealth consisteth the happiness of women as well as men. *Ibid.*

(3) Because women are sharers in the common calamities that accompany both Church and Commonwealth, when oppression is exercised over the Church and Kingdom wherein they live; and unlimited power given to the prelates to exercise authority over the consciences of women as well as men. . . . *Ibid.*

Sancta nefaria. (The nefarious Sect.) *Edicts re Jews by Roman emperors, after 326.*

Naziism is an attitude towards life. . . . Naziism does not regard people as the sum of individual citizens but as a community bound by blood ties.

Brockhaus (encyclopedia), 1937.

The foremost principle of Naziism is the *Fuehrerprinzip* (leader principle). This means victory over the parliamentary system and over majority rule in all spheres of life and consolidation of all politically and productively superior forces of the nation. *Ibid.*

The sin of man asserts itself in racial pride, racial hatreds and persecutions, and in the exploitation of other races. Against this in all its forms the Church is called by God to set its face implacably and to utter its word unequivocally, both within and without its borders.

World Conference on Church, Community, and State, Oxford, England, 1937.

Behold Simon (de Montfort), obedient, despises the loss of property, submitting himself to punishment, rather than desert truth, proclaiming to all men openly by his deeds more than by his words, that truth has nothing in common with falsehood . . . the new leader of the journey teaches to bear all that the world may inflict on account of truth, for it is this which can give perfect liberty.

The Battle of Lewes, in Political Songs, published by the Camden Society, 1839; from an original Latin poem probably written after the battle, May 14, 1264.

All constraint does not deprive of liberty, nor does every restriction take away power. . . . Therefore, that there be permitted to a king all that is good, but that he dare not do evil,—that is God's gift. *Ibid.*

Again, let him know that the people is not his but God's; and that it is profitable to him as his help; and that he who for a short period is placed over the people, soon, closed in marble, will be buried in the earth. *Ibid.*

Nor ought it properly to be named liberty, which permits fools to govern unwisely; but liberty is limited by the bounds of the law; and when those bounds are despised, it should be reputed as error. *Ibid.*

We see that God invests kings into their kingdoms, almost in the same manner that vassals are invested into their fees by their sovereign, we must conclude that kings are the vassals of God, and deserve to be deprived of the benefit they receive from their lord if they commit felony.

Vindiciae contra tyrannos, 1579; edited by H. J. Laski, 1925; sometimes credited to Huguenot leaders, and considered a landmark in human freedom.

For if God hold the place of sovereign Lord, and the king the vassal, who dare deny but that we must rather obey the sovereign than the vassal? If God commands one thing, and the king commands the contrary, what is that proud man that would term him a rebel who refuses to obey the king, when else he must disobey God?   *Ibid.*

If their assaults be verbal, their defense must be likewise verbal; if the sword be drawn against them, they may also take arms, and fight either with tongue or hand, as occasion is . . .   *Ibid.*

A whole people, that beast of many heads.   *Ibid.*

With the judgment of the angels and the sentence of the saints, we anathematize, execrate, curse and cast out Baruch de Espinosa, the whole of the sacred community assenting, in presence of the sacred books with the six hundred and thirteen precepts written therein, pronouncing against him the malediction wherewith Elisha cursed the children, and all the maledictions written in the Book of the Law.

Excommunication, July 27, 1656, of Spinoza, quoted by Will Durant, The Story of Philosophy.

Let him be accursed by day, and accursed by night; let him be accursed in his lying down, and accursed in his rising up; accursed in going out and accursed in coming in. May the Lord never more pardon or acknowledge him; may the wrath and displeasure of the Lord burn henceforth against this man, load him with all the curses written in the Book of the Law, and blot out his name from under the sky.
                                              Ibid.

Rationalism may be defined as the mental attitude which unreservedly accepts the supremacy of reason and aims at establishing a system of philosophy and ethics verifiable by experience and independent of all arbitrary assumptions of authority.

Rationalist Press Association, London, 1895; memorandum of aims and objects.

Reason unaided by revelation can prove that God exists.

Roman Catholic 1949 revised Baltimore Catechism.

Religion: a fantastic faith in gods, angels and spirits . . . a faith without any scientific foundations, Religion is being supported and maintained by the reactionary circles. It serves for the subjugation of the working people and building up the power of the exploiting bourgeois classes.

Dictionary of 20,000 foreign words and phrases, Soviet State Publishing House, quoted, Time, January 29, 1951.

Bible: A collection of fantastic legends without any scientific support . . . full of dark hints, historical mistakes and contradictions.   *Ibid.*

The Powerhouse.

A reference to the cardinal's office, Madison Avenue, New York.

The law doth punish man or woman
That steals the goose from off the
    common,
But lets the greater felon loose,
That steals the common from the goose.
                                              1764.

A rich man's war and a poor man's fight.
Slogan, draft rioters, New York, July, 1863.

Any kind of machinery used for shortening labour—except used in a cooperative society like ours—must tend to less wages, and to deprive working men of employment, and finally, either to starve them, force them into some other employment (and then reduce wages in that also), or compel them to emigrate. Now, if the working classes would socially and peacefully unite to adopt our system, no power or party could prevent their success.
*Manifesto, Cooperative Community, Ralahine, County Clare, Ireland, 1883; on introduction of the reaping machine.**

We have no rights which anyone need respect.
A sharecropper; The Nation, September 18, 1936; cf. Dred Scott decision.

We have fed you all for thousand years,
And you hail us still unfed,
Tho' there's never a dollar of all your wealth
But marks the workers' dead.
We have yielded our best to give you rest,
And you lie on crimson wool;
For if blood be the price of all your wealth,
Good God, we ha' paid in full!
Labor, a parody on a Kipling poem, quoted by Sinclair, The Cry for Justice.

Corporations have neither bodies to be kicked, nor souls to be damned.
Quoted by A. Schlesinger, Jr., The Age of Jackson.

---

* Ralahine was an Irish point of interrogation erected amidst the wilderness of capitalist thought and feudal practice, challenging both in vain for an answer. James Connolly, *Labour in Irish History.*

Marx professed to be the founder of scientific Socialism: scientists do not draw conclusions from unproved assumptions.
Hawthorn Books, 1957.

Marx (argues): just as the revolutionary bourgeoisie overthrew feudalism, so will the revolutionary proletariat overthrow the bourgeoisie; which is not logic but guesswork. *Ibid.*

Poor man's candidate and rich man's friend. *American political formula.*

Le despotism tempéré par l'assassinat
(Despotism tempered by assassination.)
A Russian noble, to Count Muenster, on the assassination of Czar Paul I, in 1800.

Peace at any price; peace and union.
Fillmore rallying cry, 1856.

No pasaran. They shall not pass.
Anti-fascist slogan, Madrid, 1936.

The cowards never started—and the weak died along the way.
Said by emigrant survivors of the Oregon trail; quoted by Bruce Catton, This Week, March 11, 1955.

Any change in whatever direction for whatever reason is strongly to be deprecated.
Credited to "a Duke of Cambridge"; quoted by Adlai Stevenson, Harper's Magazine, February, 1956.

(A liberal is) one who has both feet firmly planted in the air.

With five weapons shall we keep our land, with sword and with shield, with spade and with fork and with spear, out with the ebb, up with the flood, to fight day and night against the North-King and against the wild Viking, that all Frisians may be free, the born and the unborn, so

long as the wind from the clouds shall blow and the world shall stand.
Frisian Oath of Allegiance, quoted in New Yorker, October 21, 1956.

We . . . fraternally assembled for the public welfare, swear before high Heaven, on our hearts and on our weapons, devoted to the defense of the state, that we will remain forever united.

Abjuring every distinction of our several provinces, offering our arms and our wealth to the common country, supporting the laws which come from the National Assembly, we swear to give all possible help to each other to fulfill these sacred duties, and to fly to the help of our brothers of Paris or of any town in France which may be in danger in the cause of Liberty.
Oath of the French revolutionists, 1789. Quoted by Nicholas Halasz, Captain Dreyfus, p. 75.

Morons.—Those whose mental development is above that of an imbecile (7 years) but does not exceed that of a normal child of twelve years.
Resolutions, American Association for the Study of the Feeble-Minded, May, 1910.

A lie on the throne is a lie, still, and truth in a dungeon is truth, still; and a lie on the throne is on the way to defeat, and truth in a dungeon is on the way to victory.

Who holds the souls of children, holds the nation.

Where apathy is the master, all men are slaves.

They saye? Quhat saye they? Let them saye.
Carved over stone door, Marischal College, Aberdeen; quoted by J. D. Adams, N. Y. Times, May 12, 1937.

All mankind is divided into three classes: those that are immovable, those that are moveable, and those that move.
Arab proverb.

We are as the king, only not as rich.
Aragonese peasant saying.

The beginning of wisdom is to call things by their right names.   *Chinese proverb.*

Verité sans peur. (Truth without fear.)
French.

Wes Brot ich ess, des Lied ich sing. (Whose bread I eat, his song I sing.)
Middle High German saying.

First secure an independent income; and then practice virtue.
Greek saying quoted by Shaw, Androcles and the Lion, preface.

Gnothi seauton (Know thyself).
Meden agan (Nothing in excess).
Engraved by the Seven Wise Men, temple of Apollo, Delphi; quoted by Will Durant, Story of Philosophy.

A shipwrecked sailor, buried on this coast,
  Bids you set sail.
Full many a gallant bark, when we were
    lost,
  Weathered the gale.
Greek Anthology, quoted by William James, Pragmatism, p. 297.

The name of God is Truth.   *Hindu.*

One can stand still in a flowing stream, but not in a world of men.
Japanese proverb.

Nil credam et omnia cavebo. (Believe nothing and be on guard against everything.)   *Latin proverb.*

Vincit omnia veritas. (Truth conquers all things.)   *Ibid.*

Salus populi suprema lex esto. (The people's safety is the supreme law.) *Ibid.*

Inter arma silent leges. (In war the laws are silent.) *Ibid.*

Suppressio veri, expressio falsi. (Suppression of truth is a false representation.)
Legal maxim.

A friend is one who warns you.
Near East proverb.

The dogs bark, but the caravan passes.
Ibid.

Whoever tells the truth is chased out of nine villages. *Turkish proverb.*

Tell the truth and run.
Yugoslav proverb.

He is not an honest man who has burned his tongue and does not tell the company that the soup is hot. *Ibid.*

If you wish to know what a man is, place him in authority. *Ibid.*

St. Anselm
(1033-1109)
Archbishop of Canterbury

For I do not seek to understand that I may believe, but I believe in order to understand. For this I believe—that unless I believe, I should not understand.
Proslogium, 1.

Susan B(rownell) Anthony
(1820-1906)
American woman-suffrage advocate

Men, their rights and nothing more; women, their rights and nothing less.

Antoninus
See Marcus Aurelius Antoninus

St. Thomas Aquinas
(1225-1274)
Italian theologian

Three things are necessary for the salvation of man: to know what he ought to believe; to know what he ought to desire; and to know what he ought to do.
Two Precepts of Charity.

Law: an ordinance of reason for the common good, made by him who has care of the community. *Summa Theologica.*

Clearly the person who accepts the Church as an infallible guide will believe whatever the Church teaches. *Ibid.*

Human salvation demands the divine disclosure of truths surpassing reason. *Ibid.*

For a war to be just three conditions are necessary—public authority, just cause, right motive. *Ibid.*

That the saints may enjoy their beatitude and the grace of God more abundantly they are permitted to see the punishment of the damned in hell. *Ibid.*

If forgers and malefactors are put to death by the secular power, there is much more reason for excommunicating and even putting to death one convicted of heresy.
Ibid.

Man should not consider his material possession his own, but as common to all, so as to share them without hesitation when others are in need. *Ibid.*

God antecedently wills all men to be saved, but consequently wills some to be damned, according to the requirements of His justice. *Ibid.*

Reason in man is rather like God in the world. *Opusc. 11, 1 de Regno, 12.*

John Arbuthnot
(1667-1735)
Scottish writer, physician

All political parties die at last of swallowing their own lies.
Quoted by Garnett, Life of Emerson.

Law is a bottomless pit.
The History of John Bull, 1712.

William Archer
(1856-1924)
Scottish critic

"Theocracy" has always been the synonym for a bleak and narrow, if not a fierce and blood-stained tyranny.
Quoted in Ira L. Cardiff, What Great Men Think of Religion.

The great, dominant, all-controlling fact of this life is the innate bias of the human spirit, not towards evil, as the theologians tell us, but towards good. But for this bias, man would never have been man; he would only have been one more species of wild animal ranging a savage, uncultivated globe, the reeking battleground of sheer instinct and appetite.   *Ibid.*

Somehow and somewhere there germinated in his (man's) mind the idea that association, cooperation, would serve his ends better than unbridled egoism in the struggle for existence. Instead of "each man for himself" his motto became "each man for his family", or his tribe, or his nation, or —ultimately—"for mankind". And, at a very early stage, what made for association, cooperation, brotherhood, came to be designated a "good", while that which sinned against these upward tendencies was stigmatized as "evil."   *Ibid.*

Archimedes
(287?-212 B.C.)
Greek mathematician

Give me a lever long enough
And a prop strong enough.
I can single-handed move the world.
(Another translation: Give me a place to stand on and I will move the earth.)

R. P. Angel Maria de Arcos, S. J.
(Contemporary)
Spanish cleric

Q. What are liberal principles?
A. Those of 1789; so-called national sovereignty, freedom of religious cults, freedom of the press, freedom of instruction, universal morality, and other such.
Brief and Simple Explanation of the Catholic Catechism, imprimatur of Jacobus Vigo, S.J., with approval of the Archbishops of Granada, Spain; originally published in Boletin Oficial Eclesiastico, Vol. 54, page 28; reprinted by Administracion del Apostolado de la Prensa, translated by John Langdon-Davies, 1937.

Q. Is every Liberal government hostile to the Church?
A. Evidently, since whoever is not with Christ is against Him.   *Ibid.*

Q. Can the Church take part in politics?
A. The Church can and must take part in politics when it is a matter of faith, morals, customs, justice, and the salvation of souls.   *Ibid.*

---

* When certain British publications, finding this catechism unbelievable, libeled Langdon-Davies, he sued them and producing the originals, won his cases. *New Statesman & Nation*, November 20, 1937.

Q. Then there is no grade of Liberalism that can be good?

A. None: because Liberalism is mortal sin and anti-Christian in essence.

Q. Then whoever is liberal in politics sins?

A. Certainly; because in liberal politics there exists that Liberalism which the Church condemns.   *Ibid.*

Q. Then a Catholic must be anti-liberal?

A. Without a doubt; exactly as he must be anti-Protestant and anti-Freemason; in short, against all the contraries of Christ and his Church.   *Ibid.*

Q. What of Communism, Socialism, Modern Democracy, Anarchism, and the like sects?

A. They are contrary to Catholic faith, to justice, and to virtue, and as such condemned by the Church.   *Ibid.*

A. The liberal system is the weapon with which the accursed Jewish race makes war on our Lord Jesus Christ, on his Church, and on Christian people.   *Ibid.*

Aristotle

(384-322 B.C.)

Greek philosopher

All men naturally desire knowledge.
Metaphysics, Book A, line 1. °

Every art and every inquiry, and similarly every action and pursuit, is thought to aim at some good; and for this reason the good has rightly been declared to be that at which all things aim.   *Nicomachean Ethics.*

Anybody can become angry—that is easy; but to be angry with the right person, and to the right degree, and at the right time,

---

° "All men by nature desire to know"—translation by W. D. Ross.

and for the right purpose, and in the righ way—that is not within everybody's powe and is not easy.   *Ibid.*

As sight is in the body, so is reason i the soul.   *Ibid.*

One element in the soul is irrational an one has a rational principle.   *Ibid.*

Punishment is a sort of medicine. *Ibid.*

He does not expose himself needlessly t danger, since there are few things for whic he cares sufficiently; but he is willing, i great crises, to give even his life,—knowin that under certain conditions it is not wortl while to live.
Ethics, IV, 3. Quoted by Durant, The Story of Philosophy.

He cannot live in complaisance witl others, except it be a friend; complaisanc is the characteristic of a slave.   *Ibid.*

He is his own best friend, and take delight in privacy whereas the man of n virtue or ability is his own worst enemy and is afraid of solitude.   *Ibid.*

Man is a political animal.   *Politics, 1.*

Man, when perfected, is the best of ani mals; but when isolated he is the worst o all; for injustice is more dangerous whei armed, and man is equipped at birth witl the weapons of intelligence, and with quali ties of character which he may use for th vilest ends. Wherefore if he have not virtu he is the most unholy and savage of ani mals, full of gluttony and lust.   *Ibid.*

Men are marked out from the moment o birth to rule or be ruled.   *Ibid.*

Every state is a community of some kind and every community is established with view for some good, for men always act ir order to obtain what they think good. Bu if all communities aim at some good, the state or political organization which is the highest of all and embraces all the others, aims, and in a greater degree than any other does, at the highest good. *Ibid.*

Everyone thinks chiefly of his own, hardly ever of the public interest. *Ibid.*

A tyrant must put on the appearance of uncommon devotion to religion. Subjects are less apprehensive of illegal treatment from a ruler whom they consider godfearing and pious. On the other hand, they do less easily move against him, believing that he has the gods on his side. *Ibid.*

Revolutions are not trifles, but spring from trifles. *Ibid.*

Democracy arose from men's thinking that if they are equal in any respect, they are equal absolutely. *Ibid.*

It is characteristic of man that he alone has any sense of good and evil, or just and unjust, and the like, and the association of living things who have this sense makes a family and a state. *Ibid.*

He who is unable to live in society, or who has no need because he is sufficient for himself, must be either a beast or a god; he is no part of a state. *Ibid.*

Poverty is the parent of revolution and crime. *Ibid., bk. 2.*

The law is reason free from passion. *Ibid., bk. 3.*

The real difference between democracy and oligarchy is poverty and wealth. Wherever men rule by reason of their wealth, whether they be few or many, that is an oligarchy, and where the poor rule, that is a democracy. *Ibid.*

It is manifest that the best political community is formed by citizens of the middle class. *Ibid., bk. 4.*

Inferiors revolt in order that they may be equal, and equals that they may be superior. Such is the state of mind which creates revolutions. *Ibid., bk. 5.*

Revolutions break out when opposite parties, the rich and the poor, are equally balanced, and there is little or nothing between them; for, if either party were manifestly superior, the other would not risk an attack. *Ibid.*

All human actions have one or more of these seven causes: chance, nature, compulsions, habit, reason, passion, desire. *Rhetoric, 1.*

In democracy, liberty is to be supposed; for it is commonly held that no man is free in any other government. *Quoted by Hobbes, Leviathan.*

How many a dispute could have been deflated into a single paragraph if the disputants had dared to define their terms.

Man is by nature a social animal, and an individual who is unsocial naturally and not accidentally is either beneath our notice or more than human. Society is something in nature that precedes the individual. Anyone who either cannot lead the common life or is so self-sufficient as not to need to, and therefore does not partake of society, is either a beast or he is a god.

Woman may be said to be an inferior man.

No voice is wholly lost that is the voice of many men.

All who have meditated on the art of governing mankind have been convinced that the fate of empires depends on the education of youth.

Philosophy is the science which considers truth.

The insolence of demagogues is generally the cause of ruin in democracies. First, they calumniate the wealthy and rouse them against the government, thus causing opposite parties to unite against a common danger. Next, they produce the same result by stirring up the populace and creating a sense of insecurity. Nearly all the tyrants of old began with being demagogues.

Let men be on their guard against those who flatter and mislead the multitude: their actions prove what sort of men they are. Of the tyrant, spies and informers are the principal instruments. War is his favorite occupation, for the sake of engrossing the attention of the people, and making himself necessary to them as their leader.

The aim of art is to represent not the outward appearance of things, but their inward significance; for this, and not the external mannerism and detail, is true reality.

The artistic representation of history is a more scientific and serious pursuit than the exact writing of history. For the art of letters goes to the heart of things, whereas the factual report merely collocates details.

The good of man must be the end of the science of politics.

The tyrant, who in order to hold his power, suppresses every superiority, does away with good men, forbids education and light, controls every movement of the citizens and, keeping them under a perpetual servitude, wants them to grow accustomed to baseness and cowardice, has his spies everywhere to listen to what is said in the meetings, and spreads dissension and calumny among the citizens and impoverishes them, is obliged to make war in order to keep his subjects occupied an impose on them permanent need of a chie.

Educated men are as much superior t uneducated men as the living are to th dead.   *Quoted by Diogenes Laertius.*

Matthew Arnold
(1822-1888)
English poet, critic, essayist

Journalism is literature in a hurry.

Be neither saint nor sophist led, but b a man.

All the biblical miracles will at last dis appear with the progress of science.

The people who believe most that ou greatness and welfare are proved by ou being very rich, and who most give thei lives and thoughts to becoming rich, are just the very people whom we call Philistines. Culture says, "Consider these people then, their way of life, their habits, thei manners, the very tones of their voices, look at them attentively; observe the literature they read, the things which give them pleasure, the words which come from out of their mouths, the thoughts which make the furniture of their minds: would any amount of wealth be worth having with the condition that one has to become just like these people by having it?" And thus culture begets a dissatisfaction which is of the highest possible value in stemming the common tide of men's thoughts in a wealthy and industrial community; and which may save the future, as one may hope, from being vulgarized, even if it cannot save the present.   *Essays in Criticism.*

First and foremost of the necessary means towards man's civilization we must name *expansion*. The need of expansion is as genuine an instinct in man as the need in a plant for the light, or the need in man himself for going upright . . . The love of liberty is simply the instinct in man for expansion. *Preface, Mixed Essays, 1903.*

The armies of the homeless and unfed—
If these are yours, if this is what you are,
Then am I yours, and what you feel, I
   share.
        To a Republican Friend, 1848.

Nor will that day dawn at a human nod,
When, bursting through the network super-
   posed
By selfish occupation—plot and plan,
Lust, avarice, envy—liberated man,
All difference with his fellow mortal closed,
Shall be left standing face to face with God.
                  Ibid.

. . . that huge Mississippi of falsehood called History.
Essays. Literary Influence of Academies.

It is almost impossible to exaggerate the proneness of the human mind to take miracles as evidence, and to seek for miracles as evidence. *Literature and Dogma.*

The pursuit of perfection, then, is the pursuit of sweetness and light.
Essays on Criticism, 2nd series; Thomas Gray.

He who works for sweetness and light united, works to make reason and the will of God prevail.   *Ibid.*

And love, let us be true
To one another! for the world, which seems
To lie before us like a land of dreams,
So various, so beautiful, so new,
Hath really neither joy, nor love, nor light,
Nor certitude, nor peace, nor help for pain;
And we are here as on a darkling plain
Swept with confused alarums of struggle
   and flight,
Where ignorant armies clash by night.
             Dover Beach.

Our inequality materializes our upper class, vulgarizes our middle class, brutalizes our lower class.

Thurman (Wesley) Arnold

(1891-1969)
American lawyer, political scientist

Liberalism today has become deuces wild. It can be used to fill any hand. If I had my way, however, I would make it a criminal offense for anyone to parade under the banner of liberalism who was not conscientiously and even religiously devoted to the ideal that in an industrial democracy, freedom of opportunity is the great value that must be preserved above all others. Unless this freedom is preserved, no other freedom will be secure.
New Republic, July 22, 1946.

Arouet
See Voltaire

Asoka

(264-232 B.C.)
King of Magadha, India

It is forbidden to decry other sects; the true believer gives honor to whatever in them is worthy of honor.   *Decree.*

Astray
See Millan-Astray

Ataturk
See Kemal Ataturk

Athanasian Creed

Now the Catholic faith is this: that we worship one God in Trinity, and Trinity in Unity, neither confounding the Persons, nor dividing the substance, for there is one Person of the Father, another of the Son, and another of the Holy Ghost; but the godhead of the Father, of the Son, and of the Holy Ghost is one, the glory equal, the majesty co-eternal . . .

St. Augustine
(354-430)
Numidian Bishop of Hippo

If the thing believed is incredible, it is also incredible that the incredible should have been so believed. *The City of God.*

To confess that God exists, and at the same time to deny that He has foreknowledge of future things, is the most manifest folly. *Ibid.*

The human race we have distributed into two parts, the one consisting of those who live according to man, the other of those who live according to God. And these we also mystically call the two cities, or the two communities of men, of which the one is predestined to reign eternally with God, and the other to suffer eternal punishment with the devil. *Ibid.*

He that is good is free, though he is a slave; he that is evil is a slave, though he be a king. *Ibid., iv.*

Justice being taken away, then, what are kingdoms but great robberies? For what are robberies themselves, but little kingdoms. *Ibid.*

At the resurrection the substance of our bodies, however disintegrated, will be re-united. We maintain no fear that the omnipotence of God cannot recall all the particles that have been consumed by fire or by beasts, or dissolved into dust and ashes, or decomposed into water, or evaporated into air. *Ibid., xxii.*

Why, they ask, do not those miracles, which you preach of as past events, happen nowadays? I might reply that they were necessary before the world believed, to bring the world to believe. *Ibid.*

In fact the refutation of heretics serves to bring into light what your Church holds and what sound doctrine is. *For there must be also heresies: that they who are approved may be made manifest among the weak. Confessions.*

For you are not to suppose, brethren, that heresies could be produced through any little souls. None save great men have been the authors of heresies.
In Ps. 124, 5; quoted in The Book of Catholic Quotations.

For, were it not good that evil things should also exist, the omnipotent God would most certainly not allow evil to be, since beyond doubt it is just as easy for Him not to allow what He does not will, as it is for Him to do what He will. *Enchiridion.*

All sin is a kind of lying. *Against Lying.*

Lying is forbidden, even to the detection of heretics. *Ibid.*

Faith maintains this principle and we must believe it: Neither the soul nor the human body suffers complete annihilation; the wicked arise again for punishment beyond imagination, while the good rise again for everlasting life.
De Doctrina Christiana 1, 21, 19.

Legem non habet necessitas. (Necessity knows no law). *Soliloquium, 2.*

But those wars also are just, without doubt, which are ordained by God Him-

self, in Whom is no iniquity, and Who knows every man's merits.
Questiones in Heptateuchum.

You can force a man to enter a church, to approach the altar, to receive the Sacrament; but you cannot force him to believe.
In Joann. Evang. Tract.

No man can find salvations save in the Catholic Church. Outside the Catholic Church he can find everything save salvation.
Sermo ad Caesariensis Ecclesiae Plebem, 6.

Nothing is so much to be shunned as sex relations.   *Soliloquies, 1.*

No one sins by an act he cannot avoid.
De libero arbitrio, iii.

Salus extra ecclesiam non est. (There is no salvation outside the Church.)
De Bapt., iv.

Roma locuta est, causa finita est. (Rome has spoken, the case is ended.)
Sermons, Book I.

Understanding is the reward of faith. Therefore seek not to understand that thou mayest believe, but believe that thou mayest understand.   *On the Gospel of St. John.*

Cursed is every one who placeth his hope in man.   *On the Christian Conflict.*

The confession of evil works is the first beginning of good works.

It is a great liberty to be able not to sin; it is the greatest liberty to be unable to sin.

Faith is to believe, on the word of God, what we do not see, and its reward is to see and enjoy what we believe.

The superfluities of the rich are the necessaries of the poor. They who possess superfluities, possess the goods of others.

Neither in the confusion of paganism, nor in the defilement of heresy, nor yet in the blindness of Judaism, is religion to be sought, but among those alone who are called Catholic Christians.

All diseases of Christians are to be ascribed to demons; chiefly do they torment freshly-baptized Christians, yea, even the guiltless new-born infants.

François Émile (Gracchus) Babeuf
(1760-1797)
French revolutionist

From time immemorial it has been repeated, with hypocrisy, that *men are equal;* and from time immemorial the most degrading and the most monstrous inequality ceaselessly weighs on the human race.
Manifesto of the Equals.

We aim at something more sublime and more equitable—the common good, or the community of goods . . . We demand, we would have, the communal enjoyment of the fruits of the earth, fruits which are for everyone.   *Ibid.*

Let the revolting distinction of rich and poor disappear, once and for all, the distinction of great and small, of masters and valets, of governors and governed. Let there be no other difference between human beings than those of age and sex. Since all have the same needs and the same faculties, let there be one education for all, one food for all.   *Ibid.*

The moment has arrived for founding the Republic of Equals.   *Ibid.*

B. F. Bache
(1769-1798)
Nephew of Benjamin Franklin

If ever a nation was debauched by a man, the American nation has been debauched by Washington. If ever a nation has suffered from the improper influence of a man, the American nation has suffered from the influence of Washington. If ever a nation was deceived by a man, the American nation has been deceived by Washington. Let his conduct then be an example to future ages. Let the history of the Federal Government instruct mankind that the masque of patriotism may be worn to conceal the foulest designs against the liberties of the people.

Aurora (newspaper).

Francis Bacon
(1561-1626)
English essayist, philosopher

Liberty of Speech inviteth and provoketh liberty to be used again, and so bringeth much to a man's knowledge.
Advancement of Learning.

The sum of behaviour is to retain a man's own dignity, without intruding upon the liberty of others.   *Ibid.*

But men must know, that in this theater of man's life it is reserved only for God and the angels to be lookers on.   *Ibid.*

If a man will begin with certainties, he will end in doubts; but if he will be content to begin with doubts, he will end in certainties.   *Ibid.*

We see then how far the monuments of wit and learning are more durable than the monuments of power, or of the hands. For have not the verses of Homer continued twenty-five hundred years, or more, without the loss of a syllable or letter; during which time infinite palaces, temples, castles, cities have been decayed and demolished?
Ibid.

But this is that which will indeed dignify and exalt knowledge, if contemplation and action may be more nearly and straitly conjoined and united together than they have been; . . . that knowledge may not be as a courtesan, for pleasure and vanity only, or as a bondwoman, to acquire and gain to her master's use, but as a spouse, for generation, fruit, and comfort.   *Ibid.*

Philosophers should diligently inquire into the powers and energy of custom, exercise, habit, education, example, imitation, emulation, company, friendship, praise, reproof, exhortation, reputation, laws, books, studies, etc.; for these are the things that reign in men's morals; by these agents the mind is formed and subdued.   *Ibid.*

A little philosophy inclineth a man's mind to atheism; but depth in philosophy bringeth men's minds about to religion. For while the mind of men looketh upon second causes scattered, it may sometimes rest in them and go no further; but when it beholdeth the chain of them, confederate and linked together, it must needs fly to Providence and Deity.
Essays. On Atheism.

Custom is the principal magistrate of man's life.   *Ibid. Of Custom.*

Men commonly think according to their inclinations, speak according to their learning and imbibed opinions, but generally according to custom.   *Ibid.*

The desire of power in excess caused angels to fall; the desire of knowledge in excess caused man to fall; but in charity is no excess, neither can man or angels come into danger by it.   *Ibid. Of Goodness.*

The ways to enrich are many, and most of them foul.   *Ibid. On Riches.*

Usury is the certainest means of gain, though one of the worst; as that whereby a man doth eat his bread with sweat of another's face, and besides, doth plough upon Sundays.   *Ibid.*

I cannot call riches by a better name than the "baggage" of virtue; the Roman word is better, "impediment." For as the baggage is to an army, so are riches to virtue. It cannot be spared or left behind, and yet it hindereth the march; yea, and the care of it sometimes loseth or disturbeth the victory.   *Ibid.*

Of great riches there is no real use, except in the distribution; the rest is but conceit.   *Ibid.*

The causes and motives of sedition are, innovation in religion; taxes; alteration of laws and customs; breaking of privileges; general oppression; advancement of unworthy persons, strangers; dearths; disbanded soldiers; factions grown desperate; and whatsoever in offending a people joineth them in a common cause.
Ibid. Of Seditions and Troubles.

When any of the four pillars of the government, religion, justice, counsel, and treasure, are mainly shaken or weakened, men have need to pray for fair weather. *Ibid.*

Superstition is the reproach of the Deity.
Ibid.

Money is like muck, not good unless it be spread.   *Ibid.*

The inquiry of truth, which is the love-making or wooing of it; the knowledge of truth, which is the praise of it; and the belief of truth, which is the enjoying of it, is the sovereign good of human nature.
Ibid. Of Truth.

He that hath wife and children hath given hostages to fortune; for they are impediments to great enterprises, either of virtue or mischief.
Of Marriage and Single Life.

The mind is the man, and knowledge mind; a man is but what he knoweth.
The Praise of Knowledge.

Seek ye first the good things of the mind, and the rest will either be supplied or its loss will not be felt.   *Ibid.*

Man, being the servant and interpreter of nature, can do and understand so much and so much only as he has observed in fact or in thought of the course of nature: beyond this he neither knows anything nor can do anything.
Novum Organum, Aphorism i.

Knowledge and human power are synonymous.   *Ibid.*

One method of delivery alone remains to us; which is simply this: we must lead men to the particulars themselves; and their series and order; while men on their side must force themselves for awhile to lay their notions by and begin to familiarize themselves with facts.   *Ibid., xxxvi.*

There are four classes of idols which beset men's minds. To these for distinction's sake I have assigned names,—calling the first class *Idols of the Tribe;* the second, *Idols of the Cave;* the third, *Idols of the Market-place;* the fourth, *Idols of the Theater.*   *Ibid., xxxix.*

The Idols of the Tribe have their foundation in human nature itself, and in the tribe or race of men. For it is a false assertion that the sense of man is the measure of things. On the contrary, all perceptions, as well of the sense as of the mind, are according to the measures of the individual and not according to the measure of the universe. *Ibid., xli.*

For it is by discourse that men associate; and words are imposed according to the apprehension of the vulgar. And therefore the ill and unfit choice of words wonderfully obstructs the understanding. . . . Words plainly force and overrule the understanding, and throw all into confusion, and lead men away into numberless empty controversies and idle fancies. *Ibid., xliii.*

The human understanding is no dry light, but receives infusion from the will and affections; whence proceed sciences which may be called "sciences as one would." For what a man had rather were true he more readily believes. Therefore he rejects difficult things from impatience of research; sober things, because they narrow hope; the deeper things of nature, from superstition; the light of experience, from arrogance and pride; things not commonly believed, out of deference to the opinion of the vulgar. Numberless in short are the ways, and sometimes imperceptible, in which the affections color and infect the understanding. *Ibid., xlix.*

There are found some minds given to an extreme admiration of antiquity, others to an extreme love and appetite for novelty; but few so duly tempered that they can hold the mean, neither carping at what has been well laid down by the ancients, nor despising what is well introduced by the moderns. *Ibid., lvi.*

And generally let every student of nature take this as a rule—that whatever the mind seizes and dwells upon with peculiar

satisfaction is to be held in suspicion, and that so much the more care is to be taken in dealing with such questions to keep the understanding even and clear.

Ibid., lviii.

But the *Idols of the Market-place* are the most troublesome of all idols which have crept into the understanding through the alliances of words and names. For men believe that their reason governs words; but it is also true that words react on the understanding and this it is that had rendered philosophy and the sciences sophistical and inactive. Now words, being commonly framed and applied according to the capacity of the vulgar, follow those lines of division which are most obvious to the vulgar understanding. And whenever understanding of greater acuteness or a more diligent observation would alter those lines to suit the true divisions of nature, words stand in the way and resist the change. Whence it comes to pass that the high and formal discussions of learned men end oftentimes in disputes about words and names; with which (according to the use and wisdom of the mathematicians) it would be more prudent to begin, and so by means of definitions reduce them to order.

Ibid., lix.

It will not be amiss to distinguish the three kinds and as it were three grades of ambition in mankind. The first is of those who desire to extend their own power in their native country; which kind is vulgar and degenerate. The second is of those who labor to extend the power of their country and its dominion among men. This certainly has more dignity, though not less covetousness. But if a man endeavor to establish and extend the power and dominion of the human race itself over the universe, his ambition (if ambition it can be called) is without doubt both a more wholesome thing and a more noble than the other two. Now the empire of man over things depends wholly on the arts and sciences. For we cannot command nature except by obeying her.   *Ibid., cxxix.*

"What is truth?" said jesting Pilate and would not stay for an answer. *Essays, I.*

Nam et ipsa scientia potestas est. Knowledge itself is power.
Religious Meditations. Of Heresies.

Roger Bacon
(1214?-1292)
Franciscan theologian

There are four chief obstacles in grasping truth, which hinder every man, however learned, and scarcely allow any one to win a clear title to learning, namely, submission to faulty and unworthy authority, influence of custom, popular prejudice, and concealment of our own ignorance accompanied by an ostentatious display of our knowledge.
Opus Majus, trans. by R. B. Burke, 1928.

There are two modes of acquiring knowledge, namely by reasoning and experience. Reasoning draws a conclusion and makes us grant the conclusion, but does not make the conclusion certain, nor does it remove doubt so that the mind may rest on the intuition of truth, unless the mind discovers it by the path of experience.
Ibid.

He therefore who wishes to rejoice without doubt in regard to the truths underlying phenomena must know how to devote himself to experiment.   *Ibid.*

George F. Baer
(1842-1914)
American railroad industrialist

The rights and interests of the laboring man will be protected and cared for—not by the labor agitators, but by the Christian gentlemen to whom God has given control of the property rights of the country and upon the successful management of which so much depends.
Letter to W. F. Clark, Wilkes-Barre, Pa., during the great anthracite strike, 1902. Labor, April 1, 1950.

Baron Jacques Baeyens
(Contemporary)
French foreign office press chief

Mentir et dementir. (Lie and deny.)
Definition of a diplomatic spokesman; by the French Foreign Office press chief; Time, 1954.

Walter Bagehot
(1826-1877)
English economist

The tyranny of the commonplace, which seems to accompany civilization.
The English Constitution.

You may talk of the tyranny of Nero and Tiberius, but the real tyranny is the tyranny of your next-door neighbor. What espionage of despotism comes to your door so effectively as the eye of the man who lives at your door? Public opinion is a permeating influence. It requires us to think other men's thoughts, to speak other men's words, to follow other men's habits.
Ibid.

Nine-tenths of modern science is in this respect the same: it is the produce of men

whom their contemporaries thought dreamers—who were laughed at for caring for what did not concern them—who, as the proverb went, "walked into a well from looking at the stars"—who were believed to be useless, if anyone could be such.
Ibid.

The whole history of civilization is strewn with creeds and institutions which were invaluable at first, and deadly afterwards.
Physics and Politics.

One of the greatest pains to human nature is the pain of a new idea. *Ibid.*

So long as there are earnest believers in the world, they will always wish to punish opinions, even if their judgment tells them it is unwise and their conscience that it is wrong. *Literary Studies.*

Pascal said that most of the evils of life arose from "man's being unable to sit still in a room." *The Practical Cogitator.*

There are lies, damned lies, and church statistics. *Cf. Disraeli.*

Early law is hardly to be separated from religious ritual; it is more like the tradition of a Church than the enactments of a statute-book.
The Metaphysical Basis of Toleration, Contemporary Review, April, 1874.

Persecution in intellectual countries produces a superficial conformity, but also underneath an intense, incessant, implacable doubt. *Ibid.*

It was government by discussion that broke the bond of ages and set free the originality of mankind.
Quoted by Adlai Stevenson, Harper's, February, 1956.

Baha 'u 'llah
(1817-1892)
Religious leader

Truths for a New Day
1. The oneness of mankind.
2. Independent investigation of truth.
3. The foundation of all religions is one.
4. Religion must be the cause of unity.
5. Religion must be in accord with science and reason.
6. Equality between men and women.
7. Prejudice of all kinds must be forgotten.
8. Universal peace.
9. Universal education.
10. Spiritual solution of the economic problem.
11. A universal language.
12. An international tribunal.

Promulgated by 'Abdu'l-Bahá, in North America, 1912.

Mikhail A. Bakunin *
(1814-1876)
Russian anarchist, writer

I shall die and the worms will eat me, but I want our idea to triumph. I want the masses of humanity to be truly emancipated from all authorities and from all heroes, present and to come.
Quoted by Eugene Pyziur, The Doctrine of Anarchism of Michael A. Bakunin, 1955, p. 6.

You are mistaken if you think I do not believe in God. . . . I seek God in man,

---

* Chief opponent of Karl Marx, an influence on both Lenin and Mussolini; appears in fiction in Turgenev and probably is Dostoyevski's Prince Stavrogin in *The Possessed.*

in human freedom, and now I seek God in revolution. *Ibid., p. 50.*

Throw theory into the fire; it only spoils life. *Letter to sisters, November 4, 1842.*

The passion for destruction (is) a creative passion.°
Reaction in Germany, Ruge's Deutsche Yahrbuecher, 1842.

The liberty of man consists solely in this, that he obeys the laws of nature, because he has himself recognized them as such, and not because they have been imposed upon him externally by any foreign will whatsoever, human or divine, collective or individual.
Dieu et l'État, posthumously published, 1882.

Priests, kings, statesmen, soldiers, bankers, and public functionaries; policemen, jailers and hangmen; capitalists, usurers, business men and property-owners; lawyers, economists and politicians—all of them, down to the meanest grocer, repeat in chorus the words of Voltaire, that if there were no God it would be necessary to invent Him. *Ibid.*

All religions, with their gods, demigods, prophets, messiahs and saints, are the product of the fancy and credulity of men who have not yet reached the full development and complete personality of their intellectual powers. *Ibid.*

There are but three ways for the populace to escape its wretched lot. The first two are by the route of the wine-shop or the church; the third is by that of the social revolution. *Ibid.*

° "The desire to destroy is also a creative desire"—quoted by Edmund Wilson, *To the Finland Station, p. 267.* Also translated as "The urge to destroy is a creative urge."

All law has for its object to confirm and exalt into a system the exploitation of the workers by a ruling class. *Ibid.*

Our first work must be the annihilation of everything as it now exists. *Ibid.*

The old world must be destroyed and replaced by a new one. When you have freed your mind from the fear of God, and that childish respect for the fiction of right, then all the remaining chains that bind you—property, marriage, morality, and justice—will snap asunder like threads. *Ibid.*

It is the peculiarity of privilege and of every privileged position to kill the intellect and heart of man. The privileged man, whether he be privileged politically or economically, is a man depraved in intellect and heart.
Quoted, Encyclopaedia Britannica.

In a word, we object to all legislation, all authority, and all influence, privileged, official and legal, even when it has proceeded from universal suffrage, convinced that it must always turn to the profit of a dominating and exploiting minority, against the interests of the immense majority enslaved.
Ibid.

The revolutionist is a doomed man. He has no personal interests, no affairs, sentiments, attachments, property, not even a name of his own. Everything in him is absorbed by one exclusive interest, one thought, one passion—the revolution.
Catechism of the Revolution (The Nechaev Catechism), Article 1.

To him (the revolutionist) whatever aids the triumph of the revolution is ethical; all that which hinders it is unethical and criminal. *Ibid. Article 4.*

The revolutionist despises every sort of doctrinairism and has renounced the peaceful scientific pursuits, leaving them to future generations. He knows only one science, the science of destruction.   *Ibid. Article 5.*

Theology is the science of the divine lie, jurisprudence the science of the human lie, and metaphysics and idealistic philosophy the science of any half-lie.

Gesammelte Werke, Golos Trude edition, I, 184-5. Quoted by Pyziur.

If there is a State, then there is domination, and in turn there is slavery.

Ibid., p. 233.

They (the Marxists) say that such a yoke, the dictatorship of the state, is the inevitable but transitional remedy for achieving the maximum liberation of the people. . . . We answer that any dictatorship can have only one aim: self-perpetuation. *Ibid., p. 255.*

If there is a human being who is freer than I, then I shall necessarily become his slave. If I am freer than any other, then he will become my slave. Therefore equality is an absolutely necessary condition of freedom.

The first duty . . . is that of making every effort for the triumph of equality. . . .

This is the entire program of revolutionary socialism, of which equality is the first condition, the first word. It admits freedom only after equality, in equality and through equality, because freedom outside of equality can only create privilege.

Ibid., II, 74.

It is necessary to abolish completely, in principle and in practice, everything which may be called political power. As long as political power exists there will always be rulers and ruled, masters and slaves, exploiters and exploited.   *Ibid., III, 22.*

Revolutions are not improvised. They are not made at will by individuals. They come through the force of circumstances, and are independent of any deliberate will or conspiracy. They can be foreseen, but their explosion can never be accelerated.

Ibid., IV, 21.

Man has liberated himself (by breaking the divine commandment not to eat of the tree of knowledge), he has divided himself from animal nature and made himself man; he began his history and his human development with this act of disobedience and knowledge, i.e., with rebellion and thought.

Gesammelte Werke, I, 102.

Collective property and individual property, these two banners will be the standards under which, from now on, the great battles of the future will be fought. *Ibid., II, 67.*

From the naturalistic point of view, all men are equal. There are only two exceptions to this rule of naturalistic equality: geniuses and idiots.   *Ibid., 249.*

Freedom is the absolute right of all adult men and women to seek permission for their action only from their own conscience and reason, and to be determined in their actions only by their own will, and consequently to be responsible only to themselves, and then to the society to which they belong, but only insofar as they have made a free decision to belong to it.   *Ibid., III, 9.*

If one would make a thorough revolution, one must attack things and relationships, destroy property and the State. Then there would be no need to destroy men.

Ibid., 87.

No revolution can count on success if it does not speedily spread beyond the individual to all other nations.   *Ibid., 91.*

To my utter despair I have discovered, and discover every day anew, that there is in the masses no revolutionary idea or hope or passion.

(*Written in 1876*), *Ibid.*, 272.

The State is force; nay, it is the silly parading of force. However many pains it may take, it cannot conceal the fact that it is the legal maimer of our will, the constant negation of our liberty. Even when it commands good, it makes this valueless by commanding it, for every command slaps liberty in the face.

Polnoye Sobraniye Sochinenii, I, pp. 17-18.

Powerful states can maintain themselves only by crime, little states are virtuous only by weakness.   *Selected Works, p. 211.*

The State . . . will become nothing more than a simple business office, a sort of central bookkeeping department, devoted to the service of Society.   *Ibid., 222.*

The subordination of labor to capital is the source of all slavery: political, moral and material.   *Ibid., 265.*

1. The International claims for each worker the full product of his labor: finding it wrong that there should be in society so many men who, producing nothing at all, can maintain their insolent riches only by the work of others. The International, like the apostle St. Paul, maintains that "if any would not work, neither should he eat."

Address, Working People's International Ass'n, 1867.

6. That the proletariat ought to tend, not to the establishment of a new rule or of a new class for its own profit, but to the definitive abolition of all rule, of every class, by the organization of justice, liberty, and equality for all human beings, without distinction of race, color, nationality, or faith

—all to fully exercise the same duties and enjoy the same rights.   *Ibid.*

The human race, like all the other animal races, has inherent principles which are peculiar to it, and all these principles are summed up in or reducible to a single principle which we call Solidarity. This principle may be formulated thus: no human individual can recognize his own humanity, or, consequently, realize it in life, except by recognizing it in others and by co-operating in its realization for others. No man can emancipate himself save by emancipating with him all the men about him. My liberty is the liberty of everybody, for I am really free, free not only in idea, but in fact, only when my liberty and my right find their confirmation, their sanction, in the liberty and right of all men, my equals. *Ibid.*

(The State is) the sum of all the negations of the individual liberty of all its members; or rather that of the sacrifices which all its members make, in renouncing one portion of their liberty to the profit of the common good.

Oeuvres, Vol. I, p. 143; quoted by Adler, The Idea of Freedom, p. 374.

Where the State begins, individual liberty ceases, and vice versa.   *Ibid.*

Liberty is indivisible.   *Ibid.*

All temporal or human authority proceeds directly from spiritual or divine authority.

But authority is the negation of liberty. God, or rather the fiction of God, is thus the sanction and the intellectual and moral cause of all the slavery on earth, and the liberty of men will not be complete, unless it will have completely annihilated the inauspicious fiction of a heavenly master.

Ibid., p. 283; quoted by Adler, p. 374.

Next, and as a consequence, the revolt of each against the tyranny of men, against the authority, individual as much as social, represented and legalized by the State.

Ibid.

I have in mind the only liberty worthy of that name, liberty consisting in the full development of all the material, intellectual, and moral powers latent in every man; a liberty which does not recognize any other restrictions but those which are traced by the laws of our own nature, which, properly speaking, is tantamount to saying that there is no restriction at all, since these laws are not imposed upon us by some outside legislator standing above us, or alongside us.

The Political Philosophy of Bakunin, p. 270; quoted by Adler, op. cit., p. 395.

We wish, in a word, equality—equality in fact as corollary, or, rather, as primordial condition of liberty. From each according to his faculties, to each according to his needs; that is what we wish sincerely.

Declaration signed by forty-seven Anarchists after failure of uprising at Lyons, 1870.

Arthur J. Balfour
(1848-1930)
English statesman, essayist

His Majesty's Government views with favour the establishment in Palestine of a national home for the Jewish people, and will use their best endeavors to facilitate the achievement of this object, it being clearly understood that nothing shall be done which shall prejudice the civil and religious rights of existing non-Jewish communities in Palestine, or the rights and political status enjoyed by the Jews in any other country.

Communication, to Lord Rothschild, 1917; known as The Balfour Declaration.

John Ball
(hanged 1381)
English priest, social agitator

Whan Adam dalfe and Eve span
Who was thanne a gentil man?
Text of sermon to the rebels at Blackheath.

With ryght and with myght, with sky and with wylle, lat myght helpe ryght, and skyl go before wylle and ryght before myght than goth oure mylne aryght. And if mygh go before ryght, and wylle before skylle than is oure mylne mys adyght.

Henry Knighton, Chronicon.

John Balle, seynte Marye prist, grete wele alle maner men and byddes them in the name of the Trinity, Fadur, and Sone and Holy Gost, stonde Manylche togedyr in trewth, and helpeth trewthe and trewthe schal helpe yowe.

Prima epistola Johannis Balle.

Ah, ye good people, the matters goeth not well to pass in England, nor shall no do till everything be common, and there shall be no villeins nor gentlemen, but that we may be all united together, and that the lords be no greater masters than we be.

"How the Commons of England Rebelled Against the Noblemen" (1381), Chronicles of Froissart, 1523.

We be all come from one father and one mother, Adam and Eve: whereby can they say or shew that they be greater lords than we be, saving by that they cause us to win and labour for that they dispend? They are clothed in velvet and camlet furred with grise and we be vestured with poor cloth; they have their wines, spices and good bread and we have the drawings out of the chaff and drink water: they dwell in fair houses and we have the pain and travail, rain and wind in the fields; and by that that cometh of our labours they keep and maintain their estates: we be called their bondmen, and without we do readily them service, we be beaten; and we have no sovereign to whom we may complain, nor that will hear us nor do us right.　　*Ibid.*

Hosea Ballou
(1771-1852)
American theologian

Weary the path that does not challenge. Doubt is an incentive to truth and patient inquiry leadeth the way.

Not the least misfortune in a prominent falsehood is the fact that tradition is apt to repeat it for truth.

A religion that requires persecution to sustain it is of the devil's propagation.

The oppression of any people for opinion's sake has rarely had any other effect than to fix those opinions deeper, and render them more important.

Honoré de Balzac
(1799-1850)
French novelist

Bureaucracy is a giant mechanism operated by pygmies.

If I had remained another day in that horrible . . . United States, where there is neither hope nor faith, nor charity, I should have died without being sick.
Quoted in Life, September 12, 1955.

George Bancroft
(1800-1891)
American historian

Where the people possess no authority, their rights obtain no respect.
To the Workingmen of Northampton, Boston Courier, October 22, 1834.

Show me one instance where popular institutions have violated the rights of property, and I will show you a hundred, nay a thousand instances, where the people have been pillaged by the greedy cupidity of a privileged class.　　*Ibid.*

There is more danger from monopolies than from combinations of workingmen. There is more danger that capital will swallow up the profits of labor, than that labor will confiscate capital.　　*Ibid.*

The feud between the capitalist and laborer, the house of Have and the house of Want, is as old as social union, and can never be entirely quieted; but he who will act with moderation, prefer fact to theory, and remember that everything in this world is relative and not absolute, will see that the violence of the contest may be stilled.
Ibid.

·The cause of democracy is the cause of pure religion not less than that of justice; it is the cause of practical Christianity.
To Sylvester Judd, et al., Boston Courier, October 22, 1834.

Democracy has given to conscience absolute liberty.
Address to the Democratic Elector of Massachusetts, Boston Post, October 16, 1835.

If reason is a universal faculty, the decision of the common mind is the nearest criterion of truth.　　*Ibid.*

The exact measure of the progress of civilization is the degree in which the intelligence of the common mind has prevailed over wealth and brute force; in other words, the measure of the progress of civilization is the progress of the people.
Address, Historical Society, New York, 1854.

The best government rests on the people, and not on the few, on persons and not on property, on the free development of public opinion and not on authority.

The prejudices of ignorance are more easily removed than the prejudices of interest; the first are all blindly adopted, the second willfully preferred.

Ewald Banse
(1883-1953)
German military philosopher

Nobody should be in doubt that war stands between our prevailing need and our coming fortune. But war is today no more a fresh and frolicsome campaign, with regimental music and victorious colors and a cornucopia of decorations; it is a bloody battle, and in particular a contest of *materiel*; it is gas and plague, it is tank and aircraft horror, it is hunger and poverty, it is baseness and falsehood, it is deprivation and sacrifice. Only a nation can endure in whose every member has known for years . . . that his life belongs to the state.
Wehrwissenschaft.

Bertrand Barère de Vienzac
(1755-1841)
French revolutionist

L'arbre de la liberté ne croit qu'arrosé par le sang des tyrans. (The tree of liberty will grow only when watered by the blood of tyrants.)*
Speech, National Assembly, 1792.

Joel Barlow
(1754-1812)
Diplomat, poet, libertarian

Banish the mysticism of inequality and

---

* See Jefferson, 1787.

you banish almost all of the evils attendant on human nature.
Quoted by Justice Douglas, An Almanac of Liberty.

The tyrannies of the world, whatever be the appellation of the government under which they are exercised, are all aristocratical tyrannies. An Ordinance to plunder and murder, whether it culminate from the Vatican, or steal silently forth from the Harem; whether it come clothed in the *certain science* of a Bed of Justice, or in the legal solemnities of a bench of lawyers; whether it be purchased by the caresses of a woman, or the treasures of a nation—never confines its effects to the benefit of a single individual; it goes to enrich the whole combination of conspirators, whose business it is to dupe and to govern the nation.
Advice to the Privileged Orders.

Among beings so nearly equal in power and capacity as men of the same community are, it is impossible that a solitary tyrant should exist. Laws that are designed to operate unequally on society must offer an exclusive interest to a considerable portion of its members, to ensure their execution upon the rest. Hence has arisen the necessity of that strange complication in the governing power which has made of politics an inexplicable science; hence the reason for arming one class of our fellow creatures with the weapons of bodily destruction, and another with the mysterious artillery of the vengeance of heaven. *Ibid.*

Jerome D. Barnum
(b. 1888)
American publisher

The daily press has more power in the

shaping of public opinion than any other force in America.

Presidential address, American Newspaper Publishers Association convention, 1936.

Phineas T(aylor) Barnum
(1810-1891)
American showman

Advertising made me.
Said to President Grant, in reply to remark, "You are better known than I am"; Editor & Publisher, July 31, 1934.

A sucker is born every minute.
Quoted by Harold L. Ickes, N. Y. Post, November 24, 1947.

More persons, on the whole, are humbugged by believing nothing, than by believing too much.
Ladies' Home Journal, September, 1957.

Alan Barth
(b. 1906)
American writer

Character assassination is at once easier and surer than physical assault; and it involves far less risk for the assassin. It leaves him free to commit the same deed over and over again, and may, indeed, win him the honors of a hero even in the country of his victims.
The Loyalty of Free Men, 1951.

Loyalty in a free society depends upon the toleration of disloyalty. *Ibid.*

If tolerance of diversity involves an admitted element or risk to national unity, intolerance involves a certainty that unity will be destroyed. *Ibid.*

Thought that is silenced is always rebellious . . . Majorities, of course, are often mistaken. This is why the silencing of minorities is necessarily dangerous. Criticism and dissent are the indispensable antidote to major delusions. *Ibid.*

Tolerance of diversity is imperative, because without it, life would lose its savor. Progress in the arts, in the sciences, in the patterns of social adjustment springs from diversity and depends upon a tolerance of individual deviations from conventional ways and attitudes. *Ibid.*

Karl Barth
(1886-1968)
Swiss theologian

Conscience is the perfect interpreter of life.
The Word of God and the Word of Man, translated by Douglas Horton, 1958.

We have before us the fiendishness of business competition and the world war, passion and wrongdoing, antagonism between classes and moral depravity within them, economic tyranny above and the slave spirit below. *Ibid.*

The righteousness of God itself has slowly changed from being the surest of facts into being the highest among various high ideals; and is now at all events our very own affair. This is evident in our ability now to hang it gayly out of the window and now to roll it up again, somewhat like a flag. *Eritis sicut Deus!* You may act as if you were God, you may with ease take his righteousness under your own management. *Ibid.*

Is it not remarkable that the greatest atrocities of life—I think of the capitalistic system and of the war—can justify themselves on purely moral principles? The devil may also make use of morality. *Ibid.*

Bernard M. Baruch
(1870-1965)
American financier

We are in the midst of a cold war.
Statement, Senate War Investigating Committee, October 24, 1948.

Take the profits out of war.

Never follow the crowd.
Advice to investors; Time, February 25, 1957.

I never made a cent out of the sweat of another man.
Interview with George Seldes, for article in Who, 1936.

Whatever men attempt, they seem driven to overdo. I always repeat to myself, "Two and two still make four, and no one has ever invented a way of getting something for nothing." *Time, August 19, 1957.*

When the outlook is steeped in pessimism, I remind myself, "Two and two still make four, and you can't keep mankind down for long." *Ibid*

Society can progress only if men's labors show a profit—if they yield more than is put in. To produce at a loss must leave less for all to share.
Baruch: My Own Story, 1957.

How young she (America) is! It will be centuries before she will adopt that maturity of custom, the clothing of the grave, that some people believe she is already fitted for
Address, May 23, 1944.

The sinews of war are five—men, money materials, maintenance (food) and morale.
A Few Kind Words for Uncle Sam, Saturday Evening Post, 1930.

St. Basil
(330?-379?)
Bishop of Caesarea

Drunkenness is the ruin of reason. It is premature old age. It is temporary death.
Homilies.

The bread that you store up belongs to the hungry; the cloak that lies in your chest belongs to the naked; and the gold that you have hidden in the ground belongs to the poor. *Ibid.*

Such are the rich. Because they preoccupy common goods, they take these goods as their own. If everyone would take only according to his needs and would leave the surplus to the needy, no one would be rich, no one poor, no one in misery.

Fulgencio Batista
(1901-1973)
Former dictator of Cuba

A government needs one hundred soldiers for every guerilla it faces.
Telephone conversation with Rafael Herrera, editor, El Caribe, N.Y.C., January 1, 1959.

Vicki Baum
(1888-1960)
American writer

To be a Jew is a destiny.
And Life Goes On.

Ferdinand Christian Baur
(1792-1860)
German theologian

These Gospels (the first four of the New Testament) are spurious, and were written in the Second century.

Charles A(ustin) Beard
(1874-1948)
American historian

The germinal idea of class and group conflicts in history appeared in the writings of Aristotle, long before the Christian era, . . . It was expounded by James Madison, in No. X of *The Federalist*, written in defense of the Constitution of the United States, long before Karl Marx was born.
The Economic Interpretation of the Constitution of the United States, 1935, introduction.

The movement for the Constitution of the United States was originated and carried through principally by four groups of personal interests which had been adversely affected under the Articles of Confederation: money, public securities, manufactures, and trade and shipping. *Ibid.*

The propertyless masses under the prevailing suffrage qualifications were excluded at the outset from participation in the work of framing the Constitution.

The members of the Philadelphia conventions which drafted the Constitution were, with a few exceptions, immediately, directly, and personally interested in, and derived economic advantages from the establishment of the new system.

The Constitution was essentially an economic document. *Ibid.*

The Constitution was essentially an economic document based upon the concept that the fundamental rights of private property are anterior to government and morally beyond the reach of popular majorities.
Ibid., conclusion.

Fascism is a dictatorship, and a dictatorship is an authority possessing irresponsible power. . . . Fascism is an effort to freeze the economic crisis arising from the application of great technology—to freeze it by the pressure of military forces sustained openly or tacitly by the middle classes.

One of the best ways to get yourself a reputation as a dangerous citizen these days is to go about repeating the very phrases which our founding fathers used in the great struggle for Independence.

All despotisms, under whatever name they masquerade, are efforts to freeze history, to stop change, to solidify the human spirit.

Class and group divisions based on property lie at the basis of modern governments; and politics and constitutional law are inevitably a reflex of these contending interests.

Charles A(ustin) Beard
(1874-1948)
and
Mary R. Beard
(1876-1958)
American historians

Neither the Declaration of Independence nor the Articles of Confederation nor any of the first state constitutions had mentioned the word "republic." At the time it was like a red flag to conservatives everywhere.
Basic History of the United States, p. 121.

Pierre de Beaumarchais
(1732-1799)
French dramatist

Calumniate, calumniate; there will always be something which will stick.
Barber of Seville.

Be commonplace and creeping, and you will be a success. *Ibid.*

August Bebel
(1840-1913)
German socialist, writer

In time of war the loudest patriots are the greatest profiteers.
Speech, Reichstag, November, 1870.

All political questions, all matters of right, are at bottom only questions of might. *Ibid., July 3, 1871.*

Christianity is the enemy of liberty and of civilization. It has kept mankind in chains. *Ibid., March 31, 1881.*

Anti-Semitism is the Socialism of fools.
Antisemitismus und Sozialdemokratie, October 27, 1893.

The field of politics always presents the same struggle. There are the Right and the Left, and in the middle is the Swamp. The Swamp is made up of know-nothings, of them who are without ideas, of them who are always with the majority.
Address, Social-Democratic Party Congress, 1903.

When Socialism comes into power, the Roman Church will advocate Socialism with the same vigor it is now favoring feudalism and slavery.
Address, Social Democratic Party Congress, Jena, 1906.

If in the course of this great battle for the emancipation of the human race we should fall, those now in the rear will step forward; and we shall fall with the consciousness of having done our duty as human beings, and with the conviction that the goal will be reached, however the powers hostile to humanity may struggle or strain in resistance. *Ours is the world, despite everything; that is, for the workers and the women.*
Woman.

We aim in the domain of politics at republicanism; in the domain of economic at socialism; in the domain of what is today called religion, at atheism.
Summary of Views.

Cesare Bonesana di Beccaria
(1738?-1794)
Italian economist

It is better to prevent crimes than to punish them.
Dei Delitti e delle Pene (On Crimes and Punishments), 1764.

There are three sources of the moral and political principles which govern mankind, namely, revelation, natural law, and social conventions. . . . There are, then, three distinct kinds of virtue and vice—the religious, the natural, and the political.
Ibid.

A contradiction between the laws and the natural feelings of mankind arises from the oaths which are required of an accused, to the effect that he will be a truthful man when it is his greatest interest to be false; as if a man could really swear to contribute to his own destruction, or as if religion would not be silent with most men when their interest spoke on the other side.
Ibid.

How useless oaths are has been shown by experience, for every judge will bear me out when I say that no oath has ever yet made any criminal speak the truth; and the same thing is shown by reason, which declares all laws to be useless, and consequently injurious which are opposed to the natural sentiments of man. *Ibid.*

Happy is the nation without a history.
Ibid., introduction.

Henry Ward Beecher
(1813-1887)
American clergyman, writer

The real democratic idea is, not that every man shall be on a level with every other, but that every one shall have liberty, without hindrance, to be what God made him.   *The Dishonest Politician.*

Life represents the efforts of men to organize society; government, the efforts of selfishness to overthrow liberty.
Proverbs from Plymouth Pulpit.

The ignorant classes are the dangerous classes.   *Ibid.*

Doctrine is nothing but the skin of truth set up and stuffed.
Life Thoughts.

Is the great working class oppressed? Yes, undoubtedly it is. God has intended the great to be great and the little to be little. *New York Times, July 30, 1877.*

There is tonic in the things that men do not love to hear; and there is damnation in the things that wicked men love to hear. Free speech is to a great people what winds are to oceans and malarial regions, which waft away the elements of disease, and bring new elements of health; and where free speech is stopped miasma is bred, and death comes fast.

Perfect emancipation is effected only when the mind is permitted to form, to express, and to employ its own convictions of truth on all subjects, as it chooses.

A conservative young man has wound up his life before it was unreeled. We expect old men to be conservative but when a nation's young men are so, its funeral bell is already rung.

Greatness lies not in being strong, but in the right use of strength.

Now comes the mystery.
(on his deathbed.)

Whatever is only almost true is quite false, and among the most dangerous of errors, because being so near truth, it is the more likely to lead astray.

Precise knowledge is the only true knowledge, and he who does not teach exactly, does not teach at all.

Nothing dies so hard, or rallies so often, as intolerance.

The trade union, which originated under the European system, destroys liberty. I do not say a dollar a day is enough to support a working man, but it is enough to support a man. Not enough to support a man and five children if a man insists on smoking and drinking beer.

Lyman Beecher
(1775-1863)
American clergyman

No great advance has ever been made in science, politics, or religion, without controversy.

Max Beerbohm
(1872-1956)
English writer, caricaturist

To destroy is still the strongest instinct of our nature.   *Yet Again, 1923, p. 6.*

Every kind of writing is hypocritical.

The Nonconformist Conscience makes cowards of us all.
King George the Fourth.

Ludwig van Beethoven
(1770-1827)
German composer

Beethoven can write music, thank God—but he can do nothing else on earth.
Letter to Ferdinand Ries.

Applaud friends, the comedy is over.
(on his deathbed.)

Aphra Behn
(1640-1689)
English dramatist, novelist, poet

A brave world, Sir, full of religion, knavery and change!

He that will live in this world must be endowed with three rare qualities of dissimulation, equivocation, and mental reservation.

Clive Bell
(1881-1964)
English writer

Civilized people can talk about anything. For them no subject is taboo. . . . In civilized societies there will be no intellectual bogeys at sight of which great grownup babies are expected to hide their eyes. *Civilization, An Essay, p. 138.*

Edward Bellamy
(1850-1898)
American novelist, sociologist

The primal principle of democracy is the worth and dignity of the individual.
The inequalities of men and the lust of acquisition are a constant premium on lying.
Not higher wages, but honor and hope of men's gratitude, patriotism and the inspiration of duty, were the motives which they set before their soldiers when it was a question of dying for the nation; and never was an age of the world when these motives did not call out what is best and noblest in men.
Looking Backward, 1887.

When you come to analyze the love of money which was the general impulse to effort in your day, you find that the dread of want and desire of luxury were two of several motives which the pursuit of money represented; the others, and with many the more influential, being desire of power, of social position and reputation for ability and success. *Ibid.*

Though we have abolished poverty and the fear of it, and inordinate luxury with the hope of it, we have not touched the greater part of the motives which underlay the love of money in former times, or any of those which prompted the supremer sorts of effort. The coarser motives, which no longer move us, have been replaced by high motives wholly unknown to the mere wage earners of your age. *Ibid.*

The organization of labor and the strikes were an effect, merely, of the concentration of capital in greater masses than had ever been known before. . . . When a little capital or a new idea was enough to start a man in business for himself, workingmen were constantly becoming employers and there was no hard and fast line between the two classes. Labor unions were needless then, and general strikes out of the question. But when the era of small concerns with small capital was succeeded by that of the great aggregations of capital, all this was changed. The individual laborer, who had been relatively important to the small employer, was reduced to insignificance and powerlessness over against the great corporation, while at the same time the way upward to the grade of employer was closed to him. Self-defense drove him to union with his fellows.   *Ibid.*

The exercise of irresponsible power, by whatever means, is tyranny, and should not be tolerated. The power which men irresponsibly exercise for their private ends, over individuals and communities, through superior wealth, is essentially tyrannous, and as inconsistent with democratic principle and as offensive to self-respecting men as any form of political tyranny that was ever endured. As political equality is the remedy for political tyranny, so is economic equality the only way of putting an end to the economic tyranny exercised by the few over the many through the superiority of wealth. The industrial system of a nation, like its political system, should be a government of the people, by the people, for the people. Until the economic equality shall give a basis to political equality, the latter is but a sham.
Masthead of his weekly, The New Nation.

St. Robert Bellarmine
(1542-1621)
Italian cardinal, controversialist

God has implanted a natural tendency to the monarchial form of government not only in the hearts of men but in practically all things.   *De Romano Pontifice.*

We hold that the Pope, as Pope, although he does not have any purely temporal power, yet has in order for spiritual good, supreme power to dispose of the temporal affairs of all Christians.   *Ibid.*

The Pope may act outside the law, above the law, and against the law. (*Papa potest extra jus, super jus et contra jus.*)
De Summo Pontifice.

Political rule is so natural and necessary to the human race that it cannot be withdrawn without destroying nature itself; for the nature of man is such that he is a social animal.   *De Laicis.*

It depends on the consent of the people to decide whether kings or consuls or other magistrates are to be established in authority over them, and if there is legitimate cause, the people can change a kingdom into an aristocracy, or an aristocracy into a democracy, and vice versa, as we read was done in Rome.   *Ibid.*

Political power is delegated by the multitude to one or several, for the state cannot of itself exercise this power . . . and this authority of rulers considered thus in general is both by natural law and by divine law, nor could the entire human race assembled together decree the opposite, that is, that there should be neither rulers nor ruled.   *Ibid.*

Libertas credendi perniciosa est . . nam nihil aliud est quam libertas errandi. (Freedom of belief is pernicious, it is nothing but the freedom to be wrong.)

Hilaire Belloc
(1870-1953)
English writer

At its first inception all Collectivist Reform is necessarily deflected and evolves, in the place of what it had intended, a new thing: a society wherein the owners remain few and wherein the proletarian mass accept a security at the expense of servitude.
The Servile State, 1912.

Every major question in history is a religious question. . . . It has more effect in molding life than nationalism or a common language.

Julian Benda
(1868-1956)
French writer

La Trahison des Clercs. (The treason of the cultured classes.)
Book title.

Ruth Benedict
(1887-1948)
American anthropologist

and

Gene Weltfish
(b. 1902)
American scientist, writer

Aryans, Jews, Italians are *not* races. Aryans are people who speak Indo-European, "Aryan" languages. . . . As Hitler uses it, the term "Aryan" has no meaning, racial, linguistic, or otherwise.

Jews are people who practice the Jewish religion. They are of all races, Negro and Mongolian. European Jews are of many different biological types; physically they resemble the populations among whom they live. *The Races of Mankind.*

Benedictine Order

Laborare est orare. (To labor is to pray.)
Motto of the Order.

David Ben-Gurion
(1886-1973)
Israeli prime minister

The true right to a country—as to anything else—springs not from political or court authority, but from work.
Earning a Homeland, 1915.

The test of democracy is freedom o[f] criticism.
Quoted, McDonald, My Mission in Israel.

We don't consider manual work as [a] curse, or a bitter necessity, not even as [a] means of making a living. We consider i[t] as a high human function, as a basis o[f] human life, the most dignified thing in th[e] life of the human being, and which ough[t] to be free, creative. Men ought to be prou[d] ot it.
Statement, Anglo-American Commission of Inquiry, March 19, 1946.

James Gordon Bennett
(1795-1872)
American newspaper publisher

I tell the honest truth in my paper, and leave the consequences to God. Could [I] leave them in better hands?
Editorial, New York Morning Herald, May 10, 1836.

I may be attacked, I may be assailed, [I] may be killed, I may be murdered, but [I] never will succumb. I never will abando[n] the cause of truth, morals and virtue.
Ibid.

What is to prevent a daily newspape[r] from being made the greatest organ o[f] social life? Books have had their day—th[e] theatres have had their day—the temple o[f] religion has had its day. A newspaper ca[n] be made to take the lead of all these in th[e] great movement of human thought and o[f] human civilization.
Ibid., August 19, 1836.

Silas Bent
(1882-1945)
American writer

Harmony seldom makes a headline.
Strange Bedfellows.

Jeremy Bentham
(1748-1832)

English philosopher, economist

Will you, Sir, or will you not, concur in putting matters on such a footing, in respect to the liberty of the press, and the liberty of public discussion, that, at the hands of persons exercising the power of government, a man shall have no more fear from speaking and writing against them, than from speaking and writing for them? If his answer be yes, the government he declares in favor of, is an undespotic one; if his answer be no, the government he declares in favor of, is a despotic one.
On Liberty of the Press and Public, 1821.

Every law is an infraction of liberty.
Quoted by I. Berlin, Two Concepts of Liberty, Oxford, 1958.

Is not liberty to be evil, liberty? If not, what is it? Do we not say that it is necessary to take liberty from idiots and bad men, because they abuse it? *Ibid.*

All punishment is mischief. All punishment of itself is evil.
Principles of Morals and Legislation.

It is the greatest good to the greatest number which is the measure of right and wrong. *Works.*

No power of government ought to be employed in the endeavor to establish any system or article of belief on the subject of religion. *Constitutional Code.*

But in truth, in no instance has a system in regard to religion been ever established, but for the purpose, as well as with the effect of its being made an instrument of intimidation, corruption, and delusion, for the support of depredation and oppression in the hands of governments. *Ibid.*

Nature has placed mankind under the government of two sovereign masters, *pain* and *pleasure*. It is for them alone to point out what we ought to do, as well as to determine what we shall do. On the one hand the standard of right and wrong, on the other the chain of causes and effects, are fastened to their throne. They govern us in all we do, in all we say, in all we think: every effort we can make to throw off our subjection, will serve but to demonstrate and confirm it. *Ibid.*

Thomas Benton
(1782-1858)

American statesman

There are but two parties; there never have been but two parties . . . founded in the radical question, whether PEOPLE, or PROPERTY, shall govern? Democracy implies a government by the people . . . Aristocracy implies a government of the rich . . . and in these words are contained the sum of party distinction.
Speech, Senate; Niles Register, August 29, 1835.

Bernard Berenson
(1865-1959)

American art authority

The average European does not seem to feel free until he succeeds in enslaving and oppressing others.
N. Y. Times Book Review.

Against human nature one cannot legislate. One can only try to educate it, and that is a slow process with only a distant hope of success. *Ibid.*

There is no more suicidal doctrine than what has prevailed in my lifetime—the notion that no one has a right to interfere with the internal affairs of another country. . . . How small would have been the cost in lives and property and every kind of cultural value, if Mussolini had been nipped in the bud long before he played the part of the ape that opened the cage for the tiger Hitler. *Ibid.*

Miracles happen to those who believe in them. Otherwise why does not the Virgin Mary appear to Lamaists, Mohammedans, or Hindus who have never heard of her.
Ibid.

International affairs will be placed on a better footing when it is understood that there is no way of punishing a people for the crimes of its rulers. *Ibid.*

Governments last as long as the undertaxed can defend themselves against the overtaxed. *Rumor and Reflection.*

All of the arts, poetry, music, ritual, the visible arts, the theatre, must singly and together create the most comprehensive art of all, a humanized society, and its masterpiece, free man.
Quoted by F. H. Taylor, Atlantic Monthly, November, 1957.

José Bergamin
(b. 1895)
Spanish writer

The Church in its real role of Christian Catholic, is not under attack anywhere. But the Church as belligerent, is.
Voice of Spain, London, 1937.

We cannot help but fight the Church Fascist, the Church belligerent, because Fascism is the negation of all that is Christian. *Ibid.*

Victor Berger
(1860-1929)
Socialist leader

The herd instinct makes the average man afraid to stand alone; he is always afraid to stand alone for an idea, no matter how good, simply as a matter of prejudice. Our herd, like every other herd, when stampeded is liable to trample under its feet anybody who does not run with it.

Henri Bergson
(1859-1941)
French philosopher

The present contains nothing more than the past, and what is found in the effect was already in the cause.
Creative Evolution.

Intelligence . . . is the faculty of manufacturing artificial objects, especially tools to make tools. *Ibid.*

The animal takes its stand on the plant; man bestrides animality, and the whole of humanity, in space and time, is one immense army galloping beside and before and behind each of us in an overwhelming charge able to beat down every resistance and clear the most formidable obstacles, perhaps even death. *Ibid.*

L'élan vital. (The vital glow [or, spirit].)
Ibid., pp. 33-34.

Homo sapiens, the only creature endowed with reason, is also the only creature to pin its existence on things unreasonable.
Two Sources of Morality and Religion, 1935.

We regard intelligence as man's main characteristic, and we know that there is no superiority which intelligence cannot confer on us, no inferiority for which it cannot compensate. *Ibid., p. 171.*

Religion is to mysticism what popularization is to science.   *Ibid., p. 227.*

Europe is over-populated, the world will soon be in the same condition, and if the self-reproduction of man is not "rationalized", as its labor is beginning to be, we shall have war. In no other matter is it so dangerous to rely upon instinct. Antique mythology realized this when it coupled the goddess of love with the god of war.
Ibid., p. 279.

Sex-appeal is the keynote of our civilization.   *Ibid., p. 291.*

Alexander Berkman
(1870-suicide 1936)
American anarchist

It is economic slavery, the savage struggle for a crumb, that has converted mankind into wolves and sheep. . . . My prison-house . . . is but the intensified replica of the world beyond, the larger prison locked with the levers of Greed, guarded by the spawn of Hunger.
Prison Memoirs of an Anarchist, 1912, p. 225.

A. A. Berle, Jr.
(1895-1971)
American diplomat

When Mary Wollstonecraft Shelley's hero, Frankenstein, endowed his synthetic robot with a human heart, the monster which before had been a useful mechanical servant suddenly became an uncontrollable force. Our ancestors feared that corporations had no conscience. We are treated to the colder, more modern fear that, perhaps, they do.
The 20th Century Capitalist Revolution.

Sir Isaiah Berlin
(b. 1909)
Fellow of All Souls, Oxford

Where ends are agreed, the only questions left are those of means, and these are not political but technical, that is to say, capable of being settled by experts or machines like arguments between engineers or doctors. That is why those who put their faith in some immense, world-transforming phenomenon, like the final triumph of reason or the proletarian revolution, must believe that all political and moral problems can thereby be turned into technological ones. That is the meaning of St.-Simon's famous phrase about "replacing the government of persons by the administration of things," and the Marxist prophecies about the withering away of the state and the beginning of the true history of humanity.
Two Concepts of Liberty, Inaugural Lecture, Oxford, p. 3.

It may be that without the pressure of social forces, political ideas are stillborn: what is certain is that these forces, unless they clothe themselves in ideas, remain blind and undirected.   *Ibid., pp. 4-5.*

But to manipulate men, to propel them towards goals which you—the social reformer—see, but they may not, is to deny their human essence, to treat them as objects without wills of their own, and therefore to degrade them.   *Ibid., p. 22.*

All forms of tampering with human beings, getting at them, shaping them against their will to your own pattern, all thought control and conditioning, is, therefore, a denial of that in men which makes them men and their values ultimate.
Ibid., pp. 22-23.

The doctrine that maintains that what I cannot have I must teach myself not to desire; that a desire eliminated, or success-fully resisted, is as good as a desire satis-fied, seems to me a sublime, but unmis-takable, form of the doctrine of sour grapes: what I cannot be sure of, I cannot truly want. *Ibid., p. 24.*

The logical culmination of the process of destroying everything through which I can possibly be wounded is suicide.

Ibid., p. 25.

Passions, prejudices, fears, neuroses, spring from ignorance, and take the form of myths and illusions. *Ibid., p. 27.*

In the ideal society, composed of wholly responsible beings, laws, because I should scarcely be conscious of them, would grad-ually wither away. Only one social move-ment was bold enough to render this as-sumption quite explicit and accepts its consequences—that of the Anarchists. But all forms of liberalism founded on a ration-alist metaphysics are less or more watered-down versions of this creed.

Ibid., pp.. 33-34.

. . . the ignorant—that is, for the mo-ment, the majority of mankind—. . .

Ibid., p. 34.

One belief, more than any other, is re-sponsible for the slaughter of individuals on the altars of the great historical ideals—justice or progress or the happiness of fu-ture generations, or the sacred mission or emancipation of a nation or race or class, or even liberty itself, which demands the sacrifices of individuals for the freedom of society. This is the belief that somewhere, in the past, or in the future, in divine revelation, or in the mind of an individual thinker, in the pronouncements of history or science, or in the simple heart of an uncorrupted good man, there is a final solu-tion. *Ibid., p. 52.*

Hector Berlioz
(1803-1869)
French composer

A feeble mind, conscious of its own feebleness, grows feebler under that very consciousness. As soon as the power of fear becomes known to it, there follows the fear of fear, and, on the first perturbation, reason abandons it.

Quoted, N. Y. Times letter column, May 6, 1948.

St. Bernard
(1091-1153)
Abbot of Clairvaux

Everyone is his own enemy.

They (Christian soldiers) are to wage the war of Christ their master without fearing that they sin in killing their enemies or of being lost if they are themselves killed, since when they give or receive the death-blow, they are guilty of no crime, but all is to their glory. If they kill, it is to the profit of Christ; if they die, it is to their own.

Edward L. Bernays
(b. 1891)
American publicist

Disraeli cynically expressed the dilemma when he said: "I *must* follow the people. Am I not their leader?" He might have added: "I *must* lead the people. Am I not their servant?" *Propaganda, 1928.*

Public relations is the attempt, by in-formation, persuasion, and adjustment, to engineer public support for an activity, cause, movement, or institution.

The Engineering of Consent, 1955.

The freedom to persuade and suggest is the essence of the democratic process.
Article in Freedom & Union, October, 1947.

The key to our liberation from our jungle heritage of force and fraud lies in accelerated self-understanding. The truth shall indeed make us free when we learn, with the same control we exercise over physical nature, that it must now be the truth about ourselves.
"Why We Behave Like Inhuman Beings," Household, February, 1949.

Friedrich A. J. von Bernhardi
(1849-1930)
German general

War is a biological necessity.
Germany and the Next War.

We must rouse in our people the unanimous wish for power, together with the determination to sacrifice on the altar of patriotism, not only life and property, but also private views and preferences in the interests of the common welfare. Then alone shall we discharge our great duties of the future, grow into a world power, and stamp a great part of humanity with the impress of the German spirit.   *Ibid.*

The value of war for the political and moral development of mankind has been criticized by large sections of the modern civilized world in a way which threatens to weaken the defensive powers of States by undermining the warlike spirit of the people.   *Ibid.*

Our next war will be fought for the highest interests of our country and of mankind. This will invest it with importance in the world's history. "World power or downfall" will be our rallying cry.   *Ibid.*

The desire for peace has rendered most civilized nations anaemic, and marks a decay of spirit and political courage.   *Ibid.*

Eduard Bernstein
(1850-1932)
German socialist, author

The economic interpretation of history does not necessarily mean that all events are determined solely by economic forces. It simply means that economic facts are the ever recurring decisive forces, the chief points in the process of history.
Evolutionary Socialism.

The materialist is a Calvinist without a God.   *Ibid.*

Socialism is the legitimate heir of Liberalism, not only chronologically, but spiritually.
Ibid.

Theobald von Bethmann-Hollweg
(1856-1921)
German statesman

Whoever thinks over earnestly and objectively this question of a general disarmament, and considers it in its remotest contingencies, must come to the conviction that it is a question which cannot be solved so long as men are men, and States are States.

In order to cement peace, strength is necessary. The old proverb still holds good, that weakness will always be the booty of the stronger.

Just for a word—"neutrality", a word which in war time had so often been disregarded—just for a scrap of paper, Great Britain is going to make war on a kindred nation who desires nothing better than to be friends with her.   *August 4, 1914.*

Aneurin Bevan
(1897-1960)
British Labour Party leader

The function of parliamentary democracy, under universal suffrage, historically considered, is to expose wealth-privilege to the attacks of the people.
New York Times Magazine, October 27, 1957.

A. J. Beveridge
(1862-1927)
American historian, statesman

I must again repeat that constant touch with the people is bringing me to believe that there are very few ignorant among them. The ordinary citizen is better posted than the average Senator or Congressman —the reason is that they read more current literature. In this connection I see only one danger—and it is a grave danger—the purchase by corporations which have "interests to protect", and by enormously wealthy men who have ambitions to serve, of so many newspapers. Newspapers thus owned give the people only such information as will help their owners, suppressing all information that might injure them, on the one hand; and on the other hand, giving them information that will help the owners. This of course poisons the source of the people's information, and, so far as their influence goes, makes them a good deal worse than ignorant, because it makes them misinformed.
Letter to President Theodore Roosevelt, quoted by Claude Bowers in "Beveridge and the Progressive Era."

Francis Biddle
(1886-1968)
Former U.S. attorney general

Fear of Russia, fear of war, fear of destruction quickly resolve into fear of change and of ideas that involve change—the Fair Deal, the Welfare State, Socialism—almost anything that is unorthodox or unaccepted. The genuine desire to prevent acts of sabotage or of espionage, a highly necessary concern in the face of danger, takes the form of attempts to control and punish the spread of ideas whose radical flavor is believed to cause the acts.
The Fear of Freedom, pp. 247-8.

Ambrose Bierce
(1842-1914)
American author

Faith, n. Belief without evidence in what is told by one who speaks without knowledge, of things without parallel.
The Devil's Dictionary.

(Religion is) a daughter of Hope and Fear, explaining to Ignorance the nature of the Unknowable. *Ibid.*

Don't steal; thou'lt never thus compete Successfully in business. Cheat. *Ibid.*

Politics is the conduct of public affairs for private advantage. *Ibid.*

A saint is a dead sinner, revised and edited. *Ibid.*

Conservative: A statesman who is enamored of existing evils, as distinguished from the Liberal, who wishes to replace them with others. *Ibid.*

Labor: One of the processes by which A acquires property of B. *Ibid.*

I think that I think; therefore, I think I am. *Cogito cogito, ergo cogito sum.*
Ibid.

"Josh Billings"
(Henry Wheeler Shaw)
(1818-1885)
American humorist

If a man is right, he can't be too radical; if he is wrong, he can't be too conservative.

It ain't what a man don't know that makes him a fool, but what he does know that ain't so.

Otto von Bismarck-Schoenhausen
(1815-1898)
Prussian chancellor

Not by speeches and decisions of majorities will the greatest problems of the time be decided—that was the mistake of 1848-49—but by iron and blood.
*Impromptu speech to several ministers and deputies of the Prussian House of Delegates, September 29, 1862.**

We are perhaps too educated to put up with a constitution—we are too critical.
Ibid.

Public opinion wavers; the press is not public opinion; we know how that is made.
Ibid.

Nothing should be left to an invaded people except their eyes for weeping.
Attributed by Paul H. Loyson, The Gods in the Battle, London, 1917, p. ix; sometimes falsely attributed to General Sherman.

No one, not even the most malevolent democrat has any idea how much nullity and charlatanism there is in diplomacy.

* The nation and the kings were alarmed. Bismarck apologized. But he remained the *Blut und Eisen* chancellor in the war which followed.

Better pointed bullets than pointed speeches.   *Speech, 1850.*

The Catholic priest, from the moment he becomes a priest, is a sworn officer of the pope.
Speech, Prussian Upper House, April 12, 1886.

No work of art is worth the bones of a Pomeranian Grenadier.

History is simply a piece of paper covered with print; the main thing is still to make history, not to write it.

Die Politik ist keine exakte Wissenschaft.
Politics are not an exact science.
Prussian Chamber, December 18, 1863.

Politics is the doctrine of the possible, the attainable.
N. Y. Times, August 11, 1957.

Politics is the art of the next best.
Ibid., October 27, 1957.

Henry Campbell Black
(1860-1927)
American law author, editor

The right of revolution is the inherent right of a people to cast out their rulers, change their policy, or effect radical reforms in their system of government or institutions, by force or a general uprising, when the legal and constitutional methods of making such changes have proved inadequate, or are so obstructed as to be unavailable.
*Constitutional Law, 3rd edition, 1910, p. 10.**

* In the 4th edition, 1927, this reference to an "inherent right" was censored.

Hugo L. Black
(1886-1971)
U.S. Supreme Court justice

It is part of the established tradition in the use of juries as instruments of public justice that the jury be a body truly representative of the community. For racial discrimination to result in the exclusion from jury service of otherwise qualified groups not only violates our Constitution and the laws enacted under it, but is at war with our basic concepts of a democratic society and a representative government. . . .

If there has been discrimination, whether accomplished ingeniously or ingenuously, the conviction cannot stand.
Smith v. Texas, 1940.

Under our constitutional system, courts stand against any winds that blow as havens of refuge for those who might otherwise suffer because they are helpless, weak, outnumbered, or because they are non-conforming victims of prejudice and public excitement. . . .

No higher duty, or more solemn responsibility, rests upon this Court than that of translating into living law and maintaining this constitutional shield deliberately planned and inscribed for the benefit of every human being subject to our Constitution—of whatever race, creed or persuasion. *Chambers v. Florida, 1938.*

It was that belief (in the essential dignity of man), I think, which led Jefferson to strive unceasingly that our nation might establish, in his words, "equal and exact justice to all men of whatever state or persuasion, religious or political". A government with this faith is democracy at its best; a government without this faith leads straight to Fascism.
Speech, accepting Thomas Jefferson Award.

It will not be enough to stamp out anti democratic practices in the land of our enemies. The conditions which created Fascism there must not pass unnoticed here. Their first and most dangerous symptom is always the same everywhere: an abandonment of equal justice to all, the placing of some groups in a preferred class of citizenship at the expense of other groups. True democracy must continue to war on all such beliefs.
Ibid.

The constitutional guarantee of a free press rests on the assumption that the widest possible dissemination of information from diverse and antagonistic sources is essential to the welfare of the public, that a free press is a condition of a free society. . . .

Freedom to publish means freedom for all and not for some. Freedom to publish is guaranteed by the Constitution, but freedom to continue to prevent others from publishing is not.
Quoted, New Republic, July 2, 1945.

The "establishment of religion" clause of the First Amendment means at least this: Neither a state nor the Federal Government can set up a church. Neither can pass laws which aid one religion, aid all religions, or prefer one religion over another. Neither can force nor influence a person to go to or to remain away from church against his will or force him to profess a belief or disbelief in any religion.
Majority opinion, Everson v. Board of Education, 330 U.S. 1 (1947).

No person can be punished for entertaining or professing religious beliefs or disbeliefs, for church attendance or nonattendance.
Ibid.

No tax in any amount, large or small, can be levied to support any religious activities or institutions, whatever they may be called, or whatever form they may adopt to teach or practice religion. *Ibid.*

Neither a state nor the Federal Government can, openly or secretly, participate in the affairs of any religious organizations or groups and *vice versa*. In the words of Jefferson, the clause against establishment of religion by law was intended to erect "a wall of separation between church and state." *Ibid.*

The First Amendment has erected a wall between church and state. That wall must be kept high and impregnable. We could not approve the slightest breach.

Ibid., last words.

The interest of the people (lies) in being able to join organizations, advocate causes, and make political "mistakes" without being subjected to government penalties.

Dissent, Barenblatt case, 1959; Time, June 22, 1959.

Sir William Blackstone
(1723-1780)

English writer on law

Man was formed for society and is neither capable of living alone, nor has the courage to do it.

Commentaries on the Laws of England, 1765.

Man, considered as a creature, must necessarily be subject to the laws of his Creator. . . . This law of nature, being coeval with mankind, and dictated by God himself, is of course superior in obligation to any other. It is binding over all the globe, in all countries, and at all times: no human laws are of any validity, if contrary to this: and such of them as are valid derive all their force, and all their authority, mediately or immediately, from this original. *Ibid.*

To bereave a man of life or by violence to confiscate his estate, without accusation or trial, would be so gross and notorious an act of despotism, as must at once convey the alarm of tyranny throughout the whole nation; but confinement of the person, by secretly hurrying him to jail, where his sufferings are unknown or forgotten, is a less public, a less striking, and therefore *a more dangerous engine* of arbitrary government. *Ibid.*

It is better that ten guilty persons than one innocent suffer. *Ibid.*

That the king can do no wrong is a necessary and fundamental principle of the English constitution. *Ibid.*

No laws are binding on the human subject which assault the body or violate the conscience. *Ibid.*

To deny the possibility, nay, actual existence of witchcraft and sorcery is at once flatly to contradict the revealed word of God in various passages of both the Old and New Testament, and the thing itself is a truth to which every nation in the world has in its turn borne testimony, either by example seemingly well tested, or by prohibitory laws which at least suppose the possibility of commerce with evil spirits.

Ibid., edition of 1850, p. 59.

The liberty of the press is indeed essential to the nature of a free state, but this consists in laying no previous restraints upon publications, and not in freedom from censure for criminal matter when published.

Ibid., Vol. 2, Bk. iv.

Every free man has an undoubted right to lay what sentiments he pleases before the public; to forbid this, is to destroy the freedom of the press; but if he publishes what is improper, mischievous, or illegal, he must take the consequences of his own temerity. . . . thus the will of the individuals is still left free; and abuse only of that free-will is the object of legal punishment. Neither is any restraint hereby laid upon freedom of thought or inquiry; liberty of private sentiment is still left; the disseminating, or making public, of bad sentiments, destructive of the ends of society, is the crime which society corrects.   *Ibid.*

Every wanton and causeless restraint of the will of the subject, whether practised by a monarch, a nobility, or a popular assembly, is a degree of tyranny.   *Ibid.*

James G. Blaine
(1830-1893)
American statesman; senator

Hyperion to a satyr, Thersites to Hercules, mud to marble, dunghill to diamond, a singed cat to a Bengal tiger, a whining puppy to a roaring lion.
Speech, 1886, against Roscoe Conkling.

Eric Blair
See George Orwell

Nicholas Blake
See C. Day Lewis

William Blake
(1757-1827)
English poet, artist

The man who never alters his opinion is like standing water, & breeds reptiles of the mind. *The Marriage of Heaven and Hell.*

One Law for the Lion & Ox is Oppression.
Ibid.

Every thing possible to be believ'd is an image of truth.   *Ibid.*

Exuberance is Beauty.   *Ibid.*

Prisons are built with stones of Law, Brothels with bricks of Religion.
Ibid.: Proverbs of Hell.

As the catterpiller chooses the fairest leaves to lay her eggs on, so the priest lays his curse on the fairest joys.   *Ibid.*

The Harlot's cry from Street to Street
Shall weave Old England's winding Sheet.
Auguries of Innocence.

A truth that's told with bad intent
Beats all the Lies you can invent.   *Ibid.*

The Whore & Gambler, by the State
Licenc'd, build that Nation's Fate.   *Ibid.*

The Strongest Poison ever known
Came from Caesar's Laurel Crown.   *Ibid.*

When nations grow old the Arts grow cold,
And Commerce settles on every tree.
What is the price of Experience? do men
    buy it for a song?
Or wisdom for a dance in the street?

    No, it is bought with the price
Of all that a man hath, his house, his wife,
    his children.

A Last Judgment is Necessary because Fools flourish. Nations Flourish under Wise Rulers & are depress'd under foolish Rulers: it is the same with Individuals as Nations: works of Art can only be produc'd in Perfection where the Man is either in Affluence or is Above the Care of it.
From Blake's MS. Book concerning his picture of The Last Judgment.

A Last Judgment is not for the purpose of making Bad Men better, but for the Purpose of hindering them from opressing the Good with Poverty & Pain . . . *Ibid.*

Art is the Tree of Life. Science is the Tree of Death. God is Jesus.
Jah & His Two Sons, Satan & Adam.

The great half-truth, liberty.

Mere enthusiasm is the all in all.
Alexander Gilchrist, Life of William Blake, 1880.

To generalize is to be an idiot. *Ibid.*

I will not cease from Mental Fight,
Nor shall my Sword sleep in my hand
Till we have built Jerusalem,
In England's green & pleasant Land.
Milton, preface.

Is this a holy thing to see
In a rich and fruitful land,
Babes reduc'd to misery,
Fed with cold and usurous hand?
Songs of Experience: Holy Thursday.

I care not whether a man is Good or Evil;
all that I care
Is whether he is a Wise Man or a Fool. Go,
put off Holiness
And put on Intellect ...
Jerusalem, f. 91.

Give us day by day our Real Taxed Substantial Money bought Bread; deliver from the Holy Ghost whatever cannot be Taxed; for all is debts & Taxes between Caesar & us & one another.
Parody on Dr. Thornton's version of the Lord's Prayer, 1827.

But since the French Revolution Englishmen are all Intermeasurable One by Another. Certainly a happy state of Agreement to which I for One do not Agree, God keeps me from the Divinity of Yes & No too, The Yea Nay Creeping Jesus, from supposing Up & Down to be the same Thing.
Quoted by Prof. Thomas Parkinson, The Nation, November 30, 1957.

Elena (Petrovna) Blavatsky
(1831-1891)
Founder of theosophy

After all, his (Christ's) mission has proved scarcely less than a complete failure; two thousand years have passed and Christians do not number one-fifth part of the population of the globe.

The Christians were the first to make the existence of Satan a dogma of the church. What is the use in a Pope if there is no Devil?

There has never been a religion in the annals of the world with such a bloody record as Christianity.

There is a road steep and thorny, and beset with perils of every kind, but yet a road, and it leads to the heart of the Universe. I can tell you how to find Those who will show you the secret gateway that leads inward only, and closes fast behind the neophyte forevermore. . . . There is no danger that dauntless courage cannot conquer; there is no trial that spotless purity cannot pass through; there is no difficulty that strong intellect cannot surmount. For those who win onward, there is a reward past all telling: the power to bless and serve humanity. For those who fail, there are other lives in which success may come.

Paul Eugen Bleuler
(1857-1939)
Swiss psychiatrist

Schizophrenia (divided mind).
Word coined in 1911; Time, September 16, 1957.

Daniel Bliss
(1823-1916)
Founder Beirut University

This College is for all conditions and classes of men without regard to color, nationality, race, or religion. A man white, black, or yellow; Christian, Jew, Mohammedan, or heathen, may enter and enjoy all the advantages of this institution for three, four, or eight years, and go out believing in one God, in many gods, or in no God. But it will be impossible for anyone to continue with us long without knowing what we believe to be the truth and our reasons for that belief.

Credo for the American University of Beirut, 1871.

Tasker H. Bliss
(1853-1930)
American general

The responsibility of war is entirely upon the professing Christians of the United States. If another war like the last should come they will be responsible for every drop of blood that will be shed.

Bruce Bliven
(b. 1889)
American writer, editor

Perhaps the most important lesson the world has learned in the past fifty years is that it is not true that "human nature is unchangeable". Human nature, on the contrary, can be changed with the greatest ease and to the utmost possible extent. If in this lies huge potential danger, it also contains some of the brightest hopes that we have for the future of mankind.

Forbes Magazine, February 15, 1958.

Léon Blum
(1872-1950)
French Socialist premier

The aim of Socialism is to set up a universal society founded on equal justice for all men and equal peace for all nations.

For All Mankind, 1941.

The free man is he who does not fear to go to the end of his thought.

Ludwig Boerne
(1786-1837)
German political writer

Public opinion is a people's invincible armor.

Die Freiheit der Presse, in Baiern, 1818.

To want to be free is to be free.

Der Ewige Jude, 1821.

Nought endures but change.

Address, December 2, 1825.

Woe to the princes and people that obey the times, instead of commanding the times! The times will devour them.

Mendel der Franzosenfresser, 1836.

The difference between liberty and liberties is as great as between God and gods.

Fragmente und Aphorismen, 1840.

The Holy Roman Empire,—neither holy, nor Roman, nor an empire.

John Bogart
(1845-1921)
American journalist

When a dog bites a man, that's not news, because it happens so often. But if a man bites a dog, that is news.

Alexander A. Bogomoletz
(1881-1946)
Russian doctor, scientist

Normal longevity at the present level of human development may be scientifically determined as being 125 to 150 years. There is no reason, however, to consider

even these figures as limits to man's lifespan.
The Prolongation of Life, N. Y., 1946.

The fundamental precept of the fight for longevity is avoidance of satiation. One must not lose desires. They are mighty stimulants to creativeness, to love, and to long life. *Ibid.*

Unusual irritability, which leads to quarrels, shortens life. *Ibid.*

The scorn of death is again one of the methods of prolonging life. . . . The best way not to die too soon is to cultivate the duties of life and the scorn of death. *Ibid.*

French doctors have long said that a man is as old as his arteries. This is true. . . . The saying of the French doctors could be paraphrased: Man is as old as his connective tissue. *Ibid.*

Whether nicotine causes sclerosis of blood vessels has not been completely proved. Nicotine is unquestionably harmful to the sympathetic nervous system and the blood vessels. A spasm of arteries feeding the heart wall often is observed as the result of excessive smoking and produces the symptoms of angina pectoris. Although in medicine this angina is called "false", and its attacks stop as soon as excessive use of tobacco is discontinued, the heart muscle, nevertheless, may severely suffer for the rest of life from the interruption of nutrition. *Ibid.*

Niels Bohr
(1885-1962)
Danish physicist

Every sentence I utter must be understood not as an affirmation, but as a question.
N. Y. Times Book Review, October 20, 1957.

There are trivial truths and the great truths. The opposite of a trivial truth is plainly false. The opposite of a great truth is also true. *Ibid.*

Curtis Bok
(1897-1962)
U.S. federal judge

Truth has a way of shifting under pressure.

In the whole history of law and order the longest step forward was taken by primitive man when, as if by common consent, the tribe sat down in a circle and allowed only one man to speak at a time. An accused who is shouted down has no rights whatever.
Book Awards address, Saturday Review, February 13, 1954.

Unless people have an instinct for procedure their conception of basic human rights is a waste of effort, and wherever we see a negation of those rights it can be traced to a lack, an inadequacy, or a violation of procedure. *Ibid.*

With freedom of the press goes the freedom to read or to close the book, and it will linger so long as we retain the power to say no.

With the right of free speech goes the right of free silence, particularly when a citizen is challenged without the provision of procedure for a fair fight. And with it the duty, if we do speak to speak not only freely but fully. There would be less and better talk if this duty were observed, for the difficulty is not so much with free speech as with free truth. That slippery word must be felt rather than defined. Truth may be the temporary resting place for an enlightened judgment. Or it may be what Holmes said of it—that truth was what he couldn't help think, with the notion that his *can't helps* were not necessarily cosmic: and most of us might have to add, unhappily, that they are not necessarily legal or moral either. All that is obvious in this most stubborn of our freedoms is that there must be a battle for quality.   *Ibid.*

All that is relied upon, in a prosecution, is an indefinable fear for other people's moral standards—a fear that I regard as a democratic anomaly.

Decision, Commonwealth v. Gordon et al., 66 D & C (Pa.) 1.*

Judge Woolsey's decision [in the *Ulysses* case, 1933] may well be considered the keystone of the modern American rule, as it brings out clearly that indictable obscenity must be "dirt for dirt's sake". . . . The books before me are obvious efforts to show life as it is. . . . The effect upon the normal reader . . . would be anything but what the vice-hunters fear it might be. We are so fearful of other people's morals; they so seldom have the courage of our own convictions.   *Ibid.*

I believe that the consensus of preference today is for disclosure and not stealth, for frankness and not hypocrisy, and for public and not secret distribution. That in itself is a moral code. . . . I hold that the books before me are not sexually impure and pornographic, and are therefore not obscene.   *Ibid.*

George H. Boldt
(b. 1903)
U.S. federal judge

Ordeal by Publicity is the legitimate grandchild of Ordeal by Fire, Water and Battle. The physical harm of those ancient

* In this famous Philadelphia book seizure case authors involved included Caldwell, Farrell and Faulkner.

adjuncts of trial was more direct and severe than that of their present-day descendant but it is likely that the mental and spiritual injury to the litigant and the damage to society generally resulting from the violence of unnecessary publicity are immeasurably greater.

Address, American Bar Association, August, 1954.

The term Rule of Law, like the phrases "Love of God" and "Brotherhood of Man," is a short and simple expression of one of the few most sublime concepts that the mind and spirit of man has yet achieved.

Address, Law Day USA, Tacoma, May 1, 1958.

Jury service honorably performed is as important in the defense of our country, its Constitution and laws, and the ideals and standards for which they stand, as the service that is rendered by the soldier on the field of battle in time of war.

Concluding remarks, U.S. v. Beck, February, 1959.

Henry St. John Bolingbroke
(1678-1751)
Statesman, political and philosophical writer

Liberty is to the collective body what health is to every individual body. Without health no pleasure can be tasted by man; without liberty no happiness can be enjoyed by society.

It is a very easy thing to devise good laws; the difficulty is to make them effective. The great mistake is that of looking upon men as virtuous, or thinking that they can be made so by laws; and consequently the greatest art of a politician is to render vices serviceable to the cause of virtue.

William Bolitho (Ryall)
(1890-1930)
British (South African) writer

We will never have Fascism in England; no Englishman will dress up, not even for a revolution.
Conversation with Walter Duranty, George Seldes, and others, Paris, 1930; quoted from memory.

We, like the eagles, were born to be free. Yet we are obliged, in order to live at all, to make a cage of laws for ourselves and to stand on the perch.
Twelve Against the Gods.

Simon Bolivar
(1783-1830)
South American liberator

I plowed furrows in the ocean.

We have plowed the seas.
(translation by T. R. Ybarra.)

If Nature is against us, we shall fight Nature, and make it obey.
Quoted by Waldo Frank.

Bonaparte
See also Napoleon

Jérôme Bonaparte
(1784-1860)
King of Westphalia

Sow a Jesuit, and you reap a rebel.
Speech, Chamber of Deputies.

Louis Bonaparte
(1778-1846)
King of Holland

I will never ask for more rights than those of a French Citizen: nothing is changed in France; there is only one more Republican.
Quoted by R. Pimienta, Propaganda Bonapartista en 1848, p. 53.

Bonesana di Beccaria
See Beccaria

Boniface VIII
(1235?-1303)
Pope

1. Under the control of the Church are two swords, that is two powers, . . .
Both swords are in the power of the Church; the spiritual is wielded in the Church by the hand of the clergy; the secular is to be employed for the Church by the hand of the civil authority, but under the direction of the spiritual power.
Bull, Unam Sanctam. November 18, 1302.

The one sword must be subordinate to the other; the earthly power must submit to the spiritual authority.   *Ibid.*

This authority, although granted to man, and exercised by man, is not a human authority, but rather a Divine one, granted to Peter by Divine commission and confirmed in him and his successors. Consequently, whoever opposes this power ordained by God opposes the law of God.   *Ibid.*

Now, therefore, we declare, say, determine and pronounce that for every human creature it is necessary for salvation to be subject to the authority of the Roman pontiff.   *Ibid.*

The Book of Good Counsels

Wealth is friends, home, father, brother, title to respect, and fame;

Yes, wealth is held for wisdom—that it should be so is shame.

Sanscrit, 300 B.C.

Evangeline Booth
(1865-1950)
Salvation Army general

Drink has drained more blood,
Hung more crepe,
Sold more houses,
Plunged more people into bankruptcy,
Armed more villains,
Slain more children,
Snapped more wedding rings,
Defiled more innocence,
Blinded more eyes,
Twisted more limbs,
Dethroned more reason,
Wrecked more manhood,
Dishonored more womanhood,
Broken more hearts,
Blasted more lives,
Driven more to suicide, and
Dug more graves than any other poisoned
  scourge that ever swept its death-
  dealing waves across the world.

Good Housekeeping.

John Wilkes Booth
(1838-1865)
Actor, assassin of Lincoln

This country was formed for the *white*, not for the black man. And looking upon African slavery from the same viewpoint held by the noble framers of our Constitution, I for one have ever considered it one of the greatest blessings (both for themselves and us) that God ever has bestowed upon a favored nation.

Quoted by Bruce Catton, This Hallowed Ground, p. 395.

I have too great a soul to die like a criminal.

William E. Borah
(1865-1940)
American senator

No more fatuous chimera ever infested the brain of man than that you can control opinions by law or direct belief by statute, and no more pernicious sentiment ever tormented the human heart than the barbarous desire to do so. The field of inquiry should remain open, and the right of debate must be regarded as a sacred right. I look upon those who would deny others the right to urge and argue their position, however irksome or pernicious they may seem, as intellectual and moral cowards.

Without an unfettered press, without liberty of speech, all the outward forms and structures of free institutions are a sham, a pretense—the sheerest mockery. If the press is not free, if speech is not independent and untrammeled, if the mind is shackled or made impotent through fear, it makes no difference under what form of government you live, you are a subject and not a citizen. Republics are not in and of themselves better than other forms of government except insofar as they carry with them and guarantee to the citizens that liberty of thought and action for which they were established.

Senate speech against proposed espionage law, April 19, 1917.

England tried for two hundred years to restrain the right of discussion. She utterly failed. She is now the freest country in speech and the press under the sun—and it has more than once been her salvation. Every enlightened Englishman appreciates the value of Trafalgar Square and Hyde Park. When you drive men from the public arena, where debate is free, you send them to the cellar, where revolutions are born. "Better an uproar than a whisper".

We need not take shelter when someone cries "Radical!" If measures proposed are unsound, debate will reveal this fact better than anything else that has been discovered in the affairs of government. But if the measures are sound, we want them under whatever name they may come to us.

There is nothing that dies so hard and rallies so often as intolerance. The vices and passions which it summons to its support are the most ruthless and the most persistent harbored in the human breast. They sometimes sleep but they never seem to die. Anything, any extraordinary situation, any unnecessary controversy, may light those fires again and plant in our republic that which has destroyed every republic which undertook to nurse it.

Senate speech, April 24, 1929; quoted by Justice Douglas, An Almanac of Liberty.

The marvel of all history is the patience with which men and women submit to burdens unnecessarily laid upon them by their governments.   *Senate speech.*

G. A. Borgese
(1882-1952)
Italian-American novelist, scholar, critic

Those in the Western world who so fervently want the Pope to cast his lot with liberal democracy have forgotten the words of Metternich, a wise man who said that he could imagine anything except a liberal pope.

Cesare Borgia
(1476?-1507)
Italian Cardinal, military leader

Aut Caesar, aut nihil. (Either Caesar or nothing.)   *Motto.*

Max Born
(1882-1970)
German physicist, Nobel Prize, 1955

Since the destruction of Nagasaki and Hiroshima the atom has become a specter threatening us with annihilation.
Bulletin of the Atomic Scientists, June, 1957.

The human race has today the means for annihilating itself—either in a fit of complete lunacy, i.e., in a big war, by a brief fit of destruction, or by careless handling of atomic technology, through a slow process of poisoning and of deterioration in its genetic structure.   *Ibid.*

Only two possibilities exist: either one must believe in determinism and regard free will as a subjective illusion, or one must become a mystic and regard the discovery of natural laws as a meaningless intellectual game. Metaphysicians of the old schools have proclaimed one or the other of these doctrines, but ordinary people have always accepted the dual nature of the world.   *Ibid.*

Pierre François Joseph Bosquet
(1810-1861)
French marshal

C'est magnifique, mais ce n'est pas la guerre. (It is magnificent, but it isn't war.)
At charge of the Light Brigade, 1854.

Jacques Bénigne Bossuet
(1627-1704)
French Bishop of Meaux

There are four qualities essential to royal authority. First, the royal authority is sacred; second, it is paternal; third, it is absolute; fourth, it is submitted to reason.
Oeuvres de Bossuet, translated by Franklin Le Van Baumer, in his Main Currents of Western Thought.

We have already seen that all power comes from God. . . . Princes act then as ministers of God, and his lieutenants on earth. It is by them that he rules his empire. . . . The royal throne is not the throne of a man, but the throne of God himself.
Ibid.

The person of kings is sacred, . . . to make an attempt on their lives is a sacrilege. God causes them to be anointed by his prophets with a sacred unction, in the same way that he causes pontiffs and his ministry to be anointed. *Ibid.*

The royal authority is absolute.

In order to render this term odious and insupportable, some people try to confuse absolute with arbitrary government. But there is nothing more different, as we shall see when we speak of justice.

The prince is accountable to no one for what he orders. . . .

We must obey princes as justice itself, without which there would be no order nor purpose in human affairs.

They are gods, and participate in the divine independence. . . . *Ibid.*

The end of government is the good and conservation of the state. . . . The good constitution of the body of the state consists in two things: in religion and justice. . . . The prince must employ his authority to destroy false religions in his state. . . .

He is the protector of the public peace which depends upon religion; and he must sustain his throne, of which it is the foundation. . . . Those who would not suffer the prince to act strictly in matters of religion, because religion ought to be free, are in impious error. *Ibid.*

Bovier
See Fontenelle

Claude G. Bowers
(1878-1957)
American journalist, author, diplomat

We can at least refuse to join in the plan to suppress, distort, and mutilate the history of these days (1936-9; the war in Spain). History is the torch that is meant to illuminate the past to guard us against the repetition of our mistakes of other days. We cannot join in the rewriting of history to make it conform to our comfort and convenience. *Introduction, The United States and the Spanish Civil War, by F. Jay Taylor, 1956.*

Chester Bowles
(b. 1901)
American diplomat, author

It is the duty of the liberal to protect and to extend the basic democratic freedoms.
New Republic, July 22, 1946.

Because there can be no real individual freedom in the presence of economic insecurity, liberalism carries a heavy responsibility in fighting continuously to expand our economy and to put into effect the economic bill of rights. *Ibid.*

Fundamentally, liberalism is an attitude. The chief characteristics of that attitude are human sympathy, a receptivity to change, and a scientific willingness to follow reason rather than faith or any fixed ideas. *Ibid.*

Samuel Bowles
(1826-1878)
American newspaper editor

Journalism has already come to be the first power in the land.

William Lisle Bowles
(1762-1850)
English poet, critic, cleric

The cause of freedom is the cause of God.

William Bradford
(1590-1657)
American colonial governor

All great and honorable actions are accompanied with great difficulties, and must be both enterprised and overcome with answerable courages. The dangers were great, but not desperate; the difficulties were many, but not invincible. For though there were many of them likely, yet they were not certain; it might be sundry of the things feared might never befall; others by provident care and the use of good means, might in great measure be prevented; and all of them, through the help of God, by fortitude and patience, might either be borne or overcome.
History of the Plymouth Plantation.

Charles Bradlaugh
(1833-1891)
English reformer

Liberty's chief foe is theology.

Without free speech no search for truth is possible; without free speech no discovery of truth is useful; without free speech progress is checked and the nations no longer march forward toward the nobler life which the future holds for men. Better a thousandfold abuse of free speech than denial of free speech. The abuse dies in a day, but the denial slays the life of the people and entombs the hope of the race.

Omar N. Bradley
(1893-1981)
American general

We have grasped the mystery of the atom and rejected the Sermon on the Mount. *Address, Armistice Day, 1948.*

With the monstrous weapons man already has, humanity is in danger of being trapped in this world by its moral adolescents.
Ibid.

The world has achieved brilliance without conscience. Ours is a world of nuclear giants and ethical infants. *Ibid.*

Edward S(tuyvesant) Bragg
(1827-1912)
American soldier, congressman

They love him, gentlemen, and they respect him, not only for himself, but for his character, for his integrity and judgment and iron will; but they love him most for the enemies he has made.
Speech seconding Cleveland for President, 1884.

Berton Braley
(1882-1966)
American poet

We boast of vast achievements and of
    power,
Of human progress knowing no defeat,
Of strange new marvels, every day and
    hour—
And here's the bread line in the wintry
    street!
    The Bread Line, stanza 4.

Ten thousand years replete with every
    wonder,
Of empires risen and of empires dead;

Yet still, while wasters roll in swollen
plunder,
These broken men must stand in line
—for bread!
Ibid., 6.

Louis D. Brandeis
(1856-1941)
U.S. Supreme Court justice

Industrial democracy should ultimately
attend political democracy.
*The Employer and Trades Unions,
April 21, 1904.*

There are no short cuts in evolution.
Boston, April 22, 1904.

The function of the press is very high.
It is almost holy. It ought to serve as a
forum for the people, through which the
people may know freely what is going on.
To misstate or suppress the news is a breach
of trust.
Collier's Weekly, March 23, 1912.

Labor cannot on any terms surrender the
right to strike. *1913.*

In my opinion we are going through the
following stages: we already have had industrial despotism. With the recognition of
the unions, this is changing into a constitutional monarchy, with well-defined limitations placed upon the employer's formerly
autocratic power. Next comes profit-sharing.
This, however, is to be only a transitional,
halfway stage. Following upon it will come
the sharing of responsibility, as well as
profits. The eventual outcome promises to
be a full-grown industrial democracy. As to
this last step, the Socialists have furnished
us with an ideal full of suggestion.
Interview, La Follette's Weekly, 1913.

It is one of the greatest economic errors
to put any limitation upon production. . . .

We have not the power to produce more
than there is a potential to consume.
*Testimony, U.S. Commission on Indus-
trial Relations, 1915.*

I think all of our human experience shows
that no one with absolute power can be
trusted to give it up even in part. That
has been the experience with industrial
absolutism. Industrial democracy will not
come by gift. It has got to be won by those
who desire it. And if the situation is such
that a voluntary organization like a labor
union is powerless to bring about the democratization of a business, I think we have
in this fact some proof that the employing
organization is larger than is consistent with
public interest. I mean by larger, is more
powerful, has a financial interest too great
to be useful to the State; and the State
must in some way come to the aid of the
workingman if democratization is to be
secured. *Ibid.*

That while there are many contributing
causes of unrest, that there is one cause
which is fundamental. That is the necessary conflict—the contrast between our political liberty and our individual absolutism.
Ibid.

The social justice for which we are striving is an incident of our democracy, not the
main end. *Ibid.*

The end for which we must strive is the
attainment of rule by the people, and that
involves industrial democracy as well as
political democracy. *Ibid.*

There must be a division not only of
profits, but a division also of responsibilities
. . . We must insist upon labor sharing the
responsibilities for the result of the business.
Ibid.

Like the course of the heavenly bodies,
harmony in national life is a resultant of

the struggle between contending forces. In frank expression of conflicting opinion lies the greatest promise of wisdom in governmental action; and in suppression lies ordinarily the greatest peril.

Gilbert v. Minnesota, 254 U.S. 325 (1920).

Few laws are of universal application. It is of the nature of our law that it has dealt not with man in general, but with him in relationships.

Dissent, Truax v. Corrigan, 257 U.S. 312 (1921).

Nearly all legislation involves a weighing of public needs as against private desires; and likewise a weighing of relative social values.   *Ibid.*

Since government is not an exact science, prevailing public opinion concerning the evils and the remedy is among the important facts deserving consideration; particularly when the public conviction is both deep-seated and widespread and has been reached with deliberation.   *Ibid.*

Remedial institutions are apt to fall under the control of the enemy and to become instruments of oppression.

Letter to Robert W. Bruere, 1922.

If we would be guided by the light of reason, we must let our minds be bold.

Opinion, Jay Burns Baking Co. v. Bryan, 1924.

Those who won our independence by revolution were not cowards. They did not fear political change. They did not exalt order at the cost of liberty.

Concurring opinion, Whitney v. California, 274 U.S. 357 (1927).

To courageous, self-reliant men, with confidence in the power of free and fearless reasoning applied through the processes of popular government, no danger flowing

from speech can be deemed clear and present, unless the incidence of the evil apprehended is so imminent that it may befall before there is opportunity for full discussion. If there be time to expose through discussion the falsehoods and fallacies, to avert the evil by the process of education, the remedy to be applied is more speech, not enforced silence. Only an emergency can justify repression. Such must be the rule if authority is to be reconciled with freedom. Such, in my opinion, is the command of the Constitution.   *Ibid.*

Those who won our independence believe that the final end of the state was to make men free to develop their faculties; and that in its government the deliberative forces should prevail over the arbitrary. They valued liberty both as an end and as a means. They believe liberty to be the secret of happiness and courage to be the secret of liberty. They believed that freedom to think as you will and to speak as you think are means indispensable to the discovery and spread of political truth; that without free speech and assembly discussion would be futile; that with them, discussion affords ordinarily adequate protection against the dissemination of noxious doctrine; that the greatest menace to freedom is an inert people; that public discussion is a political duty; and that this should be a fundamental principle of the American government.   *Ibid.*

Experience should teach us to be most on our guard to protect liberty when the government's purposes are beneficent. Men born to freedom are naturally alert to repel invasion of their liberty by evil-minded rulers. The greatest dangers to liberty lurk in insidious encroachment by men of zeal, well-meaning but without understanding.

Dissenting, Olmstead v. U.S., 277 U.S. 438 (1928).

Crime is contagious. If the government becomes a law-breaker, it breeds contempt for law. *Ibid.*

To declare that in the administration of the criminal law the end justifies the means —to declare that the government may commit crimes in order to secure the conviction of a private criminal—would bring terrible retribution. Against that pernicious doctrine this Court must resolutely set its face. *Ibid.*

The makers of our Constitution undertook to secure conditions favorable to the pursuit of happiness. . . . They sought to protect Americans in their beliefs, their thoughts, their emotions and their sensations. They conferred, as against the Government, the right to be let alone—the most comprehensive of rights and the right most valued by civilized men. To protect that right, every unjustifiable intrusion by the Government upon the privacy of the individual, whatever the means employed, must be deemed a violation of the Fourth Amendment. *Ibid.*

We can have democracy in this country or we can have great wealth concentrated in the hands of a few, but we can't have both. *Labor, October 17, 1941.*

The pleas of the trades unions for immunity, be it from injunction or from liability for damages, is as fallacious as the plea of the lynchers. . . . We gain nothing by trading the tyranny of capital for the tyranny of labor.

The real fight today is against inhuman, relentless exercise of capitalistic power. First we have the struggle for independence, and the second great struggle in our history was to keep the nation whole and abolish slavery. The present struggle in which we are engaged is for social and industrial justice.

The greatest factors making for communism, socialism or anarchy among a free people are the excesses of capital. The talk of the agitator does not advance socialism one step. The great captains of industry and finance . . . are the chief makers of socialism.

This world presents enough problems if you believe it to be a world of law and order; do not add to them by believing it to be a world of miracles.

Behind every argument is someone's ignorance. Re-discover the foundation of truth and the purpose and causes of dispute immediately disappear.

Unlicensed liberty leads necessarily to despotism and oligarchy.

The main objection to the very large corporation is that it makes possible—and in many cases makes inevitable—the exercise of industrial absolutism.

Neutrality is at times a graver sin than belligerence.
The Words of Justice Brandeis, edited by Solomon Goldman, 1954.

Radicals who would take us back to the roots of things often fail because they disregard the fruit Time has produced and preserved. Conservatives fail because they would preserve even what Time has decomposed. *Ibid.*

Writs of assistance and general warrants are but puny instruments of tyranny compared to wiretapping.

There must be power in the states and nation to remould, through experimentation, our economic practices and institutions to meet changing social and economic needs.

An intolerant majority, swayed by passion or by fear, may be prone . . . to stamp as disloyal opinions with which it disagrees. Committees such as these, besides abridging freedom of speech, threaten freedom of thought and of belief.

Georg Brandes
(1842-1927)
Danish literary critic

The crowd will follow a leader who marches twenty steps in advance; but if he is a thousand steps in front of them, they do not see and do not follow him, and any literary freebooter who chooses may shoot him with impunity.

The stream of time sweeps away errors, and leaves the truth for the inheritance of humanity.   *Ferdinand Lassalle, 1881.*

W(illiam) C(owper) Brann
(1855-shot 1898)
Editor, reformer, called
"Brann the Iconoclast"

An heretic, my dear sir, is a fellow who disagrees with you regarding something neither of you knows anything about.
Quoted by Charles Carver, Brann and the Iconoclast, U. of Texas, 1958.

No man can be a patriot on an empty stomach.   *The Iconoclast.*

Joseph I. Breen
(b. 1890)
Hollywood film association executive

Deletions: All scenes of kissing.
Delete any footage which includes the idea that war is not altogether glamorous and noble.
Memorandum to film producers, quoted by Leonard Lyons, New York Post.

William J. Brennan, Jr.
(b. 1906)
U.S. Supreme Court justice

All ideas having even the slightest redeeming social importance — unorthodox ideas, controversial ideas, even ideas hateful to the prevailing climate of opinion— have the full protection of the guaranties, unless excludable because they encroach upon the limited area of more important interests. But implicit in the history of the First Amendment is the rejection of obscenity as utterly without redeeming social importance.
Opinion, Roth v. United States, 354 U.S. 476 (1957).

We hold that obscenity is not within the area of constitutionally protected speech or press.   *Ibid.*

Custom, for example, was always the common law's most cherished source. So much so, in fact, that not until well into the Seventeenth Century did English lawyers make any clear distinction between law declaring and law making. And what was declared custom but the accumulated wisdom on social problems of society itself? The function of law was to formalize and preserve this wisdom.
Gaston Lecture, Georgetown University, November 25, 1957.

The law is not an end in itself, nor does it provide ends. It is preeminently a means to serve what we think is right.   *Ibid.*

Law is here to serve! To serve what? To serve, insofar as law can properly do so, within limits that I have already stressed, the realization of man's ends, ultimate and mediate.   *Ibid.*

Law cannot stand aside from the social changes around it.   *Ibid.*

[113]

Aristide Briand
(1862-1932)
French statesman, Nobel Prize, 1926

What makes the actual situation so difficult is the fact that too many Interests are working against Peace. Those who believe that the suppression of war may affect adversely their material interests are against us. The metallurgists, the manufacturers of armaments and munitions, etc., are working against the League of Nations, against the Pact of Paris, and they support with their money Press campaigns which, at every turn, hinder our efforts. . . . The pens which write against Disarmament are made with the same steel from which guns are made.
At Geneva, September 23, 1930; quoted by Noel-Baker, The Private Manufacture of Armaments.

Harry Bridges
(b. 1900)
American labor leader

No man has ever been born a Negro hater, a Jew hater, or any other kind of hater. Nature refuses to be involved in such suicidal practices.

John Bright
(1811-1889)
English orator, statesman

If mine were a solitary voice, raised amid the din of arms and the clamours of a venal press . . .
House of Commons, December 22, 1854.

I am for "Peace, Retrenchment, and Reform," the watchword of the great Liberal Party thirty years ago.
Speech, Birmingham, April 28, 1859.

England is the Mother of Parliaments.
Ibid., January 18, 1865.

Force is not a remedy.
Ibid., November 16, 1880.

Jacques Pierre Brissot
(1754-1793)
French girondist, jurist

Exclusive property is a theft against nature.
Théorie des lois criminelles, 1780.

It is in the power of the mores rather than in the hands of the legislator that this terrible weapon of infamy rests, this type of civil excommunication, which deprives the victim of all consideration, which severs all the ties which bind him to his fellow citizens, which isolates him in the midst of society. The purer and more untouched the customs are, the greater the force of infamy.   *Ibid.*

Charlotte Bronte
(1816-1855)
English novelist

Prejudices, it is well known, are most difficult to eradicate from the heart whose soil has never been loosened or fertilized by education; they grow there, firm as weeds among stones.   *Jane Eyre.*

Conventionality is not morality. Self-righteousness is not religion. To attack the first is not to assail the last.   *Ibid.*

James Bronterre
See James O'Brien

Rupert Brooke
(1887-1915)
English poet

Honour has come back, as a king, to earth,
And paid his subjects with a royal wage;
And Nobleness walks in our ways again;
And we have come into our heritage.
The Dead.

If I should die, think only this of me:
That there's some corner of a foreign field
That is for ever England. *The Soldier.*

Phillips Brooks
(1835-1893)
American religious leader

If you limit the search for truth and forbid men anywhere, in any way, to seek knowledge, you paralyze the vital force of truth itself.

In the best sense of the word, Jesus was a radical. . . . His religion has been so long identified with conservatism—often with conservatism of the obstinate and unyielding sort—that it is almost startling for us sometimes to remember that all of the conservatism of his own times was against him; that it was the young, free, restless, sanguine, progressive part of the people who flocked to him.

Quoted, The Churchman.

Bad will be the day for every man when he becomes absolutely content with the life that he is living, with the thoughts that he is thinking, with the deeds that he is doing, when there is not forever beating at the doors of his soul some great desire to do something larger, which he knows that he was meant and made to do, because he is still, in spite of all, the child of God.

Van Wyck Brooks
(1886-1963)
American critic, translator

The American mind, unlike the English, is not formed by books, but, as Carl Sandburg once said to me, . . . by newspapers and the Bible.
The Nation, August 14, 1954.

If men were basically evil, who would bother to improve the world instead of giving it up as a bad job at the outset?
From a Writer's Notebook, 1957.

Americans are too sympathetic to provide a good milieu for the development of individuality. *Ibid.*

There is no stopping the world's tendency to throw off imposed restraints, the religious authority that is based on the ignorance of the many, the political authority that is based on the knowledge of the few. *Ibid.*

Those of our writers who have possessed a vivid personal talent have been paralyzed by a want of social background.
The Literary Life in America.

Henry Peter Brougham
(1778-1868)
Scottish statesman, historian

It was the boast of Augustus that he found Rome of brick and left it of marble. But how much nobler will be the sovereign's boast when he shall have it to say that he found law dear and left it cheap; found it a sealed book and left it a living letter; found it the patrimony of the rich and left it the inheritance of the poor; found it the two-edged sword of craft and oppression and left it the staff of honesty and the shield of innocence.
Quoted, Nieman Reports, April, 1956.

The true test of a great man—that, at least, which must secure his place among the highest order of great men—is, his having been in advance of his age.

To tyrants, indeed, and bad rulers, the progress of knowledge among the mass of mankind is a just object of terror; it is fatal to them and their designs.
Practical Observations upon the Education of the People, 1825.

Education makes people easy to lead, but difficult to drive; easy to govern, but impossible to enslave.
The Present State of the Law.

Heywood Broun
(1888-1939)
American journalist, essayist, novelist

The pursuit of happiness belongs to us, but we must climb around or over the church to get it.   *The Nation.*

Admitting the danger of generalities, I would contend that the Irish are the cry-babies of the Western world. Even the mildest quip will set them off in resolutions and protests. And still more precarious is the position of the New York newspaper man who ventures any criticism of the Catholic Church. There is not a single New York editor who does not live in mortal terror of the power of this group. It is not a case of numbers but of organization. . . . If the church can bluff its way into a preferred position, the fault lies not with the Catholics but with the editors.
Ibid., The Piece That Got Me Fired.

A newspaper is a rule unto itself. It has a soul for salvation or damnation. The intangibles of a newspaper are the men and women who make it. A newspaper can neither rise above nor fall below its staff.
Quoted, N. Y. Times, December 17, 1942.

They are too bright, we shield our eyes and kill them. We are the dead, and in us there is no feeling nor imagination nor the terrible torment of lust for justice.
A reference to Sacco and Vanzetti; New Republic, September 1, 1947.

As long as Mooney rots in jail you are not free and I am not free.
Column, N. Y. World-Telegram, November 8, 1934.

Posterity has picked practically all its heroes from the agitators. They are the saints and holy men of our religion.

For truth there is no deadline.
The Nation, December 30, 1939.

A liberal is a man who leaves a room when the fight begins.

Brotherhood is not just a Bible word. Out of comradeship can come and will come the happy life for all. The underdog can and will lick his weight in the wildcats of the world.   *Fifty-first Birthday.*

Sometimes we call a man a Fascist simply because we dislike him.
The Fight, May, 1936.

First of all we need a definition. Fascism is dictatorship from the extreme Right, or to put it a little more closely into our local idiom, a government which is run by a small group of large industrialists and financial lords.   *Ibid.*

Now one of the first steps which Fascism must take in any land in order to capture power is to disrupt and destroy the labor movement. It must rob trade unions of their power to use the strike as a weapon.
Ibid.

Business men in America, as far as our experience reaches back, have seldom been enthusiastic about trade unionism. *Ibid.*

Clarence Brown

(b. 1893)

Ohio congressman

Open each session with a prayer and close it with a probe.

Statement after Republican victory, November, 1946; Time, August 4, 1947.

David Brown

No Stamp Act, No Sedition, No Alien Bills, No Land Tax; Downfall to the Tyrants of America, peace and retirement to the President (Adams), long live the Vice-President (Jefferson) and the Minority; may moral virtue be the basis of civil government.

Quoted by Norman Thomas, The Test of Freedom, 1954.

John Brown

(1800-1859)

American abolitionist

Caution, caution, sir! It is nothing but the word of cowardice.

Quoted by Bruce Catton, Life, September 12, 1955.

I pity the poor in bondage that have none to help them; that is why I am here; not to gratify any personal animosity, revenge, or vindictive spirit. It is my sympathy with the oppressed and the wronged, that are as good as you, and as precious in the sight of God.

Quoted by Thoreau, Slavery in Massachusetts, 1859.

---

* For this inscription on a liberty pole erected at Dedham, Mass., Brown served two years in prison.

I want you to understand, gentlemen, that I respect the rights of the poorest and weakest of the colored people, oppressed by the slave system, just as much as I do those of the most wealthy and powerful. That is the idea that has moved me, and that alone.

Reply to questioning after arrest.

I will answer anything I can with honor, but not about others.

N. Y. Herald verbatim report of hearing, October 21, 1859.

In the first place, I deny everything but what I have all along admitted—the design on my part to free the slaves.

Last speech in court, November 2, 1859, N. Y. Herald, November 3.

I have another objection: and that is, it is unjust that I should suffer such a penalty. Had I interfered in the manner which I admit, and which I admit has been fairly proved—(for I admire the truthfulness and candor of the greater portion of the witnesses who have testified in this case)—had I so interfered in behalf of the rich, the powerful, the intelligent, the so-called great, or in behalf of their children, or any of that class, and suffered and sacrificed what I have in this interference, it would have been all right, and every man in this Court would have deemed it an act worthy of reward rather than punishment. *Ibid.*

This Court acknowledges, as I suppose, the validity of the Law of God. . . . I endeavored to act up to that instruction. I say, I am yet too young to understand that God is any respecter of persons. I believe that to have interfered as I have done, as I have always freely admitted I have done, in behalf of His despised poor, was not wrong, but right. Now, if it is deemed necessary that I should forfeit my life for the furtherance of the ends of justice, and

mingle my blood further with the blood of my children, and with the blood of millions in this slave country whose rights are disregarded by wicked, cruel, and unjust enactments, I submit: so let it be done!
Ibid.

I, John Brown, am now quite certain that the crimes of this *guilty land:* will never be purged away; but with Blood. I had *as I now think:* vainly flattered myself that without *very much bloodshed;* it might be done.
Last written statement, handed to a guard, December 2, 1859.

I am ready at any time. Do not keep me waiting. *Last words.*

John Mason Brown

(1900-1969)
American drama critic, author

Even when the facts are available, most people seem to prefer the legend and refuse to believe the truth when it in any way dislodges the myth. *Saturday Review.*

Nowhere are prejudices more mistaken for truth, passion for reason, and invective for documentation than in politics. That is a realm, peopled only by villains or heroes, in which everything is black or white and gray is a forbidden color.
Through These Men, 1952.

Thomas Browne

(1605-1682)
English physician, writer

To believe only possibilities, is not faith, but mere Philosophy.
Religio Medici, 1642.

Had not almost every man suffered by the Press, or were not the tyranny thereof become universal, I had not wanted reason for complaint. *Ibid., preface.*

I have ever believed, and do now know, that there are Witches. *Ibid., pt. i.*

A man may be in just possession of Truth as of a City, and yet be forced to surrender. *Ibid.*

I have tried if I could reach that great resolution . . . to be honest without a thought of Heaven or Hell. *Ibid.*

If there be any among those common objects of hatred I do condemn and laugh at, it is that great enemy of reason, virtue, and religion, the multitude; that numerous piece of monstrosity, which, taken asunder, seem men, and the reasonable creatures of God, but, confused together, make but one great beast, and a monstrosity more prodigious than Hydra. *Ibid., pt. ii, ‡1.*

Man is a noble animal, splendid in ashes, and pompous in the grave, solemnizing nativities and deaths with equal lustre, not omitting ceremonies of bravery, in the infamy of his nature.
Hydriotaphia, or Urne-Buriall, 1658.

Mummy is become merchandise, Mizraim cures wounds, and Pharaoh is sold for balsams. *Ibid.*

I could be content that we might procreate like trees, without conjunction, or that there were any way to perpetuate the world without this trivial and vulgar way of coition: it is the foolishest act a wise man commite in all his life. *Ibid., ‡9.*

There is no such thing as solitude, nor anything that can be said to be alone, and by itself, but God; who is his own circle, and can subsist by himself. *Ibid., ‡10.*

The religion of one seems madness unto another. *Ibid.*

What song the Syrens sang, or what

name Achilles assumed when he hid among women, though puzzling questions, are not beyond all conjecture.   *Ibid.*

There is a certain list of vices committed in all ages, and desclaimed against by all Authors, which will last as long as human nature; or digested into commonplaces may serve for any theme, and never be out of date until Doomsday.
Pseudoxica Epidemica, 1658.

The mortalest enemy unto knowledge, and that which hath done the greatest execution unto truth, hath been a peremptory adhesion unto authority, and especially of our belief upon the dictates of antiquities. For (as every capacity may observe) most of ages present to do so superstitiously look upon ages past that authorities of one excel the reasons of the other.

Robert Browning
(1812-1889)
English poet

You call for faith:
I show you doubt, to prove that faith exists.
The more of doubt, the stronger faith, I say,
If faith o'ercomes doubt.
Bishop Blougram's Apology.

How I shall live through centuries,
And hear the blessed mutter of the Mass,
And see God made and eaten all day long,
And feel the steady candle-flame, and taste
Good strong thick stupefying incense-smoke.
The Bishop Orders His Tomb at St. Praxed's Church.

How very hard it is to be
        A Christian!   *Easter Day.*

'Tis well averred,
A scientific faith's absurd.   *Ibid.*

Progress, man's distinctive mark alone,
Not God's, and not the beasts': God is, they are,
Man partly is and wholly hopes to be.
        A Death in the Desert.

Just for a handful of silver he left us,
    Just for a riband to stick in his coat—
Found the one gift of which fortune bereft us,
        Lost all the others she lets us devote.
        The Lost Leader*, 1845.

Shakespeare was of us, Milton was for us,
    Burns, Shelley, were with us—they watch from their graves!
He alone breaks from the van and the freeman,
    He alone sinks to the rear and the slaves!   *Ibid.*

We shall march prospering—not thro' his presence;
    Songs may inspirit us—not from his lyre;
Deeds will be done—while he boasts his quiescence,
    Still bidding crouch whom the rest bade aspire:
Blot out his name, then, record one lost soul more,
    One task more declined, one more footpath untrod,
One more devil's-triumph and sorrow for angels,
    One wrong more to man, one more insult to God!   *Ibid.*

Progress is the law of life; man is not man as yet.   *Paracelsus.*

Mothers, wives, and maids,
There be the tools wherewith priests manage men.
        The Ring and the Book, iv.

---

* A reference to Wordsworth.

Orestes A. Brownson
(1803-1876)
*American philosophical writer,
founder of Workingmen's Party*

The English laborer does not find his worst enemy in the nobility, but in the middling class.
The Laboring Classes, 1840.

The middle class is always a firm champion of equality when it concerns a class above it; but it is its inveterate foe when it concerns elevating a class below it.
Ibid.

Manfully have the British Commoners struggled against the old feudal aristocracy, and so successfully that they now constitute the dominant power in the state. To their struggles against the throne and the nobility is the English nation indebted for the liberty it so loudly boasts, and which, during the last half of the last century, so enraptured the friends of Humanity throughout Europe.

But this class has done nothing for the laboring population, the real proletarii. It has humbled the aristocracy; it has raised itself to dominion, and it is now conservative,—conservative in fact, whether it call itself Whig or Radical. From its near relation to the workingmen, its kindred pursuits with them, it is altogether more hostile to them than the nobility ever were or ever can be.
Ibid.

No one can observe the signs of the times with much care without perceiving that a crisis as to the relation of wealth and labor is approaching. It is useless to shut our eyes to the fact, and like the ostrich fancy ourselves secure because we have so concealed our heads that we see not the danger. We or our children will have to meet this crisis. The old war between the King and the Barons is well-nigh ended, and so is that between the Barons and the Merchants and Manufacturers,—landed capital and commercial capital. The business man has become the peer of my Lord. And now commences the new struggle between the operative and his employer, between wealth and labor. Every day does this struggle extend further and wax stronger and fiercer; what or when the end will be, God only knows.
Ibid.

The most dreaded of all wars, the war of the poor against the rich, a war which, however long it may be delayed, will come, and come with all its horrors.
Boston Quarterly, July, 1840.

Wages is a cunning device of the devil, for the benefit of tender consciences, who would retain all the advantages of the slave system, without the expense, trouble, and odium of being slave-holders.
Ibid.

If there must always be a laboring population distinct from proprietors and employers, we regard the slave system as decidedly preferable to the system at wages.
Ibid.

Giordano Bruno
(1548?-burned at the stake, 1600*)
Italian philosopher

There is no law governing all things.
De monade numero et figura, ii.

I hold that there is an infinite universe, which is the effect of the Infinite Divine Power, because I esteem it to be a thing unworthy of the Divine Goodness and Power that, being able to produce another world, and an infinite number of others

---

* "He turned his face away from the proffered crucifix and died in silence." Georgio de Santillana, The Age of Enlightenment.

besides this world, it should produce one finite world.   *Letter to the Inquisition.*

There is one truth and one goodness penetrating and governing all things.
Ibid.

We are surrounded by eternity and by the uniting of love. There is but one center from which all species issue, as rays from a sun, and to which all species return.
Ibid.

Truly religious and learned theologians have never challenged the freedom of philosophers; while the true, civilized and well-organized philosophers have always favored religions. Both sides are aware that religion is needed for restraining rude populations, which have to be ruled, whereas rational demonstration is for such, of a contemplative nature, as know how to rule themselves and others.
Heroic Furors, translated by L. Williams, Redway, 1887.

Doctor of a more scientific theology, professor of a purer and less harmful learning . . . a stranger with none but the uncivilized and ignoble, awakener of sleeping minds, tamer of presumptuous and obstinate ignorance who in all respects professes a general love of man, and cared not for the Italian more than for the Briton, male more than female, the mitre more than the crown, the toga more than the coat of mail, the cowled more than the uncowled; but loves who in intercourse is the more peaceable, polite, friendly and useful—
(Brunus) whom only propagators of folly and hypocrites detest, whom the honourable and studious love, whom noble minds applaud.
Card of credentials, presented to Oxford University, inviting a lectureship; quoted by Abramowitz, The Great Prisoners.

It is proof of a base and low mind for one to wish to think with the masses or majority, merely because the majority is the majority. Truth does not change because it is, or is not, believed by a majority of the people.

Bruyère
See la Bruyère

William Jennings Bryan
(1860-1925)
American orator, politician

This is not a contest between persons. The humblest citizen in all the land, when clad in the armor of a righteous cause, is stronger than all the hosts of error. I come to speak to you in defense of a cause as holy as the cause of liberty—the cause of humanity.
Speech, Democratic National Convention, 1896.

We object to bringing this question down to the level of persons. The individual is but an atom; he is born, he acts, he dies; but principles are eternal; and this has been a contest over a principle.   *Ibid.*

They tell us that this platform was made to catch votes. We reply to them that chai.ging conditions make new issues; that the principles upon which Democracy rests are as everlasting as the hills, but that they must be applied to new conditions as they arise.   *Ibid.*

If they ask us why it is that we say more on the money question than we say upon the tariff question, I reply that, if protection has slain its thousands, the gold standard has slain its tens of thousands. *Ibid.*

The question we are to decide is: Upon which side will the Democratic party fight;

upon the side of "the idle holders of idle capital" or upon the side of "the struggling masses"? . . . The sympathies of the Democratic party, as shown by the platform, are on the side of the struggling masses who have ever been the foundation of the Democratic party. There are two ideas of government. There are those who believe that, if you will only legislate to make the well-to-do prosperous, their prosperity will leak through on those below. The Democratic idea, however, has been that if you legislate to make the masses prosperous, their prosperity will find its way up through every class which rests upon them. *Ibid.*

Having behind us the producing masses of this nation, and the world, supported by the commercial interests, the laboring interests, and the toilers everywhere, we will answer their demand for a gold standard by saying to them: You shall not press down upon the brow of labor the crown of thorns, you shall not crucify mankind upon a cross of gold. *Ibid.*

The money power preys upon the Nation in times of peace and conspires against it in times of adversity. It is more despotic than monarchy, more insolent than autocracy, more selfish than bureaucracy. It denounces, as public enemies, all who question its methods, or throw light upon its crimes.

William Cullen Bryant
(1794-1878)
American poet, editor

The press, important as is its office, is but the servant of human intellect and its ministry is for good or evil, according to the character of those who direct it. The press is a mill that grinds all that is put into its hopper. Fill the hopper with poisoned grain and it will grind it to meal but there is death in the bread.
Prose writings, II, The Newspaper Press.

What was their offence? They had committed the crime of unanimously declining to go to work at the wages offered to them by their masters. They had said to one another, "Let us come out from the meanness and misery of our caste. Let us begin to do what every order more privileged and more honoured is doing every day. By the means which we believe to be the best let us raise ourselves and our families above the humbleness of our condition. We may be wrong, but we cannot help believing that we might do much if we were true brothers of each other, and would resolve not to sell the only thing which is our own, the cunning of our hands, for less than it is worth". What other things they may have done is nothing to the purpose: it was for this they were condemned; it is for this they are to endure the penalty of the law.
Editorial on the rights of workmen to organize and strike, June 13, 1836.

Can anything be imagined more abhorrent to every sentiment of generosity or justice than the law which arms the rich with the legal right to fix, by assize, the wages of the poor? If this is not SLAVERY, we have forgotten its definition. Strike the right of associating for the sale of labour from the privileges of a freeman, and you may as well at once bind him to a master, or ascribe him to the soil. If it be not in the colour of his skin, and in the poor franchise of naming his own terms in a contract for his work, what advantage has the labourer of the north over the bondman of the south? Punish by human laws a "determination not to work", make it penal by any other penalty than idleness inflicts, and it matters little whether the taskmasters be one or many, an individual or an order, the hateful scheme of slavery will have gained a foothold in the land. *Ibid.*

The right to discuss freely and openly, by speech, by the pen, by the press, all political questions, and to examine and animadvert upon all political institutions, is a right so clear and certain, so interwoven with our other liberties, so necessary, in fact, to their existence, that without it we must fall at once into despotism and anarchy. To say that he who holds unpopular opinions must hold them at the peril of his life, and that, if he expresses them in public, he has only himself to blame if they who disagree with him should rise and put him to death, is to strike at all rights, all liberties, all protection of law, and to justify or extenuate all crimes.
Editorial on the murder of Rev. E. P. Lovejoy, 1837.

Yet, mighty God, yet shall thy frown
  look forth
Unveiled, and terribly shall shake the
  earth.
Then the foul power of priestly sin and
  all
Its long-upheld idolatries shall fall.
Thou shalt raise up the trampled and
  oppressed,
And thy delivered saints shall dwell in
  rest.
    Hymn of the Waldenses, 1824.

Weep not that the world changes—did it keep a stable, changeless state, it were cause indeed to weep.

Oh Freedom, thou art not as poets dream
  A fair young girl with light and delicate
    limbs
And wavy tresses. A bearded man
  Armed to the teeth art thou. One
    mailed hand

Grasps the broad shield and one the
  sword; thy brow
Glorious in beauty though it be, is
  scarred
With tokens of old wars. . . .

James Bryce
(1838-1922)
British historian, jurist, diplomat

The tendency everywhere in America to concentrate power and responsibility in one man is unmistakable.
    The American Commonwealth.

In no other country is the ideal side of public life so ignored by the mass and repudiated by its leaders.   *Ibid.*

Towering over Presidents and State Governors, over Congress and State Legislatures, over conventions and the vast machinery of party, public opinion stands out, in the United States, as the great source of Power, the master of servants who tremble before it.   *Ibid.*

Martin Buber
(1878-1965)
Israeli theologian

Power abdicates only under stress of counter-power.
    Paths in Utopia, 1950.

Martin Bucer
(1490-1551)
German Protestant reformer

Neither the Church of Christ, nor a Christian Commonwealth, ought to tolerate such as prefer private gain to the public weal, or seek it to the hurt of their neighbors.   *De Regno Christi.*

Robert Buchanan
(1841-1901)
Scottish poet, novelist, playwright

A thousand starve, a few are fed,
  Legions of robbers rack the poor,
The rich man steals the widow's bread,
  And Lazarus dies at Dives' door;
The Lawyer and the Priest adjust
The claims of Luxury and Lust
To seize the earth and hold the soil,
  To store the grain they never reap;
Under their heels the white slaves toil,
  While children wail and women weep!
The New Rome.

The gods are dead, but in their name
Humanity is sold to shame,
While (then as now!) the tinsel'd Priest
Sitteth with robbers at the feast,
Blesses the laden blood-stain'd board,
Weaves garlands round the butcher's
  sword,
And poureth freely (now as then)
The sacramental blood of Men!
Ibid.

Pearl S. Buck
(1892-1973)
American writer, Nobel Prize, 1938

When good people in any country cease
their vigilance and struggle, then evil men
prevail.

I feel no need for any other faith than
my faith in human beings. Like Confucius
of old, I am so absorbed in the wonder of
earth and the life upon it that I cannot
think of heaven and the angels.

Be born anywhere, little embryo novelist,
but do not be born under the shadow of a
great creed, not under the burden of original sin, not under the doom of Salvation.
Advice to Unborn Novelists.

George Villiers, 2nd Duke of Buckingham
(1628-1687)
English satirist, poet, dramatist

The world is made up, for the most part,
of fools or knaves, both irreconcilable foes
to truth: the first being slaves to a blind
credulity, which we may properly call bigotry, the last too jealous of that power they
have usurped over the folly and ignorance
of the others, which the establishment of
the empire of reason would destroy.

Henry Thomas Buckle
(1821-1862)
English historian

Every new truth which has ever been
propounded has, for a time caused mischief;
it has produced discomfort, and often unhappiness; sometimes disturbing social and
religious arrangements, and sometimes merely by the disruption of old and cherished
association of thoughts. It is only after a
certain interval, and when the framework
of affairs has adjusted itself to the new
truth, that its good effects preponderate;
and the preponderance continues to increase, until at length, the truth causes
nothing but good. But, at the outset there
is always harm. And if the truth is very
great as well as very new, the harm is
serious. Men are made uneasy; they flinch;
they cannot bear the sudden light; a general restlessness supervenes; the face of
society is disturbed, or perhaps convulsed;
old interests and old beliefs have been
destroyed before new ones have been
created. These symptoms are the precursors
of revolution; they have preceded all the
great changes through which the world has
passed. *History of Civilization.*

Society prepares the crime; the criminal commits it.

Even in an advanced stage of civilization, there is always a tendency to prefer those parts of literature which favor ancient prejudices, rather than those which oppose them; and in cases where this tendency is very strong, the only effect of great learning will be to supply the materials which may corroborate old errors and confirm old superstitions. In our time such instances are not uncommon; and we frequently meet with men whose erudition ministers to their ignorance, and who, the more they read the less they know.

The Church of Rome . . . has been and still is very pliant in regard to morals and very flexible in regard to dogmas. . . . This peculiarity, though strongly marked in the Romish Church, is by no means confined to it, but is found in every religious sect which is regularly organized.

Some of the most beautiful passages in the apostolic writings are quotations from pagan authors.

To assert that Christianity communicated to man moral truths previously unknown, argues on the part of the asserter either gross ignorance or else wilful fraud. . . . The system of morals expounded in the New Testament contains no maxims which had not been previously enunciated.

Gautama Buddha
(563?-483? B.C.)
Indian philosopher

Believe nothing, O monks, merely because you have been told it . . . or because it is traditional, or because you yourselves have imagined it. Do not believe what your teacher tells you merely out of respect for the teacher. But whatsoever, after due examination and analysis, you find to be conducive to the good, the benefit, the welfare of all beings—that doctrine believe and cling to, and take it as your guide.

Those indeed are conquerors who, as I have now, have conquered the intoxications (the mental intoxications arising from ignorance, sensuality or craving after future life). Evil dispositions have ceased in me; therefore it is I that am conqueror!
Attributed; Encyclopaedia Britannica, 11th ed., vol. iv.

Bulwer-Lytton
See Lytton

John Bunyan
(1628-1688)
English religious writer, allegorist

Question: What kind of sins are the greatest?
Answer: Adultery, fornication, murder, theft, swearing, witchcraft, sedition, heresies, or any the like.
Instructions for the Ignorant, 1675.

Luther Burbank
(1849-1926)
American horticulturist

Less than fifteen per cent of the people do any original thinking on any subject. . . . The greatest torture in the world for most people is to think.

The scientist is a lover of truth for the very love of truth itself, wherever it may lead.

Men should stop fighting among themselves and start fighting insects.

We must learn that any person who will not accept what he knows to be truth, for the very love of truth alone, is very definitely undermining his mental integrity. . . . You have not been a close observer of such men if you have not seen them shrivel, become commonplace, mean, without influence, without friends and without the enthusiasm of youth and growth, like a tree covered with fungus, the foliage diseased, the life gone out of the heart with dry rot, and indelibly marked for destruction—dead, but not yet handed over to the undertaker.

The idea that a good God would send people to a burning Hell is utterly damnable to me. The ravings of insanity! Superstition gone to seed! I don't want to have anything to do with such a God. No avenging Jewish God, no satanic devil, no fiery hell is of any interest to me.

I am an infidel in the true sense of that word.

There is no personal salvation; there is no national salvation, except through science.

Our lives, as we live them, are passed on to others, whether in physical or mental forms, tinging all future lives forever. This should be enough for one who lives for truth and service to his fellow passengers on the way.

Edmund Burke
(1729-1797)
English political writer, orator

Power gradually extirpates from the mind every humane and gentle virtue.
A Vindication of Natural Society, 1756.

The whole business of the poor is to administer to the idleness of the rich; and that of the rich, in return, is to find the best methods of confirming the slavery and increasing the burthens of the poor.
Ibid.

In a state of nature it is an invariable law, that a man's acquisitions are in proportion to his labours. In a state of artificial society, it is a law as constant and as invariable, that those who labour not at all, have the greatest number of enjoyments.
Ibid.

A man is allowed sufficient freedom of thought, provided he knows how to choose his subject properly. You may criticize freely upon the Chinese constitution, and observe with as much severity as you please upon the absurd tricks or destructive bigotry of the Bonzees. But the scene is changed as you come homeward, and atheism or treason may be the names given in Britain to what would be reason and truth if asserted of China.
Ibid.

The miseries derived to mankind from superstition under the name of religion, and of ecclesiastical tyranny under the name of church government, have been clearly and usefully exposed. We begin to think and to act from reason and from nature alone.
Ibid.

But still is by far the majority in the same old state of blindness and slavery; and much is to be feared that we shall perpetually relapse, while the real productive cause of all this superstitious folly, ecclesiastical nonsense, and holy tyranny hold a reverend place in the estimation even of those who are otherwise enlightened.
Ibid.

The first accounts we have of mankind are but so many accounts of their butcheries. All empires have been cemented in blood; and, in those early periods when the races of mankind began first to form themselves into parties and combinations, the first effect of the combination, and indeed the end for which it seems purposely formed, and best calculated, is their mutual destruction.   *Ibid.*

It is no less worth observing that this artificial division of mankind into separate societies is a perpetual source in itself of hatred and dissension among them. The names which distinguish them are enough to blow up hatred and rage.   *Ibid.*

Examine history; consult present experience; and you will find that far the greater part of the quarrels between several nations had scarce any other occasion than that these nations were different combinations of people, and called by different names; to an Englishman, the name of a Frenchman, a Spaniard, an Italian, much more a Turk, or a Tartar, raises ideas of hatred and contempt.   *Ibid.*

Ask of politicians the ends for which laws were originally designed, and they will answer that the laws were designed as a protection for the poor and the weak, against the oppression of the rich and powerful. But surely no pretense can be so ridiculous; a man might as well tell me he has taken off my load, because he has changed the burden.   *Ibid.*

If the poor man is not able to support his suit according to the vexations and expensive manner established in civilized countries, has not the rich as great an advantage over him as the strong has over the weak in a state of nature?   *Ibid.*

In a state of nature it is true that a man of superior force may beat or rob me; but then it is true that I am at full liberty to defend myself, or make reprisal by surprise, or by cunning, or by any other way in which I may be superior to him. But in political society a rich man may rob me in another way. I cannot defend myself; for money is the only weapon with which we are allowed to fight. And if I attempt to avenge myself, the whole force of that society is ready to complete my ruin.
                        Ibid.

The nearer we approach to the goal of life, the better we begin to understand the true value of our existence and the real weight of our opinions. We set out much in love with both; but we leave much behind as we advance. We first throw away the tales along with the rattles of our nurses; those of the priest keep their hold a little longer; those of our governors the longest of all. But the passions which prop these opinions are withdrawn one after another; and the cool light of reason, at the setting of our life, shows us what a false splendor played upon these objects during our more sanguine seasons.   *Ibid.*

It is hard to say whether the doctors of law or divinity have made the greater advances in the lucrative business of mystery.
                            Ibid.

Party divisions, whether on the whole operating for good or evil, are things inseparable from free government.
Observations on a Late State of the Nation, 1769.

The greater the powers, the more dangerous the abuse.
Speech, Middlesex election, 1771.

Falsehood has a perennial spring.
Speech on American Taxation, 1774.

Passion for fame; a passion which is the instinct of all great souls . . .   *Ibid.*

To tax and to please, no more than to love and to be wise, is not given to men.
Ibid.

Abstract Liberty, like other mere abstractions, is not to be found. Liberty inheres in some sensible object; and every nation has formed to itself some favourite point, which by way of eminence becomes the criterion of their happiness.
Speech on Conciliation with America, March 22, 1775.

Then, Sir, from these six capital sources; of Descent; of Form of Government; of Religion in the Northern Provinces; of Manners in the Southern; of Education; of the Remoteness of Situation from the first Mover of Government; from all these causes a fierce Spirit of Liberty has grown up.
Ibid.

All government, indeed every human benefit and enjoyment, every virtue, and every prudent act, is founded on compromise and barter. We balance inconveniences; we give and take—we remit some rights that we may enjoy others. . . . Man acts from motives relative to his interests; and not on metaphysical speculations.
Ibid.

I do not know the method of drawing up an indictment against a whole people. The natural rights of mankind are indeed sacred things, and if any public measure is proved mischievously to affect them, the objection ought to be fatal to that measure, even if no charter at all could be set up against it. Only a sovereign reason, paramount to all forms of legislation and administration, should dictate.
Ibid.

I know many have been taught to think that moderation in a case like this, is a sort of treason.
Letter to the Sheriffs of Bristol, April 3, 1777.

Among a people generally corrupt liberty cannot long exist.
Ibid.

Liberty must be limited in order to be possessed.
Ibid.

People, crushed by law, have no hopes but power.
Letter to C. J. Fox, October 8, 1777.

As wealth is power, so all power must infallibly draw wealth to itself by some means or other.
Commons, February 11, 1780.

To govern according to the sense and agreement of the interests of the people is a great and glorious object of government. This object cannot be obtained but through the medium of popular election, and popular election is a mighty evil.
Speech on the Duration of Parliaments, May 8, 1780.

A spirit of innovation is generally the result of a selfish temper and confined views. People will not look forward to posterity, who never look backward to their ancestors. Besides, the people of England well know that the idea of inheritance furnishes a sure principle of conservation, and a sure principle of transmission, without at all excluding a principle of improvement. It leaves acquisition free; but it secures what it acquires.
Reflections on the Revolution in France, 1790.

Whatever each man can separately do, without trespassing upon others, he has a right to do for himself; and he has a right to a fair portion of all which society, with all its combinations of skill and force, can do in his favor. In this partnership all men have equal rights; but not to equal things.
Ibid.

Government is a contrivance of human wisdom to provide for human wants.
Ibid.

We are not converts of Rousseau; we are not the disciples of Voltaire; Helvetius has made no progress amongst us. Atheists are not our preachers; madmen are not our lawgivers. We know that *we* have made no discoveries, and we think that no discoveries are to be made, in morality,—nor many in the great principles of government, nor in the ideas of liberty. *Ibid.*

We have consecrated the state, that no man should approach to look into its defects or corruptions but with due caution, that he should never dream of beginning its reformation by its subversion; that he should approach to the faults of the state as to the wounds of a father, with pious awe and trembling solicitude. *Ibid.*

Society is, indeed, a contract. . . . It is a partnership in all science, a partnership in all art, a partnership in every virtue and in all perfection. *Ibid.*

Make the Revolution a parent of settlement, and not a nursery of future revolutions. *Ibid.*

All persons possessing a portion of power ought to be strongly and awfully impressed with an idea that they act in trust, and that they are to account for their conduct in that trust to the one great Master, Author, and Founder of society. *Ibid.*

The power of perpetuating our property in our families is one of the most valuable and interesting circumstances belonging to it, and that which tends the most to the perpetuation of society itself. *Ibid.*

Kings will be tyrants from policy, when subjects are rebels from principle. *Ibid.*

An absolute democracy no more than absolute monarchy is to be reckoned among the legitimate forms of government. *Ibid.*

In a democracy the majority of citizens is capable of exercising the most cruel oppressions upon the minority . . . and that oppression of the minority will extend to far greater numbers, and will be carried on with much greater fury, than can almost ever be apprehended from the dominion of a single sceptre. Under a cruel prince they have the plaudits of the people to animate their generous constancy under their sufferings; but those who are subjected to wrong under multitudes are deprived of all external consolation: they seem deserted by mankind, overpowered by a conspiracy of their whole species. *Ibid.*

The people never give up their liberties but under some delusion. *Speech, 1784.*

Nothing is so fatal to religion as indifference, which is, at least, half infidelity.
Letter to Wm. Smith, January 9, 1795.

The only thing necessary for the triumph of evil is for good men to do nothing.

We must all obey the great law of change. It is the most powerful law of nature.

There is but one law for all; namely, that law which governs all law—the law of our Creator, the law of humanity, justice, equity; the law of nature and of nations.

A very great part of the mischiefs that vex this world arises from words.

The tyranny of a multitude is a multiplied tyranny. *Letter to Thomas Mercer.*

Bad laws are the worst sort of tyranny.

Politics and the pulpit are terms that have little agreement.

But what is liberty without wisdom, and without virtue? It is the greatest of all possible evils; for it is folly, vice, and madness, without tuition or restraint.

I am not of the opinion of those gentlemen who are against disturbing the public repose; I like a clamour wherever there is an abuse. The fire-bell at midnight disturbs our sleep; but it keeps you from being burnt in your bed.

There are some men formed with feelings so blunt, that they can hardly be said to be awake during the whole course of their lives.
S. A. Allibone, Prose Quotations, 1876.

War never leaves where it found a nation.
Letters on a Regicide peace.

I know of nothing sublime which is not some modification of power.

Those who have once been intoxicated with power, and have derived any kind of emolument from it, even though but for one year, can never willingly abandon it.
Letter to member of National Assembly.

A nation without means of reform is without means of survival.
Quoted by Adlai E. Stevenson, Harper's Magazine, February, 1956.

The individual is foolish; the multitude, for the moment, is foolish, when they act without deliberation; but the species is wise, and, when time is given to it, as a species it always acts right.
Reform of Representation, Works, Vol. VI.

Whenever a separation is made between liberty and justice, neither, in my opinion, is safe.

The true danger is, when liberty is nibbled away, for expedients, and by parts.

Those who attempt to level never equalize. In all societies some description must be uppermost. The levellers, therefore, only change and pervert the natural order of things; they load the edifice of society by setting up in the air what the solidity of the structure requires to be on the ground.

Facts are to the mind what food is to the body. . . . The wisest in council, the ablest in debate, and the most agreeable companion in the commerce of human life, is that man who has assimilated to his understanding the greatest number of facts.

John H. Burns
(b. 1889)
American general

The military problem, psychologically speaking, resolves itself into taking every advantage of the herd instinct to integrate the mass. . . . This military processing of civilians is a purely empirical thing, but it is an eminently sound one. It has been handed down from past armies. . . . Constant repetition of the item to be inculcated unsupported by any reasons will have an immense effect on the suggestible, herd-minded human. An opinion, an idea, or a code acquired in this manner can become so firmly fixed that one who questions its essential rightness will be regarded as foolish, wicked, or insane. Suggestion, then, is the key to inculcating discipline, esprit, and morale.
Infantry Journal, December, 1928; quoted by Oswald Garrison Villard, Our Military Chaos, pp. 135-6.

Robert Burns
(1759-1796)
Scottish poet

All my fears and cares are of this world; if there is another, an honest man has nothing to fear from it.

Look abroad thro' Nature's range.
Nature's mighty law is change.
  Let Not Women E'er Complain.

The upright, honest-hearted man
Who strives to do the best he can,
Need never fear the church's ban
Or hell's damnation.

The friend of man, the friend of truth,
The friend of age, the guide of youth;
  If there's another world, he lives in
    bliss;
If there is none, he made the best of this.

God knows, I'm not the thing I should be,
Nor am I even the thing I could be,
But twenty times I rather would be
  An atheist clean,
Than under gospel colours hid be
  Just for a screen.
    Epistle to the Rev. John McMath.

Is there for honest poverty,
  That hangs his head, and a' that?
The coward slave, we pass him by,
  We daur be puir, for a' that!
    Is There for Honest Poverty, 1795.

The rank is but the guinea stamp—
  The man's the gowd for a' that.
    Ibid.

What though on hamely fare we dine,
  Wear hoddin-grey and a' that;
Gi'e fools their silks, and knaves their
    wine—
  A man's a man for a' that,
  Their tinsel show and a' that,
The honest man, though ne'er sae puir,
  Is king o' men for a' that.
    Ibid.

The man of independent mind,
  He looks and laughs at a' that.
    Ibid.

Then let us pray that come it may,
  As come it will for a' that,
That sense and worth, o'er a' the earth,
  May bear the gree and a' that.
  For a' that, and a' that,
  It's comin' yet, for a' that,
When man to man, the world o'er,
  Shall brithers be for a' that.
    Ibid.

John Burroughs
(1837-1921)
American essayist

For my part, the longer I live the less
I feel the need of any sort of theological
belief, and the more I am content to let
unseen powers go on their way with me
and mine without question or distrust.
    The Light of Day.

It is always easier to believe than to
deny. Our minds are naturally affirmative.
    Ibid.

The Kingdom of Heaven is not a place,
but a state of mind.   *Ibid.*

If we take science as our sole guide, if
we accept and hold fast that alone which
is verifiable, the old theology must go.
    Ibid.

The deeper our insight into the methods
of nature . . . the more incredible the
popular Christianity seems to us.   *Ibid.*

Science has done more for the development of western civilization in one hundred
years than Christianity did in eighteen
hundred years.   *Ibid.*

When I look up at the starry heavens at
night and reflect upon what is it that I
really see there, I am constrained to say,
"There is no God". . . . It is not the works
of some God that I see there. . . . I see no

lineaments of personality, no human traits, but an energy upon whose currents, solar systems are but bubbles. *Ibid.*

Richard Francis Burton
(1821-1890)
English explorer, archaeologist

There is no Heaven, there is no Hell;
These are the dreams of baby minds;
Tools of the wily Fetisheer,
To fright the fools his cunning blinds.
The Kasidah, VIII.

Robert Burton
(1577-1640)
English author, clergyman

A blow with a word strikes deeper than a blow with a sword.
The Anatomy of Melancholy.

One religion is as true as another. *Ibid.*

I no sooner come into the library, but I bolt the door to me, excluding lust, avarice and all such vices, whose nurse is idleness, the mother of ignorance and melancholy herself, and in the very lap of eternity, amongst so many divine souls, I take my seat, with so lofty a spirit and sweet content that I pity all our great ones and rich men that know not this happiness. *Ibid.*

It (lust) subverts kingdoms, overthrows cities, towns, families; mars, corrupts and makes a massacre of men; thunder and lightning, wars, fires, plagues, have not done that mischief as this burning lust, this brutish passion. *Ibid.*

Hermann Busenbaum
(1600-1668)
German Jesuit priest, writer

When the end is lawful, the means are also lawful. *Medulla Theologiae, 1650.*

Vannevar Bush
(b. 1890)
American scientist

It is man's mission to learn to understand.
Address, American Philosophical Society.

We have the means of removing starvation and disease. We have almost unlimited power in sight, that can make the waste lands bloom. We have the possibility of banishing disease. . . .

We know, or can know, how to learn the truth, and to tell it to one another throughout a healthy world that is secure against the ravages of nature. It is the setting for a world of peace and unity.

One thing is lacking: good will and understanding.
Address, Columbia University alumni, June 3, 1947.

Our simple survival is not worth so much that it is to be purchased at the cost of intellectual stultification. Nor would the suppression of dangerous inquiry save us. Although the achievements of science may, indeed, throw us back into barbarism, the abandonment of our search for knowledge and material betterment would only make vegetables of us.

Nicholas Murray Butler
(1862-1947)
American educator, Nobel Prize, 1931

An educated proletariat is a constant source of disturbance and danger to any nation.
Requoted in The Nation, from the N. Y. World-Telegram.

The wicked have a solid interest that the good never seem to possess. The good

are grand for one great rally. Then they go home and work at their business. The cohesive power of public plunder remains on the job.
Editor & Publisher, March 20, 1954.

The force that rules the world is conduct, whether it be moral or immoral.

Samuel Butler
(1612-1680)
English poet, satirist

Self-preservation is the first law of nature.
Remains.

Authority intoxicates,
And makes mere sots of magistrates;
The fumes of it invade the brain,
And make men giddy, proud and vain.

Religion is the interest of the churches
That sell in other worlds in this to purchase.

Samuel Butler
(1835-1902)
English writer

Though wisdom cannot be gotten for gold, still less can it be gotten without it. Gold, or the values of what is equivalent to gold, lies at the root of wisdom, and enters so largely into the very essence of the Holy Ghost that "no gold, no Holy Ghost" may pass as an axiom.
Note-Books.

An honest God's the noblest work of man.
Ibid.

Any fool can tell the truth, but it requires a man of some sense to know how to lie well.
Ibid.

There are more fools than knaves in the world, else the knaves would not have enough to live upon.
Ibid.

I don't mind lying, but I hate inaccuracy.
Ibid.

Cursed is he that does not know when to shut his mind. An open mind is all very well in its way, but it ought not to be so open that there is no keeping anything in or out of it. It should be capable of shutting its doors sometimes, or may be found a little draughty.
Ibid.

All of the animals excepting man know that the principal business of life is to enjoy it.
Ibid.

Posterity will give a man a fair hearing; his own times will not do so if he is attacking vested interests, and I have attacked two powerful sets of vested interests at once —the Church and Science.
Ibid.

The public buys its opinions as it buys its meat, or takes in its milk, on the principle that it is cheaper to do this than to keep a cow. So it is, but the milk is more likely to be watered.
Ibid.

Hell is the work of prigs, pedants and professional truth-tellers.
Ibid.

There are two great rules of life, the one general and the other particular. The first is that everyone can, in the end, get what he wants if he only tries. This is the general rule. The particular rule is that every individual is, more or less, an exception to the rule.
Ibid.

All progress is based upon the universal innate desire on the part of every organism to live beyond its income.
Ibid.

If a new edition of the Church Catechism is ever required, I should like to introduce a few words insisting on the duty of seeking all reasonable pleasure and avoiding all pain that can be honourably avoided.
Ibid.

Smedley Butler
(1881-1940)
U.S. Marine commander

I spent 33 years (in the Marines) . . . most of my time being a high-class muscle man for Big Business, for Wall Street and the bankers. In short, I was a racketeer for capitalism. . . .

I helped purify Nicaragua for the international banking house of Brown Brothers in 1909-1912. I helped make Mexico and especially Tampico safe for American oil interests in 1914. I brought light to the Dominican Republic for American sugar interests in 1916. I helped make Haiti and Cuba a decent place for the National City (Bank) boys to collect revenue in. I helped in the rape of half a dozen Central American republics for the benefit of Wall Street. . . .

In China in 1927 I helped see to it that Standard Oil went its way unmolested . . . I had . . . a swell racket. I was rewarded with honors, medals, promotions. . . . I might have given Al Capone a few hints. The best he could do was to operate a racket in three city districts. The Marines operated on three continents.

We don't want any more wars, but a man is a damn fool to think there won't be any more of them. I am a peace-loving Quaker, but when war breaks out every damn man in my family goes. If we're ready, nobody will tackle us. . . .
*The World Tomorrow, October, 1931;
N.Y. Times, August 21, 1931.*

There is no use talking about abolishing war; that's damn foolishness. Take the guns away from men and they will fight just the same.   *Ibid.*

No pacifists or Communists are going to govern this country. If they try it there will be seven million men like you rise up and strangle them. Pacifists? Hell, I'm a pacifist, but I always have a club behind my back.
Ibid.

You know very well that it (the American Legion) is nothing but a strike-breaking outfit used by capital for that purpose, and that is the reason we have all those big clubhouses and that is the reason I pulled out of it. They have been using the dumb soldiers to break strikes.
Testimony before House of Representatives' Committee, Investigation of Nazi and Other Propaganda. 1935.

Do you think it could be hard to buy the American Legion for un-American activities? You know, the average veteran thinks the Legion is a patriotic organization to perpetuate the memories of the last war, an organization to promote peace, to take care of the wounded and to keep green the graves of those who gave their lives.

But is the American Legion that? No sir, not while it is controlled by the bankers. For years the bankers, by buying big club houses for various posts, by financing its beginning, and otherwise, have tried to make a strikebreaking organization of the Legion. The groups—the so-called Royal Family of the Legion—which have picked its officers for years, aren't interested in patriotism, in peace, in wounded veterans, in those who gave their lives. . . . No, they are interested only in using the veterans, through their officers.
Speech frequently delivered after his appearance before Un-American Activities Committee.

War is a racket.
Forum magazine, September, 1934.

War, like any other racket, pays high dividends to the very few. But what does it profit the masses? . . . The cost of operations is always transferred to the people who do not profit. *Ibid.*

But there is a way to stop this racket. It cannot be smashed by disarmament conferences, by peace parleys at Geneva, by resolutions of well-meaning but impractical groups. It can be effectively smashed only by taking the profit out of war.

The only way to stop it is by conscription of capital before conscription of the nation's manhood. *Ibid.*

Let the officers and directors of our armament factories, our gun builders and munitions makers and shipbuilders all be conscripted—to get $30 a month, the same wage paid to the lads in the trenches. Give capital thirty days to think it over and you will learn by that time there will be no war. That will stop the racket—that, and nothing else. *Ibid.*

James F. Byrnes
(1879-1972)
American politician

Power intoxicates men. It is never voluntarily surrendered. It must be taken from them. The Supreme Court must be curbed. *Copyright, U.S. News; reprinted, N.Y. Times and N.Y. Herald Tribune, May 15 and 16, 1956.*

Lord Byron
(1778-1824)
English poet

Hereditary bondsmen! know ye not
Who would be free themselves must strike the blow?
By their right arms the conquest must be wrought?
Will Gaul or Muscovite redress ye? no!

True, they may lay your proud despoilers low.
But not for you will Freedom's altars flame.
Childe Harold's Pilgrimage, 1809-1817.

He who ascends to mountain tops, shall find
The loftiest peaks most wrapped in clouds and snow;
He who surpasses or subdues mankind,
Must look down on the hate of those below. *Ibid.*

Can tyrants but by tyrants conquer'd be,
And Freedom find no champion and no child
Such as Columbia saw arise when she
Sprung forth a Pallas, arm'd and undefiled? *Ibid.*

Yet, Freedom! yet the banner, torn, but flying,
Streams like the thunderstorm *against* the wind;
Thy trumpet voice, though broken now and dying,
The loudest still the tempest leaves behind. *Ibid.*

Foul superstition! howsoe'er disguised,
Idol, saint, virgin, prophet, crescent, cross,
For whatsoever symbol thou art prized,
Thou sacerdotal gain, but general loss!
Who from true worship's gold can separate the dross. *Ibid., canto ii.*

See these inglorious Cincinnati swarm,
Farmers of war, dictators of the farm;
Their ploughshare was the sword in hireling hands,
Their fields manured by gore of other lands;
Safe in their barns, these Sabine tillers sent
Their brethren out to battle—why? for rent! *The Age of Bronze, 1823.*

Year after year they voted cent. per cent.,
Blood, sweat, and tear-wrung millions—
    why? for rent!   *Ibid.*

They roar'd, they dined, they drank, they
    swore they meant
To die for England—why then live?—for
    rent!   *Ibid.*

The peace has made one general mal-
    content
Of these high-market patriots; war was
    rent!
And will they not repay the treasures
    lent?
No: down with every thing, and up with
    rent!
Their good, ill, health, wealth, joy, or
    discontent,
Being, end, aim, religion—rent, rent, rent!
      Ibid.

Eternal Spirit of the Chainless Mind!
Brightest in dungeons, Liberty! thou art,
For there thy habitation is the heart—
The heart which love of thee alone can
    bind.   *The Prisoner of Chillon.*

They never fail who die
In a great cause: the block may soak
    their gore;
Their heads may sodden in the sun; their
    limbs
Be strung to city gates and castle walls—
But still their spirit walks abroad.
      Marino Faliero.

I wish men to be free, as much from
mobs as kings—from you as me.

I do not believe in revealed religion—I
will have nothing to do with your immortality; we are miserable enough in this
life, without the absurdity of speculating
upon another. . . . The basis of your religion
is injustice: the Son of God, the pure, the
immaculate, the innocent, is sacrificed for
the guilty.
    Letter to Rev. Francis Hodgson, 1811.

And, after all, what is a lie? 'Tis but the
truth in masquerade.   *Don Juan.*

"Let there be light!" said God, "and there
    was light!"
"Let there be blood!" says man, and
    there's a sea!   *Ibid.*

Socrates and Jesus Christ were put to
death publicly as *blasphemers*, and so have
been and may be many who dare to oppose
the most notorious abuses of the name of
God and the mind of man. But persecution
is not refutation, nor even triumph: the
"wretched infidel", as he is called, is probably happier in his prison than the proudest
of his assailants.
    Quoted by V. Gollancz, From Dark-
    ness to Light.

The grand *primum mobile* of England is
cant; cant political, cant poetical, cant religious, cant moral, but always cant, multiplied through all the varieties of life.
    Letter to John Murray, February 7,
    1821.

Those who swallow their Deity, really
and truly, in transubstantiation, can hardly
find anything else otherwise than easy to
digest.
    Letter to Thomas Moore, March 8,
    1822.

He makes a solitude, and calls it—peace.
    The Bride of Abydos, ii, 1813.

Caecilius Statius
See Statius

Gaius Julius Caesar
(100-44 B.C.)
Roman general, statesman, writer

Men willingly believe what they wish.
De Bello Gallico.

Erskine Caldwell
(b. 1903)
American novelist

Tobacco Road.　　*Book title, 1932.*

Calgacus
(c. 84 A.D.)

To plunder, to slaughter, to steal, these things they misname empire; and where they make a desert, they call it peace.
Address to the Britons, quoted by Tacitus, Agricola.

John C. Calhoun
(1782-1850)
American statesman

There never has yet existed a wealthy and civilized society in which one portion of the community did not, in point of fact, live on the labor of the other. Broad and general as is this assertion, it is fully borne out by history.
Speech (defending slavery), Senate, 1837.

There is and always has been in an advanced stage of wealth and civilization, a conflict between labor and capital. The condition of society in the South exempts us from the disorders and dangers resulting from this conflict; and which explains why it is that the political condition of the slaveholding states has been so much more stable and quiet than that of the North.
Senate, January 9, 1838.

People do not understand liberty or majorities. The will of a majority is the will of a rabble. Progressive democracy is incompatible with liberty.
Jenkins, Life of John Caldwell Calhoun, p. 453.

Irresponsible power is inconsistent with liberty, and must corrupt those who exercise it.

A power has risen up in the government greater than the people themselves, consisting of many and various powerful interests, combined in one mass, and held together by the cohesive power of the vast surplus in banks. *Speech, May 27, 1836.*

Government has no right to control individual liberty beyond what is necessary to the safety and well-being of society. Such is the boundary which separates the power of the government and the liberty of the citizen or subject in the political state.
Speech, Senate, June 27, 1848.

No government based on the naked principle that the majority ought to govern, however true the maxim in its proper sense, and under proper restrictions, can preserve its liberty even for a single generation. The history of all has been the same,—violence, injustice, and anarchy, succeeded by the government of one, or a few, under which the people seek refuge from the more oppressive despotism of the many.
Works, VI, 33.

John Calvin
(1509-1564)
French Protestant reformer

The interdiction of marriage to priests was an act of impious tyranny, not only contrary to the word of God, but at war with every principle of justice.

Institutes of the Christian Religion, iv, 1536.

Beyond the bosom of the Church no remission of sins is to be hoped for, nor any salvation.

Whence is it that so many peoples, together with their innocent little children should be delivered to death eternal through the fall of Adam, unless it should please God.

Because the Papists persecute the truth should we on that account refrain from repressing error?

Simon Cameron
(1799-1889)
Republican boss of Pennsylvania

An honest politician is one who, when he is bought, will stay bought.
Quoted by Thomas B. Reed.

Tommasso Campanella
(1568-1639)
Italian philosopher

The people is a beast* of muddy brain
That knows not its own strength.
The People.

Thomas Campbell
(1777-1844)
Scottish poet, biographer, historian

The patriot's blood's the seed of Freedom's tree.   *To the Spanish Patriots.*

　　　　With its own hand it ties
And gags itself—gives death and war
For pence doled out by kings from its
　　own store.

———
*Cf. Alexander Hamilton.

Its own are all things between earth and heaven;
But this it knows not; and if one arise
To tell this truth, it kills him unforgiven.
Ibid.

Albert Camus
(1913-1960)
French novelist, essayist, playwright, Nobel Prize, 1957

Crushing truths perish by being acknowledged.
The Myth of Sisyphus, Knopf, 1955.

There is no fate that cannot be surmounted by scorn.　　　*Ibid.*

There exists an obvious fact that seems utterly moral: namely, that a man is always a prey to his truths. Once he has admitted them, he cannot free himself from them.　　　*Ibid., p. 31.*

We turn toward God only to obtain the impossible.　　　*Ibid., p. 34.*

It was previously a question of finding out whether or not life had to have a meaning to be lived. It now becomes clear, on the contrary, that it will be lived all the better if it has no meaning. *Ibid., p. 53.*

There can be no question of holding forth on ethics. I have seen people behave badly with great morality and I note every day that integrity has no need of rules.
Ibid., p. 66.

All systems of morality are based on the idea that an action has consequences that legitimize or cancel it. A mind imbued with the absurd merely judges that those consequences must be considered calmly. It is ready to pay up. In other words, there may be responsible persons, but there are no guilty ones, in its opinion. *Ibid., p. 67.*

If there is a sin against life, it consists perhaps not so much in despairing of life as in hoping for another life and in eluding the implacable grandeur of this life.

Ibid., p. 153.

Revolt and revolution both wind up at the same crossroads: the police, or folly.

The Rebel, 1952.

Every revolutionary ends by becoming either an oppressor or a heretic. *Ibid.*

We are all exceptional cases. We all want to appeal against something. Each of us insists on being innocent at all cost, even if he has to accuse the whole human race and heaven itself. *The Fall, 1957.*

Sometimes it is easier to see clearly into the liar than into the man who tells the truth. Truth, like light, blinds. Falsehood, on the contrary, is a beautiful twilight that enhances every object. *Ibid.*

In all the circumstances of his life, the writer can recapture the feeling of a living community that will justify him. But only if he accepts as completely as possible the two trusts that constitute the nobility of his calling: the service of truth and the service of freedom.

Speech, accepting Nobel Prize, N. Y. Times Book Review, December 10, 1957.

The nobility of our calling will always be rooted in two commitments difficult to observe: refusal to lie about what we know, and resistance to oppression. *Ibid.*

Truth is mysterious, elusive, ever to be won anew. Liberty is dangerous, as hard to get along with as it is exciting.

Quoted by J. Donald Adams, N. Y. Times Book Review, March 2, 1958.

Only evil can reach its limits and reign absolutely.

Exile and the Kingdom, Knopf, 1958.

Code of Canon Laws

Everywhere and with the greatest strictness the Church forbids marriage between baptized persons one of whom is a Catholic and the other a member of a schismatical or heretical sect. If there is any danger of the falling away of the Catholic party and the perversion of the children such a marriage is forbidden by the divine law also.

Canon 1060, May 19, 1918.

The Church has the right to require that the faithful shall not publish books which she has not previously officially examined, and to prohibit their publication by anybody whatsoever for just cause. The provisions of this title also apply to daily publications, periodicals, and other published writings of whatever kind, unless the contrary appear. *Canon 1384.*

The Church may acquire temporal property by every just means allowed by the natural or the positive law.

Ibid., Canon 1499.

Canute "The Great"
(994?-1035)
King of England and Denmark

I want no money raised by injustice.
Letter of state, "to all the nation of the English, both nobles and commoners," after pilgrimage to Rome, 1027.

Al Capone
(1899-1947)
American gangster

Don't get the idea that I'm one of these goddam radicals. Don't get the idea that

I'm knocking the American system.
1929 interview, quoted by Claud Cock-burn, In Time of Trouble, 1956.

My rackets are run on strictly American lines and they're going to stay that way.
Ibid.

The American system of ours, call it Americanism, call it Capitalism, call it what you like, gives each and every one of us a great opportunity if we only seize it with both hands and make the most of it.
Ibid.

Bolshevism is knocking at our gates. We can't afford to let it in. We have got to organize ourselves against it, and put our shoulders together and hold fast. We must keep America whole and safe and un-spoiled. We must keep the worker away from red literature and red ruses; we must see that his mind remains healthy.
Liberty magazine.

Benjamin N. Cardozo
(1870-1938)
U.S. Supreme Court justice

If the moral and physical fibre of its man-hood and its womanhood is not a state concern, the question is, what is?
Adler v. Deegan, 1929. 251 N. Y. Reports, 467.

The prophet and the martyr do not see the hooting throng. Their eyes are fixed on the eternities.
Law and Literature, 1931.

Property, like liberty, though immune under the Constitution from destruction, is not immune from regulation essential for the common good. What the regulation shall be, every generation must work out for itself.

Nor is the concept of the general welfare static. Needs that were narrow or parochial a century ago may be interwoven in our day with the well-being of the nation. What is critical or urgent changes with the times.
Helvering et al. v. Davis, 301 U.S. 619 (1937).

Richard Carlile
(1790-1843)
English rationalist philosopher

My whole and sole object, from first to last, from the time of putting off my leather apron to this day, has been a Free Press and Free Discussion. When I first started as a hawker of pamphlets I knew nothing of political principles, I had never read a page of Paine's writings; but I had a com-plete conviction that there was something wrong somewhere, and that the right appli-cation of the printing-press was the remedy.
The Republican (weekly journal), VII, 1819.

At a moment when Despotism displays its naked, hideous front, and finds the uni-form and unqualified support of nearly the whole clerical world, which has been always found to be one of its last props, a verdict of Not Guilty on these important questions will strike it to the ground with the force of an electric fluid, and like a violent whirl-wind tear it up root and branch . . . will destroy the remains of ignorance and super-stition, and establish the Liberty of the Press and Free Discussion with all its gen-eral influence, will give life to the literary and philosophic world which alone can perfect society.
Ibid.; preceding trial for seditious libel, 1819.

Be assured that it is pamphlet-reading that is destined to work the great necessary moral and political changes among mankind.
Ibid., V. 279, 1822.

The Printing-press may be strictly denominated a Multiplication Table as applicable to the mind of man. The art of printing is a multiplication of mind. *Ibid.*

Pamphlet-vendors are the most important springs in the machinery of Reform. *Ibid.*

Mankind in the future will owe all their social benefits to the Printing-press, and it is known to me that, where an individual addicts himself to mental improvement, he abandons the immoralities that would otherwise engage his attention. The Alehouse, I know, has charms insuperable to the great body of mechanics.
Ibid., V. 391, 1822.

The Printing-Press has become the UNIVERSAL MONARCH, and the Republic of Letters will go on to abolish all minor monarchies, and give freedom to the whole human race, by making it as one nation and one family. *Ibid., VI. 449.*

Free Discussion is the only necessary Constitution—the only necessary Law of the Constitution. *Ibid., VIII. 3, 1823.*

Thomas Carlyle
(1795-1881)
Scottish historian, critic, sociological writer

Aristocracy of Feudal Parchment has passed away with a mighty rushing; and now, by a natural course, we arrive at Aristocracy of Moneybag.
The French Revolution.

Great meanwhile is the moment, when tidings of Freedom reach us; when the long-enthralled soul, from amid its chains and squalid stagnancy, arises, were it still only in blindness and bewilderment, and swears by Him that made it, that it will be *free!* Free? Understand that well, it is the deep commandment, dimmer or clearer, of our whole being, to be *free.* Freedom is the one purport, wisely aimed at, or unwisely, of all man's struggles, toilings and sufferings, on this Earth. *Ibid.*

No iron chain, or outward force of any kind, could ever compel the soul of man to believe or to disbelieve.
Heroes and Hero-Worship.

The first duty of man is that of subduing fear. *Ibid.*

We must get rid of fear; we cannot act at all till then. A man's acts are slavish, not true but specious; his very thoughts are false, he thinks too as a slave and coward, till he have got fear under his feet. *Ibid.*

Histories are a kind of distilled newspapers. *Ibid.*

A man protesting against error is on the way toward uniting himself with all men that believe in truth. *Ibid.*

Every new opinion, at its starting, is precisely in a minority of one. *Ibid.*

Nature admits no lie.
Later-day Pamphlets.

Truth, fact, is the life of all things; falsity, "fiction", or whatever it may call itself, is certain to be the death. *Ibid.*

The three great elements of modern civilization, Gunpowder, Printing, and the Protestant Religion.
Critical and Miscellaneous Essays.

We do everything by custom, even believe by it; our very axioms, let us boast of freethinking as we may, are oftenest simply such beliefs as we have never heard questioned. *Sartor Resartus, iii.*

What is philosophy but a continual battle against custom; an ever-renewed effort to transcend the sphere of blind custom, and so become transcendental? *Ibid.*

The folly of that impossible precept, "Know Thyself"; till it be translated into this partially possible one, "Know what thou canst work at." *Ibid.*

That there should one Man die ignorant who had capacity for Knowledge, this I call tragedy, were it to happen more than twenty times in the minute, as by some computations it does. The miserable fraction of Science which our united Mankind, in a wide universe of Nescience, has acquired, why is not this, with all diligence, imparted to all? *Ibid.*

The truth is men have lost their belief in the Invisible . . . it is no longer a worship of the Beautiful and Good, but a calculation of the Profitable. *Miscellanies.*

If Jesus Christ were to come today people would not even crucify him. They would ask him to dinner, and hear what he had to say, and make fun of it.
D. A. Wilson, Carlyle at His Zenith.

Cant is itself properly a double-distilled lie, the *materia prima* of the devil, from which all falsehoods, imbecilities, and abominations body themselves, and from which no true thing can come.

We must some day, at last and forever, cross the line between Nonsense and Common Sense. And on that day we shall pass from Class Paternalism . . . to Human Brotherhood . . . ; from Political Government to Industrial Administration; from Competition in Individualism to Individu-ality in Cooperation; from War and Despotism, in any form, to Peace and Liberty.
Quoted by Upton Sinclair, The Cry for Justice.

Man seldom, or rather never for a length of time and deliberately, rebels against anything that does not deserve rebelling against. *Goethe.*

Everywhere the human soul stands between a hemisphere of light and another of darkness; on the confines of the two everlasting hostile empires, necessity and free will. *Ibid.*

Popular opinion is the greatest lie in the world.

I grow daily to honor facts more and more, and theory less and less. A fact, it seems to me, is a great thing—a sentence printed, if not by God, then at least by the Devil. *Letter to Emerson, April 29, 1836.*

The imprisoned soul of fact.

The world is a republic of mediocrities, and always was.
Letter to Emerson, May 13, 1853.

The true Church of England at this moment lies in the editors of its newspapers. These preach to the people, daily, weekly.

Mohammet is the prophet we are freest to speak of.

Just in ratio as knowledge increases, faith diminishes.

The courage we desire and prize is not the courage to die decently, but to live manfully.

"A fair day's wages for a fair day's work": it is as just a demand as governed

men ever made of governing. It is the everlasting right of man.
Past and Present, 1, 1843.

All work, even cotton-spinning, is noble;
work is alone noble. *Ibid.*

Blessed is he who has found his work;
let him ask no other blessedness. He has a
work, a life-purpose; he has found it and
will follow it. *Ibid.*

The beginning of all is to have done with
falsity—to eschew falsity as death eternal.
Journal, June 23, 1870.

What is Aristocracy? A corporation of
the best, of the bravest. *Chartism.*

Manhood begins when we have, in a
way, made truce with necessity; begins, at
all events, when we have surrendered to
necessity, as the most part only do; but
begins joyfully and hopefully only when
we have reconciled ourselves to necessity,
and thus, in reality, triumphed over it, and
felt that in necessity we are free.
Essays. Burns.

Andrew Carnegie

(1835-1919)

*American steel manufacturer,
philanthropist*

The problem of our age is the proper
administration of wealth, so that the ties
of brotherhood may still bind together the
rich and poor in harmonious relationship.
The Gospel of Wealth, 1889.

It is well, nay, essential for the progress
of the race, that the houses of some should
be homes for all that is highest and best
in literature and the arts, and for all the
refinements of civilization, rather than that
none should be so. Much better this great
irregularity than universal squalor. Without
wealth there can be no Maecenas. *Ibid.*

And while the law (of competition) may
be sometimes hard for the individual, it is
best for the race, because it insures the
survival of the fittest in every department.
We accept and welcome, therefore, as conditions to which we must accommodate
ourselves, great inequality of environment,
the concentration of business, industrial and
commercial, in the hands of a few, and the
law of competition between these, as being
not only beneficial, but essential for the
future progress of the race. *Ibid.*

The socialist or anarchist who seeks to
overturn present conditions is to be regarded as attacking the foundation upon
which civilization itself rests. . . . One who
studies this subject will soon be brought
face to face with the conclusion that upon
the sacredness of property civilization itself
depends—the right of the laborer to his
hundred dollars in the saving bank, and
equally the legal right of the millionaire to
his millions. *Ibid.*

We might as well urge the destruction
of the highest existing type of man because
he failed to reach our ideal as to favor the
destruction of Individualism, Private Property, the Law of Accumulation of Wealth,
and the Law of Competition; for these are
the highest results of human experience,
the soil in which society so far has produced the best fruit. *Ibid.*

This, then, is held to be the duty of the
man of wealth: First, to set an example of
modest, unostentatious living, shunning display or extravagance; to provide moderately
for the legitimate wants of those dependent
upon him; and after doing so consider all
surplus revenues which come to him simply
as trust funds, which he is called upon to
administer, and strictly bound as a matter
of duty to administer in the manner which,
in his judgment, is best calculated to pro-

duce the most beneficial results for the community—the man of wealth thus becoming the mere agent and trustee for his poorer brethren, bringing to their service his superior wisdom, experience, and ability to administer, doing for them better than they would or could do for themselves.

Ibid.

Those who would administer wisely must, indeed, be wise, for one of the serious obstacles to the improvement of our race is indiscriminate charity. *Ibid.*

Thus is the problem of rich and poor to be solved. The law of accumulation will be left free; the laws of distribution free. Individualism will continue, but the millionaire will be but a trustee of the poor; intrusted for a season with a great part of the increased wealth of the community, but administering it for the community far better than it could or would have done for itself. *Ibid.*

The man who dies leaving behind him millions of available wealth, which was his to administer during life, will pass away "unwept, unhonored, and unsung", no matter to what uses he leaves the dross which he cannot take with him. Of such as these the public verdict will then be: "The man who dies thus rich dies disgraced."

Such, in my opinion, is the true Gospel concerning Wealth, obedience to which is destined some day to solve the problem of the Rich and the Poor, and to bring "Peace on earth, among men Good Will." *Ibid.*

Edward Carpenter
(1844-1929)
English poet, essayist

The commercial prostitution of love is the last outcome of our whole social system, and its most clear condemnation. It flaunts in our streets, it hides itself in the garment of respectability under the name of matrimony, it eats in actual physical disease and death right through our midst; it is fed by the oppression and the ignorance of women, by their poverty and denied means of livelihood, and by the hypocritical puritanism which forbids them by millions not only to gratify but even to speak of their natural desires; and it is encouraged by the callousness of an age which has accustomed men to buy and sell for money every most precious thing—even the life-long labor of their brothers, therefore why not also the very bodies of their sisters?

Love's Coming of Age.

Here there is no solution except the freedom of woman—which means of course also the freedom of the masses of the people, men and women, and the ceasing altogether of economic slavery. There is no solution which will not include the redemption of the terms "free woman" and "free love" to their true and rightful significance. Let every woman whose heart bleeds for the sufferings of her sex, hasten to declare herself and to constitute herself, as far as she possibly can a free woman. Let her accept the term with all the odium that belongs to it; let her insist on her right to speak, dress, think, act, and above all to use her sex, as she deems best; let her face the scorn and ridicule; let her "use her own life" if she likes; assured that only so can come deliverance, and that only when the free woman is honored will the prostitute cease to exist. And let every man who really would respect his counterpart, entreat her also to act so; let him never by word or deed tempt her to grant as a bargain what can only be precious as a gift; let him see her with pleasure stand a little aloof; let him help her to gain her feet; so at last, by what slight sacrifices on his part such a course may involve, will it dawn upon him that he has gained a real companion and helpmate on life's journey.   *Ibid.*

The whole evil of commercial prostitution arises out of the domination of man in matters of sex. Better indeed were a Saturnalia of free men and women than the spectacle which as it is our great cities present at night. Here in sex, the women's instincts are, as a rule, so clean, so direct, so well-rooted in the needs of the race, that except for man's domination they would scarcely have suffered this perversion.
Ibid.

Love when felt at all deeply has an element of transcendentalism in it, which makes it the most natural thing in the world for the two lovers—even though drawn together by a passing sex-attraction —to swear eternal troth to each other; but there is something quite diabolic and mephistophelean in the practice of the Law, which creeping up behind, as it were, at the critical moment, and overhearing the two pledging themselves, claps his book together with a triumphant bang and exclaims: "There now you are married and done for, for the rest of your natural lives."
Ibid.

Real love is only possible in the freedom of society; and freedom is only possible when love is a reality. The subjection of sex-relations to legal conventions, is an intolerable bondage, but of course it is a bondage inescapable as long as people are slaves to a merely physical desire. The two slaveries in fact form a sort of natural counterpoise, the one to the other. When love becomes sufficient of a reality to hold the sex-passion as its powerful yet willing servant, the absurdity of law will be at an end.
Ibid.

These cast off clothes! The fashions, customs, opinions, desires, fears, of everyone but yourself! But what have fashion, custom, opinion, desire and fear anyhow to do with freedom?

I tell you that fashion, custom, opinion, desire and fear have nothing to do with freedom.   *Towards Democracy, 1883.*

When I see, flickering around, miserable spectrums and nostrums of reform . . . When I hear and see the droning and see-sawing of pulpits; when the vision of perfect vulgarity and commonplaceness arises upon me—of society—and of that which arrogates to itself the sacred name of England;

Of exclusiveness, and of being in the swim; of the drivel of aristocratic connections; . . . of belonging to clubs and of giving pence to crossing-sweepers without apparently seeing them; of helplessly living in houses with people who feed you, dress you, clean you, and despise you; . . . of being intellectual; of prancing about and talking glibly on all subjects on the theory of setting things right—and leaving others to do the dirty work of the world; . . . of talking about political economy and politics and never having done a single day's labour in your life; . . . of being a parson and afraid to be seen toping with Christ in public; a barrister afraid to be seen in a third class carriage; an officer and to walk with one of his own men;

When I see the sea, spreading, of infidelity—of belief in externals—in money, big guns, laws, views, accomplishments, cheap goods—town councillors, cabinet members, M.P.'s, generals, judges, bishops —all alike; . . .

O England, whither—strangled, tied and bound—whither, whither, art thou come?
Ibid.

Mutual help and combination will then have become spontaneous and instinctive: each man contributing to the service of his neighbour as inevitably and naturally as the right hand goes to help the left in the human body—and precisely for the same reason. Every man—think of it!—will do the work which he *likes* . . . without thought of wages or reward; . . . All the endless burden of the adjustments of labour and wages, of the war of duty and distaste, of want and weariness, will be thrown aside —all the huge waste of work done against the grain will be avoided; . . . Society at last will be free and the human being after long ages will have attained to deliverance.

This is the Communism which Civilization has always *hated*, as it hated Christ. Yet it is inevitable; for the cosmical man, the instinctive elemental man accepting and crowning nature, necessarily fulfils the universal law of nature. As to External Government and Law, they will disappear; for they are only the travesties and transitory substitutes of Inward Government and Order.

Civilisation: Its Cause and Cure, 1889.

Taboos and terrors still linger, many of them, in the form of conventions and morality, uneasy strivings of conscience, doubts and desperations of religion; but ultimately Man will emerge from all these things, *free*—familiar, that is, with them all, making use of all, allowing generously for the values of all, but hampered and bound by *none*. He will realize the inner meaning of the creeds and rituals of the ancient religions, and will hail with joy the fulfilment of their far prophecy down the ages—finding after all the long-expected Saviour of the world within his own breast, and Paradise in the disclosure there of the everlasting peace of the soul.

Pagan and Christian Creeds, 1920.

Over your face a web of lies is woven,
   Laws that are falsehoods pin you to
      the ground,

Labour is mocked, its just reward is
      stolen,
   On its bent back sits Idleness en-
      crowned.
      How long, while you sleep,
      Your harvest shall It reap?
Arise, O England, for the day is here!
      England, Arise, c. 1882.

Forth, then, ye heroes, patriots and lovers!
   Comrades of danger, poverty and
      scorn!
Mighty in faith of Freedom your great
      Mother!
   Giants refreshed in Joy's new-rising
      morn!
      Come and swell the song,
      Silent now so long:
England is risen!—and the day is here.
      Ibid.

Charles Carroll
(1739-1832)
*American patriot, signer of
Declaration of Independence*

When I signed the Declaration of Independence I had in view not only our independence from England but the toleration of all sects.

Letter to G. W. Parke Custis.

Grateful to Almighty God for the blessings which, through Jesus Christ our Lord, he has conferred on my beloved country in her emancipation, and on myself in permitting me under circumstances of mercy to live to the age of eighty-nine years, and to survive the fiftieth year of American Independence adopted by Congress on the 4th of July 1776, which I originally subscribed on the 2nd of August of the same year, and of which I am now the last surviving signer, I do now here recommend to the present and future generations the principles of that important document as the best earthly inheritance their ancestors could bequeath to them, and pray that the civil and religious liberties they have secured to my country may be perpetuated to the remotest posterity and extend to the whole family of man!

James Coolidge Carter
(1827-1905)
American lawyer

Justice consists in the compliance with custom in all matters of difference between men. . . . This accords with the definition of the Roman law.
Law: Its Origin, Growth and Function.

Giovanni Jacopo Casanova de Seingalt
(1725-1798)
Italian adventurer

Doubt begins only at the last frontiers of what is possible. *Mémoires, Paris, 1885.*

If there were not happiness on earth, the creation would be a monstrosity, and Voltaire would have been right when he called our planet the latrines of the universe.
Ibid.

Roger Casement
(1864-hanged 1916)
Irish rebel

Ireland has outlived the failure of all her hopes—and yet she still hopes.
Prisoner's Speech, June 29, 1916; Trial of Roger Casement, 1917.

In Ireland alone in this twentieth century is loyalty held to be a crime. If loyalty be something less than love and more than law, then we have had enough of such loyalty for Ireland or Irishmen. If we are to be indicted as criminals, to be shot as murderers, to be imprisoned as convicts because our offence is that we love Ireland more than we value our lives, then I know not what virtue resides in any offer of self-government held out to brave men on such terms. Self-government is our right, a thing born in us at birth; a thing no more to be doled out to us or withheld from us by another people than the right to life itself.
Ibid.

Ireland that has wronged no man, that has injured no land, that has sought no dominion over others—Ireland is treated today among the nations of the world as if she was a convicted criminal. If it be treason to fight against such an unnatural fate as this, then I am proud to be a rebel, and shall cling to my "rebellion" with the last drop of my blood. *Ibid.*

If there be no right of rebellion against a state of things that no savage tribe would endure without resistance, then I am sure that it is better for men to fight and die without right than to live in such a state of right as this. *Ibid.*

Where all your rights become only an accumulated wrong; where men must beg with bated breath for leave to subsist in their own land, to think their own thoughts, to sing their own songs, to garner the fruits of their own labours—and even while they beg to see things inexorably withdrawn from them—then surely it is braver, a saner and truer thing, to be a rebel in act and deed against such circumstances as these than tamely to accept it as the natural lot of men. *Ibid.*

K. K. V. Casey
(b. 1877)
American industrialist

Wars frequently begin ten years before the first shot is fired.
Testimony of DuPont director, at the Nye-Vandenberg Munitions Investigation.

Magnus Aurelius Cassiodorus
(490-575)
Roman historian

Poverty is the mother of crime.
Variae, book 9.

Fidel Castro
(b. 1926)
Liberator of Cuba

We must have teachers—a heroine in every classroom. *Time, January 26, 1959.*

Willa Cather
(1875-1947)
American novelist

The revolt against individualism naturally calls artists severely to account, because the artist is of all men the most individual: those who were not have been long forgotten. The condition every art requires is, not so much freedom from restriction, as freedom from adulteration and from the intrusion of foreign matter, considerations and purposes which have nothing to do with spontaneous invention.
On Writing.

Religion and art spring from the same root and are close kin. Economics and art are strangers. *Ibid.*

Catholic Archbishops of the United States

By treating the laborer first of all as a man, the employer will make him a better working man; by respecting his own moral dignity as a man, the laborer will compel the respect of his employer and of the community.
Pastoral Letter of the Catholic Archbishops of the United States, 1919.

Catholic Bishops of America

We express again our sympathy for labor and we appreciate the difficulties of maintaining family life with the mounting cost of living. In union with the Holy See, we have on many occasions condemned the evils of unrestrained capitalism. At the same time, in union with the Holy See, we hold that "our first and most fundamental principle, when we undertake to alleviate the condition of the masses, must be the inviolability of private property".
Statement, Crisis of Christianity, N. Y. Times, November 18, 1941.

Marcus Portius Cato, "The Censor"
(234-149 B.C.)
Roman patriot

Some have said that it is not the business of private men to meddle with government —a bold and dishonest saying, which is fit to come from no mouth but that of a tyrant or a slave.

To say that private men have nothing to do with government is to say that private men have nothing to do with their own happiness or misery; that people ought not to concern themselves whether they be naked or clothed, fed or starved, deceived or instructed, protected or destroyed.

[148]

Edith (Louisa) Cavell
(1865-1915)
English nurse; executed by the
Germans as a spy

Patriotism is not enough. I must have no hatred or bitterness toward anyone.
To the Rev. Mr. Gahan, the night before her execution by the Germans in Belgium.

Camillo di Cavour
(1810-1861)
Italian statesman

We are ready to proclaim throughout Italy the great principle of a free church in a free state.   *Address, March 27, 1861.*

I have discovered the art of deceiving diplomats. I speak the truth, and they never believe me.

You can do anything with bayonets except sit on them.

Miguel de Cervantes
(1547-1616)
Spanish novelist

The first thing I would do in my government, I would have nobody to control me. I would be absolute; and who but I: now, he that is absolute can do what he likes, can take his pleasure; he that can take his pleasure, can be content; and he that can be content, has no more to desire; so the matter's over.   *Don Quixote, pt. i*

For historians ought to be precise, truthful, and quite unprejudiced, and neither interest nor fear, hatred nor affection, should cause them to swerve from the path of truth, whose mother is history, the rival of time, the depository of great actions, the

witness of what is past, the example and instruction of the present, the monitor of the future.   *Ibid., ii.*

History is a sacred kind of writing, because truth is essential to it, and where truth is, there God himself is, so far as truth is concerned.   *Ibid., v.*

Truth may be stretched, but cannot be broken, and always gets above falsehood, as oil does above water.   *Ibid.*

There are only two families in the world, the Haves and the Have-nots.   *Ibid.*

Zechariah Chafee, Jr.
(1885-1957)
American educator

The real value of freedom is not to the minority that wants to talk, but to the majority, that does not want to listen.

What is constitutional may still be unwise.
The Nation, July 28, 1952. The Blessings of Liberty, 1956.

You make men love their government and their country by giving them the kind of government and the kind of country that inspire respect and love: a country that is free and unafraid, that lets the discontented talk in order to learn the causes of their discontent and end those causes, that refuses to impel men to spy on their neighbors, that protects its citizens vigorously from harmful acts while it leaves the remedies for objectionable ideas to counterargument and time.
Free Speech in the United States, 1942.

The majority opinions determined the cases but these dissenting opinions will determine the minds of the future.
Regarding the dissents of Justice Holmes and Justice Brandeis.

If Americanism means anything, it means free speech, right from the start. The Pilgrims came to Massachusetts to get it, and Roger Williams left Massachusetts, not only because he had his own religious views but because he attacked property rights in land not purchased from the Indians. Thomas Jefferson is usually considered a good American, but he said things about the desirability of rebellion that would make us all shudder. Alexander Hamilton argued for free speech here in New York, and James Russell Lowell called the Mexican War murder. The abolitionists, men whom we all honor today, believed in Americanism —freedom to criticize the government of their day and the institutions of property —the property in Negro slaves. I believe in private property myself, but because I believe in it I want to know why it ought to be supported.

It is advocacy of revolution by force and violence to write: "I hold a little rebellion now and then is a good thing, and as necessary in the political world as storms in the physical." (Writings of Jefferson, ed. P. L. Ford, IV, 362; see also 370 and 467). Out go the works of Thomas Jefferson. It is advocacy of change of government by assassination to say, "The right of a nation to kill a tyrant in cases of necessity can no more be doubted than to hang a robber, or kill a flea." (Works of John Adams, ed. C. F. Adams, VI, 130). Jefferson is followed by his old antagonist, John Adams, the author of the Sedition Law of 1798.

Houston Stewart Chamberlain
(1855-1927)
Anglo-German writer

Two cultures cannot exist on equal footing side by side. That is out of the question. Hellenic culture could not live under Roman influence. Roman culture disappeared. . . . The one in time must destroy the other.

The so-called unity of the human race is indeed still honored as a hypothesis, but only as a personal, subjective conviction lacking every material foundation. The ideas of the 18th century with regard to the brotherhood of nations were certainly very noble but purely sentimental in their origin; and in contrast to these ideas to which the Socialists still cling, limping on like reserves in the battle, stern reality has gradually asserted itself as the necessary result of the events and investigations of our time.
Foundations of the Nineteenth Century, 1912.

To this day these two powers—Jews and Teutonic races—stand, wherever the recent spread of the Chaos has not blurred their features, now as friendly, now as hostile, but always as alien forces face to face.
Ibid.

The Teuton is the soul of our culture.
Ibid.

The importance of each nation as a living power today is dependent upon the proportion of genuinely Teutonic blood in its population. Only Teutons sit on the thrones of Europe. *Ibid.*

Nothing is so convincing as the consciousness of the possession of Race. The man who belongs to a distinct, pure race, never loses the sense of it. The guardian angel of his lineage is ever at his side, supporting him where he loses his foothold, warning him like the Socratic Daemon where he is in danger of going astray, compelling obedience, and forcing him to undertakings which, deeming them impossible he would never have dared to attempt. *Ibid.*

Neville Chamberlain

(1869-1940)

English statesman

My good friends, this is the second time in our history that there has come back from Germany to Downing Street peace with honour. . . . I believe it is peace for our time.

Address, on return from Munich conference, September, 1938.

William Ellery Channing

(1780-1842)

American Unitarian minister, reformer

As yet Christianity has done little, compared with what it is to do, in establishing the true bond of union between man and man. The old bonds of society still continue in a great degree. They are instinct, interest, force. The true tie, which is mutual respect, calling forth mutual, growing, never-failing acts of love, is as yet little known. A new revelation, if I may so speak, remains to be made; or rather, the truths of the old revelation in regard to the greatness of human nature are to be brought out from obscurity and neglect.

We have conservatives enough.

The cry has been that when war is declared, all opposition should therefore be hushed. A sentiment more unworthy of a free country could hardly be propagated. If the doctrine be admitted, rulers have only to declare war and they are screened at once from scrutiny. . . . In war, then, as in peace, assert the freedom of speech and of the press. Cling to this as the bulwark of all our rights and privileges.

Every mind was made for growth, for knowledge; and its nature is sinned against when it is doomed to ignorance.

Great minds are to make others great. Their superiority is to be used, not to break the multitude to intellectual vassalage, not to establish over them a spiritual tyranny, but to rouse them from lethargy, and to aid them to judge for themselves.
On the Elevation of the Laboring Classes, 1840.

Of all treasons against humanity, there is no one worse than his who employs great intellectual force to keep down the intellect of his less favored brothers.   *Ibid.*

As long as it was supposed that religion is to benefit the world by laying restraints, awakening fears, and acting as a part of the system of police, so long it was natural to rely on authority and tradition as the means of its propagation; so long it was desirable to stifle thought and inquiry on the subject. But now that we have learned that the true office of religion is to awaken pure and lofty sentiments, and to unite man to God by rational homage and enlightened love, there is something monstrous in placing religion beyond the thought and the study of the mass of the human race.   *Ibid.*

If intelligence and piety may not be the foundation of a caste, on what ground shall they who have no distinction but wealth, superior costume, richer equipages, finer houses, draw lines around themselves and constitute themselves a higher class?
Ibid.

To be prosperous is not to be superior, and should form no barrier between men. Wealth ought not to secure to the prosperous the slightest consideration. The only distinctions which should be recognized are those of the soul, of strong principle, of incorruptible integrity, of usefulness, of cultivated intellect, of fidelity in seeking the truth.   *Ibid.*

Chantal
See Sévigné

Edwin Hubbel Chapin
(1814-1880)
American clergyman, writer

Neutral men are the devil's allies.

Ralph Chaplin
(1887-1961)
American writer

Mourn not the dead . . .
But rather mourn the apathetic throng—
The cowed and meek
Who see the world's great anguish and its
    wrong,
And dare not speak.

John Jay Chapman
(1862-1933)
American writer, critic

You must talk facts, you must name names, you must impute motives. You must say what is in your mind. . . . If you are not strong enough to face the issue in private life, do not dream that you can do anything for public affairs.
Practical Agitation, 1900.

The newspaper trade, as now conducted, is prostitution. It mows down the boys as they come from the colleges. It defaces the very desire for truth and leaves them without a principle to set a clock by. They grow to disbelieve in the reality of ideas.
Ibid.

In a martial age the reformer is called a mollycoddle; in a commercial age, an incompetent, a disturber of values; in a fanatical age, a heretic. If an agitator is not reviled, he is a quack. *Ibid.*

Liberty and democracy are thought to be such worthy ends that we must obtain them by any means and all ends, even by hiring mercenaries. Can we wonder that in the past men's minds were staggered by the importance of the papacy, or of some dynastic succession? Today everybody jumps to shield vice because it is called republicanism or democracy. The irony of history could go no further. *Ibid.*

Chartists

They that perish by the sword are better than they that perish by hunger.
Inscription, Chartist banner.

That all shall have a good house to live in with a garden, back or front, just as the occupier likes; good clothing to keep him warm and make him look respectable, and plenty of good food and drink to make him look and *feel* happy.
The London Democrat, 1839.

Political power our means, social happiness our end.
Slogan, quoted by Edmund Wilson, To the Finland Station, p. 138.

Stuart Chase
(b. 1888)
American writer

Semantics teaches us to watch our prejudices, and to take our exercise in other ways than jumping to conclusions. Semantics is the propagandist's worse friend.
Guides to Straight Thinking, 1956.

The pressure groups seem to be largely led by men who are ignorant of the fact that we are our brothers' keepers. They think such talk is Sunday School Stuff. They are wrong. It is the first law of modern technology.
Democracy Under Pressure, 1945.

Can people at the bottom of the economic scale, people called no-account, lazy, degraded, grasp an opportunity when a real one is offered, and rise out of their misery? This is the acid test. If they can, democracy is proved . . . I submit that this project . . . gives the lie to those who hold that the mass of the people are imprisoned in their shiftlessness from the germ plasm. It makes it impossible for an intelligent, well-informed person ever again seriously to contend that most people are incapable of self-improvement . . . Democracy, as has been said of Christianity, has never really been tried . . .   *Men at Work, 1945.*

Natural resources and inanimate energy . . . are increasingly regarded as affected with a public interest . . . Certainly they were left by God or geology to mankind and not to the Standard Oil Company of California. If this is not sound moral doctrine, I do not know what is.
The Economy of Abundance, 1934.

Words are what hold society together.
Power of Words, 1954.

Democracy . . . is a condition where people believe that other people are as good as they are.

Sanely applied advertising could remake the world.

Chasseboeuf
See Volney

Earl of Chatham
See William Pitt

Anton Chekhov
(1860-1904)
Russian author

The time has come for writers, especially those who are artists, to admit that in this world one cannot make anything out, just as Socrates once admitted it, just as Voltaire admitted it.
The Personal Papers of Anton Chekhov, Lear, 1950.

A litterateur is not a confectioner, not a dealer in cosmetics, not an entertainer. . . . He is just like an ordinary reporter. What would you say if a newspaper reporter, because of his fastidiousness or from a wish to give pleasure to his readers, were to describe only honest mayors, high-minded ladies, and virtuous railroad contractors?
Ibid.

To a chemist nothing on earth is unclean. A writer must be as objective as a chemist; he must abandon the subjective line; he must know that dung-heaps play a very respectable part in a landscape, and that evil passions are as inherent in life as good ones.   *Ibid.*

Old men (meaning Tolstoy) have always been prone to see the end of the world. The hell with the philosophy of the great of this world.
The Selected Letters of Anton Chekhov, 1955.

The power and salvation of a people lie in its intelligentzia, in the intellectuals who think honestly, who feel, and can work.
N. Y. Times, December 30, 1956.

Philip Dormer Stanhope, Fourth Earl of Chesterfield
(1694-1773)
Statesman, diplomat

One of the greatest blessings we enjoy, one of the greatest blessings a people can enjoy, is liberty; but every good in this life has its alloy of evil; licentiousness is the alloy of liberty; it is an ebullition, and ex-

crescence; it is a speck upon the eye of the political body, which I can never touch but with a gentle, with a trembling hand, lest I destroy the body, lest I injure the eye upon which it is apt to appear.
Miscellaneous Works, Vol. IV, 1779.

There is such a connection between licentiousness and liberty, that it is not easy to correct the one, without dangerously wounding the other; it is extremely hard to distinguish the true limit between them; like a changeable silk, we can easily see there are two colours, but we cannot easily discover where the one ends, or where the other begins. *Ibid.*

Let us consider that arbitrary power has seldom or never been introduced into any country at once. It must be introduced by slow degrees, and as it were step by step, lest the people should see it approach. The barriers and fences of the people's liberty must be plucked one by one, and some plausible pretences must be found for removing or hoodwinking, one after another, those sentries who are posted by the constitution of a free country for warning the people of their danger. When these preparatory steps are once made, the people may then indeed, with regret, see slavery and arbitrary power making long strides over their land; but it will be too late to think of preventing or avoiding the impending ruin. *Ibid.*

Human nature is the same all over the world.
Letters to his Son, October 2, 1747.

Every numerous assembly is *mob*, let the individuals who compose it be what they will . . . Understanding they have collectively none; but they have ears and eyes, which must be flattered and seduced.
The Letters of Lord Chesterfield, 1892, 418.

Lies and perfidy are the refuge of fools and cowards. *Ibid., 516.*

If ever the multitude deviate into the right, it is always for the wrong reason.
Ibid., 623.

Politicians neither love nor hate. Interest, not sentiment, directs them. *Ibid., 900.*

G(ilbert) K(eith) Chesterton
(1874-1936)
English essayist, novelist

Despotism can be a development, often a late development and very often indeed the end of societies that have been highly democratic. A despotism may almost be defined as a tired democracy.
The Everlasting Man.

Ireland is a country in which the political conflicts are at least genuine: they are about something. They are about patriotism, about religion, or about money: the three great realities. *George Bernard Shaw.*

To say that a man is an idealist is merely to say that he is a man. *Heretics.*

The idea of liberty has ultimately a religious root; that is why men find it so easy to die for and so difficult to define.
A Miscellany of Men.

We do not need a censorship of the press. We have a censorship of the press.
Orthodoxy.

Materialists and madmen never have doubts. *Ibid.*

Catholic theology has nothing to do with democracy, for or against, in the sense of a machinery of voting or a criticism of particular privileges. It is not committed to support what Whitman said for democracy, or even what Jefferson or Lincoln said for democracy. *The Thing.*

You can never have a revolution in order to establish a democracy. You must have a democracy in order to have a revolution.
Tremendous Trifles.

The Christian ideal has not been tried and found wanting. It has been found difficult, and left untried.
What's Wrong With the World.

From all that terror teaches,
   From lies of tongue and pen,
From all the easy speeches
   That comfort cruel men,
From sale and profanation
   Of honor and the sword,
From sleep and from damnation,
   Deliver us, good Lord.   *A Hymn.*

There is nothing the matter with Americans except their ideals. The real American is all right; it is the ideal American who is all wrong. *N.Y. Times, February 1, 1931.*

Democracy means government by the uneducated, while aristocracy means government by the badly educated.   *Ibid.*

Truths turn into dogmas the moment they are disputed.

"My country, right or wrong," is a thing that no patriot would think of saying except in a desperate case. It is like saying, "My mother, drunk or sober."
The Defendant.

Chiang Kai-shek
(1887-1975)
Chinese nationalist leader

If when I die I am still a dictator I will certainly go down into the oblivion of all dictators. If on the other hand I succeed in establishing a truly stable foundation for a democratic government, I will live forever in every home in China.

Chou En-lai
(1898-1976)
Chinese Communist leader

All diplomacy is a continuation of war by other means.°
To Edgar Snow, Saturday Evening Post, March 27, 1954.

Christian Social Action Committee

Nuclear Power . . . Our Christian Conscience demands that we lift our voice to discourage further development of this power for destructive purposes on the part of all nations.
Reported in The Gazette & Daily, York, Pa., May 7, 1954.

Alien and Domestic Totalitarian Threats. As Christian citizens we are concerned by current evidences of deterioration and decay of public morale and personal liberty. There is a growing spirit of fear and distrust among the citizens of the United States. This spirit would substitute conformity under pressure for liberty under law.
Ibid.

St. John Chrysostom
(345?-407)
Greek church father

The idea we should have of the rich and covetous—they are truly as robbers who, standing in the public highway, despoil the passersby.
Quoted in Wage Earner, American Catholic Trades Unionists.

The rich man is a thief.

Riches are not forbidden, but the pride of them is.   *Homilies, c. 388.*

―――――――
° Cf. Clausewitz; attributed by Snow to Lenin, Chou's teacher.

Nothing is more fallacious than wealth. It is a hostile comrade, a domestic enemy.
Ibid., II.

Slander is worse than cannibalism.
Ibid., III.

Hell is paved with priests' skulls.
De sacerdotio, c 390.

Winston Churchill
(1874-1965)
English statesman, writer

I have always said that if Great Britain were defeated in war I hoped we should find a Hitler to lead us back to our rightful position among the nations.
Speech, November 11, 1938; quoted by Senator Nye, Congressional Record, March 13, 1941.

He (Hitler) embodied the revolt of Germany against the hard fortunes of war. . . . Adolf Hitler is *Fuehrer* because he exemplifies and enshrines the will of Germany.
One of many quotations used by the Labour Party in attacking the Prime Minister.

I am not a bit afraid of anything I have said in a long political life.
Reply to charges he endorsed and praised Mussolini, Hitler, and Fascism. Commons, December 8, 1944.

I will not pretend that if I had to choose between Communism and Naziism, I would choose Communism.
Commons, December 8, 1944.

I have nothing to offer but blood, toil, tears and sweat. *Speech, May 13, 1940.*°

Never in the field of human conflict was so much owed by so many to so few.
Speech, July 8, 1940. A reference to British airmen in the Battle for Britain.

We shall go on to the end, we shall fight in France, we shall fight on the seas and oceans, we shall fight with growing confidence and growing strength in the air, we shall defend our island, whatever the cost may be, we shall fight on the beaches, we shall fight on the landing grounds, we shall fight in the fields and in the streets, we shall fight in the hills;° we shall never surrender, and even if, which I do not for a moment believe, this island or a large part of it were subjugated and starving, then our Empire beyond the seas, armed and guarded by the British fleet, would carry on the struggle, until, in God's good time, the New World, with all its power and might steps forth to the rescue and the liberation of the old.
Speech, House of Commons, June 4, 1940.

A shadow has fallen upon the scenes so lately lighted by the Allied victory. From Stettin in the Baltic to Trieste in the Adriatic an iron curtain°° has descended across the Continent.
Speech, Fulton, Missouri, March 5, 1946.

° A paraphrase of a famous remark by Garibaldi.

° ". . . and we will hit them over the heads with beer bottles, which is all we have really got"—aside, to Dean Hewlett Johnson, reported in *N. Y. Herald Tribune*, June 22, 1947.
°° In 1915 George W. Crile wrote in *A Mechanistic View of War and Peace*, page 69: "France . . . a nation of forty millions with a deep-rooted grievance and an iron curtain at its frontier". Dr. Goebbels on February 23, 1945, in *Das Reich* first used the phrase "iron curtain" in reference to

I have only one purpose, the destruction of Hitler, and my life is much simplified thereby. If Hitler invaded Hell, I would make at least a favourable reference to the Devil in the House of Commons.
To his private secretary, June, 1941;
N. Y. Times, February 10, 1950.

I pondered on my mission to this sullen, sinister Bolshevik State I had once tried so hard to strangle at birth, and which, until Hitler appeared, I had regarded as the mortal foe of civilized freedom.
The Hinge of Fate.

In war, Resolution; in defeat, Defiance; in victory, Magnanimity.
My Early Life: A Roving Commission.

I cannot forecast to you the action of Russia. It is a riddle wrapped in a mystery

---

Soviet Russia, according to an AP dispatch from Moscow, dated August 1, 1946 and quoting *Pravda*. On November 15, 1945, Senator Vandenberg used the phrase in a Senate speech, and when later asked where he got it replied, "I *thought* I got it out of my head", according to the *N. Y. Times*, August 21, 1949. "We are grateful to a correspondent of *The Times* (London) for providing chapter and verse to prove that the phrase 'Iron Curtain' was coined not as had been generally supposed by Mr. Churchill but by Von Krosyg, Hitler's Minister of Finance"—*Reynolds News*, August 11, 1946. The *Manchester Guardian* of February 23, 1945, published a Reuter dispatch quoting Dr. Goebbels predicting a third world war of the western world against Russia in 1948; at the end of the Second World War Goebbels said, "the whole of east and south-eastern Europe, together with the Reich, would come under Russian occupation. Behind an iron curtain, mass butcheries of people would begin...."

inside an enigma; but perhaps there is a key. That key is Russian national interest.
Statement, London, October 1, 1939.

Karl M. Chworowsky
(Contemporary)
American Unitarian minister

A Unitarian is a religious person whose ethic derives primarily from that of Jesus, who believes in one God—not the Trinity —and whose philosophy of faith and life is founded upon the principles of liberty, tolerance and fellowship.
Look, March 8, 1955.

Unitarians are firm believers in the "Church Universal". They believe that this church includes all men and women, of every race, color and creed, who seek God and worship him through *service* to their fellow men. *Ibid.*

John Ciardi
(b. 1916)
American poet, educator

A savage, after all, is simply a human organism that has not received enough news from the human race. Literature is one most fundamental part of that news.
Saturday Review, January 31, 1959.

One needs to hear Job lift his question into the wind; it is, after all, every man's question at some time. One needs to stand by Oedipus and hold the knife of his own most terrible resolution. One needs to come out of his own Hell with Dante and to hear that voice of joy hailing the sight of his own stars returned-to. One needs to run with Falstaff, roaring in his own appetites and weeping into his own pathos. What one learns from those voices is his own humanity.
Ibid.

Marcus Tullius Cicero
(106-43 B.C.)
Roman orator, statesman

The law is silent during war. (Or, Laws are dumb amidst the clash of arms.) *Silent enim leges inter arma.*   *Pro Milone.*

The safety of the people shall be the highest law.   *Laws (De Legibus).*

Of all these things respecting which learned men dispute there is none more important than clearly to understand that we are born for justice, and that right is founded not in opinion but in nature.
Ibid.

The most learned men have determined to begin with Law, and it would seem that they are right, if, according to their definition, Law is the highest reason, implanted in Nature, which commands what ought to be done and forbids the opposite. This reason, when firmly fixed and fully developed in the human mind, is Law.
Ibid.

Law is intelligence, whose natural function it is to command right conduct and forbid wrongdoing.   *Ibid.*

True law is right reason in agreement with nature; it is of universal application, unchanging and everlasting; it summons to duty by its commands, and averts from wrongdoing by its prohibitions.   *Ibid.*

Law is the security for the enjoyment of the high rank which we enjoy in the Republic; this is the foundation of liberty, this is the fountainhead of all justice; in the laws are found the will, the spirit, the prudence and the decision of the state.
Ibid.

The ministers of the law are its magistrates; the interpreters of the law are the judges; we are therefore all slaves of the Laws, that we may enjoy freedom. *Ibid.*

When you have no basis for an argument, abuse the plaintiff.   *Pro Flacco.*

Beware of ambition for wealth; for there is nothing so characteristic of narrowness and littleness of soul as the love of riches; and there is nothing more honorable or noble than indifference to money.
De Officiis, bk. 1.

In men of the highest character and noblest genius there generally exists insatiable desire of honor, command, power and glory.   *Ibid.*

Morals today are corrupted by our worship of riches.   *Ibid., bk. 2.*

Freedom suppressed and again regained bites with deeper fangs than freedom never endangered.   *Ibid.*

There is no fortress so strong that money cannot take it.   *In Verrem.*

Some prefer riches, some good health, some power, some public honors, and many even prefer sensual pleasures. . . . Again, there are those who place the "chief good" in virtue and that is really a noble view; but this very virtue is the parent and preserver of friendship and without virtue, friendship cannot exist at all.
On Friendship. Copyright, Loeb Classical Library.

For what person is there, in the name of gods and men! who would wish to be surrounded by unlimited wealth and to abound in every material blessing, on condition that he love no one and that no one love him? Such indeed is the life of tyrants —a life, I mean, in which there can be no faith, no affection, no trust in the continuance of goodwill; where every act arouses suspicion and anxiety and where friendship has no place. *Ibid.*

Can anyone love either the man whom he fears, or the man by whom he believes himself to be feared? Yet tyrants are courted under a pretence of affection, but only for a season. For when by chance they have fallen from power, as they generally do, then it is known how poor they were in friends. *Ibid.*

Wise men are instructed by reason; men of less understanding, by experience; the most ignorant, by necessity; the beasts by nature.

Taxes are the sinews of the State.

Freedom is participation in power.

I prefer the most unfair peace to the most righteous war. (Also translated: I prefer the most unjust peace to the justest war that was ever waged.) *Letters to Atticus.*

The consensus of opinion among all nations, on whatever matter, may be taken for the law of nature.
Tusculanae disputationes.

I would rather be wrong with Plato than right with such men as these. *Ibid.*

Reason is the mistress and queen of all things. *Ibid.*

Vivere est cogitare. (To think is to live.)
Ibid.

In the common people there is no wisdom, no penetration, no power of judgment.
Pro Planchio.

Our minds possess by nature an insatiable desire to know the truth.

Extreme justice is extreme injustice.

Malice is pleasure derived from another's evil which brings no advantage to oneself.

A happy life consists in tranquility of mind.

Let the soldier yield to the civilian.
Orationes Philippicae, V, c. 60 B.C.

The sinews of war are infinite money.
Ibid.

Only in states in which the power of the people is supreme has liberty any abode.
De republica, 1, c. 50 B.C.

(Freedom is) the power to live as you will. Who then lives as he wills?
Paradoxa Stoicorum, quoted by Adler, The Idea of Freedom, p. 253.

All wicked men are slaves. *Ibid.*

Superstition is a senseless fear of God.
De natura deorum, 45 B.C.

We were born to unite with our fellowmen, and to join in community with the human race. *De finibus, IV, c. 50* B.C.

Tom C. Clark
(1899-1977)
U.S. Supreme Court justice

That books, newspapers, and magazines are published and sold for profit does not prevent them from being a form of expression whose liberty is safeguarded by the First Amendment. We fail to see why operation for profit should have any different effect in the case of motion pictures.
Majority opinion, Burstyn v. Wilson, 343 U.S. 495 (1952). "The Miracle" Case.

. . . from the standpoint of freedom of speech and the press, it is enough to point out that the state has no legitimate interest in protecting any or all religions from views distasteful to them which is sufficient to justify prior restraints upon the expression of those views. It is not the business of government in our nation to suppress real or imagined attacks upon a particular religious doctrine, whether they appear in publications, speeches, or motion pictures. *Ibid.*

I am convinced that every boy, in his heart, would rather steal second base than an automobile.
Speech on juvenile delinquency; Justice Clark's favorite non-legal quotation.

James Freeman Clarke
(1810-1888)
American Unitarian clergyman, writer

The difference between a politician and a statesman is: a politician thinks of the next election and a statesman thinks of the next generation.

Claudian
(365?-408?)
Latin poet

Mobile . . . vulgus. (The fickle mob.)
Panegyricus.

He who strikes terror into others is himself in continual fear.

Karl von Clausewitz
(1780-1831)
Prussian general, military writer

We must further expressly and exactly establish the point of view, no less necessary in practice, from which war is regarded as *nothing but the continuation of state policy with other means.*
On War, prefatory note.

Defense is the stronger form with the negative object, and attack the weaker form with the positive object. *Ibid.*

Victory consists not merely in the conquest of the battlefield, but in the destruction of physical and moral forces and this is usually attained only in the pursuit after the battle is won. . . . Every attack weakens as it advances. *Ibid.*

Force, that is to say, physical force (for no moral force exists apart from the conception of a state and law), is the *means;* to impose our will upon the enemy is the *object.* To achieve this object with certainty we must disarm the enemy, and this disarming is by definition the proper aim of military action.
Ibid., Ch. 1, What is War?

Philanthropic souls might easily imagine that there is an artistic way of disarming or overthrowing our adversary without too much bloodshed and that this was what the art of war should seek to achieve. However agreeable this may sound, it is a false idea which must be demolished. In affairs so dangerous as war, false ideas proceeding from kindness of heart are precisely the worst. *Ibid.*

It is waste—and worse than a waste—of effort to ignore the element of brutality because of the repugnance it excites.
Ibid.

We see, therefore, that war is not merely a political act but a real political instrument, a continuation of political intercourse, a carrying out of the same by other means.
Ibid.

War is the province of chance. In no other sphere of human activity has such a margin to be left to this intruder, because none is in such constant contact with it on every side. It increases the uncertainty of every circumstance and deranges the course of events.
Ibid., Ch. 3, The Genius for War.

If we take a comprehensive view of the four components of the atmosphere in which war moves, *danger, physical effort, uncertainty and chance*, it is easy to understand that a great moral and mental force is needed to advance with safety and success in this baffling element, a force which, according to the different modifications arising out of circumstances, we find historians and chroniclers of military events describing as *energy, firmness, staunchness, strength of mind and character*. All these manifestations of the heroic nature might be regarded as one and the same force of will. *Ibid.*

A people's war in civilized Europe is a phenomenon of the Nineteenth century.... A people's war in general is to be regarded as a consequence of the way in which in our day the elemental violence of war has burst its old artificial barriers; as an expression and strengthening, therefore, of the whole ferment which we call war.
Ibid., Book 6, Ch. 26. Arming the Nation.

War is only caused through the political intercourse of governments and nations; . . War is nothing but a continuation of political intercourse with an admixture of other means. *Ibid.*

Does the cessation of diplomatic notes stop the political relations between different nations and governments? Is not war merely another kind of writing and language for their thought? It has, to be sure, its own grammar, but not its own logic. *Ibid.*

War can never be separated from political intercourse. *Ibid.*

The subordination of the political point of view to the military would be unreasonable, for policy has created war; policy is the intelligent faculty, war only the instrument, and not the reverse. The subordination of the military point of view to the political is, therefore, the only thing which is possible. *Ibid.*

Therefore, once more: war is an instrument of policy; it must necessarily bear the character of policy; it must measure with policy's measure. The conduct of war, in its great outlines, is, therefore, politics itself, which takes up the sword in place of the pen, but does not on that account cease to think according to its own laws. *Ibid.*

There is only one decisive victory: the last.
All that precede it, however great they may be, amount to nothing but an expenditure of energy which imperils the chances of winning the decisive final battle. *Ibid.*

The moral forces are amongst the most important subjects in war. *Ibid.*

Let us not hear of generals who conquer without bloodshed. If a bloody slaughter is a horrible sight, then that is a ground for paying more respect to war but not for making the sword we wear blunter and blunter by degrees from feelings of humanity, until some one steps in with one that is sharp and lops off the arm from our body. *Ibid.*

A conquerer is always a lover of peace. *On War; copied by Lenin in his notebook, with notation, "Ah! Ah! Witty". Lenin and Stalin were avowed students of von Clausewitz.*

(The objects of war.)
1. To conquer and to destroy the armed power of the enemy.
2. To take possession of his material and other sources of his strength.
3. To win public opinion.
To accomplish the first purpose we should always direct our principal operation

against an important portion of his forces. For only after defeating these can we pursue the other two objects successfully. In order to seize the enemy's material resources, we should direct our operations against the places where most of these resources are concentrated. On the way to these objectives we shall encounter the enemy's main forces or at least a considerable part of it.   *Op. cit.*

Henry Clay
(1777-1852)
American statesman, orator

All legislation, all government, all society is founded upon the principle of mutual concession, politeness, comity, courtesy; upon these everything is based. . . . Let him who elevates himself above humanity, above its weaknesses, its infirmities, its wants, its necessities, say, if he pleases, I will never compromise; but let no one who is not above the frailties of our common nature disdain compromises.
Quoted by Agar, The Price of Union.

An oppressed people are authorized whenever they can to rise and break their fetters.
Speech, House of Representatives, March 4, 1818.

All religions united with government are more or less inimical to liberty. All separated from government, are compatible with liberty.
House of Representatives, March 24, 1818.

Sarah N. Cleghorn
(1876-1959)
American poet

The golf links lie so near the mill
That almost any day

The laboring children can look out
And see the men at play.
The Conning Tower, N. Y. Tribune, January 1, 1915.

Georges Clemenceau
(1841-1929)
French statesman, premier

J'Accuse!
Headline over Zola article, January 13, 1898.

La guerre est une chose beaucoup trop sérieuse pour être confiée à des généraux. (War is much too serious a matter to be entrusted to generals.)
Quoted, N. Y. Times, July 14, 1944.

Le bon Dieu n'avait que dix. (The good God had only ten.)
To George Adam, journalist, who mentioned Wilson's Fourteen Points.

The Germans are in love with Death.

Archbishop of Paris (to Clemenceau): Is it really true, monsieur, you do not believe in God?
Clemenceau: And you, monsieur?

America is the only nation in history which miraculously has gone directly from barbarism to degeneration without the usual interval of civilization.
Saturday Review, December 1, 1945.

War is a series of catastrophes which result in victory.

Samuel L(anghorne) Clemens
See Twain

Clement of Alexandria *
(150?-220?)
Christian father, writer

Private property is the fruit of iniquity.

---

* Stricken from the list of saints by Pope Benedict XIV.

I know that God has given us the use of goods, but only as far as is necessary; and He has determined that the use shall be common.

It is absurd and disgraceful to live magnificently and luxuriously when so many are hungry.

The use of all things that are found in this world ought to be common to all men. Only the most manifest iniquity makes one say to the other, "This belongs to me, that to you". Hence the origin of contention among men.

Grover Cleveland

(1837-1908)

22nd and 24th President of the United States

Party honesty is party expedience.
1889.

A truly American sentiment recognizes the dignity of labor and the fact that honor lies in honest toil.

A government for the people must depend for its success on the intelligence, the morality, the justice, and the interest of the people themselves.

There is no calamity which a great nation can invite which equals that which follows a supine submission to wrong and injustice. *1895.*

Though the people support the government, the government should not support the people.

At times like the present, when the evils of unsound finance threaten us, the speculator may anticipate a harvest gathered from the misfortune of others, the capitalist may protect himself by hoarding or may even find profit in the fluctuations of values; but the wage earner—the first to be injured by a depreciated currency and the last to receive the benefit of its correction—is practically defenseless.

It is agreed that American citizenship shall be the only credential necessary to justify the claim of equality before the law, and that no condition in life shall give rise to discrimination in the treatment of the people by their Government.
Annual Message to Congress, 1888.

Communism is a hateful thing and a menace to peace and organized government; but the communism of combined wealth and capital, the outgrowth of overweening cupidity and selfishness, which insidiously undermines the justice and integrity of free institutions, is not less dangerous than the communism of oppressed poverty and toil, which, exasperated by injustice and discontent, attacks with wild disorder the citadel of rule. *Ibid.*

He mocks the people who proposes that the Government shall protect the rich and that they in turn will care for the laboring poor. *Ibid.*

Our cities are the abiding places of wealth and luxury; our manufactories yield fortunes never dreamed of by the fathers of the Republic; our business men are madly striving in the race for riches, and immense aggregations of capital outrun the imagination in the magnitude of their undertakings . . .

Upon more careful inspection we find the wealth and luxury of our cities mingled with poverty and wretchedness and unremunerative toil. *Ibid.*

The gulf between employers and employed is constantly widening, and classes are rapidly forming, one comprising the very rich and powerful, while in another are found the toiling poor. *Ibid.*

As we view the achievements of aggregated capital, we discover the existence of trusts, combinations, and monopolies, while the citizen is struggling far in the rear or is trampled to death beneath an iron heel. Corporations, which should be the restrained creatures of the law and the servants of the people, are fast becoming the people's masters. *Ibid.*

The cause for which the battle is waged is comprised within lines clearly and distinctly defined. It should never be compromised. It is the people's cause. *Ibid.*

I believe that our Great Maker is preparing the world, in His own good time, to become one nation, speaking one language. *Inaugural, March 4, 1893.*

The wage earner relies upon the ventures of confident and contented capital. This failing him, his condition is without alleviation, for he can neither prey on the misfortune of others nor hoard his labor.
Message, August 8, 1893.

The trusts and combinations—the communism of pelf. . . .
Letter to Rep. T. C. Catchings, August 1, 1894.

Voltarine de Cleyre
(1866-1912)
American radical poet, essayist

Make no laws whatever concerning speech, and speech will be free; so soon as you make a declaration on paper that speech shall be free, you will have a hundred lawyers proving that "freedom does not mean abuse, nor liberty license;" and

they will define and define freedom out of existence.

Let the guarantee of free speech be in every man's determination to use it, and we shall have no need for paper declarations.

On the other hand, so long as the people do not care to exercise their freedom, those who wish to tyrannize will do so; for tyrants are active and ardent, and will devote themselves in the name of any number of gods, religious and otherwise, to put shackles upon sleeping men.
Sinclair, The Cry For Justice.

Frank I. Cobb
(1869-1923)
Editor, New York World

It is not the powers that they conferred upon the government, but the powers that they prohibited to the government which makes the Constitution a charter of liberty.
La Follette's Magazine, January, 1920.

The Bill of Rights is a born rebel. It reeks with sedition. In every clause it shakes its fists in the face of constituted authority and thunders "Thou shalt not", and because its ultimatum is "Thou shalt not" it is the one guarantee of human freedom to the American people, unless they themselves destroy their safeguard. *Ibid.*

There is revolution in reaction, as well as in radicalism, and Toryism speaking a jargon of law and order may often be a graver menace to liberty than radicalism bellowing the empty phrases of the soapbox demagogue. *Ibid.*

Jefferson said that: "The spirit of resistance to government is so valuable on certain occasions that I wish it always to be kept alive . . ." If the author of the Declaration of Independence were to utter such a sentiment today the Post Office Department could exclude him from the mails; Grand Juries could indict him for sedition and criminal syndicalism; legislative committees could seize his private papers and search them for evidence of Bolshevism, and United States Senators would be clamoring for his deportation on the ground that he had been tainted with the ribald doctrines of the French Revolution and should be sent back to live with the rest of the terrorists. *Ibid.*

Thus the political philosophy of one generation becomes the political anathema of another. *Ibid.*

The failures of popular government have always been the failures of public opinion —mostly public opinion that was ill-informed, of public opinion that was denied the facts, of public opinion that was misguided by self-constituted masters. That will always remain a great menace, and public opinion is never to be safeguarded by trying to prevent it by law from coming into contact with political heresy. There is no surer way to give those doctrines a foothold than to proscribe them. *Ibid.*

William Cobbett
(1762-1835)
English political writer, reformer

To be poor and independent is very nearly an impossibility.
Advice to Young Men.

You hang on with unrelenting grasp; and cry "pauper" and "poacher" and "radical" and "lower orders" with as much insolence as ever! It is always thus; men like you may be convinced of error, but they never change their conduct. They never become just because they are convinced that they have been unjust; they must have a great

deal more than that conviction to make them just.
Letter to Landlords (on the hanging of two poachers). Cobbett's Weekly Register, April 6, 1822.

The agitation of this Catholic Question (Catholic Emancipation Act of 1829) serves, and can serve only, to amuse the people, and to keep them divided. If I were to choose a people to hold in a state of complete subjection, it would be a people divided into several religious sects, each condemning the others to perdition. With such a people, furnished with a suitable set of priests, a Government endued with barely common sense might do just what it pleased. *Weekly Political Register.*

If ever there was in the world a thing completely perverted from its original design and tendency, it is the Press of England; which, instead of enlightening, does, as far as it has any power, keep the people in ignorance; which, instead of cherishing notions of liberty, tends to the making of the people slaves; and which, instead of being their guardian, is the most efficient instrument in the hands of those who oppress, or wish to oppress, them. *Ibid.*

Richard Cobden
(1804-1865)
English manufacturer, radical

I took the repeal of the Corn Laws as light amusement compared with the difficult task of inducing the priests of all denominations to agree to suffer the people to be educated. *Letter to a Friend, 1846.*

Claud Cockburn
(Contemporary)
British writer

A newspaper is always a weapon in somebody's hands.
In Time of Trouble, 1956.

The hired journalist, I thought, ought to realize that he is partly in the entertainment business and partly in the advertising business—advertising either goods, or a cause, or a government. He just has to make up his mind whom he wants to entertain, and what he wants to advertise.
Ibid.

The humbug and hypocrisy of the press begin only when the newspapers pretend to be "impartial" or "servants of the public". And this becomes dangerous as well as laughable when the public is fool enough to believe it.   *Ibid.*

Erle Cocke, Jr.
(b. 1921)
American airline executive, former national commander, American Legion

I have found on an around-the-world tour that the principles of the American Legion are as good as those in the Bible.
The Nation, May 31, 1952.

Jean Cocteau
(1891-1963)
French poet, novelist, playwright

Art is not a pastime but a priesthood. *Quoted by Brooks Atkinson, N. Y. Times, September 8, 1957.*

The instinct of nearly all societies is to lock up anybody who is truly free. First, society begins by trying to beat you up. If this fails, they try to poison you. If this fails too, they finish by loading honors on your head. *Time, September 30, 1957.*

If it had to choose who is to be crucified, the crowd will always save Barabbas.

George M. Cohan
(1878-1942)
American actor-manager, playwright

Many a bum show has been saved by the flag. *Quoted in LaFollette's Progressive.*

Morris Raphael Cohen
(1880-1947)
American philosopher

The business of the philosopher is well done if he succeeds in raising genuine doubts.   *A Dreamer's Journey, 1949.*

Edward Coke
(1552-1634)
English writer on law

The common law protecteth the King. *Quod Rex non debet esse sub homine, sed sub Deo et Lege.* (The King himself should be under no man, but under God and the Law.) *Quoted in Time, August 5, 1957.*

No man, ecclesiastical or temporal, shall be examined upon secret thoughts of his heart or of his secret opinion. And the defendant must have, as in Star Chamber and Chancery, the bill (of charges) delivered unto him, or otherwise he need not answer to it.

How long soever it hath continued, if it be against reason, it is of no force in law. *Institutes. Commentary upon Littleton.*

A man's house is his castle, *et domus sua cuique est tutissimum refugium.*
Ibid.

Reason is the life of the law; nay, the Common Law itself is nothing else but reason.   *Ibid.*

No restraint, be it ever so little, but is imprisonment.   *Ibid.*

Magna Carta is such a fellow that he will have no sovereign.
House of Commons, May 17, 1628.

They (corporations) cannot commit treason, nor be outlawed, nor excommunicated, for they have no souls.
Sutton's Hospital Case.

The house of every one is to him as his castle and fortress.   *Semayne's Case.*

It appears in our books that in many cases the common law will control Acts of Parliament, and sometimes adjudge them to be utterly void: for when an Act of Parliament is against common right and reason . . . the common law will control it and adjudge such act to be void.
Dr. Bonham's Case, 1610.

Samuel Taylor Coleridge

(1772-1834)

English poet, critic, philosopher

Look through the whole history of countries professing the Romish religion, and you will uniformly find the leaven of this besetting and accursed principle of action —that the end will sanction any means.
Table Talk, August 6, 1831.

He who begins by loving Christianity better than the truth, will proceed by loving his own sect or Church better than Christianity, and end in loving himself best of all.
Cardiff, What Great Men Think of Religion.

Clergymen who publish pious frauds in the interest of the Church are the orthodox liars of God.   *Ibid.*

O ye loud Waves! and O ye Forests high!
And O ye Clouds that far above me soared!
Thou rising Sun! thou blue rejoicing Sky!
Yes, every thing that is and will be free!
Bear witness for me, wheresoe'er ye be,
With what deep worship I have still adored
That spirit of divinest Liberty.
France: An Ode, during the invasion of Switzerland, 1797.

The Sensual and the Dark rebel in vain,
Slaves by their own compulsion! In mad game
They burst their manacles and wear the name
Of Freedom, graven on a heavier chain!   *Ibid.*

All truth is a species of revelation.
Gollancz, From Darkness to Light.

To *doubt* has more of faith, even to disbelieve, than that blank negation of all such thoughts and feelings which is the lot of the herd of church-and-meeting trotters.

Not one man in a thousand has the strength of mind or the goodness of heart to be an atheist.
To Thomas Allsop, c. 1820.

Whenever philosophy has taken into its plan religion, it has ended in skepticism; and whenever religion excludes philosophy, or the spirit of free enquiry, it leads to wilful blindness and superstition.
Allsop's Letters, Conversations, and Reflections of Samuel Taylor Coleridge, 1836.

Enlist the interests of stern morality and religious enthusiasm in the cause of political liberty, as in the time of the old Puritans, and it will be irresistible.

The great ends for a statesman are, security to possessors, facility to acquirers, and liberty and hope to the people.

Charles Caleb Colton
(1780-1832)
· *English poet, essayist*

The greatest friend of truth is Time, her greatest enemy is Prejudice, and her constant companion is Humility. *The Lacon.*

Men will wrangle for religion; write for it; fight for it; die for it; anything but—live for it. *Ibid.*

He that dies a martyr proves that he was not a knave, but by no means that he was not a fool. *Ibid.*

The old ways are the safest and surest ways. *Ibid.*

Ambition is in fact the avarice of power. *Ibid.*

Bigotry murders religion to frighten fools with her ghost. *Ibid.*

Power, like the diamond, dazzles the beholder, and also the wearer; it dignifies meanness; it magnifies littleness; to what is contemptible, it gives authority; to what is low, exaltation. *Ibid.*

The only things in which we can be said to have any property is *our actions . . .* Our actions must follow us beyond the grave: with respect to them *alone* we cannot say that we shall carry nothing with us when we die, neither that we shall go naked out of the world. Our actions must clothe us with an immortality, loathsome or glorious: these are the only *title-deeds* of which we cannot be disinherited; they will have their full weight in the balance of eternity, when everything else is as nothing. *Ibid.*

Power will intoxicate the best hearts, as wine the strongest heads. No man is wise enough, nor good enough to be trusted with unlimited power.

Despotism can no more exist in a nation until the liberty of the press be destroyed than night can happen before the sun is set.

Falsehood is never so successful as when she baits her hook with truth, and no opinions so falsely mislead us as those that are not wholly wrong, as no watches so effectually deceive the wearer as those that are sometimes right.

Tyrants have not yet discovered any chains that can fetter the mind.

Calumny crosses oceans, scales mountains, and traverses deserts with greater ease than the Scythian Abaris, and, like him, rides upon a poisoned arrow.

Liberty will not descend to a people; a people must raise themselves to liberty; it is a blessing that must be earned before it can be enjoyed.

Steele observed that there is this difference between the Church of Rome and the Church of England,—that the one professes to be infallible, the other to be never in the wrong.

The three great apostles of practical atheism that make converts without persecuting, and retain them without preaching, are health, wealth, and power.

Ambition makes the same mistake concerning power, that avarice makes as to wealth. She begins by accumulating it as a means of happiness, and finishes by continuing to accumulate it as an end.

A free press is the parent of much good in the state. But even a licentious press is far less evil than a press that is enslaved. *Quoted in Free Press Anthology.*

A licentious press *may* be an evil, an enslaved press *must* be so; for an enslaved press may cause error to be more current than wisdom, and wrong more powerful than right. A licentious press cannot effect these things, for if it gives the poison, it gives also the antidote, which an enslaved press withholds.   *Ibid.*

An enslaved press is doubly fatal. It not only takes away the true light, for in that case we might stand still, but it sets up a false one, that decoys us to our destruction.
                                              Ibid.

Christopher Columbus
(1451-1506)
Genoese discoverer of America

Gold constitutes treasure, and he who possesses it has all the needs in this world, as also the means of rescuing souls from Purgatory, and restoring them to the enjoyment of Paradise.
Quoted by W. Raleigh, The English Voyages of the 16th Century, 1910.

Henry Steele Commager
(b. 1902)
American writer, educator, historian

With the Sedition and Espionage Acts . . . the "red hysteria" of the Twenties, the Alien Registration Act of 1940, the loyalty tests and purges of the mid-Forties, the establishment of un-American Activities Committees, intolerance received, as it were, the stamp of official approval. Loyalty was identified with conformity, and the American genius, which had been experimental and even rebellious, was required to conform to a pattern.
The American Mind, 1950.

Physically Americans were pioneers; in the realm of social and economic institutions, too, their tradition has been one of pioneering. From the beginning, intellectual and spiritual diversity has been as characteristic of America as racial and linguistic diversity. . . . From the beginning Americans have known that there were new worlds to conquer, new truths to be discovered. Every effort to confine Americanism to a single pattern, to constrain it to a single formula, is disloyalty to everything that is valid in Americanism.
Freedom, Loyalty, Dissent.

Loyalty . . . is a realization that America was born of revolt, flourished in dissent, became great through experimentation.
                                              Ibid.

If our democracy is to flourish, it must have criticism; if our government is to function it must have dissent.   *Ibid.*

We should not forget that our tradition is one of protest and revolt, and it is stultifying to celebrate the rebels of the past . . . while we silence the rebels of the present.   *Ibid.*

It is a gross perversion not only of the concept of loyalty but of the concept of Americanism to identify it with a particular economic system.   *Ibid.*

What is the new loyalty? It is, above all, conformity. It is the uncritical and unquestioning acceptance of America as it is—the political institutions, the social relationships, the economic practices. It rejects inquiry into the race question or socialized medicine, or public housing, or into the wisdom or validity of our foreign policy. It regards as particularly heinous any challenge to what is called "the system of private enterprise," identifying that system with Americanism. It abandons evolution, repudiates the once popular concept of progress, and

regards America as a finished product, perfect and complete.
Who is Loyal to America? Harper's Magazine, September, 1947.

Who would be cleared by their (Un-American) Committees? Not Washington, who was a rebel. Not Jefferson, who wrote that all men are created equal and whose motto was "rebellion to tyrants is obedience to God." Not Garrison, who publicly burned the Constitution; or Wendell Phillips, who spoke for the underprivileged everywhere and counted himself a philosophical anarchist; nor Seward of the Higher Law or Sumner of racial equality. Not Lincoln, who admonished us to have malice toward none, charity for all; or Wilson, who warned that our flag was "a flag of liberty of opinion as well as of political liberty"; or Justice Holmes, who said that our Constitution is an experiment and that while that experiment is being made "we should be eternally vigilant against attempts to check the expression of opinions that we loathe and believe to be fraught with death." *Ibid.*

Who are those who are really disloyal? Those who inflame race hatreds, who sow religious and class dissensions. Those who subvert the Constitution by violating the freedom of the ballot box. Those who make a mockery of majority rule by the use of the filibuster. Those who impair democracy by denying equal education facilities. Those who frustrate justice by lynch law or by making a farce of jury trials. Those who deny freedom of speech and of the press and of assembly. Those who press for special favors against the interest of the commonwealth. Those who regard public office as a source of private gain. Those who would exalt the military over the civil. Those who for selfish and private purposes stir up national antagonisms and expose the world to the ruin of war. *Ibid.*

The American people . . . have a stake in non-conformity, for they know that the American genius is non-conformist. *Ibid.*

Commission on Civil Rights
See President's Commission on Civil Rights

Commission on Freedom of the Press*

These instruments (press, radio and other means of mass communication) can spread lies faster and farther than our forefathers dreamed when they enshrined the freedom of the press in the First Amendment of the Constitution.
A Free and Responsible Press, University of Chicago Press, 1947.

The press can be inflammatory, sensational and irresponsible. *Ibid.*

One of the most effective ways of improving the press is blocked by the press itself. By a kind of unwritten law the press ignores the errors and misrepresentations, the lies and scandals of which its members are guilty. *Ibid.*

The few who are able to use the machinery of the press as an instrument of mass communications have not provided a service adequate to the needs of the society. *Ibid.*

The agencies (of mass communication) can advance the progress of civilization or they can thwart it. They can debase and vulgarize mankind. They can endanger the peace of the world. *Ibid.*

---

* Chancellor Robert Hutchins of the University of Chicago, chairman, Zechariah Chafee, Jr., professor of law at Harvard, vice chairman.

From a moral point of view, at least, freedom of expression does not include the right to lie as a deliberate instrument of policy.   *Ibid.*

The press must also be accountable. It must be accountable to society for meeting the public need and for maintaining the rights of citizens and the almost forgotten rights of speakers who have no press. It must know that its faults and errors have ceased to be private vagaries and have become public dangers.   *Ibid.*

The agencies of mass communication are big business, and their owners are big businessmen.   *Ibid.*

The public charges of distortion in the press resulting from the bias of its owners fall into the categories that might be expected. . . . Bias is claimed against consumer cooperatives, against food and drug regulations, against Federal Trade Commission orders designed to suppress fraudulent advertising, and against Federal Communications Commission regulations affecting newspaper-owned broadcasting stations.
Ibid.

The news is twisted by the emphasis on firstness, on the novel and sensational; by the personal interests of the owners; and by the pressure groups.   *Ibid.*

Karl Taylor Compton
(1887-1954)
American atomic physicist

In recent times, modern science has developed to give mankind, for the first time in the history of the human race, a way of securing a more abundant life which does not simply consist in taking away from someone else.
Address, The Social Implications of Scientific Discovery, American Philosophical Society, 1938.

Science really creates wealth and opportunity which did not exist before. Whereas the old order was based on competition, the new order of science makes possible, for the first time, a cooperative creative effort in which every one is the gainer and no one the loser . . . The advent of modern science is the most important social event in history.   *Ibid.*

Auguste Comte
(1798-1857)
French philosopher

The law is this: that each of our leading conceptions—each branch of our knowledge —passes successively through three different theoretical conditions: the Theological, or fictitious; the Metaphysical, or abstract; and the Scientific, or positive.
The Positive Philosophy.

The human mind, by its nature, employs in its progress three methods of philosophizing, the character of which is essentially different, and even radically opposed: viz., the theological method, the metaphysical, and the positive. Hence arise three philosophies, or general systems of conceptions on the aggregate of phenomena, each of which excludes the others. The first is the necessary point of departure of the human understanding; and the third is its fixed and definitive state. The second is merely a state of transition.   *Ibid.*

All good intellects have repeated, since Bacon's time, that there can be no real knowledge but which is based on observed facts.   *Ibid.*

It cannot be necessary to prove to anybody who reads this work that Ideas govern the world, or throw it into chaos; in other words, that all social mechanism rests upon Opinions.   *Ibid.*

[171]

James Bryant Conant
(1893-1978)
American educator

Those who worry about radicalism in our schools and colleges are often either reactionaries who themselves do not bear allegiance to the traditional American principles, or defeatists who despair of the success of our own philosophy in an open competition.
Education in a Divided World, 1948.

Diversity of opinion within the framework of loyalty to our free society is not only basic to a university but to the entire nation. *Ibid.*

Slogans are both exciting and comforting, but they are also powerful opiates for the conscience.
Baccalaureate, Harvard, June, 1934.

Some of mankind's most terrible misdeeds have been committed under the spell of certain magic words or phrases. *Ibid.*

Marie Jean Antoine Nicolas de Caritat, Marquis de Condorcet
(1743-1794)
French philosopher, revolutionist

There can be seen developing a new doctrine, which must give the final thrust to the tottering edifice of prejudices. It is the doctrine of the indefinite perfectibility of the human race.
Sketch for a Historical Picture of the Progress of the Human Spirit.

Nature has set no term to the perfection of human faculties; the perfectibility of man is truly indefinite; and the progress of this perfectibility, from now onwards independent of any power that might wish to halt it, has no other limits than the duration of the globe upon which nature has cast us. This progress will doubtless vary in speed, but it will never be reversed. *Ibid.*

Nature binds truth, happiness and virtue together as by an indissoluble chain. *Ibid.*

Men still preserve the errors of their childhood, of their country, and of their age long after having recognized all the truths needed to destroy them. *Ibid.*

The Confederate Constitution

Section 2 (1) The citizens of each State shall be entitled to all the privileges and immunities of citizens of the several States, and shall have the right of transit and sojourn in any State, of the Confederacy, with their slaves and other property; and the right of property in said slaves shall not be thereby impaired. *Art. VI.*

(3) The Confederate States may acquire new territory . . . In all such territory, the institution of negro slavery, as it now exists in the Confederate States, shall be recognized and protected by the Congress and by the territorial government. *Ibid.*

Confucius
(551-479 B.C.)
Chinese philosopher

Without knowing the force of words, it is impossible to know men. *Analects.*

The way of the superior man is threefold, but I am not equal to it. Virtuous, he is free from anxieties; wise, he is free from perplexities; bold, he is free from fear.
Ibid., bk. 14.

The scholar who cherishes the love of comfort, is not fit to be deemed a scholar. *Ibid.*

There were four things from which the Master was entirely free. He had no foregone conclusions, no arbitrary pre-determinations, no obstinacy, and no egoism. *Ibid.*

Tsze-kung asked what constituted the superior man. The Master said, "He acts before he speaks, and afterwards speaks according to his actions. The superior man is universally minded and no partisan. The inferior man is a partisan and not universal." *Ibid.*

The superior man thinks always of virtue; the common man thinks of comfort. *Ibid.*

The object of the superior man is truth. Food is not his object. The superior man is anxious lest he should not get truth; he is not anxious lest poverty should come upon him. *Ibid.*

Those who know the truth are not equal to those who love it. *Ibid.*

Tsze-kung asked, saying, "Is there one word which may serve as a rule of practice for all one's life?" The Master said, "Is not Reciprocity such a word? What you do not want done to yourself, do not do to others." *Ibid.*

When wealth is centralized the people are dispersed. When wealth is distributed the people are brought together. *Ibid.*

Five things constitute perfect virtue: gravity, magnanimity, earnestness, sincerity, kindness. *Ibid.*

In a country well governed poverty is something to be ashamed of. In a country badly governed wealth is something to be ashamed of. *Ibid.*

An oppressive government is more to be feared than a tiger.

The ancients who desired to illustrate illustrious virtue throughout the empire, first ordered well their own states. Wishing to order well their own states, they first regulated their families. Wishing to regulate their families, they first cultivated their own persons. Wishing to cultivate their persons, they first rectified their hearts. Wishing to rectify their hearts, they first sought to be sincere in their thoughts. Wishing to be sincere in their thoughts, they extended their knowledge to the utmost; and this extension of knowledge lay in the investigation of things.

Wou Saofong, in Treasury for the Free World, 1946.

Things being investigated, knowledge became complete. Their knowledge being complete, their thoughts were sincere. Their thoughts being rectified, their persons were cultivated. Their persons being cultivated, their families were regulated. Their families being regulated, their states were rightly governed. Their states being rightly governed, their whole empire was made tranquil and happy. From the emperor down to the mass of the people, all must consider the cultivation of the person, the root of every thing besides. *Ibid.*

I have yet to meet a man as fond of high moral conduct as he is of outward appearances.

The duties of universal obligation are five, and the moral qualities by which they are carried out are three. The duties are those between ruler and subject, between father and son, between husband and wife, between elder brother and younger, and those in the intercourse of friends. These are the five duties of universal obligation. Wisdom, compassion and courage,—these are the three universally recognized moral qualities of man.

Truth is not only the fulfilment of our own being; it is that by which things outside of us have an existence.

The fulfilment of our being is moral sense. The fulfilment of the nature of things outside of us is intellect.

These, moral sense and intellect, are the powers or faculties of our being. They combine the inner or subjective and outer or objective use of the power of the mind. Therefore, with truth, everything done is right.

Absolute truth is indestructible. Being indestructible, it is eternal. Being eternal, it is self-existent. Being self-existent, it is infinite. Being infinite, it is vast and deep. Being vast and deep, it is transcendental and intelligent.

It is man that makes truth great, not truth that makes man great.

Riches and honor are what men desire; but if they attain to them by improper ways, they should not continue to hold them. Poverty and low estate are what men dislike; but if they are brought to such condition by improper ways, they should not feel shame for it.

Ignorance is the night of the mind, a night without moon or star.

Good government consists in winning the loyalty of the people nearby and attracting the people far away.

For everyone called to the government of nations and empires there are nine cardinal directions to be attended to:
1. Cultivating his personal conduct.
2. Honoring worthy men.
3. Cherishing affection for, and doing his duty toward, his kindred.
4. Showing respect to the high ministers of state.
5. Identifying himself with the interests and welfare of the whole body of public officers.
6. Showing himself as a father to the common people.
7. Encouraging the introduction of all useful arts.
8. Indulgent treatment of men from a distance.
9. Taking interest in the welfare of the princes of the Empire.

Do to every man as thou would'st have him do to thee; and do not unto another what thou would'st not have him do to thee.   *c. 500* B.C.

The superior man understands what is right; the inferior man understands what will sell.

The superior man is liberal towards others' opinions, but does not completely agree with them; the inferior man completely agrees with others' opinions, but is not liberal towards them.

Tom Connally
(1877-1963)
American senator

Draco wrote his laws in blood; the Senate writes its laws in wind.

James Connolly
(1870-executed 1916)
Irish patriot, labor leader

One point of Catholic doctrine . . . almost forgotten and sedulously suppressed . . . that the Catholic Church is theoretically a community in which the clergy are but the officers serving the laity in a common worship and service of God, and that should the clergy at any time profess or teach doctrines not in conformity with the true teachings of Catholicity, it is not only the right, but it is the absolute duty of the laity to refuse such doctrines and to disobey such teaching. Indeed, it is this saving clause in Catholic doctrine which has again and again operated to protect the Church from the result of the mistaken attempts of the clergy to control the secular activities of the laity.

History proves that in almost every case in which the political or social aspirations of the laity came into opposition to the will of the clergy, the laity represented the best interests of the Church as a whole and of mankind in general.

Whenever the clergy succeeded in conquering political power in any country the result has been disastrous to the interests of religion and inimical to the progress of humanity.

Joseph Conrad (Korzeniowski)
(1857-1924)
Polish-English novelist

He who wants to persuade should put his trust, not in the right argument, but in the right word. The power of sound has always been greater than the power of sense. *A Personal Record.*

Do not talk to me of Archimedes' lever. He was an absent-minded person with a mathematical imagination. Mathematics command my respect, but I have no use for engines. Give me the right word and the right accent and I will move the world. *Ibid.*

For every age is fed on illusions, lest men should renounce life early, and the human race come to an end.

Remember, Razumov, that women, children and revolutionists hate irony, which is the negation of all saving instincts, of all faith, of all devotion, of all action. *Sofia, in Under Western Eyes.*

Constantine the Great
(280?-337)
Roman emperor

We have resolved to grant to all Christians as well as all others the liberty to practice the religion they prefer, in order that whatever exists of divinity or celestial power may help and favor us and all who are under our government. *Edict of Milan, 313, quoted by Adams, The Education of Henry Adams.*

Eliza Cook
(1818-1889)
English poet

Better build schoolrooms for "the boy", Than cells and gibbets for "the man". *A Song for the Ragged Schools.*

Continental Congress

The last right we shall mention, regards the freedom of the press. The importance of this consists, besides the advancement of truth, science, morality, and arts in general, in its diffusion of liberal sentiments on the administration of Government, its ready communication of thoughts between subjects, and its consequential promotion of union among them, whereby oppressive officers are shamed or intimidated, into more honourable and just modes of conducting affairs. *Letter to the inhabitants of Quebec, 1774; quoted by Justice Brennan, Roth v. U.S., U.S. 476 (1957).*

[175]

Alistair Cooke
American journalist, broadcaster
(b. 1908)

There is at least one generation of Americans growing up that not only does not have much respect for diversity of opinion but doesn't know what it is. It is only a step to believing that what is strange or unreported by fifty newspapers is somehow mischievous or "un-American." Once every man reads the same things as his neighbor, and thinks the same thought, the common man is here with a vengeance: that is to say, the mass bigot.
The Saturday Review.

Calvin Coolidge
(1872-1933)
30th President of the United States

When more and more people are thrown out of work, unemployment results.
"Immortal remark"—N. Y. Herald Tribune, September 29, 1954.

Civilization and profits go hand in hand.
Speech, N. Y. C., November 27, 1920.

Collecting more taxes than is absolutely necessary is legalized robbery.
N. Y. Times, March 6, 1955.

I think the American public wants a solemn ass as a President. And I think I'll go along with them.
To Ethel Barrymore, Time, May 16, 1955.

The political mind is the product of men in public life who have been twice spoiled. They have been spoiled with praise and they have been spoiled with abuse. With them nothing is natural, everything is artificial. A few rare souls escape these influences and maintain a vision and a judgment that are unimpaired. They are a great comfort to every President and a great service to their country. But they are not sufficient in number so that the public business can be transacted like a private business. *Autobiography.*

Progress depends very largely on the encouragement of variety. Whatever tends to standardize the community, to establish fixed and rigid modes of thought, tends to fossilize society. . . . It is the ferment of ideas, the clash of disagreeing judgments, the privilege of the individual to develop his own thoughts and shape his own character, that makes progress possible.

Well, they hired the money, didn't they? *(A reference to World 1 debts; N. Y. Times, October 20, 1947.)*

The business of America is business. *Address, Society of American Newspaper Editors, January 17, 1925.*

Business will be better or worse.

The legions which (America) sends forth are not armed with the sword but the Cross. . . . We extended our domain over distant islands in order to safeguard our own interests and accepted the consequent obligation to bestow opportunity and liberty upon less favored people.
Inaugural address.

It is only when men begin to worship that they begin to grow. *Speech, 1922.*

Prosperity is only an instrument to be used, not a deity to be worshipped.

Wealth comes from industry and from the hard experience of human toil. To dissipate it in waste and extravagance is disloyalty to humanity. This is by no means a doctrine of parsimony.

(Armaments) constitute one of the most dangerous contributing causes of international suspicion and discord, and are calculated eventually to lead to war.

After order and liberty, economy is one of the highest essentials of a free government. . . . Economy is always a guarantee of peace.   *Speech, 1923.*

I have noticed that nothing I never said ever did me any harm.
Quoted in Congressional Record, March 22, 1945.

The right of the police of Boston to affiliate, which has always been questioned, never granted, is now prohibited. There is no right to strike against the public safety by anybody, anywhere, anytime.
Letter to Samuel Gompers, AFL president, 1919.

Not long ago I happened to visit an exhibition of modern pictures. It was held in Pittsburgh and almost every nation was represented. As I looked at those pictures I felt that I could see through them, into the minds of the nations which had created them. I could see the torment out of which they had been born. If that nation's psychology was still diseased, so was its art. The traces of neuroses were unmistakable.
Quoted by Beverley Nichols.

The government of the United States is a device for maintaining in perpetuity the rights of the people, with the ultimate extinction of all privileged classes.
Address, Philadelphia, September 25, 1924.

I do not choose to run for President in nineteen twenty eight.
Written statement, to press, August 2, 1927.

Don't hesitate to be as revolutionary as science. Don't hesitate to be as reactionary as the multiplication table.

Work is not a curse, it is the prerogative of intelligence, the only means to manhood, and the measure of civilization. Savages do not work.

Our government is a government of political parties under the guiding influence of public opinion. There does not seem to be any other method by which a representative government can function.

One with the law is a majority.
Acceptance Speech, July 27, 1920.

James Fenimore Cooper
(1789-1851)
American novelist

Liberty is not a matter of words, but a positive and important condition of society. Its greatest safeguard after placing its foundations on a popular base, is in the checks and balances imposed on the public servants, and all its real friends ought to know that the most insidious attacks are made on it by those who are the largest trustees of authority, in their efforts to increase their power.
The American Democrat. On Distinctive American Principles.

Great principles seldom escape working injustice in particular things.
Ibid. On American Equality.

Liberty, like equality, is a word more used than understood. Perfect and absolute liberty is as incompatible with the existence of society, as equality of condition. It is impracticable in a state of nature even, since, without the protection of the law, the strong would oppress and enslave the weak. We are then to understand by liberty, merely such a state of the social compact as permits the members of a community to lay no more restraints on themselves, than are required by their real necessities, and obvious interests.

Ibid. On Liberty.

The principal advantage of a democracy, is a general elevation in the character of the people.

Ibid. Advantages of a Democracy.

The vulgar charge that the tendency of democracies is to levelling, meaning to drag all down to the level of the lowest, is singularly untrue, its real tendency being to elevate the depressed to a condition not unworthy of their manhood. *Ibid.*

Democracies are necessarily controlled by public opinion, and failing of the means of obtaining power more honestly, the fraudulent and ambitious find a motive to mislead, and even to corrupt the common sentiment, to attain their ends.

Ibid. On the Disadvantages of Democracy.

The tendencies of democracies are, in all things, to mediocrity, since the tastes, knowledge and principles of the majority form the tribunal of appeal. This circumstance, while it certainly serves to elevate the average qualities of a nation, renders the introduction of a high standard difficult. Thus do we find in literature, the arts, architecture and in all acquired knowledge, a tendency in America to gravitate towards the common center in this, as in other things; lending a value and estimation to mediocrity that are not elsewhere given.

Ibid.

It is a besetting vice of democracies to substitute public opinion for law. This is the usual form in which masses of men exhibit their tyranny. *Ibid.*

The peculiar office of a demagogue is to advance his own interests, by affecting a deep devotion to the interests of the people. Sometimes the object is to indulge malignancy, unprincipled and selfish men submitting but to two governing motives, that of doing good to themselves, and that of doing harm to others. The true theater of a demagogue is a democracy, for the body of the community possessing the power, the master he pretends to serve is best able to award his efforts.

Ibid. On Demagogues.

The demagogue is usually sly, a detractor of others, a professor of humility and disinterestedness, a great stickler for equality as respects all above him, a man who acts in corners, and avoids open and manly expositions of his course, calls blackguards gentlemen, and gentlemen folks, appeals to passions and prejudices rather than to reason, and is in all respects, a man of intrigue and deception, of sly cunning and management, instead of manifesting the frank, fearless qualities of the democracy he so prodigally professes.

Ibid.

In a popular government, so far from according an entire immunity from penalties to the press, its abuses are those which society is required, by its very safety, to visit with its heaviest punishments. In a democracy, misleading the publick mind, as regards facts, characters, or principles, is corrupting all that is dear to society at its source, opinion being the fountain whence justice, honors, and the laws, equally flow.

It is a misfortune that necessity has induced men to accord greater license to this formidable engine, in order to obtain liberty, than can be borne with less important objects in view; for the press, like fire is an excellent servant, but a terrible master. *Ibid. On the Press.*

The press is equally capable of being made the instrument of elevating man to the highest point of which his faculties admit, or of depressing him to the lowest. *Ibid.*

The history of the press is everywhere the same. In its infancy it is timid, distrustful, and dependent on truth for success. As it acquires confidence with force, it propagates just opinions with energy; scattering errors and repelling falsehood, until it prevails; when abuses rush in, confounding principles, truths, and all else that is estimable, until it becomes a matter of doubt, whether a community derives most good or evil, from the institution. *Ibid.*

If newspapers are useful in overthrowing tyrants, it is only to establish a tyranny of their own. The press tyrannizes over publick men, letters, the arts, the stage, and even over private life. Under the pretence of protecting publick morals, it is corrupting them to the core, and under the semblance of maintaining liberty, it is gradually establishing a despotism as ruthless, as grasping, and one that is quite as vulgar as that of any christian state known. With loud professions of freedom of opinion, there is no tolerance; with a parade of patriotism, no sacrifice of interests; and with fulsome panegyrics on propriety, too frequently, no decency. *Ibid. On the American Press.*

In a democracy, as a matter of course, every effort is made to seize upon and create publick opinion, which is, substantially, securing power.
Ibid. On Publick Opinion.

It is a mistake to suppose commerce favorable to liberty. Its tendency is to a monied aristocracy, and this, in effect, has always been the policy of every community of merchants. Commerce is an enemy of despotic power in the hands of a prince, of church influence, and of hereditary aristocracies, from which facts it has obtained its reputation of sustaining freedom; but, as a class, merchants will always be opposed to the control of majorities.
Ibid. On Commerce.

No freeman, who really loves liberty, and who has a just perception of its dignity, character, action and objects, will ever become a mere party man. He may have his preferences as to measures and man, may act in concert with those who think with himself, on occasions that require concert, but it will be his earnest endeavour to hold himself a free agent, and most of all to keep his mind untrammelled by the prejudices, frauds, and tyranny of factions.
Ibid. On Party.

The disposition of all power is to abuses, nor does it at all mend the matter that its possessors are a majority. Unrestrained political authority, though it be confided to masses, cannot be trusted without positive limitations, men in bodies being but an aggregation of the passions, weaknesses and interests of men as individuals.
Ibid. Conclusion.

Peter Cooper
(1791-1883)
American industrialist, philanthropist

Every manufacturer ought to remember that his fortune was not achieved by himself alone, but by the cooperation of his workmen. He should acknowledge their rights to share the benefits of that which could not exist without their faithful performance of duty. Not until the capitalist is just enough to recognize this truth, can he ever join a group of workmen and feel himself among his friends.

> *Quoted by A. J. Cummings, U.S. Attorney General, in letter to Samuel Gompers, read at A.F.L. convention, Philadelphia, December, 1892.*

Money is so unlike every other article that I believe a man has neither a legal or a moral right to take all that he can get.
> *Ibid.*

There is fast forming in this country an aristocracy of wealth, the worst form of aristocracy that can curse the prosperity of a nation.
> *Ibid.*

The production of wealth is not the work of any one man, and the acquisition of great fortunes is not possible without the cooperation of multitudes of men. *Ibid.*

Let the schools teach the nobility of labor and the beauty of human service: but the superstitions of ages past?—never!
> *Cardiff, What Great Men Think of Religion.*

The Dealers in money have always, since the days of Moses, been the dangerous class.

Thomas Cooper
(1759-1839)
American educator, scientist, political economist

A strong suspicion prevails that the human intellect has been kept in fetters by men who have boldly assumed superior wisdom, that their dictates might pass without inquiry—men who professedly deal in concealment, darkness, and mystery, and who fatten upon human ignorance.
> *Liberty of the Press, 1830.*

The law, unfortunately, has always been retained on the side of power; laws have uniformly been enacted for the protection and perpetuation of power. *Ibid.*

Every politician, every member of the clerical profession, ought to incur the reasonable suspicion of being an interested supporter of false doctrines, who becomes angry at opposition, and endeavors to cast an odium on free inquiry. Fraud and falsehood only dread examination. Truth invites it. . . . *Ibid.*

Indeed, no opinion or doctrine, of whatever nature it be, or whatever be its tendency, ought to be suppressed . . . *Ibid.*

Nicolaus Copernicus
(1473-1543)
Polish astronomer

In the beginning we should remark that the world is like a globe; whether because this form is the most perfect of all, as it is an integral whole and needs no joints; or because it is the figure having the greatest volume and so would be especially suitable for comprehending and conserving all things.
> *De Revolutionibus Coelestibus. On the Revolution of the Celestial Spheres, bk. 1.*

If there should chance to be any mathematicians who, ignorant in mathematics yet pretending to skill in that science, should dare, upon the authority of some passage of Scripture wrested to their purpose, to condemn and censure my hypothesis, I value them not, and scorn their inconsiderate judgment.
> *Ibid. Conclusion; dedicatory epistle to Pope Paul III.*

After I had addressed myself to this very difficult and almost insoluble problem, the suggestion at length came to me how it could be solved with fewer and much simpler constructions than were formerly used if my assumptions (which are called axioms) were granted me. They follow in this order.

1. There is no center of all the celestial circles or spheres.

2. The center of the earth is not the center of the universe, but only of gravity and of the lunar sphere.

3. All the spheres revolve about the sun as their mid-point, and therefore the sun is the center of the universe.

Commentariolus. Quoted in Edward Rosen's Three Copernican Treatises.

Charles Cornwallis

(1738-1805)

English lord, military leader

He defeated the Americans with great slaughter. *Inscription on tombstone.*

Émile Coué

(1857-1926)

French pharmacist, psychotherapist

Tous les jours, à tous points de vue, je vais de mieux en mieux. (Day by day, in every way, I am getting better and better.) *Inscription in his sanitarium, Nancy, France.*

Charles E. Coughlin

(1891-1974)

American priest

Democracy: A mockery that mouths the word and obstructs every effort on the part of an honest people to establish a government for the welfare of the people.
Social Justice, August 1, 1938.

I believe in the right of liberty of conscience and liberty of education, not permitting the state to dictate either my worship to my God or my chosen vocation in life.
Principles of the National Union for Social Justice, No. 1.

I believe not only in the right of the laboring man to organize in unions, but also in the duty of the government which that laboring man supports to facilitate and to protect these organizations against the vested interests of wealth and of intellect.
Ibid., No. 10.

I believe that in the event of a war for the defense of our nation and its liberties, there shall be a conscription of wealth as well as a conscription of men.
Ibid., No. 15.

I believe in preferring the sanctity of human rights to the sanctity of property rights. . . . *Ibid., No. 16.*

One thing is sure . . . Democracy is doomed. This is our last election.

It is Fascism or Communism. We are at the crossroads. . . . I take the road of Fascism.
Interview with Dale Kramer, Secretary, National Farm Holiday Association; reprinted in his pamphlet, Coughlin, Lemke, and the Union Party, 1936.

When an upstart dictator in the United States succeeds in making this a one-party form of government, when the ballot is useless, I shall have the courage to stand up and advocate the use of bullets.
United Press dispatch, September 25, 1936.

First Council of Arles

Concerning players, we have thought it fit to excommunicate them so long as they continue to act. *314.*

Council of Elvira (Spain)

It shall not be lawful for any woman who is either in full communion of a probationer for baptism to marry or entertain any comedians or actors; whoever takes this liberty shall be excommunicated.

Decree, 305 A.D.

Council of Trent

If anyone . . . shall deny that wonderful and singular conversion of the whole substance of the bread into the body, and of the whole substance of the wine into the blood, the outward forms of the bread and wine still remaining, which conversion the Catholic church most aptly calls transubstantiation—let him be accursed. *Canon 2.*

The Church consists principally of two parts, the one called the Church triumphant, and the other the Church militant.

Catechism, 1.

The Church triumphant is that most glorious and happy assemblage of blessed spirits, and of those souls who have triumphed over the world, the flesh and the devil, and now exempt from the troubles of this life, are blessed with the fruition of everlasting bliss.   *Ibid.*

The Church militant is the society of the faithful still dwelling on earth, and is called militant, because it wages eternal war with those implacable enemies, the world, the flesh, and the devil.   *Ibid.*

The holy synod enjoins on bishops that they diligently endeavor that the sound doctrine concerning purgatory, transmitted by the holy fathers and sacred councils, be believed, maintained, taught, and everywhere proclaimed by the faithful of Christ.

Session 25, December 3, 1563.

If anyone saith that the marriage state is to be placed above the state of virginity or of celibacy, and that it is no better and more blessed to remain in virginity or in celibacy than to be united in matrimony; let him be anathema.

Session 24, Canon 10. November 11, 1563.

The Holy Synod commands that images of Christ, of the Mother of God and of the other Saints be kept in churches, and that due honor and reverence be paid to them.

Decree XXV, 1564.

Victor Cousin
(1792-1867)
French philosopher

L'art pour l'art. (Art for art's sake.)
Lecture, Sorbonne, 1818.

All men have an equal right to the free development of their faculties; they have an equal right to the impartial protection of the state; but it is not true, it is against all the laws of reason and equity, it is against the eternal nature of things, that the indolent man and the laborious man, the spendthrift and the economist, the imprudent and the wise, should obtain and enjoy an equal amount of gods.

Justice et charité, 1848.

Norman Cousins
(b. 1912)
Editor, Saturday Review

The biggest and most pertinent lesson in history—at least for democracies—is that they cannot take their existence for granted.

Saturday Review.

War is an invention of the human mind. The human mind can invent peace with justice.   *Who Speaks for Man? 1953.*

John Cowles
(b. 1898)
American newspaper publisher

First of all, the metropolitan American newspapers have become great capitalistic business enterprises.

The American Newspapers, in America Now, edited by Harold Stearns, Scribner, 1938; p. 356.

Corruption of newspapers in any open or direct way is less common than critics of the press would have us believe. Pressure from advertisers does affect in greater or less degree many newspapers' policies in handling news, but so does pressure from other sources: pressure from religious bodies, from political machines with favors to dispense, from union labor, from groups of various kinds, as, in the '20's, in some sections, the Klan.

That the editorial and news policies of many newspapers are controlled by their business offices no one can deny.

Ibid., p. 360.

Because their newspapers are great capitalistic enterprises, it is quite understandable why many of the owners have become too conservative, and why most of their papers do not seem accurately to reflect the aspirations of the common run of people or the ideals of those who see visions of a brave new world. *Ibid., p. 369.*

In the final analysis the only Achilles heel in our present-day newspapers is that they are large capitalistic enterprises. As such some of them, when their own selfish interests are involved, are, in greater or less degree, dishonest. *Ibid.*

There's nothing much wrong with American newspapers today except us publishers.

Ibid., concluding paragraph.

Abraham Cowley
(1618-1667)
English poet, essayist

Gold begets in brethren hate;
Gold in families debate;
Gold does friendship separate;
Gold does civil wars create.
Anacreontics.

Not Oenomaus, who commits himself wholly to a Charioteer that may break his Neck; but the Man
Who governs his own Course with steddy hand,
Who does Himself with Sovereign Pow'r command;
Whom neither Death nor Poverty does fright,
Who stands not awkwardly in his own Light
Against the Truth: Who can, when Pleasures knock
Loud at his Dore, keep firm the Bolt and Lock,
Who can, though Honour at his Gate should stay
In all her masking Cloaths, send her away,
And cry, Be gone, I have no mind to Play.

This, I confess, is a Freeman . . .
An Essay of Liberty. Works, 1663.

Make an Escape; out at the Postern flee,
And get some blessed Hours of Libertie.
Ode Upon Liberty, 1663.

And steal one day out of thy life to live.
Ibid.

He's no small Prince, who every day
Thus to himself can say,
Now will I sleep, now eat, now sit, now walk,
Now meditate alone, now with acquaintance talk. *Ibid.*

Nathalia Crane
(b. 1913)
American poet

You cannot choose your battlefield,
The gods do that for you,
But you can plant a standard
Where a standard never flew.
The Colors.

Stephen Crane
(1871-1900)
American novelist

"Have you ever made a just man?"
"Oh, I have made three," answered God,
"But two of them are dead,
And the third—
Listen, listen,
And you will hear the thud of his defeat."
Lines.

These stupid peasants, who, throughout the world, hold potentates on their thrones, make statesmen illustrious, provide generals with lasting victories, all with ignorance, indifferences, or half-witted hatred, moving the world with the strength of their arms, and getting their heads knocked together, in the name of God, the king, or the stock exchange—immortal, dreaming, hopeless asses, who surrender their reason to the care of a shining puppet, and persuade some toy to carry their lives in his purse.
Death and the Child.

Every sin is the result of a collaboration.

Philosophy should always know that indifference is a militant thing. It batters down the walls of cities and murders the women and children amid the flames and the purloining of altar vessels. When it goes away it leaves smoking ruins, where lie citizens bayonetted through the throat. It is not a children's pastime like mere highway robbery.

Nelson Antrim Crawford
(1888-1963)
American writer, editor, author

Closely related to ignorance and inertia, but even more powerful in its influence against complete and impartial truth-telling by newspapers, is fear. Fear is a characteristic not simply of newspapers; it is a characteristic of the American people. It is not a physical fear; Americans have shown courage and endurance times without number. It is rather an intellectual and spiritual fear, based on nothing tangible, on nothing which affords a reasonable basis for fear. It takes most conspicuously the form of fear of and deference to the herd, the whole body of people within the nation.
The Ethics of Journalism.

Fundamentally, it is fear on the part of the reporter and employees immediately above the reporter. All, or nearly all, the newspapers that the reporter has seen, including the one on which he is working, have exhibited a conservative bias in handling the news.
Ibid.

In the United States there is no phenomenon more threatening to popular government than the unwillingness of newspapers to give the facts to their readers.
Ibid.

J. Hector St. John de Crevecoeur
(1735-1813)
French-American explorer, writer

He is an American, who, leaving behind him all his ancient prejudices and manners, receives new ones from the new mode of

life he has embraced, the new government he obeys, and the new rank he holds. He becomes an American by being received in the broad lap of our great *Alma Mater*. Here individuals of all nations are melted into a new race of men, whose labors and posterity will one day cause great changes in the world.
Letters from an American Farmer, 1782.

The American is a new man, who acts upon new principles; he must therefore entertain new ideas, and form new opinions. From involuntary idleness, servile dependence, penury, and useless labor, he has passed to toils of a very different nature, rewarded by ample subsistence.—This is an American.   *Ibid.*

Benedetto Croce
(1866-1952)
Italian philosopher, spiritual leader

It is not enough to say that history is historical judgment, it is necessary to add that every judgment is an historical judgment or, quite simply, history. . . . Historical judgment is not a variety of knowledge, but it is knowledge itself; it is the form which completely fills and exhausts the field of knowing, leaving no room for anything else.
History as the Story of Liberty, 1941.

Knowledge for the sake of knowledge, so far from having anything aristocratic or sublime about it (as some believe), would be an idiotic pastime for idiots, or for the idiotic moments which we all have in us; in reality there is no such thing, it is intrinsically impossible and the stimulus ceases with the failure of the material itself and of the end of knowledge. Those intellectuals who see salvation in the withdrawal of the artist or the thinker from the world

around him, in his deliberate non-participation in vulgar practical contests—vulgar in so far as they are practical—do without knowing it compass the death of the intellect.   *Ibid.*

In a paradisal state without work or struggle in which there were no obstacles to overcome, there could be no thought, because every motive for thought would have disappeared; neither any real contemplation, because active and poetic contemplation contains in itself a world of practical struggles and of affections.
Ibid.

Their religion was the whole intellectual patrimony of primitive peoples; our intellectual patrimony is our religion.
Aesthetic, English translation, p. 63; quoted by Durant, The Story of Philosophy.

Philosophy removes from religion all reason for existing.   *Ibid.*

Woe to the man who seeks to shed a brilliant light in a place where people want to keep in darkness and shadow.

Morality, and the ideal of freedom which is the political expression of morality, are not the property of a given party or group, but a value that is fundamentally and universally human, to diffuse and enhance which all of us must devote our efforts and good will . . . No people will be truly free till all are free.
Freedom, edited by Ruth Nanda Anshen, Harcourt, Brace & Co., 1940.

Oliver Cromwell
(1599-1658)
English general, statesman

My brethren, I beseech you, in the bowels

of Christ, think it possible that you may be mistaken.
Letter to General Assembly, Church of Scotland, before Battle of Dunbar, August 3, 1650.

No one rises so high as he who knows not whither he is going.
Quoted by William Osler in lectures to students.

As to freedom of conscience, I meddle with no man's conscience; but if you mean by that, liberty to celebrate the mass, I would have you understand that in no place where the power of the Parliament of England prevails shall that be permitted.
Quoted by Francis Biddle, The Fear of Freedom, p. 75.

That Parliaments should not make themselves perpetual is a Fundamental. Of what assurance is a *Law* to prevent so great an evil, if it lie in the same Legislature to *unlaw* it again? Is such a law like to be lasting? It will be a rope of sand; it will give no security; for the same men may unbuild what they have built.
Address, First Protectorate Parliament, September 12, 1654.

Is not Liberty of Conscience in Religion a Fundamental? So long as there is Liberty of Conscience for the Supreme Magistrate to exercise his conscience in erecting what Form of Church-Government he is satisfied he should set up, why should he not give the like liberty to others? Liberty of Conscience is a natural right; and he that would have it, ought to give it; having "himself" liberty to settle what he likes for the Public.
Ibid.

And "as for the People"—I may say it to you, I can say it: All the money of this Nation would not have tempted me to fight upon such an account as they have been engaged in, if they had not had hopes of Liberty of Conscience better than Episcopacy granted them, or than would have been afforded by a Scots Presbytery—or an English either, if it had made such steps, and been as sharp and rigid, as it threatened when first up! This, I say, is a Fundamental.
Ibid.

Rebellion to tyrants is obedience to God.
Attributed; used by Jefferson as his personal and official seal.

It will be found an unjust and unwise jealousy to deprive a man of his natural liberty upon the supposition he may abuse it.

Arbitrary power is a thing that men begin to weary of, in kings and churchmen; they juggle between them mutually to uphold civil and ecclesiastical tyranny . . . Some have cast off both and hope by the grace of God to keep it so.
Reply to the Manifesto of the Irish Bishops in 1650; Carlyle, Oliver Cromwell's Letters and Speeches, v. 2.

Laity and *clergy*. It was your pride that begat that expression, and it is for filthy lucre that you keep it up; that by making the people believe that they are not as holy as yourselves, that they might for their penny purchase some sanctity from you, and that you might bridle, saddle and ride them at your pleasure. I say this not as being troubled by your "Union"; your covenant, if you understand it, is with Death and Hell.
Ibid.

R(ichard) H(oward) S(tafford) Crossman
(b. 1907)
English writer

The main task of a free society is to civilise the struggle for power. Slavery of

the acquiescent majority to the ruthless few is the hereditary state of mankind; freedom, a (rarely) acquired characteristic.
New Statesman & Nation, April 21, 1951.

It is not power itself, but the legitimation of the lust for power, which corrupts absolutely.* *Ibid.*

Russel Crouse
See Howard Lindsay

E(dward) E(stlin) Cummings
(1894-1963)
American writer, painter

To be nobody-but-myself—in a world which is doing its best, night and day, to make you everybody else—means to fight the hardest battle which any human being can fight, and never stop fighting.
Letter to high school editor, 1955; quoted by Charles Norman, The Magic-Maker: E. E. Cummings, Macmillan, 1958.

Take the matter of being born. What does being born mean to most people? Catastrophe unmitigated. Social revolution. The cultured aristocrat yanked out of his hyperexclusively ultravoluptuous super-palazzo, and dumped into an incredibly vulgar detention camp swarming with every conceivable species of undesirable organism. Most people fancy a guaranteed birthproof safetysuit of nondestructible selflessness. If most people were to be born twice they'd probably call it dying . . .
E. E. Cummings: Poems, 1923-1954, Harcourt, Brace & Co.

---

* Cf. Lord Acton.

John Philpot Curran
(1750-1817)
Irish orator, statesman

The condition upon which God hath given liberty to man is eternal vigilance; which condition if he break, servitude is at once the consequence of his crime, and the punishment of his guilt.
Speech, Dublin, July 10, 1790.

Charles P. Curtis
(b. 1891)
American lawyer, writer, educator

There are only two ways to be quite unprejudiced and impartial. One is to be completely ignorant. The other is to be completely indifferent. Bias and prejudice are attitudes to be kept in hand, not attitudes to be avoided.
A Commonplace Book, Simon & Schuster, 1957.

Literature is a transmission of power. Text books and treatises, dictionaries and encyclopedias, manuals and books of instruction—they are communications; but literature is a power line, and the motor, mark you, is the reader. *Ibid., p. 4.*

Fraud is the homage that force pays to reason. *Ibid., p. 15.*

Guilt and sin are only a fear of the past. *Ibid., p. 191.*

If the works of God are intelligible to man, if good and evil are what we think they are, a god who is both omnipotent and benevolent is a contradiction. Humanly speaking good and evil are antithetical. *Ibid., p. 224.*

There appear to be three alternatives. God may not be wholly benevolent. If He is not, He is not worth our worship . . . Or God may not be omniscient. But if He is not, how can we be sure he is wiser than some of our wise men?

The third alternative is Plato's final conviction, that God was not coercive, but only persuasive. And is this not Christianity?
Ibid., pp. 224-5.

George William Curtis
(1824-1892)
American essayist, editor, orator

The sure foundations of the state are laid in knowledge, not in ignorance. Every sneer at education, at culture, at book learning—which is the recorded wisdom of the experiences of mankind—is the demagogue's sneer at intelligent liberty, inviting national degeneracy and ruin.
Quoted, Labor, August 14, 1954.

St. Cyprian
(200-258)
Bishop of Carthage

Whoever has been separated from the Church is yoked with an adulteress. . . . He is a stranger, he is sacrilegious, he is an enemy. Who has not the Church for mother can no longer have God for father.
On the Unity of the Catholic Church.

An ever-burning gehenna will burn up the condemned, and a punishment devouring with living flames; nor will there be any source whence at any time they may have either respite or end to their torments.
To Demetrianus the Proconsul of Africa.

Souls with their bodies will be reserved in infinite tortures of suffering. . . . The pain of punishment will then be without the fruit of penitence; weeping will be use-less, and prayer ineffectual. Too late they will believe in eternal punishment who would not believe in eternal life. *Ibid.*

Charles A. Dana
(1819-1897)
American editor, publisher

Antique civilization . . . perished because it was based on slavery. . . . Under the existing system of labor, modern society has reached the utmost development which that system will allow. New methods of industry must be established, as much superior to the wages system as that is superior to slavery, or else the doom will be pronounced and executed.
Beards, Basic History of the United States, p. 234.

There is a great disposition in some quarters to say that the newspapers ought to limit the amount of news they print; that certain kinds of news ought not to be published. I do not know how that is. I am not prepared to maintain any abstract position on that line; but I have always felt that whatever the divine Providence permitted to occur, I was not too proud to report.[*]
Final issue of The Sun, New York.

Be interesting. Get the news. Get all the news. Fight for your opinions, but do not believe they contain the whole truth, or the only truth. Above all, know that humanity is advancing; that there is progress in human life and human affairs; and that, as sure as God lives, the future will be greater and better than the present and the past. *Ibid.*

---

[*] Frequently, erroneously, quoted as: "What the Good Lord lets happen I am not ashamed to print"; also: ". . . I am not afraid to print".

Journalism consists in buying white paper at 2¢ a pound and selling it at 10¢ a pound.

Josephus Daniels
(1862-1948)
American publisher, diplomat

I advise and enjoin those who direct the paper in the tomorrows never to advocate any cause for personal profit or preferment. I would wish it always to be "the tocsin" and devote itself to the policies of equality and justice to the underprivileged. If the paper should at any time be the voice of self-interest, or become the spokesman of special privilege or selfishness, it would be untrue to its history.   *From his Will.*

As a long-time disciple of Jefferson I hold that if I had to choose between a free press and another agency, I would choose a free press; for when the press is free, no bad cause can long exist.
And by freedom of the press I mean that no influence, whether of money or power or any other thing, either directs its policy or inclines it to suppression, or advocacy, for any consideration except the common good.   *Letter to The Nation.*

A newspaper must be a militant crusader for righteous causes, and must print in its columns whatever God permits to happen in His world.   *Nieman Reports.*

Gabriele d'Annunzio
(1863-1938)
Italian writer, military leader

My aim is the re-establishment of the worship of men.

Dante Alighieri
(1265-1321)
Italian poet

Nel mezzo del cammin di nostra vita. (In the midway of this our mortal life.)
Inferno, opening line.

Lasciate ogni speranza, voi ch'entrate. (Abandon hope, all ye who enter here.)
Ibid., II.

The wretched souls of those who lived Without or praise or blame.
Ibid., Canto III.

Pride, envy, avarice—these are the sparks Have set on fire the hearts of all men.
Ibid., Canto VI.

The Church of Rome, by confounding two powers in herself, falls into the mire and fouls herself and her burden.
Purgatory, XVI, 127.

For what is liberty but the unhampered translation of will into act?   *Letters, 6.*

I affirm that gain is precisely that which comes oftener to the bad man than to the good; for illegitimate gains never come to the good at all, because they reject them. And lawful gains rarely come to the good, because, since much anxious care is needful thereto, and the anxious care of the good man is directed to weightier matters, rarely does the good man give sufficient attention thereto. Wherefore it is clear that in every way the advent of these riches is iniquitous.
The Convivio.

And what else, day by day, imperils and slays cities, countries and single persons so much as the new amassing of wealth by anyone? Which amassing reveals new longings, the goal of which may not be reached without wrong to someone.   *Ibid.*

Georges Jacques Danton
(1759-1794)
French revolutionary leader

At last I perceive that in revolutions the supreme power rests with the most abandoned.

De l'audace, et encore de l'audace, et toujours de l'audace, et la France est sauvée. (Boldness, more boldness, and always boldness, and France is saved.)
Speech, National Assembly, August, 1792.

Clarence S. Darrow
(1857-1938)
American criminal lawyer, writer

Liberty is the most jealous and exacting mistress that can beguile the brain and soul of man. From him who will not give her all, she will have nothing. She knows that his pretended love serves but to betray. But when once the fierce heat of her quenchless, lustrous eyes have burned into the victim's heart, he will know no other smile but hers.
Funeral oration for Altgeld, March 14, 1902.

It may never come, but I fancy that no man who has sympathy for the human race does not wish that sometime those who labor should have the whole product of their toil. Probably it will never come, but I wish that the time might come when the men who work in the industries would own the industries.
Address to jury, Communist trial, Chicago, 1920; quoted by Arthur Weinberg, Attorney for the Damned, Simon & Schuster.

I would like to see the proletariat rule for a while . . . Through all the past this world has been ruled by property, and if there can ever come a time when the workingman can rule it, I will say he ought to have that chance to see what he can do; and yet to tell you that is to believe in the "dictatorship of the proletariat"—well, why not?
Ibid.

As long as the world shall last there will be wrongs, and if no man objected and no man rebelled, those wrongs would last forever.
Ibid.

The objector and the rebel who raises his voice against what he believes to be the injustice of the present and the wrongs of the past is the one who hunches the world along.
Ibid.

The man who fights for his fellow-man is a better man than the one who fights for himself.
Ibid.

You can only protect your liberties in this world by protecting the other man's freedom. You can only be free if I am free.
Ibid.

Our independent American press, with its untrammeled freedom to twist and misrepresent the news, is one of the barriers in the way of the American people achieving their freedom.
Paraphrase, by Irving Stone, Clarence Darrow for the Defense.

The law (is) a horrible business.
There is no such thing as justice—in or out of court.
Interview with N. Y. Times, April 19, 1936.

I say that religion is the belief in future life and in God. I don't believe in either.
Ibid.

I don't believe in God because I don't believe in Mother Goose.
Speech, Toronto, 1930.

The origin of the absurd idea of immortal life is easy to discover; it is kept alive by hope and fear, by childish faith, and by cowardice.

I believe in the closed shop because it is only by the closed shop that the working-man can maintain his rights and secure the protection of his life.
Article in The Railroad Trainman, November, 1909.

One of the chief arguments used in support of the policy of an open shop is that every man has an inalienable and constitutional right to work. I never found that in the Constitution. If a man has a constitutional right to work, he ought to have a constitutional right to a job. . . . A man has a right to work only if he can get a job, and he has also a right not to work.
Ibid.

The employer puts his money into . . . business and the workman his life. The one has as much right as the other to regulate that business.   *Ibid.*

With all their faults, trade-unions have done more for humanity than any other organization of men that ever existed. They have done more for decency, for honesty, for education, for the betterment of the race, for the developing of character in man, than any other association of men. *Ibid.*

Some day there will come the brotherhood of man. Some day industrial warfare as well as warfare between nations, will be seen to be ridiculous and a waste of life and money. Some day men will work together in a grand co-operative scheme. But until that day the trade-union must stand as the only safeguard of the workingman, the only instrument by which he can maintain himself and his family.   *Ibid.*

I do not consider it an insult, but rather a compliment to be called an agnostic. I do not pretend to know where many ignorant men are sure—that is all that Agnosticism means. *Scopes trial, July 13, 1925.*

In spite of all the yearnings of men, no one can produce a single fact or reason to support the belief in God and in personal immortality.   *The Sign, May, 1938.* *

Chase after the truth like all hell and you'll free yourself, even though you never touch its coat-tails.

There is a soul of truth in error; there is a soul of good in evil.

None meet life honestly and few heroically.

The truth is always modern, and there never comes a time when it is safe to give it voice.   *Writing on Voltaire.*

Charles (Robert) Darwin
(1809-1882)
English biologist, writer

False facts are highly injurious to the progress of science, for they often endure long; but false views, if supported by some evidence, do little harm, for everyone takes a salutary pleasure in proving their falseness; and when this is done, one path towards error is closed and the road to truth is often at the same time opened.
The Descent of Man.

We must, however, acknowledge, as it seems to me, that man with all his noble

---

* "It is easy to answer such an extravagant and boastful defense of atheism. We point to the fact that belief in God is universal, held by all people of all times. There has never been a race of atheists."—Editor, *The Sign*

qualities . . . still bears in his bodily frame the indelible stamp of his lowly origin.
Ibid.

Man is descended from a hairy, tailed quadruped, probably arboreal in its habits . . . For my part I would as soon be descended from (a) baboon . . . as from a savage who delights to torture his enemies . . . treats his wives like slaves . . . and is haunted by the grossest superstitions.
Ibid.

Man tends to increase at a greater rate than his means of subsistence; consequently he is occasionally subjected to a severe struggle for existence.
Ibid., xxi.

All ought to refrain from marriage who cannot avoid abject poverty for their children.
Ibid.

We will now discuss in a little more detail the struggle for existence.
Ibid.

There is no fundamental difference between man and the higher animals in their mental faculties.
Ibid.

A moral being is one who is capable of reflecting on his past actions and their motives—of approving of some and disapproving of others.
Ibid.

I have called this principle, by which each slight variation, if useful, is preserved, by the term of Natural Selection.
The Origin of the Species.

The expression often used by Mr. Herbert Spencer of the Survival of the Fittest is more accurate, and is sometimes equally convenient.
Ibid.

There is good reason to believe that slight changes in the conditions of life give vigour and fertility to all organic beings. . . . A cross between the distinct individuals of the same variety, and between distinct varieties, increases the number of their offspring, and certainly gives to them increased size and vigour.
Ibid.

In the survival of favoured individuals and races, during the constantly-recurring Struggle for Existence, we see a powerful and ever-acting form of Selection.
Ibid.

More individuals are born than can possibly survive. A grain in the balance can determine which individuals shall live and which shall die.
Ibid.

Great is the power of steady misrepresentation; the history of science shows that fortunately this power does not long endure.
Ibid.

Thus, from the war of nature, from famine and death, the most exalted object which we are capable of conceiving, namely, the production of the higher animals, directly follows.
Ibid.

All parts of the organization and instincts offer, at least, individual differences . . . there is a struggle for existence leading to the preservation of profitable deviations of structure or instinct in the state of perfection of each organism.
Ibid.

Believing as I do that man in the distant future will be a far more perfect creature than he now is, it is an intolerable thought that he and all other sentient beings are doomed to complete annihilation after such long-continued slow progress. To those who fully admit the immortality of the human soul, the destruction of our world will not appear so dreadful.
Life and Letters.

The mystery of the beginning of all things is insoluble by us; and I for one must be content to remain an agnostic.
Ibid.

Another source of conviction in the existence of God, connected with the reason, and not with the feelings, impresses me as having much more weight . . . I feel compelled to look for a First Cause . . . and I deserve to be called a Theist.   *Ibid.*

I have never been an atheist in the sense of denying the existence of a God. I think that generally (& more & more so as I grow older) but not always, that an agnostic would be the most correct description of my state of mind.
Letter to Rev. J. Fordyce, July 7, 1879; quoted in The Collector, #1, 1958.

I think an Agnostic would be the more correct description of my state of mind. The whole subject (of God and morality) is beyond the scope of man's intellect.

I ought, or I ought not, constitute the whole of morality.

Erasmus Darwin
(1731-1802)
English poet, naturalist

Hear him, ye Senates, hear this truth
sublime:
He who allows oppression shares the
crime.
The Botanic Garden.

Russell D. Davenport
(1899-1934)
American writer, educator

The history of our time . . . is a history of phrases, which rise to great power and then as suddenly pass away: the "merchants of death", the "malefactors of great wealth", "monopoly", "reactionaries", "liberals", the "labor power", "America first", "cash and carry", "unconditional surrender", "peace in our time", "collective security", "bring the boys home", "disarmament", "the Red menace", "the atomic potential", etc., etc. At the time of their currency, few men have had either the courage or the resources to stand up to these tremendous shibboleths. They develop unpredictable authority.

Men are destroyed by them, and others are raised to power, and others are rallied to a fighting cause, and wars are declared, and people driven from their homes. And after all this havoc has been wreaked, suddenly the phrase disappears and is powerful no more—indeed, is lost and forgotten and replaced by something else, very likely its exact opposite. . . . It is terrifying, not just because the phrases result in so much blood and suffering, but because they raise an awful question. They raise the question of truth. Where, in all this, is truth? Or is there any such thing at all? . . .
The Dignity of Man, Harper & Bros., 1955.

John Davidson
(1857-suicide 1909)
Scottish poet, playwright, novelist

This Beauty, this Divinity, this thought,
This hallowed bower and harvest of
delight
Whose roots ethereal seemed to clutch
the stars,
Whose amaranths perfumed eternity,
Is fixed in earthly soil enriched with
bones
Of used-up workers; fattened with the
blood
Of prostitutes, the prime manure; and
dressed

With brains of madmen and the broken
    hearts
Of children.   *The Man Forbid.*

Understand it, you at least
Who toil all day and writhe and groan
    all night
With roots of luxury, a cancer struck
In every muscle: out of you it is
Cathedrals rise and Heaven blossoms
    fair;
You are the hidden putrefying source
Of beauty and delight, of leisured hours,
Of passionate loves and high imaginings;
You are the dung that keeps the roses
    sweet.   *Ibid.*

I say, uproot it; plough the land; and let
A summer-fallow sweeten all the world.
                      Ibid.

A(rthur) Powell Davies
(b. 1902)
American clergyman, author

The world is now too dangerous for anything but the truth, too small for anything
but brotherhood.
*Quoted by Adlai Stevenson, Saturday
Review, February 7, 1959.*

William H. Davies
(1871-1940)
Welsh poet, novelist

        If I cannot be free,
To do such work as pleases me,
Near woodland pools and under trees,
You'll get no work at all; for I
Would rather live this life and die
A beggar or a thief, then be
A working slave with no days free.
*No Master, from Farewell to Poesy,
and Other Poems, 1910.*

Peace makes more slaves than savage
    War,
Since tyrants, backed by their Land's
    Law—
Needing no deadly armament—
Can force a people to consent
To toil like slaves for little pay,
In shops and factories all day.
    Tyrants, from Nature Poems, 1919

Da Vinci
See Leonardo da Vinci

David Davis
(1815-1886)
U.S. Supreme Court justice

The Constitution of the United States
is a law for rulers and people, equally in
war and peace and covers with the shield
of its protection all classes of men, at all
times, and under all circumstances. No
doctrine, involving more pernicious consequences, was ever invented by the wit of
man than that any of its provisions can be
suspended during any of the great exigencies of government. Such a doctrine leads
directly to anarchy or despotism, but the
theory of necessity upon which it is based
is false, for the Government, within the
Constitution, has all the powers granted to
it, which are necessary to preserve its existence; as has been happily proved by the
result of the great effort to throw off its
just authority.
Ex Parte Milligan, 4 Wallace 2 (1866).°

° In 1864 Lambdin P. Milligan, a civilian,
was arrested on a charge that he conspired
against the government, afforded aid and
comfort to rebels, and incited the people
to insurrection. Though the civil courts in
Indiana were open and functioning at that
time, Milligan was tried by a military commission. He was sentenced to hang. . . .

Civil liberty and this kind of martial law cannot endure together; the antagonism is irreconcilable; and, in the conflict, one or the other must perish. *Ibid.*

Martial law can never exist where the courts are open, and in the proper and unobstructed exercise of their jurisdiction. *Ibid.*

Elmer Davis
(1890-1958)
American writer, commentator

What makes Western civilization worth saving is the freedom of the mind, now under heavy attack from the primitives who have persisted among us. If we have not the courage to defend that faith, it won't matter much whether we are saved or not. *But We Were Born Free, 1954.*

This Republic was not established by cowards; and cowards will not preserve it. *Ibid.*

The first and great commandment is, Don't let them scare you. *Ibid.*

This nation was conceived in liberty and dedicated to the principle—among others —that honest men may honestly disagree; that if they all say what they think, a ma-

On December 17, 1866, the Supreme Court held that the military commission had no power to try Milligan. . . . The theory was that military commissions might try civilians in theaters of war where the government was disorganized. . . . The court said that civil liberty and martial law could not endure together. "The antagonism is irreconcilable".

That decision, although much criticized by one school of thought, is an outstanding declaration of the rights of man. (*Justice Douglas, An Almanac of Liberty.*)

jority of the people will be able to distinguish truth from error; that in the competition of the market place of ideas, the sounder ideas will in the long run win out. *Ibid.*

This will remain the land of the free only so long as it is the home of the brave. *Ibid.*

Jefferson Davis
(1808-1889)
President, Confederate States of America

Neither current events nor history show that the majority rules, or ever did rule. *Letter to J. F. Jacques and J. R. Gilmore, July 17, 1864.*

All we ask is to be let alone. *Attributed; Inaugural, February 18, 1861.*

Michael Davitt
(1856-1906)
Irish revolutionary leader

The land for the people! *War slogan for the Land League, 1879.*

For names containing "de," see also the basic name.

Eugene V(ictor) Debs*
(1855-1926)
American socialist

There is nothing in our government (the ballot) cannot remove or amend. It can make and unmake presidents and congresses

* "God was feeling mighty good when He created 'Gene Debs, and He didn't have anything else to do all day."—James Whitcomb Riley.

and courts. . . . It can sweep over trusts, syndicates, corporations, monopolies and every other development of the money power.

The Cooperative Commonwealth, 1895.

The ballot . . . can give our civilization its crowning glory—the Cooperative Commonwealth. *Ibid.*

The issue is Socialism versus Capitalism. I am for Socialism because I am for humanity. *January 1, 1897.*

We have been cursed with the reign of gold long enough. Money constitutes no proper basis of civilization. The time has come to regenerate society. *Ibid.*

No strike has ever been lost.
After the Pullman strike.

There can be no defeat for the labor movement. *Ibid.*

Capitalist wars for capitalist conquest and capitalist plunder must be fought by the capitalists themselves so far as I am concerned. . . . No worker has any business to enlist in capitalist class war or fight a capitalist class battle. It is our duty to enlist in our own war and fight our own battle. *Speech, 1914.*

I have no country to fight for; my country is the earth, and I am a citizen of the world. *Ibid.*

No, I am not opposed to all wars under all circumstances, and any declaration to the contrary would disqualify me as a revolutionist. When I say I am opposed to all wars I mean ruling-class wars, for the ruling class is the only class that makes war . . . I am opposed to every war but one; I am for that war with heart and soul, and that is the world-wide war of social revolution. In that war I am prepared to fight in any way the ruling class may make

it necessary, even on the barricades. That is where I stand and I believe the Socialist Party stands, or ought to stand, on the question of war.

Address, Socialist Party convention, Canton, Ohio, June 16, 1918. Debs was arrested for this speech, tried, and imprisoned.

The master class has always brought a war and the subject class has always fought the battle. The master class has had all to gain and nothing to lose, and the subject class has had all to lose and nothing to gain. *Ibid.*

I have never advocated violence in any form, I have always believed in education, in intelligence, in enlightenment, and I have always made my appeal to the reason and to the conscience of the people.
Address to the jury, September, 1918.

When great changes occur in history, when great principles are involved, as a rule the majority are wrong. The minority are right. *Ibid.*

Years ago I began to recognize my kinship with all living beings, and I made up my mind that I was not one bit better than the meanest on earth. I said then, and I say now, that while there is a lower class I am in it; while there is a criminal element, I am of it; while there is a soul in prison, I am not free.
Address to court on being sentenced, September 14, 1918.

Great issues are not decided by courts but by the people. I have no concern in what the coterie of owned corporation lawyers in Washington may decide in my case. The court of final resort is the people, and that court will be heard from in due time.
A reference to the appeal to the Supreme Court to invalidate his sentence of 10 years; March 10, 1919.

You have got to unite in the same labor union and in the same political party and *strike and vote together,* and the hour you do that, the world is yours.

Conclusion of oft repeated speech.

To the extent that the working class has power based upon class consciousness, force is unnecessary; to the extent that power is lacking, force can only result in harm.

Liberty, divinest word ever coined by human brain or uttered by human tongue. It is the spirit of liberty that today undermines the empires of the old world, sets crowns and mitres askew, and in its onward elemental sweep is shaking the institutions of capitalism in this nation as frail weeds are shaken in the blast of the storm king's fury.

I am not a labor leader. I don't want you to follow me or anyone else. If you are looking for a Moses to lead you out of the capitalist wilderness you will stay right where you are. I would not lead you into this promised land if I could, because if I could lead you in, someone else could lead you out.

The truth has always been dangerous to the rule of the rogue, the exploiter, the robber. So the truth must be suppressed.

If it had not been for the discontent of a few fellows who had not been satisfied with their conditions, you would still be living in caves. You would never have emerged from the jungle. Intelligent discontent is the mainspring of civilization. Progress is born of agitation. It is agitation or stagnation.

The rights of one are as sacred as the rights of a million. . . . Every man has the inalienable right to work.

A scab in labor unions is the same as a traitor to his country.

Ten thousand times has the labor movement stumbled and fallen and bruised itself, and risen again; been seized by the throat and choked into insensibility; enjoined by courts, assaulted by thugs, charged by the militia, shot down by regulars, traduced by the press, frowned upon by public opinion, deceived by politicians, threatened by priests, repudiated by renegades, preyed upon by grafters, infested by spies, deserted by cowards, betrayed by traitors, bled by leeches, and sold out by leaders, but, notwithstanding all this, and all these, it is today the most vital and potential power this planet has ever known, and its historic mission of emancipating the workers of the world from the thralldom of the ages is as certain of ultimate realization as the setting of the sun.

Daniel Defoe
(1660?-1731)
English writer

I saw the world around me, one part laboring for bread, and the other part squandering in vile excess or empty pleasures, equally miserable because the end they proposed still fled from them; for the man of pleasure every day surfeited of his vice, and heaped up work for sorrow and repentance; and the man of labor spent his strength in daily struggling for bread to maintain the vital strength he labored with; so living in a daily circulation of sorrow, living but to work, and working but to live, as if daily bread were the only end of a wearisome life, and a wearisome life the only occasion of daily bread.

The Further Adventures of Robinson Crusoe.

All Men pretend the Licentiousness of the Press to be a publick Grievance, but it is much easier to say it is so, than to prove it, or prescribe a proper Remedy; nor is it the easiest Grievance to Cure.

An Essay on the Regulation of the Press, London, January 7, 1704; Luttrell Reprints, Oxford, 1948.

Whatever Party of Men obtain the Reins of Management, and have power to name the Person who shall License the Press, that Party of Men have the whole power of keeping the World in Ignorance, in all matters relating to Religion or Policy, since the Writers of that Party shall have full liberty to impose their Notions upon the World. *Ibid.*

I know no Nation in the World, whose Government is not perfectly Despotick, that ever makes preventive Laws. *Ibid.*

This I think is a just Consequence from Reason, that since the Nation is unhappily Divided into Parties, every Side ought to have an equal Advantage in the use of the Press, and this can never be the Case in Licensing; for whatsoever Party assumes the Power of placing this Paper Magistrate, will, in effect, have an Exclusive Power over the Press, to give their Friends a full liberty of *Affirming,* and to refuse the other Side the liberty of *Replying.* *Ibid.*

Laws in their Original Design are not made to draw Men into Crimes, but to prevent Crimes; *Laws are Buoys* set upon dangerous Places under Water, to warn Mankind, that such Sands or Rocks are there, and the Language of them is, *Come here at your Peril.* *Ibid.*

We do hereby declare that if the House of Commons, in breach of the Laws and Liberties of the people, do betray the trust reposed in them; and act negligently or arbitrarily and illegally: it is the undoubted Right of the People of England to call them to account for the same; and by Convention, Assembly, or Force, may proceed against them, as traitors and betrayers of their country.

Passage in the Kentist Petition, Maidstone, 1701, supporting King William III, and attacking the Tory ministry; written by Defoe.

He that opposes his own judgment against the consent of the times ought to be backed with unanswerable truths; and he that has truth on his side is a fool as well as a coward if he is afraid to own it because of other men's opinions.

And of all plagues with which mankind
  are cursed,
Ecclesiastical tyranny's the worst.
    The True-Born Englishman.

Whores and priest will never want excuse.
Fables, Ancient and Modern, introduction.

Charles de Gaulle
(1890-1970)
French general, statesman

La foule (the mob), those political animals need organization, which means simple orders and chiefs.
Quoted by T. H. White, Saturday Review, July 18, 1958.

Je suis un homme qui n'appartient à personne et qui appartient à tout le monde. (I am a man who belongs to no one and who belongs to the whole world.)
New Statesman, May 24, 1958.

How can one conceive of a one-party system in a country that has over 200 varieties of cheeses.
N. Y. Times Magazine, June 29, 1958.

I, I was France, the state, the government. I, I spoke in the name of France. I, I was the independence and sovereignty of France.
At 1954 press conference, regarding his wartime conduct. Ibid.

I always thought I was Jeanne d'Arc and Bonaparte. How little one knows oneself.
Reply to speaker who compared him to Robespierre; Requoted from Figaro Littéraire by Time, June 16, 1958.

The military corps is the most complete expression of the spirit of society.
The Sword's Edge, 1934.

The sword is the axis of the world, and grandeur is indivisible.   *Ibid.*

Men fundamentally can no more get along without direction than they can without eating, drinking, or sleeping.   *Ibid.*

Evangelical perfection cannot be conceived of without a strong dose of egoism, pride, toughness and cunning.   *Ibid.*

Dictatorship is a great adventure . . . which crumbles in misery and blood.
N. Y. Times, June 1, 1958.

For glory gives herself only to those who have always dreamed of her.   *Ibid.*

Hans Delbrueck
(1848-1929)
German historian

That nation which possesses the power of self-control to limit its daily pleasures in order to accumulate national sinews of war; which, to put it crudely, would rather drink a little less beer and smoke a few less cigars in order to procure more guns and ships, *that* nation at the time acquires the right to assert its individuality and to bequeath the mental assets which it has won for itself in the course of centuries to its own people and to humanity.

Daniel DeLeon
(1852-1914)
American socialist leader, writer

The moment religion organizes into a specific creed it becomes a political force. From Moses down to Brigham Young, every creed-founder has been a Statebuilder.
The Vatican in Politics, 1891.

The Catholic Church . . . upheld feudalism, then monarchism, warning them of growing evils and possible revolutions. In the same manner, and under the same reservations, she now upholds capitalism; but, above all things and forever, she upholds the Catholic Church.   *Ibid.*

Socialism is neither an aspiration of angels, nor a plot of devils. Socialism moves with its feet firmly planted in the ground, and its head not lost in the clouds; it takes science by the hand, asks her to lead, and goes whithersoever she points.   *Ibid.*

You will perceive the danger run by movements that—instead of accepting no leadership except such as stands squarely upon their own demands—rest content with and entrust themselves to "promises of relief": REVOLUTION, accordingly, stands on its own bottom, hence it cannot be overthrown; REFORM leans upon others, hence its downfall is certain. Of all evolutionary epochs, the present draws sharpest the line between the conflicting class interests.
Reform or Revolution.

Socialism is the logical sequence of economic and sociological development. It is the movement which overthrows the Political State; rears the Industrial Commonwealth in its place; harmonizes the system of ownership with the collective system of operating the plants of production; and abolishes economic dependency, the foundation of all slavery.   *Ibid.*

The capitalist class knows no country and no race, and any "God" suits it so that "God" approves of the exploitation of the worker.

Two Pages from Roman History, 1903.

Despite all seeming wranglings, sometimes even wars, among them the capitalist class is international, and presents a united front against the working class.   *Ibid.*

The capitalist class is interested in keeping the workingmen divided among themselves. Hence it foments race and religious animosities that come down from the past.
Ibid.

Poverty breeds lack of self-reliance.
Ibid.

Industrialism is that system of economic organization of the working class that denies that labor and the capitalist class are brothers; that recognizes the irrepressible nature of the conflict between the two; that perceives that that struggle will not, because it can not, end until the capitalist class is thrown off labor's back; that recognizes that an injury to one workingman is an injury to all; and that, consequently, and with this end in view, organizes the *whole working class into one union.*

Industrial Unionism, 1906.

The Industrial Union grasps the principle: "No Government, no organization; no organization, no cooperative labor; no cooperative labor, no abundance for all without arduous toil, hence, no freedom."
Ibid., 1913 edition.

Official economists and other pensionaries of capitalism, writhing with the cold steel of Marxian science in the vitals of their theories, hide their rage in the wrinkle of a sneer at Marx.
James Madison and Karl Marx, 1913.

Open any law book, whatever the subject be—contract, real estate, aye, even marital relations, husband and wife, father and son, guardian and ward—you will find that the picture they throw upon the mind's canvas is that of everyone's hands at everyone's throat. Capitalist law reflects the material substructure of capitalism. The theory of that substructure is war, conflict, struggle.
The Burning Question of Trades Unionism.

Every reform granted by capitalism is a concealed measure of reaction.
Quoted by Eric Hass, editor, Weekly People, January 24, 1959.*

de Lisle
See Rouget de Lisle

Joseph de Maistre
(1753-1821)
French diplomat

Toute nation a le gouvernement qu'elle mérite. (Every country has the government it deserves.)
Lettres et Opuscules Inédits, August, 1811.

Pierre de Maupertuis
(1698-1758)
French scientist, mathematician

May we not say that in the fortuitous combination of the productions of Nature,

---

* The DeLeon quotations were selected by Mr. Hass.

since only those creatures *could* survive in whose organizations a certain degree of adaptation was present, there is nothing extraordinary in the fact that such adaptation is actually found in all those species which now exist?
Quoted in MD (magazine), July, 1958.

Chance, one might say, turned out a vast number of individuals; a small proportion of these were organized in such a manner that the animals' organs could satisfy their needs. A much greater number showed neither adaptation nor order; these last have all perished . . . Thus the species which we see today are but a small part of all those that a blind destiny has produced.   *Ibid.*

Democratic Party

The Democratic Party is the friend of labor and the laboring man, and pledges itself to protect him alike against the cormorant and the Commune.
National Platform, 1880.

We favor the repeal of all laws restricting the free action of labor, and the enactment of laws by which labor organizations may be incorporated.   *Ibid., 1884.*

The interests of the people are betrayed when trusts and combinations are permitted to exist.   *Ibid., 1888.*

The Democratic Party stands for democracy; the Republican Party has drawn to itself all that is aristocratic and plutocratic. The Republican Party is the party of privilege and private monopoly.
Ibid., 1908.

Democritus
(460?-370? B.C.)
Greek philosopher

Poverty in a democracy is as much to be

preferred to what is called prosperity under despots, as freedom is to slavery.
Bertrand Russell, Philosophy and Politics, Unpopular Essays.

Opinion says hot and cold, but the reality is atoms and empty space. (In reality there is nothing but atoms and space.)
Durant, The Story of Philosophy.

Demonax
(c. 150 A.D.)

Probably all laws are useless; for good men do not want laws at all, and bad men are made no better by them.

Demosthenes
(385?-322 B.C.)
Athenian orator, statesman

Nothing is so easy as to deceive one's self; for what we wish, that we readily believe. (Another translation: We believe whatever we want to believe.)
Third Olynthiac, 348 B.C.

There is one common safeguard in the nature of prudent men, which is a good security for all, but especially for democracies against despots. What do I mean? Mistrust. Keep this, hold to this; preserve this only, and you can never be injured.
Second Philippic, 344 B.C.

Every dictator is an enemy of freedom, an opponent of law.
Oration vi, tr. by Kathleen Freeman, Fighting Words, Beacon Press, 1952.

There are all kinds of devices invented for the protection and preservation of countries: defensive barriers, forts, trenches, and the like. All these are the work of human hands aided by money. But prudent minds have as a natural gift one safeguard which is the common possession of all, and this applies especially to the dealings of democracies with dictatorships. What is this safeguard? Skepticism. This you must preserve. This you must retain. If you can keep this, you need fear no harm.   *Ibid.*

Beware lest in your anxiety to avoid war you obtain a master.   *Ibid.*

Better to die a thousand times than to do anything out of a desire to curry favor with the aggressor and to betray any of those whose counsels are in defense of your interests.   *Ibid., Oration ix.*

The Athenians of those days did not look for a statesman or a commander who would help them to enjoy a comfortable servitude. They did not think it worth while even to live, if it were not possible to do so with freedom.   *Ibid., Oration xviii.*

There is nothing, absolutely nothing which needs to be more carefully guarded against than that one man should be allowed to become more powerful than the people.
          Ibid., Oration xix.

Alfred De Musset
(1810-1857)
French writer

How glorious it is—and also how painful —to be an exception.

Thomas De Quincey
(1785-1859)
English essayist

Books, we are told, propose to *instruct* or to *amuse.* Indeed! A true antithesis to knowledge, in this case, is not *pleasure,* but *power.* All that is literature seeks to communicate power; all that is not literature, to communicate knowledge.
Letters to a Young Man, quoted by C. P. Curtis, A Commonplace Book, p. 4.

Solitude, though it may be silent as light, is like light, the mightiest of agencies; for solitude is essential to man. All men come into this world *alone;* all leave it *alone.*
Confessions of an English Opium-Eater, sequel.

René Descartes
(1596-1650)
French philosopher

After I inquired in general into what is essential to the truth and certainty of a proposition; or since I had discovered one which I knew to be true, I thought that I must likewise be able to discover the ground for this certitude. And as I observed that in the words *I think, therefore I am (Cogito, ergo sum)* there is nothing at all which gives me assurances of their truth beyond this, that I see very clearly that in order to think it is necessary to exist, I concluded that I might take, as a general rule, the principle, that all things which we clearly and distinctly conceive are true, only observing, however, that there is some difficulty in rightly determining the objects which we distinctly conceive.
Discourse on Method.

Camille Desmoulins
(1760-1794)
French revolutionist

Burning is no answer.
Reply to Robespierre's proposal to burn opposition newspapers.

My age is that of the *bon Sansculotte Jésus;* an age fatal to Revolutionists.

Before his execution; quoted by Carlyle, The French Revolution, bk. 6.

I see that power intoxicates men and they all say with Dionysius of Syracuse: "Tyranny is a fine epitaph".

Letter from prison, to wife, Lucile, April 1, 1794.

Have no more doubt of the omnipotence of a free people.

Eamon de Valera

(1882-1975)

Irish rebel, president

The killing of a human being is an awful act, but as awful when the victim is the humble worker or peasant, unknown outside his own neighborhood, as when the victim is placed in the seats of the mighty and his name known in every corner of the earth. It is characteristic of our hypocritical civilization that it is in the latter case only we are expected to cry out and express our horror and condemnation.

Robert Devereux, 2nd Earl of Essex

(1566-executed 1601)

English soldier, favorite of Queen Elizabeth

I owe to her Majesty the duty of an Earl and Lord Marshal of England. I have been content to do her Majesty the service of a clerk, but can never serve her as a villain or a slave.

Letter to Lord Keeper, Egerton; Strachey, Elizabeth and Essex.

Peter De Vries

(b. 1910)

American writer, editor

It is the final proof of God's omnipotence that he need not exist in order to save us.

Rev. Andrew Mackerel in The Mackerel Plaza, 1958.

John Dewey

(1859-1952)

American philosopher, educator

The devotion of democracy to education is a familiar fact. The superficial explanation is that a government resting upon popular suffrage cannot be successful unless those who elect and who obey their governors are educated. Since a democratic society repudiates the principle of external authority, it must find a substitute in voluntary disposition and interest; these can be created only by education.

Democracy and Education, 1916.

A democracy is more than a form of government; it is primarily a mode of associated living, of conjoint communicated experience.

Ibid.

In every new crisis it seems to be forgotten that the demand for freedom means a reaching out for mental activity, for greater scope of thought. That is the reason why the battle for freedom is never won.

Editorial, New Republic, May 5, 1920.

The reactionaries are in possession of force, in not only the army and police, but in the press and the schools.

New York World-Telegram, December 31, 1934.

Liberty is not just an idea, an abstract principle. It is power, effective power to do specific things. There is no such thing as liberty in general; liberty, so to speak, at large.

Liberty and Social Control. The Social Frontier, November, 1935.

Conflict is the gadfly of thought. It stirs us to observation and memory. It instigates to invention. It shocks us out of sheeplike passivity, and sets us at noting and contriving . . . conflict is a *sine qua non* of reflection and ingenuity.

Morals and Conduct.

Just now the favorite ideological psychological candidate for control of human activity is love of power.

Freedom and Culture, Putnam, 1939.

It is significant that human nature was taken to be strongly moved by an inherent love of freedom at the time when there was a struggle for representative government; that the motive of self-interest appeared when conditions in England enlarged the role of money, because of new methods of industrial production; that the growth of organized philanthropic activities brought sympathy into the psychological picture; and that events today are readily converted into love of power as the mainspring of human action. *Ibid.*

The demand for liberty is a demand for power, either for possession of powers of action not already possessed or for retention and expansion of powers already possessed. *Ibid.*

This relativity of liberty to the existing distribution of powers of action, while meaning that there is no such thing as absolute liberty, also means necessarily that wherever there is liberty at one place there is restraint at some other place. *The system of liberties that exists at any time is always the system of restraints or controls that*

exists at that time. No one can *do* anything except in relation to what others can do and cannot do. *Ibid.*

Historically the great movements for human liberation have always been movements to change institutions and not to preserve them intact. It follows from what has been said that there have been movements to bring about a changed distribution of power to do—and power to think and to express thought is a power to do—so that there would be a more balanced, a more equal, even, and equitable system of human liberties. *Ibid.*

Let those who are struggling to replace the present economic system by a cooperative one also remember that in struggling for a new system of social restraints and controls they are also struggling for a more equal and equitable balance of powers that will enhance and multiply the effective liberties of the mass of individuals. Let them not be jockeyed into the position of supporting social control at the expense of liberty, when what they want is another method of social control than the one that now exists, one that will increase significant human liberties. *Ibid.*

It is demonstrable that many of the obstacles to change which have been attributed to human nature are in fact due to the inertia of institutions and to the voluntary desire of powerful classes to maintain the existing status.

Monthly Review, March, 1950.

Every great advance in science has issued from a new audacity of imagination.

The Quest for Certainty.

Experience cannot deliver to us necessary truths; truths completely demonstrated by reason. Its conclusions are particular, not universal. *Ibid.*

We are all for some kind of socialism, call it by whatever name we please.

No system has ever existed which did not in some form involve the exploitation of some human beings for the advantage of others.

Education is a social process. . . . Education is growth. . . . Education is not preparation for life; education is life itself.
Quoted in Time.

There can be no doubt of our dependence upon forces beyond our control. Primitive man was so impotent in the face of these forces that, especially in an unfavorable natural environment, fear became a dominant attitude, and, as the old saying goes, fear created gods.

The mind of man is being habituated to a new method and ideal: There is but one sure road of access to truth—the road of experiment, record and controlled reflection.

Men have never fully used the powers they possess to advance the good in life, because they have waited upon some power external to themselves and to nature to do the work they are responsible for doing.

It (modern philosophy) certainly exacts a surrender of all supernaturalism and fixed dogma and rigid institutionalism with which Christianity has been historically associated.

Thomas E(dmund) Dewey
(1902-1971)

American politician

It's time for a change.
Campaign speech, September 21, 1944, San Francisco; campaign slogan.

d'Holbach
See Holbach

For names containing "di," see the basic name.

Denis Diderot
(1713-1784)

French philosopher, writer

The first step toward philosophy is incredulity. *Last conversations.*

If you want me to believe in God, you must make me touch Him.
Letters on the Blind.

Et des boyaux du dernier prêtre serrons le cou de dernier roi. (And with the guts of the last priest let us strangle the last king.)
Attributed. Ramage, Beautiful Thoughts —From French and British Authors.

Martin Dies
(1900-1972)

American congressman

(It would be safer) never to participate in anything in the future without consulting the American Legion or your local Chamber of Commerce.
Advice to Frederic March, at Un-American Committee hearing, quoted by Francis Biddle, The Fear of Freedom.

Georgi Dimitrov
(1882-1949)

Bulgarian Communist leader

Fascism in America will attempt to advance under the banner of Americanism and anti-Fascism.*

---

* These are almost the same words attributed to Huey Long.

Comrades, you remember the ancient tale of the capture of Troy . . . The attacking army . . . was unable to achieve victory until with the aid of the famous Trojan horse it managed to penetrate to the very heart of the enemy's camp. We . . . should not be shy about using the same tactics.
Address, Seventh World Congress, Communist Internationale, quoted by J. Edgar Hoover, Masters of Deceit, p. 213.

Diodorus Siculus
(c. 20 B.C.)
Greek historian

The myths about Hades and the gods, though they are pure invention, help to make men virtuous.

Diogenes ("The Cynic")
(412?-323 B.C.)
Greek philosopher

The foundation of every state is the education of its youth.

The most beautiful thing in the world is freedom of speech.
Quoted by Diogenes Laertius.

Diogenes Laertius
(c. 150 B.C.)
Greek historian, biographer

The only good is knowledge, and the only evil is ignorance.
Lives of the Philosophers (Socrates).

One of his sayings was, "Even the gods cannot strive against necessity."
Life of Pittacus, iv.

The mob is the mother of tyrants.
Antiquities of Rome, viii.

Dionysius of Halicarnassus
(c. 20 B.C.)
Greek historian

There is a written and an unwritten law. The one by which we regulate our constitutions in our cities is the written law; that which arises from custom is the unwritten law.
Plato, li.

Solon used to say that speech was the image of actions; . . . that laws were like cobwebs,—for that if any trifling or powerless thing fell into them, they held it fast; while if it were something weightier, it broke through them and was off.
Solon, x...

On one occasion Aristotle was asked how much educated men were superior to those uneducated: "As much," said he, "as the living are to the dead." *Aristotle, xi.*

Benjamin Disraeli
(1804-1881)
English statesman, novelist, poet

A conservative government is an organized hypocrisy.
Speech, House of Commons, March 3, 1845.

A precedent embalms a principle.
Ibid., February 22, 1848.

The difference of race is one of the reasons why I fear war may always exist; because race implies difference, difference implies superiority, and superiority leads to predominance.
Commons, February 1, 1849.

To tax the community for the advantage of a class is not protection: it is plunder.
Ibid., May 14, 1850.

Justice is truth in action.
Ibid., February 11, 1851.

NEWS is that which comes from the North, East, West and South, and if it comes from only one point of the compass, then it is a class publication and not news.
Ibid., March 26, 1855.

Never take anything for granted.
Ibid., October 5, 1864.

The question is this: is man an ape or an angel? I am on the side of the angels. I repudiate with indignation and abhorrence these newfangled theories.
Ibid., Oxford, November 25, 1864.

Assassination has never changed the history of the world.
Ibid., Commons, May 10, 1865; reference to Lincoln.

Change is inevitable in a progressive country. Change is constant.
Ibid., October 20, 1867.

Without publicity there can be no public support, and without public support every nation must decay. *Ibid., August 8, 1871.*

Increased means and increased leisure are the two civilizers of man.
Speech, Manchester, April 3, 1872.

Wherever is found what is called paternal government, there is found state education. *Commons, June 15, 1874.*

The best way to insure implicit obedience is to commence tyranny in the nursery.
Ibid.

Upon the education of the people of this country the fate of this country depends.
Ibid., June 15, 1874.

Peace with honor. *Speech, 1878.*

What we call public opinion is generally public sentiment. *Ibid., August 3, 1880.*

No government can long be secure without a formidable Opposition. *Coningsby.*

I have ever been of the opinion that revolutions are not to be evaded. *Ibid.*

Conservatism discards Prescription, shrinks from Principle, disavows Progress; having rejected all respect for antiquity, it offers no redress for the present, and makes no preparations for the future. *Ibid.*

The greatest of all evils is a weak government. *Ibid.*

It seems to me a barren thing, this Conservatism—an unhappy cross-breed, the mule of politics that engenders nothing.
Ibid.

When men are pure, laws are useless; when men are corrupt, laws are broken.
Contanini Fleming.

With words we govern men. *Ibid.*

Real politics are the possession and distribution of power. *Endymion.*

Religion should be the rule of life, not a casual incident in it. *Lothair.*

No man will treat with indifference the principle of race. It is the key of history.
Ibid.

I consider it a great homage to public opinion to find every scoundrel nowadays professing himself a liberal.
The Infernal Marriage.

The world is weary of statesmen whom democracy has degraded into politicians.
Ibid.

The divine right of kings may have been a plea for feeble tyrants, but the divine right of government is the keystone of human progress, and without it governments sink into police, and a nation is degraded into a mob. *Ibid., General Preface.*

In politics experiments mean revolutions.
Popanilla.

Practical politics. *Vivien Grey.*

In politics there is no honour. *Ibid.*

In politics nothing is contemptible.
Ibid.

The man who anticipates his century is always persecuted when living, and is always pilfered when dead. *Ibid.*

We are indeed a nation of shopkeepers.
The Young Duke.

A book may be as great a thing as a battle. *Memoir of Isaac D'Israeli.*

He (Gladstone) made his conscience not his guide but his accomplice.
N. Y. Times, October 20, 1947.

Damn your principles! Stick to your party. *Tribune, London.*

There are three kinds of lies: lies, damned lies, and statistics.
Attributed by Mark Twain, Autobiography.

All great events have been distorted, most of the important causes concealed, some of the principal characters never appear, and all who figure are so misunderstood and misrepresented that the result is a complete mystification. If the history of England be ever written by one who has the knowledge and the courage, the world would be astonished.

Christianity is completed Judaism, or it is nothing.

A majority is always the best repartee.

I was told that the Privileged and the People formed Two Nations.

By the aid of a few scientific discoveries, they have succeeded in establishing a society which mistakes comfort for civilization. (*a reference to the United States.*)

Milovan Djilas
(b. 1911)
Yugoslav leader, writer

In Communist revolutions, force and violence are a condition for further development and even progress. In the words of earlier revolutionaries, force and violence were only a necessary evil and a means to an end. In the words of Communists, force and violence are elevated to the lofty position of a cult and an ultimate end.
The New Class, p. 22, Praeger, 1957.

Every revolution, and even every war, creates illusions and is conducted in the name of unrealizable ideals. *Ibid., p. 30.*

Man may renounce much. But he must think, and he has a deep need to express his thoughts. It is profoundly sickening to be compelled to remain silent when there is need for expression. It is tyranny at its worst to compel men not to think as they do, to compel men to express thoughts that are not their own. The limitation of freedom of thought is not only an attack on specific political and social rights, but an attack on the human being as such. *Ibid., p. 146.*

It is necessary for the revolution not only to devour its own children, but—one might say—devour itself. *Ibid., p. 159.*

Throughout history there have been no ideal ends which were attained with non-ideal, inhumane means, just as there has been no free society which was built by slaves. Nothing so well reveals the reality and greatness of ends as the methods used to obtain them. *Ibid., p. 162.*

Contemporary Communism is that type of totalitarianism which consists of three basic factors for controlling the people. The first is power; the second, ownership; the third, ideology. They are monopolized by the one and only political party, or—according to my previous explanation and terminology—by a new class; and, at present, by the oligarchy of that party or of that class. *Ibid., p. 166.*

Power is an end in itself and the essence of contemporary Communism. *Ibid.*

Every type of power besides being a means is at the same time an end—at least for those who aspire to it. Power is almost exclusively an end in Communism, because it is both the source and the guarantee of all privileges. *Ibid., p. 170.*

J(ames) Frank Dobie
(b. 1888)
American writer

Conform and be dull.
The Voice of the Coyote, 1949.

St. Dominic
(1170-1221)
Spanish founder of Dominican Order

For many years I have exhorted you in vain, with gentleness, preaching, praying and weeping. But according to the proverb of my country, "where blessings can accomplish nothing, blows may avail." We shall rouse against you princes and prelates, who, alas, will arm nations and kingdoms against this land . . . and thus blows will avail where blessings and gentleness have been powerless.

Last discourse to heretic Albigenses, Encyclopaedia Britannica, 11th ed.

John Donne
(1573?-1631)
English poet, cleric

The Democracy of Death.

It comes equally to us all, and makes us all equal when it comes. The ashes of an Oak in the Chimney are no Epitaph of that Oak to tell me how high or large that was; it tells me not what flocks it sheltered, while it stood, nor what men it hurt when it fell. The dust of great persons' graves is speechless too, it says nothing. It distinguishes nothing: as soon as the dust of a wretch whom thou wouldest not, as of a Prince thou couldest not look upon, will trouble thine eyes, if the wind blows it thither; and when a whirlwind hath blown the dust of the Churchyard into the Church, and the man sweeps out the dust of the Church into the Churchyard, who will undertake to sift those dusts again, and to pronounce, This is the Patrician, this is the noble flower, and this the yeomanly, this the Plebeian bran. *Sermons.*

No man is an Iland, intire of it selfe. . . . every man is a peece of the Continent, a part of the maine; if a Clod bee washed away by the Sea, Europe is the lesse, as well as if a Promontorie were, as well as if a Mannor of thy friends or of thine own were; any man's death diminishes me, because I am involved in Mankinde; And therefore never send to know for whom the bell tolls; It tolls for thee.
Devotions Upon Emergent Occasions.

Ignatius Donnelly
(1831-1901)
American novelist, essayist, politician

The Democratic Party is like a mule. It has neither pride of ancestry nor hope of posterity.
Minnesota Legislature, September 13, 1860.

"Mr. Dooley"

See Finley Peter Dunne

Fyodor Dostoyevski

(1821-1881)
Russian novelist

Why are there so many lackeys among the bourgeoisie, and what is more, lackeys with a liberal and benevolent exterior? The lackey spirit is progressively corroding the nature of the bourgeois and is being increasingly regarded as a virtue.

Winter Notes.

It is not the brains that matter most, but that which guides them—the character, the heart, generous qualities, progressive ideas.
The Insulted and the Injured.

Nothing is more seductive for man than his freedom of conscience. But nothing is a greater cause of suffering.
The Brothers Karamazov, 1880.

So long as man remains free he strives for nothing so incessantly and so painfully as to find someone to worship. But man seeks to worship what is established beyond dispute, so that all men would agree at once to worship it. For these pitiful creatures are concerned not only to find what one or the other can worship, but to find something that all would believe in and worship; what is essential is that all may be *together* in it. This craving for *community* of worship is the chief misery of every man individually and of all humanity from the beginning of time. For the sake of common worship they've slain each other with the sword. They have set up gods and challenged one another, "Put away your gods and come and worship ours or we will kill you and your gods!" And so it will be to the end of the world, even when gods disappear from the earth; they will fall down before idols just the same.

Ibid.

Remember particularly that you cannot be a judge of anyone. For no one can judge a criminal, until he recognizes that he is just such a criminal as the man standing before him, and that he perhaps is more than all men to blame for that crime. When he understands that, he will be able to be a judge.

Ibid.

If you can take upon yourself the crime of the criminal your heart is judging, take it at once, suffer for him yourself, and let him go without reproach. And even if the law itself makes you his judge, act in the same spirit so far as possible, for he will go away and condemn himself more bitterly than you have done.

Ibid.

Until you have become really, in actual fact, as brother of every one, brotherhood will not come to pass.

Ibid.

I assert and venture to say that love of mankind in general, as an idea, is one of the most incomprehensible ideas for the human mind. Precisely as an idea. Sentiment alone can vindicate it. However, sentiment is possible precisely only in the presence of the accompanying conviction of the immortality of man's soul.
The Diary of a Writer, translated by Boris Brasol, Scribner's.

All the Utopias will come to pass only when we grow wings and all people are converted into angels.

Ibid.

Taking a new step, uttering a new word, is what people fear most.

(George) Norman Douglas

(1868-1952)
English writer

What is all wisdom save a collection of platitudes?

South Wind; Macmillan.

Take fifty of our current proverbial sayings—they are so trite, so threadbare, that we can hardly bring our lips to utter them. None the less they embody the concentrated experience of the race, and the man who orders his life according to their teaching cannot go far wrong. *Ibid.*

Has any man ever attained to inner harmony by pondering the experience of others? Not since the world began! He must pass through the fire. *Ibid.*

You can tell the ideals of a nation by its advertisements. *Ibid.*

Stephen A(rnold) Douglas
(1813-1861)
American statesman, orator

Abolitionism proposes to destroy the right and extinguish the principle of self-government for which our forefathers waged a seven years' bloody war, and upon which our whole system of free government is founded. *Senate, March 3, 1854.*

There can be no neutrals in this war—only patriots or traitors.
Quoted by Frank Cobb, N. Y. World, 1912.

I do not believe that the Almighty ever intended the Negro to be the equal to the white man. If He did, He has been a long time demonstrating the fact.
Quoted by Congresswoman Clare Luce, House, February 26, 1946.

William O. Douglas
(b. 1898)
U.S. Supreme Court justice

Ideas are indeed the most dangerous weapons in the world. Our ideas of freedom are the most powerful political weapons man has ever forged. If we remember that, we will never have much to fear from communism. *An Almanac of Liberty.*

Acceptance by government of a dissident press is a measure of the maturity of a nation. *Ibid.*

The right to revolt has sources deep in our history. *Ibid.*

Judges like Brandeis, Cardozo, Hughes, Murphy, Stone and Rutledge brought to the bench a libertarian philosophy and used it to shape the law to the needs of an oncoming generation. In that sense they were "activists", criticized by many. But history will honor them for their creative work. They knew that all life is change and that law must be constantly renewed if the pressures of society are not to build up to violence and revolt. *Ibid.*

The Fifth Amendment is an old friend and a good friend. It is one of the great landmarks in man's struggle to be free of tyranny, to be decent and civilized. It is our way to escape from the use of torture.
Ibid.

The press will commonly reflect (or even try to create) the view that the end justifies the means. Those of us dedicated to the law must stand before those gales.
Address, American Law Institute, 1953.

The free state offers what a police state denies—the privacy of the home, the dignity and peace of mind of the individual. That precious right to be let alone is violated once the police enter our conversations.
Ibid.

The worst provincialism of which America can be guilty is the provincialism of prejudice, racial prejudice, prejudice against new and challenging ideas.
Address, Amalgamated Clothing Workers. The Nation, May 14, 1952.

It is our attitude toward free thought and free expression that will determine our fate. There must be no limit on the range of temperate discussion, no limits on thought. No subject must be taboo. No censor must preside at our assemblies.

Address, Authors' Guild, December 3, 1952, on receiving the Lauterbach Award.

Restriction of free thought and free speech is the most dangerous of all subversions. It is the one un-American act that could most easily defeat us.   *Ibid.*

There are revolutions that are sweeping the world and we in America have been in a position of trying to stop them. With all the wealth of America, with all of the military strength of America, those revolutions cannot be stopped. Those revolutions are revolutions against a form of political and economic organization in the countries of Asia and the Middle East that are oppressive. They are revolutions against feudalism.
Ibid.

Men may believe what they cannot prove. They may not be put to the proof of their religious doctrines or beliefs. Religious experiences which are as real as life to some may be incomprehensible to others.

U.S. v. Ballard, 322 U.S. 78 (1944).

The command of the First Amendment is so clear that we should not allow Congress to call a halt to free speech except in the extreme case of peril from the speech itself. The First Amendment makes confidence in the common sense of our people and in their maturity of judgment the great postulate of our democracy. Its philosophy is that violence is rarely, if ever, stopped by denying civil liberties to those advocating resort to force.

Dissent, Dennis v. U.S., 341 U.S. 494 (1951).

The political censor has no place in our public debates. Unless and until extreme and necessitous circumstances are shown, our aim should be to keep speech unfettered and to allow the processes of law to be invoked only when the provocateurs among us move from speech to action. . . . Our faith should be that our people will never give support to these advocates of revolution, so long as we remain loyal to the purposes for which our Nation was founded.
Ibid.

Where suspicion fills the air and holds scholars in line for fear of their jobs, there can be no exercise of the free intellect. Supineness and dogmatism take the place of inquiry. A "party line"—as dangerous as the "party line" of the Communists—lays hold. It is the "party line" of the orthodox view, of the conventional thought, of the accepted approach. A problem can no longer be pursued to its edges. Fear stalks the classroom. The teacher is no longer a stimulant to adventurous thinking; she becomes instead a pipe line for safe and sound information. A deadening dogma takes the place of free inquiry. Instruction tends to become sterile; pursuit of knowledge is discouraged; discussion often leaves off where it should begin.

Dissent, Adler v. Board of Education, 342 U.S. 485 (1952).

The right to work, I had assumed, was the most precious liberty that man possesses. Man has indeed as much right to work as he has to live, to be free, to own property.

Dissent, Barsky v. Regents, April 26, 1954.

The American ideal was stated by Emerson in his essay on *Politics.* "A man has a right to be employed, to be trusted, to be loved, to be revered." It does many men little good to stay alive and free and propertied, if they cannot work.   *Ibid.*

The vitality of civil and political institutions in our society depends on free discussion. . . . (A) function of free speech under our system of government is to invite dispute. It may indeed best serve its high purpose when it induces a condition of unrest, creates dissatisfaction with conditions as they are, or even stirs people to anger. *Terminiello v. Chicago, 337 U.S. at 4.*

Only a tolerance for a host of unorthodox creeds will give us the wisdom to solve the political problem on which the chances of peace turn . . . We have frightened the people here at home so that they fear the unorthodox idea. *Friends Intelligencer (Quaker weekly).*

Fear of ideas makes us impotent and ineffective. *The Manifest Destiny of America. The Progressive, February, 1955.*

The Framers, therefore, created the federally protected right of silence and decreed that the law could not be used to pry open one's lips and make him a witness against himself . . . *Dissent (Justice Black concurring), Ullman v. U.S., 1956.*

This right of silence, this right of the accused to stand mute . . .   *Ibid.*

Government should be concerned with anti-social conduct, not with utterances. *Dissent (Justice Black concurring). Roth v. U.S., 354 U.S. 476 (1957).*

Thus, if the First Amendment means anything in this field, it must allow protests even against the moral code that the standard of the day sets for the community. In other words, literature should not be suppressed merely because it offends the moral code of the censor.   *Ibid.*

Among the liberties of citizens that are guaranteed by the Fourteenth Amendment are those contained in the First Amendment. (Five cases cited.) These include the right to believe what one chooses, the right to differ from his neighbor, the right to pick and choose the political philosophy that he likes best, the right to associate with whomever he chooses, the right to join the groups he prefers, the privilege of selecting his own path to salvation. *Douglas and Black dissenting, Lerner and Beilan cases, 1958.*

The great and invigorating influences in American life have been the unorthodox: the people who challenge an existing institution or way of life, or say and do things that make people think . . . *Mike Wallace Interview No. 3, Fund for the Republic, 1958.*

The way to combat noxious ideas is with other ideas. The way to combat falsehoods is with truth.   *Ibid.*

I think that the influences towards suppression of minority views—towards orthodoxy in thinking about public issues—have been more subconscious than unconscious, stemming to a very great extent from the tendency among Americans to conform . . . —to be safe and sound and not to deviate or depart from an orthodox point of view; to have not much original thinking; to not deviate very far from the official policy . . . ; to be safe and not get into controversial issues . . .   *Ibid.*

The great reservoir of freedom that we have is, after all, the most outstanding thing that distinguishes us from the Communist world. The Communist world, as I have seen it, would be a terrible place to live because there is no place for the spirit of man, for his soul—no place for his conscience, no place for individual utterances of dissident views. *Ibid.*

Power that controls the economy should be in the hands of elected representatives of the people, not in the hands of an industrial oligarchy.
Dissent, U.S., v. Columbia Steel Co., 334 U.S. 495.

A people who proclaim their civil liberties but extend them only to preferred groups start down the path of totalitarianism. They emulate either the dictatorship of the Right or the dictatorship of the Left. In doing this they erase a basic distinction between our system of government and totalitarianism.
Address, 100th anniversary of birth of John Peter Altgeld, who pardoned the "Haymarket Anarchists."

Frederick Douglass
(1817?-1895)
American orator, reformer

I know of no rights of race superior to the rights of humanity.

The lesson now flashed upon the attention of the American people, the lesson which they must learn, or neglect to do so at their own peril, is that "Equal Manhood means Equal Rights."
Letter to W. J. Wilson.

Slaves are generally expected to sing as well as to work. *Autobiography.*

I did not, when a slave, understand the deep meanings of those rude, and apparently incoherent songs. I was myself within the circle, so that I neither saw nor heard as those without might see and hear. They told a tale which was then altogether beyond my feeble comprehension: they were tones, loud, long and deep, breathing the prayer and complaint of souls boiling over with the bitterest anguish. Every tone was a testimony against slavery, and a prayer to God for deliverance from chains. *Ibid.*

The whole history of the progress of human liberty shows that all concessions yet made to her august claims have been born of earnest struggle. . . . If there is no struggle, there is no progress.
Letter to Gerrit Smith, March 30, 1849.

Those who profess to favor freedom, and yet depreciate agitation, are men who want rain without thunder and lightning. They want the ocean without the roar of its many waters. *Ibid.*

Power concedes nothing without a demand. It never did, and it never will. Find out just what people will submit to, and you have found out the exact amount of injustice and wrong which will be imposed upon them; and these will continue till they have resisted with either words or blows, or with both. The limits of tyrants are prescribed by the endurance of those whom they suppress. *Ibid.*

In the light of these ideas, Negroes will be hunted at the North, and held and flogged at the South, so long as they submit to those devilish outrages, and make no resistance, either moral or physical . . . If we ever get free from all the oppressions and wrongs heaped upon us, we must pay for their removal. We must do this by labor, by suffering, by sacrifice, and, if needs be, by our lives, and the lives of others. *Ibid.*

Theodore Dreiser
(1871-1945)
American novelist

Our civilization is still in a middle stage, scarcely beast, in that it is no longer wholly guided by instinct; scarcely human, in that it is not yet wholly guided by reason.
Sister Carrie.

The strongest phases of our new American philosophy . . . are the desire for enormous business, more wealth and less liberty, more despotism and less freedom of education, which always accompanies the absolute rule of the few.
Tragic America.

For 40 years the American press has been lying about me, and now it tries to ignore me.
Reference to his press interview, March, 1941.

If I were personally to define religion I would say that it is a bandage that man has invented to protect a soul made bloody by circumstance.

All forms of dogmatic religion should go. The world did without them in the past and can do so again. I cite the great civilizations of China and India.

William Drummond
(1585-1640)
Scottish historian, pamphleteer

He who will not reason is a bigot; he who cannot is a fool; and he who dares not, is a slave. *Academical Questions.*

John Dryden
(1631-1700)
English poet, dramatist, critic

For truth has such a face and such a mien,
As to be lov'd needs only to be seen.
Duke of Guise.

Some truth there was, but dash'd and
brew'd with lies,
To please the fools, and puzzle all the wise.
Ibid.

Damned Neuters, in their Middle way of
Steering,
Are neither Fish, nor Flesh, nor good Red
Herring. *Ibid.*

Never was patriot yet, but was a fool.
Absalom and Achitophel.

To die for faction is a common evil
But to be hanged for nonsense is the devil.

We find few historians who have been diligent enough in their search for truth; it is their common method to take on trust what they distribute to the public; by which means a falsehood once received from a famed writer becomes traditional to posterity.

For names containing "du," see also the basic name.

W. E. B. Du Bois
(1868-1963)
American author, editor

There can be no perfect democracy curtailed by color, race or poverty. But with all we accomplish all, even peace.

This is the modern paradox of Sin before which the Puritan stands open-mouthed and mute. A group, a nation, or a race com-

mits murder and rape, steals and destroys, yet no individual is guilty, no one is to blame, no one can be punished. The black world squirms beneath the feet of the white in impotent fury or sullen hate.
Quoted, The Nation, January 25, 1958.

Francis P. Duffy
(1871-1932)
American priest

No soldier starts a war—they only give their lives to it. Wars are started by you and me, by bankers and politicians, excitable women, newspaper editors, clergymen who are ex-pacifists, and Congressmen with vertebrae of putty. The youngsters yelling in the streets, poor kids, are the ones who pay the price.
Sermon, Joffre memorial service, New York City.

Alexandre Dumas, père
(1802-1870)
French novelist, dramatist

My father was a creole, his father a Negro, and his father a monkey; my family, it seems, begins where yours left off.
Reply to a question.

Charles François Dumouriez
(1739-1823)
French general

Les courtisans qui l'entourtent n'ont rien oublié et n'ont rien appris. (The courtiers who surround him (Louis XVIII) have forgotten nothing, and learned nothing.)

Isadora Duncan
(1877-1927)
American dancer

The whole world is absolutely brought up on lies. We are fed on nothing but lies.

We begin with lies and half our lives we live with lies. Most human beings today waste some twenty-five to thirty years of their lives before they break through the actual and conventional lies which surround them.
Dictated, Berlin, December 20, 1924, as first chapter of memoirs, but never continued. Text in This Quarter, Paris, Autumn issue, 1929.

Art is not necessary at all. All that is necessary to make this world a better place to live in is to love—to love as Christ loved, as Buddha loved.   *Ibid.*

That was the most marvellous thing about Lenin: *he* really loved mankind. Others loved themselves, money, theories, power: Lenin loved his fellow men . . . Lenin was God, as Christ was God, because God is Love and Christ and Lenin were all Love!
Ibid.

So long as little children are allowed to suffer, there is no true love in this world.
Ibid.

What I am interested in doing is finding and expressing a new form of life. The Greeks lived. People do not live nowadays —they get about ten per cent out of life.
Ibid.

Finley Peter Dunne ("Mr. Dooley")
(1867-1936)
American satirist

F'r th' lawyers ar-re too busy studyin' haby as corpus proceedin's to do annthing else, an' 'tis th' Palajeem iv our Liberties that is runnin' th' counthry an' is goin' to run it f'r a long time to come.
Mr. Dooley on the Power of the Press. American Magazine, October, 1906, p. 606.

Th' lawyers make th' law, th' judges make th' errors, but th' iditors make th' juries.   *Ibid.*

Th' printed wurrud! What can I do against it? I can buy a gun to protect me against me inimy. I can change me name to save me fr'm the gran' jury. But there's no escape fr good man or bad fr'm th' printed wurrud.   *Ibid.*

I care not who makes the laws or the money iv a counthry so long as I run th' presses.   *Ibid.*

Th' press . . . rules be findin' out what th' people want an' if they don't want annything it tells thim what it wants thim to want it to tell thim. It's against all tyrants but itsilf an' it has th' boldest if thim crookin' th' knee to it.   *Ibid.*

I wish it cud be fixed up so's that th' men that starts th' wars could do th' fightin'. Th' throuble is that all th' prelimin'ries is arranged by matchmakers an' all they'se left fr fighters is to do th' murdherin' . . .

Don't ask fr rights. Take them. An' don't let anny wan give thim to ye. A right that is handed to ye fr nawthin' has somethin' th' matter with it.   *On Woman Suffrage.*

André Dupin
(1783-1865)
French lawyer, politician

I have always belonged to France, and never to parties.
On taking office with Louis Napoleon.

The Society of Jesus is a sword, whose handle is at Rome, and the point everywhere.
1625. Ramage, Beautiful Thoughts from French and Italian Authors, p. 386.

Lammot duPont
(1880-1952)
American industrialist

People may change their minds as often as their coats, and new sets of rules of conduct may be written every week, but the fact remains that human nature has not changed and does not change, that inherent human beliefs stay the same; that fundamental rules of human conduct continue to hold.
Forbes Magazine, April 15, 1956.

Will Durant
(1885-1981)
American author

Philosophy accepts the hard and hazardous task of dealing with problems not yet open to the methods of science—problems like good and evil, beauty and ugliness, order and freedom, life and death; so soon as a field of inquiry yields knowledge susceptible of exact formulation it is called science.   *The Story of Philosophy.*

Every science begins as philosophy and ends as art.   *Ibid.*

Philosophy is a hypothetical interpretation of the unknown (as in metaphysics), or of the inexactly known (as in ethics or political philosophy); it is the front trench in the siege of truth.   *Ibid.*

When liberty becomes license, dictatorship is near.

Civilization begins with order, grows with liberty, and dies with chaos.

Jimmy Durante
(1893-1980)
American comedian

Don't put no constrictions on da people. Leave 'em ta hell alone.

Timothy Dwight
(1752-1817)
American educator, theologian, poet

If Jefferson be elected we may see our wives and daughters the victims of legal prostitution, soberly dishonored, speciously polluted, the outcasts of delicacy and virtue, the loathing of God and man.

Nieman Reports.

Max Eastman
(1883-1969)
American writer, editor

"More goods and fewer people" is the slogan I should like to see carried at the head of humanity's march into the future.
Reflections on the Failure of Socialism, 1955.

The worst enemy of human hope is not brute facts, but men of brains who will not face them. *Ibid.*

An armed seizure of power by a highly organized minority party, whether in the name of the Dictatorship of the Proletariat, the Glory of Rome, the Supremacy of the Nordics, or any other slogan that may be invented, and no matter how ingeniously integrated with the masses of the population, will normally lead to the totalitarian state. "Totalitarian state" is merely the modern name for tyranny. *Ibid.*

A false and undeliberated conception of what man is lies at the bottom, I think, of the whole bubble-castle of socialist theory. Although few seem to realize it, Marxism rests on the romantic notion of Rousseau that nature endows men with the qualities necessary to be a free, equal, fraternal, family-like living together, and our sole problem is to fix up the external conditions. All Marx did about this with his dialectical philosophy was to change the tenses in the romance: Nature *will* endow men with the qualities *as soon as* the conditions are fixed up. *Ibid.*

It was natural that idealistic people who had ceased to believe in heaven should think up some bright hope for humanity on earth. That, I think, more than any objection to "capitalism", accounts for the spread of the socialist dream, especially in Anglo-Saxon countries. *Ibid.*

The real guarantee of freedom is an equilibrium of social forces in conflict, not the triumph of any one force. In trying to build, or defend, a free society, our first concern should be to make sure that no one gang or group—neither the proletariat, nor the capitalists, nor the landowners, nor the bankers, nor the army, nor the church, nor the state itself—shall have unlimited power. *Ibid.*

Marxists profess to reject religion in favor of science, but they cherish a belief that the external universe is evolving with reliable, if not divine, necessity in exactly the direction in which they want it to go.
Marxism: Is It Science? 1940.

The only vital political difference between Marx and Lenin is that Lenin had a revolution to practice on and Marx had not. *From a letter, 1958.*

A liberal mind is a mind that is able to imagine itself believing anything.
Masses, September, 1917.

Mary Baker Eddy
(1821-1910)
American metaphysical writer, founder of Christian Science

We classify disease as error, which nothing but Truth or Mind can heal, and this Mind must be divine, not human.
Science and Health with Key to the Scriptures.

Disease is an experience of so-called mortal mind. It is fear made manifest on the body.   *Ibid.*

You command the situation if you understand that mortal existence is a state of self-deception and not the truth of being.   *Ibid.*

Christian Science explains all cause and effect as mental, not physical.   *Ibid.*

Health is not a condition of matter, but of Mind; nor can the material senses bear reliable testimony on the subject of health.   *Ibid.*

God is Mind, and God is infinite; hence all is Mind.   *Ibid.*

Truth is immortal; error is mortal.   *Ibid.*

Thomas Alva Edison
(1847-1931)
American inventive genius

I never did anything worth doing by accident; nor did any of my inventions come by accident; they came by work.

I never once made a discovery . . . I speak without exaggeration when I say that I have constructed *three thousand* different theories in connection with the electric light . . . Yet in only two cases did my experiments prove the truth of my theory.   1878.

Genius is one per cent inspiration and ninety-nine per cent perspiration.   *Newspaper interview, 1931.*

Not only will atomic power be released, but someday we will harness the rise and fall of the tides and imprison the rays of the sun.   *Newspaper interview, August 22, 1921.*

There will one day spring from the brain of science a machine or force so fearful in its potentialities, so absolutely terrifying, that even man, the fighter, who will dare torture and death in order to inflict torture and death, will be appalled, and so abandon war forever. What man's mind can create, man's character can control.   *Ibid.*

I do not believe that any type of religion should ever be introduced into the public schools of the United States.

So far as religion of the day is concerned, it is a damned fake . . . Religion is all bunk.

My mind is incapable of conceiving such a thing as a soul. I may be in error, and man may have a soul; but I simply do not believe it.   *Do We Live Again?*

There is no expedient to which a man will not go to avoid the real labor of thinking.   *Placard, in all Edison works.*

I am proud of the fact that I never invented weapons to kill.   *N. Y. Times, June 8, 1915.*

Restlessness is discontent—and discontent is the first necessity of progress. Show me a thoroughly satisfied man—and I will show you a failure.

Edward III
(1312-1377)
King of England

Honi soit qui mal y pense.
Credited to the king, 1349; motto of his Order of the Garter.

Jonathan Edwards
(1703-1758)
American clergyman, theological writer

This that you have heard is the case of every one of you that are out of Christ.

That world of misery, that lake of burning brimstone, is extended abroad under you. There is the dreadful pit of the glowing flames of the wrath of God; there is hell's wide gaping mouth open; and you have nothing to stand upon, nor anything to take hold of; there is nothing between you and hell but the air; it is only the power and mere pleasure of God that holds you up.
Sinners in the Hands of an Angry God, 1741.

The bow of God's wrath is bent, and the arrow made ready on the string, and justice bends the arrow at your heart, and strains the bow, and it is nothing but the mere pleasure of God, and that of an angry God, without any promise or obligation at all, that keeps the arrow one moment from being made drunk with your blood.   *Ibid.*

The God that holds you over the pit of hell, much as one holds a spider, or some loathsome insect over the fire, abhors you, and is dreadfully provoked: his wrath towards you burns like fire; he looks upon you as worthy of nothing else, but to be cast into the fire; he is of purer eyes than to bear to have you in his sight; you are ten thousand times more abominable in his eyes, than the most hateful venomous serpent is in ours. You have offended him infinitely more than ever a stubborn rebel did his prince; and yet it is nothing but his hand that holds you from falling into the fire every moment.   *Ibid.*

The sight of hell's torments will exalt the happiness of the saints forever.

True liberty consists only in the power of doing what we ought to well, and in not being constrained to do what we ought not to do.
Quoted in the Congressional Record, June 29, 1950.

Tryon Edwards
(1809-1894)
American theologian

Compromise is but the sacrifice of one right or good in the hope of retaining another—too often ending in the loss of both.

He that is possessed with a prejudice is possessed with a devil, and one of the worst kind of devils, for it shuts out the truth, and often leads to ruinous error.

Albert Einstein*
(1879-1955)
American (German-born) physicist, Nobel Prize, 1921

$E=mc^2$.**   *Annalen der Physik, 1905.*

---

* "I am gladly willing to review the quotations you intend sending me," Professor Einstein wrote the editor of this book October 13, 1954; "Such a review is indeed necessary. For many things which go under my name are badly translated from the German or are invented by other people." On October 24 the Ms. of the major portion of this chapter was returned: Professor Einstein had deleted the remark, "There is no hitching post in the universe," which he was supposed to have made in answer to a boat-train reporter's request for "a definition of relativity in one line."
** "The Atomic Age is built on Einstein's equation $E=mc^2$, where m is the mass of the atom, and c is the speed of light (186,-000 miles per second). You square that, and out of the atom comes quite a bit of energy!"—Stuart Chase, *Saturday Review,* January 22, 1955.
"Einstein's theory of relativity is probably the greatest synthetic achievement of the human intellect up to the present time." —Bertrand Russell, *N. Y. Times,* April 19, 1955.

Nationalism is an infantile disease. It is the measles of mankind.
Statement to G. S. Viereck, 1921.

The (American) Press, which is mostly controlled by vested interests, has an excessive influence on public opinion.
Interview, Nieuwe Rotterdamsche Courant, 1921; Ideas and Opinions of Albert Einstein, p. 6.

Everything that the human race has done and thought is concerned with the satisfaction of deeply felt needs and the assuagement of pain. One has to keep this constantly in mind if one wishes to understand spiritual movements and their development. Feeling and longing are the motive force behind all human endeavor and human creation . . . With primitive man it is above all fear that evokes religious notions—fear of hunger, wild beasts, sickness, death . . . In this sense I am speaking of a religion of fear. This, though not created, is in an important degree stabilized by the portion of a special priestly caste which sets itself up as a mediator between the people and the beings they fear, and erects a hegemony on this basis.
Religion and Science. N. Y. Times Magazine, November 9, 1930.

The religious geniuses of all ages have been distinguished by this kind of religious feeling, which knows no dogma and no God conceived in man's image; so that there can be no church whose central teachings are based on it. Hence it is precisely among the heretics of every age that we find men who were filled with this highest kind of religious feeling and were in many cases regarded by their contemporaries as atheists, sometimes also as saints. *Ibid.*

The man who is thoroughly convinced of the universal operation of the law of causation cannot for a moment entertain the idea of a being who interferes in the course of events . . . He has no use for the religion of fear and equally little for social or moral religion. A God who rewards and punishes is inconceivable to him for the simple reason that a man's actions are determined by necessity, external and internal, so that in God's eyes he cannot be responsible, any more than an inanimate object is responsible for the motions it undergoes. Science has therefore been charged with undermining morality, but the charge is unjust. A man's ethical behavior should be based effectually on sympathy, education, and social ties and needs; no religious basis is necessary. Man would indeed be in a poor way if he had to be restrained by fear of punishment and hope of reward after death. *Ibid.*

This is the problem: Is there any way of delivering mankind from the menace of war? It is common knowledge that with the advance of modern science, this issue has come to mean a matter of life and death for civilization as we know it; nevertheless, for all the zeal displayed, every attempt at its solution has ended in a lamentable breakdown.
Letter to Dr. Freud (q.v.), July 30, 1932; published by the International Institute for Cultural Cooperation, with Freud's reply, 1933.

The normal objective of my thought affords no insight into the dark places of human will and feeling. *Ibid.*

As one immune from nationalist bias, I personally see a simple way of dealing with the superficial (i.e. administrative) aspect of the problem: the setting up, by international consent, of a legislative and judicial body to settle every conflict arising between nations. Each nation would undertake to abide by the orders issued by this legislative body, to invoke its decision in every dispute, to accept its judgments unreservedly and to carry out every measure the tribunal deems necessary for the execution of its decrees. *Ibid.*

Thus I am led to my first axiom: the quest of international security involves the unconditional surrender by every nation, in a certain measure, of its liberty of action, its sovereignty that is to say, and it is clear beyond all doubt that no other road can lead to such security. *Ibid.*

The craving for power which characterizes the governing class in every nation is hostile to any limitation of the national sovereignty. *Ibid.*

The minority, the ruling class at present, has the schools and press, usually the Church as well, under its thumb. This enables it to organize and sway the emotions of the masses, and make its tool of them. *Ibid.*

How is it these devices succeed so well in rousing men to such wild enthusiasm, even to sacrifice their lives? Only one answer is possible. Because man has within him a lust for hatred and destruction. In normal times this passion exists in a latent state, it emerges only in unusual circumstances, but it is a comparatively easy task to call it into play and raise it to the power of a collective psychosis. Here lies, perhaps, the crux of all the complex of factors we are considering, an enigma that only the expert in the lore of human instincts can resolve.

And so we come to our last question. Is it possible to control man's mental evolution so as to make him proof against the psychoses of hate and destructiveness? Here I am thinking by no means only of the so-called uncultured masses. Experience proves

that it is rather the so-called "Intelligentsia" that is most apt to yield to these disastrous collective suggestions, since the intellectual has no direct contact with life in the raw, but encounters it in its easiest, synthetic form—upon the printed page. *Ibid.*

Darwin's theory of the struggle for existence and the selectivity connected with it has by many people been cited as authorization of the encouragement of the spirit of competition. Some people also in such a way have tried to prove pseudo-scientifically the necessity of the destructive economic struggle of competition between individuals. But this is wrong, because man owes his strength in the struggle for existence to the fact that he is a socially living animal. As little as a battle between single ants of an ant hill is essential for survival, just so little is this the case with the individual members of a human community.

Address, Albany, N. Y., October 15, 1936.

Great spirits have always found violent opposition from mediocrities. The latter cannot understand it when a man does not thoughtlessly submit to hereditary prejudices but honestly and courageously uses his intelligence and fulfills the duty to express the results of his thoughts in clear form.

Letter to Dr. M. I. Cohen, in Bertrand Russell affair, N. Y. World-Telegram, March 19, 1940.

In their struggle for the ethical good, teachers of religion must have the stature to give up the doctrine of a personal God, that is, give up that source of fear and hope which in the past placed such vast power in the hands of priests. In their labors they will have to avail themselves of those forces which are capable of cultivating the Good, the True, and the Beautiful in humanity itself . . .

The further the spiritual evolution of mankind advances, the more certain it seems to me that the path to genuine religiosity does not lie through the fear of life, and the fear of death, and blind faith, but through striving after rational knowledge. In this sense I believe that the priest must become a teacher if he wishes to do justice to his lofty educational mission. *Science, Philosophy and Religion, A Symposium, 1941.*

I consider it important, indeed urgently necessary, for intellectual workers to get together, both to protect their own economic status and also, generally speaking, to secure their influence in the political field. *Statement for the National Wartime Conference, May 28, 1944.*

The release of atomic energy has not created a new problem. It has merely made more urgent the necessity of solving an existing one . . . I do not believe that civilization will be wiped out in a war fought with the atomic bomb. Perhaps two-thirds of the people of the earth will be killed. *Atlantic Monthly, November, 1945.*

The secret of the bomb should be committed to a world government . . . Do I fear the tyranny of a world government? Of course I do. But I fear still more the coming of another war or wars. Any government is certain to be evil to some extent. But a world government is preferable to the far greater evil of wars. *Ibid.*

It is characteristic of the military mentality that non-human factors (atom bombs, strategic bases, weapons of all sorts, the possession of raw materials, etc.) are held essential, while the human being, his desires and thoughts—in short, the psychological factors—are considered as unimportant and secondary. Herein lies a certain resemblance to Marxism, at least in so far as its theoretical side alone is kept in view. The individual is degraded to a mere instrument; he becomes "human matériel." The normal ends of human aspiration vanish with such a viewpoint. Instead, the military mentality raises "naked power" as a goal in itself—one of the strangest illusions to which men can succumb. *The American Scholar, 1947.*

No doubt, the antagonism of economic interests within and among nations is largely responsible to a great extent for the dangerous and threatening condition in the world today. Man has not succeeded in developing political and economic forms of organization which would guarantee the peaceful co-existence of the nations of the world. *A Message to Intellectuals, 1948.*

The crippling of individuals I consider the worst evil of capitalism. Our whole educational system suffers from this evil. An exaggerated competitive attitude is inculcated into the student, who is trained to worship acquisitive success as a preparation for his future career. *Monthly Review, May, 1949.*

While it is true than an inherently free and scrupulous person may be destroyed, such an individual can never be enslaved or used as a blind tool. *Impact (Unesco), 1950.*

The discovery of nuclear chain reactions need not bring about the destruction of mankind . . . only a supranational organization, equipped with a sufficiently strong executive power, can protect us. Once we have understood that, we shall find the strength for the sacrifices necessary to ensure the future of mankind.

Message to Canadian Education Week, March, 1952.

To my mind, to kill in war is not a whit better than to commit ordinary murder.

Kaizo, Tokyo, 1952.

It gives me great pleasure indeed to see the stubbornness of an incorrigible non-conformist warmly acclaimed.

On receiving the Lord & Taylor Award, 1953.

Any power must be an enemy of mankind which enslaves the individual by terror or force, whether it arises under a fascist or communist flag. All that is valuable in human society depends upon the opportunity for development accorded the individual.

Statement, London, September 15, 1933.

I am convinced that some political and social activities and practices of the Catholic organizations are detrimental and even dangerous for the community as a whole, here and everywhere. I mention here only the fight against birth control at a time when overpopulation in various countries has become a serious threat to the health of people and a grave obstacle to any attempt to organize peace on this planet.

Letter to a reader of the Brooklyn Tablet, who questioned Dr. Einstein if he had been correctly quoted, 1954.

By academic freedom I understand the right to search for truth and to publish and teach what one holds to be true. This right implies also a duty: one must not conceal any part of what one has recognized to be true. It is evident that any restriction of academic freedom acts in such a way as to hamper the dissemination of knowledge among the people and thereby impedes national judgment and action.

Letter on 75th birthday, March 13, 1954.

In principle, everybody is equally involved in defending the constitutional rights. The "intellectuals" in the widest sense of the word are, however, in a special position since they have, thanks to their special training, a particularly strong influence on the formation of public opinion. This is the reason why those who are about to lead us toward an authoritarian government are particularly concerned with intimidating and muzzling that group.

It is therefore in the present situation especially important for the intellectuals to do their duty. I see this duty in refusing to cooperate in any undertaking that violates the constitutional rights of the individual. This holds in particular for all inquisitions that are concerned with the private life and the political affiliations of the citizens. Whoever cooperates in such a case becomes an accessory to acts of violation or invalidation of the Constitution. *Ibid.*

The existence and validity of human rights are not written in the stars . . . Those ideals and convictions which resulted from historical experience, from the craving for beauty and harmony, have been readily accepted in theory by man—and at all times, have been trampled upon by the same people under the pressures of their animal instincts. A large part of history is therefore replete with the struggle for those human rights, an eternal struggle in which a final victory can never be won. But to tire in that struggle would mean the ruin of society.

In talking about human rights today, we are referring primarily to the following demands: protection of the individual against arbitrary infringement by other individuals

or by the government; the right to work and to adequate earnings from work; freedom of discussion and teaching; adequate participation of the individual in the formation of his government. *These* human rights are nowadays recognized theoretically, although, by abundant use of formalistic, legal maneuvers, they are being violated to a much greater extent than even a generation ago.
Address, Chicago Decalogue Society, February 20, 1954.

I would rather choose to be a plumber or a peddler in the hope to find that modest degree of independence still available under present circumstances.
Letter acknowledging plumbers' union card, November, 1954.

Never do anything against conscience even if the state demands it.
Saturday Review obituary, April 30, 1955.

I cannot imagine a God who rewards and punishes the objects of his creation, whose purposes are modeled after our own—a God, in short, who is but a reflection of human frailty. Neither can I believe that the individual survives the death of his body, although feeble souls harbor such thoughts through fear or ridiculous egotisms.
N. Y. Times Obituary, April 19, 1955.

My religion consists of a humble admiration of the illimitable superior spirit who reveals himself in the slight details we are able to perceive with our frail and feeble minds. That deeply emotional conviction of the presence of a superior reasoning power, which is revealed in the incomprehensible universe, forms my idea of God.
Ibid.

What is the meaning of human life, or for that matter, of the life of any creature?

To know an answer to this question means to be religious. You ask: Does it make any sense, then, to pose this question? I answer: The man who regards his own life and that of his fellow creatures as meaningless is not merely unhappy but hardly fit for life.
N. Y. Times Magazine, April 24, 1955.

The important thing is not to stop questioning. Curiosity has its own reason for existing. One cannot help but be in awe when he contemplates the mysteries of eternity, of life, of the marvelous structure of reality. It is enough if one tries merely to comprehend a little of this mystery every day. Never lose a holy curiosity.
Personal memoir of William Miller, an editor, Life, May 2, 1955.

Try not to become a man of success but rather try to become a man of value.
Ibid.

I do not believe in the God of theology who rewards good and punishes evil.
Ibid.

The presence of a superior reasoning power . . . revealed in the incomprehensible universe, forms my idea of God.
Ibid.

If we want to resist the powers which threaten to suppress intellectual and individual freedom we must keep clearly before us what is at stake and what we owe to that freedom which our ancestors won for us after hard struggles.

Without such freedom there would have been no Shakespeare, Pasteur, or Lister. There would be no comfortable houses for the mass of the people, no railways or wireless, no protection against epidemics, no cheap books, no culture, no enjoyment of art at all. There would be no machines to relieve people from the arduous labor needed for the production of the essential necessities of life. Most people would lead a dull life of slavery just as under the ancient despotisms of Asia. It is only men who are free who create the inventions and intellectual works which to us moderns make life worth while.

Address, Albert Hall, London, quoted, N. Y. Times.

Why does this magnificent applied science, which saves work and makes life easier, bring us so little happiness? The simple answer runs: Because we have not yet learned to make sensible use of it.

Address, California Institute of Technology.

If my theory of relativity is proven successful, Germany will claim me as a German and France will declare that I am a citizen of the world. Should my theory prove untrue, France will say that I am a German, and Germany will declare that I am a Jew. *Address at the Sorbonne.*

I cannot believe that God would choose to play dice with the world . . . *Raffiniert ist der Herr Gott, aber boshaft ist Er nicht. Letter to his colleague, Prof. Max Born.*

The ideals which have lighted my way, and time after time have given me new courage to face life cheerfully, have been Kindness, Beauty, and Truth . . . The trite subjects of human efforts—possessions, outward success, luxury—have always seemed to me contemptible.

Forum & Century, vol. 84.

My political ideal is democracy. Let every man be respected as an individual and no man idolized. *Ibid.*

Force always attracts men of low morality, and I believe it to be an in-variable rule that tyrants of genius are succeeded by scoundrels. *Ibid.*

That worst outcrop of herd life, the military system, which I abhor . . . This plague-spot of civilization ought to be abolished with all possible speed. Heroism on command, senseless violence, and all the loathsome nonsense that goes by the name of patriotism—how passionately I hate them! How vile and despicable seems war to me! I would rather be hacked in pieces than take part in such an abominable business. My opinion of the human race is high enough that I believe this bogey would have disappeared long ago, had the sound sense of the people not been systematically corrupted by commercial and political interests acting through the schools and the Press. *Ibid.*

The true value of a human being is determined primarily by the measure and the sense in which he has attained liberation from the Self.

Ideas and Opinions of Albert Einstein.

The development of mechanical methods of warfare is such that human life will become intolerable if people do not discover before long a way of preventing war . . . People seek to minimize the danger by limitation of armaments and restrictive rules for the conduct of war. But war is not a parlor game in which the players obediently stick to the rules. Where life and death are at stake, rules and obligations go by the board. Only the absolute repudiation of all war can be of any use here. *Ibid.*

Anybody who really wants to abolish war must resolutely declare himself in favor of his own country's resigning a portion of its sovereignty in favor of international institutions. *Ibid.*

We cannot despair of humanity, since we are ourselves human beings.   *Ibid.*

If it (the hydrogen bomb) is successful, radioactive poisoning of the atmosphere and hence annihilation of any life on earth has been brought within the range of technical possibilities.   *Ibid.*

Judaism is not a creed: the Jewish God is simply a negation of superstition, an imaginary result of its elimination. It is also an attempt to base the moral law on fear, a regrettable and discreditable attempt. Yet it seems to me that the strong moral tradition of the Jewish nation has to a large extent shaken itself free from this fear. It is clear also that "serving God" was equated with "serving the living." The best of the Jewish people, especially the Prophets and Jesus, contended tirelessly for this. *Ibid.*

No wealth in the world can help humanity forward, even in the hands of the most devoted worker in this cause . . . Can anyone imagine Moses, Jesus, or Gandhi armed with the money-bags of Carnegie?   *Ibid.*

The attempt to combine wisdom and power has only rarely been successful and then only for a short while.
Aphorisms for Leo Baeck: Ibid.

Few people are capable of expressing with equanimity opinions which differ from the prejudices of their social environment. Most people are even incapable of forming such opinion.   *Ibid.*

Whoever undertakes to set himself up as a judge in the field of Truth and Knowledge is shipwrecked by the laughter of the gods.   *Ibid.*

I do not intend to argue with you about what inroads on human liberty may be justi-fied by reasons of state. But the pursuit of scientific truth, detached from the practical interests of everyday life, ought to be treated as sacred by every government, and it is in the highest interests of all that honest servants of truth should be left in peace.
Letter of protest to Rocco, Mussolini's Minister of Justice and Education; Ibid.

1. Those instrumental goods which should serve to maintain the life and health of all human beings should be produced by the least possible labor of all.
2. The satisfaction of physical needs is indeed the indispensable pre-condition of a satisfactory existence, but in itself it is not enough. In order to be content, men must also have the possibility of developing their intellectual and artistic powers to whatever extent accords with their personal characteristics and abilities.
On Freedom, Ibid.

Peace cannot be kept by force. It can only be achieved by understanding.
Notes on Pacifism.

Perfection of means and confusion of goals seem—in my opinion—to characterize our age.   *Out of My Later Years.*

If we desire sincerely and passionately the safety, the welfare and the free development of the talents of all men, we shall not be in want of the means to approach such a state. Even if only a small part of mankind strives for such goals, their superiority will prove itself in the long run.
Ibid.

Arrows of hate have been shot at me too; but they never hit me, because somehow they belonged to another world, with which I have no connection whatsoever.
Ibid.

Scientists can collaborate in achieving the goal of international security if they take a stand in the face of public opinion

for the establishment of an international body with both a permanent personnel and a permanent military force.
Treasury for the Free Word, Arco, 1946.

It is the duty of every citizen according to his best capacities to give validity to his convictions in political affairs.   *Ibid.*

Science without religion is lame, religion without science is blind.
The World As I See It (Philosophical Library).

The man who regards life . . . as meaningless is not merely unfortunate but almost disqualified for life.   *Ibid.*

Everybody acts not only under external compulsion but also in accordance with inner necessity.   *Ibid.*

The next World War will be fought with stones.
Quoted by John Scott, Political Warfare.

Dwight D. Eisenhower
(1890-1969)
American general, 34th President of the United States

Morale is the greatest single factor in successful wars.
N. Y. Post, June 23, 1945.

T'hell with it—I've work to do!
Reply to invitation from Lady Astor to visit Cliveden at time of preparation of African landing; newspaper report.

I am not available for and could not accept nomination.
Letter to a friend, shown to President Truman, quoted in N. Y. Times, January 23, 1948.

The necessary and wise subordination of the military to civil power will be best sustained when lifelong professional soldiers abstain from seeking high political office.
Ibid.; quoted by Truman, Memoirs, v. 2, p. 187.

Some people wanted champagne and caviar when they should have beer and hot dogs.
Speech, St. Andrews Society, N. Y. C., November 30, 1949.

If all that Americans want is security they can go to prison. They'll have enough to eat, a bed and a roof over their heads. But if an American wants to preserve his dignity and his equality as a human being, he must not bow his neck to any dictatorial government.
Speech, Galveston, December, 1949.

Don't join the book burners. Don't think you are going to conceal faults by concealing evidence that they ever existed.
Speech, Dartmouth, June 14, 1953.

Here in America we are descended in blood and in spirit from revolutionists and rebels—men and women who dare to dissent from accepted doctrine. As their heirs, we may never confuse honest dissent with disloyal subversion.
Address, Columbia University bicentennial dinner, May 31, 1954.

They (the founders) proclaimed to all the world the revolutionary doctrine of the divine rights of the common man. That doctrine has ever since been the heart of the American faith.   *Ibid.*

Without exhaustive debate, even heated debate, of ideas and programs, free government would weaken and wither. But if we allow ourselves to be persuaded that every individual or party that takes issue

with our own convictions is necessarily wicked or treasonous, then, indeed, we are approaching the end of freedom's road.
Ibid.

In this country, if someone dislikes you or accuses you, he must come up in front. He cannot hide behind the shadows, he cannot assassinate you or your character from behind without suffering the penalties an outraged citizenry will inflict.
Address, November 23, 1954

If we are going to continue to be proud that we are Americans there must be no weakening of the codes by which we have lived; by the right to meet your accuser face to face, if you have one; by your right to go to church or the synagogue or even the mosque of your own choosing; by your right to speak your mind and be protected in it.
Ibid.

One hundred and eighty-one years ago, our forefathers started a revolution that still goes on.
Speech, April 19, 1956.

Only a fool would try to deprive working men and women of the right to join the union of their choice.
Labor Scrap Book, United Rubber Workers, 1956.

The satellite . . . does not raise my apprehension one iota.
Press conference, October, 1957.

A voter without a ballot is like a soldier without a bullet.
N. Y. Times Book Review, October 27, 1957.

I hate war as only a soldier who has lived it can, only as one who has seen its brutality, its futility, its *stupidity.*
Quoted by John Gunther, Eisenhower.

"Conservatism." "Dynamic conservatism." "Progressive, dynamic conservatism." "Pro-

gressive moderation." "Moderate progressivism." "Positive and progressive."
Eisenhower policies, quoted by Eric F. Goldman, The Crucial Decade.

Kurt Eisner

(1867-assassinated 1919)
President, Bavarian Socialist Republic, journalist

Truth is the greatest of all national possessions. A state, a people, a system which suppresses the truth or fears to publish it, deserves to collapse.

Charles W. Eliot

(1834-1926)
American educator

You are in the worst job in the world. You never have time.
(to a newspaper reporter.)

George Eliot (née Mary Ann Evans Cross)

(1819-1880)
English novelist, essayist, poet

The Jews are among the aristocracy of every land; if a literature is called rich in the possession of a few classic tragedies, what shall we say to a national tragedy lasting for fifteen hundred years, in which the poets and actors were also the heroes.
Daniel Deronda.

To *fear* the examination of any proposition appears to me an intellectual and a moral palsy that will ever hinder the firm grasping of any substance whatever.
The George Eliot Letters, 1954.

Falsehood is so easy, truth so difficult.

There is a mercy which is weakness, and even treason against the common good.
Romola, bk. iii.

T(homas) S(tearns) Eliot
(1888-1965)
English (American-born) poet, essayist

We are the hollow men
We are the stuffed men
Leaning together.   *The Hollow Men.*

This is the way the world ends
Not with a bang but a whimper.   *Ibid.*

So far as we are human, what we do must be either evil or good; so far as we do evil or good, we are human; and it is better, in a paradoxical way, to do evil than to do nothing; at least, we exist.
Introduction to Baudelaire's Intimate Journals, 1930.

It is true to say that the glory of man is his capacity for damnation. The worst that can be said of most of our malefactors, from statesmen to thieves, is that they are not man enough to be damned.   *Ibid.*

The majority of mankind is lazy-minded, incurious, absorbed in vanities, and tepid in emotion, and is therefore incapable of either much doubt or much faith.
Introduction, Pascal's Pensées, 1931.

No scheme for a change of society can be made to appear immediately palatable, except by falsehood, until society has become so desperate that it will accept any change. A Christian society only becomes acceptable after you have fairly examined the alternatives.
The Idea of a Christian Society, 1939.

The Civil War is not ended: I question whether any serious civil war ever does end.   *Milton, 1947.*

We cannot, in literature any more than in the rest of life, live in a perpetual state of revolution.   *Ibid.*

We know too much, and are convinced of too little. Our literature is a substitute for religion, and so is our religion.
A Dialogue on Dramatic Poetry, 1928.

The last temptation is the greatest treason:
To do the right deed for the wrong reason.
Murder in the Cathedral, pt. 1, 1935.

Elizabeth I
(1533-1603)
Queen of England

As for my part, I care not for death; for all men are mortal, and though I be mortal, yet I have as good a courage answerable to my place as ever my father had. I am your anointed Queen. I will never be by violence constrained to do anything. I thank God I am endued with such qualities that if I were turned out of the realm in my petticoat, I were able to live in any place in Christendom.
Quoted in The Practical Cogitator.

Edward Law, 1st Baron of Ellenborough
(1750-1818)
English jurist

The greater the truth the greater the libel.

Ebenezer Elliott
(1781-1849)
English chartist leader, poet

When wilt thou save the people?
O God of mercy! when?

The people, Lord! the people!
    Not thrones and crowns, but men!
God save the people! thine they are;
Thy children, as thy angels fair;
Save them from bondage and despair!
        God save the people!
            The People's Anthem, 1827.

What is a communist? One who hath
        yearnings
    For equal division of unequal earnings.
Idler or bungler, or both, he is willing
    To fork out his copper and pocket a
        shilling.
        Poetical works. Corn Law Rhymes.

Havelock Ellis
(1859-1939)
English psychologist, writer

. . . love, a gracious and beautiful erotic art.

Sexual pleasure, wisely used and not abused, may prove the stimulus and liberator of our finest and most exalted activities.

In its accomplishment, for all spiritually evolved persons, the communion of bodies becomes the communion of souls. The outward and visible sign has been the consummation of an inward and spiritual grace.

For until it is generally possible to acquire erotic personality and to master the art of loving, the development of the individual man or woman is marred, the acquirement of human happiness and harmony remains impossible.

The greater the number of laws, the greater the number of offenses against them.

What we call "morals" is simply blind obedience to words of command.
        The Dance of Life.

The sun, the moon and the stars would have disappeared long ago, had they happened to be within reach of predatory human hands. *Ibid.*

A man must not swallow more beliefs than he can digest. *Ibid.*

The place where optimism most flourishes is the lunatic asylum. *Ibid.*

A religion can no more afford to degrade its Devil than to degrade its God.
        Impressions and Comments.

It is only the great men who are truly obscene. If they had not dared to be obscene they could never have dared to be great.
        Ibid.

So it is the dreamers, the children of genius, who for thousands of years have been whispering into the ears of Mankind that insidious delusion: *Si vis pacem para bellum.*
        Ibid.

It was thus at a late stage in social history, though still so primitive as to be prehistoric, that organized warfare developed. Warfare thus appears to owe its origin to migrant military aristocracies. These have settled in places where there is an established population producing tangible and desired forms of wealth and live the lives of social parasites . . . In short, it can be said that: Warfare is the means whereby the members of a parasitic ruling class of alien origin endeavour, while exploiting their own subjects, to dominate those surrounding peoples who produce wealth in a tangible and desired form.
        Ibid.

There can be no doubt whatever regarding the soundness of your view of "obscenity" as residing exclusively, not in the thing contemplated, but in the mind of the contemplating person.
        Letter to Theodore Schroeder, Free Press Anthology, p. 224.

I regard sex as the central problem of life.
Studies in the Psychology of Sex, v. i, preface, xxx, Random House, 1936.

And now that the problem of religion has practically been settled, and that the problem of labor has at least been placed on a practical foundation, the question of sex—with the racial questions that rest on it—stands before the coming generations as the chief problem for solution.   *Ibid.*

Sex lies at the root of life, and we can never learn to reverence life until we know how to understand sex.   *Ibid.*

That modesty—like all the closely-allied emotions—is based on fear, one of the most primitive of the emotions, seems to be fairly evident.   *Ibid., p. 36.*

Love and religion are the two most volcanic emotions to which the human organism is liable, and it is not surprising that, when there is a disturbance in one of these spheres, the vibrations should readily extend to the other. *Ibid., p. 310.*

A man's destiny stands not in the future but in the past. That, rightly considered, is the most vital of all vital facts. Every child thus has a right to choose his own ancestors.   *Ibid., v. 4, p. 1.*

In the future we cannot but have faith —for all the hope of humanity must rest on that faith—that a new guiding impulse, reinforcing natural instinct and becoming in time an inseparable accompaniment of it, will lead civilized man on his racial course. Just as in the past the race has, on the whole, been moulded by a natural, and in part sexual, selection, that was unconscious of itself and ignorant of the ends it made towards, so in the future the race will be moulded by deliberate selection,

the creative energy of Nature becoming self-conscious in the civilized brain of man.
Ibid., p. 2.

Nature accords the male but a secondary and comparatively humble place in the home, the breeding-place of the race; he may compensate himself if he will, by seeking adventure or renown in the world outside. The mother is the child's supreme parent.   *Ibid., p. 3.*

Oliver Ellsworth
(1745-1807)
Chief Justice, U.S. Supreme Court

(Jeffersonians are the) apostles of anarchy, bloodshed and atheism.
Quoted by the Beards, Basic History of the United States, 209.

Richard T. Ely
(1854-1943)
American economist

We have among us a class of mammon worshippers, whose one test of conservatism, or radicalism, is the attitude one takes with respect to accumulated wealth. Whatever tends to preserve the wealth of the wealthy is called conservatism, and whatever favors anything else, no matter what, they call socialism.
Quoted by the Beards, Basic History of the United States, 394-5.

Ralph Waldo Emerson
(1803-1882)
American essayist, poet, Unitarian minister

That is the vice,—that no one feels himself called to act for man, but only as a fraction of man.
The Reformer, lecture, Boston, January 25, 1841.

The Americans have many virtues, but they have no Faith and Hope. I know no two words whose meaning is more lost sight of. We use these words as if they were as obsolete as Selah and Amen. . . . The Americans have no faith. They rely on the power of the dollar; they are deaf to a sentiment. They think you may talk the north wind down as easily as raise society; and no class more faithless than the scholars or intellectual men.   *Ibid.*

What is a man born for but to be a Reformer, a Remaker of what man has made; a renouncer of lies; a restorer of truth and good, imitating that great Nature which embosoms us all, and which sleeps no moment on an old past, but every hour repairs herself, yielding us every morning a new day, and with every pulsation a new life?   *Ibid.*

Every great and commanding moment in the annals of the world is the triumph of some enthusiasm.   *Ibid.*

Of course, conservatism always has the worst of the argument, is always apologizing, pleading a necessity, pleading that to change would be to deteriorate; it must saddle itself with the mountainous load of the violence and vice of society, must deny the possibility of good, deny ideas, and suspect and stone the prophet; whilst innovation is always in the right, triumphant, attacking and sure of final success.
The Conservative, lecture, Boston, May 9, 1841.

Conservatism stands on man's confessed limitations; reform on his indisputable infinitude; conservatism on circumstances; liberalism on power; one goes to make an adroit member of the social frame; the other to postpone all things to the man himself.   *Ibid.*

We are reformers in spring and summer; in autumn and winter we stand by the old; reformers in the morning, conservers at night. Reform is affirmative, conservatism negative; conservatism goes for comfort, reform for truth.   *Ibid.*

Conservatism makes no poetry, breathes no prayer, has no invention; it is all memory. Reform has no gratitude, no prudence, no husbandry.   *Ibid.*

Conservatism never puts the foot forward; in the hour when it does that, it is not establishment, but reform. Conservatism tends to universal seeming and treachery, believes in a negative fate; believes that men's temper governs them; that for me, it avails not to trust in principles; they will fail me; I must bend a little; it distrusts Nature; it thinks there is a general law without a particular application—law for all that does not include any one.   *Ibid.*

Great men are they who see that spiritual is stronger than material force, that thoughts rule the world.
Phi Beta Kappa Address, July 18, 1876.

A chief event of life is the day in which we have encountered a mind that startled us.   *Character.*

We boast our emancipation from many superstitions; but if we have broken any idols, it is through a transfer of idolatry.   *Ibid.*

What have I gained, that I no longer immolate a bull to Jove or to Neptune, or a mouse to Hecate; that I do not tremble before the Eumenides, or the Catholic Purgatory, or the Calvinistic Judgment Day—if I quake at opinion, the public opinion, as we call it; or at the threat of assault, or contumely, or bad neighbours, or poverty, or mutilation, or at the rumour of revolution, or of murder? If I quake, what matters it what I quake at? *Ibid.*

No facts to me are sacred; none are profane. *Circles, 1841.*

Beware when the great God lets loose a thinker on this planet. Then all things are at risk. It is as when a conflagration has broken out in a great city, and no man knows what is safe, or where it will end. . . . The very hopes of man, the thoughts of his heart, the religion of nations, the manners and morals of mankind are all at the mercy of a new generalization.
Ibid.

If there be a country which cannot stand any one of these tests,—a country where knowledge cannot be diffused without perils of mob law and statute law; where speech is not free; where the post-office is violated, mail-bags opened and letters tampered with; where public debts and private debts outside of the State are repudiated; where liberty is attacked in the primary institution of social life; where the position of the white woman is injuriously affected by the outlawry of the black woman; where the arts, such as they have, are all imported, having no indigenous life; where the laborer is not secured in the earnings of his own hands; where suffrage is not free or equal;—that country is, in all these respects, not civil, but barbarous; and no advantages of soil, climate or coast can resist these suicidal mischiefs.
Civilization, 1862.

Morality and all the incidents of morality are essential; as, justice to the citizen, and personal liberty. Montesquieu says: "Countries are well cultivated, not as they are fertile, but as they are free"; and the remark holds not less but more true of the culture of men than of the tillage of land. And the highest proof of civility is that

the whole public action of the State is directed on securing the greatest good of the greatest number. *Ibid.*

The farmer imagines power and place are fine things. But the President has paid dear for his White House. It has commonly cost him all his peace, and the best of his manly attributes. To preserve for a short time so conspicuous an appearance before the world, he is content to eat dust before the real masters who stand behind the throne. *Compensation.*

The proverbs of all nations, which are always the literature of reason, are the statements of an absolute truth without qualification. Proverbs, like the sacred books of each nation, are the sanctuary of the intuitions. That which the droning world, chained to appearances, will not allow the realist to say in his own words, it will suffer him to say in proverbs without contradiction. And this law of laws, which the pulpit, the senate and the college deny, is hourly preached in all markets and workshops by flights of proverbs, whose teaching is as true and as omnipresent as that of birds and flies. *Ibid.*

Fear is an instructor of great sagacity and the herald of all revolutions. One thing he teaches, that there is rottenness where he appears. He is a carrion crow, and though you see not well what he hovers for, there is death somewhere. Our property is timid, our laws are timid, our cultivated classes are timid. Fear for ages has boded and mowed and gibbered over government and property. That obscene bird is not there for nothing. He indicates great wrongs which must be revised.
Ibid.

No man thoroughly understands a truth until he has contended against it. *Ibid.*

The history of persecution is a history of endeavors to cheat nature, to make water run up hill, to twist a rope of sand. *Ibid.*

The martyr cannot be dishonored. Every lash inflicted is a tongue of fame; every prison a more illustrious abode; every burned book or house enlightens the world; every suppressed or expunged word reverberates through the earth from side to side. Hours of sanity and consideration are always arriving to communities, as to individuals, when the truth is seen and the martyrs are justified. *Ibid.*

There is always some leveling circumstance that puts down the overbearing. . . . Though no checks to a new evil appear, the checks exist, and will appear. . . . The dice of God are always loaded.* *Ibid.*

If a man owns land, the land owns him. *Conduct of Life.*

Poverty demoralizes. *Ibid.*

Intellect annuls fate. So far as a man thinks, he is free. *Ibid.*

Leave this hypocritical prating about the masses. Masses are rude, lame, unmade, pernicious in their demands and influence, and need not to be flattered but schooled. *Ibid.*

All conservatives are such from personal defects. They have been effeminated by position of nature, born halt and blind, through luxury of their parents, and can only, like invalids, act on the defensive. *Ibid.*

Politics is a deleterious profession, like some poisonous handicrafts. Men in power have no opinions, but may be had cheap for any opinion, for any purpose. *Ibid.*

___
* See Einstein, Letter to Max Born.

The god of the cannibals will be a cannibal, of the crusaders a crusader, and of the merchants a merchant. *Ibid.*

The highest virtue is always against the law. *Ibid.*

The high prize of life, the crowning fortune of a man, is to be born with a bias to some pursuit, which finds him in employment and happiness. *Ibid.*

Every revolution was once a thought in one man's mind, and when the same thought occurs to another man, it is the key to that era. *History.*

Every reform was once a private opinion, and when it shall be a private opinion again it will solve the problem of the age. *Ibid.*

God offers to every mind its choice between truth and repose. Take which you please; you can never have both. Between these, as a pendulum, man oscillates. He in whom the love of repose predominates will accept the first creed, the first philosophy, the first political party he meets— most likely his father's. He gets rest, commodity, and reputation; but he shuts the door of truth. He in whom the love of truth predominates will keep himself aloof from all moorings, and afloat. He will abstain from dogmatism, and recognize all the opposite negations between which, as walls, his being is swung. He submits to the inconveniences of suspense and imperfect opinion, but he is a candidate for truth, as the other is not, and respects the highest law of his being. *Intellect.*

You must pay for conformity . . . There is alive somewhere a man whose honesty reaches to this point also, that he shall not kneel to false gods, and, on the day when you meet him, you sink into the class of counterfeits. *English Traits, 1856.*

A nation never falls but by suicide.
Journals (1861-1865).

You shall have joy, or you shall have power, said God; you shall not have both.
Ibid.

Democracy becomes a government of bullies tempered by editors. *Ibid.*

All the religion we have is the ethics of one or another holy person. *Ibid.*

Every actual State is corrupt. Good men must not obey the laws too well. What satire on government can equal the severity of censure conveyed in the word *politics* which now for ages has signified *cunning,* intimating that the State is a trick? *Ibid.*

To aim to convert a man by miracles is a profanation of the soul. *Nature.*

The first and last lesson of religion is, "The things that are seen are temporal; the things that are not seen are eternal." It puts an affront upon nature. *Ibid.*

Truth is our element of life; yet if a man fasten his attention on a single aspect of truth and apply himself to that alone for a long time, the truth becomes distorted, and not itself, but falsehood; . . . How wearisome the grammarian, the phrenologist, the political or religious fanatic, or indeed any possessed mortal, whose balance is lost by the exaggeration of a single topic. It is incipient insanity.
The Over-Soul.

This is the history of governments—one man does something which is to bind another. A man who cannot be acquainted with me, taxes me; looking from afar at me ordains that a part of my labor shall go to this or that whimsical end—not as I, but as he happens to fancy. Behold the consequence. Of all debts men are least willing to pay the taxes. What a satire is this on government! Everywhere they think they get their money's worth, except in these.
Politics.

The less government we have the better —the fewer laws, and the less confided power. The antidote to this abuse of formal government is the influence of private character, the growth of the individual; the appearance of the principal to supersede the proxy; the appearance of the wise man; of whom the existing government is, it must be owned, but a shabby imitation. *Ibid.*

A man has a right to be employed, to be trusted, to be loved, to be revered. *Ibid.*

The spirit of our American radicalism is destructive and aimless; it is not loving; it has no ulterior and divine ends; but is destructive only out of hatred and selfishness. *Ibid.*

The conservative party, composed of the most moderate, able and cultivated part of the population, is timid and merely defensive of property. It vindicates no right, it aspires to no real good, it brands no crime, it proposes no generous policy, it does not build, nor write, nor cherish the arts, nor foster religion, nor establish schools, nor encourage science, nor emancipate the slave, nor befriend the poor, or the Indian, or the immigrant. *Ibid.*

From neither party (American radical or conservative), when in power, has the world any benefit to expect in science, art or humanity, at all commensurate with the resources of the nation. *Ibid.*

Every violation of truth is not only a sort of suicide in the liar, but is a stab at the health of human society. *Prudence.*

Every hero becomes at last a bore.
Representative Men, 1850.

As there is a science of stars, called astronomy; a science of quantities, called mathematics; a science of qualities, called chemistry; so there is a science of sciences —I call it Dialectic—which is the Intellect discriminating the false and the true.

Ibid.

Who shall forbid a wise scepticism, seeing that there is no practical question on which anything more than an approximate solution can be had? *Ibid.*

Remember the open question between the present order of "competition," and the friends of "attractive and associated labour." The generous minds embrace the proposition of labour shared by all; it is the only honesty; nothing else is safe. *Ibid.*

The wise sceptic is a bad citizen; no conservative; he sees the selfishness of property and the drowsiness of institutions.

Ibid.

Great believers are always reckoned infidels, impracticable, fantastic, atheistic and really men of no account . . . He had rather stand charged with the imbecility of scepticism, than with untruth. *Ibid.*

Society everywhere is in conspiracy against the manhood of every one of its members. Society is a joint-stock company, in which the members agree, for better securing of his bread to each shareholder, to surrender the liberty and culture of the eater. *Self-Reliance.*

An institution is the lengthened shadow of one man; as, the Reformation, of Luther; Quakerism, of Fox; Methodism, of Wesley; Abolition, of Clarkson. *Ibid.*

What will you have? quoth God; pay for it and take it. *Ibid.*

If you put a chain around the neck of a slave, the other end fastens itself around your own. *Ibid.*

Whoso would be a man, must be a nonconformist. He who would gather immortal palms must not be hindered by the name of goodness, but must explore if it be goodness. Nothing is at last sacred but the integrity of your own mind. Absolve you to yourself, and you shall have the suffrage of the world . . . I am ashamed to think how easily we capitulate to badge and names, to large societies and dead institutions. *Ibid.*

For nonconformity the world whips you with its displeasure. And therefore a man must know how to estimate a sour face. The bystanders look askance on him in the public street or in the friend's parlor. If this aversion had its origin in contempt and resistance like his own he might well go home with a sad countenance; but the sour faces of the multitude, like their sweet faces, have no deep cause, but are put on and off as the wind blows and a newspaper directs. *Ibid.*

A foolish consistency is the hobgoblin of little minds, adored by little statesmen and philosophers and divines. With consistency a great soul has simply nothing to do. He may as well concern himself with his shadow on the wall. Speak what you think now in hard words and tomorrow speak what tomorrow thinks in hard words again, though it contradict every thing you said today.—"Ah, so you shall be sure to be misunderstood." Is it so bad then to be misunderstood? Pythagoras was misunderstood, and Socrates, and Jesus, and Luther, and Copernicus, and Galileo, and Newton, and every pure and wise spirit that ever took flesh. To be great is to be misunderstood.

Ibid.

I hope in these days we have heard the last of conformity and consistency. Let the words be gazetted and ridiculous henceforward. Instead of the gong for dinner, let us hear a whistle from the Spartan fife. Let us never bow and apologize more. *Ibid.*

The reliance on Property, including the reliance on governments which protect it, is the want of self-reliance. *Ibid.*

Society never advances. *Ibid.*

The virtue in most request is conformity. Self-reliance is its aversion. *Ibid.*

As man's prayers are a disease of the will, so are their creeds a disease of the intellect. *Ibid.*

We are afraid of truth, afraid of fortune, afraid of death, and afraid of each other. *Ibid.*

Men have looked away from themselves and at things so long, that they have come to esteem what they call the soul's progress, namely, the religious, learned and civil institutions, as guards of property, and they deprecate assaults on these, because they feel them to be assaults on property. They measure their esteem of each other by what each has, and not by what each is. But a cultivated man becomes ashamed of his property, ashamed of what he has, out of new respect for his being. *Ibid.*

Men love to wonder, and that is the seed of science. *Society and Solitude, 1870.*

The first farmer was the first man, and all historic nobility rests on possession and use of land. *Ibid.*

I hate this shallow Americanism which hopes to get rich by credit, to get knowledge by raps on midnight tables, to learn the economy of the mind by phrenology, or skill without study, or mastery without apprenticeship. *Ibid.*

The philosopher and lover of man have much harm to say of trade; but the historian will see that trade was the principle of liberty; that trade planted America and destroyed Feudalism; that it makes peace and keeps peace, and it will abolish slavery. We complain of its oppression of the poor, and of its building up a new aristocracy on the ruins of the aristocracy it destroys. But the aristocracy of trade has no permanence, is not entailed, was the result of toil and talent, the result of merit of some kind, and is continually falling, like the waves of the sea, before new claims of the same sort. *The Young American, 1844.*

There is a crack in everything God has made. *The Works of Ralph Waldo Emerson, 1913.*

We seldom see anybody who is not uneasy or afraid to live. *Ibid.*

The new statement is always hated by the old, and to those living in the old, comes like an abyss of scepticism. *Ibid.*

To educate the wise man, the State exists; and with the appearance of the wise man, the State expires. *Ibid.*

Though loath to grieve
The evil time's sole patriot,
I cannot leave
My honied thought
For the priest's cant,
Or statesman's rant.
Ode (inscribed to W. H. Channing), 1847.

Things are in the saddle,
And ride mankind. *Ibid.*

The philosopher, the poet, or the religious man, will, of course, wish to cast his vote with the democrat. *Quoted by the Beards, Basic History of the United States.*

The castle which conservatism is set to defend is the actual state of things, good and bad.

Quoted by A. Schlesinger, Jr., N. Y. Times Magazine, March 4, 1956.

There is a time in every man's education when he arrives at the conviction that envy is ignorance; that imitation is suicide; that he must take himself for better for worse as his portion; that though the wide universe is full of good, no kernel of nourishing corn can come to him but through his toil bestowed on that plot of ground which is given to him to till. The power which resides in him is new in nature, and none but he knows what that is which he can do, nor does he know until he has tried.

Quoted by D. D. Runes, Treasury of Philosophy.

We are of different opinions at different hours, but we always may be said at heart to be on the side of truth.

Every man is a consumer and ought to be a producer.

Most men have bound their eyes with one or another handkerchief, and attached themselves to some one of these communities of opinion. This conformity makes them not false in a few particulars, authors of a few lies, but false in all particulars.

It is easy in the world to live after the world's opinion; it is easy in solitude to live after your own; but the great man is he who in the midst of the crowd keeps with perfect sweetness the independence of solitude.

What forests of laurel we bring, and the tears of mankind, to those who stand firm against the opinions of their contemporaries! The measure of a master is his success in bringing all men 'round to his opinion twenty years later.

The law of self-preservation is surer policy than any legislation can be.

Literary history and all history is a record of the power of minorities of one.

In every work of genius we recognize our own rejected thoughts: they come back to us with a certain alienated majesty. Great works of art have no more affecting lesson for us than this. They teach us to abide by our spontaneous impression with good humored inflexibility the most when the whole cry of voices is on the other side.

Prayer as a means to effect a private end is meanness and theft.

Let me admonish you, first of all, to go alone; to refuse the good models, even those sacred in the imagination of men. . . . Imitation cannot go above its model. The imitator dooms himself to hopeless mediocrity. The inventor did it because it was natural to him, and so in him it has a charm. In the imitator, something else is natural, and he bereaves himself of his own beauty to come short of another man's.

The god of Victory is said to be one-handed, but Peace gives victory to both sides.

Fame is proof that people are gullible.

Other world! There is no other world! Here or nowhere is the whole fact.

All life is an experiment. The more experiments you make the better.

The two parties which divide the state, the party of conservatives and the party of innovators, are very old, and have disputed the possession of the world ever since it was made.

A man must consider what a rich realm he abdicates when he becomes a conformist.

Robert Emmet
(1778-hanged 1803)
Irish nationalist, rebel

A band of patriots, mindful of their oath, and faithful to their engagement as United Irishmen, have determined to give freedom to their country, and a period to the long career of English oppression . . . Countrymen of all descriptions, let us act with union and concert; . . . let each man do his duty, and remember that during public agitation, inaction becomes a crime.
Proclamation, 1803.

I have but one request to ask at my departure from this world—it is the charity of silence. Let there be no inscription on my tomb. Let no man write my epitaph.
Speech in the dock, 1803.

I am here ready to die. I am not allowed to vindicate my character; and when I am prevented from vindicating myself, let no man dare calumniate me. Let my character and motives repose in obscurity and peace, till other times and other men can do them justice.   *Ibid.*

When my country takes her place among the nations of the earth, *then* shall my character be vindicated, *then* may my epitaph be written. *Ibid., final sentence.**

Friedrich Engels**
(1820-1895)
German Socialist, associate of Marx

The organization of the working class as a class by means of the trade unions . . . is the very essential point, for this is the real class organization of the proletariat, in which it carries on its daily struggle with capital, in which it trains itself.
Letter, 1875.

The times of that superstition which attributed revolutions to the ill will of a few agitators have long passed away. Everyone knows nowadays that wherever there is a revolutionary convulsion, there must be some social want in the background, which is prevented, by outworn institutions, from satisfying itself.   *1851.*

History is about the most cruel of all goddesses.

The exploited and oppressed class—the proletariat—cannot attain its emancipation from the sway of the exploiting and ruling class—the bourgeoisie—without, at the same time, and once and for all, emancipating society at large from all exploitation, oppression, class distinction and class struggles.
Preface to The Communist Manifesto.

The basic thought underlying the Manifesto is as follows: The method of production and the organization of social life inevitably arising therefrom constitute in every historical epoch the foundation upon which is built the political and intellectual history of that epoch.
Ibid., German edition of 1883.

All history has been a history of class struggles, of struggles between dominated and dominating classes at various stages of social development.   *Ibid.*

Look at the Paris Commune. That was the dictatorship of the proletariat.
Introduction to Marx's Civil War in France, 1871.

Recently, however, since Bismarck adopted state ownership, a certain spurious socialism has made its appearance . . .

---

* Eleven or more versions of the speech exist, some cut by enemies, some "improved" by friends.
** For collaboration with Marx, *see* Marx.

which declares that *all* taking over by the state, even the Bismarckian kind, is in itself socialistic. If, however, the taking over of the tobacco trade by the state was socialistic, Napoleon and Metternich would rank among the founders of Socialism.

Anti-Duehring.

Since the emergence in history of the capitalist mode of production, the taking over of all means of production by society has often been dreamed of by individuals as well as by whole sects, more or less vaguely and as an ideal of the future. But it could not become possible, it could only become a historical necessity, when the material conditions for its realization come into existence. Like every other social advance, it becomes realizable not through the perception that the existence of classes is in contradiction with justice, equality, etc., not through the mere will to abolish these classes, but through ·ertain new economic conditions. *Ibid.*

The working class seizes state power, and then transforms the means of production into state property. But in doing this, it puts an end to itself as the working class, it puts an end to all class diffe ences and class antagonisms, it puts an end also to the state as a state. *Ibid.*

As soon as there is no longer any class of society to be held in subjection, . . . there is nothing more to be repressed, and a special repressive force, a state, is no longer necessary. *Ibid.*

The first act in which the state really comes forward as the representative of society as a whole—the seizure of the means of production in the name of society—is at the same time its last independent act as a state. *Ibid.*

Government over persons is replaced by the administration of things and the direc- tion of the processes of production. The state is not "abolished," it withers away.

Ibid.

Force, however, plays another role (other than that of a diabolical power) in history, a revolutionary role; that, in the words of Marx, it is the midwife of every old society which is pregnant with the new.

Ibid.; quoted by Lenin, State and Society.

Tradition is a great retarding force, the *vis inertiae* of history.

Socialism, Utopian and Scientific, 1891.

By it (Historical Materialism) History for the first time was placed on its real foundation: the obvious fact, hitherto totally neglectec, that first of all men must eat, drink and have shelter and clothing and therefore work, before they can struggle for supremacy or devote themselves to politics, religion, philosophy, etc., this fact at last found historical recognition. *Ibid.*

The materialist conception of history starts from the principle that production of the means to support human life, and with production the exchange of products, is the basis of every social order; that in every society which has appeared in history the distribution of the products, and with it the division of society into classes and orders, is determined by what is produced and how it is produced, and how the product is exchanged. According to this conception, the ultimate causes of all social changes and political revolutions are to be sought not in the minds of men, in their increasing insight into external truth and justice, but in changes in the mode of production and exchange; they are to be sought not in the *philosophy* but in the *economics* of the epoch concerned. *Ibid.*

According to the materialist conception of history the determining element in history is *ultimately* the production and re-production in real life. More than this neither Marx nor I have ever asserted. If therefore somebody twists this into the statement that the economic element is the *only* determining one, he transforms it into a meaningless, abstract and absurd phrase. *Ibid.*

Competition is the most extreme expression of that war of all against all which dominates modern middle-class society.
The Condition of the Working Class in England.

This struggle for existence—which in extreme cases is a life and death struggle—is waged not only between different classes of society but also between individuals within these social groups. Everybody competes in some way against everyone else and consequently each individual tries to push aside anyone whose existence is a barrier to his own advancement. *Ibid.*

What the proletarian needs he can obtain only from the bourgeoisie, which is protected in its monopoly by the power of the State. The proletarian is, therefore, in law and in fact, the slave of the bourgeoisie, which can decree his life or death. *Ibid.*

As, therefore, the "state" is only a transitory institution which is used in the struggle, in the revolution, in order to hold down one's adversaries by force, it is pure nonsense to talk of a "free people's state"; so long as the proletariat still uses the state, it does not use it in the interests of freedom but in order to hold down its adversaries, and as soon as it becomes possible to speak of freedom, the state as such ceases to exist.
Letter to August Bebel, March 18, 1875.

Just as Darwin discovered the law of evolution in organic nature, so Marx dis-

covered the law of evolution in human history.
Funeral oration for Marx, March 17, 1883.

He discovered the simple fact (heretofore hidden beneath ideological excrescences) that human beings must have food and drink, clothing and shelter, first of all, before they can interest themselves in politics, science, art, religion, and the like. This implies that the production of the immediately requisite material means of subsistence, and therewith the extant economic developmental phase of a nation or an epoch, constitute the foundation upon which the State institutions, the legal outlooks, the artistic and even the religious ideas, of those concerned, have been built up. It implies that these latter must be explained out of the former, whereas usually the former have been explained as issuing from the latter. *Ibid.*

For Marx, science was a motive force of history, was a revolutionary force. *Ibid.*

Before all else, Marx was a revolutionist. To collaborate in one way or another in the overthrow of capitalist society and of the State institutions created by that society; to collaborate in the freeing of the modern proletariat, which he was the first to inspire with a consciousness of its needs, with a knowledge of the conditions requisite for its emancipation—this was his true mission in life. Fighting was his natural element. Few men have fought with so much passion, tenacity and success. *Ibid.*

Because he was an active revolutionist, Marx was the best hated and most calumniated man of his time. He was shown the door by various governments, republican as well as absolute. Bourgeois, ultra-democrats as well as conservatives vied with one another in spreading libels about him. Yet he has gone down to his death honored, loved and mourned by millions of revolutionary workers all over the world, in Europe and Asia as far eastward as the Siberian mines, and in America as far westward as California. I can boldly assert that, while he may still have many adversaries, he has now hardly one personal enemy.

His name and his works will live through the centuries. *Ibid.*

Men make their own history, whatever its outcome may be, in that each person follows his own consciously desired end; and it is precisely the resultant of these many wills operating in different directions and of their manifold effects upon the outer world that constitutes history.

Ludwig Feuerbach and the Outcome of German Classical Philosophy, 1886. Quoted by Wilson, To the Finland Station.

A people that wants to win its independence cannot limit itself to ordinary means of war. Uprisings in mass, revolutionary war, guerillas everywhere, that is the only means through which a small nation can get the better of a big one, a less strong army be put in a position to resist a stronger and better organized one.

England—Parliament

That every Englishman, who is imprisoned by any authority whatsoever, has an undoubted right, by his agents, or friends, to apply for, and obtain a writ of *habeas corpus,* in order to procure his liberty by due course of law.

Resolution adopted by the House of Lords, February 26, 1704; and later by Commons.

En-lai
See Chou En-lai

Book of Enoch

Woe unto you who build your palaces with the sweat of others! Each stone, each brick of which it is built is a sin!
Second Century, B.C.

Epictetus
(c. 1st Century, A.D.)
Greek Stoic philosopher in Rome

Only the educated are free. *Discourses.*

Is freedom anything else than the right to live as we wish? Nothing else.
Ibid., Bk. 2.

No man who is in fear, or sorrow, or turmoil, is free, but whoever is rid of sorrows and fears and turmoils, that man is by the selfsame course rid also of slavery. *Ibid.*

Here is the beginning of philosophy:
    a recognition of the conflicts between men,
    a search for their cause,
    a condemnation of mere opinion . . .
and the discovery of a standard of judgment.
Ibid.

He is free who lives as he chooses.
Ibid., Book 4.

No bad man is free. *Ibid.*

Of all existing things some are in our power, and others are not in our power. In our power are thought, impulse, will to get and will to avoid, and, in a word, everything which is our own doing. Things not in our power include the body, property, reputation, office, and, in a word, everything which is not our own doing. Things in our power are by nature free, unhindered, untrammelled; things not in our power are weak, servile, subject to hindrance, dependent on others. *Encheiridion, or Manual.*

As a mark is not set up for men to miss it, so there is nothing intrinsically evil in the world.   *Ibid.*

Epicurus
(342?-270 B.C.)
Greek philosopher

Justice is never anything in itself, but in the dealings of men with one another in any place whatever and at any time. It is a kind of compact not to harm or be harmed.   *Principle Doctrines, xxxiii.*

XLIII. The love of money, if unjustly gained, is impious, and, if justly, shameful; for it is unseemly to be merely parsimonious even with justice on one's side.
      Fragments, Vatican Collection.

LVIII. We must release ourselves from the prison of affairs and politics.   *Ibid.*

LXVII. A free life cannot acquire many possessions, because this is not easy to do without servility to mobs or monarchs, yet it possesses all things in unfailing abundance; and if by chance it obtains many possessions, it is easy to distribute them so as to win the gratitude of neighbors.
                              Ibid.

Only the just man enjoys peace of mind.

Thus that which is the most awful of evils, death, is nothing to us, since when we exist there is no death, and when there is death we do not exist.

Desiderius Erasmus
(1465-1536)
Dutch scholar

By identifying the new learning with heresy, you make orthodoxy synonymous with ignorance.

When faith is in the mouth rather than in the heart, when the solid knowledge of Sacred Scripture fails us, nevertheless by terrorization we drive men to believe what they do not believe, to love what they do not love, to know what they do not know. That which is forced cannot be sincere, and that which is not voluntary cannot please Christ.
    From Roland H. Bainton's "Hunted Heretic."

Luther was guilty of two great crimes —he struck the Pope in his crown, and the monks in their belly.   *Colloquies.*

War is delightful to those who have had no experience of it.

The merchants, however, are the biggest fools of all. They carry on the most sordid business and by the most corrupt methods. Whenever it is necessary, they will lie, perjure themselves, steal, cheat, and mislead the public. Nevertheless, they are highly respected because of their money. There is no lack of flattering friars to kowtow to them and call them Right Honorable in public. The motive of the friars is clear enough: they are after some of the loot.
    The Praise of Folly, translated by Leonard F. Dean, 1946. (The goddess Folly is speaking.)

They may attack me with an army of six hundred syllogisms; and if I do not recant, they will proclaim me a heretic.   *Ibid.*

Next to the theologians in happiness are those who commonly call themselves "the religious" and "monks." Both are complete misnomers, since most of them stay as far away from religion as possible, and no people are seen more often in public. *Ibid.*

Finally, if the Supreme Pontiffs, who are the vicars of Christ, tried to imitate His life, His poverty, labors, teaching, His cross and contempt for life; if they stopped to consider the meaning of the title of Pope, a Father, or the epithet Most Holy, who on earth would be more overwhelmed? Who would purchase that office at the cost of every effort? Who would retain it by the sword, by poison, and by every other way?
Ibid.

If wisdom should come to Popes, what comforts it would deprive them of!
Ibid.

The only things left are the weapons and sweet benedictions of which Paul speaks. The popes are sufficiently generous with these. I mean the interdictions, excommunications, re-excommunications, anathematizations, pictured damnations, and the terrible bolt of the papal bull, which by a flicker hurls the souls of men to the depths of hell.
Ibid.

A prince who is about to assume control of the state must be advised at once that the main hope of a state lies in the proper education of its youth. *Ibid.*

The prince should try to prevent too great an inequality of wealth. I should not want to see anyone deprived of his goods, but the prince should employ certain measures to prevent the wealth of the multitude being hoarded by a few. *Ibid.*

A good prince will tax as lightly as possible those commodities which are used by the poorest members of society; e.g., grain, bread, beer, wine, clothing, and all other staples without which human life could not exist. *Ibid.*

Great abundance of riches cannot be gathered and kept by any man without sin.

Joannes Scotus Erigena
(815?-877?)
Irish-Scottish philosopher in France

The end of all motion is its beginning; for it terminates at no other end save its own beginning from which it begins to be moved and to which it tends ever to return, in order to cease and rest in it.

In the intelligible world this law is the fundamental principle of all the sciences, that is of the seven liberal arts. Grammar begins with the letter, from which all writing is derived and into which it is all resolved. Rhetoric begins with a definite question, from which the whole argument is derived and to which it returns. Dialectic begins with essence, from which the whole argument is derived and to which it returns. Arithmetic begins with unity, from which all numbers are developed and into which they are resolved. Geometry begins with the point from which all figures are developed and into which they are resolved. Astronomy begins with the moment from which all motion is developed and into which it is resolved. Metaphysics begins and ends with God.

Patrologia Latina, translated by Dr. G. B. Burch, quoted by Anne Freemantle in The Age of Belief.

Thomas Erskine
(1750-1823)
Lord chancellor of England

The Press, my Lords, is one of our great out-sentries; if we remove it, if we hood-

wink it, if we throw it in fetters, the enemy may surprise us.
Rex v. Paine, 22 Howell, 1792.

Thus I have maintained by English history, that in proportion as the Press has been free, English Government has been secure.   *1792.*

Men cannot communicate their free thoughts to one another with a lash held over their heads. It is the nature of everything that is great and useful, both in the animate and inanimate world, to be wild and irregular—and we must be content to take them with the allies which belong to them, or live without them.   *Ibid.*

The press must be free; it has always been so and much evil has been corrected by it. If Government finds itself annoyed by it, let it examine its own conduct and it will find the cause.   *Ibid.*

What is the fairest fruit of the English Tree of Liberty? The security of our rights and of the law, and that no man shall be brought to trial where there is prejudice against him.
Defense of Thomas Paine, December 20, 1792.

When men can freely communicate their thoughts and their sufferings, real or imaginary, their passions spend themselves in air, like gunpowder scattered upon the surface —but pent up by terrors, they work unseen, burst forth in a moment, and destroy everything in their course. Let reason be opposed to reason, and argument to argument, and every good government will be safe.
Ibid.

Essex
See Robert Devereux

Euripides
(484-406 B.C.)
Greek tragic dramatist

This is true liberty, when freeborn men, Having to advise the public, may speak free.   *Suppliants.*

A state has no worse foe than a tyrant, under whom can be no common laws; but one ruler, keeping the law in his own hands, so that equality perishes.   *Ibid.*

Only an upright heart and a clear conscience, they say, give a man strength to wrestle with life; while those whose hearts are evil, sooner or later—as a young girl sees the truth in her glass—so they, when Time holds up his mirror, find their own sin revealed.
Hippolytus, translated by Philip Vellacott.

He was a wise man who originated the idea of God.

Bergen Evans
(1904-1978)
American writer

There is no necessary connection between the desire to lead and the ability to lead, and even less to the ability to lead somewhere that will be to the advantage of the led. . . . Leadership is more likely to be assumed by the aggressive than by the able, and those who scramble to the top are more often motivated by their own inner torments than by any demand for their guidance.
The Spoor of Spooks and Other Nonsense, 1954.

Legislators who are of even average intelligence stand out among their colleagues.

Many Governors and Senators have to be seen to be believed. A cultured college president has become as much a rarity as a literate newspaper publisher. A financier interested in economics is as exceptional as a labor leader interested in the labor movement. For the most part our leaders are merely following out in front; they do but marshal us the way that we are going.
Ibid.

Wainwright Evans
See Ben B. Lindsey

William T. Evjue
(b. 1882)
American editor

The media of communications on which people most depend for facts and information—the press, the movies, radio and television—have been used to reduce the people to conformity and dumb acquiescence. The press, movies, radio and television bear a large share of the responsibility for the climate of fear and hysteria which has enveloped our country and which has become such a threat to our freedom.
Editorial, Capital Times, Madison, Wisconsin.

Exupéry
See Saint-Exupéry

Fabian Society

The Fabians are associated for spreading the following opinions held by them, and discussing their practical consequences.
That, under existing circumstances, wealth cannot be enjoyed without dishonor, or foregone without misery.
That it is the duty of each member of the State to provide for his or her **own** wants by his or her own Labour.
Fabian Tract No. 2 of 1884.

Denis Fahey, C.S.Sp.
(b. 1883)
Irish prelate

Liberalism is a sin . . . Liberalism is a sin of the mind and a supreme insult to God.
The Social Rights of Our Divine Lord Jesus Christ, Browne & Nolan, Dublin.

Governments rule in the name of the people, and in the name of the people the most incredible and fantastic injustices are imposed. . . . Look, for one example, at the evil resulting from the freedom of the press. How many souls are corrupted by reading bad newspapers and the immoral and impious publications which abound in every country? How many souls are eternally lost on account of the protection by which all literary, scientific and other productions are lethally surrounded? How many souls at this moment damned would not be so, if this accursed freedom of the press did not exist? It is the same with freedom of teaching.
Ibid.

James A. Farley
(1888-1976)
American politician

As Maine goes, so goes Vermont.
Comment, election day, 1936.

James T(homas) Farrell
(1904-1979)
American writer

The danger of censorship in cultural media increases in proportion to the degree to which one approaches the winning of a mass audience.

New Leader, November 5, 1949.

Literature is not, in itself, a means of solving problems; these can be solved only by action, by social and political action.

Harper's Magazine, October, 1954.

The powers of the individual will are weaker than the forces of social circumstance. *Ibid.*

Neither man nor God is going to tell me what to write.

Quoted by Murray Kempton, columnist, N. Y. Post.

William Faulkner
(1897-1962)
American author, Nobel prize, 1950

Our tragedy today is a general and universal physical fear so long sustained by now that we can even bear it . . . The basest of all things is to be afraid.

Nobel Prize acceptance speech, Stockholm, December, 1950.

I believe that man will not merely endure; he will prevail. He is immortal, not because he alone among creatures has an inexhaustible voice, but because he has a soul, a spirit capable of compassion and sacrifice and endurance. *Ibid.*

This was the American Dream: a sanctuary on the earth for individual man: a condition in which he could be free not only of the old established closed-corporation hierarchies of arbitrary power which had oppressed him as a mass, but free of that mass into which the hierarchies of church and state had compressed and held

him individually thralled and individually impotent.

On Privacy. Harper's Magazine, July, 1955.

We will have to choose not between color nor race nor religion nor between East and West either, but simply between being slaves and being free. And we will have to choose completely and for good; the time is already past now when we can choose a little of each, a little of both. We can choose a state of slavedom, and if we are powerful enough to be among the top two or three or ten, we can have a certain amount of license—until someone more powerful rises and has us machine-gunned against a cellar wall.

Harper's Magazine, June, 1956.

We cannot choose freedom established on a hierarchy of degrees of freedom, on a caste system of equality like military rank. We must be free not because we claim freedom, but because we practice it . . . *Ibid.*

Systems political or religious or racial or national—will not just respect us because we practice freedom, they will fear us because we do. *Ibid.*

No man can write who is not first a humanitarian. *Time, February 25, 1957.*

Elie Faure
(1875-1937)
French art critic, historian

The stamping out of the artist is one of the blind goals of every civilization. When a civilization becomes so standardized that the individual can no longer make an imprint on it, then that civilization is dying. The "mass mind" has taken over and another set of national glories is heading for history's scrap heap.

Quoted in Forbes Magazine.

Francisco Ferrer

(1859-executed 1909)

Spanish freethinker

Idols are created when men are praised, and this is very bad for the future of the human race.

Will, written on the wall of his cell in Barcelona prison, on the eve of his execution.

I desire that on no occasion, whether near or remote, nor for any reason whatsoever, shall demonstrations of a political or religious character be made before my remains, as I consider the time devoted to the dead would be better employed in improving the condition of the living, most of whom stand in great need of this.

Ibid.

Let no more gods or exploiters be served. Let us learn rather to love one another.

Ibid.

We must destroy all which in the present school answers to the organization of constraint, the artificial surroundings by which children are separated from nature and life, the intellectual and moral discipline made use of to impose ready-made ideas upon them, beliefs which deprave and annihilate natural bent.

The Modern School.

Governments have ever been careful to hold a high hand over the education of the people. They know, better than anyone else, that their power is based almost entirely on the school. Hence, they monopolize it more and more.

Ibid.

Oh, what have people not expected, what do they not expect still, from education! The majority of progressive men expect everything from it, and it is only in these later days that some begin to understand that it offers nothing but illusions. . . . the organization of the school, far from spreading the ideal which we imagined, has made education the most powerful means of enslavement in the hands of the governing powers today.

Ibid.

The school imprisons children physically, intellectually, and morally, in order to direct the development of their faculties in the paths desired. It deprives them of contact with nature, in order to model them after its own pattern.

Ibid.

All the value of education rests in respect for the physical, intellectual and moral will of the child. Just as in science no demonstration is possible save by facts, just so there is no real education save that which is exempt from all dogmatism, which leaves to the child itself the direction of its effort, and confines itself to the seconding of that effort.

Ibid.

I detest the shedding of blood; I labor for the regeneration of humanity, and I love the good for the good's own sake. That which violence wins for us today another act of violence may wrest from us tomorrow.

Henry Fielding

(1707-1754)

English novelist, essayist, dramatist

Let no man be sorry he has done good, because others have done evil! If a man has acted right, he has done well, though alone; if wrong, the sanction of all mankind will not justify him.

Dorothy Canfield Fisher

(1879-1958)

American writer

Freedom is not worth fighting for if it means no more than license for everyone to get as much as he can for himself. And freedom *is* worth fighting for. Because it does mean more than unrestricted grabbing. He saw in imagination those young faces looking up at him attentively, and told them, "Laugh in the faces of the Fascist priests who chant the new Black Mass, when they tell you boys and girls that democratic government means nothing but license for the money-getters."

Seasoned Timber, 1939.

John Arbuthnot Fisher

(1841-1920)

British admiral

You're the sailor who understands war. Kill your enemy or be killed yourself. I don't blame you for this submarine business. I'd have done the same thing myself, only our idiots in England wouldn't believe it when I told 'em.

Letter to Admiral von Tirpitz, March, 1916, disclosed by G. S. Viereck.

The supremacy of the British navy is the best security for the peace of the world . . . If you rub it in, both at home and abroad, that you are ready for instant war, with every unit of your strength in the first line and waiting to be first in, and hit your enemy in the belly and kick him when he is down, and boil your prisoners in oil (if you take any) and torture his women and children, then people will keep clear of you.

Written before 1914.

Vardis Fisher

(1895-1968)

American educator, writer

Do people love truth? On the contrary, mankind has employed its subtlest ingenuity and intelligence in efforts to evade or conceal it . . . Do human beings love justice? The sordid travesties in our courts year after year suggest that they love justice only for themselves. Do they love peace? Can anyone seriously ask the question? Do they love freedom? Only for those who share their views. Love of peace, freedom, justice, truth—this is a myth that has been created by the folk mind, and if the artist does not look behind the myth to the reality he will indeed wander amid the phantoms which he creates. *God or Caesar?*

Bradley A. Fiske

(1854-1942)

American admiral, inventor

Long, continuous periods of peace and prosperity have always brought about the physical, mental and moral deterioration of the individual.

John Fiske

(1842-1901)

American philosopher, historian

The persecuting spirit has its origin morally in the disposition of man to domineer over his fellow creatures; intellectually, in the assumption that one's own opinions are infallibly correct.

Lord Edward Fitzgerald*

(1763-1798)

Irish revolutionist

In the coffee houses and playhouses,

* Irish rebel; died in prison from gunshot wound resisting arrest.

every man calls the other *camarade, frère,* and with a stranger immediately begins, *"Ah, nous sommes tous frères, tous hommes; nos victoires sont pour vous, pour tout le monde."* ("Ah, we are all brothers, all men; our victories are for you, for all the world.")
Letter to mother describing Paris, 1792, after the victory of Jemappes.

F. Scott Fitzgerald
(1896-1940)
American novelist

The victor belongs to the spoils.
The Beautiful and Damned, 1921.

George Fitzhugh
(1806-1881)
Southern economist

We warn the North that every one of the leading abolitionists is agitating the negro slavery question merely as a means to attain their ulterior ends . . . a surrender to Socialism and Communism—to no private property, no church, no law; to free love, free lands, free women and free children.
From a book published in 1857; quoted by Charles A. Madison, Critics and Crusaders.

Gustave Flaubert
(1821-1880)
French novelist

Nothing great is ever done without fanaticism. Fanaticism is religion: and the eighteenth century *philosophes* who decried the former actually overthrew the latter.
The Selected Letters of Flaubert.

Fanaticism is faith, the essence of faith, active faith, the faith that works miracles. Religion is a relative conception, a thing invented by man—an idea, in sum; the other is a feeling. What has changed on earth is the dogmas, the *stories* of Vishnu, Ormuzd, Jupiter, Jesus Christ. But what has never changed is the amulet, the sacred springs, the votive offerings, etc., the brahmins, the santons, the hermits—in a word the belief in something superior to life and the need to put one's self under the protection of this force.   *Ibid.*

What artists we should be if we had never read, seen or loved anything that was not beautiful; if from the outset some guardian angel of the purity of our pens had kept us from all contamination; if we had never known fools or read newspapers.
Letter to Louise Colet

The principal thing in this world is to keep one's soul aloft.
This Week, November 3, 1957.

ABSINTHE: Extra-violent poison. One glass and you're dead. Newspaper men drink it as they write their copy.
Dictionary of Accepted Ideas.

PRINT: To see one's name in print!—some people commit a crime for no other reason.   *Ibid.*

John Fletcher
(1579-1625)
English dramatist

Speak boldly, and speak truly,
Shame the devil.
Wit Without Money, act 4.

Abraham Flexner
(1866-1959)
American educator, author

Comfort, opportunity, number, and size, are not synonymous with civilization.
Universities, 1930.

[251]

No nation is rich enough to pay for both war and civilization. *Ibid.*

We must not overlook the important role that extremists play. They are the gadflies that keep society from being too complacent, or self-satisfied; they are, if sound, the spearhead of progress.

John Florio
(1553-1625)
English writer, translator, lexicographer

Who will not suffer labor in this world, let him not be born.
N. Y. Times, Labor Day, 1957.

The Flushing Remonstrance

Therefore, if any of these said persons (Quakers, Jews, Turks and Egyptians) come in love unto us, we cannot, in conscience, lay hands upon them, but give them free egresse and regresse into our town and houses, as God shall persuade our consciences. And in this we are true subjects both of Church and State, for we are bounde by the law of God and men to doe good unto all men and evil to noe one.
To Governor Stuyvesant, December 27, 1657.

Ferdinand Foch
(1851-1929)
French marshal

Victory is a thing of the will.
Message to Marshal Joffre, 1914.

This is not Peace. This is an Armistice for twenty years.
Quoted by Winston Churchill, The Gathering Storm.

A lost battle is a battle one thinks one has lost. *Principes de Guerre.*

The military mind always imagines that the next war will be on the same lines as the last. That never has been the case and never will be. One of the great factors in the next war will obviously be aircraft. The potentialities of aircraft attack on a large scale are almost incalculable.

Our peace must be a peace of victors, not of the vanquished.

My right has been rolled up; my left has been driven back; my center has been smashed. I have ordered an advance on all fronts.
(an attribution or a paraphrase; various versions exist.)

Fontaine
See la Fontaine

Bernard Le Bovier de Fontenelle
(1657-1757)
French writer

The centuries put no natural difference between men. Nor does climate which is too much alike in Greece, Italy and France to make any sensible difference between the Greeks, the Latins, and ourselves . . . Behold, then, all are perfectly equal, Athenians and Moderns, Greeks, Latins, and Frenchmen.
Digression on the Ancients and the Moderns, 1688.

Henry Ford
(1863-1947)
American industrialist

We want to get the boys out of the trenches.
Statement to press, November, 1915, explaining the purpose of the Ford Peace Ship. Ford did not add "by Christmas."

History is more or less bunk.[*]

Court record, Chicago Tribune libel case, 1919, quoted by Samuel T. Williamson, Saturday Review, January 22, 1955.

Along about April 1, 1913, we first tried the experiment of an assembly line. *1922.*

Labor unions are the worst thing that ever struck the earth because they take away a man's independence.

From booklet distributed to Ford workmen during CIO organization drive, 1936; Time, August 20, 1945.

The voice of dissent must be heard.

From his will; quoted by Mary McCarthy, The Listener, May 14, 1953.

Money is like an arm or leg—use it or lose it. *Forbes Magazine.*

The question, "Who ought to be boss?" is like asking "Who ought to be the tenor in the quartet?" Obviously, the man who can sing tenor. *Ibid.*

There will never be a system invented which will do away with the necessity for work.

The workingmen have been exploited all the way up and down the line by employers, landlords, everybody.

Gold is the most useless thing in the world. I am not interested in money but in the things of which money is merely a symbol.

It is all one to me if a man comes from Sing Sing or Harvard. We hire a man, not his history.

---

[*] "History is a fraud, agreed upon"—Napoleon. "That huge Mississippi of falsehood called history"—Matthew Arnold.

Capital punishment is as fundamentally wrong as a cure for crime as charity is wrong as a cure for poverty.

Thinking is the hardest work there is, which is the probable reason why so few engage in it.

John Fortescue

(1394-1476)

First English constitutional lawyer, writer

O king ruling politically, rule your people also regally when the case requires, for not all cases can be embraced by the statutes and customs of your realm, and thus the remaining cases are left to your discretion; moreover, always rule all criminal matters at your will, and moderate or remit all penalties, so long as you can do this without harm to your subjects or offence against the customs and statutes of your realm. Equity, too, is left to your wisdom, lest the rigour of the words of the law, confounding its intention, injure the common good. *De Natura Legis Naturae.*

The king of England cannot at his will change the laws of his kingdom, for he rules his people by a principate not only regal, but also political. If he ruled them by a regal principate only, he could change the laws of his realm and also impose tallages and other burdens on them without consulting them; and this kind of lordship is denoted by the Civil Laws when they say, "What has pleased the prince has the force of law." But the case is very different when a king rules his people politically, since he can neither change the laws without the consent of his subjects, nor burden his subjects against their will with strange impositions; thus his people enjoy its property under the rule of the laws which it desires, and it is not despoiled by its king nor by anyone else.

De Laudibus Legum Angliae.°

Charles Fourier
(1772-1837)
French socialist

Up to the present time politicians and philosophers have not dreamed of rendering industry attractive; to enchain the mass to labor, they have discovered no other means, after slavery, than the fear of want and starvation.

The present social order is a ridiculous mechanism, in which portions of the whole are in conflict and acting against the whole. We see each class in society desire, from interest, the misfortune of the other classes, placing in every way individual interest in opposition to public good.

Jay Fox
American libertarian

Every attempt to gag the free expression of thought is an unsocial act, a crime against society. That is why judges and juries who try to enforce such laws make themselves ridiculous.

Liberty and the Great Libertarians, edited by Charles T. Sprading.

Why does the burglar use a gag? . . . He knows that he cannot convince you by argument that he is entitled to the goods and that it is really to your best interest to pass them over to him. Capitalism holds up the toilers; it robs them of their labor and is enjoying life to its fullest on the result of

---

° Quoted from "Medieval Political Ideas," by Ewart Lewis.

its plunder. Naturally it doesn't want to be deprived of its special privilege, therefore it puts the gag of the law in the mouth of anyone who attempts to make an outcry.

Ibid.

Anatole France (né Jacques-Anatole Thibault)
(1844-1924)
French novelist, critic

Burn, burn all the books which teach hatred! Exalt labor and love! Let us create rational human beings, capable of crushing under foot the futile magnificence of barbaric glories, and of resisting those bloody ambitions of nationalism and imperialism which have crushed their brothers.

Speech, Tours, August, 1919.

It is almost impossible systematically to constitute a natural moral law. Nature has no principles. She furnishes us with no reason to believe that human life is to be respected. Nature, in her indifference, makes no distinction between good and evil.

Ibid.

If it were absolutely necessary to choose, I would rather be guilty of an immoral act than of a cruel one. *Ibid.*

Religion has done love a great service by making it a sin.

What is called the triumph of Christianity is more accurately the triumph of Judaism, and to Israel fell the singular privilege of giving a god to the world. *Epigrams.*

So long as society is founded on injustice, the function of the laws will be to defend and sustain injustice. And the more unjust they are the more respectable they will seem. *Ibid.*

Crime will last as long as old and gloomy humanity. But the number of criminals has diminished with the number of the wretched. The slums of the great cities are the feeding-grounds of crime. *Ibid.*

If you have a fresh view or an original idea you will surprise the reader. And the reader doesn't like being surprised. He never looks into history for anything but the stupidities he knows already. If you try to instruct him, you only humiliate him and make him angry. Do not try to enlighten him. He will only cry out that you insult his beliefs.

I take you all to witness, all of you famous imposters, you forgers of all time, you egregious liars, distinguished tricksters, notorious creators of fictitious errors and illusions; you whose time-honored frauds have enriched literature, sacred and profane, by so many dubious volumes, the authors of apocryphal Greek, Latin, Hebrew, Syrian and Chaldean writings which have so long deceived learned and ignorant alike; you, false Pythagoras, false Hermes-Trismegistus, false Sanchoniathon, fallacious editors of the Orphic poems and the Sibylline Books; false Enoch, false Esdras, pseudo-Clement and pseudo-Timothy.

And you lord abbots who, to assure yourselves of the possession of your lands and privileges, forged in the reign of Louis IX the charters of Clotaire and Dagobert; and you, doctors of common law, who based the pretensions of the Holy See on a heap of sacred decretals composed by yourselves; and you, wholesale manufacturers of historical memoirs, Soulavie, Courchamps, Touchard-Lafosse, lying Weber, lying Bourienne; you sham executioners and sham police-agents, who wrote the sordid memoirs of Samson and Monsieur Claude; and you, Vrain-Lucas, who with your own hand traced a letter said to be written by Mary Magdalene, and a note from the Lord of Vercingetorix, I shall call you to witness; and you whose life was a work of simulations, lying Smerdis, lying Neros, lying Maid of Orleans, who would have deceived the very brothers of Joan of Arc; lying Martin Guerr, lying Demetrious and fictitious Dukes of Normandy.

I call you to witness, workers of spells, makers of miracles that seduced the mob: Simon the Magician, Apollonious of Tyana, Cagliostro, Comte de Saint-Germain; I call you to witness travelers returning from far-off countries, who had every facility for lying and took full advantage of it; you who beheld the Cyclops and the Laestrygones, the Magnetic Mountain, the Roe and the Fish-Bishop, and you, Sir John Mandeville, who saw in Asia devils vomiting fire; and you, makers of stories and fables and tales —Mother Goose, Tyl Eulenspiegel, Baron Munchausen! and you, chivalrous and picturesque Spaniards, most notable babblers, I call you to witness!—bear witness, all of you! You have not accumulated, in the long course of the centuries so many lies as Jean Coq and Jean Mouton read in their newspapers in a single day! And after that, how can we be surprised that they have so many bogies in their heads!

M. Bergeret in Paris, 1923.

To die for an idea is to place a pretty high price upon conjectures.

The Revolt of the Angels.

There is a certain impertinence in allowing oneself to be burned for an opinion.

Ibid.

People who have neither commerce or industry are not obliged to make war, but a business people is forced to adopt a policy of conquest. As soon as one of our industries fails to find a market for its products a war is necessary to open new outlets. In Third-Zealand we have killed two-thirds of the inhabitants in order to compel the remainder to buy our umbrellas and suspenders. *The Isle of Penguins.*

On croit mourir pour la patrie, on meurt pour des industriels. (You believe you are dying for the fatherland—you die for some industrialists.)

A people living under the perpetual menace of war and invasion is very easy to govern. It demands no social reforms. It does not haggle over expenditures on armaments and military equipment. It pays without discussion, it ruins itself, and that is an excellent thing for the syndicates of financiers and manufacturers for whom patriotic terrors are an abundant source of gain.

The divine law, promulgated amid fireworks in some Mt. Sinai, is never anything but the codification of human prejudice.

Free will is but an illusion.

St. Francis Xavier
(1506-1552)
Spanish Jesuit, missionary

You will generally find that everything is defiled with usurious contracts; that those very persons have got together the greater part of their money by sheer rapine, who nevertheless assert themselves so confidently to be pure from all contagion of unjust gain.
A.C.T.U. Labor Leader.

Francisco Franco
(1892-1975)
Spanish general, dictator

Strikes are a crime. . . . This is the law of jungles and primitive societies.
Time, May 21, 1951.

We have not tried to suppress true, legitimate liberty; on the contrary, we have tried to preserve it. We are for liberty, but liberty with order, the kind of liberty which will not threaten the basic principles of our nation, nor threaten its faith and unity.
Speech, Vitoria, August 9, 1953, reported by Richard Mowrer.

Democracy is not the mere formality of dropping a ballot in a wooden box or glass jar every four years. . . .
We abhor political parties. We are against political parties, and we have none.
Speech, Pamplona, 1953; quoted by Mowrer.

Felix Frankfurter
(1882-1965)
U.S. Supreme Court justice

Certainly the affirmative pursuit of one's convictions about the ultimate mystery of the universe and man's relation to it is placed beyond the reach of law. Government may not interfere with organized or individual expressions of belief or disbelief. Propagation of belief—or even of disbelief —in the supernatural is protected, whether in church or chapel, mosque or synagogue, tabernacle or meeting-house.
Majority decision, Jehovah's Witnesses case, 1940. Minersville School District v. Gobitis, 310 U.S. 586.

. . . to use loose language or undefined slogans that are part of the conventional give-and-take in our economic and political controversies—like "unfair" or "fascist" is not to falsify facts.
Cafeteria Emp. Union v. Angelos, 320 U.S. 293 (1943).

One who belongs to the most vilified and persecuted minority in history is not likely to be insensible to the freedoms guaranteed by our Constitution . . . But as judges we are neither Jew nor Gentile, neither Catholic nor agnostic. We owe equal attachment to the Constitution and are equally bound by our judicial obligations, whether we derive our citizenship from the earliest or the latest immigrants to these shores.

Dissent, W. Va. Board of Education v. Barnette, 319 U.S. 624, 647 (1943).

The great leaders of the American Revolution were determined to remove political support from every religious establishment. . . . So far as the state was concerned, there was to be neither orthodoxy nor heterodoxy. And so Jefferson and those who followed him wrote guaranties of religious freedom into our constitutions. Religious minorities as well as religious majorities were to be equal in the eyes of the political state.

Ibid., at 653

It (government) is neither business nor technology nor applied science . . . (It is) one of the subtlest of the arts . . . since it is the art of making men live together in peace and with reasonable happiness.

Quoted by J. M. Brown, Saturday Review, October 30, 1954.

There is no inevitability in history except as men make it. *Ibid.*

A judge should be compounded of the faculties that are demanded of the historian and the philosopher and the prophet. The last demand upon him—to make some forecast of the consequences of his action—is perhaps the heaviest. To pierce the curtain of the future, to give shape and visage to mysteries still in the womb of time, is the gift of the imagination. It requires poetic sensibilities with which judges are rarely endowed and which their education does not normally develop. These judges must have something of the creative artist in

them; they must have antennae registering feeling and judgment beyond logical, let alone quantitative, proof.

Address; N. Y. Times Magazine, November 28, 1954.

The core of the difficulty is that there is hardly a question of any real difficulty before the Court that does not entail more than one so-called principle. Anybody can decide a question if only a single principle is in controversy. *Ibid.*

Freedom of the press is not an end in itself but a means to the end of a free society.

Pennekamp v. Florida, concurring opinion.

Benjamin Franklin
(1706-1790)
American scientist, diplomat, writer

Without freedom of thought there can be no such thing as wisdom, and no such thing as publick liberty, without freedom of speech; which is the right of every man, as far as by it he does not hurt and control the right of another: and this is the only check it ought to suffer, and the only bounds it ought to know.

Dogwood Papers, 1722 (at age of 16). Quoted by A. Schlesinger, Jr., N. Y. Post, January 15, 1956.

In those wretched countries where a man cannot call his tongue his own, he can scarce call anything his own. Whoever would overthrow the liberty of a nation must begin by subduing the freeness of speech; a thing terrible to publick traytors.

Ibid.

Printers are educated in the belief, that when men differ in opinion, both sides ought equally to have the advantage of being heard by the publick; and that when truth and error have fair play, the former is always an overmatch for the latter.

Apology for Printers, 1731. Quoted by Carl Van Doren, Benjamin Franklin.

If all printers were determined not to print anything till they were sure it would offend nobody, there would be very little printed.   *Ibid.*

I think vital religion has always suffered when orthodoxy is more regarded than virtue. The scriptures assure me that at the last day we shall not be examined on what we thought but what we did.

Letter to his father, 1738.

We must, indeed, all hang together, or most assuredly we shall all hang separately.

In Continental Congress, before signing of the Declaration of Independence, 1776.

It is a common observation here (Paris) that our cause is *the cause of all mankind,* and that we are fighting for their liberty in defending our own.

Letter to Samuel Cooper, 1777.

Liberté, egalité, fraternité.

Suggested to French leaders as a slogan.

I wish to see the discovery of a plan, that would induce and oblige nations to settle their disputes without cutting one another's throats. When will men be convinced, that even successful wars at length become misfortunes to those who unjustly commenc'd them, and who triumph'd blindly in their success, not seeing all the consequences.   *1780.*

I have never known a peace made, even the most advantageous, that was not censured as inadequate, and the makers condemned as injudicious or corrupt. "Blessed are the peacemakers" is, I suppose, to be understood in the other world; for in this they are frequently cursed.

Letter to John Adams, Passy, October 12, 1781.

I join with you most cordially in rejoicing at the return of peace. I hope it will be lasting, and that mankind will at length, as they call themselves reasonable creatures, have reason to settle their differences without cutting throats; for, in my opinion, there never was a good war or a bad peace.

Letter to Josiah Quincy, 1783.

God grant that not only the love of liberty but a thorough knowledge of the rights of man may pervade all the nations of the earth, so that a philosopher may set his foot anywhere on its surface and say: "This is my country."

Letter to David Hartley, December 4, 1789.

Our Constitution is in actual operation; everything appears to promise that it will last; but nothing in this world is certain but death and taxes.

Letter to M. Leroy, of the French Academy of Sciences, 1789.

I wish it (Christianity) were more productive of good works . . . I mean real good works . . . not holy-day keeping, sermon-hearing . . . or making long prayers, filled with flatteries and compliments despised by wise men, and much less capable of pleasing the Deity.

Works, Vol. VII, p. 75.

When a religion is good, I conceive it will support itself; and when it does not support itself, and God does not take care to support it so that its professors are obliged to call for help of the civil power, 'tis a sign, I apprehend, of its being a bad one.   *Ibid., Vol. XIII, p. 506.*

He who will introduce into public affairs the principles of primitive Christianity, will revolutionize the world.

He does not possess wealth; it possesses him.   *Poor Richard, 1734.*

Nine men in ten are suicides.
                         Ibid., 1749.

The way to see by Faith is to shut the eye of Reason.   *Ibid., 1758.*

When knaves fall out, honest men get their goods; when priests dispute, we come at the truth.   *Ibid.*

Lighthouses are more helpful than churches.

Abuses of the freedom of speech ought to be repressed; but to whom are we to commit the power of doing it?

Even peace may be purchased at too high a price.

A ploughman on his legs is higher than a gentleman on his knees.*

If we look back into history for the character of the present sects in Christianity, we shall find few that have not in their turns been persecutors, and complainers of persecution. The primitive Christians thought persecution extremely wrong in the Pagans, but practiced it on one another. The first Protestants of the Church of England blamed persecution in the Romish Church, but practiced it upon the Puritans. They found it wrong in Bishops, but fell into the practice themselves both here (England) and in New England.

There is no kind of dishonesty into which otherwise good people more easily and

---

* See Ibarruri, and F. D. Roosevelt for similar expressions.

frequently fall than that of defrauding the government.

Sir James (George) Frazer
(1854-1941)
Scottish anthropologist

The inconsistency of acting on two opposite principles, however it may vex the soul of the philosopher, rarely troubles the soul of the common man; indeed he is seldom even aware of it. His affair is to act, not to analyze the motives of his action. If mankind had always been logical and wise, history would not be a long chronicle of folly and crime.   *The Golden Bough.*

Frederick (II) the Great
(1712-1786)
King of Prussia

All religions must be tolerated . . . for . . . every man must get to heaven in his own way.
      In re the Catholic Schools, 1740.

Religion is the idol of the mob; it adores everything it does not understand.
      Letter to Voltaire, July 6, 1737.

The greatest and noblest pleasure which we have in this world is to discover new truths, and the next is to shake off old prejudices.
      N. Y. Times Book Review, February 20, 1955.

A man who seeks truth and loves it must be reckoned precious to any human society.

If I wished to punish a province, I would have it governed by philosophers.

I begin by taking. I shall find scholars afterwards to demonstrate my perfect right.

Philip M. Freneau

(1752-1832)

American poet, journalist, rebel

If to control the cunning of a knave,
Freedom respect, and scorn the name of
slave;
If to protest against a tyrant's laws,
And arm for vengeance in a rightful cause,
Be deemed Rebellion—'tis a harmless thing:
This bugbear name, like death, has lost its
sting.   *To the Americans, 1775.*

But this great lesson teach—that kings are
vain;
That warring realms to certain ruin haste,
That kings subsist by war, and wars are
waste:
So shall our nation, form'd on Virtue's plan,
Remain the guardian of the Rights of Man,
A vast Republic, fam'd through every clime,
Without a king, to see the end of time.
To a Republican, 1795.

Sigmund Freud *

(1856-1939)

*Austrian physician, founder
of psychoanalysis*

The bit of truth behind all this—one so
eagerly denied—is that men are not gentle,
friendly creatures wishing for love, who
simply defend themselves if they are attacked, but that a powerful measure of desire for aggression has to be reckoned as
part of their instinctual endowment.
Civilization and Its Discontents.

---

* "The Freudian theory is one of the most
important foundation stones for an edifice
to be built by future generations, the dwelling of a freer and wiser humanity"—Thomas
Mann, *N. Y. Times, June 21, 1939.*

Civilized society is perpetually menaced
with disintegration through this primary
hostility of men towards one another . . .
Ibid.

The tendency to aggression is an innate,
independent, instinctual disposition in man
. . . it constitutes the most powerful obstacle to culture.   *Ibid.*

And now, it seems to me, the meaning of
the evolution of culture is no longer a riddle
to us. It must present to us the struggle between Eros and Death, between the instincts of life and the instincts of destruction, as it works itself out in the human
species. This struggle is what all life essentially consists of and so the evolution of
civilization may be simply described as the
struggle of the human species for existence.
And it is this battle of the Titans that our
nurses and governesses try to compose with
their lullaby-song of Heaven!   *Ibid.*

So in every individual the two trends,
one towards personal happiness and the
other towards unity with the rest of humanity, must contend with each other.
Ibid.

I have no concern with any economic
criticism of the communistic system; but I
am able to recognize that psychologically it
is founded on an untenable illusion. By
abolishing private property one deprives
the human love of aggression of one of its
instruments; a strong one undoubtedly, but
assuredly not the strongest. It in no way
alters the individual differences in power
and influence which are turned by aggressiveness to its own use, nor does it change
the nature of the instinct in any way.
Ibid., Chapter 5.

The different religions have never overlooked the part played by the sense of guilt
in civilization. What is more, they come

forward with a claim . . . to save mankind from this sense of guilt, which they call sin.
Ibid.

Religion is comparable to a childhood neurosis.
Future of an Illusion, 1949, p. 92.

Neurosis seems to be a human privilege.
Moses and Monotheism.

Hatred for Judaism is at bottom hatred for Christianity.   *Ibid.*

The great majority of people have a strong need for authority which they can admire, to which they can submit, and which dominates and sometimes even ill-treats them. We have learned from the psychology of the individual whence comes this need of the masses. It is the longing for the father that lives in each of us from his childhood days, for the same father whom the hero of legend boasts of having overcome.   *Ibid.*

In popular language we may say that the ego stands for reason and sanity, in contrast to the id which contains untamed passions.
New Introductory Lectures on Psycho-analysis.

The doctrine is that the universe was created by a being similar to man, but greater in every respect, in power, wisdom, and strength of passion, in fact by an idealized superman.   *Ibid.*

This God-Creator is openly called Father. Psychoanalysis concludes that he really is the father, clothed in the grandeur in which he once appeared to the small child. The religious man's picture of the creation of the universe is the same as his picture of his own creation. . . . He therefore looks back on the memory-image of the overrated father of his childhood, exalts it into a

Deity, and brings it into the present and into reality. The emotional strength of this memory-image and the lasting nature of his need for protection are the two supports of his belief in God.   *Ibid.*

The contribution of psychoanalysis to science consists precisely in having extended research to the region of the mind. *Ibid.*

Religion is an attempt to get control over the sensory world, in which we are placed, by means of the wish-world which we have developed inside us as a result of biological and psychological necessities. But it cannot achieve its end. Its doctrines carry with them the stamp of the times in which they originated, the ignorant childhood days of the human race. Its consolations deserve no trust . . . If one attempts to assign to religion its place in man's evolution, it seems not so much to be a lasting acquisition, as a parallel to the neurosis which the civilized individual must pass through on his way from childhood to maturity.
Ibid., Chapter 7.

We may suppose that the final aim of the destructive instinct is to reduce living things to an inorganic state. For this reason we call it the *death instinct.*
An Outline of Psychoanalysis, 1949.

When the superego begins to be formed, considerable amounts of the aggressive instinct become fixated within the ego and operate there in a self-destructive fashion. This is one of the dangers to health to which mankind becomes subject on the path to cultural development. The holding back of aggressiveness is in general unhealthy and leads to illness.   *Ibid.*

Confession enters into analysis, as its introduction, as it were. But it is far from being the same thing as analysis, and it cannot serve to explain its effect. In con-

fession the sinner tells what he knows, in analysis the neurotic must tell more. Besides, we have no knowledge that the system of confession has developed the power to get rid of direct symptoms of illness.
Ibid.

Conflicts of interest between man and man are resolved, in principle, by the recourse to violence. It is the same in the animal kingdom, from which man can not claim exclusion; nevertheless men are also prone to conflicts of opinion, touching on occasion, the loftiest peaks of abstract thought, which seem to call for settlement by quite another method.

Letter to Albert Einstein (q.v.) written at the suggestion of the International Institute for Cultural Cooperation, September, 1932, published in Free World, 1933.

Now, for the first time, with the coming of weapons, superior brains began to oust brute force, but the object of the conflict remained the same; one party was to be constrained, by the injury done him or impairment of his strength, to retract a claim or a refusal. This end is most effectively gained when the opponent is definitely put out of action—in other words, is killed. This procedure has two advantages: the enemy cannot renew hostilities, and, secondly, his fate deters others from following his example. Moreover the slaughter of a foe gratifies an instinctive craving. *Ibid.*

We may define "right" (i.e., law) as the might of a community. Yet, it, too, is nothing else than violence . . . it is the communal, not individual, violence that has its way. *Ibid.*

There is but one sure way of ending war and that is the establishment, by common consent, of a central control which shall have the last word in every conflict of in-

terests. For this, two things are needed: first, the creation of such a supreme court of judicature; secondly, its investment with adequate executive force. Unless the second requirement be fulfilled, the first is unavailing. *Ibid.*

We assume that human instincts are of two kinds: those that conserve and unify, which we call "erotic" (in the meaning Plato gives to *Eros* in his *Symposium*), or else "sexual" (explicitly extending the popular connotation of "sex"); and, secondly, the instincts to destroy and kill, which we assimilate as the aggressive or destructive instincts. These are, as you perceive, the well-known opposites, Love and Hate. Transformed into theoretical entities, they are, perhaps, another aspect of those eternal polarities, attraction and repulsion, which fall within your province. *Ibid.*

There is no likelihood of our being able to suppress humanity's aggressive tendencies . . . Complete suppression of man's aggressive tendencies is not in issue; what we may try is to direct it into a channel other than that of warfare. *Ibid.*

That men are divided into leaders and the led is but another manifestation of their inborn and irremediable inequality . . . Men should be at greater pains than heretofore to form a superior class of independent thinkers, unamenable to intimidation and fervent in the quest of truth, whose function it would be to guide the masses dependent on their lead. There is no need to point out how little the rule of politicians and the Church's ban on liberty of thought encourage such a new creation. *Ibid.*

Why do we, you and I and many another, protest so vehemently against war, instead of just accepting it as another of life's importunities? For it seems a natural thing enough, biologically sound and practically unavoidable . . . The answer to my query may run as follows: Because every man has a right over his own life and war destroys lives that were full of promise; it forces the individual into situations that shame his manhood, obliging him to murder fellow men, against his will; it ravages material amenities, the fruits of human toil, and much besides. Moreover, wars, as now conducted, afford no scope for acts of heroism according to the old ideals and, given the high perfection of modern arms, war today would mean the sheer extermination of one of the combatants, if not of both. This is so true, so obvious, that we can but wonder why the conduct of war is not banned by general consent.   *Ibid.*

The neuroses (are) without exception disturbances of the sexual function.
                    Time, June 26, 1939.

The mind is an iceberg—it floats with only one-seventh of its bulk above water.
Quotation in N. Y. Times obituary, September 24, 1939.

The conscious mind may be compared to a fountain playing in the sun and falling back into the great subterranean pool of the subconscious from which it rises.
                              Ibid.

It is tragic when a man outlives his body.
                              Ibid.

The goal of all life is death.
N. Y. Times Magazine, May 6, 1956.

Demons do not exist any more than gods do, being only the products of the psychic activity of man.   *Ibid.*

Men are strong only so long as they represent a strong idea. They become powerless when they oppose it.   *Ibid.*

A neurosis is the result of a conflict between the ego and the id; the person is at war with himself. A psychosis is the outcome of similar disturbance in the relation between the ego and the outside world.*
                              Ibid.

Despite my 30 years of research into the feminine soul, I have not yet been able to answer . . . the great question that has never been answered: What does a woman want?
Quoted by Dr. Ernest Jones, The Life and Works of Sigmund Freud, Vol. 2.

Science is no illusion. But it would be an illusion to suppose that we could get anywhere else what it cannot give us.

The history of the world which is still taught to our children is essentially a series of race murders.

The very emphasis of the commandment: Thou shalt not kill, makes it certain that we are descended from an endlessly long chain of generations of murderers, whose love of murder was in their blood as it is perhaps also in ours.

Love cannot be much younger than the lust for murder.

Ernst Freund
(1863-1946)
American professor of law

The constitutional guaranty of freedom of speech and press and assembly demands the right to oppose all government and to argue that the overthrow of government cannot be accomplished otherwise than by force; and the statutes referred to, in so

---

* Regarding the terms Id, Ego and Superego, David Severn writes (*Time*, May 7, 1956): "Freud used understandable terms: *es, Ich,* and *Ueber-Ich*—literally translatable as the *it,* the *I* and the *beyond-I.*"

far as they deny these rights, should consequently be considered as unconstitutional.
Police Power, 1904.

Henry Clay Frick
(1849-1919)
American industrialist

He (Theodore Roosevelt) got down on his knees before us. We bought (him) and he did not stay bought.

A reference to the 1904 campaign fund, as quoted in the N. Y. Times. An uncensored version reads: We bought the s.o.b. but he didn't stay bought.

Erich Fromm
(b. 1900)
American psychoanalyst, author

Destructiveness is the outcome of unlived lives. *Escape from Freedom, 1941.*

The lust for power is not rooted in strength but in weakness. *Ibid.*

Human history begins with man's act of disobedience which is at the same time the beginning of his freedom and development of his reason.
Psychoanalysis and Religion, 1950.

In the 19th century the problem was that God was dead; in the 20th century the problem is that man is dead.
N. Y. Post, January 15, 1956.

The danger of the past was that men became slaves. The danger of the future is that men may become robots. True enough, robots do not rebel. But given man's nature, robots cannot live and remain sane.
Ibid.

Robert Frost
(1874-1963)
American poet

I never dared to be a radical when young For fear it would make me conservative when old. **Ten Mills.**

Freedom lies in being bold.
Quoted in Time.

Why abandon a belief merely because it ceases to be true. Cling to it long enough, and . . . it will turn true again, for so it goes. Most of the change we think we see in life is due to truths being in and out of favor. *The Churchman, April 1, 1956.*

James A(nthony) Froude
(1818-1894)
English historian, essayist

One lesson, and only one, history may be said to repeat with distinctness: that the world is built somehow on moral foundations; that in the long run it is well with the good; in the long run it is ill with the wicked. But this is no science; it is no more than the old doctrine taught long ago by the Hebrew prophets.
Ladies' Home Journal, March, 1957.

Wild animals never kill for sport. Man is the only one to whom the torture and death of his fellow creatures is amusing in itself.
Oceana.

St. Fulgentius
(468-533)
Early Christian bishop

Hold most firmly and doubt not that not all the pagans, but also all Jews, heretics, and schismatics who depart from their present life outside the Catholic Church, are

custom. This hereditary taint, due to the primeval barbarism of our race, and maintained by later influences, will have to be bred out of it before our descendants can rise to the position of free members of an intelligent society.

Léon Gambetta
(1838-1882)
French statesman

Clericalism is the enemy. (Also translated: Clericalism—there is the enemy!)
The Churchman, October 15, 1947.

No one can forbid us the future.
Inscription on monument, Paris.

Mohandas Karamchand Gandhi*
(1869-1948)
Hindu nationalist leader

Non-violence does not admit of running away from danger . . . Between violence and cowardly flight I can only prefer violence to cowardice.
The Gandhi Sutras: The Basic Teachings of Mahatma Gandhi, Devin-Adair, 1950.

Much that we hug today as knowledge is ignorance pure and simple . . . It makes the mind wander and even reduces it to a vacuity.   *Ibid.*

No work done by any man, however great, will really prosper unless it has a distinct religious backing. But what is Religion? I for one would answer: "Not the Religion you will get after reading all the scriptures of the world. Religion is not what is grasped by the brain, but a heart grasp."   *N. Y. Times, March 11, 1956.*

* "A naked fakir"—Winston Churchill, *London Tribune*, January 23, 1948.

Non-violence is the first article of my faith. It is also the last article of my creed.
Defense against charge of sedition, March 23, 1922.

In my humble opinion, non-cooperation with evil is as much a duty as is cooperation with good. But in the past, non-cooperation has been deliberately expressed in violence to the evildoer. I am endeavoring to show to my countrymen that violent non-cooperation only multiplies evil and that as evil can only be sustained by violence. Withdrawal of support of evil requires complete abstention from violence. Non-violence implies voluntary submission to the penalty for non-cooperation with evil.
Ibid.

The term *Satyagraha* was coined by me . . . in order to distinguish it from the movement then going on . . . under the name of Passive Resistance.
Its root meaning is "holding on to truth", hence truth-force. I have also called it love-force or soul-force. In the application of *Satyagraha*, I discovered in the earliest stages that pursuit of truth did not permit violence being inflicted on one's opponent, but that he must be weaned from error by patience and sympathy. For what appears truth to the one may appear to be error to the other. And patience means self-suffering. So the doctrine came to mean vindication of truth, not by the infliction of suffering on the opponent, but on one's self.

Ahimsa ("harmlessness" or non-violence) means the largest love. It is the supreme law. By it alone can mankind be saved. He who believes in non-violence believes in a living God.
True Patriotism: Some Sayings of Mahatma Gandhi, edited by S. Hobhouse, published by the Peace Pledge Union, London, 1939.

If blood be shed, let it be our blood. Cultivate the quiet courage of dying without killing. For man lives freely only by his readiness to die, if need be, at the hands of his brother, never by killing him. *Ibid.*

India must conquer her so-called conquerors, by love. For us patriotism is the same as the love of humanity. *Ibid.*

Non-violence and Truth (*Satya*) are inseparable and presuppose one another. There is no God higher than Truth. *Ibid.*

All humanity is one undivided and indivisible family, and each one of us is responsible for the misdeeds of all the others. I cannot detach myself from the wickedest soul. *Ibid.*

The *willing* sacrifice of the innocent is the most powerful answer to insolent tyranny that has yet been conceived by God or man. Disobedience to be "civil" must be sincere, respectful, restrained, never defiant, and it must have no ill-will or hatred behind it. Neither should there be excitement in civil disobedience, which is a preparation for mute suffering. *Ibid.*

I have an implicit faith . . . that mankind can only be saved through non-violence, which is the central teaching of the Bible, as I have understood the Bible. *Ibid.*

God has chosen me as His instrument for presenting non-violence to India for dealing with her many ills . . . Peace will not come out of a clash of arms, but out of justice lived and done by unarmed nations in the face of odds. *Ibid.*

To a man with an empty stomach food is God.
Quoted by Edgar Snow, Journey to the Beginning, Random House, 1958.

All amassing of wealth or hoarding of wealth above and beyond one's legitimate needs is theft. There would be no occasion for theft and no thieves if there were wise regulations of wealth, and social justice. *Ibid.*

Freedom is not worth having if it does not connote freedom to err.
Saturday Review, March 1, 1959.

Where there is fear, there is no religion.

My nationalism is intense internationalism. I am sick of the strife between nations or religions.

James A. Garfield
(1831-1881)
20th President of the United States

Next in importance to freedom and justice is popular education, without which neither freedom nor justice can be permanently maintained.
Letter date lined Mentor, Ohio, accepting nomination for President.

(The President) is the last person in the world to know what the people really want and think.

My God! What is there in this place that a man should ever want to get into it?
A reference to the Presidency; Time, April 24, 1950.

A pine bench, with Mark Hopkins at one end of it and me at the other, is a good enough college for me! (Another version: "My ideal would be a log with a student at one end of it and Mark Hopkins on the other.") *Attributed; address, 1871.*

The combined power of rebellion, Catholicism, and whiskey.
Letter, 1876, referring to Tilden backers; Caldwell, James Abram Garfield, p. 251.

All free governments are party-governments.

House of Representatives, January 18, 1878.

Real political issues cannot be manufactured by the leaders of political parties. The real political issues of the day declare themselves, and come out of the depths of that deep which we call public opinion.

Speech, Boston, September 10, 1878.

A law is not a law without coercion behind it.

In the long, fierce struggle for freedom of opinion, the Press, like the Church, counted its martyrs by thousands.

I am trying to do two things—dare to be a radical, and not a fool; which, if I may judge by the exhibition around me, is a matter of no small difficulty.

Ideas are the great warriors of the world, and a war that has no idea behind it, is simply a brutality.

Whoever controls the volume of money in any country is absolute master of all industry and commerce.

Whatever helps a nation can justly afford should be generously given to aid the states in supporting common schools, but it would be unjust to our people and dangerous to our institutions to apply any portion of revenues of the nation or of the States to the support of sectarian schools.

All free governments are managed by the combined wisdom and folly of the people.

Giuseppe Garibaldi
(1807-1882)
Italian patriot

The Vatican is a dagger in the heart of Italy.   *Quoted by Mussolini.*

Masonry being the oldest bulwark of liberty and justice, and therefore the true antagonist of the papacy, which is the antithesis of progress and civilization, I implore all my brothers of all the Italian lodges to assist the poor Romans, oppressed by the immoral domination of the harsh enemy of Italy, and of humanity.

In the midst of Italy, at its heart, there is a cancer called Popery,—an imposture called Popery. Yes, young men, we still have a formidable enemy, the more formidable because it exists among the ignorant classes, where it rules by falsehood.

Address to the students of the University of Pavia.

I offer neither pay, nor quarters, nor provisions; I offer hunger, thirst, forced marches, battles and death. Let him who loves his country in his heart and not with his lips only, follow me.°

Quoted by G. M. Trevelyan, Garibaldi's Defense of the Roman Republic, p. 231.

William Lloyd Garrison
(1805-1879)
American abolitionist, editor

Our country is the world—our countrymen are all mankind.

Motto of The Liberator.

° The original of Winston Churchill's "I have nothing to offer but blood, toil, tears and sweat."

Quoted in *Reformers and Rebels:* "What I have to offer you is fatigue, danger, struggle, death . . . forced marches, dangerous watchposts, and the continual struggle with the bayonet against batteries; those who love freedom and their country may follow me," as Garibaldi's call for volunteers for the liberation of Italy.

I determined, at all hazard, to lift up the standard of emancipation in the eyes of the nation, within sight of Bunker Hill, and in the birth-place of liberty. That standard is now unfurled; and long may it float, un-hurt by the spoliations of time or the missiles of a desperate foe; yea, till every chain be broken, and every bondman set free! Let Southern oppressors tremble; let their secret abettors tremble; let their Northern apologists tremble; let all the enemies of the persecuted blacks tremble.

The Liberator, first issue, January 1, 1831.

I am aware that many object to the severity of my language; but is there no cause for severity? I will be harsh as truth, and as uncompromising as justice. On this subject I do not wish to think, or speak, or write, with moderation. No! no! Tell a man whose house is on fire to give a moderate alarm; tell him to moderately rescue his wife from the hands of the ravisher; tell the mother to gradually extricate her babe from the fire into which it has fallen; but urge me not to use moderation in a cause like the present. *Ibid.*

I am in earnest. I will not equivocate—I will not excuse—I will not retreat an inch —AND I WILL BE HEARD. The apathy of the people is enough to make every statue leap from its pedestal and to hasten the resurrection of the dead. *Ibid.*

Cost what it may, every slave on the American soil must be liberated from his chains. Nothing is to be put in competition, on the score of value, with the price of his liberty; for whatever conflicts with the rights of man must be evil, and therefore intrinsically worthless. *The Liberator.*

It (slavery) has exercised absolute mastery over the American Church. In her skirts it found "the blood of the souls of the poor innocents." With the Bible in their hands, her priesthood have attempted to prove that slavery came down from God out of heaven. They have become slaveholders and dealers in human flesh.

Ibid.

If the State cannot survive the anti-slavery agitation, then let the State perish. If the Church must be cast down by the strugglings of Humanity to be free, then let the Church fall, and its fragments be scattered to the four winds of heaven, never more to curse the earth. If the American Union cannot be maintained, except by immolating human freedom on the altar of tyranny, then let the American Union be consumed by a living thunderbolt, and no tear shed over its ashes. If the Republic must be blotted out from the roll of nations, by proclaiming liberty to the captives, then let the Republic sink beneath the waves of oblivion . . . *Ibid.*

The Party or Sect that will suffer by the triumph of justice cannot exist with safety to mankind. The State that cannot tolerate universal freedom must be despotic; and no valid reason can be given why despotism should not at once be hurled to the dust. *Ibid.*

The Church that is endangered by the proclamation of eternal truth, and that trades in slaves and souls of men, is "the habitation of devils, and the hold of every foul spirit." *Ibid.*

There must be no compromise with slavery—none whatever. Nothing is gained, everything is lost, by subordinating principle to expediency. *Ibid.*

The apologist for oppression becomes himself the oppressor. To palliate crime is to be guilty of its perpetration. To ask for a postponement of the case, till a more convenient season, is to call for a suspension of the moral law, and to assume that it is right to do wrong, under present circumstances. *Ibid.*

Nothing can take precedence of the question of liberty. No interest is so momentous as that which involves "the life of the soul"; no object so glorious as the restoration of a man to himself. *Ibid.*

He who is for forcibly stopping the mouth of his opponent, or for burning any man at the stake, or thrusting him into prison, or exacting a pecuniary fine from him, or impairing his means of procuring an honest livelihood, or treating him scornfully, on account of his peculiar view on any subject, whether relation to God, man (or sex), to time or eternity, is under the dominion of a spirit of ruffianism or cowardice, or animated by that fierce intolerance which characterized Saul of Tarsus in his zeal to exterminate the heresy of Christianity. *Free Speech and Free Inquiry.*

God never made a tyrant, nor a slave. *Address, April 15, 1865, at flag-raising exercises, Fort Sumter.*

If our Constitution does not guarantee freedom for all, it is not a Constitution I can subscribe to . . . And now, let me give the sentiment which has been, and ever will be, the governing passion of my soul: Liberty for each, for all, for ever. *Ibid.*

He who opposes the public liberty overthrows his own. *William Lloyd Garrison: The Story of His Life, p. 200.*

There is no safety where there is no strength; no strength without Union; no Union without justice; no justice where faith and truth are wanting. The right to be free is a truth planted in the hearts of men. *Ibid.*

Resolved: That the compact which exists between the North and the South is the covenant with death and an agreement with hell, involving both parties in atrocious criminality, and should be immediately annulled. *Written for and adopted by the Anti-Slavery Society, 1843.*

When I look at these crowded thousands, and see them trample on their consciences and the rights of their fellowmen at the bidding of a piece of parchment, I say, my curse on the Constitution of the United States.

Has not the experience of two centuries shown that gradualism in theory is perpetuity in practice? Is there an instance, in the history of the world, where slaves have been educated for freedom by their taskmasters?

With reasonable men, I will reason; with humane men I will plead; but to tyrants I will give no quarter, nor waste arguments where they will certainly be lost.

No person shall rule over me with my consent. I will rule over no man.

Enslave the liberty of but one human being and the liberties of the world are put in peril.

Slavery will not be overthrown without excitement, a most tremendous excitement.

Gasset
See Ortega y Gasset

Paul Gauguin
(1848-1903)
French painter

Art is either a plagiarist or a revolutionist. *James Huneker, The Pathos of Distance.*

Gaulle
See de Gaulle

Théophile Gautier
(1811-1872)
French poet, novelist, critic

All passes. Art alone
    Enduring stays to us;
The Bust outlasts the throne,—
    The Coin, Tiberius.
Ars Victrix, a translation, or "imitation", by Austin Dobson.

Emile Gauvreau
(1891-1961)
American newspaper editor

Careers, reputations, friendships, life-long labors; the sanctity of homes; confidences in business; errors long atoned for; feuds long buried; the guarded secrets of the heart; innocent pleasures, loyalties—all the things that hitherto were respected and honored in the society of men, this monster (the press) violated, ripped up, disgorged, blasted, and threw, mangled and bleeding, to the scavenging rabble, that fed ravenously on it, and clamored always for more.
Quoted in Editor & Publisher, September 10, 1932.

J. Geddes
British glassworks owner

As far as I can see, the greater amount of education which a part of the working class has employed for some years past, is an evil. It is dangerous because it makes them independent.   *1865.*

George III
(1738-1820)
King of England

Knavery seems to be so much the striking feature of its (America's) inhabitants that it may not in the end be an evil that they will become aliens to this kingdom.
                    1782.

I desire what is good; therefore, every one who does not agree with me is a traitor.

David Lloyd George
See Lloyd George

Henry George
(1839-1897)
American economist, reformer, champion of the single tax

The association of poverty with progress is the great enigma of our times—it is the riddle which the Sphinx of fate puts to our civilization, and which, not to answer, is to be destroyed.
Progress and Poverty, 1879.

So long as all the increased wealth which modern progress brings, goes but to build up great fortunes, to increase luxury, and make sharper the contest between the House of Have and the House of Want, progress is not real and cannot be permanent.   *Ibid.*

There is but one way to remove an evil —and that is, to remove its cause. Poverty deepens as wealth increases, and wages are forced down while productive power grows, because land, which is the source of all wealth and the field of all labor, is monopolized. To extirpate poverty, to make wages what justice demands they should be, the full earnings of the laborer, we must therefore substitute for the individual ownership of land a common ownership. Nothing will go to the cause of the evil—in nothing else is there the slightest hope.

This, then, is the remedy for the unjust

and unequal distribution of wealth apparent in modern civilization, and for all the evils which flow from it:

We must make land common property.

Ibid.

The law of society is, each for all, as well as all for each.

Ibid.

It is not from top to bottom that societies die; it is from bottom to top.

Ibid.

Poverty is the openmouthed relentless hell which yawns beneath civilized society. And it is hell enough.

Ibid.

What I. therefore, propose, as the simple yet sovereign remedy, which will raise wages, increase the earnings of capital, extirpate pauperism, poverty, give remunerative employment to whoever wishes it, afford free scope to human powers, lessen crime, elevate morals, taste, and intelligence, purify government and carry civilization to yet nobler heights, is—to appreciate rent by taxation.

Ibid.

What has destroyed every previous civilization has been the tendency to the unequal distribution of wealth and power. This same tendency, operating with increasing force, is observable in our civilization today, showing itself in every progressive community, and with greater intensity the more progressive the community.

Ibid.

If, while there is yet time, we turn to Justice and obey her, if we trust Liberty and follow her, the dangers that now threaten must disappear, the forces that now menace will turn to agencies of elevation. Think of the powers now wasted; of the infinite fields of knowledge yet to be explored; of the possibilities of which the wondrous inventions of this century give us but a hint. With want destroyed, with greed changed to noble passions, with

the fraternity that is born of equality taking the place of the jealousy and fear that now array men against each other, with mental power loosened by conditions that give to the humblest comfort and leisure; who shall measure the heights to which our civilization may soar?

Ibid.

Our boasted freedom necessarily involves slavery, so long as we recognize private property in land. Until that is abolished, Declarations of Independence and Acts of Emancipation are in vain. So long as one man can claim the exclusive ownership of the land from which other men must live, slavery will exist, and as material progresses on, must grow and deepen!

Ibid.

The truth is, and from this truth there can be no escape, that there is and can be no just title to an exclusive possession of the soil, and that private property in land is a bold, bare, enormous wrong, like that of chattel slavery.

Ibid.

I do not propose either to purchase or to confiscate private property in land. The first would be unjust; the second, needless. Let the individuals who now hold it still retain, if they want to, possession of what they are pleased to call their land. Let them continue to call it their land. Let them buy and sell, and bequeath and devise it. We may safely leave them the shell, if we take the kernel. It is not necessary to confiscate land; only to confiscate rent.

We already take some rent in taxation. We have only to make some changes in our modes of taxation to take it all.

Ibid.

Now, insomuch as the taxation of rent, or land values, must necessarily be increased just as we abolish other taxes, we may put the proposition into practical form by proposing—

To abolish all taxation save that upon land values.

Ibid.

How many men are there who fairly earn a million dollars?   *Ibid.*

The rise of wages, the opening of opportunities for all to make an easy and comfortable living, would at once lessen and would soon eliminate from society the thieves, swindlers, and other classes of criminals who spring from the unequal distribution of wealth . . . We would get rid, not only of many judges, bailiffs, clerks and prison keepers, but of the great host of lawyers who are now maintained at the expense of producers; and talent now wasted in legal subtleties would be turned to higher pursuits.   *Ibid.*

An equitable distribution of wealth, that would exempt all from the fear of want, would destroy the greed of wealth, just as in polite society the greed of food has been destroyed.   *Ibid.*

It is not labor in itself that is repugnant to man; it is not the natural necessity for exertion which is a curse. It is only labor which produces nothing—exertion of which he cannot see the result.

The fact is that the work which improves the condition of mankind, the work which extends knowledge and increases power and enriches literature, and elevates thought, is not done to secure a living. It is not the work of slaves, driven to their task either by the lash of a master or by animal necessities. It is the work of men who perform it for their own sake, and not that they may get more to eat or drink, or wear, or display. In a state of society where want is abolished, work of this sort could be enormously increased.   *Ibid.*

There is danger in reckless change; but greater danger in blind conservatism.
    Social Problems.

How can a man be said to have a country when he has no right to a square inch of it.   *Ibid.*

We cannot safely leave politics to politicians, or political economy to college professors.   *Ibid.*

The ideal state is not that in which each gets an equal amount of wealth, but in which each gets in proportion to his contribution to the general stock.   *Ibid.*

Industrial changes imply social changes and necessitate political changes.   *Ibid.*

Progressive societies outgrow institutions as children outgrow clothes.   *Ibid.*

No theory is too false, no fable too absurd, no superstition too degrading for acceptance when it has become imbedded in common belief. Men will submit themselves to torture and to death, mothers will immolate their children, at the bidding of beliefs they thus accept.   *Ibid.*

In this tendency to accept what we find, to believe what we are told, is at once good and evil. It is this which makes social advance possible; it is this which makes it so slow and painful. It is thus tyranny is maintained and superstition perpetuated.
    Ibid.

Capital is good; the capitalist is a helper, if he is not also a monopolist. We can safely let any one get as rich as he can if he will not despoil others in doing so.
    Ibid.

For every social wrong there must be a remedy. But the remedy can be nothing less than the abolition of the wrong.
    Ibid.

Let us first ask what are the natural rights of men, and endeavor to secure them, before we propose either to beg or to pillage. *Ibid.*

Many there are, too depressed, too embruted with hard toil, and the struggle for animal existence, to think for themselves. Therefore the obligation devolves with all the more force on those who can. If thinking men are few, they are for that reason all the more powerful. *Ibid.*

Let no man imagine that he has no influence. Whoever he may be, and wherever he may be placed, *the man who thinks* becomes a light and a power. *Ibid.*

Whoever becomes imbued with a noble idea kindles a flame from which other torches are lit, and influences those with whom he comes in contact, be they few or many. *Ibid.*

There are three ways by which an individual can get wealth—by work, by gift, and by theft. And, clearly, the reason why the workers get so little is that the beggars and thieves get so much. *Ibid.*

Great wealth always supports the party in power, no matter how corrupt it may be. It never exerts itself for reform for it instinctively fears change. *Ibid.*

Nature gives wealth to labor, and to nothing but labor. There is, and there can be no article of wealth but such as labor has got by making it, or searching for it, out of the raw material. If there were but one man in the world it is manifest that he could have no more wealth than he was able to make and to save. This is the natural order. *Ibid.*

Land itself has no value. Value arises only from human labor. It is not until the ownership of land becomes the equivalent to the ownership of laborers that any value attaches to it. And where land has a specu-lative value it is because of the expectation that the growth of society will in the future make its ownership equivalent to the ownership of laborers.
Protection or Free Trade?

Property in land is as indefensible as property in man. It is so absurdly impolitic, so outrageously unjust, so flagrantly subversive to the true right of property, that it can only be instituted by force and maintained by confounding in the popular mind the distinction between property in land and property in things that are the result of labor. *Ibid.*

That value which the growth and improvement of a community attaches to land should be taken for the use of the community. *The Single Tax Theory.*

We are in favor of raising all public revenues by a single tax upon land values.
Ibid.

The vested interests.

The ideal of Socialism is grand and noble; and it is, I am convinced, possible of realization; but such a state of society cannot be manufactured—it must grow. Society is an organism, not a machine.

Social reform is not to be secured by noise and shouting, by complaints and denunciations, by the formation of parties, or the making of revolutions, but by the awakening of thought and the progress of ideas.

Power is in the hands of the masses of men. What oppresses the masses is their ignorance, their shortsighted selfishness.

Poverty is not merely deprivation; it means shame, degradation, the searing of the most sensitive parts of our moral and mental nature, as with hot irons.

Elbridge Gerry
(1744-1814)

American statesman

The evils we experience flow from the excess of democracy. The people do not want virtue, but are the dupes of pretended patriots.　　*Madison Reports, 135.*

Edward Gibbon
(1734-1794)

English historian

All that is human must retrograde if it does not advance.
Decline and Fall of the Roman Empire.

History is little more than the register of the crimes, follies, and misfortunes of mankind.　　*Ibid.*

The various modes of worship which prevailed in the Roman world were all considered by the people as equally true; by the philosopher as equally false; and by the magistrate as equally useful.　　*Ibid*

The theologian may indulge in the pleasing task of describing Religion as she descended from heaven, arrayed in her native purity. A more melancholy duty is imposed upon the historian. He must discover the inevitable mixture of error and corruption which she contracted in a long residence upon earth, among a weak and degenerate race of beings.　　*Ibid.*

When the promise of eternal happiness was proposed to mankind, on condition of adopting the faith and of observing the precepts of the gospel, it is no wonder that so advantageous an offer should have been accepted by great numbers of every religion, of every rank, and of every province in the Roman empire.　　*Ibid.*

A state of skepticism and suspense may amuse a few inquisitive minds. But the practice of superstition is so congenial to the multitude that, if they are forcibly awakened, they still regret the loss of their pleasing vision.　　*Ibid.*

Corruption, the most infallible symptom of constitutional liberty . . .　　*Ibid.*

To a philosophic eye the vices of the clergy are far less dangerous than their virtues.　　*Ibid.*

I darted a contemptuous look at the stately monuments of superstition.
A reference to the Gothic cathedrals;
Time, November 28, 1955.

Defending nonsense by violence.
A reference to the medieval Roman Catholic Church.

James Gibbons
(1834-1921)

American Cardinal

The church is not susceptible of being reformed in her doctrines. The church is the work of an incarnate God. Like all God's works, it is perfect. It is, therefore, incapable of reform.
The Faith of Our Fathers, vii, 1876.

A civilian ruler dabbling in religion is as reprehensible as a clergyman dabbling in politics. Both render themselves odious as well as ridiculous.　　*Ibid., xii.*

To the carnal eye the priest looks like other men, but to the eye of faith he is exalted above the angels, because he exercises powers not given even to angels.
Ibid., xxviii.

Our country has liberty without license and authority without despotism.
Address, Rome, March 25, 1887.

American Catholics rejoice in our separation of Church and State, and I can conceive no combination of circumstances likely to arise which would make a union desirable for either Church or State.
North American Review, March, 1909.

Reform must come from within, not without. You cannot legislate for virtue.
Address, Baltimore, September 13, 1909.

Philip Gibbs
(1877-1962)
English novelist, journalist

It is almost impossible for public opinion to form any kind of verdict based on actual facts. Newspapers nowadays use facts merely as the raw material of propaganda. By suppression, or alteration, or overemphasis, or by the trick of false perspective, or by scare headlines and editorial comment, the "facts" are made to convey exactly the particular idea which the newspaper desires to suggest to its readers.
A. E. Mander, Public Enemy the Press, Sydney, Australia, 1944.

André Gide
(1869-1951)
French novelist, essayist

Art is a collaboration between God and the artist, and the less the artist does the better.

An anthill Utopia.
A reference to Soviet Russia; John Gunther, Inside Russia Today.

Sir W(illiam) S(chwenck) Gilbert
(1836-1911)
English dramatist, librettist

I always voted at my party's call,
And I never thought of thinking for myself at all. *H.M.S. Pinafore.*

When Wellington thrashed Bonaparte,
As every child can tell,
The House of Peers, throughout the war,
Did nothing in particular
And did it very well. *Iolanthe.*

I often think it's comical,
How nature always does contrive
That every boy and every gal
That's born into the world alive,
Is either a little Liberal,
Or else a little Conservative. *Ibid.*

Man is Nature's sole mistake.
Princess Ida.

Stephen Girard
(1750-1831)
American banker, founder of Girard College

I enjoin and require that no ecclesiastic, missionary or minister of any sect whatsoever, shall ever hold or exercise any station or duty whatsoever in the said College; nor shall any such person ever be admitted for any purpose, or as a visitor, within the premises appropriated to the purpose of the said College.
From the will, endowing Girard College.

I do not mean to cast any reflection upon any sect or person whatsoever; but as there is such a multitude of sects, and such a diversity of opinion amongst them, I desire to keep the tender minds of the orphans, who are to derive advantage from this bequest, free from the excitement which clashing doctrines and sectarian controversy are so apt to produce. *Ibid.*

Tom Girdler
(1877-1965)
U.S. steel manufacturer

I never knew a steel plant that didn't

have guns and ammunition to protect its property.

Testimony, Congressional investigating committee, requoted, Time, June 14, 1937.

George Robert Gissing
(1857-1903)
English novelist

It is because nations tend to stupidity and baseness that mankind moves so slowly; it is because individuals have a capacity for better things that it moves at all.

Josiah William Gitt
(b. 1884)
Editor, York, Pa., Gazette & Daily

A newspaper is a public servant and to be permanently successful must be faithful to the interests of the public it serves. It dare not be selfish. It dare not be mercenary. *The Nation, June 4, 1955.*

Human progress has come about through change . . . Humanity's most valuable assets have been the non-conformists. Were it not for the non-conformist, he who refuses to be satisfied to go along with the continuance of things as they are, and insists upon attempting to find new ways of bettering things, the world would have known little progress indeed.

Editorial, Gazette & Daily, February 2, 1957.

William E. Gladstone*
(1809-1898)
English statesman

A conservative revolution.

A reference to the American Revolu-

---

* "He could improvise a lifelong conviction on the spur of the moment"—said of Gladstone.

tion, North American Review, September-October, 1878.

Liberalism is trust of the people tempered by prudence; Conservatism is distrust of the people tempered by fear.

National injustice is the surest road to national downfall.

Speech, Plumstead, 1878.

In almost every one, if not in every one, of the greatest political controversies of the last 50 years, whether they affected the franchise, whether they affected commerce, whether they affected religion, whether they affected the bad and abominable institution of slavery, or what subject they touched, these leisured classes, these educated classes, these titled classes, have been in the wrong.

Sinclair, The Cry for Justice.

The common people, the toilers, the men of uncommon sense—these have been responsible for nearly all of the social-reform measures which the world accepts today.

Ibid.

We have no adequate idea of the predisposing power which an immense series of measures of preparation for war has in actually begetting war.

No more cunning plot was ever devised against the intelligence, the freedom, the happiness and virtue of mankind, than Romanism.

What do I understand by the Liberal principle? I understand, in the main, it is a principle of trust in the people only qualified by prudence. By this principle which is opposed to the Liberal principle I understand mistrust of the people, only qualified by fear. *Speech, May 31, 1865.*

Time is on our side.

House of Commons, 1866.

All the world over, I will back the masses against the classes.
Speech, Liverpool, June 28, 1866.

Mary Godwin
See Wollstonecraft

William Godwin
(1756-1836)
English novelist, biographer, philosopher

Whenever government assumes to deliver us from the trouble of thinking for ourselves, the only consequences it produces are those of torpor, imbecility.
An Enquiry Concerning Political Justice, 1793.

Whenever truth stands in the mind unaccompanied by the evidence upon which it depends, it cannot properly be said to be apprehended at all.   *Ibid.*

A virtuous man will teach himself to recollect the principle of universal benevolence as often as pious men repeat their prayers.   *Ibid.*

I have no business with factions or intrigue, but simply to promulgate the truth, and to wait the tranquil progress of conviction.   *Ibid.*

No maxim can be more pernicious than that which would teach us to consult the temper of the times, and to tell only so much (truth) as we imagine our contemporaries will be able to bear.   *Ibid.*

We retail and mangle truth. We impart it to our fellows, not with the liberal measure with which we have received it, but with such parsimony as our own miserable prudence may chance to prescribe. . . . That we may deceive others with a tranquil conscience, we begin with deceiving ourselves.   *Ibid.*

The first duty of man is, to take none of the principles of conduct upon trust; to do nothing without a clear and individual conviction that it is right to be done. He that resigns his understanding upon one particular topic, will not exercise it vigorously upon another.   *Ibid.*

Even yet how few there are that venture to examine into the foundation of Mohametanism and Christianity in those countries where those systems are established by law!
Ibid.

The proper method for hastening the decay of error is . . . by teaching every man to think for himself.   *Ibid.*

All riches, and especially all hereditary riches, are to be considered as the salary of a sinecure office, where the laborer and the manufacturer perform the duties, and the principal spends the income in luxury and idleness. Hereditary wealth is in reality a premium paid to idleness.   *Ibid.*

Our judgment will always suspect those weapons that can be used with equal prospect of success on both sides. Therefore we should regard all force with aversion.
Ibid.

Since government, even in its best state is an evil, the object principally to be aimed at is that we should have as little of it as the general peace of human society will permit.   *Ibid.*

All government corresponds in a certain degree to what the Greeks denominated a tyranny.   *Ibid.*

Society and government are different in themselves, and have different origins. Society is produced by our wants, and government by our wickedness. Society is in every state a blessing; government even in its best state but a necessary evil. *Ibid.*

Laws we sometimes call the wisdom of our ancestors. But this is a strange imposition. It was as frequently the dictate of their passion, of timidity, jealousy, a monopolizing spirit, and a lust of power that knew no bounds. Are we not obliged perpetually to renew and remodel this misnamed wisdom of our ancestors? To correct it by a detection of their ignorance, and a censure of their intolerance? *Ibid.*

Justice is the sum of all moral duty.
Ibid.

Truth, when originally presented to the mind, is powerful and invigorating; but, when attempted to be perpetuated by political institutions, becomes flaccid and lifeless. Truth in its unpatronized state improves the understanding; because in that state it is embraced only so far as it is perceived to be true. But truth when recommended by authority is weakly and irresolutely embraced. *Ibid.*

Law is an institution of the most pernicious tendency. The institution once begun, can never be brought to a close. No action of any man was ever the same as any other action, had ever the same degree of utility or injury. As new cases occur, the law is perpetually found deficient. It is therefore perpetually necessary to make new laws. The volume in which justice records her prescriptions is forever increasing, and the world would not contain the books that might be written. The consequences of the infinitude of law is its uncertainty. Law was made that a plain man might know what he had to expect, and yet the most skillful practitioners differ about the event of my suit. *Ibid.*

Every community of men, as well as every individual, must govern itself according to its ideas of justice. What I should desire is, not by violence to change its institutions, but by reason to change its ideas.
Ibid.

Governments, no more than individual men, are infallible. *Ibid.*

There is no species of reasoning in defense of the suppression of heresy which may not be brought back to this monstrous principle, that the knowledge of truth, and the introduction of right principles of policy, are circumstances altogether indifferent to the welfare of mankind. *Ibid.*

The moment government descends to wear the badge of a sect, religious war is commenced, the world is disgraced with inexpiable broils, and deluged with blood.
Ibid.

When we enter the lists of battle, we quit the sure domain of truth and leave the decision to the caprice of chance. *Ibid.*

Power is not happiness. *Ibid.*

Supposing that we should even be obliged to take democracy with all the disadvantages that were ever annexed to it, and that no remedy could be discovered for any of its defects, it would still be greatly preferable to the exclusive systems of other forms. *Ibid.*

Democracy restores to man a consciousness of his value, teaches him by the removal of authority and oppression to listen to the dictates of reason, gives him confidence to treat all other men as his fellow human beings, and induces him to regard them no longer as enemies against whom to be upon his guard, but as brethren whom it becomes him to assist. *Ibid.*

Joseph Paul Goebbels
(1897-suicide 1945)
German Nazi propaganda minister

Christ cannot possibly have been a Jew. I don't have to prove that scientifically. It is a fact.
Quoted by John Gunther, The Nation, February 6, 1935.

I know it is a sacrifice for us not to have a new war.

War is the most simple affirmation of life. Suppress war, and it would be like trying to suppress the processes of nature. These are also terrible. Every living thing is terrible.

If the day should ever come when we (the Nazis) must go, if some day we are compelled to leave the scene of history, we will slam the door so hard that the universe will shake and mankind will stand back in stupefaction.

If the German people lay down their arms the whole of Eastern and Southern Europe, together with the Reich, will come under Russian occupation. Behind an iron curtain° mass butcheries of people would begin.

The past is lying in flames. The future will rise from the flames within our hearts.
Spoken at the Nazi book-burning, May 10, 1933.

These flames . . . light up a new era. . . . Spirits are awakening, and oh, Century, it is a joy to live!   *Ibid.*

_____
° The phrase "iron curtain" was coined by either Goebbels or Von Krosyg; it was popularized, in the same sense, by Churchill in his Fulton, Missouri, speech.

It is the absolute right of the State to supervise the formation of public opinion.
Address, 1923.

Not every item of news should be published: rather must those who control news policies endeavor to make every item of news serve a certain purpose.
Diary, March 14, 1943.

Intellectual activity is a danger to the building of character. *Michael (a novel).*

We can do without butter, but . . . not without arms. One cannot shoot with butter but with guns.
Speech, Berlin, January 17, 1936.

Hermann Goering
(1893-committed suicide after being sentenced to the gallows 1946)
German Nazi politician

I determine who is a Jew.

The only motive which guided me was my ardent love for my people.
Defense, at Nuremberg trial.

Guns will make us powerful; butter will only make us fat. *Radio broadcast, 1936.*

Johann Wolfgang von Goethe
(1749-1832)
German writer

There is nothing more frightful than ignorance in action.
Criticisms, Reflections and Maxims. (Another translation: Nothing is so terrible as activity without thought.)

He who moves not forward goes backward.   *Herman and Dorothea.*

The happy do not believe in miracles.
Ibid.

Yes! To this thought I hold with firm per-
sistence;
The last result of wisdom stamps it
true:
He only earns his freedom and existence
Who daily conquers them anew.
Faust.

Capacious is the Church's belly;
Whole nations it has swallowed down,
Yet no dyspepsia 'neath its gown;
The Church alone, in jewels drest,°
Your "tainted wealth" can quite digest.
Ibid.

Your messages I hear, but faith has not
been given;
The dearest child of Faith is Miracle.
Ibid.

Das Ewig-Weibliche zieht uns hinan.
The Eternal Feminine draws us on (or,
upward). *Ibid., last line.*°°

But in general man has to grope his way.
He knows not whence he comes nor whither
he goes; he knows little of the world and
himself least of all.
*Goethe: Wisdom and Experience, Pan-
theon Books.*

Men are so inclined to content themselves with what is commonplace; the spirit
and the senses so easily grow dead to the
impressions of the beautiful and perfect,

———
° Another translation:
"The church alone beyond all question
Has for ill-gotten goods the right digestion."
°° Bayard Taylor translated this line as
"The Woman Soul leadeth us Upward and
on." He wrote he could find no English
equivalent for *Ewig-Weibliche.*

that every one should study, by all methods,
to nourish in his mind the faculty of feeling
these things. For no man can bear to be
entirely deprived of such enjoyments.
Wilhelm Meister's Apprenticeship.

One ought, every day at least, to hear a
little song, read a good poem, see a fine
picture, and, if it were possible, to speak
a few reasonable words. *Ibid.*

National hatred is something peculiar.
You will always find it strongest and most
violent where there is the lowest degree of
culture. *Goethe to Eckerman.*

If we grant freedom to man, there is an
end to the omniscience of God; for if the
Divinity knows how I shall act, I must act
so perforce. *Ibid.*

What you have inherited from your
fathers, earn over again for yourselves or it
will not be yours.
*Quoted by Adlai Stevenson, Saturday
Review, February 7, 1959.*

*Macht doch den Fensterladen in Schlaf-
gemach auf, damit mehr Licht herein
komme.* (Open the bedroom shutters and let
in more light.) *Deathbed words, 1832.*

The highest problem of every art is, by
means of appearances, to produce the illusion of a loftier reality.
Truth and Poetry.

*Man lernt nichts kennen als was man
liebt.* (A man doesn't learn to understand
anything unless he loves it.)

He who is plenteously provided for from
within, needs but little from without.

Let us not dream that reason can ever
be popular. Passions, emotions, may be
made popular, but reason remains ever the
property of the few.

None are more hopelessly enslaved than those who falsely believe they are free.

One must keep repeating the Truth. (*Man muss das Wahre immer wiederholen.*)

To a new truth there is nothing more hurtful than an old error.

It is much easier to recognize error than to find truth; error is superficial and may be corrected; truth lies hidden in the depths.

The destiny of any nation, at any given time, depends on the opinions of its young men under five-and-twenty.

There is nothing more odious than the majority. It consists of a few powerful men who lead the way; of accommodating rascals and submissive weaklings; and of a mass of men who trot after them without in the least knowing their own minds.

We know accurately only when we know little; with knowledge doubt enters.

Whatever you cannot understand, you cannot possess.   *Maxims, v. iii.*

Nature knows no pause in progress and development, and attaches her curse on all inaction.

Science and art belong to the whole world, and before them vanish the barriers of nationality.

The work of art may have a moral effect, but to demand moral purpose from the artist is to make him ruin his work.

Progress has not followed a straight ascending line, but a spiral with rhythms of progress and retrogression, of evolution and dissolution.

Everything in the world may be endured except continual prosperity.

The decline of literature indicates the decline of a nation.

The Golden Rule

Christianity: All things whatsoever ye would that men should do to you, do ye even so to them: for this is the Law and the Prophets.   *Matthew, 7, 12.*

Judaism: What is hateful to you, do not to your fellowmen. That is the entire Law; all the rest is commentary.
             Talmud, Shabbat, 31 a.

Brahmanism: This is the sum of duty: Do naught unto others which would cause you pain if done to you.
             Mahabharata, 5, 1517.

Buddhism: Hurt not others in ways that you yourself would find hurtful.
             Udana-Varga, 5, 18.

Confucianism: Surely it is the maxim of loving-kindness: Do not unto others that you would not have them do unto you.
             Analects, 15, 23.

Taoism: Regard your neighbor's gain as your own gain, and your neighbor's loss as your own loss. *T'ai Shang Kan Ying P'ien.*

Zoroastrianism: That nature alone is good which refrains from doing unto another whatsoever is not good for itself.
             Dadistan-i-dinik, 94, 5.

Islam: No one of you is a believer until he desires for his brother what which he desires for himself.   *Sunnah.*

Emma Goldman*
(1869-1940)
International anarchist

It is organized violence on top which creates individual violence at the bottom.

---

* "The Daughter of the Dream"—William Marion Reedy.

It is the accumulated indignation against organized wrong, organized crime, organized injustice, which drives the political offender to act.
Address to the jury, June 15, 1917.

We are but the atoms in the incessant human struggle towards the light that shines in the darkness—the ideal of economic, political, and spiritual liberation of mankind! *Ibid.*

Anarchy stands for the liberation of the human mind from the dominion of religion; the liberation of the human body from the dominion of property; liberation from the shackles and restraints of government. *Anarchism, 1917.*

Anarchy asserts the possibility of organization without discipline, fear or punishment, and without the pressure of property.
Living My Life, 1931.

Demonstrate before the palaces of the rich; demand work. If they do not give you work, demand bread. If they deny you both, take bread. It is your sacred right.
Public comment on Cardinal Manning's statement, "Necessity knows no law." Arrest and a year in the penitentiary resulted.

No revolution ever succeeds as a factor of liberation unless the Means used to further it be identified in spirit and tendency with the Purpose to be achieved.
My Further Disillusion, 1924.

The ultimate end of all revolutionary social change is to establish the sanctity of human life, the dignity of man, the right of every human being to liberty and well-being. *Ibid.*

The idealists and visionaries, foolish enough to throw caution to the winds and express their ardor and faith in some supreme deed, have advanced mankind and have enriched the world.

Eric F. Goldman
(b. 1915)
American writer, historian

For almost a century the modern American reformer has been the gadfly and the conscience, to a large extent the heart and the mind, of the only nation in man's history which has dared to live by the credo that any individual's rendezvous with his destiny is a rendezvous with a better tomorrow.
Rendezvous With Destiny, p. 461, Knopf, 1952.

Oliver Goldsmith
(1728-1774)
English dramatist, poet, novelist

The English laws punish vice; the Chinese laws do more, they reward virtue.

Ill fares the land, to hastening ills a prey,
Where wealth accumulates, and men decay.
The Deserted Village.

Laws grind the poor, and rich men rule the law. *The Traveller.*

The united voice of millions cannot lend the smallest foundation to falsehood.
The Vicar of Wakefield.

Samuel Goldwyn
(1882-1974)
American motion picture pioneer

No person who is enthusiastic about his work has anything to fear from life.
Words to Live By, This Week, September 30, 1956.

Victor Gollancz
(b. 1893)
British publisher, author

We shall never stop war, whatever machinery we may devise, until we have learned to think always, with a sort of desperate urgency and an utter self-identification, of single human beings.
From Darkness to Light, p. 504.

Baron Kolmar von der Goltz
(1843-1916)
German World War I marshal

As a rule, high culture and military power go hand in hand, as evidenced in the cases of Greece and Rome.

A collision of interests leads to war, but the passions of the nations decide independently of these up to what point the war shall be carried. War aids politicians in the attainment of their objects; yet for the sake of subordinate interests, it must be waged until the enemy has been completely subjected. This necessarily entails the decisive use of all means, intellectual and material alike, tending to subjugate the foe.

National egotism is inseparable from our ideas of national greatness. This egotism will always appeal to arms where other means fail.

The warlike spirit must not be allowed to die out among people, neither must the love of peace get the upper hand, for all the greater would be the consternation at the moment of awakening.

A nation which desires happiness must also be powerful and skilled in arms . . . As long as the process of reconstructing states proceeds with the changing seasons, as long as human development does not stand still, so long will there be war.

Samuel Gompers
(1850-1924)
American labor leader

More!
Reply to question, What does labor want? at a Congressional hearing.

More, more, more now.
As quoted in Editor & Publisher, November 29, 1952.

More, more, more for labor.
Charles A. Madison, American Labor Leaders.

What does Labor want? We want more schoolhouses and less jails; more books and less arsenals; more learning and less vice; more leisure and less greed; more justice and less revenge; in fact, more of the opportunities to cultivate our better natures, to make manhood more noble, womanhood more beautiful, and childhood more happy and bright.   *Labor, August 4, 1956.*

As one voice labor must speak—to reward its friends and punish its enemies. *Ibid.*

Stand faithfully by our friends and elect them; oppose our enemies and defeat them, whether they be candidates for President, for Congress, or other offices, whether executive, legislative or judicial.
Slogan for the American Federation of Labor.

Trades unions . . . were born of the necessity of workers to protect and defend themselves from encroachment, injustice and wrong. . . . To protect the workers in their inalienable right to a higher and better life; to protect them, not only as equals before the law, but also in their rights to the product of their labor; to protect their lives, their limbs, their health, their homes, their firesides, their liberties as men, as workers, as citizens; to overcome

and conquer prejudice and antagonism; to secure them the right to life, and the opportunity to maintain that life; the right to be full sharers in the abundance which is the result of their brain and brawn, and the civilization of which they are the founders and the mainstay.
Address, 1898.

There is no more demoralizing theory than that which imputes all human evils to Capitalism or any other single agency.
Seventy Years of Life and Labor, 1925.

The labor of a human being is not a commodity or article of commerce. You can't weigh the soul of a man with a bar of pig iron. *Ibid., ii, 296.*

Socialism holds nothing but unhappiness for the human race. It destroys personal initiative, wipes out national pride . . . and even plays into the hands of the autocrats.
Ibid., ii, 431.

Socialism is the end of fanatics, the sophistry of so-called intelligentsia, and it has no place in the hearts of those who would fight for freedom and preserve democracy. *Ibid.*

Show me the country in which there are no strikes and I'll show you that country in which there is no liberty.
Madison, American Labor Leaders.

Thomas Gordon
(1690-1750)
Scottish writer
and
John Trenchard
(1662-1723)
Irish political w iter

Some have said it is not the business of private men to meddle with government:

—a bold, false, and dishonest saying, which is fit to come from no mouth but that of a tyrant or a slave.
Cato's Letters, Vol. ii, No. 38, 1724.

To say that private men have nothing to do with government, is to say that private men have nothing to do with their own happiness or misery:—that people ought not to concern themselves whether they be naked or clothed, fed or starved, deceived or instructed, protected or destroyed.
Ibid.

Maxim Gorky (né Alexei Peshkoff)
(1868-1936)
Russian novelist, playwright

There is no more contemptible poison than power over one's fellow men.
Novaya Zhism. Quoted by Wendell Willkie.

Follow us to a new life, follow us in our struggle against the old order, in the work for a new form of life, for the freedom and beauty of life.

The function of the intellectual has always been confined, in the main, to embellishing the bored existence of the bourgeoisie, to consoling the rich in the trivial troubles of their life. The intelligentsia was the nurse of the capitalist class. It was kept busy embroidering white stitches on the philosophical and ecclesiastical vestments of the bourgeoisie—that old and filthy fabric, besmeared so thickly with the blood of the toiling masses.
To American Intellectuals, 1932.

It is no exaggeration to say that the press of Europe and America busies itself assiduously and almost exclusively with the task of lowering the cultural level of its readers, a level which is already sufficiently low.
Ibid.

You reproach me with "preaching hatred" and advise me to "propagate love". It would seem that you think me capable of preaching to the workers: "Love the capitalists, for they are devouring your kith and kin; . . . love the capitalists, for their church is holding you down in obscurity and ignorance." *Ibid.*

Nothing save the victory of the proletariat will be able to rid the world of hatred.
Ibid.

The one sacred thing is the dissatisfaction of man with himself and his striving to be better than he is. *Foma Gordyeeff.*

There is no one on earth more disgusting and repulsive than he who gives alms. Even as there is no one so miserable as he who accepts them. *Ibid.*

I lacked something essential to a Socialist —love of mankind, perhaps.

All this life is senseless and tragic in which the endless slaving labor of one man constantly goes to supply another with more bread than he can use.

Jay Gould
(1836-1892)
American capitalist

I needed the good will of the legislature of four states. I "formed" the legislative bodies with my own money. I found that it was cheaper that way.
Testimony, Congressional Committee; André Siegfried, America at Mid-Century.

I can hire one-half of the working class to kill the other half.
In reference to Knights of Labor strike, 1886.

Baltasar Gracián
(1601-1658)
Spanish writer, Jesuit rector

Truth is for the minority.
The Art of Worldly Wisdom, xliii, 1647.

Truth always lags behind, limping along on the arm of Time. *Ibid., cxlvi.*

What the multitude says is so, or soon will be so. *Ibid., cclxx.*

Know what is evil, no matter how worshipped it may be. Let the man of sense not mistake it, even when clothed in brocade, or at times crowned in gold, because it cannot thereby hide its hypocrisy, for slavery does not lose its infamy, however noble the master.
Gracián's Manual, 1653, tr. by Martin Fischer, 1934.

William F. ("Billy") Graham
(b. 1918)
American evangelist

Why do I believe in the Devil? *For three reasons:*
1. Because the Bible plainly says he exists.
2. Because I see his work everywhere.
3. Because great scholars have recognized his existence. *This Week, March 2, 1958.*

(Hiram) Ulysses S. Grant
(1822-1885)
18th President of the United States

Let us all labor to add all needful guarantees for the more perfect security of free thought, free speech, and free press, pure morals, unfettered religious sentiments, and of equal rights and privileges to all men, irrespective of nationality, color, or religion. *Speech, before the Army of the Tennessee, Des Moines, 1875.*

Encourage free schools, and resolve that not one dollar of money shall be appropriated to the support of any sectarian school. Resolve that neither the state nor nation, or both combined, shall support institutions of learning other than those sufficient to afford every child growing up in the land the opportunity of a good common school education, unmixed with sectarian, pagan, or atheistical tenets. Leave the matter of religion to the family altar, the church, and the private schools, supported entirely by private contributions. Keep the church and the state forever separated. *Ibid.*

I would call your attention to the importance of correcting an evil that, if permitted to continue, will probably lead to great trouble in our land before the close of the Nineteenth century. It is the acquisition of vast amounts of untaxed church property. . . . In a growing country, where real estate enhances so rapidly with time as in the United States, there is scarcely a limit to the wealth that may be acquired by corporations, religious or otherwise, if allowed to retain real estate without taxation. The contemplation of so vast a property as here alluded to, without taxation, may lead to sequestration without constitutional authority, and through blood. I would suggest the taxation of all property equally, whether church or corporation. *Message to Congress, December 7, 1875; Congressional Record, Vol. 4, part 7, page 175.*

I do not think there ever was a more wicked war than that waged by the United States in Mexico. I thought so at the time, when I was a youngster, only I had not

moral courage enough to resign. . . . It was an instance of a republic following the bad example of European monarchies, in not considering justice in their desire to acquire additional territory. *Personal Memoirs.*

The right of revolution is an inherent one. When people are oppressed by their government, it is a natural right they enjoy to relieve themselves of the oppression, if they are strong enough, whether by withdrawal from it, or by overthrowing it and substituting a government more acceptable. *Ibid.*

The United States, knowing no distinction of her own citizens on account of religion or nativity, naturally believes in a civilization the world over which will secure the same universal views. *Letter appointing Benjamin F. Peixotto U.S. Consul in Bucharest, December 8, 1870.*

I know no method to secure the repeal of bad or obnoxious laws so effective as their stringent execution. *Inaugural, March 4, 1869.*

Let no guilty man escape, if it can be avoided. No personal consideration should stand in the way of performing a public duty. *Indorsement on a letter regarding the Whiskey Ring, July 19, 1875.*

Whatever there is of greatness in the United States or indeed in any other country, is due to labor. The laborer is the author of all greatness and wealth. Without labor there would be no government, and no leading class, and nothing to preserve.

The will of the people is the best law.

Too long denial of guaranteed right is sure to lead to revolution—bloody revolution, where suffering must fall upon the innocent as well as the guilty.

I have never advocated war except as a means of peace.

There never was a time when, in my opinion, some way could not be found to prevent the drawing of the sword.

I felt like anything rather than rejoicing at the downfall of a foe who had fought so long and valiantly and had suffered so much for a cause, though that cause was, I believe, one of the worst for which a people ever fought. *On Lee's surrender.*

It was my intention, if nominated and elected, to appoint John Sherman secretary of the treasury. Now you may be certain I shall not. Not to be president of the United States would I consent that a bargain should be made.°

The Constitution does not forbid a third term, but the unwritten law does.
Statement to N. Y. Times correspondent before his death.

Horace Greeley
(1811-1872)
American educator, lecturer, political leader

Full of error and suffering as the world yet is, we cannot afford to reject unexamined any idea which proposes to improve the Moral, Intellectual or Social condition of mankind. Better incur the trouble of testing and exploding a thousand fallacies than by rejecting stifle a single beneficent Truth.
Editorial, New York Tribune, 1845.

° The result of this statement was the nomination of Garfield.

Turn the rascals out.
Slogan against "Grantism," for Greeley's Liberal Republican Party, 1872.

I never said all Democrats were saloon-keepers. What I said was that all saloon-keepers are Democrats.
c. 1860; quoted in Time.

I cannot forget that the laboring class, so-called, must, like any other, stand up for its rights, or be content to see them trampled underfoot; and that the strength given it by organization, superintended upon numbers, is its only effectual defense against the else unchecked tyranny of capital, greedy for profit and reckless of others' rights. The power developed by combination may be abused, like any other power; but labor is helpless and a prey without it.
Weekly People, April 4, 1959.

Morality and religion are but words to him who fishes in gutters for the means of sustaining life, and crouches behind barrels in the street for shelter from the cutting blasts of a winter night.

The best use of a journal is to print the largest practical amount of important truth —truth which tends to make mankind wiser, and thus happier.

But the world *does* move, and its motive power under God is the fearless thought and speech of those who dare to be in advance of their time—who are sneered at and shunned through their days of struggle as lunatics, dreamers, impracticables and visionaries; men of crotchets, vagaries, and isms. They are the masts and sails of the ship to which conservatism answers as ballast. The ballast is important—at times indispensable—but it would be of no account if the ship were not bound to go ahead.

St. Gregory I (the Great)
(540-604)
Pope

For the human mind is prone to pride even when not supported by power; how much more, then, does it exalt itself when it has that support. *Pastoral Care, 2, 6.*

Ad majorem Dei gloriam. To the greater glory of God. (Motto of the Society of Jesus.) *Dialogues, 1.*

If the work of God could be comprehended by reason, it would be no longer wonderful, and faith would have no merit if reason provided proof.
Homilies on the Gospels, 26, 1.

The earth of which they are born is common to all, and, therefore, the fruit that the earth brings forth belongs without distinction to all.

St. Gregory VII (Hildebrand)
(about 1020 to 1085)
Pope

1. The Roman Church has been founded by Christ alone.
Dictatus Papae, circa 1075, document found among his letters.

8. He alone (the Pope) may use the imperial insignia. *Ibid.*

9. The pope is the only one whose feet are kissed by princes. *Ibid.*

12. He (the pope) may depose emperors. *Ibid.*

18. His (the pope's) judgment may not be revised by anyone, and he alone may revise the judgment of others. *Ibid.*

19. He may not be judged by anyone. *Ibid.*

22. The Roman Church has never erred, and, according to Scripture, never shall err. *Ibid.*

Gregory XVI
(1765-1846)
Pope

From the polluted fountain of indifferentism flows that absurd and erroneous doctrine or rather raving (*deliramentum*) which claims and defends liberty of conscience for everyone. From this comes, in a word, the worst plague of all, namely, unrestrained liberty of opinion and freedom of speech.
Encyclical Mirari Vos.

Sir Edward Grey, 1st Viscount of Fallodon
(1862-1933)
English liberal statesman

The moral is obvious; it is that great armaments lead inevitably to war.
Twenty-Five Years.

The increase of armaments that is intended in each nation to produce consciousness of strength, and a sense of security, does not produce these effects. On the contrary, it produces a consciousness of the strength of other nations and a sense of fear. Fear begets suspicion and distrust and evil imaginings of all sorts. *Ibid.*

The enormous growth of armaments in Europe, the sense of insecurity and fear caused by them—it was these that made World War I inevitable. This, it seems to me, is the truest reading of history, and the lesson that the present should be learning from the past in the interests of future peace, the warning to be handed on to those who come after us. *Ibid.*

Alfred Whitney Griswold
(b. 1906)
*American educator, president of
Yale University*

There are certain things that we can accomplish by law and there are certain things that we cannot accomplish by law or by any process of government. We cannot legislate intelligence. We cannot legislate morality. No, and we cannot legislate loyalty, for loyalty is a kind of morality. We cannot produce these things by decrees or commissions or public inquisitions.
Essays on Education.

Books won't stay banned. They won't burn. Ideas won't go to jail. *Ibid.*

In the long run of history, the censor and the inquisitor have always lost. The only sure weapon against bad ideas is better ideas. The source of better ideas is wisdom. The surest path to wisdom is a liberal education. *Ibid.*

There are certain things in man that have to be won, not forced; inspired, not compelled. Among these are many, I should say most, of the things that constitute the good life. *Ibid.*

If Carlyle could define a university as a collection of books, Socrates might have defined it as a conversation about wisdom. *Ibid.*

Moritz Guedemann
(1835-1918)
German-Austrian rabbi

Men will sooner surrender their rights than their customs.
Geschichte des Erziehungswesens, 1888.

Albert Guérard
(b. 1880)
American educator, writer

Unanimity and stagnation are two names for a single disease, the arteriosclerosis of a society. *Testament of a Liberal, 1956.*

All ideas are to some extent inevitably subversive. . . . Christianity was subversive to paganism. *Ibid.*

Francesco Guicciardini
(1483-1540)
Italian historian, statesman

Never wage war on religion, nor upon seemingly holy institutions, for this thing has too great a force upon the minds of fools. *Ricordi Politici.*

François Pierre Guillaume Guizot
(1787-1874)
French historian, statesman

Among the masses, even in revolution, aristocracy must ever exist. Destroy it in the nobility, and it becomes centered in the rich and powerful Houses of Commons. Pull them down, and it still survives in the master and foreman in the workshop.
Mémoires pour Servir à l'Histoire de Mon Temps.

Of all the tyrants custom is that which to sustain itself stands most in need of the opinion which is entertained of its powers; its only strength lies in that which is attributed to it. A single attempt to break the yoke soon shows us its fragility.
S. A. Allibone, Prose Quotations, 1876, p. 158.

The chief property of custom is to contract our ideas, like our movements, within the circle it has traced for us; it governs us by the terror it inspires for any new and untried condition. *Ibid.*

Hunter Guthrie
President, Georgetown University

Liberty is today's major plague.
Inaugural address, N. Y. Compass, November 11, 1949.

Ha-Babli
(c. 30 B.C.)

Whatsoever thou wouldst that men should not do to thee, do not do that to them. This is the whole Law. The rest is explanation.

Ernst Haeckel
(1834-1919)
German biologist, naturalist, philosopher

Our monistic view, that the great cosmic law applies throughout the whole of nature, is of the highest moment. . . . It definitely rules out the three central dogmas of metaphysics—God, freedom, and immortality.
The Riddle of the Universe, 1901.

The enormous daily progress of natural science is irresistibly destroying the roots of all church dogmas.

I do not belong to the amiable group of "men of compromise" . . . If I seem to you to be an iconoclast, I pray you to remember that the victory of pure reason over superstition will not be achieved without a tremendous struggle.

Count Gottlieb von Haeseler
(1836-1919)
Prussian officer

It is necessary that our civilization build its temple on mountains of corpses, on an ocean of tears and on the death cries of men without number.
1893; quoted by William Shirer, N. Y. Herald Tribune.

Frank Hague
(1896-1956)
American politician, one-time mayor of Jersey City

I am the law.
N. Y. Times, November 11, 1937.

As long as I am mayor of this city the great industries are secure. We hear about constitutional rights, free speech and the free press. Every time I hear these words I say to myself, "That man is a Red, that man is a Communist". You never hear a real American talk like that.
N. Y. World-Telegram, April 2, 1938.

Haile Selassie I
See Selassie

J. B. S. Haldane
(1892-1964)
English scientist, geneticist

Scientific education and religious education are incompatible. The clergy have ceased to interfere with education at the advanced state, with which I am directly concerned, but they have still got control of that of children. This means that the children have to learn about Adam and Noah instead of about Evolution; about David who killed Goliath, instead of Koch who killed cholera; about Christ's ascent into heaven instead of Montgolfier's and Wright's. Worse than that, they are taught that it is a virtue to accept statements without adequate evidence, which leaves them a prey to quacks of every kind in later life, and makes it very difficult for them to accept the methods of thought which are successful in science.

Capitalism did not arise because capitalists stole the land or the workmen's tools, but because it was more efficient than feudalism. It will perish because it is not merely less efficient than socialism, but actually self-destructive.   *I Believe.*

George Savile, Marquess of Halifax
(1633-1695)
English statesman

There is a Soul in that great body of the People, which may for a time be drowsy and unactive, but when the Leviathan is roused, it moveth like an angry Creature, and will neither be convinced or resisted.
The Complete Works of George Savile, First Marquess of Halifax, 1912, 101.

The angry Buzz of a Multitude is one of the bloodiest Noises of the World.
Ibid., 219.

There is an accumulative Cruelty in a number of Men, though none in particular are ill-natured.   *Ibid.*

Liberty can neither be got nor kept, but by so much Care that Mankind are generally unwilling to give the Price for it.
Ibid., 224.

The best Party is but a kind of Conspiracy against the rest of the Nation.
Ibid., 225.

Ignorance maketh most Men go into a Party, and Shame keepeth them from getting out of it.   *Ibid., 227.*

Men are not hanged for stealing Horses, but that Horses may not be stolen.
Ibid., 229.

They who are of the opinion that Money will do everything, may very well be suspected to do everything for Money.
Ibid., 242.

A Man that should call every thing by its right Name, would hardly pass the Streets without being knocked down as a common enemy.   *Ibid., 246.*

A Man that doth not use his Reason, is a tame Beast; a Man that abuses it, is a wild one.   *Ibid., 254.*

Power and Liberty are respectively managed in the world in a manner not suitable to their Value and Dignity.
They are both so abused that it justifieth the Satires that are generally made upon them . . .
They are perpetually wrestling, and have had their Turns when they have been thrown, to have their Bones broken by it.
If they were not both apt to be out of Breath, there would be no living.   *Ibid.*

In a limited Monarchy, Prerogative and Liberty are as jealous of one another as any two neighboring States can be of their respective Incroachments.
Political Thoughts and Reflections, 1750.

Power is so apt to be insolent, and Liberty to be saucy, that they are very seldom upon good Terms.
They are both so quarrelsome that they will not easily enter into a fair Treaty. For indeed it is hard to bring them together; they ever quarrel at a distance.   *Ibid.*

If the People were designed to be the sole Property of the supream Magistrate, sure God would have made them of a differing and subordinate Species; as He hath the Beasts, that by the Inferiority of their Nature they might the better submit to the Dominion of Mankind.   *Ibid.*

If none were to have Liberty but those who understand what it is, there would not be many freed Men in the World.   *Ibid.*

When the People contend for their Liberty, they seldom get any thing for their Victory but new Masters.   *Ibid.*

E(velyn) Beatrice Hall
See Tallentyre

Robert Hall
(1764-1831)
English orator of the Baptist Church

The most capital advantage an enlightened people can enjoy is the liberty of discussing every subject which can fall within the compass of the human mind; while this remains, freedom will flourish; but should it be lost or impaired, its principles will neither be well understood or long retained. To render the magistrate a judge of truth, and engage his authority in the suppression of opinions, shews an inattention to the nature and designs of political society.
An Apology for the Liberty of the Press, 1793.

Turn a Christian society into an established church, and it is no longer a voluntary assembly for the worship of God; it is a powerful corporation, full of such sentiments and passions as usually distinguish those bodies: a dread of innovation, an attachment to abuses, a propensity to tyranny and oppression.   *Ibid., sect. v.*

Henry Hallam
(1777-1859)
English historian

As we find in the history of all usurping governments, time changes anomaly into system, and injury into right; examples beget custom, and custom ripens into law; and the doubtful precedent of one generation becomes the fundamental maxim of another.
The View of the State of Europe During the Middle Ages, 1818.

Henry Wager Halleck
(1815-1872)
American Union general during Civil War

The Bible nowhere prohibits war . . . Although war was raging in the world in the time of Christ and His Apostles, still they said not a word of its unlawfulness and immorality.
Military Art and Science, introduction, 1846.

Alexander Hamilton
(1757-1804)
American statesman

Why was government instituted at all? Because the passions of men will not conform to the dictates of reason and justice without restraint. *The Federalist, No. 15.*

I trust the friends of the proposed Constitution will never concur with its enemies, in questioning that fundamental principle of republican government which admits the right of the people to alter or abolish the established Constitution whenever they find it inconsistent with their happiness.
Ibid., No. 79.

Next to permanency in office, nothing can contribute more to the independence of the judges than a fixed provision for their support. The remark made in relation to the President is equally applicable here. In the general course of human nature *a power* over a man's subsistence amounts to a power over his will. *Ibid.*

History teaches that among the men who have overturned the liberties of republics, the greatest number have begun their career by paying an obsequious court to the people; commencing demagogues, and ending tyrants. *Ibid.*

It is of great importance in a republic not only to guard the society against the oppression of its rulers, but to guard one part of the society against the injustice of the other part. *Ibid., 1788.*

What signifies a declaration, that "the liberty of the press shall be inviolably preserved." What is the liberty of the press? Who can give it any definition which would not leave the utmost latitude for evasion? I hold it to be impracticable; and from this I infer that its security, whatever fine declaration may be inserted in any constitution respecting it, must altogether depend on public opinion, and on the general spirit of the people and of the government. Here, after all, must we seek for the only solid basis of our rights. *Ibid.*

To judge from the history of mankind, we shall be compelled to conclude that the fiery destructive passions of war reign in the human breast with much more powerful sway than the mild and beneficent sentiments of peace; and that to model our political systems upon speculations of lasting tranquillity, is to calculate on the weaker springs of the human character. *Ibid.*

The liberty of the press consists in the right to publish with impunity truth with good motives, for justifiable ends. To disallow it is fatal.
Quoted by Dorothie Bobbe, N. Y.

Times Magazine, January 6, 1957; incorporated in N. Y. State Constitution.

A national debt, if it is not excessive, will be to us a national blessing.*
Letter to Robert Morris, April 30, 1781.

Take mankind in general; they are vicious, their passions may be operated upon.
Speech, Federal Convention, June 22, 1787.

Great confusion about the words democracy, aristocracy, monarchy. . . . Democracy in my sense, where the whole power of the government in the people, whether exercised by themselves or by representatives, chosen by them either mediately or immediately and legally accountable to them. . . . *Consequence, the proposed government a representative democracy.* . . . Constitution revocable and alterable by the people. This representative democracy as far as is consistent with its genius has all the features of good government.
Brief of Argument on the Constitution of the United States, 1788; quoted by (Justice) Jackson, Law Society Journal, November, 1940.

All communities divide themselves into the few and the many. The first are rich and well-born, the other the mass of people. . . . The voice of the people has been said to be the voice of God; and, however generally this maxim has been quoted and

---

* At the time we were funding our national debt, we heard much about "a public debt being a public blessing"—Jefferson to John W. Epps, November 6, 1813. Cf. Andrew Jackson.

believed, it is not true in fact. The people are turbulent and changing; they seldom judge or determine right.

To Robert Morris, 1780; Lodge, Works of Alexander Hamilton, III, 332.

Give therefore, to the former class, a distinct, permanent share in the government. They will check the unsteadiness of the second, and, as they cannot receive any advantage by a change, they therefore will ever maintain good government. *Ibid.*

The interest of the State is in intimate connection with those of the rich individuals belonging to it. *Ibid., p. 338.*

If government is in the hands of a few they will tyrannize the many; if in the hands of the many, they will tyrannize over the few. It ought to be in the hands of both, and they should be separated. This separation must be permanent. Representation alone will not do; demagogues will generally prevail; and, if separated, they will need a mutual check. This check is a monarch. *Works, II, 413.*

It has been observed that a pure democracy, if it were practicable, would be the most perfect government. Experience has proved that no position in politics is more false than this. The ancient democracies, in which the people themselves deliberated, never possessed one feature of good government. Their very character was tyranny. *Ibid., II, 440.*

Unfortunately, they have truth on their side, who say that the great mass of mankind cannot be trusted with decisions for their own welfare. The decisions had better be made by those who, by birth, education, or knowledge, are better enabled to determine what is in their interest, than are the people themselves.

Congressional Record, January 1, 1950.

The people is a great beast.*
Quoted by Justice Douglas, An Almanac of Liberty, p. 164

In framing a government which is to be administered by men over men the great difficulty lies in this: You must first enable the government to control the governed, and in the next place, oblige it to control itself.

Andrew Hamilton
(?-1703)
American pioneer, colonial official

It is an old and wise caution—That when your neighbour's house is on fire, we ought to take care of our own.
Defense of Peter Zenger (1735).

We ought at the same time to be upon our guard against Power, wherever we apprehend that it may affect ourselves or our Fellow-Subjects. . . . Power may be justly compared to a great river which, while kept within its due bounds is both beautiful and useful; but when it overflows its banks, is then too impetuous to be stemmed, it bears down all before it and brings destruction and desolation wherever it goes. If this then is the nature of power, let us at least do our duty, and like wise men use our utmost care to support liberty, the only bulwark against lawless power, which in all ages has sacraficed to its wild lust and boundless ambition the blood of the best men that ever lived.
Ibid.

The question before the Court and you gentlemen of the Jury, is not of small or private concern, it is not the cause of a poor

---

* "Your people," Hamilton is reported to have said, "is a great beast." The Beards, *Basic History of the United States.*

Printer, nor of New York alone, which you are now trying: No! It may in its consequence, affect every Freeman that lives under a British Government on the main of America. It is the best cause. It is the cause of Liberty. *Ibid.*

That, to which nature and the laws of our country have given us a Right—That Liberty—both of exposing and opposing arbitrary power (in these parts of the world at least) by speaking and writing the Truth. *Ibid.*

Edith Hamilton
(1867-1963)
Greek scholar

The fundamental fact about the Greek was that he had to use his mind. The ancient priests had said, "Thus far and no farther. We set the limits of thought." The Greeks said, "All things are to be examined and called into question. There are no limits set on thought."
The Greek Way, W. W. Norton & Co.

The modern minds in each generation are the critics who preserve us from a petrifying world, who will not leave us to walk undisturbed in the ways of our fathers. *Ibid.*

Oscar Hammerstein II
(1895-1960)
American composer, librettist

All the sounds of the earth are like music.
Oklahoma!

Learned Hand
(1872-1961)
American jurist

The spirit of liberty is the spirit which is not too sure that it is right; the spirit of liberty is the spirit which seeks to understand the minds of other men and women; the spirit of liberty is the spirit which weighs their interests alongside its own without bias; the spirit of liberty remembers that not even a sparrow falls to earth unheeded; the spirit of liberty is the spirit of Him who, near two thousand years ago, taught mankind that lesson it has never learned, but has never quite forgotten: that there is a kingdom where the least shall be heard and considered side by side with the greatest. *The Faith We Fight For.*

As soon as we cease to pry about at random, we shall come to rely upon accredited bodies of authoritative dogma; and as soon as we come to rely upon accredited bodies of authoritative dogma, not only are the days of our liberty over, but we have lost the password that has hitherto opened to us the gates of success as well.
Quoted in the N. Y. Times.

God knows there is risk in refusing to act till the facts are all in; but is there not greater risk in abandoning the conditions of all rational inquiry? Risk for risk, for myself I had rather take my chance that some traitors will escape detection than spread abroad a spirit of general suspicion and distrust, which accepts rumor and gossip in place of undismayed and unintimidated inquiry.
Address to Board of Regents, University of the State of New York, Albany, October 24, 1952.

I believe that that community is already in process of dissolution where each man begins to eye his neighbor as a possible enemy, where nonconformity with the accepted creed, political as well as religious, is a mark of disaffection; where denunciation, without specification or backing, takes the place of evidence; where orthodoxy chokes freedom of dissent; where faith in the eventual supremacy of reason has become so timid that we dare not enter our convictions in the open lists to win or lose. Such fears as these are a solvent which can eat out the cement that binds the stones together; they may in the end subject us to a despotism as evil as any that we dread; and they can be allayed only in so far as we refuse to proceed on suspicion, and trust one another until we have tangible ground for misgiving.　　　*Ibid.*

The mutual confidence on which all else depends can be maintained only by an open mind and a brave reliance upon free discussion. I do not say that these will suffice; who knows but we may be on a slope which leads down to aboriginal savagery. But of this I am sure; if we are to escape, we must not yield a foot upon demanding a fair field, and an honest race, to all ideas.　　*Ibid.*

The day has clearly gone forever of societies small enough for their members to have personal acquaintance with one another, and to find their station through the appraisal of those who have any first-hand knowledge of them. Publicity is an evil substitute, and the art of publicity is a black art; but it has come to stay, and every year adds to its potency.
Address, Elizabethan Club, May, 1951.

The hand that rules the press, the radio, the screen, and the far-spread magazine rules the country; whether we like it or not, we must learn to accept it.　*Ibid.*

It is the power of reiterated suggestion and consecrated platitude that at this moment has brought our entire civilization to imminent peril of destruction. The individual is as helpless against it as the child is helpless against the formulas with which he is indoctrinated. Not only is it possible by these means to shape his tastes, his feelings, his desires, and his hopes; but it is possible to convert him into a fanatical zealot, ready to torture and destroy and to suffer mutilation and death for an obscene faith, baseless in fact, and morally monstrous.　*Ibid.*

A society in which each is willing to surrender only that for which he can see a personal equivalent is not a society at all; it is a group already in process of dissolution, and no one need concern himself to stay its inevitable end; it would be a hard choice between it and a totalitarian society. No Utopia, nothing but Bedlam, will automatically emerge from a regime of unbridled individualism, be it ever so rugged.
Quoted by Justice Frankfurter, N. Y. Times Magazine, November 24, 1954.

My thesis is that any organization of society which depresses free and spontaneous meddling is on the decline, however showy its immediate spoils; I maintain that in such a society Liberty is gone, little as its members may know it; that the Nirvana of the individual is too high a price for a collective Paradise.　　　*Ibid.*

If I am to say what are "the principles of civil liberties and human rights," I answer that they lie in habits, customs—conventions if you will—that tolerate dissent and can live without irrefragable certainties; they are ready to overhaul existing assumptions; they recognize that we never see save through a glass, darkly, and at long last we shall succeed only so far as we continue to undertake "the intolerable labor of thought"—that most distasteful of all our activities.
N. Y. Times Magazine, February 20, 1955.

In the end it is worse to suppress dissent than to run the risk of heresy.
O. W. Holmes Lecture, Harvard, 1958.

I question whether in the end men will regard that as obscene which is honestly relevant to the adequate expression of innocent ideas, and whether they will not believe that truth and beauty are too precious to society at large to be mutilated in the interests of those most likely to pervert them to base uses.

*U.S. v. Mitchell Kennerley, U.S. District Court, 1913; protest against the Hicklin rule.**

To put thought in leash to the average conscience of the time is perhaps tolerable, but to fetter it by the necessities of the lowest and least capable seems a fatal policy.   *Ibid.*

All discussion, all debate, all dissidence tends to question, and in consequence to upset existing convictions; that is precisely its purpose and its justification.

Address, January 29, 1955.

Heretics have been hateful from the beginning of recorded time; they have been ostracized, exiled, tortured, maimed and butchered; but it has generally proved impossible to smother them; and when it has not, the society that has succeeded has always declined.   *Ibid.*

Hannibal
(247?-183 B.C.)
Carthaginian general

We will either find a way or make one.

---

* Lord Chief Justice Alexander Cockburn, Queen *v.* Hicklin, 1868: "I think the test of obscenity is this, whether the tendency of the matter charged as obscenity is to deprave and corrupt those whose minds are open to such immoral influences, and into whose hands a publication of this sort may fall."

James Keir Hardie
(1856-1915)
British labor leader

That, considering the increased burden which the private ownership of land and capital is imposing upon the industrious and useful classes of the community, the poverty . . . resulting . . . from a . . . system of . . . production which aims primarily at profitmaking, the alarming growth of trusts and syndicates, able by reason of their great wealth to influence Governments and plunge peaceful nations into war to serve their interests, this House is of the opinion that such a condition of affairs constitutes a menace to the wellbeing of the realm, and calls for legislation designed to remedy the same by inaugurating a Socialist Commonwealth founded upon the common ownership of land and capital, production for use and not for profit, and equality of opportunity for every citizen.

First Socialist resolution introduced into the House of Commons, 1901.

Warren G. Harding
(1865-1923)
29th President of the United States

America's present need is not heroics but healing; not nostrums but normalcy; not revolution but restoration; not surgery but serenity, not the dramatic but the dispassionate, not experiment but equipoise, not submergence in internationality but sustainment in triumphant nationality.

Speech, Boston, May 14, 1920.

Government after all is a very simple thing.

Quoted by Justice Frankfurter, who added: "There never was a more pathetic misapprehension of responsibility than Harding's touching statement."

Normal men and back to normalcy will steady a civilization which has been fevered by the supreme upheaval of all the world.

Thomas Hardy
(1840-1928)
English novelist, poet

The beggarly question of parentage— what is it after all? What does it matter, when you come to think of it, whether a child is yours by blood or not? All the little ones of our time are collectively the children of us adults of the time, and entitled to our general care. The excessive regard of parents for their children, and their dislike of other people's is, like class-feeling, patriotism, save-your-soul-ism, and other virtues, a mean exclusiveness at bottom.

Jude the Obscure, p. 324, Modern Library.

John Marshall Harlan
(1833-1911)
U.S. Supreme Court justice

In respect of civil rights, common to all citizens, the Constitution of the United States does not, I think, permit any authority to know the race of those entitled to be protected in the enjoyment of such rights.

Sole dissent, Plessy v. Ferguson, 163 U.S. 537 (1896).

If a State can prescribe, as a rule of civil conduct, that whites and blacks shall not travel as passengers in the same railroad coach, why may it not so regulate the use of the streets of its cities and towns as to compel white citizens to keep on one side of the street and black citizens to keep on the other. *Ibid.*

The white race deems itself to be the dominant race in this country. And so it is, in prestige, in achievements, in education, in wealth, and in power. So, I doubt not, it will continue to be for all time, if it remains true to its great heritage and holds fast to the principles of constitutional liberty. But in view of the Constitution, in the eye of the law, there is in this country no superior, dominant, ruling class of citizens. There is no caste here. *Ibid.*

Our Constitution is color-blind and neither knows nor tolerates classes among citizens. *Ibid.*

The law regards man as man and takes no account of his surroundings or of his color when his civil rights as guaranteed by the supreme law of the land are involved. *Ibid.*

The sure guarantee of the peace and security of each race is the clear, distinct, unconditional recognition by our governments, National and State, of every right that inheres in civil freedom, and of the equality before the law of all the citizens of the United States without regard to race. *Ibid.*

State enactments, upon regulating the enjoyment of civil rights, upon the basis of race, and cunningly devised to defeat legitimate results of the war, under the pretense of recognizing equality of rights, can have no other results than to render permanent peace impossible, and to keep alive a conflict of races, continuance of which must do harm to all concerned. *Ibid.*

It is not within the functions of government . . . to compel any person in the course of his business and against his will, to accept or retain the personal services of another, or to compel any person, against his will, to perform personal services for another.

Adair v. U.S., 209 U.S. 161 (1908). (The Yellow Dog Contract case.)

I cannot assent to that view, if it be meant that the legislature may impair or abridge the rights of a free press and of free speech whenever it thinks that the public welfare requires that to be done. The public welfare cannot override constitutional privilege.

Patterson v. Chicago; inscribed on the Chicago Tribune Tower.

George Julian Harney

Chartist, journalist

Time was when every Englishman had a musket in his cottage, and along with it hung a flitch of bacon; now there is no flitch of bacon for there is no musket; let the musket be restored and the flitch of bacon will soon follow.

James Harrington

(1611-1677)

English political writer

The Monarchy of England was not a Government of Arms, but a Government of Laws, though imperfect and ineffectual Laws.   *Political Aphorisms.*

The People cannot see, but they can feel. The People having felt the difference between a Government of Laws and a Government of Arms, will always desire the Government of Laws, and abhor that of Arms.   *Ibid.*

Where the spirit of the People is impatient of a Government of Arms, and desirous of a Government of Laws, there the spirit of the People is not unfit to be trusted with their Liberty.   *Ibid.*

Where Civil Liberty is entire, it includes Liberty of Conscience. Where Liberty of Conscience is entire, it includes Civil Liberty.   *Ibid.*

Every man, either to his terror or consolation, has some sense of religion.

The Oceana and Other Works.

The lust of government is the greatest lust.   *Ibid.*

Treason doth never prosper: what's the reason?
Why, if it prosper, none dare call it treason.

Epigrams, bk. iv, 5; also in Alcilia.

Frank Harris

(1854-1931)

American novelist, biographer, dramatist

All the faults of the age come from Christianity and journalism.

Margot Asquith, Autobiography. Vol. 1, ch. 10.

Benjamin Harrison

(1833-1901)

23rd President of the United States

We Americans have no commission from God to police the world.   *1888.*

---

* Said to A. J. Balfour, who replied, "Christianity of course, but why journalism?"

Frederic Harrison
(1831-1923)
English philosopher, biographer, critic

Society can overlook murder, adultery or swindling; it never forgives the preaching of a new gospel.

William Henry Harrison
(1773-1841)
9th President of the United States

I have never regarded the office of Chief Magistrate as conferring upon the incumbent the power of master over the popular will, but as granting him the power to execute the properly expressed will of the people and not resist it.
N. Y. Times Magazine, January 13, 1957.

I believe and I say it is true Democratic feeling, that all the measures of the Government are directed to the purpose of making the rich richer and the poor poorer.
Speech, October 1, 1840; Schlesinger, The Age of Jackson, p. 292.

William Harvey
(1578-1657)
English physician

For true philosophers, who are only eager for truth and knowledge, never regard themselves as already so thoroughly informed, but that they welcome further information from whomsoever and from whencesoever it may come; nor are they so narrow-minded as to imagine any of the arts or sciences transmitted to us by the ancients, in such a state of forwardness or completeness, that nothing is left for the ingenuity and industry of others. Very many, on the contrary, maintain that all we know is still infinitely less than all that still remains unknown; nor do philosophers pin their faith to others' precepts in such wise that they lose their liberty, and cease to give credence to the conclusions of their proper senses. Neither do they swear such fealty to their mistress Antiquity, that they openly, and in sight of all, deny and desert their friend Truth.
On the Motion of the Heart and Blood, addressed to the Royal College of Physicians, 1628.

The heart, consequently, is the beginning of life; the sun of the microcosm, even as the sun in his turn might well be designated the heart of the world; for it is the heart by whose virtue and pulse the blood is moved, perfected, made apt to nourish, and is preserved from corruption and coagulation; it is the household divinity which, discharging its function, nourishes, cherishes, quickens the whole body, and is indeed the foundation of life, the source of all action.   *Ibid.*

William H. Hastie
(b. 1904)
American judge

Democracy is a process, not a static condition. It is becoming, rather than being. It can easily be lost, but never is fully won. Its essence is eternal struggle.

Henry O. Havemeyer
(1847-1907)
American sugar refiner, art collector

We always contribute to the funds of the political parties for their election campaigns in the states. Where the issue is too uncertain, the (sugar) trust subscribes to the funds of both parties, in order to have some influence on the winning side, whichever it may be.

André Siegfried, America at Mid-Century.

Jacquetta Hawkes
(b. 1910)
English archeologist

The discouragement of radical thought must lead to the closed society and closed mind; and so, too, may our present orthodox forms of Christianity—Catholicism through its liking for ignorance, Protestantism through its approval of money making, respectability, and the whole crowned and mitred body of the *status quo.*

New Statesman & Nation, January, 1957.

The only inequalities that matter begin in the mind. It is not income levels but differences in mental equipment that keep people apart, breed feelings of inferiority.
Ibid.

Nathaniel Hawthorne
(1804-1864)
American novelist

What we call real estate—the solid ground to build a house on—is the broad foundation on which nearly all the guilt of the world rests.
The House of the Seven Gables.

The world owes all its onward impulses to men ill at ease. The happy man inevitably confines himself within ancient limits.
Ibid.

From principles is derived probability, but truth or certainty is obtained only from facts.

How seldom a fact is accurately stated; how almost invariably when a story has passed through the mind of a third person it becomes . . . little better than a falsehood; and this, too, though the narrator be the most truth-seeking person in existence.

Labor is the curse of the world, and nobody can meddle with it without becoming proportionately brutified.
American Note-Books, August 12, 1841.

John Hay
(1838-1905)
American statesman, author

The people will come to their own at last—God is not mocked forever.
The Sphynx of the Tuileries.

For always in thine eyes, O Liberty!
Shines that high light whereby the world
  is saved;
  And, though they slay us, we will trust
  in thee.

S(amuel) I(chiye) Hayakawa
(b. 1906)
Professor of language arts, educator, writer

Motivation researchers are those harlot social scientists who, in impressive psychoanalytic and/or sociological jargon, tell their clients what their clients want to hear, namely, that *appeals to human irrationality are likely to be far more profitable than appeals to rationality.*
Etc. (publication), Spring, 1958.

Rutherford B. Hayes
(1822-1893)
19th President of the United States

He serves his party best who serves the country best.
Inaugural Address, March 5, 1877.

Arthur Garfield Hays
(1881-1954)
American lawyer, libertarian

Indignation boils my blood at the thought of the heritage we are throwing away; at the thought that, with few exceptions, the fight for freedom is left to the poor, forlorn and defenseless, and to the few radicals and revolutionaries who would make use of liberty to destroy, rather than to maintain American institutions.

William ("Big Bill") D. Haywood
(1869-1928)
American radical labor leader

This is the Continental Congress of the working class.
Address to delegates, preliminary to formation of the Industrial Workers of the World (IWW), January 2, 1905.

We are here to confederate the workers of this country into a working-class movement. The aims and objects of this organization shall be to put the working-class in possession of economic power, the means of life, in control of the machinery of production and distribution without regard to capitalist masters. *Ibid.*

There will be a new society sometime in which there will be no battle between capitalist and wage earner, but that every man will have free access to land and its resources. In that day there will be non-political government, there will be no States, and Congress will not be composed of lawyers and preachers as it is now, but will be composed of experts of the different branches of industry, who will come together for the purpose of discussing the welfare of all the people and discussing the means by which the machinery can be made the slave of the people instead of a part of the people being made the slave of machinery or of the owners of machinery.
1908; American Labor Leaders. Madison.

William Hazlitt
(1778-1830)
English essayist, critic

Principle is a passion for truth.

Prejudice is the child of ignorance.
Sketches and Essays.

One truth discovered is immortal, and entitles its author to be so; for, like a new substance in nature, it cannot be destroyed.
The Spirit of the Age.

The love of liberty is the love of others; the love of power is the love of ourselves.
Political Essays.

Man is a toad-eating animal. The admiration of power in others is as common to man as the love of it in himself; the one makes him a tyrant, the other a slave.
Ibid.

We are all of us more or less the slaves of opinion. *Ibid.*

Nothing is more unjust or capricious than public opinion. *Characteristics.*

The only vice that cannot be forgiven is hypocrisy. The repentance of a hypocrite is itself hypocrisy. *Ibid.*

There is some virtue in almost every vice, except hypocrisy; and even that, while it is a mockery of virtue, is at the same time, a compliment to it. *Ibid.*

The Public have neither shame nor gratitude. *Ibid.*

Want of principle is power.   *Ibid.*

Truth and honesty set a limit over efforts which impudence and hypocrisy easily overleap.   *Ibid.*

If mankind had wished for what is right, they might have had it long ago.
The Plain Speaker, 1826.

Indifferent pictures, like dull people, must absolutely be moral.
Criticism of Art.

The contemplation of truth and beauty is the proper object for which we were created, which calls forth the most intense desires of the soul, and of which it never tires.   *Ibid.*

The origin of science is in the desire to know causes; and the origin of all false science and imposture is in the desire to accept false causes rather than none; or, which is the same thing, in the unwillingness to acknowledge our own ignorance.
Burke and the Edinburgh Phrenologists, The Atlas, February 15, 1829.

The majority, compose them how you will, are a herd, and not a nice one.
Butts of Different Sorts, Ibid., February 8, 1829.

Mankind are an incorrigible race. Give them but bugbears and idols—it is all that they ask.   *Collected Works, xi, 557.*

When a thing ceases to be a subject of controversy, it ceases to be a subject of interest.   *Ibid., xii, 384.*

There is no more mean, stupid, dastardly, pitiful, selfish, spiteful, envious, ungrateful animal than the Public. It is the greatest of cowards, for it is afraid of itself.
Table Talk.

Words are the only things that last forever.   *Ibid.*

Great thoughts reduced to practice become great acts.   *Ibid.*

Political truth is libel; religious truth, blasphemy.

Man is the only animal that laughs and weeps; for he is the only animal that is struck with the difference between what things are and what they ought to be.
Lectures on the English Comic Writers.

A man's reputation is not in his own keeping, but lies at the mercy of the profligacy of others. Calumny requires no proof. The throwing out of malicious imputations against any character leaves a stain, which no after-refutation can wipe out. To create an unfavorable impression, it is not necessary that certain things should be *true,* but that they *have been said.* The imagination is of so delicate a texture that even words wound it.   *Selected Essays.*

William Randolph Hearst
(1863-1951)
American newspaper publisher

Please realize that the first duty of newspaper men is to get the news and PRINT THE NEWS.
Requoted in Editor & Publisher, August 12, 1944.

You furnish the pictures and I'll furnish the war.
Cable to Frederic Remington, artist, in Cuba, 1898.

We hold that the greatest right in the world is the right to be wrong, that in the exercise thereof people have an inviolable right to express their unbridled thoughts on all topics and personalities, being liable only for the abuse of that right.
Platform, Independence League; N. Y. Journal, February 1, 1924.

We hold that no person or set of persons can properly establish a standard of expression for others. *Ibid.*

What has become of the descendants of the irresponsible adventurers, the scapegrace sons, the bond servants, the redemptionists and the indentured maidens, the undesirables, and even the criminals, which made up—not all, of course, but nevertheless a considerable part of—the earliest emigrants to these virgin countries?

They have become the leaders of the thought of the world, the vanguard in the march of progress, the inspirers of liberty, the creators of national prosperity, the sponsors of universal education and enlightenment.

Communication to the American Crime Study Commission, May 19, 1929.

The NARROW-MINDED BIGOTS have given to this country and to the world freedom of speech, freedom of thought and action and religious liberty. *Ibid.*

Any man who has the brains to think and the nerve to act for the benefit of the people of the country is considered a radical by those who are content with stagnation and willing to endure disaster.

Interview, Cleveland Plain Dealer, October 24, 1932.

A politician will do anything to keep his job—even become a patriot.

Editorial, August 28, 1933.

SEVENTH, the text of a newspaper must tell the news.

The headlines must tell the news.

The pictures must tell the news.

The subheads and subtitles must tell the news.

Please see that the newspapers perform this function.

Instructions to E. D. Coblentz, March 1, 1938.

When free discussion is denied, hardening of the arteries of democracy has set in, free institutions are but a lifeless form, and the death of the republic is at hand.

"In the News," June 13, 1941.

Whatever is right can be achieved through the irresistible power of awakened and informed public opinion. Our object, therefore, is not to enquire whether a thing can be done, but whether it ought to be done, to so exert the forces of publicity that public opinion will compel it to be done.

Advertisement, N. Y. Herald Tribune, August 19, 1946.

According to American principle and practice the public is the ruler of the State, and in order to rule rightly it should be informed correctly.

N. Y. Journal-American, November 11, 1954.°

Jacques René Hébert

(1755-guillotined 1794)

French revolutionist, journalist

Everywhere and at all times men of commerce have had neither heart nor soul; their cash-box is their God. . . . They traffic in all things, even human flesh. . . . Could it ever be expected that such worthless creatures could become citizens? Above all, a freeman must be humane and disinterested; he must sacrifice everything for his country. Their country? *Foutre!* Business men have no such thing.

Le Père Duchesne, 1793.

° Hearst published a daily quotation on his editorial pages; after his death a daily quotation from his writings was published.

Ben Hecht

(1894-1964)

American journalist, author

Prejudice is a raft onto which the shipwrecked mind clambers and paddles to safety. *A Guide for the Bedevilled, 1947.*

The artist isn't made by a haberdasher and a left-wing editorial. He's made by the explosive in him that bears the label, "Beware Uniformity." *Charlie, p. 127.*

August Heckscher

(b. 1913)

American author, executive

In one sense freedom is always in crisis, just as beauty is, and honor and truth—all those things which man has made for himself as a garment against the ever-present blasts of the barbarian spirit. *Address, Kenyon College, April 4, 1957.*

Eternal vigilance is the condition, not only of liberty, but of everything which as civilized men we hold dear. *Ibid.*

Georg Wilhelm Friedrich Hegel *

(1770-1831)

German philosopher

The only Thought which Philosophy brings with it to the contemplation of History, is the simple conception of *Reason;* that Reason is the Sovereign of the World; that the history of the world, therefore, presents us with a rational process. *Philosophy of History.*

---

* "It is impossible to fully understand Marx's *Capital,* particularly its first chapter, without preliminary study and complete understanding of Hegel's *Logic*"—Lenin.

The History of the world is none other than the progress of the consciousness of Freedom. *Ibid.*

It must further be understood that all the worth which the human being possesses —all spiritual reality—he possesses only through the State. *Ibid.*

Only that which obeys law, is free; for it obeys itself—it is independent and so free. When the State or our country constitutes a community of existence; when the subjective will of man submits to laws—the contradiction between Liberty and Necessity vanishes. *Ibid.*

The State is embodied Morality. It is the ethical spirit which has clarified itself and has taken substantial shape as Will, a Will which is manifest before the world, which is self-conscious and knows its purposes and carries through that which it knows to the extent of its knowledge. *Ibid.*

Custom and Morality are the outward and visible form of the inner essence of the State. *Ibid.*

The State is Mind, *per se.* *Ibid.*

History in general, is . . . the development of Spirit in *Time,* as Nature is the development of the Idea in *Space.* *Ibid.*

Peoples and governments have never learned anything from history, or acted upon principles deducible from it. *Ibid.*

Passions, private aims, and the satisfaction of selfish desires, are on the other hand, most effective springs of action. Their power lies in the fact that they respect none of the limitations which justice and morality would impose on them; and that their natural impulses have a more direct influence over man than the artificial and tedious discipline that tends to order and self-restraint, law and morality. *Ibid.*

We may affirm absolutely that *nothing great in the World* has been accomplished without *passion*. *Ibid.*

World-historical men—the Heroes of an epoch—must, therefore, be recognized as its clear-sighted ones; *their* deeds, *their* words are the best of that time. Great men have formed purposes to satisfy themselves, not others. *Ibid.*

A World-historical individual is not so unwise as to indulge a variety of wishes to divide his regards. He is devoted to the One Aim, regardless of all else. *Ibid.*

For Truth is the Unity of the universe and subjective Will; and the Universal is to be found in the State, its laws, its universal and rational arrangements. The State is the Divine Idea as it exists on Earth. *Ibid.*

It is a dangerous and false prejudice, that the People *alone* have reason and insight, and know what justice is; for each popular faction may represent itself as the People, and the question as to what constitutes the State is one of advanced science, and not of popular decision. *Ibid.*

The State rests on Religion. *Ibid.*

Nations are what their deeds are. *Ibid.*

The State, being an end in itself, is provided with the maximum of rights against the individual citizens, whose highest duty it is to be members of the State. *Ibid.*

To the ideal of freedom, law and morality are indispensably requisite. . . . Society and the State are the very conditions in which freedom is realized. *Ibid.*

The first glance at History convinces us that the actions of men proceed from their needs, their passions, their characters and talents; and impresses us with the belief that such needs, passions and interests are the sole spring of action—the efficient agents in this scene of activity. Among these may, perhaps, be found aims of a liberal or universal kind—benevolence it may be, or noble patriotism; but such virtues and general views are but insignificant as compared with the World and its doings. *Ibid.*

Passion is regarded as a thing of sinister aspect, as more or less immoral. Man is required to have no passions. Passion, it is true, is not quite the suitable word for what I wish to express. I mean here nothing more than human activity as resulting from private interests—special, or if you will, self-seeking designs, with this qualification, that the whole energy or will and character is devoted to their attainment; that other interests . . . are sacrificed to them. *Ibid.*

Man must . . . venerate the State as a secular deity. *Philosophy of Right.*

The march of God in the world, that is what the State is. *Ibid.*

The basis of the State is the power of Reason actualizing itself as Will. *Ibid.*

In considering the idea of the State, we must not have our eyes on particular states or on particular institutions. Instead we must consider the Idea, this actual God, by itself. *Ibid.*

Robert L. Heilbroner
(b. 1919)
American writer

If one could divine the nature of the economic forces in the world, one could foretell the future.
The Worldly Philosophers, p. 305.

Heinrich Heine
(1797-1856)
German lyric poet, critic

Religion cannot sink lower than when somehow it is raised to a state religion. . . . It becomes then an avowed mistress.
Letters from Berlin, March 16, 1822.

The fundamental evil of the world arose from the fact that the good Lord has not created money enough.
English Fragments, 1828.

It must require an inordinate share of vanity and presumption, too, after enjoying so much that is good and beautiful on earth, to ask the Lord for immortality in addition to it all. *City of Lucca, 1829.*

Since the Exodus, Freedom has always spoken with a Hebrew accent.
Germany to Luther, 1834.

Whether a revolution succeeds or miscarries, men of great heart will always be its victims. *Salon, 1834.*

In these times we fight for ideas, and newspapers are our fortresses.

Human misery is too great for men to do without faith.

Be entirely tolerant or not at all; follow the good path or the evil one. To stand at the crossroads requires more strength than you possess.

Communism possesses a language which every people can understand—its elements are hunger, envy, and death.

Demagogy, the Holy Alliance of the Peoples.
Gedanken und Einfalle, Vol. 10; quoted in The Nation, February 11, 1956; translated by Mina Curtiss.

The German is like the slave who, without chains, without whip, obeys his master's merest word, his very glance. The condition of servitude is inherent in him, in his very soul; and worse than the physical is the spiritual slavery. The Germans must be set free from within. From without there is no help. *Ibid.*

Luther convulsed Germany—but Francis Drake calmed it down again. He gave us the potato. *Ibid.*

Every religion, after its own fashion, guarantees consolation in suffering. With the Jews, hope: We are in captivity, Jehovah is angry at us, but he will send a saviour. With the Mohammedans, fatalism: No man escapes his destiny. It is written above on tablets of stone. Let us bear the inevitable with resignation. *Allah il Allah.* With the Christian, spiritual contempt of pleasure and joy, morose craving for heaven; on earth temptation for the wicked, above salvation. *Ibid.*

God has given us no manifesto indicating life after death; nor did Moses speak of it. The pious are perhaps quite unfair to God in taking immortality so seriously. Perhaps with fatherly kindness, He wishes to give it to us as a surprise. *Ibid.*

In earlier religions the spirit of the time was expressed through the individual and confirmed by miracles. In modern religions the spirit is expressed through the many and confirmed by reason. Now, since physics has been perfected, there are no longer any miracles. *Ibid.*

In dark ages people are best guided by religion, as in a pitch-black night a blind man is the best guide; he knows the roads and paths better than a man who can see. When daylight comes, however, it is foolish to use blind, old men as guides. *Ibid.*

If he does it from conviction (i.e., becomes a convert), he is a fool. If he does it for convenience, he is a scoundrel.
Ibid. (Before his conversion.)

No Jew can ever believe in the divinity of any other Jew. *Ibid.*

Dieu me pardonnera; c'est son métier. (God will pardon me; it is his trade.)
February 17, 1856, the day before he died.

Lillian Hellman
(b. 1905)
American playwright

I am not willing, now or in the future, to bring bad trouble to people who, in my past association with them, were completely innocent of any talk or any action that was disloyal or subversive. . . . I cannot and will not cut my conscience to fit this year's fashions, even though I long ago came to the conclusion that I was not a political person and could have no comfortable place in any political group.
Letter to Committee on Un-American Activities, The Nation, May 31, 1952.

Claude Adrien Helvétius
(1715-1771)
French philosopher, litterateur

When a government prohibits writing on matters of administration, it makes a vow of blindness. *De l'Homme, Vol. 1, sec. 4.*

To limit the press is to insult a nation; to prohibit reading of certain books is to declare the inhabitants to be either fools or slaves. *Ibid.*

By annihilating the desires, you annihilate the mind. Every man without passions has within him no principle of action, nor motive to act.

The free man is the man who is not in irons, not imprisoned in a gaol, nor terrorized like a slave by the fear of punishment . . . it is not a lack of freedom not to fly like an eagle or swim like a whale.
Quoted by Prof. Sir Isaiah Berlin, q.v., Oxford, 1958.

Ernest Hemingway
(1898-1961)
American writer, Nobel prize, 1954

We have come out of the time when obedience, the acceptance of discipline, intelligent courage and resolution were most important, into that more difficult time when it is a man's duty to understand his world rather than simply fight for it.
Introduction to Treasury of the Free World, 1946.

It would be easy for us, if we do not learn to understand the world and appreciate the rights, privileges and duties of all other countries and peoples, to represent in our power the same danger to the world that Fascism did. *Ibid.*

No weapon has ever settled a moral problem. It can impose a solution but it cannot guarantee it to be a just one. You can wipe out your opponents. But if you do it unjustly you become eligible for being wiped out yourself. *Ibid.*

An aggressive war is the great crime against everything good in the world. A defensive war, which must necessarily turn to aggressive at the earliest moment, is the necessary great counter-crime. But never think that war, no matter how necessary, nor how justified, is not a crime. Ask the infantry and ask the dead. *Ibid.*

We have fought this war and won it. Now let us not be sanctimonious; nor hypocritical; nor vengeful; nor stupid. Let us make our enemies incapable of ever making war again, let us re-educate them, let us learn to live in peace and justice with all countries and all peoples in this world. To do this we must educate and re-educate. But first we must educate ourselves.

Ibid.

What is moral is what you feel good after and what is immoral is what you feel bad after.   *Death in the Afternoon.*

Once we have a war there is only one thing to do. It must be won. For defeat brings worse things than any that can ever happen in war.   *Men at War (anthology).*

The first panacea for a mismanaged nation is inflation of the currency; the second is war. Both bring a temporary prosperity; both bring a permanent ruin. But both are the refuge of political and economic opportunists.   *Notes on the Next War.*

There is only one form of government that cannot produce good writers, and that system is Fascism. For Fascism is a lie told by bullies. A writer who will not lie cannot live or work under Fascism.

Because Fascism is a lie, it is condemned to literary sterility. And when it is past, it will have no history, except the bloody history of murder.

Address, American Writers Congress, N.Y.C., 1937, reprinted, New Masses, June 22, 1937.

For our dead are a part of the earth of Spain now and the earth of Spain can never die.

On the American Dead in Spain. New Masses, February 14, 1939.

As long as all our dead live in the Spanish earth, and they will live as long as the earth lives, no system of tyranny ever will prevail in Spain.   *Ibid.*

The dead do not need to rise. They are a part of the earth now and the earth can never be conquered. For the earth endureth forever. . . . Those who have entered it honorably, and no men ever entered earth more honorably than those who died in Spain, already have achieved immortality.

Ibid.

Man is not made for defeat.
          The Old Man and the Sea.

Henry IV
(1553-1610)
King of France

Paris vaut bien une messe. (Paris is worth a Mass.)   *Attributed.*

Pends-toi, brave Crillon, nous avons combattu à Arques, et tu n'y etais pas. (Hang yourself, brave Crillon, we have conquered at Arques, and you were not there.)
Letter to Crillon, attributed by Voltaire, in Henriade, Chant. viii.

Je veux qu'il n'y ait si pauvre paysan en moi royaume qu'il n'ait tous les dimanches sa poule au pot. I wish that there would not be a peasant so poor in all my realm who would not have a chicken in his pot every Sunday.**
Hardovin de Perefixe, Histoire de Henri le Grand, 1681.

---

* The quotation is incorrect and a distortion of history, as it was written before Arques. Ramage, *Beautiful Thoughts from French and Italian Authors,* p. 379, gives the following text of a letter from the king to A. M. de Grillon, 1597: "Brave Grillon, hang yourself for not having been near me on Monday last, on the finest occasion that was ever seen."
** President Hoover (q.v.) denies he ever said anything about two cars in every garage and two chickens in every pot.

Henry VIII
(1491-1547)
King of England

The King, our sovereign Lord . . . shall be taken, accepted, and reputed the only supreme head in earth of the Church of England called Anglicana Ecclesia . . . and that our said Lord . . . shall have full power and authority from time to time to visit, repress, redress, redeem . . . all such errors, heresies, abuses . . . which by any manner spiritual authority or jurisdiction ought or may lawfully be reformed . . . any usage, foreign laws, foreign authority . . . to the contrary nothwithstanding.

Supremacy Act.

Patrick Henry
(1736-1799)
American Revolutionary statesman

It is natural for man to indulge in the illusions of hope. We are apt to shut our eyes against a painful truth, and listen to the song of that siren till she transforms us into beasts. Is this the part of wise men, engaged in a great and arduous struggle for liberty? Are we disposed to be of the number of those who having eyes see not, and having ears hear not, the things which so nearly concern their temporal salvation?

For my part, whatever anguish of spirit it may cost, I am willing to know the whole truth—to know the worst and to provide for it.

Speech on the Stamp Act, Virginia Convention, March 23, 1775.

I have but one lamp by which my feet are guided, and that is the lamp of experience. I know of no way of judging of the future but by the past. . . .   *Ibid.*

Suffer not yourself to be betrayed with a kiss. Ask yourselves how the gracious reception of our petition comports with those warlike preparations which cover our waters and darken our land. Are fleets and armies necessary to a work of love and reconciliation? Have we shown ourselves so unwilling to be reconciled that force must be called in to win back our love? Let us not deceive ourselves, sir. These are the implements of war and subjugation—the last arguments to which kings resort.

Ibid.

There is no longer any room for hope. If we wish to be free, if we mean to preserve inviolate those inestimable privileges for which we have been so long contending, if we mean not basely to abandon the noble struggle in which we have been so long engaged, and which we have pledged ourselves never to abandon until the glorious object of our contest shall be obtained—we must fight!

I repeat it, sir, we must fight! An appeal to arms and to the God of Hosts is all that is left us.   *Ibid.*

It is vain, sir, to extenuate the matter. Gentlemen may cry, peace, peace, peace —but there is no peace. The war is actually begun! The next gale that sweeps from the north will bring to our ears the clash of resounding arms! Our brethren are already in the field! Why stand we here idle? What is it that gentlemen wish? What would you have? Is life so dear, or peace so sweet, as to be purchased at the price of chains and slavery? Forbid it, Almighty God! I know not what course others may take, but as for me, give me liberty or give me death!

Ibid.

Is the relinquishment of trial by jury and the liberty of the press necessary for your liberty? Will the abandonment of your most sacred rights tend to anyone's security? Liberty, the greatest of all earthly blessings

—give us that precious jewel and you may take everything else. . . . Suspect everyone who approaches that jewel.

Heraclitus
(540?-475? B.C.)
Greek philosopher

Good and ill are one. . . . To God all things are fair and good and right, but men hold some things wrong and some right.
Burnet, Early Greek Philosophy, 1908.

Man's character is his fate.   *Ibid.*

It is hard to fight for one's heart's desire. Whatever it wishes to get, it purchases at the cost of soul.   *Ibid.*

Wisdom is one thing. It is to know the thought by which all things are steered through all things.   *Ibid.*

All is flux, nothing is stationary.
       Fragment.

There is nothing permanent except change.   *Ibid.*

The greatness of man consists in saying what is true, and in acting according to Nature.
Quoted by Sir Richard Livingstone, Atlantic Monthly, November, 1957.

Through strife all things arise and pass away. *Durant, The Story of Philosophy.*

War is the father and king of all: some he has made gods, and some men; some slaves, and some free.   *Ibid.*

Auberon Herbert
(1838-1906)
English political philosopher

Of all the miserable, unprofitable, inglorious wars in the world is the war against words. Let men say just what they like. Let them propose to cut every throat and burn every house—if so they like it. We have nothing to do with a man's words or a man's thoughts, except to put against them better words and better thoughts, and so to win in the great moral and intellectual duel that is always going on, and on which all progress depends.
Westminister Gazette, London, November 22, 1893.

Deny human rights, and however little you may wish to do so, you will find yourself abjectly kneeling at the feet of that old-world god, Force—that grimmest and ugliest of gods that men have ever created for themselves out of the lusts of their hearts. You will find yourself hating and dreading all other men who differ from you; you will find yourself obliged by the law of the conflict into which you have plunged, to use every means in your power to crush them before they are able to crush you; you will find yourself day by day growing more unscrupulous and intolerant, more and more compelled by the fear of those opposed to you, to commit harsh and violent actions. You will find yourselves clinging to and welcoming Force, as the one and only form of protection left to you, when you have once destroyed the rule of the great principles.   *Ibid.*

When once you have plunged into the strife for power, it is the fear of those who are seeking for power over you that so easily persuades to all the great crimes.
       Ibid.

Who shall count up the evil brood that is born from power—the pitiful fear, the madness, the despair, the overpowering craving for revenge, the treachery, the unmeasured cruelty?   *Ibid.*

[313]

George Herbert

(1593-1632)

English metaphysical poet

Prosperity destroys fools and endangers the wise. *Jacula Prudentum.*

Follow not truth too near the heels, lest it dash out thy teeth. *Ibid.*

Dare to be true. Nothing can need a lie: A fault which needs it most, grows two thereby. *Church. Porch, st. 13.*

William Herndon

(1818-1891)

American lawyer, author

He (Lincoln) soon grew into the belief of a universal law, evolution, and from this he has never deviated.

Mr. Lincoln believed in laws that imperiously ruled both matter and mind. With him there were no miracles outside the law; he held that the universe was a grand mystery and a miracle. . . . There were no accidents in his philosophy. Every event had its cause. . . . Everything to him was the result of the forces of Nature, playing on matter and mind from the beginning of time. . . . (Lincoln did not believe) that the Bible was the special divine revelation of God, as the Christian world contends.

He firmly believed in an overruling Providence, Maker, God, and the great moral of Him written in the human soul. His—late in life—conventional use of the word God must not by any means be interpreted that he believed in a personal God. I know that it is said Mr. Lincoln changed his views. There is no evidence of this.

George D. Herron

(1862-1925)

American clergyman, socialist

No man ever ruled other men for their own good; no man was ever rightly the master of the minds or bodies of his brothers; no man ever ruled other men for anything except for their undoing and for his own brutalization.
Quoted by Sinclair, The Cry for Justice.

The possession of power over others is inherently destructive both to the possessor of the power and to those over whom it is exercised. And the great man of the future, in distinction from the great man of the past, is he who will seek to create power in the people, and not gain power over them. The great man of the future is he who will refuse to be great at all, in the historic sense; he is the man who will literally lose himself, who will altogether diffuse himself in the life of humanity. *Ibid.*

All that any man can do for a people, all that any man can do for another man, is to set the man or the people free. Our work, whensoever and wheresoever we would do good, is to open to men the gates of life—to lift up the heavenly doors of opportunity. . . . Give men opportunity and opportunity will give you men. *Ibid.*

There can be no peace between the man who is down and the man who builds on his back. There can be no reconciliation between classes; there can only be an end to classes. *Ibid.*

It is idle to talk of good-will until there is first justice, and idle to talk of justice until the man who makes the world possesses the work of his own hands. *Ibid.*

[314]

The ignorance of the working-class and the superior intelligence of the privileged class are superstitions—are superstitions fostered by intellectual mercenaries, by universities and churches, and by all the centers of privilege. *Ibid.*

John Hersey
(b. 1914)
American writer

The wisdom and compassion of man, with which he tries to check his crimes and folly, are couched in print. In words pressed onto paper lie man's best hopes of doing something more than merely surviving.
Report, Fairfield (Conn.) School Study Council.

Theodor Herzl
(1860-1904)
Founder of political Zionism

A nation is a historical group of men of recognizable cohesion, held together by a common enemy. *The Jewish State, 1896.*

The wealth of a country is its working people. *Altneuland, 1902.*

Whoever would change men must change the conditions of their lives. *Diary.*

Henry Hetherington
(1792-1849)
English printer, publisher, libertarian

We shall begin by protecting and upholding this grand bulwark and defense of all our rights—this key to all our liberties—THE FREEDOM OF THE PRESS—*the Press, too, of the* IGNORANT AND THE POOR! We have taken upon ourselves its

protection, and we will never abandon our post; we will die rather.
First issue of his newspaper, The Poor Man's Guardian, 1831.

It is property which has made tyrants and not tyrants property. . . . Down then with property; the Kings, Lords, and Priests will go down of themselves.
The Poor Man's Guardian.

Hieronymus
See St. Jerome

James Higgins
(Contemporary)
Assistant editor,
York, Pa., Gazette & Daily

Democracy is a dynamic, not a constant; a means, not an absolute; its condition is freedom and its aim is truth.
Editorial, Gazette & Daily, April 12, 1956.

The intrusion of orthodoxy of whatever sort is not simply a problem for democracy. It is utterly alien to democracy. Wherever orthodoxy is settled or threatens to settle in the public domain, democracy is to the same degree removed. *Ibid.*

There is no one orthodoxy which is the enemy of democracy. All of them are.
Ibid.

Sidney Hillman
(1887-1946)
American labor leader

What labor is demanding all over the world today is not a few material things like more dollars and fewer hours of work, but a right to a voice in the conduct of industry. *Speech, 1918.*

Journalism has . . . itself become big business and in turn has become increasingly dependent upon other big business for its revenue in the form of advertising. Thus there is a present and growing danger that large sections of the press may become special pleaders for those financial interests which they represent and upon which they rely for support.

St. Louis Post-Dispatch, symposium on the press, 1938.

Politics is the science of who gets what, when, and why.

Political Primer for All Americans, 1944.

The strike is the weapon of the industrial jungle.

Josephson, Sidney Hillman, p. 142.

We want a better America—an America that will give its citizens a higher and higher standard of living, so that no child will cry for food in the midst of plenty.

Statement, 1946.

Joe Hill(strom)

(1879-executed 1915)

American labor organizer

You will eat bye and bye
In that glorious land above the sky;
Work and pray,
Live on hay,
You'll eat pie
In the sky,
When you die.

Industrial Workers of the World Song.

Don't mourn for me. Organize.

Last message. Barrie Stavis, The Man Who Never Died.

Cardinal Hinsley

(1865-1943)

Archbishop of Westminster

Fascist rule prevents worse injustice, and if Fascism—which in principle I do not approve—goes under, nothing can save the country from chaos: *God's cause goes under with it.*

Reprinted in Christian Science Monitor, from The Times, London.

Hippocrates

(460?-370? B.C.)

Greek physician, father of medicine

Life is short, art long, occasion sudden; to make experiments dangerous; judgment difficult. Neither is it sufficient that the physician do his office, unless the patient and his attendants do their duty, and that externals are likewise well ordered.

Aphorisms.

Extreme remedies are very appropriate for extreme diseases. *Ibid.*

I will not give to a woman an instrument to procure abortion. *Hippocratic oath.*

Adolf Hitler

(1889-1945)

German chancellor, leader of Nazi party

The size of the lie is a definite factor in causing it to be believed, for the vast masses of a nation are in the depths of their hearts more easily deceived than they are consciously and intentionally bad. The primitive simplicity of their minds renders them a more easy prey to a big lie than a small one, for they themselves often tell little lies but would be ashamed to tell big ones.*

Mein Kampf. British Foreign Policy Association translation, 1935.

Something therefore always remains and sticks from the most impudent lies, a fact which all bodies and individuals concerned with the art of lying in this world know only too well, and hence they stop at nothing to achieve this end.   *Ibid.*

All propaganda must be so popular and on such an intellectual level, that even the most stupid of those toward whom it is directed will understand it. Therefore, the intellectual level of the propaganda must be lower the larger the number of people who are to be influenced by it.
      Ibid., p. 197, 14th edition.

Propaganda must not serve the truth, especially not insofar as it might bring out something favorable for the opponent.
      Ibid., p. 260.

Through clever and constant application of propaganda, people can be made to see paradise as hell, and also the other way round, to consider the most wretched sort of life as paradise.   *Ibid., p. 376.*

The receptive ability of the great masses is only very limited, their understanding is small; on the other hand, their forgetfulness is great. This being so, all effective propaganda should be limited to a very few points which, in turn, should be used as slogans until even the very last man is able to imagine what is meant by such words.
      Ibid., N. Y. Times translation, 1941.

___

* Written in prison, 1923, with the aid of Hess, Rauschning, and others, whose ideas Hitler used and whose sentences he frequently incorporated without change. *Mein Kampf* is ghost-written.

No matter how skillfully propaganda is presented it will not lead to success unless a fundamental principle is considered with continually sharp attention: it has to confine itself to little and to repeat this eternally. Here, too, persistency, as in so many other things in this world, is the first and the most important condition for success.   *Ibid.*

Diplomacy has to see to it that a nation does not perish heroically but maintains itself in a practical way. Every means which leads to this end is justified. To refuse such means could only be characterized as criminal neglect of duty.
      Ibid., British F.P.A. edition, p. 693.

The German has no idea how much the people must be misled if the support of the masses is required.
      Op. cit., 1935. Omitted from later editions.

A great politician has to bother himself less with means than with the goal.
      Ibid., unexpurgated edition, p. 268.

Success is the sole earthly judge of right and wrong.   *Op. cit.*

Humanitarianism is the expression of stupidity and cowardice.   *Ibid.*

The conviction of the justification of using even most brutal weapons is always dependent on the presence of a fanatical belief in the necessity of the victory of a revolutionary new order on this globe.
      Ibid.

The whole end of education . . . is found in burning into the heart and brain of the youth entrusted to it an instinctive and comprehended sense of race.   *Ibid.*

Hate is more lasting than dislike.
      Ibid.

The victor will never be asked if he told the truth. *Ibid.*

The humanitarian and pacifist idea will perhaps be excellent on the day when the man superior to all others will have conquered and subjugated the world, in such a way that he becomes the sole master of the earth. First then, battle; and afterwards, perhaps, pacifism. *Ibid.*

The very first essential for success is a perpetually constant and regular employment of violence. *Ibid.*

Either the world will be governed according to the ideas of modern democracy and then the weight of any decision will result in favor of the numerically stronger races, or the world will be dominated in accordance with the laws of the natural order of force, and then it is the peoples of brutal will who will conquer. *Ibid.*

All who are not of good race in this world are chaff. *Ibid.*

The greatness of every mighty organization embodying an idea in this world lies in the religious fanaticism and intolerance with which, fanatically convinced of its own right, it intolerantly imposes its will against all others. *Ibid.*

(The Jew) always talks about the equality of all men, without regard of race and color. Those who are dumb begin to believe that. *Ibid.*

The democracy of the western countries is the predecessor of Marxism, which would be unthinkable without democracy. Democracy provides the nourishing soil for this word-disease; the plague spreads from this ground. *Ibid.*

The majority can never take the place of the man. It is not only the representative

of stupidity but also of cowardice at all times. *Ibid.*

Just as little as Nature desires a mating between weaker individuals and stronger ones, far less she desires the mixing of a higher race with a lower one, as in this case her entire work of higher breeding, which has perhaps taken hundreds of thousands of years, would tumble at one blow. Historical experience offers countless proofs of this. It shows with terrible clarity that with any mixing of the blood of the Aryan with lower races the result was the end of the culture-bearer. *Ibid.*

The folk-State has to start with the presumption that a man, though scientifically little educated but physically healthy, who has a sound, firm character, filled with joyous determination and will power, is of greater value to the national community than an ingenious weakling. *Ibid.*

All epoch-making revolutionary events have been produced not by the written but by the spoken word. *Ibid.*

Every world-moving idea has not only the right, but also the duty of securing those means which make possible the execution of the idea. *Ibid.*

Ideas such as "Democracy," "World Solidarity," "World Peace," "Internationality of Art," etc., disintegrate our race-consciousness, breed cowardice. *Ibid.*

(Democracy) the deceitful theory that the Jew would insinuate—namely, that theory that all men are created equal. *Ibid.*

The one means that wins the easiest victory over reason: terror and force. *Ibid.*

We stand for the maintenance of private property. . . . We shall protect free enterprise as the most expedient, or rather the sole possible economic order.

1926. Der Fuehrer, p. 287, U.S. edition.

Pacifism is simply undisguised cowardice.
Speech, Nuernberg, August 2, 1926.

The Nordic race has a right to rule the world. We must make this right the guiding star of our foreign policy.
To Otto Strasser, May 21, 1930.

It is not the neutrals or the lukewarms who make history.
Speech, Berlin, April 23, 1933.

The National Socialist (Nazi) Party is the state. *Speech, Berlin, July 6, 1933.*

The great strength of the totalitarian state is that it forces those who fear it to imitate it. *Koenigsburg, September, 1933.*

I am insulted by the persistent assertion that I want war. Am I a fool? War! It would settle nothing.
Interview with Le Matin, November 10, 1933.

I am not so senseless as to want war. We want peace and understanding, nothing else. We want to give our hand to our former enemies. . . . When has the German people ever broken its word?
Address, Berlin, November 10, 1933.

Das ist das Werk der Kommunisten. (This is the work of Communists.)
Referring to the Reichstag fire, 1933.

The Fuehrer is the Party, and the Party is the Fuehrer. Just as I feel myself only as a part of the Party, the Party feels itself only as a part of me.
Nazi Congress, 1935.

The new Reich will call into being an astounding blossoming of German art. For never has art been presented with greater duties and opportunities than in this Reich.
July 18, 1937, dedicating House of German Art, Munich.

I believe today that I am acting in the sense of the Almighty Creator. By warding off the Jews I am fighting for the Lord's work. *Speech, Reichstag, 1938.*

It was anxiety for European culture and for real civilization that compelled Germany to take sides in the fight carried on in national Spain against the Bolshevist destroyers. *Speech, January 30, 1939.*

There is a road to freedom. Its milestones are Obedience, Endeavor, Honesty, Order, Cleanliness, Sobriety, Truthfulness, Sacrifice, and Love of Fatherland.
Signed message, painted on walls of concentration camp. Life, August 21, 1939.

The occupation of Stalingrad, which will now be concluded, will become a gigantic success. . . . No human being ever shall push us away from that spot.
Speech, Berlin, September 30, 1942.

I wanted to take it (Stalingrad). And—you know we are modest—we actually have it.
Statement, November 8, 1942, Munich.

Anyone who sees and paints a sky green and pastures blue ought to be sterilized.
Quoted by Dorothy Thompson, N. Y. Post, January 3, 1944.

We shall banish want; we shall banish fear. The essence of National Socialism is human welfare. . . . National Socialism is the revolution of the common man.
Quoted in National Association of Manufacturers' organ, N.A.M. News, February 10, 1945, in attack on Wallace's "Century of the Common Man" speech (q.v.).

Natural instincts bid all living human beings not merely conquer their enemies but also destroy them. In former days it was the victor's prerogative to destroy tribes, entire peoples.
Quoted by Raphael Lemkin, Free World, April, 1945.

The curse of Mt. Sinai. . . . This is what we are fighting against: the masochistic spirit of self-torment, the curse of so-called mortals, idolized to protect the weak from the strong in the face of the immortal law of battle, the great law of divine nature. Against the so-called Ten Commandments, against them we are fighting.
Dr. Herman Rauschning, preface, The Ten Commandments.

Universal education is the most corroding and disintegrating poison that liberalism has ever invented for its own destruction.
Rauschning, The Voice of Destruction: Hitler Speaks.

If I can send the flower of the German nation into the hell of war without the smallest pity for the spilling of precious German blood, then surely I have the right to remove millions of an inferior race that breeds like vermin. *Ibid.*

The religions are all alike, no matter what they call themselves. They have no future —certainly none for Germans. Fascism, if it likes, may come to terms with the Church. So shall I. Why not? That will not prevent me from tearing up Christianity root and branch and annihilating it in Germany.
Ibid.

At a mass meeting thought is eliminated. And because this is the state of mind I require, because it secures to me the best sounding-board for my speeches, I order every one to attend the meetings, where they become a part of the mass whether they like it or not, "intellectuals" and *bourgeois* as well as workers. *Ibid.*

Anti-Semitism is a useful revolutionary expedient. My Jews are a valuable hostage given to me by democracy. *Ibid.*

Anti-Semitic propaganda in all countries is an almost indispensable medium for the extension of our political campaign. You will see how little time we shall need in order to upset the ideas and the criteria of the whole world, simply and purely by attacking Judaism. It is beyond question the most important weapon in my propaganda arsenal, and almost everywhere of deadly efficiency. *Ibid.*

We do not intend to abolish the inequality of man; on the contrary, we would deepen it and, as in ancient great civilizations, create insurmountable barriers which would turn it into law. *Ibid.*

There will be a Herren-class, an historical class tempered by battle, and welded from the most varied elements. There will be a great hierarchy of party members. They will be the new middle class. And there will be the great mass of the anonymous, the serving collective, the eternally disfranchised.
Beneath them there will still be the class of subject alien races—we need not hesitate to call them the modern slave class.
And over all of these will stand the new high aristocracy, the most deserving and the most responsible Fuehrer-personalities.
Ibid.

It is a great satisfaction for me to find myself totally foreign to the world of Christianity. I shall never believe that what is founded on lies can endure forever. I believe in truth.
Hitler's Secret Conversations, published 1953.

The organization of our press has truly been a success. Our law concerning the press is such that divergencies of opinion between members of the government are no longer an occasion for public exhibitions, which are not the newspapers' business. We've eliminated that conception of political freedom which holds that everybody has the right to say whatever comes into his head. *Ibid.*

It is enough for me to send for Lorenz and inform him of my point of view and I know that next day all the German newspapers will broadcast my ideas. I'm proud to think that with such collaborators at my side, I can make a complete about-face without anyone's moving a muscle. That's a thing that's possible in no country but ours. *Ibid.*

If in this war everything points to the fact that gold is fighting against labor; capitalism against the people; and reaction against the progress of humanity, then work, the people, and progress will be victorious. *War talk to workers, Rheinmetall-Borsig plant.*

A violently active, dominating, intrepid, brutal youth—that is what I am after. . . . I want to see in its eyes the gleam of pride and independence, of prey. I will have no intellectual training. Knowledge is ruin to my young men. *Quoted by John Gunther, The Nation.*

Confusion, indecision, fear: these are my weapons.

I am liberating man from the degrading chimera known as conscience.

The New Testament is a Jewish swindle on the part of four Evangelists, because the teaching is copied exactly from the Indian belief of Jischnu Christa.

Christianity is a religion for slaves and fools, for "the last shall be first and the first shall be last."

Thomas Hobbes

(1588-1679)

English philosopher

So that in the first place, I put for a general inclination of all mankind, a perpetual and restless desire of power after power, that ceaseth only in death. *Leviathan, 1651.*

So that in the nature of man, we find three principal causes of quarrel. First, competition; secondly, diffidence; thirdly, glory. *Ibid.*

The first maketh man invade for gain, the second, for safety; and the third, for reputation. The first cause violence, to make themselves masters of other men's persons, wives, children, and cattle; the second, to defend them; the third, for trifles, at a word, a smile, a different opinion, and any other sign of undervalue, either direct in their persons, or by reflection in their kindred, their friends, their nation, their profession, or their name.

Hereby it is manifest, that during the time men live without a common power to keep them all in awe, they are in that condition which is called war; and such a war, as is of every man, against every man. *Ibid.*

To this war of every man, against every man, this also is consequent; that nothing can be unjust. The notions of right and wrong, justice and injustice, have there no place. Where there is no common power, there is no law, no justice. Force and fraud, are in war the two cardinal virtues. *Ibid.*

[321]

The passions that incline men to peace, are fear of death; desire of such things as are necessary to commodious living; and a hope by their industry to obtain them.

Ibid.

It followeth also that there is on earth no such universal Church, as all Christians are bound to obey; because there is no power on earth to which all other commonwealths are subject. *Ibid.*

They that approve a private opinion, call it opinion; but they that mislike it, heresy; and yet heresy signifies no more than private opinion. *Ibid.*

If a man consider the origin of this great ecclesiastical dominion, he will easily perceive that the Papacy is no other than the ghost of the deceased Roman empire, sitting crowned upon the grave thereof. For so did the Papacy start up on a sudden out of the ruins of that heathen power. *Ibid.*

Desire to know why, and how, curiosity, which is a lust of the mind, that by a perseverance of delight in the continued and indefatigable generation of knowledge, exceedeth the short vehemence of any carnal pleasure. *Ibid.*

For the laws of nature, as justice, equity, modesty, mercy, and, in sum, *doing to others as we would be done to*, of themselves, without the terror of some power to cause them to be observed, are contrary to our natural passions, that carry us to partiality, pride, revenge, and the like. And covenants, without the sword, are but words, and of no strength to secure a man at all.

Leviathan, Part 2, Of Commonwealth.

Liberty, or freedom, signifieth, properly, the absence of opposition: by opposition, I mean external impediments of motion;

and may be applied no less to irrational and inanimate creatures, than to rational.

Ibid.

But as men, for the attaining of peace and conservation of themselves thereby, have made an artificial man, which we call a commonwealth; so also have they made artificial chains, called *civil laws*, which they themselves, by mutual covenants, have fastened, at one end, to the lips of that man or assembly to whom they have given the sovereign power, and at the other end to their own ears. *Ibid.*

Another doctrine repugnant to civil society, is, that *whatsoever a man does against his conscience, is sin;* and it dependeth on the presumption of making himself judge of good and evil. For a man's conscience, and his judgment is the same thing, and as the judgment, so also the conscience may be erroneous. *Ibid.*

"The right of Nature," which writers commonly call *jus naturale,* is the liberty each man hath, to use his own power, as he will himself, for the preservation of his own nature; that is to say, of his own life; and consequently, of doing anything, which in his own judgment and reason he shall conceive to be the aptest means thereunto.

Ibid.

By "liberty," is understood, according to the proper signification of the word, the absence of external impediments: which impediments may oft take away part of a man's power to do what he would; but cannot hinder him from using the power left him, according to his judgment and reason shall dictate to him. *Ibid.*

A "law of Nature," *lex naturalis,* is a precept or general rule, found out by reason. . . . For though they that speak of this subject, use to confound *jus* and *lex,* "right" and "law"; yet they ought to be distinguished; because "right," consisteth in liberty to do, or to forebear; whereas "law," determineth and bindeth to one of them; so that law and right differ as much as obligation and liberty; which in one and the same matter are inconsistent. *Ibid.*

For the nature of power is in this point, like to fame, increased as it proceeds; or like the motion of heavy bodies, which the further they go, make still the more haste. *Ibid.*

The *value,* or WORTH of a man, is as of all other things, his price; that is to say, so much as would be given for the use of his power. And as in other things, so in men, not the seller, but the buyer, determines the price. *Ibid.*

Leisure is the mother of philosophy. *Ibid.*

And according to this proper and generally received meaning of the word, a *"freeman is he that in those things which by his strength and wit he is able to do, is not hindered to do what he has a will to."* *Ibid.*

From the use of the word *free-will,* no liberty can be inferred of the will, desire, or inclination, but the liberty of the man; which consisteth in this, that he finds no stop, in doing what he has the will, desire, or inclination to do. *Ibid.*

The original of all great and lasting societies consisted not in the mutual good will men had toward each other, but in the mutual fear they had of each other. *Philosophical Rudiments Concerning Government and Society, 1651.*

Now I am about to take my last voyage, a frightful leap in the dark. *On his deathbed, December 4, 1679.*

J. A. Hobson
(1858-1940)
English economist

The domain of political and economic rulers, the spiritual and intellectual orthodoxies and authorities, the secure and comfortable lives of the luxurious and leisured classes, the pleasant illusions of the herd-mind, so "good" in themselves and so serviceable to the ruling and possessing classes, all feel themselves menaced by free-thinking and free-speaking science. *Free-Thought in the Social Sciences, Part I, Ch. V, 1926.*

The maxim, "To understand all is to forgive all" does not recommend itself to those who value the sense of sin and the hatred of offenders against the purities, sanctities, respectabilities of the established social order. *Ibid.*

The standardisation of mass-production carries with it a tendency to standardise a mass-mind, producing a willing conformity, not merely to common ways of living, but to common ways of thinking and common valuations. The worst defect of patriotism is its tendency to foster and impose this common mind, and so to stifle the innumerable germs of liberty. *Ibid.*

The tendency of all strong Governments has always been to suppress liberty, partly in order to ease the processes of rule, partly from sheer disbelief in innovation. *Ibid.*

When vested economic interests "stand in" with Governments, the sacredness of property converts all innovation into sacrilege. *Ibid.*

The creative spirit is one and indivisible. It cannot live and work under servitude or external control. Disinterested thought cannot be drawn into the physical sciences and kept out of politics and economic theory. If we are right in holding that the most urgent business of our age is to devise better laws of conduct in the arts of human government, within and beyond the limits of nationality, success depends upon stimulating in as many spots as possible the largest number and variety of independent thinkers. *Ibid.*

Those who in vague rhetoric dwell on education as the substitute for force and revolution often mean a doped, standardised, and servile education. But such education affords no safety in this dangerous world. Free-thinking alone can furnish the energy and the direction to human government, helping to bridge the chasm between physical and moral progress. *Ibid.*

The claims of modern science to open up for close and fearless scrutiny the instinct of sex and the structure of the family, the historical basis and the ethical limitations of private property and industry, the sovereignty of the State in relation to its individual members, other institutions, and other States, are subject to much obstruction, mainly from the secret or avowed fear lest the primitive taboo, improved and sublimated for modern conservative uses, should be weakened or dissolved by a subjection to impartial criticism.
Ibid., Part III, Ch. III.

(Imperialism is) the endeavor of the great controllers of industry to broaden the channel for the flow of their surplus wealth by seeking foreign markets and foreign investments to take off the goods and capital they cannot use at home. *Imperialism.**

---

* This book greatly influenced Socialists and Communists, notably Lenin.

William Ernest Hocking
(1873-1966)
American philosopher

Myths there must be, since visions of the future must be clothed in imagery. But there are myths which displace truth and there are myths which give wings to truth.
Time, September 17, 1953.

There are deeper myths, born of the permanent and universal aspirations of men, such as the dream of a future human fraternity. Such myths as these . . . are never mere mythology, because they are founded on a literal and present truth. *Ibid.*

Only the man who has enough good in him to feel the justice of the penalty can be punished; the others can only be hurt.
The Coming World Civilization, Harper, 1957.

There is no moral right to property, to liberty, to life itself, in the absence of good will. The dilemma of the state is that this condition, as a moral condition, cannot be legally administered. *Ibid.*

Where men cannot freely convey their thoughts to one another, no other liberty is secure.
Freedom of the Press, U. of Chicago Press, 1947.

Religion . . . is the forerunner of international law; because it alone can create the international spirit, the international obligation.
The Meaning of God in Human Experience, 1913.

We require a world-religion just because we do not require a world-state. *Ibid.*

The prospect of individual immortality must be gained if at all by the same painstaking scientific and metaphysical enquiries as justify our confidence in human welfare. *Ibid.*

No brave man, nor brave man-and-woman's, life goes for nothing in this world—in spite of appearances.
Letter to G. S., September 10, 1958.

Eric Hoffer
(b. 1902)
San Francisco longshoreman

When we lose our individual independence in the corporateness of a mass movement, we find a new freedom—freedom to hate, bully, lie, torture, murder, and betray without shame and remorse. Herein undoubtedly lies part of the attractiveness of a mass movement.
The True Believer, 1951.

All social disturbances and upheavals have their roots in crises of individual self-esteem, and the great endeavor in which the masses most readily unite is basically a search for pride.
The Passionate State of Mind, 1955.

It is easier to love humanity as a whole than to love one's neighbor.
N. Y. Times Magazine, February 15, 1959.

Thus blind faith is to a considerable extent a substitute for the lost faith in ourselves; insatiable desire a substitute for hope; accumulation a substitute for growth; fervent hustling a substitute for purposeful action, and pride a substitute for unattainable self-respect. *Ibid.*

Paul G. Hoffman
(b. 1891)
American industrialist

The thought control of dictatorships is imposed by force, but discussion, criticism and debate can be stifled by fear as well as by force. Persecution of public opinion can be as powerful as purges and pogroms. Frightened men are, at best, irresponsible in their actions and, at worst, dangerous. Of all the forms of t/ranny over the mind of man, none is more terrible than fear—to be afraid of being one's self among one's neighbors.
Address, Freedom House Award, 1951.

Hohenheim
See Paracelsus

Paul Henry Thiry d'Holbach
(1723-1789)
French baron, skeptic, materialistic philosopher

It is thus that for opinions, which no man can demonstrate, we see the Brahman despised; the Mohammedan hated; the Pagan held in contempt; that they oppress and disdain each with the most rancourous animosity; the Christian burns the Jew . . . because he clings to the faith of his fathers; the Roman Catholic condemns the Protestant to the flames, and makes a conscience of massacring him in cold blood; this reacts in turn; sometimes the various sects of Christians league together against the incredulous Turk, and for a moment suspend their own bloody disputes that they may chastise the enemies to the true faith; then, having glutted their revenge, return with redoubled fury, to wreak over again their infuriated vengeance on each other.
The System of Nature, 1770.

If we go back to the beginning we shall find that ignorance and fear created the gods; that fancy, enthusiasm, or deceit adorned or disfigured them; that weakness worships them; that credulity preserves them, and that custom, respect and tyranny support them in order to make the blindness of men serve its own interests. *Ibid.*

The source of man's unhappiness is his ignorance of Nature. The pertinacity with which he clings to blind opinions imbibed in his infancy, which interweave themselves with his existence, the consequent prejudice that warps his mind, that prevents his expansion, that renders him the slave of fiction, appears to doom him to continual error. *Ibid.*

The *enlightened man,* is a man in his maturity, in his perfection, who is capable of pursuing his own happiness; because he has learned to examine, to think for himself, and not to take that for truth upon the authority of others, which experience has taught him examination will frequently prove erroneous. *Ibid.*

Nature tells man to consult reason, and to take it for his guide: religion teaches him that his reason is corrupted, that it is only a treacherous guide, given by a deceitful God to lead his creatures astray. Nature tells man to enlighten himself, to search after truth, to instruct himself in his duties: religion enjoins him to examine nothing, to remain in ignorance, to fear truth. *Ibid.*

Nature tells man to be sociable, to love his fellow-creatures, to be just, peaceable, indulgent, and benevolent, to cause or suffer his associates to enjoy their opinions: religion counsels him to fly society, to detach himself from his fellow-creatures, to hate them, when their imagination does not procure them dreams comfortable to his own, to break the most sacred bonds to please his God, to torment, to afflict, to persecute, and to massacre those who will not be mad after his own manner. Nature tells man in society to cherish glory, to labor to render himself estimable, to be active, courageous, and industrious: religion tells him to be humble, abject, pusillanimous, to live in obscurity, to occupy himself with prayers, with meditations, and with ceremonies; it says to him be useful to thyself, and do nothing for others. *Ibid.*

The citizen, or the man in society, is no less depraved by religion, which is always in contradiction with sound politics. Nature says to man, *thou are free, no power on earth can legitimately deprive thee of thy rights*; religion cries out to him, that he is a slave, condemned by his God to groan all his life under the iron rod of his representatives. Nature tells man to *love the country which gave him birth,* to serve it faithfully . . . . : religion orders him to obey, without murmuring, the tyrants who oppress his country, to serve them against it. . . . Nevertheless, if the sovereign be not sufficiently devoted to his priests, religion quickly changes its language; it calls upon subjects to become rebels, it makes it a duty in them to resist their master, it cries out to them, that it is better to obey God than man. *Ibid.*

Shall it be in the revealed religions, that we shall draw up our idea of virtue? Alas! do they not all appear to be in accord in announcing a despotic, jealous, vindictive, and selfish God, who knows no law, who follows his caprice in everything, who loves or who hates, who chooses or reproves, according to his whim; who acts irrationally, who delights in carnage, rapine, and crime; who plays with his feeble subjects, who overloads them with puerile laws, who lays continual snares for them, who rigorously prohibits them from consulting their reason? What would become of morality, if men proposed to themselves such Gods as models? *Ibid.*

Nature tells princes they are men; that it is not their whim that can decide what is just, and what is unjust, that *the public will maketh the law*: religion, sometimes says to them, that they are Gods, to whom nothing in this world ought to offer resistance: sometimes it transforms them into tyrants whom enraged Heaven is desirous should be immolated to its wrath.

Ibid.

Hollweg

See Bethmann-Hollweg

John Haynes Holmes

(1879-1964)

American clergyman

Priests are no more necessary to religion than politicians to patriotism.

Sensible Man's View of Religion.

In a capitalist society all institutions are in danger of control by the counting room. Newspapers have no monopoly of this danger. It is shared, for example, by churches, always faced with the problem of money changers in the temple. I know of no escape from this danger except through the development of a code of honor to which the journalists shall be bound as the soldier to his oath.

St. Louis Post-Dispatch symposium, 1938.

Newspapermen must organize themselves into a profession . . . a group of men voluntarily under pledge to an ideal which supersedes all money considerations.

Ibid.

I await the hour when a journalist can be driven from the press room for venal practices, as a minister can be unfrocked, or a lawyer disbarred. *Ibid.*

Oliver Wendell Holmes (Sr.)

(1809-1894)

American poet, essayist, novelist

Rough work, iconoclasm, but the only way to get at truth.

We are all tattooed in our cradles with the beliefs of our tribe; the record may seem superficial, but it is indelible. You cannot educate a man wholly out of the superstitious fears which were implanted in his imagination, no matter how utterly his reason may reject them.

The longing for certainty and repose is in every human mind. But certainty is generally illusion and repose is not the destiny of man.

Don't be "consistent," but be simply true.

You never need think you can turn over any old falsehoods without a terrible squirming of the horrid little population that dwells under it.

The Pope put his foot on the neck of kings, but Calvin and his cohorts crushed the whole human race under their heels in the name of the Lord of Hosts.

I am too much in earnest for either humility or vanity, but I do entreat those who hold the keys of life and death to listen.

The history of most countries has been that of majorities—mounted majorities, clad in iron, armed with death, treading down the tenfold more numerous minorities.

Address, Massachusetts Medical Society, May 30, 1860.

Sin has many tools, but a lie is the handle that fits them all.

The Autocrat of the Breakfast Table.

We are all omnibuses in which our ancestors ride, and every now and then one of them sticks his head out and embarrasses us. *The Guardian Angel, 1867.*

Oliver Wendell Holmes (Jr.)
(1841-1935)
U.S. Supreme Court Justice

The great act of faith is when man decides that he is not God.
Letter to William James, 1907.

No Justice is God. He is a man serving men.

About seventy-five years ago I learned that I was not God. And so, when the people of the various States want to do something and I can't find anything in the Constitution expressly forbidding them to do it, I say, whether I like it or not: Damn it, let 'em do it.

I dare say that I have worked off my fundamental formula on you that the chief end of man is to frame general propositions and that no general proposition is worth a damn.
S. J. Konefsky, The Legacy of Holmes and Brandeis.

No generalization is wholly true, not even this one. *Attributed.*

As life is action and passion, it is required of a man that he should share the passion and action of his time, at peril of being judged not to have lived.
Memorial Day Address, 1884.

I do not know what is true. I do not know the meaning of the universe. But in the midst of doubt, in the collapse of creeds, there is one thing I do not doubt, that no man who lives in the world with most of us can doubt, and that is that the faith is true and adorable which leads a soldier to throw away his life in obedience to a blindly accepted duty, in a cause which he little understands, in a plan of campaign of which he has no notion, under tactics of which he does not see the use.
Address, A Soldier's Faith, Harvard, Memorial Day, 1895.

One of the eternal conflicts of which life is made up is that between the effort of every man to get the most he can for his services, and that of society, disguised under the name of capital, to get his services for the least possible return.
Dissent, Vegelahn v. Gunther, 1896 (when on Massachusetts Supreme Court).

The character of every act depends on the circumstances in which it is done. The most stringent protection of free speech would not protect a man in falsely shouting fire in a theater and causing a panic.
Schenck v. U.S., 249 U.S. 47 (1919).

The question in every case is whether the words are used in such circumstances and are of such a nature as to create a clear and present danger. *Ibid.*

Every idea is an incitement. It offers itself for belief, and if believed it is acted on unless some other belief outweighs it or some failure of energy stifles the movement at its birth. The only difference between the expression of an opinion and an incitement in the narrower sense is the speaker's enthusiasm for the result. Eloquence may set fire to reason. But whatever may be thought of the redundant discourse before us, it had no chance of starting a present conflagration. *Gitlow v. N. Y. (1925).*

I think that we should be eternally vigilant against attempts to check the expression of opinions that we loathe and believe to be fraught with death, unless they imminently threaten interference with the lawful and pressing purposes of the law that an immediate check is required to save the country. *Dissent, Abrams v. U.S. (1919).*

But when men have realized that time has upset many fighting faiths, they may come to believe even more than they believe the very foundations of their own conduct that the ultimate good desired is better reached by free trade in ideas—that the best test of truth is the power of the thought to get itself accepted in the competition of the market, and that truth is the only ground upon which their wishes safely can be carried out. That at any rate is the theory of our Constitution. *Ibid.*

All life is an experiment. *Ibid.*

I can't help an occasional semi-shudder as I remember that millions of intelligent men think that I am barred from the face of God unless I change. But how can one pretend to believe what seems to him childish and devoid alike of historical and rational foundations.
Quoted in book review, Time.

The attempt to lift up men's hearts by a belief in progress seems to me, like the wish for spiritualism or miracles, to rest on not taking a large enough view or going far enough back. *Ibid.*

The petitioner may have a constitutional right to talk politics, but he has no constitutional right to be a policeman.
New Bedford police-removal case.

It is our duty to declare lynch law as little valid when practiced by a regularly drawn jury as when administered by one elected by a mob intent on death.
Dissenting opinion, Leo Frank case.

We have to choose, and for my part I think it a less evil that some criminals should escape than that the government should play an ignoble part.
Olmstead v. U.S. (1928).

If there is any principle of the Constitution that more imperatively calls for attachment than any other it is the principle of free thought—not free for those who agree with us but freedom for the thought we hate. *Dissent, U.S. v. Schwimmer.*

A Constitution is not intended to embody a particular economic theory. . . . It is made for people of fundamentally different views, and the accident of our finding certain opinions natural and familiar, or novel and even shocking, ought not to conclude our judgment upon the question whether statutes embodying them conflict with the Constitution. *Dissent, Lochner case.*

General propositions do not decide concrete cases. *Ibid.*

The power to tax is not the power to destroy while this court sits.
Dissent, Panhandle Oil Co. v. Mississippi, 1930.

Great cases like hard cases make bad law.
Northern Securities Co. v. U.S., 1904.

It is better for all the world, if instead of waiting to execute degenerate offspring for crime, or let them starve for their imbecility, society can prevent those who are manifestly unfit from continuing their kind. The principle that sustains compulsory vaccination is broad enough to cover cutting the Fallopian tubes. . . . Three generations of imbeciles are enough.
Buck v. Bell, 274 U.S. 200 (1927).

The notion that a business is clothed with a public interest and has been devoted to the public use is little more than a fiction intended to beautify what is disagreeable to the sufferers.

Tyson v. Banton, 273 U.S. 418 (1927).

The standards of the law are standards of general application. The law takes no account of the infinite varieties of temperament, intellect, and education which make the internal characters of a given act so different in different men. It does not attempt to see men as God sees them, for more than one sufficient reason.

The Common Law and Collected Legal Papers.

The life of the law has not been logic; it has been experience. The felt necessities of the time, the prevalent moral and political theories, intentions of public policy, avowed or unconscious, even the prejudices which judges share with their fellow men, have had a good deal to do with the syllogism in determining the rules by which men should be governed. *Ibid.*

When Socialism first began to be talked about, the comfortable classes of the community were a good deal frightened. I suspect that this fear has influenced judicial action both here and in England. *Ibid.*

All I mean by truth is what I can't help thinking.

Mark DeWolfe Howe, The Shaping Years.

It is revolting to have no better reason for a rule of law than that so it was laid down in the time of Henry IV.

Ibid. (1897).

In the abstract, I have no very enthusiastic belief (in free speech), though I hope I would die for it. *Ibid.*

It is no sufficient condemnation of legislation that it favors one class at the expense of another; for much or all legislation does

that; and none the less when the bona fide object is the greatest good of the greatest number. Why should the greatest number be preferred? Why not the greatest good of the most intelligent and most highly developed?

The Mind and Faith of Justice Holmes.
Edited by Max Lerner.

The greatest good of a minority of our generation may be the greatest good of the greatest number in the long run. *Ibid.*

If the welfare of the living majority is paramount, it can only be on the ground that the majority have the power in their hands. *Ibid.*

On the whole, I am on the side of the unregenerate who affirm the worth of life as an end in itself, as against the saints who deny it. *Letter to Lady Pollock.*

To have doubted one's own first principles, is the mark of a civilized man.

To rest upon a formula is a slumber that, prolonged, means death.

Freedom of contract begins where equality of bargaining power begins.

Dirty business (re: wire-tapping).
Majority opinion, June 4, 1928.

Homer

(c. 850 B.C.)
Greek poet

Injustice, suave, erect, and unconfined,
Sweeps the wide earth, and tramples o'er
    mankind—
While prayers to heal her wrongs move slow
    behind. *The Iliad.*

Enlighten me now, O Muses, tenants of
    Olympian homes,

For you are goddesses, inside on everything,
know everything.
But we mortals hear only the news, and
know nothing at all.   *Ibid.*

Sidney Hook
(b. 1902)
American writer, philosopher

In contrast to totalitarianism, democracy
can face and live with the truth about itself.
*N. Y. Times Magazine, September 30,
1951.*

Earnest A. Hooton
(1887-1954)
American anthropologist, author

Man is still a super-age-savage, predatory,
acquisitive, primarily interested in himself.
Address, Cleveland, April 11, 1953.

Up to 30,000 years ago man could boast
a proud evolutionary record, but since then
no physical improvement has occurred in
the human species.
*N. Y. World-Telegram & Sun, obituary,
May 4, 1954.*

Mankind is in the process of a physical
and mental degeneration which is producing
a resurgence of the ape within him, and
which may plunge civilization into ultimate
chaos.   *Ibid.*

Herbert Clark Hoover
(1874-1964)
31st President of the United States

We shall soon with the help of God be
in sight of the day when poverty will be
banished from this nation. *Address, 1920.*

We in America today are nearer to the
final triumph over poverty than ever before
in the history of any land.
Campaign speech, 1928.

There are only two occasions when
Americans respect privacy, especially in
Presidents. Those are prayer and fishing.
N. Y. Herald Tribune, May 19, 1947.

Fishing is the chance to wash one's soul
with pure air. It brings meekness and inspiration, reduces our egotism, soothes our
troubles and shames our wickedness. It is
discipline in the equality of men—for all
men are equal before fish.   *Ibid.*

Criticism also comes from our native
Communists who want to overturn the system. And from the fuzzy-minded totalitarian liberals who believe that their creeping collectivism can be adopted without
destroying personal liberty and representative government.
*The Miracle of America, Woman's
Home Companion, 1947.*

Our American system has perfected the
greatest productivity of any nation on earth;
our standard of living is the highest in the
world.°   *Ibid.*

In my opinion, we are in danger of developing a cult of the Common Man, which
means a cult of mediocrity.
This Week, August 5, 1956.

Absolute freedom of the press to discuss
public questions is a foundation stone of
American liberty.
*A. P. Luncheon, N. Y. C., April 22,
1929.*

Liberalism is a force truly of the spirit
proceeding from the deep realization that
economic freedom cannot be sacrificed if
political freedom is to be preserved.
Address, N. Y. C., October 31, 1932.

° The standard of living in New Zealand
and Australia during the Labour Party
regime was higher than that of the U.S.A.

Words without action are the assassins of idealism. *Quoted in Forbes Magazine.*

It (freedom) is a thing of the spirit. Men must be free to worship, to think, to hold opinions, to speak without fear. They must be free to challenge wrong and oppression with surety of justice. Freedom conceives that the mind and spirit of man can be free only if he be free to pattern his own life, to develop his own talents, free to earn, to spend, to save, to acquire property as the security of his old age and his family. *Addresses Upon the American Road, p. 227.*

The slogan of progress is changing from the full dinnerpail to the full garage. *Speech, N. Y. C., October 22, 1928.*

J(ohn) Edgar Hoover
(1895-1972)
American lawyer, director of Federal Bureau of Investigation

When any person is intentionally deprived of his constitutional rights those responsible have committed no ordinary offense. A crime of this nature, if subtly encouraged by failure to condemn and punish, certainly leads down the road to totalitarianism. *FBI Law Enforcement Bulletin, September, 1952, quoted by Justice Frankfurter, dissent, Irvine v. California.*

Law enforcement is a protecting arm of civil liberties. Civil Liberties cannot exist

---

* "No one has ever been able to find in Mr. Hoover's speeches or writings, of which a very careful file has been kept over the years, the expression 'a chicken in every pot.' [See Henry IV.] Mr. Hoover has also never promised or even expressed his hope of two cars in every garage."—Letter to G. S. from Mr. Hoover's secretary, with proofsheet corrections, December 12, 1958.

without law enforcement; law enforcement without civil liberties is a hollow mockery. They are parts of the same whole—one without the other becomes a dead letter. *Iowa Law Review, Winter, 1952.*

Law enforcement, however, in defeating the criminal, must maintain inviolate the historic liberties of the individual. *Ibid.*

Mark Hopkins
(1802-1887)
American educator, theologian

No revolution that has ever taken place in society can be compared to that which has been produced by the words of Jesus Christ.

Horace
(c. 65 B.C.)
Roman poet

Riches either serve or govern the possessor.

Money by right means if you can; if not, by any means. *Epistles, I, i, 66.*

Gold will be slave or master. *Ibid., x, 1, 47.*

Odi profanum vulgus et arceo. (I hate the vulgar herd and hold it far.) *Odes III.*

Dulce et decorum est pro patriâ mori. (It is sweet and glorious to die for one's country.) *Ibid., III, 2, 13.*

Who so cultivates the golden mean avoids the poverty of a hovel and the envy of a palace. *Ibid., x.*

That man lives happy and in command of himself, who from day to day can say, I have lived. Whether clouds obscure, or the sun illumines the following day, that which is past is beyond recall.

Carmina, iii, 29, 41.

Who, then, is free? The wise man who can command his passions, who fears not want, nor death, nor chains, firmly resisting his appetites and despising the honors of the world, who relies wholly on himself, whose angular points of character have all been rounded off and polished.

Hoshi

See Kenkò Hoshi

Dr. Karen Horney

(1885-1952)

American psychoanalyst

A perfectly normal person is rare in our civilization. *Quoted in obituary in Time.*

A. E. Housman

(1859-1936)

English poet, essayist, scholar

The laws of God, the laws of man,
He may keep that will and can;
Not I: let God and man decree
Laws for themselves and not for me.

Laws. Last Poems.

Edgar Watson Howe

(1853-1937)

American journalist, author

Devoted to Indignation and Information.
Slogan of Ed Howe's Weekly.

That the politicians are permitted to carry on the same old type of disgraceful campaign from year to year is as insulting to the people as would be a gang of thieves coming back to a town they had robbed, staging a parade, and inviting citizens to fall in and cheer.

The scientists are the world's greatest army devoted to good works. . . . In a world filled with men who shamefully invent fables to uphold their opinions or defend their guilt, the scientists attack falseness of every kind, and accept no doctrine until the last doubt has been disposed of.

I have never been free; the world, my kin, my neighbors, have always enslaved me.

Indignations, Little Blue Books, 1934.

What we call Protestantism was really a free thought movement; a revolt against religion.

Preaching from the Audience, 1926.

Louis McHenry Howe

(1871-1936)

American presidential secretary

You cannot adopt politics as a profession and remain honest.

Address, January 17, 1933.

William Dean Howells

(1837-1920)

American author

Art, indeed, is beginning to find out that if it does not make friends with Need it must perish. It perceives that to take itself from the many and leave them no joy in their work, and to give itself to the few whom it can bring no joy in their idleness, is an error that kills.

Criticism and Fiction, 1891.

The men and women who do the hard work of the world have learned from him (Ruskin) and Morris that they have a right to pleasure in their toil, and that when justice is done them they will have it.

Ibid.

Democracy in literature is the reverse of all this. It wishes to know and tell the truth, confident that consolation and delight are there; it does not care to paint the marvelous and impossible for the vulgar many, or to sentimentalize and falsify the actual for the vulgar few.   *Ibid.*

Neither arts, nor letters, nor sciences, except as they somehow, clearly or obscurely, tend to make the race better and kinder, are to be regarded as serious interests; they are all lower than the rudest crafts that feed and house and clothe, for except they do this office they are idle; and they cannot do this except from and through the truth.   *Ibid.*

Elbert Hubbard
(1856-1915)
American writer, publisher, lecturer

This will never be a civilized country until we expend more money for books than we do for chewing gum.   *The Philistine.*

Theology is an attempt to explain a subject by men who do not understand it. The intent is not to tell the truth but to satisfy the questioner.   *Ibid.*

The only foes that threaten America are the enemies at home, and these are ignorance, superstition and incompetence.
    Ibid., vol. 20.

It is not book learning young men need, nor instruction about this and that, but a stiffening of the vertebrae which will cause them to be loyal to a trust, to act promptly, concentrate their energies, do a thing— "carry a message to Garcia."
Ibid., March, 1900; Carry a Message to Garcia.

Laws that do not embody public opinion can never be enforced.   *Epigrams.*

God will not look you over for medals, degrees or diplomas, but for scars. *Ibid.*

An idea that is not dangerous is unworthy of being called an idea at all.
    Roycroft Dictionary, 1923.

If you can't answer a man's arguments, all is not lost; you can still call him vile names.

It is the weak man who urges compromise—never the strong man.

A Miracle: An event described by those to whom it was told by men who did not see it.

A conservative is a man who is too cowardly to fight and too fat to run.

Frank McKinney Hubbard
(1868-1930)
American caricaturist, humorist

What this country needs is a good five-cent cigar.°
Abe Martin saying; often ascribed to Thomas Marshall—Editor & Publisher.

Now and then an innocent man is sent t' th' legislature.   *Abe Martin.*

Charles Evans Hughes
(1862-1948)
U.S. Supreme Court Chief Justice

The greater the importance of safeguarding the community from incitements to the overthrow of our institutions by force and

° "There are plenty of good five-cent cigars in the country. The trouble is they cost a quarter. What the country really needs is a good five-cent nickel"—F. P. Adams.

violence, the more imperative is the need to preserve inviolate the constitutional rights of free speech, free press and free assembly in order to maintain the opportunity for free political discussion, to the end that government may be responsible to the will of the people and that changes, if desired, may be obtained by peaceful means. Therein lies the security of the Republic, the very foundation of constitutional government.
DeJonge v. Oregon, 1937.

We are under a Constitution, but the Constitution is what the judges say it is.
Address, Elmira, May 3, 1907; quoted by F. D. Roosevelt, March 9, 1937.

In a number of cases dissenting opinions have in time become the law.

While democracy must have its organization and controls, its vital breath is individual liberty.

When there is muck to be raked, it must be raked, and the public must know of it, that it may mete out justice . . .
Publicity is a great purifier because it sets in action the forces of public opinion, and in this country public opinion controls the courses of the nation.
Address, Manufacturers' Association, May, 1908.

It is of the essence of the institutions of liberty that it be recognized that guilt is personal and cannot be attributed to the holding of opinions or to mere intent in the absence of overt acts.
John Lord O'Brian, Harvard Law Review, April, 1948.

Our institutions were not devised to bring about uniformity of opinion; if they had been we might well abandon hope. It is important to remember, as has well been said, "the essential characteristic of true liberty is that under its shelter many different types of life and character and opinion and belief can develop unmolested and unobstructed." *Forbes, November 1, 1957.*

Langston Hughes
(1902-1967)
American poet, writer

O, let my land be a land where Liberty
Is crowned with no false patriotic wreath,
But opportunity is real, and life is free,
Equality is in the air we breathe.

(There's never been equality for me,
Nor freedom in this "homeland of the free.")
Let America Be America Again.

I am the poor white, fooled and pushed apart,
I am the Negro bearing slavery's scars,
I am the Red man driven from the land,
I am the immigrant clutching the hope I seek—
And finding only the same old stupid plan
Of dog eat dog, of mighty crush the weak.
Ibid.

O, yes,
I say it plain,
America never was America to me.
And yet I swear this oath—
America will be! *Ibid.*

I swear to the Lord
I still can't see
Why Democracy means
Everybody but me.
The Black Man Speaks.

Victor Hugo
(1802-1885)
French poet, novelist, dramatist

By fraternity only will liberty be saved.
1870.

There is one thing stronger than all the armies in the world: and that is an idea whose time has come.*

In the twentieth century war will be dead, the scaffold will be dead, royalty will be dead, and dogmas will be dead; but man will live. For all, there will be but one country—that country the whole earth; for all, there will be but one hope—that hope the whole heaven. All hail, then, to that noble twentieth century, which shall own our children, and which our children shall inherit. *The Future of Man.*

Voltaire was more than a man; he was an epoch.

People do not lack strength, they lack will.

Poverty and wealth are comparative sins.

A republic may be called the climate of civilization. *Address, Assembly, 1851.*

The ones who live are the ones who struggle.
The ones whose soul and heart are filled with high purpose.
Yes, these are the living ones.

There is no such thing as a little country. The greatness of a people is no more determined by their number than the greatness of a man is determined by his height.

I represent a party which does not yet exist: the party of revolution, civilization. This party will make the twentieth century. There will issue from it, first, the United States of Europe, then the United States of the World.
N. Y. Post, January 29, 1948.

---

* Translated variously, including: "Nothing in this world is so powerful as an idea whose time has come."

When dictatorship is a fact, revolution becomes a right. *Time, June 3, 1957.*

The pun when it is of Aeschylus, the grimace when it is Goya's, the hump when Aesop wears it, the louse when Murillo cracks it, the flea when it bites Voltaire, the ass's jawbone when Samson wields it, hysteria when paraded empurpled in the Song of Songs, Goton at the lavatory when it pleases Rembrandt to call it Susanna at the Bath, the bulging eye when it is that of Oedipus, the plucked-out eye when it is Gloucester's, the shrieking woman when it is Hecuba, snoring when it comes from the Eumenides, a blow when it is the Cid's vengeance, spittle when Jesus receives it, coarseness when Homer uses it, savagery when it is that of Shakespeare, slang when Villon utters it, rags when worn by Iris, blows of a stick when Scapin gives them, carrion when the vulture of Salvator Rosa gnaws it, the belly when Agrippina uncovers it, the lupanar when Regnier is our guide, the meddling woman when Plautus makes use of her, the squirt when it pursues Porceaugnac, the cesspool when Tacitus drowns Nero in it and when Rabelais uses it to smear theocracy—all these are parts of this supreme taste. The hag of Moliere, the prostitute of Beaumarchais, and the bawd of Shakespeare belong to it.
Intellectual Autobiography.

Certain familiarities, intimacies of speech, insolences, if you will, which emanate only from greatness, are found in sovereign works alone and are their seal. The eagle's dung reveals the topmost heights. *Ibid.*

Hell is an outrage on humanity. When you tell me that your Deity made you in his own image, I reply that he must have been very ugly.
Cardiff, What Great Men Think About Religion.

Every step which the intelligence of Europe has taken has been in spite of the clerical party.   *Ibid.*

Revolution is the larva of civilization.

So long as there shall exist, by reason of law and custom, a social condemnation, which, in the face of civilization, artificially creates hells on earth and complicates a destiny that is divine, with human fatality; so long as the three problems of the age—the degradation of man by poverty, the ruin of women by starvation, and the dwarfing of childhood by physical and spiritual night—are not solved; so long as, in certain regions, social asphyxia shall be possible; in other words, and from a yet more extended point of view, so long as ignorance and misery remain on earth, books like this cannot be useless.

Les Misérables, preface.

I am for religion against religions.
                                    Ibid.

Would you realize what Revolution is, call it Progress; and would you realize what Progress is, call it Tomorrow.   *Ibid.*

Alexander von Humboldt
(1769-1859)
German scientist, author

Men have now arrived at such a high pitch of civilization that all institutions which act in any way to obstruct or thwart the development of individuals, and compress men together into vast uniform masses, are now far more hurtful than in earlier ages of the world.
The Sphere and Duty of Government.

In estimating the advantages arising from increased freedom of thought and the consequent wide diffusion of enlightenment, we should moreover especially guard against presuming that they would be confined to a small proportion of the people only;—that to the majority, whose energies are exhausted by cares for the physical necessaries of life, such opportunities would be useless or even positively hurtful, and that the only way to influence the masses is to promulgate some definite points of belief—to restrict the freedom of thought. *Ibid.*

There is something degrading to human nature in the idea of refusing to any man the right to be a man. There are none so hopelessly low on the scale of culture and refinement as to be incapable of rising higher; and even though the more pure and lofty views of philosophy and religion could not at once be entertained by a large portion of the community—though it should be necessary to array truth in some different garb before it could find admission to their convictions—should we have to appeal rather to their feeling and imagination than to the cold decision of reason, still, the diffusiveness imparted to all scientific knowledge by freedom and enlightenment spreads gradually downward even to them; and the happy results of perfect liberty of thought on the mind and character of the entire nation, extend their influence even to its humblest individuals.   *Ibid.*

In claiming the unity of the human race we resist the unsavory assumption of higher and lower races.
Helmut de Terra, Humboldt, Knopf.

There are no inferior races; all are destined equally to attain freedom. *Ibid.*

David Hume
(1711-1776)
Scottish philosopher, historian

Nor is it possible to explain distinctly, how the Deity can be the mediate cause of

all the actions of men, without being the author of sin and moral turpitude.
An Enquiry Concerning Human Understanding, 1748.

Custom, then, is the great guide to human life. *Ibid.*

To reconcile the indifference and contingency of human actions with prescience; or to defend absolute decrees, and yet free the Deity from being the author of sin, has been found hitherto to exceed the powers of philosophy. *Ibid.*

There is no method of reasoning more common, and yet none more blamable, than, in philosophical disputes, to endeavor the refutation of any hypothesis, by a pretense of its dangerous consequences to religion and morality. When any opinion leads to absurdities, it is certainly false; but it is not certain that an opinion is false, because it is of dangerous consequence. *Ibid.*

A wise man proportions his belief to the evidence. *Ibid., Of Miracles.*

No testimony is sufficient to establish a miracle, unless the testimony be of such a kind, that its falsehood would be more miraculous than the fact which it endeavors to establish. *Ibid.*

The Christian religion not only was at first attended with miracles, but even at this day cannot be believed by any reasonable person without one. *Ibid.*

There is not to be found, in all history, any miracle attested by a sufficient number of men, of such unquestioned good sense, education, and learning, as to place them beyond all suspicion or any design to deceive others; of such credit and reputation in the eyes of mankind, as to have a great deal to lose in case of their being detected in any falsehood. *Ibid.*

It forms a strong presumption against all supernatural and miraculous relations, that they are observed chiefly to abound among ignorant and barbarous nations; or if a civilized people has ever given admission to any of them, that people will be found to have received them from ignorant and barbarous ancestors, who transmitted them with that inviolable sanction and authority which always attend received opinions. *Ibid.*

A miracle is a violation of the laws of nature; and as a firm and unalterable experience has established these laws, the proof against a miracle, from the very nature of the fact, is as entire as any argument from experience can possibly be imagined. . . . Nothing is esteemed a miracle, if it ever happen in the common course of nature. . . . There must, therefore, be an uniform experience against every miraculous event, otherwise the event would not merit that appellation. And as an uniform experience amounts to a proof, there is here a direct and full proof, from the nature of the fact, against the existence of any miracle. *Ibid.*

The many instances of forged miracles and prophecies and supernatural events, which, in all ages, have either been detected by contrary evidence, or which detect themselves by their absurdity, prove sufficiently the strong propensity of mankind to the extraordinary and marvelous, and ought reasonably to beget a suspicion against all relations of this kind. *Ibid.*

It is apprehended that arbitrary power would steal in upon us, were we not careful to prevent its progress, and were there not an easy method of conveying the alarm from one end of the kingdom to another. The spirit of the people must frequently be roused, in order to curb the ambition of the court, and the dread of rousing this spirit must be employed to prevent that ambition.

Nothing is so effectual to this purpose as the liberty of the press, by which all the learning, wit, and the genius of the nation may be employed on the side of freedom, and every one be animated to its defense. As long, therefore, as the republican part of our government can maintain itself against the monarchical, it will naturally be careful to keep the press open, as of importance to its own preservation.

Essays, Moral, Political and Literary; Of the Liberty of the Press, 1741.

By priests I understand only the pretenders to power and dominion, and to a superior sanctity of character, distinct from virtue and good morals.   *Ibid., I.*

The slaving poor are incapable of any principles.   *Ibid., II, 1742.*

Though men be much governed by interest, yet even interest itself, and all human affairs, are entirely governed by opinion.   *Ibid., VII.*

It is harder to avoid censure than to gain applause, for this may be done by one great or wise action in an age; but to escape censure a man must pass his whole life without saying or doing one ill or foolish thing.

Edward Hunter

(b. 1902)

Author, foreign correspondent, China specialist

Brainwashing.
Translation of Hsi Nao; Brain-Washing in Red China.

John Hus

(1373?-burned to death 1415)

Bohemian reformer

They who believe in the infallibility of the pope and openly say so are blasphemers.   *De ecclesia, 1412.*

Priests who claim that they can create the body of Christ whenever they want to are blasphemers.   *Simony, published 1442.*

Whenever the papacy has waged war, its power has diminished.   *Ibid.*

Robert Maynard Hutchins

(1899-1977)

American educator, President of the Fund for the Republic

There are two ways of fighting subversive ideas. One is the policy of repression. This policy is contrary to the letter and spirit of the Constitution of this country. It cannot be justly enforced, because it is impossible to tell precisely what people are thinking; they have to be judged by their acts.

Statement, Subversive Activities Committee of Illinois, April, 1949; Tower Topics, June, 1949.

The policy of the repression of ideas cannot work and never has worked. The alternative to it is the long, difficult road of education. To this the American people have been committed.   *Ibid.*

A world community can exist only with world communication, which means something more than extensive short-wave facilities scattered about the globe. It means common understanding, a common tradition, common ideas and common ideals. . . . The task is overwhelming and the chance of success is slight. We must take the chance or die.

Quoted in N. Y. Times, October 24, 1954.

A university is a place that is established and will function for the benefit of society, provided it is a center of independent thought. It is a center of independent thought and criticism that is created in the interest of the progress of society, and the one reason that we know that every totalitarian government must fail is that no totalitarian government is prepared to face the consequences of creating free universities.

Testimony, Congressional Committee, 1952. Quoted by Justice Douglas, An Almanac of Liberty.

How is the educated man to show the fruits of his education in times like these? . . . He must keep his head, and use it. He must never push other people around, nor acquiesce when he sees it done. He must decline to be carried away by waves of hysteria. He must be prepared to pay the penalty of unpopularity. . . . He must insist that freedom is the chief glory of mankind and that to repress it is in effect to repress the human spirit.

Quoted in The Churchman.

The death of democracy is not likely to be an assassination from ambush. It will be a slow extinction from apathy, indifference, and undernourishment.

Great Books, 1954.

Human rights rest on human dignity. The dignity of man is an ideal worth fighting for and worth dying for.

Democracy and Human Nature.

The faith rests on the proposition that man is a political animal, that participation in political decisions is necessary to his fulfillment and happiness, that all men can and must be sufficiently educated and informed to take part in making these decisions, that protection against arbitrary power, though indispensable, is insufficient to make either free individuals or a free society, that such a society must make positive provisions for its development into a community learning together; for this is what political participation, government by consent, and the civilization of the dialogue all add up to.

Address on receiving Sidney Hillman Award, N. Y. C., January 21, 1959.

Anybody who feels at ease in the world today is a fool. *Ibid.*

The notion that the sole concern of a free society is the limitation of governmental authority and that that government is best which governs least is certainly archaic. Our object today should not be to weaken government in competition with other centers of power, but rather to strengthen it as the agency charged with responsibility for the common good. That government is best which governs best.

Ibid.

Hutterite Creed

We believe in community of goods, and have all our property in common; we believe in non-resistance; we do not take oaths; we do not take or hold public office; we baptize only upon profession of faith.

Quoted. Scientific American, 1953.

Aldous Huxley

(1894-1963)
English writer

The vast majority of human beings dislike and even actually dread all notions with which they are not familiar. . . . Hence it comes about that at their first appearance innovators have generally been persecuted, and always derided as fools and madmen.

Proper Studies.

That all men are equal is a proposition to which, at ordinary times, no sane individual has ever given his assent. *Ibid.*

Facts do not cease to exist because they are ignored. *Ibid.*

Success—"the bitch-goddess, Success" in William James's phrase—demands strange sacrifices from those who worship her.

Ibid.

Of all social, moral and spiritual problems, that of power is the most chronically urgent and the most difficult of solution. Craving for power is not a vice of the body, consequently knows none of the limitations imposed by a tired or satiated physiology upon gluttony, intemperance and lust. Growing with every successive satisfaction, the appetite for power can manifest itself indefinitely, without interruption by bodily fatigue or sickness.

The Perennial Philosophy.

Instead of bringing to the power lover a merciful respite from his addictions, old age is apt to intensify them by making it easier for him to satisfy his cravings on a larger scale and in a more spectacular way. That is why in Acton's words, "all great men are bad." Can we therefore be surprised if political action undertaken, in all too many cases not for the public good, but solely or at least primarily to gratify the power lusts of bad men, should prove so often either self-stultifying or downright disastrous?

Ibid.

In actual practice how many great men have ever fulfilled or are ever likely to fulfill, the conditions which alone render power innocuous to the ruler as well as to the ruled? Obviously, very few. Except by saints, the problem of power is finally insoluble. But since genuine self-government is possible only in very small groups, societies on a national or super-national scale will always be ruled by oligarchal minorities whose members come to power because they have a lust for power.

This means that the problem of power will always arise and, since it cannot be solved . . . will always make trouble. And this, in its turn, means that we cannot expect the large-scale societies of the future to be much better than were the societies of the past during the brief periods when they were at their best. *Ibid.*

The more cant there is in politics the better. Cant is nothing in itself; but attached to even the smallest quantity of sincerity, it serves like a nought after a numeral, to multiply whatever of genuine good-will may exist. Politicians who cant about humanitarian principles find themselves sooner or later compelled to put those principles into practice—and far more thoroughly than they had ever originally intended. Without political cant there would be no democracy.

Jesting Pilate, 1926.

If it were not for intellectual snobs who pay—in solid cash—the tribute which philistinism owes to culture, the arts would perish with their starving practitioners. Let us thank heaven for hypocrisy. *Ibid.*

The value, first of all, of individual freedom, based upon the facts of human diversity and genetic uniqueness; the value of charity and compassion, based upon the old familiar fact, lately rediscovered by modern psychiatry—the fact that, whatever their mental and physical diversity, love is as necessary to human beings as food and shelter; and finally the value of intelligence,

without which love is impotent and freedom unattainable.
Brave New World Revisited, Harper & Bros., 1958.

Facts are ventriloquists' dummies. Sitting on a wise man's knee they may be made to utter words of wisdom; elsewhere, they say nothing, or talk nonsense, or indulge in sheer diabolism.
Mr. Huxley "can't remember the source of this quotation."

If we must play the theological game, let us never forget that it is a game. Religion, it seems to me, can survive only as a consciously accepted system of make-believe.   *Ibid.*

Luckily the majority of nominal Christians has at no time taken the Christian ideal very seriously; if it had, the races and the civilization of the West would long ago have come to an end.
Cardiff, What Great Men Think of Religion.

There is no possibility of anyone realizing the Christian ideals. For human beings simply cannot, in the nature of things, be superhuman.   *Ibid.*

The only completely consistent people are the dead.

Money breeds insensitiveness.

Obviously the passion for power is one of the most moving passions that exists in man. All democracies are based on the proposition that power is very dangerous, and that it's extremely important not to let any one man or any one small group have too much power for too long a time. What are the British and American Constitutions except devices for limiting power?
Mike Wallace Interview, Fund for the Republic, November 4, 1958.

You can produce plenty of goods without much freedom, but the whole creative life of man is ultimately impossible without a considerable measure of individual freedom, of initiative, or creativity.   *Ibid.*

Julian Huxley
(1887-1975)
English biologist, writer

The solution . . . would seem to lie in dismantling the theistic edifice, which will no longer bear the weight of the universe as enlarged by recent science, and attempting to find new outlets for the religious spirit. God, in any but a purely philosophical, and one is almost tempted to say Pickwickian sense, turns out to be a product of the human mind. As an independent or unitary being active in the affairs of the universe, he does not exist.
Science, Religion and Human Nature, Conway Memorial Lecture, 1930.

With final realization of the universality of natural law and its automatic, inevitable workings such a god is reduced to the position of a spectator, benevolent perhaps but ineffective, of the workings of the cosmic machine. His only possible function is that he may have created the machine; and, of course, if he is all wise, he will then have known exactly how it was going to work. But for the rest, his sole occupation throughout eternity is to enjoy the verification of his predictions.

This, it appears to me, is the only logical outcome of the belief in a personal or superpersonal absolute god who is eternal to his world, when it is confronted with modern science. Instead of ruling a kingdom he merely holds a watching brief.   *Ibid.*

What has been loosely called the conflict between science and religion is just

reaching its acute phase. Up to the present the fighting has been an affair of outposts; the incidents of Galileo and Darwin were but skirmishes. The real conflict is to come: it concerns the very conception of the Deity.
Cardiff, What Great Men Think of Religion.

This brings me back to where I started —the idea of religion as an organ of destiny.
Religion Without Revelation.

It is clear, as I suggested earlier, that twentieth-century man needs a new organ for dealing with destiny, a new system of beliefs and attitudes adapted to the situation in which he and his societies now have to exist and thus an organ for the better orientation of the human species as a whole —in other words, a new religion. The most significant contribution of science in this vital field is the discovery of man's position and role in evolution.   *Ibid.*

Man is that part of reality in which and through which the cosmic process has become conscious and has begun to comprehend itself. His supreme task is to increase that conscious comprehension and to apply it as fully as possible to guide the course of events. In other words, his role is to discover his destiny as agent of the evolutionary process, in order to fulfil it more adequately.   *Ibid.*

Thomas H(enry) Huxley
(1825-1895)
English biologist

Irrationally held truths may be more harmful than reasoned errors.
The Coming of Age of the Origin of the Species.

It is the customary fate of new truths to begin as heresies and to end as superstitions.
Ibid.

If then the question is put to me, would I rather have a miserable ape for a grandfather or a man highly endowed by nature and possessing great means and influence and yet who employs those faculties and that influence for the mere purpose of introducing ridicule into grave scientific discussion—I unhesitatingly affirm my preference for the ape.
Reply to Bishop Wilberforce, who asked if he was descended from an ape on his mother's or his father's side; in Huxley letters, first published in Nature, London; N. Y. Times, November 14, 1953.

A beautiful theory, killed by a nasty, ugly, little fact.
Quoted by Francis Galton, The Practical Cogitator.

The great end of life is not knowledge but action.   *Science and Culture.*

Logical consequences are the scarecrows of fools and the beacons of wise men.
Ibid.

I neither deny nor affirm the immortality of man. I see no reason for believing in it, but, on the other hand, I have no means of disproving it.
Letter to Charles Kingsley, 1860.

The longer I live the more obvious it is to me that the most sacred act of a man's life is to say and feel "I believe such and such to be true." All the greatest rewards and all the heaviest penalties of existence cling about that act.   *Ibid.*

My business is to teach my aspirations to conform themselves to fact, not to try and make facts harmonize with my aspirations.
Ibid.

Sit down before fact as a little child, be prepared to give up every preconceived notion, follow humbly wherever and whatever abysses nature leads, or you will learn nothing.   *Ibid.*

Every great advance in natural knowledge has involved the absolute rejection of authority.   *Lay Sermons, 1870.*

A world of facts lies outside and beyond the world of words.   *Ibid.*

It is wrong for a man to say that he is certain of the objective truth of any proposition unless he can produce evidence which logically justifies that certainty. This is what agnosticism asserts.
Agnosticism and Christianity, 1889.

The church founded by Jesus has *not* made its way; has *not* permeated the world—but *did* become extinct in the country of its birth—as Nazarenism and Ebionism.   *Letter to Robert Taylor, 1889.*

The dogma of the infallibility of the Bible is no more self-evident than is that of the infallibility of the popes.
Controverted Questions, 1892.

God give me strength to face a fact though it slay me.

There is nothing of permanent value (putting aside a few human affections), nothing that satisfies quiet reflection—except the sense of having worked according to one's capacity and light, to make things clear and get rid of cant and shams of all sorts.
Trevelyan, Carlyle: An Anthology.

In this sense strict anarchy may be the highest conceivable grade of perfection of social existence; for, if all men spontaneously did justice and loved mercy, it is plain that all swords might be advantageously turned into plowshares, and that the occupation of judges and police would be gone.

Time, whose tooth gnaws away everything else, is powerless against truth.
Administrative Nihilism, 1871.

Rome is the one great spiritual organization which is able to resist and must, as a matter of life and death, the progress of science and modern civilization.
Address, Scientific Education, Liverpool, 1869.

I took thought, and invented what I conceived to be the appropriate title of "Agnostic." It came into my head as suggestively antithetic to the "Gnostic" of Church history who professed to know so much about the very things of which I was ignorant.
Agnosticism. Nineteenth Century, 1889.

Social progress means a checking of the cosmic process at every step and the substitution for it of another, which may be called the ethical process; the end of which is not the survival of those who may happen to be the fittest, in respect of the whole of the conditions which obtain, but of those who are ethically the best.
Evolution and Ethics.

I see no limit to the extent to which intelligence and will, guided by sound principles of investigation, and organized in common effort, may modify the conditions of existence, for a period longer than that now covered by history. And much may be done to change the nature of man himself. The intelligence which has converted the brother of the wolf into the faithful guardian of the flock ought to be able to do something towards curbing the instincts of savagery in civilized men.   *Ibid.*

The deepest sin against the human mind is to believe things without evidence.

Science is simply common sense at its best—that is, rigidly accurate in observation, and merciless to fallacy in logic.

That man, I think, has had a liberal education who has been so trained in youth that his body is the ready servant of his will and does with care and pleasure all the work that as a mechanism it is capable of; whose intellect is a clear cold logic engine with all its parts of equal strength and in smooth working order ready like a steam engine to be turned to any kind of work and spin the gossamers as well as forge the anchors of the mind; whose mind is stored with the great and fundamental truths of Nature and of the laws of her operations; one who, no stunted ascetic, is full of life and fire, but whose passions are trained to come to heel by a vigorous will, the servant of a tender conscience; who has learned to love all beauty, whether of nature or of art, to hate all vileness, and to respect others as himself.

Evolution and Ethics.

"Learn what is true in order to do what is right" is the summing up of the whole duty of man . . .

My belief is that no human being or society composed of human beings ever did or ever will come to much unless their conduct was governed and guided by the love of some ethical ideal.

I have no faith, very little hope, and as much charity as I can afford.

Cardiff, What Great Men Think of Religion.

What are among the moral convictions most fondly held by barbarous and semi-barbarous people? They are the convictions that authority is the soundest basis of belief; that merit attaches to readiness to believe; that the doubting disposition is a bad one,

and skepticism a sin; that when good authority has pronounced what is to be believed, and faith has accepted it, reason has no further duty. *Ibid.*

The improver of natural knowledge absolutely refuses to acknowledge authority, as such. For him, skepticism is the highest of duties; blind faith the one unpardonable sin. *Ibid.*

The man of science has learned to believe in justification, not by faith, but by verification. *Ibid.*

The only question which a wise man can ask himself is whether a doctrine is true or false. Consequences will take care of themselves. *Ibid.*

Ecclesiasticism in science is only unfaithfulness to truth. *Ibid.*

Agnosticism simply means that a man shall not say he knows or believes that for which he has no grounds for professing to believe. *Ibid.*

My fundamental axiom of speculative philosophy is that materialism and spiritualism are opposite poles of the same absurdity—the absurdity of imagining that we know anything about either spirit or matter. *Ibid.*

Agnosticism, in fact, is not a creed, but a method, the essence of which lies in the rigorous application of a single principle. That principle is of great antiquity; it is as old as Socrates; as old as the writer who said: "Try all things, hold fast by that which is good"; it is the foundation of the Reformation, which simply illustrated the axiom that every man should be able to give a reason for the faith that is in him; it is the great principle of Descartes; it is the fundamental axiom of modern science.

Positively, the principle may be expressed: In matters of the intellect, follow your reason as far as it will take you, without regard to any other consideration. And negatively: In matters of the intellect do not pretend that conclusions are certain which are not demonstrated or demonstrable. That I take to be agnostic faith, which if a man keep whole and undefiled he shall not be ashamed to look the universe in the face, whatever the future may have in store for him. *Ibid.*

Orthodoxy is the Bourbon of the world of thought. It learns not, neither can it forget. *Ibid.*

Thoughtful men, once escaped from the blinding influences of traditional prejudice, will find in the lowly stock whence man has sprung the best evidence of the splendor of his capacities, and will discern in his long progress through the past, a reasonable ground of faith in his attainment of a noble future. *Collected Essays, v. 7.*

Vicente Blasco Ibáñez
(1867-1928)
Spanish author, political agitator

The only beast in the Plaza de Toros is the crowd.

Dolores Ibarruri
(La Pasionaria)
(b. 1895)
Spanish Communist leader

Mejor morir a pie que vivir en rodillas. (Better to die on one's feet than live on one's knees.) *Address, Valencia, 1936.**

---

* F. D. Roosevelt: "We, too, born to freedom and believing in freedom, are willing to fight to maintain freedom. We, and all others who believe as deeply as we do,

It is better to be the widow of a hero than the wife of a coward. *Ibid.*

Henrik Ibsen
(1828-1906)
Norwegian dramatic poet

The minority is always in the right.
An Enemy of the People, act iv.

The most dangerous foe to truth and freedom in our midst is the compact majority. Yes, the damned, compact, liberal majority. *Ibid.*

A man should never put on his best trousers when he goes out to battle for freedom and truth. *Ibid., act v.*

The strongest man in the world is he who stands most alone. *Ibid.*

The pillars of truth and the pillars of freedom—they are the pillars of society.
The Pillars of Society, act iv.

Nora: While I was at home with father, he used to tell me his opinions, and I held the same opinions. If I had others, I concealed them, because he wouldn't have liked it. *A Doll's House.*

There are two kinds of moral law, two kinds of consciences, in men and women, and they are altogether different. The two sexes do not understand each other. But in practical life, the woman is judged by man's law, as if she were a man, not a woman.
Notes for A Doll's House, Rome, October 19, 1878.

---

would rather die on our feet than live on our knees." June 19, 1941; to a special convocation of the University of Oxford, at Cambridge, Mass.

I almost believe we are all of us ghosts! It is not only what we have inherited from our father and mother that haunts us. It is all sorts of old, dead ideas, all kinds of old, dead beliefs, and so forth. They have no life, yet they cleave to us, and we cannot shake ourselves free from them.
Ghosts.

The devil is compromise.
Gollancz, From Darkness to Light.

I hold that man is in the right who is most closely in league with the future.*
Letter to Georg Brandes, January 3, 1882.

I, on the contrary, must of necessity say, "The minority is always right." Naturally I am not thinking of that minority of stagnationists who are left behind by the great middle party, which with us is called Liberal; but I mean that minority which leads the van, and pushes on to points which the majority has not yet reached.
Ibid.

The State is the curse of the individual. With what is Prussia's political strength bought? With the absorption of the individual in the political and geographical idea. The waiter is the best soldier. And on the other hand, take the Jewish people, the aristocracy of the human race—how is it they have kept their place apart, their poetical halo, amid surroundings of coarse cruelty? By having no State to burden them. Had they remained in Palestine, they would long ago have lost their individuality in the process of their State's construction, like all other nations.
Ibid.

Away with the State! I will take part in that revolution. Undermine the whole conception of a state, declare free choice and spiritual kinship to be the only all-important conditions of any union, and you will have the commencement of a liberty that is worth something.
Ibid.

And what can be said of the attitude assumed by the press of these leaders of the people who speak and write of freedom of thought, and at the same time make themselves the slaves of the supposed opinions of their subscribers?
Ibid.

The struggle for liberty is nothing but the constant active appropriation of the idea of liberty. He who possesses liberty otherwise than as an aspiration possesses it soulless, dead. One of the qualities of liberty is that, as long as it is being striven after, it goes on expanding. Therefore, the man who stands still in the midst of the struggle and says, "I have it", merely shows by so doing that he has just lost it. Now this very contentedness in the possession of a dead liberty is characteristic of the so-called State, and, as I have said, is not a good characteristic.
Ibid.

Changes in forms of government are pettifogging affairs—a degree less or a degree more, mere foolishness. The State has its root in time, and will ripen and rot in time. Greater things than it will fall—religion, for example. Neither moral conceptions nor art forms have an eternity before them. How much are we really in duty bound to pin our faith to? Who will guarantee me that on Jupiter two and two do not make five? . . .
Ibid.

The past, with its gilt, with its hypocrisy and its hollowness, its lying conventionality, and its pitiful cowardice, shall lie behind us like a museum.
Epigrams.

It is a lie that truth always belongs to the majority! What kind of truths do the

---

* This exact quotation was used by Eisenhower in accepting the Republican nomination of 1956.

majority rally around? Truths so old that they are positively decrepit with age. When a truth is hoary with years it is in a fair way to become a lie. *Ibid.*

It is only in the realm of politics that the work of emancipation may go on? Is not the emancipation of the mind the first and greatest need? *Ibid.*

The masses are nothing but the raw material from which a people is formed.

Harold L. Ickes
(1874-1952)
American public official, writer

With rare exceptions, the attitude of that newspaper is unsocial whose publisher belongs to the moneyed class and whose primary objective is to make profits.
America's House of Lords.

While they shriek for "freedom of the press" when there is no slightest threat of that freedom, they deny to citizens that freedom *from* the press to which the decencies of life entitle them. They misrepresent, they distort, they color, they blackguard, they lie. *Ibid.*

As a matter of fact, it is the fascist-minded men of America who are the real enemies of our institutions. They have solidarity, a common interest in seizing more power and greater riches for themselves and ability and willingness to turn the concentrated wealth of America against the welfare of America. It is these men who, pretending that they would save us from dreadful communism, would superimpose upon America an equally dreaded fascism.
Address, American Civil Liberties Union, December 8, 1937.

The columnist's stock in trade is falsification and vilification. He is journalism's Public Enemy No. 1, and if the American press is to improve itself, it must get rid of him.
Statement, April 11, 1939.

I would dare to dispute the integrity of the President on any occasion my country's welfare demanded it. . . . After all, the President of the United States is neither an absolute monarch nor a descendant of a sun goddess. *Time, March 11, 1946.*

The barefoot boy from Wall Street.
A reference to Wendell Willkie, candidate for President.

Industrial Workers of the World (I.W.W.)

The working class and the employing class have nothing in common. There can be no peace so long as hunger and want are found among millions of working people, and the few who make up the employing class have all the good things of life.
Preamble, constitution, adopted at Chicago, June 27, 1905.

St. Ignatius
See Loyola

William R. Inge
(1860-1954)
English clergyman, theologian

No Christian can be a pessimist, for Christianity is a system of radical optimism.
Obituary editorial, Manchester Guardian, March 4, 1954.

Democracy is a whim and a fetish.
Ibid.

I know as much about the afterlife as you—nothing. I don't even know if there is one. . . . I have no vision of "heaven"

or a "welcoming God." I do not know what I shall find. I must wait and see.
Obituary, Time, March 8, 1954.

Lutheranism is essentially German. . . . It worships a God who is neither just nor merciful. *Time, April 1, 1946.*

Religious fanaticism, unlimited competition, and war are the murderers of freedom. We know now that they end in suicide, though they win victories. They may drive liberalism underground; they have done so before now. But we know our danger, as we did not know it in the last century. It is not too late to "stand fast in the liberty wherewith Christ hath made us free." The alternative may be the atom bomb.
The Modern Churchman.

Miracle is the bastard child of faith and reason, which neither parent can afford to own.

Experience proves that none is so cruel as the disillusioned sentimentalist.

Public opinion, a vulgar, impertinent, anonymous tyrant who deliberately makes life unpleasant for anyone who is not content to be the average man.
Outspoken Essays.

A man may build himself a throne of bayonets, but he cannot sit on it.*
Marchant, Wit and Wisdom of Dean Inge.

We are distressed because our churches are half empty; and many of them would be emptier if the Gospel were preached in them.

Patriotism varies, from a noble devotion to a moral lunacy.

---

* Cf. Cavour: "You can do anything with bayonets except sit on them."

Catholicism and Protestantism are both obsolescent phases in the evolution of the Christian religion.

Race and nationality are catchwords for which rulers find that their subjects are willing to fight, as they fought for what they called religion 400 years ago.

Robert G. Ingersoll *
(1833-1899)
American lawyer, orator, statesman

The infidels of one age have been the aureoled saints of the next. The destroyers of the old are the creators of the new.
The Great Infidels.

Heresy is what the minority believe; it is the name given by the powerful to the doctrines of the weak.
Heretics and Heresies.

Every man who expresses an honest thought is a soldier in the army of intellectual liberty. *Interview on Talmadge.*

An honest God is the noblest work of man. *Gods, pt. 1, p. 2, 1879.*

You have no right to erect your toll-gate upon the highways of thought.
The Ghosts.

Slavery includes all other crimes. It is the joint product of the kidnaper, the pirate, thief, murderer and hypocrite.
Workers Should Be Free, quoted in "Labor," January 10, 1948.

With the idea that labor is the basis of progress goes the thought that labor must be free. *Ibid.*

---

* The quotations with no source given have been verified by Joseph Lewis, Secretary of The Thomas Paine Foundation.

The laboring people should unite and should protect themselves against all idlers. You can divide mankind into classes: the laborers and the idlers, the supporters and the supported, the honest and the dishonest.
Ibid.

Every man is dishonest who lives upon the unpaid labor of others, no matter if he occupies a throne. *Ibid.*

We need free bodies and free minds—free labor and free thought, chainless hands and fetterless brains. Free labor will give us wealth. Free thought will give us truth.
Ibid.

There will never be a generation of great men until there has been a generation of free women—of free mothers. *Ibid.*

There is but one blasphemy, and that is injustice.
Speech, Chicago, September 20, 1880.

One good schoolmaster is worth a thousand priests. *Ibid., N.Y.C., May 1, 1881.*

The history of intellectual progress is written in the lives of infidels. *Ibid.*

Few rich men own their own property. The property owns them.
Ibid., October 29, 1896.

I believe in liberty, always and everywhere.

Give to every man the fruit of his own labor—the labor of his hand and of his brain.

No man should be allowed to own any land that he does not use.

A believer is a bird in a cage, a freethinker is an eagle parting the clouds with tireless wing.

In all ages hypocrites, called priests, have put crowns upon the heads of thieves, called kings.

Mental slavery is mental death, and every man who has given up his intellectual freedom is the living coffin of his dead soul.

For many centuries the sword and cross were allies. Together they attacked the rights of man. They defended each other.

Liberty is a word hated by kings—loathed by popes. It is a word that shatters thrones and altars—that leaves the crowned without subjects, and the outstretched hand of superstition without alms. Liberty is the blossom and fruit of justice—the perfume of mercy. Liberty is the seed and soil, the air and light, the dew and rain of progress, love and joy.

A government founded upon anything except liberty and justice cannot stand. All the wrecks on either side of the stream of time, all the wrecks of the great cities, and all the nations that have passed away—all are a warning that no nation founded upon injustice can stand. From the sand-enshrouded Egypt, from the marble wilderness of Athens, and from every fallen, crumbling stone of the once mighty Rome, comes a wail as it were, the cry that no nation founded upon injustice can permanently stand.

It is a blessed thing that in every age some one has had individuality enough and courage enough to stand by his own convictions—some one who had the grandeur to say his say. I believe it was Magellan who said, "The Church says the earth is flat; but I have seen its shadow on the moon, and I have more confidence even in a shadow than in the Church." On the prow of his ship were disobedience, defiance, scorn, and success.

Is it possible that an infinite God created this world simply to be the dwelling-place

[350]

of slaves and serfs? Simply for the purpose of raising orthodox Christians? That he did a few miracles to astonish them? That all the evils of life are simply his punishments, and that he is finally going to turn heaven into a kind of religious museum filled with Baptist barnacles, petrified Presbyterians, and Methodist mummies?

Surely there is grandeur in knowing that in the realm of thought, at least, you are without a chain; that you have the right to explore all heights and all depths; that there are no walls nor fences, nor prohibited places, nor sacred corners in all the vast expanse of thought; that your intellect owes no allegiance to any being, human or divine; that you hold all in fee and upon no condition and by no tenure whatever; that in the world of mind you are relieved from all personal dictation, and from the ignorant tyranny of majorities. Surely it is worth something to feel that there are no priests, no popes, no parties, no governments, no kings, no gods, to whom your intellect can be compelled to pay a reluctant homage.

The man who does not do his own thinking is a slave, and is a traitor to himself and to his fellow-men.

Every art and artifice, every cruelty and outrage has been practiced and perpetrated to destroy the rights of man. In this great struggle every crime has been rewarded and every virtue has been punished. Reading, writing, thinking, and investigating have all been crimes.

What do I mean by liberty? By physical liberty I mean the right to do anything which does not interfere with the happiness of another. By intellectual liberty I mean the right to think and the right to think wrong.

My creed:—To love justice, to long for the right, to love mercy, to pity the suffering, to assist the weak, to forget wrongs and remember benefits, to love the truth, to be sincere, to utter honest words, to love liberty, to wage relentless war against slavery in all its forms, to love wife and child and friend, to make a happy home, to love the beautiful in art, in nature, to cultivate the mind, to be familiar with the mighty thoughts that genius has expressed, the noble deeds of all the world; to cultivate courage and cheerfulness, to make others happy, to fill life with the splendor of generous acts, the warmth of loving words; to discard error, to destroy prejudice, to receive new truths with gladness, to cultivate hope, to see the calm beyond the storm, the dawn beyond the night, to do the best that can be done and then be resigned. This is the religion of reason, the creed of science. This satisfies the brain and heart.

Political rights have been preserved by traitors; the liberty of mind by heretics.

Fortunately for us, there have been traitors and there have been heretics, blasphemers, thinkers, investigators, lovers of liberty, men of genius who have given their lives to better the condition of their fellow men.

In the history of the world, the man who is ahead has always been called a heretic.
Liberty of Man, Woman and Child.

There is no slavery but ignorance. Liberty is the child of intelligence. *Ibid.*

Every science has been an outcast.
Ibid.

I had rather live with the woman I love in a world full of trouble, than to live in heaven with nobody but men. *Ibid.*

The "Sabbath" was born of asceticism, hatred of human joy, fanaticism, ignorance, egotism of priests and the cowardice of people. *Some Mistakes of Moses.*

It is said that desire for knowledge lost us the Eden of the past; but whether that is true or not, it will certainly give us the Eden of the future. *Ibid.*

To hate man and worship God seems to be the sum of all creeds. *Ibid.*

A false friend, an unjust judge, a braggart, hypocrite, and tyrant, sincere in hatred, jealous, vain and revengeful, false in promise, honest in curse, suspicious, ignorant, infamous and hideous—such is the God of the Pentateuch. *Ibid.*

There is but one blasphemy, and that is injustice. *Speech, 1880.*

What light is to the eyes—what air is to the lungs—what love is to the heart, liberty is to the soul of man. *Progress.*

Happiness is the only good, reason the only torch, justice the only worship, humanity the only religion, and love the only priest.
Eulogy at the grave of his brother, Eben.

The man who finds a truth lights a torch. *The Truth.*

Civilization was thrust into the brain of Europe on the point of a Moorish lance.

I would have all the nobility drop their titles and give their lands back to the people. I would have the pope throw away his tiara, take off his sacred vestments, and admit that he is not acting for God—is not infallible—but is just an ordinary Italian. I would have all the cardinals, archbishops, bishops, priests and clergymen admit that they know nothing about theology, nothing

about hell or heaven, nothing about the destiny of the human race, nothing about devils or ghosts, gods or angels.
What I Want for Christmas.

I would have all the professors in colleges, all the teachers in schools of every kind, including those in Sunday schools, agree that they would teach only what they know, that they would not palm off guesses as demonstrated truths. *Ibid.*

I would like to see all editors of papers and magazines agree to print the truth and nothing but the truth, to avoid all slander and misrepresentation, and to let the private affairs of the people alone. *Ibid.*

I would like to see a fair division of profits between capital and labor, so that the toiler could save enough to mingle a little June with the December of his life. *Ibid.*

I would like to see an international court established in which to settle disputes between nations, so that armies could be disbanded and the great navies allowed to rust and rot in perfect peace. *Ibid.*

I would like to see the whole world free—free from injustice—free from superstition. *Ibid.*

Innocent III
(1161-1216)
Pope

Consequently, in the name of God Almighty, by the authority of the Apostles Saints Peter and Paul, and by our Own, We reprove and condemn this Charter; under pain of anathema We forbid the King to observe it or the barons to demand its execution. We declare the Charter null and of no effect, as well as all the obligations con-

tracted to confirm it. It is Our wish that in no case should it have any force.
Condemnation of Magna Carta.

Use against heretics the spiritual sword of excommunication, and if this does not prove effective, use the material sword.

The Jews, like Cain, are doomed to wander the earth as fugitives and vagabonds, and their faces are covered with shame.
Letter to Count de Nevers, c. 1200.

International Confederation of Free Trade Unions (ICFTU)

Bread: economic security and social justice for all.
Freedom: through economic and political democracy.
Peace: with liberty, justice and dignity for all.
Manifesto, first congress, London, December, 1949.

Institute of Brothers of the Christian Church

114. Why is the (Roman Catholic) Church superior to the State? Because the end to which the Church tends is the noblest of all ends.
Manual of the Christian Doctrine, 48th edition, 1926, with imprimatur of Archbishop (later Cardinal) Dougherty of Philadelphia.

123. What name is given to the doctrine that the State has neither the right nor the duty to be united to the Church to protect it? This doctrine is called *Liberalism.* It is founded principally on the fact that modern society rests on liberty of con-

science and of worship, on liberty of speech and of the press. *Ibid.*

124. Why is Liberalism condemned? 1. Because it denies all subordination of the State to the Church; 2. Because it confounds liberty with right; 3. Because it despises the social dominion of Christ, and rejects the benefits derived therefrom.
Ibid.

The Irish Republic

We declare the right of the people of Ireland to the ownership of Ireland, and to the unfettered control of Irish destinies, to be sovereign and indefeasible. The long usurpation of that right by a foreign people and government has not extinguished the right, nor can it ever be extinguished except by the destruction of the Irish people.
Proclamation of the provisional government, Easter uprising, 1916.

Isocrates
(436-338 B.C.)
Athenian orator, rhetorician

Whom, then, do I call educated? First, those who manage well the circumstances which they encounter day by day and who possess a judgment which is accurate in meeting occasions as they arise and rarely miss the expedient course of action; next, those who are decent and honorable in their intercourse with all men, bearing easily and goodnaturedly what is unpleasant or offensive in others, and being themselves as agreeable and reasonable to their associates as it is humanly possible to be; furthermore, those who hold their pleasures always under control and are not unduly overcome by their misfortunes, bearing up under them bravely and in a manner worthy of our common nature; finally, and most important of all, those who are not spoiled by their successes and who do not desert their true selves, but hold their ground steadfastly as wise and soberminded men, rejoicing no more in the good things which have come to them through chance than in those which through their own nature and intelligence are theirs since birth. Those who have a character which is in accord, not with one of these things, but with all of them—those I maintain are educated and whole men, possessed of all the virtues of a man.   *Panathenaicus.*

The soul of a state is its constitution, which has the same power as the mind over the body: for it is that and nothing else which deliberates on everything, which tries to preserve what is good and to avoid disasters. Laws, politicians, private citizens, all must necessarily take on its likeness and act in accordance with whatever kind of constitution they live under.

Oration, vii, 14; translated by Kathleen Freeman, Fighting Words.

They were thinking not of their duties as citizens, but of their rights. They were looking upon the state to guarantee not freedom as in the old days, but privilege. Great danger lay in that course. Men bent on self interest were always short-sighted. They could rise to long views, to where they could see the good of the whole country, only when they looked beyond their own affairs, and the state in which men did not do that was doomed.

Edith Hamilton, The Echo of Greece.

One must now apologize for any success in business as if it were a violation of the moral law, so that today it is worse to prosper than to be a criminal.

Quoted in Republican News, January, 1948.

Andrew Jackson
(1767-1845)
7th President of the United States

I am one of those who do not believe that a national debt is a national blessing, but rather a curse to a republic; inasmuch as it is calculated to raise around the administration a moneyed aristocracy dangerous to the liberties of the country.°

To L. H. Colman, April 26, 1824.

To persuade my countrymen, so far as I may, that it is not in a splendid government, supported by powerful monopolies and aristocratical establishments, that they will find happiness, or their liberties protected, but in a plain system, void of pomp—protecting all, and granting favors to none.

Benton, Thirty Years' View, vol. 1; quoted by Parrington.

The authority of the Supreme Court must not . . . be permitted to control the Congress, or the Executive, when acting in their legislative capacities.   *Address, 1832.*

I consider, then, the power to annul a law of the United States, assumed by one State, *incompatible with the existence of the Union, contradicted expressly by the letter of the Constitution, unauthorized by the spirit, inconsistent with every principle on which it was founded, and destructive of the great object for which it was formed.*

Proclamation to the People of South Carolina, December 10, 1832.

The Constitution of the United States, then, forms a *government*, not a league.
                                          Ibid.

Each State, having expressly parted with so many powers as to constitute, jointly with the other States, a single nation, can not, from that period, possess any right to

---

° Cf. Alexander Hamilton.

secede, because such secession does not break a league, but destroys the unity of a nation. *Ibid.*

You are a den of vipers and thieves. I intend to rout you out, and by the eternal God, I will rout you out.
To delegation of bankers discussing Bank Renewal Bill, 1832.

Every monopoly and all exclusive privileges are granted at the expense of the public, which ought to receive a fair equivalent.
Veto, Bank Renewal Bill, July 10, 1832. (A considerable part of this message was written by Roger B. Taney.)

Mere precedent is a dangerous source of authority, and should not be regarded as deciding questions of constitutional power except where the acquiescence of the people of the States can be considered as well settled. *Ibid.*

It is to be regretted that the rich and powerful too often bend the acts of government to their selfish purposes. *Ibid.*

Distinctions in society will always exist under every just government. Equality of talents, of education or of wealth cannot be produced by human institutions. In the full enjoyment of the gifts of heaven and the fruits of superior industry, economy and virtue, every man is equally entitled to protection by law; but when the laws undertake to add to these natural and just advantages artificial distinctions, to grant titles, gratuities, and exclusive privileges, to make the rich richer and the potent more powerful, the humble members of society —the farmers, mechanics, and laborers— who have neither the time nor the means of securing like favors to themselves, have a right to complain of the injustice of their Government. *Ibid.*

There are no necessary evils in government. Its evils exist only in its abuses. If it would confine itself to equal protection, and, as Heaven does its rain, shower its favors alike on the high and on the low, the rich and the poor, it would be an unqualified blessing. *Ibid.*

If we can not at once, in justice to interests vested under improvident legislation, make our Government what it ought to be, we can at least take a stand against all new grants of monopolies and exclusive privileges, against any prostitution of our Government to the advancement of the few at the expense of the many, and in favor of compromise and gradual reform in our code of laws and systems of political economy. *Ibid.*

Many of our rich men have not been content with equal protection and equal benefits, but have besought us to make them richer by act of Congress. By attempting to gratify their desires we have in the results of our legislation arrayed section against section, interest against interest, and man against man, in a fearful commotion which threatens to shake the foundations of our Union. *Ibid.*

If a national debt is considered a national blessing, then we can get on by borrowing. But as I believe it is a national curse, my vow shall be to pay the national debt.

Peace, above all things, is to be desired, but blood must sometimes be spilled to obtain it on equable and lasting terms.

One man with courage makes a majority.

I could not do otherwise without transcending the limits prescribed by the Constitution for the President; and without feeling that I might in some degree disturb the security which religion nowadays enjoys in this country in its complete separation from the political concerns of the General Government.

Statement, refusing to proclaim a national fast day of prayers against cholera.

Robert H. Jackson
(1892-1954)
U.S. Supreme Court Justice

Our forefathers found the evils of free thinking more to be endured than the evils of inquest or suppression. This is because thoughtful, bold and independent minds are essential to wide and considered self-government.

Quoted by Z. Chafee, Jr. Atlantic Monthly, January, 1955.

A Government to perform even a minimum of service to its people, must take steps to suppress avarice, to strike down privately built-up schemes of economic exploitation or oppression, to uproot privilege, and to assure justice and economic opportunity to the masses.

Quoted in N. Y. Times obituary, October 10, 1954.

It is Mr. Mellon's credo that $200,000,000 can do no wrong. Our offense consists in doubting it. *Ibid.*

No longer may the head of a state consider himself outside the law, and impose inhuman acts on the peoples of the world.

Ibid.; explaining the Nuernberg trials.

I think under our system it is time enough for the law to lay hold of the citizen when he acts illegally, or in some rare circumstances when his thoughts are given illegal utterance. I think we must let his mind alone.

Partial dissent on non-Communist oath in Taft-Hartley Act.

The very purpose of a Bill of Rights was to withdraw certain subjects from the vicissitudes of political controversy, to place them beyond the reach of majorities and officials and to establish them as legal principles to be applied by the courts. One's right to life, liberty, and property, to free speech, a free press, freedom of worship and assembly, and other fundamental rights may not be submitted to vote; they depend on the outcome of no elections.

W. Va. State Board of Education v. Barnette, 1943. The Jehovah's Witnesses flag salute case.

Struggles to coerce uniformity of sentiment in support of some end thought essential to their time and country have been waged by many good as well as by evil men. Nationalism is a relatively recent phenomenon, but at other times and places the ends have been racial or territorial security, support of a dynasty or regime, and particular plans for saving souls. As first the moderate methods to attain unity have failed, those bent on its accomplishment must resort to an ever-increasing severity. As government pressure toward unity becomes greater, so strife becomes more bitter as to whose unity it shall be.

Ibid.

Ultimate futility of such attempts to compel coherence is the lesson of every such effort from the Roman drive to stamp out Christianity as a disturber of its pagan unity, the Inquisition as a means to religious and dynastic unity, the Siberian exiles as a means to Russian unity, down to the fast-failing efforts of our present totalitarian enemies. *Ibid.*

Those who begin coercive elimination of dissent soon find themselves exterminating dissenters. Compulsory unification of opinion achieves only the unanimity of the graveyard. *Ibid.*

We apply the limitations of the Constitution with no fear that freedom to be intellectually and spiritually diverse or even contrary will disintegrate the social organization. *Ibid.*

To believe that patriotism will not flourish if patriotic ceremonies are voluntary and spontaneous instead of a compulsory routine is to make an unflattering estimate of the appeal of our institutions to free minds. We can have intellectual individualism and the rich cultural diversities that we owe to exceptional minds only at the price of occasional eccentricity and abnormal attitudes. *Ibid.*

Freedom to differ is not limited to things that do not matter much. That would be a mere shadow of freedom. The test of its substance is the right to differ as to things that touch the heart of the existing order. *Ibid.*

If there is any fixed star in our constitutional constellation, it is that no official, high or petty, can prescribe what shall be orthodox in politics, nationalism, religion, or other matters of opinion, to force citizens to confess by word or act their faith therein. *Ibid.*

I can see in their teachings nothing but humbug, untainted by any trace of truth. But that does not dispose of the constitutional question whether misrepresentation of religious experience is prosecutable; it rather emphasizes the dangers of such prosecutions. *Dissent, U.S. v. Ballard, 1944.*

I do not know what degree of skepticism or disbelief in a religious representation amounts to actionable fraud. (William) James points out that "Faith means belief in something concerning which doubt is theoretically possible." Belief in what one may demonstrate to the senses is not faith. All schools of religious thought make enormous assumptions, generally on the basis of revelations authenticated by some sign or miracle. The appeal in such matters is to a very different plane of credulity than is invoked by representations of secular fact in commerce. Some who profess belief in the Bible read literally what others read as allegory or metaphor, as they read Aesop's fables. *Ibid.*

The chief wrong which false prophets do to their following is not financial. . . . The real harm is on the mental and spiritual plane. There are those who hunger and thirst after higher values which they feel wanting in their humdrum lives. They live in mental confusion or moral anarchy and seek vaguely for truth and beauty and moral support. When they are deluded and then disillusioned, cynicism and confusion follow. The wrong of these things, as I see it, is not in the money the victims part with half so much as in the mental and spiritual poison they get. But that is precisely the thing the Constitution put beyond the reach of the prosecutor, for the price of freedom of religion or of speech or of the press is that we must put up with, and even pay for, a good deal of rubbish. *Ibid.*

There is no reason to doubt that this Court may fall into error as may other branches of the Government. . . . The Court differs, however, from other branches of the Government in its ability to extricate itself from error. It can reconsider.[*]

Helvering v. Griffiths, Vol. 318, p. 400.

---

[*] Justice Jackson cited a long list of cases in which the Supreme Court has reversed itself.

Newspapers, in the enjoyment of their Constitutional rights, may not deprive accused persons of their right to fair trial.
Opinion, Frankfurter concurring, reversing Florida rape convictions, N. Y. Times, April 10, 1951.

The day that this country ceases to be free for irreligion it will cease to be free for religion—except for the sect that can win political power.
Zorach v. Clauson, 343 U.S. 306 (1952).

If we concede to the State power and wisdom to single out "duly constituted religious" bodies as exclusive alternatives for compulsory secular instruction, it would be logical to also uphold the power and wisdom to choose the true faith among those "duly constituted." We start down a rough road when we begin to mix compulsory public education with compulsory godliness.   *Ibid.*

I am heartened by the fact that democracy has not destroyed freedom of the press. But I am equally heartened by the fact that the press has not been able to destroy the freedom of democracy. The press, despite doing its utmost unanimous worst, has not been able to destroy a democratic government. The people know who is with them, despite all the packaged opinions handed them.
Address to N. Y. Press Association, Labor, February 8, 1958.

Joseph Jacobs
(1854-1916)
English historian

The religion of Israel freed mankind from that worship of Luck and Fate which is at the basis of all savagery.
Jewish Contributions to Civilization, 1919.

James I
(1566-1625)
King of England

I will govern according to the common weal, but not according to the common will.   *Reply to Commons, 1621.*

A custom loathsome to the eye, hateful to the nose, harmful to the brain, dangerous to the lungs, and in the black, stinking fume thereof, nearest resembling the horrible Stygian smoke of the pit that is bottomless.
A Counterblast to Tobacco, 1604.

Henry James
(1843-1916)
American author

The fatal futility of Fact.
Preface, The Spoils of Poynton.

Ideas are, in truth, forces. Infinite, too, is the power of personality. A union of the two always makes history.
Charles W. Eliot.

It is art that makes life, makes interest, makes importance.

The faculty of attention has utterly vanished from the general Anglo-Saxon mind, extinguished at its source by the big, blatant, Bayaders of Journalism, of the newspaper and the *picture* (above all) magazine.

William James
(1842-1910)
American psychologist, philosopher

The moral flabbiness born of the exclusive worship of the bitch-goddess SUCCESS. That—with the squalid cash interpretation put on the word success—is our national disease.

Letter to H. G. Wells, 1906.

I am against all big organizations as such, national ones first and foremost; against all big successes and big results; and in favor of the eternal forces of truth which always work in the individual and immediately unsuccessful way, underdogs always, till history comes, after they are long dead, and puts them on the top.

If this life be not a real fight, in which something is eternally gained for the universe by success, it is no better than a game of private theatricals from which one may withdraw at will.

The deadliest enemies of nations are not their foreign foes; they always dwell within their own borders. And from these internal enemies civilization is always in need of being saved. The nation blest above all nations is she in whom the civic genius of the people does the saving day by day, by acts without external picturesqueness; by speaking, writing, voting reasonably; by smiting corruption swiftly; by good temper between parties; by the people knowing true men when they see them, and preferring them as leaders to rabid partisans or empty quacks. Such nations have no need of wars to save them. Their accounts with righteousness are always even; and God's judgments do not have to overtake them fitfully in bloody spasms and convulsions of the race.

Memories and Studies.

Man, biologically considered, and whatever else he may be into the bargain, is the most formidable of all beasts of prey, and, indeed, the only one that preys systematically on his own species. *Ibid.*

Meaning, other than practical, there is for us none. *Pragmatism, 1907.*

There can *be* no difference anywhere that doesn't *make* a difference elsewhere— no difference in concrete fact and in conduct consequent upon that fact, imposed on somebody, somehow, somewhere, and somewhen. The whole function of philosophy ought to be to find out what definite difference it will make to you and me, at definite instances in our life, if this world-formula or that world-formula be the true one. *Ibid.*

Anti-intellectualist tendencies. *Ibid.*

No particular results then, so far, but only an attitude of orientation, is what the pragmatic method means. *The attitude of looking away from first things, principles, "categories," supposed necessities; and of looking toward last things, fruits, consequences, facts.* *Ibid.*

In the matter of belief, we are all extreme conservatives. *Ibid.*

The most violent revolutions in an individual's beliefs leave most of his old order standing. Time and space, cause and effect, nature and history, and one's own biography remain untouched. New truth is always a go-between, a smoother-over of transitions. It marries old opinions to new facts so as ever to show a minimum of jolt, a maximum of continuity. *Ibid.*

Pragmatism is uncomfortable away from facts. Rationalism is comfortable only in the presence of abstractions. . . . Objective truth must be something non-utilitarian, haughty, refined, remote, august, exalted. . . . Down with psychology, up with logic, in all this question! *Ibid.*

In this real world of sweat and dirt, it seems to me that when a view of things is "noble," that ought to count as a presumption against its truth, and as a philosophic disqualification. The prince of darkness may be a gentleman, as we are told he is, but whatever the God of earth and heaven is, he can surely be no gentleman. His menial services are needed in the dust of our human trials, even more than his dignity is needed in the empyrean.   *Ibid.*

The true is the name of whatever proves itself to be good in the way of belief, and good, too, for definite, assignable reasons.
Ibid.

The true . . . is only the expedient in the way of our thinking, just as "the right" is only the expedient in the way of our behaving.   *Ibid.*

The Tender-minded	The Tough-minded
Rationalistic (going by "principles")	Empiricist (going by "facts")
Intellectualistic	Sensationalistic
Idealistic	Materialistic
Optimistic	Pessimistic
Religious	Irreligious
Free-Willist	Fatalistic
Monistic	Pluralistic
Dogmatical	Sceptical
	Ibid.

Democracy is still upon its trial. The civic genius of our people is its only bulwark, and neither laws nor monuments, neither battleships nor public libraries, nor great newspapers, nor booming stocks; neither mechanical invention nor political adroitness, nor churches nor universities nor civil service examinations can save us from degeneration if the inner mystery be lost.

That mystery, at once the secret and the glory of our English-speaking race, consists in nothing but two common habits. . . . One of them is the habit of trained and disciplined good temper towards the opposite party when it fairly wins its innings. It was by breaking away from this habit

that the Slave States nearly wrecked our nation. The other is that of fierce and merciless resentment toward every man or set of men who break the public peace. By holding to this habit the free States saved her life.   *Ibid.*

These, then, are my last words to you: Be not afraid of life. Believe that life is worth living and your belief will help create the fact.   *The Will to Believe.*

Why does the painting of any paradise or utopia, in heaven or on earth, awaken such yawnings for nirvana and escape? The white-robed harp-playing heaven of our sabbath-schools, and the ladylike tea-table elysium represented in Mr. Spencer's Data of Ethics, as the final consummation of progress, are exactly on a par in this respect,—lubberlands, pure and simple, one and all.   *Ibid.*

If *this* be the whole fruit of the victory, we say: if the generations of mankind suffered and laid down their lives; if prophets confessed and martyrs sang in the fire, and all the sacred tears were shed for no other end than that a race of creatures of such unexampled insipidity should succeed, and protract . . . their contented and inoffensive lives,—why, at such a rate, better lose than win the battle, or at all events better ring down the curtain before the last act of the play, so that a business that began so importantly may be saved from so singularly flat a winding-up.   *Ibid.*

Science, like life, feeds on its own decay. New facts burst old rules; then newly divined conceptions bind old and new together into a reconciling law.   *Ibid.*

Religion is a monumental chapter in the history of human egotism.
The Varieties of Religious Experience.

Religious experience, in other words, spontaneously and inevitably engenders myths, superstitions, dogmas, creeds, and metaphysical theologies, and criticisms of one set of these by the adherents of another. *Ibid.*

The opposition between the men who have and the men who are is immemorial. *Ibid.*

What we now need to discover in the social realm is the moral equivalent of war; something heroic that will speak to man as universally as war does, and yet will be as compatible with their spiritual selves as war has proved to be incompatible. *Ibid.*

The prevalent fear of poverty among the educated classes is the worst moral disease from which our civilization suffers. *Ibid.*

Militarism is the great preserver of our ideals of hardihood, and human life with no use for hardihood would be contemptible. *The Moral Equivalent of War.*

The war against war is going to be no holiday excursion or camping party. The military feelings are too deeply grounded to abdicate their place among our ideals until better substitutes are offered than the glory and shame that come to nations as well as individuals from the ups and downs of politics and the vicissitudes of trade. *Ibid.*

We are all ready to be savage in some cause. The difference between a good man and a bad one is the choice of the cause. *Ladies' Home Journal, May, 1956.*

The ultimate test of what a truth means is the conduct it dictates or inspires.

The instinct of ownership is fundamental in man's nature.

There is no difference of truth that doesn't make a difference of fact somewhere.

Reason is one of the very feeblest of Nature's forces, if you take it at any one spot and moment. It is only in the very long run that its effects become perceptible.

As for the yellow (news)papers—every country has its criminal classes, and with us as in France, they have simply got into journalism as part of their professional evolution, and they must be got out. *Quoted by John Macy, Civilization in the United States.*

Greek history is a panorama of war for war's sake . . . of the utter ruin of a civilization which in intellectual respects was perhaps the highest the earth has ever seen. The wars were purely piratical. Pride, gold, women, slaves, excitement, were their only motives. *Ibid.*

The world . . . is only beginning to see that the wealth of a nation consists more than in anything else in the number of superior men that it harbors. . . . Geniuses are ferments; and when they come together, as they have done in certain lands at certain times, the whole population seems to share in the higher energy which they awaken. The effects are incalculable and often not easy to trace in detail, but they are pervasive and momentous. *Ibid.*

Karl Jaspers
(1883-1969)
German psychiatrist, philosopher

For Marxism, psychoanalysis, and ethnological theory (eugenics) have peculiarly destructive qualities! Just as Marxism assumes all spiritual life to be no more than a superstructure erected upon material foundations, so does psychoanalysis believe itself able to disclose this same spiritual life as the sublimation of repressed impulses; and what, by these lights, is still spoken of as civilization or culture, is constructed like an obsessional neurosis.

Man in the Modern Age, Doubleday, 1957.

Jean (Léon) Jaurès
(1859-assassinated 1914)
French Socialist leader

There is only one sovereign method for the achievement of Socialism—the winning of a legal majority.

Studies in Socialism, 1902.

I have no superstitious belief in legality, it has already received too many blows; but I always advise workmen to have recourse to legal means, for violence is the sign of temporary weakness.   *Ibid.*

Capitalism carries in itself war, like clouds carry rain.   *Ibid.*

When Socialism has triumphed, when conditions of peace have succeeded conditions of combat, when all men have their share of property in the immense human capital, and their share of initiative and of the exercise of free-will in the immense human activity, then all men will know the fulness of pride and joy; and they will feel that they are co-operators in the universal civilization.   *Ibid.*

Thomas Jefferson
(1743-1826)
3rd President of the United States

DOCUMENTS AND MISCELLANEOUS

Our cause is just. Our union is perfect. Our internal resources are great, and, if necessary, foreign assistance is undoubtedly attainable. . . . The arms we have been compelled by our enemies to assume we will, in defiance of every hazard, with unabating firmness and perseverance, employ for the preservation of our liberties; being with one mind resolved to die free men rather than live slaves.

Declaration of the Causes of Taking Up Arms, July 6, 1775.

We hold these truths to be sacred and undeniable; that all men are created equal and independent, that from that equal creation they derive rights inherent and inalienable, among which are the preservation of life, and liberty, and the pursuit of happiness.

Original draft of the Declaration of Independence.

He (King George III) has waged cruel war against human nature itself, violating its most sacred rights of life and liberty in the persons of a distant people who never offended him, captivating and carrying them into slavery in another hemisphere, or to incur miserable death in their transportation thither.   *Ibid.*

Well aware that the opinions and belief of men depend not on their own will, but follow involuntarily the evidence proposed to their minds; that Almighty God hath created the mind free, and manifested His supreme will that free it shall remain by making it altogether insusceptible of restraint; that all attempts to influence it by temporal punishments, or burdens, or by civil incapacitations, tend only to beget habits of hypocrisy and meanness, and are a departure from the plan of the holy author of our religion. . . .

Virginia Act for Religious Freedom, 1786.

That the impious presumption of legislature and ruler, civil as well as ecclesiastical, who, being themselves but fallible and uninspired men, have assumed dominion over the faith of others, setting up their own opinions and modes of thinking as the only true and infallible, and as such endeavouring to impose them on others, hath established and maintained false religions over the greatest part of the world and through all time.   *Ibid.*

That it is time enough for the rightful purposes of civil government for its officers to interfere when principles break out into overt acts against peace and good order.
Ibid.

And, finally, that truth is great and will prevail if left to herself; that she is the proper and sufficient antagonist to error, and has nothing to fear from the conflict unless by human interposition disarmed of her natural weapons, free argument and debate; errors ceasing to be dangerous when it is permitted freely to contradict them.
Ibid.

We, the General Assembly of Virginia do enact that no man shall be compelled to frequent or support any religious worship, place, or ministry whatsoever, nor shall be enforced, restrained, molested, or burthened in his body or goods, or shall otherwise suffer, on account of his religious opinions or belief; but that all men shall be free to profess, and by argument to maintain, their opinions in matters of religion, and that the same shall in no wise diminish, enlarge, or affect their civil capacities.   *Ibid.*

Where the preamble declares, that coercion is a departure from the plan of the holy author of our religion, an amendment was proposed by inserting the words "Jesus Christ," so that it should read, "A departure from the plan of Jesus Christ, the holy author of our religion;" the insertion was rejected by a great majority, in proof that they meant to comprehend, within the mantle of its protection, the Jew and the Gentile, the Christian and Mohammedan, the Hindoo and Infidel of every denomination.
Autobiography; a reference to the Virginia Act for Religious Freedom.

It is error alone which needs the support of government. Truth can stand by itself.
Notes on Virginia.

I tremble for my country when I reflect that God is just; that his justice cannot sleep forever; that considering numbers, nature, and natural means only, a revolution of the wheel of fortune, an exchange of situation, is among possible events; that it may become probable by supernatural interference! The Almighty has no attribute which can take side with us in such a contest.   *Ibid.*

Subject opinion to coercion: whom will you make your inquisitors? Fallible men; men governed by bad passions, by private as well as public reasons. And why subject it to coercion? To produce uniformity. But is uniformity of opinion desirable? No more than of face and stature.   *Ibid.*

Difference of opinion is advantageous in religion. The several sects perform the office of a *censor morum* over each other. *Ibid.*

Is uniformity attainable? Millions of innocent men, women, and children, since the introduction of Christianity, have been burnt, tortured, fined, imprisoned; yet we have not advanced an inch towards uniformity. What has been the effect of coercion? To make one half the world fools, and the other half hypocrites. To support roguery and error all over the earth. *Ibid.*

It does me no injury for my neighbor to say there are twenty gods, or no God.

Ibid.

Those who labor in the earth are the chosen people of God, if ever He had a chosen people.

Ibid.

But is the spirit of the people infallible —a permanent reliance? Is it government? . . . The spirit of the times may alter—will alter. Our rulers will become corrupt, our people careless. A single zealot may become persecutor, and better men become his victims.

Ibid.

No man complains of his neighbor for ill management of his affairs, for an error in sowing his land, or marrying his daughter, for consuming his substance in taverns . . . in all these he has liberty; but if he does not frequent the church, or then conform in ceremonies, there is an immediate uproar.

Ibid.

This institution will be based on the illimitable freedom of the human mind. For here we are not afraid to follow truth wherever it may lead, nor to tolerate error so long as reason is free to combat it.

To prospective teachers, University of Virginia.

All, too, will bear in mind this sacred principle, that though the will of the majority is in all cases to prevail, that will, to be rightful, must be reasonable; that the minority possess their equal rights, which equal laws must protect, and to violate which would be oppression.

First Inaugural Address, 1801.

And let us reflect that having banished from our land that religious intolerance under which mankind so long bled and suffered, we have yet gained little if we countenance a political intolerance as des-

potic, as wicked, and capable of as bitter and bloody persecutions.

Ibid.

But every difference of opinion is not a difference of principle. We have called by different names brethren of the same principle. We are all republicans—we are all federalists. If there be any among us who would wish to dissolve this Union or to change its republican form, let them stand undisturbed as monuments of the safety with which error of opinion may be tolerated where reason is left free to combat it.

Ibid.

. . . a wise and frugal government, which shall restrain men from injuring one another, which shall leave them otherwise free to regulate their own pursuits of industry and improvement, and shall not take from the mouth of labor the bread it has earned.

Ibid.

It is proper that you should understand what I deem the essential principles of our government, and consequently those which ought to shape its administration. . . . Equal and exact justice to all men, of whatever state or persuasion, religious or political; peace, commerce, and honest friendship, with all nations—entangling alliances with none; the support of the state governments in all their rights, as the most competent administrations for our domestic concerns and the surest bulwarks against antirepublican tendencies; the preservation of the general government in its whole constitutional vigor, as the sheet anchor of our peace at home and safety abroad; a jealous care of the rights of election by the people —a mild and safe corrective of abuses which are lopped by the sword of the revolution where peaceable remedies are unprovided; absolute acquiescence in the decisions of the majority—the vital principle of republics, from which there is no appeal but to force, the vital principle and immediate parent of despotism; a well disciplined militia—our best reliance in peace and for the first moments of war, till regulars may relieve them; the supremacy of the civil over the military authority; economy in the public expense, that labor may be lightly burdened; the honest payment of our debts and sacred preservation of the public faith; encouragement of agriculture, and of commerce as its handmaid; the diffusion of information and the arraignment of all abuses at the bar of public reason; freedom of religion; freedom of the press; freedom of person under the protection of the habeas corpus; and trial by juries impartially selected—these principles form the bright constellation which has gone before us, and guided our steps through the age of revolution and reformation. The wisdom of our sages and the blood of our heroes have been devoted to their attainment. They should be the creed of our political faith—the text of civil instruction—the touchstone by which to try the services of those we trust; and should we wander from them in moments of error or alarm, let us hasten to retrace our steps and to regain the road which alone leads to peace, liberty, and safety. *Ibid.*

Timid men prefer the calm of despotism to the boisterous sea of liberty.
Quoted by Brooks, From a Writer's Notebook, Dutton, p. 165.

My answer (to a letter from a mutual friend) was: "Say nothing of my religion. It is known to God and myself alone. Its evidence before the world is to be sought in my life; if that has been honest and dutiful to society the religion which has regulated it cannot be a bad one."
Letter to John Adams, Works, Vol. VII, p. 55.

I never told my own religion, nor scrutinized that of another. I never attempted to make a convert, nor wished to change another's creed. I have ever judged of others' religion by their lives . . . for it is from our lives and not from our words, that our religion must be read. *Ibid., Vol. XV.*

The whole of government consists in the art of being honest. *Ibid., VI, 186.*

Rebellion to tyrants is obedience to God. *Motto—found among his papers; supposed epitaph of John Bradshaw.*

ON FREEDOM OF THE PRESS.

Printing presses shall be subject to no other restraint than liableness to legal prosecution for false facts printed and published. *Proposed Constitution for Virginia, 1783.*

It is, however, an evil for which there is no remedy, our liberty depends on the freedom of the press, and that cannot be limited without being lost.
To Dr. J. Currie, 1786.

I am persuaded that the good sense of the people will always be found to be the best army. They may be led astray for a moment, but will soon correct themselves. The people are the only censors of their governors, and even their errors will tend to keep these to the true principles of their institutions. To punish these errors too severely would be to suppress the only safeguards of the public liberty.
To Edward Carrington, 1787.

The way to prevent these irregular interpositions of the people, is to give them full information of their affairs through the channel of the public papers, and to contrive that those papers should penetrate the whole mass of the people. *Ibid.*

The basis of our government being the opinion of the people, the very first object should be to keep that right; and were it left to me to decide whether we should have a government without newspapers, or newspapers without government, I should not hesitate a moment to prefer the latter. But I should mean that every man should receive those papers, and be capable of reading them. *Ibid.*

Our citizens may be deceived for a while, and have been deceived; but as long as the presses can be protected, we may trust them for light.

To Archibald Stuart, 1789.

Printing presses shall be free except as to false facts published maliciously, either to injure the reputation of another, whether followed by pecuniary damages or not, or to expose him to the punishment of the law.

1794.

I am for . . . freedom of the press and against all violations of the Constitution to silence by force, and not by reason, the complaints or criticisms, just or unjust, of our citizens against the conduct of their agents.

To Elbridge Gerry, January 26, 1799.

To the press alone, chequered as it is with abuses, the world is indebted for all the triumphs which have been gained by reason and humanity over error and oppression. . . .

Virginia and Kentucky Resolutions, 1799.

They (the Federalists) fill their newspapers with falsehoods, calumnies, and audacities. . . . I shall protect them in the right of lying and calumniating.

To Volney, 1802.

Indeed the abuses of the freedom of the press here have been carried to a length

never before known or borne by any civilized nation. But it is so difficult to draw a clear line of separation between the abuse and the wholesome use of the press, that as yet we have found it better to trust the public judgment, rather than the magistrate, with the discrimination between truth and falsehood. And hitherto the public judgment has performed that office with wonderful correctness. *To Pictet, 1803.*

No experiment can be more interesting than that we are now trying, and which we trust will end in establishing the fact, that man may be governed by reason and truth. Our first object should therefore be, to leave open to him all the avenues of truth. The most effectual hitherto found is the freedom of the press. It is, therefore, the first shut up by those who fear the investigation of their actions.

To Judge Tyler, 1804.

The firmness with which the people have withstood the late abuses of the press, the discernment they have manifested between truth and falsehood, show that they may safely be trusted to hear everything true and false, and to form a correct judgment between them. *Ibid.*

Conscious that there was not a *truth* on earth which I feared should be known, I have lent myself willingly on the subject of a great experiment, which was to prove that an administration, conducting itself with integrity and common understanding, cannot be battered down, even by the falsehoods of a licentious press. . . .

I have never therefore even contradicted the thousands of calumnies so industriously propagated against myself. But the fact being once established, that the press is impotent when it abandons itself to falsehood, I leave to others to restore it to its strength, by recalling it within the pale of truth.

Within that it is a noble institution, equally the friend of science & of civil liberty.

To Thos. Seymour, Jonth. Bull, and other citizens of Hartford, Conn., February 11, 1807.

It is a melancholy truth, that a suppression of the press could not more completely deprive the nation of its benefits, than is done by its abandoned prostitution to falsehood. *To J. Norvell, 1807.*

Nothing can now be believed which is seen in a newspaper. Truth itself becomes suspicious by being put into that polluted vehicle. *Ibid.*

I really look with commiseration over the great body of my fellow citizens, who, reading newspapers, live and die in the belief, that they have known something of what has been passing in the world in their time; whereas the accounts they have read in newspapers are just as true a history of any period of the world as of the present, except that the real names of the day are affixed to their fables. *Ibid.*

The man who never looks into a newspaper is better informed than he who reads them; inasmuch as he who knows nothing is nearer to truth than he whose mind is filled with falsehoods and errors. *Ibid.*

Perhaps an editor might begin a reformation in some such way as this. Divide his paper into four chapters, heading the 1st, Truths. 2d, Probabilities. 3d, Possibilities. 4th, Lies. The first chapter would be very short. *Ibid.*

At present it is disreputable to state a fact on newspaper authority; and the newspapers of our country by their abandoned spirit of falsehood, have more effectively destroyed the utility of the press than all the shackles devised by Bonaparte.

To T. Wortman, 1813. Quoted by Saul Padover, Thomas Jefferson on Democracy.

If a nation expects to be ignorant and free, in a state of civilization, it expects what never was and never will be. The functionaries of every government have propensities to command at will the liberty and property of their constituents. There is no safe deposit for these but with the people themselves; nor can they be safe with them without information. Where the press is free, and every man able to read, all is safe. *To Col. Charles Yancey, 1816.*

Advertisements contain the only truths to be relied on in a newspaper.
To Nathaniel Macon, 1819.

I read but one newspaper and that . . . more for its advertisements than its news.
To Charles Pickering, 1820.

5. Freedom of the press, subject only to liability for personal injuries. This formidable censor of the public functionaries, by arraigning them at the tribunal of public opinion, produces reform peaceably, which must otherwise be done by revolution. It is also the best instrument for enlightening the mind of man, and improving him as a rational, moral, and social being. *To Coray, 1823.*

The only security of all is in a free press. The force of public opinion cannot be resisted, when permitted freely to be expressed. The agitation it produces must be submitted to. It is necessary to keep the waters pure.
To Marquis de LaFayette, 1823.

I shall never take another newspaper of any sort.
Letter to Madison, quoted in Nieman Reports.

I do not take a single newspaper, nor read one a month, and I feel myself infinitely the happier for it.

JEFFERSON LETTERS

Merchants love nobody.
To John Langdon, 1785.

The most important bill in our whole code is that for the diffusion of knowledge among the people. No other sure foundation can be devised, for the preservation of freedom and happiness.
To George Wythe, August, 1786.

Preach, my dear sir, a crusade against ignorance; establish and improve the law for educating the common people. Let our countrymen know, that the people alone can protect us against these evils (of monarchy), and that the tax which will be paid for this purpose, is not more than a thousandth part of what will be paid to kings, priests, and nobles, who will rise up among us if we keep the people in ignorance.
Ibid.

The art of life is the avoiding of pain.
To Mrs. Cosway, 1786.

God forbid we should ever be twenty years without such a rebellion.
To Colonel William S. Smith, 1787.

The people cannot be all, and always, well informed. The part which is wrong will be discontented, in proportion to the importance of the facts they misconceive. If they remain quiet under such misconceptions, it is a lethargy, a forerunner of death to the public liberty.
Ibid.

What country before, ever existed a century and a half without a rebellion? And what country can preserve its liberties, if its rulers are not warned from time to time, that this people preserve the spirit of resistance? Let them take arms. The remedy is to set them right as to facts, pardon and pacify them. What signify a few lives lost in a century or two?
Ibid.

The tree of liberty must be refreshed from time to time, with the blood of patriots and tyrants. It is their natural manure.*
Ibid.

I will now tell you what I do not like. First, the omission of a bill of rights, providing clearly, and without the aid of sophism, for freedom of religion, freedom of the press, protection against standing armies, restriction of monopolies, the eternal and unremitting force of the habeas corpus laws, and trials by jury, in all matters of fact triable by the law of the land, and not by the laws of nations.
To James Madison, 1787.

I have a right to nothing which another has a right to take away. And Congress will have a right to take away trial by jury in all civil cases. Let me add that a bill of rights is what the people are entitled to against every government on earth, general or particular, and what no just government should refuse or rest on inference. *Ibid.*

This abomination (Negro slavery) must have an end. *To Edward Rutledge, 1787.*

Religion . . . Divest yourself of all bias in favor of novelty and singularity of opinion. Indulge them in any other subject rather than that of religion. It is too im-

---

* Barère: "The tree of liberty will grow only when watered by the blood of tyrants." 1792.

portant, and the consequences of error may be too serious.

To Peter Carr (nephew), August 10, 1787.

Shake off all the fears of servile prejudices, under which weak minds are servilely crouched. Fix reason firmly in her seat, and call on her tribunal for every fact, every opinion. Question with boldness even the existence of a God; because, if there be one, he must more approve of the homage of reason than that of blindfolded fear.

Ibid.

Do not be frightened from this inquiry by any fear of its consequences. If it ends in a belief that there is no God, you will find incitements to virtue in the comfort and pleasantness you feel in its exercise, and the love of others which it will procure you. If you find reason to believe there is a God, a consciousness that you are acting under his eye, and that he approves you, will be a vast additional incitement. *Ibid.*

The natural progress of things is for liberty to yield and government to gain ground.

To Carrington, 1788.

Every government degenerates when trusted to the rulers of the people alone. The people themselves therefore are its only safe depositories.

To Abbé Arnoud, July 19, 1789.

No society can make a perpetual constitution, or even a perpetual law.

To Madison, 1789.

That the earth belongs in usufruct to the living; that the dead have neither powers nor right over it. The portion occupied by any individual ceases to be his when he himself ceases to be, and reverts to society.

Ibid., September 6, 1789.

The republican is the only form of government which is not eternally at open or secret war with the rights of mankind.

To Hunter, 1790.

No man will ever bring out of the Presidency the reputation which carries him into it. *To Rutledge, 1796.*

Politics is such a torment that I would advise every one I love not to mix with it.

To Martha Jefferson Randolph, 1800.

They (the clergy) believe that any portion of power confided to me, will be exerted in opposition to their schemes. And they believe rightly: for *I have sworn upon the altar of God, eternal hostility against every form of tyranny over the mind of man.* But this is all they have to fear from me: and enough too in their opinion. *To Dr. Benjamin Rush, 1800.*

I contemplate with sovereign reverence that act of the whole American people which declared that their legislature should make no law respecting an establishment of religion, or prohibit the free exercise thereof, thus building a wall of separation between church and state.

To Baptists of Danbury, Conn., 1802.

It behooves every man who values liberty of conscience for himself, to resist invasions of it in the case of others.

To Dr. Rush, 1803.

I never will, by any word or act, bow to the shrine of intolerance, or admit a right in inquiry into the religious opinions of others. *To Edward Dowse, 1803.*

It is too late in the day for men of sincerity to pretend they believe in the Platonic mysticisms that three are one, and

---

* The italicized words appear on the Jefferson Memorial, Washington, D. C.

one is three; and yet that the one is not three, and the three are not one. . . . But this constitutes the craft, the power and the profit of the priests.

To John Adams, 1803.

We should all then, like the Quakers, live without an order of priests, moralize for ourselves, follow the oracle of conscience, and say nothing about what no man can understand, nor therefore believe. *Ibid.*

But a short time elapsed after the death of the great reformer of the Jewish religion, before his principles were departed from by those who professed to be his special servants, and perverted into an engine for enslaving mankind, and aggrandizing their oppressors in Church and State.

To S. Kercheval, 1810.

The purest system of morals ever before preached to man has been adulterated and sophisticated by artificial constructions, into a mere contrivance to filch wealth and power to themselves: that rational men, not being able to swallow their impious heresies, in order to force them down their throats, they raise the hue and cry of infidelity, while themselves are the greatest obstacle to the advancement of the real doctrines of Jesus, and do, in fact, constitute the real Anti-Christ. *Ibid.*

A strict observance of the written laws is doubtless *one* of the high duties of a good (officer), but it is not the *highest.* The laws of necessity, of self-preservation, of saving our country when in danger, are of higher obligation.

To John B. Colvin, 1810.

We have long suffered under base prostitution of law to party passions in one judge, and the imbecility of another.

To Governor Tyler, May 26, 1810.

There is a natural aristocracy among men. The grounds of this are virtue and talents. . . . There is also an artificial aristocracy founded on wealth and birth, without either virtue or talents; for with these it would belong to the first class. The natural aristocracy I consider as the most previous gift of nature, for the instruction, the trusts, and government of society. . . .

May we not even say, that that form of government is best, which provides the most effectually for a pure selection of these natural aristoi into the offices of government? The artificial aristocracy is a mischievous ingredient in government, and provision should be made to prevent its ascendancy. *To John Adams, 1813.*

Of all the systems of morality, ancient or modern, which have come under my observation, none appears to me so pure as that of Jesus. *To W. Canby, 1813.*

History I believe furnishes no example of a priest-ridden people maintaining a free civil government. This marks the lowest grade of ignorance, of which their political as well as religious leaders will always avail themselves for their own purpose.

To Baron von Humboldt, 1813.

You give a just outline of the theism of the three religions, when you say that the principle of the Hebrew was fear, of the Gentile the honor, and of the Christian the love of God. *To Adams, October 13, 1813.*

The earth belongs to the living, not to the dead. *To J. W. Eppes, 1813.*

We may consider each generation as a distinct nation, with a right, by the will of its majority, to bind themselves, but none to bind the succeeding generation, more than the inhabitants of another country. *Ibid.*

In every country and in every age, the priest has been hostile to liberty. He is always in alliance with the despot, abetting his abuses in return for protection to his own. It is easier to acquire wealth and power by this combination than by deserving them, and to effect this, they have perverted the purest religion ever preached to man into mystery and jargon, unintelligible to all mankind, and therefore the safer engine for their purposes.

To Horatio Spofford, 1814.

Are we to have a censor whose imprimatur shall say what books may be sold, and what we may buy? And who is thus to dogmatize religious opinions for our citizens? Whose foot is to be the measure to which ours are all to be cut or stretched? Is a priest to be our inquisitor, or shall a layman, simple as ourselves, set up his reason as the rule of what we are to read, and what we must believe?

To Dufief, Philadelphia bookseller, 1814, on the occasion of prosecution for selling De Becourt's "Sur le Création du Monde, un Système d'Organisation Primitive."

If M. de Becourt's book be false in its facts, disprove them; if false in its reasoning, refute it. But, for God's sake, let us freely hear both sides, if we choose. *Ibid.*

The doctrines that flowed from the lips of Jesus himself are within the comprehension of a child; but thousands of volumes have not yet explained the Platonisms engrafted on them; and for this obvious reason, that nonsense can never be explained.

To Adams, July 5, 1814.

We have heard it said that there is not a Quaker or a Baptist, a Presbyterian or an Episcopalian, a Catholic or a Protestant in heaven; that on entering the gate, we leave those badges of schism behind. . . . Let us not be uneasy then about the different roads we may pursue, as believing them the shortest, to that our last abode.

To Miles King, September 26, 1814.

The priests have so disfigured the simple religion of Jesus that no one who reads the sophistications they have engrafted on it, with the jargon of Plato, or Aristotle, and other mystics, would conceive these could have been fathered on the sublime preacher of the Sermon on the Mount.

To Dr. B. Waterhouse, 1815; N. Y. Public Library ms. IV, 2-3, quoted by Padover.

The question before the human race is, whether the God of Nature shall govern the world by His own laws, or whether priests and kings shall rule it by fictitious miracles.   *To John Adams, 1815.*

This loathsome combination of Church and State.   *To C. Clay, 1815.*

I am not among those who fear the people. They, and not the rich, are our dependence for continued freedom.

To S. Kercheval, 1816.

Some men look at constitutions with sanctimonious reverence and deem them like the ark of the covenant, too sacred to be touched. They ascribe to the men of the preceding age a wisdom more than human, and suppose what they did to be beyond amendment. . . . Laws and institutions must go hand in hand with the progress of the human mind. . . . As new discoveries are made, new truths disclosed, and manners and opinions change with the change of circumstances, institutions must advance also, and keep pace with the times. . . . Each generation . . . has right to choose for itself the form of government it believes the most promotive of its own happiness. . . . A solemn opportunity of doing this every 19 or 20 years should be provided by the constitution.   *Ibid.*

You judge truly that I am not afraid of priests. They have tried upon me all their various batteries, of pious whining, hypocritical canting, lying & slandering, without being able to give me one moment of pain. I have contemplated their order from the Magi of the East to the Saints of the West and I have found no difference of character, but of more or less caution, in proportion to their information or ignorance on whom their interested duperies were to be plaid off. Their sway in New England is indeed formidable. No mind beyond mediocrity dares there to develop itself.
    To Horatio G. Spofford, 1816.

There would never have been an infidel, if there had never been a priest.
    To Mrs. Harrison Smith, 1816.

I know nothing of the History of the Jesuits you mention, in four volumes. Is it a good one? I dislike, with you, their restoration, because it marks a retrogade step from light towards darkness.
To Adams, August 1, 1816; reply to letter of May 6.

Ours will be the follies of enthusiasm, not of bigotry, not of Jesuitism. Bigotry is the disease of ignorance, of morbid minds; enthusiasm of the free and buoyant. Education and free discussion are the antidotes of both. We are destined to be a barrier against the return of ignorance and barbarism.   *Ibid.*

On the dogmas of religion, as distinguished from moral principles, all mankind, from the beginning of the world to this day, have been quarreling, fighting, burning and torturing one another, for abstractions unintelligible to themselves and to all others, and absolutely beyond the comprehension of the human mind.
    To Carey, 1816; ms. IV, quoted by Padover.

If by *religion* we are to understand *sectarian dogmas,* in which no two of them agree, then your exclamation on that hypothesis is just, "that this would be the best of all possible worlds, if there were no religion in it." But if the moral precepts, innate in man, and made a part of his physical constitution, as necessary for a social being, if the sublime doctrine of philanthropism and deism taught us by Jesus of Nazareth, in which all agree, constitute true religion, then, without it, this would be, as you say, "something not fit to be named even, indeed, a hell."   *To Adams, May 5, 1817.*

I am of a sect by myself, as far as I know. I am not a Jew, and therefore do not adopt their theology, which supposes the God of infinite justice to punish the sins of the fathers upon their children, unto the third and fourth generations; and the benevolent and sublime reformer of that religion (Jesus of Nazareth) has told us only that God is good and perfect, but has not defined him.
    To Ezra Stiles (President of Yale), June 25, 1819.

But the greatest of all reformers of the depraved religion of his own country, was Jesus of Nazareth. Abstracting what is really his from the rubbish in which it is buried, easily distinguished by its lustre from the dross of his biographers, and as separable from that as the diamond from the dunghill, we have the outlines of a system of the most sublime morality which has ever fallen from the lips of man . . . The establishment of the innocent and genuine character of this benevolent morality, and the rescuing it from the imputation of imposture, which has resulted from artificial systems, invented by ultra-Christian sects* . . . is a most desirable object. *To Short, October 31, 1819.*

The genuine and simple religion of Jesus will one day be restored: such as it was preached and practised by himself. Very soon after his death it became muffled up in mysteries, and has been ever since kept in concealment from the vulgar eye.
To Van der Kemp, 1820.

It is not to be understood that I am with him (Jesus Christ) in all his doctrines. I am a Materialist; he takes the side of Spiritualism; he preaches the efficacy of repentance toward forgiveness of sin; I require a counterpoise of good works to redeem it. . . .
Among the sayings and discourses imputed to him by his biographers, I find many passages of fine imagination, correct morality, and of the most lovely benevolence; and others, again, of so much ignorance, so much absurdity, so much untruth, charlatanism and imposture, as to pronounce it impossible that such contradictions should have proceeded from the same being. I separate, therefore, the gold from the dross; restore to him the former, and leave the latter to the stupidity of some, the roguery of others of his disciples. Of this band of dupes and imposters, Paul was the great Coryphaeus, and first corruptor of the doctrines of Jesus.
To W. Short, 1820.

---

* Jefferson's footnote: "The immaculate conception of Jesus, his deification, the creation of the world by him, his miraculous powers, his resurrection and visible ascension, his corporeal presence in the Eucharist, the Trinity; original sin, atonement, regeneration, election, orders of the Hierarchy, etc. —T.J."

(I am) happy in the restoration, of the Jews, particularly, to their social rights . . . (I have) ever felt regret at seeing a sect, the parent and basis of all those of Christendom, singled out by all of them for a persecution and oppression which proved they had profited nothing from the benevolent doctrines of Him whom they profess to make the model of their principle and practice.
To De La Motte and Joseph Marx, 1820; quoted by Foner, Thomas Jefferson: Selected Writings.

My aim . . . was, to justify the character of Jesus against the fictions of his pseudo-followers, which have exposed him to the inference of being an imposter. For if we could believe that he really countenanced the follies, the falsehoods, and the charlatanisms which his biographers father upon him, and admit the misconstructions, interpolations, and theorizations of the fathers of the early, and fanatics of the latter ages, the conclusion would be irresistible by every sound mind, that he was an imposter. *To Story, August 4, 1820.*

The office of reformer of the superstitions of a nation, is ever dangerous. Jesus had to work on the perilous confines of reason and religion; and a step to right or left might place him within the grasp of the priests of the superstition, a bloodthirsty race, as cruel and remorseless as the being whom they represented as the family God of Abraham, of Isaac and of Jacob, and the local God of Israel. . . . That Jesus did not mean to impose himself on mankind as the son of God, physically speaking, I have been convinced by the writings of men more learned than myself in that lore. *Ibid.*

To give rest to my mind, I was obliged

to recur ultimately to my habitual anodyne, "I feel, therefore I exist." °
To Adams, August 15, 1820.

I hold the precepts of Jesus, as delivered by himself, to be the most pure, benevolent, and sublime which have ever been preached to man. I adhere to the principles of the first age; and consider all subsequent innovations as corruptions of this religion, having no foundation in what came from him. *To Jared Sparks, November 4, 1820.*

Our judges are as honest as other men, and not more so. They have, with others, the same passions for party, for power, and the privilege of their corps.
To William Charles Jarvis, 1820.

I know of no safe depository of the ultimate powers of society but the people themselves; and if we think them not enlightened enough to exercise their control with a wholesome discretion, the remedy is not to take it from them, but to inform their discretion by education. *Ibid., 1821.*

No one sees with greater pleasure than myself the progress of reason in its advances towards rational Christianity. When we shall have done away the incomprehensible jargon of the Trinitarian arithmetic, that three are one, and one is three . . .
To Timothy Pickering, February 27, 1821.

The religion-builders have so distorted and deformed the doctrines of Jesus, so muffled them in mysticism, fancies and falsehoods. *Ibid.*

Had there never been a commentator, there never would have been an infidel.
Ibid.

The doctrines of Jesus are simple, and tend all to the happiness of man. . . . But

___
° Cf. Descartes, *Cogito, ergo sum.*

compare with these the demoralizing dogmas of Calvin.

1. That there are three Gods.
2. That good works, or the love of our neighbor, is nothing.
3. That faith is every thing, and the more incomprehensible the proposition, the more merit the faith.
4. That reason in religion is of unlawful use.
5. That God, from the beginning, elected certain individuals to be saved, and certain others to be damned; and that no crimes of the former can damn them; no virtues of the latter save.
To Benjamin Waterhouse, June 26, 1822.

Had the doctrines of Jesus been preached always as pure as they came from his lips, the whole civilized world would now have been Christian. *Ibid.*

(Creeds) have been the bane of the Christian church . . . made of Christendom a slaughter-house. *Ibid.*

The truth is, that the greatest enemies of the doctrine of Jesus are those, calling themselves the expositors of them, who have perverted them to the structure of a system of fancy absolutely incomprehensible, and without any foundation in his genuine words. And the day will come, when the mystical generation of Jesus, by the Supreme Being as his father, in the womb of a virgin, will be classed with the fable of the generation of Minerva in the brain of Jupiter.
To Adams, April 11, 1823.

The generation which commences a revolution rarely completes it. Habituated from their infancy to passive submission of body and mind to their kings and priests, they are not qualified when called on to think and provide for themselves; and their in-experience, their ignorance and bigotry make them instruments often, in the hands of the Bonapartes and Iturbides, to defeat their own rights and purposes.

To Adams, 1823.

Men by their constitutions are naturally divided into two parties: 1. Those who fear and distrust the people and wish to draw all powers from them into the hands of the higher classes. 2. Those who identify them-selves with the people, have confidence in them, cherish and consider them as the most honest and safe, although not the most wise depository of the public interests. In every country these two parties exist, and in every one where they are free to think, speak, and write, they will declare them-selves. Call them, therefore, liberals and serviles, Jacobins and Ultras, whigs and tories, republicans and federalists, aristo-crats and democrats, or by whatever name you please, they are the same parties still, and pursue the same object. The last appel-lation of aristocrats and democrats is the true one expressing the essence of all.

To Henry Lee, 1824.

There is no truth existing which I fear, or would wish unknown to the whole world.

To Henry Lee, 1826.

May it [the Declaration of Independ-ence] be to the world what I believe it will be (to some parts sooner, to others later, but finally to all): the signal of arousing men to burst the chains under which monk-ish ignorance and superstition have per-suaded them to bind themselves and assume the blessings and security of self-govern-ment. That form which we have substituted, restores the free right of the unbounded exercise of reason and freedom of opinion. All eyes are opened or opening to the rights of man. The general spread of the light of science has already laid open to every view the palpable truth that the mass of mankind has not been born with saddles on their backs, nor a favored few booted and spurred ready to ride them legitimately by the grace of God. These are grounds of hope for others.

To Roger C. Weightman, June 24, 1826, the 50th anniversary of the Declaration; and ten days before Jef-ferson's death.

That to compel a man to furnish con-tributions of money for the propagation of opinions which he disbelieves and abhors, is sinful and tyrannical.   *Ibid.*

Francis Jeffrey
(1773-1850)
Scottish critic, essayist, jurist

Opinions founded on prejudice are always sustained with the greatest violence.

St. Jerome
(né Eusebius Hieronymus)
(340?-420)
Catholic church father

All riches come from iniquity, and unless one has lost, another cannot gain. Hence that common opinion seems to be very true, "the rich man is unjust, or the heir to an unjust one." Opulence is always the result of theft, if not committed by the actual possessor, then by his predecessor.

American Catholic Trade Union. "Labor."

I will say it boldly, though God can do all things, He cannot raise a virgin up after she has fallen.

The Virgin's Confession, c. 420.

Virginity can be lost by a thought.
Ibid.

Matrimony is always a vice, all that can be done is to excuse it and to sanctify it; therefore it was made a religious sacrament.

Joan of Arc
(1412-burned at stake 1431)
French national heroine

Yes, my voices were of God; my voices have not deceived me.
Attributed; last words, at the stake, Rouen, May 30.

The Lord will open a way for me through the midst of them. . . . For that was I born.
Lucien Fabre, Joan of Arc, McGraw-Hill.

John of Salisbury (called Parvus)
(1115?-1180)
English ecclesiastic, scholar, author

I do not, however, assert that the actor is dishonorable when he follows his profession, although it is undoubtedly dishonorable to be an actor.
Policraticus, 1, 8, 46.

The safe and cautious thing to do is to read only Catholic books. It is somewhat dangerous to expose the unsophisticated to pagan literature; but a training in both is very useful to those safe in the faith, for accurate reading on a wide range of subjects makes the scholar; careful selection of the better makes the saint.
Ibid., 7, 10, 133.

Between a tyrant and a prince there is this single or chief difference, that the latter obeys the law and rules the people by his dictates, accounting himself as but their servant. It is by virtue of the law that he makes good his claim to the foremost and chief place in the management of the affairs of the commonwealth and in the bearing of its burdens; and his elevation over others consists in this, that whereas private men are held responsible only for their private affairs, on the prince fall the burdens of the whole community. *The Statesman's Book.*

Andrew Johnson
(1808-1875)
17th President of the United States

Tyranny and despotism can be exercised by many, more rigorously, more vigorously, and more severely than by one.
Speech on the occasion of a serenade, April 8, 1866.

The Supreme Court . . . has been viewed by the people as the true expounder of their Constitution. . . . Any act which may be construed into . . . an attempt to prevent or evade its decisions on a question which affects the liberty of its citizens . . . can not fail to be attended with unpropitious consequences. *1868.*

Gerald W. Johnson
(b. 1890)
American writer

No man was ever endowed with a right without being at the same time saddled with a responsibility.
Saturday Review, July 5, 1958.

In theory our government is based on a division of powers among three coordinate branches, but in practice it is and it always has been based on Presidential leadership.
Ibid.

Nothing changes more constantly than the past; for the past that influences our lives does not consist of what actually happened but of what men believe happened. *American Heroes and Hero-Worship, 1943.*

Samuel Johnson

(1709-1784)

English lexicographer, essayist, poet

Among the calamities of war may be justly numbered the diminution of the love of truth by the falsehoods which interest dictates and credulity encourages. A peace will equally leave the warrior and the relater of wars destitute of employment; and I know not whether more is to be dreaded from streets filled with soldiers accustomed to plunder, or from garrets filled with scribblers accustomed to lie.

If nothing may be published but what civil authority shall have previously approved, power must always be the standard of truth; if every dreamer of innovations may propagate his projects, there can be no settlement; if every murmurer at Government may diffuse discontent, there can be no peace; and if every skeptic in theology may teach his follies, there can be no religion. *Lives of the English Poets.*

But as every art ought to be exercised in our subordination to the public good, I cannot but propose it as a moral question, whether they do not sometimes play too wantonly with our passions. *Ibid.*

Advertisements are now so numerous that they are very negligently perused, and it is therefore become necessary to gain attention by magnificence of promises and by eloquence sometimes sublime and sometimes pathetick. Promise—large promise—is the soul of advertising. . . . The trade of advertising is now so near perfection that it is not easy to propose any improvement. *The Idler, 1758.*

Poverty is a great enemy of human happiness; it certainly destroys liberty and it makes some virtues impracticable, and others extremely difficult. *Ibid., iv, 157.*

A newswriter is a man without virtue, who lies at home for his own profit.[*] *Ibid., November 11, 1758.*

The mental disease of the present generation is impatience of study, contempt of the great masters of ancient wisdom, and a disposition to rely wholly upon unassisted genius and natural sagacity. *The Rambler.*

That every man should regulate his actions by his own conscience, without any regard to the opinions of the rest of the world, is one of the first precepts of moral prudence. *Ibid., 23.*

There are, in every age, new errors to be rectified, and new prejudices to be opposed. *Ibid., January 12, 1751.*

I would not give half a guinea to live under one form of government rather than another. It is of no moment to the happiness of an individual. *Boswell's Life of Johnson, March 31, 1772.*

The only method by which religious truth can be established is by martyrdom. *Ibid., May 7, 1773.*

Patriotism is the last refuge of a scoundrel. *Ibid., April 7, 1775.*

It is of so much more consequence that truth should be told, than that individuals should not be made uneasy, that it is much better that the law does not restrain writ-

---

[*] Johnson's addition to Wotton's "An ambassador is an honest man, sent to lie abroad for the good of his country."

ing freely concerning the characters of the dead. . . . If a man could say nothing against a character but what he can prove, history could not be written; for a great deal is known of men of which proof cannot be brought. *Ibid., 1776.*

No man but a blockhead ever wrote except for money. *Ibid., 1776.*

A poor man has no honor.
Ibid., September 22, 1777.

The insolence of wealth will creep out.
Ibid., April 14, 1778.

We are all agreed as to our own liberty: we would have as much of it as we can get; but we are not agreed as to the liberty of others; for in proportion as we take, others must lose. I believe we hardly wish that the mob should have liberty to govern us. *Ibid., 1779.*

Clear your mind of cant.
Ibid., May 15, 1783.

Political liberty is good only so far as it produces private liberty. *Ibid., 1788.*

They make a rout about *universal* liberty, without considering that all that is to be valued, or indeed can be enjoyed by individuals, is *private* liberty. *Ibid.*

Everything that enlarges the sphere of human powers, that shows man he can do what he thought he could not do, is valuable. *Ibid., 1791.*

Every state has a right to preserve public peace and order, and therefore has a right to prohibit the propagation of opinions which have a dangerous tendency. To say the magistrate has this right is using an inadequate word; it is society for which the magistrate is agent. He may be morally or theologically wrong in restraining the

propagation of opinion which he thinks dangerous, but he is politically right.
Ibid., Clarendon Press, v. 2, p. 249.

The inevitable consequence of poverty is dependence. *Works, vii, 299.*

In sovereignty there can be no gradations. There may be limited royalty, there may be limited consulship; but there can be no limited government. There must in every society be some power or other from which there is no appeal, which admits no restrictions, which pervades the whole mass of the community, regulates and adjusts all subordination, enacts laws or repeals them, erects or annuls judicatures, extends or contracts privileges, exempt itself from question or control, and bounded only by physical necessity. *Ibid., viii.*

Power is not sufficient evidence of truth.
Ibid., p. 155.

Calumny differs from most other injuries in this dreadful circumstance. He who commits it never can repair it. A false report may spread where a recantation never reaches, and an accusation must certainly fly faster than a defence while the greater part of mankind are base and wicked.
Wit and Wisdom of Samuel Johnson, 1888.

The less is included in the greater. The power which can take away life, may seize property.
Address to electors of Great Britain, 1774.

Power is gradually stealing away from the many to the few, because the few are more vigilant and consistent.
The Adventurer.

The lust of gold succeeds the rage of conquest;

The lust of gold, unfeeling and remorse-
less!
The last corruption of degenerate man.
Irene, act 1, sc. 1.

Knowledge is more than equivalent to
force.   *Rasselas, ch. 13.*

Knowledge without integrity is dangerous and dreadful.   *Ibid., ch. 41.*

The liberty of the press is a blessing
when we are inclined to write against
others, and a calamity when we find ourselves overborne by the multitude of our
assailants.

It is more from carelessness about the
truth, than from intention of lying, that
there is so much falsehood in the world.

To build is to be robbed.

The two great movers of the human mind
are the desire for good, and the fear of evil.

Tom L. Johnson
(1854-1911)
American legislator, administrator

I believe in municipal ownership of all
public service monopolies for the same
reason that I believe in the municipal
ownership of waterworks, of parks, of
schools. I believe in the municipal ownership of these monopolies because if you do
not own them, they will in time own you.
They will rule your politics, corrupt your
institutions, and finally destroy your liberties.
*My Story; quoted by Justice Douglas,
An Almanac of Liberty.*

It was not free silver that frightened the
plutocratic leaders. What they feared then,
what they fear now, is free men.

When you see a situation you cannot
understand, look for the financial interest.

Eric A(llen) Johnston
(b. 1896)
*American motion picture executive,
diplomat*

And the word is capitalism. We are too
mealy-mouthed. We fear the word capitalism is unpopular. So we talk about the
"free enterprise system" and run to cover
in the folds of the flag and talk about the
American Way of Life.
N. Y. Times, January 26, 1958.

Hanns Johst
(b. 1890)
German dramatist, story writer

When I hear the word "Culture" I slip
back the safety catch of my revolver.[*]

Ernest Jones
(1819-1869)
Chartist poet, novelist

The Book of Kings is fast closing in the
great Bible of Humanity.
*Northern Star, March 4, 1848; abdica-
tion of Louis Philippe.*

We're low, we're low, we're very, very low,
And yet we the trumpets ring.
The thrust of a poor man's arm will go
Through the heart of the proudest king.
We're low, we're low, our place we know,
We're only the rank and file,
We're not too low to kill the foe,
But too low to touch the spoil.
Song of the Lower Classes, 1855.

Sons of poverty, assemble,
Ye whose hearts with woe are riven,

---

[*] Also given as: "When I hear the word
'Culture' I pick up my Browning."

Let the guilty tyrants tremble,
Who our hearts with woe have given.
    We will never
From the shrine of truth be driven.
                        Chartist song.

Ernest Jones
(1879-1958)
English psychoanalyst

It is the people with secret attractions to various temptations, who busy themselves with removing those temptations from other people; really they are defending themselves under the pretext of defending others, because at heart they fear their own weaknesses.
Papers on Psychoanalysis, London, 1918.

Amid the turmoil of conflicting ideas in which we live . . . there seems to be one proposition commanding nearly universal assent. *The control man has secured over nature has far outrun his control over himself.*
The Life and Work of Sigmund Freud, Vol. 3.

Man's chief enemy is his own unruly nature and the dark forces pent up within him.   *Ibid.*

Ben Jonson
(1572?-1637)
English actor, poet, dramatist

Tell troth and shame the devil.
                Tale of a Tub, II, i.

'Twas only fear first in the world made gods.   *Sejanus, II, ii.*

They set the sign of the cross over their outer doors, and sacrifice to their gut and their groin in their inner closets.
                        Explorata.

I am a printer, and a printer of news; . . . I'll give anything for a good copy now, be it true or false, so it be news.
            News from the New World.

Ambition, like a torrent, ne'er looks back;
And is a swelling, and the last affliction
A high mind can put off; being both a rebel
Upon the soul of reason, and enforceth
All laws, all conscience, treads upon religion,
And offereth violence to nature's self.
                Catiline, act iii, sc. 2.

David Starr Jordan
(1851-1931)
University President, educator

That one man or ten thousand or ten million men find a dogma acceptable does not argue for its soundness.
Cardiff, What Great Men Think of Religion.

When a dog barks at the moon, then it is religion; but when he barks at strangers, it is patriotism!   *Ibid.*

Virgil Dustin Jordan
(b. 1892)
American economist, writer

In peace time it is the accepted custom and normal manners of modern government to conceal all important facts from the public, or to lie about them; in war it is a political vice which becomes a public necessity.
Address, Investment Bankers Association, December 10, 1940.

James Joyce
(1882-1941)
Irish writer

The artist, like the God of the creation, remains within or behind or beyond or

above his handiwork, invisible, refined out of existence, indifferent, paring his finger-nails.
Portrait of the Artist as a Young Man.

Welcome, O life! I go to encounter for the millionth time the reality of experience and to forge in the smithy of my soul the uncreated conscience of my race. *Ibid.*

Carl Gustav Jung
(1875-1961)
Swiss psychologist, psychiatrist

"Education to personality" has become a pedagogical ideal that turns its back upon the standardized—the collective and normal —human being. It thus fittingly recognizes the historical fact that the great, liberating deeds of world history have come from leading personalities and never from the inert mass that is secondary at all times and needs a demagogue if it is to move at all. The paean of the Italian nation is addressed to the personality of the Duce, and dirges of other nations lament the absence of great leaders.
Lecture, The Inner Voice, Kulturbund, Vienna; 1932; The Integration of Personality, Farrar & Rinehart, N. Y., 1939.

The psychology of the creative is really feminine psychology, a fact which proves that creative work grows out of the unconscious depths, indeed out of the region of the mothers.
J. B. Priestley, Times Literary Supplement, London, August 6, 1954.

We can never legitimately cut loose from our archetypal foundations unless we are prepared to pay the price of a neurosis, any more than we can rid ourselves of our body and its organs without committing suicide. *Ibid.*

All ordinary expression may be explained causally, but creative expression which is the absolute contrary of ordinary expression, will be forever hidden from human knowledge.
Psychology and Poetry. transition, June, 1930.

For his (the artist's) life is, of necessity, full of conflicts, since two forces fight in him: the ordinary man with his justified claim for happiness, contentment, and guarantees for living on the one hand, and the ruthless creative passion on the other, which under certain conditions crushes all personal desires into the dust. *Ibid.*

There is rarely a creative man who does not have to pay a high price for the divine spark of his great gifts . . . the human element is frequently bled for the benefit of the creative element and to such an extent that it even brings out the bad qualities, as for instance, ruthless, naive egoism (so-called "auto-eroticism"), vanity, all kinds of vices—and all this in order to bring to the human I at least some life-strength, since otherwise it would perish of sheer inanition. *Ibid.*

Junius
(c. 1770)
Unidentified British author

Let it be impressed upon your minds, let it be instilled into your children, that the Liberty of the Press is the Palladium of all the civil, political and religious rights of an Englishman. *Letters, dedication.*

Justinian I
(483-565)
Byzantine emperor

Justice is the earnest and constant will to render to every man his due. The precepts of the law are these: to live honorably, to injure no other man, to render to every man his due. *The Institutes of Justinian, 533.*

Juvenal
(60?-140)
Roman rhetorician, satirical poet

Crescit amor nummi quantum ipsa pe-cunia crescit. (The love of money grows as the money itself grows.)

Panem et circenses. (Bread and circuses.)
Satires, X.

Orandum est ut sit mens sana in corpore sano. (Your prayer must be that you have a sound mind in a sound body.) *Ibid., 356.*

Poverty, bitter though it be, has no sharper pang than this, that it makes men ridiculous. *Ibid., III, 152.*

From heaven descended the precept "Know Thyself."°

Many commit the same crime with a very different result. One bears a cross for his crime; another a crown.

What man was ever content with one crime?

Humayun Kabir
(1488-1512)
Hindu religious reformer, philosopher

Men have always looked before and after, and rebelled against the existing order. But for their divine discontent men would not have been men, and there would have been no progress in human affairs.
The American Scholar, 1957.

° "Know Thyself" is inscribed on the temple of Apollo at Memphis; it is attributed to Socrates and others, notably Thales.

Franz Kafka
(1883-1924)
Austrian writer

We are sinful not merely because we have eaten of the Tree of Knowledge, but also because we have not eaten of the Tree of Life. *Paradise. Parables, 25.*

From the true antagonist illimitable cour-age is transmitted to you.
Reflections, #23, Dearest Father, 1954.

Kai-shek
See Chiang Kai-shek

H. M. Kallen
(1882-1974)
American educator

Competition is the very life of science.

It is an uncompromising devotion to the idea of equal liberty as both the means and end of life that characterizes the liberal spirit.

Persecution, wherever it occurs, estab-lishes only the power and cunning of the persecutor, not the truth and worth of his belief.

Education is the first resort as well as the last, for a world-wide solution of the problem of freedom.

All beliefs on which you bet your life are fundamentally religious beliefs, and atheism can be as much a religion as theism.
Religion and Freedom, Fund for the Republic, 1958.

Immanuel Kant
(1724-1804)
German philosopher

There are three juridical attributes that inseparably belong to the citizen by right. These are:

1. Constitutional freedom, as the right of every citizen to have to obey no other law than that to which he has given his consent or approval;

2. Civil equality, as the right of the citizen to recognize no one as a superior among the people in relation to himself. . . ; and

3. Political independence, as the right to owe his existence and continuance in society not to the arbitrary will of another, but to his own rights and powers as a member of the commonwealth.
Science of Right, 1797.

Two things fill the mind with ever new and increasing wonder and awe—the starry heavens above me and the moral law within me.   *Critique of Pure Reason.*

In whatsoever mode, or by whatsoever means, our Knowledge may relate to objects, it is at least quite clear, that the only manner in which it immediately relates to them is by means of an intuition.
Ibid.

We cannot divide ourselves between right and expedience. Policy must bow the knee before morality.

Since reason condemns war and makes peace an absolute duty, and since peace cannot be effected or guaranteed without a compact among nations, they must form an alliance of a peculiar kind, which may be called a pacific alliance (*foedus pacificum*), different from a treaty of peace (*pactum pacis*), inasmuch as it would forever terminate all wars, whereas the latter only ends one.   *Perpetual Peace, II, 1795.*

The civil constitution of every state shall be republican, and war shall not be declared except by a plebescite of all the citizens.   *Ibid.*

That kings should become philosophers, and philosophers kings, can scarcely be expected, nor is it to be wished, since the enjoyment of power inevitably corrupts the judgment of reason, and perverts its liberty.   *Ibid.*

With men, the state of nature is not a state of peace, but war; if not of open war, then at least ever ready to break out.
Ibid.

Freedom is that faculty which enlarges the usefulness of all other faculties.

I ought, therefore I can.*
Gollancz, From Darkness to Light.

Morality is not properly the doctrine of how we may make ourselves happy, but how we may make ourselves worthy of happiness. *Critique of Practical Reason.*

Virtue and happiness together constitute the possession of the *summum bonum* in a person, and the distribution of happiness in exact proportion to morality (which is the worth of the person, and his worthiness to be happy) constitute the *summum bonum* of a possible world.   *Ibid.*

Christ has brought the kingdom of God nearer to earth; but he has been misunderstood; and in place of God's kingdom the kingdom of the priest has been established among us.
H. S. Chamberlain, Immanuel Kant, Vol. 1, p. 510.

So act as to treat humanity, whether in thine own person or in that of another, in

---

* Cf. Descartes, "*Cogito, ergo sum.*"

every case as an end, never only as a means.[*]
Metaphysics of Morals, London, 1909.

Enlightenment is man's release from his self-incurred tutelage. Tutelage is man's inability to make use of his understanding without direction from another. Self-incurred is this tutelage when its cause lies not in lack of reason but in lack of resolution and courage to use it without direction from another. *Sapere aude!* (Dare to know). "Have courage to use your own reason!"—that is the motto of enlightenment. *Ibid.*

Seek not the favor of the multitude; it is seldom got by honest and lawful means. But seek the testimony of the few; and number not voices, but weigh them.

The death of dogma is the birth of morality.

The function of the true State is to impose the *minimum* restrictions and safeguard the *maximum* liberties of the people, and it never regards the person as a thing.

Nobody can compel me to be happy in his own way. Paternalism is the greatest despotism.
Quoted by Isaiah Berlin, Two Concepts of Liberty, 1958.

The human heart refuses to believe in a universe without a purpose.
Quoted, Ladies' Home Journal, September, 1957.

There is but one categorical imperative: Act only on that maxim whereby thou canst

___
[*] Another translation: "Every man is to be respected as an absolute end in himself; and it is a crime against the dignity that belongs to him as a human being, to use him as a means for some external purpose"
—Will Durant, *The Story of Philosophy.*

at the same time will that it should become a universal law.
Fundamental Principles, tr. by A. D. Lindsay.

A true policy will not take a step without first paying its homage to morality. United to morals, politics is no longer a difficult and complicated art; morality cuts the knot that a policy is unable to untie.

Peter L. Kapitza
(b. 1894)
Russian physicist

To talk of atomic energy in terms of atomic bombs is like talking of electricity in terms of the electric chair.
Reynolds News, London, interview with Gordon Schaffer, editor.

Karl Kautsky
(1854-1938)
German Socialist leader

Freedom of education and of scientific investigation from the fetters of capitalist dominion; freedom of the individual from the oppression of exclusive, exhaustive physical labor; displacement of capitalist industry in the intellectual production of society by the free unions—along this road proceeds the tendency of the proletarian regime. *The Social Revolution and After.*

Regulation of social chaos and liberation of the individual—these are the two historical tasks that capitalism has placed before society. They appear to be contradictory, but they are simultaneously soluble because each of them belongs to a different sphere of social life. *Ibid.*

Communism in material production, anarchism in intellectual. This is the type of the Socialist productive system which will arise from the dominion of the proletariat. *Ibid.*

John Keats
(1795-1821)
English poet

Works of genius are the first things in this world.
Letters. To G. and F. Keats, January 13, 1818.

The excellency of every art is its intensity, capable of making all disagreeables evaporate, from their being in close relationship with beauty and truth.
Ibid., December 21, 1817.

All great poetry should produce the instantaneous conviction, this is true.
Edith Hamilton, Witness to the Truth, 1949.

To bear all naked truths,
And to envisage circumstance, all calm;
That is the top of sovereignty.
Hyperion, bk. 2.

"Beauty is truth, truth beauty,"—that is all
Ye know on earth, and all ye need to know.
Ode to a Grecian Urn.

I am certain of nothing but of the holiness of the heart's affections, and the truth of Imagination. What the Imagination seizes as Beauty must be Truth, whether it existed before or not. *Letters.*

Estes Kefauver
(1903-1963)
American politician

Liberalism means an intelligent effort to keep the political and economic develop-ment of our nation abreast of the responsibilities that come from the atomic age. It means an extension of the use of our resources for the common good, the solving of the problem of maintaining democratic principles and free competitive enterprise in a day of Big Business, Big Unions and Big Government.
New Republic, June 22, 1946

Private profit by public servants at the expense of the general welfare is corrupt period.

Sir Arthur Keith
(1866-1927)
Scottish anthropologist

No two human beings have made, or ever will make, exactly the same journey in life.

As long as man remains an inquiring animal, there can never be a complete unanimity in our fundamental beliefs. The more diverse our paths, the greater is likely to be the divergence of beliefs.

Like other conservative-minded men, I tried to empty the new knowledge of science into the time-revered biblical bottles . . . but to my eye the biblical bottles, when modified to hold the wine of modern science, bear no resemblance to the scriptural originals. To say they are the same is to prostitute truth.

If men believe, as I do, that this present earth is the only heaven, they will strive all the more to make heaven of it.

The course of human history is determined, not by what happens in the skies, but by what takes place in the hearts of men.

[385]

Helen Keller
(1880-1968)

American writer

There is no king who has not had a slave among his ancestors, and no slave who has not had a king among his.

Story of My Life.

Security is mostly a superstition. It does not exist in nature, nor do the children of men as a whole experience it. Avoiding danger is no safer in the long run than outright exposure. Life is either a daring adventure, or nothing.

The Open Door, Doubleday.

Serious harm, I am afraid, has been wrought to our generation by fostering the idea that they would live secure in a permanent order of things. They have expected stability and have found none within themselves or in their universe. Before it is too late they must learn and teach others that only by brave acceptance of change and all-time crisis-ethics can they rise to the heights of superlative responsibility.

Ibid.

Step by step my investigation of blindness led me into the industrial world. And what a world it is! I must face unflinchingly a world of facts—a world of misery and degradation, of blindness, crookedness, and sin, a world struggling against the elements, against the unknown, against itself.

Sinclair, The Cry for Justice.

How reconcile this world of fact with the bright world of my imagining? My darkness has been filled with the light of intelligence, and, behold, the outer day-lit world was stumbling and groping in social blindness. *Ibid.*

Kemal Ataturk
(1881-1938)

Turkish liberator, dictator

Those who are inclined to compromise never make a revolution.

Mathilda von Kemnitz
(b. 1877)

German writer

Since the fundamental principle of eroticism imperiously governs every human life, since the manner of the first erotic happiness determines in a far-reaching manner the laws of the individual's eroticism throughout his entire life, the majority of men have become entirely incapable of concentrating their erotic will consistently on one human being; therefore they have become incapable of monogamy.

Quoted by Havelock Ellis.

The man experiences the highest unfolding of his creative powers not through asceticism, but through sexual happiness.

Ibid.

Kempis
See Thomas à Kempis

William Mitchell Kendall
(1856-1941)

American architect

Neither snow nor rain nor heat nor gloom of night stays these couriers from the swift completion of their appointed rounds.

Inscription, N. Y. Post Office, a paraphrase of Herodotus; N. Y. Times, April 15, 1957.

Kenkò Hoshi
(14th Century)
Japanese Buddhist

It is desirable for a ruler that no man should suffer from cold and hunger under his rule. Man cannot maintain his standard of morals when he has no ordinary means of living.   *Sinclair, The Cry for Justice.*

So long as people, being ill-governed, suffer from hunger, criminals will never disappear. It is extremely unkind to punish those who, being sufferers from hunger, are compelled to violate laws.   *Ibid.*

George F. Kennan
(b. 1904)
American diplomat

This fear of the untypical, this quest for security within the walls of secular uniformity—these are traits of our national character we would do well to beware of and to examine for their origins.
Address, Notre Dame University, May 15, 1953.

The immense impact of commercial advertising and the mass media of our lives is—let us make no mistake about it—an impact that tends to encourage passivity, to encourage acquiescence and uniformity, to place handicaps on individual contemplativeness and creativeness.   *Ibid.*

Rockwell Kent
(1882-1971)
American artist, writer

Art must unquestionably have a social value; that is, as a potential means of communication it must be addressed, and in comprehensible terms, to the understanding of mankind.
It's Me O Lord: The Autobiography of Rockwell Kent.

Vaster is Man than his works.
Caption for illustration, Architectonics.

We *do*, to what extent of freedom we have earned or are allowed by others and ourselves, what we most want to do. We *say*—speak, paint, carve, write, express ourselves . . . as we damn please. And in both the *doing* of things and the talking about them—which together seem to me to sum up life—we so crave freedom or liberty or whatever one may choose to call it as to justify our Declaration's romantically terming it an unalienable right of Man, bestowed on Man by his Creator.
This Is My Own, p. 130.

While reasonable men will ungrudgingly submit to such curtailment of their liberties as will promote at least the greater liberty of all, to the exact degree to which curtailment may become *unreasonable* will the enforcement of it have to rest on force. Force against reason: reason, because it has the power of enlisting force to fight for it, will win. From the recognition of that truth has come democracy.   *Ibid.*

Robert Kett
(Hanged 1549)
English rebel

The pride of great men is now intolerable, but our condition is miserable.
These abound in delights; and compassed with the fulness of all things, and consumed with vain pleasures, thirst only after gain, inflamed with the burning delights of their desires.
But ourselves, almost killed with labour and watching, do nothing all our life long but sweat, mourn, hunger, and thirst. Which things, though they seem miserable and base (as they are indeed most miserable), yet might be borne howsoever, if they which are drowned in the boiling seas of

evil delights did not pursue the calamities and miseries of other men with too much insolent hatred.

The Rebels' Complaint, in Nevylle's De Furoribus Norfolcensium Ketto Duce, 1575.

The present condition of possessing land seemeth miserable and slavish—holding it all at the pleasure of great men; not freely, but by prescription, and, as it were, at the will and pleasure of the lord. For as soon as any man offend any of these gorgeous gentlemen he is put out, deprived, and thrust from all his goods.   *Ibid.*

We can no longer bear so much, so great, and so cruel injury; neither can we with quiet minds behold so great covetousness, excess, and pride of the nobility. We will take up arms, and mix Heaven and earth together, than endure so great cruelty.
      Ibid.

We desire liberty, and an indifferent (equal) use of all things. This will we have. Otherwise these tumults and our lives shall only be ended together.   *Ibid.*

C(harles) F(ranklin) Kettering
(1876-1958)
American industrialist

It is man's destiny to ponder on the riddle of existence and, as a byproduct of his wonderment, to create a new life on this earth.

Time, obituary, December 8, 1958.

The world hates change, yet it is the only thing that has brought progress.

Ellen Key
(1849-1926)
Swedish feminist, writer

Love has been in perpetual strife with monogamy.

Instead of defending "free love," which is a much-abused term capable of many interpretations, we ought to strive for the freedom of love; for while the former has come to imply freedom for any sort of love, the latter must only mean freedom for a feeling which is worthy the name of love. This feeling, it may be hoped, will gradually win for itself the same freedom in life as it already possesses in poetry.

Sprading, Liberty and the Great Libertarians, 1913.

A great poet has seldom sung of lawfully wedded happiness, but often of free and secret love; and in this respect, too, the time is coming when there will no longer be one standard of morality for poetry and another for life. To anyone tender of conscience, the ties formed by a free connection are stronger than the legal ones, since in the former case he has made a choice more decisive to his own and the other's personality than if he had followed law and custom.   *Ibid.*

Francis Scott Key
(1779-1843)
American poet

The land of the free, and the home of the brave.   *The Star-Spangled Banner.*

John Maynard Keynes
(1883-1946)
English economist

Both of the two opposed errors of pessimism which now make so much noise in the world will be proved wrong in our time —the pessimism of the revolutionaries who think that things are so bad that nothing can save us but violent change, and the pessimism of our reactionaries who consider the balance of our economic and so-

cial life so precarious that we must risk no experiments.
Quoted by Gilbert Seldes, Against Revolution, 1932.

The ideas of economists and political philosophers, both when they are right and when they are wrong, are more powerful than is commonly understood. Indeed, the world is ruled by little else.
The General Theory of Employment, Interest and Money, 1947.

Practical men, who believe themselves to be quite exempt from any intellectual influences, are usually the slaves of some defunct economist. Madmen in authority, who hear voices in the air, are distilling their frenzy from some academic scribbler of a few years back. I am sure that the power of vested interests is vastly exaggerated compared with the gradual encroachment of ideas. *Ibid.*

But, soon or late, it is ideas, not vested interests, which are dangerous for good or evil. *Ibid.*

The moral problem of our day is concerned with the love of money, with the habitual appeal to the money motive in nine-tenths of the activities of life, with the universal striving after individual economic security as the prime objects of endeavour, with the social approbation of money as the measure of constructive success, and with the social appeal of the hoarding instinct as the foundation of the necessary provision for the family and for the future.

Hermann Alexander von Keyserling
(1880-1946)
German scientist, philosopher

The majority of great men are the offspring of unhappy marriages.

Marriage is primarily a matter of mutual destiny. . . . Marriage sets up an indissoluble state of tension, and its very existence depends upon the preservation of this state. Man and woman, both as individuals and as types, are fundamentally different, incompatible and essentially solitary. In marriage they form an indissoluble unit of life, based upon fixed distance.

Man and woman should never endeavor to be completely merged in one another; on the contrary, the more intimate they are, the more strictly should they cherish their own individuality.

Where conjugal happiness has been achieved it outweighs all possible suffering.

Nikita S. Khrushchev
(1894-1971)
Former Soviet Russian premier

Revolutionary theory is not a collection of petrified dogmas and formulas, but a militant guide to action in transforming the world, in building Communism.
Report to Central Committee, February 14, 1956.

Marxism-Leninism teaches us that a theory isolated from practice, is dead, and practice which is not illumined by revolutionary theory is blind. *Ibid.*

Our enemies like to depict us Leninists as advocates of violence, always and everywhere. True, we recognize the need for the revolutionary transformation of capitalist society into socialist society. It is this which distinguishes the revolutionary Marxist from the reformist, the opportunist. There is no doubt that in a number of capitalist countries the violent overthrow of the dictatorship of the bourgeoisie and the sharp aggravation of class struggle are inevitable. *Ibid.*

Leninism teaches us that the ruling classes will not surrender their power voluntarily. *Ibid.*

A Communist has no right to be a mere onlooker. *Ibid.*

Creative work in literature and art must be permeated with the spirit of a struggle for communism, it must instil buoyancy and firm conviction in people's hearts and minds, cultivate a socialist mentality and a comradely sense of duty. Particular attention must be devoted to enhancing further the part played by the press in all aspects of ideological, political, and organizational work. *Ibid.*

On a hungry stomach, Marxist-Leninism may be difficult to understand. It is not wrong to throw in a piece of bacon and a piece of butter in the course of improving the theory of Marx.
Speech in Prague. Time, July 22, 1957.

The press is our chief ideological weapon. Its duty is to strike down the enemies of the working class, the foes of the working people.
N. Y. Times Magazine, September 29, 1957.

Just as an army cannot fight without arms, so the party cannot do ideological work successfully without such a sharp and militant weapon as the press. We cannot put the press in unreliable hands. It must be in the hands of the most faithful, most trustworthy, most politically steadfast people devoted to our cause. *Ibid.*

One of the major principles is that Soviet literature and art must be inseverably linked with the policy of the Communist Party. *Ibid.*

The supreme social mission of literature and art is to raise the people to struggle for new victories in Communist construction. *Ibid.*

We declare war upon the United States in the peaceful field of trade.
W. R. Hearst, Jr., interview, November, 1957.

We declare that however acute the ideological differences between the two systems —the Socialist and the capitalist—we must solve questions in dispute among states not by war, but by peaceful negotiation.
Address, Supreme Soviet, Moscow, December 21, 1957.

The history of a social system will be decided not by rockets, not by atomic and hydrogen bombs, but by the fact of which system ensures greater material and spiritual benefits to man. *Ibid.*

Life is short; live it up.
N. Y. Times Magazine, August 3, 1958.

The Communist Party . . . supports those authors . . . who, with the people, are glad in the success of the nation in building Communism and find bright colors to show these successes. *Life, November 3, 1958.*

It is not true that we regard violence and civil war as the only way to remake society. . . . The Communist system must be based on the will of the people, and if the people should not want that system, then that people should establish a different system.
John Gunther, Inside Russia Today, Harper & Bros., 1958.

Once you pledge, don't hedge. *Ibid.*

Call it what you will, incentives are what get people to work harder.
Reply to Senator Humphrey's charge of capitalism; New Republic, January 5, 1959.

Indeed, there is freedom in the capitalist countries, but for whom? Of course not for the working people, who are forced to hire themselves out to the capitalists on any conditions just to avoid finding themselves in the ranks of the huge army of people who are "free from work."
Speech to 21st Party Congress, N. Y. Times, February 1, 1959.

"Freedom" in capitalist countries exists only for those who possess money and who consequently hold power.   *Ibid.*

Alfred von Kiderlen-Waechter
(1852-1912)
German foreign minister

A press campaign of four months will convince the German people of the rightness of any idiocy you like to suggest.
Quoted by Senator Wiley, Congressional Record.

Sören Kierkegaard
(1813-1855)
Danish philosopher, theologian

All essential knowledge relates to existence, or only such knowledge as has an essential relationship to existence is essential knowledge.
Concluding Unscientific Postscript.

Christendom has done away with Christianity without being quite aware of it.
Time, December 16, 1946.

In an unpermissible and unlawful way people have become *knowing* about Christ, for the only permissible way is to be *believing.*   *Ibid.*

What one especially praises in Christ is precisely what one would be most embittered by if one were contemporary with it.
Ibid.

Man is spirit. But what is spirit? Spirit is the self. But what is the self? The self is a relation which relates itself to its own self or it is that (which accounts for it) that the relation relates itself to its own self; the self is not the relation but (consists in the fact) that the relation relates itself to its own self.
Quoted in The Freeman, May 4, 1953, p. 567.

The present state of the world and the whole of life is diseased. If I were a doctor and were asked for my advice, I should reply: Create silence.
N. Y. Times Magazine, April 6, 1958.

Harley M. Kilgore
(1893-1956)
American politician

What good does it do the world for the governments to sit down at peace tables and to work out fine political mechanisms if they leave the instruments of economic and technical power in the hands of unrestrained private individuals and corporations?

Charles Kingsley
(1819-1875)
English founder of Christian Socialism

To be discontented with the divine discontent, and to be ashamed with the noble shame, is the very germ of the first upgrowth of all virtue.
Health and Education.

Down, down, down and down,
With idler, knave and tyrant.
Why for sluggards stint and moil?
He that will not live by toil
Has no right on English soil,
God's word or warrant.
Alton Locke (Chartist novel), 1848.

Up, up, up and up!
　　Face your game and play it!
The night is past, behold the sun!
The idols fall, the lie is done!
The Judge is set, the doom begun!
　　Who shall stay it?　　　　*Ibid.*

Society has not given me my rights. And woe unto the man on whom that idea, true or false, rises lurid, filling all his thoughts with stifling glare, as of the pit itself. Be it true, be it false, it is equally a woe to believe it; to have to live on a negation; to have to worship for our only idea, as hundreds of thousands of us have this day, the hatred of the things which are.　　*Ibid.*

Here lies your iniquity; you have given the laborer nothing but his daily food—not even his lodgings; the pigs were not stinted of their wash to pay for their sty-room, the man was; and his wages, thanks to your competitive system, were beaten down deliberately and conscientiously (for was it not according to political economy, and the laws thereof?) to the minimum on which he could or would work, without the hope or the possibility of saving a farthing.
　　　　　　　　　　　　Ibid.

But let, secondly, a dozen, or fifty, or a hundred journeymen say to one another: It is competition that is ruining us, and competition is division, disunion, every man for himself, every man against his brother. The remedy must be in association, coopperation, self-sacrifice for the sake of one another.
Cheap Clothes and Nasty, by "Parson Lot", 1849.

Regulations as to police, order, and temperance, the workmen must, and, if they are worthy of the name of free men, they can, organize for themselves. Let them remember that an association of labor is very different from an association of capital. The capitalist only embarks his money on the venture; the workman embarks his time—that is, much at least of his life. Still more different is the operatives' association from the single capitalist, seeking only to realize a rapid fortune, and then withdraw. The association knows no withdrawal from business; it must grow in length and in breadth, outlasting rival shopsellers, swallowing up all association similar to itself, and which might end by competing with it. "Monopoly!" cries a free-trader, with hair on end. Not so, good friend; there will be no real free trade without association.　　*Ibid.*

George R. Kirkpatrick
(1867-1937)
Socialist writer, lecturer

Nature gave men two ends—one to sit on and one to think with. Ever since then man's success or failure has been dependent on the one he used most.

Rudolf Kjellen
(1864-1922)
Swedish geographer

Lebensraum. (Living space.)*

Knights of Labor

An injury to one is the concern of all.
　　　　　　　　　　　　Motto.

Labor is noble and holy. To defend it from degradation; to divest it of the evils of body, mind, and estate, which ignorance has imposed; to rescue the toiler from the grip of the selfish—is the work worthy of the noblest and best of our race.
　　Card issued to all new members.

---

* Generally attributed to Prof. Karl Haushofer, who appropriated it.

John Knox
(1505?-1572)
Scottish reformer

Queen Mary: Think ye that subjects, having the power, may resist their princes?

Knox: If their princes exceed their bounds, Madam, no doubt they may be resisted, even by power.

History of the Reformation in Scotland.

Arthur Koestler
(1905-1983)
Hungarian novelist, journalist

The ultimate truth is penultimately a falsehood.   *Darkness at Noon.*

People don't mind if you betray humanity, but if you betray your club, you are considered a renegade.

The Age of Longing, 1951.

The Koran*

Give tidings, O Mohammed, of painful doom to those who disbelieve . . . Slay the idolaters wherever ye find them . . . And fight them until persecution is no more, and religion is all for Allah.

Marry such women as seem good to you, two, three or four, but if you fear you will not be equitable, then only one.

Justice is an unassailable fortress, built on the brow of a mountain which cannot be overthrown by the violence of torrents, nor demolished by the force of armies.

Whatever ye put out at usury to increase it with the substance of others shall have no increase from God; but whatever ye shall give in alms, as seeking the face of God, shall be doubled to you.

---

* See also, Mohammed.

It beseemeth not the majesty of Allah that he should beget a son.   *xix.*

They who believe not shall have garments of fire fitted unto them; boiling water shall be poured on their heads; their bowels shall be dissolved thereby, and also their skins, and they shall be beaten with maces of iron.   *xxii.*

Thaddeus Kosciusko
(1756-1817)
Polish patriot, general

Should I make no other testamentary disposition of my property in the United States . . . authorize my friend Thomas Jefferson to employ the whole thereof in purchasing Negroes from among his own as any others and giving them liberty in my name, in giving them an education in trades and otherwise, and in having them instructed for their new condition in the duties of morality which may make them good neighbors, good fathers or mothers, husbands or wives, and in their duties as citizens, teaching them to be defenders of their liberty and country and of the good order of society and in whatsoever may make them happy and useful.

Will, dated Fifth Day of May, 1798.

Lajos Kossuth
(1802-1894)
Hungarian patriot, orator

A fool only can think that nations desire disorder. No, oppression is disorder, liberty is order. Slaves are turbulent, freemen love peace. If Europe be a volcano, it is because it is oppressed. Remove oppression, and the volcano shall cease to boil, or else it never will.   *1848.*

I am a man of peace. God knows, how I love peace. But I hope I shall never be such a coward as to mistake oppression for peace.

The era of Christianity—peace, brotherhood, the Golden Rule as applied to governmental matters—is yet to come, and when it comes, then and then only, will the future of nations be sure.

Alfred Kreymborg
(b. 1883)
American poet, dramatist

Satan the envious said with a sigh:
Christians know more about their hell than I.
Envious Satan.

Peter A. Kropotkin
(1842-1921)
Russian prince, philosophical anarchist

A revolution must from its inception be an act of justice towards the ill-treated and the oppressed, and not a promise to perform this act of reparation later on. If not, it is sure to fail.   *Tribune (London).*

It rests with you either to palter continually with your conscience, and in the end to say, one fine day: "Perish humanity, provided I can have plenty of pleasures and enjoy them to the full so long as the people are foolish enough to let me." Or, once more the inevitable alternative, to take part with the Socialists and work with them for the complete transformation of society.   *An Appeal to the Young.*

Individualism, narrowly egotistic, is incapable of inspiring anybody. There is nothing great or gripping in it. Individuality can attain its supreme development only in the highest common social order.
Mutual Aid.

If plenty for all is to become a reality, this immense capital—cities, houses, pastures, arable lands, factories, highways, education—must cease to be regarded as private property, for the monopolist to dispose of at his pleasure . . . There must be Expropriation. The well-being of all—the end; expropriation—the means.   *Ibid.*

Sociability is as much a law of nature as mutual struggle.   *Ibid.*

If we resort to an indirect test, and ask Nature: "Who are the fittest: those who are continually at war with each other, or those who support one another?" we at once see that those animals which acquire habits of mutual aid are undoubtedly the fittest. They have more chances to survive, and they attain, in their respective classes, the highest development of intelligence and bodily organization.   *Ibid.*

Mutual aid is as much a law of animal life as mutual struggle . . . as a factor of evolution, it most probably has a far greater importance, inasmuch as it favors the development of such habits and characters as insure the maintenance and further development of the species, together with the greatest amount of welfare and enjoyment of life for the individual, with the least waste of energy.   *Ibid.*

As soon as we study animals—not in laboratories and museums only, but in the forest and prairies, in the steppe and in the mountains—we at once perceive that though there is an immense amount of warfare and extermination going on amidst various species, and especially amidst various classes of animals, there is, at the same time, as much, or perhaps more, of mutual support, mutual aid, and mutual defense amidst animals belonging to the same species, or, at least, to the same society. *Ibid.*

The origin of the state, and its reason for existence, lie in the fact that it works in favor of the propertied minority and against the propertyless.

Paroles d'un révolté, 1884.

The word *state* is identical with the word *war.* *Ibid.*

Freedom of the press, freedom of association, the inviolability of domicile, and all the rest of the rights of man are respected only so long as no one tries to use them against the privileged class. On the day they are launched against privilege they are thrown overboard. *Ibid.*

The law is an adroit mixture of customs that are beneficial to society, and could be followed even if no law existed, and others that are of advantage to a ruling minority, but harmful to the masses of men, and can be enforced on them only by terror. *Ibid.*

The law has no claim to human respect. It has no civilizing mission; its only purpose is to protect exploitation. *Ibid.*

Anarchism is he ame given to a principle or theory of l'e and conduct under which society is conceived without government—harmony in such a society being obtained not by submission to law or by obedience to any authority, but by free agreements concluded between the various groups, territorial and professional, freely contributed for the sake of protection and consumption, as also for the satisfaction of the infinite variety of needs and aspirations of a civilized being.

Contribution to Encyclopaedia Britannica, 11th ed., I, 914.

Nadezhda K. Krupskaya
(1869-1939)
Russian comrade and wife of Lenin

People must grow both in mind and heart. And on the basis of this individual growth of each person, there will finally take shape a new type of collective in which "I" and "we" will merge into one indissoluble whole. Such a collective can grow up only on the basis of a profound ideological unity and of an equally profound emotional concord and mutual understanding.

For names containing "la," see also the basic name.

Jean de la Bruyère
(1645-1696)
French moralist, author

There are but three general events which happen to mankind: birth, life, and death. Of their birth they are insensible, they suffer when they die, and neglect to live.

Characters of Men.

If poverty is the mother of crimes, want of sense is the father of them.

Les Charactères, c. 11.

The exact contrary of what is generally believed is often the truth. *Ibid., c. 12.*

When a book raises your spirit and inspires you with noble and courageous feelings, seek no other rule to judge the event by; it is good and made by a good workman.

A purchased slave has but one master; an ambitious man must be a slave to all who may conduce to his aggrandisement.

Avoid law suits beyond all things; they influence your conscience, impair your health, and dissipate your property.

Laertius

See Diogenes Laertius

Paul Lafargue

(1842-1911)
French political leader

Rise up, study the economic forces which oppress you; they have emerged from the hand of man just as the gods emerged from his brain. You can control them: if you will it, the machine, this dreadful instrument of torture, will turn into god who emancipates man from arduous work and gives him the leisure to enjoy physical and mental happiness.

Robert M. LaFollette, Sr.

(1855-1925)
American politician, reform leader

The setting up of a new, invisible and all powerful government in this country, within the last twenty years, in open violation of fundamental and statutory law, could not have been accomplished under the steady fire of a free and independent press.

Fooling the People as a Fine Art. La Follette's Magazine, April, 1918.

Where public opinion is free and uncontrolled, wealth has a wholesome respect for the law.   *Ibid.*

Except for the subserviency of most of the metropolitan newspapers, the great corporate interests would never have ventured upon the impudent, lawless consolidation of business, for the suppression of competition, the control of production, markets and prices.

Except for this monstrous crime, 65 per cent of all the wealth of this country would not now be centralized in the hands of 2 per cent of all the people.   *Ibid.*

To control the American market is to own America.   *Ibid.*

When the Morgan and Rockefeller interests harmonized to consummate the great wrong, they well understood that they could not achieve their purpose against a hostile press. Hence they "took over" the newspapers.

This does not necessarily mean the ownership of all newspapers. The perfection of the modern combination is little less than a Fine Art. Here again control is better than outright ownership. And control can be achieved through that community of interests, that interdependence of investment and credits which ties the publisher up to the banks, the advertisers, and special interests.   *Ibid.*

It has been well said that: "An enslaved press is doubly fatal; it not only takes away the true light; for in that case we might stand still, but it sets up a false light that decoys us to our destruction."   *Ibid.*

To befool and mislead the people, to falsify public opinion, is to pervert and destroy a republican form of government.
                                    Ibid.

Free government is government by public opinion. Upon the soundness and integrity of public opinion depends the destiny of our democracy.   *Ibid.*

The supreme issue, involving all others, is the encroachment of the powerful few upon the rights of the many.

Jean de la Fontaine

(1621-1695)
French writer

Every newspaper editor owes tribute to

the devil. (*Tout faiseur de journeaux doit tribut au Malin.*)
Letter to M. Simon de Troyes, 1686.

Francis J. Lally
(b. 1918)
American Monsignor; Editor, The Pilot

The Church cannot be restricted to the sanctuary. The Church isn't just a preaching Church, a sacramental Church, but is involved in the total life of the human being, which is another way of saying religion has implications in society.
Mike Wallace Interview, Fund for the Republic, 1958.

The Church doesn't believe in book-burning, but it believes in restricting the use of dangerous books among those whose minds are unprepared for them. *Ibid.*

The Church has, through the centuries, understood that ideas are really more dangerous than other weapons. Their use should be restricted. *Ibid.*

James Fintan Lalor
(1807-1849)
Irish revolutionary leader

Mankind will yet be masters of the earth.
The Irish Felon.

The right of the people to make the laws —this produced the first great modern earthquake, whose distant shocks, even now, are heaving in the hearts of the world. The right of the people to own the land—this will produce the next. *Ibid.*

Train your hands, and your sons' hands, gentlemen of the earth, for you and they will yet have to use them. *Ibid.*

Any man who tells you that an act of armed resistance—even if offered by ten men only—even if offered by men armed only with stones—any man who tells you that such an act of resistance is premature, imprudent, or dangerous—any and every such man should at once be spurned and spat at. For remark you this, *somewhere, somehow, and by somebody, a beginning* must be made and that the first act of resistance is always, and must be ever, premature, imprudent, and dangerous. *Ibid.*

Alfred M. Landon
(b. 1887)
American politician, businessman

A government is free in proportion to the rights it guarantees to the minority.
Kansas Day address, October, 1936.

Walter Savage Landor
(1775-1864)
English writer

Delay in justice is injustice.

A want of the necessaries of life in peasants or artisans, when the seasons have been favorable, is a certain sign of defect in the constitution, or of criminality in the administration.
Sinclair, The Cry for Justice.

There is nothing on earth divine except humanity.
Cardiff, What Great Men Think of Religion.

The most pernicious of absurdities is that weak, blind, stupid faith is better than the constant practice of every human virtue.
Ibid.

The Papal power is the most monstrous and by far the most degrading imposition that ever outraged and deformed the human intellect. *Ibid.*

Lao-Tse
(c. 565 B.C.)
Chinese philosopher

A leader is best
When people barely know he exists.
Not so good when people obey and acclaim him,
Worse when they despise him.
"Fail to honor people,
They fail to honor you";
But of a good leader, who talks little,
When his work is done, his aim fulfilled,
They will say, "We did this ourselves."
The Way of Life According to Lao-Tzu (sic), an American version, by Witter Bynner.

By the accident of fortune a man may rule the world for a time, but by virtue of love he may rule the world forever.
The Simple Way.

With virtue and quietness one may conquer the world. *Ibid.*

Let there be no putting of the best people into office: this will stop vicious rivalry among the people. Let there be no prizing of rare merchandise; this will stop robbing among the people. Let nothing desirable be visible; this will save the people's minds from moral confusion.
Runes, Treasury of Philosophy.

La Pasionaria
See Dolores Ibarruri

François de La Rochefoucauld
(1613-1680)
French moralist, writer

Truth does not do so much good in the world as the appearance of it does evil.
Réflexions, ou sentences et maximes morales.

However brilliant an action it should not be esteemed great unless the result of a great motive. *Ibid.*

Although men flatter themselves with their great actions, they are usually the result of chance and not of design. *Ibid.*

Men would not live long in society were they not the dupes of each other.
Ibid., 87.

L'hypocrisie est un hommage que le vice rend à la vertu. (Hypocrisy is the homage vice pays to virtue.) *Ibid., 218.*

Envy is more implacable than hatred.
Translated by Constantine FitzGibbon, 1958.

Harold J(oseph) Laski
(1893-1950)
English political scientist

Men live by their routines; when these are called into question, they lose all power of normal judgment. . . . Discussion becomes a challenge; new ideas seem to be a threat. Men are gripped by fear, and fear, by its nature, is the enemy of thought. So that when men are too fearful to understand, they move to suppress, because they dare not stay to examine. . . . Invited to experiment, they act like children who are terrified of the dark. . . . They will listen to nothing save the echo of their own voices; all else becomes dangerous thoughts.
Quoted, The Nation.

Those who know the normal life of the poor . . . will realize well enough that, without economic security, liberty is not worth having. *Quoted by Max Eastman.*

The instruments which shape the minds of citizens are not freely at the disposal of anyone who wishes to operate them. They

are controlled, for the most part, by men or bodies who can afford either to create or to employ them. And, for the most part, they are controlled by the vested interests which dwarf altogether the individual and leave him helpless, save as he can find some other association which makes it possible to express his experience of life.
The American Democracy.

There are some half a score of nationally known columnists in the United States of whom, perhaps, the late Arthur Brisbane was the most notorious, who act as what it is difficult not to call the permanent gangsters of Big Business. *Ibid., p. 642.*

Dependent upon advertisers, who are themselves a part of Big Business, the newspaper owners must work within a framework which the advertisers largely define. The real guardian of their interests in the paper is then shifted from the editorial to the business side; and stages are presently reached when the news columns of the journal differ from the advertisement columns only in that they have a different commodity to sell. *Ibid., p. 645.*

Because each of these three media (press, cinema, radio) is a branch of Big Business, its object is not the communication of truth, but the making of profits; and the truth it can afford is rarely the whole truth, but so much of it as is compatible with profit-making. *Ibid.*

The only real security for social well-being is the free exercise of men's minds.
Authority in the Modern State, 1919.

Everyone who considers the relation of liberty to the institutions of a State will, I think, find it difficult to resist the conclusion that without democracy there cannot be liberty. *Ibid.*

Men cannot, as Rousseau claimed, be forced into freedom. They do not, as Hegel insisted, find their liberty in obedience to law. They are free when the rules under which they live leave them without a sense of frustration in realms they deem significant. They are unfree whenever the rules to which they have to conform compel them to conduct which they dislike and resent.
Ibid.

The only permanent safeguard of democratic government is that the unchanging and ultimate sanction of intellectual decision should be the conscience. We have here a realm within which the state can have no rights and where it is well that it should have none. *Ibid.*

No state, in truth, is ever firmly grounded that has not . . . won the consent of its members to its action. . . . It is patent to the world that the inexhaustible well-spring of democratic resource, as against any other form of government, is that no unfree system can be certain of itself. *Ibid.*

It is only by freeing ourselves from the tyranny of things that we can enter into our real heritage. That freedom is impossible so long as the division of property is not referable to the principles of justice.
Socialism and Freedom, 1921.

Freedom cannot live where there is injustice since it can flourish only where the souls of men are regarded as of a worth too eminent to be degraded by a mean struggle for bread. *Ibid.*

No method but ruthless dictatorship (could have achieved the Socialist revolution in the Soviet Union). . . . Historically means cannot be separated from ends: they enter them and transform their nature.
The Secret Battalion, quoted by Sidney Hook, N. Y. Times Book Review, July 12, 1953.

Every nation prepares, through its government, to equip itself with the power to hurl death upon its fellow-nations. No people seeks that power; it is governments that seek it.

Plan or Perish. The Nation, December 15, 1945.

We live under a system by which the many are exploited by the few, and war is the ultimate sanction of that exploitation.
Ibid.

Either we must have power in the hands of men who use scarcity as the means of compulsion, or we must give it to men who find abundance is the instrument of freedom. There is no middle way. Free enterprise and the market economy mean war; socialism and planned economy mean peace. We must plan our civilization or we must perish. *Ibid.*

War is the outcome of the exercise by governments of unlimited sovereignty. Unlimited sovereignty is essential to the preservation of those legal relations which subdue all human behavior to their service. We shall get rid of war as we get rid of those legal relations and the evil power politics they involve. We shall not get rid of it on any other terms. *Ibid.*

It is not by accident that our schools and colleges, our universities and foundations, even the churches, are the instruments of big business. It is not accident that the press is now a branch of big business too. It would be madness to let the purposes or the methods of private enterprise set the habits of the age of atomic energy. *Ibid.*

A people without reliable news is, sooner or later, a people without the basis of freedom. *A Grammar of Politics.*

Ferdinand Lassalle
(1825-1864)
German socialist

For the bourgeoisie the sole duty of the State is to protect the personal liberty and property of the individual. It looks upon the State as the image of the policeman, whose sole duty is, theoretically, to prevent theft and burglary.
Arbeiter-Programm, 1862.

Workingmen we all are so far as we have the desire to make ourselves useful to human society in any way whatever. *Ibid.*

There is nothing more dangerous than a principle which appears in false and perverted form. *Ibid.*

Labor is the source of all wealth and all culture. *Ibid., preamble.*

Our principal enemy, the principal enemy of any healthy development of the German spirit and of the German people today, is the press! The press, at the stage of its evolution which it has now reached, is the true enemy of the people, an enemy all the more dangerous by reason of its many disguises.
Speech, General Union of German Workers, September 26, 1863.*

Daily new lies; lies by means of pure fact alone, lies by means of invented facts, lies by means of facts distorted into their opposites—such were the weapons with which we were fought! And to cap the climax of this shameful business, the newspapers in most cases even refused to print a correction. *Ibid.*

---

* Lassalle served two terms in prison for delivering this address; it was judged seditious.

Nothing is more sacred than the publishers' capital! . . . With the aid of that shameless process of distorting all conceptions which has so long been the prerogative of our newspapers, it was now argued that it was the actual duty of the newspapers to do nothing that might incur a monetary loss. . . . It is as if a soldier—and the newspapers ought to be soldiers, champions of liberty, and claim to be such—should regard it as his first duty under no circumstances to expose himself to the danger of being hit by a bullet.   *Ibid.*

If a man makes money by publishing a newspaper, by poisoning the wells of information, by feeding the people a daily spiritual death, he is the greatest criminal I can conceive.
Ibid., Duesseldorf, September 28, 1863.

With my soul full of sadness, I do not hesitate to say that unless a complete transformation of our press can be accomplished, if this newspaper pestilence shall continue for fifty years more, the intelligence of our people will be destroyed!   *Ibid.*

Hold fast and zealously, therefore, to the slogan I now ask you to make your own: hatred and contempt, death and destruction, to the press of today!   *Ibid.*

Hugh Latimer
(1485?-burned for heresy 1555)
English prelate, reformer

Say the truth and shame the devil.
Sermons, 1552, p. 506.

The poor man hath title to the rich man's goods; so that the rich man ought to let the poor man have part of his riches to help and to comfort him withal.
Sermons, Everyman edition, p. 336.
Quoted by Tawney, Religion and the Rise of Capitalism.

Be of good comfort, Master Ridley. Play the man! We shall this day light such a candle, by God's grace, in England, as I trust shall never be put out.
To Nicholas Ridley, at the stake, October 16, 1555.*

Owen Lattimore
(b. 1900)
American Orientalist, author

I believe in my right to be wrong, and still more in my right to be right.
Gazette & Daily, York, Pa., January 7, 1956.

L'Aulne
See Turgot

Emile Louis Victor de Lavelaye
(1822-1892)
Belgian economist

If Christianity were taught and understood conformable to the spirit of its Founder, the existing social organism could not exist a day.

Edward Law
See Ellenborough

D. H. Lawrence
(1885-1930)
English writer

The world fears a new experience more than it fears anything. Because a new ex-

---

* Another version: "Be of good cheer, brother, we shall this day kindle such a torch in England, as, I trust in God, shall never be extinguished."

perience displaces so many old experiences. . . . The world doesn't fear a new idea. It can pigeon-hole any idea. But it can't pigeon-hole a real new experience.
Studies in Classic American Literature, 1922; written in 1915.

Art-speech is the only truth. An artist is usually a damned liar, but his art, if it be art, will tell you the truth of his day. And that is all that matters. Away with eternal truth. Truth lives from day to day, and the marvellous Plato of yesterday is chiefly bosh today.   *Ibid.*

The land of the free! This the land of the free! Why, if I say anything that displeases them, the free mob will lynch me, and that's my freedom. Free? Why I have never been in any country where the individual has such an abject fear of his fellow countrymen. Because, as I say, they are free to lynch him the moment he shows he is not one of them.   *Ibid.*

The only justice is to follow the sincere intuition of the soul, angry or gentle. Anger is just, and pity is just, but judgment is never just.   *Ibid.*

Sin is a queer thing. It isn't the breaking of divine commandments. It is the breaking of one's own integrity.   *Ibid.*

Men fight for liberty and win it with hard knocks. Their children, brought up easy, let it slip away again, poor fools. And their grandchildren are once more slaves.

If a woman hasn't got a tiny streak of a harlot in her, she's a dry stick as a rule.
Pornography and Obscenity, This Quarter (Paris), 1929.

Every man has a mob self and an individual self, in varying proportions. *Ibid.*

The public, which is feebleminded like an idiot, will never be able to preserve its individual reactions from the tricks of the exploiter. The public is always exploited and always will be exploited. . . . Why? Because the public has not enough wit to distinguish between mob-meanings and individual-meanings. The mass is forever vulgar, because it can't distinguish between its own original feelings and feelings which are diddled into existence by the exploiter.   *Ibid.*

The public is always profane, because it is controlled from the outside, by the trickster, and never from the inside, by its own sincerity. The mob is always obscene, because it is always second-hand.   *Ibid.*

So we can dismiss the idea that sex appeal in art is pornography. It may be so to the grey Puritan, but the grey Puritan is a sick man, soul and body sick, so why should we bother about his hallucinations?   *Ibid.*

This is the great pornographical class— the really common men-in-the-street and women-in-the-street. They have as great a hate and contempt of sex as the greyest Puritan, and when an appeal is made to them, they are always on the side of the angels. They insist that a film-heroine shall be a neuter, a sexless thing of washed-out purity. They insist that real sex-feeling shall only be shown by the villain or villainess . . . they have the grey disease of sex-hatred, coupled with the yellow disease of dirt-lust.   *Ibid.*

The great mass of humanity should never learn to read or write.
N. Y. Times Magazine, December 30, 1956.

My great religion is a belief in the blood, the flesh, as being wiser than the intellect.
The Letters of D. H. Lawrence, edited by Aldous Huxley, Viking, 1957.

We can go wrong in our minds, but what our blood feels and believes and says is always true. The intellect is only a bit and a bridle. What do I care about knowledge? All I want is to answer to my blood, direct, without fribbling intervention of mind, of moral, or what-not. *Ibid.*

I conceive a man's body as a kind of flame, like a candle flame, forever upright and yet flowing: and the intellect is just the light that is shed on to the things around. *Ibid.*

My mother was a superior soul
A superior soul was she,
Out to play a superior role
  In the god-damn bourgeoisie.
                Red Herring.

When men think they are like gods they are usually much less than men, being conceited fools. *Men Like Gods.*

T. E. Lawrence (Lawrence of Arabia)
(1888-1935)
English archaeologist, soldier, writer

We lived many lives in those whirling campaigns, never sparing ourselves any good or evil; yet when we had achieved, and the new world dawned, the old men came out again, and took from us our victory and remade it in the likeness of the former world they knew. Youth could win, but had not learned to keep, and was pitiably weak against age. We stammered that we had worked for a new heaven and a new earth, and they thanked us kindly, and made their peace. When we are their age, no doubt we shall serve our children so.

I have convinced myself that progress today is made not by the single genius, but the common people. . . . The genius raids but the common people occupy and possess. *Quoted in London Tribune.*

For names containing "le," see also the basic name.

Henry Charles Lea
(1825-1909)
American publisher, author

One of the conditions (for escaping the stake) was that of stating all they knew of other heretics and apostates, which proved an exceedingly fruitful source of information as, under the general terror, there was little hesitation in denouncing not only friends and acquaintances, but the nearest and dearest kindred—parents and children, and brothers and sisters.
History of the Inquisition of Spain, Vol. 1, p. 165.

League of Nations

(1) That armament firms have been active in fomenting war scares and in persuading their own countries to increase their armaments.

(2) That armament firms have attempted to bribe government officials both at home and abroad.

(3) That armament firms have disseminated false reports concerning the military and naval programs of various countries in order to stimulate armament expenditure in others.

(4) That armament firms have sought to influence public opinion through the control of newspapers in their own and foreign countries.

(5) That armament firms have organized international armament rings through which the armament race has been accentuated by playing off one country against another.

Conclusions of the commission to inquire into the private manufacture of arms, 1921.

Gustave LeBon
(1841-1931)
French physician, social psychologist

Reason creates science; sentiments and creeds shape history.

The sudden political revolutions which strike the historian most forcibly are often the least important. The great revolutions are those of manners and thought. The true revolutions, those which transform the destinies of people, are most frequently accomplished so slowly that the historians can hardly point to their beginnings. Scientific revolutions are by far the most important.

W. E. H. Lecky
(1838-1903)
Irish historian, essayist

In proportion to its power, Protestantism has been as persecuting as Catholicism.
Cardiff, What Great Men Think of Religion.

There is no wild beast so ferocious as Christians who differ concerning their faith
Ibid.

The question, What is truth? has certainly no prospect of obtaining a speedy answer; but the question, What is the spirit of truth? may be discussed with a greater prospect of agreement.
By the spirit of truth I mean that frame of mind by which men who acknowledge their own fallibility, and who desire above all things to discover what is true, should adjudicate between conflicting arguments. . . . Reason, reason alone, should determine their opinions.
A History of Rationalism, 1900.

There is scarcely a disposition that marks the love of abstract truth and scarcely a

rule which reason teaches as essential for its attainment, that theologians did not for centuries, stigmatize as offensive to the Almighty. *Ibid.*

In one age the persecutor burned the heretic; in another, he crushed him with penal laws; in a third, he withheld from him places of emolument and dignity; in a fourth, he subjected him to excommunication of society. Each stage of advancing toleration marks a stage in the decline of the spirit of dogmatism and of the increase of the spirit of truth. *Ibid.*

It is so much easier to assume than to prove; it is so much less painful to believe than to doubt; there is such a charm in the repose of prejudice, when no discordant voice jars upon the harmony of belief; there is such a thrilling pang when cherished dreams are scattered, and old creeds abandoned, that it is not surprising that men close their eyes to the unwelcome light.
Ibid.

Liberty, which is often very unfavorable to theological systems, is always in the end favorable to morals; for the most effectual method that has been devised for diverting men from vice is to give free scope to a higher ambition.
A History of European Morals.

Robert E. Lee
(1807-1870)
American soldier, educator

In this enlightened age there are few, I believe, but what will acknowledge that slavery as an institution is a moral and political evil in any country. It is useless to expatiate on its disadvantages. I think it, however, a greater evil to the white than to the black race, and while my feelings

are strongly enlisted in behalf of the latter, my sympathies are more strong for the former.
Letter to Mrs. Lee, December 6, 1856.

The blacks are immeasurably better off here than in Africa, morally, socially, and physically. . . . How long their subjugation may be necessary is known and ordered by a wise Merciful Providence.
Ibid., December 27, 1856.

The Abolitionist . . . must see that he has neither the right or power of operating except by moral means and suasion. . . .
Ibid.

It has been evident for years that the country was doomed to run the full length of democracy. *Ibid., January 23, 1861.*

It is well that war is so terrible—we should grow too fond of it.
To James Longstreet, December 13, 1862.

True patriotism sometimes requires of men to act exactly contrary, at one period, to that which it does at another.
N. Y. Times, January 19, 1957.

Abandon your animosities and make your sons Americans.

Richard Le Gallienne
(1866-1947)
English journalist, author

War I abhor, and yet how sweet
The sound along the marching street
Of drum and fire, and I forget
Wet eyes of widows, and forget
Broken old mothers, and the whole
Dark butchery without a soul.
The Illusion of War.

Organized Christianity has probably done more to retard the ideals that were its founder's than any other agency in the world.

William Leggett
(1801-1839)
American journalist, editor, libertarian

It was to guard against the encroachments of power, the insatiate ambition of wealth that this government was instituted, by the people themselves.
Rich and Poor, editorial, N. Y. Evening Post, 1834.

The rich perceive, acknowledge, and act upon a common interest, and why not the poor? Yet the moment the latter are called upon to combine for the preservation of their rights, forsooth the community is in danger! Property is no longer secure, and life in jeopardy. This cant has descended to us from those times when the poor and labouring classes had no stake in the community, and no rights except such as they could acquire by force. But the times have changed, though the cant remains the same. The scrip nobility of this Republic have adopted towards the free people of this Republic the same language which the Feudal Barons and the despots who contested with them the power of oppressing the people used towards serfs and villains, as they were opprobriously called. *Ibid.*

What and where is the danger of a combination of the labouring classes in vindication of their political principles, or in defence of their menaced rights? Have they not the right to act in concert, when their opponents act in concert? Nay, is it not their bounden duty to combine against the only enemy they have to fear as yet in this free country, monopoly and a great paper system that grinds them to the dust? Truly,

this is strange republican doctrine, and this is a strange republican country, where men cannot unite in one common effort, in one common cause, without rousing the cry of danger to the rights of person and property.
Ibid.

A CONCENTRATED MONEY POWER; a usurper in the guise of a benefactor; an agent exercising privileges which his principal never possessed; an impostor who, while he affects to wear chains, is placed above those who are free; a chartered libertine, that pretends to be manacled only that he may the more safely pick our pockets, and lord it over our rights. This is the enemy that we are now to encounter and overcome, before we can expect to enjoy the substantial realities of freedom.
Ibid.

We are menaced by our old enemies, avarice and ambition, under a new name and form. The tyrant is changed from a steel-clad feudal baron, or a minor despot, at the head of thousands of ruffian followers, to a mighty civil gentleman, who comes mincing and bowing to the people with a quill behind his ear, at the head of countless millions of magnificent *promises*. He promises to make everybody rich; he promises to pave cities with gold, and he promises to pay. In short he is made up of promises. He will do wonders, such as never were seen or heard of, provided the people will only allow him to make his promises equal to silver and gold, and human labour, and grant him the exclusive benefits of all the great blessings he intends to confer on them. He is the sly, selfish, grasping and insatiable tyrant the people are now to guard against. *Ibid.*

Legion of Decency

I acknowledge my obligation to form a right conscience about pictures that are dangerous to my moral life . . . I pledge myself to remain away from them. I promise, further, to stay away altogether from places of amusement which show them as a matter of policy.
Pledge taken once a year by American Catholics.

Herbert H. Lehman
(1878-1963)
American politician

The threat to democracy lies, in my opinion, not so much in revolutionary change, achieved by force or violence. Its greatest danger comes through gradual invasion of constitutional rights with the acquiescence of an inert people, through failure to discern that constitutional government cannot survive where the rights guaranteed by the Constitution are not safeguarded even to those citizens with whose political and social views the majority may not agree.

Gottfried Wilhelm von Leibnitz
(1656-1716)
German philosopher

There are two kinds of truth: those of reasoning and those of fact. The truths of reasoning are necessary and their opposite is impossible; the truths of fact are contingent and their opposite is possible.
The Monadology, xxxiii, 1714.

V. I. Lenin (né Vladimir Ilyich Ulyanov)
(1870-1924)
Russian revolutionist, statesman

"Freedom" is a grand word, but under the banner of Free Trade the most predatory

[406]

wars were conducted; under the banner of "free labor" the toilers were robbed.

What Is To Be Done? 1902.

Without a revolutionary theory there can be no revolutionary movement. *Ibid.*

Since there can be no talk of an independent ideology being developed by the masses of the workers in the process of their movement then *the only choice is*: Either bourgeois or Socialist ideology. There is no middle course (for humanity has not created a "third" ideology, and, moreover, in a society torn by class antagonisms there can never be a non-class or above-class ideology.) *Ibid.*

The history of all countries shows that the working class, exclusively by its own effort, is able to develop only trade union consciousness, i.e., the conviction that it is necessary to combine in unions, fight the employers, and strike to compel the government to pass necessary labor legislation, etc. *Ibid.*

The spontaneous working class movement is trade unionism, and trade unionism means the enslavement of the workers by the bourgeoisie. Hence our task is . . . to *divert* the working class . . . to bring it under the wing of revolutionary Social Democracy.

Ibid.

The theory of Socialism, however, grew out of the philosophical, historical and economic theories that were elaborated by the educated representatives of the propertied classes, the intellectuals. According to their social status, the founders of modern scientific Socialism, Marx and Engels, themselves belonged to the bourgeois intellectuals.

Ibid.

This (proposed) newspaper would become a part of an enormous bellows that would blow every spark of class struggle and popular indignation into a general conflagration. *Ibid.*

Literature must become a *part* of the proletarian cause as a *whole*, a "little wheel and screw" in the great one-and-indivisible Social-Democratic mechanism set into motion by the whole conscious vanguard of the whole working class. Literature must become an integral part of the organized, planned, unified work of the Social-Democratic Party (later known as the Bolshevik Party).

Party Organization and Party Literature, Novaya Zhizn (New Life). November 13, 1905.

Literature is the last thing to lend itself to mechanical equalization, to levelling, to domination of the majority over the minority. There can be no doubt that in this field it is absolutely necessary that the widest latitude be assured to personal initiative and individual inclinations, to thought and imagination, to form and content.

All this is beyond dispute, but all this proves only that the literary aspect of the work of a proletarian party cannot be identified in a stereotyped manner with the other aspects of its work. All this does not refute the principle that literature must necessarily and inevitably become an inextricable part of the work of the Social Democratic Party.

Ibid.

This absolute freedom is nothing but a bourgeois or anarchist phrase (for ideologically an anarchist is just a bourgeois turned inside out). It is impossible to live in a society and yet be free from it. The freedom of the bourgeois writer, artist, or actress is nothing but a self-deceptive (or hypocritically deceiving) dependence upon the money bags, upon bribery, upon patronage.

And we socialists expose this hypocrisy,

we tear away this false front—not in order to attain a classless art and literature (that will be possible only in a socialist, classless society), but in order to oppose to a literature hypocritically free, and in reality allied with the bourgeoisie, a literature truly free, *openly* allied with the proletariat. *Ibid.*

Mankind can pass directly from capitalism into Socialism, i.e., into social ownership of the means of production and the distribution of products according to the work of the individual. Our party looks further ahead than that: Socialism is bound sooner or later to ripen into Communism, whose banner bears the motto: "From each according to his ability, to each according to his needs." *The Task of the Proletariat, 1917.*

We shall now proceed to construct the Socialist order.
Address, Congress of the Soviets, November 8, 1917.

History will not forgive delay by revolutionists who could at once be victorious.
Letter to Central Committee on eve of October Revolution; Wilson, To the Finland Station, p. 451.

If Socialism can only be realized when the intellectual development of all the people permits it, then we shall not see Socialism for at least five hundred years.
November 27, 1917; Reed, Ten Days That Shook the World, Modern Age, pp. 303-4.

If Compromise continues, the Revolution disappears. *Ibid., p. 304.*

Capitalists are no more capable of self-sacrifice than a man is capable of lifting himself by his own bootstraps.
Letters from Afar, 1917.

The bloody capitalists cannot conclude an honorable peace. They can conclude only a dishonorable peace, based upon a division of spoils. *Ibid.*

There are no more reactionary people in the world than judges.
Political Parties and the Proletariat, 1917.

Imperialism, in a sense, is the transition stage from capitalism to socialism. . . . It is capitalism dying, not dead.
Materials Relating to the Revision of the Party Program, 1917.

The Jewish bourgeoisie are our enemies, not as Jews but as bourgeoisie. The Jewish worker is our brother.
Speech, Council of Peoples Commissars, August 9, 1918.

That which the Socialists do not understand, which constitutes their theoretic nearsightedness, their submission to bourgeois prejudices and their political treason with respect to the proletariat, is the following: . . . There can be no middle course between dictatorship of the bourgeoisie and dictatorship of the proletariat.
Report on Bourgeois Proletarian Democracies. Pravda, Petrograd, March 8, 1919.

Comrades, either the louse defeats Socialism or Socialism defeats the louse.
Speech, Congress of the Soviets, November, 1919, during typhus epidemic.

In the last analysis victory in war depends on the morale of the masses which are shedding their blood on the battlefield. The conviction of fighting a just war and the willingness to give one's own life for one's brothers, therein lies the morale of the soldier.
1921; reprinted, Pravda, February 1, 1942.

Only Communism renders the state absolutely unnecessary, for there is *no one to* be suppressed—"no one" in the sense of a *class*. . . .

The fundamental social cause of excesses which consists in violating the rules of social life is the exploitation of the masses, their want and their poverty. With the removal of this chief cause, excesses will inevitably begin to "wither away." We do not know how quickly and in what succession, but we know that they will wither away. With their withering away, the state will also *wither away*.

State and Revolution, New York, 1932.

Democracy is of great importance for the working class in its struggle for freedom against capitalists. But democracy is by no means a limit one may not overstep; it is only one of the stages in the course of development from feudalism to capitalism, and from capitalism to Communism. *Ibid.*

Only now can we appreciate the full correctness of Engels' remarks in which he mercilessly ridiculed all the absurdity of combining the words "freedom" and "state." While the state exists there is no freedom. When there is freedom, there will be no state. *Ibid.*

The economic basis for the complete withering away of the state is that high stage of development of Communism when the antagonism between mental and physical labor disappears, that is to say, when one of the principal sources of modern *social* inequality disappears—a source, moreover, which it is impossible to remove immediately by the mere conversion of the means of production into public property, by the mere expropriation of the capitalists. *Ibid.*

It will become possible for the State to wither away completely when society adopts the rule: "From each according to his ability, to each according to his needs," i.e., when people have become so accustomed to observing the fundamental rules of social life and when their labor becomes so productive that they will voluntarily work *according to their ability*. *Ibid.*

Here we have, expressed in all its clearness, the basic idea of Marxism on the question of the historical role and meaning of the state. The state is the product and the manifestation of the *irreconcilability* of class antagonisms. The state arises when, where, and to the extent that the class antagonisms *cannot* be objectively reconciled And, conversely, the existence of the state proves that the class antagonisms *are* irreconcilable. *Ibid.*

The freedom of the press throughout the world where the capitalists rule, is the freedom to buy up papers, the freedom to buy writers, to buy and manufacture public opinion in the interests of the capitalists. *1921.*

Religion is one of the forms of spiritual oppression which everywhere weigh upon the masses who are crushed by continuous toil for others, by poverty and loneliness. *Religion, N. Y., 1933.*

Religion teaches those who toil in poverty all their lives to be resigned and patient in this world, and consoles them with the hope of reward in heaven. As for those who live upon the labor of others, religion teaches them to be charitable in earthly life, thus providing a cheap justification for their whole exploiting existence and selling them at a reasonable price tickets to heavenly bliss. "Religion is the opium of the people." (Marx.) Religion is a kind of spiritual intoxicant, in which the slaves of capital drown their humanity and blunt their desires for some sort of decent human existence. *Ibid.*

A slave who has become conscious of his slavery, and who has risen to the height of fighting for his emancipation, has half ceased to be a slave. *Ibid.*

The modern proletariat ranges itself on the side of Socialism, which, with the help of science, is dispersing the fog of religion and is liberating the workers from their faith in a life after death, by rallying them to the present-day struggle for a better life here upon earth. *Ibid.*

We demand that religion be regarded as a private matter as far as the State is concerned, but under no circumstances can we regard it as a private matter with regard to our own Party. *Ibid.*

Our program necessarily includes the propaganda of atheism. *Ibid.*

Is there such a thing as Communist ethics? Is there such a thing as Communist morality? . . . In what sense do we deny ethics, morals?

In the sense in which they are preached by the bourgeoisie, a sense which deduces these morals from god's commandments. *Ibid.*

Of course, we say that we do not believe in god. We know perfectly well that the clergy, the landlords, and the bourgeoisie all claimed to speak in the name of god, in order to protect their own interests as exploiters. *Ibid.*

The old society was based on the oppression of all the workers and peasants by the landlords and capitalists. We had to destroy this society. We had to overthrow these landowners and capitalists. But to do this, organization was necessary. God could not create such organization. *Ibid.*

The helplessness of the exploited classes in their struggle against the exploiters in-evitably generates a belief in a better life after death, even as the helplessness of the savage in his struggle with nature gives rise to a belief in gods, devils, miracles, etc. *Ibid.*

Dictatorship is power, based directly upon force, and unrestricted by any laws. *Quoted in The Proletarian Revolution and the Renegade Kautsky, International Publishers, N. Y., 1934.*

The revolutionary dictatorship of the proletariat is power won and maintained by the violence of the proletariat against the bourgeoisie, power that is unrestricted by any laws. *Ibid.*

World capitalism has at the present time, i.e., about the beginning of the 20th century, reached the stage of imperialism. . . . Imperialist wars, i.e., wars for the mastery of the world, for markets, for bank capital and for the strangulation of small nations, are inevitable under such a state of affairs. *Selected Works, Vol. VI.*

The dictatorship of the proletariat is nothing else than power based upon force and limited by nothing—by no law and by absolutely no rule. *Complete Works (French edition), Vol. XVIII, p. 361.*

The means of production are not private property any more. They belong to the entire society. Every member of society, when he fulfills a certain socially necessary part of work, receives a certificate from the society that he has completed this or that quantity of work. On the basis of such a certificate he obtains from public storages the corresponding quantity of products. . . . The state withers away; since the capitalists have disappeared, classes no longer exist. *Sochineniya (Works), 4th ed., Moscow, 1949, Vol. 25, pp. 437, 439; Political Science Quarterly, Vol. LXXI.*

That which is called Socialism, Marx named the first, or the lower, phase of Communism.   *Ibid., p. 442.*

The history of modern, civilized America opens with one of those great wars which are really emancipatory, really revolutionary, of which there have been so few among the great mass of robber wars. . . . That was the war of the American people against the British robbers who were oppressing and keeping America in colonial slavery.

A Letter to the American Workers.

We understand the impossibility of eliminating wars without eliminating classes and creating Socialism, and in that we fully recognize the justice, the progressivism and the necessity of civil wars, i.e., wars of an oppressed class against the oppressor, of slaves against the slaveholders, of serfs against the landowners, of wage-workers against the bourgeoisie.

The Imperialist War, p. 219.

Our generation achieved something of amazing significance for history. The cruelty which the conditions of our lives made necessary will be understood and vindicated.   *Quoted by Maxim Gorki.*

The press should be not only a collective propagandist and a collective agitator, but also a collective organizer of the masses.

C. L. Sulzberger, N. Y. Times, December 26, 1955.

Every "peace program" is a deception of the people and a piece of hypocrisy unless its principal object is to explain to the masses the need for a revolution.

Ibid., June 11, 1956.

In the end, one or the other will triumph —a funeral dirge will be sung over the Soviet Republic or over world capitalism.

Ibid.

When people talk to us about morality we say: for the Communist, morality consists entirely of compact united discipline and conscious mass struggle against the exploiters. We do not believe in eternal morality.   *Ibid., June 13, 1956.*

We say that our morality is entirely subordinated to the interests of the class struggle.   *Ibid.*

The strictest loyalty to the ideas of communism must be combined with the ability to make all the necessary practical compromises, to tack, to make agreements, zigzags, retreats, and so on, in order to accelerate coming into power.   *Ibid.*

If you are not able to adapt yourself, if you are not inclined to crawl in the mud on your belly, you are not a revolutionary but a chatterbox.   *Ibid.*

There can be a question only of utilizing bourgeois state institutions with the object of destroying them. . . . The Communist Party enters such institutions not in order to do constructive work, but in order to direct the masses to destroy from within the whole bourgeois state machine and parliament itself.   *Ibid.*

Soviet power is a new type of state in which there is no bureaucracy, no police, no standing army.   *Ibid.*

Can a nation be free if it oppresses other nations? It cannot.   *Ibid.*

We must be ready to employ trickery, deceit, law-breaking, withholding and concealing truth. We can and must write in the language which sows among the masses

hate, revulsion, scorn, and the like, toward those who disagree with us.
Max Eastman, Reflections on the Failure of Socialism, p. 87.

History is a cruel stepmother, and when it retaliates, it stops at nothing.
To Gorki; Edmund Wilson, To the Finland Station.

War as a part of a whole, and that whole —politics.* *Time, November 17, 1947.*

There are no morals in politics; there is only expedience. A scoundrel may be of use to us just because he is a scoundrel.
Ibid.

Give me four years to teach the children and the seed I have sown will never be uprooted.
Walter Duranty, N. Y. Times Magazine.

Why should freedom of speech and freedom of the press be allowed? Why should a government which is doing what it believes is right allow itself to be criticized? It would not allow opposition by lethal weapons. Ideas are much more fatal things than guns.
Nieman Reports, January, 1956.

Only after the Proletariat has disarmed the Bourgeoisie will it be able, without destroying its world historical mission, to throw all armaments on the scrap heap.
Time, August 9, 1954.

Only when the country is electrified, when industry, agriculture and transport are placed on a technical basis of modern large-scale production—only then will our victory be complete.
Address to party congress.

---

* Cf. Clausewitz.

Soviet Russia equals socialism plus electrification.*
Gunther, Soviet Russia Today, Harper, 1958.

The true leader must submerge himself in the fountain of the people. *Ibid.*

Outside of Socialism there is no salvation of mankind from war, hunger, and the further destruction of millions and millions of human beings.

Support this state that I represent, this beastly political bureaucracy; it is needed now to make wars, civil and foreign. But observe that alongside this thing that I bid you hate and obey, temporarily, we are building an organization of all industry and when that is ready, then smash the state. . . .

To hell with Fate!

Fascism is Capitalism in decay.

Crime is a product of social excess.

Capitalism is hell compared to Socialism, but heaven compared to Feudalism.

It is necessary . . . to go the whole length of any sacrifice, if need be to resort to strategy and adroitness, illegal proceedings, reticence and subterfuge, to do anything in order to penetrate into the trade unions, remain in them, at any cost.
Weekly People, August 6, 1960

Leo XIII
(1810-1903)
Pope

To despise legitimate authority, no matter

---

* "Socialism is electrification plus Soviet power"—*Time*, September 8, 1947; "Communism is Soviet Authority plus electrification"—*Time*, January 23, 1956.

in whom it is invested, is unlawful; it is rebellion against God's will.

Immortale Dei (On the Christian Constitution of States). November 1, 1885.

Just as the end at which the Church aims is by far the noblest of all ends, so is its authority the most exalted of all authority, nor can it be looked upon as inferior to the civil power, or in *any manner* dependent upon it. *Ibid.*

Inciting to revolution is treason, not only against man, but also against God. *Ibid.*

To exclude the Church, founded by God Himself, from life, from laws, from the education of youth, from domestic society, is a grave and fatal error. A state from which religion is banished can never be well regulated. *Ibid.*

It is not lawful for the State, any more than for the individual, either to disregard all religious duties, or to hold in equal favor different kinds of religion. *Ibid.*

The liberty of thinking and publishing whatsoever each one likes, without any hindrances, is not in itself an advantage over which society can wisely rejoice. On the contrary, it is the fountainhead and origin of many evils. *Ibid.*

All public power proceeds from God. *Ibid.*

The equal toleration of all religions . . . is the same thing as atheism. *Ibid.*

All Catholics must make themselves felt as active elements in daily political life in the countries where they live. They must penetrate, wherever possible, in the administration of civil affairs; must constantly

exert the utmost vigilance and energy to prevent the usages of liberty from going beyond the limits fixed by God's law. *Ibid.*

All Catholics should do all in their power to cause the constitutions of states and legislation to be modeled on the principles of the true Church. *Ibid.*

The Church deems it unlawful to place all the religions on the same footing as the true religion. *Ibid.*

Catholicism cannot be reconciled with materialism or rationalism. *Ibid.*

That civilization which conflicts with the doctrine of Holy Church is but a worthless imitation and a hollow name.
Inscrutabili, 1878.

From what has been said it follows that it is in no way lawful to demand, to defend, or to grant, unconditional freedom of thought, of speech, of writing, or of religion, as if they were so many rights that nature has given to man.
Libertas Praestantissimum, 1888.

Whatever the Roman pontiffs have handed down or will later hand down is to be held with unwavering belief and publicly professed as often as circumstances permit. *Ibid.*

Liberty will ever be more free and secure, in proportion as license is kept in restraint. *Ibid.*

Liberty belongs only to those who have the gift of reason. *Ibid.*

The highest duty is to respect authority. *Ibid.*

The fatal theory of the separation of Church and State . . . *Ibid.*

It would be very erroneous to draw the conclusion that in America is to be sought the type of the most desirable status of the Church, or that it would be universally expedient for State and Church to be as in America, dissevered and divorced.

Longinque Oceani, January 6, 1895.

The books of apostates, heretics, schismatics, and all writers whatsoever, defending heresy or schism, or in any way attacking the foundations of religion, are altogether prohibited. Moreover, the books of non-Catholics, *ex professo* treating of religion, are prohibited, unless they clearly contain nothing contrary to the Catholic faith.

Officiorum ac Munerum, January 25, 1897.

We hold upon this earth the place of Almighty God.

Praeclara Gratulationis Publicae, June 20, 1894.

Inequality of rights and power proceeds from the very Author of nature, *from whom all paternity in heaven and earth is named.*
Quod Apostolici Muneris, December 28, 1878.

Socialists, Communists, and Nihilists . . . strive to uproot the foundations of civilized society.   *Ibid.*

These monstrous views (i.e., Socialism) . . . these venomous teachings.   *Ibid.*

The Church has never neglected to adapt itself to the genius of nations.
Rerum Novarum,* May 15, 1891.

The great mistake made in regard to the matter now under consideration, is the no-

tion that class is naturally hostile to class, and that the wealthy and the workmen are intended by nature to live in mutual conflict. So irrational and so false is this view, that the direct contrary is the truth. *Ibid.*

We may lay it down as a general and lasting law that working-men's associations should be so organized and governed as to furnish the best and most suitable means for attaining what is aimed at, that is to say, for helping each individual member to better his condition to the utmost in body, soul, and property.   *Ibid.*

It is ordained by nature that . . . classes should dwell in harmony and agreement, so as to maintain the balance of the body politic.   *Ibid.*

The first and most fundamental principle, therefore, if one would undertake to alleviate the condition of the masses, would be the inviolability of private property. *Ibid.*

Wages ought not to be insufficient to support a frugal and well-behaved wage-earner.   *Ibid.*

This great labor question cannot be solved except by assuming as a principle that private property must be held sacred and inviolable.   *Ibid.*

The main tenet of Socialism, namely, the community of goods, must be rejected without qualification, for it would injure those it pretends to benefit, it would be contrary to the natural rights of man, and it would introduce confusion and disorder into the commonwealth.   *Ibid.*

A small number of the very rich have been able to lay upon the teeming masses a yoke little better than that of slavery itself.   *Ibid.*

If the working people can be encouraged to look forward to obtaining a share in the land, the consequence will be that the gulf between vast wealth and sheer poverty will

---

* This encyclical was influenced by Cardinal Manning, according to the *Encyclopaedia Britannica*, 11th edition.

be bridged over and respective classes will be brought nearer to one another.   *Ibid.*

If the laws of the state are openly at variance with the laws of God—if they inflict injury upon the Church—or set at naught the authority of Jesus Christ which is vested in the Supreme Pontiff, then indeed it becomes a duty to resist them, a sin to render obedience.

Encyclical, 1890; quoted by Upton Sinclair, The Profits in Religion, 117-8.

The first law of history is not to dare to utter falsehood; the second, not to fear to speak the truth.

On the Opening of the Vatican Archives, August 18, 1883.

The main principle and foundation of liberalism is the rejection of the divine law. . . . It rejects and destroys all authority and divine law.

Letter to the Archbishop of Bogota, April 6, 1900.

Nothing is more important than to war on war.

It is impossible to reduce civil society to one dead level. Socialists may in that intent do their utmost, but all striving against nature is in vain.

People differ in capacity, skill, health, strength; and unequal fortune is a necessary result of unequal condition. Such inequality is far from being disadvantageous either to the individual or the community.

Leonardo da Vinci
(1452-1519)
Florentine painter, sculptor, architect, engineer

Iron rusts from disuse, stagnant water loses its purity, and in cold weather be-

comes frozen; even so does inaction sap the vigors of the mind.
                              Notebooks, c. 1500.

Man has great power of speech, but the greater part thereof is empty and deceitful. The animals have little, but that little is useful and true; and better is a small and certain thing than a great falsehood. *Ibid.*

Necessity is the mistress and guide of nature. Necessity is the theme and artificer of nature, the bridle and eternal law.

Ibid., Jonathan Cape; Reynal & Hitchcock, 1938.

Falsehood is so utterly vile that though it should praise the great works of God it offends against His divinity; truth is of such excellence that if it praise the meanest things they become ennobled.   *Ibid.*

Max Lerner
(b. 1902)
American educator, political scientist

The Seven Deadly Press Sins:

1. Concentrated Power of the Big Press.

2. Passing of competition and the coming of monopoly.

3. Governmental control of the press.

4. Timidity, especially in the face of group and corporate pressures.

5. Big Business mentality.

6. Clannishness among the newspaper publishers that has prevented them from criticizing each other.

7. Social blindness.

Actions and Passions, Simon & Schuster, 1949.

The American press today is ninety per cent a class monopoly. That means it responds to the pressures and compulsions to which other big business enterprises respond.

St. Louis Post-Dispatch Symposium, December, 1938.

So long as our society is dominated by the spirit of the counting house, so long will the press continue to express that spirit. In fact, the press is the most class-conscious segment of big business, since its stock in trade consists of the legends and folklore of capitalism. *Ibid.*

Men have always found it easy to be governed. What is hard is for them to govern themselves.

Of the many things we have done to democracy in the past, the worst has been the indignity of taking it for granted.

Alain René Le Sage
(1668-1747)

French novelist, dramatist

Facts are stubborn things.
Gil Blas, bk. x, ch. i.

Gotthold Ephraim Lessing
(1729-1781)

German critic, dramatist

I have never admitted any principle of authority in religion.

I can no longer accept the Orthodox notions of the Deity. I cannot swallow them.

Sir Roger L'Estrange
(1616-1704)

English pamphleteer

Live and let live is the rule of common Justice. *Fables of Aesop, 127.*

George Henry Lewes
(1817-1878)

English philosopher, writer

A philosophic creed is impossible. The true function of philosophy is to educate us in the principles of reasoning and not to put an end to further reasoning by the introduction of fixed conclusions.
The Biographical History of Philosophy.

C. Day Lewis (pseudonym of Nicholas Blake)
(1904-1972)

English poet, critic

Freedom . . . is mortal, we know, and made
In the image of simple men who have no taste for carnage
But sooner kill and are killed than see that image betrayed.

John L(lewellyn) Lewis
(1880-1969)

American labor leader

No tin hat brigade of goose-stepping vigilantes or Bible-babbling mob of blackguarding and corporation-paid scoundrels will prevent the onward march of labor.
Time, September 9, 1937.

Freedom of the press . . . we regard as a corner stone of democracy . . .
The integrity of the news is essential to freedom of the press.
St. Louis Post-Dispatch symposium, December, 1938.

You can't dig coal with bayonets.
Testimony before Congressional Committee. N. Y. Post, March 1, 1956.

It is a sad commentary upon our form of government when every decision of the Supreme Court seems designed to fatten capital and starve and destroy labor.
Speech on the Guffey Act.

The struggle today is not one between communism and fascism; it is the struggle between tolerance and bigotry—bigotry preached equally by communism and fascism. Here in this country the worst Fascists are those who, disowning fascism, preach enslavement to capitalism under the cloak of liberty and the Constitution. They steal not only wages but honor.
It Won't Happen Here, N. Y. Times Magazine.

It rests with the liberals and the tolerant to preserve our civilization. Everything of importance in this world has been accomplished by the free inquiring spirit and the preservation of that spirit is more important than any social system. That spirit must prevail. So long as it does it won't happen here. *Ibid.*

Organize the unorganized.
Slogan for unionization campaign, 1935.

The future of labor is the future of America. *Labor Day address, 1936.*

The genesis of this campaign against labor in the House of Representatives is not hard to find. . . . It runs across to the Senate of the United States and emanates there from a labor-baiting, poker-playing, whiskey-drinking, evil old man whose name is (Vice-President) Garner.
Statement, Congressional committee, August, 1939.

If we must grind up human flesh and bones in an industrial machine—in the industrial machine that we call modern America—then, before God, I assert that those who consume coal, and you and I who benefit from that service—because we live in comfort—owe protection to those men first, and we owe security to their families after, if they die. I say it! I voice it! I proclaim it! And I care not who in heaven or hell oppose it.
Statement, House Labor Committee, April 3, 1947.

The Taft-Hartley Statute is the first ugly, savage thrust of fascism in America. It came into being through an alliance between industrialists and the Republican majority in Congress, aided and abetted by those Democratic legislators who still believe in the institution of human slavery.
Address, AFL convention, San Francisco, 1947.

There are those who profess to fight communism who are secretly hoping that the alternative of communism as they see it, in some form of fascist type of government, will eventually triumph in America. There are rich men in America who are so fearful for the preservation of their wealth and privileges, who profess to be so alarmed at the rising strength of the common man as exemplified in our modern labor organizations, that they would willingly trade to accept the regulations and the proscriptions of a possible man on horseback.
Closing address, United Mine Workers, 1948 Convention.

Joseph Lewis
(b. 1889)
President, Freethinkers of America

The burning of an author's books, imprisonment for opinion's sake, has always been the tribute that an ignorant age pays to the genius of its time.
Voltaire: The Incomparable Infidel.

Only when a man ceases to be a child, only when he emancipates himself completely from the fetishes of religion, and gives up his silly and childish ideas concerning the existence of a God, will he be able to rise to that commanding position and station in life when he can be truly called a Man!
Lecture, Community Church, N. Y. C.,
April 20, 1930.

Faith and Prayers are no substitute for Knowledge and Courage.
Age of Reason Magazine, April, 1958.

Superstition is the poison of the mind.
Ibid., September, 1958.

I do not believe that if there is a God of this vast universe that such a God would create a hell to torment to all eternity helpless and innocent human beings. I defend the God of the religionists against the libels of his own believers.
Answer to Preacher Jack Coe, Station
WMIE, Miami, March 21, 1956.

If I had the power that the New Testament Narrative says that Jesus had, I would not cure one person of blindness, I would make blindness impossible; I would not cure one person of leprosy, I would abolish leprosy.   *Ibid.*

Sinclair Lewis
(1885-1951)
American novelist, playwright

It Can't Happen Here.
Book title, Doubleday, 1935. °

On the whole, with scandalous exceptions, Democracy has given the ordinary worker more dignity than he ever had.
It Can't Happen Here.

° A reference to Fascism or Naziism.

Cure the evils of Democracy by the evils of Fascism! Funny therapeutics! I've heard of their curing syphilis by giving the patient malaria, but I've never heard of their curing malaria by giving the patient syphilis.
Ibid.

Intellectually I know that America is no better than any other country; emotionally I know she is better than every other country.
Interview, Berlin, December 29, 1930.

God give me unclouded eyes and freedom from haste. God give me quiet and relentless anger against all pretense and all pretentious work and all work left slack and unfinished. God give me a restlessness whereby I may neither sleep nor accept praise until my observed results equal my calculated results, or, in pious glee, I discover and assault my error. God give me strength not to trust to God.
Arrowsmith (scientist's credo).

Advertising is a valuable economic factor because it is the cheapest way of selling goods, particularly if the goods are worthless.   *N. Y. Times, April 18, 1943.*

That nation is proudest and noblest and most exalted which has the greatest number of really great men.
This Week, August 5, 1956.

Every compulsion is put upon writers to become safe, polite, obedient, and sterile.
Letter declining the Pulitzer Prize,
1926.

Robert Ley
(1890-suicide 1945)
Chief of Nazi German Labor Front

We begin with the child of three. As soon as he begins to think, we press a little

flag into his hand. Then comes school, Hitler Youth, the Storm Troops, military service. We do not leave him alone for one minute. When all that is over, the Labor Front comes and takes possession of him again, and does not let him go until death.
(U.S.) *Army Talks, April 24, 1945.*

Trygve Lie

(1896-1968)
Norwegian, First Secretary General, United Nations

Wars occur because people prepare for conflict, rather than for peace.
Labor, September 6, 1947.

War can be abolished forever by providing clothing, food, and housing, instead of bombers, destroyers and rockets. *Ibid.*

Francis Lieber

(1800-1872)
American historian, originator of Encyclopedia Americana

He (the student) ought, lastly, to present clearly to his mind the psychologic processes by which liberty has been lost—by gratitude, hero-worship, impatience, indolence, permitting great personal popularity to overshadow institutions and laws, hatred against opposite parties or classes, denial of proper power to government, the arrogation of more and more power, and the gradual transition into absolutism; by local jealousies, by love of glory and conquest, by passing unwise laws against a magnified and irritating evil—laws which afterwards serve to oppress all, by recoiling oppression

of a part, by poverty and by worthless use of wealth, by sensuality and that indifference which always follows in its train.
On Civil Liberty and Self-Government, revised ed., 1859.

Karl Liebknecht

(1871-assassinated 1919)
German Socialist politician

Der Feind steht im eigenen Lager—The main enemy is at home.
Speech at outbreak of war, 1914.

In the bourgeois revolutions, bloodshed, terror and murder were indispensable weapons in the hands of the rising classes. The proletarian revolution does not stand in need of terror to achieve its aims; it hates and despises murder. It does not stand in need of such weapons because it fights institutions, not individuals, and because it does not enter the arena with naive illusions whose disappointment it would have to avenge by blood. It is not the desperate attempt of a minority to model the world according to its own idea; it is the action of the millions of the people who are called upon to fulfil the mission of history and to transform historical necessity into reality.
Spartacist proclamation, Berlin, December 14, 1918; quoted by Rudolf Coper, Failure of a Revolution, 1955.

Wilhelm Liebknecht

(1826-1900)
German politician, journalist

The essence of revolution lies not in the means, but in the ends. Violence has been for thousands of years a reactionary factor.

John Lilburne

(1614-1657)

English agitator, Puritan pamphleteer

They may talk of *freedom*, but what freedom indeed is there, so long as they stop the Presse, which is indeed, and hath been so accounted in all free Nations, the most essential part thereof.
The Second Part of England's New-Chains Discovered, 1648.

We the People of England to whom God hath given hearts, means and opportunity to effect the same (the restoration of "the true fundamentall Laws and common Freedomes of the People") do with submission to his wisdom, in his name and desiring the equity thereof may be to his praise and glory: Agree to ascertain our Government, to abolish all arbitrary Power, and to set bounds and limits both for our Supreme, and all Subordinate Authority, and to remove all known Grievances.
An Agreement of the Free People of England, Tendered as a Peace-Offering to this distressed Nation. By Lieutenant Colonel John Lilburne, Master William Welwyn, Master Thomas Prince, and Master Richard Overton, Prisoners in the Tower of London, May the 1st, 1649.

X. That we do not empower or entrust our said Representatives to continue in force, or to make any Lawes, Oathes, or Covenants whereby to compell by penalties or otherwise any person to anything in or about matters of faith, Religion, or God's worship, or to restrain any person from the profession of his faith, or exercise his Religion according to his Conscience, nothing having caused more distractions, and heart burning, in all ages, than persecution and molestation for matters of Conscience in or about Religion.   *Ibid.*

XI. We do not empower them to impress or constrain any person to serve in war by Sea or Land every man's Conscience being to be satisfied in the justness of that cause whereto he hazards his own life or may destroy an other's.   *Ibid.*

XVI. That it shall not be in the power of any Representative to punish, or cause to be punished, any person or persons for refusing to answer to questions against themselves in Criminall cases.   *Ibid.*

XXI. That it shall not be in their power to make or continue any Law, for taking away any man's life, except for murther, or other the like hainous offence destructive to humane society.   *Ibid.*

XXII. That it shall not be in their power to continue or make any Law, to deprive any person in case of Tryalls for Life, Limb, Liberty, or Estate from the benefit of Witnesses on his or their behalf. *Ibid.*

David E. Lilienthal

(1899-1981)

American industrial executive

Methods can be developed—methods I have described as grass-roots democracy—which do create an opportunity for greater happiness and deeper experience, for freedom, in the very course of technical progress. . . . Far from forcing the surrender of individual freedom and the things of the spirit to the machine, the machine can be made to promote those very ends.
Democracy on the March, 1944.

I believe—and I conceive the Constitution of the United States to rest, as does religion, upon the fundamental proposition of the integrity of the individual; and that all government and all private institutions must be designed to promote and protect and defend the integrity and the dignity of the individual; that that is the essential meaning of the Constitution and the Bill of Rights, and it is essentially the meaning of religion.

Testimony, Joint Congressional Committee, February 4, 1947, which investigated his fitness as head of the Atomic Energy Commission.

Any form of government, therefore, and any other institutions which make men means rather than ends, which exalt the state or any other institutions above the importance of men, which place arbitrary power over men as a fundamental tenet of government are contrary to that conception, and, therefore, I am deeply opposed to them.   *Ibid.*

It is very easy to talk about being against communism. It is equally important to believe those things which provide a satisfying and effective alternative. Democracy is that satisfying, affirmative alternative.
Ibid.

We believe in man not merely as production units, but as the child of God. We believe that the purpose of our society is not primarily to assure the "safety of the State" but to safeguard human dignity and the freedom of the individual.   *Ibid.*

Abraham Lincoln
(1809-1865)
16th President of the United States

Upon the subject of education, not presuming to dictate any plan or system respecting it, I can only say that I view it as the most important subject which we, as a people, can be engaged in. . . .

First public speech; to the people of Sangamon Co., March 9, 1832.

I go for all sharing the privileges of the government who assist in bearing its burdens. Consequently I go for admitting all whites to the right of suffrage who pay taxes or bear arms (by no means excluding females).

Letter to Sangamon Journal, dated New Salem, June 13, 1836.

These capitalists generally act harmoniously and in concert, to fleece the people.
Speech, Illinois Legislature, January, 1837.

As the patriots of Seventy-six did to the support of the Declaration of Independence, so to the support of the Constitution and the Laws let every American pledge his life, his property, and his sacred honor; let every man remember that to violate the law is to trample on the blood of his father, and to tear the charter of his own and his children's liberty.

Address, The Perpetuation of Our Political Institutions, Young Men's Lyceum, Springfield, Illinois, January 27, 1837.

Let me not be understood as saying that there are no bad laws, or that grievances may not arise for the redress of which no legal provisions have been made. I mean to say no such thing. But I do mean to say that although bad laws, if they exist, should be repealed as soon as possible, still, while they continue in force, for the sake of example they should be religiously observed.
Ibid.

If we take habitual drunkards as a class, their heads and their hearts will bear an advantageous comparison with those of any other class. There seems ever to have been a proneness in the brilliant and warm-blooded to fall into this vice. The demon of intemperance ever seems to have delighted in sucking the blood of genius and generosity.

Address, Washington Temperance Society, Springfield, February 22, 1842.

There was, too, the strangest combination of church influence against me. Baker (his opponent in the Congressional race) is a Campbellite; and therefore, as I suppose, with few exceptions, got all that church. My wife has some relations in the Presbyterian churches, and some with the Episcopal churches; and therefore, wherever it would tell, I was set down as either the one or the other, while it was everywhere contended that no Christian ought to go for me, because I belonged to no church, was suspected of being a deist, and had talked about fighting a duel. . . .

Letter to Martin M. Morris, Springfield, March 26, 1843.

Any people anywhere being inclined and having the power, have the right to rise up and shake off the existing government, and form a new one that suits them better. This is a most valuable, a most sacred right—a right which we hope and believe is to liberate the world.

Speech, House, in reply to President Polk on Mexico, 1848.

This declared indifference, but, as I must think, real, covert zeal, for the spread of slavery, I cannot but hate. I hate it because of the monstrous injustice of slavery itself. I hate it because it deprives our republican example of its just influence in the world, enables the enemies of free institutions with plausibility to taunt us as hypocrites, causes the real friends of freedom to doubt our sincerity, and especially because it forces so many good men amongst ourselves into an open war with the very fundamental principles of civil liberty, criticizing the Declaration of Independence, and insisting that there is no right principle of action but self-interest.

Reply to Senator Douglas, Peoria, Illinois, October 16, 1854.

As labor is the common burden of our race, so the effort of some to shift their share of the burden on to the shoulders of others is the great durable curse of the race.

Speech, c. July 1, 1854.

The Autocrat of all the Russias will resign his crown and proclaim his subjects free republicans sooner than will our American masters voluntarily give up their slaves.

Letter, 1855, quoted in Higginson, Contemporaries, 1889.

I now do no more than oppose the extension of slavery. I am not a Know-nothing; that is certain. How could I be? How can anyone who abhors the oppression of Negroes be in favor of degrading classes of white people? Our progress in degeneracy appears to me to be pretty rapid. As a nation, we began by declaring that *all men are created equal.* We now practically read it, *all men are created equal except Negroes.* When the Know-nothings get control, it will read, *all men are created equal except Negroes and foreigners and Catholics.* When it comes to this I shall prefer emigrating to some country where they make no pretense of loving liberty—to Russia, for instance, where despotism can be taken pure, and without the base alloy of hypocrisy.

Letter to Joshua F. Speed, August 24, 1855.

Be not deceived. Revolutions do not go backward.   *Speech, May 19, 1856.*

We will make converts day by day; we will grow strong by the violence and injustice of our adversaries. And, unless truth be a mockery and justice a hollow lie, we will be in the majority after a while, and then the revolution which we will accomplish will be none the less radical from being the result of pacific measures. The battle of freedom is to be fought out on principle. *Ibid.*

The ballot is stronger than the bullet. *1856.*

I think the authors of that notable instrument (Declaration of Independence) intended to include all men, but they did not intend to declare all men equal in all respects. They did not mean to say all men were equal in color, size, intellect, moral developments, or social capacity. They defined with tolerable distinctness in what respects they did consider all men created equal—equal with "certain unalienable rights among which are life, liberty and the pursuit of happiness." This they said, and this they meant. They did not mean to assert the obvious untruth that all were then actually enjoying that equality, or yet that they were about to confer it immediately upon them. In fact, they had no power to confer such a boon. They meant simply to declare the right, so that enforcement of it might follow as fast as circumstances should permit.
Speech on Dred Scott decision, Springfield, June 26, 1857.

The assertion that "all men are created equal" was of no practical use in effecting our separation from Great Britain and it was placed in the Declaration not for that, but for future use. Its authors meant it to be—as thank God, it is now proving itself—a stumbling-block to all those who in after times might seek to turn a free people back into the hateful paths of despotism. They knew the proneness of prosperity to breed tyrants, and they meant when such should reappear in this fair land and commence their vocation, they should find left

for them at least one hard nut to crack. *Ibid.*

In the right to eat the bread . . . which his own hand earns, he (the Negro) is my equal and the equal of Judge Douglas, and the equal of any living man.
Lincoln-Douglas Debate, August 2, 1858.

The fight must go on. The cause of civil liberty must not be surrendered at the end of one or even one hundred defeats.
Letter to H. Asbury, November 19, 1858.

We are now a mighty nation: we are thirty, or about thirty, millions of people. . . . We have, besides these men—descended by blood from our ancestors—among us, perhaps half our people who are not descendants at all of these men; they are men who have come from Europe—German, Irish, French, and Scandinavian, —men who have come from Europe themselves, or whose ancestors have come hither and settled here, finding themselves our equal in all things. If they look back through this history, to trace their connection with those days of blood, they find they have none; they cannot carry themselves back into that glorious epoch and make themselves feel that they are part of us; but when they look through that old Declaration of Independence, they find that those old men say that "we hold these truths to be self-evident, that all men are created equal," and then they feel that that moral sentiment taught in that day evidences their relation to those men, that it is the father of all moral principle in them, and that they have a right to claim it as though they were blood of the blood, and flesh of the flesh, of the men who wrote that Declaration; and so they are.
Reply to Douglas on Popular Sovereignty, July 10, 1858.

Wise statesmen as they were, they knew the tendency of posterity to breed tyrants; and so they established these great self-evident truths, that when in the distant future, some man, some faction, some interest, should set up the doctrine that none but rich men, or none but white men, or none but Anglo-Saxons, were entitled to life, liberty, and the pursuit of happiness, their posterity might look up again to the Declaration of Independence, and take courage to renew the battle which their fathers began.

Campaign Speech, Senate race, 1858; The Rail Splitter, October 10, 1860.

Those arguments that are made, that the inferior race are to be treated with as much allowance as they are capable of enjoying; that as much is to be done for them as their condition will allow, what are these arguments? They are the arguments that kings have made for enslaving the people in all the ages of the world. You will find that all the arguments in favor of kingcraft were of this class; they always bestrode the necks of the people—not that they wanted to do it, but because the people were better off for being ridden. That is their argument; and this argument of the Judge (Douglas) is the same old serpent, that says, "You work, and I eat; you toil, and I will enjoy the fruits of it." Turn it whatever way you will,—whether it come from the mouth of a king, an excuse for enslaving the people of his country, or from the mouth of men of one race as a reason for enslaving the men of another race,—it is all the same old serpent. *Ibid.*

What constitutes the bulwark of our own liberty and independence? It is not our frowning battlements, our bristling sea coasts, our army and our navy. These are not our reliance against tyranny. All of these may be turned against us without making us weaker for the struggle.

Our reliance is in the love of liberty which God has planted in us. Our defense is in the spirit which primed liberty as the heritage of all men, in all lands everywhere. Destroy this spirit and you have planted the seeds of despotism at your door. Familiarize yourselves with the chains of bondage and you prepare your own limbs to wear them.

Accustomed to trample on the rights of others, you have lost the genius of your own independence and become the fit subjects of the first cunning tyrant who rises among you.

Speech, Edwardsville, September 13, 1858.

I am for the people of the whole nation doing just as they please in all matters which concern the whole nation; for that of each part doing just as they choose in all matters which concern no other part; and for each individual doing just as he chooses in all matters which concern nobody else. *Speech, October 8, 1858.*

The right of peaceable assembly and of petition, and by Article Fifth of the Constitution, the right of amendment, is the constitutional substitute for revolution. Here is our Magna Carta, not wrested by barons from King John, but the free gift of states to the nation they create.

To Alexander H. Stephens, January 19, 1859.

No law is stronger than is the public sentiment where it is to be enforced. Free speech and discussion, and immunity from whip and tar and feathers, seem implied by the guarantee to each state of "a republican form of government."

Crittenden letter, December 22, 1859.

According to this theory, a blind horse upon a tread mill is a perfect illustration of what a laborer should be—all the better for being blind—that he could not kick understandingly.

According to this theory, the education of labor is not only useless but pernicious and dangerous. In fact, it is, in some sort, deemed a misfortune that laborers should have heads at all. These same heads are regarded as explosive material, only to be safely kept in damp places, as far as possible from that peculiar sort of fire which ignites them.

A Yankee who could invent a strong-handed man without a head would receive the everlasting gratitude of these "Mudsill advocates."

Address, Wisconsin Agricultural Society, Milwaukee, September 30, 1859.

I am glad to see that a system of labor prevails in New England under which laborers can strike when they want to, where they are not obliged to work under all circumstances, and are not tied down and obliged to labor whether you pay them or not. I like the system which lets a man quit when he wants to, and wish it might prevail everywhere.

Speech, New Haven, Conn., March 6, 1860.

I do not mean to say we are bound to follow implicitly in whatever our fathers did. To do so, would be to discard all the lights of current experience—to reject all progress, all improvement.

Address, Cooper Institute, N. Y., February 27, 1860.

Neither let us be slandered from our duty by false accusations against us, nor frightened from it by menaces of destruction to the government, nor of dungeons to ourselves. Let us have faith that right makes right, and in that faith let us to the end dare to do our duty as we understand it.   *Ibid.*

The love of property and consciousness of right or wrong have conflicting places in our organization, which often makes a man's course seem crooked, his conduct a riddle.

Hartford, Conn., March 5, 1860.

Mr. Lincoln thanked God that we have a system of labor where there can be a strike. Whatever the pressure, there is a point where the workmen may stop. He didn't pretend to be familiar with the subject of the shoe strike—probably knew as little about it as Senator Douglas himself.

Shall we stop making war upon the South? We never have made war upon them. If any one has, he had better go and hang himself and save Virginia the trouble. If you give up your convictions and call slavery right, as they do, you let slavery in upon you—instead of white laborers who can strike, you'll soon have black laborers who can't strike.

Indirect quotation as reported in the press, March 6, 1860, of Hartford, Conn., speech.

I do but quote from one of those speeches when I declare that "I have no purpose, directly or indirectly, to interfere with the institution of slavery in the States where it exists. I believe I have no lawful right to do so, and I have no inclination to do so." Those who nominated and elected me did so with full knowledge that I had made this and many similar declarations, and had never recanted them.

First Inaugural Address, March 4, 1861.

Why should there not be a patient confidence in the ultimate justice of the people? Is there any equal hope in the world?   *Ibid.*

I hold that, in contemplation of universal law and of the Constitution, the Union of these States is perpetual. Perpetuity is implied, if not expressed, in the fundamental law of all national governments. It is safe to assert that no government proper ever had a provision in its organic law for its own termination.   *Ibid.*

If by the mere force of numbers a majority should deprive a minority of any clearly written constitutional right, it might, in a moral point of view, justify revolution —certainly would if such a right were a vital one.   *Ibid.*

A majority held in restraint by constitutional checks and limitations, and always changing easily with deliberate changes of popular opinions and sentiments, is the only true sovereign of a free people. Whoever rejects it does, of necessity, fly to anarchy or to despotism. Unanimity is impossible; the rule of a minority, as a permanent arrangement, is wholly inadmissible; so that, rejecting the majority principle, anarchy or despotism in some form is all that is left.   *Ibid.*

This country, with its institutions, belongs to the people who inhabit it. Whenever they shall grow weary of the existing Government, they can exercise their constitutional right of amending it, or their revolutionary right to dismember or overthrow it. I cannot be ignorant of the fact that many worthy and patriotic citizens are desirous of having the National Constitution amended. While I make no recommendation of amendments, I fully recognize the rightful authority of the people over the whole subject, to be exercised in either of the modes prescribed in the instrument itself; and I should, under existing circumstances, favor rather than oppose a fair opportunity being afforded the people to act upon it. *Ibid.*

The better angels of our nature. *Ibid.*

It is now for them to demonstrate to the world that those who can fairly carry an election can also suppress a rebellion; that ballots are the rightful and peaceful successors of bullets; and that when ballots have fairly and constitutionally decided, there can be no successful appeal back to bullets.

First message to Congress, special session, July 4, 1861.

It is not needed nor fitting here that a general argument should be made in favor of popular institutions; but there is one point, with its connections, not so hackneyed as most others, to which I ask a brief attention. It is the effort to place capital on an equal footing with, if not above, labor, in the structure of government. It is assumed that labor is available only in connection with capital; that nobody labors, unless somebody else, owning capital, somehow, by the use of it, induces him to labor.

Message to Congress, regular session, December 3, 1861.

Now, there is no such relation between capital and labor as assumed, nor is there any such thing as a free man being fixed for life in the condition of a hired laborer. Both these assumptions are false, and all inferences from them are groundless.

Ibid.

Labor is prior to and independent of capital. Capital is only the fruit of labor, and could never have existed if labor had not first existed. Labor is the superior of capital, and man deserves much the higher consideration. Capital has its rights, which are as worthy of protection as any other rights. Nor is it denied that there is, and probably always will be, a relation between labor and capital, producing mutual bene-fits. The error is in assuming that the whole labor of the community exists within that relation. A few men own capital, and that few avoid labor themselves, and with their capital hire or buy another few to labor for them. A large majority belong to neither class—neither work for others, nor have others work for them. *Ibid.*

No men living are more worthy to be trusted than those who toil up from poverty, none less inclined to take or touch aught which they have not honestly earned. Let them beware of surrendering a political power which they already possess, and which, if surrendered, will surely be used to close the door of advancement against such as they, and to fix new disabilities and burdens upon them, till all of liberty shall be lost.* *Ibid.*

I admit that slavery is at the root of the rebellion, or at least its sine qua non.
Ibid.

Fellow-citizens, we cannot escape history. We of this Congress and this Administration will be remembered in spite of ourselves. No personal significance or insignificance can spare one or another of us. The

---

* Carl Sandburg: "An extraordinary little treatise on what Lincoln considered the basic point of the American economic and political system as related to the common man. . . . This passage is a rough-hewn sketch of American society, placing the farmer and the free laborer as the living and controlling element in a government of the people."

fiery trial through which we pass will light us down, in honor or dishonor, to the latest generation. . . .
Annual message to Congress, December 1, 1862.

I recommend the adoption of the following. . . . The President of the United States shall deliver to every such State bonds of the United States bearing interest at the rate of ___ per cent per annum to an amount equal to the aggregate sum of ___ for each slave shown to have been therein by the Eighth census . . . *Ibid.*

We, even we here, hold the power and bear the responsibility. In giving freedom to the slave, we assure freedom to the free, —honorable alike in what we give and what we preserve. We shall nobly save or meanly lose the last, best hope of earth. *Ibid.*

And by virtue of the power and for the purpose aforesaid, I do order and declare that all persons held as slaves within said designated states and parts of states are, and henceforward shall be, free; and that the executive government of the United States, including the military and naval authorities thereof, will recognize and maintain the freedom of said persons.
Emancipation Proclamation, January 1, 1863.

Only those generals who gain successes can set up dictators. What I now ask of you is military success, and I will risk the dictatorship.
Letter, January 26, 1863, to General Hooker, who assailed Lincoln, said the country needed a dictator.

I know the trials and woes of working men, and I have always felt for them. I know that in almost every case of strikes, the men have a just cause for complaint.

To delegation from the Machinists' and Blacksmiths' Union, 1863.

Of those who were slaves at the beginning of the rebellion, fully one hundred thousand are now in the United States military service, about one-half of which number actually bear arms in the ranks; thus giving the double advantage of taking so much labor from the insurgent cause and supplying the places which otherwise must be filled with so many white men. So far as tested, it is difficult to say they are not as good soldiers as any.

Annual message to Congress, December 8, 1863.

The strongest bond of human sympathy outside the family relation should be one uniting all working people of all nations and tongues and kindreds.

Letter to New York Workingmen's Association, 1864.

The world has never had a good definition of the word "liberty", and the American people, just now, are much in want of one. We all declare for liberty; but in using the same word, we do not all mean the same thing. With some, the word "liberty" may mean for each man to do as he pleases with himself and the product of his labor; while with others, the same word may mean for some men to do as they please with other men and the product of other men's labor. Here are two, not only different, but incompatible things, called by the same name, —liberty. And it follows that each of the things is, by the respective parties, called by two different and incompatible names,— liberty and tyranny.

Address, Sanitary Fair, Baltimore, April 18, 1864.

The shepherd drives the wolf from the sheep's throat, for which the sheep thanks the shepherd as his liberator, while the wolf denounces him for the same act as the destroyer of liberty, especially as the sheep was a black one. Plainly, the sheep and the wolf are not agreed upon a definition of the word "liberty"; and precisely the same difference prevails today, among us human creatures, even in the North, and all professing to love liberty. Hence we behold the process by which thousands are daily passing from under the yoke of bondage hailed by some as the advance of liberty, and bewailed by others as the destruction of liberty. *Ibid.*

Whenever there is a conflict between human rights and property rights, human rights must prevail.

Quoted in Congressional Record, May 12, 1944.

My earlier views of the unsoundness of the Christian scheme of salvation and the human origin of the scriptures, have become clearer and stronger with advancing years and I see no reason for thinking I shall ever change them.

To Judge J. S. Wakefield, after the death of Willie Lincoln.

If I were to try to read, much less answer, all the attacks made on me, this shop might as well be closed for any other business.

I am a firm believer in the people. If given the truth, they can be depended upon to meet any national crisis. The great point is to bring them the real facts.

Politicians are a set of men who have interests aside from the interests of the people and who, to say the most of them, are, taken as a mass, at least one step removed from honest men.

When a white man governs himself, that is self government. But when he governs himself and also governs some other men, that is worse than self government—that is despotism. What I do mean to say is that no man is good enough to govern another man without that other's consent.

Friends, I agree with you in Providence; but I believe in the Providence of the most men, the largest purse, and the longest cannon.

Public opinion is everything. With public sentiment nothing can fail; without it, nothing can succeed. Consequently, he who moulds public opinion goes deeper than he who enacts statutes or pronounces decisions.

Our government rests on public opinion. Whoever can change public opinion can change the government practically as such.

Public opinion, though often formed upon a wrong basis, yet generally has a strong underlying sense of justice.

Anne Morrow Lindbergh
(b. 1906)
American writer

Somehow the leaders in Germany, Italy and Russia have discovered how to use new economic forces. . . . They have felt the wave of the future and they have leapt upon it.

Charles A. Lindbergh (Sr.)
(1859-1924)
American congressman

A radical is one who speaks the truth.
Labor, June 15, 1957.

Under the Federal Reserve Act panics are scientifically created: the present one is the first scientifically created one worked out as we figure a mathematical problem.
1920.

Charles A. Lindbergh (Jr.)
(1902-1974)
American aviator

Oriental guns are turning westward. Asia presses towards us on the Russian border, all foreign races stir restlessly. It is time to turn from our quarrels and to build our White ramparts again. The alliance with foreign races means nothing but death for us.
Aviation, Geography and Race. Also, Readers Digest, November, 1939.

It is our turn to guard our heritage from Mongol, and Persian and Moor, before we become engulfed in a limitless foreign sea.
Ibid.

The three most important groups which are pressing this country toward war are the British, the Jewish and the Roosevelt Administration. . . .
They planned, first to prepare the United States for foreign war under the guise of American defense; second, to involve us in the war, step by step, without our realization; third, to create a series of incidents which would force us into the actual conflict.
Only the creation of sufficient "incidents" yet remains; and you see the first of these already taking place, according to plan—a plan that was never laid before the American people for their approval.
Address, Des Moines, September 11, 1941; A. P. dispatch in newspapers of September 12.

Science, freedom, beauty, adventure: What more could you ask of life? Aviation combined all the elements I loved. . . . I began to feel that I lived on a higher plane than the skeptics of the ground; one that was richer because of its very association with the element of danger they dreaded, because it was freer of the earth to which they were bound. In flying I tasted the wine of the gods of which they could know nothing. . . .   *1953.*

Robert M(itchell) Lindner
(1915-1956)
American psychiatrist, writer

Man is a rebel. He is committed by his biology not to conform.
Must You Conform? Rinehart, 1956.

Unlike other creatures of earth, man cannot submit, cannot surrender his birthright of protest, for rebellion is one of his essential dimensions. He cannot deny it and remain man. In order to live he must rebel.
                                        Ibid.

Non-conformity, as it is now conceived, is largely exhibited as psychosis, neurosis, crime and psychosomatic illness; or it appears as pitifully hopeless, vain little defiances of convention and custom, in dress, manner, opinion and taste. All of these ways are negative, unproductive, totally inadequate to meet the situation and face it.
                                        Ibid.

In the time of their demise, it has been characteristic of all peoples that they have surrendered to pressures put upon them by their power-mad leaders, by their insane religions, and by their misguided philosophies, to conform.   *Ibid.*

Abroad in the world today is a monstrous falsehood, a consummate fabrication, to which all social agencies have loaned themselves and into which most men, women and children have been seduced . . . "the Eleventh Commandment"; for such, indeed, has become the injunction: You Must Adjust!   *Ibid.*

You must adjust . . . This is the legend imprinted in every schoolbook, the invisible message on every blackboard. Our schools have become vast factories for the manufacture of robots.   *Ibid.*

"Must we conform?" The answer is a resounding No! No . . . not only because in the end we are creatures who cannot conform and who are destined to triumph over the forces of conformity; but No because there is an alternate way of life available to us here and now. It is the way of positive rebellion, the path of creative protest, the road of productive revolt.   *Ibid.*

The answer . . . lies in the mobilization and implementation of the instinct of rebellion. We must, in short, become acquainted with our protestant nature and learn how to use it in our daily lives, how to express it ourselves, how to infuse it throughout all levels of our culture, and how to nourish it in our young.   *Ibid.*

Howard Lindsay
(1889-1968)
American playwright, producer, actor
and
Russel Crouse
(1893-1966)
American writer

Every so often, we pass laws repealing human nature.
Quoted by John Crosby, N. Y. Herald Tribune, November 21, 1954.

(Nicholas) Vachel Lindsay
(1879-1931)
American poet

Let not young souls be smothered out before
    They do quaint deeds and fully flaunt
        their pride.
It is the world's one crime its babes grow
    dull,
    Its poor are ox-like, limp and leaden-
        eyed.
Not that they starve, but starve so dream-
    lessly,
Not that they sow, but that they seldom
    reap,
Not that they serve, but have no gods to
    serve,
Not that they die, but that they die like
    sheep.   *The Congo and*
Other Poems,   Macmillan, 1933, p. 65.

I am unjust, but I can strive for justice.
    My life's unkind, but I can vote for
        kindness.
I, the unloving, say life should be lovely.
    I, that am blind, cry out against my
        blindness.
        Why I Voted the Socialist Ticket.

And must the Senator from Illinois
    Be this squat thing, with blinking, half-
        closed eyes?
This brazen gutter idol, reared to power
    Upon a leering pyramid of lies?
        To the United States Senate.
        (*A reference to William Lorimer.*)

What will you trading frogs do on a day
    When Armageddon thunders thro' the
        land;
When each sad patriot rises, mad with
    shame,
    His ballot or his musket in his hand?
        Ibid.

Where is Roosevelt, the young dude cow-
    boy,

Who hated Bryan, then aped his way?
Gone to join the shadows with mighty
    Cromwell
And tall King Saul, till the Judgment Day.
        Bryan, Bryan, Bryan.

Where is Altgeld, brave as the truth,
Whose name the few still say with tears?
Gone to join the ironies with Old John
    Brown,
Whose fame sings loud for a thousand years.
        Ibid.

Where is that boy, that Heaven-born Bryan,
That Homer Bryan, who sang from the
    West?
Gone to join the shadows with Altgeld the
    Eagle,
Where the kings and the slaves and the
    troubadours rest.   *Ibid.*

Ben B. Lindsey
(1869-1943)
American judge, reformer
and
Wainwright Evans

We still put a blight on the "illegitimate" child, though we have never defined how he differs from ordinary children. We still make outcasts of mothers who are not parties to the (legal) marriage contract, though in what respect unmarried maternity as maternity, differs from other maternity—especially as to the rights of the child, is not clear.
The Revolt of Modern Youth, Boni & Liveright, 1925.

Motherhood is so honorable a thing that nothing—no convention—can possibly make it dishonorable; and from the standpoint of the right of the child, the unborn—the unmarried mother should be granted by society the same reverence and regard as the married mother. *Ibid., p. 168.*

I am for children first, because I am for Society first, and the children of today are the Society of tomorrow. I insist, therefore, on the right of the child to be born, and that there be no "illegitimate" children.
Ibid., p. 220.

I demand for the unmarried mother, as a sacred channel of life, the same reverence and respect as for the married mother; for Maternity is a cosmic thing, and once it has come to pass our conventions must not be permitted to blaspheme it. *Ibid.*

. . . our sex taboos, saturated as they are with superstitions, are a trap that destroys human happiness. They are no more rational than . . . witch-hangings. *Ibid., p. 277.*

At present our notion of preserving what we think to be the truth is to gag all who do not think it's the truth. We win our arguments by forbidding argument.
Ibid., p. 280.

The churches used to win their arguments against atheism, agnosticism, and other burning issues by burning the ismists, which is fine proof that there is a devil but hardly evidence that there is a God. *Ibid.*

I cannot admit that any man born of woman has either the knowledge or authority to tell other men, as a statement of ascertained fact, what God's purposes are in this or any other matter. *Ibid., p. 285.*

Carl E. Lindstrom
(b. 1896)
American editor, educator

We have a reasonably free press in this country, but there are far too many captive editors who cannot even be heard to rattle their chains.

Ralph Linton
(1893-1953)
American anthropologist

The human capacity for being bored, rather than man's social or natural needs, lies at the root of man's cultural advance.
The Study of Man, 1936.

In a time when change in certain aspects of "human nature" has become necessary to the survival of our species, it is comforting to know that it can be done and has been done. The problem of the scientist is to find out how. *Ibid.*

Walter Lippmann
(1889-1974)
American editor, author

Men who are "orthodox" when they are young are in danger of being middle-aged all their lives. *Harvard Monthly.*

A political revolution is in progress: the state as policeman is giving place to the state as producer. *A Preface to Politics.*

Those who deplore the use of force in the labor struggle should ask themselves whether the ruling class of any country could be depended upon to inaugurate a program of reconstruction which would abolish the barbarism that prevails in industry. . . . Fight labor's demands to the last ditch and there will come a time when it seizes the whole of power, makes itself sovereign and takes what it used to ask.
Ibid.

The world has been slow to recognize the work of the Socialist Party in transmuting dumb mutterings into a civilized program. *Ibid.*

Civilization has much to fear from blind class antagonism; but the preaching of "class consciousness," far from being a fomenter of violence, must be recognized as the civilizing influence of culture upon economic interests. *Ibid.*

The writers who have nothing to say are the ones you can buy; the others have too high a price. *Ibid.*

It has been the fashion to speak of the conflict between human rights and property rights, and from this it has come to be widely believed that the use of private property is tainted with evil and should not be espoused by rational and civilized men. In so far as these ideas refer to plutocratic property, to great impersonal corporate properties, they make sense. These are not in reality private properties. They are public properties privately controlled, and they have either to be reduced to genuinely private properties or to be publicly controlled. But the issue between the giant corporations and the public should not be allowed to obscure the truth that the only dependable foundation of personal liberty is the personal economic security of private property. *The Good Society.*

Private property was the original source of freedom. It still is its main bulwark. *Ibid.*

No official yet born on this earth is wise enough or generous enough to separate good ideas from bad ideas, good beliefs from bad beliefs.
Free Speech and Free Press, Bulletin, League of Free Nations Association, March, 1920.

The reactionaries have been winning the battles and losing the war.

The compelling reason why, if liberty of opinion did not exist, we should have to invent it, why it will eventually have to be restored in all civilized countries where it is now suppressed, is that we must protect the right of our opponents to speak because we must hear what they have to say.
The Indispensable Opposition, Atlantic Monthly, August, 1939.

The opposition is indispensable. A good statesman, like any other sensible human being, always learns more from his opponents than from his fervent supporters. *Ibid.*

The demagogue, whether of the Right or Left, is consciously or unconsciously, an undetected liar.

The unexamined life, said Socrates, is unfit to be lived by man. This is the virtue of liberty, and the ground on which we may justify our belief in it, that it tolerates error in order to serve truth.

When men are brought face to face with their opponents, forced to listen and learn and mend their ideas, they cease to be children and savages and begin to live like civilized men. Then only is freedom a reality, when men may voice their opinions because they must examine their opinions.

In the blood of the Martyrs to intolerance are the seeds of unbelief.

Men cannot be made free by laws unless they are in fact free because no man can buy and no man can coerce them. That is why the Englishman's belief that his home is his castle and that the king cannot enter it, like the American's conviction that he must be able to look any man in the eye and tell him to go to hell, are the very essence of the free man's way of life.

This, perhaps, is the testament of Liberalism. For underlying all the specific projects which men espouse who think of themselves as Liberals there is always, it seems to me, a deeper concern. It is fixed upon the importance of remaining free in mind and action before changing circumstances.

This is why Liberalism has always been associated with a passionate interest in freedom of thought and freedom of speech, in scientific research, in experiment, in the liberty of teaching, in an independent and unbiased press, in the right of men to differ in their opinions and to be different in their conduct. . . .

Lisle
See Rouget de Lisle

Maxim Litvinov
(1876-1951)
Russian politician, diplomat

Food is a weapon.
To Walter Lyman Brown of the Hoover Mission, Riga, 1921.

Complete lack of confidence on one side; absolute distrust on the other.
Ibid.; explaining failure of U.S.-Soviet understanding.

Peace is indivisible.
Geneva, League of Nations session, 1934.

International diplomacy has never done anything which Hitler disliked.

Titus Livius Livy
(59 B.C.-17 A.D.)
Roman historian

In great straits and when hope is small, the boldest counsels are the safest.

Avarice and luxury, those pests which have ever been the ruin of every great state.

It is said that truth is often eclipsed but never extinguished.

Vae victis. (Woe to the vanquished.)
History, V.

Henry Demarest Lloyd
(1847-1903)
American journalist, industrial reformer

The wealth created by a thousand men under the motive power of the self-interest of the capitalist is not, and cannot be, equal to the wealth that will be created by the same men under the motive power of co-operation or democracy.
Man, the Social Creator.

Private property being individualism, and its abolition being socialism, the two are correlative and must yield to each other just as rapidly as experience and necessity dictate. Civilization is a growth both ways —an intensification of private property in certain ways, an abolition of it in others.
Ibid.

The higher the individualism, the higher must be the socialism. The resultant of these opposing forces of socialism and individualism must be determined by each age for itself.
Ibid.

The system which comes nearest to calling out all the self-interests and using all the faculties and sharing all the benefits will outcompete any system that strikes a lower level of motive, faculty and profit. The capitalists are the cooperators that were; the people are the cooperators that will be.
Ibid.

Monopoly is business at the end of its journey.
Wealth Against Commonwealth, 1894.

Churches come and go, but there has ever been but one religion. The only religion is conscience in action.

David Lloyd-George
(1863-1945)

English statesman, prime minister

We are fighting Germany, Austria and drink, and as far as I can see, the greatest of these three deadly foes is drink.
Speech, March 29, 1915.

What is our task? To make Britain a fit country for heroes to live in.
Speech, Wolverhampton, November 24, 1918.

Sweating, slums, the sense of semi-slavery in labour, must go. We must cultivate a sense of manhood by treating men as men. *Election speech, 1919.*

A New Deal for everyone.
Ibid.; election slogan.

Wars are precipitated by motives which the statesmen responsible for them dare not publicly avow. A public discussion would drag these motives in their nudity into the open, where they would die of exposure to the withering contempt of humanity.

Liberty has restraints but no frontiers.

Liberty is not merely a privilege to be conferred; it is a habit to be acquired.

No quarrel ought ever to be converted into a policy.

John Locke
(1632-1704)

English philosopher

New opinions are always suspected, and usually opposed, without any other reason but because they are not already common. *An Essay Concerning Human Understanding, 1690.*

It is one thing to show a man he is in error, and another to put him in possession of the truth. *Ibid.*

The necessity of pursuing true happiness (is) the foundation of our liberty. *Ibid.*

As therefore the highest perfection of intellectual nature lies in a careful and constant pursuit of true and solid happiness; so the care of ourselves that we mistake not imaginary for real happiness, is the necessary foundation of our liberty. *Ibid.*

If men are for a long time accustomed only to one sort or method of thoughts, their minds grow stiff in it, and do not readily turn to another . . . I do not propose . . . a variety and stock of knowledge, but a variety and freedom of thinking . . . an increase of the powers and activity of the mind, not . . . an enlargement of its possessions. *Ibid.*

1. *According to reason* are such propositions whose truth we can discover by examining and tracing those ideas we have from sensation and reflection; and by natural deduction find to be true or probable.

2. *Above reason* are such propositions whose truth or probability we cannot by reason derive from those principles.

3. *Contrary to reason* are such propositions as are inconsistent with or irreconcilable to our clear and distinct ideas. Thus the existence of one God is according to reason; the existence of more than one God, contrary to reason; the resurrection of the dead, above reason. *Ibid.*

Reason, therefore, here, as contradistinguished to *faith*, I take to be the discovery of the certainty or probability of such propositions or truths, which the mind arrives at by deduction made from such ideas, which it has got by the use of its natural faculties: viz., by sensation or reflection.

Faith, on the other side, is the assent to any proposition, not thus made out by the deductions of reason, but upon the credit of the proposer, as coming from God, in some extraordinary way of communication. This way of discovering truths to men, we call *revelation.* *Ibid.*

Nothing that is contrary to, and inconsistent with, the clear and self-evident dictates of reason, has a right to be urged or assented to as a matter of faith, wherein reason hath nothing to do. *Ibid.*

So that, in effect, religion, which should most distinguish us from beasts, and ought most peculiarly to elevate us, as rational creatures, above brutes, is that wherein men often appear most irrational, and more senseless than beasts themselves. *Credo, quia impossibile est:* I believe, because it is impossible, might, in a good man, pass for a sally of zeal; but would prove a very ill rule for men to choose their opinions or religion by. *Ibid.*

For he that thinks absolute power purifies men's blood, and corrects the baseness of human nature, need read but the history of this, or any age, to be convinced to the contrary.

Two Treatises on Government, 1690.

The great question which, in all ages, has disturbed mankind, and brought on them the greatest part of these mischiefs which have ruined cities, depopulated countries, and disordered the peace of the world, has been, not whether there be power in the world, nor whence it came, but who should have it. *Ibid.*

Political power, then, I take to be a right of making laws with penalties of death, and consequently all less penalties, for the regulating and preserving of property, and of employing the force of the community in the execution of such laws, and in the defense of the commonwealth from foreign injury, and all this only for the public good.
Ibid., Ch. 1.

The state of nature has a law of nature to govern it, which obliges everyone; and reason, which is that law, teaches all mankind who will but consult it, that, being all equal and independent, no one ought to harm another in his life, health, liberty or possessions. *Ibid., Ch. 2.*

The natural liberty of man is to be free from any superior power on earth, and not to be under the will or legislative authority of man, but to have only the law of nature for his rule. The liberty of man in society is to be under no other legislative power but that established by consent in the commonwealth; nor under the dominion of any will or restraint of any law, but what that legislative shall enact according to the trust put in it. *Ibid.*

But freedom of men under government is to have a standing rule to live by, common to every one of that society, and made by the legislative power erected in it. A liberty to follow my own will in all things where that rule prescribes not, not to be subject to the inconstant, uncertain, unknown, arbitrary will of another man, as freedom of nature is to be under no other restraint but the law of Nature.
Ibid., Ch. 4, Of Slavery.

This freedom from absolute, arbitrary power is so necessary to, and closely joined with, a man's preservation, that he cannot part with it but by what forfeits his preservation and life together. For a man, not having the power of his own life, cannot by compact or his own consent enslave himself to any one, nor put himself under the absolute, arbitrary power of another to take away his life when he pleases.

Ibid.

Nor is it so strange, as perhaps before consideration it may appear, that the property of labor should be able to overbalance the community of land. For it is labor indeed that puts the difference of value on everything. . . . Of the products of the earth useful to the life of man nine-tenths are the effects of labor; nay, if we will rightly estimate things as they come to our use, and cast up the several expenses about them—what in them is purely owing to nature, and what to labor—we shall find that in most of them ninety-nine hundredths are wholly to be put on the account of labor. *Ibid., Ch. 5.*

Man being born, as has been proved, with a title to perfect freedom, and an uncontrolled enjoyment of all the rights and privileges of the law of nature equally with any other man or number of men in the world, hath by nature a power not only to preserve his property—that is, his life, liberty, and estate—against the injuries and attempts of other men, but to judge of and punish the breaches of that law in others as he is persuaded the offense deserves, even with death itself, in crimes where the heinousness of the fact in his opinion requires it. *Ibid., Ch. 7.*

The great and chief end, therefore, of men's uniting into commonwealths, and putting themselves under government, is the preservation of their property; to which in the state of nature there are many things wanting. *Ibid., Ch. 9.*

The reason why men enter into society is the preservation of their property; and the end while they choose and authorize a legislature is that there may be laws made, and rules set, as guards and fences to the properties of all the society.

Ibid., Ch. 19, Of the Dissolution in Government.

Whenever the legislators endeavour to take away and destroy the property of the people, or to reduce them to slavery under arbitrary power, they put themselves into a state of war with the people, who are thereupon absolved from any farther obedience, and are left to the common refuge which God hath provided for all men against force and violence. Whensoever, therefore, the legislative shall transgress this fundamental rule of society, and either by ambition, fear, folly, or corruption, endeavour to grasp themselves, or put into the hands of any other, an absolute power over the lives, liberties, and estates of the people, by this breach of trust they forfeit the power the people had put into their hands for quite contrary ends, and it devolves to the people, who have a right to resume their original liberty, and by the establishment of a new legislative (such as they shall think fit) provide for their own safety and security, which is the end for which they are in society. *Ibid.*

All wealth is the product of labor.

The love of truth for truth's sake is the principal part of human perfection in this world, and the seed-plot of all other virtues.

But there is only one thing which gathers people into seditious commotions, and that is oppression.

Four Letters of Toleration in Religion, 1689.

Truth, whether in or out of fashion, is the measure of knowledge, and the business of the understanding.

Jack London
(1876-1916)
American writer

I took with me certain simple criteria with which to measure. That which made for more life, for physical and spiritual health, was good; that which made for less life, which hurt, dwarfed and distorted life, was bad.　*People of the Abyss.*

The unfit and the unneeded! The miserable and despised and forgotten, dying in the social shambles. The progeny of prostitution—of the prostitution of men and women and children, of flesh and blood, and sparkle and spirit; in brief the prostitution of labor. If this is the best that civilization can do for the human, then give us howling and naked savagery.　*Ibid.*

Times change, and men's minds with them. Down the past, civilizations have exposited themselves in terms of power, of world-power or of other-world power. No civilization has yet exposited itself in terms of love-of-man.
　The Cry For Justice, Introduction.

He, who by understanding becomes converted to the gospel of service, will serve truth to confute liars and make of them truthtellers; will serve kindness so that brutality will perish; will serve beauty to the erasement of all that is not beautiful. He will devote his strength, not to the debasement or the defilement of his weaker fellows, but to the making of opportunity for them to make themselves into men rather than into slaves and beasts.　*Ibid.*

After God had finished the rattlesnake, the toad, the vampire, He had some awful substance left with which He made a scab. *"A Scab." C.I.O. News, September 13, 1946.*

A scab is a two-legged animal with a corkscrew soul, a waterlogged brain, a combination backbone of jelly and glue. Where others have hearts, he carries a tumor of rotten principles.　*Ibid.*

No man has a right to scab so long as there is a pool of water to drown his carcass in, or a rope long enough to hang his body with. Judas Iscariot was a gentleman compared with a scab. For betraying his master, he had character enough to hang himself. A scab has not.　*Ibid.*

Esau sold his birthright for a mess of pottage. Judas Iscariot sold his Savior for thirty pieces of silver. Benedict Arnold sold his country for a promise of a commission in the British Army. The modern strikebreaker sells his birthright, his country, his wife, his children and his fellow men for an unfulfilled promise from his employer, trust or corporation.　*Ibid.*

Esau was a traitor to himself; Judas Iscariot was a traitor to his God; Benedict Arnold was a traitor to his country; a strikebreaker is a traitor to his God, his country, his wife, his family and his class.　*Ibid.*

Life was a matter of food and shelter. In order to get food and shelter men sold things. The merchant sold shoes, the politician sold his manhood, and the representative of the people, with exceptions, of course, sold his trust; while nearly all sold their honor. Women, too, whether on the street or in the holy bond of wedlock, were prone to sell their flesh. All things were commodities, all people bought and sold. The one commodity that labor had to sell was its muscle. The honor of labor had no

price in the market-place. Labor had muscle, and muscle alone, to sell.
What Life Means to Me, 1906.

Huey P. Long
(1893-1935)

*American politician, governor
and senator from Louisiana*

If Fascism came to America it would be on a program of Americanism.
Army Talk, Orientation Fact Sheet 64, U.S. War Department, March 24, 1945.°

Henry Wadsworth Longfellow
(1807-1882)

American poet

Were half the power that fills the world
with terror,
Were half the wealth bestowed on
camps and courts,
Given to redeem the human mind from
error,
There were no need of arsenals nor
forts. *The Arsenal at Springfield.*

The warrior's name would be a name
abhorred!
And every nation, that would lift again
Its hand against a brother, on his forehead
Would wear forevermore the curse of
Cain! *Ibid.*

Big words do not smite like war clubs,
Boastful breath is not a bow-string,
Taunts are not so sharp as arrows,
Deeds are better things than words are,
Actions mightier than boastings.
Hiawatha.

Buried was the bloody hatchet;
Buried was the dreadful war-club;
Buried were all warlike weapons,
And the war-cry was forgotten.
There was peace among the nations.
Ibid.

Write on your doors the saying wise and
old,
"Be bold! be bold!" and everywhere, "Be
bold;
Be not too bold!" Yet better the excess
Than the defect; better the more than less;
Better like Hector in the field to die,
Than like a perfumed Paris turn and fly.
Morituri Salutamus.

In the world's broad field of battle,
In the bivouac of Life,
Be not like dumb, driven cattle!
Be a hero in the strife!
A Psalm of Life, st. 5.

How strange it seems! These Hebrews in
their graves,
Close by the streets of this fair seaport
town,
Silent beside the never-silent waves,
At rest in all this moving up and down!

. . . .

How came they here? What burst of Christian hate,
What persecution, merciless and blind,
Drove o'er the sea—that desert desolate—
These Ishmaels and Hagars of mankind?
The Jewish Cemetery at Newport.

Louis XIV
(1638-1715)

King of France

How much more legitimate is it to say with the wise Plato, that the perfect felicity

° Another version: "Sure we'll have Fascism, but it will come disguised as Americanism."

of a kingdom consists in the obedience of the subjects to their prince, and of the prince to the laws, and in the laws being just and constantly directed to the public good.

Of the Rights of the Most Christian Queen over various States of the Monarchy of Spain, 1667; quoted by Rousseau, The Social Contract.

L'État c'est moi. (I am the state.)

Attributed; said to have been spoken before Parlement de Paris, April 13, 1655.

It is legal because I wish it.

Elijah P. Lovejoy
(1802-1837)
American abolitionist, editor

As long as I am an American citizen and as long as American blood runs in these veins, I shall hold myself at liberty to speak, to write, and to publish whatever I please, being amenable to the laws of my country for the same.

Inscription on Lovejoy Monument.

If the civil authorities refuse to protect me, I must look to God; and if I die, I have determined to make my grave in Alton. I have sworn eternal opposition to slavery and by the blessing of God I will never turn back.

I am impelled to the course I have taken because I fear God. As I shall answer to God in the great day, I dare not abandon my sentiments, or cease in all proper ways to propagate them. With God I can cheerfully rest my cause. I can die at my post but I cannot desert it.

Speech to the mob, Alton, Illinois, November 3, 1837; Lovejoy was shot to death by the mob November 7.

George Loveless*
(19th Century)
English labor leader

God is our Guide: From field, from wave,
From plough, from anvil, and from loom,
We come, our country's rights to save,
And speak the tyrant faction's doom;
We raise the watchword Liberty—
We will, we will, we will be free.

(*verse written while in prison.*)

James Russell Lowell
(1819-1891)
American poet, critic

The foolish and the dead alone never change their opinions.
My Study Windows.

Where Church and State are habitually associated it is natural that minds, even of a high order, should unconsciously come to regard religion as only a subtler mode of police.
Literary Essays, Dryden, Vol. III, p. 186.

Toward no crimes have men shown themselves so cold-bloodedly cruel as in punishing differences of belief.
Ibid., Witchcraft, Vol. II, p. 374.

If there are men who regret the Good Old Times, without too clear a notion of what they were, they should at least be thankful that we are rid of that misguided energy of faith which justifies conscience in making men unrelentingly cruel.
Ibid., p. 395.

---

* Sentenced to seven years' transportation (a form of exile) in 1834, for administering an oath to laborers joining his trade union at Tolpuddle, Dorset, England.

He who is firmly seated in authority soon learns to think security, and not progress, the highest lesson of statecraft.

Among My Books.

From the summit of power men no longer turn their eyes upward, but begin to look about them. Aspiration sees only one side of every question; possession, many. *Ibid.*

But it was in making education not only common to all, but in some sense compulsory on all, that the destiny of the free republics of America was practically settled.

Ibid. New England Two Centuries Ago.

Simple as it seems, it was a great discovery that the key of knowledge could turn both ways, that it could open, as well as lock, the door of power to the many.

Ibid.

Puritanism, believing itself quick with the seed of religious liberty, laid, without knowing it, the egg of democracy.   *Ibid.*

The capacity of indignation makes an essential part of the outfit of every honest man.

On a Certain Condescension in Foreigners, 1869.

Both of them (Breckenridge and Douglas, Lincoln's opponents) mean that Labor has no rights which Capital is bound to respect, —that there is no higher law than human interest and cupidity.

The Elections in November 1860.

Whatever be the effect of slavery upon the States where it exists, there can be no doubt that its moral influence upon the North has been most disastrous. It has compelled our politicians into that first fatal compromise with their moral instincts and hereditary principles which makes all consequent ones come easy; it has accustomed us to makeshifts instead of statesmanship, to subterfuge instead of policy, to party-platforms for opinions, and to a defiance of the public sentiment of the civilized world of patriotism.   *Ibid.*

One of the most curious of these frenzies of exclusion was that against the emancipation of the Jews. All share in the government of the world was denied for centuries to perhaps the ablest, certainly the most tenacious, race that had ever lived in it— the race to whom we owed our religion and the purest spiritual stimulus and consolation to be found in all literature—a race in which ability seems as natural and hereditary as the curve of their noses, and whose blood, furtively mingling with the bluest bloods in Europe, has quickened them with its own indomitable impulsion.

Democracy. Address, Birmingham, England, October 6, 1884.

What people are afraid of in democracy is less the thing itself than what they conceive to be its necessary adjuncts and consequences. It is supposed to reduce all mankind to a dead level of mediocrity in character and culture, to vulgarize men's conceptions of life, and therefore their code of morals, manners and conduct—to endanger the rights of property and possession.

Ibid.

The real gravamen of the charges (against democracy) lies in the habit it has of making itself generally disagreeable by asking the Powers that Be at the most inconvenient moment whether they are the powers that ought to be.   *Ibid.*

All free governments, whatever their name, are in reality governments by public

opinion, and it is on the quality of this public opinion that their prosperity depends.
Ibid.

Communism means barbarism, but Socialism means, or wishes to mean, cooperation and community of interests, sympathy, the giving to the hands not so large a share as to the brains, but a larger share than hitherto in the wealth they must combine to produce—means, in short, the practical application of Christianity to life, and has in it the secret of an orderly and benign reconstruction. *Ibid.*

It is not the insurrections of ignorance that are dangerous, but the revolts of intelligence.
Democracy and Other Addresses.

The pressure of public opinion is like the pressure of the atmosphere; you can't see it—but, all the same, it is sixteen pounds to the square inch.
Interview with Julian Hawthorne.

The traitor to humanity is the traitor most accursed;
Man is more than Constitutions; better rot beneath the sod,
Than to be true to Church and State while we are doubly false to God!
On the Capture of . . . Fugitive Slaves.

Great truths are portions of the soul of man;
Great souls are portions of eternity.
Sonnets, vi.

Once to every man and nation comes the moment to decide,
In the strife of Truth with Falsehood, for the good or evil side;
Some great cause, God's new Messiah offering each the bloom or blight,
Parts the goats upon the left hand, and the sheep upon the right;

And the choice goes by forever 'twixt that darkness and that light.
The Present Crisis.

Then to side with Truth is noble when we share her wretched crust,
Ere her cause brings fame and profit, and 'tis prosperous to be just;
Then it is the brave man chooses, while the coward stands aside,
Doubting in his abject spirit, till his Lord is crucified. *Ibid.*

Truth forever on the scaffold, wrong forever on the throne. *Ibid.*

New occasions bring new duties; Time makes ancient good uncouth;
They must upward still, and onward, who would keep abreast with Truth. *Ibid.*

New times demand new measures and new men;
The world advances, and in time outgrows
The laws which in our father's times were best;
And doubtless, after us, some purer scheme
Will be shaped out by wiser men than we,
Made wiser by the steady growth of truth.
A Glance Behind the Curtain.

No man is born into the world whose work
Is not born with him; there is always work,
And tools to work withal, for those who will;
And blessed are the horny hands of toil.
Ibid.

They are slaves who fear to speak
For the fallen and the weak;
They are slaves who will not choose
Hatred, scoffing, and abuse,
Rather than in silence shrink
From the truth they needs must think;
They are slaves who dare not be
In the right with two or three.
Stanzas for Freedom.

Men! Whose boast it is that ye
Come of fathers brave and free,
If there breathe on earth a slave,
Are ye truly free and brave?
If ye do not feel the chain,
When it works a brother's pain,
Are ye not base slaves indeed,
Slaves unworthy to be freed?   *Ibid.*

Is true Freedom but to break
Fetters for our own dear sake,
And, with leathern hearts, forget
That we owe mankind a debt?
No! True Freedom is to share
All the chains our brothers wear,
And, with heart and hand, to be
Earnest to make others free!   *Ibid.*

They talk about their Pilgrim blood,
    Their birthright high and holy!
A mountain-stream that ends in mud
    Methinks is melancholy.
            Interview with Miles Standish.

Earth gets its price for what Earth gives us;
    The beggar is taxed for a corner to die
        in,
The priest hath his fee who comes and
        shrives us,
    We bargain for the graves we lie in:
At the devil's booth are all things sold,
    Each ounce of dross costs its ounce of
        gold.
            Vision of Sir Launfal, Prelude 1.

Laborin' man an' laborin' woman
    Hev one glory an' one shame.
Ev'y thin' thet's done inhuman
    Injers all of 'em the same.
            The Biglow Papers.

Ez fer war, I call it murder,—
    There you hev it plain an' flat;
I don't want to go no furder
    Than my Testament fer that;

God hez sed so plump an' fairly,
    It's ez long ez it is broad,
An' you've gut to git up airly
    Ef you want to take in God.   *Ibid.*

Ef you take a sword an' dror it,
    An' go stick a feller thru,
Guv'mint ain't to answer for it,
    God'll send the bill to you.   *Ibid.*

'Tain't by turnin' out to hack folks
    You're agoin' to git your right,
Nor by lookin' down on black folks
    Coz you're put upon by white;
Slavery ain't o'nary color,
    'Tain't the hide thet makes it wus,
All it keers fer in a feller
    'S jest to meke him fill its pus.   *Ibid.*

I du believe in Freedom's cause,
    Ez fur away ez Payris is;
I love to see her stick her claws
    In them infarnal Phayrisees;
It's wal enough agin a king
    To dror resolves an' triggers,—
But libbaty's a kind o' thing
    Thet don't agree with niggers.
            *The Pious Editor's Creed, Bigelow
            Papers, VI.*

I du believe with all my soul
    In the gret Press's freedom,
To pint the people to the goal
    An' in the traces lead 'em;
Palsied the arm thet forges yokes
    At my fat contracts squintin',
An' withered be the nose thet pokes
    Inter the gov'ment printin'!   *Ibid.*

In short, I firmly du believe
    In Humbug generally,
Fer it's a thing thet I perceive
    To hev a solid vally;
This heth my faithful shepherd ben,
    In pasturs sweet heth led me,

An' this'll keep the people green
    To feed ez they have fed me.   *Ibid.*

We will speak out, we will be heard,
    Though all earth's systems crack;
We will not bate a single word,
    Nor take a letter back.
Let liars fear, let cowards shrink,
    Let traitors turn away;
Whatever we have dared to think
    That dared we also say.
We speak the truth, and what care we
    For hissing and for scorn,
While some faint gleamings we can see
    Of Freedom's coming morn.

Compromise makes a good umbrella, but a poor roof; it is a temporary expedient, often wise in party politics, almost sure to be unwise in statesmanship.

The devil loves nothing better than the intolerance of reformers, and dreads nothing so much as their charity and patience.

Wealth may be an excellent thing, for it means power, it means leisure, it means liberty.

Men in earnest have no time to waste in patching fig leaves for the naked truth.

St. Ignatius of Loyola
(1491-1556)
*Spanish founder of the
Society of Jesus*

We should always be disposed to believe that that which appears white is really black, if the hierarchy of the Church so decides.   *Exercitia spiritualia, 1541.*

Lucan (Marcus Annaeus Lucanus)
(39-65)
Roman poet, born in Spain

Never so long as earth supports sea, or air supports earth, or the sun makes his perennial journey through the signs of the Zodiac, or night follows day—never will loyalty be found among fellow-despots. It is a law of Nature that every great man inevitably resents a partner in greatness.
    *Lucan : Pharsalia, tr. Robert Graves,
    Penguin.*

F(rank) L(aurence) Lucas
(1894-1967)
English scholar, novelist

Hardly any critics have ever admitted, or perhaps ever will admit, even in theory, what seems to me this simple truth—that esthetic tastes are merely subjective. Men's desire of forcing their own opinions on other men remains too incorrigible.
    The Search for Good Sense, Macmillan.

The only hope I can see for the future depends on a wiser and braver use of the reason, not a panic flight from it.   *Ibid.*

"Intellectuals," no doubt, are often tiresome enough, because they are often pseudo-intellectuals—ingenious fools too clever to be wise, though brilliant at inventing the most ingenious reasons for their fatuous beliefs. But, tiresome as intellectuals can be, even they are probably much less menacing and pernicious to the world than anti-intellectuals.   *Ibid.*

The two World Wars came in part, like much modern literature and art, because men, whose nature is to tire of everything in turn, as the Athenians tired even of the goodness of Aristides, had tired of common sense and civilization.   *Ibid.*

Clare Boothe Luce
(b. 1903)
American playwright, politician, diplomat

Lying increases the creative faculties, ex-

pands the ego, lessens the friction of social contacts. . . . It is only in lies, wholeheartedly and bravely told, that human nature attains through words and speech the forbearance, the nobility, the romance, the idealism, that—being what it is—it falls so short of in fact and in deed.
"Vanity Fair," October, 1930.

The Democratic Party has a vested interest in depression at home and war abroad. Its leaders are always troubadours of trouble; crooners of catastrophe. Public confusion on vital issues is Democratic weather. A Democratic President is doomed to proceed to his goals like a squid, squirting darkness all about him.
New York Times, February 27, 1959.

Henry Robinson Luce
(1898-1967)
American editor, publisher

Clement Attlee often observed that British Socialism owed more to Christ than Marx.   *The Fabulous Future, 1956.*

Newspapers and magazines should not be run from the counting room. . . . It is to the counting room's advantage that the counting room not edit. . . . It is too often forgotten that the press is a profit-making institution. Like other private enterprise it has to make money to exist. If the press were not self-supporting who would support it? The alternatives are subsidy and control, contemporary examples of which are at hand. It is easy to get subsidies for propaganda, pink, red, or black, but who is going to subsidize honest journalism?
St. Louis Post-Dispatch symposium, December, 1938.

Lucian
(120-180)
Greek satirist

The God from the machine.[*]
Hermotimus, 86.

Lucretius
(96?-55 B.C.)
Roman poet

The greatest wealth is to live content with little, for there is never want where the mind is satisfied.
De Rerum Natura, 57 B.C.

How many evils have flowed from religion.   *Ibid.*

Fear was the first thing on earth to make gods.

The vain crowds, wandering blindly, led by lies.

Erich von Ludendorff
(1865-1937)
German general, World War

I decline Christianity because it is Jewish, because it is international, and because, in cowardly fashion, it preaches Peace on Earth. *Belief in German God.*

Raymond Lully
(1235-1313)
Majorcan, Christian martyr

The office of a knight is to have a castle and horse for to keep the highways, and for to defend them that labor on the lands

---

[*] Usually given in its Latin form, *Deus ex machina.*

and the earth, and they ought to have towns and cities for to hold right to the people, and for to assemble in a place men of many diverse crafts, which be much necessary to the ordinance of this world to keep and maintain the life of man and woman.

The Book of the Order of Chivalry, 1276.

Ferdinand Lundberg

(b. 1902)

American writer

If there is one general judgment that will hold about the American public it is that it is lacking in the fundamental seriousness of outlook necessary to the working of a true democracy, that it is extremely juvenile, not to say infantile, in its attitudes . . .

Martin Luther

(1483-1546)

Leader of German Reformation

An earthly kingdom cannot exist without inequality of persons. Some must be free, some serfs, some rulers, some subjects.

Werke, Vol. xviii, p. 327; quoted by Tawney, Religion and the Rise of Capitalism.

There can be no better instructions in . . . all transactions in temporal goods than that every man who is to deal with his neighbor present to himself these commandments:

"What ye would that others should do unto you, do ye also unto them", and "Love thy neighbor as thyself."

If these were followed out, then everything would instruct and arrange itself; then no law books nor courts nor judicial actions would be required; all things would quietly

and simply be set to rights, for everyone's heart and conscience would guide him.

Ibid., Vol. vi, p. 49.

It will be asked, "Who then can be saved, and where shall we find Christians?" . . . Christians are rare people on earth.

Ibid., Vol. xv, p. 302.

No one need think that the world can be ruled without blood. The civil sword shall and must be red and bloody.   *Ibid.*

Heretics are not to be disputed with, but to be condemned unheard, and whilst they perish by fire, the faithful ought to pursue the evil to its source, and bathe their hands in the blood of the Catholic bishops, and of the Pope, who is the devil in disguise.

Riffel, Kirchengeschichte, II, 9; quoted by Lord Acton, The Protestant Theory of Persecution.

Superstition, idolatry, and hypocrisy have ample wages, but truth goes a begging.

Table Talk, 53.

For where God built a church there the Devil would also build a chapel. They imitated the Jews in this, namely, that as the Most Holiest was dark, and had no light, even so and after the same manner did they make their shrines dark where the Devil made answer. Thus is the Devil ever God's ape.   *Ibid., 67.*

In our sad condition, our only consolation is the expectancy of another life. Here below all is incomprehensible. *Ibid., 132.*

I confess that mankind has a free will, but it is to milk kine, to build houses, etc., and no further.   *Ibid., 165.*

The Mass is the greatest blasphemy of God, and the highest idolatry upon earth, an abomination the like of which has never been in Christendom since the time of the Apostles. *Ibid., 171.*

Jews and papists are ungodly wretches; they are two stockings made of one piece of cloth. *Ibid., 275.*

Antichrist is the pope and the Turk together. A beast full of life must have a body and soul. The spirit or soul of Antichrist is the pope, his flesh or body the Turk. *Ibid., 329.*

Reason is the greatest enemy that faith has: it never comes to the aid of spiritual things, but—more frequently than not—struggles against the divine Word, treating with contempt all that emanates from God. *Ibid., 353.*

It is imperative for the Christian and true church to subsist without the shedding of blood, for her adversary, the Devil, is a liar and a murderer. The church grows and increases through blood; she is sprinkled with blood. *Ibid., 371.*

The Pope derives his institutions neither from divine nor from human right, but is a self-chosen human creature and intruder. *Ibid., 415.*

The Devil begat darkness, darkness begat ignorance . . . the mass-offering begat unbelief . . . ambition begat simony; simony begat the pope and his brethren. *Ibid., 500.*

The ungodly papists prefer the authority of the Pope far above God's Word; a blasphemy abominable and not to be endured; void of all shame and piety they spit in God's face. *Ibid., 581.*

The hound of Hell, in Greek is called Cerberus; in Hebrew, Scorphur; he has three throats—sin, the law, and death. *Ibid., 626.*

Men have broad and large chests, and small narrow hips, and are more understanding than women, who have but small and narrow chests, and broad hips, to the end they should remain at home, sit still, keep house, and bear and bring up children. *Ibid., 725.*

On what pretense can man have interdicted marriage, which is a law of nature? 'Tis as though we were forbidden to eat, to drink, to sleep. 'Tis the most certain sign of God's enmity of popedom that He has allowed it to assail the conjugal union of the sexes. *Ibid., 728.*

This, then is the question: Whether the papacy at Rome, possessing the actual power over all Christendom (as they say), is of divine or of human origin, and this being decided, whether it is possible for Christians to say that all other Christians in the world are heretics and apostates, even if they agree with us in holding to the same baptism, Sacrament, Gospel, and all the articles of faith, but merely do not have their priests and bishops confirmed by Rome, or, as it is now, buy such confirmation with money and let themselves be mocked and made fools of like the Germans.

The Papacy at Rome, 1520.

Now the greater part of the Roman communion, and even some of the popes themselves, have forsaken the faith wantonly and without struggle, and live under the power of Satan, as is plainly to be seen, and thus the papacy often has been under the dominion of the gates of hell. And should I speak quite openly, this same Roman authority, ever since the time it has presumed to soar over all Christendom, not only has never attained its purpose, but has become the cause of nearly all the apostasy, heresy, discord, sects, unbelief and misery in Christendom, and has never freed itself from the gates of hell. *Ibid.*

And if there were no other passage to prove that Roman authority was of human and not of divine right, this passage alone would be sufficient, where Christ says, the gates of hell shall not prevail against His building on the rock. Now the gates of hell ofttimes had the papacy in their power, at times the pope was not a pious man, and the office was occupied by a man without faith, without grace, without good works; which God would never have permitted if the papacy were meant in Christ's word concerning the rock. For then He would not be true to His promise, nor fulfil His own word; therefore the rock, and the building of Christ founded upon it, must be something entirely different from the papacy and its external Church. *Ibid.*

But when a prince is in the wrong, are his people bound to follow him then too? I answer, No, for it is not one's duty to do wrong.
Secular Authority: To What Extent It Should Be Obeyed.

Peace, if possible, but the truth at any rate.

Hier steh' Ich, Ich kann nicht anders. (Here I stand, I cannot do otherwise.)
Declaration, Diet of Worms, April 18, 1521.

The prosperity of a country depends, not on the abundance of its revenues, nor on the strength of its fortifications, nor on the beauty of its public buildings; but it consists in the number of its cultivated citizens, in its men of education, enlightenment and character.

I, Martinus Luther, D., do by these indentures acknowledge and testify that I have received this angry fiction concerning my death on the 21st day of March, and that I have read it with considerable pleasure and joy, except the blasphemous portion of the document in which this lie is attributed to the exalted Majesty of God. Otherwise I felt quite tickled on my knee-cap and under my left heel at this evidence how cordially the Devil and his ministers, the Pope and the papists, hate me. May God turn them from the Devil!
Comment appended to letter of the Italian Ambassador to the King of France, stating Luther had died after begging for and receiving "the Holy Sacrament of the Body of our Lord Jesus Christ."

Rosa Luxemburg
(1880-1919)
German Socialist, revolutionary leader

Be prepared for the day when Socialism will ask not only for your vote but for your life itself.

Civil war is only another name for class war.

The revolution of November 9th (1918) was chiefly a political revolution, whereas the real revolution must be chiefly an economic one.

I hope to die at my post; on the street or in prison.* *Letter to Sonia Liebknecht.*

Freedom for supporters of the government only, for the members of one party only—no matter how big its membership may be—is no freedom at all. Freedom is always freedom for the man who thinks differently.
Die Russische Revolution, quoted in Paul Froelich's biography of her, London, 1940.

---

* Rosa Luxemburg was assassinated on the street, in Berlin, in 1919.

The suppression of political life throughout the country must gradually cause the vitality of the Soviets themselves to decline. Without general elections, without freedom of the press, freedom of speech, freedom of assembly, without the free battle of opinions, life in every public institution withers away, becomes a caricature of itself, and bureaucracy rises as the only deciding factor.   *Ibid.*

No one can escape the workings of this law. Public life gradually dies, and a dozen party leaders with inexhaustible energy and boundless idealism direct and rule . . . In the last resort, clique-ism develops into a dictatorship, but not the dictatorship of the proletariat: the dictatorship of a handful of politicians, i.e., a dictatorship in the bourgeois sense, in the Jacobin sense.   *Ibid.*

He who renounces the struggle for Socialism renounces both the labor movement and democracy.
Slogan in numerous Socialist publications.

Matthew Lyon
(1746-1822)
American congressman

I cannot say that I am descended from the bastards of Oliver Cromwell, or his courtiers, or from the Puritans who punish their horses for breaking the Sabbath, or from those who persecuted the Quakers and burned the witches.

Trofim Lysenko
(1898-1976)
Russian scientist

The conversion of one species into another takes place by a leap.
The Science of Biology Today, N. Y., 1948.

A science which fails to give practical workers a clear perspective, the power of finding their bearings and confidence that they can achieve practical aims, does not deserve to be called science.   *Ibid.*

We must firmly remember that *science is the enemy of chance.* That is why Michurin, who was the transformer of nature, put forward the slogan: "We must not wait for favors (*i.e.,* lucky chances—T.L.) from nature; our task is to wrest them from her."
Ibid.

Lord George Lyttleton
(1709-1773)
English literary patron, writer

To argue against any breach of liberty from the ill use that may be made of it, is to argue against liberty itself, since all is capable of being abused.

Edward George Bulwer-Lytton
(1803-1873)
English novelist, poet, dramatist

The principle is this—that you ought not in a free country to lay a tax on the expression of political opinion—a tax on the diffusion of that information on public affairs which the spirit of our constitution makes the interest and concern of every subject in the State. Still more, you should not, by means of that tax, create such an artificial necessity for capital that you secure the monopoly of thought upon the subjects that most interest the public at large to a handful of wealthy and irresponsible oligarchs.
Speech on the act abolishing taxes on newspapers.

Revolutions are not made with rose-water.
The Parisians, bk. 5, ch. 7.

When the people have no tyrant, their own public opinion becomes one.
Ernest Maltravers, vi.

A reform is a correction of abuses; a revolution is a transfer of power.
Speech, House of Commons, 1866.

Beneath the rule of men entirely great
The pen is mightier than the sword.
Richelieu.

Mac
See also Mc

Douglas MacArthur
(1880-1964)
American general

Wars are caused by undefended wealth.

Men will not fight and die without knowing what they are fighting and dying for.

A warlike spirit, which alone can create and civilize a state, is absolutely essential to national defense and to national perpetuity.
Infantry Journal, March, 1927, pp. 328-9.

The more warlike the spirit of the people, the less need for a large standing army, as in such a community every ablebodied man should be willing to fight on all occasions whenever the nation demands his services in the field.   *Ibid.*

In a free country like our own where everything depends upon the individual action of the citizen, every male brought into existence should be taught from infancy that the military service of the Republic carries with it honor and distinction, and his very life should be permeated with the ideal that even death itself may become a boon when a man dies that a nation may live and fulfill its destiny.   *Ibid.*

Blank cartridges should never be used against a mob, nor should a volley be fired over the heads of the mob even if there is little danger of hurting persons in the rear. Such things will be regarded as an admission of weakness, or an attempt to bluff, and may do much more harm than good.
Basic Field Manual, Vol. VII, part 3. Domestic Disturbances, War Department, August 1, 1935. (An edition for National Guards was titled: Military Aid to Civil Authorities.)

Military alliances, balances of power, leagues of nations, all in turn failed, leaving the only path to be by way of the crucible of war. The utter destructiveness of war now blocks out this alternative. We have had our last chance. If we will not devise some greater and more equitable system, Armageddon will be at our door.
On the deck of the "Missouri," Tokyo Bay, September 2, 1945.

I know war as few other men now living know it, and nothing to me is more revolting. I have long advocated its complete abolition, as its very destructiveness on both friend and foe has rendered it useless as a method of settling international disputes.
Address to Congress, April 19, 1951.

In war there is no substitute for victory.
Ibid.

Thomas Babington Macaulay
(1800-1859)
English historian, essayist, statesman

We say, and we say justly, that it is not by mere numbers, but by property and intelligence, that the nation ought to be governed. Yet, saying this, we exclude all share in the government great masses of property and intelligence, great numbers of those who are most interested in preserving tranquillity, and who know best how to preserve it. We do more. We drive over to the side of revolution those whom we shut out from power.

Speech on the Reform Bill, Commons, March 2, 1831.

There is a change in society. There must be a corresponding change in the government. We are not, we cannot, in the nature of things, be, what our fathers were.

Speech on The Reform Bill, September 20, 1831.

Agitations of the public mind, so deep and long continued as those which we have witnessed, do not end in nothing. In peace or in convulsion, by the law or in spite of the law, through Parliament, or over the Parliament, Reform must be carried. Therefore be content to guide the movement which you cannot stop.   *Ibid.*

We treat them (the Jews) as slaves, and wonder that they do not regard us as brethren. We drive them to mean occupations, and then reproach them for not embracing honourable professions. We long forbade them to possess land; and we complain that they chiefly occupy themselves in trade. We shut them out of all the paths of ambition; and then we despise them for taking refuge in avarice.

Speech, On Civil Disabilities of the Jews, April 17, 1833.

During many ages we have, in all our dealings with them (the Jews), abused our immense superiority of force, and then we are disgusted because they have recourse to that cunning which is the natural and universal defence of the weak against the violence of the strong.   *Ibid.*

In the infancy of civilisation, when our island was as savage as New Guinea, when letters and arts were still unknown to Athens, when scarcely a thatched hut stood on what was afterwards the site of Rome, this condemned people (the Jews) had their fenced cities and cedar palaces, their splendid Temple, their fleets of merchant ships, their schools of sacred learning, their great statesmen and soldiers, their natural philosophers, their historians and their poets. What nation ever contended more manfully against overwhelming odds for its independence and religion? What nation ever, in its last agonies, gave such signal proofs of what may be accomplished by a brave despair?   *Ibid.*

Let us do justice to them (the Jews). Let us open to them the doors of the House of Commons. Let us open to them every career in which ability and energy can be displayed. Till we have done this, let us not presume to say that there is no genius among the countrymen of Isaiah, no heroism among the descendants of the Maccabees.   *Ibid.*

When the sceptre shall have passed away from England; when, perhaps, travellers from distant regions shall in vain labor to decipher on some mouldering pedestal the name of our proudest chief; shall hear savage hymns chanted to some misshapen idol, over the ruined dome of our proudest temple; and shall see a single naked fisherman wash his nets in the river of the ten thousand masts; her (Athens') influence and her glory will still survive, fresh in eternal youth.

Knight's Quarterly Magazine, 1829; critique of Mitford's "Greece."

She (the Roman Catholic Church) saw the commencement of all the governments and of all the ecclesiastical institutions that now exist in the world; and we feel no assurance that she is not destined to see the end of them all. She was great and respected before the Saxon had set foot in Britain, before the Frank had crossed the Rhine, when Grecian eloquence still flourished in Antioch, when idols were still worshipped in the temple of Mecca. And she may still exist in undiminished vigour when some traveler from New Zealand shall, in the midst of a vast solitude, take his stand on a broken arch of London Bridge to sketch the ruins of St. Paul's.

Essay, On Ranck's "History of the Popes," 1840.

What are laws but the expressions of the opinion of some class which has power over the rest of the community? By what was the world ever governed but by the opinion of some person or persons? By what else can it ever be governed?

Southey's Colloquies, 1830.

Every sect clamors for toleration when it is down.

Sir John Macintosh's History of the Revolution, 1835.

The doctrine which, from the very first origin of religious dissensions, has been held by bigots of all sects, when condensed into a few words and stripped of rhetorical disguise, is simply this: I am in the right, and you are in the wrong. When you are the stronger, you ought to tolerate me; for it is your duty to tolerate truth. But when I am the stronger I shall persecute you; for it is my duty to persecute error. *Ibid.*

The Roman Church is filled with men who are led into it merely by ambition, who, though they might have been useful and respectable as laymen, are hypocritical and immoral. *Letter from Rome, 1838.*

For political and intellectual freedom, and for all the blessings which political and intellectual freedom have brought in their train, she (England) is chiefly indebted to the great rebellion of the laity against the priesthood.

History of England, 1848-1855.

Thus our democracy was, from an early period, the most aristocratic, and our aristocracy the most democratic in the world. *Ibid.*

In every age the vilest specimens of human nature are to be found among demagogues. *Ibid.*

The . . . spirit which made the Jesuit regardless of his ease, of his liberty, and of his life, made him also regardless of truth and of mercy. No means which could promote the interests of his order seemed to him unlawful. . . . In the most atrocious plots recorded in history his agency could be distinctly traced. . . . He was in some countries the most dangerous enemy of freedom. *Ibid.*

The Puritan hated bear-baiting, not because it gave pain to the bear, but because it gave pleasure to the spectators. *Ibid.*

I have not the slightest doubt that, if we had a purely democratic government here, the effect would be the same. Either the poor would plunder the rich, and civilisation would perish, or order and property would be saved by a strong military government, and liberty would perish.

Letter to Henry S. Randall, an American friend, May 23, 1857.

I have long been convinced that institutions purely democratic must, sooner or

later, destroy liberty, or civilization, or both.
Ibid.

Either some Caesar or Napoleon will seize the reins of government with a strong hand; or your republic will be as fearfully plundered and laid waste by barbarians in the Twentieth century as the Roman Empire was in the Fifth—with this difference ... that your Huns and Vandals will have been engendered within your own country by your own institutions. *Ibid.*

American democracy must be a failure because it places the supreme authority in the hands of the poorest and most ignorant part of society. In England there is plenty of grumbling in bad years, and sometimes a little rioting, but it matters little, for here the sufferers are not the rulers. The supreme power is in the hands of a select class, deeply interested in the security of property and the maintenance of order.
Accordingly, the malcontents are firmly restrained. The bad time is got over without robbing the wealthy to relieve the indigent.
Quoted by F. D. Roosevelt, August, 1937.

There is no malice like the malice of the renegade.

In truth, of all the intellectual weapons which have been wielded by man, the most terrible was the mockery of Voltaire. Bigots and tyrants, who had never been moved by the wailings and cursing of millions, turned pale at his name.

Even the law of gravitation would be brought into dispute were there a pecuniary interest involved.

Many politicians of our time are in the habit of laying it down as a self-evident proposition, that no people ought to be free till they are fit to use their freedom. The maxim is worthy of the fool in the old story,

who resolved not to go into the water till he had learned to swim. If men are to wait for liberty till they become wise and good in slavery, they may indeed wait forever.

Niccolò Machiavelli*
(1469-1527)
Italian statesman, political writer

Hence it comes about that all armed Prophets have been victorious, and all unarmed Prophets have been destroyed.
The Prince (Il Principe), ch. 6.

In taking possession of a state the conqueror should well reflect as to the harsh measures that may be necessary, and then execute them at a single blow. ... Cruelties should be committed all at once.
Ibid., ch. 8.

From this arises the question whether it is better to be loved rather than feared, or feared rather than loved. It might perhaps be answered that we should wish to be both: but since love and fear can hardly exist together, if we must choose between them, it is far safer to be feared than loved. *Ibid.*

A prince, then, should have no other thought or object so much at heart, and make no other thing so much his special study, as the art of war and the organization and discipline of his army; for this is the only art that is expected of him who commands. *Ibid.*

It is essential for a prince to be on a friendly footing with his people, since, otherwise, he will have no resource in adversity. *Ibid.*

---

* "I affirm that the doctrine of Machiavelli is more alive today than it was four centuries ago." Mussolini, 1924.

Let no one quote against me the old proverb, "He who builds on the people builds on sand," for that may be true of a private citizen who presumes on his favor with the people, and counts on being rescued by them when overpowered by his enemies or by the magistrates. But a prince who is a man of courage and is able to command, who knows how to preserve order in his state, need never regret having founded his security on the affection of the people. *Ibid.*

It may be said of men in general that they are ungrateful and fickle, dissemblers, avoiders of danger, and greedy of gain. So long as you shower benefits upon them, they are all yours; they offer you their blood, their substance, their lives and their children, provided the necessity for it is far off; but when it is near at hand, then they revolt. *Ibid., ch. 17.*

The prince who relies upon their words, without having otherwise provided for his security, is ruined; for friendships that are won by awards, and not by greatness and nobility of soul, although deserved, yet are not real, and cannot be depended upon in time of adversity. *Ibid.*

Men have less hesitation in offending one who makes himself beloved than one who makes himself feared; for love holds by a bond of obligation which, as mankind is bad, is broken on every occasion whenever it is for the interest of the obliged party to break it. But fear holds by the apprehension of punishment, which never leaves men. *Ibid.*

A sagacious prince then cannot and should not fulfill his pledges when their observance is contrary to his interest, and when the causes that induced him to pledge his faith no longer exist. If men were all good, then indeed this precept would be bad; but as men are naturally bad, and will not observe their faith towards you, you must, in the same way, not observe yours to them; and no prince ever yet lacked legitimate reasons with which to color his want of good faith. *Ibid., ch. 18.*

It is necessary that the prince should know how to color his nature well, and how to be a great hypocrite and dissembler. For men are so simple, and yield so much to immediate necessity, that the deceiver will never lack dupes. *Ibid.*

A prince then should look mainly to the successful maintenance of his state. The means which he employs for this will always be accounted honorable, and will be praised by everybody; for the common people are always taken by appearances and by results, and it is the vulgar mass that constitutes the world. *Ibid.*

I judge impetuosity to be better than caution; for Fortune is a woman, and if you wish to master her, you must strike and beat her. *Ibid.*

The Church has ever kept and keeps our country divided.
Discourses on the First Ten Books of Titus Livius.

Politics have no relation to Morals.
Ibid.

Our religion has glorified those of meek and contemplative character rather than those of action. Further, it places the highest good in humility, lowliness, and the contempt for worldly things. . . . This manner of life, then, seems to have rendered the world weak, and to have given it over as a prey to wicked men. *Ibid.*

Those Princes or Republics that would save themselves from growing corrupt should above all else keep uncorrupted the ceremonies of religion, holding them always in veneration. For there can be no surer sign of decay in a country than to see the rites of religion held in contempt. *Ibid.*

In the opinion of all who have written about civil government, and according to the experience of all history, whoever prepares to establish a commonwealth and prescribe laws, must presuppose all men naturally bad, and that they will yield to their innate evil passions, as often as they can do so with safety; and though those passions may lie concealed for a time, they spring up from some hidden cause, of which we can give no account; but Time then discovers them, and is therefore justly called the "Father of Truth." *Ibid., i, c. 3.*

It is therefore the duty of princes and heads of republics to uphold the foundations of the religion of their countries, for then it is easy to keep their people religious, and consequently well conducted and united. And therefore everything that tends to favor religion (even though it were believed to be false) should be received and availed of to strengthen it; and this should be done the more, the wiser the rulers are, and the better they understand the natural course of things. *Ibid., i, 12.*

And certainly, if the Christian religion had from the beginning been maintained according to the principles of its founder, the Christian states and republics would have been much more united and happy than what they are. Nor can there be a better proof of its decadence than to witness the fact that the nearer people are to the Church of Rome, which is the head of our religion, the less religious are they. *Ibid.*

The evil example of the court of Rome has destroyed all piety and religion in Italy. *Ibid.*

And as the strict observance of religious worship is the cause why states rise to eminence, so contempt for religion brings ruin on them. For where the fear of God is wanting, destruction is sure to follow, or else it must be sustained by the fear felt for their prince, who may thus supply the want of religion in his subjects. Whence it arises that the kingdoms, that depend only on the virtue of a mortal, have a short duration; it is seldom that the virtue of the father survives in the son. *Ibid., i, c. 11.*

The records of ancient history furnish many examples to show how difficult it is for a people brought up under a prince to preserve its liberty, if by accident it is attained . . . and not by reason; for the people resemble a wild beast,* which, naturally fierce, and accustomed to live in the woods has been brought up, as it were, in a prison and in servitude, and having by accident got its liberty, not being accustomed to search for its food, and not knowing where to conceal itself, easily becomes the prey of the first who seeks to incarcerate it again. *Ibid., i, c. 16.*

He who desires or attempts to reform the government of a state, and wishes to have it accepted and capable of maintaining itself to the satisfaction of everybody, must at least retain the semblance of the old forms; so that it may seem to the people that there has been no change in the institutions, even though in fact they are entirely different from the old ones. *Ibid., c. 25.*

For the great majority of mankind are satisfied with appearances, as though they were realities, and are often more influenced by the things that seem than by those that are. *Ibid.*

---

* Cf., Campanella, Alexander Hamilton.

It is well observed by writers on civil policy that those people are more cruel and vindictive who have lost and recovered their liberty, than those who have preserved it as handed down by their fathers.
Ibid., i, c. 28.

Whenever men are not obliged by necessity to fight, they fight from ambition.
Ibid., i, c. 37.

He who takes upon himself a tyranny, and does not slay Brutus, and he who makes a free state, and does not slay the sons of Brutus, maintains his work only for a short time. *Ibid., iii, c. 3.*

It seldom happens that men rise from low conditions to high rank without employing either force or fraud, unless that rank should be attained either by gift or inheritance. *Ibid., c. 13.*

Nor do I believe that there was ever a man who from obscure condition arrived at great power by merely employing open force; but there are many who have succeeded by fraud alone. *Ibid.*

Though fraud in all other actions be odious, yet in matters of war it is laudable and glorious, and he who overcomes his enemies by stratagem is as much to be praised as he who overcomes them by force. *Ibid., iii. c. 40.*

For when on the decision to be taken wholly depends the survival of one's country, no consideration should be given either to justice or injustice, to kindness or cruelty, or to its being praiseworthy or ignominious, but rather, any other thought being set aside, that alternative should be followed utterly which will save its existence and preserve its freedom.
Op. cit., quoted by Giorgio de Santillana, The Age of Adventure.

You cannot govern states with words.*

How perilous it is to free a people who prefer slavery.

Before all else, be armed.

When the material (the people, or masses) is corrupt, it is easy for the Prince to act.

Domestic revolutions are most commonly occasioned by people who have property, because the fear of losing what they have begets in them the same passions that burn in the hearts of those who desire to seize property, because men think they own securely only those things that they have taken or defended successfully from others.

You do not know the unfathomable cowardice of humanity . . . servile in the face of force, pitiless in the face of weakness, implacable before blunders, indulgent before crimes . . . and patient to the point of martyrdom before all the violences of bold despotism.

One of the great secrets of the day is to know how to take possession of popular prejudices and passions, in such a way as to introduce a confusion of principles which makes impossible all understanding between those who speak the same language and have the same interests.

Never was anything great achieved without danger.

For *our* country, wrong is right.

Men, yron, money and bread be the strengthe of the warre, but of these fower, the first two be most necessarie; because men and yron fynde money and bread; but bread and money fynde not men and yron.
The Art of War, English translation, 1586.

---

* "With words we govern men." Disraeli.

Sir Halford (John) Mackinder

(1861-1947)

English writer

Who rules East Europe commands the Heartland: Who rules the Heartland commands the World-Island: Who rules the World-Island commands the World.
Democratic Ideals and Reality, Constable, 1919.

Archibald MacLeish

(1892-1982)

American poet

The remedy in the United States is not less liberty but real liberty—an end to the brutal intolerance of churchly hooligans and flag-waving corporations and all the rest of the small but bloody despots who have made the word Americanism a synonym for coercion and legal crime.
The Nation, December 4, 1937.

The dissenter is every human being at those moments of his life when he resigns momentarily from the herd and thinks for himself.
In Praise of Dissent. N. Y. Times Book Review, December 16, 1956.

What is freedom? Freedom is the right to choose: the right to create for oneself the alternatives of choice. Without the possibility of choice and the exercise of choice a man is not a man but a member, an instrument, a thing.
A Declaration of Freedom, written for Freedom House.

How shall freedom be defended? By arms when it is attacked by arms; by truth when it is attacked by lies; by democratic faith when it is attacked by authoritarian dogma.

Always, and in the final act, by dedication and faith. *Ibid.*

Freedom is the right to one's dignity as a man. *Ibid.*

The complete freedom of the dissenting spirit to be heard . . .
Ed Murrow TV interview, December, 1958.

The perversion of the mind is only possible when those who should be heard in its defense are silent.
The Irresponsibles, 1940.

Man can live his truth, his deepest truth, but he cannot speak it. It is for this reason that love becomes the ultimate human answer to the ultimate human question.
Time, December 22, 1958.

Love in reason's terms, answers nothing. We say that *Amor vincit omnia* but in truth love conquers nothing—certainly not death—certainly not chance. *Ibid.*

What love does is to arm. It arms the worth of life in spite of life . . . *Ibid.*

The infantile cowardice of our time which demands an external pattern, a non-human authority . . .

We have no choice but to be guilty. God is unthinkable if we are innocent.
J. B., 1958.

Guilt matters. Guilt must always matter. Unless guilt matters the whole world is Meaningless. *Ibid.*

God help that country where informers thrive!
Where slander flourishes and lies contrive:—
Kill truth by whispers and keep fraud alive.
N. Y. Herald Tribune.

Henry Dunning Macleod
(1821-1902)
Scottish economist

Gresham's Law (i.e., Bad money drives out good).
Phrase coined in 1857, in the mistaken impression that Sir Thomas Gresham had explained it in 1558.

John (Albert) Macy
(1877-1932)
American critic, biographer

The Old Testament is tribal in its provinciality; its god is a local god, and its village police and sanitary regulations are erected into eternal laws.
The Spirit of American Literature.

Salvador de Madariaga
(1886-1978)
Spanish writer

He is free . . . who knows how to keep in his own hands the power to decide, at each step, the course of his life, and who lives in a society which does not block the exercise of that power.
N. Y. Times, January 29, 1957.

No one has ever succeeded in keeping nations at war except by lies.

Charles A. Madison
(b. 1895)
American writer, editor

Marx's great achievement was to place the system of capitalism on the defensive.
Critics and Crusaders, p. 447.

A radical may be many things and he may be moved by complex motives, but in the last analysis he is an idealist who feels impelled to right existing wrongs. His rebelliousness may be a form of compensation for suffering from authority or poverty, from thwarted ambition or personal maladjustment. But while others who are similarly conditioned, yet lack the noble impulse, become gangsters or millionaires, clowns or cranks, the radical is driven by a messianic urge to remake the world.
Ibid., p. 529.

James Madison
(1751-1836)
4th President of the United States

The most common and durable source of faction has been the various and unequal distribution of property.
The Federalist, No. 10.

Those who hold and those who are without property have ever formed distinct interests in society.   *Ibid.*

A landed interest, a manufacturing interest, a mercantile interest, a money interest, with many lesser interests, grow up of necessity in civilized nations and divide them into different classes actuated by different sentiments and views. The regulation of these various and interfering interests forms the principal task of modern legislation . . .   *Ibid.*

The apportionment of taxes on the various descriptions of property is an act which seems to require the most exact impartiality; yet there is, perhaps, no legislative act in which greater opportunity and temptation are given to a predominant party to trample on the rules of justice.   *Ibid.*

A pure democracy, by which I mean a society consisting of a small number of citizens, who assemble and administer the government in person, can admit of no cure for the mischiefs of faction. *Ibid.*

However small the republic may be, the representatives must be raised to a certain number, in order to guard against the cabals of a few; and that, however large it may be, they must be limited to a certain number, in order to guard against the confusion of a multitude. In an equal degree does the increased variety of parties comprised within the Union, increase this security. *Ibid.*

From the protection of different and unequal faculties of acquiring property, the possession of different degrees and kinds of property immediately results; and from the influence of these on the sentiments and views of the respective proprietors, ensues a division of the society into different interests and parties. *Ibid.*

The two great points of difference between a democracy and a republic are: first, the delegation of the government, in the latter, to a small number of citizens, elected by the rest; secondly, the greater number of citizens, and greater sphere of country, over which the latter may be extended. *Ibid.*

In a democracy the people meet and exercise the government in person; in a republic they assemble and administer it by their representatives and agents. A democracy, consequently, will be confined to a small spot. A republic may be extended over a large region. *Ibid., No. 14.*

As treason may be committed against the United States, the authority of the United States ought to be enabled to punish it. But as newfangled and artificial treasons have been the great engines by which violent factions, the natural offspring of free government, have usually wreaked their alternate malignity on each other, the convention have, with great judgment, opposed a barrier to this peculiar danger, by inserting a constitutional definition of the crime, fixing the proof necessary for conviction of it, and restraining the Congress, even in punishing it, from extending the consequences of guilt beyond the person of its author. *Ibid., No. 43.*

Justice is the end of government. It is the end of civil society. It ever has been and ever will be pursued until it is obtained, or until liberty be lost in the pursuit.
Ibid., No. 51.

We hold it for a fundamental and undeniable truth "that religion, or the duty which we owe our Creator, and the manner of discharging it, can be directed only by reason and conviction, not by force or violence." The religion, then, of every man must be left to the conviction and conscience of every man: and it is the right of every man to exercise it as these may dictate.
A Memorial and Remonstrance, addressed to the General Assembly of the Commonwealth of Virginia, 1785.

It is proper to take alarm at the first experiment on our liberties. We hold this prudent jealousy to be the first duty of citizens, and one of the noblest characteristics of the late Revolution. The freedom of America did not wait till usurped power had strengthened itself by exercise and entangled the question in precedents. They saw all the consequences in the principle, and they avoided the consequences by denying the principle. *Ibid.*

Who does not see that the same authority which can establish Christianity in exclusion of all other religions may establish, with the same ease, any particular sect of

Christians in exclusion of all other sects? That the same authority which can force a citizen to contribute threepence only of his property for the support of any one establishment may force him to conform to any other establishment in all cases whatsoever?
Ibid.

Experience witnesseth that ecclesiastical establishments, instead of maintaining the purity and efficacy of religion, have had a contrary operation. During almost fifteen centuries has the legal establishment of Christianity been on trial. What has been its fruits? More or less, in all places, pride and indolence in the clergy; ignorance and servility in the laity; in both, superstition, bigotry and persecution. *Ibid.*

What influence, in fact, have ecclesiastical establishments had on society? In some instances they have been seen to erect a spiritual tyranny on the ruins of the civil authority; on many instances they have been seen upholding the thrones of political tyranny; in no instance have they been the guardians of the liberties of the people. Rulers who wish to subvert the public liberty may have found an established clergy convenient auxiliaries. A just government, instituted to secure and perpetuate it, needs them not. *Ibid.*

I believe there are more instances of the abridgment of the freedom of the people by gradual and silent encroachments of those in power than by violent and sudden usurpations.
Address, Virginia Convention, June 16, 1788.

On a candid examination of history, we shall find that turbulence, violence, and abuse of power, by the majority, have produced factions and commotions which, in republics, have, more frequently than any other cause, produced despotism. *Ibid.*

A popular Government, without popular information, or the means of acquiring it, is but a Prologue to a Farce or a Tragedy; or, perhaps both.
Letter to W. T. Barry, August 4, 1832.

In the Papal System, Government and Religion are in a manner consolidated, and that is found to be the worst of Government.
To "the Reverend Adams," 1832.

To the press alone, chequered as it is with abuses, the world is indebted for all the triumphs which have been gained by reason and humanity over error and oppression.
Justice Douglas, An Almanac of Liberty.

The truth is that all men having power ought to be mistrusted. *Tribune, London.*

We are free today substantially, but the day will come when our Republic will be an impossibility. It will be an impossibility because wealth will be concentrated in the hands of a few. A Republic cannot stand upon bayonets, and when the day comes, when the wealth of the nation will be in the hands of a few, then we must rely upon the wisdom of the best elements in the country to readjust the laws of the nation to the changed conditions.
Quoted, New York Post.

Maurice Maeterlinck
(1862-1949)
Belgian dramatist, essayist

Every progressive spirit is opposed by a thousand men appointed to guard the past. . . . The least that the most timid among us can do is not to add to· the immense deadweight (conservatism) that nature drags along.

Il n'y a pas de morts. (There are no dead.)
The Blue Bird, iv, ii.

Ferdinand Magellan
(1480?-1521)
Portuguese navigator

The church says the earth is flat, but I know that it is round, for I have seen the shadow on the moon, and I have more faith in a shadow than in the church.
Cardiff, What Great Men Think of Religion.

Magna Carta

39. No freeman shall be taken, or imprisoned, or outlawed, or exiled, or in any way harmed, nor will we go upon him nor will we send upon him, except by the legal judgment of his peers or by the law of the land.
40. To none will we sell, to none deny or delay, right or justice.

The Mahabharata
Hindu epic poem

This is the sum of all true righteousness: deal with others as thou wouldst thyself be dealt by. Do nothing to thy neighbor which thou wouldst not have him do to thee hereafter.

Alfred Thayer Mahan
(1840-1914)
American naval historian and theorist

Self-interest is not only a legitimate but a fundamental cause for national policy, one which needs no cloak of hypocrisy.
Quoted in Society and Thought in Modern America.

Governments are corporations and corporations have no souls . . . Commercial and industrial predominance forces a nation to seek markets, and where possible to control them to its own advantage by prepondering force, the ultimate expression of which is possession.
The Interest of America in International Conditions, 1908.

An inevitable link in a chain of logical sequences: industry, markets, control, navy bases. *Ibid.*

Force is never more operative than when it is known to exist but is not brandished.
Time, August 4, 1958.

Norman Mailer
(b. 1923)
American writer

The natural role of twentieth-century man is anxiety.
General Cummings, in The Naked and the Dead.

. . . the indispensable requirement for a good newspaperman—as eager to tell a lie as the truth.
N. Y. Times Book Review, January 27, 1956.

Maistre
See de Maistre

Bronislaw Malinowski
(1884-1942)
Anglo-Polish anthropologist

Speaking in terms of evolution, we find that war is not a permanent institution of mankind. If we define war as an instrument of national policy, as an effective way of obtaining the fruits of victory by means of organized force, war has not always been in existence. The chaotic brawls, the internecine fighting of the lowest savages have nothing in common with the institution of war.

Address, Phi Beta Kappa, Harvard, September 17, 1936.

Is war a biological necessity? As regards the earliest cultures the answer is emphatically negative. The blow of the poisonous dart from behind a bush, to murder a woman or a child in their sleep, is not pugnacity. Nor is head-hunting, body-snatching, or killing for food instinctive or natural. *Ibid.*

Turning to the wars of today and tomorrow, can we say that today man is pitting his strength, skill, courage or endurance against man? Certainly not! War has become a contest between machines, industrial enterprises and financial organizations.
Ibid.

The hero of the next war, the man who from the air destroys a whole peaceful township in its sleep with poison gas, is not expressing any biological characteristics of his organism, or showing any moral virtues.
Ibid.

André Malraux
(1901-1976)
French writer

The great mystery is not that we should have been thrown down here at random between the profusion of matter and that of the stars; it is that, from our very prison, we should draw from our own selves images powerful enough to deny our nothingness.
Man's Fate.

A break in the established order is never

the work of chance. It is the outcome of a man's resolve to turn life to account.
Ibid.

If man is not ready to risk his life, where is his dignity? *Ibid.*

A man becomes truly Man only when in quest of what is most exalted in him. True arts and cultures relate Man to duration, sometimes to eternity and make of him something other than the most favored denizen of a universe founded on absurdity.
Voices of Silence, 1953.

All art is a revolt against man's fate.
Ibid.

Culture is the sum of all the forms of art, of love and of thought, which, in the course of centuries, have enabled man to be less enslaved.
N. Y. Times, September 8, 1957.

The total sacrifice to a cause beyond his comprehension restored a richness to man.
Ibid.

Art is anti-destiny. *Ibid.*

Each of the masterpieces is a purification of the world, but their common message is that of their existence and the victory of each individual artist over his servitude, spreading like ripples on the sea of time, implementing art's eternal victory over the human situation. *Ibid.*

The next century's task will be to rediscover its gods. *Time, July 18, 1955.*

Communism destroys democracy. Democracy can also destroy Communism.
Interview, C. L. Sulzberger, N. Y. Times, June 23, 1958.

Thomas Robert Malthus
(1766-1834)
English minister, economist

Population, when unchecked, increases in a geometrical ratio.
Essay on the Principle of Population, 1798.

Subsistence only increases in an arithmetical ratio.   *Ibid.*

Hard as it may appear in individual cases, dependent poverty ought to be held disgraceful.   *Ibid.*

First, that food is necessary to the existence of man; Secondly, that the passion between the sexes is necessary, and will remain nearly in its present state. *Ibid.*

. . . that the power of population is indefinitely greater than the power in the earth to produce subsistence for man.
Ibid.

Other circumstances being the same, it may be affirmed that countries are populous according to the quantity of human food which they produce or can acquire, and happy according to the liberality with which this food is divided, or the quantity which a day's labour will purchase. *Ibid.*

Corn countries are more populous than pasture countries, and rice countries more populous than corn countries. But their happiness does not depend upon their being thinly or fully inhabited, upon their poverty or their richness, their youth or their age, but on the proportion which the population and the food bear to each other.   *Ibid.*

There is one right, which man is generally thought to possess, which I am confident he neither does, nor can, possess, a right to subsistence when his labour will not fairly purchase it. Our laws indeed say that he has this right, and bind the society to furnish employment and food to those who cannot get them in the regular market; but in so doing, they attempt to reverse the laws of nature.   *Ibid.*

Almost everything that has been hitherto done for the poor, has tended, as if with solicitous care, to throw a veil of obscurity over this subject and to hide from them the true cause of their poverty. When the wages of labour are hardly sufficient to maintain two children, a man marries and has five or six.   *Ibid.*

It is to the established administration of property, and to the apparently narrow principle of self-love, that we are indebted for all the noblest exertions of human genius, all the finer and more delicate emotions of the soul, for everything, indeed, that distinguishes the civilised man from the savage state.   *Ibid.*

Famine seems to be the last, the most dreadful resource of nature. The power of population is so superior to the power of the earth to provide subsistence . . . that premature death must in some shape or other visit the human race. The vices of mankind are active and able ministers of depopulation. . . . But should they fail in this war of extermination, sickly seasons, epidemical pestilence, and plague advance in terrible array, sweep off their thousands and tens of thousands. Should success still be incomplete, gigantic inevitable famine stalks in the rear, and with one mighty blow, levels the population with the food of the world.   *Ibid.*

Horace Mann
(1796-1859)
American educator

Be ashamed to die until you have won some victory for humanity.
Commencement oration, Antioch, 1859.

[463]

The Common School is the greatest discovery ever made by man.
Inscribed on bust, Hall of Fame.

If any man seeks for greatness, let him forget greatness and ask for truth, and he will find both. *On Achieving Greatness.*

Republics, one after another . . . have perished from a want of intelligence and virtue in the masses of the people. . . . If we do not prepare children to become good citizens; if we do not develop their capacities, if we do not enrich their minds with knowledge, imbue their hearts with love of truth and duty, and a reverence for all things sacred and holy, then our republic must go down to destruction, as others have gone before it; and mankind must sweep through another vast cycle of sin and suffering, before the dawn of a better era can arise upon the world.
N. Y. Times, September 15, 1953.

A human being is not, in any proper sense, a human being till he is educated.

Thomas Mann
(1875-1955)
German novelist, essayist

Every reasonable human being should be a moderate Socialist.
N. Y. Times, June 18, 1950.

Opinions cannot survive if one has no chance to fight for them.

But self-examination, if it is thorough enough, is nearly always the first step toward change. I was to discover that no one who learns to know himself remains just what he was before.

A harmful truth is better than a useful lie. *Quoted by Arthur Koestler.*

To be poised against fatality, to meet adverse conditions gracefully, is more than simple endurance; it is an act of aggression, a positive triumph. *Death in Venice.*

Nor is it possible to devote oneself to culture and declare that one is "not interested" in politics.
Freedom, edited by Ruth Nanda Anshen, Harcourt, 1940.

It was left for the Germans to bring about a revolution of a character never seen before: a revolution without ideas, opposed to ideas, to everything higher, better, decent, opposed to liberty, truth, and justice. Nothing like it has ever occurred in human history.
Diary; requoted, Treasury for the Free World, Arco, 1946.

That the whole of art is inclined to lead to the bottomless pit is only too certain. But art, in spite of its connection with death and beauty, is still a wonderful way associated with life, and finds in itself the antitoxin; friendliness and benevolence toward life make up the artist's fundamental instinct. He must possess to a certain degree the sense of citizenship in life and ethics, in spite of art and virtue having so little in common, if he is to be at all eligible for social intercourse. The artist, so it seems to me, is in reality the (ironical!) mediator between the realms of death and life . . .

An artist who has not a moral feeling for life is an impossibility . . . even when it produces a work which is furthest remote from life.

Henry Edward Manning
(1808-1892)
English Cardinal

Either Rome or license of thought and will.
Letter to Hope-Scott, Britannica, 11th ed.

Every man has a right to work or to bread. *Ibid.*

I acknowledge no civil power; I am subject of no prince; I claim more than this —I claim to be the supreme judge and director of the conscience of men—of the peasant that tills the field, and of the prince that sits upon the throne; of the household of privacy, and legislator that makes laws for kingdoms; I am the sole, last supreme judge of what is right and wrong.

Sermon, Pro-Cathedral at Kensington; quoted by Sinclair, The Profits of Religion, p. 118.

A starving man has a natural right to his neighbor's bread.

Politics are a part of morals.

The future of Catholicism is in America.

A forced faith is a hypocrisy hateful to God and man. *Statement, to Gladstone.*

William Murray, 1st Earl of Mansfield
(1705-1793)
Lord Chief Justice of England

The air of England has long been too pure for a slave, and every man is free who breathes it. Every man who comes to England is entitled to the protection of English law, whatever oppression he may heretofore have suffered, and whatever may be the colour of his skin.

Case of James Somersett, a Negro, 1772.

The constitution does not allow reasons of state to influence our judgment. God forbid it should! We must not regard political consequences, however formidable they might be; if rebellion were the certain consequence, we are bound to say, *"Justitia fiat, ruat coelum."* °

Rex v. Wilkes (publisher of the North Briton).

Katherine Mansfield
(1888-1932)
English writer, critic

Risk! Risk anything! Care no more for the opinion of others, for those voices. Do the hardest thing on earth for you. Act for yourself. Face the truth. *Journals.*

Manu
(c. 1200 B.C.)
Hindu poet

Iniquity, committed in this world, produces not fruit immediately, but, like the earth, in due season, and advancing by little and little, it eradicates the man who committed it.

He grows rich for a while through unrighteousness; then he beholds good things; then it is that he vanquishes his foes; but he perishes at length from his whole root upwards.

Justice, being destroyed, will destroy; being preserved, will preserve; it must never therefore be violated.

Mao Tse-tung
(1893-1976)
Chinese Communist leader

Armament is an important factor in war, but not the decisive factor. . . . Man, not material, forms the decisive factor.

Lecture, 1938. The Nation, April 16, 1955.

° "Let justice be done though the heavens fall." The usual quotation is *Fiat justitia, ruat coelum.*

War cannot be divorced from politics for a single moment. *Ibid.*

We are always revolutionists and never reformers.
To Edgar Snow; The Battle for Asia, 1941.

The people are like water and the army is like fish.
Aspects of China's Anti-Japanese Struggle, Bombay, 1948.

Communism is not love. Communism is a hammer which we use to crush the enemy.
Time, December 18, 1950.

Revolution is not a dinner party, nor an essay, nor a painting, nor a piece of embroidery; it cannot be advanced softly, gradually, carefully, considerately, respectfully, politely, plainly and modestly.
Ibid.

A revolution does not march a straight line. It wanders where it can, retreats before superior forces, advances wherever it has room, attacks whenever the enemy retreats or bluffs and, above all, is possessed of enormous patience.
Richard Hughes, N. Y. Times Magazine, September 21, 1958.

The policy of letting a hundred flowers blossom and a hundred schools of thought contend is designed to promote the flourishing of the arts and the progress of science; it is designed to enable a socialist culture to thrive in our land.
On the Correct Handling of Contradictions Among the People, February 27, 1957.

The main form of struggle is war, the main form of organization is the army. . . . Without armed struggle there would be no place for the proletariat, there will be no place for the people, there will be no place for the Communist Party, and there will be no victory in revolution.
25 Years of the Chinese Liberation Army, Peking, 1952.

Our determined policy is 70% self-development, 20% compromise and 10% fight the Japanese. *Time.*

Learn from the masses, and then teach them.

Jean Paul Marat
(1743-1793)
French Revolutionary leader

Of what use is political liberty to those who have no bread? It is of value only to ambitious theorists and politicians.
Letter to C. Desmoulins, June 24, 1790.

They accuse me of being cruel, who cannot even see an insect suffer, but when I find that, in order to spare a few drops of blood people risk shedding floods of it, I am indignant in spite of myself at our false maxims of humanity, and at our foolish regard for our cruel enemies; fools that we are, we fear to cause them a scratch. Let them but be masters one day and you will soon see them overrun the provinces, fire and sword in hand, striking down all those who offer them any resistance, massacring the friends of the country, slaughtering women and children, and reducing our cities to ashes. *Ami du Peuple, 121.*

Marcus Aurelius Antoninus
(121-180)
Roman emperor, philosopher

Opinion is the main thing which does good or harm in the world. It is our false opinions of things which ruin us.
Meditations.

We are born for cooperation, as are the feet, the hands, the eyelids, and the upper and lower jaws. *Ibid.*

I cannot comprehend how any man can want anything but the truth. *Ibid.*

In the whole constitution of man, I cannot see any virtue contrary to justice, whereby it may be resisted and opposed. *Ibid.*

Never value anything as profitable to thyself which shall compel thee to break thy promise, to lose thy self-respect, to hate any man, to suspect, to curse, to act the hypocrite, to desire anything which needs walls and curtains. *Ibid.*

The best way of avenging thyself is not to become like the wrong-doer. *Ibid.*

Everything that exists is in a manner the seed of that which will be. *Ibid.*

Live with the gods. *Ibid., iv, 27.*

Observe constantly that all things take place by change, and accustom thyself to consider that the nature of the Universe loves nothing so much as to change the things which are, and to make new things like them. *Ibid., 36.*

Do not think that what is hard for thee to master is impossible for man; but if a thing is possible and proper to man, deem it attainable by thee. *Ibid., vi, 19.*

One Universe made up of all that is; and one God in it all, and one principle of Being, and one Law, the Reason, shared by all thinking creatures, and one Truth. *Ibid., vii, 9.*

Men exist for the sake of one another. Teach them then or bear with them. *Ibid., viii, 59.*

Take heed lest thou become a Caesar indeed; lest the purple stain thy soul. *To his adopted father, the Emperor Antoninus Pius.*

William Learned Marcy
(1786-1857)
American lawyer, statesman

They see nothing wrong in the rule, that to the victors belong the spoils of the enemy.* *U.S. Senate, January, 1832.*

Victor Margueritte
(1866-1942)
French novelist

The Fascists cannot argue, so they kill.** *Oration, French Academy.*

Jacques Maritain
(1882-1973)
French philosopher, writer

"There must be religion for the people": this formula expresses in an exact though inverted form the same conception as the phrase of Marx that religion is the opiate of the people. Atheist communism is only bourgeois deism turned the other way round. *Freedom in the Modern World.*

Absolute atheism starts in an act of faith in reverse gear and is a full-blown religious commitment. Here we have the first internal inconsistency of contemporary atheism: it proclaims that all religion must necessarily vanish away, and it is itself a religious phenomenon. *The Range of Reason.*

---

* Origin of the phrase, "the spoils system."
** Another translation: "The Fascists kill because they cannot argue."

True civilization knows the price of human life but makes the imperishable life of man its transcendent supreme value. It does not fear death, it confronts death, it accepts risk, it requires self-sacrifice—but for aims that are worthy of human life, for justice, for truth, for brotherly love.

Man's Destiny in Eternity, Beacon Press.

Lester Markel

(1894-1977)

New York Sunday Times editor

What you *see* is news, what you *know* is background, what you *feel* is opinion.

While You Were Gone, 1946.

Edwin Markham

(1852-1940)

American poet

By a divine paradox, wherever there is one slave there are two. So in the wonderful reciprocities of being, we can never reach the higher levels until all our fellows ascend with us.

1902. Quoted in N.Y. Times Magazine.

There is no true liberty for the individual except as he finds it in the liberty of all. There is no true security for the individual except as he finds it in the security for all.

Ibid.

Tyrants, the tools begin to think;
And the long bondage, link by link,
Is breaking. Out of the ancient night
A new world rises, fast with might
A star breaks on the chaos—lo,
The shapes of the dark begin to go!

The Man With a Hope. Written for "Labor," Labor Day, 1922.

Behold, O World, the Toiling Man,
Breaking at last the ancient ban.
Behold, his brains!—so long his lack—
Must lift his burden from his back.
The hammers of thought within his brain
Must break at last the ancient chain. *Ibid.*

We are all blind until we see
    That in the human plan
Nothing is worth the making if
    It does not make the man.
                    Man-Making.

Why build these cities glorious
    If man unbuilded goes?
In vain we build the world unless
    The builder also grows.   *Ibid.*

Bowed by the weight of centuries he leans
Upon his hoe and gazes on the ground,
The emptiness of ages in his face,
And on his back the burden of the world.
Who made him dead to rapture and despair,
A thing that grieves not and that never
    hopes,
Stolid and stunned, a brother to the ox?
Who loosened and let down this brutal jaw?
Whose was the hand that slanted back this
    brow?
Whose breath blew out the light within this
    brain?

The Man With the Hoe, st. 1. (Copyright, Doubleday, Page & Co., 1899.)

Is this the thing the Lord God made and
    gave
To have dominion over sea and land;
To trace the stars and search the heavens
    for power;
To feel the passion of Eternity?
Is this the dream He dreamed who shaped
    the suns
And marked their ways upon the ancient
    deep?
Down all the stretch of Hell to its last gulf

There is no shape more terrible than this—
More tongued with censure of the world's
    blind greed—
More filled with signs and portents for the
    soul—
More fraught with menace to the universe.
               Ibid., st. 2.

What gulfs between him and the seraphim!
Slave of the wheel of labor, what to him
Are Plato and the swing of Pleiades?
               Ibid., st. 3.

Through this dread shape humanity
    betrayed,
Plundered, profaned and disinherited,
Cries protest to the Judges of the World,
A protest that is also prophecy.   *Ibid.*

O masters, lords and rulers in all lands,
How will the Future reckon with this Man?
How answer his brute question in that hour
When whirlwinds of rebellion shake the
    world?   *Ibid., st. 5.*

How will it be with kingdoms and with
    kings—
With those who shaped him to the thing
    he is—
When this dumb Terror shall reply to God,
After the silence of the centuries? *Ibid.*

Christopher Marlowe
(1564-1593)
English dramatist

I cannot read, and wish all books were
burnt. I am lean with seeing others eat. O,
that there would come a famine through all
the world, that all might die, and I live
alone! Then thou shoulds't see how fat I
would be.   *Envy, in "Faustus."*

Thinkst thou that I who saw the face of
God,

And tasted the eternal joys of heaven,
Am not tormented with ten thousand hells
In being deprived of everlasting bliss.
               Op. cit., i, 312.

Was this the face that launched a thousand
    ships,
And burned the topless towers of Ilium?
             Ibid., i, 1328.

I count religion but a childish toy,
And hold there is no sin but ignorance.
          The Jew of Malta, i, 14.

Accurst be he that first invented war.
    Conquests of Tamburlaine, i, 664.

Jean François Marmontel
(1723-1799)
French author

It is true you are not allowed to go out
of here, but inside the Bastille you are as
free as any man in the world.
    Quoting the Bastille governor.

George Catlett Marshall
(1880-1959)
American general, diplomat

In a democracy such as ours military
policy is dependent on public opinion.
    Yank, January 28, 1943.

Our policy is directed not against any
country or doctrine but against hunger,
poverty, desperation and chaos. Its purpose
should be the revival of a working economy
in the world so as to permit the emergence
of political and social conditions in which
free institutions can exist.
    *Address, Harvard, later known as "The
Marshall Plan."*

[469]

Wars are bred by poverty and oppression. Continued peace is possible only in a relatively free and prosperous world.

N. Y. Times Magazine.

John Marshall

(1755-1835)

Chief Justice, U.S. Supreme Court

The government of the United States has been emphatically termed a government of laws, and not of men. It will certainly cease to deserve this high appellation, if the laws furnish no remedy for the violation of a vested legal right.

Marbury v. Madison, 1 Cranch 137, 1803.

That the people have an original right to establish for their future government, such principles as, in their opinion, shall most conduce to their own happiness, is the basis in which the whole American fabric has been erected. *Ibid.*

The Constitution is either a superior, paramount law, unchangeable by ordinary means, or it is on a level with ordinary legislative acts, and like other acts, is alterable when the legislature shall please to alter it . . . Certainly all those who have framed written constitutions contemplate them as forming the fundamental and paramount law of the nation, and consequently the theory of every such government must be that an act of the legislature, repugnant to the constitution, is void. *Ibid.*

That the power to tax involves the power to destroy; that the power to destroy may defeat and render useless the power to create; that there is a plain repugnance, to confer on one government power to control the constitutional measures of another, which other, with respect to those very measures, is declared to be supreme over that which exerts the control, are propositions not to be denied.

McCulloch v. Maryland, 4 Wheaton 316 (1819).

(The states) have no power, by taxation or otherwise, to retard, impede, burden or in any manner control the operations of the constitutional laws enacted by Congress. *Ibid.*

A corporation is an artificial being, invisible, intangible, and existing only in the contemplation of the law. Being the mere creature of the law, it possesses only those properties which the charter of its creation confers on it, either expressly, or as incidental to its very existence. These are such as are supposed best calculated to effect the object for which it was created. Among the most important are immortality, and, if the expression be allowed, individuality; properties by which a perpetual succession of many persons are considered the same, and may act as a single individual.

Dartmouth College v. Woodward, 4 Wheaton 518 (1819).

This is a contract, the obligation of which can not be impaired without violating the Constitution of the United States. *Ibid.*

America was chosen to be, in many respects, and to many purposes, a nation; and for all these purposes, her government is complete; to all these objects, it is competent. The people have declared that in the exercise of all powers given for these objects it is supreme. It can, then, in effecting these objects legitimately control all individuals or governments within the American territory.

Cohens v. Virginia, 6 Wheaton 264 (1821).

The Constitution and laws of a State, so far as they are repugnant to the Constitution and laws of the United States, are absolutely void. These states are constituent parts of the United States; they are members of one great empire—for some purposes sovereign, for some purposes subordinate.

Ibid.

The principle which entitles the United States to the testimony of every citizen and the principle by which every witness is privileged not to accuse himself can neither of them be disregarded.

N. Y. Times report on the Fifth Amendment, April 1, 1956.

"Abe Martin"

See Frank McKinney Hubbard

Karl Marx

(1818-1883)

German Socialist, journalist

Dynamic principle.
Doctor's thesis, quoted by Edmund Wilson, To the Finland Station.

Philosophy makes no secret of the fact. Her creed is the creed of Prometheus—"In a word, I detest all the gods." This is her device against all deities of heaven or earth who do not recognize as the highest divinity the human self-consciousness itself. *Ibid.*

Religion is the sigh of the oppressed creature, the feeling of a heartless world, just as it is the spirit of unspiritual conditions. It is the opium of the people.°
Introduction, Critique of the Hegelian Philosophy of Right, Deutsch-Franzoesische Yahrbuecher, 1844.

° Another translation: "Religion is the soul

The first requisite for the people's happiness is the abolition of religion.   *Ibid.*

The emancipation of the Jews in its last significance is the emancipation of mankind from Judaism.
On the Jewish Question, 1844.

History does nothing; it "possesses *no* colossal riches"; it "fights no fight". It is rather *man*—real, living man—who acts, possesses and fights in everything. . . . History is *nothing* but the activity of man in pursuit of his ends.
The Holy Family (in collaboration with Engels), 1845.

XI. The philosophers have only *interpreted* the world in various ways; the point, however, is to *change* it.
Theses on Feuerbach, 1845 (published 1888).

Men's ideas are the most direct emanations of their material state.
The German Ideology, 1846.

A spectre is haunting Europe—the spectre of Communism. All the powers of old

of soulless conditions, the heart of a heartless world, the opium of the people."
The German text: *"Die Religion . . . ist das Opium des Volkes."*
In Russian, at the entrance of the Red Square: *"Religia opium dlya naroda."*
"Marx's position is widely misunderstood . . . When the essay in question was written opium was used in Europe almost exclusively for relieving pain . . . Marx was using the word 'opium' in *this* sense and *not* in the sense that religion is a stupefier deliberately administered to the people by agents of the ruling class"—*Weekly People* (official organ, Socialist Labor Party), January 31, 1959.

Europe have entered into a holy alliance to exorcise this spectre: Pope and Czar, Metternich and Guizot, French Radicals and German police-spies.

Manifesto of the Communist Party,
1848. °

The history of all hitherto existing society is the history of class struggles.   *Ibid.*

The bourgeoisie, wherever it has got the upper hand, has put an end to all feudal, patriarchal, idyllic relations. It has pitilessly torn asunder the motley feudal ties that bound man to his "natural superiors," and has left no other bond between man and man than naked self-interest, than callous "cash payment."   *Ibid.*

Lumpenproletariat.° °   *Ibid.*

The bourgeoisie has played a most revolutionary role in history.   *Ibid.*

The "dangerous class," the social scum, that passively rotting mass thrown off by the lower layers of old society, may, here and there, be swept into the movement by a proletarian revolution; its conditions of life, however, prepare it far more for the part of a bribed tool of reactionary intrigue.   *Ibid.*

Law, morality, religion, are to him (the proletarian) so many bourgeois prejudices, behind which lurk in ambush just as many bourgeois interests.   *Ibid.*

Modern bourgeois private property is the final and most complete expression of the system of producing and appropriating products that is based on class antagonisms, on the exploitation of the many by the few.

° In collaboration with Friedrich Engels.
° ° Literally "ragged," but translated as "stupid" proletariat, or "social scum."

In this sense, the theory of the Communists may be summed up in the single sentence: Abolition of private property.
    Ibid.

Our bourgeois, not content with having the wives and daughters of their proletarians at their disposal, not to speak of common prostitutes, take the greatest pleasure in seducing each other's wives.   *Ibid.*

Bourgeois marriage is in reality a system of wives in common.   *Ibid.*

Capital is therefore not a personal, it is a social power.   *Ibid.*

In proportion as the antagonism between the classes vanishes, the hostility of one nation to another will come to an end.
    Ibid.

Christian Socialism is but the holy water with which the priest consecrates the heartburnings of the aristocrat.   *Ibid.*

1. Abolition of property in land and application of all rents of land to public purposes.
2. A heavy progressive or graduated income tax.
3. Abolition of all right of inheritance.
4. Confiscation of the property of emigrants and rebels.
5. Centralization of credit in the hands of the state. . . .
6. Centralization of the means of communication and transport in the hands of the state.
7. Extension of factories and instruments of production owned by the state. . . .
8. Equal obligation to work. Establishment of industrial armies, especially for agriculture.
9. Combination of agriculture with manufacturing industries; gradual abolition of the distinction between town and country. . . .

10. Free education for all children in public schools. Abolition of child factory labor in its present form. Combination of education with industrial production, etc.
Ibid.

The Communists disdain to conceal their views and aims. They openly declare that their ends can be attained only by the forcible overthrow of all existing social conditions. Let the ruling classes tremble at a Communist revolution. The proletarians have nothing to lose but their chains. They have a world to win.
Workingmen of all countries, unite!
Ibid.

The demands of the workers will thus everywhere have to be guided by the concessions and measures of the democrats . . . Their battle cry must be: The Permanent Revolution.
Address, Communist League, March, 1850.

The honor does not belong to me for having discovered the existence either of classes in modern society or of the struggle between the classes. Bourgeois historians a long time before me expounded the historical development of this class struggle, and bourgeois economists the economic anatomy of classes.
Letter to Joseph Wedemeyer, March 5, 1852.

What was new on my part, was to prove the following:
1. that the existence of classes is connected only with certain historical struggles which arise out of the development of production;
2. that class struggle necessarily leads to the dictatorship of the proletariat;
3. that this dictatorship itself is only a

transition to the *abolition of all classes* and to a *classless society.* *Ibid.*

Hegel remarks somewhere that all great, historical facts and personages occur as it were, twice. He forgets to add: the first time as tragedy, the second as farce.
The Eighteenth Brumaire of Louis Bonaparte, 1852.

Men make their own history, but they do not make it just as they please; they do not make it under circumstances chosen by themselves, but under circumstances directly found, given, and transmitted from the past. *Ibid.*

The tradition of all the dead generations weighs like an incubus on the brain of the living.° *Ibid.*

The profound hypocrisy and inherent barbarism of bourgeois civilization lies unveiled before our eyes, turning from its home, where it assumes respectable forms, to the colonies, where it goes naked.
The British Rule in India, contribution, N. Y. Tribune,°° June 25, 1853.

All our inventions have endowed material forces with intellectual life, and degraded human life into a material force.
Speech, 1856.

History is the judge;—its executioner, the proletarian.
Speech to English Chartists, 1856, quoted by Wilson, To the Finland Station.

° Two other translations use the word "Alp" or "nightmare" for incubus.
°° "I have . . . pawned the last thing pawnable . . . I have no resources beyond the income from *The Tribune*, you will understand my situation." Letter to Engels, 1853.

The method of production of the material things of life generally determines the social, political and spiritual currents of life.
A Contribution to the Critique of Political Economy, 1859.

Art is always and everywhere the secret confession and, at the same time, the immortal movement of its time.   *Ibid.*

The writer must earn money in order to be able to live and to write, but he must by no means live and write for the purpose of making money.   *Herr Vogt, 1860.*

The freedom of the press consists primarily in not being a trade. The writer who degrades it by making it a material means deserves, as a punishment for his inner slavery, outer slavery—censorship; or rather his existence is already his punishment.
Ibid.

From the commencement of the titanic struggle in America, the working men of Europe felt instinctively that the Star Spangled Banner carried the destiny of their class.
Letter to Lincoln, November 29, 1865.

When an oligarchy of 300,000 Slaveholders dared to inscribe, for the first time in the annals of the World, Slavery on the banner of Armed Revolt, when on the very spots where hardly a century ago the idea of one great democratic Republic had first sprung up, whence the first declaration of the Rights of Man was issued, and the first impulse given to the European Revolution of the 18th Century, when on those very spots counter revolution . . . maintained "Slavery to be a beneficial institution, indeed, the only solution of the great problem of the relation of Labor and Capital," and cynically proclaimed property in Man "the corner-stone of the new Edifice," then

the Working Classes of Europe understood at once . . . that for the Men of Labor, with their hopes for the future, even their past conquests were at stake in that tremendous conflict on the other side of the Atlantic.   *Ibid.*

The Working Men of Europe feel sure that as the American War of Independence initiated a new era of ascendency for the Middle Class, so the American Anti-Slavery War will do for the Working Classes. They consider it an earnest of the epoch to come that it fell to the lot of Abraham Lincoln, the single-minded Son of the Working Class, to lead his Country through the matchless struggle for the rescue of the enchained Race and the Reconstruction of a Social World.   *Ibid.*

(What is your favorite virtue?) Simplicity.
(Your outstanding characteristic?) Singleness of purpose.
(Your idea of happiness?) To struggle.
(The vice you detest most?) Servility.
(Your favorite maxim?) *Homo sum, et humani nihil a me alienum puto.* Terence's: I am a man and nothing pertaining to man is alien to me.
(Your favorite motto?) *De omnibus dubitandum.* One must doubt everything.
Answers to questionnaire prepared by Marx's daughters, 1865.

Capital is dead labor, that vampire-like, only lives by sucking living labor.
Capital, 1867, published in 1887.

Capitalist production begets, with the inexorability of a law of nature, its own negation.   *Ibid.*

Follow your own bent, no matter what people say.   *Ibid.*

The road to Hell is paved with good intentions.   *Ibid.*

The establishment of a normal working day is the outcome of centuries of struggle between capitalist and worker. *Ibid.*

Within the ruling-classes themselves, a foreboding is dawning, that the present society is no solid crystal, but an organism capable of change, and is constantly changing. *Ibid.*

Capitalist production is not merely the production of commodities; it is essentially the production of surplus value. *Ibid.*

All surplus value, whatever particular (profits, interest, or rent) it may subsequently crystallize into, is in substance the materialization of unpaid labor. *Ibid.*

The secret of the self-expansion of capital resolves itself into having the disposal of a definite quantity of other people's unpaid labor. *Ibid.*

They mutilate the laborer into a fragment of a man, degrade him to the level of an appendage of a machine, destroy every remnant of charm in his work and turn it into a hated toil. *Ibid.*

They distort the conditions under which he works, subject him during the labor process to a despotism the more hateful for its meanness; they transform his lifetime into working time, and drag his wife and child beneath the wheels of the Juggernaut of capital. *Ibid.*

Labor in a white skin cannot be free as long as labor in a black skin is branded. *Ibid.*

Now the capitalist system buys children and young persons under age. Previously, the workman sold his own labor-power, which he disposed of nominally as a free agent. Now he sells wife and child. He has become a slave dealer.
Ibid., Moore and Aveling translation, 1887.

The separation of the intellectual powers of production from the manual labor, and the conversion of those powers into the might of capital over labor, is, as we have already shown, finally completed by modern industry erected on the foundation of machinery. *Ibid.*

Along with the constantly diminishing number of the magnates of capital, who usurp and monopolize all advantages of this process of transformation, grows the mass of misery, oppression, slavery, degradation, exploitation; but with this too grows the revolt of the working-class, a class always increasing in numbers, and disciplined, united, organized by the very mechanism of the process of capitalist production itself. The monopoly of capital becomes a fetter upon the mode of production, which has sprung up and flourished along with, and under it. Centralization of the means of production and socialization of labor at last reach a point where they become incompatible with their capitalist integument. This integument is burst asunder. The knell of capitalist private property sounds. The expropriators are expropriated. *Ibid.*

The policy of Russia is changeless. . . . Its methods, its tactics, its maneuvers may change, but the polar star of its policy—world domination—is a fixed star. *1867.*

Anyone who knows anything of history knows that great social changes are impossible without the feminine ferment. Social progress can be measured exactly by the social position of the fair sex (the ugly ones included.) *Letter, 1868.*

On that point I cannot speak in the name of the society (The International Association.) I myself am an Atheist.
Statement to R. Landor, N. Y. World, July 18, 1871.

In a higher phase of Communist society, when the enslaving subordination of the individual in the division of labor has disappeared, and with it also the antagonism between mental and physical labor; when labor has become not only a means of living, but itself the first necessity of life; when, along with the all-around development of individuals, the productive forces too have grown, and all the springs of social wealth are flowing more freely—it is only at that stage that it will be possible to pass completely beyond the narrow horizon of bourgeois rights, and for society to inscribe on its banners: *Jeder nach seinen Faehigkeiten, jedem nach seinen Beduerfnissen.* From each according to his abilities, to each according to his needs.*
Critique of the Gotha Program, 1875.

Philosophy stands in the same relation to the study of the actual world as onanism to sexual love.
Wilson, To the Finland Station, p. 190.

Those passions which are at once the most violent, the basest and the most abominable of which the human breast is capable: the furies of personal interest.
Ibid., p. 290.

I hope the bourgeoisie as long as they live will have cause to remember my carbuncles. *Letter to Engels, Ibid., p. 312.*

I, I am not a Marxist.
Ibid.; also, Reflex, November, 1917, p. 43.

---

* In 1848 Louis Blanc, the French Socialist, wrote: "From each according to his abilities, to each according to his needs."

The daily press and the telegraph which in a moment spreads inventions over the whole world, fabricate more myths . . . in a day than could have formerly been done in a century.   *Letter to Kugelmann.*

The conscience of man does not determine his existence; rather does his social existence determine his consciousness.
Quincy Howe, ACLU Bulletin, September, 1953.

Jenny! If we can but weld our souls together,
  then with contempt shall I fling my glove in the world's face,
then shall I stride through the wreckage a creator!*
    Poem, to Jenny von Westphalen.

The imaginary flowers of religion adorn man's chains. Man must throw off the flowers, and also the chains.
The Wisdom of Karl Marx, Simon Emler, editor, 1948.

The criticism of religion is the basis of all criticism.   *Ibid.*

Man makes religion, religion does not make man.   *Ibid.*

Religion is man's self-consciousness and self-estimation while he has not found his feet in the universe.   *Ibid.*

The abolition of religion, as the illusory happiness of the people, is the demand for their real happiness.   *Ibid.*

---

* Another version:
If we two can but weld our souls together,
Then with contempt I shall fling my glove in the world's face;
Then I, a creator, shall stride through the wreckage!

[476]

The machinery of labor strikes down the laborer. *Ibid.*

I have got so far that I could be finished with the whole economic crap in five weeks . . . This is beginning to bore me.
Ibid. (A reference to "Capital.")

Following is a short outline of the first part. The whole *Scheisse* is to be divided into six books. *Ibid.*

Force is the midwife of every old society pregnant with a new one.
Quoted by J. E. Hoover, Masters of Deceit, p. 345.

The existence of the State is inseparable from the existence of slavery.
Weekly People (S.L.P.), April 4, 1959.

The reactionary lusts and prejudices of the workers. *Quoted in Tribune, London.*

Capitalism will kill competition.

The rich will do everything for the poor but get off their backs.

He fears a great victory more than a great defeat.
(a reference to General McClellan.)

To say that the newspaper press represents public opinion is to administer insult to intelligent men. It is the property of speculators, political leaders, large contractors and railway directors.

Can we expect the truth through channels of falsehood, light from regions of darkness, or fairness from those whose business it is to calumniate, pervert and deceive? Certainly not. Hence the need of an organ that should be beyond taint of corruption, invulnerable against attacks and inspired by men who feel it their mission to teach the truth that they have acquired by hard toil and bitter suffering.

We do not say to the world: Cease struggling—your whole struggle is futile. All we do is to provide it with a true slogan of the struggle.

Maryland Colonial Assembly

By this Law, (1.) Blasphemy against GOD, denying our Saviour JESUS CHRIST to be the Son of GOD, or denying the Holy TRINITY, or the Godhead of any of the Three Persons, &c. was to be Punished with Death, and Confiscation of Lands and Goods to the Lord Proprietary.
An Act concerning Religion, passed April 21, 1649.

(2.) Persons using any reproachful Words or Speeches concerning the Blessed Virgin *Mary*, Mother of our Saviour, or the Holy Apostles or Evangelists, or any of them, for the 1st Offence to forfeit 5 £ Sterling to the Lord Proprietary; or, in default of Payment, to be publicly Whipped, and Imprisoned at the Pleasure of his Lordship, or his Lieut. General. *Ibid.*

(3.) Persons reproaching any other within the Province by the Name or Denomination of Heretic, Schismatic, Idolater, Puritan, Independent, Presbyterian, Popish Priest, Jesuit, Jesuited Papist, Lutheran, Calvinist, Anabaptist, Brownist, Antinomian, Barrowist, Round-Head, Separatist, or any other Name or Term, in a reproachful Manner, relating to matters of Religion, to forfeit 10 s. Sterling for each Offence; one half to the Person reproached, the other half to his Lordship: Or, in default of Payment, to be publicly Whipped, and suffer Imprisonment without Bail or Mainprize, until the Offender shall satisfy the Party reproached,

by asking him or her respectively Fore-
giveness publicly for such Offence. *Ibid.*

(5.) And whereas the enforcing of the
Conscience in Matters of Religion, hath
frequently fallen out to be of dangerous
Consequence in those Common Wealths
where it had been practiced, and for the
more quiet and peaceable Government of
this Province, and the better to preserve
mutual Love and Unity among the Inhabitants, &c. No person or Persons whatsoever,
within this Province, or the Islands, Ports,
Harbours, Creeks, or Havens, thereunto belonging, professing to believe in JESUS
CHRIST, shall from henceforth be any
Ways troubled, molested, or discounten-
anced, for, or in respect to his or her Religion, nor in the free exercise thereof,
within this Province, or the Islands thereunto belonging, nor any Way compelled to
the Belief or Exercise of any other Religion,
against his or her Consent, so as they be not
unfaithful to the Lord Proprietary, or molest
or conspire against the Civil Government
established, or to be established, in this
Province, under him or his Heirs. *Ibid.*

Thomas G. Masaryk
(1850-1937)
Czech patriot, first President

Dictators always look good until the last
minutes.

John Masefield
(1878-1967)
English writer

Man with the burning soul
Has but an hour of breath
To build a ship of truth
On which his soul may sail—
Sail on the sea of death,
For death takes toll

Of beauty, courage, youth,
Of all but truth.
> *Truth. Philip the King and Other
> Poems, Heinemann, 1914.*

Stripped of all purple robes,
Stripped of all golden lies,
I will not be afraid,
Truth will preserve through death.
Ibid.

Not of the princes and prelates with peri-
wigged charioteers
Riding triumphantly laurelled to lap the
fat of the years,
Rather the scorned—the rejected—the men
hemmed in with the spears;

The men of the tattered battalion which
fights till it dies,
Dazed with the dust of the battle, the din
and the cries,
The men with the broken heads and the
blood running into their eyes.
A Consecration.

Not the ruler for me, but the ranker, the
tramp of the road,
The slave with the sack on his shoulders
pricked on with the goad,
The man with too weighty a burden, too
weary a load. *Ibid.*

Others may sing of the wine and the wealth
and the mirth,
The portly presence of potentates goodly
in girth;—
Mine be the dirt and the dross, the dust
and the scum of the earth! *Ibid.*

Theirs be the music, the color, the glory,
the gold;
Mine be a handful of ashes, a mouthful of
mould.
Of the maimed, of the halt and the blind
in the rain and the cold.

Of these shall my songs be fashioned, my
tale be told.

AMEN.

Ibid.

Commonplace people dislike tragedy because they dare not suffer and cannot exult.
The Tragedy of Nan, preface.

The truth and rapture of man are holy
things, not lightly to be scorned. A carelessness of life and beauty marks the glutton,
the idler, and the fool in their deathy path
across history. *Ibid.*

O Lord, the sin,
Done for the things there's money in.

Success is the brand on the brow of the
man who has aimed too low.

George Mason

(1725-1792)

American Revolutionary leader

All men are created equally free and independent, and have certain inherent rights,
of which they cannot, by any compact, deprive or divest their posterity: among which
are the enjoyment of life and liberty, with
the means of acquiring and possessing property, and pursuing the obtaining happiness
and safety.
*First draft, Virginia Declaration of
Rights.*

That government is, or ought to be instituted for the common benefit, protection,
and security of the people, nation, or community; . . . and that when any government shall be found inadequate or contrary to these purposes, a majority of the
community hath an indubitable, unalienable, and indefeasible right to reform, alter

or abolish it, in such manner as shall be
judged conducive to the publick weal.
Ibid.

Freedom of the press is one of the bulwarks of liberty and can never lie restrained
but by despotic government.
Virginia Bill of Rights, 1776.

That all power is vested in, and consequently derived from, the people; that
magistrates are their trustees and servants,
and at all times amenable to them. *Ibid.*

That religion, or the duty which we owe
to our Creator, and the manner of discharging it, can be directed only by reason
and conviction, not by force or violence;
and therefore all men are equally entitled
to the free exercise of religion, according
to the dictates of conscience; and that it is
the mutual duty of all to practice Christian
forbearance, love, and charity towards each
other. *Ibid.*

André Masson

(b. 1896)

French artist

That which goes contrary to the prevailing taste is, for me, the most precious of
things . . . Whatever is scorned, despised
or not understood by the society in which
one lives has prospects for the future.
*1953; quoted, Atlantic Monthly, April,
1958.*

Edgar Lee Masters

(1868-1950)

American writer

Here! You sons of the men
Who fought with Washington at Valley
Forge,
And whipped Black Hawk at Starved Rock,

Arise! Do battle with the descendants of
those
Who bought land in the Loop when it was
waste land
And sold blankets and guns to the army of
Grant,
And sat in legislatures in the early days,
Taking bribes from the railroads!
    *English Thornton, in "Spoon River
    Anthology."*

Arise! Do battle with the fops and bluffs
The pretenders and figurantes of the society
    column
And the yokel souls whose daughters marry
    counts;
And the parasites on great ideas,
And the noisy riders of great causes,
And the heirs of ancient thefts.   *Ibid.*

He stripped off the armor of institutional
    friendships
To dedicate his soul
To the terrible deities of Truth and Beauty!
        Poem for R. G. Ingersoll.

He is sent to school
Little or much, where he imbibes the rule
Of safety first and comfort; in his youth
He joins the church and ends the quest of
    truth.
    *The Typical American? The Great
    Valley, Macmillan, 1916.*

            . . . upon my wall
I woke to see these words: he only wins
His freedom and existence who each day
Conquers them newly.
        The Radical's Message, ibid.

Henri Matisse
(1869-1954)
French post-impressionist painter

There is an inherent truth which must be
disengaged from the outward appearance
of the object to be represented. This is the
only truth that matters. . . . Exactitude is
not truth.
    *Preface to catalogue of exhibit, quoted
    in "Time."*

J. B. Matthews
(b. 1894)
American writer
and
R. E. Shallcross
(b. 1906)
American writer

In business, plunder is of the essence.
The springs of thought as well as the source
of physical life for the masses are poisoned
when poisoning is profitable, adulterated
when adulteration is profitable, and otherwise exploited in ways that blight and
despoil.
    *Partners in Plunder, copyright, Covici,
    Friede.*

Business is a . . . series of frauds, utilizing
methods, both in its production and distribution, which are indistinguishable in
spirit and effects from the practices of
gangsterism.   *Ibid.*

Advertising, in its spirit and purpose, is
germinal fascism. Hitler was the first European politician who saw the significance of
the techniques of commercial advertising
for politics. In *Mein Kampf* he uses the
distinctly commercial word "Reklame"—advertising—to describe his political method.
        Ibid.

T(homas) S(tanley) Matthews
(b. 1901)
American editor, writer

The Press is not our daily bread but our
daily sugar pill.
    *The Sugar Pill, Simon & Schuster,
    1959.*

W(illiam) Somerset Maugham
(1874-1965)
English novelist, dramatist

What mean and cruel things men do for the love of God. *A Writer's Notebook.*

Men are mean, petty, muddle-headed, ignoble, bestial from their cradles to their death-beds; ignorant, slaves now of one superstition, now of another, and illiberal; selfish and cruel. *Ibid.*

Art, if it is to be reckoned as one of the great values of life, must teach men humility, tolerance, wisdom and magnanimity. The value of art is not beauty, but right action. *Ibid.*

There are two good things in life—freedom of thought and freedom of action. *Of Human Bondage.*

Money is like a sixth sense—and you can't make use of the other five without it. *N. Y. Times Magazine, October 18, 1958.*

If a nation values anything more than freedom, it will lose its freedom; and the irony of it is that if it is comfort or money that it values more, it will lose that too. *Strictly Personal.*

Guy de Maupassant
(1850-1893)
French writer

We live always under the weight of the old and odious customs ... of our barbarous ancestors. *Sur l'Eau.*

Military men are the scourges of the world. *Ibid.*

Since governments take the right of death over other people, it is not astonishing if the people should sometime take the right of death over governments. *Ibid.*

Any government has as much of a duty to avoid war as a ship's captain has to avoid a shipwreck. *Ibid.*

Patriotism is a kind of religion; it is the egg from which wars are hatched. *My Uncle Sosthenes.*

Maupertuis
See de Maupertuis

François Mauriac
(1885-1970)
French novelist

Liberty, Equality, Fraternity, or *Death. Letters, 1944; quoted by A. J. Liebling, New Yorker, June 21, 1958.*

André Maurois
(1885-1967)
French writer

Men fear silence as they fear solitude, because both give them a glimpse of the terror of life's nothingness. *Quoted, N. Y. Times Magazine.*

Sergei Mayakovsky
(1893-suicide 1930)
One-time Soviet poet-laureate

Enough of living by laws
That Adam and Eve have left.
Hustle old history's horse
Left! Left! Left!
Quoted by Mark Gayn, The Nation, March 3, 1956.

Charles H. Mayo
(1865-1939)
American surgeon

Worry affects the circulation, the heart, the glands, the whole nervous system. I have never known a man who died from overwork, but many who died from doubt.
Quoted, American Mercury.

Giuseppe Mazzini
(1805-1872)
Italian Risorgimento leader

Your first duties—first as regards importance—are, as I have already told you, towards Humanity. You are *men* before you are either citizens or fathers. If you do not embrace the whole human family in your affection, if you do not bear witness to your belief in the Unity of that family, consequent upon the Unity of God . . . if, wheresoever a fellow-creature suffers, or the dignity of human nature is violated by falsehood or tyranny—you are not ready, if able, to aid the unhappy, and do not feel called upon to combat, if able, for the redemption of the betrayed or oppressed—you violate your law of life, you comprehend not that Religion which will be the guide and blessing of the future.
On the Duties of Man, 1844-58.

Country is not a mere zone of territory. The true country is the Idea to which it gives birth; it is the Thought of love, the sense of communion which unites in one all the sons of that territory. *Ibid.*

So long as a single one amongst your brothers has no vote to represent him in the development of the national life, so long as a single man, able and willing to work, languishes in poverty through want of work to do, you have no country in the sense in which country ought to exist—the country of all and for all. *Ibid.*

So long as you are ready to die for Humanity, the life of your country is immortal. *Ibid.*

Inexorable as to principles, tolerant and impartial as to persons.
Watchword for the Roman Republic, 1849.

The epoch of individuality is concluded, and it is the duty of reformers to initiate the epoch of association. Collective man is omnipotent upon the earth he treads. *Ibid.*

Mc
See also Mac

Joseph M. McCabe
(1867-1957)
English rationalist philosopher

Any body of men who believe in hell will persecute whenever they have the power.
What Gods Cost Men. Little Blue Books, #1732.

No Pope ever condemned slavery.
Christianity and Slavery. Ibid., #1127.

Not material or economic conditions in the ordinary sense, but perverse religious ideas explain the suspension of civilization in Europe from the 5th to the 12th century, and in the Mohammedan world after the 15th century.
Great Ideas Made Simple.

Mary McCarthy
(b. 1912)
American writer

The vast growth of the social life, steadily encroaching on both private and public life, has produced the eerie phenomenon of mass society, which rules everybody anonymously, just as bureaucracy, the rule of no one, has become the modern form of despotism.

The New Yorker, October 18, 1958.

David J. McDonald
(1902-1979)
*President, United Steelworkers
of America*

Democratic capitalism, combined with industrial democracy, is unquestionably the best way of life for mankind.

N. Y. Post, October 30, 1957.

Carl McGee
Editor, Albuquerque Tribune

Give Light and the People Will Find Their Own Way.

Slogan for Scripps-Howard papers. *

Claude McKay
(1890-1948)
American writer

O kinsmen; we must meet the common foe!
Though far outnumbered let us show us
    brave,
And for their thousand blows deal one
    death-blow!
What though before us lies the open grave?
Like men, we'll face the murderous,
    cowardly pack.
Pressed to the wall, dying, but fighting
    back!   *If We Must Die, 1919.*

---

* A paraphrase of Dante's *Purgatory*, XXII 67-69:
*Facesti come quei che va di notte
che porta il lume dietro
e a se no giova
ma dopo se fa le persone dotte.*

Although she feeds me bread of bitterness,
And sinks into my throat her tiger's tooth,
Stealing my breath of life, I will confess
I love this cultured hell that tests my youth.

America, 1921.

Ruth McKenney
(1911-1972)
American writer

Man has no nobler function than to defend the truth. *Letter to George Seldes.*

If modern civilization had any meaning it was displayed in the fight against Fascism.   *Ibid.*

William McKinley
(1843-1901)
25th President of the United States

War should never be entered upon until every agency of peace has failed.

Inaugural address, March 4, 1897.

You understand, Messrs. ambassadors, when we go to war it will be for humanity's sake.   *1898.*

For labor a short day is better than a short dollar.

Letter to Henry Cabot Lodge, September 8, 1900.

Lesley James McNair
(1883-1944)
American general

We must hate with every fiber . . . We must lust for battle; our object in life must be to kill; we must scheme and plan night and day to kill. There need be no pangs of conscience, for our enemies have lighted the way to faster, surer, crueler killing.

Time, December 7, 1942.

Carey McWilliams
(b. 1905)
American writer, editor of The Nation

I equate the function of critical journals of opinion with the spirit and method of science. Dissent is the journalist's way of asking the scientist's question: "Who says so?" "Can you prove it?" or, simply, "I don't believe it." It is the way by which individuals and societies protect themselves not only against oppressive orthodoxies but against foolish fallacies.

Gazette & Daily, January 19, 1957.

Modern secular societies are not without their own special tribal idols and their own brands of fetishism. Present-day advertising constitutes a form of sorcery that is often successful in inducing even well-educated people to believe that the moon is made of green cheese.   *Ibid.*

The value of dissent is not purely negative; it does more than protect us from error. It often points to the truth. One could make a good case for the proposition that the heroes of science, the arts, and the professions have been dissenters.   *Ibid.*

Margaret Mead
(1901-1978)
American anthropologist

The readings of history and anthropology in general give us no reason to believe that societies have built-in self-preservative systems. And therefore we can't say that man will be sensible enough not to destroy himself. He never has been sensible enough not to destroy himself, but he lived in small groups so that when he destroyed himself he didn't destroy everybody. So the necessity for new inventions for the conduct of the world cannot possibly be over-emphasized.

Conversation with Henry Brandon, New Republic, June 23, 1958.

George Meany
(b. 1894)
American labor leader

Sam Gompers once put the matter succintly. When asked what the labor movement wanted, he answered "More". If by a better standard of living we mean not only more money but more leisure and a richer cultural life, the answer remains "More." *

American labor has always championed academic freedom . . . Our fight here has been honest, not demagogic. Our motto here has been: intellectual heresy, yes; political conspiracy, no!

Address, Phi Beta Kappa Alumni, N. Y. C., March 13, 1957.

Communism of every type and stripe brings with it an ideological straightjacket. Thought control, brain-washing, censorship, imprisonment, exile, mental and physical torture are the indispensable weapons of Communist rule. Totalitarianism is soulless. That is why one of the brightest and most significant chapters in the history of the American labor movement is its unswerving policy of unrelenting opposition to all forms of totalitarianism—Naziism, Fascism, Falangism, Peronism and Communism—as the mortal enemies of human dignity, decency and freedom.   *Ibid.*

---

* Mr. Meany could not pinpoint this quotation; it is similar to a paragraph in his Phi Beta Kappa Alumni address.

Alexander Meiklejohn
(b. 1872)
American educator

In our popular discussions, unwise ideas must have a hearing as well as wise ones, dangerous ideas as well as safe, unAmerican as well as American.

Testimony, Hennings subcommittee of Senate Committee on Constitutional Liberties, November 14, 1955.

Whatever may be the immediate gains and losses, the dangers to our safety arising from political suppression are always greater than the dangers to that safety arising from political freedom. Suppression is always foolish. Freedom is always wise.   *Ibid.*

Richard B. Mellon
American industrialist
(1858-1933)

You can't mine coal without machine guns.

Testimony before Congressional Committee, quoted, Time, June 14, 1937.

Herman Melville
(1819-1891)
American novelist

Of all the preposterous assumptions of humanity over humanity, nothing exceeds most of the criticisms made on the habits of the poor by the well-housed, well-warmed, and well-fed.

Poor Man's Pudding and Rich Man's Crumbs. Harper's Magazine, 1854.

We Americans are the peculiar, chosen people—the Israel of our time—we bear the ark of liberties of the world.
White Jacket.

We are the pioneers of the world; the advance guard sent on through the wilderness of untried things to break a new path in the New World that is ours. In our youth is our strength; in our inexperience, our wisdom.   *Ibid.*

Yea and Nay—
Each hath his say;
But God He keeps the middle way.
N. Y. Times, February 18, 1951.

What plays the mischief with the truth is that men will insist upon the universal application of a temporary feeling or opinion.

They talk of the dignity of work. Bosh. The dignity is in leisure.

There is something in the contemplation of the mode in which America has been settled that, in a noble breast, should forever extinguish the prejudices of national dislikes.

Settled by the people of all nations, all nations may claim her for their own. You can not spill a drop of American blood without spilling the blood of the whole world. Be he Englishman, German, Dane, or Scot; the European who scoffs at an American, calls his own brother *Raca*, and stands in danger of the judgment.

We are not a narrow tribe of men . . . No: our blood is as the flood of the Amazon, made up of a thousand noble currents all pouring into one.

We are not a nation so much as a world.
Redburn.

There are certain queer times and occasions in this strange mixed affair we call life when a man takes his whole universe for a vast practical joke.   *Moby Dick.*

Menander
(342?-291? B.C.)
Greek comic dramatist

Marriage, to tell the truth, is an evil, but a necessary evil.   *Fragment.*

Everything is destroyed by its own particular vice: the destructive power resides within. Rust destroys iron, moths destroy clothes, the worm eats away the wood; but greatest of all evils is envy, impious habitant of corrupt souls, which ever was, is, and shall be a consuming disease.
Fragment 557; translated by Kathleen Freeman, Beacon Press.

No man to me is an alien, if he be good. Nature is one for all men, and it is character that creates kinship.
Ibid., Fragment 602.

Mencius (Meng-tse)
(372?-289? B.C.)
Chinese philosopher

To act without clear understanding, to form habits without investigation, to follow a path all one's life without knowing where it really leads—such is the behavior of the multitude.

H(enry) L(ouis) Mencken
(1880-1956)
American editor, writer

The smallest atom of truth represents some man's bitter toil and agony; for every ponderable chunk of it there is a brave truth-seeker's grave upon some lonely ash-heap and a soul roasting in hell.
Prejudices. First Series.

The one permanent emotion of the inferior man is fear—fear of the unknown, the complex, the inexplicable. What he wants beyond everything else is safety.
Ibid. Second Series.

No man ever quite believes in any other man.   *Ibid. Third Series.*

It doesn't take a majority to make a rebellion; it takes only a few determined leaders and a good cause.
Ibid. Fifth Series.

To die for an idea: it is unquestionably noble. But how much nobler it would be if men died for ideas that were true!
Ibid.

The thing constantly overlooked by those hopefuls who talk about abolishing war is that it is by no means an evidence of decay but rather a proof of health and vigor.
Minority Report: H. L. Mencken's Notebooks.

Human beings never welcome the news that something they have long cherished is untrue: they almost always reply to that news by reviling its promulgator.   *Ibid.*

The average man never really thinks from end to end of his life. The mental activity of such people is only a mouthing of clichés. What they mistake for thought is simply repetition of what they have heard. My guess is that well over 80% of the human race goes through life without having a single original thought. Whenever a new one appears the average man shows signs of dismay and resentment.
Ibid.

There is no possibility whatsoever of reconciling science and theology, at least in Christendom. Either Jesus arose from the dead or He didn't. If He did, then Christianity becomes plausible; if He did not, then it is sheer nonsense. I defy any genuine scientist to say that he believes in the Resurrection, or indeed in any other cardinal dogma of the Christian system. *Ibid.*

Only a country that is rich and safe can afford to be a democracy, for democracy is the most expensive and nefarious kind of government ever heard of on earth.
Ibid.

Government is actually the worst failure of civilized man. There has never been a really good one, and even those that are most tolerable are arbitrary, cruel, grasping and unintelligent. Indeed, it would not be far wrong to describe the best as the common enemy of all decent citizens.
Ibid.

Metaphysics is almost always an attempt to prove the incredible by an appeal to the unintelligible. *Ibid.*

The difference between religions is a difference in their relative content of agnosticism. The most satisfying and ecstatic faith is almost purely agnostic. It trusts absolutely without professing to know at all.
The Vintage Mencken, edited by Alistair Cooke, Knopf.

For the habitual truth-teller and truth-seeker, indeed, the whole world has very little liking. He is always unpopular, and not infrequently his unpopularity is so excessive that it endangers his life. Run your eye back over the list of martyrs, lay and clerical: nine-tenths of them, you will find, stood accused of nothing worse than honest efforts to find out and announce the truth.
Ibid., p. 72.

The men the American people admire most extravagantly are the most daring liars; the men they detest most violently are those who try to tell them the truth.
Ibid., p. 73.

A Galileo could no more be elected president of the United States than he could be elected Pope of Rome. Both high posts are reserved for men favored by God with an extraordinary genius for swathing the bitter facts of life in bandages of self-illusion.
Ibid.

There is only one honest impulse at the bottom of Puritanism, and that is the impulse to punish the man with a superior capacity for happiness—to bring him down to the miserable level of "good" men, i.e., of stupid, cowardly, and chronically unhappy men. *Ibid., p. 76.*

To the best of my knowledge and belief, the average American newspaper, even of the so-called better sort, is not only quite as bad as Upton Sinclair says it is, but ten times worse—ten times as ignorant, ten times as unfair and tyrannical, ten times as complaisant and pusillanimous, and ten times as devious, hypocritical, disingenuous, deceitful, pharisaical, pecksniffian, fraudulent, slippery, unscrupulous, perfidious, lewd and dishonest.
Review of "The Brass Check," requoted. The American Guardian, June 21, 1941.

The average newspaper, especially of the better sort, has the intelligence of a hillbilly evangelist, the courage of a rat, the fairness of a prohibitionist boob-jumper, the information of a high-school janitor, the taste of a designer of celluloid valentines, and the honor of a police-station lawyer.
Ibid.

A good one (politician) is quite as unthinkable as an honest burglar.
Newsweek, September 12, 1955.

Faith may be defined briefly as an illogical belief in the occurrence of the improbable.
New York Times Magazine, September 11, 1955.

I believe that religion, generally speaking, has been a curse to mankind. *Ibid.*

The curse of man, and the cause of nearly all his woe, is his stupendous capacity for believing the incredible.
Cardiff, What Great Men Think of Religion.

This magazine is committed to the policy of the return of the American saloon.
Letter to Upton Sinclair, Money Writes, p. 35.

The Booboisie.

All government, of course, is against liberty.

No one ever went broke underestimating the taste of the American public.

Men become civilized, not in proportion to their willingness to believe, but in proportion to their readiness to doubt.

The demagogue is one who preaches doctrines he knows to be untrue to men he knows to be idiots.

The Catholic clergy seldom bother to make their arguments plausible; it is plain that they have little respect for human intelligence, and indeed little belief in its existence.

The whole drift of our law is toward the absolute prohibition of all ideas that diverge in the slightest from the accepted platitudes, and behind the drift of law there is a far more potent force of growing custom, and under that custom there is a national philosophy which erects conformity into the noblest of virtues and the free functioning of personality into a capital crime against society.

The truth is, as everyone knows, that the great artists of the world are never puritans, and seldom ever ordinarily respectable. No virtuous man—that is, virtuous in the YMCA sense—has ever painted a picture worth looking at, or written a symphony worth hearing, or a book worth reading, and it is highly improbable that the thing has ever been done by a virtuous woman.

Aubrey Menen
(b. 1912)
English writer

There are three things which are real. God, human folly, and laughter. Since the first two pass our comprehension, we must do what we can with the third.
Time, March 9, 1959.

Meng-tse
See Mencius

Karl Menninger
(b. 1893)
American psychiatrist

It is a strange and dismal thing that in a world of such need, such opportunity and such variety as ours, the search for an illusory peace of mind should be so zealously pursued and defended, while truth goes languishing.
This Week, October 16, 1958.

Unrest of spirit is a mark of life. *Ibid.*

The voice of the intelligence is soft and weak, said Freud. It is drowned out by the roar of fear. It is ignored by the voice of desire. It is contradicted by the voice of shame. It is hissed away by hate, and extinguished by anger. Most of all it is silenced by ignorance.
The Progressive, October, 1955.

William C. Menninger
(1889-1966)
American psychiatrist

Throughout history people have used a series of . . . objects on which to project their insecurity: werewolves, incubi, witches, mental patients, Christians, Jews, Catholics, Negroes and many other innocent victims . . . This insecurity is a fear . . . of being conquered by (a) horde that is different in some way . . . Through any means of . . . persecution . . . we maintain our security.
Psychiatry in a Troubled World.

Gian Carlo Menotti
(b. 1911)
American composer

We pretend truth. We know the impossibility in ourselves of being completely truthful. Even so, we expect truth and we resent in the beloved our own pretense.
Notebook jottings for "Maria Golovin."

I know of no better definition of love than the one given by Proust—"Love is space and time measured by the heart."
Ibid.

Love is born of faith, lives on hope, and dies of charity. *Ibid.*

Jean Messelier
(18th Century)

Je voudrais que le dernier des rois fût étranglé avec les boyaux du dernier prêtre.
(I would like to see the last king strangled with the guts of the last priest.)
From his will, 1733, published by Voltaire.

Methodist Episcopal Church

The delegates of the annual conference are decidedly opposed to modern Abolitionism, and wholly disclaim any right, wish, or intention to interfere in the civil and political relation between master and slave as it exists in the slave-holding states of the union.
General Conference, Cincinnati, May, 1836.

Republic of Mexico

Religious institutions known as churches, irrespective of creed, shall in no case have legal capacity to acquire, hold or administer real property. *Constitution, 1917.*

Places of worship are the property of the nation, as represented by the Federal Government, which shall determine which may continue to be devoted to their present purpose; . . . no religious education may be imparted without the consent of the Government and no foreign priest may hold a living in Mexico. *Ibid.*

Jules Michelet
(1798-1874)
French historian

He who knows how to be poor knows everything. *History of the Revolution.*

John Stuart Mill
(1806-1873)
English political economist, philosopher

The struggle between liberty and authority is the most conspicuous feature in the portions of history with which we are earliest familiar, particularly in that of Greece, Rome and England.

On Liberty, Chapter I, 1859.

To prevent the weaker members of the community from being preyed upon by innumerable vultures, it was needed that there should be an animal of prey stronger than the rest, commissioned to keep them down. But as the king of the vultures would be no less bent upon preying on the flock than any of the minor harpies, it was indispensable to be in a perpetual attitude of defense against his beak and claws. The aim, therefore, of patriots was to set limits to the power which the ruler should be suffered to exercise over the community; and this limitation was what was meant by liberty.   *Ibid.*

The will of the people, moreover, practically means the will of the most numerous or the most active *part* of the people; the majority, or those who succeed in making themselves accepted as the majority: the people, consequently *may* desire to oppress a part of their number, and precautions are as much needed against this as against any other abuse of power. *Ibid.*

Protection, therefore, against the tyranny of the magistrate is not enough: there needs protection also against the tyranny of the prevailing opinion and feeling; against the tendency of society to impose, by other means than civil penalties, its own ideas and practices as rules of conduct on those who dissent from them . . .   *Ibid.*

Like other tyrannies, the tyranny of the majority was at first, and is still vulgarly, held in dread chiefly as operating through the acts of the public authorities. But reflecting persons perceived that when society is itself the tyrant—society collectively over the separate individuals who compose it—its means of tyrannizing are not restricted to the acts which it may do by the hands of its political functionaries.   *Ibid.*

There is a limit to the legitimate interference of collective opinion with individual independence; and to find that limit, and maintain it against encroachment, is as indispensable to a good condition of human affairs, as protection against political despotism.   *Ibid.*

Wherever there is an ascendant class, a large portion of the morality of the country emanates from its class interests, and its feelings of class superiority.   *Ibid.*

All that makes existence valuable to anyone, depends on the enforcement of restraints upon the action of other people.
Ibid.

Another grand determining principle of the rules of conduct, both in act and forbearance, which have been enforced by law or opinion, has been the servility of mankind towards the supposed preferences or aversions of their temporal masters or of their gods.   *Ibid.*

The great writers to whom the world owes what religious liberty it possesses, have mostly asserted freedom of conscience as an indefeasible right, and denied absolutely that a human being is accountable to others for his religious belief. Yet so natural to mankind is intolerance in whatever they really care about, that religious freedom has hardly anywhere been practically realized, except where religious indifference, which dislikes to have its peace disturbed by theological quarrels, has added its weight to the scale. *Ibid.*

The sole end for which mankind are warranted, individually or collectively, in interfering with the liberty of action of any of their number, is self-protection. . . . The only purpose for which power can be rightfully exercised over any member of a civilized community, against his will, is to prevent harm to others. *Ibid.*

The only part of the conduct of anyone, for which he is amenable to society, is that which concerns others. In the part which merely concerns himself, his independence is, of right, absolute. Over himself, over his own body and mind, the individual is sovereign. *Ibid.*

A person may cause evil to others not only by his actions but by his inaction, and in either case he is justly accountable to them for the injury. *Ibid.*

This then, is the appropriate region of human liberty. It comprises, *first,* the inward domain of consciousness; demanding liberty of conscience in the most comprehensive sense; liberty of thought and feeling; absolute freedom of opinion and sentiment on all subjects, practical or speculative, scientific, moral, or theological. The liberty of expressing and publishing opinions may seem to fall under a different principle, since it belongs to that part of the conduct of an individual which concerns other people; but, being almost of as much importance as the liberty of thought itself, and resting in great part on the same reasons, is practically inseparable from it. *Secondly,* the principle requires liberty of tastes and pursuits; of framing the plan of our life to suit our own character; of doing

as we like, subject to such consequences as may follow: without impediment from our fellow-creatures, so long as what we do does not harm them, even though they should think our conduct foolish, perverse, or wrong. *Thirdly,* from this liberty of each individual, follows the liberty, within the same limits, of combination among individuals; freedom to unite, for any purpose not involving harm to others: the persons combining being supposed to be of full age, and not forced or deceived. *Ibid.*

The only freedom deserving the name, is that of pursuing our own good in our own way, so long as we do not attempt to deprive others of theirs, or impede their efforts to obtain it. Each is the proper guardian of his own health, whether bodily, or mental and spiritual. Mankind are greater gainers by suffering each other to live as seems good to themselves, than by compelling each to live as seems good to the rest. *Ibid.*

The engines of moral repression have been wielded more strenuously against divergence from the reigning opinion in self-regarding, than even in social matters; religion, the most powerful of the elements which have entered into the formation of moral feeling, having always been governed by the ambition of a hierarchy, seeking control over every department of human conduct, or by the spirit of Puritanism. *Ibid.*

There is also in the world at large an increasing inclination to stretch unduly the powers of society over the individual, both by the force of opinion and even by that of legislation. . . . The disposition of mankind, whether as rulers or as fellow-citizens, to impose their own opinions and inclinations as a rule of conduct on others, is so energetically supported by some of the best and by some of the worst feelings incident to human nature, that it is hardly ever kept under restraint by anything but want of power; and as the power is not declining, but growing, unless a strong barrier of moral conviction can be raised against the mischief, we must expect, in the present circumstances of the world, to see it increase. *Ibid.*

If all mankind minus one were of one opinion, and only one person were of the contrary opinion, mankind would be no more justified in silencing that one person, than he, if he had the power, would be justified in silencing mankind.

Ibid., Chapter II.

The peculiar evil of silencing the expression of an opinion is, that it is robbing the human race: posterity as well as the existing generation; those who dissent from the opinion, still more than those who hold it. If the opinion is right, they are deprived of the opportunity of exchanging error for truth; if wrong, they lose, what is almost as great a benefit, the clearer perception and livelier impression of truth, produced by its collision with error. *Ibid.*

We can never be sure that the opinion we are endeavoring to stifle is a false opinion; and if we were sure, stifling it would be an evil still. *Ibid.*

All silencing of discussion is an assumption of infallibility. *Ibid.*

Ages are no more infallible than individuals; every age having held many opinions which subsequent ages have deemed not only false but absurd; and it is certain that many opinions now general will be rejected by future ages, as it is that many, once general, are rejected by the present. *Ibid.*

That miscellaneous collection of a few wise and many foolish individuals, called the public. *Ibid.*

The most intolerant of churches, the Roman Catholic Church, even at the canonization of a saint, admits, and listens patiently to, a "devil's advocate." The holiest of men, it appears, cannot be admitted to posthumous honors, until all that the devil could say against him is known and weighed. *Ibid.*

The dictum that truth always triumphs over persecution is one of those pleasant falsehoods which men repeat after one another till they pass into commonplaces, but which all experience refutes. History teems with instances of truth put down by persecution. If not suppressed forever, it may be thrown back for centuries. *Ibid.*

Men might as well be imprisoned, as excluded from the means of earning their bread. *Ibid.*

The peculiarity of the evidence of mathematical truths is that all the argument is on one side. *Ibid.*

The fatal tendency of mankind to leave off thinking about a thing when it is no longer doubtful, is the cause of half their errors. A contemporary author has well spoken of "the deep slumber of a decided opinion." *Ibid.*

It can do truth no service to blink the fact, known to all who have the most ordinary acquaintance with literary history, that a large portion of the noblest and most valuable teaching has been the work, not only of men who did not know, but of men who knew and rejected, the Christian faith. *Ibid.*

Unmeasured vituperation employed on the side of the prevailing opinion really does deter people from professing contrary opinions, and from listening to those who profess them. *Ibid.*

Complete liberty of contradicting and disproving our opinion is the very condition which justifies us in assuming its truth for purposes of action; and on no other terms can a being with human faculties have any rational assurance of being right. *Ibid.*

Wrong opinions and practices gradually yield to fact and argument; but facts and arguments, to produce any effect on the mind, must be brought before it. *Ibid.*

Very few facts are able to tell their own story, without comments to bring out their meaning. The whole strength and value, then, of human judgment, depending on the one property, that it can be set right when it is wrong, reliance can be placed on it only when the means of setting it right are kept constantly at hand. *Ibid.*

It is a piece of idle sentimentality that truth, merely as truth, has any inherent power denied to error of prevailing against the dungeon and the stake. *Ibid.*

Men are not more zealous for truth than they often are for error, and a sufficient application of legal or even social penalties will generally succeed in stopping the propagation of either. *Ibid.*

The real advantage which truth has, consists in this, that when an opinion is true, it may be extinguished once, twice, or many times, but in the course of ages there will generally be found persons to rediscover it, until some one of its reappearances falls on a time when from favorable circumstances it escapes persecution until it has made such head as to withstand all subsequent attempts to suppress it. *Ibid.*

Never when controversy avoided the subjects which are large and important enough to kindle enthusiasm, was the mind of a people stirred up from its foundations, and the impulse given which raised even persons of the most ordinary intellect to something of the dignity of thinking beings.
Ibid.

Popular opinions, on subjects not palpable to sense, are often true, but seldom or never the whole truth. . . . Heretical opinions, on the other hand, are generally some of these suppressed and neglected truths, bursting the bonds which kept them down, and either seeking reconciliation with the truth contained in the common opinion, or fronting it as enemies, and setting themselves up, with similar exclusiveness, as the whole Truth. *Ibia.*

In politics, again, it is almost a commonplace, that a party of order or stability, and a party of progress or reform, are both necessary elements of a healthy state of political life; until the one or the other shall have so enlarged its mental grasp as to be a party equally of order and of progress, knowing and distinguishing what is fit to be preserved from what ought to be swept away. *Ibid.*

We have now recognized the necessity to the mental well-being of mankind (on which all their other well-being depends) of freedom of opinion, and freedom of the expression of opinion, on four distinct grounds; which we will now briefly recapitulate.

First, if any opinion is compelled to silence, that opinion may, for aught we can certainly know, be true. To deny this is to assume our own infallibility.

Secondly, though the silenced opinion be an error, it may, and very commonly does, contain a portion of truth; and since the general or prevailing opinion on any subject is rarely or never the whole truth, it is only by the collision of adverse opinions that the remainder of the truth has any chance of being supplied.

Thirdly, even if the received opinion be not only true, but the whole truth; unless it is suffered to be, and actually is, vigorously and earnestly contested, it will, by most of those who receive it, be held in the manner of a prejudice, with little comprehension or feeling of its rational grounds.
Ibid.

An opinion that corn-dealers are starvers of the poor, or that private property is robbery, ought to be unmolested when simply circulated through the press, but may justly incur punishment when delivered orally to an excited mob assembled before the house of a corn-dealer, or when handed about among the same mob in the form of a placard. . . . The liberty of the individual must be thus far limited; he must not make himself a nuisance to other people.
Ibid., Chapter III.

The majority, being satisfied with the ways of mankind as they now are (for it is they who make them what they are), cannot comprehend why those ways should not be good enough for everybody; and what is more, spontaneity forms no part of the ideal of the majority of moral and social reformers, but is rather looked on with jealousy, as a troublesome and perhaps rebellious obstruction to the general acceptance of what these reformers, in their own judgment, think would be best for mankind.
Ibid.

Even despotism does not produce its worst effects, so long as individuality exists under it; and whatever crushes individuality is despotism, by whatever name it may be called, and whether it professes to be enforcing the will of God or the injunctions of men.
Ibid.

The mass do not now take their opinions from dignitaries in Church or State, from ostensible leaders, or from books. Their thinking is done for them by men much like themselves, addressing them or speaking in their name, on the spur of the moment, through the newspapers.
Ibid.

The progressive principle, however, in either shape, whether as the love of liberty or of improvement, is antagonistic to the sway of custom, involving at least emancipation from that yoke; and the contest between the two constitutes the chief interest of the history of mankind.
Ibid.

The maxims are, first, that the individual is not accountable to society for his actions, in so far as these concern the interests of no person but himself. Advice, instruction, persuasion, and avoidance by other people if thought necessary by them for their own good, are the only measures by which society can justifiably express its dislike or disapprobation of his conduct. Secondly, that for such actions as are prejudicial to the interests of others, the individual is accountable, and may be subjected either to social or to legal punishment, if society is of opinion that the one or the other is requisite for its protection.
Ibid., Chapter V.

There is always need of persons not only to discover new truths, and point out when what were once truths are true no longer, but also to commence new practices, and set the example of more enlightened conduct, and better taste and sense in human life.
Ibid.

The general tendency of things throughout the world is to render mediocrity the ascendant power among mankind. *Ibid.*

At present individuals are lost in the crowd. In politics it is almost a triviality to say that public opinion now rules the world. *Ibid.*

Precisely because the tyranny of opinion is such as to make eccentricity a reproach, it is desirable, in order to break through that tyranny, that people should be eccentric. Eccentricity has always abounded when and where strength of character has abounded; and the amount of eccentricity in a society has generally been proportional to the amount of genius, mental vigor, and moral courage it contained. That so few dare to be eccentric marks the chief danger of the time. *Ibid.*

The despotism of custom is everywhere the standing hindrance to human advancement, being in unceasing antagonism to that disposition to aim at something better than customary, which is called, according to circumstances, the spirit of liberty, or that of progress or improvement. *Ibid.*

Trade is a social act. Whoever undertakes to sell any description of goods to the public, does what affects the interest of other persons, and of society in general; and thus his conduct, in principle, comes within the jurisdiction of society. *Ibid.*

Any sentiment of freedom which can exist in a man whose nearest and dearest intimacies are with those of whom he is absolute master, is not the genuine or Christian love of freedom, but, what the love of freedom generally was in the ancients and in the Middle Ages—an intense feeling of the dignity and importance of his own personality; making him disdain a yoke for himself, of which he has no abhorrence whatever in the abstract, but which he is abundantly ready to impose on others for his own interest or glorification.

The Subjugation of Women, Ch. II, 1869.

Where liberty cannot be hoped for, and power can, power becomes the grand object of human desire. . . . The love of power and the love of liberty are in eternal antagonism. Where there is least liberty, the passion for power is the most ardent and unscrupulous. The desire of power over others can only cease to be a depraving agency among mankind, when each of them individually is able to do without it: which can only be where respect for liberty in the personal concerns of each is an established principle.

Ibid., Ch. IV.

The world would be astonished if it knew how great a proportion of its brightest ornaments, of those most distinguished even in popular estimation for wisdom and virtue, are complete skeptics in religion.

Cardiff, What Great Men Think of Religion.

But it is not the minds of heretics that are deteriorated most by the ban placed on all inquiry which does not end in orthodox conclusions. The greatest harm is to those who are not heretics, and whose whole mental development is cramped and their reason cowed by the fear of heresy. Who can compute what the world loses in the multitude of promising intellects combined with timid characters who dare not follow out any bold, vigorous, independent train of thought lest it should land them in something which would admit of being considered irreligious or immoral? *Ibid.*

There have been, and may again be, great individual thinkers in a general atmosphere of mental slavery. But there never has been and never will be, in that atmosphere, an intellectually active people.

Ibid.

It is conceivable that religion may be morally useful without being intellectually sustainable. *Ibid.*

No one can be a great thinker who does not recognize that as a thinker it is his first duty to follow his intellect to whatever conclusions it may lead. *Ibid.*

Truth gains more even by errors of one who, with due study and preparation, thinks for himself than by the true opinions of those who only hold them because they do not suffer themselves to think. *Ibid.*

Not that it is solely or chiefly to form great thinkers that freedom of thinking is required. On the contrary, it is as much and even more indispensable to enable average human beings to attain the mental stature which they are capable of. *Ibid.*

The people who think it a shame when anything goes wrong—who rush to the conclusion that the evil could or ought to have been prevented, are those who, in the long run, do most to make the world better.

Representative Government, III, 1861.

Unearned increment.
Dissertations and Discussions, Essay on Coleridge, 1859, Vol. 4, p. 299.

Art necessarily presupposes knowledge.
System of Logic, introduction.

General Millan-Astray
(Contemporary)
Spanish fascist leader

Mort à l'intelligence et vive la mort.

(Death to intelligence, and long live death.)
Shouted while breaking up lecture of Unamuno, Salamanca University; quoted in Vendredi (Paris), January 8, 1937.

Robert A. Millikan
(1868-1953)
American physicist, Nobel Prize, 1923

If, then, you ask me to put into one sentence the cause of that recent, rapid, and enormous change and the prognosis for the achievement of human liberty, I should reply, *It is found in the discovery and utilization of the means by which heat energy can be made to do man's work for him.*
Freedom, edited by Ruth Nanda Anshen, Harcourt Brace, 1940.

Civilization consists in the multiplication and refinement of human wants. *Ibid.*

Three ideas stand out above all others in the influence they have exerted and are destined to exert upon the development of the human race: The idea of the Golden Rule, the idea of natural law, and the idea of age-long growth, or evolution.

Forbes Magazine.

John Milton
(1608-1674)
English poet

For books are not altogether dead things, but do contain a progeny of life in them to be as active as that soul was whose progeny they are.
Areopagitica: A Speech for the Liberty of Unlicensed Printing, 1644.

And yet, on the other hand, unless wariness be used, as good almost kill a man as kill a good book: who kills a man kills a reasonable creature, God's image; but he who destroys a good book, kills reason itself, kills the image of God, as it were, in the eye.   *Ibid.*

Many a man lives a burden to the earth; but a good book is the precious lifeblood of a master spirit, imbalmed and treasured up on purpose to a life beyond life.   *Ibid.*

It is true, no age can restore life, whereof, perhaps there is no great a loss; and revolutions of ages do not oft recover the loss of a rejected truth, for the want of which whole nations fare the worse. *Ibid.*

We should be wary, therefore, what persecution we raise against the living labors of public men, how we spill that seasoned life of man, preserved and stored up in books; since we see a kind of homicide may be thus committed, sometimes a martyrdom; and if it extend to the whole impression, a kind of massacre, whereof the execution ends not in the slaying of an elemental life, but strikes at the ethereal and fifth essence, the breath of reason itself; slays an immortality rather than a life.   *Ibid.*

As therefore the state of man now is, what wisdom can there be to choose, what continence to forebear, without the knowledge of evil? He that can apprehend and consider vice with all her baits and seeming pleasures, and yet abstain, and yet distinguish, and yet prefer that which is truly better, he is the true wayfaring Christian.
Ibid.

We do not see that while we still affect by all means a rigid stupidity, a stark and dead congealment of "wood and hay and stubble" forced and frozen together, which is more to the sudden degenerating of a church than many sub-dichotomies of petty schisms.   *Ibid.*

I cannot praise a fugitive and cloistered virtue unexercised and unbreathed, that never sallies out and seeks her adversary, but flings out of the race, where that immortal garland is to be run for, not without dust and heat.   *Ibid.*

Well knows he who uses to consider, that our faith and knowledge thrive by exercise, as well as our limbs and complexion. Truth is compared in Scripture to a streaming fountain; if her waters flow not in a perpetual progression, they sicken into a muddy pool of conformity and tradition.   *Ibid.*

A man may be a heretic in the truth; and if he believe things only because his pastor says so, or the assembly so determines, without knowing other reason, though his belief be true, yet the very truth he holds becomes his heresy.   *Ibid.*

And though all the winds of doctrine were let loose to play upon the earth, so truth be in the field, we do injuriously by licensing and prohibiting to misdoubt her strength. Let her and falsehood grapple; who ever knew truth put to the worse, in a free and open encounter?   *Ibid.*

For who knows not that truth is strong, next to the Almighty; she needs no policies, nor strategems, nor licensings to make her victorious; those are the shifts and the defences that error uses against her power: give her but room, and do not bind her when she sleeps.   *Ibid.*

Give me the liberty to know, to utter, and to argue freely according to conscience, above all liberties.   *Ibid.*

Tolerated popery, as it extirpates all religious and civil supremacies, so itself should be extirpated, provided first that all charitable and compassionate means be used to win and regain the weak and the misled. *Ibid.*

Truth . . . never comes into the world, but like a Bastard, to the ignominy of him that brought her forth.
A Complete Collection of the Historical, Political, and Miscellaneous Works of John Milton, I, 276.

The greatest burden in the World is Superstition, not only of Ceremonies in the Church, but of imaginary and scarecrow Sins at home. *Ibid., I, 277.*

It being thus manifest, that the power of kings and magistrates is nothing else but what is only derivative, transferred, and committed to them in trust from the people to the common good of them all, in whom the power yet remains fundamentally, and cannot be taken from them, without a violation of their natural birthright.
The Tenure of Kings and Magistrates.

If men within themselves would be governed by reason, and not generally give up their understanding to a double tyranny, of custom from without and blind affections within; they would discern better what it is to favour and uphold the tyrant of a nation. Being slaves within doors, no wonder that they strive so much to have the public state conformably governed to the inward vicious rule, by which they govern themselves. *Ibid.*

Unless that liberty, which is of such a kind as arms can neither procure nor take away, which alone is the fruit of piety, of justice, of temperance, and unadulterated virtue, shall have taken deep root in your minds and hearts, there will not long be wanting one who will snatch from you by treachery what you have acquired by arms.
The Second Defence of the People of England.

He alone is worthy of the appellation who either does great things, or teaches how they may be done, or describes them with a suitable majesty when they have been done. *Ibid.*

Those only are great things which tend to render life more happy, which increase the innocent enjoyments and comforts of existence, or which pave the way to a state of future bliss more permanent and more pure. *Ibid.*

Truth is as impossible to be soiled by any outward touch as the sunbeam.
The Doctrine and Discipline of Divorce.

Romanism is less a religion than a priestly tyranny armed with the spoils of civil power which, on the pretext of religion, it hath seized against the command of Christ Himself. *Treatise on Civil Power, 1659.*

For what can war but endless war still breed? *Of General Fairfax.*

Fear and dull disposition, lukewarmness and sloth, are not seldom wont to cloak themselves under the affected name of Moderation.
An Apology for Smectymnuus, 1642.

Our country is wherever we are well off.
Letter to P. Heinbach, August 15, 1666.

Men of most renowned virtue have sometimes by transgressing most truly kept the law. *Tetrachordon.*

The mind is its own place, and in itself
Can make a heaven of Hell, a hell of
   Heaven. *Paradise Lost, bk. i, 253.*

Here we may reign secure; and in my
   choice

To reign is worth ambition, though in hell.
Better to reign in hell than serve in heaven.
Ibid., 263.

Who overcomes
By force, hath overcome but half his foe.
Ibid., 648.

For neither man nor angel can discern
Hypocrisy, the only evil that walks
Invisible, except to God alone,
By his permissive will, through Heaven
and Earth.   *Ibid.*, *iii*, 682.

And with necessity,
The tyrant's plea, excused his devilish deeds.
Ibid., *iv*, 393.

Wherefore with thee
Came not all hell broke loose.
Ibid., 917.

And what the people but a herd confus'd,
A miscellaneous rabble, who extol
Things vulgar, and, well weigh'd, scarce
worth the praise.
Paradise Regained, bk. iii, 49.

Fame is the spur that the clear spirit doth
raise
(That last infirmity of noble mind).
Lycidas, 70.

But what more oft in Nations grown
corrupt,
And by their vices brought to servitude,
Than to love Bondage more than Liberty,
Bondage with ease than strenuous
Liberty . . . ?   *Samson Agonistes.*

Just are the ways of God
And justifiable to men,
Unless there be who think not God at all.
Ibid.

Iskander Mirza
(b. 1899)
President of Pakistan

My authority is revolution.
Proclamation on abolition of parliament; Time, October 20, 1958.

Democracy requires breeding. These illiterate peasants certainly know less about running a country than I do . . . There has to be someone to prevent the people from destroying themselves.   *Ibid.*

Democracy without education is hypocrisy without limitation.   *Ibid.*

Mohammed*
(570-632)
Arab founder of Mohammedanism

He is the best of men who dislikes power.

The ink of the scholar is more sacred than the blood of the martyr.

Jean Baptiste Molière
(1622-1673)
French dramatist

There is no rampart that will hold out against malice.   *Tartuffe.***

I prefer an accommodating vice to an obstinate virtue.   *Amphitryon, I, 1668.*

Helmuth von Moltke
(1800-1891)
Prussian field marshal

Eternal peace is a dream, and not even a beautiful one, and war is a part of God's

---

* *See also* The Koran.
** Also translated: "There is no protection against slander."

world order. In it are developed the no-blest virtues of man, courage and abnega-tion, dutifulness and self-sacrifice at the risk of life. Without war the world would sink into materialism.
Letter to Bluntschli, December 11, 1880.

Every war is a national misfortune.
Public declaration, 1880.

James Monroe

(1758-1831)
5th President of the United States

That the American continents, by the free and independent condition which they have assumed and maintained, are henceforth not to be considered as subjects for future colonization by any European powers.
Message to Congress, December 2, 1823.

In the wars of the European Powers in matters relating to themselves we have never taken any part, nor does it comport with our policy so to do.   *Ibid.*

It is only when our rights are invaded or seriously menaced that we resent in-juries or make preparation for our defense. With the movements in this hemisphere we are of necessity more immediately connected and by causes which must be obvious to all enlightened and impartial observers. The political system of the allied powers is essentially different in this respect from that of America. This difference proceeds from that which exists in their respective Governments. And to the defense of our own, which has been achieved by the loss of so much blood and treasure, and ma-tured by the wisdom of their most en-lightened citizens, and under which we

have enjoyed unexampled felicity, this whole nation is devoted.   *Ibid.*

We owe it, therefore, to candor and to the amicable relations existing between the United States and those powers to declare that we consider any attempt on their part to extend their system to any portion of this hemisphere as dangerous to our peace and safety. With the existing colonies or dependencies of any European power we have not interfered and shall not interfere.
Ibid.

Our policy in regard to Europe . . . remains the same, which is, not to inter-fere in the internal concerns of any of its Powers; to consider the government de facto as the legitimate government for us; to cultivate friendly relations with it, and to preserve those relations by a frank, firm and manly policy, meeting in all instances the just claims of every Power, submitting to injuries from none.   *Ibid.*

Preparation for war is a constant stimulus to suspicion and ill will.
Declaration, April 28, 1818, on sign-ing Rush-Bagot pact with Britain.

Michel de Montaigne

(1533-1592)
French philosopher, essayist

The thing in the world I am most afraid of is fear, and with good reason; that pas-sion alone, in the trouble of it, exceeding all other accidents.   *Essays.*

No man can profit except by the loss of others, and by this reasoning all manner of profit must be condemned.   *Ibid.*

If you have known how to compose your life, you have accomplished a great deal more than the man who knows how to compose a book. Have you been able to take your stride? You have done more than the man who has taken cities and empires.   *Ibid.*

There are some defeats more triumphant than victories.   *Ibid.*

The great and glorious masterpiece of man is to live to the point. All other things —to reign, to hoard, to build—are, at most, but inconsiderate props and appendages.   *Ibid.*

I speak truth, not so much as I would, but as much as I dare; and I dare a little more as I grow older.   *Ibid.*

Stubborn and ardent clinging to one's opinion is the best proof of stupidity.   *Ibid.*

The laws keep up their credit, not by being just, but because they are laws; 'tis the mystic foundation of their authority; they have no other, and it well answers their purpose. They are often made by fools; still oftener by men who, out of hatred to equality, fail in equity; but always by men, vain and irresolute authors.   *Ibid.*

Man is certainly stark mad. He cannot make a flea, and yet he will be making gods by the dozen.   *Ibid.*

Philosophy is doubt.   *Ibid.*

How many things served us yesterday for articles of faith, which today are fables to us!   *Ibid.*

Nothing is so firmly believed as that which we least know.   *Ibid.*

There is nothing so much, nor so grossly, nor so ordinarily faulty, as laws. Whoever obeys them because they are just, does not justly obey them as he ought.   *Ibid.*

It is an absolute perfection, and as it were divine, to know how, in all sincerity, to get the very most out of one's own individuality (*de savoir jouir loyalement de son être*).   *Ibid.*

Of all the benefits which virtue confers on us, the contempt of death is one of the greatest.   *Ibid., I.*

All general judgments are loose and imperfect.   *Ibid., III.*

There is no man so good, who, were he to submit all his thoughts and actions to the laws, would not deserve hanging ten times in his life.   *Ibid.*

There is no course of life so weak and sottish as that which is managed by orders, method, and discipline.   *Ibid.*

The souls of emperors and cobblers are cast in the same mould . . . The same reason that makes us wrangle with a neighbor causes a war betwixt princes.
          Apology for Raimond Sebond.

What do I know? (*Que sais-je?*)
          (*motto.*)

On the most exalted throne in the world, nothing but our arse.
          Quoted, Practical Cogitator, p. 389.

Claude G. Montefiore
(1858-1938)
English scholar

How anyone can believe in eternal punishment . . . or in any soul which God has made being "lost", and also believe in the love, nay, even in the justice, of God, is a mystery indeed.

Liberal Judaism, 1903, p. 58.

Charles de Secondat, Baron de la Brède et de Montesquieu

(1689-1755)

French jurist, philosopher

As virtue is necessary in a republic, and honor in a monarchy, fear is what is required in a despotism. As for virtue, it is not at all necessary, and honor would be dangerous there.

De l'Esprit des Lois (The Spirit of the Laws), iii. c. 9.

Republics come to an end by luxurious habits; monarchies by poverty.*

Ibid., vii. c. 4.

Democracy has two excesses to avoid: the spirit of inequality, which leads to an aristocracy, or to the government of a single individual; and the spirit of extreme equality, which conducts it to despotism, as the despotism of a single individual finishes by conquest. *Ibid., viii. c. 2.*

Experience constantly proves that every man who has power is impelled to abuse it.

Ibid., xi. c. 4.

Important maxim: we ought to be very cautious and circumspect in the prosecution of magic and heresy. The attempt to put down these two crimes may be extremely perilous to liberty. *Ibid., xii. c. 5.*

---

* *Les républiques finissent par le luxe; les monarchies par la pauvreté.* Another translation: "Republics end through luxury; monarchies through poverty."

Men who are knaves individually, are in the mass very honorable people.

Ibid., xxv. c. 2.

But the general rule always holds good. In constitutional states liberty is a compensation for the heaviness of taxation. In despotic states the equivalent for liberty is the lightness of taxation. *Op. cit.*

Society is the union of men but not men themselves; the citizen may perish, but man remains. *Ibid.*

The tyranny of a prince in an oligarchy is not so dangerous to the public welfare as the apathy of a citizen in a democracy.

Ibid.

In the state of nature, indeed, all men are born equal, but they cannot continue in this equality. Society makes them lose it, and they recover it only by the protection of the laws. *Ibid.*

A nation may lose its liberties in a day, and not miss them for a century. *Ibid.*

Power should be a check to power.

Ibid.

The political liberty of the subject is a tranquility of mind arising from the opinion each person has of his safety. In order to have this liberty, it is requisite the government be so constituted as no man need be afraid of another. *Ibid.*

The great advantage of representatives is, their capacity of discussing public affairs. For this, the people collectively are extremely unfit, which is one of the chief inconveniences of a democracy. *Ibid.*

To prevent the executive power from being able to oppress, it is requisite that the armies with which it is intrusted should consist of the people, and have the same spirit as the people.   *Ibid.*

If there should be a standing-army composed chiefly of the most despicable part of the nation, the legislative power should have a right to disband them as soon as it pleased: the soldiers should live in common with the rest of the people; and no separate camp, barracks, or fortress, should be suffered.   *Ibid.*

Laws, in their most general signification, are the necessary relations arising from the nature of things. In this sense, all beings have their laws; the Deity his laws, the material world its laws, the intelligences superior to man their laws, the beasts their laws, man his laws.   *Ibid.*

Law in general is human reason, inasmuch as it governs all the inhabitants of the earth; the political and civil laws of each nation ought to be only the particular cases in which human reason is applied.

They should be adapted in such a manner to the people for whom they are framed, that it is a great chance if those of one nation suit another.   *Ibid.*

Democratic and aristocratic states are not in their own nature free. Political liberty is to be found only in moderate governments; and even in these it is not always found. It is there only when there is no abuse of power; but constant experience shows us that every man invested with power is apt to abuse it, and to carry his authority as far as it will go. Is it not strange, though true, to say, that virtue itself has need of limits?   *Ibid.*

When the legislative and executive powers are united in the same person, or in the same body of magistrates, there can be no liberty; because apprehensions may arise, lest the same monarch or senate should enact tyrannical laws, to execute them in a tyrannical manner.   *Ibid.*

Again, there is no liberty if the judiciary power be not separated from the legislative and executive. Were it joined with the legislative, the life and liberty of the subject would be exposed to arbitrary control; for the judge would be then the legislator. Were it joined to the executive power, the judge might behave with violence and oppression.

There would be an end to every thing, were the same man, or the same body, whether of the nobles or of the people, to exercise those three powers, that of enacting laws, that of executing the public resolutions, and of trying the causes of individuals.   *Ibid.*

History is full of religious wars; but, we must take care to observe, it was not the multiplicity of religions that produced these wars, it was the intolerating spirit which animated that one which thought she had the power of governing.

Persian Letters, No. 65.

If I knew something useful to my nation which would be ruinous to another, I would not propose it to my prince, because I am a man before I am a Frenchman, or (better still) because I am necessarily a man, and only by chance a Frenchman.   *Pensée.*

Maria Montessori
(1870-1952)
Italian educator

The pedagogical method of observation has for its base the liberty of the child; and liberty is activity.

The Montessori Method.

Discipline must come through liberty. Here is a great principle which it is difficult for followers of the common-school methods to understand. How shall one obtain discipline in a class of free children? Certainly in our system we have a concept of discipline very different from that commonly accepted. If discipline is founded upon liberty, the discipline itself must necessarily be *active*. We do not consider an individual disciplined only when he has been rendered as artificially silent as a mute and as immovable as a paralytic. He is an individual *annihilated*, not *disciplined*. *Ibid.*

The liberty of the child should have as its *limit* the collective interest; as its form, what we universally consider good breeding. We must therefore check in the child whatever offends or annoys others, or whatever tends toward rough or ill-bred acts. But all the rest—every manifestation having a useful scope, whatever it be, and under whatever form it expresses itself—must not only be permitted, but must be observed by the teacher. *Ibid.*

Here lies the essential point; from her scientific preparation, the teacher must bring not only the capacity, but the desire to observe natural phenomena. In our system, she must become a passive, much more than an active, influence, and her passivity shall be composed of anxious scientific curiosity, and of absolute respect for the phenomenon which she wishes to observe. The teacher must understand and feel her position of observer; the activity must lie in the phenomenon. *Ibid.*

Humanity shows itself in all its intellectual splendour during this tender age as the sun shows itself at the dawn, and the flower in the first unfolding of the petals; and we must respect religiously, reverently, these first indications of individuality. If any educational act is to be efficacious, it will be only that which tends to help toward the complete unfolding of this life. To be thus helpful it is necessary rigorously to avoid the arrest of spontaneous movements and the imposition of arbitrary tasks. It is, of course, understood that here we do not speak of useless or dangerous acts, for these must be suppressed, destroyed.

Ibid.

The first idea that the child must acquire, in order to be actively disciplined, is that of the difference between good and evil; and the task of the educator lies in seeing that the child does not confound good with immobility, and evil with activity, as often happens in the case of the oldtime discipline. And all this because our aim is to discipline for activity, for work, for good; not for immobility, not for passivity, not for obedience. *Ibid.*

The child, because of the peculiar characteristics of helplessness with which he is born, and because of his qualities as a social individual, is circumscribed by bonds which limit his activity.

An educational method that shall have liberty as its basis must intervene to help the child to a conquest of these various obstacles. In other words, his training must be such as shall help him to diminish, in a rational manner, the social bonds which limit his activity. *Ibid.*

Henri de Montherlant
(1893-1972)
French novelist

One puts into one's art what one has not been capable of putting into one's existence. It is because he was unhappy that God created the world.

Costals and the Hippogriff.

George Moore
(1852-1933)
Irish novelist, essayist

God is a great expense but government would be impossible without Him.

The mind petrifies if a circle be drawn around it, and it can hardly be denied that dogma draws a circle round the mind.

I don't care how the poor live; my only regret is that they live at all.
Confessions of a Young Man, xii.

Sir Thomas More
(1478-beheaded 1535)
English judge, writer

They have but few lawes. For to people so instructe and institute very fewe do suffice. Yea this thing they chiefly reprove among other nations, that innumerable bokes of lawes and expositions upon the same be not sufficient. But they think it against all right and justice that men shoulde be bound to those lawes, which either be in number more than be able to read, or els blinder and darker, then that anye man can well understande them.
Utopia, Book II, 1516.

Furthermore they utterlie exclude and banishe all attorneis, proctours, and sergeaunts at the lawe; whiche craftelye handell matters, and subtelly dispute of the lawes. For they thinke it moste meete, that every man should pleade his own matter, and tel the same tale before the judge that he wold tel to his man of law. So shal there be lesse circumstaunce of wordes, and the trueth shal soner come to light, whiles the judge with a discrete judgement doeth waye the woordes of him whom no lawyer hath instructe with deceit, and whiles he helpeth and beareth out simple wittes against the false and malicious circumventions of craftie children. *Ibid.*

This is one of the ancientest lawes among them: that no man shall be blamed for resoninge in the maintenaunce of his own religion. For kyng Utopus, even at the firste beginning, hearing that the inhabitauntes of the land wer before his coming thether, at continuall dissention and strife amonge themselves for their religions . . . he made a decree, that it should be lawfull for everie man to favoure and folow what religion he would, and that he mighte do the best he could to bring other to his opinion, so that he did it peaceablie, gentelie, quietly, and soberlie, without hastie and contentious rebuking and invehing against other. *Ibid.*

Whereof he durst define and determine nothing unadvisedlie, as douting whether god desiering manifolde and diverse sortes of honour, would inspire sondry men with sondrie kindes of religion. And this suerly he thought a very unmete and folish thing, and a point of arrogant presumption, to compell all other by violence and thrateninges to agre to the same, that thou belevest to be trew. *Ibid.*

When I consider and way in my mind all these common wealthes, which now a dayes any where do florish, so god helpe me, I can perceave nothing but a certain conspiracy of riche men procuringe theire owne commodities under the name and title of the common wealth. They invent and devise all meanes and craftes, first how to kepe safely, without feare of losing, that they have unjustly gathered together, and next how to hire and abuse the worke and laboure of the poore for as litle money as may be. *Ibid.*

Every man has by the law of nature a right to such a waste portion of the earth as is necessary for his subsistence. *Ibid.*

Is not this an unjust and an unkynde publyque weale, whych gyveth great fees and rewardes to gentlemen, as they call them, and to goldsmythes, and to suche other, which be either ydle persones, or els onlye flatterers, and devysers of vaine pleasures: And of the contrary parte maketh no gentle provision for poore plowmen, coliars, laborers, carters, yronsmythes, and carpenters: without whome no common wealthe can continewe? *Ibid.*

They marveile also that golde, whych of the owne nature is a thinge so unprofytable, is nowe amonge all people in so hyghe estimation, that man him selfe, by whome, yet and for the use of whom it is so much set by, is in muche lesse estimation, then the golde it selfe. *Ibid.*

Henry Morgan
(b. 1915)
American comedian

Any man with ambition, integrity—and $10,000,000—can start a daily newspaper.

J(ohn) Pierpont Morgan
(1837-1913)
American financier

Remember, my son, that any man who is a bear on the future of this country will go broke.

Quoted by his son, Chicago Club, December 10, 1908.

Question: Do you consider $10 a week enough for a longshoreman with a family to support?

Answer: If that's all he can get, and he takes it, I should say it's enough.

Testimony, U.S. Commission on Industrial Relations.

Anybody has a right to evade taxes if he can get away with it. No citizen has a moral obligation to assist in maintaining the government. If Congress insists on making stupid mistakes and passing foolish tax laws, millionaires should not be condemned if they take advantage of them.

Statement to reporters. Requoted, "Labor," June 15, 1957.

Congress should know how to levy taxes, and if it doesn't know how to collect them, then a man is a fool to pay the taxes.

N. Y. Times, March 6, 1955.

Of all forms of tyranny the least attractive and the most vulgar is the tyranny of mere wealth, the tyranny of plutocracy.

Autobiography, p. 437.

I commit my soul into the hands of my Savior, in full confidence that having redeemed it and washed it in His most precious blood He will present it faultless before the throne of my Heavenly Father, and I entreat my children to maintain and defend, at all hazard, and at any cost of personal sacrifice, the blessed doctrine of the complete atonement for sin through the blood of Jesus Christ, once offered, and through that alone. *Will, 1913.*

Lewis Henry Morgan
(1818-1881)
American ethnologist

Centralize property in the hands of a few and the millions are under bondage to property—a bondage as absolute and deplorable as if their limbs were covered with manacles. Abstract all property from the hands of labor and you thereby reduce labor to dependence; and that dependence becomes as complete a servitude as the master could fix upon his slave.

Lecture, Diffusion Against Centralization, 1852.

The time will come when human intelligence will rise to the mastery of property.

Ancient Society.

The interests of society are paramount to individual interests, and the two must be brought into just and harmonious relations. A mere property career is not the final destiny of mankind, if progress is to be the law of the future as it has been of the past.　　　　　　　*Ibid.*

The dissolution of society bids fair to become the termination of a career of which property is the end and aim, because such a career contains the elements of self-destruction. Democracy in government, brotherhood in society, equality in rights and privileges, and universal education, foreshadow the next higher plane of society to which experience, intelligence and knowledge are steadily tending.　　*Ibid.*

Hans J. Morgenthau
(b. 1904)
American political scientist

Man is born to seek power, yet his actual condition makes him a slave to the power of others.

Christopher Morley
(1890-1957)
American writer

There is only one success—to be able to spend your life in your own way.

Where the Blue Begins.

John Morley
(1838-1923)
English statesman

It has been often said that he who begins life by stifling his convictions is in a fair way for ending it without any convictions to stifle. We may, perhaps, add that he who sets out with the notion that the difference between truth and falsehood is a thing of no consequence to the vulgar, is very likely sooner or later to come to the kindred notion that it is not a thing of any supreme concern to himself.

On Compromise, 1874; Ch. 3, Intellectual Responsibility and the Political Spirit.

As to those who deliberately and knowingly sell their intellectual birthright for a mess of pottage, making a brazen compromise with what they hold despicable, lest they should have to win their bread honourably. Men need to expend no declamatory indignation upon them. They have a hell of their own; words can add no bitterness to it.　　　　　　　*Ibid.*

It is no light thing to have secured a livelihood on condition of going through life masked and gagged. To be compelled, week after week, and year after year, to recite the symbols of ancient faith and lift up his voice in the echoes of old hopes, with the blighting thought in his soul that the faith is a lie, and the hope no more than the folly of the crowd; to read hundreds of times in a twelve month with solemn unction as the inspired word of the Supreme what to him are meaningless as the Abracadabras of the conjuror in the booth; to go to the end of his days administering to the simple folk holy rites of commemoration and solace, when he has in his mind at each phrase what dupes are these simple folk and how wearisomely counterfeit their rites: and to know through all that this is really to be the one business of his prostituted life, that so dreary and hateful a piece of play-acting will make the desperate retrospect of his last hours—of a truth here is the very . . . abomination of desolation of the human spirit indeed. *Ibid.*

It is the worst of political blunders to insist on carrying an ideal set of principles into execution, where others have right of dissent . . . But to be afraid or ashamed of holding such an ideal set of principles in one's mind in their highest and most abstract expression, does more than any one other cause to stunt or petrify those elements in character to which life should owe most of its savour. *Ibid.*

Theology has borrowed, and coloured for her own use, the principles which were first brought into vogue in politics. If in the one field it is the fashion to consider convenience first and truth second, in the other there is a corresponding fashion of placing truth second and emotional comfort first. *Ibid.*

If there are some who compromise their real opinions, or the chance of reaching truth, for the sake of gain, there are far more who shrink from giving their intelligence free play, for the sake of keeping undisturbed certain luxurious spiritual sensibilities. *Ibid.*

The law of things is that they who tamper with veracity, from whatever motive, are tampering with the vital force of human progress. *Ibid.*

You have not converted a man, because you have silenced him. *Ibid.*

Opinion and force belong to different elements. To think that you are able by social disapproval or other coercive means to crush a man's opinion, is as one who fires off a blunderbuss to put out a star. *Ibid.*

The fatal French saying about small reforms being the worst enemies of great reforms, is in the sense in which it is commonly used, a formula of social ruin. On the other hand, let us not forget that there is a sense in which the very saying is profoundly true. A small and temporary improvement may really be the worst enemy of a great and permanent improvement, unless the first is made on the lines and in the direction of the second . . . The small reform may become the enemy of the great one. *Ibid.*

Liberalism, too, would be something more generous, more attractive—yes, and more practically effective, if its professors and champions could allow their sense of what is feasible to be refreshed and widened by a more free recognition, however private and undemonstrative, of the theoretic ideas which give their social creed whatever life and consistency it may have. *Ibid.*

Contented acquiescence in the ordering that has come down to us from the past is selfish and anti-social, because amid the ceaseless change that is inevitable in a growing organism, the institutions of the past demand progressive re-adaptations. *Ibid.*

Improvements are most likely to be secured in the greatest abundance by limiting the sphere of authority, extending that of free individuality . . . ; that progress on its political side means more than anything else the substitution of Justice as a governing idea, instead of Privilege, and that the best guarantee for justice in public dealings is the participation in their own government of the people most likely to suffer from injustice. *Ibid.*

Now compromise, in view of the foregoing theory of social advance, may be of two kinds, and of these two kinds one is legitimate and the other not . . . It may mean the deliberate suppression or mutilation of an idea, in order to make it congruous with the traditional idea or the current prejudice on the given subject, whatever that may be. Or else it may mean a rational acquiescence in the fact that the bulk of your contemporaries are not yet prepared either to embrace the new idea, or to change their ways of living in conformity to it. The first prolongs the duration of the empire of prejudice, and retards the arrival of improvement. The second does his best to abbreviate the one and to hasten to make definite the other, yet he does not insist on hurrying changes which, to be effective, would require the active support of numbers of persons not yet ripe for them. *Ibid.*

And what is this smile of the world, to win which we are bidden to sacrifice our moral manhood; this frown of the world, whose terrors are more awful than the withering of truth, and the slow going out of light within the souls of us?
N. Y. Herald Tribune, January 1, 1949.

We liberals have tried patience for twenty years. I vote we now try "courage" . . . We have principles we believe in, we have faith, we have great traditions, and we have a great cause behind us and before us.

All religions die of one disease, that of being found out.

Book of Mormon

For it must needs be that there is an opposition in all things.

If not so . . . righteousness could not be brought to pass; neither wickedness; neither holiness nor misery; neither good nor bad.
2 Nephi 1: 81-82.

A lake of fire and brimstone whose flames are unquenchable and whose smoke ascendeth up forever and ever.
Jacob, vi, 10.

Gouverneur Morris
(1752-1816)
American statesman

Nine-tenths of the people are at present freeholders . . . The time is not distant when this country will abound with mechanics and manufacturers (i.e., artisans) who will receive their bread from their employers. Will such men be the secure and faithful guardians of liberty? (He thought not.) Give the votes to people who have no property, and they will sell them to the rich who will be able to buy them.
Speech, August 7, 1787, in favor of the "Patricians."

William Morris
(1834-1896)
English artist, writer

What I mean by Socialism is a condition of society in which there should be neither rich nor poor, neither master nor master's man, neither idle nor overworked, neither brain-sick brain workers, nor heart-sick hand workers, in a word, in which all men would be living in equality of condition, and would manage their affairs unwastefully, and with the full consciousness that harm to one would mean harm to all—the realization at last of the meaning of the word COMMON-WEALTH.
Written for "Justice." 1884.

If you want a golden rule that will fit everybody, this is it:

Have nothing in your houses that you do not know to be useful, or believe to be beautiful.   *The Beauty of Life, 1880.*

Any art which professes to be founded on the special education or refinement of a limited body or class must of necessity be unreal and short-lived. ART IS MAN'S EX-PRESSION OF HIS JOY IN LABOUR.

Art Under Plutocracy, 1883.

When Socialism comes, it may be in such a form that we won't like it.

No man is good enough to be another's master.

What is this, the sound and rumour? What is this that all men hear,
Like the wind in hollow valleys when the storm is drawing near,
Like the rolling on of ocean in the eventide of fear?
    'Tis the people marching on.
The March of the Workers, in "Chants for Socialists," published by the Socialist League, 1885.

Many a hundred years passed over have they laboured, deaf and blind;
Never tidings reached their sorrow, never hope their toil might find.
Now at last they've heard and hear it, and the cry comes from the wind,
And their feet are marching on. *Ibid.*

O ye rich men, hear and tremble! for with words the sound is rife:
"Once for you and death we laboured; changed henceforward is the strife.
We are men, and we shall battle for the world of men and life,
And our host is marching on."
Ibid.

"On we march, then, we the workers,
    and the rumour that ye hear
Is the blended sound of battle and deliv'-rance drawing near;
For the hope of every creature is the banner that we bear,
    And the world is marching on".
Ibid.

I heard men saying, Leave tears and praying,
The sharp knife heedeth not the sheep;
Are we no stronger than the rich and the wronger,
When day breaks over dreams and sleep?
Come shoulder to shoulder ere the world grows older!
Help lies in naught but thee and me.
The Voice of Toil.

Dwight W(hitney) Morrow
(1873-1931)
American banker, diplomat

Any party which takes credit for the rain must not be surprised if its opponents blame it for the drought.

Wayne Morse
(1900-1974)
American senator, educator

Liberalism cannot be defined in the abstract in any helpful way. Liberalism in politics can best be defined in terms of specific issues. Political liberalism should also be defined in terms of objectives. A major objective is the protection of the economic weak and doing it within the framework of a private-property economy. The liberal, emphasizing the civil and property rights of the individual, insists that the individual must remain so supreme as to make the state his servant.
New Republic, July 22, 1946.

James F. Morton
(1870-1941)
American curator

In all ages, the truest lovers of mankind have toiled to imbue their fellows with the spirit of open-mindedness.

The cause of free speech numbers the most glorious martyrs in history. Socrates, whose name we hold in reverence today, was murdered by the Athenian people, for seeking to lead them to think for themselves.

Bruno in death and Galileo in imprisonment paid the penalty of loving truth more than public opinion. Roger Bacon upheld the cause of scientific research against unnumbered persecutions. Milton perceived that no error was so fatal as the suppression of thought, and penned his glorious Areopagitica, which remains to this day an unanswerable argument to all who, either from mental weakness or from a tyrannous disposition, seek to set bounds to human speculation or expression.

Voltaire, Paine and a host of others have followed in demonstrating that free minds and free lips were necessary, in order that men might grow and learn.

In our own land, Elijah Lovejoy gave his life for the principle of freedom of the press; and from his martyrdom was born the grand apostleship of Wendell Phillips in the cause of freedom.

We stand indeed on holy ground when we approach the sublime company of those who, through the ages, have striven to secure, not only for themselves, but for all mankind, the right of unfettered utterance on every theme. Well for us, if we are found worthy to tread in their footsteps, and to bear the most humble part in this great work.

Herbert J. Muller
(b. 1905)
American writer, critic, scholar

The Russian dictatorship of the proletariat has made a farce of the whole Marxist vision: developing a powerful, privileged ruling class to prepare for a classless society, setting up the most despotic state in history so that the state may "wither away," establishing by force a colonial empire to combat imperialism and unite the workers of the world.
Saturday Review, November 1, 1958.

Max Muller
(1823-1900)
English philologist, essayist, philosopher

All truth is safe, and nothing else is safe; and he who keeps back the truth or withholds it from men, from motives of expedience, is either a coward or a criminal, or both.
Chips from a German Workshop, 1867.

To me an ethnologist who speaks of Aryan race, Aryan blood, Aryan eyes and hair, is as great a sinner as a linguist who speaks of a dolichocephalic or a brachycephalic grammar.
Biographies of Words, 1888.

Lewis Mumford
(b. 1895)
American critic, writer

Man's chief purpose . . . is the creation and preservation of values: that is what gives meaning to our civilization, and the participation in this is what gives significance, ultimately, to the individual human life.   *Faith for Living, 1940.*

The fundamental values of a true community are elsewhere: in love, poetry, disinterested thought, the free use of the imagination, the pursuit of non-utilitarian activities, the production of non-profitmaking goods, the enjoyment of non-consumable wealth—here are the sustaining values of a living culture. *Ibid.*

A community whose life is not irrigated by art and science, by religion and philosophy, day upon day, is a community that exists half alive. *Ibid.*

The segregation of the spiritual life from the practical life is a curse that falls impartially upon both sides of our existence. A society that gives to one class all the opportunities for leisure, and to another all the burdens of work, dooms both classes to spiritual sterility. *Ibid.*

Let us confess it: the human situation is always desperate. *In the Name of Sanity.*

Today, all the normal mischances of living have been multiplied, a million-fold, by the potentialities for destruction, for an unthinking act of collective suicide, which man's very triumphs in science and invention have brought about. In this situation the artist has a special task and duty: the task of reminding men of their humanity and the promise of their creativity. *Ibid.*

George William Mundelein
(1872-1939)
American Cardinal

The trouble with us in the past has been that we were too often drawn into an alliance with the wrong side.
Address, Holy Name Society, Chicago, January 2, 1938. N. Y. Times, January 3, 1938.

Selfish employers of labor have flattered the Church by calling it the great conservative force, and then called upon it to act as a police force while they paid but a pittance of wages to those who worked for them. *Ibid.*

Our place is beside the poor, behind the working man. They are our people; they build our churches, they occupy their pews, their children crowd our schools, our priests come from their sons. *Ibid.*

(George) Gilbert (Aimé) Murray
(1866-1957)
British classical scholar

The enemy has no definite name, though in a certain degree we all know him. He who puts always the body before the spirit, the dead before the living; who makes things only in order to sell them; who has forgotten that there is such a thing as truth, and measures the world by advertisement or by money; who daily defiles the beauty that surrounds him and makes vulgar the tragedy.
N. Y. Post, March 27, 1949.

If we were to lose all of our liberties, the liberty of the press would bring them all back again. The liberty of the press, and the liberty of the country, must stand or fall together.

Thomas E. Murray
(b. 1891)
American business executive, former Atomic Energy Commissioner

Man now has the power to put an end to his own history.
Washington Post, November 18, 1955.

William Murray

See Lord Mansfield

Musset

See De Musset

Benito Mussolini

(1883-1945)
Italian fascist dictator

When we claim that "God does not exist", we mean to deny by this declaration the personal God of theology, the God worshipped in various ways and divers modes by believers the world over, that God who from nothing created the universe, from chaos matter, that God of absurd attributes who is an affront to human reason.

L'Homme et la Divinité, published by Bibliotheque Internationale de propagande rationalist, Chene-Bourg, Geneva, July, 1904. Chapter titled Dieu N'existe Pas. First published writing. Quoted in Sawdust Caesar, pp. 387-390.

Science is now in the process of destroying religious dogma. The dogma of the divine creation is recognized as absurd. "Religion is the opium of the people"—Karl Marx. *Ibid.*

Religious morality shows the original stigmata of authoritarianism precisely because it pretends to be the revelation of divine authority. In order to translate this authoritarianism into action and impose it upon humanity, the priestly caste of revealers has sprung up and with it the most atrocious intolerance. *Ibid.*

Religion has shown itself in the open as the institution whose aim is political power by which to externalize the exploitations and the ignorance of the people. *Ibid.*

The mass, whether it be a crowd or an army, is vile.
Pagine Libere, January 1, 1911.

If you acquit me you make me rejoice, for then I can return to work and the community of human society. If you sentence me you honor me, for then you will be condemning not a criminal, but a follower of the Ideal, an agitator according to his conscience, a Soldier of the Truth.
November 23, 1911; address to judge after first arrest as Socialist agitator.

Attempted assassinations are the accidents of kings, just as falling chimneys are the accidents of masons. If we must weep, let us weep for the masons.
Socialist Congress, Reggio Emilia, July, 1912.

Journalism is not a profession but a mission. Our newspaper is our party, our ideal, our soul, and our banner which will lead us to victory.
Editorial, "Avanti!" (Socialist Party organ), 1912.

Italy is the only country in all Europe which in the past hundred years has not had a revolution. Italy has need of a blood bath. (*L'Italia ha bisogno di un bagno di sangue.*) And you, Social Democrats and leaders of the Syndicalists, are the major obstacles against the establishment of such a fact.
To Bruno Buozzi, head of the labor unions, 1913; Sawdust Caesar, p. 91.

O Youth, Youth of Italy, I fling you my call, which will resound into the Future. This call is but one word, a word which I have never pronounced in time of order, but which I pronounce today, boldly, without reservation, without irresolution, with

clear voice and strong faith: a word rebellious and terrifying: W A R!
Popolo d'Italia, November 13, 1914.

Blood alone moves the wheels of history.
Speech, Parma, December 13, 1914.

Socialism is a fraud, a comedy, a phantom, a blackmail.   *Milan, July 22, 1919.*

The proletariat should therefore train
for the great historic struggle in which it
will be able to settle accounts with its adversaries: for the Italian proletariat *needs
a bath of blood* for its force to be renewed.
*Editorial, Popolo d'Italia, 1920 general
strike.*

Revolution is not a surprise packet which
can be opened by all. I do not carry it in
my pocket. Revolution will be accomplished
with the army, not against the army; with
arms, not without them; with trained forces,
not with undisciplined mobs called together
in the streets. It will succeed when it is
surrounded by a halo of sympathy or by the
majority, and if it has not all that, it will
fail.
*Speech, Milan, 1920, when accused of
failing to aid D'Annunzio in Fiume.*

Down with the State, the State of yesterday, today and tomorrow, the Bourgeois
State and the Socialist State. There remains
for me now nothing but the consoling religion of Anarchism.
Popolo d'Italia, April 6, 1920.°

The Italy of 1921 is fundamentally different from that of 1919 . . . To say that
the Bolshevik danger still exists in Italy is
equivalent to trying to exchange for reasons

of self-interest, fear against truth. Bolshevism is conquered.°
Popolo d'Italia, July 2, 1921.

Today Italian Fascism . . . has need of
a corpus of doctrine . . . The request is
somewhat great: but I wish that within
two months . . . there shall be created a
philosophy of Fascism.
*Letter to Michele Bianchi, August 27,
1921. Messagi e Proclami, Milan, 1929,
pp. 38-9.*

There is a violence that liberates, and a
violence that enslaves; there is a violence
that is moral and a violence that is immoral.
Speech, Udine, September 20, 1922.

I see the world as it really is: that is to
say, as a world of unleashed egotism.
*Chamber of Deputies, February 16,
1923. Scritti e Discorsi, V. iii, p. 61.*

Liberty is not an end, it is a means. As
a means it needs to be controlled and dominated. Here we come to the question of
force!   *Ibid.*

Liberalism is not the last word; it does
not represent any final and decisive formula in the art of government . . . Today the
most striking of post-war experiences, those
that are taking place before our eyes, are
marked by the defeat of Liberalism.
*March, 1923 issue of Gerarchia; trans-
lations by N. Y. World, 1923; and
Mme. Sarfatti in her biography of
Mussolini.*

Communism and Fascism have nothing
to do with Liberalism.   *Ibid.*

° Mussolini's father was a follower of Bakunin, the Anarchist philosopher and rival
of Karl Marx.

° In 1925, when Mussolini received a loan
from J. P. Morgan & Co., public relations
agents in America revived the myth of
the Bolshevik danger in Italy.

I beg my friends the Liberals to tell me if ever in all history there was a Government which was based exclusively upon the consent of the people, and which was ready to dispense altogether with the use of force.

There has never been and will never be such a Government. *Ibid.*

The consent of the people is as mutable as the sands of the seashore. The consent of the people is never complete, never permanent. *Ibid.*

There never was a Government that made all the governed happy . . . There must always be malcontents . . . How shall you prevent their feelings from growing and from becoming a danger to the State? You must have recourse to force. *Ibid.*

Fascism now throws the noxious theories of so-called Liberalism upon the rubbish heap. When a group or a party is in power, it is its duty to fortify and defend itself against all. *Ibid.*

The truth, apparent to everyone whose eyes are not blinded by dogmatism, is that men are perhaps weary of liberty. They have had a surfeit of it. Liberty is no longer the virgin, chaste and severe, fought for by the generations of the first half of the past century. For the intrepid youth who present themselves at this new dawn of history, there are other words which move them more deeply; these words are: Order, Hierarchy, Discipline. *Ibid.*

Fascism, which was not afraid to call itself reactionary . . . does not hesitate to call itself illiberal and anti-liberal. *Ibid.*

Know then, once and for all, that Fascism recognizes no idols, worships no fetishes. It has already passed over the more or less decayed body of the Goddess of Liberty, and is quite prepared, if necessary, to do so once more. *Ibid.*

You know what I think about violence. For me it is profoundly moral, more moral than compromises and transactions.
Augesteo speech, August, 1925, reported to Chicago Tribune by G. S.

The bullets pass; Mussolini remains.
Remark when shot by Violet Gibson, 1925.

It is necessary to be very intelligent in the work of repression. All opposition journals have been suppressed and all the anti-fascist organizations dissolved.
Speech, May 26, 1926.

The 18th and 19th centuries experimented with democracy. The 20th century will be the century of Fascism.
Interview with G. S. Viereck, N. Y. World, January 24, 1927.

Let us have a dagger between our teeth, a bomb in our hands, and an infinite scorn in our hearts. *Speech, 1928.*

Democracy is beautiful in theory; in practice it is a fallacy.
N. Y. Times interview, 1928.

The struggle between the two worlds (Fascism and Democracy) can permit of no compromises . . . Either We or They.
Address from balcony of Palazzo Venezia, October 27, 1930.

I repeat that so long as there are cannon they will always be more beautiful than beautiful but often false *words.*
Time, October 27, 1930.

Fortunately the Italian people is not habituated to eating several times a day.

Fortunamente il popolo italiano non e ancora abituato a mangiare molte volte al giorno.
> Chamber of Deputies, December 12, 1930.

It was only one life. What is one life in the affairs of state?
> *To Cornelius Vanderbilt, when their automobile killed a child; repeated by General Smedley Butler, who was court-martialed, 1931.*

Fascism is a religious conception in which man is seen in his immanent relationship with a superior law and with an objective Will that transcends the particular individual and raises him to conscious membership of a spiritual society. Whoever has seen in the religious politics of the Fascist regime nothing but mere opportunism has not understood that Fascism besides being a system of government is also, and above all, a system of thought.
> *The Doctrine of Fascism, Italian Encyclopedia, 1932.*

There is no concept of the State which is not fundamentally a concept of life: philosophy or intuition, a system of ideas which develops logically or is gathered up into a vision or into a faith, but which is always, at least virtually, an organic conception of the world.
> *Ibid.*

The world seen through Fascism is not this material world which appears on the surface, in which man is an individual separated from all others and is standing by himself, and in which he is governed by a natural law that makes him instinctively live a life of selfish and momentary pleasure. The man of Fascism is an individual who is nation and fatherland, which is a moral law, binding together individuals and the generations into a tradition and a mission, suppressing the instinct for a life enclosed within the brief round of pleasure in order to restore within duty a higher life free from the limits of time and space: a life in which the individual, through the denial of himself, through the sacrifice of his own private interests, through death itself, realizes that completely spiritual existence in which his value as a man lies.
> *Ibid.*

It (Fascism) is opposed to classical Liberalism, which arose from the necessity of reacting against absolutism, and which brought its historical purpose to an end when the State was transformed into the conscience and will of the people. *Ibid.*

And if liberty is to be the attribute of the real man, and not of that abstract puppet envisaged by individualistic Liberalism, Fascism is for liberty. And for the only liberty which can be a real thing, the liberty of the State and of the individual within the State. Therefore, for the Fascist, everything is in the State, and nothing human or spiritual exists, much less has value, outside the State. In this sense Fascism is totalitarian, and the Fascist State, the synthesis and unity of all values, interprets, develops and gives strength to the whole life of the people. *Ibid.*

Against individualism, the Fascist conception is for the State; and it is for the individual in so far as he coincides with the State, which is the conscience and universal will of man in his historical existence.
> *Ibid.*

Liberalism denied the State in the interests of the particular individual; Fascism reaffirms the State as the true reality of the individual. *Ibid.*

The Fascist State, the highest and most powerful form of personality, is a force but a spiritual force, which takes over all the forms of the moral and intellectual life of man. It cannot therefore confine itself simply to the functions of order and supervision as Liberalism desired. It is not simply a mechanism which limits the sphere of the supposed liberties of the individual. It is the form, the inner standard and the discipline of the whole person; it saturates the will as well as the intelligence. *Ibid.*

Fascism, in short, is not only the giver of laws and the founder of institutions, but the educator and promoter of spiritual life. It wants to remake, not the forms of human life, but its content, man, character, faith. And to this end it requires discipline and authority that can enter into the spirits of men and there govern unopposed. *Ibid.*

Fascism, the more it considers and observes the future and the development of humanity, quite apart from political considerations of the moment, believes neither in the possibility nor the utility of perpetual peace.
Article for the Encyclopedia Italiana,
N. Y. Times, January 11, 1935.

War alone brings up to its highest tension all human energy, and puts the stamp of nobility upon the peoples who have the courage to meet it. All other trials are substitutes, which never really put men into the position where they have to make the great decision—the alternatives of life or death. *Ibid.*

Fascism conceives of the State as an absolute, in comparison with which all individuals or groups are relative, only to be conceived of in their relation to the State. *Ibid.*

The individual in the Fascist State is not annulled, but rather multiplied just in the same way a soldier in a regiment is not diminished but rather increased by the number of his comrades. *Ibid.*

The Fascist State organizes the nation, but leaves a sufficient margin of liberty to the individual. The latter is deprived of all useless and possibly harmful freedom, but retains what is essential. The deciding power in this question cannot be the individual, but the State alone. *Ibid.*

If every age has its own characteristic doctrine, there are a thousand signs which point to Fascism as the characteristic doctrine of our time. Fascism has henceforth in the world the universality of all those doctrines which, in realizing themselves, have represented a stage in the history of the human spirit. *Ibid.*

This holiday (Christmas) which reminds one only of the birth of a Jew who gave the world debilitating and devitalizing theories, and who especially contrived to trick Italy through the disintegrating power of the Popes.
1941. Ciano's Hidden Diary, Dutton, 1953.

The Italian race is a race of sheep . . . To make a people great you have to send them into battle even if you have to kick them in the pants. *Ibid.*

Only a base, vile, insignificant country can be democratic. A strong and heroic people tends to aristocracy. *Ibid.*

This is the epitaph I want on my tomb: "Here lies one of the most intelligent animals who ever appeared on the face of the earth." *Ibid.*

Three cheers for war! May I be permitted to raise this cry? Three cheers for

Italy's war, noble and beautiful above all, with its 500,000 dead who are our surest wealth. And three cheers for war in general.
Sawdust Caesar. Appendix 16: Volte-face Caesar.

Mine is a policy of peace.
Ibid. Autobiography.

Our formula is this: everything within the State, nothing outside the State, nothing against the State.   *Ibid.*

My program is simple: I want to govern.
Ibid.

One is born a Fascist.   *Ibid.*

Fascism is a religion.   *Ibid.*

It is not possible to transform one's mind. Socialism is part of my flesh. *Ibid.*

War is to man what maternity is to a woman. From a philosophical and doctrinal viewpoint, I do not believe in perpetual peace.   *Ibid.*

Our motto must be to lie in order to conquer.
Instructions to Fernando Mezzasoma; Roman Dombrowski, "Mussolini: Twilight and Fall," 1956.

The vanquished have no friends. *Ibid.*

Se avanzo seguitemi. Se indietreggio uccidetemi. Se muoio Vendicatemi. (If I advance, follow me; if I retreat, cut me down; if I die, avenge me.)
*Poster, signed Mussolini.**

---

* In 1793 La Rochejaquelin said: "If I advance, follow me! If I retreat, kill me! If I die, avenge me!"

Napoleon Bonaparte
(1769-1821)
Emperor of France

A nation must have a religion, and that religion must be under the control of the government.
To Count Thibaubeau, June, 1801.

What a beautiful fix we are in now; peace has been declared.
March 7, 1802; Treaty of Amiens.

If they want peace, nations should avoid the pin-pricks that precede cannon-shots.
To Czar Alexander, Tilsit, June 22, 1807.

I am the state—I alone am here the representative of the people.   *Senate, 1814.*

If I had believed in a God of rewards and punishments, I might have lost courage in battle.
To Gaspard Gourgaud, St. Helena, 1815.

The Society of Jesus is the most dangerous of orders, and has done more mischief than all the others.
To Barry E. O'Meara, St. Helena, November 2, 1816.

All religions have been made by men.
To Gourgaud, January 28, 1817.

I am neither an atheist nor a rationalist; I believe in God and am of the religion of my father. I was born a Catholic, and will fulfill all the duties of that church.
St. Helena, April 18, 1821.

There are only two forces in the world, the sword and the spirit. In the long run the sword will always be conquered by the spirit. *Frederiks, Maxims of Napoleon.*

A journalist is a grumbler, a censurer, a giver of advice, a regent of sovereigns, a tutor of nations. Four hostile newspapers are more to be feared than a thousand bayonets.[*]   *Sayings of Napoleon.*

In war morale counts for three quarters, the balance of man-power counts for only one quarter.
>   *Correspondence de Napoleon.*

Nothing of the kind; Providence is always on the side of the last reserve.
>   *Reply, when someone remarked, "God is always on the side of the largest battalions." Ramage, Beautiful Thoughts from French and Italian Authors, p. 346.*

The Bourbons might have preserved themselves if they had controlled writing materials. The advent of cannon killed the feudal system; ink will kill the modern social organization.
>   *Bertaut, Napoleon in His Own Words, p. 63.*

If I had to choose a religion, the sun as the universal giver of life would be my god.
>   *Cardiff, What Great Men Think of Religion.*

How can you have order in a state without religion? For, when one man is dying of hunger near another who is ill of surfeit, he cannot resign himself to this difference unless there is an authority which declares "God wills it thus." Religion is excellent stuff for keeping common people quiet.
>   *American Freeman.*

---

[*] Sometimes given as "ten thousand bayonets." Another version: "I fear the *Cologne Gazette* more than ten thousand bayonets."

L'Angleterre est une nation de boutiquiers. (England is a nation of little shopkeepers.)
>   *O'Meara, Napoleon at St. Helena.*

Revolution is an idea which has found its bayonets.
>   *Quoted by Mussolini, masthead of Popolo d'Italia.*

Revolutions are like the most noxious dungheaps, which bring into life the noblest vegetables.

What is history but a fable agreed upon? *Attributed.*

War is the business of barbarians. *Ibid.*

Ignatz Leo Nascher

(1863-1944)
American writer

Geriatrics.
>   *Book title, 1914; invented word.*

Ogden Nash

(1902-1971)
American writer

They take the paper and they read the headlines,
So they've heard of unemployment and they've heard of breadlines,
And they philanthropically cure them all
By getting up a costume charity ball.
>   *Pride Goeth Before a Raise.*

A man is quite dishonorable to sell himself
For anything other than quite a lot of pelf.
>   *Tide, November 8, 1946.*

Gamal Abdel Nasser

(1918-1970)
President, United Arab Republic

Fate does not jest and events are not a

matter of chance—there is no existence out of nothing.

The Philosophy of the Revolution, 1954. Time, August 27, 1956.

Within the Arab circle there is a role wandering aimlessly in search of a hero. For some reason it seems to me that this role is beckoning to us—to move, to take up its lines, put on its costume and give it life. Indeed, we are the only ones who can play it. The role is to spark the tremendous latent strengths in the region surrounding us to create a great power, which will then rise up to a level of dignity and undertake a positive part in building the future of mankind. *Ibid.*

I have been a conspirator for so long that I mistrust all around me.

Time, July 28, 1958.

George Jean Nathan
(1882-1958)

American author, editor, critic

Patriotism is often an arbitrary veneration of real estate above principles.

Testament of a Critic.

The path of sound credence is through the thick forest of skepticism.

Materia Critica, 1924.

The great problems of the world—social, political, economic and theological—do not concern me in the slightest . . . If all the Armenians were to be killed tomorrow and if half of Russia were to starve to death the day after, it would not matter to me in the least. What concerns me alone is myself and the interests of a few close friends.

Living Authors, H. W. Wilson, 1932.

National Association of Manufacturers

Now, more than before, strikes are being won or lost in the newspapers and over the radio. The swing of public opinion has always been a major factor in labor disputes, but with the settlement of strikes being thrown more and more into the laps of public officials, the question of public opinion becomes of greater importance. For it is public opinion—what the voters think —that moves those elected to action along one course or another.

Senate Report No. 6, part 6, 76th Congress, 1st Session. Violations of Free Speech and Rights of Labor, Part III.

National Catholic Alumni Federation

Man as we know him in the whole of recorded human history is, and ever has been, of an unchanging and unchangeable nature.

Resolutions, 1936.

Scott Nearing
(b. 1883)

American sociologist

Through the ages, this question of distribution has been answered by the struggle between men and men—the struggle for wealth, income, privilege, security and power.

Those who have taken part in this historic struggle over the division of property and income fall into one of two classes:

1. The workers, who perform productive and useful labor.

2. The robbers, who appropriate the products of labor under the slogan, "You toil—we eat."

From Capitalism to Communism, 1945.

The robbers may be subdivided into (1) grabbers who take an active part in appropriating the wealth produced by the workers—bankers, pirates, bandits, real estate operators, stockbrokers, corporation lawyers, hijackers, kidnappers, oil magnates, coal barons, steel kings, and (2) grafters, who merely consume without taking any active part in the economic struggle —absentee landlords, stock, bond and mortgage holders, owners of annuities, kept families and other economic parasites.

Ibid.

During the whole period of written history, it is not the workers but the robbers who have been in control of the world.

Ibid.

In a pinch the liberals can always be counted on to back up the principles of the established order—private property in the implements of production, special privileges, and the more moderate and lucrative phases of imperialism.

Modern Monthly, July, 1950.

Jawaharlal Nehru

(1889-1964)

Indian prime minister

The basic fact of today is the tremendous pace of change in human life.

Credo; circulated to friends; reprinted in N. Y. Times Magazine, September 7, 1958.

We see the growing contradictions within the rigid framework of communism itself. Its suppression of individual freedom brings about powerful reactions. Its contempt for what might be called the moral and spiritual side of life not only ignores something that is basic in man but also deprives human behavior of standards and values. Its unfortunate association with violence encourages a certain evil tendency in human beings.

Ibid.

Communism became too closely associated with the necessity for violence and thus the idea which it placed before the world became a tainted one. Means distorted ends.

Ibid.

Democracy and socialism are means to an end, not the end itself.

Ibid.

The law of life should not be the competition of acquisitiveness, but cooperation, the good of each contributing to the good of all.

Ibid.

The forces of a capitalist society, if left unchecked, tend to make the rich richer and the poor poorer.

Ibid.

Socialism is basically a different approach from that of capitalism . . . Socialism is, after all, not only a way of life, but a certain scientific approach to social and economic problems.

Ibid.

Imperialism, or colonialism, suppressed, and suppresses, the progressive social forces. Inevitably, it aligns itself with certain privileged groups or classes because it is interested in preserving the social and economic *status quo*.

Ibid.

I want nothing to do with any religion concerned with keeping the masses satisfied to live in hunger, filth and ignorance. I want nothing to do with any order, religious or otherwise, which does not teach people that they are capable of becoming happier and more civilized, on this earth, capable of becoming true *man*, master of his fate and captain of his soul. To attain this I would put priests to work, also, and turn the temples into schools.

Edgar Snow, Journey to the Beginning, p. 77. Random House, 1958.

Inevitably we are led to only one possible solution—the establishment of a Socialist order, first within national boundaries, and eventually in the world as a whole, with a controlled production and distribution of wealth for the public good . . . If political institutions or social institutions stand in the way of such a change, they have to be removed. *Ibid., p. 411.*

You don't change the course of history by turning the faces of portraits to the wall. *To Khrushchev; quoted by Leonard Lyons, N. Y. Post, April 1, 1959.*

Grownups have a strange way of putting themselves in compartments and groups. They build up barriers . . . of religion, of caste, of color, of party, of nation, of province, of language, of custom and of wealth and poverty. Thus they live in prisons of their own making. *India News, quoted Gazette & Daily, York, Pa., February 10, 1958.*

The spectacle of what is called religion, or at any rate organized religion, in India and elsewhere, has filled us with horror, and I have frequently condemned it and wished to make a clean sweep of it. *Cardiff, What Great Men Think of Religion.*

Slogans are apt to petrify man's thinking . . . every slogan, every word almost, that is used by the socialist, the communist, the capitalist. People hardly think nowadays. They throw words at each other.

The French Revolution of 150 years ago gradually ushered in an age of political equality, but the times have changed, and that by itself is not enough today. The boundaries of democracy have to be widened now so as to include economic equality also. This is the great revolution through which we are all passing. *Glimpses of World History, 1939.*

Horatio Nelson

(1758-1805)
British admiral

Nelson confides that every man will do his duty. *Proposed signal, Battle of Trafalgar.*

New Hampshire

Article 10. Right of Revolution: Government being instituted for the common benefit, protection, and security of the whole community and not for the interests or emoluments of any one man, family, or class of men; therefore, whenever the ends of government are perverted, and public liberty manifestly endangered, and all other means of redress ineffectual, the people may, and of right ought to, reform the old, or establish a new government. The doctrine of non-resistance against arbitrary power and oppression is absurd, slavish, and destructive of the good and happiness of mankind. *Article X, New Hampshire Bill of Rights, 1784.*

John Henry Newman**

(1801-1890)
English Cardinal, writer

In the corrupt papal system we have the very cruelty, the craft and the ambition of

---

* Captain Blackwood proposed substituting England for Nelson; Lieutenant Pasco substituted expects for confides; according to George Fielding Eliot, N. Y. Times, October 5, 1958.

** Newman's writings, until 1843 when he

[522]

the Roman Republic; its cruelty in its un-sparing sacrifice of the happiness and virtue of individuals to a phantom of public ex-pedience, in its forced celibacy within, and its persecutions without; its craft in its false-hoods, its deceitful deeds and lying won-ders; and its grasping ambition in the very structure of its policy, in the assumption of universal dominion: old Rome is still alive; nowhere have its eagles lighted, but it still claims the sovereignty under another pre-tense. The Roman Church I will not blame, but pity—she is, as I have said, spellbound, as if by an evil spirit, she is in thralldom.
The Development of Christian Doc-trine, 1834.

In truth, she is a Church beside herself, abounding in noble gifts and rightful titles, but unable to use them religiously; crafty, obstinate, wilful, malicious, cruel, unnat-ural, as madmen are. Or rather, she may be said to resemble a demoniac, pos-sessed with principles, thoughts and ten-dencies not her own.
1837; English Churchman, March 3, 1910.

We must deal with her (Rome) as we would towards a friend who is visited by derangement; in great affliction, with all affectionate, tender thought, with tearful regret and a broken heart, but still with a steady eye and a firm hand.
Lectures on the Prophetical Office of the Church, 1837, p. 101.

published a retraction, were anti-Roman Catholic. The Encyclopaedia Britannica, 11th edition, states that "the tone of his mind was at this date (1816) evangelistical and Calvinistic, and he held that the pope was Anti-Christ." In 1845 Newman was received into the Roman Catholic Church. The quotations here are given chronologi-cally.

Moreover, there is this harm, too, and one of vast extent, and touching men gen-erally, that by insincerity and lying, faith and truth are lost, which are the firmest bonds of human society, and when they are lost supreme confusion follows in life, so that men seem in nothing to differ from devils.   *Apologia pro Vita Sua, 1864.*

There are but two ways, the way of Rome and the way of atheism.   *Ibid.*

It would be a gain to the country were it vastly more superstitious, more bigoted, more gloomy, more fierce in its religion than at present it shows itself to be.
Ibid.

The Catholic Church claims, not only to judge infallibly on religious questions, but to animadvert on opinion in secular matters which bear upon religion, on matters of phi-losophy, of science, of literature, of history, and it demands our submission to her claim.
Ibid.

By liberalism I mean false liberty of thought, or the exercise of thought upon matters, in which, from the constitution of the human mind, thought cannot be brought to any successful issue, and there-fore is out of place. Among such matters are first principles of any kind; and of these the most sacred and momentous are espe-cially to be reckoned the truths of revela-tion.   *Ibid., Note A.*

From the age of fifteen, dogma has been the fundamental principle of my religion: I know no other religion; I cannot enter into the idea of any other sort of religion; religion, as a mere sentiment, is to me a dream and a mockery.   *Op. cit.*

Such, then, is popular Protestantism, con-sidered in its opposition to Catholics. Its

[523]

truth is establishment by law; its philosophy is theory; its faith is prejudice; its facts are fiction; its reasoning fallacies; and its security is ignorance about those it is opposing.

The law says that white is black; ignorance says, why not? Theory says it ought to be; fallacy says it must be; fiction says it is, and prejudice says it shall be.
Present Position of Catholics.

(The Church) holds that it were better for sun and moon to drop from heaven, for the earth to fail, and for all the many millions who are upon it to die of starvation in the extremest agony, as far as temporal affliction goes, than that one soul . . . should commit one single venial sin, should tell one wilful untruth.
Lecture on Anglican Difficulties.

I do not see much difference between avowing that there is no God, and implying that nothing definite can for certain be known about Him. *Historical Sketches, 3.*

No one can dislike the democratic principle more than I do.
Letter to the Duke of Norfolk.

Reason is one thing and faith is another and reason can as little be made a substitute for faith, as faith can be made a substitute for reason.
Discourse to Mixed Congregations.

A liberal education is the education which gives a man a clear, conscious view of his own opinions and judgments, a truth in developing them, an eloquence in expressing them, and a force in urging them. It teaches him to see things as they are, to go right to the point, to disentangle a skein of thought, to detect what is sophistical, and to discard what is irrelevant. . . .

He is at home in any society, he has common ground with every class; he knows when to speak and when to be silent.
Saturday Review of Literature, November 21, 1953.

Clergymen are bound to form and pronounce an opinion. It is sometimes said in familiar language, that a clergyman should have nothing to do with politics. That is true if it be meant that he should not aim at secular objects, should not side with a political party as such, should not be ambitious of popular applause, or the favor of great men . . .
Priests in Politics, reprinted in "Social Justice."

But if it means that he should not express an opinion and exert an influence one way rather than another, it is plainly unscriptural . . . *Ibid.*

If indeed, this world's concerns could be altogether disjoined from those of Christ's kingdom, then indeed all Christians (laymen as well as clergy) should abstain from the thought of temporal affairs, and let the worthless world pass down the stream of events till it perishes; but if (as is the case) what happens in nations must affect the cause of religion in those nations, since the Church may be seduced and corrupted by the world . . . therefore it is our duty to stand as a beacon on a hill, to cry aloud and spare not, to lift up our voice like a trumpet, and show the people their transgression, and the house of Jacob its sins.

All this may be done without injury to our Christian gentleness and humbleness, though it is difficult to do it. We need not be angry nor use contentious words, and yet may firmly give our opinion, in proportion as we have the means of forming one, and be zealous towards God in all active good service, and scrupulously and pointedly keep aloof from the bad men whose evil arts we fear. *Ibid.*

Nothing great is done without suffering, without humiliation . . . I believe, O my God, that poverty is better than riches, pain better than pleasure, obscurity and contempt better than name, and ignominy and reproach better than honor . . .

I will never have faith in riches, rank, power or reputation. I will never set my heart on worldly success, or on worldly advantages. I will never wish for what men call the prizes of life . . .

Isaac Newton
(1642-1727)
English philosopher, mathematician

Every body preserves in its state of rest or of uniform motion in a straight line, except in so far as it is compelled to change that state by impressed forces.
Principia (First Law of Motion).

The Supreme God is a Being eternal, infinite, absolutely perfect; but a being, however perfect, without dominion, cannot be said to be Lord God.
Principia, second edition.

It is the dominion of a spiritual being which constitutes a God: a true, supreme, or imaginary dominion makes a true, supreme or imaginary God. And from his true dominion it follows that the true God is a living, intelligent, and powerful Being; and from his other perfections, that he is supreme, or most perfect. *Ibid.*

A god without dominion, providence, and final causes, is nothing else but Fate and Nature. *Ibid.*

I seem to have been only like a boy playing on the seashore and diverting myself in now and then finding a smoothe pebble or a prettier shell than ordinary whilst the great ocean of truth lay all undiscovered before me. *Brewster, Memoirs of Newton.*

New York State

And whereas, We are required by the benevolent principles of rational liberty, not only to expel civil tyranny, but also to guard against that spiritual oppression and intolerance . . . the free exercise and enjoyment of religious profession and worship, without discrimination or preference, shall forever hereafter be allowed within this state to all mankind.
First Constitution, 1777.

No school . . . in which any religious sectarian doctrine shall be taught . . . shall receive any portion of the school moneys.
Bill passed by legislature, April 11, 1842.

Nicholas of Cusa
(1401-1464)
Roman Catholic prelate,
mathematician, philosopher

The greatest danger against which most men have warned us is that which comes from communicating intellectual secrets to minds become subservient to the authority of an inveterate habit, for such is the power of a long-lasting observance, that most men prefer death to giving up their way of life.
De Docta Ignorantia (Learned Ignorance).

All we know of the truth is that the absolute truth, such as it is, is beyond our reach. *Ibid.*

George Nicholas
(1754?-1799)
American soldier, pioneer, politician

The liberty of the press ought to be left where the Constitution has placed it, without any power in Congress to abridge it; that if they abridge it, they will destroy it; and that whenever that falls, all our liberties must fall with it.

Letter to a friend in Virginia, 1798.

Among those principles deemed sacred in America; among those sacred rights considered as forming the bulwark of their liberty, which the government contemplates with *awful reverence,* and would approach only with the most *cautious circumspection,* there is none of which the importance is more deeply impressed on the public mind than the liberty of the press. That this liberty is often carried to excess, that it has sometimes degenerated to licentiousness, is seen and is lamented; but the remedy has not yet been discovered. Perhaps it is an evil inseparable from the good with which it is allied: perhaps it is a shoot which cannot be stripped from the stalk *without wounding vitally the plant from which it is torn.* *Ibid.*

Reinhold Niebuhr
(1892-1971)
American theologian

Socialism and Communism may be brothers; if so, they are as the late Socialist leader Kurt Schumacher observed, like Cain and Abel.

There is no basis for the Marxist hope that an "economy of abundance" will guarantee social peace; for men may fight as desperately for "power and glory" as for bread.

Man's capacity for justice makes democracy possible; but man's inclination to injustice makes democracy necessary.
Children of Light and Children of Darkness.

Dietrich von Nieheim (also known as Niem and Nyem)
(1340?-1418)
German historian, papal official

When its existence is threatened, the Church is freed of moral edicts. Unity as an aim blesses all means: perfidy, treachery, tyranny, simony, prisons, and death. For every holy order exists because of the aims of society, and personality must be sacrificed to the general good.
Quoted by Djilas, The New Class, p. 150.

Friedrich Nietzsche
(1844-1900)
German philosopher

So long as the priest, that professional negator, slanderer and poisoner of life, is regarded as a superior type of human being, there cannot be any answer to the question: What is truth? *The Antichrist.*

Neither as an ethical code nor as a religion has Christianity any point of contact with things as they actually are. *Ibid.*

The Christian religion grew upon a soil of such utter falsification, where the deepest instincts of the ruling factions were opposed to nature and natural values to such an extent, that Christianity became a death struggle against reality which has never been surpassed. *Ibid.*

There is no need to deck out Christianity in fine trappings; for it has waged war to the death against this higher type of man; it has laid a ban upon all the basic instincts of this type, it has distilled evil and the voice of evil out of those very instincts, rebuking the strong man as a wrong-doer.
Ibid.

With every extension of Christianity to wider and ruder masses, who were increasingly less able to grasp its essentials, the need arose to vulgarize and barbarize Christianity more and more. It absorbed the teachings and rites of all the subterranean cults of the *Imperium Romanum*, and the rot of all kinds of sickly reasoning. *Ibid.*

Nothing is more pathological in our pathological modernity than this disease of Christian pity. *Ibid.*

What is good? All that elevates the feeling of power, the will to power, the power itself in man. *Ibid., sect. 2.*

What is bad? All that proceeds from weakness. *Ibid.*

What is happiness? The feeling that power *increases*—that resistance is being overcome. *Ibid.*

The Christian, that *ultimo ratio* of lying, is the Jew all over again—he is threefold the Jew. *Ibid.*

Life is an instinct of growth, for survival, for the accumulation of forces, for power. *Ibid., 6.*

Great intellects are skeptical. *Ibid., 10.*

Definition of Protestantism: hemiplegic paralysis of Christianity—and of reason. *Ibid.*

The preponderance of pain over pleasure is the cause of our fictitious morality and religion. *Ibid., 15.*

Anti-Semitism is the last consequence of Judaism. *Ibid., 24.*

"Sins" are indispensable to every society organized on an ecclesiastical basis; they are the only reliable weapons of power; the priest lives upon sins; it is necessary to him that there be "sinning." *Ibid., 26.*

Morality is the best of all devices for leading mankind by the nose. *Ibid., 44.*

Woman was God's second mistake. *Ibid., 48.*

It is all up with priests and gods when man becomes scientific. *Ibid.*

Whom do I hate most among the rabble of the present day? The Socialist rabble, the Chandala apostles, who undermine the workingman's instinct, his delight, his feeling of contentedness with his petty existence—who make him envious and teach him revenge. *Ibid., 57.*

Wrong never lies in unequal rights, **it** lies in the pretension of equal rights. *Ibid.*

I call Christianity the one great curse, one great intrinsic depravity, and the one great instinct of revenge, for which no means are venomous enough, or secret, subtler and small enough—I call it the one immortal blemish on the human race. *Ibid., 62.*

Beyond Good and Evil. Book title.

There is Master-Morality and Slave-Morality. *Beyond Good and Evil.*

The Jews—"a people born to slavery," as Tacitus and the whole ancient world say of them . . . performed the miracle of the inversion of values . . . Their prophets fused the terms "rich," "godless," "evil," "violent," and "sensuous," into one idea, and for the first time coined the expression "world" as a term of reproach. In this inversion of values (in which is also included the term "poor" as a synonym with "saint"

and "friend") which the Jewish people have brought about, their significance as a people is to be found; it is with them that the *slave insurrection in morals commences.*
                                    Ibid.

A married philosopher is a comic character.   *Ibid.*

Inasmuch as in all ages, as long as mankind has existed, there have also been human herds (family alliances, communities, tribes, peoples, states, churches), and always a great number who obey in proportion to the small number who command —in view, therefore of the fact that obedience has been most practised and fostered among mankind hitherto, one may reasonably suppose that, generally speaking, the need thereof is now innate in every one, as a kind of *formal conscience* which gives the command: "Thou shalt unconditionally do something, unconditionally refrain from something"; in short, "Thou shalt."   *Ibid.*

A herd of blond beasts of prey, a race of conquerors and masters, with military organization, with the power to organize, unscrupulously placing their fearful paws upon a population perhaps vastly superior in numbers . . . this herd founded the State.
*The Genealogy of Morals. Also called,
The Natural History of Morals.*

Napoleon, the synthesis of *brute* and *Superman.*   *Ibid.*

Wherever the religious neurosis has appeared on the earth so far, we find it connected with three dangerous prescriptions as to regimen: solitude, fasting, and sexual abstinence—but without its being possible to determine with certainty which is cause and which is effect, or *if* any relation at all of cause and effect exists there.   *Ibid.*

The *universal degeneracy of mankind* to the level of the "man of the future"—as idealised by the socialistic fools and shallowpates—this degeneracy and dwarfing of man to an absolutely gregarious animal (or as they call it, to a man of "free society"), this brutalising of man into a pigmy with equal rights and claims, is undoubtedly possible!
                                    Ibid.

The philosopher, as a man *indispensable* for tomorrow and the day after the morrow, has ever found himself, and has been *obliged* to find himself, in contradiction to the day in which he lives; his enemy has always been the ideal of his day.   *Ibid.*

Success has always been a great liar.
                                    Ibid.

Life itself is *Will to Power;* self-preservation is only one of the indirect and most frequent *results* thereof.   *Ibid.*

The noble soul has reverence for itself.
                                    Ibid.

Fear is the mother of morality.   *Ibid.*

The Christian faith from the beginning, is sacrifice: the sacrifice of all freedom, all pride, all self-confidence of spirit; it is at the same time subjection, self-derision, and self-mutilation.   *Ibid.*

At the bottom of all distinguished races the beast of prey is not to be mistaken, the magnificent *blond beast,* roaming wantonly in search of prey and victory.   *Ibid.*

The Philosopher has to be the bad conscience of his age.
            The Case of Wagner. Preface.

In the sphere of so-called moral valuations, there is no greater contrast than that between *master-morality* and the mo-

rality of *Christian* conceptions of worth: the latter having grown upon a thoroughly morbid soil; while reversely, master-morality (Roman, heathen, classical, Renaissance morality) is the symbolic language of well-constitutedness, of *ascending* life, of the Will to Power as the principle of life.
Ibid.

Master morality *affirms*, just as instinctively as Christian morality *denies*. ("God," "the other world," and "self-renunciation" are nothing but negations.) *Ibid.*

All idealism is falsehood in the face of necessity. *Ecce Homo.*

Human, All Too Human. Book title.

There are no eternal facts, as there are no absolute truths.
Human, All Too Human.

Nobody dies nowadays of fatal truths: there are too many antidotes to them.
Ibid.

One's belief in truth begins with a doubt of all the truths one has believed hitherto.
Ibid.

I teach you the Superman. Man is something that is to be surpassed. What have you done to surpass him?
Thus Spake Zarathustra.

What is the ape to man? A ridicule, or a grievous shame. And that is just what man is to be to the Superman—a ridicule, or a grievous shame. *Ibid.*

All the gods are dead; so we now want the Superman to live. *Ibid.*

You say that a good cause will even sanctify war! I tell you, it is the good war that sanctifies every cause! *Ibid.*

In the mountains of truth you never climb in vain. *Ibid.*

If there were gods, how could I bear to be no god? *Consequently* there are no gods.
Ibid.

I conjure you, my brethren, remain faithful to earth, and do not believe those who speak unto you of superterrestrial hopes! Poisoners they are, whether they know it or not. *Ibid.*

He who must be a creator in good and evil—verily, he must first be a destroyer, and break values into pieces. *Ibid.*

Let us speak thereon, ye wisest men, however bad it be. To be silent is worse; all unuttered truths become poisonous.
Ibid.

Wherever I found a living creature, there I found the will to power. *Ibid.*

Jesus died too soon. He would have repudiated His doctrine if he had lived to my age. *Ibid.*

Two great European narcotics, alcohol and Christianity.
The Twilight of the Gods (also translated as The Twilight of the Idols).

What is it: is man only a blunder of God, or God only a blunder of man?
Ibid.

Out of the very love one bears to life one should wish death to be free, deliberate, and a matter neither of chance or of surprise. *Ibid.*

Freedom denotes that the virile instincts which rejoice in war and victory, prevail over other instincts. *Ibid.*

The man who has won his freedom . . tramples ruthlessly upon that contemptible kind of comfort which tea-grocers, Christians, cows, women, Englishmen, and other democrats worship in their dreams. *Ibid.*

The Will to Power.   *Book title.*°

The Germans are responsible for everything that exists today, for the sickliness and stupidity that oppose culture, the neurosis, called nationalism, from which Europe suffers; they have robbed Europe itself of its meaning and its intelligence. They have led it into a blind alley.
Quoted by Prof. Irwin Edman as an illustration of Nietzsche's opinion of his people. N. Y. Times, October 15, 1944.

The Germans are like women. You can never fathom their depths. They have none. What is called "deep" in Germany is an instinctive uncleanliness in one's self. Might I not suggest that the word German as an international epithet be used to indicate this psychological depravity? The Germans have no idea of how vulgar they are, which is itself the very acme of vulgarity.
Ibid.

Not only have the German historians completely lost the broad view, which is banned by them. First and foremost, according to them, a man must be "German", he must belong to the "race". "I am a German" con-

stitutes an argument; *"Deutschland ueber Alles"* a principle.   *Ibid.*

What fails to kill me makes me only stronger.°

Convictions are more dangerous enemies of truth than lies.
The Portable Nietzsche, 1954.

The surest way to corrupt a youth is to instruct him to hold in higher esteem those who think alike than those who think differently.   *Ibid.*

One has to pay dearly for immortality; one has to die several times while one is still alive.   *Ibid.*

The Aryan influence perverted the whole world . . . Mixed races are the sources of great civilizations . . . Maxim: never speak to a man who believes in the race fraud.

How refreshing it is to see a Jew among the Germans! All this dullness, all these flaxen heads, these blue eyes; the absence of *esprit* in their faces, words, demeanor; their lazy sprawling, the German need for "recuperating" that stems not from overwork but from their repulsive habit of stimulating themselves with alcohol . . . The anti-Semites do not forgive the Jews for having "spirit" and money. Anti-Semites —another name for "failures".

The world is beautiful, but has a disease called Man.

The Christian resolve to find the world evil and ugly has made the world evil and ugly.

° This book was compiled from literary remains by Nietzsche's sister, Frau Foerster-Nietzsche. In 1958 Prof. Karl Schlechta in a new introduction to Nietzsche's work showed that there was no such book, that in addition to using notebook jottings, Frau Foerster-Nietzsche, a notorious anti-Semite, forged 30 letters and committed other frauds in the volume she published, for the purpose of making her brother appear a racist, pan-German, and premature Nazi.

° Used as motto by Nazis at Ordensburg Vogelsang, training center of selected Hitler Youth leaders.

It is more convenient to follow one's conscience than one's intelligence, for at every failure, conscience finds an excuse and an encouragement in itself. That is why there are so many conscientious and so few intelligent people.

Robert Georges Nivelle

(1856-1924)

French general

Ils ne passeront pas. (They shall not pass.) *To Castelnau, at Verdun, February, 1916; mistakenly attributed to Pétain.*

Kwame Nkrumah

(1909-1972)

Founder and prime minister of Ghana

Seek ye first the political kingdom and all things shall be added unto you.
Inscribed on his statue at Accra; Kenneth Love in N. Y. Times Magazine, July 20, 1958.

We prefer self-government with danger to servitude with tranquillity. *Ibid.*

What other countries have taken three hundred years or more to achieve, a once dependent territory must try to accomplish in a generation if it is to survive. *Op. cit.*

Capitalism is too complicated a system for a newly independent nation, hence the need for a socialistic society. But even a system based on social justice and a democratic constitution may need backing up, during the period following independence, by emergency measures of a totalitarian kind. *Ibid.*

Alfred Nobel

(1833-1896)

Swedish munitions manufacturer, philanthropist

A mere increase in the deadliness of armaments would not bring peace. The difficulty is that the action of explosives is too limited; to overcome this deficiency war must be made as deadly for all the civilians back home as for the troops on the front lines. . . . War will instantly stop if the weapon is bacteriology.
Robert Shaplen, New Yorker profile, March 22, 1958.

Great accumulations of property should go back to the community and common purposes. *Ibid.*

The only true solution would be a convention under which all the governments would bind themselves to defend collectively any country that was attacked. *Ibid.*

Such persons should be especially considered (for the Nobel peace prize) as are successful in word and deed in combatting the peculiar prejudices still cherished against the inauguration of a European peace tribunal. *Ibid., Second will, 1893.*

To the person who shall have done the best work for fraternity among nations, for the abolition or reduction of standing armies and promotion of peace congresses. *Ibid., Final will, 1895.*

Perhaps my dynamite plants will put an end to war sooner than your congresses. On the day two army corps can annihilate each other in one second all civilized nations will recoil from war in horror.
To Bertha von Suttner, at a pacifist congress, in Switzerland, August, 1892.

Max Nordau (né Sudfeld)
(1849-1923)
German writer, physician

Conventional Lies of Our Civilization.
Book title.

Historical investigations have revealed to us the origin and growth of the Bible. We know that by this name we designate a collection of writings as radically unlike in origin, character and contents, as if the Nibelungen Lied, Mirabeau's speeches, Heine's love poems and a manual of zoology had been printed and mixed up promiscuously, and then bound into one volume.

We find collected in this book the superstitious beliefs of the ancient inhabitants of Palestine, with indistinct echoes of Indian and Persian fables, mistaken imitations of Egyptian theories, and customs, historical chronicles as dry as they are unreliable, and miscellaneous poems, amatory, human and Jewish-national, which are rarely distinguished by beauties of the highest order, but frequently by superfluity of expression, coarseness, bad taste, and genuine Oriental sensuality.

As a literary monument the Bible is of much later origin than the Vedas; as a work of literary value it is surpassed by everything written in the last two thousand years by authors even of the second rank, and to compare it seriously with the productions of Homer, Sophocles, Dante, Shakespeare or Goethe would require a fanaticized mind that had entirely lost its power of judgment. Its conception of the universe is childish, and its morality revolting, as revealed in the malicious vengeance attributed to God in the Old Testament and in the New, the parable of the laborers of the eleventh hour and the episodes of Mary Magdalen and the woman taken in adultery.

Frank Norris
(1870-1902)
American novelist

If there is much pain in life, all the more reason that it should appear in a class of literature which, in its highest form, is a sincere transcription of life. It is the complaint of the coward, this cry against the novel with a purpose, because it brings the tragedies and griefs of others to notice.
Essays on Authorship.

The Muse is a teacher, not a trickster.
Ibid.

She is a Child of the People, this Muse of our Fiction of the future . . . Believe me, she will lead you far from the studios and the aesthetes, the velvet jackets and the uncut hair, far from the sexless creatures who cultivate their little art of writing as the fancier cultivates his orchid. Tramping along, then, with a stride that will tax your best paces, she will lead you—if you are humble with her and honest with her—straight into a World of Working Men, crude of speech, swift of action, strong of passion, straight to the heart of a new life, on the borders of a new time, and there and there only, will you learn to know the stuff of which must come the American fiction of the future.
Ibid.

It is all very well to jeer at the People and at the People's misunderstanding of the arts, but the fact is indisputable that no art that is not in the end understood by the People can live or ever did live a single generation. In the larger view, in the last analysis, the People pronounce the final judgment.
Ibid.

Sincerity, sincerity, and again sincerity.
Ibid.

The people have a right to the truth as they have a right to life, liberty and the pursuit of happiness.   *Ibid.*

George W. Norris
(1861-1944)
*American senator, sponsor of
20th Amendment*

Mr. President, we are gradually reaching a time, if we have not already reached that period, when the business of the country is controlled by men who can be named on the fingers of one hand, because these men control the money of the Nation, and that control is growing at a rapid rate. There is only a comparatively small part of it left for them to get, and when they control the money, they control the banks, they control the manufacturing institutions, they control the aviation companies, they control the insurance companies, they control the publishing companies; and we have had some remarkable instances of the control of the publishing companies presented before a subcommittee of the Committee on the Judiciary.

Speech, Senate, reprinted in Congressional Record, November 30, 1944.

These corporations forget nothing. We have had illustrations given us where a magazine would start out on a particular line, but would find itself called on the carpet by some one from one of these great institutions. They were told what the policy must be. Absolute failure stared them in the face unless they obeyed. Through the control of advertising, which, incidentally, to a great extent, is handled by corporations which this money trust controls, they control the avenues of publicity.   *Ibid.*

I have fought the good fight with all that was in me. Now there is no strength left. Other hands must take up the burden. Remember, the battle against injustice is never won.

Quoted by Justice Douglas in An Almanac of Liberty.

State of North Carolina

No person who shall deny the being of God, or the truth of the Christian religion, shall be capable of holding any office or place of trust or profit.

Constitution, 1836.

Northwest Ordinance

Religion, morality, and knowledge being necessary to good government, and the happiness of mankind, schools and the means of education shall forever be encouraged.

1787.

Charles Eliot Norton
(1827-1908)
American educator, humanitarian

"There never was a good war," said Franklin. There have indeed been many wars in which a good man must take part, and take part with grave gladness to defend the cause of justice, to die if need be, a willing sacrifice, thankful to give life for what is dearer than life, and happy that even by death in war he is serving the cause of peace. But if a war be undertaken for the most righteous end, before the resources of peace have been tried and proved vain to secure it, that war has no defence, it is a national crime.

Address, Cambridge, Mass., June 7, 1898, denouncing the Spanish-American War.

The voice of protest, of warning, of appeal is never more needed than when the clamour of fife and drum, echoed by the press and too often by the pulpit, is bidding all men fall in and keep step and obey in silence the tyrannous word of command. Then, more than ever, it is the duty of the good citizen not to be silent, and spite of obloquy, misrepresentation and abuse, to insist on being heard, and with sober counsel to maintain the everlasting validity of the principles of the moral law.   *Ibid.*

So confused are men by false teaching in regard to national honour and the duty of the citizen that it is easy to fall into the error of holding a declaration of war, however brought about, as a sacred decision of the national will, and to fancy that a call to arms from the Administration has the force of a call from the lips of the country, of the America to whom all her sons are ready to pay the full measure of devotion.
Ibid.

Richard Oastler
(1789-1861)
British reformer

Let the truth speak out, appalling as the statements may appear. Thousands of our fellow-creatures and fellow-subjects . . . are at this very moment existing in a state of slavery more horrid than are the victims of that hellish system, colonial slavery . . . Thousands of little children . . . are daily compelled to labor from 6 o'clock in the morning to 7 o'clock in the evening with only—British, blush while you read it—with only 30 minutes allowed for eating and recreation.
Slavery in Yorkshire. Leeds Mercury, 1830.

James O'Brien (James Bronterre)
(1805-1864)
Irish Chartist leader

The desire of one man to live on the fruits of another's labor is the original sin of the world.

Sean O'Casey
(b. 1884)
Irish dramatist

God be my judge that I hate fighting. If I be damned for anything, I shall be damned for keeping the two-edged sword of thought tight in the scabbard when it should be searching the bowels of fools and knaves.
To Mrs. G. B. Shaw. "Life," July, 1954.

The bells of the world have tolled long enough for death, let them now ring out for life . . . A dead youth is a blasphemy against the God of Life. No one desires war but a fool or a madman, and there is no longer room in the world for madmen or fools. We deny the infallibility of the atom bomb; we affirm the infallibility of the brotherhood of man the world over.

Adolph Simon Ochs
(1858-1935)
American newspaper publisher

To give the news impartially, without fear or favor, regardless of any party, sect or interest involved.
Credo for N. Y. Times, August 19, 1896.

All the News That's Fit to Print.
Slogan for N. Y. Times.

Advertising in the final analysis should be news. If it is not news it is worthless.
N. Y. Times Magazine, March 9, 1958.

Daniel O'Connell
(1775-1847)
Irish nationalist

Bigotry has no head and cannot think; no heart and cannot feel. When she moves it is in wrath; when she pauses it is amid ruin. Her prayers are curses, her god is a demon, her communion is death, her vengeance is eternity, her decalogue written in the blood of her victims, and if she stops for a moment in her infernal flight it is upon a kindred rock to whet her vulture fang for a more sanguinary desolation.

I am a Catholic, but not a papist.

William Henry O'Connell
(1859-1944)
American Cardinal

Capital has a right to a just share of the profits, but only to a just share.
Pastoral Letter on the Laborer's Rights, November 23, 1912.

Feargus O'Connor
(1794-1855)
Irish Chartist leader

A great revolution . . . must, in the first instance, be productive of hazard, vicissitudes, and perhaps calamity. But the question is for you, whether or no it is not worth while to pass through the ordeal of temporary suffering to establish permanent liberty?   *Northern Star, 1848.*

Liam O'Flaherty
(b. 1896)
Irish novelist

It's impossible for a creative artist to be either a Puritan or a Fascist, because both are a negation of the creative urge. The only things the creative artist can be opposed to are ugliness and injustice. In Ireland today we have the rising of a lower middle class created by the Sinn Fein revolution. They correspond rather to the igno-

rant people here who go in for 100 per cent Americanism. In Ireland today you have a Catholic Fascism which takes the form of a sentimental nationalism . . . My sympathies are Left.
Interview with May Cameron, N. Y. Post, November 27, 1937.

Omar I
(581?-644)
2nd Caliph, captor of Jerusalem

Burn the libraries, for their value is in this one book (the Koran).
At the capture of Alexandria; quoted by Emerson, Representative Men.

Eugene O'Neill
(1888-1953)
American playwright

If a person is to get the meaning of life he must learn to like the facts about himself—ugly as they may seem to his sentimental vanity—before he can learn the truth *behind* the facts. And the truth is never ugly.
N. Y. Herald Tribune, September 9, 1956.

We talk about the American Dream, and want to tell the world about the American Dream, but what is that dream, in most cases, but the dream of material things? I sometimes think that the United States for this reason, is the greatest failure the world has ever seen.
Give Me Liberty and . . . (unpublished play).

Poverty—the most deadly and prevalent of all diseases.

One should be either sad or joyful. Contentment is a warm sty for eaters and sleepers.

James Oppenheim
(1882-1932)
American poet, novelist

They set the slave free, striking off his
  chains. . . .
Then he was as much a slave as ever.
                            The Slave.

He was still bound by fear and superstition,
By ignorance, suspicion and savagery . . .
His slavery was not in his chains,
But in himself.   *Ibid.*

They can only set free men free . . .
And there is no need of that:
Free men set themselves free.   *Ibid.*

J. Robert Oppenheimer
(1904-1967)
American physicist

In some crude sense, which no vulgarity,
no humor, no overstatement can quite extinguish, the physicists have known sin and
this is a knowledge which they cannot lose.
            Lecture, November 25, 1947.

You can certainly destroy enough of humanity so that only the greatest act of
faith can persuade you that what's left will
be human.
  *To Ed Murrow, CBS program, January
  4, 1955.*

The world cannot endure half-darkness
and half-light.
  *Journal of the Atomic Scientists, Sep-
  tember, 1956.*

In a free world, if it is to remain free,
we must maintain, with our lives if need
be, but surely by our lives, the opportunity
for a man to learn anything.   *Ibid.*

There must be no barriers to freedom of
inquiry. There is no place for dogma in
science. The scientist is free, and must be
free to ask any question, to doubt any assertion, to seek for any evidence, to correct any errors. *Life, October 10, 1949.*

As long as men are free to ask what they
must, free to say what they think, free to
think what they will, freedom can never be
lost, and science can never regress. *Ibid.*

John Boyle O'Reilly
(1844-1890)
Irish-American journalist, poet

The thirsty of soul soon learn to know
The moistureless froth of the social show,
The vulgar sham of the pompous feast
Where the heaviest purse is the highest
  priest;
The organized charity, scrimped and iced,
In the name of a cautious, statistical Christ.
                            In Bohemia.

Origen
(185?-254?)
Alexandrian theologian

This also is clearly defined in the teaching of the Church, that every rational soul
is possessed of freewill and volition; that it
has a struggle to maintain with the devil
and his angels, and opposing influences, because they strive to burden it with sins.
                  De Principiis, Proem. 5.

The power of choosing good and evil is
within the reach of all.   *Ibid., 2.*

Without the church no one is saved.

José Clemente Orozco
(1883-1949)
Mexican painter

Errors and exaggerations do not matter.
What matters is boldness in thinking with

a strong-pitched voice, in speaking out about things as one feels them in the moment of speaking; in having the temerity to proclaim what one believes to be true without fear of the consequences. If one were to await the possession of the absolute truth, one must be either a fool or a mute. If the creative impulse were muted, the world would then be stayed on its march.   *Letter to a friend.*

José Ortega y Gasset
(1883-1955)
Spanish philosopher, politician

Our firmest convictions are apt to be the most suspect, they mark our limitations and our bounds. Life is a petty thing unless it is moved by the indomitable urge to extend its boundaries.
The Dehumanization of Art and Notes on the Novel.

Our horizon is a biological line, a living part of our organism. In times of fullness of life it expands. . . . When the horizon stiffens it is because it has become fossilized and we are growing old.   *Ibid.*

The mass crushes beneath it everything that is different, everything that is excellent, individual, qualified, and select. Anybody who is not like everybody, who does not think like everybody, runs the risk of being eliminated. *Revolt of the Masses.*

I am I plus my circumstances.
Time, October 31, 1955.

In times of great passion the duty of the intellectual is to remain silent, because in times of passion one has to lie and the intellectual has no right to lie.   *Ibid.*

I am here, but I do not exist here.
Ibid.; a reference to the Franco dictatorship.

George Orwell (né Eric Blair)
(1903-1950)
English novelist, essayist

All animals are equal but some animals are more equal than others. *Animal Farm.*

Orthodoxy means not thinking—not needing to think. Orthodoxy is unconsciousness.
Nineteen Eighty-four.

The past is whatever the records and the memories agree upon. And since the party is in full control of all records, and in equally full control of the minds of its members, it follows that the past is whatever the party chooses to make it. Six means eighteen, two plus two equals five, war is peace, freedom is slavery, ignorance is strength.   *Ibid.*

Most revolutionaries are potential Tories, because they imagine that everything can be put to rights by altering the *shape* of society.   *Ibid.*

In a society in which there is no law, and in theory no compulsion, the only arbiter of behaviour is public opinion. But public opinion, because of the tremendous urge to conformity in gregarious animals, is less tolerant than any system of law. When human beings are governed by "thou shalt not," the individual can practice a certain amount of eccentricity: when they are supposedly governed by "love" or "reason," he is under continuous pressure to make him behave exactly the same way as everyone else.
Orwell Reader, edited by Richard H. Rovere, pp. 292-3. Politics vs. Literature.

Saints should always be judged guilty until they are proved innocent.
Ibid., p. 328. Reflections on Gandhi.

Many people genuinely do not wish to be saints, and it is probable that some who achieve or aspire to sainthood have never felt much temptation to be human beings.
Ibid.

One must choose between God and Man, and all "radicals" and "progressives," from the mildest liberal to the most extreme anarchist, have in effect chosen Man.
Ibid., p. 332.

In our age there is no such thing as "keeping out of politics." All issues are political issues, and politics itself is a mass of lies, evasions, folly, hatred, and schizophrenia.
Ibid., pp. 363-4. Politics and the English Language.

The Communism of the English intellectual is something explicable enough. It is the patriotism of the deracinated.
A Collection of Essays, 1954.

Fairfield Osborn
(b. 1887)
American writer

Warfare as practiced by man has no parallel in nature. That is to say that within the more highly developed animal populations of this earth there is not now nor has there ever been similar destruction within a species itself.
Our Plundered Planet, Little, Brown & Co.

William Osler
(1849-1919)
British physician

The desire to take medicine is perhaps the greatest feature which distinguishes man from the animals.
Hal Boyle, Boston Globe, January 22, 1957.

No human being is constituted to know the truth, the whole truth, and nothing but the truth; and even the best of men must be content with fragments, with partial glimpses, never the full fruition.
The Student Life.

Study until twenty-five, investigation until forty, profession until sixty, at which age I would have him retired on a double allowance.

In the life of every successful physician there comes the temptation to toy with the Delilah of the Press—daily and otherwise. There are times when she can be courted with satisfaction, but beware! Sooner or later she is sure to play the harlot, and has left many a man shorn of his strength, namely the confidence of his professional brethren.

John O'Sullivan
(1813-1895)
American journalist, diplomat

Our manifest destiny to overspread the continent allotted by Providence for the free development of our yearly multiplying millions.
U.S. Magazine and Democratic Review, Vol. xvii, p. 5.

James Otis
(1725-1783)
American patriot, pamphleteer

Let the origin of government be placed where it may, the end of it is manifestly the good of *the whole. Salus populi suprema lex esto* is the law of nature, and part of that grand charter given the human race (though too many of them are afraid to assert it) by the only monarch in the universe who has a clear and indisputable right to *absolute* power; because he is the *only* One who is *omniscient* as well as *omnipotent*.

The Rights of the British Colonies Asserted and Proved, 1764.

Kingcraft and priestcraft have fell out so often, that 'tis a wonder this grand and ancient alliance is not broken off forever. Happy for mankind will it be when such a separation shall take place.   *Ibid.*

The end of the government being the good of mankind points out its great duties: it is above all things to provide for the security, the quiet, the happy enjoyment of life, liberty, and property.   *Ibid.*

If life, liberty, and property could be enjoyed in as great perfection in solitude as in society, there would be no need of government.   *Ibid.*

The colonists are by the law of nature free-born, as indeed all men are, white or black. . . . It is a clear truth that those who every day barter away other men's liberty will soon care little for their own.   *Ibid.*

Taxes are not to be laid on the people but by their consent in person or by deputation.   *Ibid.*

Now, one of the most essential branches of English liberty is the freedom of one's house. A man's house is his castle; and whilst he is quiet, he is as well guarded as a prince in his castle.

Argument, Boston Court, February 24, 1761, on Writs of Assistance.*

---

* "Then and there the child Independence was born." John Adams.

Taxation without representation is tyranny.

Attributed, by John Adams, and others.

Harry A. Overstreet
(b. 1875)
American writer

All through man's history, there has been a competition between the safe and the adventurous; the fully informed and the to-be-informed; between the "pattern set for all men" and the glimmer of a gleam for men to follow.

Contribution, Saturday Review.

Exactly as in the great humanistic religions of Lao-tse, Buddha, Isaiah, Jesus, so in psychoanalysis, the aim is to free the individual from his various enslavements so that he is able "to see the truth, to love, to become free and responsible, and to be sensitive to the voice of his conscience."

Review in N. Y. Times of Erich Fromm's "Psychoanalysis and Religion."

Ovid
(43 B.C.-18 A.D.)
Roman poet

Through all the air the eagle may roam
The whole earth is father-land to the brave.
Fragment 866.

Expedit esse deos, et, ut expedit, esse putemus. (It is expedient that there should be gods, and as it is expedient, let us believe that they exist.) *Art of Love, bk. i.*

Robert Owen
(1771-1858)
English Socialist, philanthropist

The people are the only sovereigns of any country.

Man is the creature of circumstances.
Biography.

Men of industry, producers of wealth and knowledge, and of all that is truly valuable in society! Unite your powers now to create a wise and righteous state of human existence—a state in which the only contest shall be, who shall produce the greatest amount of happiness for the human race. *Legacy to the World, 1834.*

Finding that no religion is based on facts and cannot therefore be true, I began to reflect what must be the condition of mankind trained from infancy to believe in errors.
Cardiff, What Great Men Think of Religion.

What divisions, hatreds, miseries, and dreadful physical and mental sufferings have been produced by the names of Confucius, Bramah, Juggernaut, Moses, Jesus, Mohammed, Penn, Joe Smith, Mother Lee, etc.! *Ibid.*

I propose to prove . . . that all the religions of the world have been founded upon the ignorance of mankind; that they are directly opposed to the never-changing laws of our nature; that they have been, and are, the real source of vice, disunions, and the misery of every description; that they are now the only real bar to the formation of a society of virtue, of intelligence, of charity in its most extended sense, and of sincerity and kindness among the whole human family; and that they can be no longer maintained except through the ignorance of the mass of the people and the tyranny of the few over the mass. *Ibid.*

Alvin M. Owsley
(b. 1888)
American lawyer, diplomat

If ever needed, the American Legion stands ready to protect our country's institutions and ideals as the Fascisti dealt with the destructionists who menaced Italy.

(Questioned, whether that meant taking over the government.)

Exactly that. The American Legion is fighting every element that threatens our democratic government—soviets, anarchists, I.W.W., revolutionary socialists and every other "red.". . . Do not forget that the Fascisti are to Italy what the American Legion is to the United States.
N.E.A. Interview 1923; confirmed in letter to the present editor, 1937.

G(arfield) Bromley Oxnam
(1891-1963)
American Methodist Bishop

Self-appointed illiterates have organized agencies under high-sounding names for the alleged purpose of saving our schools from subversion . . . and in the name of subversion have themselves contributed to undermining the very bastion of the free way of life.
N. Y. Times, November 14, 1954.

We talk of free enterprise, and rightly, and I think with proper pride . . . Personally, I do not wish the collective ownership or the democratic management of the principal means of production, distribution, and exchange that was advocated by the Socialist of a generation ago, but I must face the fact that there is something radically wrong with so-called "free enterprise."
Methodist National Convocation on Urban Life, February 20, 1958.

I am fearful of stumbling capitalism as well as of creeping socialism. *Ibid.*

Pierre van Paassen

(1895-1968)

American Unitarian minister, writer

For years philosophers and sociologists in their role as awakeners of men's consciences have pointed to the exact spot and the precise hour where history went wrong —or, rather, where man turned up the wrong way. Long before the industrial system had reached its zenith there were men who warned that it had been built up, as Bishop Gore once said, "in a profound revolt against the central law of Christian morality: Thou shalt love thy neighbor as thyself." There are, in fact, few things in history more astonishing than the silent acquiescence of the Christian world in the radical betrayal of its ethical foundation.

Thomas Paine*

(1737-1809)

American Revolutionary writer

I believe in one God, and no more; and I hope for happiness beyond this life.
The Age of Reason.

I believe in the equality of man; and I believe that religious duties consist in doing justice, loving mercy, and endeavoring to make our fellow-creatures happy. *Ibid.*

I do not believe in the creed professed by the Jewish church, by the Roman church, by the Greek church, by the Turkish church, by the Protestant church, nor by any church

---

* "At the time of his death Tom Paine had accomplished more for human freedom, for the abolition of physical and mental slavery, and for the brotherhood of mankind, than any other American then living." Woodward, *Tom Paine: America's Godfather*, p. 341.

that I know of. My own mind is my own church. *Ibid.*

The adulterous connection of church and state . . . *Ibid*

The declaration which says that God *visits the sins of the fathers upon the children* is contrary to every principle of moral justice. *Ibid.*

The event that served more than any other to break the first link in this long chain of despotic ignorance is that known by the name of the Reformation by Luther. *Ibid.*

Any system of religion that has anything in it that shocks the mind of a child, cannot be a true system. *Ibid.*

The true Deist has but one Deity, and his religion consists in contemplating the power, wisdom, and benignity of the Deity in his works, and in endeavoring to imitate him in everything moral, scientifical, and mechanical. *Ibid.*

Whenever we read the obscene stories, the voluptuous debaucheries, the cruel and tortuous executions, the unrelenting vindictiveness, with which more than half the Bible is filled it would be more consistent that we call it the word of a demon than the word of God. It is a history of wickedness that has served to corrupt and brutalize mankind. *Ibid.*

All national institutions of churches, whether Jewish, Christian or Turkish, appear to me no other than human inventions, set up to terrify and enslave mankind, and monopolize power and profit. *Ibid.*

The story of the whale swallowing Jonah, though a whale is large enough to do it, borders greatly on the marvelous; but it would have approached nearer to the idea of a miracle if Jonah had swallowed the whale. *Ibid.*

It is impossible to calculate the moral mischief, if I may so express it, that mental lying has produced in society. When a man has so corrupted and prostituted the chastity of his mind as to subscribe his professional belief to things he does not believe, he has prepared himself for the commission of every other crime. *Ibid.*

It is certain that, in one point, all the nations of the earth and all religions agree—all believe in a God; the things in which they disagree, are the redundancies annexed to that belief; and, therefore, if ever a universal religion should prevail, it will not be by believing anything new, but in getting rid of redundancies, and believing as man believed at first.

Ibid. Conclusion, part 1.

The notion of a Trinity of Gods has enfeebled the belief of one God. A multiplication of beliefs acts as a division of belief; and in proportion as anything is divided it is weakened. *Ibid. Conclusion, part 2.*

The only religion that has not been invented, and that has in it the evidence of divine originality, is pure and simple Deism . . . But pure and simple Deism does not answer the purpose of despotic governments. They cannot lay hold of religion as an engine, but by mixing it with human inventions, and making their own authority a part; neither does it answer the avarice of priests, but by incorporating themselves and their functions with it, and becoming, like the government, a party to the system. *Ibid.*

Infidelity does not consist in believing or in disbelieving; it consists in professing to believe what one does not believe. *Ibid.*

These are the times that try men's souls. The summer soldier and the sunshine patriot will, in this crisis, shrink from the service of his country; but he that stands it NOW, deserves the love and thanks of man and woman.

The American Crisis, No. 1, December 19, 1776.

Tyranny, like hell, is not easily conquered; yet we have this consolation with us, that the harder the conflict, the more glorious the triumph. What we obtain too cheap, we esteem too lightly:—'Tis dearness only that gives every thing its value. Heaven knows how to set a proper price upon its goods; and it would be strange indeed, if so celestial an article as FREEDOM should not be highly rated. *Ibid.*

I have as little superstition in me as any man living, but my secret opinion has ever been, and still is, that GOD Almighty will not give up a people to military destruction, or leave them unsupportedly to perish, who had so earnestly and so repeatedly sought to avoid the calamities of war, by every decent method which wisdom could invent. *Ibid.*

Those who expect to reap the blessings of freedom, must, like men, undergo the fatigue of supporting it. *Ibid.*

The times that tried men's souls are over—and the greatest and completest revolution the world ever knew, gloriously and happily accomplished.

The Crisis Papers, 1783.

Never, I say, had a country so many openings to happiness as this. . . . Her cause was good. Her principles just and liberal. Her temper serene and firm. . . . The remembrance then of what is past, if it operates rightly, must inspire her with the most laudable of an ambition, that of adding to the fair fame she began with. The world has seen her great in adversity. . . . Let then, the world see that she can bear prosperity; and that her honest virtue in time of peace is equal to the bravest virtue in time of war.   *Ibid.*

Society in every state is a blessing, but government, even in its best state is but a necessary evil; in its worst state, an intolerable one.   *Common Sense.*

When we are planning for posterity, we ought to remember that virtue is not hereditary.   *Ibid.*

We have it in our power to begin the world over again. A situation, similar to the present, hath not happened since the days of Noah until now. The birthday of a new world is at hand, and a race of man . . . are to receive their portion of freedom from the events of a few months. The reflection is awful, and in this point of view, how trifling, how ridiculous, do the little paltry cavilings of a few weak or interested men appear, when weighed against the business of a world.   *Ibid.*

The more perfect civilization is, the less occasion has it for government.   *Ibid.*

A long habit of not thinking a thing *wrong*, gives it a superficial appearance of being *right*, and raises at first a formidable outcry in defense of custom.   *Ibid.*

Time makes more converts than reason.   *Ibid.*

I fully believe that it is the will of the Almighty that there should be a diversity of religious opinion among us. I look upon the various denominations among us as children of the same family, differing only in what is called their Christian names.   *Ibid.*

We hold the moral obligation of providing for old age, helpless infancy, and poverty, is far superior to that of supplying the invented wants of courtly extravagance.

Declaration of the Friends of Universal Peace and Liberty, 1791.

Monarchy would not have continued so many ages in the world had it not been for the abuses it protects. It is the master fraud, which shelters all others.

The Rights of Man.

It will be proper to take a review of the several sources from which governments have arisen, and on which they have been founded.

They may be all comprehended under three heads—1st, Superstition; 2d, Power; 3d, the common interests of society, and the common rights of man.

The first was a government of priestcraft, the second of conquerors, and the third of reason.   *Ibid.*

Every age and generation must be free to act for itself, *in all cases,* as the ages and generations which preceded it. The vanity and presumption of governing beyond the grave is the most ridiculous and insolent of all tyrannies.   *Ibid.*

Man has no property in man; neither has any generation a property in the generations which are to follow.   *Ibid.*

Toleration is not the *opposite* of intoleration, but is the *counterfeit* of it. Both are despotisms. The one assumes to itself the right of withholding the liberty of conscience, and the other of granting it.   *Ibid.*

Persecution is not an original feature in *any* religion; but is always the strongly marked feature of all law-religions, or religions established by law.   *Ibid.*

Governments thus established (by the sword) last as long as the power to support them lasts; but that they might avail themselves of every engine in their favor, they united fraud with force, and set up an idol they called *divine right,* and which, in imitation of the pope who affects to spiritual and temporal, and in contradiction to the founder of the Christian church, twisted itself afterwards into an idol of another shape, called *church and state.* The key of St. Peter and the key of the treasury became quartered on one another, and the wondering cheated multitude worshipped the invention. *Ibid.*

When wealth and splendor, instead of fascinating the multitude, excite emotions of disgust; when, instead of drawing forth admiration, it is beheld as an insult upon wretchedness; when the ostentatious appearance it makes serves to call the right of it in question, the case of property becomes critical, and it is only in a system of justice that the possessor can contemplate security. *Ibid.*

The Bible has been received by the Protestants on the authority of the Church of Rome, and on no other authority. It is she that has said it is the Word of God. We do not admit the authority of that Church with respect to its pretended *infallibility,* its manufactured miracles, its setting itself up to forgive sins, its amphibious doctrine of transubstantiation, etc.; and we ought to be watchful with respect to any book introduced by her, or her ecclesiastical councils, and called by her the Word of God: and the more so, because it was by propagating that belief and supporting it by fire and faggot that she kept up her temporal power.

Contribution (unsigned) to The Prospect, 1804.

Deism is the only profession of religion that admits of worshipping and reverencing God in purity . . . God is almost forgotten in the Christian religion. Everything, even the creation, is ascribed to the son of Mary.

"To Mr. Moore of New York, commonly called Bishop Moore," The Prospect, 1804.

Religion has two principal enemies, fanaticism and infidelity, or that which is called atheism. The first requires to be combated by reason and morality, the other by natural philosophy.

Address, Society of Theophilanthropists, Paris, 1797.

It is wrong to say that God made rich and poor; He made only male and female, and He gave them the whole earth for their inheritance.

The United States of America will sound as pompously in the world or in history as The Kingdom of Great Britain.°

Second issue of "The Crisis," addressed to Lord Howe.

Belief in a cruel God makes a cruel man.

One good schoolmaster is of more use than a hundred priests.

'Tis the business of little minds to shrink; but he whose heart is firm, and whose conscience approves his conduct, will pursue his principles unto death.

° "To Paine, also belongs the honor of naming our country the 'United States of America.' He was the first to use the name in print, and it was his own creation." Woodward, *Tom Paine: America's Godfather.*

Moderation in temper is always a virtue; but moderation in principle is always a vice.

All hereditary government is in its nature tyranny. . . . To inherit a government is to inherit the people as though they were flocks and herds.

One of eight quotations from Paine on which the British Government indicted him for seditious libel.

It is an affront to treat falsehood with complaisance.

You will do me the justice to remember, that I have always strenuously supported the right of every man to his opinion, however different that opinion may be to mine. He who denies to another this right, makes a slave of himself to his present opinion, because he precludes himself the right of changing it. The most formidable weapon against errors of every kind is reason. I have never used any other, and I trust I never shall.

Letter to "My fellow-citizens," dated Luxembourg, 8th Pluvoise, Second Year of the French Republic.

The trade of governing has always been monopolized by the most ignorant and the most rascally individuals of mankind.

Give to every other human being every right that you claim for yourself—that is my doctrine.

Reason obeys itself; and ignorance submits to whatever is dictated to it.

As to religion, I hold it to be the indispensable duty of all government to protect all conscientious professors thereof, and I know of no other business which government hath to do therewith.

Henry John Temple, Lord Palmerston
(1784-1865)
English statesman

England has no permanent friends; she has only permanent interests.
N. Y. Times Magazine, May 20, 1956.

Happy the country where an honest man speaks as loud as a scoundrel.

Christabel Pankhurst
(1880-1958)
British militant suffragist

We are here to claim our rights as women, not only to be free, but to fight for freedom. It is our privilege, as well as our pride and our joy, to take some part in this militant movement, which, as we believe, means the regeneration of all humanity. Nothing but contempt is due to those people who ask us to submit to unmerited oppression. We shall not do it.
Speech, March 23, 1911.

Be ready when the hour comes, to show that women are human and have the pride and dignity of human beings. Through such resistance our cause will triumph. But even if it does not, we fight not only for success, but in order that some inward feeling may have satisfaction. We fight that our pride, our self-respect, our dignity may not be sacrificed in the future as they have been in the past. *Ibid.*

Women must stand erect now and for ever more. Then, even if they should not win success—and we know that they will win it—at least they will deserve success, and that is what matters more than all beside. *Ibid.*

Philippus Aureolus Paracelsus, Theophrastus Bombastus von Hohenheim

(1493-1541)

Swiss physician

Thoughts are free and are subject to no rule. On them rests the freedom of man, and they tower above the light of nature. *Selected Writings, ed. by Jolande Jacobi, tr. by Norbert Huterman, Pantheon, 1951.*

Thoughts give birth to a creative force that is neither elemental nor sidereal . . . Thoughts create a new heaven, a new firmament, a new source of energy, from which new arts flow. *Ibid.*

When a man undertakes to create something, he establishes a new heaven, as it were, and from it the work that he desires to create flows into him . . . For such is the immensity of man that he is greater than heaven and earth. *Ibid.*

Poison is in everything, and no thing is without poison. The dosage makes it either a poison or a remedy.
Time, March 9, 1959.

Alton B. Parker

(1852-1926)

American jurist

A man has a right to pass through this world, if he wills, without having his picture published, his business enterprises discussed, his successful experiments written up for the benefit of others, or his eccentricities commented upon, whether in handbills, circulars, catalogues, newspapers or periodicals.
Decision, Roberson v. Rochester Folding Box Co., 1901.

Dorothy Parker

(1893-1967)

American writer, poet

Art is a form of catharsis. **Art.**

Theodore Parker

(1810-1860)

American preacher, abolitionist

. . . The American idea . . . a democracy, —that is, a government of all the people, by all the people, for all the people; of course, a government of the principles of eternal justice, the unchanging law of God: for shortness sake, I will call it the idea of Freedom. *Speech, Boston, May 20, 1850.*

Slavery is a flagrant violation of the institutions of America—direct government—over all the people, by all the people, for all the people. *Sermon, 1858.*

Democracy means not "I am as good as you are" but "You are as good as I am."

Manual labor, though an unavoidable duty, though designed as a blessing, and naturally both a pleasure and a dignity, is often abused, till, by its terrible excess, it becomes really a punishment and a curse. It is only a proper amount of work that is a blessing. Too much of it wears out the body before its time; cripples the mind, debases the soul, blunts the senses, and chills the affections. It makes a man a spinning-jenny, or a ploughing-machine, and not "a being of a large discourse, that looks before and after." He ceases to be a man, and becomes a thing.
Thoughts on Labour, 1841.

Neither the democratic nor the despotic idea is fully made real anywhere in the world. There is no perfect democracy, nor

perfect aristocracy. There are democrats in every actual aristocracy; despots in every actual democracy. But in the Northern States the democratic idea prevails extensively and chiefly, and we have made attempts at establishing a democratic government. In the Southern States the despotic idea prevails extensively and chiefly, and they have made attempts to establish an aristocratic government.
Sermon, Thanksgiving Day, 1850.

In an aristocracy there are two classes: the people to be governed, and the governing class, the nobility which is to govern. This nobility may be moveable, and depend on wealth; or immoveable, and depend on birth. In the Southern States the nobility is immoveable, and depends on color.
Ibid.

Look at these ancient States, and queenliest queens of earth. There is Rome, the widow of two civilizations—the Pagan and the Catholic . . . the Niobe of Nations, she boasted that her children were holier and more fair than all the pure ideas of justice, truth, and love, the offspring of the eternal God. *Ibid.*

Do you know how empires find their end? Yes, the great States eat up the little. . . . But how do the great States come to an end? By their own injustices, and no other cause. They would make unrighteousness their law, and God wills not that it be so. *Ibid.*

We are a rebellious nation. Our whole history is treason; our blood was attainted before we were born; our creeds are infidelity to the mother church; our Constitution, treason to our fatherland. What of that? Though all the governors of the world bid us commit treason against man,

and set the example, let us never submit.
Quoted by H. S. Commager, Harper's, September, 1947.

I think lightly of what is called treason against a government. That may be your duty today, or mine. But treason against the people, against mankind, against God, is a great sin not lightly to be spoken of.
Speech denouncing Mexican War, 1846.

Vernon Louis Parrington
(1871-1929)
American historian, educator

Your Tory is always a Fascist at heart.
Main Currents in American Thought, 1927-1931.

The driving force of the new (Jacksonian) Democracy was the class-feeling that had done service a generation before, the will to destroy the aristocratic principle in government. This conscious class-feeling had been strengthened by the spread of the dogma of equalitarianism through the frontier. *Ibid.*

The battle seemed to lie between homespun and broadcloth for control of government, and this serves to explain the odium that quickly attached to Jacksonian Democracy in polite circles. *Ibid.*

Old Hickory . . . was our first great popular leader, our first man of the people . . . He was one of our few Presidents whose heart and sympathy were with the plain people, and who clung to the simple faith that government must deal as justly with the poor as with the rich. *Ibid.*

Learning their lesson from Jackson, the Whig politicians outdid him in democratic professions. They had discovered that business has little to fear from a skilfully guided electorate; that quite the safest way, indeed, to reach into the public purse is to do it in the sacred name of the majority will. *Ibid.*

Perhaps the rarest bit of irony in American history is the later custodianship of democracy by the middle class, who while perfecting their tariffs and subsidies, legislating from the bench, exploiting the state and outlawing all political theories but their own, denounce all class consciousness as unpatriotic and all agrarian or proletarian programs as undemocratic. But it was no fault of Andrew Jackson if the final outcome of the great movement of Jacksonian democracy was so untoward; it was rather the fault of the times that were not ripe for democracy. *Ibid.*

One far-reaching result survived the (Jacksonian) movement, the popularization of the name of democracy and the naive acceptance of the belief that the genius of America was democratic. *Ibid.*

You see the dilemma in which I find myself. We must have a political state powerful enough to deal with corporate wealth, but how are we going to keep that state with its augmenting power from being captured by the force we want it to control?
(statement, to a friend.)

A dramatic discovery . . . when the corruption of American politics was laid on the threshold of business—like a bastard on the doorstep of his father—a tremendous disturbance resulted.

There would be no adequate civilization, no Christianity, until cooperation displaced competition, and women were become equal in economic rights as they were in franchise rights.

Albert Parsons

(1848-hanged 1887)

*American anarchist,
principal in Haymarket trial*

Let the voice of the people be heard.
Last words, at execution.

Of my life and the cause of my unnatural and cruel death, you will learn from others. Your father is a self-offered sacrifice upon the altar of Liberty and Happiness. To you I leave the legacy of an honest name and duty done. Preserve it, emulate it. Be true to yourselves; you cannot then be false to others.
Last letter to his children.

There was *no evidence* that any one of the eight doomed men knew of, or advised, or abetted the Haymarket tragedy. But what does that matter? The privileged class *demands a victim,* and we are offered a sacrifice to appease the hungry yells of an infuriated mob of millionaires who will be contented with nothing less than our lives. Monopoly triumphs! Labor in chains ascends the scaffold for having dared to cry out for liberty and right!
*Letter to his wife, August 20, 1886:
The Life of Albert Parsons, 1889.*

I have one request to make of you: Commit no rash act to yourself when I am gone, but take up the great cause of Socialism where I am compelled to lay it down.
Ibid.

Parvus
See John of Salisbury

Blaise Pascal
(1623-1662)
French geometrician, philosopher, writer

If man is not made for God, why is he happy only in God? If man is made for God, why is he opposed to God?

Pensées.

You must wager; this depends not on your will, you are embarked in the affair. Which will you choose? . . . Since you must needs choose, your reason is no more wounded in choosing one than the other. Here is one point cleared up, but what of your happiness? Let us weigh the gain and loss in choosing "heads" that God is. Let us weigh the two cases: if you gain, you gain all; if you lose, you lose nothing. Wager then unhesitatingly that He is. . . .

Ibid.

Man is but a reed, the most feeble thing in nature; but he is a thinking reed. (*L'homme n'est qu'un roseau, le plus faible de la nature; mais c'est un roseau pensant.*)

Ibid.

The entire universe needs not arm itself to crush him. A vapor, a drop of water, suffices to kill him. But, if the universe were to crush him, man would still be more noble than that which killed him because he knows that he dies and the advantage which the universe has over him; the universe knows nothing of this.

Ibid.

All our dignity consists, then, in thought. It is the heart which experiences God, and not reason. This, then, is faith: God felt by heart, not by reason.

Ibid.

Le coeur a ses raisons que la raison ne connaît point. (The heart has its reasons which reason does not understand.) *Ibid.*

Force and not opinion is the queen of the world; but it is opinion that uses force.

Ibid.

Men never do evil so completely and cheerfully as when they do it from religious conviction.

Ibid.

What reason have atheists for saying that we cannot rise again? Which is the more difficult—to be born, or to rise again? That what has never been, should be, or that what has been, should be again? Is it more difficult to come into being than to return to it?

Ibid.

Theft, incest, infanticide, patricide, have all had a place among virtuous actions. Can anything be more ridiculous than that a man should have the right to kill me because he lives on the other side of the water, and because his ruler has a quarrel with mine, though I have none with him?

Ibid.

We know truth, not only by reason, but also by the heart, and it is from this last that we know first principles; and reason, which has nothing to do with it, tries in vain to combat them. The skeptics who desire truth alone labor in vain.

Ibid.

Atheism is a sign of mental strength, but only up to a certain point.

Ibid.

Nothing is thoroughly approved but mediocrity. The majority has established this, and it fixes its fangs on whatever gets beyond it either way.

Ibid.

All the troubles of man come from his not knowing how to sit still.

Ibid.

In the just and unjust we find hardly anything which does not change its character in changing its climate. Three degrees of elevation of the pole reverse the whole of jurisprudence. A meridian is decisive of truth, or a few years of possession. Fundamental laws change! Right has its epochs! A pleasant justice, that, which a river or a mountain limits. Truth on this side of the Pyrenees, may be heresy on the other!

Ibid.

Thought makes the whole dignity of man; therefore, endeavor to think well, that is the only morality. *Ibid.*

Justice without power is inefficient; power without justice is tyranny. Justice without power is opposed, because there are always wicked men. Power without justice is soon questioned. Justice and power must therefore be brought together, so that whatever is just may be powerful, and whatever is powerful may be just. *Ibid.*

The incredulous are the most credulous. They believe the miracles of Vespasian that they may not believe those of Moses.

Ibid., ch. 2.

Montaigne (bk. 1, ch. 22) is wrong in declaring that custom ought to be followed simply because it is custom, and not because it is reasonable or just. *Ibid., ch. 4.*

Justice is what is established; and thus all our established laws will be regarded as just, without being examined, since they are established. *Ibid., ch. 7.*

To carry piety to the extent of superstition is to destroy it. *Ibid., ch. 14.*

Had it not been for miracles, there would have been no sin in not believing in Jesus Christ. *Ibid., ch. 22.*

Tous nos malheurs viennent de ne pouvoir être seuls. (All our troubles come from not being able to be alone.)

Boris Pasternak
(1890-1960)
*Russian writer, Nobel Prize
for literature, 1959*

Man is born to live and not to prepare to live.
Doctor Zhivago, Copyright, Pantheon Books, 1958.

To run true to type is the extinction of a man, his condemnation to death. If he cannot be assigned to a category, if he is not a model of something, a half of what is needed is there. He is still free from himself, he has acquired an atom of immortality. *Ibid.*

Gregariousness is always the refuge of mediocrities, whether they swear by Soloviev or Kant or Marx. Only individuals seek the truth, and they shun those whose sole concern is not the truth. *Ibid.*

How many things in the world deserve our loyalty? Very few indeed. I think one should be loyal to immortality, which is another word for life, a stronger word for it. One must be true to immortality—true to Christ. *Ibid.*

It is possible to be an atheist, it is possible not to know whether God exists, or why, and yet believe . . . that history as we know it now began with Christ, and that Christ's gospel is its foundation.
Ibid.

The two basic ideas of modern man (are in the Gospels)—without them he is unthinkable—the idea of free personality and the idea of life as sacrifice. *Ibid.*

Marxism is too uncertain of its grounds to be a science. I do not know a movement more self-centered and further removed from the facts than Marxism. *Ibid.*

As for the men in power, they are so anxious to establish the myth of their infallibility that they do their utmost to ignore truth. *Ibid.*

No single man makes history. History cannot be seen, just as one cannot see grass growing. *Ibid.*

Wars and revolutions, kings and Robespierres, are history's organic agents, its yeast. But revolutions are made by fanatical men of action with one-track minds, geniuses in their ability to confine themselves to a limited field. They overturn the old order in a few hours or days, the whole upheaval takes a few weeks or at most years, but the fanatical spirit that inspired the upheavals is worshipped for decades thereafter, for centuries. *Ibid.*

Now what is history? It is the centuries of systematic explorations of the riddle of death, with a view of overcoming death. *Ibid.*

I think that if the beast in man could be held down by threats—any kind of threat, whether of jail or of retribution after death —then the highest emblem of humanity would be the lion tamer in the circus with his whip, not the prophet who sacrificed himself. But don't you see this is just the point—what for centuries raised man above the beast is not the cudgel but an inward music; the irresistible power of unarmed truth, the powerful attraction of its example. *Ibid.*

Reshaping life! People who can say that have never understood a thing about life —they have never felt its breath, its heartbeat, however much they may have seen or done. They look on it as a lump of raw material that needs to be processed by them, to be ennobled by their touch. But life is never a material, a substance to be molded . . . Life is constantly renewing and remaking itself. *Ibid.*

The great majority of us are required to live a life of constant duplicity. Your health is bound to be affected if, day after day, you say the opposite of what you feel, if you grovel before what you dislike and rejoice at what brings you nothing but misfortune. *Ibid.*

I stand alone. All else is swamped by
    Pharisaism.
To live life to the end is not a childish task. *Ibid.*

In every generation there has to be some fool who will speak the truth as he sees it.
H. N. Taylor interview, N. Y. Times, February 2, 1959.

In this era of world wars, in this atomic age, values have changed. We have learned that we are the guests of existence, travelers between two stations. We must discover security within ourselves.
Nils Nillson of "The Reporter"; This Week, February 22, 1959.

Louis Pasteur
(1822-1895)
French chemist, bacteriologist

Two opposing laws seem to me now in contest. The one a law of blood and death, opening out each day new modes of destruction, forces nations to be always ready for battle.

The other, a law of peace, work and health, whose only aim is to deliver man from the calamities which beset him. The one seeks violent conquest, the other the relief of mankind.

Which of these two laws will prevail, God only knows. *A.P. dispatch, 1888.*

Walter Pater
(1839-1894)
English critic, essayist

How shall we pass most swiftly from point to point and be present always at the focus where the greatest number of vital forces unite in their purest energy? To burn always with this hard, gemlike flame, to maintain this ecstasy, is success in life. *The Renaissance.*

Joseph Medill Patterson
(1879-1946)
American newspaper publisher

I am talking about myself, the type of the idle, rich young man, not myself the individual. I have an income of between ten and twenty thousand dollars a year. I spend all of it. I produce nothing.

Confessions of a Drone. There are four versions in the N. Y. Public Library: SFC p.v. 57; SFC p.v. 53; SFC p.v. 70; CX p.v. 23.

My income doesn't descend upon me like manna from heaven. It can be traced. Some of it comes from the profits of a daily newspaper, some of it from Chicago real estate, some from the profits made by the Pennsylvania and other railroads, some from the profits of the U.S. Steel Corporation, some from the profits of the American Tobacco Company . . .

It takes to support me just about twenty times as much as it takes to support an average working man or farmer. And the funny thing about it is that these working men and farmers work hard all year round, while I don't work at all. *Ibid.*

The work of the working people, and nothing else, produces the wealth, which, by some hocus-pocus arrangement, is transferred to me, leaving them bare. While they support me in splendid style, what do I do for them? Let the candid upholder of the present order answer, for I am not aware of doing anything for them. *Ibid.*

Newspapers start when their owners are poor and take the side of the people, and so they build up a large circulation, and presently, as a result, advertising. That makes them rich, and they begin most naturally to associate with other rich men —they play golf with one and drink whisky with another, and their son marries the daughter of a third. They forget about the people.

Brand, in play, "The Fourth Estate."

Linus Pauling
(b. 1901)
American scientist, Nobel Prize for chemistry, 1954

The power to destroy the world by the use of nuclear weapons is a power that cannot be used—we cannot accept the idea of such monstrous immorality.

The time has now come for morality to take its proper place in the conduct of world affairs; the time has now come for the nations of the world to submit to the just regulation of their conduct by international law.

No More War, Dodd, Mead & Co., 1958.

Ivan Pavlov
(1849-1936)
Russian physiologist, Nobel Prize for physiology and medicine, 1904

There isn't any science of revolution, and there won't be for a long time. There **is** only a groping of the life force, partly guided empirically.

Letter to Max Eastman.

Gradualness, gradualness and gradualness. From the very beginning of your work, school yourself to severe gradualness in the accumulation of knowledge.

Bequest to the Academic Youth of Soviet Russia, February 27, 1936.

School yourself to demureness and patience. Learn to inure yourself to drudgery in science. Learn, compare, collect the facts!

Ibid.

Facts are the air of scientists. Without them you never can fly. *Ibid.*

Learning, experimenting, observing, try not to stay on the surface of facts. Do not become the archivists of facts. Try to penetrate to the secret of their occurrence, persistently search for the laws which govern them. *Ibid.*

Science demands from a man all his life.

Ibid.

Only science, exact science about human nature itself, and the most sincere approach to it by the aid of the omnipotent scientific method, will deliver man from his present gloom, and purge him from his contemporary shame in the sphere of interhuman relations.

1928. Quoted by Henry A. Wallace, address, Great Barrington, Mass., April 25, 1954.

Thomas Love Peacock
(1785-1866)
English writer

Where the Greeks had modesty, we have cant; where they had poetry, we have cant;

where they had patriotism, we have cant; where they had anything that exalts, delights, or adorns humanity, we have nothing but cant, cant, cant. *Crochet Castle.*

Raymond Pearl
(1879-1940)
American biologist, educator

After each actual war the surviving and disillusioned combatants . . . and the youths too young at the time of the war to have been combatants . . . exhibit almost invariably and universally the psychological reaction epitomized in the phrases "There must never be another war" and "Never again so far as we are concerned" . . The explanation of this recurring volte-face is found in the effects of propaganda.

Some Biological Considerations About War, American Journal of Sociology, January, 1941.

Padraic Pearse
(1879-1916)
Irish poet, revolutionary

Blood is a cleansing and sanctifying thing, and the nation that regards it as the final horror has lost its manhood . . . There are many things more horrible than bloodshed, and slavery is one of them!

And I say to my people's masters: Beware, Beware of the thing that is coming, beware
of the risen people,
Who shall take what ye would not give.

The Rebel.

Hesketh Pearson
(b. 1887)
American writer

You cannot serve God without Mammon.

Biography of G. B. Shaw.

Robert Peel
(1788-1850)
English statesman

Public opinion is a compound of folly, weakness, prejudice, wrong feeling, right feeling, obstinacy and newspaper paragraphs.

Westbrook Pegler
(1894-1969)
American syndicated columnist

As one member of the rabble, I will admit that I said "Fine, that is swell," when the papers came up that recent day, telling of the lynching of the two men who killed the young fellow in California, and that I haven't changed my mind yet for all the storm of right-mindedness which has blown up since. I know how storms of right-mindedness are made.
N. Y. World-Telegram, December 13, 1933.

I am a reactionary, that is what I am, and I would like to see a political reaction get off to a good start in our largest city.
Ibid., October 31, 1941.

I must not mix champagne, whiskey and gin. (Repeated fifty times to fill column.)
Quoted, Time, June 23, 1947.

Charles S. Peirce
(1839-1914)
American physicist, mathematician, logician

The essence of belief is the establishment of a habit.
Popular Science Monthly, January, 1878.

Where different faiths flourish side by side, renegades are looked upon with contempt even by the party whose belief they adopt; so completely has the idea of loyalty replaced that of truth-seeking.   *Ibid.*

The opinion which is fated to be ultimately agreed to by all who investigate, is what we mean by the truth, and the object represented in this opinion is the real. That is the way I would explain reality. *Ibid.*

In the matter of ideas the public prefer the cheap and nasty.   *Ibid.*

It is the man of science, eager to have his every opinion regenerated, his every idea rationalized, by drinking at the fountain of fact, and devoting all the energies of his life to the cult of truth, not as he understands it, but as he does not yet understand it, that ought properly to be called a philosopher.
Annual Report, Smithsonian Institution, June 30, 1900.

To an earlier age knowledge was power, merely that and nothing more; to us it is life and the *summum bonum.*   *Ibid.*

We all know what morality is: it is behaving as you were brought up to behave; that is, to think you ought to be punished for not behaving. But to believe in thinking as you were brought up to think defines conservatism. It needs no reasoning to perceive that morality is conservatism. But conservatism again means, as you will surely agree, not trusting to one's reasoning powers. To be a moral man is to obey the traditional maxims of your community without hesitation or discussion. Hence, ethics, which is reasoning out an explanation of morality, is—I will not say immoral, that would be going too far—composed of the very substance of immorality.
N. Y. Times Book Review.

José Pemartin
(Contemporary)
Spanish Minister of Education

Spanish Fascism must be Catholic Fascism. *Qué es "Lo Nuevo"?*

William Penn
(1644-1718)
*English leader of Society of Friends,
founder of Pennsylvania*

The humble, meek, merciful, just, pious and devout souls everywhere are of one religion and when death has taken off the mask, they will know one another, though the diverse liveries they wore here make them strangers. *Some Fruits of Solitude.*

Government has many Shapes: But 'tis *Sovereignty*, tho' not Freedom, in all of them. *Ibid.*

Rex & Tyrannus are very different Characters: One rules his People by Laws, to which they consent; the other by his absolute Will and Power. That is call'd *Freedom*, This *Tyranny*.
The first is endanger'd by the Ambition of the *Popular*, which shakes the Constitution: The other by an ill Administration, which hazards the Tyrant and his Family.
It is great Wisdom in Princes of both sorts, not to *strain* Points too high with their People: For whether the People have a Right to oppose them or not, they are ever sure to attempt it, when things are carried too far; though the Remedy oftentimes proves worse than the Disease. *Ibid.*

Let the People think they Govern and they will be Govern'd. This cannot fail if Those they Trust, are Trusted. *Ibid.*

Religion is nothing else but love of God and man. *Ibid.*

Inquiry is human; blind obedience brutal. Truth never loses by the one but often suffers by the other. *Ibid.*

To do evil that good may come of it is for bunglers in politics as well as morals. *Ibid.*

Equivocation is half-way to Lying, and Lying the whole way to Hell. *Ibid.*

Governments, like clocks, go from the motions men give them, and as governments are made and moved by men, so by them are they ruined too. Wherefore governments rather depend upon men than men upon governments.
Preface to The Frame of Government of Pennsylvania, 1682.

First, By Liberty of Conscience, we understand not only a mere Liberty of the Mind, in believing or disbelieving this or that principle or doctrine; but "the exercise of ourselves in a visible way of worship, upon our believing it to be indispensably required at our hands, that if we neglect it for fear or favour of any mortal man, we sin, and incur divine wrath."
The Great Cause of Liberty of Conscience, Preface, 1670. (Written in Newgate.)

Secondly, By imposition, restraint, and persecution, we do not only mean the strict requiring of us to believe this to be true, or that to be false; and upon refusal to incur the penalties enacted in such cases; but by those terms we mean thus much, "any coercive lett or hindrance to us, from meeting together to perform those religious exercises which are according to our faith and persuasion." *Ibid.*

We meet on the broad pathway of good faith and good will; no advantage shall be

taken on either side, but all shall be openness and love.
Addressed to Lenni-Lenape tribes, November 30, 1682, at Shackamaxon (now North Philadelphia).

It is certain that the most natural and human government is that of consent, for that binds freely . . . when men hold their liberty by true obedience to rules of their own making.
Essay Towards the Present and Future Peace of Europe, 1693.

If we will not be governed by God, we must be governed by tyrants.

In all debates, let Truth be the aim, not Victory, or an unjust interest: And endeavor to gain, rather than to expose thy Antagonist.

State of Pennsylvania

Every citizen may freely speak, write or print on any subject, being responsible for the abuse of that liberty.   *Constitution.*

Boies Penrose
(1860-1921)
American politician, senator

Public office is the last refuge of a scoundrel. *Collier's Weekly, February 14, 1931.*

Claude Pepper
(b. 1900)
American lawyer, politician

One has the right to be wrong in a democracy.
Congressional Record, May 27, 1946.

If more politicians in this country were thinking about the next generation instead of the next election, it might be better for the United States and the world.
Orlando Sentinel-Star, December 29, 1946.

Pericles
(495?-429 B.C.)
Athenian statesman, orator

Our form of government does not enter into rivalry with the institutions of others. We do not copy our neighbors, but are an example to them. It is true that we are called a democracy, for the administration is in the hands of the many and not of the few. But while the laws secure equal justice to all alike in their private disputes, the claim of excellence is also recognized; and when a citizen is in any way distinguished he is preferred to the public service, not as a matter of privilege, but as the reward of merit.

Neither is poverty a bar, for a man may benefit his country whatever be the obscurity of his condition. There is no exclusiveness in our public life, and in our private intercourses we are not suspicious of one another, nor angry with our neighbor if he does what he likes; we do not put on sour looks at him, which, though harmless, are not pleasant.

While we are thus unconstrained in our private intercourse, a spirit of reverence pervades our public acts; we are prevented from doing wrong by respect for authority and for the laws, having an especial regard to those which are ordained for the protection of the injured, as well as to those unwritten laws which bring upon the transgressor of them the reprobation of the general sentiment.

Thucydides, Hist. ii 37. Funeral oration over Athenians fallen in the Peloponnesian War.

Remember that prosperity can be only for the free, and that freedom is the sure possession of those alone who have the courage to defend it.   *Ibid.*

Périgord

See Talleyrand-Périgord

Juan Domingo Perón

(1895-1974)

Ex-President of Argentina

Let us establish as permanent conduct for our movement: he who . . . tries to disturb order in opposition to the established authorities or contrary to the law of the Constitution, may be slain by any Argentine.

Speech, September, 1955; The Nation, September 10, 1955.

The order of the day for every Peronist . . . is to answer a violent action with another action still more violent. And when one of our people falls, five of them will fall.   *Ibid.*

Ralph Barton Perry

(1876-1957)

American philosopher, educator

There are at least seven meanings of liberty which are relevant to democracy. There is positive versus negative liberty; and there is primitive versus moral liberty. These are all fundamental meanings, prior to government. The introduction of government generates three additional meanings: legal liberty, or liberty *under* government; civil liberty, or liberty *against* government; and political liberty, or liberty *for* government.

Freedom, ed. by Ruth Nanda Anshen, Harcourt Brace, 1940.

John J. Pershing

(1860-1948)

American general

(Reduction of armaments) would be a long step towards the prevention of war.

Chemical warfare should be abolished among nations as abhorrent to civilization. It is a cruel, unfair and improper use of science. It is fraught with the gravest danger to non-combatants and demoralizes the better instincts of humanity . . .

Scientific research may discover a gas so deadly that it will produce instant death. To sanction the use of gas in any form would be to open the way for the use of the most deadly gases and the possible poisoning of whole populations of non-combatant men, women and children. The contemplation of such a result is shocking to the senses. It is unthinkable that civilization should deliberately decide upon such a course.

Johann Heinrich Pestalozzi

(1746-1827)

Swiss educational reformer

I learned that no man in God's wide earth is either willing or able to help any other man.

Quoted by Emerson, The American Scholar.

Thinking leads men to knowledge. One may see and hear and read and learn as much as he pleases; he will never know any of it except that which he has thought over, that which by thinking he has made the property of his mind. Is it then saying too much if I say that man by thinking only becomes truly great?

Peter I (Peter the Great)
(1672-1725)
Czar of Russia

Approach as near as possible to Constantinople and India. Whoever governs there will be the true sovereign of the world. *Testament.*

Theodore Peterson
(b. 1918)
American writer

The themes of 20th century criticism, in general, have been these:
1. The press has wielded its enormous power for its own ends. The owners have propagated their own opinions, especially in matters of politics and economics, at the expense of opposing views.
Four Theories of the Press, pp. 78-9.

2. The press has been subservient to big business and at times has let advertisers control editorial policies and editorial content. *Ibid.*

3. The press has resisted social change. *Ibid.*

7. The press is controlled by one socio-economic class, loosely the "business class," and access to the industry is difficult for the newcomer; therefore, the free and open market of ideas is endangered. *Ibid.*

James Louis Petigru
(1789-1863)
American statesman

Unawed by Opinion,
Unseduced by Flattery:
Undismayed by disaster,
He confronted Life with antique Courage:
And Death with Christian Hope:

In the great Civil War
He withstood his People for his Country ...
Inscribed on tombstone, Charleston, S. C., quoted by Jonathan Daniels. This Week, May 30, 1948.

Petronius Arbiter
(suicide 66? A.D.)
Roman writer

It is fear that first brought gods into the world. *Satyricon.*

Alphonse Peyrat
(1812-1891)

Le cléricalisme, voilà l'ennemi. (Clericalism: that is the enemy.)
Address, French Legislative Assembly, 1859; quoted by Gambetta, Grenoble, September 26, 1872.

Wendell Phillips
(1811-1884)
American orator, abolitionist

The time has been when it was the duty of the reformer to show cause why he appeared to disturb the quiet of the world. But during the discussion of the many reforms that have been advocated, and which have more or less succeeded, one after another, freedom of the lower classes, freedom of food, freedom of the press, freedom of thought, reform in penal legislation, and a thousand other matters, it seems to me to have been proved conclusively that government commenced in usurpation and oppression; that liberty and civilization, at present, are nothing else than the fragments of rights which the scaffold and stake have wrung from the strong hands of the usurpers.
Speech, Woman's Rights, 1851.

Every step of progress the world has made has been from scaffold to scaffold, and from stake to stake.   *Ibid.*

All the great truths relating to society and government have been first heard in the solemn protests of martyred patriotism, or the loud cries of crushed and starving labor. The law has been always wrong. Government began in tyranny and force, began in the feudalism of the soldier and the bigotry of the priest; and the ideas of justice and humanity have been fighting their way, like a thunder-storm, against the organized selfishness of human nature.
Ibid.

In every great reform, the majority have always said to the claimant, no matter what he claimed, "You are not fit for such a privilege." Luther asked of the Pope liberty for the masses to read the Bible. The reply was that it would not be safe to trust the common people with the word of God. "Let them try!" said the great reformer; and the history of three centuries of development and purity proclaim the result.
Ibid.

Eternal vigilance is the price of liberty.
Speech, 1852.

Revolutions are not made: they come. A revolution is as natural a growth as an oak. It comes out of the past. Its foundations are laid far back.
Address, Anti-Slavery Society, Boston, January 28, 1852.

The manna of popular liberty must be gathered each day, or it is rotten.   *Ibid.*

The hand entrusted with power becomes, either from human depravity or *esprit de corps,* the necessary enemy of the people.
Ibid.

Only by unintermitted agitation can a people be kept sufficiently awake to principle (,) not to let liberty be smothered in material prosperity.   *Ibid.*

The best use of good laws is to teach men to trample bad laws under their feet.
Speech, April 12, 1852.

Insurrection of thought always precedes insurrection of arms.
Speech on John Brown, Harper's Ferry, November 1, 1859.

One, of God's side, is a majority.
Ibid.

Every man meets his Waterloo at last.
Ibid.

Whether in chains or in laurels, liberty knows nothing but victories.   *Ibid.*

You can always get the truth from an American statesman after he has turned seventy, or given up all hope of the Presidency.   *Speech, November 7, 1860.*

Governments exist to protect the rights of minorities. The loved and the rich need no protection,—they have many friends and few enemies.
Address, Boston, December 21, 1860.

Aristocracy is always cruel.
Address, Toussaint L'Ouverture, 1861.

Revolutions never go backward.
Speech, Boston, February 17, 1861.

The community which dares not protect its humblest and most hated member in the free utterance of his opinions, no matter how false or hateful, is only a gang of slaves. If there is anything in the universe that can't stand discussion, let it crack.
Speech, 1863.

When you have convinced thinking men that it is right, and humane men that it is just, you will gain your cause. Men always lose half of what is gained by violence. What is gained by argument, is gained forever.

Orations, Speeches, Lectures and Letters, published 1863.

Law has always been wrong. Government is the fundamental Ism of the soldier, bigot, and priest. *Ibid.*

It is easy to be independent when all behind you agree with you, but the difficulty comes when nine hundred and ninety-nine of your friends think you wrong. *Ibid.*

Nothing but Freedom, Justice, and Truth is of any permanent advantage to the masses of mankind. To these society, left to itself, is always tending. *Ibid.*

To hear some men talk of the government, you would suppose that Congress was the law of gravitation, and kept the planets in their places. *Ibid.*

Let History close the record. Let her show that "on the side of the oppressor there was power"—power "to frame mischief by a law;" that on that side were all the *forms* of law, and behind these forms, most of the elements of control: wealth, greedy of increase and anxious for order at any sacrifice of principle—priests prophesying smooth things and arrogating to themselves the name of Christianity,—ambition, baptizing itself statesmanship,—and that unthinking patriotism, child of habit and not of reason, which mistakes government for liberty, and law for justice. *Ibid.*

I rejoice at every effort working-men make to organize; I do not care on what basis they do it. Men sometimes say to me,

"Are you an Internationalist?" I say, "I do not know what an Internationalist is;" but they tell me it is a system by which the working men from London to Gibraltar, from Moscow to Paris can clasp hands. Then I say, God speed to that or any similar movement.

Labor-Reform Convention, Worcester, Mass., September 4, 1870.

Only organize, and stand together. Claim something together, and at once; let the nation hear a united demand from the laboring voice, and then, when you have got that, go on after another; but get something. *Ibid.*

If there is any one feature which we can distinguish in all Christendom, under different names—trades-unions, cooperation, and internationals—under all flags, there is one great movement. It is for the people peaceably to take possession of their own. *Ibid.*

No reform, moral or intellectual, ever came from the upper class of society. Each and all came from the protest of martyr and victim. The emancipation of the working people must be achieved by the working people themselves. *Ibid.*

We affirm, as a fundamental principle, that labor, the creator of wealth, is entitled to all it creates.

Resolution, presented to Labor-Reform Convention.

Affirming this, we avow ourselves willing to accept the final results of the operation of a principle so radical—such as the overthrow of the whole profit-making system, the extinction of all monopolies, the abolition of privileged classes, universal education and fraternity, perfect freedom of exchange, and, best and grandest of all, the final obliteration of that foul stigma upon our so-called Christian civilization—the poverty of the masses.   *Ibid.*

Therefore, Resolved, That we declare war with the wages system, which demoralizes the life of the hirer and the hired, cheats both, and enslaves the workingman; war with the present system of finance, which robs labor, and gorges capital, makes the rich richer and the poor poorer, and turns a republic into an aristocracy of capital; war with these lavish grants of the public lands to speculating companies; and whenever in power we pledge ourselves to use every just and legal means to resume all such grants heretofore made; war with the system of enriching capitalists by the creation and increase of public interest-bearing debts.   *Ibid.*

Our fathers, when they prevented entail, when they provided for the distribution of estates, thought they had erected a bulwark against the money power that had killed Great Britain. They forgot that money could combine; that a moneyed corporation was like the papacy,—a succession of persons with a unity of purpose; that it never died; that it never by natural proclivity became imbecile.

The Foundation of the Labor Movement, 1871.

The grandson of a king is necessarily one third an idiot; but the third generation of a money corporation is wiser for the experience of predecessors, and preserves the same unity of purpose.   *Ibid.*

The land of England has ruled it for six hundred years. The corporations of America mean to rule it in the same way, and unless some power more radical than that of ordinary politics is found, will rule it inevitably.   *Ibid.*

The Labor movement means just this: It is the last noble protest of the American people against the power of incorporated wealth.   *Ibid.*

The motto of the working-men of the United States . . . "Short hours, better education, co-operation in the end, and in the meantime a political movement that will concentrate the thought of the country upon this thing."   *Ibid.*

Wealth, with you, governs; but its power is, I suppose, somewhat masked, sometimes countervailed or checked by other forces. With us it rules, bare, naked, shameless, undisguised. Our *incorporated* wealth, often wielded by a single hand, is feared with direct, and still more with indirect, power.
Letter to an English Friend.

It is momentous, yes, a fearful truth, that the millions have no literature, no school and almost no pulpit but the press. Not one in ten reads books . . . But every one of us, except the very few helpless poor, poisons himself every day with a newspaper. It is parent, school, college, pulpit, theater, example, counselor, all in one. Every drop of our blood is colored by it.

We live under a government of men and morning newspapers.

Let me make the newspapers and I care not what is preached in the pulpit or what is enacted in Congress.

The Declaration of Independence establishes, what the heart of every American acknowledges, that the people—mark you, the *people*—have always an inherent, paramount, inalienable right to change their governments, whenever they think that it will minister to their happiness. That is a revolutionary right.

Agitation prevents rebellion, keeps the peace, and secures progress.

Governments exist to protect the rights of minorities. The Government is only a necessary evil, like other go-carts and crutches.

What gunpowder did for war, the printing press has done for the mind; the statesman is no longer clad in the steel of special education, but every reading man is his judge.

Write on my gravestone, "Infidel, Traitor"—infidel to every church that compromises with the strong; traitor to every government that oppresses the people.

Christianity is a battle, not a dream.

Philo

(20? B.C.-40? A.D.)
Hellenistic Jewish philosopher
of Alexandria

Money, it has been said, is the cause of good things to a good man, of evil things to a bad man. *Noah's Work as a Planter.*

The demagogue, mounting the platform, like a slave in the market, is a slave . . . and because of the honors which he seems to receive, is the slave of ten thousand masters. *Joseph.*

Pablo Picasso

(1881-1973)
Spanish painter, sculptor

My whole life as an artist has been nothing more than a continuous struggle against Reaction and the death of art.
Message to North American Committee to Aid Spanish Democracy, 1937.

We all know that art is not truth. Art is the lie that makes us realize truth—at least the truth that is given us to understand.
The Arts, 1923; requoted by Genêt, The New Yorker, March 9, 1957.

What do you think an artist is? An imbecile who has only his eyes if he is a painter, or his ears if a musician, or a lyre at every level of his heart throbs if he is a poet, or, if he is merely a boxer, only his muscles? On the contrary, he is at the same time a political being, constantly on the alert to the heart-rending, burning, or happy events in the world, molding himself in their likeness.
Genêt, The New Yorker, March 16, 1957.

How could it be possible to feel no interest in other people and, because of an ivory-tower indifference, detach yourself from the life they bring with such open full hands? No, painting is not made to decorate apartments. It is an instrument of war, for attack and defense against the enemy. *Ibid.*

The people who make art their business are mostly imposters. *Quoted in "Time."*

One must act in painting as in life, directly.
Quoted in N. Y. Post, September 8, 1953.

I have tried to penetrate deeper into a knowledge of the world and of men so that this knowledge might free us. In my own way I have always said what I considered most true, most just and best and, therefore, most beautiful. But during the oppression and the insurrection (in Spain) I felt that that was not enough, that I had to fight not only with painting but with my whole being. Previously, out of a sort of "innocence," I had not understood this. *Statement issued on joining French Communist Party.*

Jozif Pilsudski
(1867-1935)
Polish statesman

You accuse me of having betrayed Socialism. It is this way, gentlemen: We rode together in a streetcar marked *Socialism,* but I got off at the stop "Independent Poland." *Time, August 14, 1933.*

William Pitt (Sr.),
1st Earl of Chatham
(1708-1778)
English statesman, orator

Unlimited power is apt to corrupt the minds of those who possess it. *House of Lords, January 9, 1770.*

The poorest man may in his cottage bid defiance to the forces of the Crown. It may be frail—its roof may shake—the wind may blow through it—the storm may enter—the rain may enter—but the King of England cannot enter—all his force dares not cross the threshold of the ruined tenement! *House of Lords; quoted, Brougham's Statesmen in the Time of George III.*

The press is like the air, a chartered libertine. *Letter to Lord Greville, 1757.*

Where law ends, tyranny begins. *Lords, defense of John Wilkes, January 9, 1770.*

We have a Calvinistic creed, a Popish liturgy, and an Arminian clergy. *Quoted, Prior's Life of Burke, 1790.*

William Pitt (Jr.)
(1759-1806)
English statesman

Necessity is the argument of tyrants; it is the creed of slaves. *Speech on the India Bill, November 1783.*

Pittacus of Lesbos
(650?-569? B.C.)
Greek politician, poet

The best state is that in which bad men are not allowed to hold office, and good men are not allowed to refuse office. *Plutarch, Septem Sapientem Convivum, tr. by Kathleen Freeman.*

Pius IV
(1499-1565)
Pope

We order that each and every Jew of both sexes in our temporal dominions, and in all the cities, lands, places and baronies subject to them, shall depart completely out of the confines thereof within the space of three months and after these letters shall have been made public. *Decree.*

Pius IX
(1792-1878)
Pope

The Church is not a true and perfect society, entirely free; nor is she endowed with proper and perpetual rights of her own, conferred upon her by her divine Founder; but it belongs to the civil power to define what the rights of the Catholic

Church are and the limits within which she may exercise these rights.

Condemned proposition, Syllabus of Errors, 1867.

The Church does not have the power to use force, nor does she have any temporal power direct or indirect. *Ibid.*

In the case of conflicting laws enacted by the two powers (lay and clerical), the civil law prevails. *Ibid.*

Every man is free to embrace and profess that religion which, guided by the light of reason, he considers to be true.
Ibid.

All the truths of religion proceed from the innate strength of human reason; hence reason is the ultimate standard by which man can and ought to arrive at the knowledge of all truths of every kind. *Ibid.*

The Church ought to be separated from the state, and the state from the Church.
Ibid.

The Roman pontiff can and ought to reconcile himself, and come to terms, with progress, liberalism, and modern civilization. . . *Ibid.*

The Church has no innate and legitimate right to acquire and possess property.
Ibid.

Protestantism is nothing else than another form of the same true Christian religion, in which form it is possible to please God equally as much as in the Catholic Church. *Ibid.*

Human reason, without any reference whatsoever to God, is the sole arbiter of truth and falsehood, and of good and evil; it is law to itself, and suffices by its natural force to secure the welfare of men and of nations. *Ibid.*

Pius X

(1835-1914)

Pope

Let Catholic writers take care when defending the cause of the proletariat and the poor not to use language calculated to inspire among the people aversion to the upper classes of society.

Letter to the Bishops of Italy on Catholic Social Action, December 18, 1903.

Human society, as established by God, is composed of unequal elements, just as parts of the human body are unequal; to make them all equal is impossible, and would mean the destruction of human society itself. *Ibid.*

Pius XI

(1857-1939)

Pope

Education belongs pre-eminently to the Church.

Encyclical on Education, December 31, 1929.

The Church is independent of earthly sovereignty both in origin and the exercise of its educational mission. *Ibid.*

The Church therefore has the independent right to judge whether any other system or method of education is helpful or harmful to Christian education. *Ibid.*

The Church, being a perfect society, has independent rights on all means to its end, and because every system of teaching, just like any action, has certain relations with the ultimate aim of man, and cannot therefore escape the rules of Divine Law of which the Church is the infallible custodian, interpreter, and teacher. *Ibid.*

Where education is concerned, it is the right, or rather duty, of the State to protect with its laws the prior rights . . . of families over the Christian education of their offspring. As a consequence, it is the duty of the State to respect the supernatural rights of the Church over Christian education. *Ibid.*

From this it follows that the so-called neutral or lay schools from which religion is excluded are contrary to the fundamental principles of education. *Ibid.*

We repeat and confirm their (Pius IX and Leo XIII) declarations, together with the prescriptions of the sacred canons by which attendance at non-Catholic, neutral, or mixed schools or of schools, that is to say, indifferently open to Catholics and non-Catholics without distinction, is forbidden to Catholic children and can only be tolerated at the discretion of Bishops in special circumstances of place and time and under special precautions. *Ibid.*

Any use whatsoever of matrimony exercised in such a way that the act is deliberately frustrated in its natural power to generate life is an offence against the law of God and of nature, and those who indulge in such are branded with the guilt of a grave sin.
Casti Connubii, December 31, 1930.

However we may pity the mother whose health and even life is imperiled by the performance of her natural duty, there yet remains no sufficient reason for condoning the direct murder of the innocent. *Ibid.*

The Church accommodates itself to all forms of government and civil institutions provided the rights of God and the Christian conscience are left intact.
Dilectissimi nobis, 1933.

The mutual relations between capital and labor must be determined according to the laws of the strictest justice, called commutative justice, supported however by Christian charity.
Quadragesimo Anno, May 15, 1931.

Free competition and still more economic domination must be kept within just and definite limits, and must be brought under the effective control of the public authority, in matters appertaining to this latter's competence. *Ibid.*

The chair of Peter, that sacred repository of truth . . . *Ibid.*

Whenever possible the wage-contract should be modified by a partnership-contract, whereby the wage-earner is made to share in the ownership, the management, or the profits. *Ibid.*

Socialism . . . is drifting toward truths which the Christian tradition has always supported. Indeed, it cannot be denied that its progress often comes close to the just demands of Christian reformers. *Ibid.*

No one can be, at the same time, a sincere Catholic and a true Socialist.
Ibid.

"Religious Socialism," "Christian Socialism," are expressions implying a contradiction in terms. *Ibid.*

It violates right order whenever capital so employs the working or wage-earning classes as to divert business and economic activity entirely to its own arbitrary will and advantage, without any regard to the human dignity of the workers, the social character of economic life, social justice, and the common good. *Ibid.*

Man's natural right of possessing and transmitting property by inheritance must remain intact and cannot be taken away by the state. *Ibid.*

The wage paid to the working man must be sufficient for the support of himself and of his family. *Ibid.*

Everyone knows that damage is done to the soul by bad motion pictures.
Vigilanti cura, July 2, 1936.

The more marvelous is the progress of the motion picture art and industry, the more pernicious and deadly has it shown itself to morality, to religion, and even to the very decencies of human society.
Ibid.

Mussolini . . . a gift of Providence, a man free from the prejudices of the politicians of the liberal school.
February, 1929, signing the Lateran Pact.

Refute stoutly and skilfully these doctrines:
1. Vigor of race and purity of blood must be conserved and fostered at any cost.
Letter of instructions to Catholic teachers, August, 1938.

2. It is from blood, wherein the genius of the race is contained, that all intellectual and moral qualities derive as from their most potent source. *Ibid.*

It is not possible for Christians to take part in anti-Semitism.
Address to pilgrims, September, 1938; Time, November 14, 1938.

Pius XII
(1876-1958)
Pope

Always moved by religious motives, the Church has condemned the various forms of Marxist Socialism; and she condemns them today, because it is her permanent right and duty to safeguard men from currents of thought and influence that jeopardize their eternal salvation.
Christmas broadcast, 1942.

An erroneous doctrine affirms that you—representatives of labor—and you—representatives of capital—are, almost by a law of nature, forced to battle each other in bitter and implacable struggle, and that industrial pacification cannot be reached except at this price.
Speech, N. Y. Herald Tribune, January 26, 1946.

To obtain the desired harmony between labor and capital, professional organizations and unions have been devised, both of which are intended, not as a weapon directed exclusively toward defensive and offensive war, which causes reactions and reprisals, nor as an overflowing river, which is divided, but as a bridge which unites.
Ibid.

We must take an open and firm stand against errors of this kind. The power of the Church is not bound by limits of "matters strictly religious" as they say, but by the whole matter of natural law. Its foundation, its interpretation, and its application, so far as moral aspects are concerned, are within the Church's power.
Address to prelates and theologians, November 2, 1954.

Plato

(427?-347? B.C.)
Greek philosopher

The rulers of the State are the only ones who should have the privilege of lying, either at home or abroad; they may be allowed to lie for the good of the State.°
The Republic, b. 3. (Tr. Jowett.)

There seem to be two causes of the deterioration of the arts . . . wealth . . . and poverty. . . . Wealth, I said, and poverty; the one is the parent of luxury and indolence, and the other of meanness and viciousness, and both of discontent.
Ibid., b. 4.

For that is, and ever will be, the best of sayings, *That the useful is the noble and the hurtful is the base. Ibid., b. 5.*

I think, I said, that there might be a reform of the State, if only one change were made . . .
Until philosophers are kings, or the kings and princes of this world have the spirit and power of philosophy, and political greatness and wisdom meet in one, and those commoner natures who pursue either to the exclusion of the other are compelled to stand aside, cities will never have rest from their evils,—no, nor the human race, as I believe,—and then only will this our State have a possibility of life and behold the light of day.°° Ibid.

° "An ambassador is an honest man sent to lie abroad for the good of his country." Sir Henry Wotton.
°° Another translation: "The human race would never see the end of trouble until true lovers of wisdom should come to hold political power, or the holders of political power should, by some divine appointment, become true lovers of wisdom."

He said: Who then are the true philosophers?
Those, I said, who are lovers of the vision of truth. *Ibid.*

But, whether true or false, my opinion is that in the world of knowledge the idea of good appears last of all, and is seen only with an effort; and, when seen, is also inferred to be the universal author of all things beautiful and right, parent of light and of the lord of light in this visible world, and the immediate source of reason and truth in the intellectual; and that this is the power upon which he who would act rationally either in public or private life must have his eye fixed. *Ibid., b. 7.*

A man must take with him into the world below an adamantine faith in truth and right, that there too he may be undazzled by the desire of wealth or the other allurements of evil, lest coming upon tyrannies and similar villainies, he do irremediable wrongs to others and suffer yet worse himself; but let him know how to choose the mean and avoid the extremes on either side, as far as possible, not only in this life but in all that which is to come. For this is the way of happiness. *Ibid.*

Any ordinary city is in fact two cities, one the city of the poor, the other of the rich, each at war with the other; and in either division there are smaller ones—you would make a great mistake if you treated them as single states. *Ibid., section 423.*

In every case the guilt of war is confined to a few persons, and the many are friends.
Ibid., sect. 471.

The elements of instruction . . . should be presented to the mind in childhood, but not with any compulsion. *Ibid., sect. 536.*

Knowledge which is acquired under compulsion has no hold on the mind. Therefore do not use compulsion, but let early education be rather a sort of amusement; this will better enable you to find out the natural bent of the child. *Ibid.*

. . . And yet the true creator is necessity, which is the mother of our invention.
Ibid., b. 2.

Without determining as yet whether war does good or harm, this much we may affirm, that now we have discovered war to be derived from causes which are also the cause of almost all the evils in States, private as well as public. *Ibid.*

Then the first thing will be to establish a censorship of the writers of fiction, and let the censors receive any tale of fiction which is good, and reject the bad; and we will desire mothers and nurses to tell their children the authorized ones only. *Ibid.*

The people always have some champion whom they set over them and nurse into greatness . . . This and no other is the root from which a tyranny springs. When he first appears above ground he is a protector. In the early days of his career he is full of smiles, and he salutes everyone he meets—he is to be called a tyrant, who is making promises in public and also in private; liberating debtors and distributing land to the people and his followers, and wanting to be so kind and good to everyone! But when he has disposed of foreign enemies by conquest or treaty, and there is nothing to fear from them, then he is always stirring up some war or other, in order that the people may require a leader. He has another object, which is that they may be impoverished by payment of taxes and thus compelled to devote themselves to their daily wants and therefore less likely

to conspire against him. And if any of them are suspected by him of having notions of freedom and of resistance to his authority, he will have a good pretext for destroying them by placing them at the mercy of the enemy; and for all these reasons the tyrant must always be getting up a war.
Ibid., b. 8.

Neither do the ignorant seek after wisdom. For herein is the evil of ignorance, that he who is neither good nor wise is nevertheless satisfied with himself: he has no desire for that of which he feels no want.
Symposium.

As to the people, they have no understanding, and only repeat what their rulers are pleased to tell them. *Protagoras, 317.*

He was a wise man who invented God.
Sisyphus.

Wonder is the feeling of a philosopher, and philosophy begins in wonder.
Theaetetus.

Evil, Theodorus, can never pass away, for there must always be an opposite to good. It has no place in heaven, so of necessity it haunts the mortal nature of this earthly sphere. Therefore we ought to escape from earth to heaven as quickly as we can; and the way to escape is to become like God, as far as this is possible; and the way to become like him is to become holy, good and wise. *Ibid.*

Even the gods love their jokes.
Cratylus.

Punishment brings wisdom; it is the healing art of wickedness. *Gorgias.*

Renouncing the honors at which the world aims, I desire only to know the truth,

and to live as well as I can, and, when I die, to die as well as I can.
Quoted by Gollancz, From Darkness to Light.

I exhort you also to take part in the great combat, which is the combat of life, and greater than every other earthly conflict. *Ibid.*

For no man is voluntarily bad; but the bad becomes bad by reason of an ill disposition of the body and bad education, things which are hateful to every man and happen to him against his will. *Ibid.*

Every king springs from a race of slaves, and every slave had kings among his ancestors.

Freedom in a democracy is the glory of the State, and, therefore, in a democracy only will the freeman of nature deign to dwell.

All men are by nature equal, made, all, of the same earth by the same Creator, and however we deceive ourselves, as dear to God is the poor peasant as the mighty prince.

Titus Maccius Plautus
(254?-184 B.C.)
Roman comic dramatist

The gods play games with men as balls.[*]
Captivi.

George Plekhanov
(1857-1918)
*Russian revolutionist,
political philosopher*

A great man is great not because his personal qualities give individual features to great historical events, but because he possesses qualities which make him most capable of serving the great social needs of his time, needs which arose as a result of general and particular causes.
The Role of the Individual in History.

It has long been observed that great talents appear everywhere, whenever the social conditions favorable to their development exist. This means that every man of talent who actually appears, every man of talent who becomes a social force, is the product of social relations. Since this is the case, it is clear why talented people can, as we have said, change only individual features of events, but not their general trends; they are themselves the products of this trend; were it not for that trend they would never have crossed the threshold that divides the potential from the real.
Ibid.

Pliny the Elder
(23-79)
Roman naturalist

It is ridiculous to suppose that the great head of things, whatever it be, pays any regard to human affairs. *Natural History.*

The world, and whatever that be which we call the heavens, by the vault of which all things are enclosed, we must conceive to be a deity, to be eternal, without bounds, neither created nor subject at any time to destruction. To inquire what is beyond it is no concern of man; nor can the human mind form any conjecture concerning it.
Ibid.

Pliny the Younger
(62-113)
Latin author

No one has deceived the whole world, nor has the whole world ever deceived any one. *Panegyricus, lxii.*

[*] See Einstein, letter to Max Born.

George Washington Plunkitt

(1842-1924)

American politician; one-time chief,
Tammany Hall

The politician who steals is worse than a thief. He is a fool. With the grand opportunities all around for a man with political pull, there's no excuse for stealin' a cent.   *Quoted, Time, August 22, 1955.*

Plutarch

(46-120)

Greek historian

When men are arrived at the goal, they should not turn back.

Of the Training of Children.

"Those Macedonians," said he, "are a rude and clownish people, they call a spade a spade."

Apothegms of Great Commanders, Philip.

Those persons who live in obedience to reason are worthy to be accounted free: They alone live as they will, who have learned what they ought to will.

Quoted by John Wise, A Vindication of the Government of New England Churches, Boston, 1772.

Socrates said he was not an Athenian or a Greek, but a citizen of the world.

On Banishment.

The first destroyer of the liberties of a people is he who first gave them bounties and largesses.

He who first called money the sinews of affairs seems to have said this with special reference to war.

They are wrong who think that politics is like an ocean voyage or a military campaign, something to be done with some particular end in view, something which leaves off as soon as that end is reached. It is not a public chore, to be got over with. It is a way of life. It is the life of a domesticated political and social creature who is born with a love for public life, with a desire for honor, with a feeling for his fellows; and it lasts as long as need be.

It is an observation no less just than common, that there is no stronger test of a man's real character than power and authority, exciting as they do every passion, and discovering every latent vice.

Edgar Allan Poe

(1809-1849)

American writer

The idea of God stands for the possible attempt at an impossible conception. We know nothing about the nature of God.

Notes. The Raven and Other Poems, 1845, p. 28.

James Knox Polk

(1795-1845)

11th President of the United States

Thank God, under our Constitution there was no connection between Church and State, and that in my action as President of the United States I recognized no distinction of creeds in my appointments to office. *To a Presbyterian minister caller.*

I have a great veneration and regard for Religion and sincere piety, but a hypocrite or a bigoted fanatic without reason I cannot bear.

Diary, edited by M. M. Quaife, II, 187.

Polybius

(204?-122? B.C.)

Greek historian

Since the masses of the people are inconsistent, full of unruly desires, passionate, and reckless of consequence, they must be filled with fears to keep them in order. The ancients did well, therefore, to invent gods, and the belief in punishment after death.
Histories, vi, c. 125 B.C.

Jeanne Antoinette Poisson le Normant d'Étoiles, Marquise de Pompadour

(1721-1764)

Chief mistress of Louis XV of France

Après nous le déluge.
Attributed, by Mirabeau, in pamphlet, Lettre du Comte de Mirabeau à M. La Couteulx de la Noraye . . .

Arthur Ponsonby

(1871-1946)

English diplomat, writer

When war is declared, Truth is the first casualty.
Falsehood in Wartime, Dutton, 1928.

Alexander Pope

(1688-1744)

English poet

But vindicate the ways of God to man.
Essay on Man. Epistle i. l.16.

All nature is but art, unknown to thee;
All chance, direction, which thou canst not see;

All discord, harmony not understood;
All partial evil, universal good;
And spite of pride, in erring reason's spite,
One truth is clear, Whatever is, is right.
Ibid., l.289.

Know then thyself, presume not God to scan;
The proper study of mankind is man.
Ibid., ii. l.1.

Vice is a monster of so frightful mien,
As, to be hated, needs but to be seen;
Yet seen too oft, familiar with her face,
We first endure, then pity, then embrace.
Ibid., l.217-20.

For forms of government let fools contest;
Whate'er is best administer'd is best;
For modes of faith let graceless zealots fight;
He can't be wrong whose life is in the right.
Ibid., iii. l.303.

See Cromwell damn'd to everlasting fame.
Ibid., iv. l.281.

Slave to no sect, who takes no private road,
But looks through Nature up to Nature's God.
Ibid., l.331.

The people are a many-headed beast.
The First Epistle of the First Book of Horace.

"Give me again my hollow Tree,
A crust of Bread and Liberty."
Second Book of Horace.

Damn with faint praise, assent with civil leer,
And, without sneering, teach the rest to sneer;
Willing to wound, and yet afraid to strike,
Just hint a fault, and hesitate dislike.
Satires and Epistles. Prologue to Dr. Arbuthnot.

Populist Party

The conditions which surround us best justify our cooperation; we meet in the midst of a nation brought to the verge of moral, political and material ruin. Corruption dominates the ballot box, the legislatures, the Congress, and touches even the ermine of the bench.

Preamble, first party platform, 1892.

The newspapers are largely subsidized or muzzled, public opinion silenced, business prostrated, homes covered with mortgages, labor impoverished, and the land concentrating in the hands of capitalists. The urban workmen are denied the right to organize for self-protection, imported pauperized labor beats down their wages, a hireling standing army, unrecognized by our laws, is established to shoot them down, and they are rapidly degenerating into European conditions. *Ibid.*

The fruits of the toil of millions are boldly stolen to build up colossal fortunes for a few, unprecedented in the history of mankind; and the possessors of those, in turn, despise the republic and endanger liberty. From the same prolific womb of governmental injustice we breed the two great classes—tramps and millionaires. *Ibid.*

Wealth belongs to him who creates it, and every dollar taken from industry without an equivalent, is robbery. "If they will not work, neither shall they eat." The interests of rural and civic labor are the same; their enemies are identical. *Ibid., plank 2.*

We believe that the time has come when the railroad corporations will either own the people, or the people must own the railroads. *Ibid., plank 3.*

We demand free and unlimited coinage of silver and gold at the present legal ratio of 16 to 1. *Ibid.*

Eugene Pottier

(1816-1887)

French writer

Arise, ye pris'ners of starvation!
　Arise, ye wretched of the earth,
For Justice thunders condemnation,
　A better world's in birth.
The Internationale.

No more tradition's chains shall bind us.
　Arise, ye slaves! No more in thrall!
The earth shall rise on new foundations,
　We have been naught, we shall be all.
Ibid.

'Tis the final conflict,
　Let each stand in his place,
The International Party
　Shall be the human race.
Ibid., refrain.

Arise, ye toilers of all nations
Condemned to misery and woe;
To Hell with humbleness and patience,
Give deadly battle to your foe!
Wipe out the ruling wealthy classes,
Arise and slash your thralldom chains,
Let power be wielded by the masses,
Let those who labor hold the reins!
Ibid., first verse, present Soviet version.

Terence V. Powderly

(1849-1924)

American labor leader

Conscious of the justice of my cause I am willing to face hell itself in defense of it. So that if the die must be cast and the Church arrays itself on the side of wealth, usury, monopoly and oppression, I will array myself where I stand, on the side of God's poor alongside of those for whom Christ died.

Letter to Dan O'Donoughue: Madison, American Labor Leaders.

The wage system, as I see it, has broken down all over the world. . . . My belief that cooperation shall one day take the place of the wage system remains unshaken. The fundamentals of cooperation will be taught in our schools yet.

Autobiography.

President's Commission on Civil Rights

The central theme in our American heritage is the importance of the individual person. *To Secure These Rights, 1947.*

We abhor the totalitarian arrogance which makes one man say that he will respect another man as his equal only if he has "*my* race, *my* religion, *my* political views, *my* social position". In our land men are equal, but they are free to be different. From these very differences among our people has come the great human and national strength of America. *Ibid.*

Four basic rights have seemed important to this Commission and have influenced its labors . . .

The Right to Safety and Security of Person
The Right to Equality of Opportunity
The Right to Citizenship and its Privileges
The Right to Freedom of Conscience and Expression. *Ibid.*

Joseph Priestley
(1733-1804)
English clergyman, nonconformist philosopher

Since every man retains, and can never be deprived of his natural right (founded on a regard to the general good) of relieving himself from all oppression, that is, from everything that has been imposed upon him without his own consent; this must be the only true and proper foundation of all the governments subsisting in the world, and that to which the people who compose them have an unalienable right to bring them back.

The First Principles of Government, Section II, "Of Political Liberty," 1771.

In the largest states, if the abuses of government should, at any time, be great and manifest; if the servants of the people, forgetting their *masters*, and their masters' interest, should pursue a separate one of their own; . . . in the name of God, I ask, what principles are those, which ought to restrain an injured and insulted people from asserting their natural rights, and from changing, or even punishing their governors, that is their *servants*, who had abused their trust; or from altering the whole form of their government, if it appeared to be of a structure so liable to abuse? *Ibid.*

Governors will never be awed by the voice of the people, so long as it is a mere voice, without overt acts. *Ibid.*

If the power of government be very extensive, and the subjects of it have, consequently, little power over their own actions, that government is tyrannical, and oppressive; whether, with respect to its

form, it be a monarchy, an aristocracy, or even a republic.
Ibid., III, "Of Civil Liberty."

For the government of the temporary magistrates of a democracy, or even the laws themselves may be as tyrannical as the maxims of the most despotic monarchy, and the administration of the government may be as destructive of private happiness. The only consolation that a democracy suggests in those circumstances is, that every member of the state has a chance of arriving at a share in the chief magistracy, and consequently of playing the tyrant in his turn; and as there is no government in the world so perfectly democratical, as that every member of the state, without exception, has a right of being admitted into the administration, great numbers will be in the same condition as if they had lived under the most absolute monarchy; and this is, in fact, almost universally the case with the poor, in all governments. *Ibid.*

All hereditary Government is in its nature tyranny. An heritable crown, or an heritable throne, or by what other fanciful name such things may be called, have no other significant explanation than that mankind are heritable property. To inherit a Government, is to inherit the people, as if they were flocks and herds.
The Rights of Man, 1791.

Matthew Prior
(1664-1721)
English poet, diplomat

The end must justify the means.
Hans Carvel, l.67.

Progressive Party

Every generation must wage a new war

for freedom against new forces which seek through new devices to enslave mankind.
Party Platform, 1924.

Protagoras of Adera
(481?-411? B.C.)
Greek philosopher

Man is the measure of all things, of things that are that they are, and of things that are not that they are not.
Quoted by Plato, Theaetetus.

Pierre Joseph Proudhon
(1809-1865)
French Socialist

La propriété, c'est la vol. (Property is theft.)   *Qu'est-ce la propriété? 1840.*

The ideal republic is a positive anarchy. It is liberty free from all shackles, superstitions, prejudices, sophistries, usury, authority; it is reciprocal liberty and not limited liberty; liberty not the daughter but the Mother of Order.   *Ibid.*

Government of man by man in every form is oppression.
Encyclopaedia Britannica, 11th ed., xxii, p. 490.

The highest perfection of society is found in the union of order and *anarchy.*
Ibid.

All parties without exception, when they seek power, are varieties of absolutism.
Confessions of a Revolutionaire, 1849.

No more parties, no more authority, absolute liberty of man and citizen—that is my political and social confession of faith.
Ibid.

To feel and to assert the dignity of man, first in everything in connection with ourselves, then in the person of our neighbor, and that without a shadow of egoism, without any consideration either of divine or communal sanction—therein lies Right. To be ready to defend that dignity in every circumstance with energy, and, if necessary, against ourself, that is Justice.
Quoted by Georges Sorel, Reflections on Violence.

Then you will know what a revolution is, that has been set going by lawyers, accomplished by artists, and conducted by novelists and poets . . . *Ibid.*

Les grands ne sont grands que parce que nous sommes à genoux; relevons nous. (The great are only great because we are on our knees; let us arise.)
Revolutions de Paris. Motto.

Les journaux sont les cimetières des idées. (The newspapers are the cemeteries of ideas.)

For God's sake, after we have demolished all the dogmatisms *a priori*, let us not of all things attempt in our turn to instil another kind of doctrine into the people.
Letter to Karl Marx.

But simply because we are at the head of a new movement, let us not set ourselves up as the leaders of a new intolerance, let us not pose as the apostles of a new religion—even though this religion be the religion of logic, the religion of reason itself. Let us welcome, let us encourage all the protests; let us condemn all the exclusions, all the mysticisms; let us never regard a question as closed, and even after we have exhausted our last argument, let us begin again, if necessary with eloquence and irony. *Ibid.*

Communism is a society where each one works according to his ability and gets according to his needs.

To be governed is to be watched, inspected, spied, directed, law-ridden, regulated, penned up, indoctrinated, preached at, checked, appraised, seized, censured, commanded by beings who have neither title nor knowledge nor virtue.

To be governed is to have every operation, every transaction, every movement noted, registered, counted, rated, stamped, measured, numbered, assessed, licensed, refused, authorized, indorsed, admonished, prevented, reformed, redressed, corrected.

To be governed is, under pretext of public utility and in the name of the general interest, to be laid under contribution, drilled, fleeced, exploited, monopolized, extorted from, exhausted, hoaxed and robbed; then, upon the slightest resistance, at the first word of complaint, to be repressed, fined, vilified, annoyed, hunted down, pulled about, beaten, disarmed, bound, imprisoned, shot, mitrailleused, judged, condemned, banished, sacrificed, sold, betrayed, and, to crown all, ridiculed, derided, outraged, dishonored.

Marcel Proust
(1871-1922)
French novelist

The great quality of true art is that it rediscovers, grasps and reveals to us that reality far from which we live, from which we get farther and farther away as the conventional knowledge we substitute for it becomes thicker and more impermeable . . .
The Maxims of Marcel Proust, edited by Justin O'Brien, Columbia University Press.

Everything great in the world comes from neurotics. They alone have founded our religions and composed our masterpieces. Never will the world know all it owes to them nor all that they have suffered to enrich us. We enjoy lovely music, beautiful paintings, a thousand intellectual delicacies, but we have no idea of their cost, to those who invented them, in sleepless nights, tears, spasmodic laughter, rashes, asthmas, epilepsies, and the fear of death, which is worse than all the rest.

Ibid., Le Coté de Guermantes.

Publilius Syrus

(c. 1st century, B.C.)
Latin writer

Necessity knows no law except to conquer. *Maxim 553.*

Every day should be passed as if it were to be our last. *Maxim 633.*

Keep the golden mean between saying too much and too little. *Maxim 1072.*

Honesta turpitudo est pro causa bona. (Crime is honest in a good cause.)

Joseph Pulitzer

(1847-1911)
American newspaper publisher

Our republic and its press will rise or fall together.
Quotation used on U.S. 3¢ stamp, 1947.

An able, disinterested, public-spirited press, with trained intelligence to know the right and courage to do it, can preserve that public virtue without which popular government is a sham and a mockery. A cynical, mercenary, demagogic press will produce in time a people as base as itself. The power to mould the future of the Republic will be in the hands of the journalism of future generations.
Conclusion of above quotation.

Nothing less than the highest ideals, the most scrupulous anxiety to do right, the most accurate knowledge of the problems it has to meet, and a sincere sense of moral responsibility will save journalism from a subservience to business interests, seeking selfish ends, antagonistic to public welfare.
The College of Journalism, contribution, North American Review, May, 1904.

Publicity, *publicity*, PUBLICITY, is the greatest moral factor and force in our public life.
To his editors, N. Y. World, December 29, 1895.

I know that my retirement will make no difference in its cardinal principles; that it will always fight for progress and reform, never tolerate injustice or corruption, always fight demagogues of all parties, never belong to any party, always oppose privileged classes and public plunderers, never lack sympathy with the poor, always remain devoted to the public welfare; never be satisfied with merely printing news; always be drastically independent; never be afraid to attack wrong, whether by predatory plutocracy or predatory poverty.
Statement of policy of the St. Louis Post-Dispatch, April 10, 1907.

Nathan M. Pusey

(b. 1907)
American educator, president of Harvard University

It is our task not to produce "safe" men, in whom our safety can never in any case lie, but to keep alive in young people the courage to dare to seek the truth, to be free, to establish in them a compelling desire to live greatly and magnanimously, and to give them the knowledge and awareness, the faith and the trained facility to get on with the job. Especially the faith . . .

Time, March 1, 1954.

Alexander Pushkin
(1799-1837)
Russian writer

The heavy hanging chains shall fall,
    The walls shall crumble at the word,
And Freedom greet you with the light
    And brothers give you back the sword.

The Decembrists.

John Pym
(1584-1643)
English statesman

Shall it be treason to embase the king's coin, though but a piece of sixpence, and not a greater treason to embase the spirit of his subjects, to set a stamp and character of servitude upon them?

If they (the Jesuits) should once obtain a connivance, they will press for a toleration; from thence to an equality, from an equality to a superiority, from a superiority to an extirpation of all contrary religions.

Quoted, The Churchman, July, 1956.

Pyrrhus
(318?-272 B.C.)
King of Epirus, general

Another such victory and we are undone.

Pythagoras
(1592-1644)
Greek philosopher, mathematician

It is only necessary to make war with five things: with the maladies of the body, the ignorances of the mind, with the passions of the body, with the seditions of the city, and the discords of families.

As soon as laws are necessary for men, they are no longer fit for freedom.

Francis Quarles
(1592-1644)
English poet

Let the greatest part of the news thou hearest be the least part of what thou believest, lest the greater part of what thou believest be the least part of what is true. Where lies are easily admitted the father of lies will not easily be excluded.

Enchiridion.

Matt(hew Stanley) Quay
(1833-1904)
Political boss

If you have a weak candidate and a weak platform, wrap yourself up in the American flag and talk about the Constitution.

1886.

Quincey
See De Quincey

Josiah Quincy
(1744-1775)
American lawyer, Revolutionary patriot

Blandishments will not fascinate us, nor will threats of a "halter" intimidate. For, under God, we are determined that wheresoever, whensoever, or howsoever we shall be called to make our exit, we will die free men.

Observations on the Boston Port Bill, 1774.

Quintilian
(35?-95?)
Roman rhetorician

What in some is called liberty, in others is called licence.

De institutione oratoria, III.

Though ambition is itself a vice, it is often the parent of virtues.

For there is absolutely no foundation for the complaint that but few men have the power to take in the knowledge that is imparted to them, and that the majority are so slow of understanding that education is a waste of time and labor.

On the contrary, you will find that most are quick to reason and ready to learn. Reasoning comes as naturally to man as flying to birds, speed to horses, and ferocity to beasts of prey; our minds are endowed by nature with such activity and sagacity that the soul is believed to be produced from heaven.

Those who are dull and unteachable are as abnormal as prodigious births and monstrosities, and are but few in number.

François Rabelais
(1495?-1553?)
French satirist

I am going to seek a great perhaps. Draw the curtain; the farce is played out.
Last words.

Rabutin-Chantal
See Sévigné

Arthur W. Radford
(b. 1896)
U.S. admiral

The things that will destroy America are prosperity at any price, peace at any price, safety first instead of duty first, the love of soft living and the get-rich-quick feeling of living.

Speech, Cincinnati, January 30, 1959; the N. Y. Times "Quotation of the day"; but see Theodore Roosevelt.

Matyas Rakosi
(1892-1963)
Communist dictator of Hungary

I expect to see all of Asia and even parts of Africa under the communist banner long before there is even a radical labor movement in America.

Interview with the editor of this volume.

Sir Walter Raleigh
(1552-executed 1618)
English courtier, colonizer, poet

Men well governed should seek after no other liberty, for there can be no greater liberty than a good government.

Go tell the Court it glows
    And shines like rotten wood;
Go tell the Church it shows
    What's good, but does no good;
      If Court and Church reply
      Give Court and Church the lie.
        The Lie, 1592.

Tell men of high condition,
    That rule affairs of state,
Their purpose is ambition:
    Their practice only hate:
      And if they do reply,
      Then give them all the lie.
        Ibid.

Philip Lee Ralph
(Contemporary)
American historian

When civilizations fail, it is almost always man who has failed—not in his body, not in his fundamental equipment and capacities, but in his will, spirit and mental habits. . . . Men—and civilization—live by their beliefs and die when their beliefs pass over into doubt.
The Story of Our Civilization, 1954.

Heresy hunters are intolerant not only of unorthodox ideas; worse than that, they are intolerant of ideas—of any ideas which are really alive and not empty cocoons.
Ibid.

John Randolph
(1773-1833)
American politician, orator

You may cover whole skins of parchment with limitations, but power alone can limit power.

(It is impossible) to divorce property from power.

I am an aristocrat. I love liberty; I hate equality.
Bruce, Randolph of Roanoke, Vol. ii, p. 203.

Otto Rank
(1884-1939)
Austrian psychoanalyst

For the only therapy is life. The patient must learn to live, to live with his split, his conflict, his ambivalence, which no therapy can take away, for if it could, it would take with it the actual spring of life.

John J. Raskob
(1879-1950)
American industrialist

If a man saves $15 a week and invests in good common stocks and allows the dividends and rights to accumulate, at the end of twenty years he will have at least $80,000. He will have an income from investments of around $400 a month. He will be rich. And because income can do that, I am firm in my belief that anyone not only can be rich but ought to be rich
1928; quoted in N. Y. Times.

Walter Rathenau
(1867-assassinated 1922)
German industrialist, statesman, author

When a Jew says he's going hunting to amuse himself he lies.
Quoted by Albert Einstein, Mein Weltbild, 1934.

John Reed
(1887-1920)
American journalist, poet

Ten Days That Shook the World.
Book title.

In the last analysis the property-owning class is loyal only to its own property.
The Liberator.

The property owning class will never readily compromise with the working class. The masses of the workers are not only capable of great dreams but have in them the power to make dreams come true.
Ibid.

War means an ugly mob-madness, crucifying the truthtellers, choking the artists, sidetracking reforms, revolutions, and the working of social forces.

Whose War? 1917.

Thomas B. Reed
(1839-1902)
American lawyer, politician

One, with God, is always a majority, but many a martyr has been burned at the stake while the votes were being counted.
W. A. Robinson, Life of Thomas B. Reed.

Theodore (Roosevelt), if there is one thing more than another for which I admire you, it is your original discovery of the Ten Commandments.   *Ibid.*

The best system is to have one party govern and the other party watch.
House of Representatives, April 22, 1880.

The only justification of rebellion is success.   *Ibid., April 12, 1878.*

Lizette Woodworth Reese
(1856-1935)
American writer

The old faiths light their candles all
about,
But burly Truth comes by and puts
them out.   *Truth.*

Henry Reeve
(1813-1895)
*English writer; foreign editor,
London Times*

To find out the true state of facts, to report them with fidelity, to apply to them strict and fixed principles of justice, humanity, and law; to inform as far as possible the very conscience of nations, and to call down the judgment of the world on what is false, or base, or tyrannical, appear to me to be the first duties of those who write.

Reply to Napoleon III's attack on "The Times." 1852.

George A. Reid
(1841-1913)
Scottish writer

Probably in all history there is no instance of a society in which ecclesiastical power was dominant which was not at once stagnant, corrupt and brutal.

Theodor Reik
(1888-1969)
*Austrian-American psychoanalyst,
writer*

He (Freud) would often say three things were impossible to fulfill completely: healing, educating, governing. He limited his goals in analytic treatment to bringing a patient to the point where he could *work* for a living, and learn to *love*.

Of Love and Lust, 1957.

Work and love—these are the basics. Without them there is neurosis.

Ibid., conclusion.

Freud told us, his circle of students in Vienna, that only those convictions are lasting and valuable which one acquires after overcoming doubts and objections; and added, "Convictions and women one can get easily are not highly appreciated."

Letter to G. S., January 20, 1959.

Thomas Devin Reilly
(1824-1854)
Irish revolutionary writer

The social system in which a man, willing to work, is compelled to starve, is a blasphemy, an anarchy, and no system.
The Irish Felon, 1848.

(Joseph) Ernest Renan
(1823-1890)
French philologist, historian

Jesus remains for humanity an inexhaustible principle of moral regeneration. Philosophy, for the majority, is not enough; they must have sainthood.
Edmund Wilson, To the Finland Station.

It is through Christianity that Judaism has really conquered the world. Christianity is the masterpiece of Judaism, its glory and the fullness of its evolution.
History of Israel.

Even in this remote epoch, the Semite shepherd bore upon his forehead the seal of the absolute God, upon which was written, "This race will rid the earth of superstition." *Ibid.*

Religion is a necessary imposture. Even the most obvious ways of throwing dust in people's eyes cannot be neglected when you are dealing with a race as stupid as the human species, a race created for error, which, when it does admit the truth, never does it for the right reasons. It is necessary, then, to give it the wrong ones.
Ibid., Vol. 4, pp. 105-6.

No miracle has ever taken place under conditions which science can accept. Experience shows, without exception, that miracles occur only in times and in countries in which miracles are believed in, and in the presence of persons who are disposed to believe them.
Introduction, Vie de Jésus, 1863.

O Lord—if there is a Lord; save my soul —if I have a soul. Amen.
Prayer of a Skeptic.

Republican Party

Free soil, free men, free speech, Frémont.
Slogan, 1856 campaign.

We declare our opposition to all combinations of capital, organized as trusts or otherwise. *National Platform, 1888.*

The trend of Democracy is toward Socialism, while the Republican party stands for a wise and regulated individualism. Socialism would destroy wealth; Republicanism would prevent its abuse. *Ibid., 1908.*

Walter P. Reuther
(1907-1970)
American labor leader

No labor leader can deliver the vote. If any labor leader says he can deliver the vote he is kidding you or himself. He can influence and try to mobilize his people around issues, and they will deliver the vote. *The Nation, December 3, 1952.*

The conflict in America is between two kinds of planning. It is privately planned economic scarcity by companies for profits or publicly planned economic abundance for people. This is really the struggle.

Cecil Rhodes
(1853-1902)
English colonial statesman

We are the first race in the world, and the more of the world we inherit the better it is for the human race.

My cherished idea is a solution for the actual problem; i.e., in order to save the 40,000,000 inhabitants of the United Kingdom from a bloody civil war, we colonial statesmen must acquire new lands to settle the surplus population, to provide new markets for the goods produced by them in the factories and mines. The Empire, as I have always said, is a bread and butter question.

Press interview.

The extension of British rule throughout the world . . . the ultimate recovery of the United States of America as an integral part of the British Empire . . . and finally, the foundation of so great a power as to hereafter render wars impossible and promote the best interests of humanity.

First will; Cecil Rhodes, by Basil Williams. Holt, 1921.

David Ricardo*
(1772-1823)
English political economist

Taxation under every form presents but a choice of evils.

Principles of Political Economy and Taxation.

Capital is that part of the wealth of a country which is employed in production,

---

* "Ricardo and company assumed: (1) poverty for the majority; (2) inequality enforced by the iron law of wages; (3) insecurity for both entrepreneur (the risk taker) and worker; (4) the beneficence of private production in any amount and any variety; (5) the insatiability of human wants; and (6) the necessity of free competition to insure maximum output, government to act as arbiter only"—Stuart Chase, *The Reporter,* June, 1958.

and consists of food, clothing, tools, raw materials, machinery, etc., necessary to give effect to labour.

Ibid.

The natural price of labour is that price which is necessary to enable the labourers, one with another, to subsist and to perpetuate the race, without either increase or diminution.

Ibid.

It is a truth which admits no doubt, that the comforts and well being of the poor cannot be permanently secured without some regard on their part, or some effort on the part of the legislature, to regulate the increase of their numbers, and to render less frequent among them early and improvident marriages.

Ibid.

Labour, like all other things which are purchased and sold . . . has its natural and its market price.

Ibid.

The market price of labour is the price which is really paid for it, from the natural operation of the proportion of the supply to the demand.

Ibid.

Like all other contracts, wages should be left to the fair and free competition of the market and should never be controlled by the interference of the legislature.

Ibid.

There is no way of keeping profits up but by keeping wages down.

On Protection to Agriculture, 1820.

The interest of the landlords is always opposed to the interest of every other class in the community.

1815.

The last point for consideration is the supposed disposition of the people to interfere with the rights of property. So essential does it appear to me, to the cause of good government, that the rights of property should be held sacred, that I would agree to deprive those of the elective franchise against whom it could justly be alleged that they considered it their interest to invade them.

Observations on Parliamentary Reform, The Scotsman, April 24, 1824.

H. M. Richardson

Editor, Reynolds News, London

Were the press of the world resolutely and unanimously determined not in any circumstances to support a war policy or any policy provocative of war, then peace would be assured.

Memorandum, May 2, 1932, on behalf of the National Union of Journalists, to the Disarmament Conference, League of Nations.

Armand Jean du Plessis, Duc de Richelieu

(1585-1642)

French Cardinal, statesman

If you give me six sentences written by the most innocent of men, I will find something in them with which to hang him.

Savoir dissimuler est le savoir des rois. (Dissimulation is the art of kings.)
Mirame (attributed play).

David Riesman

(b. 1909)

American educator, social scientist

The society of high growth potential develops in its typical members a social character whose conformity is insured by their tendency to follow tradition: these I shall term *tradition-directed* people.

The Lonely Crowd (with Nathan Glazer and Reuel Denney), Anchor Books, 1953, p. 23.

The society of transitional population growth develops in its typical members a social character whose conformity is insured by their tendency to acquire early in life an internalized set of goals. These I shall term *inner-directed.* *Ibid.*

The society of incipient population decline develops in its typical members a social character whose conformity is insured by their tendency to be sensitized to the expectations and preferences of others. These I shall term *other-directed* people. *Ibid.*

Jacob Riis

(1849-1914)

American reformer, writer

The slum is the measure of civilization.

Paul Robeson

(1898-1976)

American singer, actor

The war has given us a name for the enslavement of the masses of people by a few with an insane greed for power. That name is Fascism, and we must fight it with all our power.

If Negro freedom is taken away, or that of any minority group, the freedom of all the people is taken away.

Some fight Fascism with guns. Some fight it with the labor of their hands. Others fight it with words and song and brush.

But all of us who want to live as free men and women, no matter what the color of our skins, or our religious belief, or our politics, must fight it in some way—fight it to the death.

Maximilien de Robespierre
(1758-guillotined 1794)
French Revolutionist

It is with regret that I pronounce the fatal truth: Louis ought to perish rather than a hundred thousand virtuous citizens; Louis must die that the country may live.
Speech, National Convention, 1792.

We desire a state of things wherein all base and cruel passions shall be enchained, all generous and beneficent passions awakened by the laws; wherein ambition should be the desire of glory, and glory the desire of serving the country; wherein distinctions should arise but from equality itself; wherein the citizen should submit to the magistrate, the magistrate to the people, and the people to justice; wherein the country assures the welfare of every individual; wherein every individual enjoys with pride the prosperity and glory of his country; wherein all minds are enlarged by the continual communication of republican sentiments and by the desire of meriting the esteem of a great people; wherein arts should be the decorations of that liberty which they ennoble, and commerce the source of public wealth and not the monstrous opulence of some few houses.
Speech before the Convention, February 5, 1794.

We desire to substitute morality for egotism, probity for honor, principles for usages, duties for functions, the empire of reason for the tyranny of fashions, the scorn of vice for the scorn of misfortune, pride for insolence, greatness of soul for vanity, the love of glory for the love of money, good citizens for good society, merit for intrigue, genius for cleverness, truth for splendor, the charm of happiness for the ennui of voluptuousness, the grandeur of man for the pettiness of the great, a magnanimous people, powerful, happy, for a people amiable, frivolous, and miserable; that is to say, all the virtues and all the miracles of a republic for all the vices and all the follies of a monarchy.   *Ibid.*

Democracy is that state in which the people, guided by laws that are its own work, executes for itself all that it can well do, and, by its delegates, all that it cannot do itself.   *Ibid.*

The great purity of the French Revolution, the sublimity even of its object, is precisely that which makes our force and our weakness. Our force, because it gives us the ascendency of truth over imposture, and the rights of public interest over private interest. Our weakness, because it rallies against us all the vicious; all those who in their hearts meditate the robbery of the people; all those who, having robbed them, seek impunity; all those who have rejected liberty as a personal calamity; and those who have embraced the Revolution as a trade, and the Republic as a prey.   *Ibid.*

We must crush both the interior and exterior enemies of the Republic, or perish with her. And in this situation, the first maxim of our policy should be to conduct the people by reason, and the enemies of the people by terror.   *Ibid.*

If the spring of popular government during peace is virtue, the spring of popular government in rebellion is at once both virtue and terror: virtue, without which terror is fatal! terror, without which virtue is powerless!   *Ibid.*

Terror is nothing else than justice, prompt, secure and inflexible.   *Ibid.*

The government of a revolution is the despotism of liberty against tyranny.
Ibid.

Until when will the fury of tyranny continue to be called justice, and the justice of the people barbarity and rebellion?
Ibid.

I conceive that it is easy for the league of the tyrants of the world to overwhelm a man.
Last speech to the Convention, July 26, 1794.

O people, you who are feared—whom one flatters; you who are despised, you who are acknowledged sovereign and are ever being treated as a slave; remember that wherever justice does not reign it is the passions of the magistrates that reign instead, and that the people have changed their chains but not their destinies!
Ibid.

Know, then, that any man who will rise to defend public right and public morals will be overwhelmed with outrage and proscribed by the knaves! Know, also, that every friend of liberty will ever be placed between duty and calumny; that those who cannot be accused of treason will be accused of ambition; that the influence of uprightness and principles will be compared to tyranny and the violence of factions; that your confidence and your esteem will become certificates of proscription for all your friends; that the cries of oppressed patriotism will be called cries of sedition; and that, as they do not dare to attack you

in mass, you will be proscribed in detail in the person of all good citizens, until the ambitious shall have organized their tyranny.   *Ibid.*

What can be objected to a man who is in the right and knows how to die for his country?   *Ibid.*

I was created to battle against crime, not to govern it. The time has not come when upright men may serve their country with impunity! The defenders of liberty will be but outlaws so long as a horde of knaves shall rule!   *Ibid.; last words.*

James Harvey Robinson
(1863-1936)
American historian

We are incredibly heedless in the formation of our beliefs, but find ourselves filled with an illicit passion for them when anyone proposes to rob us of their companionship. It is obviously not the ideas themselves that are dear to us, but our self-esteem, which is threatened. We are by nature stubbornly pledged to defend our own from attack, whether it be our person, our family, our property, or our opinion.
The Mind in the Making.

Few of us take the pains to study the origins of our cherished convictions; indeed, we have a natural repugnance to so doing. We like to continue to believe what we have been accustomed to accept as true, and the resentment aroused when doubt is cast upon any of our assumptions leads us to seek every manner of excuse for clinging to them. The result is that most of our so-called reasoning consists in finding arguments for going on believing as we already have.   *Ibid.*

Alfredo Rocco
(1875-1925)
Fascist Minister of Justice

Fascism is, above all, action and sentiment . . . it is the unconscious reawakening of our profound racial instinct.
The Political Doctrine of Fascism.

For Liberalism, the individual is the end, and society the means. . . . For Fascism, society is the end, individuals the means, and its whole life consists in using individuals as instruments for its social ends.
Ibid.

The fundamental problem of society in the old doctrine is the question of the rights of individuals. It may be the right of freedom as the Liberals would have it; or the right to the government of the commonwealth as the Democrats claim it, or the right to economic justice as the Socialists contend; but in every case it is the right of individuals, or groups of individuals (classes). Fascism on the other hand faces squarely the problem of the right of the State and of the duty of individuals. Individual rights are only recognized in so far as they are implied in the rights of the State. In this preeminence of duty we find the highest ethical value of Fascism.
Ibid.

James Jeffrey Roche
(1847-1908)
American editor

The net of law is spread so wide,
No sinner from its sweep may hide.
Its meshes are so fine and strong,
They take in every child of wrong.
O wondrous web of mystery!
Big fish alone escape from thee!
The Net of Law.

John P. Roche
(b. 1923)
Professor of political science, Haverford

In a healthy democracy the majority and the non-conformist depend upon each other, and each supplies a vital component to the whole. Stability is provided by the majority, while vitality flows from the non-conformist. Consequently, the democrat protects the rights of the non-conformist not merely as an act of decency, but more significantly as an imperative for himself and the whole society.
A Sane View of Non-Conformity, New Republic, February 6, 1956.

Rochefoucauld
See La Rochefoucauld

John D. Rockefeller (Sr.)
(1839-1937)
American capitalist, philanthropist

The good Lord gave me my money, and how could I withhold it from the University of Chicago?
Address, first graduating class.

The growth of a large business is merely a survival of the fittest.
Quoted by W. J. Ghent, Our Benevolent Feudalism; and Richard Hofstadter, Social Darwinism in American Thought.

The American Beauty rose can be produced in the splendor and fragrance which brings cheer to its beholder only by sacrificing the early buds which grow up around it. This is not an evil tendency in business. It is merely the working out of a law of nature and a law of God. *Ibid.*

The best philanthropy is a search for cause, an attempt to cure evils at their source. *Quoted in "Time."*

John D. Rockefeller (Jr.)
(1874-1960)
American capitalist, philanthropist

I believe in the supreme worth of the individual and in his right to life, liberty and the pursuit of happiness.
Credo. Time, July 21, 1941.

I believe that every right implies a responsibility; every opportunity, an obligation; every possession, a duty. *Ibid.*

I believe that the law was made for man and not man for the law; that government is the servant of the people and not their master. *Ibid.*

I believe in the dignity of labor, whether with head or hand; that the world owes no man a living but that it owes every man an opportunity to make a living. *Ibid.*

I believe that thrift is essential to well-ordered living. *Ibid.*

Will Rogers
(1879-1935)
American humorist

All I know is what I read in the papers.

I hope we never live to see the day when a thing is as bad as some of our newspapers make it.
Reference to 1934 San Francisco strike reporting.

I never knew a man I didn't like.
Quoted on U.S. postage stamp.

The United States never lost a war or won a conference. *Life, July 18, 1949.*

About all I can say for the United States Senate is that it opens with prayer and closes with an investigation.
N. Y. Times Magazine, January 1, 1956.

There is no more independence in politics than there is in jail.
Ibid., September 8, 1946.

I tell you folks, all politics is apple sauce.
The Illiterate Digest.

There is only one thing that can kill the Movies, and that is education . . . Some say, what is the salvation of the Movies? I say, run 'em backwards. It can't hurt 'em and it's worth a trial.
Autobiography of Will Rogers, edited by Donald Day.

The American Animal . . . is nothing but the big Honest Majority, that you might find in any country. He is no politician, he is not a 100% American, he is not any organization, either uplift or downfall . . . In fact, all I can find out about him is that he is just normal . . . This normal breed is so far in the majority that there is no use to worry about the others. They are a lot of mavericks and strays.
Quoted in N. Y. Times.

Mme. Jeanne (Manon) Roland
(1754-guillotined 1793)
French girondist

Liberty! It is for noble minds, who despise death, and who know how upon occasion to give it to themselves. It is not for those weak beings who enter into a composition with guilt, who cover their selfishness and cowardice with the name of prudence. . . .

It is for the wise people who delight in humanity, praise justice, despise their flatterers, and respect the truth.

As long as you are not such a people, O my fellow citizens! you will talk in vain of liberty.

Defense, written at the Conciergerie, the night after cross-examination.

O liberté! O liberté! que de crimes on commet en ton nom!
Attributed by Lamartine, Histoire des Girondins.

The feeble tremble before opinion, the foolish defy it, the wise judge it, the skillful direct it.

Romain Rolland

(1866-1944)
French writer

It requires a bold courage to dare, when one is alone, to attack the monster, the new Minotaur, to which the entire world renders tribute: the Press.
Letter to Upton Sinclair, re "The Brass Check," 1920.

Error struggling on toward the living truth is more fruitful than dead truth.
Gollancz, From Darkness to Light.

Skepticism and faith are no less necessary. Skepticism, riddling the faith of yesterday, prepared the way for the faith of tomorrow.   *Ibid.*

There is an age in life when . . . we must make a clean sweep of all the admiration and respect got at second-hand, and deny everything—truth and untruth—everything which we have not of ourselves known for truth.   *Ibid.*

This must be put bluntly: every man who has more than is necessary for his livelihood and that of his family, and for the normal development of his intelligence, is a thief and a robber. If he has too much, it means that others have too little.
Jean-Christophe.

They have no opinions, except in so far as they disapprove of all enthusiastic opinion: but if man is to be independent he must stand alone, and how many men are there who are capable of that? How many men are there, even amongst the most clear sighted, who will dare to break free from the bondage of certain prejudices, certain postulates which cramp and fetter all the men of the same generation?   *Ibid.*

Every man, every art, has its hypocrisy. The world is fed with little truth and many lies.   *Ibid.*

The human mind is feeble: pure truth agrees with it but ill: its religion, its morality, its states, its poets, its artists must all be presented to it swathed in lies. These lies are adapted to the mind of each race: they vary from one to the other: it is they that make it so difficult for nations to understand each other, and so easy for them to despise each other.   *Ibid.*

Truth is the same for all of us; but every nation has its own lie, which it calls its idealism; every creature therein breathes it from birth to death; it has become the condition of life; there are only a few men of genius who can break free from it through heroic moments of crisis, when they are alone in the free world of their thoughts.   *Ibid.*

You who have more than your share of the wealth of the world are rich at the cost of our suffering and poverty. That troubles you not at all: you have sophistries and to spare to reassure you: the sacred right of property, the fair struggle for life, the supreme interests of that Moloch, the State of Progress, that fabulous monster, that problematical Better for which men sacrifice the Good—the Good of other men. But for all that, the fact remains, and all of your sophistries will never manage to deny it: "You have too much to live on. We have not enough." *Ibid.*

The heroic lie is a cowardice. There is only one heroism in the world: to see the world as it is and to love it.
Quoted by Josué de Castro, The Geography of Hunger.

Never tire of protesting.

France fell because there was corruption without indignation.   *1940.*

Eleanor Roosevelt
(1884-1962)
American diplomat, writer

A democratic form of government, a democratic way of life, presupposes free public education over a long period; it presupposes also an education for personal responsibility that too often is neglected.
Let Us Have Faith in Democracy. Land Policy Review, Department of Agriculture, January, 1942.

Democracy cannot be static. Whatever is static is dead.   *Ibid.*

A mature person is one who does not think only in absolutes, who is able to be objective even when deeply stirred emotionally, who has learned that there is both good and bad in all people and in all things, and who walks humbly and deals charitably with the circumstances of life,

knowing that in this world no one is all-knowing and therefore all of us need both love and charity. *It Seems To Me, 1954.*

Our family, like my husband and myself, have been amongst the very privileged people in this country because we have had great opportunities. That does not mean, however, that we will not range ourselves in the battle of the future on the side of the many, because the understanding of democracy is strong in us all.
Ladies' Home Journal, May, 1942.

I don't know what kind of a future life I believe in but I believe that all that we go through here must have some value.*

I think if the people of this country can be reached with the truth, their judgment will be in favor of the many, as against the privileged few. *Ladies' Home Journal.*

Wars frequently have been declared in the past with the backing of the nations involved because public opinion had been influenced through the press and through other mediums, either by the governments themselves or by certain powerful interests which desire war. *This Troubled World.*

It is very difficult to have a free, fair, and honest press anywhere in the world. In the first place, as a rule, papers are largely supported by advertising, and that immediately gives the advertisers a certain hold over the medium which they use.
If You Ask Me, p. 51; reply to question by G. S.

The only hope for a really free press is for the public to recognize that the press

---

* The foregoing, clipped from *Time*, was corrected by Mrs. Roosevelt; all others were found correct.

should not express the point of view of the owners and the writers but be factual; whereas the editorials *must* express the opinions of owners and writers.   *Ibid.*

If they (the public) really want to get at the truth, they can read a variety of publications whose owners and writers have different points of view and in so doing they will be able to decide where they themselves stand.   *Ibid., p. 52.*

Q. President Roosevelt once said, "If I worked in a factory, the first thing I would do would be to join a union." If you had to work in a department store, let us say, would you join a union?

A. I certainly would. I do belong to a union in my own field—the American Newspaper Guild, CIO—and I would urge every woman who works' to join the union of her industry.

"CIO News" interview. York Gazette & Daily, February 22, 1955.

Franklin D(elano) Roosevelt *
(1882-1945)
32nd President of the United States

We often hear it said that government operation of anything under the sun is socialistic. If that is so, our postal service is socialistic, so is the parcel post which has largely taken the place of the old express companies; so are the public highways which took the place of the toll roads.

Hyde Park, September 22, 1928.

These unhappy times call for the building of plans that rest upon the forgotten,

the unorganized but indispensable units of economic power, for plans like those of 1917 that build from the bottom up and not from the top down, that put their faith once more in the forgotten man at the bottom of the economic pyramid.

Radio address, April 7, 1932.

I pledge you, I pledge myself, to a new deal for the American people.°

Acceptance speech, July 2, 1932.

So first of all let me assert my firm belief that the only thing we have to fear is fear itself—nameless, unreasoning, unjustified terror which paralyzes needed efforts to convert retreat into advance.°°

First Inaugural, March 4, 1933.

Our Constitution is so simple and practical that it is possible always to meet extraordinary needs by changes in emphasis and arrangement without loss of essential form.   *Ibid.*

Practices of the unscrupulous money changers stand indicted in the court of public opinion, rejected by the hearts and minds of men . . . The money changers have fled from their high seats in the temple of our civilization. We may now restore the temple to the ancient truths.   *Ibid.*

The measure of the restoration lies in the extent to which we apply social values more noble than mere monetary profit.   *Ibid.*

° "A New Deal for everyone." Lloyd George, 1919.

°° "Nothing is to be feared but fear." Francis Bacon, *De Augmentis Scientiarum: Fortitudo.* "Nothing is so much to be feared as fear—Thoreau, unpublished manuscript, quoted by Emerson at funeral service; see Adams, *N. Y. Times Book Review*, January 11, 1948.

---

* "The work that was put in on these speeches was prodigious, for Roosevelt with his acute sense of history knew that all of those words would constitute the bulk of the estate that he would leave to posterity." Robert E. Sherwood.

No business which depends for its existence on paying less than living wages to its workers has any right to continue in this country. By living wages I mean more than a bare subsistence level—I mean the wages of decent living.
Statement, June 16, 1933.

The freedom guaranteed by the Constitution is freedom of expression and that will be scrupulously respected—but it is not freedom to work children, or to do business in a fire trap, or violate the laws against obscenity, libel and lewdness.
Statement to publishers, signing Newspaper Code, February, 1934.

I am not for a return of that definition of liberty under which for many years a free people were being gradually regimented into the service of the privileged few. *Fireside chat, September 30, 1934.*

The royalists of the economic order have conceded that political freedom was the business of the government, but they have maintained that economic slavery was nobody's business.
Acceptance speech, Democratic National Convention, June 27, 1936.

We stand committed to the proposition that freedom is no half-and-half affair. If the average citizen is guaranteed equal opportunity in the polling place, he must have equal opportunity in the market place.
Ibid.

Concentration of economic power in all-embracing corporations . . . represents private enterprise become a kind of private government which is a power unto itself—a regimentation of other people's money and other people's lives. *Ibid.*

I believe in individualism . . . up to the point where the individualist starts to operate at the expense of society. *Ibid.*

Concentration of wealth and power has been built upon other people's money, other people's business, other people's labor. Under this concentration, independent business was allowed to exist only on sufferance. It has been a menace to . . . American democracy. *Ibid.*

The economic royalists complain that we seek to overthrow the institutions of America. What they really complain of is that we seek to take away their power. Our allegiance to American institutions requires the overthrow of this kind of power.
Ibid.

The gains of education are never really lost. Books may be burned and cities sacked, but truth, like the yearning for freedom, lives in the hearts of humble men.
Ibid.

I see an America where the workers are really free and through their great unions, undominated by any outside force or any dictator within, can take their proper place in the council tables with the owners and managers of business; where the dignity and security of the working man and woman are guaranteed by their strength and fortified by the safeguards of law.
Ibid.

In the spring of 1933, we faced a crisis . . . We were against revolution. And, therefore, we waged war against those conditions which make revolution—against the inequalities and resentments that breed them.
Democratic State Convention, Syracuse, September 30, 1936.

The true conservative seeks to protect the system of private property and free enterprise by correcting such injustices and inequalities as arise from it. The most serious threat to our institutions comes from those who refuse to face the need for change. Liberalism becomes the protection for the far-sighted conservative.   *Ibid.*

I see millions of families trying to live on incomes so meager that the pall of family disaster hangs over them day by day.

I see millions whose daily lives in city and on farm continue under conditions labeled indecent by a so-called polite society half a century ago.

I see millions denied education, recreation, and the opportunity to better their lot and the lot of their children.

I see millions lacking the means to buy the products of farm and factory and by their poverty denying work and productiveness to many other millions.

I see one-third of a nation ill-housed, ill-clad, ill-nourished.

Second Inaugural Address, January 20, 1937.

We have, therefore, reached the point as a nation where we must take action to save the Constitution from the (Supreme) Court and the Court from itself. We must find a way to take an appeal from the Supreme Court to the Constitution itself. We want a Supreme Court which will do justice under the Constitution—not over it. In our courts we want a government of laws and not of men.

Radio address, March 9, 1937.

Remember always that all of us, and you and I especially, are descended from immigrants and revolutionists.

Speech to Daughters of the American Revolution. N. Y. Times, April 21, 1938.

Unhappy events abroad have retaught us two simple truths about the liberty of a democratic people.

The first truth is that the liberty of a democracy is not safe if the people tolerate the growth of private power to a point where it becomes stronger than their democratic State itself. That, in its essence, is fascism—ownership of government by an individual, by a group, or by any other controlling private power.

Message to Congress proposing the Monopoly Investigation, 1938.

The liberty of a democracy is not safe if its business system does not provide employment and produce and distribute goods in such a way as to sustain an acceptable standard of living.   *Ibid.*

Among us today a concentration of private power without equal in history is growing.

This concentration is seriously impairing the economic effectiveness of private enterprise as a way of providing employment for labor and capital and as a way of assuring a more equitable distribution of income and earnings among the people of the nation as a whole.   *Ibid.*

Private enterprise is ceasing to be free enterprise.   *Ibid.*

The arts cannot thrive except where men are free to be themselves and to be in charge of the discipline of their own energies and ardors. The conditions for democracy and for art are one and the same. What we call liberty in politics results in freedom of the arts. There can be no vitality in the works gathered in a museum unless there exists the right of spontaneous life in the society in which the arts are nourished.

Address, dedication, Museum of Modern Art, N. Y. C., May 10, 1939.

A world turned into a stereotype, a society converted into a regiment, a life translated into a routine, make it difficult for either art or artists to survive. Crush individuality in society and you crush art as well. Nourish the conditions of a free life and you nourish the arts, too.   *Ibid.*

A radical is a man with both feet firmly planted in the air.
Radio address, October 26, 1939.

A conservative is a man with two perfectly good legs who, however, has never learned how to walk forward.   *Ibid.*

A reactionary is a somnambulist walking backward.   *Ibid.*

We are a nation of many nationalities, many races, many religions—bound together by a single unity, the unity of freedom and equality. Whoever seeks to set one nationality against another, seeks to degrade all nationalities. Whoever seeks to set one race against another seeks to enslave all races. Whoever seeks to set one religion against another seeks to destroy all religion.
Address, New York, November 1, 1940.

We must always be wary of those who with sounding brass and a tinkling cymbal preach the "ism" of appeasement.
We must especially beware of that small group of selfish men who would clip the wings of the American eagle in order to feather their own nests.
The Four Freedoms Speech, Message to Congress, January 6, 1941.

Certainly this is no time for any of us to stop thinking about the social and economic problems which are the root cause of the social revolution which is today a supreme factor in the world.
For there is nothing mysterious about the foundations of a healthy and strong democracy. The basic things expected by our people of their political and economic systems are simple. They are:
Equality of opportunity for youth and others.
Jobs for those who can work.
Security for those who need it.
The ending of special privilege for the few.
The preservation of civil liberties for all.
The enjoyment of the fruits of scientific progress in a wider and constantly rising standard of living.   *Ibid.*

In the future days, which we seek to make secure, we look forward to a world founded upon four essential human freedoms.
The first is freedom of speech and expression—everywhere in the world.
The second is freedom of every person to worship God in his own way—everywhere in the world.
The third is freedom from want—which, translated into world terms, means economic understanding, which will secure to every nation a healthy peacetime life for its inhabitants everywhere in the world.
The fourth is freedom from fear, which translated into world terms means a worldwide reduction of armaments to such a point and in such a thorough fashion that no nation will be in a position to commit an act of physical aggression against any neighbor—anywhere in the world.   *Ibid.*

Democracy alone, of all forms of government, enlists the full force of men's enlightened will. . . .
It is the most humane, the most advanced and in the end the most unconquerable of all forms of human society.
The democratic aspiration is no mere recent phase of human history. It is human history.
Third Inaugural, January 20, 1941.

We . . . would rather die on our feet than live on our knees.° *Ibid.*

We all know that books burn—yet we have the greater knowledge that books cannot be killed by fire. People die, but books never die. . . . No man and no force can put thought in a concentration camp forever. No man and no force can take from the world the books that embody men's eternal fight against tyranny of every kind. . . . In this war we know books are weapons. And it is a part of your dedication to make them weapons for man's freedom.

Message to American Booksellers Association, April 23, 1941, on the anniversary of the Nazi book-burning.

We shall not be able to claim that we have gained total victory in this war if any vestige of Fascism in any of its malignant forms is permitted to survive anywhere in the world.

Message to Congress, September 17, 1943.

I believe now, as I have all my life, in the right of workers to join unions and to protect their unions.

Radio address, May 2, 1943.

We have accepted, so to speak, a second bill of rights under which a new basis of security and prosperity can be established for all, regardless of station, race or creed. Among these are:

The right to a useful and remunerative job in the industries or shops or farms or mines of the nation.

The right of every farmer to raise and sell his products at a return which will give him and his family a decent living.

The right of every business man, large and small, to trade in an atmosphere of freedom from unfair competition and domination by monopolies at home or abroad.

The right of every family to a decent home.

The right to adequate medical care and the opportunity to achieve and enjoy good health.

The right to adequate protection from the economic fears of old age, sickness, accident and unemployment.

The right to a good education.

Message to Congress, January 11, 1944.

Clear it with Sidney.°

July 15-17, 1944, quoted by James F. Byrnes, All in One Lifetime, Harper, 1958.

I believe in free enterprise—and always have. I believe in the profit system—and always have.

Speech, Chicago, October 28, 1944.

The basic proposition of the worth and dignity of man is the strongest, the most creative force now present in the world.

Quoted in "Army Talks," Vol. IV, No. 24.

The system of party responsibility in America requires that one of its parties be the liberal party and the other the conservative party. This has been the division by which the major parties in American history have identified themselves when-

---

° See Dolores Ibarruri (La Pasionaria).

° Arthur Krock reported July 25, 1944, Roosevelt saying "Clear everything with Sidney" (Hillman), regarding his choice of a Vice-President in 1944. This was officially denied. Hillman was head of the Political Action Committee, C.I.O.

ever crises have developed which required definite choice of direction.

Introduction, Vol. 7, The Public Papers and Addresses of Franklin D. Roosevelt.

The liberal party—no matter what its particular name was at the time—believed in the wide wisdom and efficacy of the will of the great majority of the people, as distinguished from the judgment of a small minority of either education or wealth.
Ibid.

The liberal party is a party which believes that, as new conditions and problems arise beyond the power of men and women to meet as individuals, it becomes the duty of the government itself to find new remedies with which to meet them. *Ibid.*

I have always believed, and I have frequently stated, that my own party can succeed at the polls only so long as it continues to be the party of militant liberalism. *Ibid.*

It (the war effort) must not be impeded by those who put their own selfish interests above the interest of the nation.

It must not be impeded by a few bogus patriots who use the sacred freedom of the press to echo the sentiments of the propagandists in Tokyo and Berlin.

And above all, it shall not be imperiled by the handful of noisy traitors—betrayers of America, betrayers of Christianity itself —would-be dictators who in their hearts and soul have yielded to Hitlerism and would have this republic do likewise.

If the fires of freedom and civil liberties burn low in other lands, they must be made brighter in our own. If in other lands the press and books and literature of all kinds are censored, we must redouble our efforts here to keep them free. If in other lands

the eternal truths of the past are threatened by intolerance, we must provide a safe place for their perpetuation.

Theodore Roosevelt
(1858-1919)
26th President of the United States

That filthy little atheist . . .*
Gouverneur Morris, 1888.

Our country calls not for the life of ease, but for the life of strenuous endeavor. The twentieth century looms before us big with the fate of many nations.
Speech, The Strenuous Life, Chicago, 1899.

If we stand idly by, if we seek merely swollen, slothful ease, and ignoble peace, if we shrink from the hard contests where men must win at hazard of their lives and at the risk of all they hold dear, then the bolder and stronger peoples will pass us by and will win for themselves the domination of the world. *Ibid.*

No man is justified in doing evil on the ground of expedience. *Ibid.*

It was my good fortune at Santiago to serve beside colored troops. A man who is good enough to shed his blood for the country is good enough to be given a square deal afterward. More than that no man is entitled to, and less than that no man shall have.
1903; quoted by Herman Hagedorn, N. Y. Times Magazine, October 27, 1957.

If elected, I shall see to it that every man has a square deal, no less and no more.
Speech, November, 1904.

---

* A reference to Tom Paine, who was neither filthy, nor little, nor an atheist.

Power invariably means both responsibility and danger. *1905; Hagedorn.*

The men with the muckrakes are often indispensable to the well-being of society; but only if they know when to stop raking the muck.
Address, Washington, April 14, 1906.

Every time they (judges) interpret contract, property, vested right . . . they necessarily enact into laws parts of a system of social philosophy. . . . The decisions of the courts on economic and social questions depend on their economic and social philosophy.
Message to Congress, December 8, 1908.

Americanism is a question of principle, of purpose, of Idealism, of Character; it is not a matter of birthplace or creed or line of descent.
Address, Washington, D. C., 1909.

The true friend of property, the true conservative, is he who insists that property shall be the servant and not the master of the commonwealth; who insists that the creature of man's making shall be the servant and not the master of the man who made it. The citizens of the United States must effectively control the mighty commercial forces which they have themselves called into being.
The New Nationalism, 1910.

There can be no effective control of corporations while their political activity remains. To put an end to it will be neither a short nor an easy task, but it can be done.
Ibid.

No man should receive a dollar unless that dollar has been fairly earned. Every dollar received should represent a dollar's worth of service rendered—not gambling in stocks, but service rendered. The really big fortune, the swollen fortune, by the mere fact of its size acquires qualities which differentiate it in kind as well as in degree from what is possessed by men of relatively small means. Therefore, I believe in a graduated income tax on big fortunes, and in another tax which is far more easily collected and far more effective—a graduated inheritance tax on big fortunes, properly safeguarded against evasion and increasing rapidly in amount with the size of the estate.
Ibid.

Nothing is more true than that excess of every kind is followed by reaction; a fact which should be pondered by reformer and reactionary alike. We are face to face with new conceptions of the relations of property to human welfare, chiefly because certain advocates of the rights of property as against the rights of men have been pushing their claims too far. The man who wrongly holds that every human right is secondary to his profit must now give way to the advocate of human welfare, who rightly maintains that every man holds his property subject to the general right of the community to regulate its use to whatever degree the public welfare may require it.
Ibid.

I believe in shaping the ends of government to protect property as well as human welfare. Normally, and in the long run, the ends are the same; but whenever the alternative must be faced, I am for men and not for property.
Ibid.

I am far from underestimating the importance of dividends; but I rank dividends below human character.
Ibid.

Power undirected by high purpose spells calamity; and high purpose by itself is utterly useless if the power to put it into effect is lacking.
1911; Hagedorn.

Labor organizations are like other organizations, like organizations of capitalists; sometimes they act very well, and sometimes they act very badly. We should consistently favor them when they act well, and as fearlessly oppose them when they act badly. *Ibid.*

I wish to see labor organizations powerful; and the minute any organization becomes powerful it becomes powerful for evil as well as for good; and when organized labor becomes sufficiently powerful the state will have to regulate the collective use of labor just as it must regulate the collective use of capital. *Ibid.*

I took the canal zone and let Congress debate, and while the debate goes on the canal does also.
Speech, Berkeley, Calif., March 23, 1911.

My hat's in the ring. The fight is on and I'm stripped to the buff. *1912.*

It is essential that there should be organizations of labor. This is an era of organization. Capital organizes and therefore labor must organize.
Speech, Milwaukee, October 14, 1912.

Every reform movement has a lunatic fringe. *Autobiography, 1913.*

There is no room in this country for hyphenated Americanism. *1915.*

Everything is un-American that tends either to government by a plutocracy or government by a mob. *1917; Hagedorn.*

To divide along the lines of section or caste or creed is un-American. *Ibid.*

All privileges based on wealth, and all enmity to honest men merely because they are wealthy, are un-American. *Ibid.*

A pacifist is as surely a traitor to his country and to humanity as is the most brutal wrongdoer.
Speech, Pittsburgh, July 27, 1917.

A great democracy must be progressive or it will soon cease to be a great democracy.
T. Roosevelt quotation used by F. D. Roosevelt at the dedication of the Theodore Roosevelt Memorial.

The relations of capital and labor, and especially of organized capital and organized labor, to each other and to the public at large, come second in importance only to the intimate questions of family life.
Ibid.

The corporation has come to stay, just as the trade union has come to stay. Each can do and has done great good. Each should be favored as long as it does good, but each should be sharply checked where it acts against law and justice. *Ibid.*

If I were a factory employee, a working man on the railroads, or a wage earner of any sort, I would undoubtedly join the union of my trade. If I disapproved of its policy, I would join in order to fight that policy; if the union leaders were dishonest, I would join in order to put them out. I believe in the union and I believe that all men who are benefitted by the union are morally bound to help to the extent of their powers in the common interests advanced by the union.

I want to see you shoot the way you shout.

If I were asked to name the three influences which I thought were most dangerous to the perpetuity of American institutions, I should name corruption, in business and politics alike; lawless violence; and mendacity, especially used in connection with slander.

We Americans are children of the crucible.

The more we condemn unadulterated Marxian Socialism, the stouter should be our insistence on thorough-going social reforms.

I am in every fiber of my body a radical.

In no other country was such power held by the men who had gained these fortunes, the mighty industrial overlords. . . . The Government was practically impotent. . . . Of all forms of tyranny the least attractive and the most vulgar is the tyranny of mere wealth. *Quoted in The Saturday Review.*

I believe in power; but I believe that responsibility should go with power.
Time, March 3, 1958 (100th anniversary).

Americanism means the virtues of courage, honor, justice, truth, sincerity and hardihood—the virtues that made America. The things that will destroy America are prosperity-at-any-price, peace-at-any-price, safety-first instead of duty-first, the love of soft living and the get-rich-quick theory of life. *Ibid.*

Elihu Root
(1845-1937)
American lawyer, statesman

Never forget that men who labor cast the votes, set up and pull down governments.

Alfred Rosenberg
(1893-1946)
Nazi politician, editor

The racial interpretation of history is an insight which will soon become self-evident.
Der Mythus der 20. Jahrhunderts, translated by Franklin Le Van Baumer. Main Currents of Western Thought, 1952.

Today there awakens a new faith: the myth of blood, the belief that to defend blood is to defend the divine nature of man: the faith, embodied in clearest knowledge, that the nordic blood represents that mystery which has replaced and overcome the old sacraments. *Ibid.*

Germanic Europe presented the world with the brightest ideal of manhood: the teaching of the value of character as the foundation of all morality, the paean of praise to the highest value of the nordic nature, to the idea of freedom of conscience and honor. *Ibid.*

The Negro problem in the United States is vital to the country's future existence. If means are not taken to suppress the Negroes . . . they, in their capacity as Bolshevik combatants, will prepare the doom of white America. *Ibid.*

The idea of National Socialism is an accomplishment of the human soul that ranks with the Parthenon, the Sistine Madonna, and the Ninth Symphony of Beethoven.
Quoted by John Gunther. The Nation, February 6, 1935.

A new peace shall make Germany master of the globe, a peace not hanging on the palm fronds of pacifist womenfolk, but established by the victorious sword of a master-race that takes over the world.

Edward Alsworth Ross
(1866-1951)
American sociologist

There is one deadly, damning count against the daily newspaper as it is coming to be; namely, it doesn't give the news.

The religion a hierarchy ladles out to its dupes is chloroform.

Claude Joseph Rouget de Lisle
(1760-1836)
French army officer

Allons, enfants de la Patrie
  Le jour de gloire est arrivé!
Contre nous de la tyrannie
  L'étendard sanglant est levé ...
            La Marseillaise, 1792.

Ye sons of freedom, wake to glory!
  Hark! hark! what myriads bid you rise!
Your children, wives and grandsires hoary,
  Behold their tears and hear their cries ...

Aux armes, citoyens,
  Formez vos bataillons!
Marchons! marchons! Qu'un sang impur
  Abreuve nos sillons. (*Chorus*)

To arms! to arms! ye brave!
  The avenging sword unsheathe!
March on! march on! all hearts resolved
  On victory or death!

With luxury and pride surrounded,
  The vile, insatiate despots dare,
Their thirst for gold and power unbounded,
  To mete and vend the light and air.
            Ibid.

But Man is Man, and who is More?
            Ibid.

O Liberty! can man resign thee,
  Once having felt thy generous flame?
Can dungeons' holds and bars confine thee,
  Or whips thy noble spirit tame? *Ibid.*

Too long the world has wept bewailing,
  That Falsehood's dagger tyrants wield;
But Freedom is our sword and shield,
  And all their arts are unavailing! *Ibid.*

Jean Jacques Rousseau
(1712-1778)
French writer, philosopher

General and abstract ideas are the source of the greatest errors of mankind.
            Émile.

With children use force, with men reason; such is the natural order of things. The wise man requires no law.   *Ibid.*

I believe, therefore, that the world is governed by a wise and powerful *Will*.
            Ibid.

Liberty is not to be found in any form of government; she is in the heart of the free man; he bears her with him everywhere. The vile man bears his slavery by himself; the one would be a slave in Geneva, the other free in Paris.
Ibid., quoted by Adler, The Idea of Freedom.

Supreme happiness consists in self-content; that we may gain this self-content we are placed upon this earth and endowed with freedom, we are tempted by our passions and restrained by conscience. What more could divine power itself have done in our behalf?   *Ibid.*

While I, overwhelmed with misfortune of all kinds, was destined one day to serve as a warning to all who, inspired solely by love of justice and the public welfare and trusting to the strength of their innocence alone, have the courage to tell the truth openly to the world, without the support of cabals, and without having formed a party to protect them.
Confessions. Modern Library edition.

I have always felt that the position of an author is not and cannot be distinguished or respectable, except in so far as it is not a profession. It is too difficult to think nobly, when one thinks only in order to live. In order to be able to venture to utter great truths, one must not be dependent upon success. *Ibid.*

Laws are always useful to those who own, and injurious to those who do not. . . . Laws give the weak new burdens, and the strong new powers; they irretrievably destroyed natural freedom, established in perpetuity the law of property and inequality, turned a clever usurpation into an irrevocable right, and brought the whole future race under the yoke of labor, slavery and money . . .
Contrat Social (The Social Contract).

Nothing is more dangerous than the influence of private interests on public affairs . . . *Ibid.*

Man is born free; and everywhere he is in chains. One thinks himself the master of others, and still remains a greater slave than they. *Ibid.*

Nothing can be more certain than that every man born in slavery is born for slavery. Slaves lose everything in their chains, even their desire of escaping from them;

they love their servitude, as the comrades of Ulysses loved their brutish condition.
Ibid.

Since no man has a natural authority over his fellow, and force creates no right, we must conclude that conventions form the basis of all legitimate authority among men. *Ibid.*

To renounce liberty is to renounce being a man, to surrender the rights of humanity and even its duties. *Ibid.*

Whoever dares to say: "Outside the Church is no salvation," ought to be driven from the State. *Ibid.*

The social order is a sacred right which is the basis of all other rights. Nevertheless, this right does not come from nature, and must therefore be founded on conventions.
Ibid.

The first (the religion of man), which has neither temples, nor altars, nor rites, and is confined to the purely internal cult of the supreme God and the eternal obligations of morality, is the religion of the Gospel pure and simple, the true theism, which may be called natural divine right or law. *Ibid.*

The other (the religion of the citizen), which is codified in a single country, gives it its gods, its own tutelary patrons; it has its dogmas, its rites, and its external cult prescribed by law; outside the single nation that follows it, all the world is in its sight infidel, foreign, and barbarous; the duties and rights of man extend for it only as far as its own altars. *Ibid.*

There remains therefore the religion of man or Christianity—not the Christianity of today, but that of the Gospel, which is entirely different. By means of this holy, sublime, and real religion all men, being children of one God, recognize one another as brothers, and the society that unites them is not dissolved even at death.   *Ibid.*

But I am mistaken in speaking of a Christian republic; the terms are mutually exclusive. Christianity preaches only servitude and dependence. Its spirit is so favorable to tyranny that it always profits by such a regime. True Christians are made to be slaves, and they know it and do not much mind: this short life counts for too little in their eyes.   *Ibid.*

An antisocial being.   *Ibid.*

Those who distinguish civil from theological intolerance are, to my mind, mistaken. The two forms are inseparable. It is impossible to live at peace with those we regard as damned; to love them would be to hate God who punishes them; we positively must either reclaim or torment them.   *Ibid.*

If there were a people consisting of gods, they would be governed democratically. So perfect a government is not suitable to men.   *Ibid.*

Liberty is obedience to the law which one has laid down for oneself.   *Ibid.*

All the articles of the social contract will, when clearly understood, be found reducible to this single point—*the total alienation of each associate, and all his rights, to the whole community.* For every individual gives himself up entirely—the condition of every person is alike; and being so, it would not be the interest of any one to render himself offensive to others.   *Ibid.*

The first man who, having enclosed a piece of ground, bethought himself of saying *This is mine,* and found people simple enough to believe him, was the real founder of civil society. From how many crimes, wars and murders, from how many horrors and misfortunes might not anyone have saved mankind, by pulling up the stakes, or filling up the ditch, and crying to his fellows, "Beware of listening to this impostor; you are undone if you once forget that the fruits of the earth belong to us all, and the earth itself to nobody."

A Discourse on the Origin of Inequality, 1754.

But from the moment one man began to stand in need of the help of another; from the moment it appeared advantageous to any one man to have enough provisions for two, equality disappeared, property was introduced, work became indispensable, and vast forests became smiling fields, which man had to water with the sweat of his brow, and where slavery and misery were soon seen to germinate and grow up with the crops.   *Ibid.*

Civilized man, on the other hand, is always moving, sweating, toiling and racking his brains to find still more laborious occupations: he goes on in drudgery to his last moment, and even seeks death to put himself in a position to live, or renounces life to acquire immortality. He pays his court to men in power, whom he hates, and to the wealthy, whom he despises; he stops at nothing to have the honor of serving them; he is not ashamed to value himself on his own meanness and their protection; and, proud of his slavery, he speaks with disdain of those, who have not the honor of sharing it.   *Ibid.*

As there is hardly any inequality in the state of nature, all the inequality which now prevails owes its strength and growth to the development of faculties and the advance of the human mind, and becomes at last permanent and legitimate by the establishment of property and laws. *Ibid.*

Moral inequality, authorized by positive right alone, clashes with natural right, whenever it is not proportionate to physical inequality; a distinction which sufficiently determines what we ought to think of that species of inequality which prevails in all civilized countries; since it is plainly contrary to the law of nature, however defined, that children should command old men, fools wise men, and that the privileged few should gorge themselves with superfluities, while the starving multitude are in want of the bare necessities of life. *Ibid.*

Get rid of the miracles and the whole world will fall at the feet of Jesus Christ.

Quoted by Shaw, preface, Androcles and the Lion.

de Rouvroy

See Saint-Simon

Josiah Royce

(1855-1916)

American philosophical writer, psychologist

Philosophy, in the proper sense of the term, is not a presumptuous effort to explain the mysteries of the world by means of any superhuman insight or extraordinary cunning, but has its origin and value in an attempt to give a reasonable account of our own personal attitude toward the more serious business of life.

The Spirit of Philosophy, quoted in N. Y. Times, December 2, 1945.

You philosophize when you reflect critically upon what you are actually doing in your world. What you are doing is, of course, in the first place, living. And life involves passions, faiths, doubts and courage. The critical inquiry into what these things mean and imply is philosophy.

Ibid.

We have our faith in life; we want reflectively to estimate that faith. We feel ourselves in a world of law and significance. Yet why we feel this home-like sense of the reality and the worth of our world is a matter for criticism. Such criticism of life, made elaborate and thoroughgoing, is a philosophy. *Ibid.*

Richard Rumbold

(1622-executed 1685)

English conspirator, rebel

I never would believe that Providence had sent a few men into the world, ready booted and spurred to ride, and millions ready saddled and bridled to be ridden.[*]

Statement on scaffold. Macaulay's History of England, v. 1.

Karl Rudolf Gerd von Rundstedt

(1875-1953)

Nazi officer, World War II

One of the great mistakes of 1918 was to spare the civil life of the enemy countries,

---

[*] "Things are in the saddle and ride mankind"—Emerson. "I hold that if the Almighty had ever made a set of men that should do all the eating and none of the work, He would have made them with mouths only and no hands; and if He had ever made another class that He intended should do all the work and no eating, He would have made them with hands only and no mouths"—Lincoln.

for it is necessary for us Germans to be always at least double the numbers of the people of the contiguous countries. We are therefore obliged to destroy at least a third of their inhabitants. The only means is organized underfeeding, which in this case is better than machine guns.

Address, Reich War Academy, Berlin, 1943; Free World, April, 1945.

Benjamin Rush
(1745-1813)
Signer of the Declaration of Independence, American physician

The Constitution of the Republic should make provision for medical freedom as well as religious freedom. To restrict the art of healing to one class of men and deny equal privilege to others will constitute the Bastille of medical science.

There is but one method of preventing crimes, and of rendering a republican form of government durable, and that is, by disseminating the seeds of virtue and knowledge through every part of the state by means of proper places and modes of education, and this can be done effectively only by the interference and aid of the Legislature.

John Ruskin
(1819-1900)
English writer

Labour without joy is base. Labour without sorrow is base. Sorrow without labour is base. Joy without labour is base.
Time and Tide, letter 5.

To make your children capable of honesty is the beginning of education.
Ibid., letter 8.

The first duty of a state is to see that every child born therein shall be well housed, clothed, fed, and educated, till it attains years of discretion. *Ibid., letter 13.*

Government and cooperation are in all things the law of life; anarchy and competition the laws of death. *Unto This Last.*

Whereas it has been known and declared that the poor have no right to the property of the rich, I wish it also to be known and declared that the rich have no right to the property of the poor. *Ibid.*

There is no wealth but life. *Ibid.*

That country is the richest which nourishes the greatest number of noble and happy human beings. *Ibid.*

Race is precisely of as much consequence in man as it is in any animal.
Modern Painters, 1860.

He is the greatest artist who has embodied, in the sum of his works, the greatest number of the greatest ideas. *Ibid.*

Distribute the earth as you will, the principal question remains inexorable—Who is to dig it? Which of us, in brief word, is to do the hard and dirty work for the rest, and for what pay? Who is to do the pleasant and clean work, and for what pay? Who is to do no work, and for what pay?
Sesame and Lilies.

Even if you are a slave, forced to labour at some abominable and murderous trade for bread—as iron-forging, for instance, or gunpowder-making—you can resolve to deliver yourself, and your children after you, from the chains of that hell, and from the domination of its slave-masters, or to die. That is Patriotism: and true desire of Free-

dom, or Franchise. What Egyptian bondage do you suppose . . . was ever so cruel as a modern English forge, with its steel hammers? What Egyptian worship of garlic or crocodile ever so damnable as modern English worship of money?
Fors Clavigera, letter 46, 1871.

The treacherous phantom which men call liberty . . .
The Seven Lamps of Architecture.

In a community regulated by laws of demand and supply, but protected from open violence, the persons who become rich are, generally speaking, industrious, resolute, proud, covetous, prompt, methodical, sensible, unimaginative, insensitive, and ignorant.   *Ad Valorem.*

The persons who remain poor are the entirely foolish, the entirely wise, the idle, the reckless, the humble, the thoughtful, the dull, the imaginative, the sensitive, the well-informed, the improvident, the irregularly and impulsively wicked, the clumsy knave, the open thief, and the entirely merciful, just, and godly person.   *Ibid.*

It is physically impossible for a well-educated, intellectual, or brave man to make money the chief object of his thoughts; as physically impossible as it is for him to make his dinner the principal object of them.   *The Crown of Wild Olive.*

Men of business rarely know the meaning of the word "rich." At least if they know, they do not in their reasonings allow for the fact, that it is a relative word, implying its opposite "poor" as positively as the word "north" implies its opposite "south."   *The Veins of Wealth.*

The art of making yourself rich, in the ordinary mercantile economic sense, is

therefore equally and necessarily the art of keeping your neighbour poor.   *Ibid.*

The power of the press in the hands of highly-educated men, in independent position, and of honest purpose, may indeed become all that it has been hitherto vainly vaunted to be.   *Ibid.*

Education is the leading of human souls to what is best, and making what is best out of them; and these two objects are always attainable together, and by the same means. The training which makes men happiest in themselves also makes them most serviceable to others.
Stones of Venice, 1853.

Education does not mean teaching people what they do not know. It means teaching them to behave as they do not behave. It is not teaching the youth the shapes of letters and the tricks of numbers, and leaving them to turn their arithmetic to roguery and their literature to lust. It means, on the contrary, training them into the perfect exercise and kingly continence of their bodies and souls. It is a painful, continual, and difficult work to be done by kindness, by watching, by warning, by precept, and by praise, but above all—by example.   *Ibid.*

You may either win your peace or buy it; win it by resistance to evil; buy it by compromise with evil.   *The Two Paths.*

I have seen, and heard, much of the cockney impudence before now; but never expected to hear a coxcomb ask 200 guineas for flinging a pot of paint in the public's face.
(attack on Whistler; subject of a libel action.)

Lord Russell

(1872-1970)

English mathematician, philosopher

Men fear thought as they fear nothing else on earth—more than ruin, more even than death.

Selected Papers of Bertrand Russell.

Thought is subversive and revolutionary, destructive and terrible; thought is merciless to privilege, established institutions, and comfortable habit. Thought looks into the pit of hell and is not afraid. Thought is great and swift and free, the light of the world, and the chief glory of man.

Ibid.

But if thought is to become the possession of many, not the privilege of the few, we must have done with fear. It is fear that holds men back—fear lest they should prove less worthy of respect than they have supposed themselves to be.   *Ibid.*

Should the working man think freely about property? Then what will become of us the rich? Should soldiers think freely about war? Then what will become of military discipline? Away with thought! Back into the shades of prejudice, lest property, morals, and war should be endangered!   *Ibid.*

Conventional people are roused to fury by departure from convention, largely because they regard such departure as a criticism of themselves.

The Conquest of Happiness.

One should respect public opinion in so far as is necessary to avoid starvation and to keep out of prison, but anything that goes beyond this is voluntary submission to an unnecessary tyranny, and is likely to interfere with happiness in all kinds of ways.   *Ibid.*

Drunkenness is temporary suicide; the happiness that it brings is merely negative, a momentary cessation of unhappiness.

Ibid.

Love as a relation between men and women was ruined by the desire to make sure of the legitimacy of children.

Marriage and Morals.

To fear love is to fear life, and those who fear life are already three parts dead.

Ibid.

Dark terror and misfortunes in the life to come oppressed the Egyptians and Etruscans, but never reached their full development until the victory of Christianity. Gloomy saints who abstained from all pleasures of sense, who lived in solitude in the desert, denying themselves meat and wine and the society of women, were, nevertheless, not obliged to abstain from all pleasures. The pleasures of the mind were considered to be superior to those of the body, and a high place among the pleasures of the mind was assigned to the contemplation of the eternal tortures to which the pagans and heretics would hereafter be subjected.

Ideas That Have Harmed Mankind, Haldeman-Julius, 1946.

Most of the greatest evils that man has inflicted upon man have come through people feeling quite certain about something which, in fact, was false.   *Ibid.*

The reformative effect of punishment is a belief that dies hard, chiefly I think, because it is so satisfying to our sadistic impulses.   *Ibid.*

Change is one thing, progress is another. "Change" is scientific, "progress" is ethical; change is indubitable, whereas progress is a matter of controversy.

Unpopular Essays. Philosophy and Politics.

The essence of the Liberal outlook lies not in *what* opinions are held, but in *how* they are held: instead of being held dogmatically, they are held tentatively, and with a consciousness that new evidence may at any moment lead to their abandonment. This is the way opinions are held in science, as opposed to the way in which they are held in theology. *Ibid.*

Dogma demands authority, rather than intelligent thought, as the source of opinion; it requires persecution of heretics and hostility to unbelievers; it asks of its disciples that they should inhibit natural kindliness in favor of systematic hatred. *Ibid.*

Since argument is not recognized as a means of arriving at truth, adherents of rival dogmas have no method except war by means of which to reach a decision. And war, in our scientific age, means, sooner or later, universal death. *Ibid.*

Before the end of the present century, unless something quite unforeseeable occurs, one of three possibilities will have been realized. These three are:

I. The end of human life, perhaps of all life on our planet.

II. A reversion to barbarism after a catastrophic diminution of the population of the globe.

III. A unification of the world under a single government, possessing a monopoly of all the major weapons of war.
Ibid., The Future of Mankind.

If war no longer occupied men's thoughts and energies, we would, within a generation, put an end to all serious poverty throughout the world. *Ibid.*

All movements go too far.
Ibid., On Being Modern-Minded.

There is no evidence that there is any advantage in belonging to a pure race. The purest races now in existence are the Pygmies, the Hottentots, and the Australian aborigines; the Tasmanians, who were probably even purer, are extinct. They were not the bearers of a brilliant culture. The ancient Greeks, on the other hand, emerged from an amalgamation of northern barbarians and an indigenous population; the Athenians and Ionians, who were the most civilized, were also the most mixed. The supposed merits of racial purity, are, it would seem, wholly imaginary.
Ibid., An Outline of Intellectual Rubbish.

There is no nonsense so arrant that it cannot be made the creed of the vast majority by adequate governmental action.
Ibid.

Man can be scientifically manipulated.
Ibid.

If all governments taught the same nonsense, the harm would not be so great. Unfortunately each has its own brand, and the diversity serves to produce hostility between the devotees of different creeds. If there is ever to be peace in the world, governments will have to agree either to inculcate no dogmas, or all to inculcate the same. *Ibid.*

The most savage controversies are those about matters as to which there is no good evidence either way. Persecution is used in theology, not in arithmetic. *Ibid.*

Fear is the main source of superstition, and one of the main sources of cruelty. *Ibid.*

To conquer fear is the beginning of wisdom. *Ibid.*

All human activity is prompted by desire.
The Springs of Human Action. Atlantic Monthly, January, 1952.

There is a wholly fallacious theory advanced by earnest moralists to the effect that it is possible to resist desire in the interests of duty and moral principle. I say this is fallacious, not because no man ever acts from a sense of duty, but because duty has no hold on him unless he desires to be dutiful. If you wish to know what men will do, you must know not only, or principally, their material circumstances, but rather the whole system of their desires with their relative strength. *Ibid.*

Undoubtedly the desire for food has been, and still is, one of the main causes of great political events. *Ibid.*

The pursuit of knowledge is, I think, mainly actuated by love of power. *Ibid.*

But schools are out to teach patriotism; newspapers are out to stir up excitement; and politicians are out to get re-elected. None of the three, therefore, can do anything whatever toward saving the human race from reciprocal suicide. *Ibid.*

Much that passes as idealism is disguised hatred or disguised love of power. *Ibid.*

Man, even if he does not commit scientific suicide, will perish ultimately through failure of water or air or warmth. It is difficult to believe that Omnipotence needed so vast a setting for so small and transitory a result.

Apart from the minuteness and brevity of the human species, I cannot feel that it is a worthy climax to such an enormous prelude.
The Faith of a Rationalist. BBC Broadcast, 1953.

Religions that teach brotherly love have been used as an excuse for persecution, and our profoundest scientific insight is made into a means of mass destruction.

I can imagine a sardonic demon producing us for his amusement, but I cannot attribute to a Being who is wise, beneficent, and omnipotent the terrible weight of cruelty, suffering, and ironic degradation of what is best that has marred the history of man in increasing measure as he has become more master of his fate. *Ibid.*

Men tend to have the beliefs that suit their passions.
Cruel men believe in a cruel God and use their belief to excuse their cruelty. Only kindly men believe in a kindly God, and they would be kindly in any case. *Ibid.*

If a conquering dogmatic Marxism were to replace Christianity, it might be as great an obstacle to scientific progress as Christianity has been.
Cardiff, What Great Men Think of Religion.

I say quite deliberately that the Christian religion, as organized by its churches, has been and still is, the principal enemy of moral progress in the world. *Ibid.*

Morally, a philosopher who uses his professional competence for anything except a disinterested search for truth is guilty of a kind of treachery.
A History of Western Philosophy, Simon & Schuster; Allen & Unwin, 1945.

Ever since Plato most philosophers have considered it part of their business to produce "proofs" of immortality and the existence of God. They have found fault with the proofs of their predecessors—Saint Thomas rejected Saint Anselm's proofs, and Kant rejected Descartes'—but they have supplied new ones of their own. In order to make their proofs seem valid, they have had to falsify logic, to make mathematics

mystical, and to pretend that deepseated prejudices were heaven-sent intuitions.
Ibid.

Power is sweet; it is a drug, the desire for which increases with a habit.
Review of Crossman's The God That Failed, Saturday Review, 1951.

Those who have seized power, even for the noblest of motives, soon persuade themselves that there are good reasons for not relinquishing it. This is particularly likely to happen if they believe themselves to represent some immensely important cause. They will feel that their opponents are ignorant and perverse; before long they will come to hate them . . . The important thing is to keep their power, not to use it as a means to an eventual paradise. And so what were means become ends, and the original ends are forgotten except on Sundays.
Ibid.

The Communist theory of the dictatorship assumes that ultimate success in achieving the goal is certain—so certain as to justify a generation at least of poverty, slavery, hatred, spying, forced labor, extinction of independent thought, and refusal to cooperate in any way with the nations that have heretical governments.
Ibid.

It is preoccupation with possession, more than anything else, that prevents men from living freely and nobly.
Principles of Social Reconstruction.

Real life is, to most men, a long second-best, a perpetual compromise between the ideal and the possible.
The Study of Mathematics.

Mathematics takes us into the region of absolute necessity, to which not only the actual world, but every possible world, must conform.
Ibid.

It is clear that thought is not free if the profession of certain opinions makes it impossible to earn a living.
Sceptical Essays.

William James used to preach the "will to believe." For my part, I should wish to preach the "will to doubt" . . . What is wanted is not the will to believe, but the wish to find out, which is the exact opposite.
Ibid.

The infliction of cruelty with a good conscience is a delight to moralists. That is why they invented Hell.
Ibid.

Freedom in general may be defined as the absence of obstacles to the realization of desires.
Freedom, edited by Ruth Nanda Anshen, Harcourt Brace, 1940.

The first step in a fascist movement is the combination under an energetic leader of a number of men who possess more than the average share of leisure, brutality, and stupidity. The next step is to fascinate fools and muzzle the intelligent, by emotional excitement on the one hand and terrorism on the other.
Ibid.

Freedom of opinion is important for many reasons, especially because it is a necessary condition of all progress, intellectual, moral, political and social. Where it does not exist, the *status quo* becomes stereotyped, and all originality, even the most necessary, is discouraged.
Ibid.

Freedom of opinion can only exist when the government thinks itself secure. *Ibid.*

There are certain things that our age needs, and certain things that it should avoid. It needs compassion and a wish that mankind should be happy; it needs the desire for knowledge and the determination to eschew pleasant myths; it needs above all courageous hope and the impulse to creativeness. The things that it must avoid and that have brought it to the brink of catastrophe are cruelty, envy, greed, competitiveness, search for irrational subjective certainty, and what Freudians call the death wish. *The Impact of Science on Society.*

The root of the matter is a very simple and old-fashioned thing, a thing so simple that I am almost ashamed to mention it, for fear of the derisive smile with which wise cynics will greet my words. The thing I mean—please forgive me for mentioning it —is love, Christian love, or compassion. If you feel this, you have a motive for existence, a guide for action, a reason for courage, an imperative necessity for intellectual honesty. *Ibid.*

Life on this planet is almost certainly temporary. The earth will grow cold, or the atmosphere will gradually fly off, or there will be an insufficiency of water, or, as Sir James Jeans genially prophesies, the sun will burst and all the planets will be turned into gas. Which of these will happen first, no one knows; but in any case the human race will ultimately die out. Of course, such an event is of little importance from the point of view of orthodox theology, since men are immortal, and will continue to exist in heaven and hell when none are left on earth.
An Outline of Intellectual Nonsense.

Every advance in civilization has been denounced as unnatural while it was recent. *Ibid.*

Other passions besides self-esteem are common sources of error; of these perhaps the most important is fear. . . . Fear has many forms—fear of death, fear of the dark, fear of the unknown, fear of the herd, and the vague generalized fear that comes to those who conceal from themselves their own specific terrors. *Ibid.*

Until you have admitted your own fears to yourself, and have guarded yourself by a difficult effort of will against their myth-making power, you cannot hope to think truly about many matters of great importance, especially those with which religious beliefs are concerned. *Ibid.*

Fear is the main source of superstition, and one of the main sources of cruelty. To conquer fear is the beginning of wisdom, in the pursuit of truth as in the endeavor after a worthy manner of life. *Ibid.*

To abandon the struggle for private happiness, to expel all eagerness of temporary desire, to burn with passion for eternal things—this is emancipation, and this is the free man's worship. And this liberation is effected by a contemplation of Fate; for Fate itself is subdued by the mind which leaves nothing to be purged by the purifying fire of Time.
The Free Man's Worship, Philosophical Essays, 1903.

Science can help us to get over this craven fear in which mankind has lived for so many generations. Science can teach us, and I think our own heart can teach us, no longer to look around but rather to look to our own efforts here below to make this world a fit place to live in, instead of the sort of place that the churches in all these centuries have made it. *Ibid.*

Dora Russell
(b. 1894)
English writer

Marriage laws, the police, armies and navies are the mark of human incompetence. *The Right to Be Happy.*

George W. Russell (AE)
(1867-1935)
Irish writer, poet, essayist, journalist

When steam first began to puff and wheels go round at so many revolutions per minute, the wild child humanity, who had hitherto developed his civilization in picturesque unconsciousness of where he was going, and without any set plan, was caught and put in harness. What are called business habits were invented to make the life of man run in harmony with the steam engine, and his movements rival the train in punctuality. The factory system was invented, and it was an instantaneous success. Men were clothed with cheapness and uniformity. Their minds grew numerously alike, cheap and uniform also.
Co-operation and Nationality.

The relation of landlord and tenant is not an ideal one, but any relations in a social order will endure if there is infused into them some of that spirit of human sympathy which qualifies life for immortality.
An Open Letter to the Employers, Dublin Times, 1913 general strike.

Despotisms endure while they are benevolent, and aristocracies while *"noblesse oblige"* is not a phrase to be referred to with a cynical smile. Even an oligarchy might be permanent if the spirit of human kindness, which harmonizes all things otherwise incompatible, were present. *Ibid.*

Those who have economic power have civil power also. *Ibid.*

There was autocracy in political life, and it was superseded by democracy. So surely will democratic power wrest from you the control of industry. *Ibid.*

Democracy in economics, aristocracy in thought.
Quoted, Van Wyck Brooks, A Writer's Notebook.

The journalist holds up an umbrella, protecting society from the fiery hail of conscience.

Intellectual and moral victories are the only ones which do not leave the victor bankrupt and desolate in spirit when the goal is won.

Bernhard Rust
(b. 1883)
Nazi minister of education

The end of it (personal liberty) will always be . . . a dictatorship of the masses. Believe me, behind that word "freedom" demons lurk.
Address at Goettingen, press report, 1937.

Nicola Sacco
(1891-1927)
American anarchist

Help the weak ones that cry for help, help the prosecuted and the victim . . . they are the comrades that fight and fall . . . for the conquest of the joy of freedom for all the poor workers. In this struggle of life you will find more love and you will be loved. *Letter to his son, Dante.*

Antoine de Saint-Exupéry
(1900-1944)
French writer, aviator

I know but one freedom and that is the freedom of the mind.
The Wisdom of the Sands, Harcourt, 1950.

[610]

Norman St. John-Stevas
(b. 1930)
American educator

Whoever is responsible, the image of the Catholic Church which has been created in the American mind is not an image of the Church of Christ. It is largely an image of a power structure.
Religion and Freedom. Fund for the Republic, 1958.

Claude Henri de Rouvroy, Comte de Saint-Simon
(1760-1825)
Founder of French socialism

Princes! hear the voice of God, which speaks to you through my mouth: Become good Christians again; throw off the belief that hired armies, the nobility, the heretical clergy, the corrupt judges, constitute your principal supporters; unite in the name of Christianity and learn to accomplish the duties which Christianity imposes on the powerful; remember that Christianity commands them to devote their energies to bettering as rapidly as possible the lot of the very poor.
The New Christianity, 1825.

Antonio de Oliveira Salazar
(1889-1970)
Dictator of Portugal

Authority and liberty are two incompatible ideas . . . Liberty diminishes in proportion as man progresses and becomes civilized.
Salazar, Le Portugal et son Chef, official biography by Antonio Ferro, Paris, 1934.

Liberalism, Materialism, Class Warfare or Internationalism have no place whatever in our regime or in our land; they are rejected by the national mentality, by the laws, by public and private institutions, in a word by the life of the nation.
Father Richard S. Devane, S. J., Irish Ecclesiastical Record, 1937; Diario da Manha, June 3, 1937.

In the newspapers I often read this pitiful sentence: "The people must be taught to read," and I say to myself, What shall they read? It is education and undesirable literature, these are our enemies.
N. Y. Post, August 10, 1938.

Salisbury
See John of Salisbury

Coluccio Salutati
(c. 1390)
Florentine humanist, chancellor

Do not believe, my friend, that to flee the crowd, to avoid the sight of beautiful things, to shut oneself up in a cloister, is the way to perfection. In fleeing from the world you may topple down from heaven to earth, whereas I, remaining among earthly things, shall be able to lift my heart securely to heaven.   *Letter.*

Carl Sandburg
(1878-1967)
American poet, author

Tell them too much money has killed men
and left them dead years before burial:
and quest of lucre beyond a few easy needs
has twisted good enough men
sometimes into dry thwarted worms.
The People, Yes. Copyright, Harcourt, Brace & Co., 1936.

When have the people been half as rotten as what the panderers to the people dangle before crowds?   *Ibid.*

The people will live on.
The learning and blundering people will
    live on.
    They will be tricked and sold and again
      sold
And go back to the nourishing earth for
    rootholds,
    The people so peculiar in renewal and
      comeback,
    You can't laugh off their capacity to take
      it.
The mammoth rests between his cyclonic
    dramas.   *Ibid.*

Man is a long time coming.
Man will yet win.
Brother may yet line up with brother;
In the darkness with a great bundle of grief
    the people march.
In the night, and overhead a shovel of stars
    for keeps, the people march:
      Where to? what next?   *Ibid.*

When I, the People, learn to remember,
    when I, the
    People, use the lessons of yesterday and
      no longer
    forget who robbed me last year, who
      played me for
    a fool—then there will be no speaker in
      all the world
    say the name: "The People", with any
      fleck of a
    sneer in his voice or any far-off smile of
      derision.
The mob—the crowd—the mass—will arrive
    then.
I am the People-from "Chicago Poems."
Copyright 1916, Henry Holt & Co.

In the average newspaper there is not a complete suppression of stories the sacred cows don't want printed. But rather what happens is that the stories get printed with stresses, colorations and emphasis that favor the sacred cows.
To his biographer, Karl Detzer; Editor & Publisher, September 27, 1941.

George Santayana
(1863-1952)
Spanish-born philosopher

Wisdom comes by disillusionment.
    Reason in Common Sense.

Fanaticism consists in redoubling your effort when you have forgotten your aim.
Life of Reason, vol. 1. (Quoted by Gen. Eisenhower, campaign speech, October 16, 1952· N. Y. Times, March 19, 1956.)

That life is worth living is the most necessary of assumptions, and, were it not assumed, the most impossible of conclusions.
    The Life of Reason.

That fear first created the gods is perhaps as true as anything so brief could be on so great a subject.   *Ibid.*

The fact of having been born is a bad augury for immortality.   *Ibid.*

It is pathetic to observe how lowly are the motives that religion, even the highest, attributes to the deity, and from what a hard-pressed and bitter existence they have been drawn. To be given the best morsel, to be remembered, to be praised, to be obeyed blindly and punctiliously—these have been thought points of honor with the gods, for which they would dispense favors and

punishments on the most exorbitant scale.
Ibid.

Revolutions are ambiguous things. Their success is generally proportionate to their power of adaptation and to the reabsorption within them of what they rebelled against. *Ibid.*

A thousand reforms have left the world as corrupt as ever, for each successful reform has founded a new institution, and this institution has bred its new and congenial abuses. *Ibid.*

To call war the soil of courage and virtue is like calling debauchery the soil of love.
Reason in Society.

The glories of war are all blood-stained, delirious, and infected with crime; the combative instinct is a savage prompting by which one man's good is found in another's evil. *Ibid.*

Great thoughts require a great mind and pure beauties a profound sensibility. To attempt to give such things a wide currency is to be willing to denaturalize them in order to boast that they have been propagated. Culture is on the horns of this dilemma: if profound and noble it must remain rare, if common it must become mean. These alternatives can never be eluded until some purified and high-bred race succeeds the promiscuous bipeds that now blacken the planet. *Ibid.*

There is no tyranny so hateful as a vulgar and anonymous tyranny. It is all-permeating, all-thwarting; it blasts every budding novelty and sprig of genius with its omnipresent and fierce stupidity.
Ibid; The Sense of Beauty.

Christianity persecuted, tortured, and burned. Like a hound it tracked the very scent of heresy. It kindled wars, and nursed furious hatreds and ambitions. It sanctified, quite like Mohammedanism, extermination and tyranny. All this would have been impossible if, like Buddhism, it had looked only to peace and the liberation of souls. It looked beyond; it dreamt of infinite blisses and crowns it should be crowned with before an electrified universe and an applauding God.
Reason in Science.

Moreover, the Life of Reason is an ideal to which everything in the world should be subordinated; it establishes lines of moral cleavage everywhere and makes right eternally different from wrong.
Reason in Religion.

Even the heretics and atheists, if they have had profundity, turn out after a while to be forerunners of some new orthodoxy. What they rebel against is a religion alien to their nature; they are atheists only by accident, and relatively to the convention which inwardly offends them, but they yearn mightily in their souls after the religious acceptance of a world interpreted in their own fashion. *Ibid.*

Each religion, so dear to those whose life it sanctifies, and fulfilling so necessary a function in the society that has adopted it, necessarily contradicts every other religion, and probably contradicts itself. *Ibid.*

What religion a man shall have is a historical accident, quite as much as what language he shall speak. *Ibid.*

Scepticism is the chastity of the intellect.
Scepticism and Animal Faith.

The brute necessity of believing something so long as life lasts does not justify any belief in particular. *Ibid.*

Catholicism is the most human of religions, if taken humanly: it is paganism spiritually transformed and made metaphysical. *Persons and Places, p. 91.*

My atheism, like that of Spinoza, is true piety towards the universe and denies only gods fashioned by men in their own image, to be servants of their human interests; and that even in this denial I am no rude iconoclast, but full of secret sympathy with the impulses of idolaters.
Soliloquies in England, 1922.

This liberty to discover and pursue a natural happiness, this liberty to grow wise and live in friendship with the gods and with one another, was the liberty vindicated at Thermopylae by martyrdom and at Salamis by victory. *Ibid., 1925.*

It is not worldly ecclesiastics that kindle the fires of persecution, but mystics who think they hear the voice of God.
New Republic, January 15, 1916.

Words are weapons, and it is dangerous in speculation, as in politics, to borrow them from the arsenal of the enemy.
Obiter Scripta.

For Shakespeare, in the matter of religion, the choice lay between Christianity and nothing. He chose nothing.
The Absence of Religion in Shakespeare.

There is joy in jettisoning useless, troublesome commitments that burden our lives. How genial public life becomes when reduced entirely to cordiality and platitudes. The leaders in such a society need not be superior to the crowd in knowledge or virtue; they must be simply quicker. They must be the first to name, and loudest to

demand, something that, for the moment, will appeal to the average man. This is no machination on the leaders' part; those will succeed best who are sincere and have divined the people's instinct by passionately trusting their own.
New Republic, February 25, 1957.

George Sarton
(1884-1955)
American authority on history of science

There are but few saints among scientists, as among other men, but truth itself is a goal comparable to sanctity.
History of Science.

There is sanctity in pure knowledge, as there is in pure beauty, and the disinterested quest of truth is perhaps the greatest purification. *Ibid.*

Attempts at religious reform aroused popular anger because the inborn conservativeness of man is nowhere stronger than in the field of religion. The religion of his fathers must not be criticized, even if his own profession of it is but an outward show. The most malicious kind of hatred is that which is built upon a theological foundation. *Ibid.*

Conservative people are undoubtedly right in their distrust and hatred of science, for the scientific spirit is the very spirit of innovation and adventure—the most reckless kind of adventure into the unknown. And such is its aggressive strength that its revolutionary activity can neither be restrained nor restricted within its own field. Sooner or later it will go out to conquer other fields and to throw floods of light into all the dark places where superstition and injustice are still rampant.
Ibid.

[614]

Jean-Paul Sartre
(1905-1980)
French existentialist, writer

There are two kinds of existentialist; first those who are Christian . . . and on the other hand the atheistic existentialists, among whom . . . I class myself. What they have in common is that they think that existence precedes essence, or, if you prefer, that subjectivity must be the turning point. *Existentialism, 1947.*

The existentialist says at once that man is anguish. *Ibid.*

Atheistic existentialism . . . states that if God does not exist, there is at least one being in whom existence precedes essence, a being who exists before he can be defined by any concept and that this being is man, or, as Heidegger says, human reality. What is meant here by saying that existence precedes essence? It means that, first of all, man exists, turns up, appears on the scene, and, only afterwards, defines himself. *Ibid.*

If man, as the existentialist conceives him, is indefinable, it is because at first he is nothing. Only afterward will he be something, and he himself will have made what he will be. Thus there is no human nature, since there is no God to conceive it. Not only is man what he conceives himself to be, but he is also only what he wills himself to be after this thrust toward existence. *Ibid.*

The existentialist is strongly opposed to a certain kind of secular ethics which would like to abolish God with the least possible expense. *Ibid.*

The existentialist . . . thinks it very distressing that God does not exist, because all possibility of finding values in a heaven of ideas disappears along with Him; there can no longer be an *a priori* Good, since there is no infinite and perfect consciousness to think it. Nowhere is it written that the Good exists, that we must be honest, that we must not lie; because the fact is we are on a plane where there are only men. Dostoevsky said, "If God didn't exist, everything would be possible." That is the very starting point of existentialism. Indeed, everything is permissible if God does not exist, and as a result man is forlorn, because neither within him nor without does he find anything to cling to. *Ibid.*

Man is condemned to be free; because once thrown into the world, he is responsible for everything he does. *Ibid.*

Existentialism is nothing less than an attempt to draw all the consequences of a coherent atheistic position. It isn't trying to plunge man into despair at all. But if one calls every attitude of unbelief despair, like the Christians, then the word is not being used in its original sense. Existentialism isn't so atheistic that it wears itself out showing that God doesn't exist. Rather, it declares that even if God did exist, that would change nothing. There you've got our point of view. Not that we believe that God exists, but we think that the problem of His existence is not the issue. In this sense existentialism is optimistic, a doctrine of action, and it is plain dishonesty for Christians to make no distinction between their own despair and ours and then to call us despairing. *Ibid.*

Should I betray the proletariat to serve truth or betray truth in the name of the proletariat?
Quoted in "Time," July 18, 1955.

George Savile
See Halifax

Girolamo Savonarola
(1452-burned and hanged 1498)
Italian religious reformer

In the primitive church the chalices were of wood, the prelates of gold. In these days the church hath chalices of gold and prelates of wood.

If Rome be against me, know that she is not against me, but Christ.

Your holiness holds the place of God on earth.   *Addressed to Pope Alexander VI.*

Friedrich Schiller
(1759-1805)
German dramatist, poet, historian

Men show no mercy and expect no mercy, when honor calls, or when they fight for their idols or their gods.
The Maid of Orleans, I, 5.

Mit der Dummheit kaempfen Goetter selbst vergebens. (Against stupidity the very gods fight in vain.)   *Ibid., III, 6.*

Arthur M. Schlesinger, Sr.
(1888-1965)
American historian, educator

History has generally shown the radical in the role of an active proponent of change and has cast the conservative for the part of the stalwart defender of things as they are.
New Viewpoints in American History, Macmillan, 1922.

The radical is a person who, in contrast to the conservative, favors a larger participation of the people in the control of government and society and in the benefits accruing from such control . . . The conservative, on the other hand, is skeptical of the capacity of the mass of the people to protect their own interests intelligently; and believing that social progress in the past has always come from the leadership of wealth and ability, he is the consistent opponent of the unsettling plans of the radical.   *Ibid.*

The thinking conservative finds his chief allies in the self-complacency of comfortable mediocrity, in the apathy and stupidity of the toil-worn multitudes, and in the aggressive self-interest of the privileged classes.   *Ibid.*

All those who dread uncertainty either because of timidity or from conventionalmindedness or for fear of material loss are enlisted under the conservative standard.
Ibid.

Arthur M. Schlesinger, Jr.
(b. 1917)
American educator, historian

Like every great democratic movement in American history, Jacksonian democracy eventually collided with the courts, running up sharply against their inclination to devise new guarantees for property and throw up new obstacles to popular control.
The Age of Jackson, p. 322.

Arthur Schnitzler
(1882-1931)
Austrian dramatist, physician

Without our faith in free will the earth would be the scene not only of the most horrible nonsense but also of the most intolerable boredom.
Buch der Sprueche und Bedenken, 1927.

[616]

Martyrdom has always been a proof of the intensity, never of the correctness of a belief. *Ibid.*

Arthur Schopenhauer
(1788-1860)
German philosopher

Nothing is to be had for gold but mediocrity.
The World as Will and Idea, preface, 2nd ed.

Life is short, but truth works far and lives long; let us speak the truth. *Ibid.*

Life swings like a pendulum backward and forward between pain and boredom.
Ibid., b. I.

"The world is my idea":—this is a truth which holds good for everything that lives and knows, though man alone can bring it into reflective and abstract consciousness.
Ibid.

As the world is in one aspect entirely *idea*, so in another it is entirely *will. Ibid.*

To desire immortality is to desire the eternal perpetuation of a great mistake.
Ibid., b. II.

The amount of noise which anyone can bear undisturbed stands in inverse proportion to his mental capacity, and may therefore be regarded as a pretty fair measure of it. . . . Noise is a torture to all intellectual people. *Ibid.*

The greatest intellectual capacities are only found in connection with a vehement and passionate will. *Ibid.*

All religions promise a reward . . . for excellences of the *will* or heart, but none for excellences of the head or understanding. *Ibid.*

Eros is the first, the creator, the principle from which all things proceed. The relation of the sexes . . . is really the invisible central point of all action and conduct, and peeps out everywhere in spite of all veils thrown over it. It is the cause of war and the end of peace; the basis of what is serious, and the aim of the jest; the inexhaustible source of wit, the key of all illusions, and the meaning of all mysterious hints.
Ibid., quoted by Durant, The Story of Philosophy.

I hold this thought—that the world is will —to be that which has long been sought under the name of philosophy, and the discovery of which is therefore regarded, by those who are familiar with history, as quite as impossible as the discovery of the philosopher's stone. *Ibid.*

For as the phenomenon of will becomes more complete, the suffering becomes more and more apparent . . . Thus, in proportion as knowledge attains to distinctness, as consciousness ascends, pain also increases, and reaches its highest degree in man. And then, again, the more distinctly a man knows—the more intelligent he is—the more pain he has; the man who is gifted with genius suffers most of all.
Counsels and Maxims, quoted by Durant.

Everything else can satisfy only *one* wish, *one* need; . . . Money alone is absolutely good, because it is not only a concrete satisfaction of one need in particular; it is an abstract satisfaction of all.
Aphorismen zur Lebensweisheit, tr. by T. Bailey Saunders.

Every miserable fool who has nothing at all of which he can be proud, adopts, as a last resource, pride in the nation to which he belongs; he is ready and glad to defend all its faults and follies tooth and nail, thus reimbursing himself for his own inferiority. *Ibid.*

There is but one thing to be done, though how difficult!—the foolish must become wise—and that they can never be. The value of life they never know; they see with the outer eye but never with the mind, and praise the trivial because the good is strange to them. *Ibid.*

Whatever be the form which excellence takes, mediocrity, the common lot of by far the greatest number, is leagued against it in a conspiracy to resist, and if possible, to suppress it. The pass-word of this league is *à bas le mérite.* *Ibid.*

No child under the age of fifteen should receive instruction in subjects which may possibly be the vehicle of serious error, such as philosophy or religion, for wrong notions imbibed early can seldom be rooted out, and of all the intellectual faculties, judgment is the last to arrive at maturity.
On Education, 1851.

Man is at bottom a wild, terrific animal. We know him only in connection with the taming and training, which is called civilization.
Parerga und Paralipomena, II, 178.

To form a judgment intuitively is the privilege of the few; authority and example lead the rest of the world. They see with the eyes of others, they hear with the ears of others. Therefore it is easy to think as all the world now think; but to think as all the world will think thirty years hence, is not in the power of every one.
Grundprobleme der Ethic, 28.

Truth that has merely been learned is like an artificial limb, a false tooth, a waxen nose; it adheres to us only because it is put on. But truth acquired by thought of our own is like a natural limb; it alone really belongs to us.
N. Y. Times Magazine, September 8, 1957.

Patriotism is the passion of fools and the most foolish of passions.
The American Freeman.

A man can be himself only so long as he is alone; and, if he does not love solitude, he will not love freedom; for it is only when he is alone that he is really free.

There is no absurdity so palpable but that it may be firmly planted in the human head if only you begin to inculcate it before the age of five, by constantly repeating it with an air of great solemnity.

Olive Schreiner
(1863?-1920)
South African writer

Our women's movement resembles strongly the gigantic religious and intellectual movement which for centuries convulsed the life of Europe, and had, as its ultimate outcome, the final emancipation of the human intellect and the freedom of the human spirit.
Woman and Labor, Stokes, 1911.

We have in us the blood of a womanhood that was never bought and never sold; that wore no veil and had no foot bound; whose realized ideal of marriage was sexual companionship and an equality in duty and labor. *Ibid.*

We are women of a breed whose racial ideal was no Helen of Troy, passed passively from male hand to male hand, as men pass gold or lead; but that Brynhild whom Segurd found, clad in helm and byrne, the warrior maid, who gave him counsel "the deepest that ever yet was given to living man" and "wrought on him to the performing of great deeds." *Ibid.*

We demand that, in that strange new world that is arising alike upon man and the woman, where nothing is as it was, and all things are assuming new shapes and relations, that in this new world we also shall have our share of honored and socially useful human toil, our full half of the labor of the Children of Woman. We demand nothing more than this, and will take nothing less. *This is our* "WOMAN'S RIGHT"! *Ibid.*

Theodore Schroeder
(b. 1864)
American libertarian

Unto the lewd all things are lewd.
A Challenge to the Sex Censors, privately printed, New York, 1938.

Obscenity has no objective existence. It is neither a quality that inheres in or emanates from a book, picture or play. On the contrary, obscenity is wholly an attitude or predisposition of the viewing and accusing mind, which is only delusionally read into, or ascribed to, that which is accused of being obscene. *Ibid.*

Unto the lewd all things are lewd, and their profession of much purity is a mask for much lewdness, since even their minds and conscience are defiled. I know and am persuaded that there is nothing unclean in itself, but to him that esteemeth anything to be unclean, well it showeth him to be obsessed by his own lewdness.
Ibid.

All despotisms should be considered problems of mental hygiene, and all support of censorship should be considered as problems of abnormal psychology. *Ibid.*

Obscenity is not a quality inherent in a book or picture, but solely and exclusively a contribution of the reading mind, and hence cannot be defined in terms of the qualities of a book or picture. *Ibid.*

Obscenity is never a ponderable quality of any book, picture or play. Neither is it ever an imponderable force for evil, which emanates from that which is accused.
Ibid.

Like witchcraft, obscenity will disappear, as we grow more healthily minded, mentally more mature, and more intelligent about sexual psychology. *Ibid.*

And yet when men ceased to believe in witches, they ceased to be, and so when men shall cease to believe in the "obscene" they will also cease to find that. Obscenity and witches exist only in the minds and emotions of those who believe in them, and, neither dogmatic judicial dictum nor righteous vituperation can ever give to them any objective existence. *Ibid.*

Obscenity is always and exclusively in the shame-psychology of the accusing persons. Their sensitiveness is a product of their own past "guilty" experiences. They may be wholly unaware of that fact and honestly deny it. Always their guilty feelings are delusionally read into those external facts, which only made them conscious of their own shameful predisposition. . . . *Unavoidably, they must believe infallibly, that the obscenity which embarrasses and distresses them exists only in that which they see and hear, and not in themselves.* *Ibid.*

Once let the public become sufficiently clean-minded to allow every adult access to all that is to be known about the psychology, physiology, hygiene and ethics of sex, and in two generations we will have a new humanity, with more health and joy, fewer wrecked nerves, and almost no divorces.

All morbid curiosity will then be dispelled, and thus the dealer in bawdy art and literature will be bankrupted. Our sanitariums and hospitals and insane asylums in that day will be uninhabited by those hundreds of thousands of inmates who are now there because of compulsory ignorance of their own sex nature. All these present evils are the outgrowth of that enforced sexual ignorance resulting from our legalized prudery, brought about by our general acquiescence in the "obscene" superstition.   *Ibid.*

Censorship always protects and perpetuates every horror of the prevailing forms of oppression. With us, its subtle disguises increase its evils by creating delusions of safety, liberty and democracy. It precludes that intelligence which is necessary to hasten a wholesome and natural social evolution. By that same ignorance it makes revolutions by violence more certain, more bloody, and less useful.

Intellectual Slavery, broadside pasted into copies of Schroeder's Free Press Anthology.

Tyrant wrongs and rebel vengeance will continue their vicious rounds, until our minds are freed from their emotional adherence to conventions, traditions, superstitions, pious slogans, mob delusions, high toned demagogues, and the psycho-neurotic leaders of our moron civilization.   *Ibid.*

Carl Schurz

(1829-1906)

German-American statesman, journalist

If you want to be free, there is but one way; it is to guarantee an equally full measure of liberty to all your neighbors. There is no other.

Albert Schweitzer

(1875-1965)

Physician, organist, philosopher

How strong would Christian truth now stand in the world of today, if its relation to the truth of history were in every respect what it should be! Instead of allowing this truth its rights, piety treated it, whenever it caused her embarrassment, in various ways, conscious or unconscious, but always by either evading, or twisting, or suppressing it.

Out of My Life and Thought, Mentor, p. 45.

Today the condition of Christianity is such that hard struggles are now required to make possible that coming to terms with historical truth which has been so often missed in the past.   *Ibid.*

Late on the third day, at the very moment when, at sunset, we were making our way through a herd of hippopotamuses, there flashed upon my mind, unforeseen and unsought, the phrase, "Reverence for Life." The iron door had yielded: the path in the thicket had become visible. Now I had found my way to the idea in which affirmation of the world and ethics are contained side by side; Now I knew that the ethical acceptance of the world and of life, together with the ideals of civilization contained in this concept, has a foundation in thought.   *Ibid., p. 124.*

Descartes makes thinking start from the sentence "I think; so I must exist" (*Cogito, ergo sum*), and with his beginning thus chosen he finds himself irretrievably on the road to the abstract. Out of this empty, artificial act of thinking there can result, of course, nothing which bears on the relation of man to himself, and to the universe.
                    Ibid., p. 125.

To think means to think something. The most immediate fact of man's consciousness is the assertion: "I am life which wills to live, in the midst of life which wills to live," and it is as will-to-live in the midst of will-to-live that man conceives himself during every moment that he spends in meditating on himself and the world around him.
                    Ibid.

Affirmation of life is the spiritual act by which man ceases to live unreflectively and begins to devote himself to his life with reverence in order to raise it to its true value. To affirm life is to deepen, to make more inward, and to exalt the will-to-live.
                    Ibid., p. 126.

At the same time the man who has become a thinking being feels a compulsion to give to every will-to-live the same reverence for life that he gives to his own. He experiences that other life in his own. He accepts as being good: to preserve life, to promote life, to raise to its highest value life which is capable of development; and as being evil: to destroy life, to injure life, to repress life which is capable of development. This is the absolute, fundamental principle of the moral, and it is a necessity of thought.   *Ibid.*

The idea of Reverence for Life offers itself as the realistic answer to the realistic question of how man and the world are related to each other.   *Ibid., p. 178.*

Any profound view of the world is mysticism. It has, of course, to deal with life and the world, both of which are nonrational entities.   *Ibid., p. 182.*

Christianity has need of thought that it may come to the consciousness of its real self. For centuries it treasured the great commandment of love and mercy as traditional truth without recognizing it as a reason for opposing slavery, witch burning, torture, and all the other ancient and medieval forms of inhumanity. It was only when it experienced the influence of the thinking of the Age of Enlightenment that it was stirred into entering the struggle for humanity. The remembrance of this ought to preserve it forever from assuming any air of superiority in comparison with thought.
                    Ibid., p. 183.

Because I have confidence in the power of truth and of the spirit, I believe in the future of mankind.   *Op. cit.*

The spiritual and material misery to which mankind of today is delivering itself through its renunciation of thinking and of the ideals which spring therefrom . . .
                    Ibid.

One belief of my childhood I have preserved with the certainty that I can never lose it: belief in truth. I am confident that the spirit generated by truth is stronger than the force of circumstances. In my view no other destiny awaits mankind than that which, through its mental and spiritual disposition, it prepares for itself. Therefore, I do not believe that it will have to tread the road to ruin to the end.   *Ibid.*

If men can be found who revolt against the spirit of thoughtlessness, and who are personalities sound enough and profound enough to let the ideals of ethical progress radiate from them as a force, there will start an activity of the spirit which will be strong enough to evoke a new mental and spiritual disposition in mankind.   *Ibid.*

Truth has no special time of its own. Its hour is now—always. . . .   *Ibid.*

The city of truth cannot be built on the swampy ground of scepticism.   *Ibid.*

Our age is bent on trying to make the barren tree of scepticism fruitful by tying fruits of truth on its branches.   *Ibid.*

Jesus no doubt fits his teaching into the late-Jewish messianic dogma. But he does not think dogmatically. He formulates no doctrine. He is far from judging any man's belief by reference to any standard of dogmatic correctness. Nowhere does he demand of his hearers that they shall sacrifice thinking to believing.   *Ibid.*

Ethics is the maintaining of life at the highest point of development—my own life and other life—by devoting myself to it in help and love, and both these things are connected. And this ethic, profound, universal, has the significance of a religion. It is religion.   *Ibid., epilogue.*

The fundamental idea of good is thus that it consists in preserving life, in favoring it, in wanting to bring it to its highest value, and evil consists in destroying life, doing it injury, hindering its development.   *Saturday Review, June 13, 1953.*

Reverence for life affords me my fundamental principle of morality.
N. Y. Times Magazine, January 1, 1956.

The term Reverence for Life is larger and at the same time dimmer than the term Love. But it bears within itself the same potentialities. The essential philosophical notion of Good has the advantage of being more complete than the notion of Love . . .
Atlantic Monthly, November, 1958.

By having reverence for life, we enter into a spiritual relation with the world.
Ibid.

By practicing reverence for life we become good, deep, and alive.   *Ibid.*

Reverence for life . . . does not allow the scholar to live for his science alone, even if he is very useful to the community in so doing. It does not permit the artist to exist only for his art, even if he gives inspiration to many by its means. It refuses to let the business man imagine that he fulfills all legitimate demands in the course of his business activities. It demands from all that they should sacrifice a portion of their own lives for others.
N. Y. Times Magazine, January 9, 1955 (celebrating Schweitzer's 80th birthday).

One truth stands firm. All that happens in world history rests on something spiritual. If the spiritual is strong, it creates world history. If it is weak, it suffers world history.   *Ibid.*

Every ethic has something absolute about it, just as soon as it ceases to be mere social law . . . Take the question of man's duty to his neighbor. The ethic cannot be fully carried out, without involving the possibility of complete sacrifice of self. Yet, Philosophy has never bothered to take due notice of the distinction.   *Ibid.*

The fundamental rights of man are, first, the right to habitation; secondly, the right to move freely; thirdly, the right to the soil and the subsoil, and to the use of it; fourthly, the right to freedom of labor and exchange; fifthly, the right to justice; sixthly, the right to live within a natural, national organization; and seventhly, the right to education. *Ibid.*

Man has become a superman . . . because he not only disposes of innate, physical forces, but because he is in command . . . of latent forces in nature and because he can put them to his service . . . But the essential fact we must surely all feel in our hearts . . . is that we are becoming inhuman in proportion as we become supermen.
On receiving the Nobel peace prize, 1954.

What is important is that we should recognize jointly that we are guilty of inhumanity. The horror of this experience (the two world wars) should shake us out of our torpor, so that we turn our will and our hopes toward the coming of an era in which war will be no more. That will and that hope can have only one result: The attainment, by a new spirit, of that higher reason which would deter us from making deadly use of the power which is at our disposal. *Ibid.*

We are living today under the sign of the collapse of civilization. The situation has not been produced by the war; the latter is only a manifestation of it. The spiritual atmosphere has solidified into actual facts, which again react on it with disastrous results in every respect.
The Philosophy of Civilization, 1947.

Rosika Schwimmer
(1877-1948)
American pacifist

I am an uncompromising pacifist . . . I have no sense of nationalism, only a cosmic consciousness of belonging to the human family.
Court testimony, citizenship hearings, 1928.

Women's rights, men's rights—human rights—all are threatened by the ever-present spectre of war so destructive now of human, material and moral values as to render victory indistinguishable from defeat.
Address, centennial celebration of Seneca Falls Convention on Women's Rights, July, 1948.

We who successfully freed one half of the human race without violence must now undertake with equal devotion, perseverance and intelligence the supreme act of human statesmanship involved in the creation of institutions of government on a world scale. *Ibid.*

Woman's function of home-maker, we once dreamed, would extend into politics and economics our highest creative and conserving instincts. Let us go back to the task of building that safe, decent and wholesome home for the entire human family to which we once pledged ourselves. *Ibid.*

E(dward) W(yllis) Scripps
(1854-1926)
American press lord

I believe that few people aside from myself have any idea of the tremendous, the almost invincible power and force of the daily press. I am one of those who believe that at least in America the press rules the country; it rules its politics, its religion, its social practice.
Damned Old Crank. Harper, 1951.

Why is it that the daily press of the United States is almost invariably plutocratic or dishonest? I can answer this question very easily. There is no more valuable and substantial property in the world than a successful newspaper. In every community the property value of the most successful newspaper in that community is greater, perhaps, than the property value of any other single business institution in the locality . . . One cannot own a newspaper that is worth several millions without owning many more million dollars worth of property. A newspaper cannot be a very great and successful newspaper without being worth several millions of dollars. The publisher who has succeeded, then, is necessarily a capitalist. *Ibid.*

God damn the rich, God help the poor. Our papers desire to be the poor man's advocate and they desire to win and hold the respect of the poor and rich alike, because of their perfect truthfulness in the matter of news and their fairness and good intentions in really trying to serve the interests of the humble people who are our principal clients.
Lusty Scripps, by Gilson Gardner, p. 73.

In fact, I have not a whole series of journalistic principles. I have only one principle, and that is represented by an effort to make it harder for the rich to grow richer and easier for the poor to keep from growing poorer.
E. W. Scripps, by Negley Cochrane.

The press of this country is now and always has been so thoroughly dominated by the wealthy few of the country that it cannot be depended upon to give the great mass of the people that correct information concerning political, economical, and social subjects which it is necessary that the mass of the people shall have, in order that they shall vote and in all ways act in the best way to protect themselves from the brutal force and chicanery of the ruling and employing class. I have sought to give these people all the information which will strengthen them in their unequal contest with their masters. *Ibid.*

Our paper (the adless *Chicago Day Book*) is to be the poor man's advocate and friend, whether the poor man be right or wrong. *Ibid.*

I want no one connected with the paper who is not willing to carry out my ideas and who does not fully and completely believe in my method so that he would do the same thing that I want done even if he were furnishing all the money. *Ibid.*

The writers who are employes of newspaper owners have, necessarily, points of view that differ from those of their employers. The owner of the newspaper, the employer, requires his employees to write those things which the employer either believes or wants his readers to believe. As he is human, he will not allow his newspaper to be used to controvert his own opinions. Nor will he pay to the writers wages to produce matter which he does not want to appear in his paper.
History of Cooperative News-Gathering, Rosewater, p. 354.

There is not only a community of interest, but a community of social feeling between the capitalists of any locality, section or country. The successful journalist, that is to say, when he owns his own paper, is a wealthy man, a capitalist by necessity. His associates are necessarily other capitalists . . . A social capitalistic class quickly crystallizes and solidifies into a social caste. *Ibid.*

I knew that at least ninety per cent of my fellows in American journalism were capitalistic and conservative. I knew that, at that time at least, unless I came into the field with a new service, it would be impossible for the people of the United States to get correct news through the medium of the Associated Press . . . I have made it impossible for the men who control the Associated Press to suppress the truth, or successfully to disseminate falsehood.   *Ibid.*

Pedro Segura y Saenz
(b. 1880)
Archbishop of Seville, Spain

The universal aspiration of the present time may be summed up in one magical word, which has succeeded in seducing people—liberty.

The worst type of freedom of thought is proclaimed as representing a positive achievement of our times. This is true of freedom of thought, learning, and the press . . . actually liberties of perdition, whose origin is a poisoned fount giving birth to the great evils of the world.

Diocesan bulletin, September 17, 1952.

Haile Selassie
(1891-1975)
Emperor of Ethiopia

It is my duty to inform the Governments of the deadly peril which threatens them . . . It is a question of trust in international treaties and of the value of promises to small States that their integrity shall be respected. In a word, it is international morality that is at stake. Apart from the Kingdom of God, there is not on this earth any nation that is higher than any other . . . God and history will remember your judgment.

Speech, League of Nations, Geneva, June 30, 1936.

John Selden
(1584-1654)
English jurist, oriental scholar

Scrutamini scripturas. (Let us look at the scriptures.) These two words have undone the world.

Table Talk, first published in 1689.

He was a wise pope (Julius III) that, when one that used to be merry with him before he was advanced to the popedom refrained afterwards to come at him (presuming he was busy in governing the Christian world), sent for him, bade him come again, and (says he) we will be merry as we were before, for thou little thinkest what a little foolery governs the whole world.

Ibid., Pope.

Ignorance of the law excuses no man; not that all men know the law, but because 'tis an excuse every man will plead, and no man can tell how to refute him.

Ibid., Law.

Gilbert Seldes
(1893-1970)
American journalist, writer

The Seven Lively Arts.
Book title, 1924.

The Public Arts.   *Book title, 1956.*

The Great God Bogus . . .
The Seven Lively Arts.

Comedy is the last refuge of the nonconformist mind.
Book review. New Republic, December 20, 1954.

Nothing is inevitable—not even revolution.   *Against Revolution, 1932.*

Marx predicted that the great industrial countries would be the first to advance, or collapse, into communistic socialism. His success as an economist in Russia was, in effect, his annihilation as a prophet. *Ibid.*

Change is the great enemy of revolution. *Ibid.*

Revolutions appeal to those who have not; they have to be imposed on those who have. *Ibid.*

The charity system is outworn. But the charity of the rich to the poor is not the only one. There is the appalling charity of the poor to the rich. On the great lists of charitable contributions from the rich to the poor only a few items are anonymous; on the infinitely longer list of charity which the poor have given to the rich no names occur. The unmonied ones have had the exquisite tact to keep their benevolence a secret. The rich have given to the poor a little food, a little drink, a little shelter and a few clothes. The poor have given to the rich palaces and yachts, and an almost infinite freedom to indulge their doubtful taste for display, and bonuses and excess profits, under which cold and forbidding terms have been hidden the excess labor and extravagant misery of the poor. *Ibid.*

Inevitable revolutions which fail go down as footnotes in history under the names of treason and riot. *Ibid.*

There is nothing more old-fashioned than the radical revolutionary; revolution as a method is five thousand years old and one hundred years too old. *Ibid.*

As long as the means of (mass) communication are not available for criticism of themselves, as long as we are prevented from thinking about the process by which we are hypnotized into not thinking, we remain at the mercy of our simplest appetites, our immediate and most childish sensations, and these can be exploited—for the arts most useful to the public are essentially those which can be most effectively turned against the public good.

The Public Arts.

Seneca (the Younger)
(4? B.C.-65 A.D.)
Latin moralist, stoic philosopher

A hungry people listens not to reason, nor cares for justice, nor is bent by any prayers. *De Brevitate Vitae, i. 18.*

The greater part of progress is the desire to progress. *Epistulae ad Lucilium.*

What is freedom? It means not being a slave to any circumstance, to any restraint, to any chance; it means compelling Fortune to enter the lists on equal terms. *Ibid.*

Thou inquirest what liberty is? To be slave to nothing, to no necessity, to no accident, to keep fortune at arm's length. *Ibid.*

Vivere, mi Lucili, militare est. (Life is a warfare.) *Ibid.*

To strive with an equal is a doubtful thing to do; with a superior, a mad thing; with an inferior, a vulgar thing. *De Ira.*

Veritatem dies aperit. (Time discovers the truth.) *Ibid.*

Time heals what reason cannot. *Agamemnon.*

There is no genius without a mixture of madness. *De Tranquillitate Animi.*

Moreover, there are three kinds of life, and it is a common question as to which

of them is best. One is devoted to pleasure, a second to contemplation, a third to action.
Moral Essays on Leisure, Basore's translation, Loeb.

Worse than war is the fear of war.
Thyestes.

Si vis tibi omnia subjicere, subjice te rationi. (If you would subject all things to yourself, subject yourself to reason.)
Durant, The Story of Philosophy.

We are members of one great body. Nature planted in us a mutual love, and fitted us for a social life. We must consider that we were born for the good of the whole.

All cruelty springs from weakness.

A kingdom founded on injustice never lasts.

It is proof of a bad cause when it is applauded by the mob.

We become wiser by adversity; prosperity destroys our appreciation of the right.

The language of truth is simple.

Religion is regarded by the common people as true, by the wise as false, and by the rulers as useful.

I am not born for one corner; the whole world is my native land.

The Germans, a race eager for war.

We punish murderers and massacres among private persons. What do we do respecting wars, and the glorious crime of murdering whole nations? The love of conquest is a murderess. Conquerors are scourges not less harmful to humanity than floods and earthquakes.

Robert W. Service
(1874-1958)
Canadian poet, novelist

When we, the Workers, all demand:
  "What are WE fighting for?"
Then, then we'll end that stupid crime,
  That Devil's madness—WAR.
Weekly People, March 28, 1959.

Robert W. Seton-Watson
(1879-1951)
English historian

In our Victorian dislike of the practice of calling a spade a bloody shovel, it is not necessary to go to the opposite extreme of calling it an agricultural implement.

Eric Sevareid
(b. 1912)
American journalist, commentator

The bigger the information media, the less courage and freedom they allow. Bigness means weakness.
The Press and the People, No. 7, TV Program, 1959.

Marie de Rabutin-Chantal, Marquise de Sévigné
(1626-1696)
French letter-writer

Fortune is always on the side of the largest battalions.°

———

° See Voltaire, letter to M. le Riche, 1770; also, Tacitus, *Deos fortioribus adesse.* (The gods are on the side of the stronger.)

William H. Seward
(1801-1872)
American statesman

I know, and all the world knows, that revolutions never go backwards.
Speech on The Irrepressible Conflict, Rochester, October, 1858.

There is a higher law than the Constitution. *Senate, March 11, 1850.*

Ben Shahn
(1898-1969)
American artist

All art is based on non-conformity.
Atlantic Monthly, September, 1957.

Every great historic change has been based upon non-conformity, has been bought either with the blood or with the reputation of non-conformists. *Ibid.*

To create anything at all in any field, and especially anything of outstanding worth, requires non-conformity, or a want of satisfaction with things as they are. *Ibid.*

R. E. Shallcross
See J. B. Matthews

George Bernard Shaw
(1856-1950)
Irish dramatist, critic

Why not give Christianity a trial? The question seems a hopeless one after 2000 years of resolute adherence to the old cry of "Not this man, but Barabbas." . . . "This man" has not been a failure yet; for nobody has ever been sane enough to try his way.
Preface, Androcles and the Lion, 1912.

The moneyed, respectable, capable world has been steadily anti-Christian and Barabbasque since the crucifixion; and the specific doctrine of Jesus has not in all that time been put into political or general social practice. *Ibid.*

Christ, though rejected by his posterity as an unpractical dreamer, and executed by his contemporaries as a dangerous anarchist and blasphemous madman, was greater than his judges. *Ibid.*

It is not disbelief that is dangerous in our society: it is belief. The moment it strikes you (as it may any day) that Christ is not the lifeless harmless image he has hitherto been to you, but a rallying centre for revolutionary influences which all established States and Churches fight, you must look to yourselves; for you have brought the image to life; and the mob may not be able to bear that horror. *Ibid.*

The conversion of Paul was no conversion at all: it was Paul who converted the religion that has raised one man above sin and death into a religion that delivered millions of men so completely into their dominion that their own common nature became a horror to them, and the religious life became a denial of life. *Ibid.*

No sooner had Jesus knocked over the dragon of superstition than Paul boldly set it on its legs again in the name of Jesus. *Ibid.*

There is not one word of Pauline Christianity in the characteristic utterances of Jesus. *Ibid.*

There has really never been a more monstrous imposition perpetrated than the imposition of the limitations of Paul's soul upon the soul of Jesus. *Ibid.*

The followers of Paul and Peter made Christendom, whilst the Nazarenes were wiped out.   *Ibid.*

All great truths begin as blasphemies.
                    Annajanska.

The worst sin towards our fellow creatures is not to hate them, but to be indifferent to them: that's the essence of inhumanity.   *The Devil's Disciple, act 2.*

Twentieth-century sociologists must begin with an emphatic repudiation of the Eighteenth-century Rousseau-Jefferson-and pre-Marxian delusion that all men are born free. They must rub in the fact that we are all born in a slavery to nature which compels us to work hours a day, as cows are compelled to graze, on pain of death by hunger, thirst, cold and exposure.
    Everybody's Political What's What?

Honest education is dangerous to tyranny and privilege: the systems like the capitalist system, kept in vogue by popular ignorance, churches which depend on it for priestly authority, privileged classes, and ambitious conquerors and dictators who have to instil royalist idolatry and romantic hero-worship, all use both ignorance and education as underpinnings for general faith in themselves as rulers.   *Ibid.*

It cannot be too thoroughly understood that Socialism is not charity nor loving-kindness, nor sympathy with the poor, nor popular philanthropy . . . but the economist's hatred of waste and disorder, the aesthete's hatred of ugliness and dirt, the lawyer's hatred of injustice, the doctor's hatred of disease, the saint's hatred of the seven deadly sins.   *Ibid.*

The Fabian knows that property does not hesitate to shoot, and that now, as always, the unsuccessful revolutionist may expect calumny, perjury, cruelty, judicial and military massacre without mercy.
                    Fabian Essays, 1908.

That under existing circumstances wealth cannot be enjoyed without dishonor or foregone without misery.   *Fabian Manifesto.*

Instead of sympathizing with the poor and abolishing the rich, we must ruthlessly abolish the poor by raising their standard of life.
    Intelligent Woman's Guide to Socialism.

Capitalism has destroyed our belief in any effective power but that of self interest backed by force.   *Ibid.*

My way of joking is to tell the truth. It's the funniest joke in the world.
                    John Bull's Other Island.

The irresistible natural truth which we all abhor and repudiate: to wit, that the greatest of our evils, and the worst of our crimes is poverty, and that our first duty . . . is not to be poor.
                    Preface, Major Barbara, 1907.

The universal regard for money is the one hopeful fact in our civilization. *Ibid.*

Money is the most important thing in the world. It represents health, strength, honor, generosity and beauty as conspicuously as the want of it represents illness, weakness, disgrace, meanness and ugliness.   *Ibid.*

The crying need of the nation is not for better morals, cheaper bread, temperance, liberty, culture, redemption of fallen sisters and erring brothers, nor the grace, love and fellowship of the Trinity, but simply for enough money. And the evil to be attacked is not sin, suffering, greed, priestcraft, kingcraft, demagogy, monopoly, ignorance,

drink, war, pestilence, nor any of the consequences of poverty, but just poverty itself.
Ibid.

Morals being mostly only social habits and circumstantial necessities.   *Ibid.*

Churches are suffered to exist only on condition that they preach submission to the State as at present capitalistically organized.
Ibid.

I am, and have always been, and shall now always be, a revolutionary writer, because our laws make law impossible; our liberties destroy all freedom; our property is organized robbery; our morality is an impudent hypocrisy; our wisdom is administered by inexperienced or malexperienced dupes, our power wielded by cowards and weaklings, and our honor false in all its points. I am an enemy of the existing order.   *Ibid.*

Hatred is the coward's revenge for being intimidated.   *Ibid.*

The greatest of evils and the worst of crimes is poverty . . . All the other crimes are virtues beside it: all the other dishonors are chivalry itself by comparison. Poverty blights whole cities; spreads horrible pestilence; strikes at the soul of all of those who come within sight, sound or smell of it.   *Ibid.*

The seven deadly sins . . . Food, clothing, firing, rent, taxes, respectability and children. Nothing can lift those seven milestones from man's neck but money; and the spirit cannot soar until the milestones are lifted.   *Ibid.*

What you call crime is nothing; a murder here and a theft there, a blow now and a curse then, what do they matter? They are only the accidents and illnesses of life; there

are not fifty genuine professional criminals in London. But there are millions of poor people, abject people, dirty people, ill-fed, ill-clothed people.   *Ibid.*

I had rather be a thief than a pauper. I had rather be a murderer than a slave. I don't want to be either, but if you force the alternative on me, then, by heaven, I'll choose the braver and more moral one. I hate poverty and slavery worse than any other crimes whatsoever. And let me tell you this. Poverty and slavery have stood up for centuries to your sermons and leading articles; they will not stand up to my machineguns. Don't preach at them! Don't reason with them. Kill them.   *Ibid.*

Every man is a revolutionist concerning the thing he understands. For example, every person who has mastered a profession is a sceptic concerning it, and consequently a revolutionist.
Man and Superman. The Revolutionist's Handbook. 1903.

All who achieve real distinction in life begin as revolutionists. The most distinguished persons become more revolutionary as they grow older, although they are commonly supposed to become more conservative owing to their loss of faith in conventional methods of reform.   *Ibid.*

Any person under the age of thirty, who, having any knowledge of the existing social order, is not a revolutionist, is an inferior.
Ibid.

Revolutions have never lightened the burden of tyranny: they have only shifted it to another shoulder.   *Ibid.*

No doubt it is easy to demonstrate that property will destroy society unless society destroys it. No doubt, also, property has hitherto held its own and destroyed all the empires. *Ibid.*

National Christianity is impossible without a nation of Christs. *Ibid.*

Every genuine religious person is a heretic and therefore a revolutionist. *Ibid.*

The only fundamental and possible Socialism is the socialization of the selective breeding of Man: in other terms, of human evolution. We must eliminate the Yahoo, or his vote will wreck the commonwealth. *Ibid.*

The golden rule is that there is no golden rule.
Ibid., Maxims for Revolutionists.

The art of government is the organization of idolatry. *Ibid.*

Democracy substitutes selection by the incompetent many for appointment by the corrupt few. *Ibid.*

Nothing can be unconditional: consequently nothing can be free. *Ibid.*

Liberty means responsibility. That is why most men dread it. *Ibid.*

Beware of the man whose god is in the skies. *Ibid.*

A moderately honest man with a moderately faithful wife, moderate drinkers both, in a moderately healthy house: that is the true middle class unit. *Ibid.*

The man who listens to Reason is lost: Reason enslaves all whose minds are not strong enough to master her. *Ibid.*

Do not waste your time on Social Questions. What is the matter with the poor is

Poverty: what is the matter with the rich is Uselessness. *Ibid.*

Lack of money is the root of all evil. *Ibid.*

All censorships exist to prevent any one from challenging current conceptions and existing institutions. All progress is initiated by challenging current conceptions, and executed by supplanting existing institutions. Consequently the first condition of progress is the removal of censorships.
Mrs. Warren's Profession, preface.

You'll never have a quiet world till you knock the patriotism out of the human race.
O'Flaherty, V. C.

A gentleman of our days is one who has money enough to do what every fool would do if he could afford it: that is, consume without producing.
The Quintessence of Ibsenism, 1891.

If the Englishman had not repudiated the duty of absolute obedience to his king, his political progress would have been impossible. If women had not repudiated the duty of absolute submission to their husbands, and defied public opinion as to the limits set by modesty to their education, they would never have gained the protection of the Married Women's Property Act or the power to qualify themselves as medical practitioners. If Luther had not trampled on his duty to the head of his Church and on his vow of chastity, our priests would still have to choose between celibacy and profligacy. There is nothing new, then, in the defiance of duty by the reformer: every step of progress means a duty repudiated. and a scripture torn up. And every reformer is denounced accordingly, Luther as an apostate, Cromwell as a traitor, Mary Wollstonecraft as an unwomanly virago, Shelley as a libertine, and Ibsen as all the things enumerated in the *Daily Telegraph. Ibid.*

It is necessary for the welfare of society that genius should be privileged to utter sedition, to blaspheme, to outrage good taste, to corrupt the youthful mind, and, generally to scandalize one's uncles.
The Sanity of Art.

Karl Marx made a man of me. Socialism made a man of me. Otherwise I should be like so many of my literary colleagues who have just as much literary ability as I have. Socialism made a man of Mr. Wells, and he has done something. But look at the rest of the literary people and you will understand why I am inordinately proud of being a socialist.
James Fuchs, The Socialism of Shaw. (From an address to guests, 80th birthday.)

I myself have been particularly careful never to say a civil word to the United States. I have scoffed at their inhabitants as a nation of villagers. I have defined the 100% American as 99% an idiot. And they adore me.
*Remarks, 1930, on Sinclair Lewis receiving the Nobel prize.**

---

* Asked for a confirmation of this (and other) quotations, Shaw wrote, December 10, 1937: "Dear Mr. Seldes: I cannot remember the exact wording of the statement to which you allude; but what I meant was that in my experience a man who calls himself a 100% American and is proud of it, is generally 150% an idiot politically. But the designations may be good business for war veterans. Having bled for their country in 1861 and 1918, they have bled it all they could consequently. And why not? G. Bernard Shaw."

Food and houses and clothes can be produced by human labor, but when they are produced they can be stolen ... What you do to a horse or a bee, you can also do to a man or a woman or a child. You can get the upper hand of them by force, or trickery of any sort, or even by teaching them that it is their religious duty to sacrifice their freedom to ours.
BBC broadcast, weekly series on Freedom; CBS June 18, 1935; reprinted in The Nation, July 10, 1935 with editorial note stating newspapers omitted it.

Naturally, the masters in parliaments, in schools, and in newspapers make the most desperate efforts to prevent us from realizing our slavery. From our earliest years we are taught that our country is the land of the free. *Ibid.*

I have never smoked in my life and look forward to a time when the world will look back with amazement and disgust to a practice so unnatural and offensive. To employ idle hours men could knit as women do. *N. Y. Herald Tribune, April 14, 1946.*

Power does not corrupt men; fools, however, if they get into a position of power, corrupt power.
Stephen Winsten, Days with Bernard Shaw.

I hold with Adolf Hitler that our political democracy is a lie ... There is no antithesis between authoritarian government and democracy. All government is authoritarian; and the more democratic a government is the more authoritative it is; for with the people behind it, it can push its authority further than any Tsar or foreign despot dare do.
Letter to The New Republic, April 14, 1937.

There is only one sort of genuine Socialism, the democratic sort, by which I mean the organization of society for the benefit of the whole people.

Eighty-fifth birthday interview, N. Y. Times, July 25, 1941.

No American newspaper will print anything contrary to its own interests.

To Morris Watson, Associated Press correspondent; confirmed in letter to G. S., November 21, 1941.

Patriotism is a pernicious, psychopathic form of idiocy.   *L'Esprit Français, Paris.*

Henry Wheeler Shaw
See "Josh Billings"

Fulton J. Sheen
(b. 1895)
American radio priest

Nothing has so much contributed to egotism, pride, conceit, swellheadedness and braggadocio as the assumption that an "inferiority complex" is always wrong. If the failure to assert oneself . . . is the mark of a psychic disease, then satanic pride is on the throne.   *Way to Inner Peace.*

One of the greatest disasters that happened to modern civilization was for democracy to inscribe "liberty" on its banners instead of "justice". Because "liberty" was considered the ideal it was not long until some men interpreted it as meaning "freedom from justice"; then when religion and decent government attempted to bring them back to justice, organized into "freedom groups" they protested that their constitutional and natural rights were being violated.

The industrial and social injustice of our era is the tragic aftermath of democracy's overemphasis on freedom as the "right to do whatever you please". No, freedom means the right to do what you *ought*, and *ought* implies law, and law implies justice, and justice implies God. So too in war, a nation that fights for freedom divorced from justice has no right to war, because it does not know why it wants to be free, or why it wants anyone else to be free.

Catholic Hour broadcast, January 5, 1941.

Percy Bysshe Shelley
(1792-1822)
English poet

Men of England, Heirs of Glory,
Heroes of unwritten story,
Nurslings of one mighty mother,
Hope of her, and one another,

Rise, like lions after slumber,
In unvanquishable number,
Shake your chains to earth like dew,
Which in sleep had fall'n on you.
   The Masque of Anarchy, 1819.

What is Freedom? Ye can tell
That which Slavery is too well,
For its very name has grown
To an echo of your own.

'Tis to work and have such pay
As just keeps life from day to day
In your limbs, as in a cell
For the tyrants' use to dwell:

So that ye for them are made,
Loom, and plough, and sword, and spade;
With or without your own will, bent
To their defence and nourishment.
   Ibid.

What art thou, Freedom? Oh! could Slaves
Answer from their living graves
This demand, tyrants would flee
Like a dream's dim imagery.   *Ibid.*

For the laborour thou art bread,
And a comely table spread,
From his daily labour come,
In a neat and happy home.

Thou art clothes, and fire, and food
For the trampled multitude . . .   *Ibid.*

For the rich thou art a check,
When his foot is on the neck
Of his victim . . .

Thou art Justice—ne'er for gold
May thy righteous laws be sold,
As laws are in England:—thou
Shield'st alike the high and low.   *Ibid.*

Thou art Wisdom—Freedom never
Dreams that God will damn for ever
All who think those things untrue,
Of which priests make such ado.   *Ibid.*

Thou art Peace—never by thee
Would blood and treasure wasted be,
As tyrants wasted them, when all
Leagued to quench thy flame in Gaul.
                                   Ibid.

What if English toil and blood
Was pour'd forth, even as a flood!
It avail'd,—oh Liberty!
To dim—but not extinguish thee.   *Ibid.*

Thou art Love—the rich have kist
Thy feet, and like him following Christ,
Give their substance to the free,
And through the rough world follow thee.
                                   Ibid.

Thrones, altars, judgment-seats; wherein,
And beside which, by wretched men were
      borne

Sceptres, tiaras, swords, and chains, and
      tomes
Of reason'd wrong, glozed on by ignorance,
Were like those monstrous and barbaric
      shapes,
The ghost of a no more remember'd fame,
Which, from their unworn obelisks, look
      forth
In triumph o'er the palaces and tombs
Of those who were their conquerors:
      mouldering round
Those imaged to the pride of kings and
      priests,
A dark yet mighty faith, a power as wide
As is the world it wasted, and are now
But an astonishment; even so the tools
And emblems of its last captivity,
Amid the dwellings of the peopled earth,
Stand, not o'erthrown, but unregarded now.
            Prometheus Unbound, 1820.

The painted veil, by those who were, called
      life,
Which mimick'd, as with colours idly
      spread,
All men believed and hoped, is torn aside;
The loathsome mask has fall'n, the man
      remains
Sceptreless, free, uncircumscribed, but man
Equal, unclass'd, tribeless, and nationless,
Exempt from awe, worship, degree, the king
Over himself; just, gentle, wise: but man
Passionless, no; yet free from guilt or pain,
Which were, for his will made or suffer'd
      them,
Nor yet exempt, tho' ruling them like slaves,
From chance, and death, and mutability.
                                   Ibid.

Blind Love, and equal Justice, and the
      Fame
      Of what has been, the Hope of what
      will be?
O Liberty! if such could be thy name
      Wert thou disjoin'd from these, or they
      from thee:

If thine or theirs were treasures to be
  bought
By blood or tears, have not the wise and
  free
Wept tears, and blood like tears?
                    Ode to Liberty, c. 1820.

O that the wise from their bright minds
Such lamps within the dome of this dim
  world would kindle,
That the pale name of priest might shrink
  and dwindle
Till human thoughts might kneel alone,
Each before the judgment throng,
Of his own aweless soul, or of the power
  unknown.   *Ibid.*

  O cease! must hate and death return?
      Cease! must men kill and die?
  Cease! drain not to its dregs the urn
      Of bitter prophecy.
  The world is weary of the past,
  O might it die or rest at last!
                    Hellas, 1821.

Fear not that the tyrants rule forever,
    Or the priests of the bloody faith;
They stand on the brink of the mighty river
    Whose waves they have tainted with
      death.
And their swords and their scepters, I
    floating see
Like wrecks on the surge of eternity.
                    Rosalind and Helen.

War is the statesman's game, the priest's
    delight,
The lawyer's jest, the hired assassin's trade.
                    Queen Mab.

Power, like a desolating pestilence,
Pollutes whate'er it touches; and obedience,
Bane of all genius, virtue, freedom, truth,
Makes slaves of men, and of the human
    frame
A mechanized automaton.   *Ibid.*

Hence Commerce springs, the venal inter-
    change
Of all that human Art or Nature yield.
                    Ibid.

Commerce! beneath whose poison-breathing
    shade
No solitary virtue dares to spring,
But Poverty and Wealth with equal hand
Scatter their withering curses.   *Ibid.*

A brighter dawn awaits the human day . . .
When poverty and wealth, the thirst of
    fame,
The fear of infamy, disease and woe,
War with its million horrors, and fierce hell
Shall live but in the memory of time.
                    Ibid.

Man is soul and body, formed for deeds,
Of high resolve.   *Ibid., iv.*

Gold is a living god.   *Ibid., v.*

Necessity, thou mother of the world!
                    Ibid., vi.

Priests dare babble of a God of peace,
Even whilst their hands are red with guilt-
    less blood,
Murdering the while, uprooting every germ
Of truth, exterminating, spoiling all,
Making the earth a slaughter-house.
                    Ibid., vii.

How ludicrous the priest's dogmatic roar!
The weight of his exterminating curse,
How light! and his affected charity,
To suit the pressure of the changing times,
What palpable deceit!—but for thy aid,
Religion! but for thee, prolific fiend,
Who peoplest earth with demons, hell with
    men,
And heaven with slaves!
Thou taintest all thou look'st upon!

Men of England, wherefore plough
For the lords who lay you low?
Wherefore weave with toil and care
The rich robes your tyrants wear?
> *Song to the Men of England.*

Sow seed—but let no tyrant reap;
Find wealth—but let no imposter heap;
Weave robes—let not the idle wear;
Forge arms—in your defense to bear.
> *Ibid.*

That which is incapable of proof itself is no proof of anything else.

A man has a right to unrestricted liberty of discussion. Falsehood is a scorpion that will sting itself to death.

The same means that have supported every popular belief have supported Christianity. War, imprisonment, assassination and falsehood; deeds of unexampled and incomparable atrocity have made it what it is. *Queen Mab, Notes, 1813.*

There is no real wealth but the labor of man. *Ibid.*

A system could not well have been devised more studiously hostile to human happiness than marriage. *Ibid.*

Wealth is a power usurped by the few, to compel the many to labor for their benefit. *Ibid.*

If there had never been war there could never have been tyranny in the world.
A Philosophical View of Reform, 1819.

All that miserable tale of the Devil and Eve, and an Intercessor with the childish mummeries of the God of the Jews, is irreconcilable with the knowledge of the stars.

The plurality of worlds—the indefinite immensity of the universe—is a most awful subject of contemplation. He who rightly feels its mystery and grandeur is in no danger of seduction from the falsehoods of religious systems or of defying the principle of the universe.

The crime of inquiry is one which religion never has forgiven.

Richard Brinsley Sheridan
(1751-1816)
Irish dramatist, orator, statesman

Give them a corrupt House of Lords, give them a venal House of Commons, give them a tyrannical Prince, give them a truckling Court, and let me have but an unfettered Press. I will defy them to encroach a hair's breadth upon the liberties of England.
Speech, Commons, February 6, 1810; Cobbett's Parliamentary Debates, 15, cols. 341-3.

Give me but the liberty of the press, and I will give to the minister a venal House of Commons—I will give him the full sway of patronage of office—I will give him the whole host of ministerial influence—I will give him all the power that place can confer upon him to purchase up submission and overawe resistance; and yet, armed with the Liberty of the Press, I will go forth to meet him undismayed; I will attack the mighty fabric he has reared with that mightier engine; I will shake down from its height corruption and bury it beneath the ruins of the abuses it was meant to shelter. *Ibid.*

What was it that had caused the downfall of all the nations of Europe? Was it the Liberty of the Press? No; it was the want of that salutary control upon their governments, that animating source of public spirit and national exertion. *Ibid.*

William Tecumseh Sherman
(1820-1891)
American Union general

Vox populi, vox humbug. (The voice of the people is the voice of humbug.)
Letter to his wife, June 2, 1863.

I begin to regard the death and mangling of a couple thousand men as a small affair, a kind of morning dash—and it may be well that we become so hardened.
Ibid., July 1864.

You cannot qualify war in harsher terms than I will. War is cruelty, and you cannot refine it.
Letter to James M. Calhoun and others, Atlanta, September 12, 1864.

I would not if I could modify or abolish slavery. I don't know that I would materially change the actual political relation of master and slave.
Memoirs of William T. Sherman, 1875; reissued by U. of Indiana, 1958; letter to brother-in-law.

Negroes in the great numbers that exist here must of necessity be slaves. Theoretical notions of humanity and religion cannot shake the commercial fact that their labor is of great value and cannot be dispensed with. *Ibid.*

Talk thus to the Marines, but not to me.
Ibid., Letter to General Hood, denying accusations.

I am publishing my own memoirs, not *theirs,* and we all know that no three honest witnesses of a brawl can agree on all the details. How much more likely will be the difference in a great battle covering a vast space of broken ground, when each division, brigade, regiment, and even company, naturally and honestly believes that it was the focus of the whole affair! Each of them won the battle. None ever lost. That was the fate of the old man who unhappily commanded. *Ibid., preface, 2nd edition.*

There is many a boy here today who looks on war as all glory, but, boys, it is all hell. You can bear this warning voice to generations yet to come. I look upon war with horror.
Address, G. A. R. Convention, August 11, 1880.

There will soon come an armed contest between capital and labor. They will oppose each other, not with words and arguments, but with shot and shell, gun-powder and cannon. The better classes are tired of the insane howling of the lower strata and they mean to stop them.
Attributed, 1885; "Labor," March 4, 1944.

If forced to choose between the penitentiary and the White House for four years, I would say the penitentiary, thank you.
Letter to H. W. Halleck, September, 1864.

If nominated I will not accept; if elected I will not serve.
Telegram to Republican National Convention, 1884.

Siculus
See Diodorus Siculus

Seymour Siegel
(Contemporary)
Teacher, Jewish Theological Seminary

The central problem of Christianity is: if the Messiah has come why is the world so evil? For Judaism, the problem is: if the world is so evil, why does the Messiah not come? *Saturday Review, March 28, 1959.*

André Siegfried
(1875-1959)
French economist, historian

How is it that the American, once he has attained his majority, appears to us as the perfect conformist. It is, perhaps, because he has exhausted during his childhood and adolescence practically all his indiscipline and anarchy, so that he has no difficulty later in life in integrating himself into a collective society, which he himself fully accepts.
America at Mid-Century, Harcourt, 1955.

The United States is par excellence a country where public opinion plays an important role, inspiring, orienting, and controlling the policy of the nation. Nothing can be achieved or endure without it, and its veto is final. It is characterized by the fact that it is both more spontaneous than anywhere else in the world and also more easily directed by efficient propaganda technique than in any other country.
Ibid.

There appears to be in the American labor movement an indefinable lack of spirit . . . no mystical feeling of class consciousness, no revolutionary apostolate, but merely the vocabulary of businessmen.
Ibid.

Emmanuel Joseph Sieyès
(1748-1836)
French abbé, statesman, publicist

J'ai vécu. (Translated: I lived, or, I got through, or, I survived, or, I existed.°)
Mignet, Notices Historiques, 1, 81.

Ignazio Silone
(1900-1978)
Italian novelist

Liberty is the possibility of doubting, the possibility of making a mistake, the possibility of searching and experimenting, the possibility of saying "No" to any authority —literary, artistic, philosophic, religious, social, and even political.
The God That Failed.

The final struggle will be between the Communists and the ex-Communists.°°
Merle Miller, N. Y. Herald Tribune, January 8, 1950.

Every means tends to become an end. To understand the tragedy of history it is necessary to grasp that fact. Machines, which ought to be man's instruments, enslave him, the state enslaves religion, parliament enslaves democracy, institutions enslave justice, academies enslave art, the party en-

---

° In reply to the question what he did during the Reign of Terror, the Abbé Sieyès replied, according to Ramage, *Beautiful Thoughts from French and Italian Authors,* p. 384, "Ce qui j'ai fait, j'ai vécu." He had in fact resolved the most difficult problem of the time, that of not perishing.
°° "The decisive battles will be between the communists and ex-communists." *N. Y. Times Book Review,* September 7, 1952.

slaves the cause, the dictatorship of the proletariat enslaves Socialism.
Tribune, London.

Deriving from the cult of state, of party, of power, politics are always sacrificing the interests and aspirations of man for a multi-headed monster, for an idol.
To Marc Slonim, N. Y. Times Book Review, August 24, 1958.

The individual is right when he negates the mass production of souls and hearts and conceives life as a creative design and not as a pre-fabricated pattern.   *Ibid.*

Good faith is inconceivable to the Russian communist.
Gunther, Inside Russia Today.

Upton Sinclair
(1878-1968)
American author, Socialist

Comrade Jesus.   *Singing Jailbirds.*

Fascism is Capitalism plus Murder.
Ibid.

When you pick up your morning or evening newspaper and think you are reading the news of the world, what you are really reading is a propaganda which has been selected, revised, and doctored by some power which has a financial interest in you.
The Brass Check.

Journalism in America is the business and practice of presenting the news of the day in the interest of economic privilege.
Ibid.

We offer you a new way of life, in which any normal man can find happiness and peace. No matter how rich you may be, and how well satisfied with your world, you will be better off and a better man in a cooperative commonwealth.
The Way Out.

Is it altogether a Utopian dream, that once in history a ruling class might be willing to make the great surrender, and permit social change to come about without hatred, turmoil, and waste of human life?   *Ibid.*

Or consider Christmas—could Satan in his most malignant mood have devised a worse combination of graft plus buncombe than the system whereby several hundred million people get a billion or so of gifts for which they have no use, and some thousands of shop-clerks die of exhaustion while selling them, and every other child in the western world is made ill from overeating —all in the name of the lowly Jesus?
Money Writes! Boni, 1927.

Pessimism is mental disease. It is whatever and under whatever circumstances it appears, in art and philosophy, in everyday life. It means illness in the person who voices it, and in the society which produces that person.   *Ibid.*

All truly great art is optimistic. The individual artist is happy in his creative work, and in its reception by the public. *Ibid.*

The fact that practically all great art is tragic does not in any way change the above thesis.   *Ibid.*

Capitalist art, when produced by artists of sincerity and intelligence, is pessimistic because capitalism is dying; it has no morals, and can have none, being the negation of morality in social affairs.   *Ibid.*

Proletarian art is optimistic, because it is only by hope that the workers can act, or dream of acting. Proletarian art has a morality of brotherhood and service, because it is only by these qualities that the masses can achieve their freedom. *Ibid.*

Grant Singleton
(b. 1890)
American writer

Fascism is big business armed with bayonets.   *Letter to the present editor.*

The road to Fascism is paved with socialist pretensions.   *Ibid.*

The love of money is the root of all Fascism.   *Ibid.*

I do not know of any reactionary who is not a liar.   *Ibid.*

Most persons are conformists; they follow, they never create; the non-conformist alone is a creative person.   *Ibid.*

History in the making is always censored.   *Ibid.*

The apathy of the born freeman is worse than the docility of the born slave.
Unpublished manuscript.

This nation has mistaken comfort for culture, conveniences for civilization. *Ibid.*

Art is elevation.   *Ibid.*

All our liberties, everything that mankind has fought and struggled for in modern times, have been won and maintained with the aid of the press. We admit that the press is the most powerful force in the world—both the free world and the dictated world. Its chief function should be to safeguard the people from their rulers.
Ibid.

Mr. Hoover was never president of the United States; he was for four years chairman of the board.   *Ibid.*

John Sloan
(1871-1951)
American artist

Consistency is the quality of a stagnant mind.
John Sloan, by Van Wyck Brooks, 1955.

It may be taken as an axiom that the majority is always wrong in cultural matters . . . Politically I believe in democracy, but culturally, not at all . . . Whenever a cultural matter rolls up a majority, I know it is wrong.   *Ibid.*

Adam Smith
(1723-1790)
Scottish moralist, political economist

Science is the great antidote to the poison of enthusiasm and superstition.
The Wealth of Nations, 1776.

No society can surely be flourishing and happy, of which the far greater part of the members are poor and miserable.   *Ibid.*

All systems either of preference or of restraint, therefore, being thus completely taken away, the obvious and simple system of natural liberty establishes itself of its own accord. Every man, as long as he does not violate the laws of justice, is left perfectly free to pursue his own interest in his own way, and to bring both his industry and capital into competition with those of any other man, or order of men.   *Ibid.*

In order to make every man feel himself perfectly secure in the possession of every right that belongs to him, it is not only necessary that the judicial should be separated from the executive power, but that it should be rendered as much as possible independent of that power.   *Ibid.*

To found a great empire for the sole purpose of raising up a people of customers may, at first sight, appear a project fit only for a nation of shopkeepers.   *Ibid.*

We rarely hear, it has been said, of the combination of masters; though frequently of those of workmen. But whoever imagines, upon this account, that masters rarely combine, is as ignorant of the world as of the subject. Masters are always and everywhere in a sort of tacit, but constant and uniform, combination, not to raise the wages of labor above the actual rate.   *Ibid.*

The masters, being fewer in number, can combine much more easily; and the law, besides, authorizes, or at least does not prohibit their combinations, while it prohibits those of the workmen.   *Ibid.*

We have no acts of parliament against combining to lower the price of work; but many against combining to raise it. *Ibid.*

The capricious ambition of kings and ministers has not, during the present and the preceding century, been more fatal to the repose of Europe than the impertinent jealousy of merchants and manufacturers. The violence and injustice of the rulers of mankind is an ancient evil, for which, I am afraid, the nature of human affairs can scarce admit of a remedy. But the mean rapacity, the monopolising spirit of manufacturers, who neither are, nor ought to be, the rulers of mankind, though it cannot perhaps be corrected, may very easily be prevented from disturbing the tranquillity of anybody but themselves.   *Ibid.*

The real price of everything, what every thing really costs to the man who wants to

acquire it, is the toil and trouble of acquiring it.   *Ibid.*

People of the same trade seldom meet together but the conversation ends in a conspiracy against the public, or in some diversion to raise prices.   *Ibid.*

With the great part of rich people, the chief employment of riches consists in the parade of riches, which in their eye is never so complete as when they appear to possess those decisive marks of opulence which nobody can possess but themselves.* *Ibid.*

Every man is rich or poor according to the degree in which he can afford to enjoy the necessities, conveniences, and amusements of human life. But after the division of labour has once thoroughly taken place, it is but a very small part of these with which a man's own labour can supply him. The far greater part of them he must derive from the labour of other people, and he must be rich or poor according to the quantity of what labour which he can command, or which he can afford to purchase.   *Ibid.*

The value of any commodity, therefore, to the person who possesses it, and who means not to use or consume it himself, but to exchange it for other commodities, is equal to the quantity of labour which it enables him to purchase or command. Labour, therefore, is the real measure of the exchangeable value of all commodities.   *Ibid.*

Labour was the first price, the original purchase-money that was paid for all things. It was not by gold or by silver, but by labour, that all wealth of the world was originally purchased; and its value, to those

---

* See Veblen.

who possess it, and who want to exchange it for some new productions, is precisely equal to the quantity of labour which it can enable them to purchase or command.

Ibid.

Alfred E. Smith

(1873-1944)
American politician

All the ills of democracy can be cured by more democracy.

Speech, Albany, June 27, 1933.

If unpopular minorities are to be deprived by any such device as this of their basic rights to representation upon the ballot, they will, indeed, have conferred upon them a just claim to political martyrdom. The very evils of ultra-radicalism which are feared by the opponents of this measure would, in my opinion, be definitely enhanced if the bill became law.

Veto message, 1920, N. Y. Legislature; quoted by Justice Douglas, An Almanac of Liberty, p. 256.

No matter to what extent we may disagree with our neighbor, he is entitled to his own opinion, and, until the time arrives when he seeks by violation of law to urge his opinion upon his neighbor, he must be left free not only to have it but to express it. In a State, just as in a legislative body, the majority needs no protection, for they can protect themselves. Law, in a democracy, means the protection of the rights and liberties of the minority . . . It is a confession of the weakness of our own faith in the righteousness of our cause when we attempt to suppress by law those who do not agree with us. *Ibid.*

It is the right of our people to organize to oppose any law and any part of the Constitution with which they are not in sympathy.

Address, League of Women Voters, December 2, 1927.

I believe in absolute separation of Church and State . . . I believe in the support of the public school.

Presidential campaign statement, 1928.

Let's look at the record.

Quoted by John O'Donnell, N. Y. Daily News, October 9, 1947.

You don't shoot Santa Claus. *Ibid.*

Bernard Smith

(b. 1906)
American writer

The words men fight and die for are the coins of politics, where by much usage they are soiled and by much manipulating debased. That has evidently been the fate of the word "democracy." It has come to mean whatever anyone wants it to mean.

Introduction, The Democratic Spirit, 1941.

Democracy is a very simple principle, and those who speculate about its meaning are those who are not quite willing to accept it. The dictionary defines it as "the rule of the people." Not much more need be said about it. *Ibid.*

A significant factor in our history has been the effort, on the one hand, of minority groups to prevent the people from ruling, and, on the other hand, of the people to express their will and to have it applied rationally. The people's desire to rule has been simply a desire for greater opportunities to get more of the good things of life—food, shelter, leisure, education, security, pleasure. Occasionally their will has been deliberately thwarted; usually they have been misinformed as to what their will should be and how they should attempt to satisfy it. *Ibid.*

The people are in general inadequately educated and have little experience in philosophical and political reasoning, and so it is possible to misinform, divert, and delude them. But not forever and not about everything. They learn. *Ibid.*

E. Harold Smith
American Catholic priest

If we had followed the social program that was ours, we should be today in the vanguard of the social movement, instead of battling in many places for our very lives, with the doubtful help of Fascist and reactionary allies.
Commonweal. January 1, 1937, p. 261.

Captain John Smith
(1580-1631)
President, Colony of Virginia

He that will finde Truth, must seek it with a free judgement, and a sanctified minde: he that thus seeks, shall finde; he shall live in Truth, and that shall live in him; it shall be like a stream of living waters issuing out of his own Soule; he shall drink of the waters of his own cisterne, and be satisfied; he shall every morning finde this Heavenly Manna lying upon the top of his own Soule, and be fed with it to eternal life; he will finde satisfaction within, feeling himself in conjunction with Truth, though all the World should dispute against him.

Quoted, Gollancz, From Darkness to Light.

Lillian Smith
(b. 1897)
American writer

Faith and doubt both are needed—not as antagonists but working side by side—to take us around the unknown curve.
The Journey, 1954.

To believe in something not yet proved and to underwrite it with our lives: it is the only way we can leave the future open. Man, surrounded by facts, permitting himself no surprise, no intuitive flash, no great hypothesis, no risk, is in a locked cell. Ignorance cannot seal the mind and imagination more securely. *Ibid.*

To find the point where hypothesis and fact meet; the delicate equilibrium between dream and reality; the place where fantasy and earthy things are metamorphosed into a work of art, the hour when faith in the future becomes knowledge of the past; to lay down one's power for others in need; to shake off the old ordeal and get ready for the new; to question, knowing that never can the full answer be found; to accept uncertainties quietly, even our incomplete knowledge of God: this is what man's journey is about, I think. *Ibid.*

Sydney Smith
(1771-1845)
English writer, clergyman

Every law which originated in ignorance and malice, and gratifies the passions from which it sprang, we call the wisdom of our ancestors. *Peter Plymley Letters.*

Truth is its (justice's) handmaid, freedom is its child, peace is its companion, safety walks in its steps, victory follows in its train; it is the brightest emanation from the gospel; it is the attribute of God.

Lady Holland's Memoir.

In the four quarters of the globe, who reads an American book? or goes to an American play? or looks at an American picture or statue? What does the world yet owe to American physicians or surgeons? What new substances have their chemists discovered? or what old ones have they analyzed? What new constellations have been discovered by the telescopes of Americans? What have they done in mathematics? Who drinks out of American glasses? or eats from American plates? or wears American coats or gowns? or sleeps in American blankets? Finally, under which of the old tyrannical governments of Europe is every sixth man a slave, whom his fellow-creatures may buy, and sell, and torture?
Edinburgh Review, January, 1820.

Men who prefer any load of infamy, however great, to any pressure of taxation, however light. . . *On American Debts.*

Tobias Smollett

(1721-1771)

English novelist

Hark ye, Clinker, you are a most notorious offender. You stand convicted of sickness, hunger, wretchedness, and want.
Humphry Clinker.

Edgar Snow

(1905-1972)

American writer

No one can rule guiltlessly, and least of all those whom history compels to hurry.
Journey to the Beginning, Random House, 1958.

In Russia religion is the opium of the people; in China opium is the religion of the people.

Socialist Labor Party

We hold that man cannot exercise his right to life, liberty, and the pursuit of happiness without the ownership of the land and the tools with which to work. Deprived of these, his life, his liberty and his fate fall into the hands of the class that owns those essentials for work and production. This ownership is today held by the minority in society, the capitalist class, exercising through this ownership and control an economic despotism without parallel in history.
Declaration of Fundamental Principles, adopted, national convention, N.Y.C., April 29, 1940.

Having outlived its social usefulness, capitalism must give way to a new social order—a social order wherein government shall rest on industry, on the basis of useful occupations, instead of resting on territorial (political) representation. This new system can only be the Socialist Industrial Union form of Government if the needs of the vast majority are to be served and if progress is to be the law of the future as it has been in the past. Upon the despoiled workers rests the duty of effecting this revolutionary change in a peaceful, civilized manner, using the ballot and all that thereby hangs in order to effect the change.
Ibid.

Society of Friends

The Christian faith, which we believe is the hope of our troubled world, is a revolutionary faith. It is rooted in inward experience, but, wherever it is genuine, it leads to radical changes in the ways in which men live and act. We rejoice in the movements, appearing in many parts of the world at once, which are inspired by the desire for social justice, equal rights for all races, and the dignity of the individual person. These changes can neither be achieved nor prevented by war.

Declaration, world conference, Oxford, England, 1952, in commemoration of their 300th anniversary.

War leads to a vicious circle of hatred, oppression, subversive movements, false propaganda, rearmament and new wars. An armament race cannot bring peace, freedom or security. We call upon peoples everywhere to break this vicious circle, to behave as nations with the same decency as they would behave as men and brothers, to substitute the institutions of peace for the institutions of war. *Ibid.*

Let us join together throughout the world to grow more food, to heal and prevent disease, to conserve and develop the resources of the good earth to the glory of God and the comfort of man's distress.
Ibid.

Socrates*

(470?-399 B.C.)
Greek philosopher

The unexamined life is not worth living.
Plato's Apology.

I shall never act differently, even if I have to die for it many times. *Ibid.*

Do not be angry with me if I tell you the truth. *Ibid.*

---

* "Of Socrates we have nothing genuine but in the Memorabilia of Xenephon; for Plato makes him one of his Collocutors merely to cover his own whimsies under the mantle of his name"—Jefferson, to William Short, October 31, 1819.

No man will ever be safe who stands up boldly against you, or any other democracy, and forbids the many sins and crimes that are committed in the State; the man who is to fight for justice—if he is to keep his life at all—must work in private, not in public.
Ibid.

So, my judges, face death with a good hope, and know for certain that no evil can happen to a good man, either in life or after death. *Ibid.*

If you kill me you will not easily find a successor to me who will be, if I may use such a ludicrous figure of speech, a sort of gadfly, attached to the state by God, and the state is a great and noble horse who is rather sluggish owing to his very size and requires to be stirred into life.
I am that gadfly which God has attached to the state, and all day long and in all places am always fastening upon you, arousing and persuading and reproaching you.
Ibid.

I do nothing but go about persuading you all, old and young alike, not to take thought for your persons or your properties, but first and chiefly to care about the greatest improvement of the soul. I tell you that virtue does not come from money, but that from virtue comes money and every other good of man, public as well as private.
Ibid.

For know that if you kill me, I being such a man as I am, you will not injure me so much as yourselves; for neither Meletus nor Anytus could injure me; that would be impossible, for I believe it is not God's will that a better man be injured by a worse.
Ibid. Fowler's translation, Loeb Classical Library.

I think I have sufficient witness that I speak the truth, namely, my poverty.
Ibid.

And what do I deserve to suffer or to pay, because in my life I did not keep quiet, but neglecting what most men care for— money-making and property, and military offices, and public speaking, and the various offices and plots and parties that come up in the state . . .   *Ibid.*

If you put me to death in spite of my declared innocence, you will do me less harm than you do yourselves. Heaven, I believe, does not permit a good man to be harmed by his inferior. The latter can kill him, no doubt, or drive him into exile, or deprive him of his rights as a citizen, and will think, with others, that he is thereby inflicting great harm on him. But I disagree. I believe that conduct like my accuser's, directed towards depriving a man unjustly of his life, brings down on its author a far greater hurt.

Ibid., tr. by Kathleen Freeman, Fighting Words, Beacon Press, 1952.

To fear death, gentlemen, is nothing other than to think oneself wise when one is not; for it is to think one knows what one does not know. No man knows whether death may not even turn out to be the greatest of blessings for a human being; and yet people fear it as if they knew for certain that it is the greatest of evils.
                                        Ibid.

In battle it is often obvious that a man can escape death if he will drop his weapons and beg for mercy from his pursuers; and there are plenty of devices for shunning death in every kind of danger if a man sticks at nothing in word or deed. But, perhaps, gentlemen, the difficulty does not lie so much in avoiding death as in avoiding dishonor. For she runs faster than death.
                                        Ibid.

Be of good hope in the face of death. Believe in this one truth for certain, that no evil can befall a good man either in life or death, and that his fate is not a matter of indifference to the gods.   *Ibid.*

And now the time has come when we must depart: I to my death, you to go on living. But which of us is going to the better fate is unknown to all except God.
                                        Ibid.

The beginning of wisdom is the definition of terms.

How much there is in the world I do not want.
(on seeing articles of luxury on sale.)

Brehon Somervell
(b. 1892)
American general

We fight for simple things, for the little things that are all-important. We fight for the right to lock our house doors and be sure that no bully with official sanction will break the lock.
Address, N. Y. Post, March 9, 1944.

We fight for town meetings, for the soapbox in the public square, for the high school debating team, for open doors to cathedral and church and synagogue.   *Ibid.*

We fight for the country editor and for the metropolitan daily and for the editor's right to say the wrong thing if he thinks it's right.   *Ibid.*

Sophocles
(496?-406 B.C.)
Greek tragic poet

A lie never lives to be old.
                        Acrisius. Fragment 59.

Laws can never be enforced unless fear supports them.   *Ajax.*

No such device
Ever appeared, as money to mankind:
This is that sacks cities, this routs out
Men from their homes, and trains and turns
     astray
The minds of honest mortals, setting them
Upon base actions; this revealed to men
Habits of his misdoing, and cognizance
Of every work of wickedness. *Antigone.*

Of all the foul growths current in the world,
The worst is money. Money drives men
     from home,
Plunders proud cities, and perverts honest
     minds
To shameful practice, godlessness and
     crime.   *Ibid.; another translation.*

For money you would sell your soul. *Ibid.*

In a really just cause the weak conquer the
     strong.   *Oedipus Coloneus.*

Truth is always the strongest argument.
                            Phaedra.

Let every man in mankind's frailty,
Consider his last day, and let none
Presume on his good fortune until he find
Life, at his death, a memory without pain.
                     Oedipus Tyrannus.

Georges Sorel
(1847-1922)
French journalist, syndicalist

The strike is a phenomenon of war.
     Reflections on Violence. *

The proletariat has none of the servile instincts of democracy . . . the men who

----

* A book Mussolini credited with much of his ideology, notably the Syndicalist State.

devote themselves to the revolutionary cause know that they must always remain poor.
                            Ibid.

It is to violence that Socialism owes those high ethical values by means of which it brings *salvation* to the modern world.
                            Ibid.

Syndicalists do not propose to reform the State, as the men of the 18th century did; they want to destroy it, because they wish to realize this idea of Marx's that the Socialist revolution ought not to culminate in the replacement of one governing minority by another minority.   *Ibid.*

Proletarian violence, carried on as a pure and simple manifestation of the sentiment of the class war, appears thus as a very fine and very heroic thing; it is at the service of the immemorial interests of civilization; it is not perhaps the most appropriate method of obtaining immediate material advantages, but it may save the world from barbarism.   *Ibid.*

Syndicalism claims to create a real proletarian ideology, and, whatever the middle class professors say of it, historical experience . . . tells us that . . . out of it may come the salvation of the world.   *Ibid.*

Proletarian acts of violence have no resemblance to these proscriptions (the Inquisition, *Ancien Régime,* Robespierre); they are purely and simply acts of war; they have the value of military demonstrations, and serve to mark the separation of classes.
                            Ibid.

Every time that we attempt to obtain an exact conception of the ideas behind proletarian violence we are forced to go back to the notion of the general strike. . . . The Syndicalists (concentrate) the whole of Socialism in the drama of the general strike.
                            Ibid.

The general strike is indeed what I have said: the *myth* in which Socialism is wholly comprised, *i.e.*, a body of images capable of evoking instinctively all the sentiments which correspond to the different manifestations of the war undertaken by Socialism against modern society. Strikes have engendered in the proletariat the noblest, deepest, and most moving sentiments that they possess. *Ibid.*

It would serve no purpose to explain to the poor that they ought not to feel sentiments of jealousy and vengeance against their masters; these feelings are too powerful to be suppressed by exhortations; it is on the widespread prevalence of these feelings that democracy chiefly founds its strength. *Ibid.*

Herbert Spencer
(1820-1903)
English philosopher

Liberty of action being the first essential to the exercise of faculties, and therefore the first essential to happiness; and the liberty of each limited by the like liberties of all, being the form which this first essential assumes when applied to many instead of one; it follows that this liberty of each, limited by the like liberties of all, is the rule in conformity with which society must be organized. *Social Statics, 1850.**

As one of our living writers puts it—the tyrant is nothing but a slave turned inside out. *Ibid.*

We constantly observe that those who fawn upon the great are overbearing to

---

* This, and the following quotations, are from the chapter *The Right to Ignore the State*, which was omitted from later editions.

their inferiors. That "emancipated slaves exceed all other owners (of slaves) in cruelty and oppression," is a truth established by numerous authorities. *Ibid.*

Nay, indeed, have we not seen that government is essentially immoral? Is it not the offspring of evil, having about it all the marks of its parentage? Does it not exist because crime exists? Is it not strong, or, as we say, despotic, when crime is great? Is there not more liberty—that is, less government—as crime diminishes? And must not government cease when crime ceases, for very lack of objects on which to perform its functions? *Ibid.*

Not only does magisterial power exist *because* of evil, but it exists *by* evil. Violence is employed to maintain it; and all violence involves criminality. Soldiers, policemen, and jailers; swords, batons, and fetters,—are instruments for inflicting pain; and all infliction of pain is, in the abstract, wrong. The state employs evil weapons to subjugate evil, and is alike contaminated by the objects with which it deals and the means by which it works. *Ibid.*

The freest form of government is only the least objectionable form. The rule of the many by the few we call tyranny: the rule of the few by the many is tyranny also, only of a less intense kind. *Ibid.*

What is the meaning of Dissent? The time was when a man's faith and his mode of worship were as much determinable by law as his secular acts; . . . Thanks to the growth of a Protestant spirit, however, we have ignored the State in this matter—wholly in theory, and partly in practice. *Ibid.*

Feudalism, serfdom, slavery, all tyrannical institutions, are merely the most vigorous kind of rule, springing out of, and necessary to, a bad state of man. The progress from these is in all cases the same—less government. *Ibid.*

What a cage is to the wild beast, law is to the selfish man. *Ibid.*

Were there no thieves and murderers, prisons would be unnecessary. It is only because tyranny is yet rife in the world that we have armies. Barristers, judges, juries, all the instruments of law, exist simply because knavery exists. Magisterial force is the sequence of social vice, and the policeman is but the complement of the criminal. Therefore it is that we call government "a necessary evil." *Ibid.*

Whatever fosters militarism makes for barbarism; whatever fosters peace makes for civilization. *Ibid.*

We do not commonly see in a tax a diminution of freedom, and yet it clearly is one. The money taken represents so much labor gone through, and the product of that labor being taken away, either leaves the individual to go without such benefit as was achieved by it or else to go through more labor. *Ibid.*

A man's liberties are none the less aggressed upon because those who coerce him do so in the belief that he will be benefitted. *Ibid.*

Aggression which is flagitious when committed by one, is not sanctioned when committed by a host. *Ibid.*

Hero-worship is strongest where there is least regard for human freedom. *Ibid.*

The chief faculty of self-rule being the moral sense, the degree of freedom in their institutions which any given people can bear, will be proportionate to the diffusion of this moral sense among them. And only when its influence greatly predominates can so large an instalment of freedom as a democracy implies become possible.

Op. cit. This, and the following quotations, appear in all editions.

The man of genuinely democratic feeling loves liberty as a miser loves gold, for its own sake and quite irrespective of its apparent advantages. What he thus highly values he sleeplessly watches; and he opposes aggression the moment it commences. *Ibid.*

Progress, therefore, is not an accident, but a necessity . . . It is part of nature. *Ibid.*

No one can be perfectly free till all are free; no one can be perfectly moral till all are moral; no one can be perfectly happy till all are happy. *Ibid.*

Conservatism defends those coercive arrangements which a still-lingering savageness makes requisite. Radicalism endeavours to realize a state more in harmony with the character of the ideal man. *Ibid.*

Ethical truth is as exact and peremptory as physical truth. *Ibid.*

Opinion is ultimately determined by the feelings, and not by the intellect. *Ibid.*

Society exists for the benefit of its members; not the members for the benefit of society. *Principles of Ethics.*

Science is organized knowledge. *Education.*

Absolute morality is the regulation of conduct that pain shall not be inflicted. *Essays, 1891.*

[649]

The Republican form of government is the highest form of government; but because of this it requires the highest type of human nature—a type nowhere at present existing.   *Ibid. The Americans.*

The socialist speculation is vitiated by an assumption like that which vitiates the speculations of the "practical" politician. It is assumed that officialism will work as it is intended to work, which it never does. *Man Versus the State. The Coming Slavery. 1884.*

The machinery of Communism, like existing social machinery, has to be framed out of existing human nature; and the defects of existing human nature will generate in the one the same evils as in the other. The love of power, the selfishness, the injustice, the untruthfulness, which often in comparatively short time bring private organizations to disaster, will inevitably, where their effects accumulate from generation to generation, work evils far greater and less remediable.   *Ibid.*

All Socialism involves slavery.   *Ibid.*

Life is the continuous adjustment of internal relations to external relations. *Principles of Biology, 1872.*

Our lives are universally shortened by our ignorance.   *Ibid.*

This survival of the fittest, which I have here sought to express in mechanical terms, is that which Mr. Darwin has called "natural selection, or the preservation of favoured races in the struggle for life."   *Ibid.*

There is a principle which is a bar against all information, which is a proof against all argument, and which cannot fail to keep a man in everlasting ignorance—that principle is condemnation before investigation.

Oswald Spengler

(1880-1936)
German philosopher, historian

We have entered upon the age of world wars. It began in the 19th Century and will outlast the present and probably the next.   *The Hour of Decision.*

The world economic crisis . . . is not, as the world supposes, the temporary consequence of war, revolution, inflation, and payment of debts. It has been willed. In all essentials it is the product of the deliberate work of the leaders of the proletariat.   *Ibid.*

It is from the intellectual "mob", with the failures from all academic professions, the spiritually unfit and the morally inhibited, at its head, that the gangsters of Liberal and Bolshevist risings are recruited.   *Ibid.*

If few can stand a long war without deterioration of soul, none can stand a long peace.   *Ibid.*

Let it for once be said outright, though it is a slap in the face for the vulgarity of the age: property is not a vice, but a *gift*, and a gift such as few possess.   *Ibid.*

Liberty has always been the liberty of those who wish to obtain the power, not to abolish it. *Ibid.*

Christian theology is the grandmother of Bolshevism. *Ibid.*

Socialism is nothing but the capitalism of the lower classes. *Ibid.*

All the great leaders in history go "Right", however low the depths from which they have climbed. *Ibid.*

The peace of 1918 . . . the first great triumph of the colored world . . . There remains as a formative power only the warlike, "Prussian" spirit—everywhere and not in Germany alone . . . He whose sword compels victory here will be lord of the world. The dice are there ready for this stupendous game. *Who dares to throw them?* *Ibid.*

Cultures are organisms, and world-history is their collective biography. Morphologically, the immense history of the Chinese or of the Classical Culture is the exact equivalent of the petty history of the individual man, or of the animal, or the tree, or the flower . . . In the destinies of the several Cultures that follow upon one another, grow up with one another, touch, overshadow, and suppress one another, is compressed the whole content of human history. *Decline of the West.*

The men of the "New Order" upon whom every decline-time founds such hopes . . . They are the fluid megalopolitan Populace, the rootless city-mass (*oi polloi,* as Athens called it) that has replaced the People, the Culture-folk that was sprung from the soil and peasantlike even when it lived in towns. They are the market-place loungers of Alexandria and Rome, the newspaper-readers of our own corresponding time; the "educated" man who then and now makes a cult of intellectual mediocrity and a church of advertisement; the man of the theatres and places of amusement, of sport and "best-sellers". It is this late-appearing mass of *not* "mankind" that is the object of Stoic and Socialist propaganda, and one could match it with equivalent phenomena in the Egyptian New Empire, Buddhist India and Confucian China. *Ibid.*

Benedict (Baruch) Spinoza
(1632-1677)
Dutch philosopher

Avarice, ambition, lust, etc. are species of madness. *Ethics, 1677.*

True virtue is life under the direction of reason. *Ibid.*

Men who are governed by reason . . . desire for themselves nothing which they do not also desire for the rest of mankind. *Ibid.*

The man who is guided by reason is more free in a state, where he lives under a general system of law, than in solitude, where he is independent. *Ibid.*

There is no such thing as free will. The mind is induced to wish this or that by some cause, and that cause is determined by another cause, and so on back to infinity. *Ibid.*

Those who wish to seek out the causes of miracles, and to understand the things of nature as philosophers, and not to stare at them in astonishment like fools, are soon considered heretical and impious, and proclaimed as such by those whom the mob adore as the interpreters of nature and the gods. *Ibid., part i, appendix.*

Desire is the very essence of man.
Ibid., part iv.

Sin cannot be conceived in a natural state, but only in a civil state, where it is decreed by common consent what is good or bad. *Ibid.*

Man is a social animal. *Ibid.*

Whatever hinders man's perfecting of his reason and capability to enjoy the rational life, is alone called evil.
Ibid., appendix v.

Everyone has as much right as he has might.
Theologico-Political Treatise, 1670.

Men are especially intolerant of serving and being ruled by, their equals.
Ibid., ch. 5.

How blest would our age be if it could witness a religion freed from all the trammels of superstition! *Ibid., ch. 11.*

Philosophy has no end in view save truth; faith looks for nothing but obedience and piety. *Ibid., ch. 14.*

He alone is free who lives with free consent under the entire guidance of reason.
Ibid., ch. 16.

I believe democracy to be of all forms of government the most natural, and the most consonant with individual liberty. In it no one transfers his natural rights so absolutely that he has no further voice in affairs, he only hands it over to the majority of a society, whereof he is a unit. Thus all men remain, as they were in the state of nature, equals. *Ibid.*

The fickle disposition of the multitude almost reduces those who have experience of it to despair; for it is governed solely by emotions, and not by reason.
Ibid., ch. 17.

The most tyrannical governments are those which make crimes of opinions, for everyone has an inalienable right to his thoughts. *Ibid., ch. 18.*

Freedom is absolutely necessary for progress in science and the liberal arts.
Ibid., ch. 20.

The ultimate end of the state is not to dominate man, nor to restrain them by fear; rather it is so to free each man from fear that he may live and act with full security and without injury to himself or his neighbor. *Ibid.*

The end of the state, I repeat, is not to make rational beings into brute beasts and machines. It is to enable their bodies and their minds to function safely. It is to lead men to live by, and to exercise, a free reason; that they may not waste their strength in hatred, anger and guilt, nor act unfairly toward one another. Thus the end of the state is real liberty. *Ibid.*

Laws directed against opinions affect the generous-minded rather than the wicked, and are adapted less for coercing criminals than for irritating the upright . . . What greater misfortune for a state than that honorable men should be (treated) like criminals . . . ?
Quoted by Zechariah Chafee. Atlantic Monthly, January, 1955.

Whatever comes to pass, comes to pass according to laws and rules which involve eternal necessity and truth.
Ethica ordine geometrica demonstrata.

As nature preserves a fixed and immutable order; it must clearly follow that mira-

cles are only intelligible as a relation to human opinions, and merely mean events of which the natural cause cannot be explained by a reference to any ordinary occurrence, either by us, or at any rate, by the writer and narrator of the miracle.
Ibid.

Men do all things for an end, namely, for that which is useful to them, and which they seek. *Ibid.*

There is no rational life, therefore, without intelligence and things are good only in so far as they assist man to enjoy that life of the mind which is determined by intelligence.
The Foundations of the Moral Life.

I take a totally different view of God and Nature from that which the later Christians usually entertain, for I hold that God is the immanent, and not the extraneous, cause of all things. I say, All is in God; all lives and moves in God. *Epistle 21.*

I do not know how to teach philosophy without becoming a disturber of established religion.
C. 1670, on being offered a Heidelberg professorship.

Lysander Spooner
(1808-1887)
American lawyer, libertarian

All restraints upon men's natural liberty, not necessary for the simple maintenance of justice, are of the nature of slavery, and differ from each other only in degree.
Trial by Jury.

All governments, the worst on earth and the most tyrannical on earth, are free governments to that portion of the people who voluntarily support them. *Ibid.*

If the jury have no right to judge of the justice of a law of the government, they plainly can do nothing to protect the people against the oppressions of the government; for there are no oppressions which the government may not authorize by law.
Ibid.

"The trial by jury" is a trial by the country—that is, by the people—as distinguished from a trial by the government. *Ibid.*

The conclusion, therefore, is that any government that can, for a day, enforce its own laws, without appealing to the people (or a tribunal fairly representing the people) for their consent is, in theory, an absolute government, irresponsible to the people, and can perpetuate its power at pleasure.
Ibid.

It is perfectly self-evident that, where there is no legal right to resist the oppression of government, there can be no legal liberty. And here it is all-important to notice that, practically speaking, there can be no legal right to resist the oppressions of the government unless there be some legal tribunal other than the government, and wholly independent of and above the government, to judge between the government and those who resist its oppression; in other words, to judge what laws of the government are to be obeyed and what held for naught.

The only tribunal known to our laws for this purpose is a jury. If a jury have not the right to judge between the government and those who disobey its laws, the government is absolute, and the people, legally speaking, are slaves. *Ibid*

Charles T. Sprading
(Contemporary)
American libertarian writer

The history of civilized man is the history of the incessant conflict between liberty and authority.

Introduction, Liberty and the Great Libertarians.

The first great struggle for liberty was in the realm of thought. The Libertarians reasoned that freedom of thought would be good for mankind; it would promote knowledge, and increased knowledge would advance civilization. But the Authoritarians protested that freedom of thought would be dangerous; that people would think wrong; that a few were divinely appointed to think for the people, that these had books which contained the whole truth, and that further search was unnecessary and forbidden. The powers of Church and State were arrayed against the Libertarians; but, after the sacrifice of many great men, freedom in thought was won. *Ibid.*

Ethical right is largely abstract; legal right is mostly concrete. Ethical right the just man wishes to be established; legal right is already established. Ethical right and legal right mutually exclude each other; where one prevails, the other cannot endure. One is founded on power, on might; the other on justice, on equality. One appeals to the sword to settle matters, the other appeals to the judgment of men. *Ibid.*

The Law of Equal Liberty is the principle that is offered by Libertarians as a substitute for these conflicting and unjust customs of the past. This law has been well formulated by that great philosopher and sociologist, Herbert Spencer. Here it is in brief: that every man may claim the fullest liberty to exercise his faculties compatible with the possession of like liberty by every other man. This gives us a basis for justice in perfect harmony with the idea of equity. Equal liberty is the essence of equity, and

is not equity just? If there are to be laws in a free society, they must be based upon equal liberty or they will be unjust. *Ibid.*

The greatest violator of the principle of equal liberty is the State. Its functions are to control, to rule, to dictate, to regulate, and in exercising these functions it interferes with and injures individuals who have done no wrong. *Ibid.*

Governments cannot accept liberty as their fundamental basis for justice, because governments rest upon authority and not upon liberty. To accept liberty as the fundamental basis is to discard authority; that is, to discard government itself; as this would mean the dethronement of the leaders of government, we can expect only those who have no economic compromise to make to accept equal liberty as the basis of justice. *Ibid.*

The Libertarians say: Let those who believe in religion have religion; let those who believe in government, have government; but let those who believe in liberty, have liberty, and do not compel them to accept a religion or a government they do not want. *Ibid.*

It is as unjust to force one's government upon another, as it is unjust to force one's religion upon another. *Ibid.*

We no longer believe that it is just for one man to govern two men, but we have yet to outgrow the absurd belief that it is just for two men to govern one man. *Ibid.*

The power to command and the weakness to obey are the essence of government and the quintessence of slavery. *Ibid.*

Most crimes are offenses against property. The struggle for property leads to depredations and infractions of the principles of equal liberty in various ways. Greed on the one side and poverty on the other, is the cause of so-called crime. To cure crime, it is necessary to remove its cause. The disease of greed may not be curable but its baneful results can be obviated by destroying special privileges, out of which ensues poverty, that in turn breeds crime. *Ibid.*

Economists are agreed that there are four methods by which wealth is acquired by those who do not produce it. These are: interest, profit, rent and taxes, each of which is based upon special privilege, and all are gross violations of the principle of equal liberty.   *Ibid.*

Knowledge consists in understanding the evidence that establishes the fact, not in the belief that it is a fact.   *Ibid.*

Joseph Stalin (né Joseph Vissarionovich Djugashvili)

(1879-1953)

Communist dictator, U.S.S.R.

The press is the only weapon with whose aid the party every day speaks to the working class in the language of the party. You cannot find in the world another such flexible apparatus as the press, and there are no other means through which the party can so well connect its ideological threads with the working class.

Pravda, Petrograd, c. 1917.

Whereas private property and capital inevitably disunite people, inflame national enmity and intensify national oppression, collective property and labor just as inevitably bring people closer and undermine national oppression.   *Speech, 1921.*

As soon as classes have been abolished, and the dictatorship of the proletariat has been done away with, the Communist Party will have fulfilled its mission and can be allowed to disappear.

Speech, April, 1924.

To put it briefly: the dictatorship of the proletariat is the domination of the proletariat over the bourgeoisie, untrammelled by law and based on violence and enjoying the sympathy and support of the toiling and exploited masses.

April, 1924; Speech, Sverdloff University; reprinted, Foundations of Leninism, International Publishers, N. Y. C., 1934.

What is the difference between revolutionary tactics and reformist tactics? Some are of the opinion that Leninism is opposed to reforms, opposed to compromises and to agreements in general. That is absolutely untrue. Bolsheviks know as well as anybody else that in a certain sense "every little helps," that under certain conditions reforms, in general, and compromises and agreements, in particular, are necessary and useful.   *Ibid.*

We guarantee the right of every citizen to combat by argument, propaganda, and agitation any and all religion. The Communist Party cannot be neutral toward religion. It stands for science, and all religion is opposed to science.

Declaration to an American labor delegation, September 7, 1927.

Being the highest phase of capitalist development, imperialism . . . draws within the orbit of finance-capital, exploits all colonies, all races and all nations.

Speech, Third Internationale, 1928.

The basic contradiction of capitalism is expressed in the contradiction between the colossal growth in the productive capacity of capitalism, calculated to secure the maximum of capitalist profit, and the relative reduction of purchasing power of millions of toilers whose standards of living the capitalists are all the time trying to keep within the limits of the lowest possible minimum.
Report to 16th Congress, C.P.S.U., June, 1930.

But surely no capitalist would ever agree to the complete abolition of unemployment, to the abolition of the reserve army of unemployed, the purpose of which is to bring pressure on the labor market, to ensure a supply of cheap labor.
Stenogram of Stalin interview with H. G. Wells, July 23, 1934; from copy given by Mr. Wells to G. S.

Without getting rid of the capitalists, without abolishing the principle of private property in the means of production, it is impossible to create planned economy.
Ibid.

Theoretically, of course, the possibility of marching gradually, step by step, under the conditions of capitalism, towards the goal which you call Socialism in the Anglo-Saxon meaning of the word, is not precluded. But what will this "Socialism" be? At best, bridling to some extent the most unbridled of individual representatives of capitalist profit, some increase in the application of the principle of regulation in national economy. That is all very well. But as soon as Roosevelt, or any other captain in the contemporary bourgeois world, proceeds to undertake something serious against the foundation of capitalism, he will inevitably suffer utter defeat. *Ibid.*

Mankind is divided into rich and poor, into property owners and exploited; and to abstract oneself from this fundamental division and from the antagonism between poor and rich means abstracting oneself from fundamental facts. I do not deny the existence of intermediate, middle strata which, either take the side of one or other of these two conflicting classes, or else take up a neutral or semi-neutral position in this struggle. But, I repeat, to abstract oneself from this fundamental division in society and from the fundamental struggle between the two main classes means ignoring facts.
Ibid.

You, Mr. Wells, evidently start out with the assumption that all men are good. I, however, do not forget that there are many wicked men. I do not believe in the goodness of the bourgeoisie. *Ibid.*

(Wells: You of all people know something about revolutions, Mr. Stalin, from the practical side. Do the masses ever rise? Is it not an established truth that all revolutions are made by a minority?)
(Stalin) To bring about a revolution a leading revolutionary minority is required: but the most talented, devoted and energetic minority would be helpless if it did not rely upon the at least passive support of millions.
(Wells: At least passive? Perhaps subconscious?)
(Stalin) Partly also the semi-instinctive and semi-conscious, but without the support of millions, the best minority is impotent. *Ibid.*

Capitalism is decaying, but it must not be compared simply with a tree which has decayed to such an extent that it must fall to the ground of its own accord. No, revolution, the substitution of one social system for another, has always been a struggle, a painful and a cruel struggle, a life and death struggle. *Ibid.*

Obsolete classes do not voluntarily abandon the stage of history. . . . Dying classes take to arms and resort to every means to save their existence as a ruling class.

(Wells: But were there not a few lawyers at the head of the Great French Revolution?)

(Stalin) I don't deny the role of the intelligentsia in revolutionary movements.
Ibid.

The rich experience of history teaches that up to now not a single class has voluntarily made way for another class. *Ibid.*

(Wells: It seems to me insurrection against the old order, against the law, is obsolete; old fashioned.)

(Stalin) In order to achieve a great object, an important social object, there must be a main force, a bulwark, a revolutionary class. *Ibid.*

Education is a weapon, whose effect depends on who holds it in his hands and at whom it is aimed. *Ibid.*

The export of revolution is nonsense. Every country makes its own revolution if it wants to, and if it does not want to, there will be no revolution.
Interview with Roy Howard, 1936. Problems of Leninism, 1940.

We have not built this society in order to cramp human freedom. We have built it in order that human personality might feel itself actually free. We built it for the sake of genuine freedom, freedom without quotation marks. *Ibid.*

What can be the "personal freedom" of an unemployed person who goes hungry and finds no use for his toil? *Ibid.*

Only where exploitation is annihilated, where there is no oppression of some by others, no unemployment, no beggary, and no trembling for fear that a man may on the morrow lose his work, his habitation, and his bread—only there is true freedom found. *Ibid.*

The proletarian state is a machine for the suppression of the bourgeoisie.
Foundations of Leninism, International Publishers, N.Y., 1939.

Dialectical materialism is the world outlook of the Marxist-Leninist party. It is called dialectical materialism because its approach to the phenomena of nature, its method of studying and apprehending them, is *dialectical*, while its interpretation of the phenomena of nature, its conception of these phenomena, its theory, is *materialistic*.
Dialectical and Historical Materialism, 1940.

I believe in one thing only, the power of the human will.
Duranty, "Stalin & Co."

It is not heroes that make history, but history that makes heroes. It is not heroes who create a people, but the people who create heroes and move history forward.
Attributed, in Short History of the Communist Party of the Soviet Union.

Leaders come and go, governments rise and fall; only the people endure, only the people are eternal.
Max Eastman, The New Leader, December 9, 1944.

The victory of socialism in one country is not a self-sufficient task. The revolution which has been victorious in one country must regard itself not as a self-sufficient entity, but as an aid, a means for hastening the victory of the proletariat in all countries.

N. Y. Times quotations from writings and speeches, published with obituary.

If any foreign minister begins to defend to the death a "peace conference" you can be sure his Government has already placed its orders for new battleships and airplanes.

Ibid.

The Government of the U.S.S.R. considers that, despite the differences in the economic systems and ideologies, the co-existence of these systems and a peaceful settlement of differences between the U.S.S.R. and the United States are not only possible, but also doubtless necessary in the interests of general peace. *Ibid.*

No important political or organizational problem is ever decided by our soviets and other mass organizations without directives from our Party. In this sense we may say that the dictatorship of the proletariat is, substantially, the dictatorship of the party, as the force which effectively guides.

Quoted by Edgar Snow, Saturday Evening Post, March 24, 1945.

Our Soviet society has succeeded in achieving socialism, in the main, and has created a socialist order, i.e., has achieved what is otherwise called among Marxists the first or lower phase of Communism. It is known that the fundamental principle of this phase of Communism is the formula: "From each according to his abilities; to each according to his deeds".

But Soviet society has not yet succeeded in bringing about the higher phase of Communism, where the ruling principle will be the formula: "From each according to his abilities; to each according to his needs".

New Soviet Constitution, p. 11.

Words must have no relation to action—otherwise what kind of diplomacy is it? Words are one thing, actions another. Good words are a mask for concealment of bad deeds. Sincere diplomacy is no more possible than dry water or wooden iron.

Quoted by the Committee on Un-American Affairs, report, May 29, 1956, p. 33.

You cannot make a revolution with silk gloves.

Quoted by John Gunther, Soviet Russia Today.

The writer is an engineer of the human soul. *Ibid.*

How many divisions has the Pope?

Quoted by C. L. Sulzberger, N. Y. Times, October 8, 1958, who also quotes Napoleon saying "Treat the Pope as though he had an army of 200,000 men."

A single death is a tragedy, a million deaths is a statistic.

Quoted by Anne Freemantle, N. Y. Times Book Review, September 28, 1958.

Lenin never became a prisoner of the majority. Lenin without hesitating would resolutely take the side of principle against the majority of the Party.

It is time to realize that of all the valuable capital the world possesses, the most valuable and most decisive is people.

The inevitability of wars between capitalist countries remains in force.

Last public statement, 1952.

Stanhope
See Chesterfield

Elizabeth Cady Stanton
(1815-1902)
American reformer

The memory of my own suffering has prevented me from ever shadowing one young soul with the superstitions of the Christian religion.
Eight Years and More, p. 26.

I found nothing grand in the history of the Jews nor in the morals inculcated in the Pentateuch. I know of no other books that so fully teach the subjection and degradation of women.   *Ibid., p. 395.*

The Bible and Church have been the greatest stumbling blocks in the way of women's emancipation.
Free Thought Magazine, Vol. XIV, September, 1896.

The whole tone of Church teaching in regard to woman is, to the last degree, contemptuous and degrading.
Ibid., November, 1896.

The religious superstitions of women perpetuate their bondage more than all other adverse influences.

To no form of religion is woman indebted for one impulse of freedom, as all alike have taught her inferiority and subjection.

Throughout this protracted and disgraceful assault on American womanhood the clergy baptized each new insult and act of injustice in the name of the Christian religion, and uniformly asked God's blessing on proceedings that would have put to shame an assembly of Hottentots.*

Harold E. Stassen
(b. 1907)
American lawyer, politician

Whoever kindles the flames of intolerance in America is lighting a fire underneath his own home.
Where I Stand, Doubleday, 1947.

Caecilius Statius
(220-168 B.C.)
Roman comic poet

Primus in orbe deos facit timor. (Fear created the first gods in the world.)
Thebais, iii.

Vilhjalmur Stefansson
(1879-1962)
American explorer, anthropologist

The most striking contradiction of our civilization is the fundamental reverence for truth which we profess and the thoroughgoing disregard for it which we practice.
The Standardization of Error.

Lincoln Steffens
(1866-1936)
American writer, muckraker

I have been over into the future, and it works.**   *Autobiography, 1931.*

---

* Signed by Mrs. Stanton, Mrs. Gage, Mrs. Susan B. Anthony.
** Reply to Bernard Baruch, who asked, "So you've been over into Russia?" Usually misquoted: "I have seen the future and it works."

We in America are fighting the money power; but if men can elsewhere get the power without money, what do they care about money? Power is what men seek, and any group that gets it will abuse it. It is the same old story.

In re Soviet Russia; to Upton Sinclair. Exposé, February, 1956.

Convictions were what I was afraid of. I tried to steer him (Jack Reed) away from convictions, that he might play; that he might play with life; and see it all, love it all, live it all, tell it all; that he might be it all, but all, not any one thing.

Under the Kremlin. The Freeman Magazine, 1920.

You sell 'em out; you turn over the whole thing—the city, its property, and its people —to Business, to the big fellows; to the business leaders of the people. You deliver not only franchises, privileges, private rights and public property, and values, Boss: you—all of you together—have delivered the government itself to these men, so that today this city, this State, and the national government represent, normally, not the people, not the great mass of common folk, who need protection, but—Business; preferably bad business; privileged business; a class, a privileged class. *The Dying Boss.*

That's the system. It's an organization of social treason, and the political boss is the chief traitor . . . They can't buy the people —too many of them; so they buy the people's leaders, and the disloyalty of the political boss is the key to the whole thing.
Ibid.

It is privilege that causes evil in the world, not wickedness, and not men.

It is no cynical joke, it is literally true, that the Christian churches would not recognize Christianity if they saw it.

It is dangerous to think. The thoughtless knowers will call you a red or a communist or a capitalist or some name that expresses their aversion to any mental activity. But somebody must take a chance. The monkeys did who became men, and the monkeys who didn't are still jumping around in the trees making faces at the monkeys who did.
Lincoln Steffens Speaking.

Gertrude Stein
(1874-1946)
American writer

You are a lost generation.
Quoted by Hemingway.

As a cousin of mine once said about money, money is always there but the pockets change; it is not in the same pockets after a change, and that is all there is to say about money.

John Steinbeck
(1902-1968)
American writer

The King said, "Power does not corrupt. Fear corrupts, perhaps the fear of a loss of power." *The Short Reign of Pippin IV.*

The fields were fruitful, and starving men moved on the roads. The granaries were full and the children of the poor grew up rachitic, and the pustules of pellagra swelled on their side. The great companies did not know that the line between hunger and anger is a thin line.
The Grapes of Wrath.

A red is any son of a bitch who wants thirty cents when we're paying twenty-five.
Ibid.

I'm learnin' one thing good. Learnin' it all a time, ever' day. If you're in trouble, or hurt or need—go to the poor people. They're the only ones that'll help—the only ones. *Ibid*

It is wonderful that even today, with all competition of records, of radio, of television, of motion pictures, the book has kept its precious character.

A book is somehow sacred. A dictator can kill and maim people, can sink to any kind of tyranny and only be hated, but when books are burned the ultimate in tyranny has happened. This we cannot forgive. . . .

People . . . automatically believe in books. This is strange but it is so. Messages come from behind the controlled and censored areas of the world and they do not ask for radios, for papers and pamphlets. They invariably ask for books. They believe books when they believe nothing else.

Charles P(roteus) Steinmetz
(1865-1923)
American inventor, engineer

No human being should engage in an unsocial act. I believe that laws of behavior can be so arranged that man can develop to the utmost, and yet under such conditions as shall make an unsocial act highly improbable. At present, we seem unable to develop except at the expense of others.

I am a firm believer in socialism and I know that the quicker you have monopoly in this country the quicker we will have socialism.
Congressional Record, January 27, 1949.

In the realm of science, all attempts to find any evidence of supernatural beings, of metaphysical conceptions, as God, immortality, infinity, etc., thus have failed, and

if we are honest, we must confess that in science there exists no God, no immortality, no soul or mind as distinct from the body.
American Freeman, July, 1941.

Wilhelm Stekel
(1868-1940)
Austrian psychoanalyst, writer

The mark of the immature man is that he wants to die nobly for a cause, while the mark of a mature man is that he wants to live humbly for one.
Quoted in "Ladies' Home Journal."

Truth is not always the best basis for happiness . . . There are people who perish when their eyes are opened.
Autobiography, 1950, p. 260.

Fervid atheism is usually a screen for repressed religion. *Ibid.*

Stephanus V
(9th Century)
Pope

The popes, like Jesus, are conceived by their mothers through the overshadowing of the Holy Ghost. All popes are a certain species of man-gods, for the purpose of being the better able to conduct the functions of mediator between God and mankind. All powers in Heaven, as well as on earth, are given to them.

Alexander H. Stephens
(1812-1883)
American statesman, Vice-President of the Confederacy

With Lincoln the Union rose to the sublimity of religious mysticism.

Our new government's foundations are laid, its cornerstone rests, upon the great truth that the Negro is not equal to the white man, that slavery—subordination to the superior race—is his natural and normal condition.

Speech, Savannah, March 21, 1861.

John Sterling
(1806-1844)
English poet, author

There is no lie that many men will not believe; there is no man who does not believe many lies; and there is no man who believes only lies. *Essays and Tales.*

Yates Sterling
(1873-1942)
American rear admiral

. . . War, you have become the foundation of all human virtues. . . .

Nations have found cohesion in war and dispersion in peace;
Wisdom in war and deception in peace.
Training in war and betrayal in peace.

Nations have been born in war and expire in peace.

You teach men how to die, while peace shows them only how to live.
You cleanse the world; Peace litters it with corruption.

Read before the New Netherlands Chapter, Daughters of the American Revolution, New York.

Laurence Sterne
(1713-1768)
English writer

Of all the cants which are canted in this canting world, though the cant of hypo-crites may be the worst, the cant of criticism is the most tormenting.

Tristram Shandy.

The Republic of letters. *Ibid.*

Thaddeus Stevens
(1792-1868)
American statesman

I have done what I deemed best for humanity. It is easy to protect the interests of the rich and powerful. But it is a great labor to protect the interests of the poor and downtrodden. It is the eternal labor of Sisyphus forever to be renewed.

If there be anything for which I have entire indifference, perhaps I might say contempt, it is the public opinion which is founded on popular clamor.

Adlai E. Stevenson
(1900-1965)
Ex-governor of Illinois; American lawyer, politician

(I am) considerably concerned when I see the extent to which we are developing a one-party press in a two-party country. *Campaign Speech, Portland, Oregon, 1952.*

Let's talk sense to the American people. Let's tell them the truth. . . . Better we lose the election than mislead the people. *Accepting nomination, July, 1952.*

Communism is the death of the soul. It is the organization of total conformity—in short, of tyranny—and it is committed to making tyranny universal. *Ibid.*

Because we have always thought of government as friendly, not as brutal, character assassins and slanderers in the Congress of the United States have a free hand in the methods they use. We never foresaw that the cult of thought control and of the Big Lie would come to America. So if their conscience permits, they can say almost anything . . .   *Ibid.*

I venture to suggest that patriotism is not a short and frenzied outburst of emotion but the tranquil and steady dedication of a lifetime.
Address, American Legion Convention, August, 1952.

A hungry man is not a free man.
Campaign speech, September 6, 1952.

The time to stop a revolution is at the beginning, not the end.
Ibid., September 11.

It is a common heresy and its graves are to be found all over the earth. It is the heresy that says you can kill an idea by killing a man, defeat a principle by defeating a person, bury truth by burying its vehicle.
Man may burn his brother at the stake, but he cannot reduce truth to ashes; he may murder his fellow man with a shot in the back, but he does not murder justice; he may slay armies of men, but as it is written, "truth beareth off the victory."
At dedication of Lovejoy memorial tablet, November 9, 1952.

Some in America today would limit our freedom of expression and of conscience. In the name of unity, they would impose a narrow conformity of ideas and opinion . . .
Only a government which fights for civil liberties and equal rights for its own people can stand for freedom in the rest of the world.
Speech, Jefferson-Jackson Day, February 14, 1953.

All progress has resulted from people who took unpopular positions.
Speech, Princeton, March 22, 1954.

If there is anything that the whole idea of liberalism contradicts, it is the notion of competitive indoctrination. I believe that if we really want human brotherhood to spread and increase until it makes life safe and sane, we must also be certain that there is no one true faith or path by which it may spread.
But it is not easy to banish the notion that there can be universal brotherhood just as soon as everybody gives up his faith and accepts ours. That day may never come, for the richness of human diversity cannot be abolished any more than Mars or Jupiter. Difference is the nature of life, it is part of our moral Universe. Without difference, life would become lifeless. So I reject the idea of conformity, compulsory or complacent, the faith that is swallowed like pills, whole and at once, with no questions asked.
This I Believe, edited by E. R. Murrow.

After lots of people who go into politics have been in it for a while they find that to stay in politics they have to make all sorts of compromises to satisfy their supporters and that it becomes awfully important for them to keep their jobs because they have nowhere else to go.
Mike Wallace Interview, Fund for the Republic, 1958.

We simply have to develop better methods of communication with the people because we know that there is no better system of ultimate reliance on the discriminating choice of the people. But they have to be informed. The first responsibility is information, is truth.   *Ibid.*

We have to serve the truth as candidates for public office and not mislead, misguide, misdirect the people merely to provoke emotional responses and win votes that way.   *Ibid.*

Robert Louis Stevenson
(1850-1894)
Scottish essayist, novelist, poet

To tell the truth, rightly understood, is not to state the true facts, but to convey a true impression; truth in spirit, not truth to the letter, is the true veracity.
Virginibus Puerisque.

The cruelest lies are often told in silence.
Ibid.

The price we have to pay for money is paid in liberty.
Familiar Studies of Men and Books.

Joseph W. Stilwell
(1883-1946)
American general

Don't let the bastards grind you down.[*]

Max Stirner (né Johann Kaspar Schmidt)
(1806-1856)
German writer

Freedom cannot be granted. It must be taken.
Der Einzige und sein Eigentum—The Ego and His Own.

Individually free is he who is responsible to no *man*.   *Ibid.*

The great are great only because we are on our knees. Let us rise!   *Ibid.*

_____
[*] His own translation of *Illegitimati non carborundum.*

The men of future generations will yet win many a liberty of which we do not even feel the want.   *Ibid.*

A race of altruists is necessarily a race of slaves. A race of free men is necessarily a race of egoists.   *Ibid.*

The State seeks to hinder every free activity by its censorship, its supervision, its police, and holds this hindering to be its duty, because it is in truth a duty of self-preservation. The State wants to make something out of man, therefore there live in it only made men; everyone who wants to be his own self is its opponent.   *Ibid.*

If the Church had deadly sins, the State has capital crimes; if the one had heretics, the other has traitors; the one ecclesiastical penalties, the other criminal penalties; the one inquisitorial processes, the other fiscal; in short, there sins, here crimes, there sinners, here criminals, there inquisition and here—inquisition.   *Ibid.*

A fig for good and evil! I am I, and I am neither good nor evil. Neither has any meaning for me.   *Ibid.*

The godly is the affair of God, and the human that of humanity. My concern is neither the Godly nor the Human, is not the True, the Good, the Right, the Free, etc., but simply my own self, and it is not general, it is individual, as I myself am individual. For me there is nothing above myself.   *Ibid.*

Property exists by force of the law. It is not a fact, but a legal fiction.   *Ibid.*

The state calls its own violence law, but that of the individual crime.   *Ibid.*

The state always has the sole purpose to limit, tame, subordinate, the individual—to make him subject to some generality of order.   *Ibid.*

The object of the State is always the same: to limit the individual, to tame him, to subordinate him, to subjugate him.
Ibid., another translation.

Joseph Story
(1779-1845)
U.S. Supreme Court justice

Here shall the Press the People's right maintain,
Unaw'd by influence and unbrib'd by gain;
Here patriot Truth her glorious precepts draw,
Pledg'd to Religion, Liberty, and Law.
Motto of the Salem Register, 1802.

The poor man may possess as much patriotism as the rich; but it is unjust to suppose that he necessarily possesses more.
Journal of Debates and Proceedings in the Convention Chosen to Revise the Constitution of Massachusetts, 1820.

Patriotism and poverty do not necessarily march hand in hand; nor is wealth that monster which some imaginations have depicted, with a heart of adamant, and a sceptre of iron. *Ibid.*

Government indeed stands upon a combination of interests and circumstances. *Ibid.*

It is a mistaken theory, that government is founded for one object only. It is organized for the protection of life, liberty and property, and all the comforts of society. *Ibid.*

Harriet Beecher Stowe
(1811-1896)
American novelist, humanitarian

Private opinion is weak, but public opinion is almost omnipotent.

The Negro is an exotic of the most gorgeous and superb countries of the world, and he has deep in his heart a passion for all that is splendid, rich and fanciful.

John Strachey
(1901-1963)
English writer, politician

Fascism denies every one of the assumptions upon which the progressive movement is based. Fascism proclaims, as it will be easy to establish both from Fascist words and Fascist deeds, that the whole great hope, by the light of which the peoples of the West have lived for a century, is a delusion; that democracy is a decaying corpse; international peace a coward's dream; equality of opportunity a chimera; the conquest of poverty a futile dream.
The Menace of Fascism.

Above all, Fascism proclaims the necessity and the excellence of war. War, and preparation of war are to be one of the most sacred duties of human life. Men must find death and mutilation the true purpose of their lives, and women must rejoice to exhaust themselves in childbirth that every new generation of men may take their places upon the battlefield. *Ibid.*

The besetting sin of democrats has been complacency.
Contemporary Capitalism, N. Y., 1956.

Our danger is that the virtual monopolization of the media of mass expression by big capital will distort and finally abort the democratic process. *Ibid., p. 321.*

The drop in the number and increase in the size of firms have reached a point at which it has produced a new and easily recognized industrial pattern . . . The pattern is usually referred to as "oligopoly," or few sellers, by the economists.*

> *Ibid., p. 19.*

The purpose of Fascism is to defend by violence the private ownership of the means of production, even though our modern civilization has become incompatible with a social system based upon private ownership.

Gustav Stresemann
(1878-1929)
*German chancellor, winner
Nobel Prize, 1926*

Sometimes you think you hear the voice of Almighty God, and it is only that of a Privy Councillor.**

> *To the present editor, 1925.*

Luigi Sturzo
(1871-1959)
Italian priest, founder Popular Party

Democracy has two fundamental elements. They are: freedom, as opposed to despotism, and a society in which there are no special classes, castes or interests. Freedom must be total or else it is not freedom.

> *Time, March 8, 1954.*

Peter Stuyvesant
(1592-1672)
Governor of New Netherlands

To give liberty to the Jews will be very

---

* Oligopoly, according to Strachey, traces back to More's *Utopia*. More wrote of few sellers: "If we cannot call them a monopoly they are certainly an oligopoly."
** "It is the folly of too many to mistake the echo of a London coffeehouse for the voice of the kingdom." Swift.

detrimental . . . Giving them liberty, we cannot refuse the Lutherans and Papists.

> *New York Times Magazine.*

Arthur Hays Sulzberger
(1891-1968)
President, publisher, New York Times

Along with responsible newspapers we must have responsible *readers*. No matter how conscientiously the publisher and his associates perform their work, they can do only half the job. Readers must do the rest. The fountain serves no useful purpose if the horse refuses to drink.

> *Address, Southern Newspaper Publishers' Association, October 4, 1955.*

Perhaps we ought to ask ourselves just what freedom of the press really is. Whose freedom is it? Does it merely guarantee the right of the publisher to do and say whatever he wishes, limited only by the laws of libel and decency? Is it only a special license to those who manage the units of the press? The answer, of course, is no. Freedom of the press—or, to be more precise, the *benefit* of freedom of the press belongs to everyone—to the citizen as well as the publisher. The publisher is not granted the privilege of independence simply to provide him with a more favored position in the community than is accorded to other citizens. He enjoys an explicitly defined independence because it is the only condition under which he can fulfill his role, which is to inform fully, fairly and comprehensively. The crux is *not* the publisher's "freedom to print"; it is rather, the citizens' "right to know." *Address, August 28, 1956.*

Charles Sumner
(1811-1874)
American statesman

Judges are but men, and in all ages have shown a fair share of frailty. Alas! Alas! The worst crimes of history have been perpetrated under their sanction, the blood of martyrs and patriots, crying from the ground, summons them to judgment.

Address, Massachusetts Republican Convention, September 7, 1854.

Where Slavery is there Liberty cannot be; and where Liberty is there Slavery cannot be.
Speech, Slavery and the Rebellion.

The true grandeur of nations is in those qualities which constitute the true greatness of the individual.

The true grandeur of humanity is in moral elevation, sustained, enlightened and decorated by the intellect of man.

From the beginning of our history the country has been afflicted with compromise. It is by compromise that human rights have been abandoned.

War crushes, with bloody heel, all justice, all happiness, all that is God-like in man. *Speech, Boston, July 4, 1845.*

Nothing from man's hands, no law, nor constitution, can be final. Truth alone is final. *Senate, August 26, 1852.*

William Graham Sumner
(1840-1910)

American economist, sociologist

If you want war, nourish a doctrine. Doctrines are the most frightful tyrants to which men ever are subject, because doctrines get inside of a man's reason and betray himself against himself. Civilized men have done their fiercest fighting for doctrines.
War, 1903.

The four great motives which move men to social activity are hunger, love, vanity, and fear of superior powers. *Ibid.*

When the earth is underpopulated and there is an economic demand for men, democracy is inevitable. That state of things cannot be permanent. Therefore democracy cannot last. It contains no absolute and "eternal" truth. *1906.*

Industry, self-denial, and temperance are the laws of prosperity for men and states; without them advance in the arts and in wealth means only corruption and decay through luxury and vice. With them progress in the arts and increasing wealth are the prime conditions of an advancing civilization which is sound enough to endure.
The Challenge of Facts and Other Essays, 1914.

Wealth comes only from production, and all that the wrangling grabbers, loafers and jobbers get to deal with comes from somebody's toil and sacrifice. Who, then, is he who provides it all? The Forgotten Man . . . delving away in patient industry, supporting his family, paying his taxes, casting his vote, supporting the church and the school . . .
Speech, The Forgotten Man, 1883.

William A. (Billy) Sunday
(1862-1935)

American evangelist

I have studied the Bible from Genesis to Revelation, I have read everything that Bob Ingersoll ever spouted from one end of the land to the other, and I have read it carefully. And if Bob Ingersoll isn't in hell, God is a liar and the Bible isn't worth the paper it is printed on.
Courier, Jacksonville, Illinois, October 27, 1908.

[667]

I don't believe your old bastard theory of evolution either; I believe it's pure jackass nonsense.°

When the consensus of scholarship says one thing and the Word of God another, the consensus of scholarship can go plumb to hell for all I care.

I say, with Waite of Colorado, that the rivers of America will run with blood filled to their banks before we will submit to them taking the Bible out of our schools.

If a minister believes and teaches evolution, he is a skunk, a hypocrite and a liar.

Sun Tzu Wu
(fl. 500 B.C.)
Army commander of King of Wu

Therefore, in your deliberations, when seeking to determine the military conditions, let them be made the basis of a comparison, in this wise:—
(1) Which of the two sovereigns is imbued with the Moral law? (2) Which of the two generals has most ability? (3) With whom lie the advantages derived from Heaven and Earth? (4) On which side is discipline most rigorously endorced? (5) Which army is the stronger? (6) On which side are officers and men more highly trained? (7) In which army is there the greater constancy both in reward and punishment?
By means of these seven considerations I can forecast victory or defeat.

Art of War, translated by Lionel Giles, Luzac & Co., London, 1910. pp. 3-4.

° This, and the following, are quotations from various revival meetings, several reported by the present editor in 1912.

All warfare is based on deception.
Ibid., p. 6.

There is no instance of a country having benefited from prolonged warfare.
Ibid., p. 12.

Hence to fight and conquer in all our battles is not supreme excellence; supreme excellence consists in breaking the enemy's resistance without fighting. *Ibid., p. 17.*

Thus we may know that there are five essentials for victory: (1) He will win who knows when to fight and when not to fight. (2) He will win who knows how to handle both superior and inferior forces. (3) He will win whose army is animated by the same spirit throughout all the ranks. (4) He will win who, prepared himself, waits to take the enemy unprepared. (5) He will win who has military capacity and is not interfered with by his sovereign. Victory lies in the knowledge of these five points.
Ibid., pp. 23-4.

Rapidity is the essence of war.
Ibid., p. 122.

Prohibit the taking of omens, and do away with superstitious doubts. Then, until death itself comes, no calamity need be feared.
Ibid., p. 126.

Place your army in deadly peril, and it will survive; plunge it into desperate straits, and it will come off in safety.
Ibid., p. 143.

Sun Yat-sen
(1866-1925)
Founder of the Kuomintang

To understand is hard. Once one understands, action is easy.

George Sutherland
(1862-1942)
U.S. Supreme Court justice

The liberty of the individual to do as he pleases, even in innocent matters, is not absolute. It must frequently yield to the common good.
Adkins v. Children's Hospital, 261 U.S. 525 (1925).

It is impossible to concede that by the words "freedom of the press" the framers of the amendment intended to adopt merely the narrow view then reflected by the law of England that such freedom consisted only in immunity from previous censorship; for this abuse had then permanently disappeared from English practice. It is equally important to believe that it was not intended to bring within the reach of these words such modes of restraint as were embodied in the two forms of taxation already described . . .
The tax here involved is bad . . . because, in the light of history and of its present setting, it is seen to be a deliberate and calculated device in the guise of a tax to limit the circulation of information to which the public is entitled in virtue of the constitutional guarantees.
Grosjean v. American Press Co., 297 U.S. 233 (1936).

And since informed public opinion is the most potent of all restraints upon mis-government, the suppression or abridgement of publicity afforded by a free press cannot be regarded otherwise than with grave concern.   *Ibid.*

A free press stands as one of the great interpreters between men and government and the people. To allow it to be fettered is to fetter ourselves.   *Ibid.*

Emanuel Swedenborg
(1688-1772)
Swedish theologian, scientist

Conscience is God's presence in man.
Arcana Coelesta.

Since angels are men, and live together in society like men on earth, therefore they have garments, houses and other things familiar to those which exist on earth, but, of course infinitely more beautiful and perfect.

The garments of the angels correspond to their intelligence. The garments of some glitter as with flame, and those of others are resplendent as with light: others are of various colors, and some white and opaque.

The angels of the inmost heaven are naked, because they are in innocence and nakedness corresponds to innocence. It is because garments represent states of wisdom that they are so much spoken of in the Word, in relation to the Church and good men.

To be able to discern that what is true is true, and that what is false is false; this is the mark and character of intelligence.

Jonathan Swift
(1667-1745)
English satirist

When a true genius appears in this world you may know him by the sign that the dunces are all in confederacy against him.
Thoughts on Various Subjects.

We have enough religion to make us hate, but not enough to make us love one another.
Ibid.

Politics, as the word is commonly understood, are nothing but corruptions. *Ibid.*

Arbitrary power is the natural object of temptation to a prince, as wine and women to a young fellow, or a bribe to a judge, or avarice to old age, or vanity to a woman.
Ibid.

The love and torrent of power prevailed.
The Drapier's Letters, v, 1723.

For in reason, all government without the consent of the governed is the very definition of slavery.   *Ibid.*

But in fact, eleven men well armed will certainly subdue one single man in his shirt.
Ibid.

It will sometimes happen, I know not how in the course of human affairs, that a man shall be made liable to legal animadversions, where he has nothing to answer for, either to God or his country; and condemned at Westminster-hall for what he will never be charged with at the Day of Judgment.
Ibid., VI.

It is a maxim among lawyers, that whatever hath been done before may legally be done again: and therefore they take special care to record all the decisions formerly made against common justice and the general reason of mankind. These, under the name of precedents, they produce as authorities, to justify the most iniquitous opinions; and the judges never fail of directing accordingly.   *Gulliver's Travels.*

It is likewise to be observed that this society (of lawyers) hath a peculiar chant and jargon of their own, that no other mortal can understand, and wherein all their laws are written, which they take special care to multiply; whereby they have wholly confounded the very essence of truth and falsehood.   *Ibid.*

The first I shall mention relateth to informers. All crimes against the state are punished here with the utmost severity; but if the person accused make his innocence plainly to appear upon his trial, the accuser is immediately put to an ignominious death; and out of his goods or lands the innocent person is quadruply recompensed for the loss of his time, for the danger he underwent, for the hardship of his imprisonment, and for all the charges he hath been at in making his defence.
Ibid., A Journey to Lilliput.

Poor nations are hungry, and rich nations are proud; and pride and hunger will ever be at variance. For these reasons, the trade of a soldier is held the most honourable of all others; because a soldier is a *Yahoo* hired to kill in cold blood as many of his own species, who have never offended him, as possibly he can.
Ibid., IV, A Voyage to the Houyhnhnms, Ch. IV, 1726.

Liberty of conscience is nowadays not only understood to be the liberty of believing what men please, but also of endeavoring to propagate that belief as much as they can.
Sermon on the Testimony of Conscience, c. 1715.

Tell truth, and shame the devil.
Mary the Cookmaid's Letter.

I have ever hated all nations, professions and communities, and all my love is towards individuals . . . But principally I hate and detest that animal called man; although I heartily love John, Peter, Thomas, and so forth.
Letter to Pope, September 29, 1725.

There is no more inward value in the greatest emperor than in the meanest of his subjects. His body is composed of the same substance, the same parts, and with the same, or greater, infirmities. His education is generally worse, by flattery, and idleness, and luxury, and those evil dispositions that early power is apt to give. It is therefore against common sense, that his private personal interest, or pleasure, should be put in the balance with the safety of millions, every one of which is his equal by nature, equal in the sight of God, equally capable of salvation; and it is for their sakes, not his own, that he is entrusted with the government over them.

Sermon, The Martyrdom of King Charles I, 1725.

Algernon Charles Swinburne

(1837-1909)

English poet

O sorrowing hearts of slaves,
  We hear you beat from far!
We bring the light that saves,
  We bring the morning star;
Freedom's good things we bring you, whence
  all good things are.

             A Marching Song.

Rise, ere the dawn be risen;
  Come, and be all souls fed;
From field and street and prison
  Come, for the feast is spread;
Live, for the truth is living; wake, for night
  is dead.   *Ibid.*

The tree of faith ingraft by priests
  Puts its foul foliage out above thee,
And round it feed man-eating beasts
  Because of whom we dare not love thee;
Though hearts reach back and memories
  ache,
We cannot praise thee for their sake.

            Before a Crucifix.

Not with dreams, but with blood and with
  iron
Shall a nation be moulded to last.
         A Word for the Country.

We have done with the kisses that sting,
The thief's mouth red from the feast,
The blood on the hands of the King,
And the lie on the lips of the priest.

John Swinton

(1830-1901)

American editor

There is no such thing in America as an independent press, unless it is in the country towns. You know it and I know it.

There is not one of you who dare to write his honest opinions, and if you did you know beforehand they would never appear in print.

I am paid $150 a week for keeping my honest opinions out of the paper I am connected with. Others of you are paid similar salaries for doing similar things. If I should permit honest opinions to be printed in one issue of my paper, like Othello, before twenty-four hours, my occupation would be gone.

Five-minute Talk, "Journalists' Gathering," Twilight Club, N.Y.C., April 12, 1883.

The business of the New York journalist is to destroy the truth, to lie outright, to pervert, to vilify, to fawn at the feet of Mammon, and to sell his race and his country for his daily bread.   *Ibid.*

You know this and I know it, and what folly is this to be toasting an "independent press". We are the tools and vassals of rich men behind the scenes. We are the jumping-jacks; they pull the strings and we dance. Our talents, our possibilities and our lives are all the property of other men. We are intellectual prostitutes.   *Ibid.*

Herbert Bayard Swope
(1882-1958)
American editor

Let us not be deceived—today we are in the midst of a cold war.*
Ghost-written speech for B. M. Baruch, Columbia, South Carolina, April 16, 1947.

The First Duty of a newspaper is to be Accurate. If it be Accurate, it follows that it is Fair.
Letter to N. Y. Herald Tribune, March 16, 1958.

Syrus
See Publilius Syrus

Tacitus
(55?-120?)
Roman historian, orator

Ubi solitudinem faciunt, pacem appelant.
(They make a desert and call it peace.)
Agricola, 30.

We are corrupted by prosperity.
History, b. 1.

Lust of power is the most flagrant of all the passions. *Annals.*

A bad peace is even worse than war.
Ibid., iii.

The supremacy of the people tends to liberty. *Ibid.*

When the state is corrupt then the laws are most multiplied.

---

* Swope had used the phrase a year earlier; Walter Lippmann popularized it in his syndicated column.

The lust of fame is the last that a wise man shakes off.

License, which fools call liberty.
De Oratoribus, xl.

William Howard Taft
(1857-1930)
27th President of the United States

Anti-Semitism is a noxious weed that should be cut out. It has no place in America. *Speech, 1920.*

Rabindranath Tagore
(1861-1941)
Indian philosopher, Nobel prize for literature, 1913

Where the mind is without fear and the head
    is held high;
Where knowledge is free; . . .
Where the clear stream of reason has not lost
    its way into the dreary desert sand of
    dead habit; . . .
Into that heaven of freedom, my Father, let
    my country awake. *Prayer; Gitanjali.*

Man has been able to make his pursuit of power easier today by his art of mitigating the obstructive forces that come from the higher regions of his humanity. With his cult of power and his idolatry of money he has, in a great measure, reverted to his primitive barbarism, a barbarism whose path is lit up by the lurid light of intellect.
Gollancz, From Darkness to Light.

He only has freedom who ideally loves freedom himself and is glad to extend it to others. He who cares to have slaves must chain himself to them. He who builds walls to create exclusion for others builds walls across his own freedom. He who distrusts freedom in others loses his moral right to it. Sooner or later he is lured into the meshes of physical and moral servility.   *Ibid.*

S. G. Tallentyre (née Evelyn Beatrice Hall)
(b. 1868)
English writer

I disapprove of what you say, but I will defend to the death your right to say it.*
The Friends of Voltaire, London, 1906, p. 199.

Charles Maurice de Talleyrand-Périgord
(1754-1838)
French political leader

C'est pire qu'une crime, c'est un bêtise. (It is worse than a crime, it is a blunder.)
A reference to Napoleon's murder of the Duke of Enghien.

Ils n'ont rien appris, ni rien oublié. (They have learned nothing and forgotten nothing.)
A reference to the Bourbons, attributed by Chevalier de Parat, 1796.

War is much too serious a thing to be left to military men.
Quoted by Briand to Lloyd George; also spoken by Clemenceau as his own.

An important art of politicians is to find new names for institutions which under old names have become odious to the public.

---

* In a letter dated July 20, 1935, Miss Hall wrote: "I believe I did use the phrase as a description of Voltaire's attitude . . . I did not intend to imply that Voltaire used these words verbatim." *Editor & Publisher,* August 25, 1956.

Since the masses are always eager to believe *something,* for their benefit nothing is so easy to *arrange* as facts.

The Talmud

Who can protest and does not, is an accomplice in the act.   *Sabbath, 54 b.*

Power buries those who wield it.
Yoma, 86 b.

Ambition destroys its possessor.   *Ibid.*

We presume none sins unless he stands to profit by it   *Baba Metzia, 5 b.*

The fire of Gehenna is sixty times as hot as the fire of earth.   *Berachoth.*

H. H. Tammen
(1892-1924)
American editor, publisher

Rats! We are out after the stuff.
Answer to a question on commercialism vs. idealism in journalism.

A dog fight on Champa Street is more important than a war in Europe.
Life, March, 1954.

Roger B. Taney
(1777-1864)
U.S. Supreme Court justice

The question is simply this: Can a Negro, whose ancestors were imported into this country, and sold as slaves, become a member of the political community formed and brought into existence by the Constitution of the United States, and as such become entitled to all the rights, and privileges, and immunities, guaranteed by that instrument?

One of which rights is the privilege of suing in a court of the United States in cases specified by the Constitution.

Dred Scott v. Sanford, 1857.°

The question before us is, whether the class of persons described in the plea in abatement compose a portion of this people, and are constituent members of this sovereignty. We think they are not. *Ibid.*

They were at that time considered as a subordinate and inferior class of beings . . . they had no rights which the white man was bound to respect. *Ibid.*

He was bought and sold and treated as an ordinary article of merchandise whenever a profit could be made by it. This opinion was at that time fixed and universal in the civilized portion of the white race.

Ibid.

Congress has no power to abolish or prevent slavery in any of its territories.

Ibid.

The right of property in a slave is distinctly and expressly affirmed in the Constitution. The right to traffic in it, like an ordinary article of merchandise and property, was guaranteed to the citizens of the United States, in every State that might desire it, for twenty years. . . . *Ibid.*

No word can be found in the Constitution which gives Congress a greater power over slave property, or which entitles property of that kind to less protection than property of any other description. The only power conferred is the power coupled with the duty of guarding and protecting the owner in his rights. *Ibid.*

° "Probably the most unworthy, ill-advised opinion in its long history"–Justice Douglas on the Dred Scott decision.

Upon these considerations, it is the opinion of the Court that the Act of Congress which prohibited a citizen from holding and owning property of this kind in the territory of the United States north of the line therein mentioned, is not warranted by the Constitution, and is therefore void; and that neither Dred Scott himself, nor any of his family, were made free by being carried into this territory; even if they had been carried there by the owner, with the intention of becoming a permanent resident.

Ibid.

Allen Tate

(1899-1979)

American poet

The purpose of education is not happiness; it is not social integration, or political system. Its purpose is at once the discipline of the mind for its own sake; these ends are to be achieved through the mastery of fundamental subjects which cluster around language and number, the two chief instruments by which man knows himself and understands his relation to the world.

To entering class, University of Minnesota, 1958.

Richard H. Tawney

(1880-1962)

English educator, economist

In every human soul there is a socialist and an individualist, an authoritarian and a fanatic for liberty, as in each there is a Catholic and a Protestant. The same is true of the mass movements in which men marshal themselves for common action.

Religion and the Rise of Capitalism, 1926, ch. 4.

There was in Puritanism an element which was revolutionary; a collectivism which grasped at an iron discipline, and an individualism which spurned the savorless mess of human ordinances; a sober prudence which would garner the fruits of this world, and a divine recklessness which would make all things new. *Ibid.*

Practically, the Church was an immense vested interest, implicated to the hilt in the economic fabric, especially on the side of agriculture and land tenure. Itself the greatest of landowners, it could no more quarrel with the feudal structure than the Ecclesiastical Commission, the largest of mineral owners today, can lead a crusade against royalties. *Ibid.*

It is probable that democracy owes more to Nonconformity than to any other single movement. *Ibid.*

All revolutions are declared to be natural and inevitable, once they are successful, and capitalism, as the type of economic system prevailing in Western Europe and America, is clothed today with the unquestioned respectability of the triumphant fact. But in youth it was a pretender, and it was only after centuries of struggle that its title was established. For it involved a code of economic conduct and a system of human relations which were sharply at variance with venerable conventions, with the accepted scheme of social ethics, and with the law, both of the Church and of most European states. *Ibid.*

What is significant, in short, is not the strength of the motive of economic self-interest, which is the commonplace of all ages and demands no explanation. It is the change of moral standards which converted a natural frailty into an ornament of the spirit, and canonized as the economic virtues habits which in earlier ages had been denounced as vices. The force which produced it was the creed associated with the name of Calvin. Capitalism was the social counterpart of Calvinist theology. *Ibid.*

The foundation of democracy is the sense of spiritual independence which nerves the individual to stand alone against the powers of the world. *Ibid.*

Societies, like individuals, have their moral crises and their spiritual revolutions.
Ibid., ch. 5.

Mankind may wring her secrets from nature; and use their knowledge to destroy themselves. *Ibid.*

Both the existing economic order, and too many of the projects advanced for reconstructing it, break down through their neglect of the truism that, since even quite common men have souls, no increase in material wealth will compensate them for arrangements which insult their self-respect and impair their freedom. A reasonable estimate of economic organization must allow for the fact that, unless industry is to be paralyzed by recurrent revolts on the part of outraged human nature, it must satisfy criteria which are not purely economic. *Ibid.*

The distinctions made by the philosophers of classical antiquity between liberal and servile occupations, the medieval insistence that riches exist for man, not man for riches, Ruskin's famous outburst, "there is no wealth but life," the argument of the Socialist who urges that production should be organized for service, not for profit, are but different attempts to emphasize the instrumental character of economic activities by reference to an ideal which is held to express the true nature of man. *Ibid.*

"Modern capitalism," wrote Mr. Keynes, "is absolutely irreligious, without internal union, without much public spirit, often, though not always, a mere congeries of possessors and pursuers." It is that whole system of appetites and values, with its deification of the life of snatching to hoard, and hoarding to snatch, which now, in the hour of its triumph, while the plaudits of the crowd still ring in the ears of the gladiators and the laurels are still unfaded on their brows, seems sometimes to leave a taste as of ashes on the lips of a civilization which has brought to the conquest of its material environment resources unknown in earlier ages, but which has not yet learned to master itself. *Ibid.*

The certainties of one age are the problems of the next. *Ibid.*

Capitalism, in the sense of great individual undertakings, involving the control of large financial resources, and yielding riches to their masters as a result of speculation, money-lending, commercial enterprise, buccaneering, and war, is as old as history. Capitalism, as an economic system, resting on the organization of legally free wage-earners, for the purpose of pecuniary profit, by the owners of capital or his agents, and setting its stamp on every aspect of society, is a modern phenomenon.

Baptized in the bracing, if icy, waters of Calvinist theology, the life of business, once regarded as perilous to the soul— *summa periculosa est emptionis et venditionis negotiatio*—acquires a new sanctity. Labor is not merely an economic means: it is a spiritual end. Covetousness, if a danger to the soul, is a less formidable menace than sloth. So far from poverty being meritorious, it is a duty to choose the more profitable occupation. So far from there being an inevitable conflict between money-making and piety, they are natural allies, for the virtues incumbent on the elect—diligence, thrift, sobriety, prudence—are the most re-

liable passport to commercial prosperity. Thus the pursuit of riches, which once had been feared as the enemy of religion, was now welcomed as its ally. *Ibid.*

The Prince of Darkness has a right to a courteous hearing and a fair trial, and those who will not give him his due are wont to find that, in the long run, he turns the tables by taking his due and something over. *Ibid.*

The rise of a naturalistic science of society, with all its magnificent promise of fruitful action and of intellectual light; the abdication of the Christian Churches from departments of economic conduct and social theory long claimed as their province; the general acceptance by thinkers of a scale of ethical values, which turned their desire for pecuniary gain from a perilous, if natural, frailty into the idol of philosophers and the mainspring of society—such movements are written large over the history of the tempestuous age which lies between the Reformation and the full light of the eighteenth century. *Ibid.*

Revolutions, as a long and bitter experience reveals, are apt to take their color from the regime they overthrow.
The Acquisitive Society, Harcourt, Brace & Co., Harvest Books, 1920, p. 28.

Wealth in modern societies is distributed according to opportunity; and while opportunity depends partly upon talent and energy, it depends still more upon birth, social position, access to education and inherited wealth; in a word, upon property. *Ibid., pp. 33-34.*

The true cause of industrial warfare is as simple as the true cause of international warfare. It is that if men recognize no law superior to their desires, then they must fight when their desires collide.

Ibid., p. 42.

Men may use what mechanical instruments they please and be none the worse for their use. What kills their souls is when they allow their instruments to use *them.*

Ibid., p. 45.

Nationalism is in fact, the counterpart among nations of what individualism is within them . . . So the perversion of nationalism is imperialism, as the perversion of individualism is industrialism.

Ibid., pp. 48-49.

The journalist who says that "private property is the foundation of civilization" agrees with Proudhon, who said it was theft, in this respect at least that, without further definition, the words of both are meaningless. *Ibid., p. 54.*

Property is not theft, but a good deal of theft becomes property. *Ibid., p. 70.*

Functionless property is the greatest enemy of legitimate property itself.

Ibid., p. 81.

A society is rich when material goods, including capital, are cheap, and human beings dear: indeed the word "riches" has no other meaning. The interests of those who own the property used in industry . . . is that their capital should be dear and human beings cheap. *Ibid., p. 98.*

When men have gone so far as to talk as though their idols have come to life, it is time that some one broke them. Labor consists of persons, capital of things. The only use of things is to be applied to the service of persons. *Ibid., p. 99.*

For slavery will work—as long as the slaves will let it; and freedom will work when men have learned to be free; but what will not work is a combination of the two. *Ibid., p. 144.*

For ultimately, if by slow degrees, power follows the ability to wield it; authority goes with function. *Ibid., p. 160.*

Jeremy Taylor
(1613-1667)
English divine, author

Whoever persecutes a disagreeing person, armes all the world against himselfe, and all pious people of his owne perswasion, when the scales of authority return to his adversary, and attest his contradictory; and then, what can he urge for mercy for himselfe, or his party that sheweth none to other?

The Liberty of Prophesying, XIII, "Of the deportment to be used towards persons disagreeing. . . ."

And it is not only lawfull to tollerate disagreeing perswasions, but the authority of God onely is competent to take notice of it, and infallible to determine it, and fit to judge, and therefore no humane authority is sufficient to doe all those things which can justifie the inflicting temporall punishments upon such as doe not conforme in their perswasions to a rule or authority which is not only fallible, but supposed by the disagreeing person to be actually deceived.

Ibid., XVI, "Whether it be lawful for a Prince to give toleration to severall Religions."

See all things in one. *Via Pacis.*

Ignorance is the mother of devotion.
To a Person Newly Converted to the Church of England, 1657.

A great fear, when it is ill-managed, is the parent of superstition; but a discreet and well-guided fear produces religion.

The Rule and Exercises of Holy Living, 1654.

Henry John Temple

See Palmerston

Alfred, Lord Tennyson

(1809-1892)

English poet

It is the land that freemen till,
  That sober-suited Freedom chose,
  The land, where girt with friends or foes
A man may speak the thing he will.
                              To J. S., 1833.

A land of settled government,
  A land of just and old renown,
  Where Freedom slowly broadens down
From precedent to precedent.   *Ibid.*

Her open eyes desire the truth.
  The wisdom of a thousand years
Is in them. May perpetual youth
  Keep dry their light from tears;

That her fair form may stand and shine,
  Make bright our days and light our
    dreams,
Turning the scorn with lips divine
  The falsehood of extremes!   *Ibid.*

Cursed be the social wants that sin against
    the strength of youth!
Cursed be the social ties that warp us from
    the living truth!
Cursed be the sickly forms that err from
    honest nature's rule!
Cursed be the gold that gilds the straighten'd
    forehead of the fool.
                              Locksley Hall.

Men my brothers, men the workers, ever
    reaping something new,
That which they have done but earnest of
    the things that they shall do. *Ibid.*

I myself must mix with action lest I wither
    by despair.   *Ibid.*

Till the war drums throbbed no
    longer and the battle flags were furled
In the Parliament of Man, the Federation
    of the world.   *Ibid.*

Why do they prate of the blessings of peace?
    we have made them a curse, . . .
And lust for gain, in the spirit of Cain, is it
    better or worse
Than the heart of the citizen hissing in
    war . .   *Maud, I.*

The year is going, let him go;
Ring out the false, ring in the true.
        In Memorium, Part CVI, stanza 2.

Ring out the feud of rich and poor.
Ring in redress of all mankind.
                        Ibid., stanza 3.

Ring out a slowly dying cause,
And ancient forms of party strife.
                        Ibid., stanza 4.

Ring out false pride in place and blood,
    The civic slander and the spite;
    Ring in the love of truth and light,
Ring in the common love of good.
                        Ibid., stanza 6.

Ring out old shapes of foul disease;
  Ring out the narrowing lust of gold;
  Ring out the thousand wars of old,
Ring in the thousand years of peace.
                        Ibid., stanza 7.

Ring in the valiant man and free,
The larger heart, the kindlier hand;
Ring out the darkness of the land,
Ring in the Christ that is to be.
Ibid., stanza 8.

That a lie which is half a truth is ever the
blackest of lies;
That a lie which is all a lie may be met and
fought with outright;
But a lie which is part a truth is a harder
matter to fight.
The Grandmothers, stanza 8.

The old order changeth, yielding place to
new;
And God fulfils himself in many ways,
Lest one good custom should corrupt the
world.   *The Passing of Arthur.*

O purblind race of miserable men,
How many among us at this very hour
Do forge a lifelong trouble for ourselves,
By taking true for false, or false for true!
Geraint and Enid.

Terence
(180-159 B.C.)
Latin playwright

*Homo sum, et humani nihil a me alienum
puto.* (I am a man, and nothing pertaining to
man is alien to me.)
Heauton Timorumenos, act 1.

The golden rule is moderation in all things.
Andria.

No man was ever endowed with a judgment so correct and judicious in regulating
his life but that circumstances, time and experience would teach him something new,
and apprise him that of those things with
which he thought himself the best acquainted
he knew nothing; and that those ideas which

in theory appeared the most advantageous,
were found, when brought into practice, to
be altogether inapplicable.
Forbes Magazine.

Tertullian (Quintus Septimus Florens Tertullianus)
(180?-230?)
Church writer

It is a fundamental human right, a privilege of nature, that every man should worship according to his own convictions: one
man's religion neither harms nor helps another man. It . . . is certainly no part of religion to compel religion. *To Scapula, 2.*

So we, who are united in mind and soul,
have no hesitation about sharing property.
All is common among us—except our wives.
Apology, 39.

Christians have no matters and no Christian shall be bound for bread and raiment.
Ibid.

The land is no man's inheritance; none
shall possess it as property.   *Ibid.*

Prevention of birth is a precipitation of
murder.   *Ibid.*

Certum est quia impossibile est. It is certain, because it is impossible. (The probable
origin of the phrase, *"Credo quia impossibile,"* I believe because it is impossible.)
De Carne Christi, v.

Semen est sanguis Christianorum. The
blood of Christians is seed. (Usually quoted
as: "The blood of the martyrs is the seed of
the Church.")   *Ibid., 197.*

---

* Condemned in the syllabus of Pope Pius
IX sixteen centuries later.

Nothing that is God's is obtainable by money. *The Christian Defence.*

Fear is the foundation of safety.
De Cultu Feminarum. Women's Dress, c. 220.

A woman's appearance depends upon two things: the clothes she wears and the time she gives to her toilet . . . Against the first we bring the charge of ostentation, against the second of harlotry. *Ibid.*

The judgment of God upon your sex endures even today; and with it inevitably endures your position of criminal at the bar of justice. *Ibid.*

Do you know that each of you women is an Eve? The sentence of God on this sex of yours lives in this age; the guilt must necessarily live too. You are the gate of Hell, you are the temptress of the forbidden tree; you ᵖre the first deserter of the divine law.
Ibid.

William Makepeace Thackeray
(1811-1863)
English novelist

Ah, ye knights of the pen! May honor be your shield, and truth tip your lances! Be gentle to women. Be tender to children. And as for the Ogre Humbug, out sword, and have at him. *Roundabout Papers.*

People dare not be happy for fear of Snobs. People dare not love for fear of Snobs. People pine away lonely under the tyranny of Snobs. Honest kindly hearts dry up and die. Gallant generous lads, blooming with hearty youth, swell into bloated old bachelorhood, and burst and tumble over. Tender girls wither into shrunken decay, and perish solitary, from whom Snob-bishness has cut off the common claim to happiness and affection with which Nature endowed us all. *The Book of Snobs.*

Of the Corporation of the Goosequill—of the Press, . . . of the fourth estate . . . There she is—the great engine—she never sleeps. She has her ambassadors in every quarter of the world—her courtiers upon every road. Her officers march along with armies, and her envoys walk into statesmen's cabinets. They are ubiquitous.
Pendennis, ch. 30.

Third International

The ultimate aim of the Communist Internationale is to replace world economy by a world system of Communism. Communist Society, the basis for which has been prepared by the whole course of historical development, is mankind's only way out, for it alone can abolish the contradictions of the capitalist system which threaten to degrade and destroy the human race. *Program, 1928.*

Thomas à Kempis
(Thomas Hammerken)
(1380-1471)
German canon and writer

O quam cito transit gloria mundi! (How swiftly passes the glory of the world!)
Of the Imitation of Christ.

Homo proponet sed Deus diponit. (Man proposes, but God disposes.) *Ibid.*

If thou wilt stand firm and grow as thou oughtest, esteem thyself as a pilgrim and stranger upon earth. *Ibid.*

Thou must be contented for Christ's sake to be esteemed as a fool in this world, if thou desire to lead the life of a monk.
Ibid.

Dress and tonsure profit little; but change of heart and perfect mortification of the passions make a true monk.　　*Ibid.*

Norman Thomas

(1884-1968)

American socialist leader

The very existence of armaments and great armies psychologically accustoms us to accept the philosophy of militarism. They inevitably increase fear and hate in the world.

Address, League of Industrial Democracy.

Madariaga has pointed out, nations never prepare for war but for *a* war. It is the business of the general staffs to have particular enemies in mind . . . To get their citizens to support huge armaments, it is always necessary to play up this fear.

He who would save liberty must put his trust in Democracy.

Peace will never be entirely secure until men everywhere have learned to conquer poverty without sacrificing liberty or security.

The alternative to the totalitarian state is the cooperative commonwealth.

Dorothy Thompson

(1894-1961)

American journalist, author

The United States is the only great and populous nation-state and world power whose people are not cemented by ties of blood, race or original language. It is the only world power which recognizes but one nationality of its citizens—American—while lacking the ties of blood, tribal kinship, original language, long-established culture, which contribute so much to national cohesion. How can such a union be maintained except through some idea which involves loyalty?

Ladies' Home Journal, October, 1954.

But I do not think that communism as a belief, apart from overt and illegal actions, can be successfully combatted by police methods, persecution, war or a mere anti spirit. The only force that can overcome an idea and a faith is another and better idea and faith, positively and fearlessly upheld.

Ibid.

The United States is not a nation of people which in the long run allows itself to be pushed around.　　*On the Record.*

They have not wanted *Peace* at all; they have wanted to be spared war—as though the absence of war was the same as peace.

Ibid.

Of all forms of government and society, those of free men and women are in many respects the most brittle. They give the fullest freedom for activities of private persons and groups who often identify their own interests, essentially selfish, with the general welfare.　　*Ibid., May, 1958.*

It is not the fact of liberty but the way in which liberty is exercised that ultimately determines whether liberty itself survives.

Ibid.

When liberty is taken away by force it can be restored by force. When it is relinquished voluntarily by default it can never be recovered. *Ibid., August, 1958.*

Henry David Thoreau
(1817-1862)
American writer, libertarian

The mass of men lead lives of quiet desperation.°   *Walden.*

The civilized man is a more experienced and wiser savage.   *Ibid.*

Why should we be in such desperate haste to succeed, and in such desperate enterprises? If a man does not keep pace with his companions, perhaps it is because he hears a different drummer.   *Ibid.*

It is never too late to give up your prejudices.   *Ibid.*

No way of thinking or doing, however ancient, can be trusted without proof. What everybody echoes or in silence passes by as true today may turn out to be falsehood tomorrow, mere smoke of opinion, which some had trusted for a cloud that would sprinkle fertilizing rain on their fields.   *Ibid.*

Man's capacities have never been measured; nor are we to judge of what he can do by any precedents, so little has been tried.   *Ibid.*

Trade curses everything it handles; and though you trade in messages from Heaven, the whole curse of trade attaches to the business.   *Ibid.*

Most of the luxuries and many of the so-called comforts of life are not only not indispensable, but positive hindrances to the elevation of mankind.   *Ibid.*

There are a thousand hacking at the branches of evil to one who is striking at the root.   *Ibid.*

—————
° "Thoreau's most famous single remark." Charles Poore, N. Y. *Times, April 4, 1956.*

Superfluous wealth can buy superfluities only.   *Ibid.*

Rather than love, than money, than fame, give me truth.   *Ibid.*

To be a philosopher is not merely to have subtle thoughts, nor even to found a school, but so to love wisdom as to live according to its dictates, a life of simplicity, independence, magnanimity, and trust. *Ibid.*

I heartily accept the motto, "That government is best which governs least"; and I should like to see it acted up to more rapidly and systematically. Carried out, it finally amounts to this, which also I believe—"That government is best which governs not at all"; and when men are prepared for it, that will be the kind of government which they will have. Government is at best but an expedient; but most governments are sometimes, inexpedient.

On the Duty of Civil Disobedience, 1849.

A government in which the majority rule in all cases cannot be based on justice, even as far as men understand it. Can there not be a government in which majorities do not virtually decide right and wrong, but conscience?—in which majorities decide only those questions to which the rule of expedience is applicable? Must the citizen ever for a moment, or in the least degree, resign his conscience to the legislator?   *Ibid.*

We should be men first, and subjects afterward. It is not desirable to cultivate a respect for the law, so much as for the right.   *Ibid.*

It is truly enough said that a corporation has no conscience; but a corporation of conscientious men is a corporation *with* a conscience. Law never made men a whit more just; and, by means of their respect for it, even the well-disposed are daily made the agents of injustice. A common and natural result of an undue respect for law is, that you may see a file of soldiers, colonels, captains, corporals, privates, powder-monkeys, and all, marching in admirable order over hill and dale to the wars, against their wills, ay, against their common sense and conscience, which makes it very steep marching indeed, and produces a palpitation of the heart.   *Ibid.*

All men recognize the right of revolution; that is, the right to refuse allegiance to, and to resist, the government, when its tyranny or its inefficiency are great and unendurable. But almost all say that such is not the case now. But such was the case, they think, in the Revolution of '75.   *Ibid.*

The American has dwindled into an Odd Fellow—one who may be known by the development of his organ of gregariousness, and a manifest lack of intellect and cheerful self-reliance.   *Ibid.*

A wise man will not leave the right to the mercy of chance, nor wish it to prevail through the power of the majority. There is little of virtue in the action of masses of men. When the majority shall at length vote for the abolition of slavery, it will be because they are indifferent to slavery, or because there is but little slavery left to be abolished by their vote. *They* will then be the only slaves. Only *his* vote can hasten the abolition of slavery who asserts his own freedom by his vote.   *Ibid.*

Those who, while they disapprove of the character and measures of a government, yield to it their allegiance and support are undoubtedly its most conscientious supporters, and so frequently the most serious obstacles to reform.   *Ibid.*

Unjust laws exist: shall we be content to obey them, or shall we endeavor to amend them, and obey them until we have succeeded, or shall we transgress them at once?
                                                Ibid.

Men, generally, under such a government as this, think that they ought to wait until they have persuaded the majority to alter them. They think that, if they should resist, the remedy would be worse than the evil. But it is the fault of the government itself that the remedy *is* worse than the evil. *It* makes it worse. Why is it not more apt to anticipate and provide for reform? Why does it not cherish its wise minority? Why does it cry and resist before it is hurt? Why does it not encourage its citizens to be on the alert to point out its faults, and *do* better than it would have them? Why does it always crucify Christ, and excommunicate Copernicus and Luther, and pronounce Washington and Franklin rebels?   *Ibid.*

Under a government which imprisons any unjustly, the true place for a just man is also a prison.   *Ibid.*

The opportunities for living are diminished in proportion as what are called the "means" are increased.   *Ibid.*

I did not see why the schoolmaster should be taxed to support the priest, and not the priest the schoolmaster.   *Ibid.*

Is a democracy, such as we know it, the last improvement possible in government? Is it not possible to take a step further towards recognizing the rights of man? There will never be a free and enlightened State until the State comes to recognize the individual as a higher and independent power, from which all its own power and authority are derived, and treats him accordingly.
                                                Ibid.

I please myself with imagining a State at last which can afford to be just to all men, and to treat the individual with respect as a neighbor; which even would not think it inconsistent with its own repose if a few were to live aloof from it, not meddling with it, not embraced by it, who fulfilled all the duties of neighbors and fellowmen. A State which bore this kind of fruit, and suffered it to drop off as fast as it ripened, would prepare the way for a still more perfect and glorious State, which also I have imagined, but not yet anywhere seen.   *Ibid.*

Any man more right than his neighbor, constitutes a majority of one.   *Ibid.*

What is the price-current of an honest man and patriot today? They hesitate, and they regret, and sometimes they petition; but they do nothing in earnest and with effect. They will wait well disposed, for others to remedy the evil, that they may no longer have it to regret. At most, they give only a cheap vote, and a feeble countenance and God-speed, to the right, as it goes by them. There are nine hundred and ninety-nine patrons of virtue to one virtuous man.   *Ibid.*

But the rich man—not to make any invidious comparison—is always sold to the institution which makes him rich. Absolutely speaking, the more money, the less virtue; for money comes between a man and his objects, and obtains them for him; and it was certainly no great virtue to obtain it.   *Ibid.*

They who know of no purer sources of truth, who have traced up its stream no higher, stand, and wisely stand, by the Bible and the Constitution, and drink at it there with reverence and humility; but they who behold where it comes trickling into this lake or that pool, gird up their loins once more,

and continue their pilgrimage toward its fountain-head.   *Ibid.*

Thus the State never intentionally confronts a man's sense, intellectual or moral, but only his body, his senses. It is not armed with superior wit or honesty, but with superior physical strength. I was not born to be forced.   *Ibid.*

The mass never comes up to the standard of its best member, but on the contrary degrades itself to the level with the lowest.
The Heart of Thoreau's Journal, edited by Odell Shepard, Houghton Mifflin. March 14, 1839.

All this worldly wisdom was once the unamiable heresy of some wise man.
Ibid., July 6, 1840.

Things do not change; we change.
Ibid., October, 1850.

The man for whom law exists—the man of forms, the conservative—is a tame man.
Ibid., March 30, 1851.

How rarely I meet with a man who can be free, even in thought! We all live according to rule. Some men are bed-ridden; all world-ridden.   *Ibid., May 12, 1857.*

Talk about slavery! It is not the peculiar institution of the South. It exists wherever men are bought and sold, wherever a man allows himself to be made a mere thing or tool, and surrenders his inalienable rights of reason and conscience.
Journal, December 4, 1860.

Blessed are they who never read a newspaper, for they shall see Nature, and through her, God.   *Essays and Other Writings.*

There is something servile in the habit of seeking after a law which we may obey . . . A successful life knows no law.
Excursions, Poems and Familiar Letters.

As for conforming outwardly, and living your own life inwardly, I do not think much of that.
Ibid. To Harrison Blake, August 9, 1850.

The law will never make men free; it is men who have got to make the law free. They are the lovers of law and order who observe the law when the government breaks it. *Slavery in Massachusetts, 1854.*

I hear many condemn these men because they were so few. When were the good and the brave ever in a majority?
A Plea for Captain John Brown, 1859.

So we defend ourselves and our hen-roosts, and maintain slavery. *Ibid.*

Is it not possible that an individual may be right and a government wrong? Are laws to be enforced simply because they are made? or declared by any number of men to be good, if they are *not* good? *Ibid.*

A man is rich in proportion to the number of things he can afford to let alone.
Where I Live.

Thucydides
(471?-401? B.C.)
Athenian historian

I shall be content if those shall pronounce my History useful who desire to give a view of events as they did really happen, and as they are very likely, in accordance with human nature, to repeat themselves at some future time—if not exactly the same, yet very similar. *Historia, bk. 1.*

War is a matter not so much of arms as of expenditure, through which arms may be made of service. *Ibid.*

To admit poverty is no disgrace to a man, but to make no effort to escape it is indeed disgraceful. *Ibid., bk. 2.*

Our constitution does not copy the laws of neighboring states; we are rather a pattern to others than imitators ourselves. Its administration favors the many instead of the few; this is why it is called a democracy.
Ibid., Pericles' Ideal.

The secret of Happiness is Freedom, and the secret of Freedom, Courage.
Funeral Speech for Pericles.

War is a bad thing: but to submit to the dictation of other states is worse . . . Freedom, if we hold fast to it, will ultimately restore our losses, but submission will mean permanent loss of all that we value . . . To you who call yourselves men of peace, I say: You are not safe unless you have men of action at your side. *Quoted in "Time."*

Samuel J. Tilden
(1814-1886)
American statesman, lawyer

The capitalist class has banded together all over the world and organized the *modern dynasty of associated wealth*, which maintains an unquestioned ascendency over most of the civilized portions of our race.
John Bigelow, Life of Samuel J. Tilden.

Paul Tillich
(1886-1965)
American philosopher

Protestantism is a continuous history of the breaking of images.
Religion and Freedom, Fund for the Republic, 1958.

John Tillotson
(1630-1694)
English archbishop

Ignorance and inconsideration are the two great causes of the ruin of mankind.
Quoted by John Adams, Dissertation on the Canon and the Feudal Law.

Josef Broz Tito
(1892-1980)
President of Yugoslavia

Any movement in history which attempts to perpetuate itself, becomes reactionary.
Tito, by Vladimir Dedijer, p. 431.

An intelligent man cannot accept the theory that personalities create history. In my opinion, men make history and plan a considerable part in it only if they understand the people's needs and wishes, and insofar as they become part of the people themselves.
Quoted by Eleanor Roosevelt, Chicago Sun-Times, April 7, 1953.

Communism really exists nowhere, least of all in the Soviet Union. Communism is an ideal that can be achieved only when people cease to be selfish and greedy and when everyone receives according to his needs from communal production. But that is a long way off.
Eleanor Roosevelt, On My Own, Harper, 1958.

Our road is Socialism and we shall build a socialist state here . . . The methods are not fixed but the goal is . . . It is true democracy which can be achieved only through Socialism.
Interview with George Seldes, York, Pa., Gazette & Daily, February 7, 1957.

Alexis de Tocqueville
(1805-1859)
French writer, statesman

Justice is the end of government, it is the end of civil society. It has ever been and ever will be pursued, until it either will be obtained or until liberty be lost in the pursuit. *Democracy in America.*

There is an amazing strength in the expression of the will of a people; and when it declares itself, even the imagination of those who wish to contest it is overawed. *Ibid.*

The health of a democratic society may be measured by the quality of functions performed by private citizens. *Ibid.*

There is, in fact, a manly and lawful passion for equality that incites men to wish all to be powerful and honored. This passion tends to elevate the humble to the rank of the great; but there exists also in the human heart a depraved taste for equality, which impels the weak to attempt to lower the powerful to their own level and reduces men to prefer equality in slavery to inequality with freedom. Not that those nations whose social condition is democratic naturally despise liberty; on the contrary, they have an instinctive love of it. But liberty is not the chief and constant object of their desires; equality is their idol; they make rapid and sudden efforts to obtain liberty and, if they miss their aim, resign themselves to their disappointment; but nothing can satisfy them without equality, and they would rather perish than lose it. *Ibid.*

In a state where the citizens are all practically equal, it becomes difficult for them to preserve their independence against aggressions of power. *Ibid.*

In the principle of equality I discern two tendencies: the one leading the mind of every man to untried thoughts; the other prohibiting him from thinking at all.

Americans are so enamored of equality that they would rather be equal in slavery than unequal in freedom. *Ibid.*

I know of no country in which there is so little independence of mind and real freedom of discussion as in America. *Ibid.*

The will of man is not shattered, but softened, bent, and guided; men are seldom forced by it (majority opinion) to act, but they are constantly restrained from acting. Such a power does not destroy, but it prevents existence; it does not tyrannize, but it compresses, enervates, extinguishes, and stupefies a people. *Ibid.*

The majority no longer says: You shall think as I do or you shall die (but says) You are free to think differently from me and to retain your life, your property, and all that you possess; but you are henceforth a stranger among your people. You may retain your civil rights, but they will be useless to you, for you will never be chosen by your fellow citizens if you solicit their votes; and they will affect to scorn you if you ask for their esteem.
You will remain among men, but you will be deprived of the rights of mankind. Your fellow creatures will shun you like an im-

pure being; and even those who believe in your innocence will abandon you, lest they should be shunned in their turn. Go in peace! I have given you your life, but it is an existence worse than death. *Ibid.*

But men will never establish any equality with which they can be contented. Whatever efforts a people may make, they will never succeed in reducing all the conditions of society to a perfect level; and even if they unhappily attained that absolute and complete equality of position, the inequality of minds would still remain, which, coming directly from the hand of God, will forever escape the laws of man. *Ibid.*

There is no philosopher in the world so great but that he believes a million things on the faith of other people and accepts a great many more truths than he demonstrates. *Ibid.*

If it should happen that the men of some one period were agreed upon . . . rules, that would prove nothing for the following period; for among democratic nations each new generation is a new people. *Ibid.*

Ernst Toller
(1893-1939)
German dramatist, poet

As a rule people are afraid of truth. Each truth we discover in nature or social life destroys the crutches on which we used to lean.
Saturday Review of Literature, May 20, 1944.

What people fear most is that they may have to put into practice truths which wise men have discovered. Many people have to surrender old privileges and everybody has to give up old customs without which life may seem hardly worth living. The old penalty for heretics was dramatic: death. The modern penalty is less drastic: boycott and social ruin. *Ibid.*

The writer is forced to proclaim truth in spite of all hostilities. We shall never reach a solution without the will and courage to truth. Truth is a passion. One cannot learn it; one must possess it. The foundation on which true writing can grow is spiritual freedom. *Ibid.*

The basis of democracy is freedom and reason. Acceptance of the democratic ideology is not compulsory. The basis of fascism is blind belief and a contempt for reason . . . Fascism exploits the fear of reason which lives secretly in the conscious and subconscious minds of many people. Reason means facing life and its facts. *Ibid.*

Leo N(icholaevich) Tolstoy
(1828-1910)
Russian writer

The injustice of the seizure of the land as property has long ago been recognized by thinking people, but *only since* the teaching of Henry George has it become clear *by what means* this injustice can be abolished.
Message to Single Tax League of Australia, September 15, 1908, published in "Standard," November 15, 1908.

This problem, i.e., the abolition of property in land, at the present time everywhere demands its solution as insistingly, as half a century ago the problem of *slavery* demanded its solution in Russia and America. *Ibid.*

The supposed right of landed property now lies at the *foundation* not only of economic misery, but also of political disorder, and above all, the moral deprivation of the people. *Ibid.*

Christianity, with its doctrine of humility, of forgiveness, of love, is incompatible with the state, with its haughtiness, its violence, its punishment, its wars.
The Kingdom of God Is Within You, 1893.

The Christian churches and Christianity have nothing in common save in name: they are utterly hostile opposites. The churches are arrogance, violence, usurpation, rigidity, death; Christianity is humility, penitence, submissiveness, progress, life. *Ibid.*

Laws . . . are the product of selfishness, deception, and party prejudice. True justice is not in them, and cannot be in them. *Ibid.*

Property is based on violence and slaying and threat thereof. *Ibid.*

In order to obtain and hold power a man must love it. Thus the effort to get it is not likely to be coupled with goodness, but with the opposite qualities of pride, craft and cruelty. *Ibid.*

Without hypocrisy, lying, punishments, prisons, fortresses and murders, no new power can arise and no existing one hold its own. *Ibid.*

If patriotism is good, then Christianity, which gives peace, is an idle term, and the sooner this teaching is eradicated, the better. But if Christianity really gives peace, and we really want peace, patriotism is a survival from barbarous times, which must not be evoked and educated, as we now do, but which must be eradicated by all means.
Letter to Manson, 1896.

Money is a new form of slavery, and distinguishable from the old simply by the fact that it is impersonal—that there is no human relation between master and slave.

What Shall We Do?

The essence of all slavery consists in taking the produce of another's labor by force. It is immaterial whether this force be founded upon ownership of the slave or ownership of the money that he must get to live. *Ibid.*

We will do anything for the poor man, anything but get off his back.

Quoted by Huntingdon, Philanthropy and Morality.

Error is the force that welds men together; truth is communicated to men only by deeds of truth. *My Religion.*

One may say with one's lips: "I believe that God is one, and also three;"—but no one can believe it, because the words have no sense. *What Is Religion?*

"Resist not evil" means "Do not resist the evil man," which means "Do no violence to another," which means "Commit no act that is contrary to love."

What I Believe, 1884.

Only those live who do good.

My Confession, ch. 5.

Anti-Semitism is . . . a pathological condition, a peculiar form of sexual perversion . . . Among all disgraceful phenomena, it is the most disgusting and abominable.

Letter to I. Tenoromo, 1889.

We have met here to fight against war. The truth is that one may not and should not in any circumstances or under any pretext kill his fellow man.

Address, Swedish Government Congress Peace Conference, 1909; Saturday Review, August 9, 1958.

We must repudiate one of the two, either Christianity with its love of God and one's neighbor, or the state with its armies and wars. *Ibid.*

We must say what everybody knows but does not venture to say. We must say that by whatever name men may call murder —murder always remains murder and a criminal and shameful thing. And it is only necessary to say that clearly, definitely, and loudly, as we can say it here, and men will cease to see what they thought they saw and will see what is really before their eyes. They will cease to see the service of their country, the heroism of war, military glory, and patriotism, and will see what exists: the naked, criminal business of murder! *Ibid.*

Three things I hate: autocracy, orthodoxy, and militarism.

I believe Christ was a man like ourselves; to look upon him as God would seem to me the greatest of sacrileges.

The government in which I believe is that which is based on the mere moral sanction of men. Buddha, Moses, Plato, Socrates, Schopenhauer are to me the real sovereigns. Just as I hate a hereditary potentate, so do I hate a cheap parliament. A political party has never accomplished anything for humanity. Individuals and geniuses have been the pioneers of every reform and of progress. The real law lives in our hearts. If our hearts are empty, no law or political reform can fill them.

Man has received direct from God only one instrument wherewith to know himself and to know his relation to the universe—he has no other—and that instrument is reason.

Every man is gifted with reason, and by that reason the law he should follow is revealed to each man. That law is hidden only from those who do not wish to follow it, and who, in order not to obey the law, reject reason, and instead of using the reason given to them wherewith to discern truth, accept on faith the guidance of others who have also rejected reason.

Man must not check reason by tradition, but contrariwise, must check tradition by reason.

Every kind of oppression of man by man rests on the possibility which a man has of taking another's life and, by keeping a threatening attitude, compelling his obedience.

When in the ancient world the entire economic fabric rested on personal slavery, the greatest minds could not see it. To Xenophon and Plato, and Aristotle, and the Romans it seemed that things could not be different, and that slavery was the inevitable and natural result of wars, without which, in turn, humanity was inconceivable.

There has long existed and still exists a terrible superstition, which has done men more harm, perhaps, than the most awful religious superstitions, and it is this superstition, which with all its might and perseverance the so-called political science upholds. The superstition is similar in every respect to religious superstitions. It consists in the affirmation that, besides the duties of man to man, there are still more important obligations to an imaginary being. In theology the imaginary being is God, and in political sciences the imaginary being is Government.

Things to which men must be driven by force, cease to be, thanks to the force, for the common good.

The abolition of slavery has gone on for a long time. Rome abolished slavery, America abolished it, and we did, but only the words were abolished, not the thing.

Slavery means the freeing themselves, by some, of the necessity of labor for the satisfaction of their needs and the throwing of this labor upon others by means of physical force; and where there is a man who does not labor because another is compelled to work for him, there slavery is.

What is it that renders it possible for people to make laws? The same thing makes it possible to establish laws as enforce obedience to them—organized violence.

The robber generally plundered the rich, the governments generally plunder the poor and protect those rich who assist in their crimes. The robber doing his work risked his life, while the governments risk nothing, but base their whole activity on lies and deceptions.

Slavery results from laws, laws are made by governments, and, therefore, people can only be freed from slavery by the abolition of governments . . . All attempts to get rid of governments by violence have hitherto, always and everywhere, resulted only in this: that in place of the deposed governments new ones established themselves, often more cruel than those they replaced.

The age for the veneration for governments, notwithstanding all the hypnotic influence they employ to maintain their position, is more and more passing away. And it is time for people to understand that governments not only are not necessary, but are harmful and most highly immoral institutions, in which a self-respecting, honest man cannot and must not take part, and the advantages of which he cannot and should not enjoy. And as soon as people clearly understand that, they will naturally cease to take part in such deeds—that is, cease to give the governments soldiers and money. And as soon as a majority of people ceases to do this the fraud which enslaves people will be abolished. Only in this way can people be freed from slavery.

Wolfe Tone
(1763-1798)
Irish revolutionist

The Greatest Happiness of the Greatest Number—on the rock of this principle let this society rest, and by this let it judge and determine every political question, and whatever is necessary for this and let it not be accounted hazardous, but rather our interest, our duty, our glory, and our common religion. The Rights of Man are the Rights of God, to vindicate the one is to maintain the other. We must be free in order to serve him whose service is perfect freedom.

Manifesto to the Friends of Freedom in Ireland, written by Wolfe Tone with the aid of others, June, 1791.

Arnold J. Toynbee
(1889-1975)
English historian

A life which does not go into action is a failure; and this is just as true of a prophet's, a poet's, or a scholar's life as it is true of the life of a "man of action", in the conventionally limited popular usage of the term.

A Study of History.

Of the living civilizations every one has already broken down and is in process of disintegration except our own.

And what of our Western Civilization? It has manifestly not yet reached the stage of a universal state . . . the universal state is not the first stage in disintegration any more than

it is the last. It is followed by what we have called an "interregnum," and preceded by what we have called a "time of troubles," which seems usually to occupy several centuries; and if we in our generation were to permit ourselves to judge by the purely subjective criterion of our own feeling about our own age, the best judges would probably declare that our "time of troubles" had undoubtedly descended upon us.

A Study of History, Somervell abridgement, 1946.

We are already far advanced in our time of troubles; and, if we ask what has been our most conspicuous and specific trouble in the recent past, the answer clearly is: nationalistic internecine warfare, reinforced, . . . by the combined "drive" of energies generated by the recently released forces of Democracy and Industrialism.   *Ibid.*

The Gospels and Herodotus made me aware of the divine irony in human affairs; the most tremendous of all the lessons of history.

Saturday Review, October 2, 1954.

Edmunds Travis
(b. 1890)
Editor, Austin (Texas) Tribune

A free press is the protagonist and preserver of all rights, the foe and destroyer of all tyrannies. It insures every good cause a hearing and every false doctrine a challenge. It is the servant of Religion, Philosophy, Science and Art, the agent of truth, justice and civilization. Possessing it, no people can be held in intellectual or political bondage. Without it none can be secure against any form of enslavement.

Cornerstone inscription.

Heinrich von Treitschke
(1834-1896)
German military philosopher

The State is the people, legally united as an independent entity. By the word "people" we understand briefly a number of families permanently living side by side. This definition implies that the State is primordial and necessary, that it is as enduring as history, and no less essential to mankind than speech.
"Politics," London, 1916.

It is quite inaccurate to call the State a necessary evil. We have to deal with it as a lofty necessity of Nature.   *Ibid.*

Ultramontanes and Jacobins both start with the assumption that the legislation of the modern State is the work of sinful man. They thus display their total lack of reverence for the objectively revealed Will of God, as unfolded in the life of the State.   *Ibid.*

It is a false conclusion that wars are waged for the sake of material advantage. Modern wars are not fought for the sake of booty. Here the high moral ideal of national honor is a factor handed down from one generation to another, enshrining something positively sacred, and compelling the individual to sacrifice himself to it.   *Ibid.*

War and the administration of justice are the chief tasks of even the most barbaric States. But these tasks are only conceivable where a plurality of States are found existing side by side. Thus the idea of one universal empire is odious—the ideal of a State coextensive with humanity is no ideal at all.   *Ibid.*

The features of history are virile, unsuited to sentimental or feminine natures. Brave people alone have an existence, an evolution or a future; the weak and cowardly perish, and perish justly. The grandeur of history lies in the perpetual conflict of nations, and it is simply foolish to desire the suppression of their rivalry.   *Ibid.*

Means only exist to serve an end. *Ibid.*

The State is no academy of arts, nor yet a stock exchange; it is a power, and therefore it denies its very nature when it neglects its army.   *Ibid.*

The next essential function of the State is the conduct of war. The long oblivion into which this principle has fallen is a proof of how effeminate the science of government had become in civilian hands.   *Ibid.*

Without war no State could be. All those we know of arose through war, and the protection of their members by armed force remains their primary and essential task. War, therefore, will endure to the end of history, as long as there is a multiplicity of States.
Ibid.

It is indeed political idealism which fosters war, whereas materialism rejects it. What a perversion of morality to want to banish heroism from human life.   *Ibid.*

The Bible states expressly that the man in authority shall wield the sword. *Ibid.*

We have learned to recognize as the civilizing majesty of war precisely what appears to the superficial observers to be brutality and inhumanity. . . . Man must not only be ready to sacrifice his life, but also the natural deeply rooted feelings of the human soul; he must devote his whole *ego* for the furtherance of a great patriotic idea: that is the moral sublimity of war.   *Ibid.*

Those who know history know also that it would be a curtailment of human nature to wish to banish war from the world. There is no freedom without a military power which is ready to sacrifice itself for freedom . . . If a State neglects its physical strength in favor of its mental, it comes to grief.   *Ibid.*

The Jews are our misfortune.
Ein Wort ueber unser Judentum.

John Trenchard
See Thomas Gordon

Leon Trotsky (né Lev Davidovich Bronstein)
(1879-assassinated 1940)
Soviet Russian leader

The permanent revolution.
Fortune, February, 1951.

Where force is necessary, there it must be applied boldly, decisively and completely.
What Next? 1932.

Fascism is nothing but capitalist reaction; from the point of view of the proletariat the difference between the types of reaction is meaningless.   *Ibid.*

Not believing in force is the same as not believing in gravitation.   *Ibid.*

The dictatorship of the Communist Party is maintained by recourse to every form of violence.
Terrorism and Communism, Paris, 1924, p. 71.

The powerful force of competition . . . will not disappear in a socialist Society, but . . . will be sublimated.
Literature and Revolution, 1925.

To accept the workers' Revolution in the name of a high ideal means not only to reject it but to slander it. All the social illusions which mankind has raved about in religion, poetry, morals or philosophy. served only the purpose of deceiving and blinding the oppressed . . . The Revolution is strong to the extent to which it is realistic, strategic and mathematical.

Terror as the demonstration of the will and strength of the working class, is historically justified, precisely because the proletariat was able thereby to break the political will of the Intelligentzia, pacify the professional men of various categories and work, and gradually subordinate them to its own aims within the field of their specialties.
Izvestia, January 10, 1919; quoted by Walling, Sovietism.

The personality of Stalin and his career are different. It is not Stalin who created the machine. The machine created Stalin. But a machine, like a pianola, cannot replace human creative power. Bureaucracy as bureaucracy is impregnated through and through with the spirit of mediocrity. Stalin is the most outstanding mediocrity of the Soviet bureaucracy. His strength lies in the fact that he expresses the instinct of self-preservation of the ruling caste more firmly more decisively, and more pitilessly than anyone else.   *Life, October 2, 1939.*

Harry S Truman
(1884-1972)
33rd President of the United States

If we see that Germany is winning we ought to help Russia, and if we see Russia is winning, we ought to help Germany, and that way let them kill as many as possible.
Senate speech, "U.S. Week," July 5, 1941.

Of course I believe in free enterprise but in my system of free enterprise, the demo-

cratic principle is that there never was, never has been, never will be, room for the ruthless exploitation of the many for the benefit of the few.
Congressional Record, May 9, 1944.

Last night the moon, the stars and all the planets fell on me. If you fellows ever pray, pray for me.
Statement to press, April 13, 1945.

It is an atomic bomb. It is a harnessing of the basic power of the universe.
Statement to the press, July 28, 1945.

In presenting this scroll . . . I am rewarding "a good public servant." I hope that will be my epitaph.   *September 7, 1945.*

At the present moment in world history nearly every nation must choose between alternative ways of life . . . One way of life is based upon the will of the majority . . . The second way of life is based upon the will of the minority forcibly imposed upon the majority. It relies upon terror and oppression, a controlled press and radio, fixed elections, and the suppression of personal freedom.

I believe that it must be the policy of the United States to support free peoples who are resisting subjugation by armed minorities or by outside pressure.
Address to Congress, March, 1947; "The Truman Doctrine."

I would rather have peace in the world than be President.
Truman Christmas greeting, 1948.

Communism is based on the belief that man is so weak and inadequate that he is unable to govern himself, and therefore requires the rule of strong masters.

Democracy is based on the conviction that man has the moral and intellectual capacity,

as well as the inalienable right, to govern himself with reason and justice.
Inaugural address, January 20, 1949.

Communism holds that the world is so deeply divided into opposing classes that war is inevitable.

Democracy holds that free nations can settle differences justly and maintain lasting peace.   *Ibid.*

In my opinion eight years as President is enough and sometimes too much for any man to serve in that capacity.

There is a lure in power. It can get into a man's blood just as gambling and lust for money have been known to do.
Memorandum, written for himself, April 16, 1950; Life and N. Y. Times, February 20, 1956.

Once a government is committed to the principle of silencing the voice of opposition, it has only one way to go, and that is down the path of increasingly repressive measures, until it becomes a source of terror to all its citizens and creates a country where everyone lives in fear.
Message to Congress, August 8, 1950.

I think a publisher, or any newspaperman, who doesn't have a sense of responsibility and prints a lot of lies and goes around slandering without any basis in fact—I think that sort of fellow actually can be called a traitor.
Interview with John Hersey. The New Yorker, April 7, 1951.

The opportunities afforded by the Vice Presidency, particularly the Presidency of the Senate, do not come—they are there to be seized. Here is one instance in which it is the man who makes the office, not the office the man.
Memoirs; Years of Decisions, vol. 1, 1955.

I'm going to fight hard. I'm going to give them hell.
To Senator Barkley; Memoirs; Years of Trial and Hope, Doubleday, 1956.

I've got the most awful responsibility a man ever had.
N. Y. Times Magazine, January 13, 1957.

I never did give anybody hell. I just told the truth and they thought it was hell.
To Ed Murrow, See It Now, CBS-TV; Time, February 10, 1958.

As long as I was in the White House I ran the executive branch of the government, and no one was ever allowed to act in the capacity of President of the United States except the man who held that office . . . I had no intention of being an "acting President."
Democratic Digest, March, 1958.

A person who is fundamentally honest doesn't need a code of ethics. The Ten Commandments and the Sermon on the Mount are all the ethical code anybody needs. *AP dispatch, July 10, 1958.*

Men make history and not the other way 'round. In periods where there is no leadership, society stands still. Progress occurs when courageous, skillful leaders seize the opportunity to change things for the better.
This Week, February 22, 1959.

When a leader is in the Democratic Party he's a boss; when he's in the Republican Party he's a leader.
Lecture, Columbia University, April 28, 1959.

When even one American—who has done nothing wrong—is forced by fear to shut his mind and close his mouth, then all Americans are in peril. *N. Y. Times Magazine.*

In the cause of freedom we have to battle for the rights of people with whom we do not agree; and whom, in many cases, we may not like . . . If we do not defend their rights, we endanger our own.

Our goal must be—not peace in our time —but peace for all time.

Tse-tung
See Mao Tse-tung

Ivan (Sergeyevich) Turgenev
(1818-1883)
Russian novelist

A Nihilist is a man who does not bow down before any authority; who does not take any principle on faith, whatever reverence that principle may be enshrined in.
Fathers and Sons.

Anne Robert Jacques Turgot (Baron de l'Aulne)
(1727-1781)
French statesman, economist

The Pagans tolerated every opinion, the Chinese do the same; Prussia excludes no sect, Holland includes all, and these nations have never experienced a religious war. England and France have wished to have but one religion, and London and Paris have seen the blood of their inhabitants flowing in streams. *Le Conciliateur.*

Everywhere the strong have made the laws and oppressed the weak; and, if they have sometimes consulted the interests of society, they have always forgotten those of humanity.

Mark Twain
(Samuel Langhorne Clemens)
(1835-1910)
American novelist, essayist

I have no race prejudices, and I think I have no color prejudices nor creed prejudices. Indeed, I know it. I can stand any society. All I care to know is that a man is a human being—that is enough for me; he can't be any worse.
> *Concerning the Jews.*

The Jews are members of the human race—worse I can say of no man.
> *Quoted by Columnist Dorothy Thompson.*

Anti-Semitism . . . is the swollen envy of pygmy minds—meanness, injustice.
> *Quoted by Clara Clemens, My Husband Gabrilowitsch.*

If Christ were here now there is one thing he would not be—a Christian.
> *Notebook, 1935.*

There are two forces that can carry light to all corners of the globe—the sun in the heavens and the Associated Press down here.
> *Speech, New York City, September 19, 1906.*

Religion had its share in the changes of civilization and national character, of course. What share? The lion's. In the history of the human race this has always been the case, will always be the case, to the end of time, no doubt; or at least until man by the slow process of evolution shall develop into something really fine and high —some billions of years hence, say.
> *Europe and Elsewhere.*

The methods of the priest and the parson have been very curious; their history is very entertaining. In all the ages the Roman Church has owned slaves, bought and sold slaves, authorized and encouraged her children to trade in them. Long after some Christian peoples had freed their slaves the Church still held on to hers. If any could know, to absolute certainty, that all this was right, and according to God's will and desire, surely it was she since she was God's specially appointed representative in the earth and sole authorized and infallible expounder of his Bible. There were the texts; there was no mistaking their meaning; she was right, she was doing in all this thing what the Bible had mapped out for her to do. So unassailable was her position that in all the centuries she had no word to say against human slavery.
> *Ibid.*

Yet now at last, in our immediate day, we hear a Pope saying slave trading is wrong, and see him sending an expedition to Africa to stop it. The texts remain; it is the practice that has changed. Why? Because the world has corrected the Bible. The Church never corrects it; and also never fails to drop in at the tail of the procession—and take the credit of the correction. As she will presently do in this instance.
> *Ibid.*

In England an illegitimate Christian rose against slavery. It is curious that when a Christian rises against a rooted wrong at all, he is usually an illegitimate Christian, member of some despised and bastard sect.
> *Ibid.*

During many ages there were witches. The Bible said so. The Bible commanded that they should not be allowed to live. Therefore the Church, after doing its duty in but a lazy and indolent way for 800 years, gathered up its halters, thumbscrews, and firebrands, and set about its holy work in earnest. She worked hard at it night and day during nine centuries and imprisoned, tortured, hanged, and burned whole hordes and armies of witches, and washed the Christian world clean with their foul blood.

Then it was discovered that there was no such thing as witches, and never had been. One does not know whether to laugh or to cry. Who discovered that there was no such thing as a witch—the priest, the parson? No, these never discover anything. At Salem, the parson clung pathetically to his witch text after the laity had abandoned it in remorse and tears for the cruelties it had persuaded them to do. The parson wanted more blood, more shame, more brutalities; it was the unconsecrated laity that stayed his hand. *Ibid.*

There are no witches. The witch text remains; only the practice has changed. Hell fire is gone, but the text remains. Infant damnation is gone, but the text remains. More than 200 death penalties are gone from the law books, but the texts that authorized them remain. *Ibid.*

Is it not well worthy of note that of all the multitude of texts through which man has driven his annihilating pen he has never once made the mistake of obliterating a good and useful one? It does certainly seem to suggest that if man continues in the direction of enlightenment, his religious practice may, in the end, attain some semblance of human decency. *Ibid.*

One of the most striking differences between a cat and a lie is that a cat has only nine lives. *Pudd'nhead Wilson's Calendar.*

Truth is the most valuable thing we have. Let us economize it. *Ibid.*

There are 869 different forms of lying, but only one of them has been squarely forbidden. Thou shalt not bear false witness against thy neighbor. *Ibid.*

When in doubt, tell the truth. *Ibid.*

It is by the goodness of God that in our country we have those three unspeakably precious things: freedom of speech, freedom of conscience, and the prudence never to practice either of them. *Ibid.*

Whoever has lived long enough to find out what life is, knows how deep a debt of gratitude we owe to Adam, the first great benefactor of our race. He brought death into the world. *Ibid.*

The crowned beasts of Europe. *(referring to Leopold II of Belgium and the Congo atrocities.)*

Prosperity is the surest breeder of insolence I know.

Loyalty to petrified opinion never yet broke a chain or freed a human soul.

Get your facts first, and then you can distort them as much as you please. *Quoted by Rudyard Kipling, From Sea to Sea.*

I have been reading the morning paper. I do it every morning—well knowing that I shall find in it the usual depravities and basenesses and hypocrisies and cruelties that make up civilization, and cause me to put in the rest of the day pleading for the damnation of the human race. *Letter to W. D. Howells.*

Hain't we got all the fools in town on our side? And hain't that a big enough majority in any town? *Huckleberry Finn.*

(An Englishman is) a person who does things because they have been done before. (An American is) a person who does things because they haven't been done before.

Vast material prosperity always brings in its train conditions which debase the morals and enervate the manhood of a nation—then the country's liberties come into the market and are bought, sold, squandered, thrown away, and a popular idol is carried to the throne upon the shields or shoulders of the worshipping people and planted there in permanency. . . . It is curious—curious that physical courage should be so common in the world, and moral courage so rare. *Mark Twain in Eruption.*

Almost any man worthy of his salt would fight to defend his home, but no one ever heard of a man going to war for his boarding house. *Ibid.*

We are discreet sheep; we wait to see how the drove is going, and then go with the drove. We have two opinions: one private, which we are afraid to express; and another one—the one we use—which we force ourselves to wear to please Mrs. Grundy, until habit makes us comfortable in it, and the custom of defending it presently makes us love it, adore it, and forget how pitifully we came by it. Look at it in politics. *Ibid.*

There is no other life; life itself is only a vision and a dream for nothing exists but space and you. If there was an all-powerful God, he would have made all good, and no bad. *Ibid.*

There never was a just one, never an honorable one—on the part of the instigator of the war. I can see a million years ahead, and this rule will never change in so many as half a dozen instances. The loud little handful—as usual—will shout for the war. The pulpit will—warily and cautiously—object—at first, the great dull bulk of the nation will rub its sleepy eyes and try to make out why there should be a war and

will say earnestly and indignantly, "It is unjust and dishonorable and there is no necessity for it". Then the handful will shout louder. A few fair men on the other side will argue and reason against the war with speech and pen, and at first will have a hearing and be applauded; but it will not last long; those others will outshout them, and presently the anti-war audiences will thin out and lose popularity. Before long you will see this curious thing: the speakers stoned from the platform and free speech strangled by hordes of furious men who in their secret hearts are still at one with those stoned speakers—as earlier—but do not dare to say so. And now the whole nation—pulpit and all—will take up the war-cry and shout itself hoarse, and mob any honest man who ventures to open his mouth; and presently such mouths will cease to open. Next the statesmen will invent cheap lies putting the blame upon the nation that is attacked; and every man will be glad of those conscience-soothing falsities, and will diligently study them and refuse to examine any refutations of them; and thus he will by and by convince himself that the war is just and will thank God for the better sleep he enjoys after this process of grotesque self-deception.

(Satan speaking.) The Mysterious Stranger, Harper & Bros., 1916.

There were two "Reigns of Terror", if we would but remember it and consider it; the one wrought murder in hot passion, the other in heartless cold blood; the one lasted mere months, the other had lasted a thousand years; the one inflicted death upon ten thousand persons, the other upon a hundred millions; but our shudders are all for the "horrors" of the minor Terror, the momentary Terror, so to speak; whereas, what is the horror of swift death by the ax compared with lifelong death from hunger, cold, insult, cruelty, and heartbreak? What is swift death by lightning compared with death by slow fire at the stake?

A Connecticut Yankee in King Arthur's Court, 1889.

I said I had seen one (a nation of people ... with a free vote in every man's hand) —and that it would last until it had an Established Church. *Ibid.*

My kind of loyalty was loyalty to one's country, not to its institutions or its office-holders. The country is the real thing, the substantial thing, the eternal thing; it is the thing to watch over, and care for, and be loyal to; institutions are extraneous, they are its mere clothing, and clothing can wear out, become ragged, cease to be comfortable, cease to protect the body from winter, disease, and death. To be loyal to rags, to shout for rags, to worship rags, to die for rags—that is a loyalty of unreason, it is pure animal; it belongs to monarchy, was invented by monarchy; let monarchy keep it. I was from Connecticut, whose Constitution declares "that all political power is inherent in the people, and all free governments are founded on their authority and instituted for their benefit; and that they have *at all times* an undeniable and indefeasible right to *alter their form of government* in such a manner as they may think expedient." *Ibid.*

The citizen who thinks he sees that the commonwealth's political clothes are worn out, and yet holds his peace and does not agitate for a new suit, is disloyal; he is a traitor. That he may be the only one who thinks he sees this decay, does not excuse him; it is his duty to agitate anyway, and it is the duty of others to vote him down if they do not see the matter as he does. *Ibid.*

William Marcy ("Boss") Tweed
(1823-1878)
American demagogue, political boss

As long as I count the votes what are you going to do about it? *The Ballot in 1871.*

The way to have power is to take it.
Attributed.

William Tyndale
(1484?-executed 1536)
English religious reformer

Let every man of whatsoever craft or occupation he be of, whether brewer, baker, tailor, victualler, merchant or husbandman, refer his craft and occupation unto the common wealth, and serve his brethren as he would do Christ himself.
The Parable of the Wicked Mammon.

John Tyndall
(1820-1893)
English physicist

Superstition is . . . religion which has grown incongruous with intelligence.
Fragments of Science for Unscientific People, 1871.

The brightest flashes in the world of thought are incomplete until they have been proved to have their counterparts in the world of fact. *Ibid.*

It is as fatal as it is cowardly to blink facts because they are not to our taste.
Lecture, Belfast, August 19, 1874.

Miguel de Unamuno
(1864-1936)
Spanish writer, educator

True Science teaches, above all, to doubt, and to be ignorant.
The Tragic Sense of Life.

That which the Fascists hate above all else, is intelligence.

Quoted in "Vendredi," Paris, January 8, 1937.

United Nations

Everyone shall have the right to freedom of thought and expression. This shall include freedom to hold opinions without interference and to seek, receive and impart information and ideas by any means and regardless of frontiers.

Paragraph 1, program presented by U.S. delegate William Benton, at Geneva.

Art. 1. All human beings are born free and equal in dignity and rights.

Declaration of Human Rights, December 10, 1948.

Art. 2. Everyone is entitled to all the rights of freedom set forth in this Declaration, without distinction of any kind, such as race, colour, sex, language, religion, political or other opinion, national or social origin, property, birth or other status.　　*Ibid.*

Art. 18. Everyone has the right to freedom of thought.　　*Ibid.*

Art. 19. Everyone has the right to freedom of opinion and expression.　　*Ibid.*

Since wars begin in the minds of men, it is in the minds of men that the defenses of peace must be constructed.

Constitution of UNESCO (United Nations Educational, Scientific and Cultural Organization).

United States Army

Democracy: A government of the masses. Authority derived through mass meeting or any other form of direct expression. Results in mobocracy. Attitude toward property is communistic . . . negating property rights. Attitude toward law is that the will of the majority shall regulate, whether it is based upon deliberation or governed by passion, prejudice, and impulse, without restraint or regard to consequences. Result is demagogism, license, agitation, discontent, anarchy.

Army Training Manual No. 2000-25 (1928-1932)*.

Democracy, simply stated, is a form of society wherein government rests with the majority of people. There is no better definition for it than that expressed by Lincoln—"A government of the people, by the people, and for the people". It would be wrong and useless to deny that the implications and full development of Democracy have never been reached in our country. However, it is our job to see that the issues of the War are so personalized in the mind of each soldier that he is fully conscious of his own stake in the world for which we are fighting. The terms "Political Democracy" and "Economic Democracy" are not empty phrases. They are inherent in our very form of government and represent fundamental objectives for which not only we Americans but all of the Allies are fighting.

"Classes in Citizenship and War Issues," issued during the Second World War.

Fascism is a political, social and economic form of society wherein by virtue of a merger which has been accomplished between certain powerful financial interests and a military machine, the entire nation is under the dictatorship of this oligarchy. Individuality

---

* This manual was withdrawn after an article exposing it was published by the editor of this volume.

and freedom are suppressed "in the interests of the state" which happens to be none other than the dictating oligarchy. Since so radical a change in a form of government is not very easily accomplished, the transition to Fascism is, at first, made easier by demagogic political agitation of the kind which is described as "We are all things to all men". To gain the backing of powerful industrialists . . . a form of society is offered which will protect their objective; disunity is created by playing political groups against each other, religious groups against each other, social and economic groups against each other. A confused and disunited people can offer no effective resistance to the seizure of power by this newly-merged oligarchy.   *Ibid.*

The informed soldier fights best.
Army Orientation booklets.

Fascism is not the easiest thing to identify and analyze; nor, once in power, is it easy to destroy. . . Points to stress are: (1) Fascism is more apt to come to power in time of economic crisis; (2) Fascism inevitably leads to war; (3) it can come in any country; (4) we can best combat it by making our democracy work.
Army Talk, Orientation Fact Sheet 64, March 24, 1945.

Fascism is government by the few and for the few. The objective is seizure and control of the economic, political, social and cultural life of the state.   *Ibid.*

The United States also has its native Fascists who say that they are "100 percent American". . .
At various times in our history, we have had sorry instances of mob sadism, lynchings, vigilantism, terror, and suppression of civil liberties. We have had our hooded gangs, Black Legions, Silver Shirts, and racial and religious bigots. All of them, in the name of Americanism, have used undemocratic methods and doctrines which experience has shown can be properly identified as "fascist".
Ibid.

An American Fascist seeking power would not proclaim that he is a Fascist. Fascism always camouflages its plans and purposes. . . . Any fascist attempt made to gain power in America would not use the exact Hitler pattern. It would work under the guise of "super-patriotism" and "super-Americanism". Fascist leaders are neither stupid nor naive. They know that they must hand out a line that "sells". Huey Long is said to have remarked that if Fascism came to America it would be on a program of "Americanism".
Ibid.

What is true of America is true of the world. The germ of Fascism cannot be quarantined in a Munich Brown House or a balcony in Rome. If we want to make certain that Fascism does not come to America, we must make certain that it does not thrive anywhere in the world.   *Ibid.*

United States Congress

The labor of a human being is not a commodity or article of commerce.
Clayton Act, section 6.

(A fine not exceeding $2,000 and imprisonment not exceeding two years is imposed on anyone who should) write, print, utter or publish . . . any false, scandalous, and malicious writing or writings against the government of the United States or the President of the United States, with intent . . . to bring them . . . into contempt or disrepute.
Sedition Act.

The inequality of bargaining power between employees who do not possess full freedom of association or actual liberty of contract, and employers who are organized in the corporate or other forms of ownership association, substantially burdens and affects the flow of commerce and tends to aggravate recurrent business depressions, by depressing wage rates and the purchasing power of wage earners in industry and by preventing the stabilization of competitive wage rates and working conditions within and between industries. *Wagner Labor Act, Section 1.*

Experience has proved that protection by law of the right of employees to organize and bargain collectively safeguards commerce from injury, impairment or interruption, and promotes the flow of commerce by removing certain recognized sources of industrial strife and unrest, by encouraging practices fundamental to the friendly adjustment of industrial disputes arising out of differences as to wages, hours, or other working conditions, and by restoring equality of bargaining power between employers and employees. *Ibid.*

Through the press, public opinion, and pressure groups it is possible to influence the political process. While all three of these factors have played a part in the process since our beginnings as a nation, the extent and consciousness of their use has grown inordinately. They are employed by all contestants in the struggle for control, but reflect the viewpoint of business more accurately than that of others.
Monopoly Investigation — Temporary National Economic Committee, Investigation of Concentration of Economic Power, 76th Congress, 3d Session, Monograph 26.

The revolution in communications, produced by American ingenuity and promoted by American business, makes the press, the radio, and other opinion-forming instruments far more important in the political process than ever before. Both press and radio are, after all, "big business", and even when they possess the highest integrity, they are the prisoners of their own beliefs.   *Ibid.*

Through the American Newspaper Publishers Association the country's daily newspapers join their strength for business and against government.   *Ibid.*

Business exerts its influence on industrial relations policy through the National Association of Manufacturers, its members and affiliates and other sympathetic organizations . . .
The American Bar Association has, by framing and pushing legislative proposals designed to achieve this purpose (opposition to the Wagner Act) indicated its fundamental community of interest with business. The American Newspaper Publishers Association shares a similar community of interest.
     Ibid.

United States Supreme Court *

If one race be inferior to the other socially, the Constitution of the United States cannot put them on the same plane.**
     Plessy v. Ferguson, 1896.

Separate educational facilities are inherently unequal. Therefore we hold that . . . (those segregated are) deprived of the equal protection of the laws. *May 17, 1954.****

The doctrine of "separate but equal" (facilities) has no place . . . Segregation is a denial of the equal protection of the laws.
     Ibid.

---

* For other decisions (and dissents), see under names of Justices.
** See dissent by Justice Harlan.
*** See Earl Warren.

It is no longer open to doubt that the liberty of the press, and speech, is within the liberty safeguarded by the due process clause of the Fourteenth Amendment from invasion of State action. It was found impossible to conclude that the essential personal liberty of the citizen was left unprotected by the general guaranty of fundamental rights of person and property.

Near v. Minnesota ex rel, 283 U.S. 697 (1931), p. 707.

The publisher of a newspaper has no special immunity from the application of the general laws.

Associated Press v. NLRB, 301 U.S. 103 (1937); known as "the Watson case."

The "establishment of religion" clause of the First Amendment means at least this: Neither a state nor the Federal Government can set up a church. Neither can pass laws which aid one religion, aid all religions, or prefer one religion over another... No tax in any amount, large or small, can be levied to support any religious activities or institutions, whatever they may be called, or whatever form they may adopt to teach or practice religion. Neither a state nor the Federal Government can, openly or secretly, participate in the affairs of any religious organizations or groups and *vice versa*. In the words of Jefferson, the clause against establishment of religion by law was intended to erect "a wall of separation between Church and State".

People ex rel. McCullom v. Board of education of Champaign, Illinois. 333 U.S. 203 (1948).

We cannot have it both ways. Religious teaching cannot be a private affair when the state seeks to impose regulations which infringe on it indirectly, and a public affair when it comes to taxing citizens of one faith to aid another, or those of no faith at all. If these principles seem harsh in prohibiting aid to Catholic education, it must not be forgotten that it is the same Constitution that alone assures Catholics the right to maintain these schools at all when predominant local sentiment would forbid them.

Pierce v. Society of Sisters, 268 U.S. 510.

What is good literature, what has educational value, what is refined public information, what is good art, varies with individuals as it does from one generation to another. There doubtless would be a contrariety of views concerning Cervantes' *Don Quixote*, Shakespeare's *Venus and Adonis*, or Zola's *Nana*. But a requirement that literature or art conform to some norm prescribed by an official smacks of an ideology foreign to our system ... To withdraw the second-class rate from this publication today because its contents seemed to one official not good for the public would sanction withdrawal of the second-class rate tomorrow from another periodical whose social or economic views seemed harmful to another official.

The Esquire case, quoted by Justice Douglas, An Almanac of Liberty.

Long ago we stated the reason for labor organizations. We said that union was essential to give laborers opportunity to deal on an equality with their employer.

N.L.R.B. v. Jones & Laughlin, 301 U.S. 1.

Louis Untermeyer

(1885-1977)

American poet

Ever insurgent let me be,
  Make me more daring than devout:

From sleek contentment keep me free,
And fill me with a buoyant doubt.
Prayer.

From compromise and things half-done,
Keep me, with stern and stubborn pride;
And when, at last, the right is won,
God, keep me still unsatisfied. *Ibid.*

Harold C(layton) Urey
(1893-1981)
*American scientist, Nobel Prize
for chemistry, 1934*

Life is not a miracle. It is a natural phenomenon, and can be expected to appear whenever there is a planet whose conditions duplicate those of the earth.
Time, November 24, 1952.

U.S.S.R. (Union of Soviet Socialist Republics)

In conformity with the interests of the working people, and in order to strengthen the socialist system, the citizens of the U.S.S.R. are guaranteed by law:
(a) Freedom of Speech;
(b) Freedom of the Press;
(c) Freedom of assembly, including the holding of mass meetings;
(d) Freedom of street processions and demonstrations.
Constitution of the U.S.S.R.

These civil rights are ensured by placing at the disposal of the working people and their organizations, printing presses, stocks of paper, public buildings, the streets, communications, facilities and other material requisites for the exercise of these rights.
Ibid.

The U.S.S.R. declares labor the duty of all citizens of the republic. *Ibid.*

Among the noble qualities of the Soviet citizen is class hatred. It is a sage and profound feeling of organic hatred toward the enemy—toward all the filthy, abominable remnants of the old world, its wolfish laws and fetid life . . . Irreconcilable, inflexible, untamable hate should be nourished by every worker, by every collective farm worker, by every soldier and office employee, by every teacher and artist, because this hate is a great, heroic, sacred hate which belongs to the proletariat.
Komsomolskaya Pravda, quoted in Time, October 7, 1935.

Alan Valentine
(b. 1901)
American writer

Most Americans want to be cultivated, but only comfortably cultivated. They dabble with the intellectual just enough to avoid being lowbrow and escape being highbrow. Middlebrowism looks like cultivation because it is so clearly superior to vulgarity, but to be satisfied with it is to make the good the enemy of the best. It merely dresses and domesticates the commonplace.
The Age of Conformity, Regnery.

Valera
See de Valera

Paul Valéry
(1871-1945)
French poet, academician

Two dangers constantly threaten the world: order and disorder.
The Nation, January 5, 1957.

The world acquires value only through its extremes and endures only through moderation; extremists make the world great, the moderates give it stability.   *Ibid.*

All politicians have read history; but one might say that they read it only in order to learn from it how to repeat the same calamities all over again.   *Saturday Review.*

History is the most dangerous of all the products of the chemical laboratory of our mind. It stimulates dreaming, it intoxicates nations, it generates in them false memories, exaggerates their reflexes, irritates their old wounds, deprives them of peace and infects them with megalomania or mania of persecution.

For names containing "van," see also the basic name.

Martin Van Buren
(1782-1862)
8th President of the United States

The second, sober thought of the people is seldom wrong, and always efficient.
Letter, 1829; Schlesinger, The Age of Jackson, p. 392.

From the first institution of government to the present time there has been a struggle going on between capital and labor for a fair distribution of profits resulting from their joint capacities.

Cornelius Vanderbilt
(1794-1877)
American capitalist

What do I care about the law. Hain't I got the power?
R. L. Heilbroner, The Worldly Philosophers.

Gentlemen: You have undertaken to ruin me. I will not sue you, for law takes too long. I will ruin you. Sincerely, Cornelius Vanderbilt.   *Letter to associates.*

William H. Vanderbilt
(1821-1885)
American railroad president

The public be damned.
Quoted by Melville E. Stone, head of the Associated Press, Fifty Years a Journalist.

Where Vanderbilt sits, there is the head of the table. I teach my son to be rich.
Quoted by Mr. Justice Holmes, The Soldier's Faith, 1895.

When I want to buy up any politicians I always find the anti-monopolists the most purchaseable. They don't come so high.
To reporters on special train nearing Chicago, October 8, 1882; Chicago Daily News, October 9.

William K. Vanderbilt
(1849-1920)
American railroad president

Inherited wealth is a big handicap to happiness. It is as certain death to ambition as cocaine is to morality.   *Interview, 1905.*

Frank Vanderlip
(1864-1937)
American financier

Anyone who tries to understand the money question goes crazy.   *Attributed.*

Carl Van Doren
(1885-1950)
American editor, historian, critic

The race of men, while sheep in credulity, are wolves for conformity.
Why I Am an Unbeliever.

[705]

Mark Van Doren
(1894-1972)
American poet, critic, novelist

An ancient sentence about liberal education says it is the education worthy of a free man, and the converse is equally ancient: the free man is the one who is worthy of a liberal education. Both sentences remain true, the only difficulty being to know how many men are capable of freedom.
Liberal Education, Henry Holt & Co.

To say that truth is better than falsehood is not to speak vaguely. It is more powerful, it is more interesting, and it is less lonely ... It is the love of truth that makes men free in the common light of day.   *Ibid.*

"Respect for the truth is an acquired taste," and the recovery of it may take a long time, for it involves an understanding that freedom has its own compulsions, and it requires a discipline in the adjustment of thought to thought which only the liberal arts can teach.   *Ibid.*

No society can succeed henceforth unless its last citizen is as free to become a prince and a philosopher as his powers permit. The greatest number of these is none too many for democracy, nor is the expense of producing them exorbitant.   *Ibid.*

Vincent van Gogh
(1853-1890)
Dutch painter

I can very well do without God both in my life and in my painting, but I cannot, suffering as I am, do without something which is greater than I, which is my life —the power to create.
Letter to Theo. Art News Annual, 1950.

Hendrik Van Loon
(1882-1944)
American historian, biographer

The history of the world is the record of man in quest of his daily bread and butter.
          The Story of Mankind.

Loneliness is part of the penalty every true artist pays for being different from the rest of his fellow men.   *Beethoven.*

Start a political upheaval and let yourself be caught, and you will hang as a traitor. But place yourself at the head of a rebellion and gain your point, and all future generations will worship you as the Father of their Country.

Bartolomeo Vanzetti
(1888-executed 1927)
American anarchist

If it had not been for this thing, I might have live out my life talking at street corners to scorning men. I might have die unmarked, unknown, a failure. Now we are not a failure. This is our career and our triumph. Never in our full life could we hope to do such work for tolerance, for justice, for man's understanding of man, as now we do by accident.

Our words—our lives—our pains: nothing! The taking of our lives—lives of a good shoemaker and a poor fish peddler—all! That last moment belongs to us—that agony is our triumph.   *Letter to his son, April, 1927.*

What I wish more than all in this last hour of agony is that our case and our fate may be understood in their real being and serve as a tremendous lesson to the forces of freedom so that our suffering and death will not have been in vain.
Letter to his defense committee, on the eve of his execution; inscribed by Gutzon Borglum on the memorial tablet.

[706]

It is incredible the insult made to the liberty, to the life, to the dignity of the human beings, by other human beings. And it is humiliating, for he who feels the common humanity that ties together all the men, good and bad, to think that all the committed infamies have not produced in the crowd an adequate sense of rebellion, of horrors, of disgust. It is humiliating to human beings, the possibility of such ferocity, of such cowardness.

Letter to "Dear Comrade Blackwell," Charlestown Prison, April 14, 1923.

This is the great danger, the danger of the tomorrow; the danger, I mean, that, after the Fascismo, declined from internal dissolution or by external attack, may have to follow a period of insensate violences, of sterile vendettas, which would exhaust in little episodes of blood that energy which should be employed for a radical transformation of the social arrangements such to render impossible the repetition of the present horrors.

Ibid.

The Fascisti's methods may be good for who inspires to become a tyrant. They are certainly bad for he who will make "opera" of a liberator, for he who will collaborate to raise all humanity to a dignity of free and conscient men.

We remain as always we were, the partisans of the liberty, of all the liberty.

Ibid.

I still hope, and we will fight until the last moment, to revindicate our right to live and to be free, but all the forces of the State and of the money and reaction are deadly against us because we are libertarians or Anarchists.

Letter to Dante Sacco.

Sacco's name will live in the hearts of the people, when your name, your laws, institutions, and your false god are but a dim remomoring of a cursed past in which man was wolf to the man.

Last speech in Massachusetts court.

Vatican Council

If any one shall say that human reason is so independent that faith cannot be enjoined upon it by God; let him be anathema.

Session 3, Canon 1.

If any one shall assert it to be possible that sometimes, according to the progress of science, a sense is to be given to doctrines propounded by the Church different from that which the Church has understood and understands; let him be anathema.

Ibid. Canon 3, April 24, 1870.

If any one shall say that miracles are impossible, and therefore that all the accounts regarding them, even those contained in Holy Scripture, are to be dismissed as fabulous or mythical; or that miracles can never be known with certainty, and that the divine origin of Christianity is not rightly proved by them; let him be anathema.   *Ibid. Canon 4.*

We teach and define that it is a dogma divinely revealed: that the Roman pontiff, when he speaks *ex cathedra*, that is, when in discharge of the office of pastor and doctor of all Christians, by virtue of his supreme apostolic authority he defines a doctrine regarding faith or morals to be held by the universal Church, by the divine assistance promised him in blessed Peter, is possessed of that infallibility with which the divine Redeemer willed that his Church should be endowed for defining doctrine regarding faith and morals; and that therefore such definitions of the Roman pontiff

are irreformable of themselves, and not from the consent of the Church.
Ibid. Session 4. Dogmatic Constitution.

Thorstein Veblen
(1857-1929)
American social scientist, economist

Into the cultural and technological system of the modern world, the patriotic spirit fits like dust in the eyes and sand in the bearings. Its net contribution to the outcome is obscuration, distrust, and retardation at every point where it touches the fortunes of modern mankind. Yet it is forever present in the counsels of the statesman and in the affections of the common man, and it never ceases to command the regard of all men as the prime attribute of mankind and the final test of the desirable citizen. It is scarcely an exaggeration to say that no other consideration is allowed in abatement of the claims of patriotic loyalty, and that such loyalty will be allowed to cover any multitude of sins.
The Nature of Peace, 1919.

The ultimate ground of validity for the thinking of the business classes is the natural-rights ground of property—a conventional, anthropomorphic fact having an institutional validity, rather than a matter-of-fact validity such as can be formulated in terms of material cause and effect.
The Theory of Business Enterprise.

The business classes are conservative, on the whole, but such a conservative bent is, of course, not peculiar to them. These occupations are not the only ones whose reasoning prevailingly moves on a conventional plane. Indeed, the intellectual captivity of other classes, such as soldiers, politicians, the clergy, and men of fashion, moves on a plane of still older conventions; so that if the training given by business employments is to be characterized as conservative, that given by these other, more archaic employments should be called reactionary. Extreme conventionalization means extreme conservatism. Conservatism means the maintenance of conventions already in force. On this head, therefore, the discipline of modern business life may be said simply to retain something of the complexion which marks the life of the higher barbarian culture, at the same time that it has not retained the disciplinary force of the barbarian culture in so high a state of preservation as some of the other occupations just named.
Ibid.

The possession of goods, whether acquired aggressively by one's own exertion or passively by transmission through inheritance from others, becomes a conventional basis of reputability. The possession of wealth, which was at the outset valued simply as an evidence of efficiency, becomes, in popular apprehension, itself a meritorious act. Wealth is now itself intrinsically honorable and confers honor on its possessor.
The Theory of the Leisure Class, Macmillan, 1899; Mentor, p. 37.

In order to gain and to hold the esteem of men it is not sufficient merely to possess wealth or power. The wealth or power must be put in evidence, for esteem is awarded only on evidence.
Ibid., p. 42.

The archaic theoretical distinction between the base and the honorable in the manner of a man's life retains very much of its ancient force even today. So much so that there are few of the better class who are not possessed of an instinctive repugnance for the vulgar forms of labor.
Ibid.

Abstention from labor is the conventional evidence of wealth and is therefore the conventional mark of social standing; and this insistence on the meritoriousness of wealth leads to a more strenuous insistence on leisure. *Ibid., p. 44.*

The forces which count toward a re-adjustment of institutions in any modern industrial community are chiefly economic forces; or more specifically, these forces take the form of pecuniary pressure. Such a readjustment as is here contemplated is substantially a change in men's views as to what is good and right, and the means through which a change is wrought in men's apprehension of what is good and right is in large part the pressure of pecuniary exigencies. *Ibid., pp. 135-6.*

Any change in men's views as to what is good and right in human life makes its way but tardily at the best. Especially is this true of any change in the direction of what is called progress; that is to say, in the direction of divergence from the archaic position—from the position which may be accounted the point of departure at any step in the social evolution of the community. *Ibid., p. 136.*

The office of the leisure class in social evolution is to retard the movement and to conserve what is obsolescent. This proposition is by no means novel; it has long been one of the commonplaces of popular opinion. *Ibid., p. 137.*

The opposition of the (wealthy) class to changes in the cultural scheme is instinctive, and does not rest primarily on an interested calculation of material advantages; it is an instinctive revulsion at any departure from the accepted way of doing and of looking at things—a revulsion common to all men and only to be overcome by stress of circumstances. *Ibid.*

All change in habits of life and of thought is irksome. The difference in this respect between the wealthy and the common run of mankind lies not so much in the motive which prompts to conservatism as in the degree of exposure to the economic forces that urge a change. *Ibid., pp. 137-8.*

This conservatism of the wealthy class is so obvious a feature that it has even come to be recognized as a mark of respectability. Since conservatism is a characteristic of the wealthier and therefore more reputable portion of the community, it has acquired a certain honorific or decorative value. It has become prescriptive to such an extent that an adherence to conservative views is comprised as a matter of course in our notions of respectability; and it is imperatively incumbent on all who would lead a blameless life in point of social repute. *Ibid.*

Conservatism, being an upper-class characteristic, is decorous; and conversely, innovation, being a lower-class phenomenon, is vulgar. *Ibid.*

The fact that the usages, actions, and views of the well-to-do leisure class acquire the character of a prescriptive canon of conduct for the rest of society, gives added weight and reach to the conservative influence of that class. It makes it incumbent upon all reputable people to follow their lead. *Ibid.*

By virtue of its high position as the avatar of good form, the wealthier class comes to exert a retarding influence upon social development far in excess of that which the simple numerical strength of the class would assign it. Its prescriptive example acts to greatly stiffen the resistance of all other classes against any innovation, and to fix men's affections upon the good institutions handed down from an earlier generation. *Ibid.*

The nation, being in effect a licensed predatory concern, is not bound by the decencies of that code of laws and morals that governs private conduct.

Absentee Ownership, 1923.

Born in iniquity, and conceived in sin, the spirit of nationalism has never ceased to bend human institutions to the service of dissension and distress. *Ibid.*

A protective tariff is a typical conspiracy in restraint of trade.

The Engineers and the Price System, 1921.

Conservatism is the maintenance of conventions already in force.

Bolshevism is a menace to absentee ownership. That is its unpardonable sin . . . Bolshevism . . . is the sin against the Holy Ghost of established Law and Order.

Socialism is a dead horse.

The highest achievement in business is the nearest approach in getting something for nothing . . . The less any given business concern can contrive to give for what it gets, the more profitable its own traffic will be. Business success means "getting the best of the bargain."

A spirit of quietism, caution, compromise, collusion, and chicanery.

Veblen's description of the conduct of universities by their presidents and trustees, as business enterprises.

Pierre Victurnien Vergniaud
(1753-1793)
French revolutionist

The revolution, like Saturn, successively devours all its children.

Lamartine, Histoire des Girondins.

Vincent C. Vickers
(1879-1935)
British munitions maker; director, Bank of England

In the progress of time, and through our own base carelessness and ignorance, we have permitted the money-industry, by the virtue of its business, to gradually attain a political and economic influence so powerful that it has actually undermined the authority of the State and usurped the power of Democratic government.

Economic Tribulation.

The existing (world money) system . . . creates poverty . . . and is the root cause of war. *Ibid.*

Peter Viereck
(b. 1916)
American educator, writer, poet

In a free democracy the only justified aristocracy is that of the lonely creative bitterness, the artistically creative scars of the fight for the inner dimension against outer mechanization:—the fight for the private life.

Saturday Review, November 1, 1958.

The Economic Man of Smith and Marx, with its famous Economic Motives, has never existed . . . In place of the economic, capitalistic philosophy of Adam Smith and its parallel, the socialist philosophy of Marx, the world through trial and error will come to see *the economic necessity of an anti-economic philosophy*, the material necessity of antimaterialism. Pragmatism is unpragmatic; it won't work. *Ibid.*

Pancho Villa
(1877-1923)
Mexican revolutionary hero

I, like you, think the greatest enemy of our

progress and liberty is the corrupting clergy, who for so long have dominated our country.
Telegram to General Villareal, governor of the State of Nuevo Leon; press report.

George Villiers
See Buckingham

Vinci
See Leonardo da Vinci

Fred M. Vinson
(1890-1953)
Chief Justice, U.S. Supreme Court

Overthrow of the Governent by force and violence is certainly a substantial enough interest for the Government to limit speech. Indeed, this is the ultimate value of any society, for if a society cannot protect its very structure from armed internal attack, it must follow that no subordinate value can be protected.
For the majority, Dennis v. U.S., 341 U.S. 494 (1951).

Whatever theoretical merit there may be to the argument that there is a "right" to rebellion against dictatorial governments is without force where the existing structure of the government provides for peaceful and orderly change.   *Ibid.*

Virgil
(70-19 B.C.)
Roman poet

Timeo Danaos et dona ferentes. (I fear the Greeks, even when they bring gifts.)
Aeneid, ii.

Diis aliter visum. (The gods have judged otherwise.)   *Ibid.*

Possunt quia posse videntur. (They can because they think they can.)   *Ibid., v.*

Mens agitat molem. (Mind moves matter.)
Ibid., vi.

Labor omnis vincit. (Labor conquers all things.)   *Georgics, i.*

Felix qui potuit rerum cognoscere causas,
Quique metus omnes, et inexorabile fatum,
Subjecit pedibus, strepitumque Acherontis avari.

(Happy the man who has learned the causes of things, and has put under his feet all fears, and inexorable fate, and the noisy strife of the hell of greed.)
Quoted by Bacon, The Advancement of Learning; requoted, Durant, The Story of Philosophy.

Now the last age is coming . . .
A new line is sent down to us from the skies
For whom they will beat their swords into
          ploughshares,
For whom the golden race will rise, the
          whole world new.   *Fourth Eclogue.*

Curst greed of gold, what crimes thy tyrant power has caused!

Who asks whether the enemy were defeated by strategy or valor?

Fear is the proof of a degenerate mind.

Andrei (Yanuarievich) Vishinsky
(1883-1954)
Soviet diplomat

In our state, naturally, there is and can be no place for freedom of speech, press, and so on for the foes of socialism.
The Law of the Soviet State, 1938; N.Y., 1948; quoted by Justice Douglas, dissent, Dennis v. U.S.

Freedom of speech, of the press, of assembly, of meetings, of street parades, and of demonstrations are the property of all the citizens of the U.S.S.R., fully guaranteed by the state upon the single condition that they be utilized in accord with the interests of the toilers and to the end of strengthening the socialist social order. *Ibid.*

The Soviet State is the welding of coercion and persuasion. *Time, September 8, 1947.*

Many people love democracy but do not know how to defend it. They take democracy for a lovely lady instead of seeing it as a vigorous comrade.
Address to Resistance lawyers, Palace of Justice, Paris, May, 1946; Time, May 27, 1946.

Democracy is sometimes called the dictatorship of the proletariat. Dictatorship of the proletariat in fact is democracy in action . . . As long as dictatorship acts in the name of the people for the welfare of the fatherland, it is sacred. When it acts against the people, it is criminal. In Russia, our regime is one of democratic dictatorship. *Ibid.*

After all, what is democracy if not the power of the people? . . . As Lenin said, every worker of our nation should be able to direct the state, and every cook should be able to govern. Democracy in the Soviet Union is in fact the participation of tens of millions of people in the government. *Ibid.*

Elio Vittorini
(1879-1947)
Italian educator

Communism has become what the Catholic Church was in the Middle Ages—a force

which makes use of history, which plays up to history, which is part of history, which makes history, but which nevertheless arrests or obstructs the real current of history.
The Nation, December 6, 1952.

Vivekananda
(1863-1902)
Indian Swami

This "I and mine" causes the whole misery. With the sense of possession comes selfishness or thought of selfishness and selfishness brings on misery. Every act of selfishness or thought of selfishness makes us attached to something, and immediately we are made slaves.
Published by Advaita Ashrama, India; quoted by Gollancz, From Darkness to Light.

Every wave in the Chitta that says "I and mine" immediately puts a chain around us and makes us slaves; and the more we say "I and mine" the more slavery grows, the more misery increases. Therefore, Karma-Yoga tells us to enjoy the beauty of all the pictures of the world but not to identify ourselves with any of them. *Ibid.*

Comte de Volney, Constantin François de Chasseboeuf
(1757-1820)
French scholar

Man, discontented with the present, imagines for the past a perfection that never existed. He praises the dead out of contempt for the living, and beats the children with the bones of their ancestors.

Voltaire (né François Marie Arouet)*
(1694-1778)
French philosopher

The public is a ferocious beast; one must either chain it up or flee from it.
Letter to Mlle. Quinault, August 16, 1738.

Great crimes are always committed by great ignoramuses.
Letter to Rousseau, August 30, 1755; Voltaire in His Letters, Putnam, 1919.

Opinion has caused more trouble on this little earth than plagues or earthquakes.
Letter (to unknown), January 5, 1759.

Je voudrais que vous écrasassiez l'infâme. (I wish that you would crush this infamy.)
Letter to Jean d'Alembert, June 23, 1760.°°

When we hear news we should always wait for the sacrament of confirmation.
To Count d'Argental, August 28, 1760.

You seem solicitous about that pretty thing called soul. I do protest I know nothing of it, nor whether it is, nor what it is, nor what it shall be. Young scholars and priests know all

---

* "Voltaire conquered. Voltaire waged the splendid kind of warfare, the war of one alone against all. . . . The war of thought against matter, the war of reason against prejudice, the war of the just against the unjust, the war of the oppressed against the oppressor." Victor Hugo, *Oration on Voltaire.*
°° The reference variously interpreted to mean superstition, clericalism, or ecclesiasticism. *Écrasez l'infâme* remained Voltaire's motto.

of that perfectly. For my part I am but a very ignorant fellow.
To James Boswell, February 11, 1765.

When the people undertake to reason, all is lost.   *Correspondence, April 1, 1766.*

His Sacred Majesty, Chance, decides everything.   *Ibid., February 26, 1767.*

For seventeen hundred years the Christian sect has done nothing but harm.
Letter to Frederick the Great, April 6, 1767.

In the midst of all the doubts which we have discussed for 4000 years in 4000 ways, the safest course is to do nothing against one's conscience. With this secret, we can enjoy life and have no fear from death.
Ibid.

Doubt is not a pleasant condition, but certainty is an absurd one.   *Ibid.*

There are truths which are not for all men, nor for all time.
To Cardinal de Bernis, April 23, 1761.

The number of the wise will always be small. It is true that it has been largely increased, but it is nothing in comparison with the number of fools, and unfortunately they say that God always favors the heaviest battalions.
To M. le Riche, February 6, 1770.

Tout est pour le mieux dans le meilleur des mondes possible. (All is for the best in the best of possible worlds.)   *Candide.°*

In the best of possible worlds the chateau of Monseigneur the baron was the most

---

° This phrase, spoken by Dr. Pangloss, was Voltaire's ironic criticism of the Pollyanna philosophy of Leibnitz.

beautiful of chateaux, and madame the best of possible baronesses. *Ibid.*

Dans ce pays-ci il est bon de tuer de temps en temps un amiral pour encourager les autres. [In this country (England) it is well from time to time to kill an admiral to encourage the others.] *Ibid.*

Si Dieu n'existait pas, il faudrait l'inventer. (If God did not exist, it would be necessary to invent him.)
*Epître a l'auteur du nouveau livre des trois imposteurs, 1769.**

This agglomeration which was called and which still calls itself the Holy Roman Empire is neither holy, nor Roman, nor an empire.
Essay on the Morals and the Spirit of Nations.

The history of the great events of this world are scarcely more than the history of crimes. *Ibid.*

History in general is a collection of crimes, follies, and misfortunes among which we have now and then met with a few virtues, and some happy times. *Ibid.*

Every man is the creature of the age in which he lives; very few are able to raise themselves above the ideas of the times. *Ibid.*

The poor man is never free; he serves in every country. *Les Guèbres, act 3.*

War is the greatest of all crimes; and yet there is no aggressor who does not color his crime with the pretext of justice.
The Ignorant Philosopher.

---

* Voltaire to M. Saurin, November 10, 1770: "I am rarely satisfied with my lines, but I confess that I have a father's tenderness for that one."

History is but the register of crimes and misfortunes. *L'Ingénu, ch. x.*

Ancient histories, as one of our wits has said, are but fables that have been agreed upon. *Jeannot et Colin.*

Whoever serves his country well has no need of ancestors. *Mérope, 1. 3.*

Would you believe that while the flames were consuming these innocent victims, the inquisitors and the other savages were chanting *our* prayers? These pitiless monsters were invoking the God of mercy . . . while committing the most atrocious crime.
Sermon du Rabbin Akib, Nouveaux Mélanges, iii, 1765.

Nothing can be more contrary to religion and the clergy than reason and common sense. *Philosophical Dictionary, 1764.*

If it were permitted to reason consistently in religious matters, it is clear that we all ought to become Jews, because Jesus Christ our Saviour was born a Jew, lived a Jew, died a Jew, and He said expressly that He was fulfilling the Jewish religion. *Ibid.*

Which is more dangerous, fanaticism or atheism? Fanaticism is certainly a thousand times more deadly; for atheism inspires no bloody passion, whereas fanaticism does; it is not opposed to crime, but fanaticism causes crimes to be committed. *Ibid.*

Man is a free agent; were it otherwise, the priests could not damn him. *Ibid.*

Chance is a word void of sense; nothing can exist without a cause. *Ibid.*

Le mieux est l'ennemi du bien. (The best is the enemy of the good.) *Ibid.*

Religion, you say, has produced countless misfortunes; say rather the superstition which reigns on our unhappy globe. This is the cruelest enemy of the pure worship due the Supreme Being. Let us detest this monster which has always torn the bosom of its mother; those who combat it are the benefactors of the human race; it is a serpent which chokes religion in its embrace; we must crush its head without wounding the mother whom it devours.   *Ibid.; God.*

As a rule there is no comparison between the crimes of great men, who are always ambitious, and the crimes of the people, who always want, and can only want, liberty and equality. These two sentiments, Liberty and Equality, do not lead straight to calumny, rapine, assassination, poisoning, to devastation of one's neighbor's lands, etcetera. But ambitious might and the mania for power plunge men into all these crimes, whatever the time, whatever the place.
Ibid.; Democracy.

Will is wish, and liberty is power.
Ibid.; Free Will.

Liberty, then, about which so many volumes have been written is, when accurately defined, only the power of acting. *Ibid.*

We have a natural right to make use of our pens as of our tongue, at our peril, risk and hazard.   *Ibid.; Liberty of the Press.*

I know many books which have bored their readers, but I know of none which has done real evil.   *Ibid.*

Prejudice is an opinion without judgment.
Ibid.; Prejudices.

Every sect of every kind, is a rallying-point for doubt and error. Scotist, Thomist, Realist, Nominalist, Papist, Calvinist, Molinist, and Jansenist, are only pseudonyms.
Ibid.; Sect.

There are no sects in geometry. *Ibid.*

Well, to what dogma do all minds agree? To the worship of a God, and to honesty.
Ibid.

All the philosophers of the world who had a religion have said in all ages: "There is a God; and one must be just." That, then, is the universal religion established in all ages and throughout mankind. The point in which they all agree is therefore true, and the systems through which they differ are therefore false.   *Ibid.*

One does not speak of a Euclidian, an Archimedean. When truth is evident, it is impossible for parties and factions to arise. There never has been a dispute as to whether there is daylight at noon.   *Ibid.*

Sect and *error* are synonymous. *Ibid.*

This is the character of truth: it is for all men, it has only to show itself to be recognized, and one cannot argue against it. A long dispute means that *both parties are wrong.*   *Ibid.*

The superstitious man is to the rogue what the slave is to the tyrant.
Ibid.; Superstition.

Superstition, born of paganism, and adopted by Judaism, invested the Christian Church from earliest times. All the fathers of the Church, without exception, believed in the power of magic. The Church always condemned magic, but she always believed in it: she did not excommunicate sorcerers as madmen who were mistaken, but as men who were really in communication with the devil.   *Ibid.*

One distinguishes tyranny of one man and that of many. . . . A despot always has his good moments; an assembly of despots never.
Ibid.; Tyranny.

It is forbidden to kill; therefore all murderers are punished unless they kill in large numbers and to the sound of trumpets.
Ibid.; War.

It is with books as with men: a very small number play a great part.
Ibid., miscellaneous.

The truths of religion are never so well understood as by those who have lost their power of reasoning.　*Ibid.*

The individual who persecutes a man, his brother, because he is not of the same opinion, is a monster.　*Ibid.*

To succeed in chaining the multitude, you must seem to wear the same fetters. *Ibid.*

There is but one morality, as there is but one geometry.　*Ibid.*

It requires ages to destroy a popular opinion.　*Ibid.*

The true character of liberty is independence, maintained by force.　*Ibid.*

Man is not born wicked: he becomes so as he becomes sick.　*Ibid.*

The theist is a man firmly persuaded of the existence of a supreme being as good as he is powerful, who has formed all things . . . ; who punishes, without cruelty, all crimes, and recompenses with goodness all virtuous actions.　*Ibid., Theism.*

He (the Theist) does not join any of the sects which all contradict one another. His religion is the most ancient and the most widespread; for the simple worship of a God preceded all the systems of the world . . . To do good is his worship, to submit to God is his creed. The Mohammedan cries out to him, "Beware if you fail to make the pilgrimage to Mecca!"—the priest says to him, "Curses on you if you do not make the trip to Notre Dame de Lorette!" He laughs at Lorette and at Mecca: but he succors the indigent and defends the oppressed.　*Ibid.*

Most of the great men of this world live as if they were atheists. Every man who has lived with his eyes open, knows that the knowledge of a God, his presence, and his justice, has not the slightest influence over the wars, the treaties, the objects of ambition, interest, or pleasure, in the pursuit of which they are wholly occupied.
Op. cit., London edition, 1824.

Atheism and fanaticism are two monsters, which may tear society to pieces; but the atheist preserves his reason, which checks his propensity to mischief, while the fanatic is under the influence of a madness which is constantly urging him on.　*Ibid.*

The people of all nations, whether actuated by desires or fears, have invoked the assistance of the Divinity. Philosophers, however, more respectful to the Supreme Being, and rising more above human weakness, have been habituated to substitute, for prayer, resignation.　*Ibid.*

It is lamentable, that to be a good patriot we must become the enemy of the rest of mankind.　*Ibid.*

A married priest would run the risk of having interests in common with his fellow-citizens, a state of things not at all in keeping with the profound and sacred views of the Holy Catholic Church, Apostolic and Roman.　*Pocket Theology.*

Theology: A science profound, supernatural, and divine, which teaches us to reason on that which we don't understand and to get our ideas mixed up on that which we do. Thus it is evident that theology is the noblest and most valuable science there is, all the others confining themselves to known and consequently despicable objects. Without theology empires could not subsist, the church would perish, and the nations would not know what to think about wars, gratuitous predestinations, and the Bull Unigenitus, concerning which last it is of vital importance that people have the most precise conception.   *Ibid.*

Superstition: Any practice or form of religion to which we are not accustomed. Any worship that is not offered up to the true God is false and superstitious. The only true God is the God of our priests; the only true worship is that which seems the most fitting to them; and to which they have accustomed us from our earliest childhood; any other worship is clearly superstitious, false, and even ridiculous.   *Ibid.*

The man who says to me, "Believe as I do, or God will damn you," will presently say, "Believe as I do, or I shall assassinate you."   *Selected Works, p. 65.*

Books rule the world, or at least those nations which have a written language; the others do not count.
Quoted by Durant, The Story of Philosophy.

I am tired of hearing it declared that twelve men sufficed to establish Christianity, and I want to prove to them that it only needs one to destroy it.
Quoted in "Voltaire," by Maurois.

You must have the devil in you to succeed in any of the arts.
Quoted by Tallentyre, Life of Voltaire, 3rd ed., p. 145.

I die adoring God, loving my friends, not hating my enemies, and detesting supersti-

tion. (Signed) Voltaire, February 28, 1778.
Ibid., p. 538.

It is difficult to free fools from the chains they revere.

As long as people believe in absurdities they will continue to commit atrocities.

The right of persecution is therefore absurd and barbarous; it is the right of tigers, tho' so much the more horrid, as the tigers have a plea of hunger, and devour men with a view to make them a prey; while men destroy each other for the sake of mere paragraphs.

All men are born with a nose and ten fingers, but no one was born with a knowledge of God.

Our wretched species is so made that those who walk on the well-trodden path always throw stones at those who are showing a new road.

For names containing "von," see the basic name.

Vries
See De Vries

Richard Wagner
(1813-1883)
German composer, poet

I am the secret of perpetual youth, the everlasting creator of life; where I am not, death rages. I am the comfort, the hope, the dream of the oppressed. I destroy what exists; but from the rock whereon I light, new life begins to flow. I come to you to break all chains which bear you down; to free you from the embrace of death, and instil a new life into your veins. All that exists must perish; that is the eternal condition of life, and I, the all destroying, fulfill that law to create a fresh new existence.

The Creative Force, 1849. [*]

I will dissipate every delusion which has mastery over the human race. I will destroy the authority of the one over the many; of the lifeless over the living; of the material over the spiritual. I will break in pieces the authority of the great; OF THE LAW OF PROPERTY. Let the will of each be master of mankind, one's own desires fashion laws, one's own strength be one's own property, for the freeman is the sacred man, and there is nothing sublimer than he.   *Ibid.*

Let the delusion be trampled under foot which gives one individual power over millions; which reduces millions to the subjection of one; which would teach that one possesses the power to make others happy
      Ibid.

Let the delusion be destroyed which provides for the mastery of death over life, of the past over the future. The law of the dead, that is their own law; it shares their lot and dies with them—it must not prevail over life. Life is in itself a law. And since law is for the living and not for the dead, and since you are the living, there exists no one who dare master you; thus you alone are the law, your own free will the single sublime law, and therefore I will destroy the mastery of the dead over the living.   *Ibid.*

Destroyed by the delusion which makes mankind the slave of his own work, of his own property.   *Ibid.*

I will destroy the order of things which makes millions the slaves of the few, and

those few the slaves of their own power, of their own wealth. I will destroy the order of things which severs enjoyment from labor, which turns labor into a burden and enjoyment into a vice, which makes one man miserable through want and another miserable through super-abundance. I will destroy this order of things which consumes the vigor of manhood in the service of the dead, of inert matter, which sustains one part of mankind in idleness or useless activity, which forces thousands to devote their sturdy youth to the indolent pursuit of soldiery, officialism, speculation and usury, and the maintenance of such like despicable conditions, while the other half, by excessive exertion and sacrifice of all enjoyment of life, bears the burden of the whole infamous structure. I will destroy even the very memory and trace of this delirious order of things which, pieced together out of force, falsehood, trouble, tears, sorrow, suffering, need, deceit, hypocrisy and crime, is shut up in its own reeking atmosphere, and never received a breath of pure air, to which no ray of pure joy ever penetrates.   *Ibid.*

Arise then, ye people of the earth, arise, ye sorrow stricken and oppressed. Ye, also, who vainly struggle to clothe the inner desolation of your hearts with the transient glory of riches, arise! . . . There are but two people henceforth on earth—the one which follows me, and the one which resists me. The one I will lead to happiness, but the other I will crush in my progress. For I am Revolution, I am the new creating force. I am the divinity which discerns all life, which embraces, revives and rewards.   *Ibid.*

Man's work is his true life, the living must not be beholden to the lifeless, must not be made subject to it. Therefore, DESTROYED BE THE DELUSION WHICH HAMPERS

* Written before his exile to France for participation in the 1848-49 uprisings.

[718]

ENJOYMENT AND LIMITS FREE WILL, which elevates property over man, and degrades him to become the slave of his own work. *Ibid.*

I will destroy the existing order of things which divides the one humanity into hostile peoples, into strong and weak, into privileged and outlawed, into rich and poor, for that makes unfortunate creatures of one and all.

Let everything be destroyed which oppresses you and makes you suffer, and from the ruins of the old let there arise a new undreamed of happinesss. Let no hatred, envy, jealousy, animosity remain among you. You must recognize as brothers and sisters all who live; and free to will, free to act, free to enjoy, you shall know the worth of existence. *Ibid.*

Morrison R. Waite
(1816-1888)
Chief Justice, U.S. Supreme Court

Laws are made for the government of actions, and while they cannot interfere with mere religious beliefs and opinions, they may with practices.
Reynolds v. U.S., 980 U.S. 145 (1879): upholding convictions of Mormons practicing polygamy.

Property does become clothed with a public interest when used in a manner to make it of public consequence.
Munn v. Illinois, 94 U.S. 113 (1877).

When, therefore, one devotes his property to a use in which the public has an interest, he in effect grants to the public an interest in that use, and must submit to be controlled by the public for the common good, to the extent of the interest he has thus created. *Ibid.*

Selman A. Waksman
(1888-1973)
"Father of Antibiotics", Nobel Prize for Medicine, 1952

It is usually not recognized that for every injurious or parasitic microbe there are dozens of beneficial ones. Without the latter, there would be no bread to eat nor wine to drink, no fertile soils and no potable waters, no clothing and no sanitation. One can visualize no form of higher life without the existence of the microbes. They are the universal scavengers. They keep in constant circulation the chemical elements which are so essential to the continuation of plant and animal life.
My Life with the Microbes, Simon & Schuster, 1954.

Microbes affect man's life in many ways, from the day of his birth to the day of his death, and even thereafter, since they attack and destroy his mortal remains. Microbes are always with us, in our food and our bodies, in our clothing and in our habitation, in the soil under our feet, and in the water we drink and bathe in. They are always ready to help us or to destroy us. Only circumstances decide which it shall be. *Ibid.*

Mary Edwards Walker
(1832-1919)
American physician, feminist

If men were really what they profess to be they would not compel women to dress so that the facilities for vice would always be so easy. *Quoted in Saturday Review, 1953.*

Alfred Russel Wallace
(1823-1913)
English scientist

The theory of natural selection rests on two main classes of facts which apply to all organized beings without exception, and which thus take rank as fundamental principles or laws. The first is, the power of rapid multiplication in a geometrical progression; the second, that the offspring always vary slightly from the parents, though generally very closely resembling them. From the first fact or law there follows, necessarily, a constant struggle for existence; because, while the offspring always exceed the parents in number, generally to an enormous extent, yet the total number of living organisms in the world does not, and cannot, increase year by year. *Darwinism, 1889.*

We cannot doubt that, on the whole, any beneficial variations will give the possessors of it a greater probability of living through the tremendous ordeal they have to undergo. There may be something left to chance, but on the whole the *fittest will survive. Ibid.*

Compared with our wondrous progress in physical science and practical applications, our system of government, of administering justice, of national education, and our whole social and moral organization, remains in a state of barbarism. . . . The wealth and knowledge and culture of *the few* do not constitute civilization, and do not of themselves advance us toward the "perfect social state." *The Malay Archipelago, 1869.*

Henry A(gard) Wallace

(1888-1965)
American statesman

Everywhere the common people are on the march.
Address, Century of the Common Man.

We who live in the United States may think there is nothing very revolutionary about freedom of religion, freedom of expression, and freedom from the fear of secret police. But when we begin to think about the significance of freedom from want for the average man, then we know that the revolution of the past 150 years has not been completed, either here in the United States or in any other nation in the world. We know that this revolution cannot stop until freedom from want has actually been attained. *Ibid.*

The march of freedom of the past 150 years has been a long-drawn-out people's revolution. In this Great Revolution of the people, there was the American Revolution of 1775, the French Revolution of 1792, the Latin-American revolutions of the Bolivarian era, the German Revolution of 1848, and the Russian Revolution of 1917. Each spoke for the common man in terms of blood on the battlefield. *Ibid.*

Reactionaries call the tune and the daily press dances to it.
Editorial statement on assuming editorship of the "New Republic."

My field is the world. My strength is my conviction that a progressive America can unify the world and a reactionary America must divide it. My enemy is blind reaction, placing profit before production, depression before effective government, and war ahead of a rising standard of living for the peoples of the backward areas. *Ibid.*

One of our most precious freedoms is the right to learn the truth. The common man is in danger of losing that right when 90 percent of his mental food is prepared for him every day by those who select the news to prove a point—and that point either reactionary or Marxist.
Editorial, New Republic.

We who fight in the people's cause will never stop until that cause is won.
Address, May 8, 1942.

For the combating of "racism" before it sinks its poison fangs deep in our body politic, the scientist has both a special motive and a special responsibility. His motive comes from the fact that when personal liberty disappears scientific liberty also disappears. His responsibility comes from the fact only he can give the people the truth. Only he can clean out the falsities which have been masquerading under the name of science in our colleges, our high schools and our public prints. Only he can show how groundless are the claims that one race, one nation, or one class has any God-given right to rule.

Department of Agriculture Year Book.

In some ways, certain books are more powerful by far than any battle.

Horace Walpole, 4th Earl of Orford
(1717-1797)
English politician, writer

Our supreme governors, the mob.
Letter to Sir Horace Mann, September 7, 1743.

Sir Robert Walpole, 1st Earl of Orford
(1676-1745)
Prime Minister of England

All those men have their price.
W. Coxe, Memoirs of Walpole, 1798.

The balance of power.
House of Commons, February 13, 1741.

William Walwyn
(fl. 1649)
English agitator

Shew me thy faith by thy workes; if I have all faith and have not luve, I am as sounding brass, or as a tinckling cymball, if faith workes, it workes by luve.
Quoted by Harold J. Laski.

Wang-An-Shih
(11th Century)
Chinese statesman

The State should take the entire management of commerce, industry, and agriculture into its own hands, with a view of succoring the working classes and preventing their being ground to the dust by the rich.
Quoted, Sinclair, The Cry for Justice.

James P. Warburg
(1896-1969)
American banker, author

We shall have World Government whether or not we like it. The only question is whether World Government will be achieved by conquest or consent.
On the Senate floor, February 17, 1950.

Joseph Ward
(1838-1889)
American Congregationalist clergyman, educator

I want to tell you what a newspaper means. It's a serious, sacred business. The least smell of corruption, fear, or favoritism must never creep into its news columns. . . . A newspaper, like Caesar's wife, must be above suspicion. Avoid even the appearance of evil.
Quoted by Gene Fowler, A Solo in Tom-Toms, Viking Press.

To get the news, you may kill, steal, burn, cheat, lie; but never sell out your paper in thought or deed. A newspaper doesn't belong to the men who run it or to those who own the plant. The press belongs to the public, to the people. It is their voice, their shield, their champion. And to keep it free, we ourselves must stay free, sincere, honest.

Ibid.

Nathaniel Ward
(1578-1652)
English minister, writer

He that is willing to tolerate any unsound opinion that his own may be tolerated, hangs God's Bible at the Devil's Girdle.

Ervin Wardman
(1865-1923)
American journalist

Yellow Journalism.°

Earl Warren
(1891-1974)
Chief Justice, U.S. Supreme Court

Liberty—not Communism—is the most contagious force in the world. It will permeate the Iron Curtain. It will eventually abide everywhere. For no people of any race will long remain slaves. Our strength is in our diversity. Our power is in freedom of thought and research.

Address, Columbia University, 1954.

We come then to the question presented: Does segregation of children in public schools solely on the basis of race, even though the physical facilities and other "tangible" factors may be equal, deprive the children of the minority group of equal educa-

---

° Outcault's comic strip, *The Yellow Kid*, had appeared the previous year, 1895.

tional opportunities? We believe that it does.

Unanimous court decision, Brown v. The Board of Education, May 17, 1954.

We conclude that in the field of public education the doctrine of "separate but equal" has no place. Separate educational facilities are inherently unequal. *Ibid.*

If Bob LaFollette's idea (direct primary, state civil service, utility regulation, statutory collective bargaining, corrupt practice prohibition, etc.) was radical, it was only in the sense that freedom itself was radical. And it was so considered when the Founding Fathers brought our nation into existence. It was radical only if government "of the people, by the people, for the people" is radical.

Address, LaFollette celebration, Wisconsin, June, 1955.

It is the spirit and not the form of law that keeps justice alive.

Fortune, November, 1955.

Our judges are not monks or scientists, but participants in the living stream of our national life, steering the law between the dangers of rigidity on the one hand and of formlessness on the other. Our system faces no theoretical dilemma but a single continuous problem: how to apply to ever-changing conditions the never-changing principles of freedom. *Ibid.*

We are going through a world war of ideas . . . The extent to which we maintain the spirit of our Constitution with its Bill of Rights will in the long run do more to make it both secure and the object of adulation than the number of hydrogen bombs we stockpile. *Ibid.*

Our Bill of Rights, the most precious part of our legal heritage, is under subtle

and pervasive attacks . . . In the struggle between our world and Communism, the temptation to imitate totalitarian security methods must be resisted day by day . . . When the rights of any individual or group are chipped away, the freedom of all erodes.
Ibid.

But the power to investigate, broad as it may be, is also subject to recognized limitations. It cannot be used to inquire into private affairs unrelated to a valid legislative purpose. Nor does it extend to an area in which Congress is forbidden to legislate. Similarly, the power to investigate must not be confused with any of the powers of law enforcement; those powers are assigned under our Constitution to the Executive and the Judiciary. Still further limitations on the power to investigate are found in the specific individual guarantees of the Bill of Rights, such as the Fifth Amendment's privilege against self-incrimination which is in issue here.
Quinn v. U.S., 349 U.S. 155 (1955).

To impose any strait jacket upon the intellectual leaders in our colleges and universities would imperil the future of our nation. . . . Scholarship cannot flourish in an atmosphere of suspicion and distrust. Teachers and students must always remain free to inquire, to study and to evaluate, to gain new maturity and understanding: otherwise our civilization will stagnate and die.
Sweezey v. New Hampshire, 1957.

All political ideas cannot and should not be channelled into the programs of our two major parties. History has amply proved the virtue of political activity by minority, dissident groups, who innumerable times have been in the vanguard of democratic thought and whose programs were ultimately accepted.
Ibid.

Mere unorthodoxy or dissent from the prevailing mores is not to be condemned. The absence of such voices would be a symptom of grave illness in our society.
Ibid.

We have no doubt that there is no congressional power to expose for the sake of exposure. The public is, of course, entitled to be informed concerning the workings of its government. That cannot be inflated into a general power to expose where the predominant result can only be an invasion of the private rights of individuals.
Watkins v. U.S.

Josiah Warren
(1798?-1874)
American inventor, social philosopher

Who does not wish to preserve his liberty to act according to the peculiarities or individualities of future cases, and to sit in judgment on the merits of each, and to change or vary from time to time with new developments and increasing knowledge? Each individual being thus at liberty at all times, would be sovereign of himself. No greater amount of liberty can be conceived —any less would not be liberty!
Equitable Commerce, 1855.

Liberty, then, is the sovereignty of the individual, and never shall man know liberty until each and every individual is acknowledged to be the only legitimate sovereign of his or her person, time and property, each living and acting at his own cost; and not until we live in society where each can exercise his right of sovereignty at all times without clashing with or violating that of others.
Ibid.

To require conformity in the appreciation of sentiments or the interpretation of language, or uniformity of thought, feeling, or action, is a fundamental error in human legislation—a madness which would be only equalled by requiring all to possess the same countenance, the same voice or the same stature. *Ibid.*

The disconnection of Church and State was a master stroke for freedom and harmony. The great moving power, the very soul of the Protestant Reformation, was that it left every one free to interpret the Scriptures according to his own Individual views.
Ibid.

Children are principally the creatures of example—whatever surrounding adults do, they will do. If we strike them, they will strike each other. If they see us attempting to govern each other they will imitate the same barbarism. If we habitually admit the right of sovereignty in each other and in them, they will become equally respectful of our rights and of each other's. All these propositions are probably self-evident, yet not one of them is practicable under the present mixture of the interests and responsibilities between adults and between parents and children. To solve the problem of education, children must be surrounded with equity and must be equitably treated, and each and every one, parent or child, must be understood to be an individual, and must have his or her individual rights equitably respected. *Ibid.*

Booker T. Washington
(1856-1915)
American Negro leader

I beg of you to remember that wherever our life touches yours we help or hinder . . . wherever your life touches ours, you make us stronger or weaker . . . There is no escape—man drags man down, or man lifts man up. *The American Standard, 1896.*

I have learned that success is to be measured not so much by the position that one has reached in life as by the obstacles which he has overcome while trying to succeed.
Up from Slavery.

There are two ways of exerting one's strength: one is pushing down, the other is pulling up.
Quoted by Basil Matthews, Booker T. Washington.

You can't hold a man down without staying down with him.
N. Y. Times Magazine, February 20, 1955.

I shall never permit myself to stoop so low as to hate any man.

George Washington
(1732-1799)
1st President of the United States

The matter I allude to is the exorbitant price exacted by the merchants and vendors of goods for every necessary they dispose of. I am sensible the trouble and risk in importing give the adventurers a right to a generous price, and that such, from the motives of policy, should be paid; but yet I cannot conceive that they, in direct violation of every principle of generosity, of reason and of justice, should be allowed, if it is possible to restrain 'em, to avail themselves of the difficulties of the times, and to amass fortunes upon the public ruin.
Letter to the President of Congress, from Neshamini Camp, August 16, 1777.

It is a maxim founded on the universal experience of mankind that no nation is to be trusted farther than it is bound by its interest. *Letter to Henry Laurens, 1778.*

Our conflict is not likely to cease so soon as every good man would wish. The measure of iniquity is not yet filled . . . Speculation, production, engrossing, forestalling . . . affording too many melancholy proofs of the decay of public virtue . . . and too glaring instances of its being the interest and desire of too many who would wish to be thought friends, to prolong the war.

Letter to a friend, March 31, 1779.

Is the paltry consideration of a little dirty pelf to individuals to be placed in competition keeping with the essential rights and liberties of the present generation, and of millions yet unborn?

Shall a few designing men for their own aggrandizement, and to gratify their own avarice, overset the goodly fabric we have been rearing at the expense of so much time, blood and treasure? And shall we at last become the victims of our own abominable lust for gain? *Ibid.*

Our cause is noble, it is the cause of mankind! And the danger to it is to be apprehended from ourselves. *Ibid.*

I wish the Constitution, which is offered, had been made more perfect; but I sincerely believe it is the best that could be obtained at this time. And, as a constitutional door is opened for amendment hereafter, the adoption of it, under the present circumstances of the Union, is in my opinion desirable.

Letter to Patrick Henry, from Mount Vernon, September 24, 1787.

As for instance on the ineligibility of the same person for President, after he should have served a certain course of years, I confess I differ widely myself from Mr. Jefferson and you as to the necessity or expedience of rotation in that appointment. There cannot, in my opinion, be the least danger that the President will, by any intrigue, ever be able

to continue himself one moment in office, much less perpetuate himself in it. Under an extended view of part of this subject, I can see no propriety in precluding ourselves from the service of any man, who, in some great emergency, shall be deemed universally most capable of serving the public.

Letter to Lafayette, April 28, 1788; quoted by Senator Wright Patman, May 15, 1944, Congressional Record, in defense of a fourth term.

The administration of justice is the firmest pillar of government.

Letter to Randolph, 1789.

The liberty enjoyed by the people of these States of worshipping Almighty God, agreeably to their consciences, is not only among the choicest of their *blessings,* but also of their *rights. Message to Quakers, 1789.*

As mankind becomes more liberal, they will be more able to allow that those who conduct themselves as worthy members of the community are equally entitled to the protection of civil government. I hope ever to see America among the foremost nations in examples of justice and liberality.

Message to Catholics, 1789.

The Citizens of the United States of America have a right to applaud themselves for having given to mankind examples of an enlarged and liberal policy—a policy worthy of imitation. All possess alike liberty of conscience and immunities of citizenship. It is now no more that toleration is spoken of, as if it was by the indulgence of one class of people that another enjoyed the exercise of their inherent natural rights. For happily the government of the United States, which gives to bigotry no sanction, to persecution no assistance, requires only that they who live under its protection should demean themselves as good citizens in giving it on all occasions their effectual support.

To the Jewish Congregation, New Port, Rhode Island, August, 1790.

May the children of the Stock of Abraham, who dwell in this land, continue to merit and enjoy the good will of the other inhabitants, while every one shall sit in safety under his own vine and fig-tree, and there shall be none to make them afraid. *Ibid.*

Of all the animosities which have existed among mankind, those which are caused by a difference of sentiments in religion appear to be the most inveterate and distressing, and ought most to be deprecated. I was in hopes that the enlightened and liberal policy, which has marked the present age, would at least have reconciled Christians of every denomination so far that we should never again see their religious disputes carried to such a pitch as to endanger the peace of society.

Letter to Edward Newenham, October 20, 1792.

It is substantially true, that virtue or morality is a necessary spring of popular government. The rule indeed extends with more or less force to every species of free government. Who that is a sincere friend to it, can look with indifference upon attempts to shake the foundation of the fabric.

Promote then as an object of primary importance, institutions for the general diffusion of knowledge. In proportion as the structure of a government gives force to public opinion, it is essential that public opinion be enlightened.

Farewell Address to the People of the United States, September, 1796.°

___
° This address was never delivered; it was published in *Claypole's Daily Advertiser.* The general ideas were Washington's, but Jefferson, Madison, and Hamilton, notably Hamilton, were said to have written parts.

The nation, which indulges towards another an habitual hatred, or an habitual fondness, is in some degree a slave. It is a slave to its animosity or to its affection, either of which is sufficient to lead it astray from its duty and its interest. *Ibid.*

The great rule of conduct for us, in regard to foreign nations is, in extending our commercial relations to have with them as little *political* connection as possible. *Ibid.*

It is our true policy to steer clear of permanent alliances, with any portion of the foreign world. *Ibid.*

It is folly in one nation to look for disinterested favors from another. *Ibid.*

Guard against the impostures of pretended patriotism. *Ibid.*

The basis of our political systems is the right of the people to make and to alter their constitutions of government. *Ibid.*

All obstructions to the execution of the laws, all combinations and associations under whatever plausible character, with the real design to direct, control, counteract, or awe the regular deliberations and action of the constituted authorities, are destructive of this fundamental principle, and of fatal tendency. *Ibid.*

I never mean, unless some particular circumstance should compel me to do it, to possess another slave by purchase, it being among my first wishes to see some plan adopted by which slavery in this country may be abolished by law. *Ibid.*

Against the insidious wiles of foreign influence, (I conjure you to believe me fellow-citizens) the jealousy of a free people ought to be constantly awake; since history and experience prove that foreign influence is one of the most baneful foes of republican government. *Ibid.*

Europe has a set of primary interests, which to us have none, or a very remote relation. Hence she must be engaged in frequent controversies, the causes of which are essentially foreign to our concerns. Hence therefore it must be unwise in us to implicate ourselves, by artificial ties, in the ordinary vicissitudes of her politics, or the ordinary combinations and collisions of her friendships, or enmities.   *Ibid.*

There can be no greater error than to expect, or calculate upon real favors from nation to nation. It is an illusion which experience must cure, which a just pride ought to discard.   *Ibid.*

Liberty, when it begins to take root, is a plant of rapid growth.   *Moral Maxims.*

Few men have virtue to withstand the highest bidder.   *Ibid.*

To persevere in one's duty and be silent is the best answer to calumny.   *Ibid.*

Arbitrary power is most easily established on the ruins of liberty abused to licentiousness.

Rather than quarrel about territory let the poor, the needy and oppressed of the Earth, and those who want Land, resort to the fertile plains of our western country, the second Promise, and there dwell in peace, fulfilling the first and great commandment.

Overgrown military establishments are under any form of government inauspicious to liberty, and are to be regarded as particularly hostile to republican liberty.

My first wish is to see this plague of mankind, war, banished from the earth.

Some day, taking its pattern from the United States, there will be founded a United States of Europe.

Government is not reason, it is not eloquence—it is force! Like fire it is a dangerous servant and a fearful master; never for a moment should it be left to irresponsible action.

If to please the people, we offer what we ourselves disapprove, how can we afterward defend our work? Let us raise a standard to which the wise and honest can repair. The event is in the hands of God.

Robert W. Seton-Watson
See Seton-Watson

John B(roadus) Watson
(1878-1958)
Founder, behaviorist school of psychology

Behaviorism.
Psychology as the Behaviorist Views It, 1913.

Sidney Webb (Lord Passfield)
(1859-1947)
English socialist leader, writer

The main stream which has borne European society towards Socialism during the past 100 years is the irresistible progress of Democracy.
Fabian Essays in Socialism, copyright by G. B. Shaw, 1931.

The inevitable outcome of Democracy is the control by the people themselves, not only of their own political organization, but, through that, also of the main instruments of wealth production; the gradual substitution of organized cooperation for the anarchy of the competitive struggle. . . . The economic side of the democratic ideal is, in fact, Socialism itself.   *Ibid.*

With the masses painfully conscious of the failure of Individualism to create a decent social life for four-fifths of the people, it might have been foreseen that Individualism could not survive their advent to political power. If private property in land and capital necessarily keeps the many workers permanently poor (through no fault of their own) in order to make the few idlers rich (from no merit of their own), private property in land and capital will inevitably go the way of the feudalism which it superseded. *Ibid.*

The inevitability of gradualness.*
Presidential address, Labour party, 1920.

Daniel Webster
(1782-1852)
American statesman, lawyer, orator

A free government with arbitrary means to administer it is a contradiction; a free government without adequate provision for personal security is an absurdity; a free government, with an uncontrolled power of military conscription, is a solecism, at once the most ridiculous and abominable that ever entered into the head of man. *Speech, 1811.*

An unlimited power to tax involves, necessarily, the power to destroy.**
Argument before Supreme Court, 1819, McCullough v. Maryland.

---

* "The phrase in which was summed up the Fabian Socialists' recipe for saving the world from the ills of capitalism." *N. Y. Times,* October 20, 1947.
** Cf. Justice Marshall's answer in decision: "That the power to tax involves the power to destroy . . . (is) not to be denied." Also cf. Justice Holmes, 1930: "The power to tax is not the power to destroy while this court sits."

Power *naturally* and *necessarily* follows property.
Address, Massachusetts Convention, 1820.

A representative form of government rests no more on political contributions than on those laws which regulate the descent and transmission of property. *Ibid.*

In the nature of things, those who have no property and see their neighbors possess much more than they think them to need, cannot be favorable to laws made for the protection of property. When this class becomes numerous, it grows clamorous. It looks on property as its prey and plunder, and is naturally ready, at time, for violence and revolution. *Ibid.*

It would seem, then, to be the part of political wisdom to found government on property; and to establish such distribution of property, by the laws which regulate its transmission and alienation, as to interest the great majority of society in the protection of the government.
Ibid. (Partly quoted in Justice Douglas' An Almanac of Liberty.)

There is not a more dangerous experiment than to place property in the hands of one class, and political power in those of another. . . . If property cannot retain the political power, the political power will draw after it the property.
North American Review, July, 1820.

Labor is the great producer of wealth: it moves all other causes.
House of Representatives, April 2, 1824.

If the true spark of religious and civil liberty be kindled, it will burn. Human agency cannot extinguish it. Like the earth's central fire, it may be smothered for a time; the ocean may overwhelm it; mountains may press it down; but its inherent and unconquerable force will heave both the ocean and the land, and at some time or other, in some place or other, the volcano will break out and flame up to heaven.

Address, June 17, 1825, at Bunker Hill Monument Cornerstone laying.

Let us cultivate a true spirit of union and harmony. In pursuing the great objects our condition points out to us, let us act under a settled conviction and an habitual feeling that these twenty-four States are one country. *Ibid.*

Let our object be, OUR COUNTRY, OUR WHOLE COUNTRY, AND NOTHING BUT OUR COUNTRY. And, by the blessing of God, may that country itself become a vast and splendid monument, not of oppression and terror, but of wisdom, of peace, and of liberty, upon which the world may gaze with admiration forever. *Ibid.*

The inherent right in the people to reform their government I do not deny; and they have another right, and that is to resist unconstitutional laws without overturning the government.

Second reply to Hayne, January 26, 1830.

The proposition that, in case of a supposed violation of the Constitution by Congress, the states have a constitutional right to interfere and annul the law of Congress is the proposition of the gentleman. I do not admit it. If the gentleman had intended no more than to assert the right of revolution for justifiable cause, he would have said only what all agree to. But I cannot conceive that there can be a middle course, between submission to the laws, when regularly pronounced constitutional, on the one hand, and

open resistance, which is revolution or rebellion, on the other. I say the right of a state to annul a law of Congress cannot be maintained but on the ground of the inalienable right of man to resist oppression; that is to say, upon the ground of revolution. I admit that there is an ultimate violent remedy, above the Constitution and in defiance of the Constitution, which may be resorted to when a revolution is to be justified. But I do not admit that, under the Constitution and in conformity with it, there is any mode in which a state government, as a member of the Union, can interfere and stop the progress of the general government, by force of her own laws, under any circumstances whatever. *Ibid.*

If the government of the United States be the agent of the state governments, then they may control it, provided they can agree in the manner of controlling it; if the agent of the people, then the people alone can control it, restrain it, modify, or reform it. . . . It is, Sir, the people's Constitution, the people's government, made for the people, made by the people, and answerable to the people. The people of the United States have declared that this Constitution shall be the supreme law. We must either admit the proposition or dispute their authority. *Ibid.*

We are all agents of the same supreme power, the people. *Ibid.*

On the diffusion of education among the people rest the preservation and perpetuation of our free institutions.

Address, Madison, Indiana, June 1, 1837.

Let it be borne on the flag under which we rally in every exigency, that we have one country, one constitution, one destiny.

Address, March 15, 1837.

When honored and decrepit age shall lean against the base of this monument, and troops of ingenuous youth shall be gathered round it, and when the one shall speak to the other of its objects, the purposes of its construction, and the great and glorious events with which it is connected, there shall rise from every youthful breast the ejaculation, "Thank God, I–I also–AM AN AMERICAN!"

Address, completion of Bunker Hill Monument, June 17, 1843.

Justice, sir, is the great interest of man on earth. It is the ligament which holds civilized beings and civilized nations together.

Funeral Oration for Justice Story, September 12, 1845.

Liberty exists in proportion to wholesome restraint; the more restraint on others to keep off from us, the more liberty we have.

Speech, Charleston, S. C., May 10, 1847.

I shall know but one country. The ends I aim at shall be my country's, my God's, and Truth's. I was born an American; I live an American; I shall die an American.

Speech, July 17, 1850.

I shall oppose all slavery extension and all increase of slave representation in all places, at all times, under all circumstances, even against all inducements, against all supposed limitations of great interests, against all combinations, against all compromises.

Senate address, Oregon debate, quoted by Kennedy, Profiles in Courage.

The people's government made for the people, made by the people, and answerable to the people.

Second speech on Foot's resolution.

It is, sir, as I have said, a small college —and yet there are those who love it . . .

Attributed by Chauncy Goodrich, 35 years later, and sent to Rufus Choate, who quoted it, July 27, 1853.

If the people can attain a fair compensation for their labor, they will have good homes, good clothing and good food. The great interest of this country is labor.

Quoted in C.I.O. News, May 5, 1941.

A disordered currency is one of the greatest political evils. It undermines the virtues necessary for the support of the social system, and encourages propensities destructive to its happiness. It wars against industry, frugality, and economy, and it fosters the evil spirits of extravagance and speculation. Of all the contrivances for cheating the laboring classes of mankind, none has been more effectual than that which deludes them with paper money. This is the most effectual of inventions to fertilize the rich man's field by the sweat of the poor man's brow. Ordinary tyranny, oppression, excessive taxation, these bear lightly on the happiness of the mass of the community, compared with fraudulent currencies and the robberies committed by depreciated paper. Our own history has recorded for our instruction enough, and more than enough, of the demoralizing tendency, the injustice, and the intolerable oppression on the virtuous and well disposed, of a degraded paper currency, authorized by law, or any way countenanced by government.

Quoted in Congressional Record, March 4, 1946.

The contest for ages has been to rescue liberty from the grasp of executive power.
Quoted by Forbes (magazine).

You need not fear that I shall vote for any compromise or do anything inconsistent with the past.
Quoted by Senator Kennedy, Profiles in Courage.

Labor is one of the great elements of society—the great substantial interest on which we all stand.

No feudal service or the irksome drudgery of one race subjected, on account of their color, to another, but labor—intelligent, manly, independent, thinking and acting for himself, and earning its own wages, accumulating those wages for his capital, educating childhood, maintaining worship, claiming the right of the elective franchise and helping to uphold the great fabric of the state. That is American labor, and all my sympathies with it and my voice 'til I am dumb will be for it.
Quoted in "Labor," March 9, 1946.

The freest government cannot long endure when the tendency of the law is to create a rapid accumulation of property in the hands of a few, and to render the masses poor and dependent.
Quoted by Sinclair, The Cry for Justice.

Given a free press, we may defy open or insidious enemies of liberty. It instructs the public mind and animates the spirit of patriotism. Its loud voice suppresses everything which would raise itself against the public liberty, and its blasting rebuke causes incipient despotism to perish in the bud.

Noah Webster
(1758-1843)
American lexicographer

The distinction of rich and poor does exist, and must always exist; no human power or device can prevent it.
Letter to the Hon. Daniel Webster on the political affairs of the United States.

The man who has half a million of dollars in property . . . has a much higher interest in the government, than the man who has little or no property. *Ibid.*

Power is always right, weakness always wrong. Power is always insolent and despotic.

The liberty of the press, trial by jury, the Habeas Corpus Writ, even Magna Carta itself, although justly deemed the palladia of freedom, are all inferior considerations, when compared with the general distribution of real property among every class of people.

Let the people have property and they will have power—a power that will forever be exerted to prevent the restriction of the press, the abolition of trial by jury, or the abridgment of any other privilege.

Charles E. Weller
(1840-1925)
Typewriter expert, historian

We were then in the midst of an exciting political campaign (Autumn, 1867), and it was then for the first time that the well-known sentence was inaugurated—"Now is the time for all good men to come to the aid of the party."
The Early History of the Typewriter.

Arthur Wellesley,
Duke of Wellington
(1769-1852)
English military leader, statesman

I should like much to tell the truth; but if

I did, I should be torn to pieces, here and abroad.
Attributed by Samuel Rogers, Recollections.

A conqueror, like a cannon-ball, must go on; if he rebounds, his career is over.

The whole art of war consists in getting at what is on the other side of the hill.
To J. W. Croker, c. 1845.

H(erbert) G(eorge) Wells
(1866-1946)
English novelist, historian

A war to end war.
Attributed by Bertrand Russell, Portraits from Memory, 1956.

Human history becomes more and more a race between education and catastrophe.
Tribune, London.

The idea of individual liberty is one that has grown in importance and grows with every development of modern thought. To the classical Utopists freedom was relatively trivial. Clearly they considered virtue and happiness as entirely separable from liberty, and as being altogether more important things. But the modern view, with its deepening insistence upon individuality and upon the significance upon its uniqueness, steadily intensifies the value of freedom, until at last we begin to see liberty as the very substance of life, that indeed it is life, and that only the dead things, the choiceless things, live in absolute obedience to law.
A Modern Utopia.

To have free play for one's individuality is, in the modern view, the subjective triumph of existence, as survival in creative work and offspring is its objective triumph.
Ibid.

Our true nationality is mankind.
The Outline of History.

There is no way out of the present chaotic state of human affairs but a world-wide revolutionary movement on an equalitarian, socialistic basis.
Associated Press dispatch, credited "Excelsior," Mexico, during World War II.

The great trouble with you Americans is that you are still under the influence of that second-rate—shall I say third-rate?—mind, Karl Marx.
Statement to Sinclair Lewis, Dorothy Thompson, Kyle Crichton, H. and G. Seldes, Bronxville, N. Y., 1935.

Socialism . . . ceased to be a creative movement and it became an outlet of passionate expression for the inferiority complex of the disinherited.

Moral indignation is jealousy with a halo.
The Wife of Sir Isaac Harman.

The path of social advancement is, and must be, strewn with broken friendships.
Kipps.

Sooner or later mankind must come to one universal peace, unless our race is to be destroyed by the increasing power of its own destructive inventions; and that universal peace must needs take the form of a government, that is to say, a law-sustaining organization, in the best sense of the word religious—a government ruling men through the educated co-ordination of their minds in a common conception of human history and human destiny.
Crux Ansata, Copyright 1944, Agora Publishing Co., p. 11.

"The fatherhood of God" that Jesus of Nazareth preached was overlaid almost from the beginning by the doctrines and ceremonial traditions of an earlier age, and of an intellectually inferior type. Christianity early ceased to be purely prophetic and creative, with Mithraic blood-cleansing, with priestcraft as ancient as human society, and with elaborate doctrines about the structure of the divinity. The gory entrail-searching forefinger of the Etruscan *pontifex maximus* presently overshadowed the teachings of Jesus of Nazareth. *Ibid., p. 12.*

Heresies are experiments in man's unsatisfied search for truth. *Ibid., p. 14.*

It is no longer a geographically determined warfare of the governments, nations and peoples, but the world-wide struggle of our species to release itself from the strangling octopus of Catholic Christianity. Everywhere the Church extends its tentacles and fights to prolong the Martyrdom of Man. . . . It dominates the policy of the British War Office and Foreign Office, and through these the B.B.C. and the press; by a disciplined Catholic vote, a casting vote in endless elections and a sustained organization of menace and boycott, it silences the frank discussion of its influence in America.
Ibid., p. 99.

There is no more evil thing in this present world than race prejudice, none at all. I write deliberately—it is the worst single thing in life now. It justifies and holds together more baseness, cruelty, and abomination than any other sort of error in the world.
N. Y. Times Magazine, February 20, 1955.

Without the idea of progress life is a corrupting marsh.

Power—gigantic power—has come to us and we can use it only in mutual injury according to the methods of the warring past.

Plenty overwhelms us and we do not know how to distribute or use the wealth we can now produce . . . Invention and scientific knowledge have taken our hearts and imaginations by surprise. Our social and political ideas, our morals, our ambitions, our courage have had as yet no corresponding expansion.

Man is today a challenged animal. He has to respond, he has to respond successfully to the challenge, or he will be overwhelmed—like any other insufficiently adaptable animal.

It is a fact in history that the teaching of Jesus of Nazareth had in it something profoundly new and creative; he preached a new kingdom of heaven in the hearts and in the world of men. There was nothing in his teaching, so far as we can judge it at this distance of time, to clash or interfere with any discovery or expansion of the history of the world and mankind. But it is equally a fact in history that St. Paul and his successors added to, or completed, or imposed upon, or substituted another doctrine for—as you may prefer to think—the plain and profound revolutionary teachings of Jesus by expounding a subtle and complex theory of salvation, a salvation which could be attained very largely by belief and formalities, without any serious disturbance of the believer's ordinary habits and occupations, and that this Pauline teaching did involve very definite beliefs about the history of the world and man.

Gene Weltfish
(b. 1902)
American scientist, writer

I pledge that I will use my knowledge for the good of humanity and against the destructive forces of the world and the ruthless intent of man; and that I will work together with my fellow scientists of whatever nation, creed or color, for these, our common ends.

Oath proposed for scientists; Scientific Monthly, September, 1945.

See also Ruth Benedict

Franz Werfel
(1890-1945)
Aust: ian novelist, poet, playwright

The basic formula of all sin is: frustrated or neglected love.

Between Heaven and Earth, 1944, p. 189.

John Wesley
(1703-1791)
Founder of Methodism

Act as if the whole election depended on your single vote, and as if the whole Parliament (and therein the whole nation) on that single person whom you now choose to be a member of it.

A Word to a Freeholder, 1748.

I look upon the world as my parish.
Quoted in Time.

Opinion is not religion, not even right opinion. *Quoted in Life.*

Think and let think. *Ibid.*

If I leave behind me ten pounds for which I have no use I am a thief and a robber.

Fierce and poisonous animals were created for terrifying man, in order that he might be made aware of the final judgment in Hell.

Grover A. Whalen
(1886-1962)
American businessman, politician

There is plenty of law at the end of a nightstick.

Richard Whately
(1787-1863)
English prelate

Party spirit enlists a man's virtues in the cause of his vices.

Every one wishes to have truth on his side, but it is not every one that sincerely wishes to be on the side of truth.

E. B. White
(b. 1899)
American writer, editor

Democracy, if I understand it at all, is a society in which the unbeliever feels undisturbed and at home. If there were only half a dozen unbelievers in America, their well-being would be a test of our democracy, their tranquility would be a proof.
The New Yorker, February 18, 1956.

Democracy is itself a religious faith. For some it comes close to being the only formal religion they have.

Ibid.

To disagree with anybody or anything is to run the risk of taking oneself out of the money. All this in a country that was born of controversy—a country that wrote controversy into its Constitution, and set up its legislative bodies on the theory of controversy, that established its free press in the belief that controversy is vital to information, and that created a system of justice of which controversy is the heart and soul.
Quoted in The Churchman.

William Allen White
(1868-1944)
Editor, Emporia Gazette;
Republican politician

Fifty years ago and more . . . journalism

was passing out of its status as a trade and becoming a profession. As a profession it lasted for a generation or two. And in that period what once ideally might have been called a noble calling was transformed into a fairly safe 6 per cent investment.
Address, A Free Press in a Machine Age. Wharton Assembly, University of Pennsylvania, May 2, 1938; The Nation, June 18, 1938.

Often his editorial policy was a nice compromise between blackmail and begging.
Ibid.

The merchandising of the news for a long while to come will be affected as it is now with a strong property interest. It will require machinery to assemble the news. It will require capital to distribute the news. And capital today or tomorrow always has a lively sense of its own advantage. Capital is instinctively, for all the noble intentions of us capitalists, class conscious. It is that class consciousness which is discrediting the press of the world today.   *Ibid.*

The owners of newspaper investments, whether they be bankers, stockholders of a corporation, or individuals, feel a rather keen sense of financial responsibility, and they pass their anxiety along to newspaper operatives whether these operatives be superintendents known as managing editors, foremen known as city editors, or mere wage-earners known as editorial writers, copydesk men, reporters, or what not. The sense of property goes thrilling down the line. It produces a slant and a bias that in time becomes—unconsciously and probably in all honesty—a prejudice against any man or any thing or any cause that seriously affects the right, title, or interest of all other capital, however invested.   *Ibid.*

It is not the advertising department that controls the news. Newspapermen may lean over backward in their upright attitude toward the obviously unfair demands of advertisers and the moronic prejudices of subscribers, and still may be poor miserable sinners when they discuss problems affecting the stability of institutions that are founded entirely upon the economic status quo.
Ibid.

We editors realize that we have lost caste with the American people . . . Labor as a class distrusts us. It wouldn't distrust us entirely without reason.   *Ibid.*

The deficiencies of American journals in treating the news of what we might as well frankly if regretfully call the class struggle in this country are found largely in unconscious political attitudes. It is so easy to "policy" the news. Indeed, it is so hard not to policy the news when the news is affected with a vital bread-and-butter interest to the capitalist who controls a newspaper, great or small.   *Ibid.*

And strangely and sadly enough, capital is so fluid that a threat to the safety of any investment seems to be a threat to all investments. Therefore newspapers which represent sizable investments are tempted to shy off and shiver when in Congress, in the legislature, or in the City Hall a man or a group threatens an investment in any kind of patent medicine, in any kind of holding company, in any kind of misbranded food, in any kind of railroad security, in any kind of banking affiliate, good or bad. It is no longer the advertiser who puts on the pressure. It is not even the boss back of the pay roll who begins to quake. It is the whole middle and upper structure of society.   *Ibid.*

Sooner or later the truth about any social abuse is gladly received by the middle class and by those who own and control newspaper investments. But off the bat, the newspapers representing the innate conservatism of property interests which crystallize middle-class psychology are sometimes unfair in their treatment of men or movements that threaten to disturb property in any form. *Ibid.*

A decade or so ago it seemed likely that the direct pressure of large advertisers, as for instance department stores, might affect the press with a bias. Probably that danger is decreasing . . . But today we are faced with a new menace to the freedom of the press, a menace in this country vastly more acute than the menace from government. And this menace may come through the pressure not of one group of advertisers but of a wide sector of newspaper advertisers. These advertising agencies undertake to protect their clients from what the clients and agents may regard as real dangers from inimical social, political, or industrial influences. As advisers the advertising agencies may exercise unbelievably powerful pressure upon the newspapers. There is grave danger that in the coming decade, as social, industrial, and economic problems become more and more acute, this capacity for organized control of newspaper opinion by the political advisers of national advertisers may constitute a major threat to a free press. *Ibid.*

The people have a keen and accurate sense that much of editorial anxiety about the freedom of the press rises out of editorial greed. *Ibid.*

But I suppose in the end newspapers cannot be free, absolutely free in the highest and best sense, until the whole social and economic structure of American life is open to the free interplay of democratic processes. *Ibid.*

Frank Munsey, the great publisher, is dead.

Frank Munsey contributed to the journalism of his day the talent of a meat-packer, the morals of a money-changer, and the manners of an undertaker. He and his kind have about succeeded in transforming a once-noble profession into an 8 per cent security. May he rest in trust.

Liberty is the only thing you cannot have unless you are willing to give it to others.

The D.A.R. has yanked the Klan out of the cow pasture and set it down in the breakfast room of respectability, removing its hood and putting on a transformation.
Quoted in N. Y. Times.

As a matter of fact, insofar as newspapers are influenced in their social and economic politics, the influence comes more insidiously than from direct business office orders. That fact stems largely from the fact that newspapers are profitable concerns. They pay good salaries. They land their employees smack into the middle class from printers and pressmen to managing editors, advertising salesmen and copy desk men and regular men in the news department and circulation department. A middle class complex colors the men who do the writing and editing of the American newspapers.
Contribution to St. Louis Post-Dispatch Symposium, December, 1938.

You can have no wise laws nor free enforcement of wise laws unless there is free expression of the wisdom of the people—and, alas, their folly with it. But if there is freedom, folly will die of its own poison, and the wisdom will survive. That is the history of the race. It is the proof of man's kinship with God.
The Editor and His People, 1924.

You say that freedom of utterance is not for time of stress, and I reply with the sad truth that only in time of stress is freedom of utterance in danger . . . Only when free utterance is suppressed is it needed, and when it is needed it is most vital to justice. *Ibid.*

Put fear out of your heart. This nation will survive, this state will prosper, the orderly business of life will go forward if only men can speak in whatever way given them to utter what their hearts hold—by voice, by posted card, by letters or by press. Reason never has failed men. Only force and oppression have made the wrecks in the world.
Ibid.

Alfred North Whitehead
(1861-1947)
English philosopher

There are no whole truths: all truths are half-truths. It is trying to treat them as whole truths that plays the devil.
Dialogues of Alfred North Whitehead.
As recorded by Lucien Price. Atlantic Monthly Press, 1954.

Responsibility for a social system is the groundwork of civilization. Without a society in which life and property are to some extent secure, existence can continue only at the lowest levels—you cannot have a good life for those you love, nor can you devote your energies to activity on the higher level.
Ibid.

I consider Christian theology to be one of the great disasters of the human race . . . It would be impossible to imagine anything more un-Christlike than Christian theology. Christ probably couldn't have understood it.
Ibid.

The Reformation was one of the most colossal failures in history; it threw overboard what makes the Church tolerable and even gracious; namely, its esthetic appeal; but kept its barbarous theology. *Ibid.*

The vitality of thought is in adventure. *Ideas won't keep.* Something must be done about them. When the idea is new, its custodians have fervor, live for it, and, if need be, die for it. *Ibid.*

An aristocracy that shirks its leadership is done for. Its only excuse for existence is that it takes the lead. *Ibid.*

Your diffusion of literacy and average comfort and well-being among the masses, in my opinion, is one of the major achievements in human history . . . With all its limitations, life in America is better and kinder than anywhere on earth that I have ever heard of. *Ibid.*

Art flourishes where there is a sense of adventure, a sense of nothing having been done before, of complete freedom to experiment; but when caution comes in you get repetition, and repetition is the death of art. *Ibid.*

What is morality in any given time or place? It is what the majority then and there happen to like and immorality is what they dislike. *Ibid.*

My main thesis is that a social system is kept together by the blind force of instinctive actions, and of instinctive emotions clustered around habits and prejudices. It is therefore not true that any advance in the scale of culture inevitably tends to the preservation of society. On the whole, the contrary is more often the case, and any survey of nature confirms this conclusion. A new element in life renders in many ways the operation of the old instincts unsuitable. . . . Mankind misses its opportunities, and its failures are a fair target for ironic criticism. But the fact that reason too often fails does not give fair ground for the hysterical conclusion that it never succeeds.

The Practical Cogitator.

The aim of science is to seek the simplest explanation of complex facts. We are apt to fall into the error of thinking that the facts are simple because simplicity is the goal of our quest. The guiding motto in the life of every natural philosopher should be, "Seek Simplicity and distrust it."

Concept of Nature, p. 163.

The Gospel of Force is incompatible with a social life. By force, I mean antagonism in its most general sense.

Science and the Modern World, Macmillan.

As Society is now constituted a literal adherence to the moral precepts scattered throughout the Gospels would mean sudden death. *N. Y. Herald Tribune book section.*

The art of progress is to preserve order amid change and to preserve change amid order. *Forbes, December 1, 1957.*

Religion is what the individual does with his own solitariness.

If you have had your attention directed to the novelties of thought in your own lifetime, you will have observed that almost all really new ideas have a certain aspect of foolishness when they are first produced, and almost any idea which jogs you out of your current abstractions may be better than nothing. *Adventures of Ideas.*

A pure race is likely to be stupid—the Lacedaemonians—but mix the native Attic stock with the Dorian invaders or the Ionians with Asiatics, and the results are brilliant. I think the one place where I have been that is most like ancient Athens is the University of Chicago. You see, I am looking for your American equivalent of the Aegean, and I believe it is the Mid-west.

Religion is the last refuge of human savagery.

Philosophy asks the simple question: What is it all about?

Advance or decadence are the only choices offered to mankind. The pure conservative is fighting against the essence of the universe.

Walt Whitman
(1819-1892)
American poet

The eager and often inconsiderate appeals of reformers and revolutionists are indispensable to counterbalance the inertness and fossilism making so large a part of human institutions.

Democratic Vistas, 1870.

The People! Like our huge earth itself, which, to ordinary scansion, is full of vulgar contradictions and offence, man, viewed in the lump, displeases, and is a constant puzzle and affront to the merely educated classes. *Ibid.*

But the People are ungrammatical, untidy, and their sins gaunt and ill-bred. *Ibid.*

Literature, strictly considered, has never recognized the people, and, whatever may be said, does not today . . . I know nothing more rare, even in this country, than a fit scientific estimate and reverent appreciation of the People—of their measureless wealth of latent worth and capacity, their vast, artistic contrasts of lights and shades—with, in

America, their entire reliability in emergencies, and a certain breadth of historic grandeur, of peace or war, far surpassing all the vaunted samples of book-heroes, or any *haut ton* coteries, in all the records of the world.
                                        Ibid.

The great poems, Shakespeare's included, are poisonous to the idea of the pride and dignity of the common people, the life-blood of democracy.   **Ibid.**

Did you, too, O friend, suppose democracy was only for elections, for politics, and for a party name? I say democracy is only of use there that it may pass on and come to its flower and fruit in manners, in the highest forms of interaction between men, and their beliefs—in religion, literature, colleges, and schools—democracy in all public and private life, and in the army and navy.   *Ibid.*

There is no week nor day nor hour when tyranny may not enter upon this country, if the people lose their supreme confidence in themselves,—and lose their roughness and spirit of defiance—Tyranny may always enter—there is no charm, no bar against it —the only bar against it is a large resolute breed of men.
Furness, Walt Whitman's Workshop,
p. 58.

And you, paid to defile the People—you liars, mark!
Not for numberless agonies, murders, lusts,
For court thieving in its manifold mean
    forms, working from this simplicity the
    poor man's wages,
For many a promise sworn by royal lips and
    broken and laugh'd at in the breaking,
Then in their power not for all these did the
    blows strike revenge, or the heads of
    the nobles fall;
The people scorn'd the ferocity of kings.
Europe. The 72nd and 73d Years of
These States. (1848-1849.)

Those corpses of young men,
Those martyrs that hang from the gibbets,
    those hearts pierc'd by the gray lead,
Cold and motionless as they seem live else-
    where with unslaughter'd vitality.
They live in other young men, O kings!
They live in brothers again ready to defy you,
They are purified by death, they were
    taught and exalted.   *Ibid.*

Not a grave of the murder'd for freedom
    but grows seed for freedom, in its turn
    to bear seed,
Which the winds carry afar and re-sow, and
    the rains and the snows nourish. *Ibid.*

Not a disembodied spirit can the weapons of
    tyrants let loose,
But it stalks invisibly over the earth, whis-
    pering, counseling, cautioning.
Liberty, let others despair of you—I never
    despair of you.   *Ibid.*

Liberty is poorly served by men whose good intent is quelled from one failure or two failures or any number of failures, or from the casual indifference or ingratitude of the people, or from the sharp show of the rushes of power, or the bringing to bear of soldiers and cannon or any penal statutes. Liberty relies upon itself, invites no one, promises nothing, sits in calmness and light, is positive and composed, and knows no discouragement.
Leaves of Grass, preface, 1872 edition.

And I say to mankind, Be not curious about God. For I, who am curious about each, am not curious about God—I hear and behold God in every object, yet understand God not in the least.   *Ibid., p. 90.*

The United States themselves are essentially the greatest poem . . . Here at last is something in the doings of man that corresponds with the broadcast doings of the day and night. *Op. cit.*

Whoever degrades another degrades me,
And whatever is done or said returns at
    last to me. *Ibid.*

Each of us inevitable;
Each of us limitless—each of us with his or
    her right upon the earth;
Each of us allow'd the eternal purports of
    the earth;
Each of us here as divinely as any is here.
                Salut au Monde!

A great city is that which has the greatest
    men and women,
If it be a few ragged huts, it is still the
    greatest city in the whole world.
            Song of the Broad-Axe.

I see those who in any land have died for a
    good cause,
The seed is spare, nevertheless the crop shall
    never run out.
(Mind you, O foreign kings, O priests, the
    common seed shall never run out.)
                    Ibid.

Courage yet, my brother and my sister!
Keep on—Liberty is to be subserv'd what-
    ever occurs.
    To a Foil'd European Revolutionaire.

There is nothing that is quell'd by one or two
    failures, or any number of failures,
Or by the indifference or ingratitude of the
    people, or by any unfaithfulness,
Or the show of the rushes of power, soldiers,
    cannon, penal statutes. *Ibid.*

(Not songs of loyalty alone are these,
But songs of insurrection also,
For I am the sworn poet of every dauntless
    rebel the world over,

And he going with me leaves peace and
    routine behind him,
And stakes his life to be lost at any moment.)
                    Ibid.

When Liberty goes out of a place it is not the
    first to go, nor the second or third to go,
It waits for all the rest to go, it is the last.
                    Ibid.

When there are no more memories of heroes
    and martyrs,
And when all life and all the souls of men
    and women are discharged from any
    part of the earth,
Then only shall liberty or the idea of liberty
    be discharged from that part of the
    earth,
And the infidel come into full possession.
                    Ibid.

To the States or any one of them, or any city
    of the States, *Resist much, obey little,*
Once fully enslaved, no nation, state, city of
    this earth, ever afterward resumes its
    liberty. *To the States.*

Who are they, as bats and night-bogs, askant
    in the Capitol?
Are those really Congressmen? *Ibid.*

There is to me something profoundly af
fecting in large masses of men following the
lead of those who do not believe in men.

I give the password primeval, I give the
sign of democracy. By God, I will accept
nothing that all cannot have on equal terms.

There is no greater fallacy on earth than
the doctrine of force, as applied to government.

I say discuss all and expose all—I am for
    every topic openly;

I say there can be no safety for these States
without innovators—without free
tongues, and ears willing to hear the
tongues;
And I announce as a glory of these States,
that they respectfully listen to propositions, reforms, fresh views and doctrines, from successions of men and
women.

Each age with its own growth!
I see not America only, not only Liberty's
nation but other nations preparing,
I see tremendous entrances and exits, new
combinations, the solidarity of races.

I see Freedom, completely arm'd and
victorious and very haughty, with Law
on one side and Peace on the other,
A stupendous trio all issuing forth against
the idea of caste.

I see men marching and countermarching
by swift millions,
I see the frontiers and boundaries of the old
aristocracies broken,
I see the landmarks of European kings
removed,
I see this day the People beginning their
landmarks, (all others give way);
Never was average man, his soul, more
energetic, more like a God,
Lo, how he urges and urges, leaving the
masses no rest!

John Greenleaf Whittier *
(1809-1892)
American poet, abolitionist

Shall tongue be mute, when deeds are
wrought

Which well might shame extremest hell?
Shall freemen lock the indignant thought?
Shall Pity's bosom cease to swell?
Shall Honor bleed?—shall Truth succumb?
Shall pen, and press, and soul be dumb?
Stanzas for the Times, 1835.

Rail on, then, brethren of the South,
Ye shall not hear the truth the less;
No seal is on the Yankee's mouth,
No fetters on the Yankee's press!
From our Green Mountains to the sea,
One voice shall thunder, We are free!
Ibid.

Woe, then, to all who grind
Their brethren of a common Father down!
To all who plunder from the immortal mind
Its bright and glorious crown!

Woe to the priesthood! woe
To those whose hire is with the price of
blood;
Perverting, darkening, changing, as they go,
The searching truths of God!
Clerical Oppressors. *

"Great peace in Europe! Order reigns
From Tiber's hills to Danube's plains!"
So say her kings and priests; so say
The lying prophets of our day.
The Peace of Europe.

Speak, Prince and Kaiser, Priest and Czar!
If this be Peace, pray what is War? *Ibid.*

Stern herald of thy better day,
Before thee, to prepare thy way,

---

* "In the quarter-century before the Civil
War he was *the* anti-slavery poet of America
—the prophet of the Abolitionists, the scourge

of the compromising clergy, the champion of
law-breakers on behalf of freedom." Bernard
Smith, *The Democratic Spirit.*
* The clergy of all denominations who sanc-
tioned a pro-slavery meeting in Charleston,
S. C.

The Baptist Shade of Liberty,
Gray, scarred and hairy-robed, must press
With bleeding feet the wilderness!
Oh that its voice might pierce the ear
Of princes, trembling while they hear
A cry as of the Hebrew seer:
Repent! God's kingdom draweth near!
Ibid.

The age is dull and mean. Men creep,
  Not walk; with blood too pale and tame
  To pay the debt they owe to shame;
Buy cheap, sell dear; eat, drink, and sleep
  Down-pillowed, deaf to moaning want;
Pay tithes for soul-insurance; keep
  Six days to Mammon, one to Cant.
For Righteousness' Sake, 1855.

God's ways seem dark, but, soon or late,
  They touch the shining hills of day;
  The evil cannot brook delay,
The good can well afford to wait.
  Give ermined knaves their hour of crime;
Yet have the future grand and great,
  The safe appeal of Truth to Time! *Ibid.*

So fallen! So lost! the light withdrawn
  Which once he wore!
The glory from his gray hairs gone for
    evermore!   *Ichabod.**

Of all we loved and honored, naught
  Save power remains—
A fallen angel's power of thought,
  Still strong in chains . . .   *Ibid.*

All else is gone: from those great eyes
  The soul has fled:
When faith is lost, when honor dies,
  The man is dead!   *Ibid.*

---

* This is Whittier's attack on Daniel Webster who in a speech, March 7, 1850, appealed for Southern presidential votes and disillusioned his Northern abolitionist followers.

Then pay the reverence of old days
  For his dead fame;
Walk backward, with averted gaze
  And hide his shame.   *Ibid.*

From the death of the old the new proceeds,
And the life of truth from the death of creeds.
The Preacher.

Norbert Wiener
(1894-1964)
American mathematician, writer

We have decided to call the entire field of control and communication theory, whether in the machine or in the animal, by the name of *Cybernetics*.
Cybernetics, p. 191, John Wiley & Sons, 1948.

This new development (automation) has unbounded possibilities for good and for evil.   *Ibid.*

Many a missionary has fixed his own misunderstanding of a primitive language as law eternal in the process of reducing it to writing. There is much in the social habits of a people which is dispersed and distorted by the mere act of making inquiries about it. In another sense from that in which it is usually stated, traduttore traditore.   *Ibid., p. 190.*

Ella Wheeler Wilcox
(1850-1919)
American popular poet

O man bowed down with labor,
  O woman young yet old,
O heart oppressed in the toiler's breast
  And crushed by the power of gold—
Keep on with your weary battle against triumphant might;

No question is ever settled until it is settled right.

Quoted—("immortalized")—by Bryan in the 1896 campaign.

The splendid discontent of God
  With chaos, made the world . . .
And from the discontent of man
  The world's best progress springs.
                              Discontent.

Lady Jane Francesca Wilde ("Speranza")
(1826-1896)
English poet

Weary men, what reap ye?—"Golden corn
  for the stranger."
What sow ye?—"Human corpses that await
  for the Avenger."
Fainting forms, all hunger-stricken, what
  see you in the offing?
"Stately ships to bear our food away amid
  the stranger's scoffing."
There's a proud array of soldiers—what do
  they round your door?
"They guard our master's granaries from the
  thin hands of the poor."
                      Ballad on the Irish Famine.

Oscar (Fingal O'Flahertie Wills) Wilde
(1854-1900)
English writer

Democracy means simply the bludgeoning of the people by the people for the people.
        The Soul of Man Under Socialism.

In old days men had the rack. Now they have the press.   *Ibid.*

In America the president reigns for four years, and journalism governs for ever and ever.   *Ibid.*

Disobedience, in the eyes of any one who has read history, is man's original virtue. It is through disobedience that progress has been made, through disobedience and through rebellion.   *Ibid.*

The fact is, that civilization requires slaves. The Greeks were quite right there. Unless there are slaves to do the ugly, horrible, uninteresting work, culture and contemplation become almost impossible. Human slavery is wrong, insecure, and demoralizing. On mechanical slavery, on the slavery of the machine, the future of the world depends.   *Ibid.*

Charity creates a multitude of sins. *Ibid.*

While to the claims of charity a man may yield and yet be free, to the claims of conformity no man may yield and remain free at all.   *Ibid.*

An individual who has to make things for the use of others, and with reference to their wants and their wishes, does not work with interest, and consequently cannot put into his work what is best in him. Upon the other hand, whenever a community or a powerful section of a community, or a government of any kind, attempts to dictate to the artist what he is to do, Art either entirely vanishes, or becomes stereotyped, or degenerates into a low and ignoble form of craft.   *Ibid.*

A work of art is the unique result of a unique temperament. Its beauty comes from the fact that the author is what he is. It has nothing to do with the fact that other people want what they want. Indeed, the moment that an artist takes notice of what other people want, and tries to supply the demand, he ceases to be an artist, and becomes a dull or an amusing craftsman, an honest or dishonest tradesman. He has no further claim to be considered as an artist.   *Ibid.*

Art is the most intense mode of individualism that the world has known. *Ibid.*

Art is this intense form of individualism that makes the public try to exercise over it an authority that is as immoral as it is ridiculous, and as corrupting as it is contemptible. It is not quite their fault. The public has always, and in every age, been badly brought up. They are continually asking Art to be popular, to please their want of taste, to flatter their absurd vanity, to tell them what they have been told before, to show them what they ought to be tired of seeing, to amuse them when they feel heavy after eating too much, and to distract their thoughts when they are wearied of their own stupidity. Now Art should never try to be popular. The public should try to make itself artistic.
Ibid.

The one thing that the public dislikes is novelty. Any attempt to extend the subject-matter of art is extremely distasteful to the public; and yet the vitality and progress of art depends in a large measure on the continual extension of subject-matter. The public dislikes novelty because it is afraid of it. It represents to them a mode of Individualism, an assertion on the part of the artist that he selects his own subject, and treats it as he chooses. *Ibid.*

In Art, the public accepts what has been because they cannot alter it, not because they appreciate it. They swallow their classics whole, and never taste them. They endure them as the inevitable, and, as they cannot mar them, they mouth them. . . . A fresh mode of Beauty is absolutely distasteful to them, and whenever it appears they get so angry and bewildered that they always use two stupid expressions—one is that the work of art is grossly unintelligible; the other, that the work of art is grossly immoral. *Ibid.*

A true artist takes no notice whatever of the public. The public is to him non-existent. He has no poppied or honeyed cakes through which to give the monster sleep or sustenance. *Ibid.*

It is only fair to state, with regard to modern journalists, that they always apologize to one in private for what they have written against one in public. *Ibid.*

People sometimes inquire what form of government is most suitable for an artist to live under. To this question there is only one answer. The form of government that is most suitable to the artist is no government at all. Authority over him and his art is ridiculous. *Ibid.*

The Pope may be cultivated. Many popes have been; the bad popes have been. The bad popes loved Beauty almost as passionately, nay, with as much passion as the good popes hated Thought. To the wickedness of the papacy humanity owes much. The goodness of the papacy owes a terrible debt to humanity. Yet, though the Vatican has kept the rhetoric of its thunders and lost the rod of its lightning, it is better for the artist not to live with popes. *Ibid.*

The only thing that one really knows about human nature is that it changes. Change is the one quality we can predicate on it. The systems that fail are those that rely on the permanency of human nature, and not on its growth and development. The error of Louis XIV was that he thought human nature would always be the same. The result of his error was the French Revolution. It was an admirable result. All the results of the mistakes of government are quite admirable.
Ibid.

The true perfection of man lies not in what man has, but in what man is. Private property has crushed true Individualism, and set up an Individualism that is false. It has debarred one part of the community from being individual by starving them. It has debarred the other part of the community from being individual by putting them on the wrong road, and encumbering them.   *Ibid.*

Alone, without any reference to his neighbors, without any interference, the artist can fashion a beautiful thing; and if he does not do it solely for his own pleasure, he is not an artist at all.   *Ibid.*

An idea that is not dangerous is unworthy of being called an idea at all.
The Epigrams of Oscar Wilde, edited by Alvin Redman, 1954.

Starvation, and not sin, is the parent of modern crime.   *Ibid.*

Patriotism is the virtue of the vicious.
                              (in conversation.)

Modern journalism by giving us the opinions of the uneducated, keeps us in touch with the ignorance of the community.
                        The Critic as Artist.

Truth, in matters of religion, is simply the opinion that has survived.   *Ibid.*

As long as war is regarded as wicked, it will always have its fascination. When it is looked upon as vulgar, it will cease to be popular.   *Ibid.*

There is no sin except stupidity.   *Ibid.*

There is no such thing as a moral or an immoral book. Books are well written, or badly written. That is all.
                    The Picture of Dorian Gray.

Discontent is the first step in the progress of a man or a nation.
                    A Woman of No Importance.

For Man's grim Justice goes its way,
    And will not swerve aside:
It slays the weak, it slays the strong,
    It has a deadly stride:
With iron heel it slays the strong,
    The monstrous parricide.
                    The Ballad of Reading Gaol.

For he who lives more lives than one
More deaths than one must die.   *Ibid.*

Yet each man kills the thing he loves,
    By each let this be heard,
Some do it with a bitter look,
    Some with a flattering word,
The coward does it with a kiss,
    The brave man with a sword!   *Ibid.*

I know not whether Laws be right,
    Or whether Laws be wrong;
All that we know who lie in jail
    Is that the wall is strong;
And that each day is like a year,
    A year whose days are long.   *Ibid.*

But this I know, that every Law
    That men have made for Man,
Since first Man took his brother's life,
    And the sad world began,
But straws the wheat and saves the chaff
    With a most evil fan.   *Ibid.*

This too I know—and wise it were
    If each could know the same—
That every prison that men build
    Is built with bricks of shame,
And bound with bars lest Christ should see
    How men their brothers maim.   *Ibid.*

The vilest deeds like poison weeds
    Bloom well in prison-air:

It is only what is good in Man
  That wastes and withers there:
Pale Anguish keeps the heavy gate,
  And the Warder is Despair.   *Ibid.*

Religions die when they are proved true.
Science is the record of dead religions.
  *Phrases and Philosophies for the Use
  of the Young, 1894.*

Nothing makes one so vain as being told
that one is a sinner. Conscience makes ego-
tists of us all.

There are three kinds of despots. There
is the despot who tyrannizes over the body.
There is the despot who tyrannizes over the
soul. There is the despot who tyrannizes
over the soul and the body alike. The first is
called Prince. The second is called the Pope.
The third is called the People.

All authority is quite degrading.

A thing is not necessarily true because a
man dies for it.
  *Written 1904, under the name "Sebas-
  tian Melmoth."*

To disagree with three-fourths of the
British public on all points is one of the first
elements of sanity, one of the deepest consolations in all moments of spiritual doubt.

The books that the world calls immoral
are books that show the world its own shame.

The man who sees both sides of a question
is a man who sees absolutely nothing.

Anybody can make history; only a great
man can write it.

Wilhelm II
(1859-1941)
German Kaiser

Recruits! Before the altar and the servant
of God you have given me the oath of allegi-

ance ... You have sworn fidelity to me, you
are the children of my guard, you are my
soldiers, you have surrendered yourself to
me, body and soul.

Only one enemy can exist for you—my
enemy. With the present Socialist machina-
tions, it may happen that I shall order you
to shoot your own relatives, your brothers,
or even your parents—which God forbid—
and then you are bound in duty implicitly to
obey my orders.   *Speech, 1891.*

Remember, the German people are the
chosen of God. On me the German Emperor, the spirit of God has descended. I am
His sword, His weapon, and His vice-regent.
       To soldiers, August 4, 1914.

The newspapers mostly create public
opinion ... More dangerous, and at the same
time loathsome, is that part of the press
which writes what it is paid for. The scoundrels who do such dirty work are in no fear
of starving. They will always incite the hostility of one nation against the other, and
when at last by their hellish devices they
have brought about the much desired collision they sit down and watch the fight
which they organized, resting well assured
that the profit will be theirs, no matter what
the issue may be. In this way, in 99 cases
out of 100, what is vulgarly called "public
opinion" is a mere forgery.
  *Quoted by S. B. Fay, The Origins of
  the World War, vol. 1, p. 268.*

Germany must have her place in the sun.

It is the soldier and the army, not Parliamentary Majorities and votes, that have
welded the German Empire together. My
confidence rests with the army.

Lord Northcliffe won the war.[*]

---

[*] Sometimes also quoted as "The *Daily Mail*
won the war."

Friedrich Wilhelm Victor August Ernst
(1882-1951)
German Crown Prince

If we study the pages of history we find that they are traversed as with a red thread by the doctrine of the necessity of warlike capacity in a people.

But just as lightning equalizes the tension in two differently charged strata of the air, so will the sword always be, and remain till the end of the world, the finally decisive factor.

William the Silent
(1533-1584)
Prince of Orange

Two tremendous forces have come into moral clash in our time—the newly awakened spirit of liberty and the mighty and ancient spirit of tyranny. The latter undeniably has its seat and stronghold in the Roman system, with its kingcraft and priestcraft and its established control over the motions of men's souls. To it I can no longer adhere . . .

You may not see yet what you will see as you live deeper into this time of ours, that the cause of the Huguenots in France is the cause . . . of Protestants everywhere. There will be a long struggle, fought out now on one field and now on the other, but the cause is one. A wider question is at stake and a deeper one than many see—not merely a question between the Mass and the Bible, but a question of the freedom of the human spirit for all time to come . . .

Roger Williams
(1603?-1683)
Founder of Rhode Island

First, that the blood of so many hundred thousand souls of Protestants and Papists, spilt in the wars of present and former ages for their respective consciences, is not required by Jesus Christ the Prince of Peace.

Secondly, pregnant scriptures and arguments are throughout the work proposed against the doctrine of persecution for the cause of conscience.

The Bloody Tenet of Persecution for Cause of Conscience, Preface, 1644.

Sixthly, it is the will and command of God that (since the coming of his Son the Lord Jesus) a permission of the most Paganish, Jewish, Turkish, or Antichristian consciences and worships be granted to all men in all nations and countries: and they are only to be fought against with that sword which is only (in soul matters) able to conquer: to wit, the sword of God's spirit, the word of God. *Ibid.*

Eighthly, God requireth not a uniformity of religion to be enacted and enforced in any civil state; which enforced uniformity (sooner or later) is the great occasion of civil war, ravishing of conscience, persecution of Jesus Christ in his servants, and of the hypocrisy and destruction of millions of souls. *Ibid.*

Tenthly, an enforced uniformity of religion throughout a nation or civil state confounds the civil and religious, denies the principles of Christianity and civility, and that Jesus Christ is come in the flesh. *Ibid.*

Eleventhly, the permission of other consciences and worships than a state professeth, only can (according to God) procure a firm and lasting peace. *Ibid.*

We must not let go for all the fleabitings of the present afflictions, etc.; having bought truth dear, we must not sell it cheap, not the least grain of it for the whole world, no, not for the saving of souls, though our own most precious; least of all for the bitter sweetening of a little vanishing pleasure. *Ibid., To Every Courteous Reader.*

For the broken bags of riches on eagles' wings, for a dream of these, any or all of these which on our death-bed vanish and leave tormenting stings behind them: oh, how much better it is from the love of truth, from the love of the Father of lights, from whence it comes, from the love of the son of God, who is the Way and the Truth, to say as he (John xviii. 37): For this end I was born, and for this end came I unto the world, that I might bear witness to the truth. *Ibid.*

Sovereigne, originall and foundation of civill power lies in the people.
Quoted in An Almanac of Liberty, by Justice Douglas.

There goes many a ship to sea with many hundred souls in one ship, whose weal and woe is common, and is a true picture of a commonwealth or a human combination or society. It hath fallen out sometimes, that both Papists and Protestants, Jews and Turks, may be embarked in one ship; upon which proposal I affirm that all the liberty of conscience that ever I pleaded for, turns upon these two hinges—that none of the Papists, Protestants, Jews or Turks be forced to come to the ship's prayer or worship nor compelled from their own particular prayer or worship, if they practice any. I further add that I never denied, that notwithstanding this liberty, the commander of this ship ought to command that justice, peace and sobriety be kept and practised, both among the seamen and all the passengers.
Letter to the Town of Providence, 1654.

Wendell L. Willkie
(1892-1944)
American industrialist, politician

A good catchword can obscure analysis for fifty years. *Town Hall debate, 1938.*

The glory of the United States is business. *Time, September 30, 1940.*

When we talk of freedom and opportunity for all nations, the mocking paradoxes in our own society become so clear they can no longer be ignored. If we want to talk about freedom, we must mean freedom for others as well as ourselves, and we must mean freedom for everyone inside our frontiers as well as outside. *One World.*

To suppress minority thinking and minority expression would tend to freeze society and prevent progress . . . Now more than ever we must keep in the forefront of our minds the fact that whenever we take away the liberties of those whom we hate, we are opening the way to loss of liberty for those we love. *Ibid.*

Our way of living together in America is a strong but delicate fabric. It is made up of many threads. It has been woven over many centuries by the patience and sacrifice of countless liberty-loving men and women. It serves as a cloak for the protection of poor and rich, of black and white, of Jew and Gentile, of foreign and native born. Let us not tear it asunder. For no man knows, once it is destroyed, where or when man will find its protective warmth again. *Ibid.*

Freedom is an indivisible word. *Ibid.*

I believe the moral losses of expediency always far outweigh the temporary gains. *Ibid.*

No man has a right in America to treat any other man "tolerantly" for tolerance is the assumption of superiority. Our liberties are equal rights of every citizen.

Quoted by Ben Raeburn, editor, Treasury for the Free World, Arco, 1946.

Our whole purpose today is, with our allies, to defeat Fascism. But all the forces of Fascism are not with our enemies . . . The desire to deprive some of our citizens of their rights—economic, civic or political, has the same basic motivation as actuates the fascist mind when it seeks to dominate whole people and whole nations.

I consider Anti-Semitism in America as a possible criminal movement and every anti-Semite as a possible traitor to America.

Statement to a Jewish newspaper, beginning of campaign of 1940.

The society of excess profits for some and small returns for others, the society in which a few prey upon the many, the society in which a few took great advantage and many took great disadvantage, must pass.

Campaign speech, Springfield, Ill., October 18, 1940.

We must unleash the energies of men, but we must in our revolution save this free way of life, bring well-being to a larger and larger number of people.   *Ibid.*

Every drop of blood saved through expedience will be paid for by twenty drawn by the sword.

Today it is not big business that we have to fear. It is big government.

Charles E. Wilson
(1895-1961)
American industrialist

What is good for the country is good for General Motors, and what's good for General Motors is good for the country.

Testimony, Senate Armed Forces Committee, 1952.

You can be social minded without being a socialist.

Address, Dartmouth College, May 5, 1959.

Edmund Wilson
(1895-1972)
American author, critic

The human imagination has already come to conceive the possibility of recreating human society.

(Thomas) Woodrow Wilson
(1856-1924)
28th President of the United States

The great monopoly in this country is the money monopoly. So long as it exists, our old variety of freedom and individual energy of development are out of the question.

1911; quoted by Justice Brandeis, Other People's Money.

A great industrial nation is controlled by its system of credit. Our system of credit is concentrated. The growth of the nation, therefore, and all our activities are in the hands of a few men, who, even if their actions be honest and intended for the public interest, are necessarily concentrated upon the great undertaking in which their own money is involved and who, necessarily, by every reason of their own limitations, chill and check and destroy genuine economic freedom.   *Ibid.*

By "radical" I understand one who goes too far; by "conservative" one who does not

go far enough; by "reactionary" one who won't go at all.
Speech, New York City, January 29, 1911.

I suppose I must be a "progressive," which I take to be one who insists on recognizing the facts, adjusting policies to facts and circumstances as they arise. *Ibid.*

America is not a mere body of traders; it is a body of free men. Our greatness is built upon our freedom—is moral, not material. We have a great ardor for gain; but we have a deep passion for the rights of man. *Ibid.*

The man with power but without conscience, could, with an eloquent tongue, if he cared for nothing but his own power, put this whole country into a flame, because this whole country believes that something is wrong, and is eager to follow those who profess to be able to lead it away from its difficulties.
Address, Kansas City, May 6, 1911.

Do we conceive social betterment to be in the pitiless use of irresistible power? Or do we conceive it to arise out of the irresistible might of a body of free men? Has justice ever grown in the soil of absolute power? Has not justice always come from the press of the heart and the spirit of men who resist power?
Address, New York Press Club, May 9, 1912.

Liberty has never come from government. Liberty has always come from the subjects of government. The history of liberty is the history of resistance.* *Ibid.*

---

* Theodore Roosevelt picked up this, and the following quotation, and apparently not knowing that Thomas Jefferson had used similar words and certainly believed in these

The history of liberty is a history of the limitations of governmental power, not the increase of it. *Ibid.*

When we resist . . . concentration of power, we are resisting the powers of death, because concentration of power is what always precedes the destruction of human liberties. *Ibid.*

No one can worship God or love his neighbor on an empty stomach.
Speech, New York City, May 23, 1912.

There is no indispensable man. The Government will not collapse and go to pieces if any one of the gentlemen who are seeking to be entrusted with its guidance should be left at home.
1912; quoted in 100th anniversary article, N. Y. Times Magazine, June 10, 1956.

There was a time when corporations played a minor part in our business affairs, but now they play the chief part, and most men are the servants of corporations.
1912-13 speeches; The New Freedom, Doubleday & Co., 1913.

The truth is, we are all caught in a great economic system which is heartless. *Ibid.*

The masters of the government of the United States are the combined capitalists and manufacturers of the United States. *Ibid.*

American industry is not free, as once it was free; American enterprise is not free;

---

ideas, attacked Wilson as a dangerous radical. Many newspapers, including the *N. Y. Tribune,* which claimed they were publishing the "full text" of the address, omitted the introductory quotation.

the man with only a little capital is finding it harder to get into the field, more and more impossible to compete with the big fellow. Why? Because the laws of this country do not prevent the strong from crushing the weak. *Ibid.*

There has come over the land that un-American set of conditions which enables a small number of men who control the Government to get favors from the Government; by those favors to exclude their fellows from equal business opportunity; by those favors to extend a network of control that will presently dominate every industry in the country, and so make men forget the ancient time when America lay in every hamlet, when America was to be seen in every fair valley. *Ibid.*

We stand in the presence of a revolution—not a bloody revolution; America is not given to the spilling of blood—but a silent revolution, whereby America will insist upon recovering in practice those ideals which she has always professed, upon securing a government devoted to the general interest and not the special interests. *Ibid.*

The Roman Catholic Church was then, as it is now, a great democracy. There was no peasant so humble but that he might not become a priest, and no priest so obscure that he might not become Pope of Christendom; and every chancellery in Europe, every court in Europe, was ruled by these learned, trained and accomplished men—the priesthood of that great and dominant body. What kept government alive in the Middle Ages was this constant rise of the sap from the bottom, from the rank and file of the great body of the people through the open channels of the priesthood. *Ibid.*

Today, when our government has so far passed into the hands of special interests . . .

today, supremely, does it behoove this nation to remember that a people shall be saved by the power that sleeps in its own deep bosom, or by none; shall be renewed in hope, in conscience, in strength, by waters welling up from its own sweet, perennial springs. Not from above; not by the patronage of its aristocrats. *Ibid.*

I tell you the so-called radicalism of our times is simply the effort of nature to release the generous energies of our people. *Ibid.*

This great American people is at bottom just, virtuous, and hopeful; the roots of its being are in the soil of what is lovely, pure, and of good report, and the need of the hour is just that radicalism that will clear a way for the realization of the aspirations of a sturdy race. *Ibid.*

Our liberties are safe until the memories and experiences of the past are blotted out and the Mayflower with its band of pilgrims forgotten; until our public-school system has fallen into decay and the Nation into ignorance; until legislators have resigned their functions to ecclesiastical powers and their prerogatives to priests.
Public Papers of Woodrow Wilson (Authorized Edition), Part I, Vol. 1, page 62.

Liberty does not consist, my fellow citizens, in mere declarations of the rights of man. It consists in the translation of those declarations into definite actions.
Address, July 4, 1914.

There is such a thing as a man being too proud to fight. There is such a thing as a nation being so right that it does not need to convince others by force that it is right.
Address, May 10, 1915.

It must be a peace without victory. . . . Victory would mean peace forced upon the

loser; a victor's terms imposed upon the vanquished. It would be accepted in humiliation, under duress, at an intolerable sacrifice,
and would leave a sting, a resentment, a bitter memory upon which terms of peace would
rest not permanently, but only as upon quick-
sand. Only a peace between equals can last:
only a peace, the very principle of which is
equality, and a common participation in a
common benefit.
*Address to U. S. Senate, January 22,
1917.*

The world must be made safe for democracy. Its peace must be planted upon the
tested foundations of political liberty. We
have no selfish ends to serve. We desire no
conquests, no dominion. We seek no in-
demnities for ourselves, no material compensation for the sacrifices we shall freely
make. We are but one of the champions of
the rights of mankind. We shall be satisfied
when those rights have been made as secure
as the faith and the freedom of nations can
make them.
War Message to Congress, April 2, 1917.

I firmly believe in Divine Providence.
Without belief in Providence I think I should
go crazy. Without God the world would be
a maze without a clue.   *Address, 1919.*

I have always been among those who believed that the greatest freedom of speech
was the greatest safety, because if a man
is a fool, the best thing to do is to encourage him to advertise the fact by speaking.
It cannot be so easily discovered if you allow
him to remain silent and look wise, but if you
let him speak, the secret is out and the world
knows that he is a fool.
*Address, Institute of France, Paris, May
10, 1919.*

At the front of this great treaty is put the
Covenant of the League of Nations. . . .

Unless you get the united, concerted purpose
and power of the great Governments of the
world behind this settlement, it will fall
down like a house of cards. There is only
one power to put behind the liberation of
mankind, and that is the power of mankind.
It is the power of the united moral forces of
the world, and in the Covenant of the League
of Nations the moral forces of the world are
mobilized.   *Address at Pueblo, 1919.*

You will see that international law is revo-
lutionized by putting morals into it. *Ibid.*

Why, my fellow citizens, is there any man
here or any woman—let me say is there any
child here—who does not know that the seed
of war in the modern world is industrial and
commercial rivalry?
*Speech, St. Louis, September 5, 1919;
Congressional Record, September 8,
1919, p. 5006.*

The real reason that the war we have just
finished took place was that Germany was
afraid her commercial rivals were going to
get the better of her, and the reason why
some nations went into the war against Germany was that they thought Germany would
get the commercial advantage of them. The
seed of the jealousy, the seed of the deep-
seated hatred, was hot successful commercial
and industrial rivalry. . . .   *Ibid.*

This war was a commercial and industrial
war. It was not a political war.   *Ibid.*

Sometimes people call me an idealist.
Well, that is the way I know I am an American. America is the only idealist nation in
the world.
*Speech, Sioux Falls, September 8,
1919.*

Some Americans need hyphens in their
names, because only part of them has come
over; but when the whole man has come

over, heart and thought and all, the hyphen drops of its own weight out of his name.

I believe in democracy because it releases the energy of every human being.

The trouble with the Republican Party is that it has not had a new idea for thirty years.

This is the only country in the world which experiences this constant and repeated rebirth. Other countries depend upon the multiplication of their own native people. This country is constantly drinking strength out of new sources by the voluntary association with it of great bodies of strong men and forward-looking women out of other lands. And so by the gift of the free will of independent people it is being constantly renewed from generation to generation by the same process by which it was originally created. It is as if humanity had determined to see to it that this great nation, founded for the benefit of humanity, should not lack for the allegiance of the people of the world.

Address, to American citizens of foreign birth.

My urgent advice to you would be, not only to think first of America, but always, also, to think first of humanity. *Ibid.*

Only free people can hold their purpose and their honor steady to a common end and prefer the interests of mankind to any narrow interest of their own.

If there is one thing we love more than another in the United States, it is that every man should have the privilege, unmolested and uncriticized, to utter the real convictions of his mind.

N. Y. Times Magazine, July 3, 1949.

We have forgotten the very principle of our origin if we have forgotten how to ob-

ject, how to resist, how to agitate, how to pull down and build up, even to the extent of revolutionary practices, if it is necessary to readjust matters. *Ibid.*

The President is at liberty, both in law and in conscience, to be as big a man as he can.

John Wise
(1652-1725)
New England minister, libertarian

I shall consider man in a state of natural being, as a freeborn subject under the crown of Heaven, and owing homage to none but God himself. It is certain civil government in general is a very desirable result of Providence, and an incomparable benefit to mankind, yet must needs be acknowledged to be the effect of human free-compacts and not of divine institution; it is the produce of man's reason, of human and rational combinations, and not from any direct orders of infinite wisdom, in any positive law wherein is drawn up this or that scheme of civil government.

A Vindication of the Government of New England Churches, 1717.

The second great immunity of man is an original liberty enstamped upon his rational nature. He that intrudes upon this liberty violates the law of nature. *Ibid.*

The third capital immunity belonging to man's nature is an equality amongst men, which is not to be denied by the law of nature till man has resigned himself with all his rights for the sake of a civil state, and then his personal liberty and equality is to be cherished and preserved to the highest degree as will consist with all just distinctions amongst men of honor and shall be agreeable with the public good. *Ibid.*

[753]

The first human subject and original of civil power is the people. For as they have a power every man over himself in a natural state, so upon a combination they can and do bequeath this power unto others, and settle it according as their united discretions shall determine. For that this is very plain, that when the subject of sovereign power is quite extinct, that power returns to the people again. And when they are free, they may set up what species of government they please; or if they rather incline to it, they may subside into a state of natural being if it be plainly for the best.

Ibid.

A democracy. This is a form of government which the light of nature does highly value, and often directs to as most agreeable to the just and natural prerogatives of human beings. This was of great account in the early times of the world. And not only so, but upon the experience of several thousand years, after the world had been tumbled and tossed from one species of government to another, at a great expense of blood and treasure, many of the wise nations of the world have sheltered themselves under it again; or at least have blendished and balanced their governments with it. *Ibid.*

Man's original liberty after it is resigned (yet under due restrictions) ought to be cherished in all wise governments; or otherwise a man in making himself a subject, he alters himself from a freeman into a slave, which to do is repugnant to the law of nature. Also the natural equality of men amongst men must be duly favored; in that government was never established by God or nature to give one man a prerogative to insult over another; therefore in a civil as well as in a natural state of being, a just equality is to be indulged so far as that every man is bound to honor every man, which is agreeable both with nature and religion (I Pet. ii. 17): *Honor all men.*—The end of all good government is to cultivate humanity, and promote the happiness of all, and the good of every man in all his rights, his life, liberty, estate, honor, etc., without injury or abuse done to any. *Ibid.*

Humbert Wolfe
(1885-1940)
English poet

You cannot hope to bribe or twist
    Thank God! the British journalist.
But, seeing what the man will do
    Unbribed, there's no occasion to.

Thomas Wolfe
(1900-1938)
American novelist

I believe that we are lost here in America, but I believe we shall be found. And this belief, which mounts now to the catharsis of knowledge and conviction, is for me—and I think for all of us—not only our own hope, but America's everlasting, living dream. I think the life which we have fashioned in America, and which has fashioned us—the forms we made, the cells that grew, the honeycomb that was created—was self-destructive in its nature, and must be destroyed. I think these forms are dying, and must die, just as I know that America and the people in it are deathless, undiscovered, and immortal, and must live.

You Can't Go Home Again, Harper & Bros., 1940.

I think the true discovery of America is before us. I think the true fulfillment of our spirit, of our people, of our mighty and immortal land, is yet to come. I think the true discovery of our own democracy is still before us. And I think that all these things are certain as the morning, as inevitable as noon. I think I speak for most men living when I say that our America is Here, is Now, and beckons us, and that this glorious assurance is not only our living hope, but our dream to be accomplished. *Ibid.*

I think the enemy is here before us . . . I think the enemy is simple selfishness and compulsive greed...I think the enemy is old as Time, and evil as Hell, and that he has been here with us from the beginning. I think he stole our earth from us, destroyed our wealth, and ravaged and despoiled our land. I think he took our people and enslaved them, that he polluted the fountains of our life, took unto himself the rarest treasures of our own possession, took our bread and left us with a crust, and, not content, for the nature of the enemy is insatiate—tried finally to take from us the crust. *Ibid.*

Go, seeker, if you will, throughout the land and you will find us burning in the night . . . To every man his chance, to every man, regardless of his birth, his shining golden opportunity—to every man the right to live, to work, to be himself, and to become whatever thing his manhood and his vision can combine to make him—this, seeker, is the promise of America.
Ibid.

The whole conviction of my life now rests upon the belief that loneliness, far from being a rare and curious phenomenon, peculiar to myself and to a few other solitary men, is the central and inevitable fact of human existence.
The Anatomy of Loneliness, American Mercury, October, 1941.

The surest cure for vanity is loneliness.
Ibid.

And the eternal paradox of it is that if a man is to know the triumphant labor of creation, he must for long periods resign himself to loneliness, and suffer loneliness to rob him of the health, the confidence, the belief and joy which are essential to creative work. *Ibid.*

What Christ is saying always, what he never swerves from saying, what he says a thousand times and in a thousand different ways, but always with a central unity of belief, is this: "I am my Father's son, and you are my brothers." And the unity that binds us all together, that makes this earth a family, and all men brothers and so the sons of God, is love. *Ibid.*

And Christ himself, who preached the life of love, was yet as lonely as any man that ever lived. *Ibid.*

A billion men have since professed his (Christ's) way and never followed it. *Ibid.*

W. Beran Wolfe
(1900-1935)
American psychiatrist

Freud found sex an outcast in the outhouse, and left it in the living room an honored guest.

Mary Wollstonecraft (Godwin)
(1759-1797)
English writer, feminist

Contending for the rights of women, my main argument is built on this simple principle, that if she be not prepared by education to become the companion of man, she will stop the progress of knowledge, for truth must be common to all, or it will be inefficacious with respect to its influence on general practice.

Vindication of the Rights of Women, 1792.

Make them free . . . or the injustice which one half of the human race are obliged to submit to, retorting on their oppressors, the virtue of men will be worm-eaten by the insects whom he keeps under his feet.

Ibid.

What unheard of misery have thousands suffered to purchase a cardinal's hat for an intriguing adventurer who longed to be ranked with princes, or lord it over them by seizing the triple crown.   *Ibid.*

Thomas Wolsey
(1475?-1530)
English Cardinal, statesman

This new invention of printing has produced various effects of which Your Holiness cannot be ignorant. If it has restored books and learning, it has also been the occasion of those sects and schisms which daily appear. Men begin to call in question the present faith and tenets of the Church; the laity read the Scriptures and pray in their vulgar tongue. Were this suffered, the common people might come to believe that there was not so much use of the clergy. If men were persuaded that they could make their own way to God, and in their ordinary language as well as Latin, the authority of the Mass would fall, which would be very prejudicious to our ecclesiastical orders. The mysteries of religion must be kept in the hands of the priests.

Woman's Rights Convention

The history of mankind is a history of repeated injuries and usurpations on the part of man toward woman, having in direct object the establishment of a tyranny over her.

Manifesto, Seneca Falls, 1848.

Virginia Woolf
(1882-1941)
English author

To make ideas effective, we must be able to fire them off. We must put them into action. . . . "I will not cease from mental fight," Blake wrote. Mental fight means thinking against the current, not with it. The current flows fast and furious. It issues a spate of words from the loudspeakers and the politicians. Every day they tell us that we are a free people fighting to defend freedom. That is the current that has whirled the young airman up into the sky and keeps him circulating there among the clouds. Down here, with a roof to cover us and a gas mask handy, it is our business to puncture gas bags and discover the seeds of truth.

New Republic, October 21, 1940.

If you do not tell the truth about yourself you cannot tell it about other people.

The Moment and Other Essays, Harcourt, Brace.

John M. Woolsey
(1877-1945)
U.S. District Court judge

Whilst in many places the effect of "Ulysses" undoubtedly is somewhat emetic, nowhere does it tend to be aphrodisiac.

Decision, December 6, 1933, freeing James Joyce's Ulysses, one of the great victories over censorship.

William Wordsworth
(1770-1850)
English poet

One great society alone on earth:
The noble living and the noble dead.
The Prelude, 1805.

Great God! I'd rather be
A Pagan, suckled in a creed outworn;
So might I, standing on the pleasant lea,
Have glimpses that would make me less
forlorn;
Have sight of Proteus rising from the sea,
Or hear old Triton blow his wreathed horn.
*Miscellaneous Sonnets. The World Is
Too Much With Us.*

To think that now our life is only drest
For show; mean handy-work of craftsman,
cook,
Or groom!—We must run glittering like a
brook
In the open sunshine, or we are unblest;
The wealthiest man among us is the best;
No grandeur now in nature or in book
Delights us. Rapine, avarice, expense,
This is idolatry; and these we adore;
Plain living and high thinking are no more.
Written in London, September, 1802.

We must be free or die, who speak the tongue
That Shakespeare spake; the faith and morals
hold
Which Milton held.
It Is Not to Be Thought Of.

An accursed thing it is to gaze on prosperous tyrants with a dazzled eye.

Stern Daughter of the Voice of God!
O Duty! if that name thou love
Who art a light to guide, a rod
To check the erring, and reprove;

Thou, who at victory and law
When empty terrors overawe;
From vain temptations dost set free;
And calm'st the weary strife of frail
humanity! *Ode to Duty.*

Milton! thou should'st be living at this hour;
England hath need of thee: she is a fen
Of stagnant waters: altar, sword, and pen,
Fireside, the heroic wealth of hall and
bower,
Have forfeited their ancient English power
Of inward happiness. We are selfish men;
Oh! raise us up, return to us again;
And give us manners, virtue, freedom,
power. *Sonnet, London, 1802.*

Tunis Wortman
(?-1822)
American lawyer

It has been practically maintained by the
advocates of mystery that a people can be
governed only by strategem and imposture.
. . . But by what unheard-of arguments can
it be maintained that the exercise of the rational faculties is criminal or prejudicial to
the general welfare? Until this extraordinary
position is established, no human legislature
can deny our right to the most unbounded
latitude of investigation.
*Treatise Concerning Political Inquiry
and Liberty of the Press, 1800.*

If government is the instrument . . . for
the promotion of general good; if it is the
creature in which they invested the powers
of effecting the benevolent design for social
felicity . . . the government which attempts
to coerce the progress of opinion, or abolish
freedom of investigation in political affairs,
materially violates the most essential principles of the social state. *Ibid.*

To invest the public magistrate with the
power of restricting public opinion, would

be to trust the progress of Information to the mercy and pleasure of a Government. More formidable dangers are justly to be apprehended from arming the constituted organs of Authority with a power to arrest the career of Human Intellect, than from all the evil attributes of Licentiousness. *Ibid.*

The formation of general opinion upon correct and salutary principles, requires the unbiased exercise of individual intellect; neither prejudice, authority, or terror, should be suffered to impede the liberty of discussion; no undue influence should tyrannize over mind; every man should be left to the independent exercise of his reflections; all should be permitted to communicate their ideas with the energy and ingenuousness of truth. *Ibid.*

There is no species of tyranny more pernicious in its consequences than that which is exerted to impede the progress of intellect . . . Slavery will inevitably produce mental debility and degradation. Unless the mind is conscious of liberty to reflect and expatiate, it will be wholly incapable of sublime and energetic exertion. *Ibid.*

Without establishing the liberty of inquiry, and the right of disseminating our opinions, it must always be our position to remain in a state of barbarism, wretchedness, and degradation. . . . It is impossible that the imagination should conceive a more horrible and pernicious tyranny than that which should restrain Intercourse of Thought.
Ibid.

Prejudice may boast of her fascination, and Tyranny may exult in his claims; Superstition may administer the slumbering opiate, and Delusion may continue to practice her magical artifices: the Rays of Intellectual Light will still proceed to brighten and increase, and the days of Liberty and Science succeed to the gloomy night of Ignorance and Despotism. *Ibid.*

Sir Henry Wotton
(1568-1639)
English author, diplomat

How happy. is he born and taught
That serveth not another's will;
Whose armour is his utmost thought,
And simple truth his utmost skill!
Character of a Happy Life, 1614.

This man is freed from servile bonds
Of hope to rise or fear to fall;
Lord of himself, though not of lands,
And having nothing, yet hath all. *Ibid.*

An ambassador is an honest man, sent to lie abroad for the good of his country.
Written in 1604 in the album of Christopher Fleckmore; acknowledged in letter to Velserus, 1612.*

Tell the truth, and so puzzle and confound your adversaries.

Frank Lloyd Wright
(1869-1959)
American architect

Ugliness is a sin.
Newspaper interview, 1955.

Truth against the world. *Motto.*

If capitalism is fair then unionism must be. If men have a right to capitalize their

---

* Samuel Johnson wrote in *The Idler*, November 11, 1758: "A newswriter is a man without virtue, who writes lies at home for his own profit." Cf. Plato.

ideas and the resources of their country, then that implies the right of men to capitalize their labor.

Obituary editorial, Labor, May 2, 1959.

I should like to see our country unionized to the hilt.   *Ibid.*

A new space-concept is needed . . . A definite phase of this new ideal comes in what we call organic architecture—the *natural* architecture of the democratic spirit in this age of the machine.

The Living City.

Only human values are life-giving values. No organic values are ever life-taking. When man builds "natural" buildings naturally, he builds his very life into them —inspired by intrinsic Nature in this interior sense we are here calling "organic."

Ibid.

Humanity to me is not a mob. A mob is a degeneration of humanity. A mob is humanity going the wrong way.

Mike Wallace Asks (TV interviews), Simon & Schuster, 1958.

Government can be a kind of gangsterism and is in Russia and is likely to be here if we don't take care of ourselves pretty carefully.   *Ibid.*

Wu Ting-fang
(1842-1922)
Chinese statesman

The account of the creation of the world and the story of Adam and Eve and the Garden of Eden, seem to me funny.

John Wycliffe
(1324?-1384)
English reformer

Lords devour poor men's goods in glut-

tony and waste and pride, and they perish for mischief and thirst and cold, and their children also . . . And so in a manner they eat and drink poor men's flesh and blood.

I believe that in the end the truth will conquer. *To the Duke of Lancaster, 1381.*

This Bible is for the government of the people, by the people, and for the people.

Preface to translation of the Bible by Wycliffe and Hereford.

Xavier
See St. Francis Xavier

Xenophanes
(570?-480? B.C.)
Greek philosopher, poet

If oxen and lions had hands, and could paint with their hands, and produce works of art as men do, horses would paint the forms of the gods like horses, and oxen like oxen.

Xenophon
(434?-355? B.C.)
Greek historian, essayist

The despot, be assured, lives night and day like one condemned to death by the whole of mankind for his wickedness.

Hiero, vii, n. 10, translated by Kathleen Freeman, Fighting Words.

To fear a crowd, and yet fear solitude, to fear to go unguarded, to fear the very guards themselves; to be unwilling to dispense with an armed escort, and yet to feel displeasure at the sight of one's attendants carrying arms: what a hateful predicament.

Ibid., ii, n. 8.

Leon R. Yankwich
(b. 1888)
U.S. District judge

There are no illegitimate children—only illegitimate parents.
Zipkin v. Mozon, June, 1928.

William Butler Yeats
(1865-1939)
Irish writer

All empty souls tend to extreme opinion. It is only in those who have built up a rich world of memories and habits of thought that extreme opinions affront the sense of probability. Propositions, for instance, which set all the truth upon one side can only enter rich minds to dislocate and strain, if they can enter at all, and sooner or later the mind expels them by instinct.
The Autobiography of William Butler Yeats.

Evil comes to us men of the imagination wearing as its mask all the virtues. I have certainly known more men destroyed by the desire to have a wife and child and to keep them in comfort than I have seen destroyed by drink and harlots.
Quoted by Murray Kempton, in "Part of Our Time."

A statesman is an easy man,
He tells his lies by rote;
A journalist makes up his lies
And takes you by the throat;
So stay at home and drink your beer
And let the neighbours vote.
Atlantic Monthly, April, 1954.

Brigham Young
(1801-1877)
American Mormon leader

Our religion is simply the truth. It is all said in this one expression—it embraces all truth, wherever found in all the works of God and man.

Edward Young
(1683-1765)
English poet

One to destroy is murder by the law,
And gibbets keep the lifted hand in awe;
To murder thousands takes a specious name,
War's glorious art, and gives immortal fame.
Love of Fame.

What is a miracle?—'Tis a reproach,
'Tis an implicit satire on mankind;
And while it satisfies, it censures too.
Ibid.

Israel Zangwill
(1864-1926)
English writer

Take from me the hope that I can change the future, and you will send me mad.
The Melting Pot, 1920.

America is God's Crucible, the great Melting-Pot where all the races of Europe are melting and reforming. *Ibid.*

If the press diffuses light, it can also—as Bismarck discovered—diffuse darkness. If Science as the maid-of-all-work is a success, Science as an interpreter of the mystery of the Universe is a dismal failure. Even her immense practical boons only serve to amplify our senses and increase our speed: they cannot increase our happiness. Giants suffer as well as dwarfs, and the soul may sit lonely and sad, surrounded by mechanical miracles.

Scratch the Christian and you will find the pagan—spoiled.
Children of the Ghetto.

Every dogma has its day, but ideals are eternal. *Address, November 13, 1892.*

It is a tragic paradox when the path of righteousness becomes the road to lawlessness. But the right to rebel is an elemental human right, just as the right to repress rebellion is an elemental public right.
Address, Woman Suffrage, March 28, 1912.

It is an asset of the State that prisoners shall be held in contempt and statesmen in reverence. It is an injury to the State when prisoners are held in reverence and statesmen in contempt. And by tens of thousands of women Holloway (gaol) is now held in more honour than Downing Street. *Ibid.*

The free souls are in revolt. And you cannot meet a Revolution with a Referendum.
Ibid.

The Jews are a frightened people. Nineteen centuries of Christian love have broken down their nerves.

So long as our conceptions remain radically unchanged, so long as no new world religion flames into being with a new passionate sense of brotherhood and a new scale of human values, so long shall we cry peace, peace, where there is no Peace.

John Peter Zenger
(1697-1746)
Colonial American printer, publisher

The Liberty of the Press is a Subject of the greatest Importance, and in which every Individual is as much concern'd as he is in any other Part of Liberty.
The New-York Weekly Journal, November 12, 1733. [*]

There are two Sorts of Monarchies, an absolute and a limited one. In the first, the Liberty of the Press can never be maintained, it is inconsistent with it; for what absolute Monarch would suffer any Subject to animadvert to his Actions, when it is in his Power to declare the Crime, and to nominate the Punishment? *Ibid.*

In an absolute Monarchy, the Will of the Prince being the Law, a Liberty of the Press to complain of Grievances would be complaining against the Law, and the Constitution, to which they have submitted, or have been obliged to submit; and therefore, in one Sense, may be said to deserve Punishment, So that under an absolute Monarchy, I say, such a Liberty is inconsistent with the Constitution, having no proper Subject in Politics, on which it might be exercis'd, and if exercis'd would incur a certain Penalty.
Ibid.

The loss of liberty in general would soon follow the suppression of the liberty of the press; for it is an essential branch of liberty, so perhaps it is the best preservative of the whole. *Ibid., November 19, 1733.*

No nation ancient or modern ever lost the liberty of freely speaking, writing, or publishing their sentiments, but forthwith lost their liberty in general and became slaves. *Ibid.*

[*] Four issues of this newspaper were ordered burned by the public hangman. Zenger was arrested. Andrew Hamilton (*q.v.*) defended him.

Georgi Zhukov
(1894-1974)
Soviet Russian general

(War is) a science, a series of mathematical problems, to be solved through proper integration and coordination of men and weapons in time and space.

Quoted in Life magazine.

Johann Georg von Zimmermann
(1728-1795)
Swiss physician, writer

In fame's temple there is always a niche to be found for rich dunces, importunate scoundrels, or successful butchers of the human race.

Hans Zinsser
(1878-1940)
American bacteriologist

It seems that somewhere in the legendary past of louse history, an offspring of a free living form, not unlike our book louse, found that life could be infinitely simplified, if instead of having to grub for food in straw, under tree bark, in moss, or lichen, in decaying cereals and vegetables, it could attach itself to some food-supplying host and sit tight.

Rats, Lice and History, copyright, Little, Brown.

The louse, by adapting itself to parasitism, has attained the ideal of bourgeois civilization, though its methods of getting food, shelter, and clothing are more direct than those of business and banking, and its source of nourishment is not its own species. *Ibid.*

The questions of immortality of the soul and freedom of the will, though they have called forth libraries of controversial literature, continue to appear not only utterly beyond any possibility of satisfactory proof but, instead, trivial in being so definitely personal, once the principle of an all-pervading and ordering force is accepted. And the conception of a God so constituted that we are, as individuals, of direct concern to Him appears both presumptuous—considering our individual insignificance in the scheme as a whole—and unnecessary for that feeling of helpless reverence in face of the universal order which is the essence of religious experience. Moreover, paleontologically considered, one would have to assume that such a "personal" God existed long before the evolution of man. "Why did He wait so long to create man?" asked Diderot. Yet reward, punishment, immortality of the soul in the theological sense, could have no meaning whatever until there had developed creatures possessing a nervous organization capable of abstract thinking and of spiritual suffering. One cannot imagine such a God occupied through millions of years, up to the Pleistocene, with personal supervision, reward and punishment, of amoebae, clams, fish, dinosaurs, and sabre-toothed tigers; then, suddenly, adjusting His own systems and purposes to the capacities of the man-ape He had allowed to develop.

As I Remember Him. Little, Brown.

Émile Zola
(1840-1902)
French novelist

Since they have dared, I too shall dare. I shall tell the truth because I pledged myself to tell it if justice regularly empowered, did not do so fully, unmitigatedly. My duty is to speak; I have no wish to be an accomplice.

J'Accuse! L'Aurore, January 13, 1898.

When truth is buried underground it grows, it chokes, it gathers such an explosive force that on the day it bursts out, it blows up everything with it.   *Ibid.*

I have one passion only, for light, in the name of humanity which has borne so much and has a right to happiness.   *..Ibid.*

I do not despair in the least of ultimate triumph. I repeat with more intense conviction: the truth is on the march and nothing will stop it. *(La verité est en marche et rien ne l'arrêtera.)*   *Ibid.*

The *bourgeoisie,* wielding power, would relinquish naught of the sovereignty which it has conquered, wholly stolen; while the people, the eternal dupe, silent so long, clenched its fists and growled, claiming its legitimate share.   *Paris.*

Huldreich Zwingli

(1484-1531)

Swiss Reformation leader

In the things of this life, the laborer is most like to God.

1525; quoted by Tawney, Religion and the Rise of Capitalism.

Index

INDEX

A

Abolition, Abolitionism
S. A. Douglas, 211
Lee, 405
Methodist Church, 489

Abortion
Hippocrates, 316
O. W. Holmes (Jr.), 329

Absolution
John Adams, 42

Act, Action
Acton, 38
Amiel, 55
Colton, 168
Farrell, 248
O. W. Holmes (Jr.), 328
E. Hubbard, 334
T. H. Huxley, 343
La Rochefoucauld, 398
Longfellow, 439
K. Mansfield, 465
Mencius, 486
Sun Yat-sen, 668
Tennyson, 678
Toynbee, 691

Actors
Council of Arles, 181
Council of Elvira, 182
John of Salisbury, 376

Adultery
Bunyan, 125

Advertising
F. Allen, 52

Anonymous, 59
P. T. Barnum, 83
Chase, 153
Cockburn, 166
Cowles, 183
N. Douglas, 211
Jefferson, 367
S. Johnson, 377
Kennan, 387
La Follette, 396
Laski, 399
S. Lewis, 418
Matthews-Shallcross, 480
McWilliams, 484
G. Murray, 512
Ochs, 534
Patterson, 552
Peterson, 558
E. Roosevelt, 589
W. A. White, 735, 736

Age
Bogomoletz, 103
Nascher, 519
Osler, 538

Aggression
A. Adler, 49
Evans, 246
Freud, 260, 262

Agitate, Agitator, Agitation
Baer, 75
Broun, 116
Chapman, 152
Douglass, 214

Agnostic, Agnosticism
  Darrow, 191
  C. Darwin, 192, 193
  Frankfurter, 257
  T. H. Huxley, 344, 345, 346
  Lindsey, 432
  Mencken, 487

Alcohol (see Drink, Drunk)

Alliances
  Jefferson, 364
  G. Washington, 726, 727

Ambition
  Bacon, 74
  Colton, 168
  Jonson, 380
  La Bruyère, 395
  Lecky, 404
  Machiavelli, 456
  Quintilian, 578
  Raleigh, 578
  Spinoza, 651
  Talmud, 673
  W. K. Vanderbilt, 705

America (see People, American; Union, United States; United States)
  H. B. Adams, 40
  John Adams, 43
  John Quincy Adams, 46
  E. Allen, 52
  American Legion, 54
  Amiel, 55
  Angell, 58
  Anonymous, 59
  Balzac, 81
  Bryce, 123
  Capone, 140
  Carroll, 146
  Chafee, 150
  Chesterton, 155
  Clemenceau, 162
  Cleveland, 163
  Commager, 169
  Cooke, 176
  J. F. Cooper, 178

  Dimitrov, 205
  Disraeli, 208
  W. O. Douglas, 212
  Dreiser, 215
  Emerson, 233, 238
  Faulkner, 248
  George III, 272
  Eric F. Goldman, 283
  B. Harrison, 301
  Hillman, 316
  Mencken, 488
  Monroe, 500
  O'Neill, 535
  T. Parker, 546
  Parrington, 548
  President's Commission, 573
  Radford, 578
  Rakosi, 578
  Scripps, 623, 624
  Siegfried, 638
  S. Smith, 644
  Steffens, 660
  H. A. Wallace, 720
  Washington, 725
  Wells, 732
  Whitehead, 737
  Whitman, 741
  O. Wilde, 743
  Willkie, 748
  W. Wilson, 750, 751, 752, 753
  T. Wolfe, 754, 755
  Zangwill, 760

American, Americans
  Cornwallis, 181
  Crawford, 184
  Crèvecoeur, 184, 185
  Eisenhower, 228
  Lundberg, 446
  Rogers, 587
  Thompson, 681
  Thoreau, 683
  Tocqueville, 687
  Truman, 695
  Twain, 697
  Valentine, 704

D. Webster, 730

Americanism; American Way
Capone, 140
L. Hughes, 335
Ickes, 348
LaFollette, 396
Lenin, 411
Leo XIII, 414
S. Lewis, 418
Lowell, 441
Macaulay, 453
Manning, 465
J. Marshall, 470
Marx, 474
McKay, 483
Melville, 485
Commager, 169
Johnston, 379
Long, 439
MacLeish, 457
T. Roosevelt, 596, 597, 598
Shaw, 632
U.S. Army, 70

American Legion
Smedley Butler, 134
Cocke, 166
Dies, 205
Owsley, 540

Anarchist, Anarchism, Anarchy
John Adams, 45
S. Adams, 47
Altgeld, 53
Arcos, 66
Bakunin, 76
Berlin, 94
Brandeis, 112
Carnegie, 143
Ellsworth, 232
Emma Goldman, 283
T. H. Huxley, 344
Kautsky, 384
Kropotkin, 395
Lenin, 407
Mussolini, 514

Owsley, 540
Proudhon, 574
Shaw, 628
Vanzetti, 707
Webb, 727

Anathema
Anonymous, 61
Erasmus, 245
Vatican Council, 707

Ancestors
Ellis, 232
O. W. Holmes (Sr.), 327
Lincoln, 423
Lowell, 443
Lyon, 443
S. Smith, 644
Voltaire, 714

Angel, Angels
F. Bacon, 72
Lincoln, 426
Swedenborg, 669

Animals
C. Darwin, 192
Kropotkin, 394

Anti-Christian, Anti-Christianity
Arcos, 66
Jefferson, 370
Luther, 447
Williams, 747

Anti-Semitism
V. Adler, 50
Bebel, 86
Hitler, 320
Nietzsche, 527, 530
Pius XI, 566
Taft, 672
Tolstoy, 689
Twain, 696
Willkie, 749

Anxiety
Mailer, 461

Apathy
Anonymous, 63

Brandeis, 111
N. M. Butler, 133
Chaplin, 152
Cleveland, 163
S. Crane, 184
Garrison, 270
Hutchins, 340
Montesquieu, 502
Singleton, 640

Ape
T. H. Huxley, 343
Nietzsche, 529
Zinsser, 762

Archetypal
Jung, 381

Argument
Cicero, 158
Phillips, 560

Aristocracy
John Adams, 46
Barlow, 82
Benton, 91
Carlyle, 143
Chesterton, 155
P. Cooper, 180
Guizot, 291
Alexander Hamilton, 295
Hitler, 320
A. Jackson, 354
Jefferson, 370
T. Parker, 547
Phillips, 559
Randolph, 579
Viereck, 710
Whitehead, 737
Whitman, 741
W. Wilson, 751

Armaments
H. B. Adams, 41
Coolidge, 177
Einstein, 226
Grey, 290
League of Nations, 403

Lenin, 412
Machiavelli, 456
Mao Tse-tung, 465
Nobel, 531
Pershing, 557
Society of Friends, 645
Thomas, 681

Armistice
Foch, 252

Army
M. Arnold, 69
Montesquieu, 503
Sun Tzu, 668
Wilhelm II, 746

Arse
Montaigne, 501

Art, Artist
Amiel, 55
Aristotle, 68
F. Bacon, 75
Bismarck, 97
Blake, 100, 101
Cather, 148
Cocteau, 166
Coolidge, 177
Cousin, 182
Duncan, 216
Durant, 217
Emerson, 239
Erigena, 245
Faure, 248
Gauguin, 271
Gautier, 272
Gide, 277
Goethe, 283
Hippocrates, 316
Hitler, 318, 319
Howells, 333
A. Huxley, 341
H. James, 358
S. Johnson, 377
Joyce, 380
Jung, 381
Keats, 385

Kent, 387
Khrushchev, 390
D. H. Lawrence, 402
Lenin, 407, 408
Malraux, 462
T. Mann, 464
Mao Tse-tung, 466
Marx, 474
Maugham, 481
Mencken, 488
Mill, 496
Montherlant, 504
W. Morris, 510
Mumford, 512
O'Flaherty, 535
D. Parker, 546
Picasso, 562
Plato, 567
Pope, 571
Proust, 575
Robespierre, 584
F. D. Roosevelt, 592, 593
Ruskin, 603, 604
Seldes, 625, 626
Shahn, 628
Sinclair, 639
Singleton, 640
Spinoza, 652
W. G. Sumner, 667
U.S. Supreme Court, 703
Van Loon, 706
Voltaire, 717
Whitehead, 737
O. Wilde, 743, 744, 745
Xenophanes, 759

Aryan
American Anthropological Association, 54
Benedict, 90
Hitler, 318
Müller, 511
Nietzsche, 530

Assassin, Assassination
Anonymous, 62
Disraeli, 207

Mussolini, 513

Associate, Association
Acton, 35
Archer, 65
F. Bacon, 74
Bryant, 122
W. O. Douglas, 213
Kingsley, 392
Mazzini, 482

Atheism
F. Bacon, 72
Bebel, 86
Burke, 126, 129
R. Burns, 131
Coleridge, 167
Colton, 168
Darwin, 193
Einstein, 221
Ellsworth, 232
Kallen, 382
Lenin, 410
Leo XIII, 413
Lindsey, 432
Maritain, 467
Marx, 476
Napoleon, 518
Newman, 523, 524
Paine, 542, 544
Pascal, 549
Pasternak, 550
Santayana, 613, 614
Sartre, 615
Stekel, 661
Voltaire, 714, 716

Atom
Born, 107
Bradley, 109
Christian Action, 155
Democritus, 201
Edison, 219
Einstein, 220, 223
Inge, 349
Kapitza, 384
Kefauver, 385

Khrushchev, 390
Laski, 400
Mumford, 512
T. E. Murray, 512
O'Casey, 534
Oppenheimer, 536
Pasternak, 551
Pauling, 552
Truman, 694

Authority
Acton, 35, 36, 37, 38
John Adams, 42
Anonymous, 61, 64
R. Bacon, 75
Bakunin, 76, 77, 79
Bancroft, 81
Bossuet, 107, 108
V. W. Brooks, 115
Browne, 118
Samuel Butler, 133
Freud, 261
Galton, 266
T. H. Huxley, 344, 345
Keynes, 389
Leo XIII, 412, 413
Lowell, 441
Macaulay, 453
MacLeish, 457
Mill, 490
Mirza, 499
J. Morley, 508
Peron, 557
Salazar, 611
Sprading, 654
Taylor, 677
Turgenev, 695
O. Wilde, 744, 746

Automation
Wiener, 742

Avarice
M. Arnold, 69
Dante, 189

Aviation
C. A. Lindbergh (Jr.), 429

B

Ballot
Debs, 195
Eisenhower, 229
Lincoln, 423, 426
V. Lindsay, 431

Bank, Bankers
Smedley Butler, 134
Calhoun, 137
A. Jackson, 355

Bastard
Anonymous, 59
Hardy, 300
Lindsey, 431, 432
Lyon, 449
Milton, 498
Stilwell, 664
Twain, 696
Yankwich, 760

Battle
Foch, 252
Ibsen, 346

Bayonet
Cavour, 149
Inge, 349
John L. Lewis, 416
J. Madison, 460

"Bear"
J. P. Morgan, 506

Beast
Anonymous, 61
Alexander Hamilton, 296
Ibañez, 346
W. James, 359
Machiavelli, 455
Nietzsche, 528
Pasternak, 551
Voltaire, 713

Beauty, Beautiful
Blake, 100
Carlyle, 142
Einstein, 226
Flaubert, 251

Hand, 299
Hazlitt, 305
Keats, 385
C. A. Lindbergh (Jr.), 429
Masters, 480
W. Morris, 510
O. Wilde, 744

Behavior, Behaviorism
A. Adler, 49
F. Bacon, 72
Watson, 727

Belief, Believe, Believer
Anonymous, 63, 64
Aquinas, 64
Asoka, 69
Augustine, 70, 71
F. Bacon, 74
Bagehot, 76
P. T. Barnum, 83
Bellarmine, 89
Hugo L. Black, 98
Blake, 100
Borah, 106
Buddha, 125
Burroughs, 131
Caesar, 137
Carlyle, 141
Demosthenes, 201
W. O. Douglas, 213
Ellis, 231
Emerson, 237
Erasmus, 244
France, 255
Frankfurter, 256
Frost, 264
H. George, 274
O. W. Holmes (Sr.), 327
T. H. Huxley, 343
Ibsen, 347
R. H. Jackson, 357
W. James, 359, 360
Kallen, 382
Keith, 385
Lecky, 404

Lowell, 440
Loyola, 444
Mencken, 488
Mill, 490
Montaigne, 501
Paine, 542
Peirce, 554
Ralph, 579
Robinson, 585
E. Roosevelt, 589
Santayana, 613
Shaw, 628
Tertullian, 679
Voltaire, 717

Betray, Betrayal
Browning, 119
Koestler, 393

Bible
John Adams, 42
Anonymous, 61
M. Arnold, 68
V. W. Brooks, 115
Cocke, 166
Graham, 287
Halleck, 294
Herndon, 314
T. M. Huxley, 344
R. H. Jackson, 357
Keith, 385
Macy, 458
Nordau, 532
Paine, 541, 544
Stanton, 659
Sunday, 667, 668
Thoreau, 684
Treitschke, 692
Twain, 696
N. Ward, 722
William the Silent, 747
Wu Ting-fang, 759
Wycliffe, 759

Big Business
Commission on Freedom, 171
Hillman, 316

Kefauver, 385
Laski, 399, 400
Lerner, 415, 416
G. W. Norris, 533
Peterson, 558
Rockefeller (Sr.), 586
Singleton, 640
Willkie, 749

Bigness
W. James, 359

Bigotry
John Adams, 44
Buckingham, 124
Colton, 168
Drummond, 215
Hearst, 306
Jefferson, 372
Macaulay, 452, 453
Newman, 523
D. O'Connell, 534
G. Washington, 725

Bill of Rights
R. H. Jackson, 356
Jefferson, 368
F. D. Roosevelt, 594
E. Warren, 722, 723

Birth
Cummings, 187
La Bruyère, 395

Birth Control
Einstein, 224
Pius XI, 565
Ricardo, 582
Tertullian, 679

Blasphemers
Bryan, 136

Blindness
Keller, 386

Blond
Nietzsche, 528

Blood, Bloodshed
S. Adams, 47
Anonymous, 60, 62

Barère, 82
John Brown, 118
Burke, 127
Byron, 136
Churchill, 156
Clausewitz, 160, 161
Ferrer, 249
Gandhi, 268
Harvey, 302
A. Jackson, 355
D. H. Lawrence, 402, 403
Luther, 446, 447
Marat, 466
Müller, 511
Mussolini, 513, 514
Pearse, 553
Pius XI, 566
Rosenberg, 598
Swinburne, 671
Tennyson, 678
Williams, 747

Blood and Iron
Bismarck, 97
Swinburne, 671

Blood and Treasure
S. Adams, 47
Shelley, 634
G. Washington, 725

Bold, Boldness
Danton, 190
Longfellow, 439

Bolshevism (see Communism)
A. Adler, 49
Capone, 140
Churchill, 157
Cobb, 165
Mussolini, 514
Spengler, 650, 651
Veblen, 710

Booboisie
Mencken, 488

Book, Books
John Adams, 46
F. Bacon, 72

Bok, 103
Canon Law, 139
Disraeli, 208
Griswold, 291
E. Hubbard, 334
Jefferson, 371
John of Salisbury, 376
La Bruyère, 395
Leo XIII, 414
Milton, 496, 497
S. Smith, 644
Steinbeck, 661
U.S. Supreme Court, 703
Voltaire, 715, 716, 717
H. A. Wallace, 721
O. Wilde, 745, 746
Woolsey, 756
Book-burning (see Censorship)
John Adams, 46
Akiba, 50
Eisenhower, 228
Emerson, 235
France, 254
Goebbels, 281
Griswold, 291
Lally, 397
Joseph Lewis, 417
Marlowe, 469
Omar, 535
F. D. Roosevelt, 591, 594

Bore, Bored, Boredom
Linton, 432
Schopenhauer, 617

Bourbon
Napoleon, 519
Talleyrand, 673

Bourgeois (see Middle Class)
Anonymous 61, 62
Dostoyevsky, 210
Engels, 240, 242
Gorky, 286
Hitler, 320
Khrushchev, 389
Lassalle, 400

D. H. Lawrence, 403
Lenin, 407, 408, 410
K. Liebknecht, 419
Marx, 471, 473, 476
Mussolini, 514
Stalin, 656, 657
Zinsser, 762
Zola, 763
Boy
Clark, 160
Brainwashing
Hunter, 339
Meany, 484
Brave
F. S. Key, 388
Ovid, 539
Bread
Anonymous, 63
Braley, 109, 110
Defoe, 197
Emma Goldman, 283
Gorky, 287
ICFTU, 353
Juvenal, 382
Laski, 399
Manning, 465
Marat, 466
Mill, 492
Shelley, 634
Van Loon, 706
Bribe
Masters, 480
W. H. Vanderbilt, 705
H. Wolfe, 754

Brotherhood
Archer, 65
Broun, 116
R. Burns, 131
Carlyle, 142
H. S. Chamberlain, 150
Darrow, 191
A. P. Davies, 194
Dostoyevski, 210
E. Fitzgerald, 251

A. E. Stevenson, 663
T. Wolfe, 755
Zangwill, 761
Brutality
Clausewitz, 160
Hitler, 317, 318, 321
Bryan
V. Lindsay, 431
Bullets
Coughlin, 181
Lincoln, 423, 426
Bureaucracy
Balzac, 81
McCarthy, 483
Trotsky, 693
Business
Franklin P. Adams, 40
Ameringer, 54
Bakunin, 77
K. Barth, 83
Bierce, 96
Brandeis, 110
Broun, 116
Brownson, 120
Smedley Butler, 134
Cleveland, 163
Coolidge, 176
Cowles, 183
Darrow, 191
Dreiser, 215
Epicurus, 244
Erasmus, 244
France, 255, 256
Hébert, 306
O. W. Holmes (Jr.), 329
Isocrates, 354
Matthews-Shallcross, 480
Parrington, 548
G. W. Russell, 610
Steffens, 660
U.S. Congress, 702
Veblen, 708, 710
Willkie, 748

C

Caesar
Borgia, 107
Marcus Aurelius, 467
Calumny
Acton, 37
Aristotle, 68
Beaumarchais, 85
Colton, 168
Emmet, 240
Engels, 242
Hazlitt, 305
Jefferson, 366
G. Washington, 727
Calvin
O. W. Holmes (Sr.), 327
Jefferson, 374
Tawney, 675, 676
Canon Law
John Adams, 42
Cant
Byron, 136
Carlyle, 142
A. Huxley, 341
T. H. Huxley, 344
S. Johnson, 378
Leggett, 405
Peacock, 553
Sterne, 662
Whittier, 742
Capital, Capitalist, Capitalism
B. Adams, 39
H. B. Adams, 41
Altgeld, 53
Angell, 57, 58
Anonymous, 62
Bakunin, 77
K. Barth, 83
Bellamy, 88
Brandeis, 112
Brownson, 120
Bryan, 122
Smedley Butler, 134, 135

Calhoun, 137
Capone, 140
Catholic Bishops, 148
Cleveland, 163
P. Cooper, 179
Cowles, 183
Debs, 196
De Leon, 200
Eastman, 218
Einstein, 223
Engels, 240
Fox, 254
H. George, 274
Gompers, 286
Gorky, 286, 287
Greeley, 289
Haldane, 293
Haywood, 304
Hitler, 321
J. H. Holmes, 327
O. W. Holmes (Jr.), 328
Jaurès, 362
Johnston, 379
Kautsky, 384
Khrushchev, 389, 390, 391
Kingsley, 392
Lenin, 408, 409, 410, 411
Lerner, 416
Lincoln, 421, 426
H. D. Lloyd, 434
C. A. Madison, 458
Marx, 472, 474, 477
McDonald, 483
Nehru, 521, 522
Nkrumah, 531
W. H. O'Connell, 535
Oxnam, 540
Phillips, 561
Pius XII, 566
Populist Party, 572
Republican Party, 581
Ricardo, 582
T. Roosevelt, 597
Sinclair, 639
Socialist Labor Party, 644

Spengler, 651
Stalin, 655, 656, 658
Tawney, 675, 676
Third International, 680
Tilden, 685
Webb, 728
W. A. White, 735, 736
W. Wilson, 750, 751
Wright, 758

Capital and Labor
Acton, 37
American Federation of Labor, 54
Bakunin, 79
Bancroft, 81
Brandeis, 112
Ingersoll, 352
John L. Lewis, 417
Lincoln, 426, 427
Lowell, 441
Marx, 474
Pius XI, 565, 566
Ricardo, 582
T. Roosevelt, 597
Shaw, 629, 630
Sherman, 637
Van Buren, 705

Castle
Coke, 167
Otis, 539

Categorical Imperative
Kant, 384

Catholic, Catholicism
Acton, 36, 38
John Adams, 43, 44, 45
S. Adams, 47
E. Allen, 52
Arcos, 65, 66
Athanasian Creed, 69
Augustine, 71
Bergamin, 92
Bismarck, 97
Broun, 116
Canon Laws, 139
Chesterton, 154

Cobbett, 165
Connolly, 174
Council of Trent, 182
De Leon, 199
Einstein, 224
Emerson, 233
Frankfurter, 257
Galileo, 266
Garfield, 268
Gibbon, 276
Gibbons, 277
Hawkes, 303
d'Holbach, 325
T. H. Huxley, 344
Inge, 349
Institute of Brothers of the Christian
    Church, 353
John of Salisbury, 376
Lecky, 404
Leo XIII, 413
Lincoln, 422
Luther, 446
Macaulay, 452
Manning, 465
Mencken, 488
W. C. Menninger, 489
Mill, 492
Napoleon, 518
Newman, 523
D. O'Connell, 535
O'Flaherty, 535
Pemartin, 555
Pius IX, 563
St. John-Stevas, 611
Santayana, 614
Tawney, 674
U.S. Supreme Court, 703
Vittorini, 712
Voltaire, 716
Wells, 733
W. Wilson, 751

Cause, Causation
    John Adams, 45
    Bergson, 92
    Bryan, 121

Byron, 136
Cleveland, 164
Einstein, 221
W. James, 361
Rockefeller (Sr.), 587
Sophocles, 647
Stekel, 661
Virgil, 711
Whitman, 740

Cause and Effect
    W. James, 359
    Veblen, 708

Celibacy
    Council of Trent, 182

Censorship (see Book-burning)
    Breen, 113
    Canon Law, 139
    Chesterton, 154
    Dana, 188
    W. O. Douglas, 212, 213
    Farrell, 247
    Griswold, 291
    Jefferson, 365, 371
    Lally, 397
    Meany, 484
    Plato, 568
    F. D. Roosevelt, 595
    Schroeder, 619, 620
    Shaw, 631
    Singleton, 640

Chance
    Anonymous, 62
    Aristotle, 67
    Clausewitz, 160, 161
    Lysenko, 449
    Malraux, 462
    Pascal, 549
    Voltaire, 713, 714
    T. Wolfe, 755

Change
    Anonymous, 62
    F. Bacon, 74
    C. A. Beard, 85
    Behn, 88
    Blake, 100

Boerne, 102
C. Bowles, 108
Brandeis, 111, 112
Bryant, 123
Buckle, 124
Burke, 129
R. Burns, 131
Cardozo, 140
Chafee, 150
J. Dewey, 204
T. E. Dewey, 205
Disraeli, 207
W. O. Douglas, 211
H. George, 274
Gitt, 278
Heraclitus, 313
Herzl, 315
Keller, 386
Kettering, 388
Lowell, 440
Macaulay, 451
Marcus Aurelius, 467
Marx, 471, 475
J. Morley, 508
Nehru, 521
Pascal, 549, 550
B. A. Russell, 605
Schlesinger (Sr.), 616
Seldes, 626
Sinclair, 639
Tennyson, 679
Thoreau, 684
Veblen, 709
Vinson, 711
Whitehead, 738
O. Wilde, 744
Zangwill, 760

Character
Amiel, 55
A. Barth, 83
Dostoyevsky, 210
Heraclitus, 313

Charity
F. Bacon, 72

Carnegie, 144
Nash, 519
O'Reilly, 536
Seldes, 626
O. Wilde, 743

Chicken
Henry IV, 311
H. C. Hoover, 332

Child, Children
Anonymous, 63
F. Bacon, 73
Davidson, 194
Duncan, 216
Ellis, 232
Ferrer, 249
Hand, 298
Hardy, 300
Lenin, 412
Ley, 418
Lindsey, 431, 432
H. Mann, 464
Marx, 473, 475
Montessori, 503, 504
Paine, 541
Ruskin, 603
B. A. Russell, 605, 609
Schopenhauer, 618
Vergniaud, 710
Volney, 712
J. Warren, 724
Yankwich, 760

Christ (see Jesus Christ)

Christian, Christianity
John Adams, 43, 44, 45
E. Allen, 51
Amiel, 55
Augustine, 71
Baer, 75
Bebel, 86
Bergamin, 92
Blavatsky, 101
T. H. Bliss, 102
Browning, 119
Buckle, 125

Burroughs, 131
Channing, 151
Chase, 153
Chesterton, 155
Coleridge, 167
C. P. Curtis, 188
J. Dewey, 205
Disraeli, 208
T. S. Eliot, 230
France, 254
Franklin, 258, 259
Freud, 261
Garrison, 271
Godwin, 279
Guérard, 291
Harris, 301
Heine, 309
Hitler, 320, 321
d'Holbach, 325
Hume, 338
A. Huxley, 342
Inge, 348, 349
Ingersoll, 351
Jefferson, 363, 370, 374
Kierkegaard, 391
Kossuth, 394
Kreymborg, 394
de Lavelaye, 401
Lecky, 404
Le Gallienne, 405
Lincoln, 422, 428
Longfellow, 439
Lowell, 442
Ludendorff, 445
Luther, 446, 447
Machiavelli, 455
J. Madison, 459, 460
Mencken, 486
W. C. Menninger, 489
Mill, 492, 495
Newman, 524
Nietzsche, 526, 527, 528, 529, 530
Van Paasen, 541
Paine, 541
Parrington, 548

Phillips, 560, 561, 562
Renan, 581
Rousseau, 600, 601
B. A. Russell, 605, 607
Saint-Simon, 611
Santayana, 613, 614
Sartre, 615
Schweitzer, 620, 621
Shaw, 628, 631
Shelley, 636
Siegel, 638
Society of Friends, 644
Spengler, 651
Stanton, 659
Steffens, 660
Tertullian, 679
Tolstoy, 688, 689
Twain, 696, 697
Voltaire, 713, 715, 717
G. Washington, 726
Wells, 733
Whitehead, 737
Williams, 747
Zangwill, 761

Christian Science
Eddy, 219

Christmas
Franklin P. Adams, **40**
Sinclair, 639

Church
Acton, 36, 38
H. B. Adams, 41
E. Allen, 52
Amiel, 55
Anonymous, 60
Aquinas, 64
Arcos, 65
Augustine, 70, **71**
Bagehot, 76
Bakunin, 77
Bergamin, 92
Boniface VIII, 105
Broun, 116
Bucer, 123

Buckle, 125
R. Burns, 131
Samuel Butler, 133
Calvin, 138
Connolly, 175
Council of Trent, 182
Cyprian, 188
Einstein, 222
Franklin, 259
Freud, 262
Garrison, 270
Gibbons, 276
Goethe, 282
Grant, 288
Gregory VII, 290
Hall, 294
Henry VIII, 312
Hobbes, 322
Ingersoll, 350
Jefferson, 364
Lally, 397
Leo XIII, 413, 414
Lincoln, 422
Lindsey, 432
Loyola, 444
Machiavelli, 453, 454
Magellan, 461
Masters, 480
Mexico, 489
Mill, 492, 494
Milton, 498
Mundelein, 512
Newman, 523, 524
von Nieheim, 526
Origen, 536
Paine, 541
Pius IX, 563, 564
Pius XI, 564, 565
Pius XII, 566
Powderly, 573
Raleigh, 578
Rousseau, 600
Savonarola, 616
Shaw, 628, 629, 630, 631
Stanton, 659

Tawney, 675, 676
Tertullian, 679
Tolstoy, 688
Twain, 696, 699
U.S. Supreme Court, 703
Vatican Council, 707, 708
Wells, 733
Whitehead, 737
Wolsey, 756

Church and State
Amiel, 55
Hugo L. Black, 99
Boniface VIII, 105
Cavour, 149
Clay, 162
Connolly, 175
Faulkner, 248
Frankfurter, 257
Gibbons, 277
Grant, 288
Institute of Brothers of the Christian
    Church, 353
A. Jackson, 356
Jefferson, 370, 371
Leo XIII, 413, 414, 415
Lowell, 440, 442
Mexico, 489
Mill, 494
Napoleon, 518
New York State, 525
Otis, 539
Paine, 541, 544
Pius IX, 564
Polk, 570
Reid, 580
Alfred E. Smith, 642
Sprading, 654
U.S. Supreme Court, 703
J. Warren, 724

Cigar
Franklin P. Adams, 40
F. M. Hubbard, 334

Circumstance
Ortega, 537

Owen, 540
Civilization
 Addams, 48
 Angell, 58
 M. Arnold, 68
 Bagehot, 75, 76
 Bancroft, 81
 Bebel, 86
 Bell, 88
 Bennett, 90
 Bergson, 93
 Burroughs, 131
 Carnegie, 143
 Coolidge, 176
 E. Davis, 195
 De Valera, 203
 Disraeli, 208
 Dreiser, 215
 Durant, 217
 Einstein, 223
 Faure, 248
 Flexner, 251, 252
 Hugo, 336, 337
 Ingersoll, 352
 Leo XIII, 413
 Lippmann, 433
 Lucas, 444
 Macaulay, 453
 Maritain, 468
 Millikan, 496
 Mumford, 511
 Nordau, 532
 Ralph, 579
 Riis, 583
 Schweitzer, 623
 Toynbee, 691
 A. R. Wallace, 720
Civil Liberty, Civil Rights (see Liberty)
 Anonymous, 59
 D. Davis, 195
 W. O. Douglas, 212, 213
 Hand, 298
 Harlan, 300
 Harrington, 301
 J. E. Hoover, 332

 Lincoln, 423
 F. D. Roosevelt, 593, 595
 A. E. Stevenson, 663
 Tocqueville, 687
 U.S.S.R., 704
 D. Webster, 728
Class, Classes (also, Ruling, Leisure, Upper, Lower, etc.)
 Abu'l-Ala, 35
 Acton, 36, 37
 A. Adler, 49
 Altgeld, 53
 American Legion, 54
 Anonymous, 61, 63
 M. Arnold, 69
 Bakunin, 77, 79
 K. Barth, 83
 C. A. Beard, 85
 H. W. Beecher, 87
 Bellamy, 88
 Benda, 90
 Channing, 151
 Cleveland, 163
 Coolidge, 177
 Debs, 196
 Djilas, 209
 Engels, 240
 Fourier, 254
 Gladstone, 278, 279
 Harlan, 300
 Herron, 314
 Hitler, 320
 O. W. Holmes (Jr.), 330
 Jefferson, 375
 Jones, 379
 Khrushchev, 390
 Lenin, 407, 409, 411
 Leo XIII, 414
 Lerner, 416
 Lieber, 419
 Lincoln, 422
 Lippmann, 432, 433
 Macaulay, 453
 J. Madison, 458
 Marx, 472, 473

Mill, 490
T. Parker, 547
Parrington, 547, 548
Parsons, 548
Pius X, 564
Pottier, 572
Rumbold, 602
Scripps, 624
Shaw, 631
Sherman, 637
Stalin, 655, 656, 657
Veblen, 708, 709
D. Webster, 728
W. A. White, 735

Class-Conscious, Class Struggle
Engels, 240
Khrushchev, 389
Marx, 472, 473
Parrington, 547, 548
W. A. White, 735

Clergy
John Adams, 42
Coleridge, 167
Cromwell, 186
Gibbon, 276
Haldane, 292
Jefferson, 369
Mencken, 488
Newman, 524
Stanton, 659
Villa, 711
Voltaire, 714
Whittier, 741

Clericalism
Gambetta, 267
Hugo, 337
Peyrat, 558
Voltaire, 713

Cliché
Mencken, 486

Closed Shop
Darrow, 191

Coal
John L. Lewis, 416, 417
Mellon, 485

"Cogito, ergo sum"
Bierce, 96
Descartes, 202
Jefferson, 374
Kant, 383
Schweitzer, 621, 622

Cold War
Baruch, 84
Swope, 672

Collectivism
Belloc, 89
Hand, 298
Krupskaya, 395
Mazzini, 482

College
Acton, 36
D. Bliss, 101
Conant, 172
Garfield, 268
D. Webster, 730

Colonists (American)
S. Adams, 47
Nehru, 521

Columnist
Ickes, 348
Laski, 399

Comedy
Seldes, 625

Comfort
Confucius, 172, 173
Demosthenes, 202
Disraeli, 208
Flexner, 251
Thoreau, 682
Yeats, 760

Commerce, Commercialism
John Adams, 45
Altgeld, 53
Blake, 100

Browne, 118
J. F. Cooper, 179
Shelley, 635
Sherman, 637
Tammen, 673
W. Wilson, 752

Common Law
Brennan, 113

Common Man
Angell, 58
Frazer, 259
Hitler, 319
H. C. Hoover, 331
Veblen, 708

Common People
A. Adler, 49
Cicero, 159
Confucius, 174
Gladstone, 278
Halifax, 293, 294
Jefferson, 368, 369
T. E. Lawrence, 403
Machiavelli, 454
Masefield, 479
H. A. Wallace, 720
Whitman, 739

Commonplace
Bagehot, 75
Beaumarchais, 85
Goethe, 282

Common Sense
John Adams, 42
Carlyle, 142
Lucas, 444

Commonwealth
Acton, 36
Ball, 80
Clement, 163
Hardie, 299
Hobbes, 322
W. Morris, 509
Sinclair, 639
Thomas, 681

Tyndale, 699
Williams, 748

Commune
Democratic Party, 201

Communication (see Media)
Erskine, 246
Evjue, 247
A. E. Stevenson, 663
U.S. Congress, 702
Wiener, 742

Communism (see Bolshevism)
Arcos, 66
Brandeis, 112
Smedley Butler, 134
Capone, 140
Carpenter, 146
Churchill, 156
Cleveland, 163, 164
Coughlin, 181
Djilas, 208, 209
W. O. Douglas, 211, 212, 214
Einstein, 224
Elliott, 231
Engels, 240
Fitzhugh, 251
Freud, 260
Hague, 292
Heine, 309
Hitler, 319
H. C. Hoover, 331
Kautsky, 384
Khrushchev, 389, 390
Lenin, 408, 409, 410, 411
Leo XIII, 414
John L. Lewis, 417
Lilienthal, 421
Lowell, 442
Malraux, 462
Mao Tse-tung, 466
Maritain, 467
Marx, 471, 472, 473, 476
Meany, 484
Mussolini, 514

Nehru, 521, 522
Niebuhr, 526
Orwell, 537, 538
Proudhon, 575
B. A. Russell, 608
Silone, 638, 639
Spencer, 650
Spengler, 650, 651
A. E. Stevenson, 662
Third International, 680
Thompson, 681
Tito, 686
Trotsky, 693
Truman, 694
U.S. Army, 700
Vittorini, 712
E. Warren, 722, 723

Competition
Carnegie, 143
Engels, 242
Hobbes, 321
Inge, 349
Kallen, 382
Kingsley, 392
Marx, 477
Overstreet, 539
Trotsky, 693

Compromise
Burke, 128
Clay, 162
Cleveland, 164
T. Edwards, 220
Garrison, 270
Haeckel, 292
E. Hubbard, 334
Ibsen, 347
Kemal, 386
Lenin, 408, 411
Lowell, 444
Mao Tse-tung, 466
J. Morley, 507, 508, 509
Mussolini, 515
Ruskin, 604

C. Sumner, 667
Untermeyer, 704
Veblen, 710
D. Webster, 731

Compulsion
Aristotle, 67
Einstein, 228
Plato, 567, 568

Conduct
J. D. Adams, 42
N. M. Butler, 133
Godwin, 279

Confession
Augustine, 71
Freud, 261

Conflict
Brandeis, 111
J. Dewey, 204
Freud, 262

Conformity
Bagehot, 76
Boerne, 102
Commager, 169
Dobie, 209
W. O. Douglas, 213
Emerson, 235, 237, 238, 239
Evjue, 247
Hobson, 323
R. H. Jackson, 356
Jefferson, 363
Lindner, 430
Mencken, 488
Milton, 497
J. Morley, 507, 509
Nietzsche, 530
Ortega, 537
Orwell, 537
Riesman, 583
F. D. Roosevelt, 592, 593
B. A. Russell, 605
Schopenhauer, 618
Siegfried, 638
Singleton, 640

A. E. Stevenson, 662, 663
Thoreau, 684, 685
Twain, 698
Valentine, 704
C. Van Doren, 705
Voltaire, 717
J. Warren, 723
O. Wilde, 743

Congress
C. Brown, 117
Gompers, 285
Lincoln, 427
J. Madison, 459
J. Marshall, 470
T. Roosevelt, 597
A. E. Stevenson, 662
E. Warren, 723
D. Webster, 729
Whitman, 740

Conquer, Conqueror, Conquest
Acton, 35
Buddha, 125
Byron, 135
Clausewitz, 161
Wellington, 732

Conscience
Acton, 36
S. Adams, 47
St. Ambrose, 54
Amiel, 55
Bagehot, 76
K. Barth, 83
Beerbohm, 87
Blackstone, 99
Bradley, 109
Cromwell, 186
Disraeli, 208
Dostoyevski, 210
Einstein, 225
Gregory XVI, 290
Hitler, 321
Hobbes, 322
S. Johnson, 377

Joyce, 381
Laski, 399
Lilburne, 420
Lloyd, 435
Manning, 465
Marx, 476
Mill, 490, 491
Milton, 497
Nietzsche, 531
Overstreet, 539
Penn, 555
President's Commission on Civil Rights, 573
Swedenborg, 669
Swift, 670
Twain, 697
Voltaire, 713
G. Washington, 725
Williams, 747, 748

Consequences
T. H. Huxley, 343, 344

Conservative, Conservatism
Beard, C. A. and M. R., 85
H. W. Beecher, 87
Bierce, 96
Billings, 97
Brandeis, 112
P. Brooks, 115
Brownson, 120
Channing, 151
Cowles, 183
Crawford, 184
Disraeli, 206, 207
Eisenhower, 229
Ely, 232
Emerson, 233, 235, 236, 239
Frost, 264
H. George, 274
Gilbert, 277
Gladstone, 278
Greeley, 289
E. Hubbard, 334
Maeterlinck, 460

Peirce, 554
F. D. Roosevelt, 591, 593, 594
T. Roosevelt, 596
Sarton, 614
Schlesinger (Sr.), 616
Scripps, 624
Spencer, 649
Thoreau, 684
Veblen, 708, 709, 710
W. A. White, 736
Whitehead, 738
W. Wilson, 749

Consistency
Emerson, 237
O. W. Holmes (Sr.), 327
A. Huxley, 342
Sloan, 640

Conspiracy
H. B. Adams, 41
Nasser, 520

Constitution
Acton, 36
John Quincy Adams, 46
American Legion, 54
C. A. Beard, 85
Bismarck, 97
Brandeis, 112
Chafee, 149
Cobb, 164
Commager, 170
D. Davis, 194
Franklin, 258
Garrison, 271
Grant, 289
Alexander Hamilton, 294
Harlan, 300
O. W. Holmes (Jr.), 328, 329
C. E. Hughes, 335
Hutchins, 339
Isocrates, 354
A. Jackson, 354, 355
R. H. Jackson, 357

Jefferson, 371
Lehman, 406
Leo XIII, 413
Lilienthal, 420
Lincoln, 421, 425
J. Marshall, 470, 471
F. D. Roosevelt, 590, 592
Seward, 628
Alfred E. Smith, 642
Taney, 673
Thoreau, 684
U.S. Supreme Court, 702
E. Warren, 722, 723
G. Washington, 725
D. Webster, 729

Contract
O. W. Holmes (Jr.), 330
J. Marshall, 470

Controversy
L. Beecher, 87
Hazlitt, 305
Mill, 493
E. B. White, 734

Convention, Conventional
Beccaria, 86
Bronte, 114
Duncan, 216
Ibsen, 347
Rousseau, 600
B. A. Russell, 605
Veblen, 708, 710

Convert
Heine, 310
J. Morley, 508

Conviction
Hand, 299
Ingersoll, 350
J. Morley, 507
Nietzsche, 530
Ortega, 537
Reik, 580
Robinson, 585

B. A. Russell, 605
Steffens, 660

Cooperate, Cooperation
Anonymous, 62
Archer, 65
Carpenter, 145
Commission on Freedom of the Press, 171
Darrow, 191
Debs, 196
J. Dewey, 204
Kingsley, 392
Lloyd, 434
Marcus Aurelius, 467
Nehru, 521
Powderly, 573
Sinclair, 639
Thomas, 681

Corporation, Corporations
John Adams, 46
Anonymous, 62
Berle, 93
Beveridge, 96
Brandeis, 112
Coke, 167
Kilgore, 391
J. Marshall, 470
G. W. Norris, 533
Parrington, 548
Populist Party, 572
F. D. Roosevelt, 591
T. Roosevelt, 596
Thoreau, 682
U.S. Congress, 702
W. Wilson, 750

Corrupt, Corruption
Acton, 36
S. Anderson, 56
Burke, 128
Gibbon, 276
Pope, 572
Rolland, 589

R. Walpole, 721
G. Washington, 725

Couéism
Coué, 181

Counting Room
H. R. Luce, 445
W. A. White, 736

Country
Acton, 35, 36, 37
John Adams, 43
Addison, 48
E. Allen, 52
American Legion, 54
F. Bacon, 74
Chafee, 149
Chesterton, 155
Debs, 196
de Maistre, 200
Demosthenes, 201
Franklin, 258
Garibaldi, 269
Hayes, 303
Lincoln, 426
Machiavelli, 456
Mazzini, 482
Milton, 498
J. P. Morgan, 506
Robespierre, 584, 585
Twain, 699
D. Webster, 729, 730
C. E. Wilson, 749
Wotton, 758

Court, Courts (see Supreme Court)
Altgeld, 53
Hugo L. Black, 98
D. Davis, 194
Freud, 262
Ingersoll, 352
Raleigh, 578
Schlesinger (Jr.), 616

Coward, Cowardice
Anonymous, 62
John Brown, 117

E. Davis, 195
Garrison, 271
Ibarruri, 346

Creation, Creative
Alfonso X, 51
Jung, 381
Wagner, 718
Wu Ting-fang, 559

Credit
Acton, 37
W. Wilson, 749

Creed, Credo
B. Adams, 39
Bagehot, 76
Emerson, 238
Ingersoll, 351
Jefferson, 374
Lewes, 416
Nehru, 521
Pitt (Sr.), 563
Pulitzer, 576
Rockefeller (Jr.), 587
B. A. Russell, 606
Tertullian, 679
Whittier, 742

Crillon
Henry IV, 311

Crime, Criminal (see Punishment)
Acton, 35
John Adams, 42
A. Adler, 49
Aristotle, 67
Beccaria, 86
Brandeis, 112
Buckle, 125
Cassadorus, 148
Defoe, 198
Dostoyevski, 210
Ford, 253
France, 255
Hemingway, 310
O. W. Holmes (Jr.), 329
Juvenal, 382

Kenko, 387
La Bruyère, 395
Lenin, 412
Publilius Syrus, 576
Spencer, 648, 649
Sprading, 655
Talleyrand, 673
Voltaire, 713, 714, 715

Cross
John Adams, 45
Coolidge, 176
Ingersoll, 350, 351
Jonson, 380

Cross-breeding
C. Darwin, 192

Crowd
Brandes, 113
Cocteau, 166
Ibañez, 346

Crucify
S. Anderson, 57

Cruel, Cruelty
Kett, 388
Machiavelli, 453, 456
Marat, 466
Maugham, 481
Seneca, 627

Culture (Kultur)
M. Arnold, 68
H. S. Chamberlain, 150
von der Goltz, 285
Johst, 379
Lassalle, 400
Linton, 432
Malraux, 462
Mumford, 512
Santayana, 613
Sloan, 640
Spengler, 651

Curiosity
Einstein, 225

Custom
Acton, 35
F. Bacon, 72, 73
R. Bacon, 75
Baruch, 84
Brennan, 113
Brissot, 114
Carlyle, 141, 142
Carpenter, 145
Diogenes, 206
Galton, 267
Guedemann, 291
Guizot, 291
Hallam, 294
Hegel, 307
Hume, 338
Kropotkin, 395
Maupassant, 481
Mencken, 488
Mill, 494, 495
Milton, 498
Pascal, 550
Tennyson, 679

Cybernetics
Wiener, 742

D

Danger (Dangerous Thoughts)
Bradford, 109
Brandeis, 111
Clausewitz, 161
O. W. Holmes (Jr.), 328
Lalor, 397
Laski, 398
C. A. Lindbergh (Jr.), 430
Machiavelli, 456
Meiklejohn, 485
O. Wilde, 745

Death
E. Allen, 52
Aquinas, 64

Basil, 84
Bergson, 92
Bogomoletz, 103
Campbell, 138
Clemenceau, 162
Cowley, 183
Donne, 209
Elizabeth I, 230
Epicurus, 244
Franklin, 258
Freud, 260, 261, 263
Froude, 264
Garrison, 271
von Haeseler, 292
Hobbes, 322
Horace, 333
La Bruyère, 395
Laski, 400
MacLeish, 457
Maeterlinck, 460
Maritain, 468
Masefield, 478
Mauriac, 481
Millan-Astray, 496
Montaigne, 501
Nietzsche, 529
Rouget de Lisle, 599
B. A. Russell, 605, 606, 609
Sherman, 637
Socrates, 645, 646
Stalin, 658
Twain, 697
Voltaire, 713
Wagner, 717, 718

Debt
Alexander Hamilton, 295
A. Jackson, 354

Deception
Pliny, 569
Richelieu, 583
Sun Tzu, 668

Declaration of Independence
Beard, C. A. and M. R., 85
Carroll, 146

Cobb, 164
Jefferson, 375
Lincoln, 421, 422, 423, 424

Defeat
A. Adler, 49
Montaigne, 501
Virgil, 711

Defection
Browning, 119

Defense
Clausewitz, 160
Hobbes, 321

Define, Definition
Aristotle, 67
F. Bacon, 74

Deist, Deism, Deity
E. Allen, 51
F. Bacon, 72, 73
Hume, 337, 338
J. Huxley, 343
Lessing, 416
Lincoln, 422
Paine, 541, 542, 544
Pliny the Elder, 569

Demagogue
Aristotle, 68
J. F. Cooper, 178
G. W. Curtis, 188
Alexander Hamilton, 295, 296
Heine, 309
Jung, 381
Lippmann, 433
Macauley, 452, 453
Mencken, 488
Philo, 562
Plato, 568

Democracy
Acton, 36
B. Adams, 39
John Adams, 46
S. Adams, 47
Altgeld, 53

American Legion, 54
Angell, 58
Arcos, 66
Aristotle, 67, 68
Bancroft, 81
H. W. Beecher, 87
Bellamy, 88
Ben-Gurion, 90
Benton, 91
Hugo L. Black, 98
Borgese, 107
Brandeis, 112
Bryan, 121
Burke, 129
Chapman, 152
Chase, 153
Chesterton, 154, 155
Chiang Kai-shek, 155
Commager, 169
J. F. Cooper, 177, 178
Coughlin, 181
Cousins, 182
Democratic Party, 201
J. Dewey, 203
Donne, 209
Du Bois, 215
Duncan, 216
Einstein, 226
Emerson, 236, 238
France, 256
Gerry, 276
Godwin, 280
Alexander Hamilton, 295, 296
Hastie, 302
Higgins, 315
Hitler, 318
Hook, 331
Howells, 333
C. E. Hughes, 335
L. Hughes, 335
Hutchins, 340
Inge, 348
R. H. Jackson, 358
W. James, 360

La Follette, 396
Laski, 399
Lee, 405
Lehman, 406
Lenin, 409
Lerner, 416
John L. Lewis, 416
S. Lewis, 418
Lilienthal, 420, 421
Lloyd, 434
Lowell, 441
Lundberg, 446
Macauley, 452, 453
J. Madison, 458, 459
Malraux, 462
G. C. Marshall, 469
Mencken, 487
Mirza, 499
Montesquieu, 502, 503
Mussolini, 515, 517
Nehru, 521, 522
Newman, 524
Niebuhr, 526
T. Parker, 546
Parrington, 547, 548
Pepper, 556
Pericles, 556
Perry, 557
Priestley, 574
Robespierre, 584
E. Roosevelt, 589
F. D. Roosevelt, 592, 593
T. Roosevelt, 597
G. W. Russell, 610
Schlesinger (Jr.), 616
Shaw, 631, 632
Sheen, 633
Alfred E. Smith, 642
B. Smith, 642
Socrates, 645
Spinoza, 652
Strachey, 665
Sturzo, 666
W. G. Sumner, 667

Tawney, 675
Thomas, 681
Thoreau, 683
Thucydides, 685
Tocqueville, 686
Toller, 688
Toynbee, 691
Truman, 694
U.S. Army, 700
Viereck, 710
Vishinsky, 712
Webb, 727
E. B. White, 734
Whitman, 739, 740
O. Wilde, 743
W. Wilson, 752, 753
Wise, 754
T. Wolfe, 754

Democrat, Democratic, Democratic Party
Democratic Party, 201
Donnelly, 209
Greeley, 289
Jefferson, 375
John L. Lewis, 417
C. B. Luce, 445
Truman, 695

Desire
Aquinas, 64
Aristotle, 67
Bogomoletz, 103
Carpenter, 144
Helvetius, 310
S. Johnson, 379
B. A. Russell, 606, 607, 608
Spinoza, 652

Despot, Despotism
Addison, 48
Anonymous, 62
C. A. Beard, 85
Chesterton, 154
A. Johnson, 376
Lucan, 444
G. W. Russell, 610
Xenophon, 759

Destiny
  Heine, 309
  J. Huxley, 343
Destroy, Destruction
  Bakunin, 77, 78
  Beerbohm, 87
  Bismarck, 97
  Burke, 127
  Clausewitz, 160
  Einstein, 222
  Freud, 260, 261, 262
  Fromm, 264
  Alexander Hamilton, 295
  Hitler, 320
  MacArthur, 450
  Mead, 484
  Mumford, 512
  Oppenheimer, 536
  Pasteur, 551
  Pauling, 552
  Wagner, 717, 718, 719
Devil
  H. B. Adams, 41
  K. Barth, 83
  Blavatsky, 101
  Churchill, 157
  Ellis, 231
  Fletcher, 251
  Graham, 287
  Jonson, 380
  La Fontaine, 397
  Latimer, 401
  Luther, 446, 447, 448
  Mill, 492
  Swift, 670
  Tawney, 676
  Voltaire, 717
Dialectic, Dialectical Materialism
  Aiken, 50
  Emerson, 237
  Erigena, 245
  Stalin, 657
Dictator, Dictatorship
  Bakunin, 78

Chiang Kai-shek, 155
Coughlin, 181
De Gaulle, 199
Demosthenes, 201, 202
W. O. Douglas, 214
Durant, 217
Eastman, 218
Engels, 240
Hoffman, 325
Hugo, 336
Laski, 399
Lenin, 408, 410
Lincoln, 427
Luxemburg, 449
Marx, 473
Masaryk, 478
Muller, 511
Plato, 568
Rust, 610
Stalin, 655, 657, 658
Steinbeck, 661
Thucydides, 685
Vishinsky, 712

Dignity
  John Adams, 43
  F. Bacon, 72
  Bellamy, 88
  Ben-Gurion, 90
  Emma Goldman, 283
  Hutchins, 340
  Malraux, 462
  Mill, 495
  Pascal, 550
  Society of Friends, 645
Diplomat, Diplomacy
  Baeyens, 75
  Bismarck, 97
  Cavour, 149
  Chou En-lai, 155
  Clausewitz, 161
  Litvinov, 434
  Stalin, 658
  Wotton, 758

Disarmament
Bethmann-Hollweg, 95
Briand, 114
Disbelief
Hugo L. Black, 98
Carlyle, 141
Frankfurter, 256
Discipline
Montessori, 504
Mussolini, 515
Discontent
Debs, 197
Edison, 219
Kabir, 382
Kingsley, 391
Wilcox, 743
O. Wilde, 745
Discussion
Bagehot, 76
Brandeis, 111
Disease
Bush, 132
Eddy, 218, 219
Hippocrates, 316
Disobedience
Bakunin, 78
Fromm, 264
O. Wilde, 743
Dispute
Action, 35
Aristotle, 67
Dissent, Dissenters
John Adams, 46
A. Barth, 83
Chafee, 149
Commager, 169
Eisenhower, 228
Ford, 253
Hand, 298, 299
C. E. Hughes, 335
R. H. Jackson, 356, 357
MacLeish, 457
McWilliams, 484

Mill, 490, 491, 492
J. Morley, 507
Spencer, 648
Taylor, 677
E. Warren, 723
E. B. White, 734
Divine, Divinity
Acton, 37
Bruno, 120
Doctrine
H. W. Beecher, 87
T. Cooper, 180
Milton, 497
Monroe, 500
W. G. Sumner, 667
Dogma
John Adams, 46
Haeckel, 292
Hand, 297
Hugo, 336
W. James, 360, 361
Jefferson, 372
D. S. Jordan, 380
Kant, 384
Moore, 505
Mussolini, 513
Newman, 523
Oppenheimer, 536
Proudhon, 575
B. A. Russell, 606
Schweitzer, 622
Vatican Council, 707
Voltaire, 715
Doubt
Amiel, 55
F. Bacon, 72
Bagehot, 76
Ballou, 81
Browning, 119
Casanova, 147
Chesterton, 154
Cohen, 166
Coleridge, 167

Disraeli, 207
T. S. Eliot, 230
Goethe, 283
T. H. Huxley, 345
Lecky, 404
Marx, 474
Mencken, 488
Montaigne, 501
Ralph, 579
B. A. Russell, 608
L. Smith, 643
Thoreau, 685
Unamuno, 699
Untermeyer, 704
Drink (see Alcohol)
E. Booth, 106
Lincoln, 421
Lloyd George, 435
Pegler, 554
Yeats, 760
Drunk, Drunkard, Drunkenness
A. Adler, 49
Anonymous, 59
Bakunin, 77
Basil, 84
B. A. Russell, 605
Duty
Acton, 35
Nelson, 522
Wordsworth, 757
Dynamic
Marx, 471

E

Earth
Copernicus, 181
Galileo, 265, 266
Rousseau, 601
Ruskin, 603
Eccentric
Greeley, 289
Mill, 495

Ecclesiastic
Defoe, 198
Girard, 277
T. H. Huxley, 345
J. Madison, 460
Reid, 580
Voltaire, 713
W. Wilson, 751
Economy, Economics, Economic System
B. Adams, 39
M. Anderson, 56
Baha'u'llah, 76
C. A. Beard, 85
Bellamy, 89
Bernstein, 95
C. Bowles, 108
Carpenter, 144
Commager, 169
Coolidge, 177
W. O. Douglas, 214
Engels, 242
Heilbroner, 308
Keynes, 388, 389
Kingsley, 392
Laforgue, 396
Lincoln, 427
Luxemburg, 448
G. C. Marshall, 469
Nathan, 520
Tawney, 675, 676
Viereck, 710
W. Wilson, 749, 750
Editor
Carlyle, 142
Dunne, 217
Ingersoll, 352
La Fontaine, 396
Lindstrom, 432
Reeve, 580
Somervell, 646
W. A. White, 735, 736
Education
H. B. Adams, 40
Aristotle, 67, 68

Babeuf, 71
F. Bacon, 72
Baha'u'llah, 76
Bronte, 114
Brougham, 116
Cobden, 165
J. Dewey, 203, 205
Diogenes ("The Cynic"), 206
Dionysius, 206
Disraeli, 207
Epictetus, 243
Erasmus, 245
Ferrer, 249
Garfield, 268
Haldane, 292
Hemingway, 311
Hitler, 320
Hutchins, 339, 340
Isocrates, 353
Kallen, 382
Lincoln, 421
Lowell, 441
Luther, 448
Horace Mann, 464
Marx, 473
Montessori, 504
Newman, 524
Pius XI, 564, 565
Plato, 567, 568
Quintilian, 578
E. Roosevelt, 589
Rush, 602
Ruskin, 602, 603
Salazar, 611
Stalin, 657
Tate, 674
M. Van Doren, 706
J. Warren, 724
D. Webster, 729

Ego, Egotism
Archer, 65
Confucius, 173
De Gaulle, 199
Freud, 261, 263

von der Goltz, 285
Jung, 381
Kropotkin, 394
C. B. Luce, 445
Mussolini, 514
Stirner, 664
O. Wilde, 746

Election
Burke, 128
Havemeyer, 302
Wesley, 734

Electricity
Lenin, 412

Emancipation
M. J. Adler, 49
Bebel, 86
H. W. Beecher, 87
Debs, 197
Garrison, 270
Ibsen, 348

Emigrant, Emigrants
Hearst, 306
Lincoln, 423
Melville, 485

Ends and Means (see Means)
Acton, 36
Berlin, 93
Brandeis, 111
Brennan, 113
Busenbaum, 132
Chapman, 152
Coleridge, 167
Djilas, 208, 209
W. O. Douglas, 211
Emma Goldman, 283
Hitler, 317
Kallen, 382
Kant, 384
Laski, 399
W. Liebknecht, 419
Lilienthal, 421
Macaulay, 452
Nehru, 521

von Nieheim, 526
Pius XI, 564
Prior, 574
Silone, 638
Treitschke, 692
Enemy, Enemies
Abd-el-Raham, 35
Acton, 35
Aesop, 50
Bernard, 94
Bragg, 109
J. A. Fisher, 250
Gompers, 285
Herzl, 315
W. James, 359
K. Liebknecht, 419
G. Murray, 512
Sun Tzu, 668
T. Wolfe, 755
Energy
B. Adams, 39
Einstein, 220
Millikan, 496
Engels
M. J. Adler, 49
Lenin, 407, 409
England
Brooke, 115
Byron, 136
Carpenter, 145, 146
Carroll, 146
Harvey, 301
Harrington, 301
Latimer, 401
Macaulay, 451, 452, 453
Mansfield, 465
Napoleon, 519
Palmerston, 545
Pitt (Sr.), 563
Rhodes, 581, 582
Shelley, 633, 634, 636
Sheridan, 636
Voltaire, 714
Wordsworth, 757

Enlightenment
Kant, 384
Schweitzer, 621
Enthusiasm
Blake, 101
Emerson, 233
Goldwyn, 283
Envy
M. Arnold, 69
Dante, 189
La Rochefoucauld, 398
Epitaph
Emmet, 240
Truman, 694
Equality
Acton, 36
Aristotle, 67
Babeuf, 71
Baha'u'llah, 76
Bakunin, 78, 79, 80
Ball, 80
Burke, 130
Cousin, 182
S. A. Douglas, 211
Douglass, 214
Fontenelle, 252
H. George, 273
Gregory I, 290
Harlan, 300
A. Huxley, 341
A. Jackson, 355
Jefferson, 362
Kant, 383
Kett, 388
Lincoln, 422, 423
Nietzsche, 527
Orwell, 537
Paine, 541
Pius X, 564
Plato, 569
President's Commission on Civil Rights, 573
Randolph, 579

Tocqueville, 686, 687
United Nations, 700
Voltaire, 715
Wise, 753

Equity
Acton, 37
J. Dewey, 204
Fortesque, 253
J. Warren, 724

Eros, Eroticism
Freud, 260, 262
von Kemnitz, 386
Schopenhauer, 617

Error (see False)
Acton, 37, 38
Amiel, 55
Calvin, 138
Carlyle, 141
Condorcet, 172
Eddy, 218, 219
Godwin, 279
Goethe, 283
T. H. Huxley, 343
Jefferson, 363
S. Johnson, 377
Longfellow, 439
Mill, 492, 493, 494, 496
Rolland, 588

Eternal Feminine
Goethe, 282

Ethics
Anonymous, 61
Bakunin, 77
Camus, 138
Schweitzer, 621, 622
Sprading, 654

Eugenics
Jaspers, 361
Shaw, 631

Europe
Mackinder, 457
Monroe, 500

Washington, 727
Whittier, 741

Evidence
Acton, 38
Haldane, 292
Hume, 338

Evil
Ambrose, 54
Archer, 65
Augustine, 70
Bentham, 90
V. W. Brooks, 115
Burke, 129
Camus, 139
Chekhov, 153
Edward III, 219
Epictetus, 244
Euripides, 246
Gracián, 287
Mill, 491
Milton, 497
Spencer, 648, 649
Thoreau, 682
Tolstoy, 689

Evolution
Brandeis, 110
Engels, 242
Herndon, 314
Hooton, 331
J. Huxley, 343
Millikan, 496
Shaw, 631
Sunday, 668

Excommunication
S. Adams, 47
Anonymous, 61
Aquinas, 64
Erasmus, 245
Lecky, 404
Voltaire, 715

Executive
Montesquieu, 502, 503

Existence
Kettering, 388
Kierkegaard, 391

Existentialist
Sartre, 615

Expedience
T. Roosevelt, 595
Thoreau, 682
Willkie, 748, 749

Experience
R. Bacon, 75
N. Douglas, 211
D. H. Lawrence, 401, 402

Experiment, Experimentation
R. Bacon, 75
Brandeis, 112
Commager, 170
J. Dewey, 205
Disraeli, 208
Emerson, 239
Harding, 299
Hippocrates, 316
O. W. Holmes (Jr.), 329
Keynes, 389
Whitehead, 737

Exploitation
M. J. Adler, 49
Bakunin, 77, 78
Baruch, 84
J. Dewey, 205
Enoch, 243
Ferrer, 249
Ford, 253
R. H. Jackson, 356
Kropotkin, 395
Laski, 400
D. H. Lawrence, 402
Lenin, 409, 410
Stalin, 657
Truman, 694

Expose
Brandeis, 111

E. Warren, 723
Whitman, 740

Expropriation
Kropotkin, 394
Lenin, 409
Marx, 475

Extremists
Flexner, 252
Yeats, 760

F

Fact, Facts
F. Bacon, 73
Bancroft, 81
Burke, 130
Carlyle, 141, 142
Chapman, 152
Cobb, 165
Comte, 171
Crawford, 184
C. Darwin, 191
Eastman, 218
Emerson, 234
Gibbs, 277
Hand, 297
Hawthorne, 303
A. Huxley, 341, 342
T. H. Huxley, 343
H. James, 358
W. James, 359, 360, 361
Jefferson, 368
Leibnitz, 406
Le Sage, 416
Lincoln, 428
Mill, 493
O'Neill, 535
Pavlov, 553
Peirce, 554
Reeve, 580
L. Smith, 643
Sprading, 655
Talleyrand, 672

Twain, 697
Tyndall, 699
Whitehead, 738
W. Wilson, 750

Failure
A. Adler, 49
Whitman, 739, 740

Faith
Acton, 37, 38
H. B. Adams, 41
Alcuin, 51
Amiel, 55, 56
Athanasian Creed, 69
Augustine, 70, 71
Bierce, 96
Browne, 118
Browning, 119
Buck, 124
Carlyle, 142
T. S. Eliot, 230
Emerson, 233
Erasmus, 244
Flaubert, 251
Goethe, 282
Gregory I, 290
Heine, 309
Hoffer, 325
C. W. Holmes (Jr.), 328, 329
R. H. Jackson, 357
Landor, 397
Lecky, 404
Joseph Lewis, 418
Lilburne, 420
Locke, 435, 436
Lowell, 440
Luther, 447
Manning, 465
Mencken, 488
Montaigne, 501
Newman, 523, 524
Peirce, 554
Pope, 571
Reese, 580
Royce, 602

L. Smith, 643
Spinoza, 652
Thompson, 681
U. S. Supreme Court, 703
Vatican Council, 707
Walwyn, 721
Whittier, 742

False, Falsity, Falsehood
(see Error; True and False)
Amiel, 55
Anonymous, 60
M. Arnold, 69
Ballou, 81
H. W. Beecher, 87
Bohr, 103
Burke, 127
Camus, 139
Carlyle, 143
Cervantes, 149
Colton, 168
T. Cooper, 180
C. Darwin, 191
W. O. Douglas (Jr.), 213
Dryden, 215
G. Eliot, 229
Emerson, 236
Goldsmith, 283
Hawthorne, 303
Hazlitt, 305
O. W. Holmes (Sr.), 327
E. W. Howe, 333
Jefferson, 367
S. Johnson, 377
Koestler, 393
Leonardo, 415
Lowell, 442
Mencken, 486
Milton, 497
Paine, 545
Tennyson, 678, 679

Fame
Burke, 127
Emerson, 239
Milton, 499

Pope, 571
Tacitus, 672

Family
Aristotle, 67
Hobson, 324

Famine
Malthus, 463

Fanaticism
Acton, 37
Flaubert, 251
Hitler, 318
Inge, 349
Santayana, 612
Voltaire, 714, 716

Fascism
Ameringer, 54
C. A. Beard, 85
Bergamin, 92
Hugo L. Black, 98
Bolitho, 105
Broun, 116
Churchill, 156
Coughlin, 181
Dimitrov, 205
Einstein, 224
D. C. Fisher, 250
Frankfurter, 256
Hemingway, 310, 311
Hinsley, 316
Hitler, 320
Ickes, 348
Lenin, 412
John L. Lewis, 417
S. Lewis, 418
Long, 439
Margueritte, 467
Matthews-Shallcross, 480
McKenney, 483
Meany, 484
Mussolini, 514, 515, 516, 517, 518
O'Flaherty, 535
Owsley, 540
Parrington, 547

Pemartin, 555
Robeson, 583
Rocco, 586
F. D. Roosevelt, 592, 594
B. A. Russell, 608
Sinclair, 639
Singleton, 640
Strachey, 665, 666
Toller, 688
Trotsky, 693
Unamuno, 700
U. S. Army, 700, 701
Vanzetti, 707
Willkie, 749

Fate
Camus, 138
Lenin, 412
Malraux, 462
Thomas Mann, 464
Nasser, 519

Father
Freud, 261

Fear
B. Adams, 39
Addison, 48
Amiel, 55
Angell, 57
Anonymous, 63
Bakunin, 77
Berger, 92
Berlin, 94
Berlioz, 94
Blum, 102
R. Burns, 130
Carlyle, 141
Carpenter, 145
Claudian, 160
Confucius, 172
Crawford, 184
J. Dewey, 205
Dostoyevski, 210
W. O. Douglas (Jr.), 213
Einstein, 221, 227
G. Eliot, 229

Ellis, 232
Emerson, 234
Epictetus, 243
Faulkner, 248
Fourier, 254
Gandhi, 268
Grey, 290
A. Herbert, 313
Hitler, 321
Hobbes, 322, 323
Hoffman, 325
d'Holbach, 325
O. W. Holmes (Sr.), 327
S. Johnson, 379
Jonson, 380
Laski, 398
D. H. Lawrence, 401, 402
Lucretius, 445
Machiavelli, 453, 454
Mencken, 486
K. Menninger, 489
W. C. Menninger, 489
Montaigne, 500
Nietzsche, 528
Oppenheim, 536
Petronius, 558
F. D. Roosevelt, 590, 593
B. A. Russell, 605, 606, 609
Santayana, 612
Sophocles, 647
Statius, 659
Steinbeck, 660
Taylor, 678
Tertullian, 680
Toller, 687
Virgil, 711
W. A. White, 737
Xenophon, 759

Feudal, Feudalism
John Adams, 42, 46
Anonymous, 62
Bebel, 86
W. O. Douglas, 212
Lenin, 412

Fifth Amendment
W. O. Douglas, 211
Lincoln, 424
J. Marshall, 471
E. Warren, 723

Fight
H. B. Adams, 41
Blake, 101
Bolivar, 105
Burbank, 125
Churchill, 156
Darrow, 190
Hays, 304
Hemingway, 310
Henry, 312
W. James, 359
McKay, 483
O'Casey, 534
Picasso, 562
T. Roosevelt, 597
Sun Tzu, 668
H. A. Wallace, 720
W. Wilson, 751

Fishing
H. C. Hoover, 331

Flag
Cohan, 166

Flux
Heraclitus, 313

Food
Acton, 35
Babeuf, 71
Baruch, 84
Litvinov, 434
Malthus, 463
B. A. Russell, 607

Fool, Fools, Foolish
Blake, 100
Buckingham, 124
Samuel Butler, 133
Colton, 168
Drummond, 215
Voltaire, 713, 717

Force, Forces
Acton, 37, 38
B. Adams, 39
H. B. Adams, 40, 41
Augustine, 71
Bakunin, 79
Bancroft, 81
Berlin, 93
Bernays, 95
Bright, 114
Clausewitz, 160
Djilas, 208
Einstein, 226
Engels, 241
Godwin, 279
Herbert, 313
Hitler, 318
Hobbes, 321
C. E. Hughes, 334
Lenin, 410
Machiavelli, 456
Mahan, 461
Marx, 477
Milton, 499
Pascal, 549
Stalin, 657
Tolstoy, 690
Trotsky, 693
G. Washington, 727
Whitehead, 738
Whitman, 740

Fornication
Bunyan, 125

Fortune
F. Bacon, 73
Sévigné, 627

Founding Fathers
C. A. Beard, 85
Eisenhower, 228

France
De Gaulle, 199
Dupin, 217
Rolland, 589

Fraud
Hobbes, 321
Machiavelli, 456
J. B. Matthews, 480

Free (see Freedom)
Acton, 35
John Adams, 46
Andreyev, 57
Aristotle, 67
Augustine, 70
Berenson, 91, 92
Blackstone, 100
Blum, 102
Boerne, 102
W. L. Bowles, 109
Broun, 116
Bruno, 121
Byron, 135
Carlyle, 141, 143
Carpenter, 146
Cocteau, 166
Confucius, 173
Croce, 185
W. H. Davies, 194
E. Davis, 195
Dostoyevski, 210
Douglass, 214
Einstein, 226
Epictetus, 243
Faulkner, 247
Hand, 298
Helvetius, 310
Henry, 312
Horace, 333
E. Hubbard, 334
Ingersoll, 352
Jefferson, 362
F. S. Key, 388
Laski, 399
D. H. Lawrence, 402
Lippmann, 433
Madariaga, 458
Marmontel, 469
Oppenheimer, 536

Pusey, 577
Quincy, 578
Republicans, 581
Rousseau, 599
Sartre, 615
Schurz, 620
Shaw, 629, 631
Spinoza, 652
A. E. Stevenson, 663
Stirner, 664
United Nations, 700
Wagner, 719
W. A. White, 736
Whittier, 741
Wordsworth, 757
Wotton, 758

Freedom

Acton, 35, 36, 37
S. Adams, 46, 47
T. S. Adams, 47
M. J. Adler, 49
Angell, 58
T. Arnold, 69
Bakunin, 77, 78
Blackstone, 100
Bryant, 123
Byron, 135
Camus, 139
Carlile, 141
Carlyle, 141
Carpenter, 146
Cather, 148
Cervantes, 149
Chafee, 149
Cicero, 158, 159
Coleridge, 167
E. Davis, 195
Demosthenes, 202
J. Dewey, 203
W. O. Douglas, 211
Eastman, 218
D. C. Fisher, 250
V. Fisher, 250
Frost, 264

Gandhi, 268
Goethe, 282
Haeckel, 292
Hays, 304
Heckscher, 307
Hegel, 307
Heine, 309
Helvetius, 310
Hitler, 319
H. C. Hoover, 331, 332
Hutchins, 340
A. Huxley, 341, 342
Ibarruri, 346
Ibsen, 346
ICFTU, 353
Kant, 383
Kautsky, 384
Kent, 387
Khrushchev, 391
Lenin, 406, 407, 409
C. D. Lewis, 416
Lilburne, 420
Lincoln, 423
C. A. Lindbergh (Jr.), 429
Lippmann, 433
Lowell, 443
Luxemburg, 448
Macaulay, 452
MacLeish, 457
J. Madison, 460
Masters, 480
Maugham, 481
Meiklejohn, 485
Mill, 491, 495
Morton, 511
Nietzsche, 529
Paine, 542
T. Parker, 546
Penn, 555
Pericles, 557
Plato, 569
Progressives, 574
Pushkin, 576
F. D. Roosevelt, 591, 593

Rouget de Lisle, 599
Ruskin, 603
Sacco, 610
St. Exupéry, 610
Seneca, 626
Shelley, 633, 634
Spencer, 649
Stalin, 657
Stirner, 664
Swinburne, 671
Tagore, 672
Tennyson, 678
Thucydides, 685
Truman, 695
Vanzetti, 706
H. A. Wallace, 720
E. Warren, 722
Wells, 732
Whitman, 739, 741
William the Silent, 747
Willkie, 748
W. Wilson, 749, 750
Woolf, 756
Wordsworth, 757

Freedom of the Press
John Adams, 43
Anonymous, 59
Bentham, 91
Hugo L. Black, 98
Blackstone, 99
Bok, 103
Borah, 106
Carlile, 140
Channing, 151
Clark, 159
Colton, 168
Continental Congress, 175
Daniels, 189
Fahey, 247
Frankfurter, 257
Freund, 263
Grant, 287
Alexander Hamilton, 295
Harlan, 301

Henry, 312
Hetherington, 315
H. C. Hoover, 331
C. E. Hughes, 335
Hume, 339
Ickes, 348
R. H. Jackson, 358
Jefferson, 365, 366, 367, 368
S. Johnson, 379
Junius, 381
Kropotkin, 395
Lenin, 409, 412
John L. Lewis, 416
Lindstrom, 432
Lowell, 443
Luxemburg, 449
Marx, 474
Mason, 479
Morton, 511
G. Murray, 512
G. Nicholas, 525, 526
Phillips, 558, 562
F. D. Roosevelt, 595
Sheridan, 636, 637
Sulzberger, 666
Sutherland, 669
U.S.S.R., 704
Vishinsky, 711, 712
D. Webster, 731
N. Webster, 731
W. A. White, 736
Wortman, 757, 758
Zenger, 761

Freedom of Thought
(see Freethinkers)
John Adams, 43, 44
S. Adams, 47
Altgeld, 53
Burke, 126
Fox, 254
Franklin, 257
Grant, 287
Greeley, 289
Humboldt, 337

Ingersoll, 350
R. H. Jackson, 356
Leo XIII, 413
Locke, 435
Maugham, 481
Newman, 523
Oppenheimer, 536
Segura, 625
United Nations, 700
E. Warren, 722
Willkie, 748
W. Wilson, 753
Free Enterprise
Commager, 169
Hitler, 318
Johnston, 379
Kefauver, 385
Laski, 400
Oxnam, 540
Pius XI, 565
Ricardo, 582
F. D. Roosevelt, 591, 592, 594
Truman, 693
W. Wilson, 750
Free Love
Carpenter, 144
Fitzhugh, 251
E. Key, 388
Freeman, Free Man
Cowley, 183
Hobbes, 323
M. Van Doren, 706
Whittier, 741
W. Wilson, 750
Wise, 754
Freemason
Arcos, 66
Garibaldi, 269
Free Silver
T. L. Johnson, 379
Populist Party, 572
Free Speech (see Speech)
H. W. Beecher, 87
Bentham, 91

Bok, 103
Borah, 106
Bradlaugh, 109
Brandeis, 111
Carlile, 140
Chafee, 149
Channing, 151
Clark, 159
de Cleyre, 164
W. O. Douglas, 212, 213
Eisenhower, 229
Emerson, 234
Euripides, 246
Franklin, 257, 259
Freund, 263
Grant, 287
Greeley, 289
Gregory XVI, 290
Hall, 294
Hand, 298
Harlan, 301
Hearst, 305, 306
A. Herbert, 313
Hobson, 323
O. W. Holmes (Jr.), 328, 330
C. E. Hughes, 335
R. H. Jackson, 357
Lenin, 412
Leo XIII, 413
Lincoln, 424
Lippmann, 433, 434
Lovejoy, 440
Lowell, 444
Luxemburg, 449
Mill, 493
Morton, 511
Norton, 534
Oppenheimer, 536
Orozco, 437
Palmerston, 545
State of Pennsylvania, 556
Republican Party, 581
F. D. Roosevelt, 593
Tallentyre, 672

Tennyson, 678
Tocqueville, 687
Twain, 697
U.S.S.R., 704
Vinson, 711
Vishinsky, 711, 712
W. A. White, 737
Willkie, 748
W. Wilson, 752

Freethinker (see Freedom of Thought)
E. Allen, 51
Carlyle, 142
W. O. Douglas, 212
Erskine, 246
Hobson, 323, 324
O. W. Holmes (Jr.), 329
E. Hubbard, 334
Ingersoll, 350

Free Will (see Will)
Born, 107
Carlyle, 142
France, 256
Hobbes, 323
W. James, 360
Luther, 446
Origen, 536
Schnitzler, 616
Spinoza, 651
Wagner, 719
W. Wilson, 753
Zinsser, 762

Freud
Reik, 580
W. B. Wolfe, 755

Friend, Friends
Acton, 36
H. B. Adams, 40
Anonymous, 64
Aristotle, 66
F. Bacon, 72
Gompers, 285

Fuehrer
Hitler, 319

Future
Andreyev, 57
Henry, 312
Ibsen, 347
A. M. Lindbergh, 429

G

Gadfly
Flexner, 252
Eric F. Goldman, 283
Socrates, 645

Galileo
J. Huxley, 343

Gallant
Anonymous, 63

Gambler
Blake, 100

Generalization
O. W. Holmes (Jr.), 328, 329
Montaigne, 501

Generalize
Blake, 101

Generals
Clausewitz, 161
Clemenceau, 162

General Welfare (see Welfare)
Cardozo, 140
Harlan, 301
Wortman, 757

Generation
Stein, 660

Genius
Bakunin, 78
Edison, 219
Emerson, 239
W. James, 361
Keats, 385
Mill, 495
Seneca, 626
Shaw, 632
Swift, 669

Genocide
Rundstedt, 602, 603
Seneca, 627

Gentile
Frankfurter, 257
Jefferson, 363
Willkie, 748

Gentleman
John Ball, 80
W. James, 360
Leggett, 406
More, 506
Shaw, 631

Geopolitics
Mackinder, 457

Geriatrics
Nascher, 519

Germans
Clemenceau, 162
Heine, 309
Hitler, 317, 319, 320
Inge, 349
Kiderlen-Waechter, 391
T. Mann, 464
Nietzsche, 530
Rosenberg, 598
Rundstedt, 603
Seneca, 627
Spengler, 651
Truman, 693
Wilhelm II, 746
W. Wilson, 752

Ghost
Ibsen, 347

Ghost-writing
Amory, 56

Glory
de Gaulle, 199
Gregory I, 290
Hobbes, 321
Masefield, 478
Robespierre, 584

Rouget de Lisle, 599
Sherman, 637
Thomas à Kempis, 680

God
Acton, 36
Francis Adams, 39
John Adams, 42, 43, 44
Agathon, 50
Alcuin, 51
E. Allen, 52
Amalric, 53
American Legion, 54
Anonymous, 59, 60, 61, 63
Aquinas, 64
M. Arnold, 69
Athanasian Creed, 69
Augustine, 70, 71
F. Bacon, 72
Baer, 75
Bakunin, 76, 77, 79
K. Barth, 83
H. W. Beecher, 87
Bellarmine, 89
Bennett, 90
Boniface VIII, 105
Bossuet, 108
John Brown, 117
Browning, 119
Burbank, 126
Burroughs, 131
Samuel Butler, 133
Byron, 136
Camus, 138
Chworowsky, 157
Clemenceau, 162
Coughlin, 181
S. Crane, 184
C. P. Curtis, 187, 188
Cyprian, 188
Darrow, 190
C. Darwin, 191, 193
DeLeon, 200
De Vries, 203
Diderot, 205

Eddy, 219
J. Edwards, 220
Einstein, 221
Emerson, 235, 238
Erigena, 245
Euripides, 246
Farrell, 248
Freud, 261
Fromm, 264
Gandhi, 267, 268
Garrison, 271
Goethe, 282
Gregory I, 290
Haeckel, 292
Halifax, 293
Hegel, 308
Heine, 309, 310
Herndon 314
Hinsley, 316
d'Holbach, 326, 327
O. W. Holmes (Jr.), 328, 329, 330
Hausman, 333
J. Huxley, 342
Inge, 349
Ingersoll, 349, 350, 352
Jefferson, 362, 364, 365, 369, 370, 374
Jerome, 375
Joan of Arc, 376
Joyce, 380
Lenin, 410
Leo XIII, 413, 414, 415
Joseph Lewis, 418
S. Lewis, 418
Lincoln, 423, 425
Lindsey, 432
Locke, 435, 437
London, 438
Lovejoy, 440
Lowell, 442, 443
Lucian, 445
Luther, 446, 447, 448
Machiavelli, 455
MacLeish, 457
Macy, 458

Marlowe, 469
Maryland Assembly, 477
Maugham, 481
Melville, 485
Menen, 488
Milton, 497, 499
Montefiore, 502
Montherlant, 504
Moore, 505
Mussolini, 513
Napoleon, 518
Newton, 525
Nietzsche, 527, 529
Nordau, 532
North Carolina, 533
Orwell, 538
Paine, 541, 542, 544
Pascal, 549, 550
Pasternak, 550
Pearson, 553
Plato, 568, 569
Poe, 570
Pope, 571
Rockefeller (Sr.), 586
F. D. Roosevelt, 593
Santayana, 613, 614
Sartre, 615
Selassie, 625
Shaw, 631
Sheen, 633
Shelley, 634, 635, 636,
L. Smith, 643
Society of Friends, 645
Spinoza, 653
Steinmetz, 661
Stresemann, 666
Sunday, 667, 668
Tertullian, 680
Thomas à Kempis, 680
Thoreau, 684
Tolstoy, 689, 690
Twain, 696, 697, 698
Van Gogh, 706
Vanzetti, 707

[809]

Voltaire, 714, 715, 716, 717
G. Washington, 725, 727
Wells, 732
Whitman, 739, 740, 741
Wilhelm II, 746
Williams, 747, 748
W. Wilson, 750, 752
Wise, 733, 754
Zinsser, 762
Zwingli, 763

Gods
Aeschylus, 50
M. Anderson, 56
Aristotle, 67
Bakunin, 77
Buchanan, 124
J. Dewey, 205
Diodorus, 206
Diogenes, 206
Dostoyevski, 210
Ellis, 231
Emerson, 235
Ferrer, 249
France, 254
Freud, 263
d' Holbach, 325
Jefferson, 364
Jonson, 380
D. H. Lawrence, 403
V. Lindsay, 431
Lucretius, 445
Macy, 458
Malraux, 462
Marcus Aurelius, 467
Marx, 471
Mill, 490
Ovid, 539
Petronius, 558
Plautus, 569
Polybius, 571
Santayana, 612, 614
Schiller, 616
Socrates, 646
Statius, 659

Virgil, 711
Whittier, 741, 742

Gold
Bryan, 121
Samuel Butler, 133
Columbus, 169
Cowley, 183
Debs, 196
Horace, 332
S. Johnson, 378
Lowell, 443
Masefield, 478
More, 506
Shelley, 635
Tennyson, 678
Virgil, 711
Wilcox, 742

Golden Mean (see Mean)
Plato, 567
Publilius Syrus, 576

Golden Rule
Confucius, 173, 174
Christian, 283
Talmud, 283
Brahman, 283
Buddhist, 283
Taoist, 283
Zoroastrian, 283
Islamic, 283
Ha-Babli, 292
Hobbes, 322
Kossuth, 394
Luther, 446
Mahabharata, 461
Millikan, 496
W. Morris, 510
van Paasen, 541
Shaw, 631
Terence, 679

Good, Goodness
Acton, 35
E. Allen, 52
Archer, 65

Aristotle, 66, 67, 68
Augustine, 70
Babeuf, 71
F. Bacon, 73
Bentham, 91
Blake 100
Bruno, 121
N. M. Butler, 132
Carlyle, 142
Dante, 189
J. Dewey, 205
G. Eliot, 230
Ferrer, 249
Griswold, 291
Heraclitus, 313
Nietzsche, 527
Sartre, 615
Schweitzer, 622
Veblen, 709

Good and Evil
Archer, 65
Aristotle, 67
Augustine, 71
Blake, 101
Buck, 124
C. P. Curtis, 187
Darrow, 191
Diogenes, 206
Durant, 217
T. S. Eliot, 230
Flushing Remonstrance, 252
France, 254
George II, 272
Hobbes, 322
R. H. Jackson, 356
T. E. Lawrence, 403
Lippmann, 433
London, 438
Lowell, 442
Montessori, 504
Mormons, 509
G. Nicholas, 526
Nietzsche, 527, 529
Origen, 536

Penn, 555
Philo, 562
Pittacus, 563
Plato, 568
Pope, 571
E. Roosevelt, 589
T. Roosevelt, 597
Spinoza, 652
Stirner, 664

Goods
Augustine, 71
Cousin, 182
Eastman, 218
Hutterite Creed, 340
Veblen, 708

Good, True, Beautiful
Einstein, 223, 226
Plato, 567

Good Will
Bush, 132
Hocking, 324
Penn, 555

Gospel
Baur, 84
Gibbon, 276
F. Harrison, 302
Inge, 349
Pasternak, 550
Rousseau, 600
Toynbee, 691
Whitehead, 738

Government
Acton, 36, 37
John Adams, 43, 45
M. Anderson, 56
Aristotle, 67, 68
F. Bacon, 73
Bagehot, 76
Bancroft, 82
H. W. Beecher, 87
Berenson, 92
Borah, 107
Bossuet, 108

Brandeis, 111, 112
Burke, 128, 129
Cato, 148
Chafee, 150
Cleveland, 163
Confucius 173, 174
Coolidge, 177
de Maistre, 200
Disraeli, 207
Einstein, 225
Eisenhower, 228
Emerson, 236
Frankfurter, 257
Franklin, 259
Freund, 263
Garfield, 269
Godwin, 279, 280
Emma Goldman, 283
Gordon, 286
Alexander Hamilton, 294, 296
Harding, 299
Harrington, 301
Helvetius, 310
Hobson, 323, 324
Hutchins, 340
A. Jackson, 354, 355
R. H. Jackson, 356
James I, 358
Jefferson, 363, 365, 369, 370
S. Johnson, 377, 378
Virgil Jordan, 380
LaFollette, 396
Landon, 397
Laski, 400
Leggett, 405
Lerner, 416
Lilienthal, 420, 421
Lincoln, 421, 425, 429
Locke, 436
Lowell, 441
Machiavelli, 455
J. Madison, 459, 460
J. Marshall, 470
Mason, 479

Maupassant, 481
Mencken, 487, 488
Mussolini, 515, 518
New Hampshire, 522
Otis, 538, 539
Paine, 543, 544, 545
Penn, 555, 556
Pericles, 556
Pope, 571
Priestley, 573, 574
Proudhon, 574, 575
Raleigh, 578
Ruskin, 603
B. A. Russell, 606
Shaw, 631
Spencer, 648, 649, 650
Spinoza, 652
Spooner, 653
Sprading, 654
Story, 665
Swift, 670, 671
Thompson, 681
Thoreau, 682, 685
Tocqueville, 686
Tolstoy, 690, 691
Twain, 699
Vinson, 711
A. R. Wallace, 720
Warburg, 721
G. Washington, 725, 726, 727
D. Webster, 728, 729, 730
N. Webster, 731
Wells, 732, 733
Whitman, 740
O. Wilde, 744
Willkie, 749
W. Wilson, 750, 751
Wise, 753, 754
Wortman, 757
Wright, 759

Gradualism
Garrison, 271
Pavlov, 553
Webb, 728

Great, Greatness
  H. W. Beecher, 87
  Brougham, 116
  Chekhov, 153
  Emerson, 237
  Hugo, 336
  A. Huxley, 341
  Kett, 387
  S. Lewis, 418
  Lucan, 444
  H. Mann, 464
  Milton, 498
  Plekhanov, 569
  Proudhon, 575

Greece, Greeks
  Acton, 36
  Macaulay, 451
  B. A. Russell, 606
  Virgil, 711
  O. Wilde, 743

Greed
  B. Adams, 39
  Berkman, 93
  Markham, 469
  Virgil, 711
  T. Wolfe, 755

Guerilla
  Batista, 84

Guilt
  C. P. Curtis, 187
  Freud, 260
  Grant, 288
  MacLeish, 457

H

Habeas Corpus
  England, 243
  Jefferson, 365, 368

Habit
  Aristotle, 67

F. Bacon, 72
Nicholas of Cusa, 525

Happiness
  Abd-el-Raham, 35
  Acton, 37
  Robert Burton, 132
  Casanova, 147
  Emerson, 235
  Freud, 260
  Jefferson, 362
  Kant, 383, 384
  Keyserling, 389
  Locke, 435
  J. Marshall, 470
  Marx, 471, 474
  Mencken, 487
  Milton, 498
  Owen, 540
  Paine, 541, 542
  Rousseau, 599
  B. A. Russell, 605, 608
  Socialist Labor Party, 644
  Thucydides, 685
  Tone, 691
  Zola, 763

Harlot
  Blake, 100
  D. H. Lawrence, 402
  Tertullian, 680
  Yeats, 760

Hate, Hatred
  Bridges, 114
  Burke, 127
  Cavell, 149
  Einstein, 222, 227
  Freud, 262
  Goethe, 282
  Gorky, 287
  Hitler, 317
  Kett, 388
  Lenin, 412
  Marcus Aurelius, 467
  McNair, 483
  Shaw, 630

U.S.S.R., 704
B. T. Washington, 724
G. Washington, 726

Have (and have not)
Bancroft, 81
Cervantes, 149
H. George, 272

Health
Eddy, 219

Heart
Harvey, 302
Keats, 385
Keith, 385
Krupskaya, 395
Pascal, 549

Heaven
John Adams, 42
Browne, 118
Burroughs, 131
Richard Burton, 132
W. James, 360
Marlowe, 469
Milton, 498, 499

Hebrew, Hebrews
John Adams, 43, 45
Heine, 309
Jefferson, 370
Longfellow, 439

Hegel
Marx, 473

Hell
John Adams, 43, 45
Aquinas, 64
Browne, 118
Burbank, 126
R. Burns, 131
Richard Burton, 132
Samuel Butler, 133
Chrysostom, 156
Ciardi, 157
Cyprian, 188
Diodorus, 206
J. Edwards, 220

Fulgentius, 265
Garrison, 271
Hugo, 336
Kreymborg, 394
Joseph Lewis, 418
Luther, 447, 448
Marlowe, 469
Marx, 474
McCabe, 482
Milton, 498, 499
Book of Mormon, 509
B. A. Russell, 608
Sherman, 637
Sunday, 667, 668
Talmud, 673
Tertullian, 680
Truman, 695
Twain, 697
Wesley, 734
T. Wolfe, 755

Herd (Human)
Berger, 92
J. H. Burns, 130
Crawford, 184
Einstein, 226
Hazlitt, 305
Horace, 332
MacLeish, 457
Milton, 499
Nietzsche, 528

Heretic, Heretics, Heresy
Acton, 36
John Adams, 46
S. Adams, 47
E. Allen, 52
Aquinas, 64
Augustine, 70, 71
Brann, 113
Bunyan, 125
Dominic, 209
Einstein, 221
Erasmus, 244
Fulgentius, 264
Galileo, 266

Godwin, 280
Hand, 298, 299
Hobbes, 322
T. H. Huxley, 343
Ingersoll, 349, 451, 353
The Koran, 393
H. E. Lea, 403
Lecky, 404
Leo XIII, 414
Luther, 446, 447
Maryland Assembly, 477
Meany, 484
Mill, 493, 495
Milton, 497
Montesquieu, 502
Ralph, 579
Santayana, 613
Shaw, 631
Spinoza, 651
Thoreau, 684
Toller, 688

Hero
Bakunin,76
Emerson, 236
Hegel, 308
Lieber, 419
Lloyd George, 435
Longfellow, 439
Nasser, 520
Spencer, 649
Stalin, 657

History
Acton, 36, 37, 38
H. B. Adams, 40, 41
Aristotle, 68
C. A. Beard, 85
Beccaria, 86
Bernstein, 95
Bismarck, 97
Bowers, 108
Cervantes, 149
Croce, 185
Disraeli, 208
Einstein, 224, 225

Engels, 240, 241, 243
Ford, 253
Frankfurter, 257
Gibbon, 276
Hegel, 307, 308
S. Johnson, 378
Jung, 381
Le Bon, 404
Lenin, 407, 408, 409, 411, 412
Lincoln, 427
Marx, 471, 473, 475
Montesquieu, 503
Napoleon, 519
Nehru, 522
Pasternak, 551
Sherman, 637
Snow, 644
Thucydides, 685
Tito, 686
Toynbee, 691
Treitschke, 692
Truman, 695
Valéry, 705
Van Loon, 706
Vittorini, 712
Voltaire, 714
Wells, 732, 733
O. Wilde, 746
Wilhelm (Crown Prince) 747

Hitler
Benedict-Weltfish, 90
Berenson, 92
Churchill, 156, 157
Anne Lindbergh, 429
Litvinov, 434
Thomas Mann, 464
Matthews-Shallcross, 480
F. D. Roosevelt, 595
Shaw, 632

Holy Ghost
Athanasian Creed, 70
John Ball, 80
Samuel Butler, 133

Stephanus V, 661
Veblen, 710

Holy Roman Empire
Boerne, 102
Voltaire, 714

Honor
Abd-el-Raham, 35
Brooke, 115
Confucius, 174

Hope
Dante, 189
Emerson, 233

Hostages
F. Bacon, 73

**Human, Humanitarian, Humanity, Human
Nature, Human Race**
John Adams, 42
A. Adler, 48
Amiel, 55
Babeuf, 71
F. Bacon, 73, 74
Bagehot, 76
Bakunin, 76, 79
Barlow, 82
Bebel, 86
Bellarmine, 89
Berenson, 91
Bergson, 92
Blavatsky, 101
Bliven, 102
Bradley, 109
Bryan, 121
Buchanan, 124
Burke, 129
Chesterfield, 154
Ciardi, 157
Cicero, 159
Condorcet, 172
J. Dewey, 204
Douglass, 214
DuPont, 217
Einstein, 226, 227
Faulkner, 248

Gandhi, 268
Gibbon, 276
Gollancz, 285
Herron, 314
Hitler, 317, 318
Hoffer, 325
Humboldt, 337
T. H. Huxley, 344
S. Johnson, 378
Jones, 379
Koestler, 393
Landor, 397
Lindsay-Crouse, 430
London, 432
Lowell, 442
Machiavelli, 456
H. Mann, 463
Markham, 469
Mazzini, 482
Melville, 485
Mumford, 512
Nietzsche, 529
Renan, 581
Spencer, 650
Stevens, 662
C. Sumner, 667
Thucydides, 685
Treitschke, 692
Turgot, 695
Twain, 696
Vanzetti, 707
Weltfish, 733
O. Wilde, 744
E. Wilson, 749
W. Wilson, 753
Wordsworth, 757
Wright, 759
Zola, 763

Human Rights
Einstein, 224, 225
Hutchins, 340
Tertullian, 679

Humbug
Barnum, 83

Sherman, 637
Thackeray, 680

Hunger
H B. Adams, 41
Berkman, 93
Chartists, 152
Kenko, 387
Kett, 387
Seneca, 626
J. F. Wilde, 743
W. Wilson, 750

Hydrogen Bomb
Einstein, 227

Hypocrisy
Beerbohm, 87
Bok, 104
Carpenter, 145
Hazlitt, 304
Ibsen, 347
La Rochefoucauld, 398
Machiavelli, 454
Marcus Aurelius, 467
Milton, 499
Rolland, 588

I

Iconoclast
Haeckel, 292
O. W. Holmes (Sr.), 327

Id
Freud, 261, 263

Idea, Ideas
Acton, 38
Bagehot, 76
Bakunin, 76
Brennan, 113
Comte, 171
Dostoyevski, 210
W. O. Douglas, 211, 213
France, 255
Freud, 263
Garfield, 269
H. George, 275

Greeley, 289
Hand, 298
Heine, 309
Hitler, 318
O. W. Holmes (Jr.), 328
E. Hubbard, 334
Hugo, 336
Hutchins, 339
Ibsen, 347
H. James, 358
Keynes, 389
Lally, 397
D. H. Lawrence, 402
Mencken, 486
Ralph, 579
Rousseau, 599
Schopenhauer, 617
Terence, 679
Thompson, 681
E. Warren, 722
Whitehead, 737, 738
O. Wilde, 745
Woolf, 756

Ideal, Idealism
H. B. Adams, 40
K. Barth, 83
Berlin, 94
Chesterton, 154, 155
W. O. Douglas, 212
Emma Goldman, 283
C. A. Madison, 458
Nietsche, 529
W. Wilson, 751, 752
Zangwill, 761

Ideology
John Adams, 44
Aiken, 50
Lenin, 407

Idiot
Bakunin, 78
Blake, 101

Idol
Acton, 38

F. Bacon, 73, 74
Dostoyevski, 210
Emerson, 233
Ferrer, 249
Hazlitt, 305
Kingsley, 392
The Koran, 393,
Schiller, 616
Tawney, 677
Wordsworth, 757

Ignorance
Acton, 35
H. B. Adams, 40
John Adams, 42
Berlin, 94
Brandeis, 112
Carlile, 140
Confucius, 174
Diogenes, 206
Emerson, 239
Goethe, 281
E. Hubbard, 334
Taylor, 677
Tillotson, 686

Illegitimate
Lindsey, 431, 432
Yankwich, 760

Imitation
F. Bacon, 72
Emerson, 239

Immaculate Conception
Jefferson, 373

Immortality
H. B. Adams, 41
Addison, 48
Byron, 136
Camus, 139
Darrow, 191
C. Darwin, 192
Dostoyevski, 210
Einstein, 225
Haeckel, 292
Heine, 309

Hocking, 324
T. H. Huxley, 343
Inge, 348
Keith, 385
Luther, 446
Mencken, 486
Nietzsche, 530
Paine, 541
Pascal, 549
Pasternak, 550
B. A. Russell, 607
Santayana, 612
Steinmetz, 661
Twain, 698
T. Wolfe, 754
Zinsser, 762

Imperialism
France, 254
Hobson, 324
Lenin, 408, 410
Nehru, 521
Stalin, 655

Incredible, Incredibility
Augustine, 70

Increment
Mill, 496

Independent
Cobbett, 165
Einstein, 225
Kant, 383
Lincoln, 424
Mill, 490

Index Expurgatorius
John Adams, 46

Indictment
Burke, 128

Indignation
Rolland, 84
Lowell, 441
Wells, 732

Individual, Individualism, Individuality
A. Adler, 48, 49
Bakunin, 79, 80

Baruch, 84
Bellamy, 88
Berlin, 94
Brandeis, 110
V. W. Brooks, 115
Burke, 130
Calhoun, 137
Carlyle, 142
Carnegie, 143, 144
Cather, 148
Cummings, 187
De Musset, 202
Einstein, 223, 225
Gissing, 278
Hand, 298
Hoffer, 325
J. E. Hoover, 332
C. E. Hughes, 335
Humboldt, 337
A. Huxley, 341, 342
Ibsen, 346, 347
R. H. Jackson, 357
Keyserling, 389
Kropotkin, 394
Lilienthal, 420, 421
Lincoln, 424
Lloyd, 434
Markham, 468
Mill, 490, 491, 494, 495, 496
Montaigne, 501
Montessori, 504
J. Morley, 508
Mussolini, 516, 517
Pasternak, 550
President's Commission on Civil Rights, 573
Rocco, 586
Rolland, 588
F. D. Roosevelt, 591
Silone, 639
Stirner, 664, 665
C. Sumner, 667
Sutherland, 669
Tawney, 674, 675, 676, 677

J. Warren, 723
Webb, 728
Wells, 732
O. Wilde, 744, 745

Indoctrination
Hand, 298

Industrial Democracy
T. Arnold, 69
Brandeis, 110
DeLeon, 200
McDonald, 483

Industry
S. Anderson, 57
Dana, 188
Hillman, 315
Keller, 386
John L. Lewis, 417
Mahan, 461
G. W. Russell, 610
U.S. Army, 701
W. Wilson, 750, 752

Inequality
M. Arnold, 69
Babeuf, 71
Barlow, 82
Bellamy, 88
Hitler, 320
Leo XIII, 414
Luther, 446

Infallibility
Acton, 38
E. Allen, 52
Aquinas, 64
Colton, 168
Gregory VII, 290
Hus, 339
T. H. Huxley, 344
Mill, 492, 493
Newman, 523
Paine, 544
Pasternak, 551
Pius XI, 565
Vatican Council, 707

Infamy
  Voltaire, 713
Inferiority
  A. Adler,48, 49
  American Anthropological Association, 54
  Aristotle, 67
  Confucius, 173, 174
  Schopenhauer, 618
  Seneca, 626
  Shaw, 630
  Sheen, 633
  Taney, 674
  U.S. Supreme Court, 702
  Wells, 732
Infidel
  E. Allen, 52
  Burbank, 126
  Byron, 136
  Ingersoll, 349, 350
  Jefferson, 372, 374
Inflation
  Hemingway, 311
  D. Webster, 730
Information
  John Adams, 42
  E. W. Howe, 333
  Lassalle, 401
Informers
  Aristotle, 68
  John Brown, 117
  W. O. Douglas, 213
  Hand, 297
  Lea, 403
  MacLeish, 457
  Swift, 670
Injustice
  Canute, 139
  France, 254
  Gladstone, 278
  Emma Goldman, 283
  Homer, 330
  Ingersoll, 350, 352

  Landor, 397
  G. W. Norris, 533
  Seneca, 627
Inquisition
  B. Adams, 39
  John Adams, 46
  R. H. Jackson, 356
  Lea, 403
  Voltaire, 714
Institution, Institutions
  Acton, 36
  Bagehot, 76
  Emerson, 237
  Lincoln, 426
  Machiavelli, 455
Intellect, Intelligence, Intelligent, Intellectual, Intelligentsia
  Abu'l-Ala, 35
  B. Adams, 39
  A. Adler, 49
  Amiel, 55
  Bakunin, 77
  Benda, 90
  Bergson, 92
  Channing, 151
  Chekhov, 153
  Confucius, 174
  T. Cooper, 180
  Croce, 185
  Einstein, 222, 223, 224, 227
  Emerson, 235
  Goebbels, 281
  Gorky, 286
  Griswold, 291
  Hitler, 320
  W. James, 359
  D. H. Lawrence, 403
  Lenin, 407, 408
  Lucas, 444
  Macaulay, 451, 452
  Marx, 475
  K. Menninger, 489
  Millan-Astray, 496
  Ortega, 537

Spengler, 650, 651
Spinoza, 653
Stalin, 657
Trotsky, 693
Unamuno, 700
Valentine, 704
E. Warren, 723

Interest, Vested
H. B. Adams, 41
Angell, 57

International
Angell, 58
Baha 'u'llah, 76
Bakunin, 79
Einstein, 221, 222
Gandhi, 268
Pottier, 572
Third International 680

Intolerance
H. W. Beecher, 87
Borah, 107
Garrison, 271
Hitler, 318
Jefferson, 364
Lippmann, 433
Mill, 490
Proudhon, 575
Rousseau, 601
Stassen, 659

Investigate
E. Warren, 723
Wortman, 757

Ireland, Irish
Brown, 116
Casement, 147
Chesterton, 154

Iron Curtain
Churchill, 156
Goebbels, 281
E. Warren, 722

Irony
Conrad, 175

Ism
Phillips, 560
F. D. Roosevelt, 593

Israel
France, 254
Jacobs, 358
Jefferson, 373

Ivory Tower
Croce, 185
Picasso, 562
Salutati, 611

J

Jefferson
Dwight, 218
Ellsworth, 232
Kosciusko, 393

Jesuit, Jesuits
John Adams, 44
J. Bonaparte, 105
Dupin, 217
Jefferson, 372
Macaulay, 452
Maryland Assembly, 477
Napoleon, 518
Pym, 577

Jesus Christ
B. Adams, 39
Francis Adams, 39
A. Adler, 49
S. Anderson, 57
Arcos, 65, 66
Bernard, 94
Blake, 101
Blavatsky, 101
P. Brooks, 115
Bucer, 123
Byron, 136
Carlyle, 142
Carpenter, 145, 146
Chworowsky, 157
Council of Trent, 182

Cromwell, 186
Desmoulins, 203
Einstein, 227
Goebbels, 281
Halleck, 294
Hitler, 321
Hopkins, 332
Hugo, 336
Hus, 339
T. H. Huxley, 344
Jefferson, 363, 370, 371, 372, 373, 374
Kant, 383
Kierkegaard, 391
de Lavelaye, 401
Le Gallienne, 405
Joseph Lewis, 418
London, 438
H. R. Luce, 445
Luther, 448
Maryland Assembly, 477, 478
Mencken, 486
Milton, 498
J. P. Morgan, 506
Nietzsche, 529
Owen, 540
Paine, 544
Pascal, 550
Pasternak, 550
Renan, 581
Rousseau, 602
Schweitzer, 622
Shaw, 628, 631
Shelley, 634
Sinclair, 639
Tennyson, 679
Thoreau, 683
Tolstoy, 689
Twain, 696
Voltaire, 714
Wells, 732, 733
Whitehead, 737
O. Wilde, 745
Roger Williams, 747
T. Wolfe, 755

Jew, Jews
John Adams, 43, 44
V. Adler, 50
Anonymous, 60
Arcos, 66
Balfour, 80
Baum, 84
Benedict-Weltfish, 90
Bridges, 114
Burbank, 126
H. S. Chamberlain, 150
Einstein, 226, 227
George Eliot, 229
Flushing Remonstrance, 252
Frankfurter, 257
Fulgentius, 264
Galsworthy, 266
Goebbels, 281
Goering, 281
Heine, 310
Hitler, 318, 319, 320, 321
d'Holbach, 325
Ibsen, 347
Ingersoll, 353
Jefferson, 363, 372, 373
Lenin, 408
C. A. Lindbergh (Jr.), 429
Lowell, 441
Ludendorff, 445
Luther, 446, 447
Macaulay, 451
Marx, 471
W. C. Menninger, 489
Mussolini, 517
Nietzsche, 527, 528, 530
Nordau, 532
Pius IV, 563
Rathenau, 579
Renan, 581
Schweitzer, 622
Shelley, 636
Stanton, 659
Stuyvesant, 666
Treitschke, 693

Twain, 696
Voltaire, 714
G. Washington, 726
Williams, 747, 748
Willkie, 748
Zangwill, 761

Journalist, Journalism
Anonymous, 59
M. Arnold, 68
S. Bowles, 108
Cockburn, 166
Dana, 189
Harris, 301
Hillman, 316
J. H. Holmes, 327
H. James, 358
W. James, 361
H. R. Luce, 445
Mussolini, 513
Napoleon, 519
Pulitzer, 576
G. W. Russell, 610
Scripps, 624
Swinton, 671
Wardman, 722
W. A. White, 734, 736
O. Wilde, 743, 744, 745
Yeats, 760

Judaism
Augustine, 71
Disraeli, 208
Einstein, 227
France, 254
Freud, 261
Renan, 581
Siegel, 638
Voltaire, 715

Judge, Judiciary, Judgment
Acton, 38
Blake, 100
Cicero, 158
Dostoyevski, 210
Frankfurter, 257

Jefferson, 370, 374
Lenin, 408
Montesquieu, 503
T. Roosevelt, 596
C. Sumner, 666
Terence, 679
E. Warren, 722
Wesley, 734

Jury
Boldt, 104
Henry, 312
Jefferson, 365
Spooner, 653

Just, Justice
Acton, 37
John Quincy Adams, 46
Addison, 48
Angell, 58
Aristotle, 67
Augustine, 70
F. Bacon, 73
Bakunin, 77
Hugo L. Black, 98
Blum, 102
Broun, 116
Burke, 130
Carter, 147
Cicero, 158, 159
Darrow, 190
Disraeli, 207
Epicurus, 244
V. Fisher, 250
Galsworthy, 266
Godwin, 280
Herron, 314
Ingersoll, 350, 351
Justinian, 381
The Koran, 393
Laski, 399
D. H. Lawrence, 402
Lincoln, 425
V. Lindsay, 431
J. Madison, 459
Magna Carta, 461

Lord Mansfield, 465
Manu, 465
Marcus Aurelius, 467
More, 505
Pascal, 550
Robespierre, 584, 585
Sheen, 633
Shelley, 634
S. Smith, 644
Tocqueville, 686
Vanzetti, 706
Voltaire, 714
G. Washington, 725
D. Webster, 730
O. Wilde, 745

K

Kill, Killing
Freud, 262, 263
Froude, 264
Gandhi, 268
Gould, 287
McNair, 483
Milton, 496, 497
Nietzsche, 530
Pascal, 549
Voltaire, 714, 716
O. Wilde, 745

King, Kingdom
Acton, 36
John Adams, 43
Anonymous, 61
Augustine, 70
Bakunin, 77
Blackstone, 99
Bossuet, 108
Byron, 136
Coke, 166
Diderot, 205
Fortescue, 253
Freneau, 260
Henry VIII, 312

Hetherington, 315
Jones, 379
Kant, 383
Keller, 386
Messelier, 489
Plato, 567, 569
Richelieu, 583
Shelley, 634
Swift, 670
Whitman, 739

Knave
Buckingham, 124
S. Butler, 133

Know, Knowledge
John Adams, 42
Amiel, 55
Anonymous, 63
Aristotle, 66
F. Bacon, 72, 73, 75
R. Bacon, 75
Bakunin, 78
H. W. Beecher, 87
Billings, 97
P. Brooks, 115
Brougham, 116
Bush, 132
Carlyle, 142
Confucius, 173
Croce, 185
G. W. Curtis, 188
De Quincy, 202
Diogenes, 206
Einstein, 224
Gandhi, 267
Harvey, 302
Hitler, 321
Hobbes, 322
Ingersoll, 352
Jefferson, 368
S. Johnson, 379
Kafka, 382
Kant, 383
Kierkegaard, 391
Horace Mann, 464

Montaigne, 501
Peirce, 554
Tagore, 672
G. Washngton, 726

Know-Nothing
Lincoln, 422

Know Thyself
Anonymous, 63
Carlyle, 142
Juvenal, 382
T. Mann, 464
Pope, 571

Kultur (see Culture)

L

Labor
H. B. Adams, 41
T. S. Adams, 47
Altgeld, 53
A. F. L., 54
Anonymous, 62
Baer, 75
Ball, 81
Baruch, 84
Bellamy, 88
Benedictine Order, 90
Bierce, 96
Brandeis, 110
Brownson, 120
Bryan, 122
Calhoun, 137
Catholic Archbishops, 148
Cleveland, 163
Dana, 188
Darrow, 190
Debs, 196
Defoe, 197
Emerson, 234, 237
Evans, 247
Fabian Society, 247
Florio, 252

Fourier, 254
H. George, 274, 275
Gompers, 285, 286
Greeley, 289
Hawthorne, 303
Hillman, 315
Hitler, 321
Ingersoll, 349, 350
A. Jackson, 355
Jefferson, 364, 365
Kett, 387
Kingsley, 392
Knights of Labor, 392
Lassalle, 400
Lenin, 407, 409
Leo XIII, 414
J. L. Lewis, 416, 417
Lincoln, 422, 425, 426, 427
Lippmann, 432
Lloyd George, 435
Locke, 437
London, 438
Lowell, 443
Lully, 445
Malthus, 463
Markham, 468, 469
Marx, 474, 476, 477
McKinley, 483
Meany, 484
More, 505, 506
L. H. Morgan, 507
Mundelein, 512
Nearing, 520
Oastler, 534
O'Brien, 534
T. Parker, 546
Parsons, 548
Phillips, 559, 560, 561
Pius XII, 566
Pottier, 572
Rakosi, 578
Reuther, 581
Ricardo, 582
Rockefeller (Jr.), 587

T. Roosevelt, 597
Root, 598
Ruskin, 603
Schweitzer, 623
Shelley, 634, 636
Siegfried, 638
Adam Smith, 641
Stalin, 655, 656
Tawney, 676, 677
Tolstoy, 689, 690
U.S. Congress, 701
U.S. Supreme Court, 703
U.S.S.R., 704
Veblen, 708
Virgil, 711
Wagner, 718
D. Webster, 728, 730, 731
W. A. White, 735, 736
Wilcox, 742
Wright, 759
Zwingli, 763

Ladies
A. Adams, 39

Laity
Macaulay, 452

Land
Davitt, 195
Emerson, 235, 238
H. George, 272, 273, 275
Hardie, 299
Hawthorne, 303
Haywood, 304
Ingersoll, 350, 352
Jefferson, 369
Kett, 388
Kingsley, 391
Lalor, 397
Leo XIII, 415
Locke, 437
J. Madison, 458
Marx, 472
Masters, 480
More, 506
Rhodes, 582

Rousseau, 601
Schweitzer, 623
Socialist Labor Party, 644
Spencer, 650
Tawney, 675
Tertullian, 679
Tolstoy, 688
G. Washington, 727
Webb, 728

Landlords, Owners
Byron, 136
Cobbett, 165
Eastman, 218
Ford, 253
Lenin, 410
Nearing, 521
Ricardo, 582
G. W. Russell, 610

Law, Lawyers
Acton, 37
B. Adams, 39
John Adams, 45
Altgeld, 53
Anacharsis, 56
Anonymous, 60, 64
Aquinas, 64
Arbuthnot, 65
Aristotle, 67
Augustine, 70
F. Bacon, 72, 73
Bagehot, 76
Bakunin, 77, 80
Barlow, 82
Bellarmine, 89
Bentham, 91
Berlin, 94
Blackstone, 99
Blake, 100
Bok, 103
Boldt, 104
Bolingbroke, 104
Bolitho, 105
Brandeis, 111
Brennan, 113

Brougham, 115
Buchanan, 124
Burke, 127, 129
Carpenter, 146
Cicero, 158
Coke, 166
Coolidge, 177
Darrow, 190
DeLeon, 200
Democratic Party, 201
Demonax, 201
Dionysius, 206
Disraeli, 207
W. O. Douglas, 211
Dunne, 216, 217
Ellis, 231
Emerson, 234
Fortesque, 253
France, 254
Garfield, 269
H. George, 273, 274
Godwin, 280
Grant, 288
Hague, 292
Harlan, 300
Hegel, 307
Herndon, 314
Hobbes, 322, 323
O. W. Holmes (Jr.), 329, 330
J. E. Hoover, 332
Housman, 333
A. Jackson, 355
Jefferson, 370
Justinian, 382
Kant, 383
La Bruyère, 395
Lieber, 419
Lincoln, 421, 424
Lindsay-Crouse, 430
Lippmann, 433
Locke, 436
Louis XIV, 440
Lowell, 442
Magna Carta, 461

Marcus Aurelius, 467
J. Marshall, 470, 471
Marx, 472
Mayakovsky, 481
Mill, 490
Millikan, 496
Montaigne, 501
Montesquieu, 503
More, 505
Otis, 538
Pascal, 550
Phillips, 559, 560
William Pitt (Sr.), 563
Pythagoras, 577
J. P. Roche, 586
Rousseau, 599, 600, 602
D. Russell, 609
Selden, 625
S. Smith, 643
Sophocles, 647
Spencer, 649
Spinoza, 652
Swift, 670
Tacitus, 672
Thoreau, 682, 683, 684, 685
Tolstoy, 688, 690
C. Vanderbilt, 705
Veblen, 710
E. Warren, 722
Washington, 726
Whalen, 734
W. A. White, 736
Wiener, 742

Lead, Leader, Leadership
Anonymous, 60
Aristotle, 68
Bernays, 94
Brandes, 113
Browning, 119
Bryce, 123
Debs, 197
Evans, 246, 247
Lao-Tse, 398
Lenin, 412

Lindner, 430
Luxemburg, 449
Plato, 568
Reuther, 581
Spengler, 651
Truman, 695
Whitman, 740

League of Nations
MacArthur, 450
Nobel, 531
Richardson, 583
W. Wilson, 752

Learning
F. Bacon, 72

Lebensraum
Kjellen, 392

"Left"
Bebel, 86
Mayakovsky, 481
O'Flaherty, 535

Legal, Legality
Acton, 37

Legislate
Gould, 287
Montesquieu, 503

Leisure
Disraeli, 207
Gladstone, 278
Hobbes, 323
Hobson, 323
Melville, 485
Mumford, 512
Veblen, 709

Lenin, Leninism
Duncan, 216
Eastman, 218
Khrushchev, 389, 390
Stalin, 658

Lever
Archimedes, 65

Libel
Ellenborough, 230

Liberal, Liberalism
Acton, 36
Anonymous, 62
Arcos, 65, 66
T. Arnold, 69
Berlin, 94
C. Bowles, 108
Broun, 116
Disraeli, 207
Eastman, 218
Evans, 247
Fahey, 247
Gilbert, 277
Gladstone, 278
Hitler, 320
H. Hoover, 331
T. H. Huxley, 345
Ibsen, 346, 347
Institute of Christian Brothers, 353
Jefferson, 375
Kefauver, 385
Leo XIII, 415
John L. Lewis, 417
Lippmann, 434
J. Morley, 508
Morse, 510
Mussolini, 514, 515, 516, 517
Nearing, 521
Newman, 523
Pius IX, 564
F. D. Roosevelt, 592, 594, 595
B. A. Russell, 606
Salazar, 611
A. E. Stevenson, 663
G. Washington, 725

Libertarian
W. O. Douglas, 211
Sprading, 654
Vanzetti, 707

Liberty (see Civil Liberty)
Acton, 35, 36, 37, 38
John Adams, 42, 45
John Quincy Adams, 46
S. Adams, 46, 47

Addison, 48
M. J. Adler, 49
E. Allen, 52
Altgeld, 53
A.C.L.U., 54
Amiel, 55
Andreyev, 57
Anonymous, 59, 60
Aristotle, 67
M. Arnold, 69
Augustine, 71
F. Bacon, 72
Bakunin, 77, 79, 80
Barère, 82
Barlow, 82
Bebel, 86
Bentham, 91
Blackstone, 100
Blake, 101
Boerne, 102
Bolingbroke, 104
Bradlaugh, 109
Brandeis, 111, 112
Burke, 128, 129, 130
Byron, 136
Calhoun, 137
Camus, 139
Carpenter, 146
Carroll, 147
Chapman, 152
Chesterfield, 153, 154
Chesterton, 154
Christian Action, 155
Cicero, 158
Cleghorn, 162
Coleridge, 167
Colton, 168
Coolidge, 176
J. F. Cooper, 177, 178
Coughlin, 181
Cowley, 183
Cromwell, 186
Curran, 187
Dante, 189

Darrow, 190
Debs, 197
Defoe, 198
J. Dewey, 203, 204
J. Edwards, 220
Emerson, 238
Erskine, 246
Euripedes, 246
Franco, 256
Franklin, 257, 258
Garrison, 271
Gibbons, 276
Emma Goldman, 283
Gompers, 286
Gregory XVI, 290
Guthrie, 292
Halifax, 293, 294
Andrew Hamilton, 297
Hand, 297, 298
Hay, 303
Hazlitt, 304
Hearst, 306
Heckscher, 307
Hegel, 307
Henry, 312
Hobbes, 322
Hobson, 323
Hocking, 324
C. E. Hughes, 335
L. Hughes, 335
Ibsen, 347
Ingersoll, 349, 350, 351
Jefferson, 362, 364, 368, 369, 371
S. Johnson, 377, 378
Kallen, 382
Kent, 387
Kett, 388
Kossuth, 393
Laski, 398, 399
D. H. Lawrence, 402
Lecky, 404
Leo XIII, 413
Lieber, 419
Lincoln, 423, 424, 427, 428

Lippmann, 433
Lloyd George, 435
Locke, 435, 436, 437
Loveless, 440
Lyttleton, 449
Macaulay, 453
Machiavelli, 456
MacLeish, 457
J. Madison, 459, 460
Marat, 466
Markham, 468
Mason, 479
Melville, 485
Mencken, 488
Mill, 490, 491, 493, 495
Millikan, 496
Milton, 497, 498, 499
Montesquieu, 502, 503
Montessori, 503, 504
Mussolini, 514, 516
G. Nicholas, 526
O'Connor, 535
Otis, 539
Parsons, 548
Perry, 557
Phillips, 559
Plutarch, 570
Pope, 571
Proudhon, 574
Quintilian, 578
Robespierre, 584, 585
Rockefeller (Jr.), 587
Roland, 587, 588
F. D. Roosevelt, 591, 592
Rouget de Lisle, 599
Rousseau, 599, 600, 601
Ruskin, 604
Rust, 610
Salazar, 611
Segura, 625
Shaw, 631
Sheen, 633
Shelley, 634, 636
Silone, 638

Adam Smith, 640
Socialist Labor Party, 644
Spencer, 648, 649
Spengler, 651
Spinoza, 652
Spooner, 653
Sprading, 654
Stirner, 664
C. Sumner, 667
Sutherland, 669
Tacitus, 672
Thompson, 681
Tocqueville, 686
Vanzetti, 707
Villa, 711
Voltaire, 715, 716
E. Warren, 722
J. Warren, 723
G. Washington, 725, 727
D. Webster, 730, 731
Wells, 732
W. A. White, 736
Whitman, 739, 740
William the Silent, 747
Willkie, 748, 749
W. Wilson, 750, 751, 752
Wise, 753, 754
Wortman, 758
Zenger, 761

License
Chesterfield, 153, 154
D. C. Fisher, 250
Tacitus, 672

Lie, Lying
H. B. Adams, 41
A. Adler, 49
Anonymous, 59, 63
Arbuthnot, 65
Augustine, 70
Baeyens, 75
Bagehot, 76
Bakunin, 78
Bellamy, 88
Blake, 100

Samuel Butler, 133
Byron, 136
Camus, 139
Carlyle, 141
Chesterfield, 154
Chesterton, 155
Commission on Freedom, 170
Disraeli, 208
Dreiser, 215
Duncan, 216
France, 255
G. Herbert, 314
Hitler, 316, 317
O. W. Holmes (Sr.), 327
Ibsen, 348
Kingsley, 392
Lassalle, 400
V. Lindsay, 431
C. B. Luce, 444
Madariaga, 458
Mencken, 487
Mussolini, 518
Nordau, 532
Penn, 555
Plato, 567
Rolland, 588, 589
Sophocles, 646
J. Sterling, 662
A. E. Stevenson, 663
R. L. Stevenson, 664
Tennyson, 679
Twain, 697
Wotton, 758
Yeats, 760

Life, Living
H. B. Adams, 41
S. Adams, 47
A. Adler, 49
S. Anderson, 57
Anonymous, 59
Aristotle, 66
Bogomoletz, 102, 103
Burbank, 126
Samuel Butler, 133

Camus, 138, 139
Cicero, 159
Conrad, 175
Cowley, 183
Dante, 189
J. Dewey, 205
Duncan, 216
Einstein, 225, 228
Euripides, 246
Ferrer, 249
Freud, 260, 263
Goldwyn, 283
Gorky, 286
Harvey, 302
Hippocrates, 316
Hocking, 325
Horace, 332
Ibarruri, 346
W. James, 360
Jefferson, 362, 370
Joyce, 381
Kafka, 382
Keith, 385
Keller, 386
Kent, 387
Khrushchev, 390
La Bruyère, 395
Lenin, 412
L'Estrange, 416
London, 438
Longfellow, 439
Malraux, 462
Mason, 479
Melville, 485
Montaigne, 501
Nietzsche, 527
Norris, 532
O'Neill, 535
Ortega, 537
Pasternak, 551
Pater, 552
Pavlov, 553
Plato, 569
Rank, 579

T. Roosevelt, 595
Royce, 602
Ruskin, 603
B. A. Russell, 605, 608
Santayana, 612
Schopenhauer, 617
Schweitzer, 620, 621, 622
Seneca, 626
Socialist Labor Party, 644
Socrates, 645, 646
Spencer, 650
Thoreau, 682, 685
Tolstoy, 689
Toynbee, 691
Twain, 698
Urey, 704
Van Gogh, 706
Vanzetti, 706, 707
Voltaire, 713
Wagner, 717, 718
Waksman, 719
Whitehead, 737
O. Wilde, 745
Zwingli, 763

Life and Death
Einstein, 221
Engels, 242
O. W. Holmes (Sr.), 327
La Bruyère, 395
T. Mann, 464
Sophocles, 647
O. Wilde, 745

Light
Anonymous, 59
M. Arnold, 69
Croce, 185
Goethe, 282
Latimer, 401
McGee, 483

Lincoln
Herndon, 314
Marx, 474
Stephens, 661

Literature
M. Arnold, 68
Ciardi, 157
C. P. Curtis, 187
Goethe, 283
Khrushchev, 390
Lenin, 407, 408

Longevity
Bogomoletz, 102, 103

Louse
Lenin, 411
Zinsser, 762

Love
A. Adler, 48
Amiel, 55
M. Arnold, 69
Bergson, 93
Bruno, 121
Carpenter, 144, 145
Cicero, 158
Ellis, 231, 232
Freud, 262, 263,
Gandhi, 268
Goethe, 282
Gorky, 287
A. Huxley, 341, 342
E. Key, 388
Lao-Tse, 398
Machiavelli, 453, 454
MacLeish, 457
Menotti, 489
Reik, 580
B. A. Russell, 605
Shelley, 634
Tolstoy, 689
Walwyn, 721
Werfel, 734
T. Wolfe, 755

Loyal, Loyalty
A. Barth, 83
Casement, 147
Commager, 169
Griswold, 291

E. Hubbard, 334
Twain, 697, 699

Lust
B. Adams, 39
Aristotle, 66
M. Arnold, 69
Buchanan, 124
Robert Burton, 132
D. H. Lawrence, 402
Spinoza, 651

Luther, Lutheran, Lutheranism
Erasmus, 244
Heine, 309
Inge, 349
Paine, 541
Shaw, 631
Thoreau, 683

Luxury
Augustine, 71
Bellamy, 88
Buchanan, 124
Clement, 163
Cleveland, 163
Einstein, 226
Livy, 434
Montesquieu, 502
Thoreau, 682

Lynch, Lynching
D. H. Lawrence, 402
Pegler, 554
U.S. Army, 701

M

Machiavelli
Acton, 38
Mussolini, 453

Machine
Anonymous, 62
Haywood, 304
Lafargue, 396
Lilienthal, 420

Lucian, 445
Marx, 475, 477
O. Wilde, 743
Wright, 759

Magazine
Hand, 298
Ingersoll, 352
H. James, 358
H. R. Luce, 445

Magna Carta
Coke, 167
Lincoln, 424
N. Webster, 731

Majority
Acton, 35, 36
A. Barth, 83
C. A. Beard, 85
Berlin, 94
Brandeis, 113
Bruno, 121
Burke, 126
Calhoun, 137
Chafee, 149
Crossman, 187
J. Davis, 195
Debs, 196
Disraeli, 208
Goethe, 283
Guérard, 291,
Hazlitt, 305
Hitler, 318
O. W. Holmes (Sr.), 327
O. W. Holmes (Jr.), 330
Aldous Huxley, 340
Ibsen, 346
Ingersoll, 351
A. Jackson, 355
Jaurès, 362
Jefferson, 364
Lehman, 406
Lincoln, 426
Machiavelli, 455
J. Madison, 460
Mencken, 486

Mill, 490, 494
Phillips, 559
T. B. Reed, 580
James P. Roche, 586
Sloan, 640
Stalin, 658
Thoreau, 682, 684, 685
Tocqueville, 687
Tolstoy, 691
Truman, 694
Twain, 697
U. S. Army, 700
D. Webster, 728
Whitehead, 737
O. Wilde, 746
Wilhelm II, 746

Malice
Cicero, 159
Molière, 499

Mammon
Pearson, 553
Whittier, 742

Man, Mankind
Abu'l-Ala, 35
Acton, 36
H. B. Adams, 40, 41
John Adams, 43, 44
S. Adams, 47
Addams, 48
A. Adler, 48
M. J. Adler, 49
E. Allen, 51, 52
Amiel, 55
Andreyev, 57
Anonymous, 63
Anthony, 64
Archer, 65
Aristotle, 66, 67
M. Arnold, 68, 69
Augustine, 71
F. Bacon, 72, 73, 74
Bagehot, 76
Baha' u' llah, 76
Bakunin, 76, 77, 78

Baruch, 84
Bentham, 91
Berkman, 93
Berlin, 93
Blackstone, 99
Blum, 102
Brougham, 116
Browne, 118
Bruno, 121
Bryan, 122
Burke, 127, 128
R. Burns, 131
Cicero, 159
Condorcet, 172
Cowley, 183
d'Annunzio, 189
Darwin, 191, 192, 193
Disraeli, 207
Donne, 209
Dostoyevski, 210
Einstein, 223, 224, 227
T. S. Eliot, 230
Emerson, 232, 238
Erskine, 246
Faulkner, 248
Fontenelle, 252
Franklin, 258
Freud, 260
Fromm, 264
Garrison, 269
Gissing, 278
Emma Goldman, 283
Alexander Hamilton, 295
Hawthorne, 303
Hazlitt, 305
Hemingway, 311
Hersey, 315
d'Holbach, 326, 327
Horton, 331
Humboldt, 337
W. James, 359, 361
Jefferson, 375
Jones, 380
Kent, 387

Kierkegaard, 391
Kirkpatrick, 392
Lalor, 397
Joseph Lewis, 418
Lilienthal, 421
Lindner, 430
Machiavelli, 454, 455, 456
Malraux, 462
Marcus Aurelius, 467
Markham, 468
Masefield, 478
Maugham, 481
Mead, 484
Menander, 486
Mencken, 486
Mill, 492, 494, 495
Milton, 497, 498
T. E. Murray, 512
National Catholic Federation, 520
Nietzsche, 528
Orwell, 538
Paine, 541, 543
Paracelsus, 546
Pascal, 549, 550
Pasternak, 550
Pasteur, 551, 552
Pestalozzi, 557
Plekhanov, 569
Plutarch, 570
Pope, 571
Protagoras, 574
Proudhon, 575
Richelieu, 583
F. D. Roosevelt, 590, 594
Rouget de Lisle, 599
B. A. Russell, 605, 606, 607
Sandburg, 611, 612,
Sartre, 615
Schopenhauer, 618
Schweitzer, 621, 623
Shelley, 633, 634, 635, 636
L. Smith, 643
Socialist Labor Party, 644
Spinoza, 652

Steinmetz, 661
W. G. Sumner, 667
Swift, 670
Tawney, 675, 677
Tennyson, 678
Terence, 679
Thomas à Kempis, 680
Thoreau, 682, 683, 684, 685
Tillotson, 686
Tocqueville, 687
Vanzetti, 706, 707
Veblen, 708, 709
Volney, 712
Wagner, 718
B. T. Washington, 724
G. Washington, 724, 725, 727
Wells, 732, 733
Whitehead, 737, 738
O. Wilde, 745, 746
W. Wilson, 752
Wise, 753

Manifest Destiny
O'Sullivan, 538

Manufacturer
C. A. Beard, 85
P. Cooper, 179
France, 256
Adam Smith, 641
W. Wilson, 750

Marines
Smedley Butler, 134
Sherman, 637

Market, Marketplace
Acton, 37
Anacharsis, 56
F. Bacon, 73, 74
E. Davis, 195
France, 256
Mahan, 461
Ricardo, 582

Marriage
Anonymous, 59
Bakunin, 77

Calvin, 137
Canon Laws, 139
Carpenter, 145
Council of Trent, 182
Darwin, 192
Jerome, 376
E. Key, 388
Keyserling, 389
The Koran, 393
Lindsey, 431
Luther, 447
Malthus, 463
Marx, 472
Menander, 486
Nietzsche, 528
Pius XI, 565
Ricardo, 582
Shelley, 636

Martial Law
D. Davis, 195

Martyr
Cardozo, 140
Colton, 168
Emerson, 235
S. Johnson, 377
Mencken, 487
Phillips, 559
Schnitzler, 617
Tertullian, 679
Whitman, 739

Marx, Marxism
M. J. Adler, 49
Anonymous, 62
Bakunin, 78
C. A. Beard, 85
Berlin, 93
DeLeon, 200
Eastman, 218
Einstein, 223
Engels, 241, 242
Hitler, 318
Jaspers, 361
Khrushchev, 389, 390
Lenin, 407, 409, 411

H. R. Luce, 445
C. A. Madison, 458
Maritain, 467
Marx, 476
Muller, 511
Niebuhr, 526
Pasternak, 550, 551
Pius XII, 566
T. Roosevelt, 598
B. A. Russell, 607
Seldes, 626
Shaw, 632
Sorel, 647
Viereck, 710
H. A. Wallace, 720
Wells, 732

Mass (The)
Cromwell, 186
D. C. Fisher, 250
Henry IV, 311
Luther, 446, 447
William the Silent, 747
Wolsey, 756

Mass Communication
Commission on Freedom, 170, 171
Seldes, 626
Strachey, 665

Masses
American Legion, 54
Bakunin, 76, 79
C. A. Beard, 85
Brougham, 116
Browne, 118
Browning, 119
Bruno, 121
Bryan, 122
Bryce, 123
Burke, 129
J. H. Burns, 130
Smedley Butler, 134
Calhoun, 137
Carpenter, 144
Catholic Bishops, 148

Chase, 153
Chesterfield, 154
J. F. Cooper, 179
Einstein, 222
Emerson, 235
Freud, 261, 262
H. George, 275
Gladstone, 279
Alexander Hamilton, 295, 296
Hitler, 317, 320
Hoffer, 325
Horace, 332
Humboldt, 337
Ibsen, 348
R. H. Jackson, 356
Jung, 381
D. H. Lawrence, 402
Leo XIII, 414
Machiavelli, 454, 456
Mao Tse-tung, 466
McCarthy, 483
Montesquieu, 502
Mussolini, 513
Ortega, 537
Owen, 540
Polybius, 571
Pottier, 572
Sandburg, 612
Stalin, 655
Talleyrand, 672
Thoreau, 682, 683, 684
U.S. Army, 700
Whitehead, 737
Whitman, 740

Master
Acton, 36
M. J. Adler, 49
Ball, 80
Debs, 196
Demosthenes, 202

Material, Materiel
Banse, 82
Baruch, 84
Clausewitz, 161, 162

Materialism, Materialist
H. B. Adams, 41
Bernstein, 95
Engels, 241
Jefferson, 373
Marx, 471
Moltke, 500
Treitschke, 692

Mean (The Golden) (see Golden Mean)
F. Bacon, 74
Horace, 332

Means (see Ends and Means)
Disraeli, 207
Hitler, 318
Thoreau, 683

Means of Production
M. J. Adler, 49
Engels, 241
Lenin, 408, 410
Oxnam, 540
Strachey, 666

Media (see Communication)
Evjue, 247
Farrell, 247
Kennan, 387
Laski, 399
Seldes, 626
Sevareid, 627
U.S. Congress, 702

Medicine
Aristotle, 66
Osler, 538
Rush, 603

Mediocrity
Acton, 36
Carlyle, 142
J. F. Cooper, 178
Einstein, 222
Mill, 495
Pascal, 549
Schopenhauer, 617, 618

Melting-Pot
Zangwill, 760

Merchants
  J. F. Cooper, 179
  Erasmus, 244
  Jefferson, 368
  Adam Smith, 641
  G. Washington, 724, 725

Merchants of Death
  Briand, 114
  Smedley Butler, 135
  Davenport, 193
  League of Nations, 403

Metaphysics
  Bakunin, 78
  Comte, 171
  Erigena, 245
  Mencken, 487

Microbes
  Waksman, 719

Middle Class (see Bourgeois)
  Aristotle, 67
  M. Arnold, 69
  Brownson, 120

Might (see Power)
  Ball, 80
  Bebel, 86

Military, Militarism, Military Mind
  Acton, 37
  J. H. Burns, 130
  D. Davis, 194
  de Gaulle, 198
  Eisenhower, 228
  Foch, 252
  von der Goltz, 285
  W. James, 361
  MacArthur, 450
  Maupassant, 481
  D. Russell, 609
  Spencer, 649
  Sun Tzu, 668
  G. Washington, 727
  D. Webster, 728
  Zimmerman, 761

Mind
  B. Adams, 39
  H. B. Adams, 40, 41
  John Adams, 42
  Alcott, 51
  Amiel, 55
  M. Arnold, 68, 69
  F. Bacon, 72, 73, 74
  Bakunin, 77
  H. W. Beecher, 87
  Blake, 100
  Brandeis, 111
  V. W. Brooks, 115
  Bruno, 121
  R. Burns, 131
  Burroughs, 131
  Richard F. Burton, 132
  Samuel Butler, 133
  Byron, 136
  Channing, 151
  Colton, 168
  Confucius, 174
  Coolidge, 176
  Eddy, 218, 219
  Edison, 219
  Emerson, 233
  Freud, 261
  E. Hamilton, 297
  Hawkes, 303
  Ingersoll, 350
  R. H. Jackson, 356
  W. James, 360
  Jefferson, 364
  Juvenal, 382
  Krupskaya, 395
  Lao-Tse, 398
  Laski, 399
  Leonardo, 415
  Lucretius, 445
  MacLeish, 457
  Tocqueville, 687
  Virgil, 711
  Wortman, 758

Minority
Acton, 35, 36
A. Barth, 83
D. Brown, 117
Carlyle, 141
Debs, 196
W. O. Douglas, 213
Eastman, 218
Einstein, 222
Emerson, 239
Alexander Hamilton, 295
O. W. Holmes (Sr.), 327
O. W. Holmes (Jr.), 330
Ibsen, 346, 347
Jefferson, 364
Landon, 397
Lincoln, 426
Phillips, 559, 562
Alfred E. Smith, 642
B. Smith, 642
Thoreau, 683
E. Warren, 723
Willkie, 748

Miracle, Miracles
John Adams, 43
E. Allen, 52
Amiel, 56
M. Arnold, 68
Augustine, 70
Berenson, 92
Brandeis, 112
Emerson, 236
Goethe, 282
Heine, 309
Herndon, 314
O. W. Holmes (Jr.), 329
E. Hubbard, 334
Hume, 338
Inge, 349
Jefferson, 371, 373
Lincoln, 427
Paine, 541, 544
Pascal, 550
Renan, 581

Rousseau, 602
Spinoza, 651, 653
Urey, 704
Vatican Council, 707
E. Young, 760

Mistake
Cromwell, 186

Mob, Mobs
Byron, 136
Chesterfield, 154
Claudian, 160
de Gaulle, 198
Diogenes, 206
Frederick II, 259
Galton, 266
D. H. Lawrence, 402
Lucretius, 445
MacArthur, 450
Mencius, 486
Mill, 494
Seneca, 627
H. Walpole, 721
Wright, 759

Moderation
Burke, 128
Milton, 498
Terence, 679
Valéry, 705

Mohammedan
John Adams, 45
Voltaire, 716

Monarch, Monarchy
Acton, 36, 37
Bellarmine, 89
Alexander Hamilton, 295, 296
Montesquieu, 502
Paine, 543
Zenger, 761

Money
Franklin P. Adams, 40
H. B. Adams, 40, 41
Agassiz, 50
S. Anderson, 56

Angell, 58
F. Bacon, 73
Baruch, 84
C. A. Beard, 85
Bellamy, 88
Blake, 101
Bryan, 121, 122
Canute, 139
Carlyle, 141
Chesterton, 154
Cicero, 158, 159
Coolidge, 176
P. Cooper, 180
Debs, 196
Epicurus, 244
Ford, 253
Francis Xavier, 256
Garfield, 269
H. George, 274
Halifax, 293
Heine, 309
J. H. Holmes, 327
Horace, 332
A. Huxley, 342
R. H. Jackson, 356
S. Johnson, 378
Juvenal, 382
Keynes, 389
Khrushchev, 391
Leggett, 406
Macauley, 453
Machiavelli, 456
Macleod, 458
J. Madison, 458
Marx, 474
Masefield, 479
Maugham, 481
More, 505
G. Murray, 512
Nash, 519
Phillips, 561
Philo, 562
Plutarch, 570
Raskob, 579

Rockefeller (Sr.), 586
F. D. Roosevelt, 590, 591
T. Roosevelt, 596
Ruskin, 604
Sandburg, 611
Schopenhauer, 617
Shaw, 629, 630, 631
Singleton, 640
Socrates, 645
Sophocles, 647
Steffens, 660
Stein, 660
R. L. Stevenson, 664
Tagore, 672
Tertullian, 680
Thoreau, 682, 684
Tolstoy, 688, 691,
Vanderlip, 705
Vanzetti, 707
Veblen, 709
Vickers, 710
D. Webster, 730
E. B. White, 734
W. Wilson, 749

Monism
Haeckel, 292
W. James, 360
Monks
Erasmus, 244, 245
Thomas à Kempis, 680, 681
Monogamy
von Kemnitz, 386
E. Key, 388
Monopoly
Bancroft, 81
Carnegie, 143
Cleveland, 164
A. Jackson, 354, 355
Jefferson, 368
T. L. Johnson, 379
Kingsley, 392
Kropotkin, 394
Lerner, 415
H. D. Lloyd, 434

Marx, 475
G. W. Norris, 533
Parsons, 548
Adam Smith, 641
Strachey, 666
W. Wilson, 749, 751

Moral, Morals, Morality
Acton, 37, 38
John Adams, 42
Addison, 48
F. Bacon, 72
Bakunin, 77
K. Barth, 83
Bennett, 90
Bok, 103
Camus, 138
Cardozo, 140
Christian Action, 155
Confucius, 173, 174
Croce, 185
C. Darwin, 192, 193
Ellis, 231
Emerson, 234
Froude, 264
Greeley, 289
Griswold, 291
Hazlitt, 305
Hegel, 307
Hemingway, 310, 311
Hume, 338
Kant, 383, 384
Kenkò, 387
Lecky, 404
Legion of Decency, 406
Lenin, 410, 411
Machiavelli, 454
Manning, 465
Marx, 472
Nietzsche, 527
Pauling, 552
Peirce, 554
Spencer, 649
Vatican Council, 707
Voltaire, 716

Morale
Baruch, 84
Clausewitz, 161
Eisenhower, 228
E. Key, 388
Lenin, 408
Napoleon, 519
Morons
Anonymous, 63
Mother, Motherhood
Ellis, 232
Jung, 381
Lindsey, 431, 432
Motion Pictures
Clark, 159
Evjue, 247
Hand 298
Laski, 399
Pius XI, 566
Rogers, 587
Motivation
Hayakawa, 303
La Rochefoucauld, 398
W. G. Sumner, 667
Muck, Muckrakers
F. Bacon, 73
C. E. Hughes, 335
T. Roosevelt, 596
Murder
Acton, 37
A. Adler, 49
Bunyan, 125
Einstein, 224
Freud, 263
Tolstoy, 689
E. Young, 760
Music
Beethoven, 88
Hammerstein, 297
Mussolini
Berenson, 92
Churchill, 156
Jung, 381

A. M. Lindbergh, 429
Pius XI, 566

Mutual Aid
Kropotkin, 394

Mystery
Amiel, 56
Burke, 127
Malraux, 462

Mysticism
Schweitzer, 621

Myth
John Mason Brown, 118
V. Fisher, 250
Hocking, 324
W. James, 361
B. A. Russell, 609

N

Name, Names
Anonymous, 63
F. Bacon, 74
Chapman, 152
Halifax, 293
E. Hubbard, 334

Napoleon
John Adams, 44
Nietzsche, 528

Nation, Nationality
Acton, 37
John Adams, 45
Addison, 48
Addington, 51
Angell, 58
Aonymous, 63
Banse, 82
Barlow, 82
Beccaria, 86
D. Bliss, 102
Burke, 130
Delbrueck, 199
Einstein, 221

Emerson, 236
France, 254
Goethe, 283
Harding, 299
Hegel, 308
Herzl, 315
W. James, 359
Kant, 383
Leo XIII, 414
Melville, 485
Montesquieu, 502, 503
O'Flaherty, 535
F. D. Roosevelt, 592
Selassie, 625
Swift, 670
Treitschke, 692
Truman, 694
Veblen, 710
G. Washington, 727

National Association
U.S. Congress, 702

National Debt
Alexander Hamilton, 295
A. Jackson, 354

National Resources
Chase, 153

Nature, Natural Law
John Adams, 44
S. Adams, 47
Aristotle, 67
F. Bacon, 73, 74, 75
Bakunin, 77
Beccaria, 86
Beerbohm, 87
Bolivar, 105
Samuel Butler, 133
Condorcet, 172
Darwin, 192
Hobbes, 322
d'Holbach, 326, 327
Jones, 380
Kirkpatrick, 392
Locke, 436, 437

Lysenko, 449
Pope, 571
Rousseau, 600, 601, 602
Shaw, 629
Spinoza, 653
Thoreau, 684
Wright, 759

Natural Selection
C. Darwin, 192
Ellis, 232
A. R. Wallace, 719

Navy
Mahan, 416

Naziism
Ameringer, 54
Anonymous, 60
Churchill, 156
Goebbels, 281
Hitler, 319
S. Lewis, 418
Meany, 484
Rosenberg, 598

Necessity
Aeschylus, 50
Augustine, 70
Carlyle, 142, 143
Diogenes, 206
Einstein, 221
Hegel, 307
Jefferson, 370
Landor, 397
Leonardo, 415
Milton, 499
Pitt (Jr.), 563
Plato, 568
Publilius Syrus, 576
Shelley, 635
Spinoza, 652

Need, Needs
Bakunin, 80
Basil, 84
Einstein, 221, 227

Negro
Benedict-Weltfish, 90
J. W. Booth, 106
Bridges, 114
John Brown, 117,
S. A. Douglas, 211
DuBois, 215, 216
Fitzhugh, 251
Harlan, 300
L. Hughes, 335
Jefferson, 368
Kosciusko, 393
Lee, 405
Lincoln, 422, 423, 425, 428
Lowell, 443
Marx, 475
W. L. Menninger, 489
Robeson, 583
T. Roosevelt, 595
Rosenberg, 598
Sherman, 637
Stephens, 662
Stowe, 665
Taney, 673, 674
U.S. Supreme Court, 702
E. Warren, 722
G. Washington, 726
D. Webster, 731
Whittier, 741

Neighbor
A. Adler, 48
Bagehot, 75

Neurosis, Neurotic
A. Adler, 49
Berlin, 94
Freud, 261, 262, 263
Jaspers, 362
Jung, 381
Lindner, 430
Proust, 576
Reik, 580

Neutral, Neutrality
Brandeis, 112
Chapin, 152

S. A. Douglas, 211
Dryden, 215
Hitler, 319

New Deal
Lloyd George, 435
F. D. Roosevelt, 590

New Order
Hitler, 317

News
Bogart, 102
Brandeis, 110
Ciardi, 157
Commission on Freedom, 171
Dana, 188
Darrow, 190
Disraeli, 207
Goebbels, 281
Hearst, 305, 306
Homer, 331
Jonson, 380
Laski, 400
John L. Lewis, 416
Markel, 468
Ochs, 534
Quarles, 577
Ross, 599
Sinclair, 639
Tammen, 673
Voltaire, 713
H. A. Wallace, 720
J. Ward, 721
W. A. White, 735

Newspaper
John Adams, 43
Ameringer, 54
Anonymous, 59
Bennett, 90
Bent, 90
Beveridge, 96
V. W. Brooks, 115
Broun, 116
Carlyle, 141, 142
Chapman, 152

Chekhov, 153
Cockburn, 165
J. F. Cooper, 179
Cowles, 183
Crawford, 184
Dana, 188
Daniels, 189
Desmoulins, 202
Flaubert, 251
France, 255
Gibbs, 277
Gitt, 278
Greeley, 289
Hearst, 305, 306
Heine, 309
Hitler, 321
J. H. Holmes, 327
Ickes, 348
Ingersoll, 352
R. H. Jackson, 358
H. James, 358
W. James, 361
Jefferson, 365, 366, 367, 368
La Follette, 396
Lassalle, 400, 401
League of Nations, 403
Leggett, 405
Lenin, 407
Lerner, 415
H. R. Luce, 445
Mailer, 461
Marx, 477
Mencken, 487
Mill, 494
H. Morgan, 506
Mussolini, 513
Napoleon, 519
Nash, 519
N.A.M., 520
A. B. Parker, 546
Patterson, 552
Phillips, 561
Populist Party, 572
Proudhon, 575

Rogers, 587
Ross, 599
Sandburg, 612
Scripps, 624
Shaw, 632, 633
Sinclair, 639
Sulzberger, 666
Swope, 672
Tammen, 673
Thoreau, 684
Truman, 694
Twain, 697
U.S. Congress, 702
U.S. Supreme Court, 703
J. Ward, 721, 722
W. A. White, 735, 736
Wilhelm II, 746

New Testament
Buckle, 125
Hitler, 321

Nihilist
Turgenev, 695

Noise
Schopenhauer, 617

Non-conformity
Beerbohm, 87
Hugo L. Black, 98
Commager, 170
Coolidge, 176
W. O. Douglas, 213
Einstein, 224
Emerson, 237
Gitt, 278
Hand, 297
Hecht, 307
Hobson, 324
C. E. Hughes, 335
R. H. Jackson, 356
Lindner, 430
V. Lindsay, 431
Luxemburg, 448
Masson, 479
Pasternak, 550

John P. Roche, 586
Seldes, 625
Shahn, 628
Williams, 747
Woolf, 756

Non-cooperation
Gandhi, 267

Non-resistance
Hutterites, 340
New Hampshire, 522

Non-violence
Gandhi, 267, 268

Nordic
Hitler, 319
Rosenberg, 598

Normal, Normalcy
Harding, 299, 300
Horney, 333

Nothingness
Malraux, 462
Nuclear Power

Nuclear Power
Christian Action, 155
Einstein, 223
Pauling, 552

O

Oath
Anonymous, 63
Beccaria, 86
Emmett, 240
Hutterites, 340
R. H. Jackson, 356
Weltfish, 734
Wilhelm, 746

Obedience
Emerson, 236
Wilhelm II, 746

Obscenity
Bok, 103
Brennan, 113

Ellis, 231
Hand, 299
Schroeder, 619
Woolsey, 756

Opinion
Acton, 35, 36, 38
F. Bacon, 72, 74
Bagehot, 76
Ballou, 81
Bancroft, 82
Blake, 100
Borah, 106
Brandeis, 111
Brennan, 113
Bryant, 123
Burke, 127
Samuel Butler, 133
Carlyle, 141
Carpenter, 145
Chafee, 149
Cicero, 159
Cobb, 165
Coke, 166
Comte, 171
Conant, 172
Confucius, 174
Cooke, 176
T. Cooper, 180
Defoe, 198
Einstein, 227
Emerson, 239
Epictetus, 243
France, 255
Goethe, 283
Gregory XVI, 290
Hazlitt, 304
Hitler, 321
d'Holbach, 325, 326
O. W. Holmes (Jr.), 328
C. E. Hughes, 335
Hume, 339
Ibsen, 346, 347
R. H. Jackson, 356, 357
Jefferson, 363, 365, 375

Jeffrey, 375
S. Johnson, 377, 378
Lippmann, 433
Locke, 435
Lowell, 440
Lucas, 444
Lytton, 449
Macaulay, 452
T. Mann, 464,
Marcus Aurelius, 466
Markel, 468
Melville, 485
Mill, 490, 491, 492, 493, 494, 495, 496
Montaigne, 501
J. Morley, 508
Paine, 545
Pascal, 549
Petigru, 558
Phillips, 559
Roland, 588
B. A. Russell, 608
Alfred. E. Smith, 642
Spencer, 649
Spinoza, 652
Turgot, 695
Twain, 697
United Nations, 700
Voltaire, 713, 716
N. Ward, 722
Wortman, 757, 758
Yeats, 760

Opposition
Acton, 35
Disraeli, 207
Galsworthy, 266
Hobbes, 322
W. James, 360
Lippmann, 433
Mussolini, 515
Truman, 694

Oppression
Acton, 36
F. Bacon, 73
John Brown, 117

E. Darwin, 193
Garrison, 270
Kossuth, 393, 394
Locke, 437

Optimism
Ellis, 231
Sinclair, 639

Order
Bok, 103
Mussolini, 515
Valéry, 704
Veblen, 710
Wagner, 718, 719
Whittier, 714

Organize, Organization
Hill, 316
Kingsley, 392
John D. Lewis, 417

Orthodoxy
Franklin, 258
Hand, 297
Higgins, 315
T. H. Huxley, 346
Ingersoll, 351
R. H. Jackson, 357
Lessing, 416
Lippmann, 432
Orwell, 537

P

Pacifist, Pacifism
Smedley Butler, 134
Hitler, 318, 319
T. Roosevelt, 597
Schwimmer, 623

Pagan, Paganism
Augustine,71
Wordsworth, 757

Pain
Bentham, 91
Einstein, 221

Jefferson, 368
Nietzsche, 527
Schopenhauer, 617
Spencer, 648, 649

Papacy (See Pope)
S. Adams, 47
Calvin, 138
Chapman, 152
Hobbes, 322
Hus, 339
Landor, 397
Luther, 447, 448
J. Madison, 460
Newman, 522
Williams, 747, 748
Wollstonecraft, 756

Parasite
Masters, 480
Zinsser, 762

Parliament
Bright, 114
Cromwell, 186
Sheridan, 636

Party
Acton, 36
Arbuthnot, 65
Benton, 91
Burke, 127
Cleveland, 163
Coolidge, 177
J. F. Cooper, 179
Defoe, 198
de Gaulle, 198
Disraeli, 208
Emerson, 236
Franco, 256
Garfield, 269
H. George, 275
Gilbert, 277
Halifax, 293
Havemeyer, 302
Hayes, 303
Hitler, 319

Hugo, 336
Morrow, 510
T. B. Reed, 580
A. E. Stevenson, 662
E. Warren 723
Weller, 731
Whately, 734

Passion
Aristotle, 67
Bakunin, 77
Berlin, 94
Hegel, 308
Helvetius, 310
Hobbes, 322
O. W. Holmes (Jr.), 328
Horace, 333
Jung, 381
Thomas à Kempis, 681

Past
Andreyev, 57
Bergson, 92
Browne, 119
Henry, 312
G. W. Johnson, 376
Volney, 712

Patriotism (also, Super-patriotism)
Acton, 37
Aldington, 51
B. F. Bache, 72
Bebel, 86
Bellamy, 88
Bernhardi, 95
Brann, 113
Bryan, 136
Campbell, 138
Cavell, 149
Chesterton, 154, 155
Dryden, 215
Einstein, 226
Emmet, 240
Gerry, 276
Hobson, 323
L. Hughes, 335
Inge, 349

R. H. Jackson, 357
Jefferson, 368
S. Johnson, 377
D. S. Jordan, 380
Lee, 405
Le Gallienne, 405
Maupassant, 481
Nathan, 520
Paine, 542
Quay, 577
Ruskin, 603
Schopenhauer, 617, 618
Shaw, 631, 633
A. E. Stevenson, 663
Story, 665
Tolstoy, 688, 689
Treitschke, 692
U. S. Army, 701
Veblen, 708
G. Washington, 726
W. A. White, 736
O. Wilde, 745

St. Paul
Jefferson, 373
Shaw, 628, 629
Wells, 733

Peace
Acton, 37
Angell, 57
M. Arnold, 69
Baha' u' llah, 76
Bernhardi, 95
Bethmann-Hollweg, 95
Blum, 102
Briand, 114
Bright, 114
Bryan, 136
Calgacus, 137
Chamberlain, 151
Cicero, 159
Cousins, 182
Disraeli, 207
Einstein, 227
Epicurus, 244

J. A. Fisher, 250
V. Fisher, 250
B. A. Fiske, 250
Franklin, 258, 259
von der Goltz, 285
Henry, 312
Hobbes, 322
I.C.F.T.U., 353
W. James, 360
Kant, 383
Kossuth, 393
Lenin, 411
Libby, 419
Litvinov, 434
Longfellow, 439
Ludendorff, 445
Luther, 448
G. C. Marshall, 470
K. Menninger, 488
Mussolini, 517, 518
Napoleon, 518
Nobel, 531
Radford, 578
T. Roosevelt, 595
Rosenberg, 598
Y. Sterling, 662
Tacitus, 672
Tennyson, 678
Truman, 695
United Nations, 700
Wells, 732
Whitman, 741
Whittier, 741
W. Wilson, 752
Zangwill, 761

People
Acton, 37
John Adams, 43, 44, 45
S. Adams, 46
Alcuin, 51
Alfonso X, 51
Altgeld, 53
S. Anderson, 56
Angell, 58

Anonymous, 60, 61, 64
Bancroft, 81, 82
Barlow, 82
Bellarmine, 89
Benton, 91
Berenson, 92
Burbank, 125
Burke, 129
Campanella, 138
Cato, 148
Cicero, 158
Clausewitz, 161
Cleveland, 163
Colton, 168
Cromwell, 186
Davitt, 195
Debs, 196
Demosthenes, 202
Desmoulins, 203
Disraeli, 208
Durante, 217
Eastman, 218
Elliott, 231
Fahey, 247
Grant, 288
Harrington, 301
Hay, 303
Hegel, 308
Herron, 314
Hugo, 336
Ireland, 353
Jefferson, 364, 374, 375
Lao-Tse, 398
Macaulay, 453
Machiavelli, 453, 454, 455, 456
J. Madison, 460
Mao Tse-tung, 466
J. Marshall, 470
Mason, 479
McGee, 483
Milton, 499
Montesquieu, 502
G. Morris, 509
W. Morris, 510

Mussolini, 513, 515
F. Norris, 532
Owen, 539
Parrington, 547
Parsons, 548
Pearse, 553
Philipps, 561
Plato, 568
Priestley, 573, 574
Reuther, 581
Robespierre, 584, 585
B. Smith, 642, 643
Spengler, 651
Stalin, 657, 658
Tocqueville, 686
Treitschke, 692
Van Buren, 705
Voltaire, 713, 715
G. Washington, 727
D. Webster, 729
Whitman, 738, 739, 741
O. Wilde, 743, 746
Williams, 748
W. Wilson, 751, 753
Wise, 754
T. Wolfe, 754, 755
Wycliffe, 759

People (American) (see America)
John Adams, 44
S. Adams, 46
Lincoln, 424, 425, 428
Sandburg, 612

Persecution
Acton, 37
Bagehot, 76
Emerson, 235
J. Fiske, 250
Franklin, 259
Kallen, 382
Taylor, 677
Voltaire, 717

Persuasion
Bernays, 95

Pervert
A. Adler, 49
Philistine
M. Arnold, 68
Philosophy
Amiel, 55, 56
Anonymous, 61
Aristotle, 68
F. Bacon, 72, 74
Bakunin, 78
Browne, 118
Bruno, 121
Cohen, 166
Comte, 171
S. Crane, 184
Croce, 185
Diderot, 205
Durant, 217
Epictetus, 243
Frederick II, 259
Harvey, 302
W. James, 359
Kant, 383
Keynes, 389
Lewes, 416
Marx, 471, 476
Montaigne, 501
Mussolini, 514
Nietzsche, 528
Peirce, 554
Plato, 567, 568
Royce, 602
Schopenhauer, 618
Spinoza, 652, 653
Whitehead, 738
Pie (in the Sky)
Hill, 316
Pilate
F. Bacon, 75
Platitudes
N. Douglas, 210
Hand, 298
Mencken, 488
Santayana, 614

Pleasure
  Abd-el-Raham, 35
  Bentham, 91
  Samuel Butler, 133
  Kropotkin, 394
Plutocracy
  J. P. Morgan, 506
Poison
  Blake, 100
  Paracelsus, 546
Policy
  Clausewitz, 160, 161
  Lloyd George, 435
Politics, Political, Politician
  Acton, 36, 38
  H. B. Adams, 40
  Ameringer, 55
  Arbuthnot, 65
  Arcos, 65
  Aristotle, 66, 67, 68
  Bakunin, 77
  C. A. Beard, 85
  Bebel, 86
  Bellarmine, 89
  Bierce, 96
  Bismarck, 97
  John Mason Brown, 118
  Burke, 129
  Cameron, 138
  Chesterfield, 154
  Clarke, 160
  Clausewitz, 160, 161
  Cobb, 165
  Coleridge, 167
  Disraeli, 207, 208
  Emerson, 235, 236
  Epicurus, 244
  Franco, 256
  Garfield, 269
  Henry George, 274
  Gibbons, 276
  Alexander Hamilton, 296
  Havemeyer, 302
  Hazlitt, 305

  Hearst, 306
  Hellman, 310
  Hillman, 316
  E. W. Howe, 333
  L. M. Howe, 333
  Hutchins, 340
  A. Huxley, 341
  Jefferson, 369
  Kant, 384
  Lenin, 412
  Leo XIII, 413
  Lincoln, 427, 428
  Lowell, 444
  Machiavelli, 454
  T. Mann, 464
  Manning, 465
  Mao Tse-tung, 466
  Mencken, 488
  Mill, 493
  Monroe, 500
  Nathan, 520
  Nkrumah, 531
  Orwell, 538
  Parrington, 548
  Penrose, 556
  Pepper, 556
  Plunkitt, 570
  Plutarch, 570
  Quay, 577
  Rogers, 587
  T. Roosevelt, 598
  Silone, 639
  Steffens, 660
  A. E. Stevenson, 663
  Swift, 669
  Talleyrand, 673
  Valéry, 705
  W. H. Vanderbilt 705
  G. Washington, 726
Polygamy
  The Koran, 393
Poor
  Acton, 35, 36
  M. Arnold, 69

John Brown, 117
Cobbett, 165
S. Johnson, 378
Moore, 505
More, 505
Saint-Simon, 611
Sorel, 648
Steinbeck, 660, 661
Tolstoy, 689
Voltaire, 714

Pope, Popery
Acton, 36, 38
John Adams, 46
S. Adams, 47
E. Allen, 52
Bellarmine, 89
Blavatsky, 101
Boniface VIII, 105
Erasmus, 244, 245
T. Fuller, 265
Garibaldi, 269
Gregory VII, 290
O. W. Holmes (Sr.), 327
Hus, 339
T. H. Huxley, 344
Ingersoll, 350, 352
Leo XIII, 413
Luther, 446, 447, 448
McCabe, 482
Milton, 497
Phillips, 559
Pius IX, 564
Savonarola, 616
Selden, 625
Stalin, 658
Stephanus, 661
Twain, 696
Vatican Council, 707
O. Wilde, 744, 746
W. Wilson, 751

Population
Bergson, 93
Einstein, 224
Malthus, 463

Possessions
Einstein, 226
Epicurus, 244
Vivekananda, 712

Poverty
John Adams, 43
M. J. Adler, 49
Aristotle, 67
Bellamy, 88
R. Burns, 131
Carpenter, 144
Cassiodorus, 148
Cleveland, 163
Confucius, 173, 174
Cowley, 183
C. Darwin, 192
DeLeon, 200
Democritus, 201
Emerson, 235
H. George, 272, 273, 275
H. C. Hoover, 331
W. James, 361
S. Johnson, 377, 378
Juvenal, 382
La Bruyère, 395
Lincoln, 427
Malthus, 463
Michelet, 489
Montesquieu, 502
Newman, 524
O'Neill, 535
Paine, 543
F. D. Roosevelt, 592
Shaw, 630
Shelley, 635
Adam Smith, 640
Socrates, 645
Story, 665
Tawney, 676
Thomas, 681
Thucydides, 685
Vickers, 710

Power (see Might)
Abd-el-Raham, 35

Acton, 35, 36, 37, 38
B. Adams, 39
H. B. Adams, 40, 41
John Adams, 43, 44
Addison, 48
A. Adler, 49
Aesop, 50
Alfonso X, 51
Amiel, 55
Angell, 57
Anonymous, 60
Aristotle, 68
F. Bacon, 72, 73, 74, 75
Bakunin, 78
J. D. Barnum, 82
C. A. Beard, 85
Bellamy, 88, 89
Bellarmine, 89
Bernhardi, 95
Bismarck, 97
Boniface VIII, 105
Bossuet, 108
Brandeis, 110, 112
Broun, 116
Bruno, 120
Bryce, 123
Buber, 123
Burke, 126, 127, 128, 129, 130
Byrnes, 135
Calhoun, 137
Chartists, 152
Chesterfield, 154
Cicero, 158
Colton, 168
J. F. Cooper, 179
T. Cooper, 180
Cromwell, 186
Crossman, 186, 187
Demosthenes, 202
De Quincey, 202
Desmoulins, 203
J. Dewey, 203, 204
Disraeli, 207
Djilas, 209

F. Douglass, 214
Eastman, 218
Einstein, 222, 227
Emerson, 235, 236
Engels, 241
Epictetus, 243, 244
Fromm, 264
Galsworthy, 266
H. George, 273, 275
Godwin, 280
Gorky, 286
Gregory I, 290
Halifax, 293
Andrew Hamilton, 296
Hazlitt, 304, 305
Herbert, 313
Herron, 314
Hobbes, 321, 323
Hume, 338
Hutchins, 340
A. Huxley, 341, 342
A. Jackson, 355
Jefferson, 374
S. Johnson, 378
Kant, 383
Khrushchev, 391
Kilgore, 391
Knox, 393
Laski, 400
Leggett, 405
Lenin, 410, 411
Leo XIII, 413
Lieber, 419
Lilburne, 420
Lincoln, 427
V. Lindsay, 431
Lippmann, 432
Locke, 436
London, 438
Longfellow, 439
Lowell, 441, 444
Macaulay, 451
J. Madison, 459, 460
Mason, 479

Menander, 486
Mill, 490, 491, 492, 495
Milton, 498
Mohammed, 499
Montesquieu, 502, 503
Morgenthau, 507
Nasser, 520
Newman, 525
Niebuhr, 526, 527
Otis, 539
Paine, 543
Pascal, 550
Phillips, 559, 560
Pitt (Sr.), 563
Plato, 567
Plutarch, 570
Proudhon, 574
Randolph, 579
F. D. Roosevelt, 591, 592
T. Roosevelt, 596, 598
B. A. Russell, 607, 608
G. W. Russell, 610
St. John-Stevas, 611
Shaw, 632
Shelley, 635
Spencer, 650
Steffens, 660
Steinbeck, 660
Swift, 670
Tacitus, 672
Tagore, 672
Talmud, 673
Tawney, 677
Tolstoy, 688
Treitschke, 692
Truman, 694
Twain, 699
Tweed, 699
C. Vanderbilt, 705
Veblen, 708
Vishinsky, 712
Voltaire, 715
Wagner, 718
F. Walpole, 721

G. Washington, 727
D. Webster, 728, 731
N. Webster, 731
Wells, 733
Whitman, 739, 740
Whittier, 742
Williams, 748
W. Wilson, 750, 752
Wise, 754
Wordsworth, 757
Zola, 763

Powerhouse
   H. B. Adams, 40
   Anonymous, 61

Pragmatism
   W. James, 359
   Viereck, 710

Praise
   Acton, 38
   Pope, 571

Pray, Prayers
   Benedictine Order, 90
   Emerson, 238, 239
   Joseph Lewis, 418

Precedent
   Disraeli, 206
   Hallam, 294
   A. Jackson, 355
   Swift, 670

Prejudice
   Acton, 36
   Amiel, 55
   R. Bacon, 75
   Bancroft, 82
   Berlin, 94
   Bronte, 114
   John Mason Brown, 118
   Buckle, 125
   C. P. Curtis, 187
   W. O. Douglas, 211
   T. Edwards, 220
   Erskine, 246
   France, 256

Frederick II, 259
Hazlitt, 304
Hecht, 307
T. H. Huxley, 346
Jefferson, 369
Jeffrey, 375
S. Johnson, 377
Thoreau, 682
Twain, 696
Voltaire, 715
Wells, 733
Whitehead, 737
President, Presidency
  B. Adams, 39
  H. B. Adams, 40
  Coolidge, 176, 177
  Emerson, 234
  Garfield, 268
  Gompers, 285
  Grant, 289
  Alexander Hamilton, 294
  W. H. Harrison, 302
  H. C. Hoover, 331
  Ickes, 348
  A. Jackson, 355
  Jefferson, 369
  G. W. Johnson, 376
  C. B. Luce, 445
  Mencken, 487
  Phillips, 559
  Sherman, 637
  Singleton, 640
  Truman, 694, 695
  G. Washington, 725
  O. Wilde, 743
  W. Wilson, 753
Press
  H. B. Adams, 41
  John Adams, 43, 44, 46
  Borah, 106
  Brandeis, 110
  Briand, 114
  Bright, 114
  Browne, 118

Bryant, 122, 123
Carlile, 140
Chesterton, 154
Cockburn, 166
Colton, 168, 169
Commission on Freedom, 170, 171
J. F. Cooper, 178, 179
Darrow, 190
Debs, 197
Defoe, 198
J. Dewey, 203
W. O. Douglas, 211
Dreiser, 215
Dunne, 216, 217
Einstein, 221, 222
Erskine, 245, 246
Garfield, 269
Evjue, 247
Gauvreau, 272
Gorky, 286
Hand, 298
Helvetius, 310
Hillman, 316
Hitler, 321
Ibsen, 347
Ickes, 348
Institute of Brothers of the Christiar
    Church, 353
Jefferson, 365, 366, 367
Khrushchev, 390
Kiderlen-Waechter, 391
La Follette, 396
Laski, 399, 400
Lassalle, 400, 401
Lenin, 411
Lerner, 415
Libby, 419
Lilburne, 420
J. Madison, 460
Marx, 476, 477
T. S. Matthews, 480
Mill, 494
Osler, 538
Peterson, 558

Phillips, 561, 562
Pitt (Sr.), 563
Pulitzer, 576
Richardson, 583
Rolland, 588
E. Roosevelt, 589, 590
Ruskin, 604
Scripps, 623, 624
Segura, 625
Sheridan, 636, 637
Singleton, 640
Stalin, 655
A. E. Stevenson, 662
Story, 665
Sutherland, 669
Swinton, 671
Thackeray, 680
Travis, 691
Twain, 696
U. S. Congress, 702
U. S. Supreme Court, 703
Henry Wallace, 720
J. Ward, 722
Wells, 733
E. B. White, 734
O. Wilde, 743
Wilhelm II, 746
Zangwill, 760
Pressure, Pressure Groups
Chase, 152
Commission on Freedom, 171
Lindner, 430
U. S. Congress, 702
W. A. White, 736
Price
Hobbes, 323
Adam Smith, 641
R. Walpole, 721
G. Washington, 724
Pride
Dante, 189
W. Wilson, 751
Priest, Priestcraft, Priesthood
B. Adams, 39

John Adams, 42, 43, 44, 46
E. Allen, 52
Bakunin, 77
Bismarck, 97
Blake, 100
Browning, 119
Bryant, 123
Buchanan, 124
Burke, 127
Calvin, 137
Cobbett, 165
Cobden, 165
Connolly, 174, 175
Debs, 197
Defoe, 198
Diderot, 205
Einstein, 221, 222, 223
Emersor., 238
D. C. Fisher, 250
Franklin, 259
Gibbons, 276
E. Hamilton, 297
Hetherington, 315
J. H. Holmes, 327
Hume, 339
Hus, 339
Ingersoll, 350, 352
Jefferson, 370, 371, 372, 373
Kant, 383
Lowell, 443
Macaulay, 452
Messelier, 489
Mexico, 489
Milton, 498
Mussolini, 513
Nehru, 521
Newman, 524
Nietzsche, 526. 527
Otis, 539
Paine, 544
Phillips, 559, 560
Shelley, 634, 635
Swinburne, 671
Thoreau, 683

Twain, 696
Voltaire, 713, 714, 716, 717
Wells, 733
Whittier, 741
William the Silent, 747
W. Wilson, 751
Wolsey, 756
Prince
John of Salisbury, 376
Knox, 393
Machiavelli, 453, 454
O. Wilde, 746
Principle
John Quincy Adams, 46
A. Adler, 49
Bakunin, 79
Bryan, 121
Burke, 129
J. F. Cooper, 177
Disraeli, 206, 208
Frankfurter, 257
Godwin, 279
Hazlitt, 304, 305
O. W. Holmes (Jr.), 330
Hume, 339
W. James, 360
Lassalle, 400
J. Morley, 508, 509
Paine, 544, 545
Scripps, 624
Print, Printers, Printing
John Adams, 43, 46
Anonymous, 58
Carlile, 141
Carlyle, 141
Flaubert, 251
Franklin, 257
Andrew Hamilton, 297
Jonson, 380
Napoleon, 519
State of Pennsylvania, 556
Wolsey, 756
Prison
Blake, 100

Debs, 196
Thoreau, 683
O. Wilde, 745
Privacy
Brandeis, 112
Coke, 166
Jefferson Davis, 195
W. O. Douglas, 211
H. C. Hoover, 331
A. B. Parker, 546
Somervell, 646
Viereck, 710
T. Wolfe, 755
Privilege
F. Bacon, 73
Bakunin, 77, 78
Bancroft, 81
Bevan, 96
Democratic Party, 201
Disraeli, 208
Isocrates, 354
E. Roosevelt, 589
F. D. Roosevelt, 591, 593
Procreate
Browne, 118
Product, Production
Brandeis, 110
Engels, 241, 242
Haywood, 304
Hobson, 323
Profit (Profit and Loss)
Alfonso X, 51
Baruch, 84
Bebel, 86
Brandeis, 110
Bucer, 123
Smedley Butler, 135
Carlyle, 142
Coolidge, 176
Ingersoll, 352
Kefauver, 385
Montaigne, 500
Patterson, 552

Phillips, 560
Reuther, 581
Ricardo, 582
F. D. Roosevelt, 594
T. Roosevelt, 596
Talmud, 673
Taney, 674
Veblen, 710

Progress, Progressive
Acton, 38
M. Arnold, 68
Browning, 119
Samuel Butler, 133
Carnegie, 143
Coolidge, 176
Disraeli, 207
Dostoyevski, 210
Douglass, 214
H. George, 272, 274
Goethe, 283
O. W. Holmes (Jr.), 329
H. C. Hoover, 332
Hugo, 337
Kabir, 382
Kettering, 388
T. E. Lawrence, 403
Maeterlinck, 460
Mill, 493, 495
Phillips, 559
Pius IX, 564
B. A. Russell, 605
Seneca, 626
Shaw, 631
Spencer, 649
Spinoza, 652
A. E. Stevenson, 663
Veblen, 709
Wells, 733
Whitehead, 738
Wilcox, 743
W. Wilson, 750

Proletariat
Anonymous, 62
Bakunin, 79

Belloc, 89
Berlin, 93
Brownson, 120
N. M. Butler, 132
Darrow, 190
Eastman, 218
Engels, 240, 242
Gorky, 287
Kautsky, 384, 385
Lenin, 407, 408, 410
K. Liebknecht, 419
Luxemburg, 449
Marx, 471, 473
Muller, 511
Mussolini, 514
Parrington, 548
Pius X, 564
Sartre, 615
Silone, 639
Sinclair, 639
Sorel, 647
Spengler, 650
Stalin, 655, 657, 658
Trotsky, 693
U.S.S.R. 704
Vishinsky, 712

Propaganda
S. Anderson, 57
Gibbs, 277
Hitler, 317
Pearl, 553
Siegfried, 638

Property
Acton, 37
H. B. Adams, 41
John Adams, 42, 45, 46
S. Adams, 47
Ambrose, 54
Anonymous, 59, 60
Aquinas, 64
Baer, 75
Bakunin, 77, 78
Bancroft, 81, 82
C. A. Beard, 85

Brissot, 114
Burke, 126, 129
Canon Law, 139
Cardozo, 140
Carnegie, 143
Catholic Bishops of America, 148
Cnafee, 150
Clemenceau, 162
Clement, 163
Confederate States, 172
Coughlin, 181
Darrow, 190
Emerson, 234, 237, 238
Epictetus, 243
Freud, 260
H. George, 273, 275
Girdler, 278
Emma Goldman, 283
Hetherington, 315
Hitler, 318
Hobson, 324
Hocking, 324
Hutterite Creed, 340
Ingersoll, 350
W. James, 361
Juarès, 362
S. Johnson, 378
Kropotkin, 395
Laski, 399
Lassalle, 400
Leggett, 405
Lenin, 409
Leo XIII, 414
Lincoln, 425, 428
Lippmann, 433
Lloyd, 434
Locke, 436, 437
Lowell, 441
Macaulay, 451, 452, 453
Machiavelli, 456
J. Madison, 458, 459
Malthus, 463
J. Marshall, 470
Marx, 472

Mason, 479
Mill, 494
L. H. Morgan, 506, 507
G. Morris, 509
Morse, 510
Nearing, 520, 521
Nobel, 531
Otis, 539
Paine, 543, 544
Pius IX, 564
Pius XI, 566
Proudhon, 574
Randolph, 579
J. Reed, 579
Ricardo, 582
Robinson, 585
Rolland, 589
F. D. Roosevelt, 591
T. Roosevelt, 596
Rousseau, 600, 601
Ruskin, 603
B. A. Russell, 605, 608
Schlesinger (Jr.), 616
Scripps, 624
Shaw, 629, 630
Socrates, 645, 646
Spencer, 650
Spengler, 650
Sprading, 654
Stalin, 655, 656
Stirner, 664
Taney, 674
Tawney, 677
Tertullian, 679
Tolstoy, 688
U. S. Army, 700
Veblen, 708
Vivekananda, 712
Wagner, 718, 719
D. Webster, 728, 731
N. Webster, 731
W. A. White, 735, 736
Whitehead, 737
O. Wilde, 745

Prophecy, Prophet
Cardozo, 140
R. H. Jackson, 357
Machiavelli, 453

Prosper, Prosperity, Prosperous
Acton, 36
Coolidge, 176
B. A. Fiske, 250
Goethe, 283
G. Herbert, 314
Paine, 543
Radford, 578
Seneca, 627
Tacitus, 672
Twain, 697, 698

Prostitute
A. Adler, 49
Carpenter, 144, 145
Chapman, 152
Davidson, 193
Dwight, 218
London, 438
Marx, 472
Swinton, 671

Protest
Norton, 533
Rolland, 589
Talmud, 673

Protestant
John Adams, 46
ᴌ. Allen, 52
Arcos, 66
Carlyle, 141
Hawkes, 303
d'Holbach, 325
E. Hubbard, 334
Inge, 349
Lecky, 404
Newman, 523
Nietzsche, 527
Pius IX, 564
Tawney, 674
Tillich, 686

William the Silent, 747
Williams, 747, 748

Providence
H. B. Adams, 41
John Adams, 45

Psychoanalysis
Freud, 261
Jaspers, 361
Overstreet, 539
Reik, 580

Psychology
Jung, 381

Psychotic
A. Adler, 49

Public
Anonymous, 59
Hazlitt, 304, 305
Hearst, 306
D. H. Lawrence, 402
Mill, 492
W. H. Vanderbilt, 705
Voltaire, 713
O. Wilde, 744

Publicity
Boldt, 104
Disraeli, 207
Hand, 298
C. E. Hughes, 335
Pulitzer, 576

Public Opinion
Angell, 57
Bagehot, 75
J. D. Barnum, 83
Bismarck, 97
Boerne, 102
Brandeis, 111
Carlyle, 142
Clausewitz, 161
Coolidge, 177
J. F. Cooper, 178, 179
Debs, 197
Disraeli, 207
Einstein, 221, 224

Emerson, 233
Garfield, 269
Gibbs, 277
Goebbels, 281
Hazlitt, 304
Hearst, 306
Hoffman, 325
E. Hubbard, 334
Inge, 349
Jefferson, 367
LaFollette, 396
League of Nations, 403
Lincoln, 429
Lowell, 441, 442
Lytton, 450
G. C. Marshall, 469
Marx, 477
Mill, 495
Morton, 511
N.A.M., 520
Orwell, 537
Peel, 554
Populist Party, 572
B. A. Russell, 605
Siegfried, 638
Stevens, 662
Stowe, 665
Sutherland, 669
U. S. Congress, 702
G. Washington, 726
Wilhelm II, 746
Wortman, 757, 758

Public Ownership
T. L. Johnson, 379

Public Relations
Bernays, 94
Bryce, 123

Publish, Publisher, Publishing
John Adams, 43
Canon Law, 139
Cowles, 183
Evans, 247
Halifax, 293

Ickes, 348
S. Johnson, 377
La Follette, 396
Lassalle, 401
Libby, 419
Mill, 491
~ulzberger, 666
Truman, 694
U. S. Congress, 702
U. S. Supreme Court, 703

Punishment (see Crime)
Aristotle, 66
Beccaria, 86
Bentham, 91
Hocking, 324
Lilburne, 420
Montefiore, 501
Plato, 568
B. A. Russell, 605

Purgatory
Council of Trent, 182
Emerson, 233

Puritan, Puritanism
John Adams, 42
Carpenter, 144
D. H. Lawrence, 402
Lowell, 441
Macaulay, 452
Mencken, 487, 488
Mill, 491
O'Flaherty, 535
Tawney, 674

Q

Quaker, Quakers
B. Adams, 39
Flushing Remonstrance, 252
Jefferson, 370

Questions
Browne, 119

R

Race

Acton, 37
H. B. Adams, 40, 41
J. Donald Adams, 42
American Anthropological Association, 54
Anonymous, 60
Augustine, 70
Hugo L. Black, 98
D. Bliss, 102
Burke, 127
H. S. Chamberlain, 150
Crevecoeur, 185
Disraeli, 206, 207
N. Douglas, 211
Harlan, 300
Hitler, 317, 318, 319, 321
Humboldt, 337
C. A. Lindbergh (Jr.), 429
Müller, 511
Nietzsche, 528, 530
Pius XI, 566
Rosenberg, 598
Ruskin, 603
B. A. Russell, 606
U.S. Supreme Court, 702
H. A. Wallace, 721
E. Warren, 722
Whitehead, 738
Whitman, 741
Zangwill, 760

Racket, Racketeer

Smedley Butler, 134
Capone, 140

Radical, Radicalism

Biddle, 96
Josh Billings, 97
Borah, 107
Brandeis, 112
P. Brooks, 115
Capone, 139
Cobb, 164
Cobbett, 165

Conant, 172
Emerson, 236
Frost, 264
Garfield, 269
Hawkes, 303
Hays, 304
Hearst, 306
C. A. Lindbergh (Sr.), 429
C. A. Madison, 458
Rakosi, 578
F. D. Roosevelt, 593
T. Roosevelt, 598
Schlesinger (Sr.), 616
Seldes, 626
Alfred E. Smith, 642
Society of Friends, 644
Spencer, 649
E. Warren, 722
W. Wilson, 749, 751

Radio

Commission on Freedom, 170
Evjue, 247
Hand, 298
Laski, 399
U.S. Congress, 702

Rascals

Greeley, 289

Rational

Anonymous, 61
Leo XIII, 413

Reaction, Reactionary

Anonymous, 61
Cobb, 164
Conant, 172
Coolidge, 177
DeLeon, 200
J. Dewey, 203
Hitler, 321
Keynes, 388
Lenin, 408
Lippmann, 433
Mussolini, 515
Pegler, 554

Picasso, 562
F. D. Roosevelt, 593
Singleton, 640
Tito, 686
Trotsky, 693
Vanzetti, 707
H. A. Wallace, 720
W. Wilson, 750

Reason
Acton, 38
E. Allen, 51, 52
Amiel, 55
Anonymous, 61
Aquinas, 64
Aristotle, 66, 67
M. Arnold, 69
F. Bacon, 74
R. Bacon, 75
Baha'u'llah, 76
Bancroft, 81
Basil, 84
Bergson, 92
Berlin, 93
C. Bowles, 108
Brandeis, 111
Burke, 127
Cicero, 158, 159
Coke, 166, 167
C. P. Curtis, 187
Debs, 196
Dreiser, 215
Drummond, 215
Erskine, 246
Franklin, 259
Fromm, 264
Garrison, 271
Goethe, 282
Gregory I, 290
Haeckel, 292
Hegel, 307, 308
Ingersoll, 351, 352
W. James, 361
Jefferson, 369
Kant, 384

Kent, 387
Le Bon, 404
Lecky, 404
Leibnitz, 406
Locke, 435, 436
Lucas, 444
Luther, 447
Marcus Aurelius, 467
Milton, 498
Newman, 524
Paine, 545
Pascal, 549
Pius IX, 564
Plutarch, 570
Pym, 577
Quintilian, 578
Robespierre, 584
Rousseau, 599
Santayana, 613
Seneca, 626, 627
Shaw, 631
Spinoza, 651, 652
Tagore, 672
Tolstoy, 689, 690
Vatican Council, 707
Voltaire, 714
Whitehead, 738

Rebel, Rebellion
A. Adams, 39
B. Adams, 39
H. B. Adams, 41
S. Adams, 47
Bakunin, 78
Carlyle, 142
Casement, 147
Chafee, 150
Clay, 162
Cobb, 164
Cromwell, 186
Darrow, 190
Defoe, 198
Eisenhower, 228
Freneau, 260
Garfield, 268

Jefferson, 368
Lalor, 397
Lincoln, 422, 4⁹5
Lindner, 430
Markham, 469
T. Parker, 547
Peron, 557
T. B. Reed, 580
Vinson, 711
Untermeyer, 703
Van Loon, 706
Whitman, 740
O. Wilde, 743
Zangwill, 761

"Red"
Capone, 140
Commager, 169
Hague, 292
Owsley, 540
Steffens, 660
Steinbeck, 660

Reform, Reformers
Altgeld, 53
Belloc, 89
Berlin, 93
Bright, 114
Carlile, 141
Carpenter, 145
Chapman, 152
DeLeon, 199
Emerson, 233, 235
H. George, 275
Gibbon, 276, 277
Eric Goldman, 283
Lowell, 444
Lytton, 450
Macaulay, 451
Mao Tse-tung, 466
Mill, 493
J. Morley, 508
Phillips, 558, 559, 560
T. Roosevelt, 597
Santayana, 613
Stalin, 655

D. Webster, 729
Whitman, 738, 741

Reformation, The
John Adams, 44, 46
T. H. Huxley, 345
Paine, 541
J. Warren, 724
Whitehead, 737

Religion
Abu'l-Ala, 35
Acton, 35, 37
H. G. Adams, 41
John Adams, 43, 44, 45
S. Adams, 47
Alcuin, 51
E. Allen, 52
Amiel, 56
Anonymous, 61
Aristotle, 67
Augustine, 71
F. Bacon, 72, 73
Baha' u 'ullah, 76
Bakunin, 77
Ballou, 81
Bancroft, 81
Beccaria, 86
Behn, 88
Belloc, 89
Bentham, 91
Bergson, 93
Bierce, 96
Hugo L. Black, 98
Blavatsky, 101
D. Bliss, 102
Bossuet, 108
Browne, 119
Bruno, 121
Burke, 126, 129
Robert Burton, 132
Samuel Butler, 133
Byron, 136
Carpenter, 146
Cather, 148
Channing, 151

Chesterton, 154
Clark, 159
Coleridge, 167
Colton, 168
Croce, 185
Cromwell, 186
Darrow, 190
DeLeon, 199
Disraeli, 207
W. O. Douglas, 212
Dreiser, 215
Edison, 219
Einstein, 221, 225, 228
T. S. Eliot, 230
Emerson, 236
Flaubert, 251
France, 254
Franklin, 258
Frederick II, 259
Freud, 260, 261
T. Fuller, 265
Gandhi, 267, 268
Gibbon, 276
Emma Goldman, 283
Grant, 288
Greeley, 289
Guicciardini, 291
Harrington, 301
Hegel, 308
Heine, 309
Hitler, 320
Hocking, 324
d'Holbach, 326, 327
E. Hubbard, 334
Hugo, 337
Hume, 338
A. Huxley, 342
J. Huxley, 342, 343
Ibsen, 347
Ingersoll, 351, 352
A. Jackson, 355
R. H. Jackson, 357
W. James, 360, 361
Jefferson, 363, 365, 368, 369, 372

S. Johnson, 377
D. S. Jordan, 380
Lally, 397
D. H. Lawrence, 402
Lenin, 409, 410
Leo XIII, 413, 414
Lessing, 416
Joseph Lewis, 418
Lilburne, 420
Lilienthal, 420
Lindner, 430
Locke, 436
Lowell, 440
Lucretius, 445
Machiavelli, 454, 455
J. Madison, 459
Maritain, 467
Marlowe, 469
Marx, 471, 472, 476
Maryland, 477, 478
McCabe, 482
Mencken, 487, 488
Mexico, 489
Mill, 490, 496
Montesquieu, 503
More, 505
J. Morley, 509
Mumford, 512
Mussolini, 513
Napoleon, 518, 519
Nehru, 521, 522
Newman, 523, 524
New York State, 525
Neitzsche, 526, 528
North Carolina, 533
Owen, 540
Paine, 541, 542, 543, 544, 545
Penn, 555
Pius IX, 564
Pius XI, 565
Polk, 570
Renan, 581
F. D. Roosevelt, 593
Ross, 599

Rousseau, 600, 601
B. A. Russell, 607
Santayana, 612, 613
Sarton, 614
Schopenhauer, 617, 618
Seneca, 627
Shaw, 628, 631, 632
Shelley, 636
Snow, 644
Spinoza, 652, 653
Stalin, 655
Swift, 669
Taylor, 678
Tertullian, 679
Turgot, 695
Twain, 696
U.S. Supreme Court, 703
Voltaire, 714, 715, 716
G. Washington, 726
D. Webster, 728
Wells, 732
Wesley, 734
E. B. White, 734
Whitehead, 738
O. Wilde, 745, 746
Williams, 747
Wolsey, 756
B. Young, 760

Rent
Byron, 135, 136
H. George, 273, 275
Marx, 472

Repetition
J. H. Burns, 130
Goethe, 283
Hand, 298
Hitler, 317
Schopenhauer, 618

Republic
C. A. and M. R. Beard, 85
Borah, 106
E. Davis, 195
Hugo, 336
Jefferson, 369, 375

J. Madison, 459, 460
H. Mann, 464
Montesquieu, 502
Spencer, 650
Sterne, 662

Republican Party
John L. Lewis, 417
Truman, 695
W. Wilson, 753

Resistance
Camus, 139
Lalor, 397

Resurrection
Augustine, 70

Revelation
E. Allen, 52
Beccaria, 86
Herndon, 314
Newman, 523

Reverence
Lindsey, 432
Nietzsche, 528
Schweitzer, 620, 621, 622

Revolution
Acton, 37
Angell, 58
Aristotle, 67
Bakunin, 77, 79
Berlin, 93
Hugo L. Black, 97
Blake, 101
Borah, 106
Buckle, 124
Burke, 129
Camus, 139
Chafee, 150
Chesterton, 155
Cobb, 164
Commager, 169
Coolidge, 177
Danton, 190
DeLeon, 199
Desmoulins, 203

Disraeli, 207
Djilas, 208
W. O. Douglas, 211, 212
Eisenhower, 229
T. S. Eliot, 230
Emerson, 234, 235
Engels, 240, 241, 242
Gauguin, 271
Emma Goldman, 283
Grant, 288
Harding, 299
Heine, 309
Hugo, 336, 337
Jefferson, 364, 374
Kemal, 386
Keynes, 388
Khrushchev, 389
Kropotkin, 394
Le Bon, 404
Lenin, 407, 408, 410, 411
Leo XIII, 413
K. Liebknecht, 419
W. Liebknecht, 419
Lincoln, 422, 426
Lowell, 442
Luxemburg, 448
Lytton, 449, 450
Macaulay, 451
Machiavelli, 456
Mao Tse-tung, 466
Marx, 473
Mirza, 499
Mussolini, 514
Napoleon, 519
Nehru, 522
New Hampshire, 522
O'Connor, 535
Orwell, 537
Pasternak, 551
Pavlov, 552
Phillips, 559, 561
J. Reed, 580
Robespierre, 585
F. D. Roosevelt, 591, 592

Santayana, 613
Seldes, 625, 626
Seward, 628
Shaw, 628, 629, 630, 631
Society of Friends, 644
Sorel, 647
Stalin, 655, 656, 657
A. E. Stevenson, 663
Tawney, 674, 675, 676
Thoreau, 683
Trotsky, 693
Vergniaud, 710
Wagner, 718
H. A. Wallace, 720
D. Webster, 729
Wells, 732, 733
Whitman, 738
Willkie, 749
W. Wilson, 751, 753
Zangwill, 761
Revolution (American)
John Adams, 44
Bakunin, 78
Eisenhower, 228
Frankfurter, 257
Gladstone, 278
H. A. Wallace, 720
Revolution (French)
John Adams, 44
Blake, 101
Burke, 128, 129
Cobb, 165
Nehru, 522
Robespierre, 584
H. A. Wallace, 720
O. Wilde, 744
Rich, Riches
Abd-el Raham, 35
Acton, 36
John Adams, 42
Aga Khan, 50
Ambrose, 53
Anacharsis, 56
Anonymous, 63

M. Arnold, 68
F. Bacon, 72, 73
John Brown, 117
Chrysostom, 155
Cicero, 158
Confucius, 174
Dante, 189
Erasmus, 245
Godwin, 279
Alexander Hamilton, 295, 296
Horace, 332
A. Jackson, 355
Jerome, 375
John L. Lewis, 417
W. Morris, 510
Newman, 525
Patterson, 552
Raskob, 579
Shelley, 634
Adam Smith, 641
Thoreau, 684
W. K. Vanderbilt, 705
Wagner, 718
Wang-An-Shih, 721
Zimmerman, 762

Rich and Poor
John Adams, 45
Ambrose, 53
Ameringer, 55
Anonymous, 62
Aristotle, 67
Augustine, 71
Babeuf, 71
Ball, 80
Basil, 84
Brownson, 120
Bryant, 122
Buchanan, 124
Burke, 126
Calhoun, 137
Carnegie, 144
Cleveland, 163
France, 254
Goldsmith, 283

Alexander Hamilton, 295
W. H. Harrison, 302
A. Jackson, 355
Latimer, 401
Leggett, 405
Leo XIII, 415
Macaulay, 452, 453
Marx, 477
Melville, 485
Nehru, 521
Newman, 525
Paine, 544
Phillips, 561
Plato, 567
Populist Party, 572
Rolland, 588, 589
Ruskin, 603, 604
Scripps, 624
Seldes, 626
Shaw, 629
Adam Smith, 641
Stalin, 656
Story, 665
Tennyson, 678
Tolstoy, 690
Wagner, 719
Webb, 728
D. Webster, 731
N. Webster, 731
J. F. Wilde, 743
Willkie, 748
Wycliffe, 759

Right, Rights
Acton, 37
John Adams, 43, **44**
Altgeld, 53
Angell, 58
Anonymous, 62
Anthony, 64
Bakunin, 77
Ball, 80
Bancroft, 81
Bebel, 86
Bok, 103

L. Bonaparte, 105
Brandeis, 112
Brown, 116
Burke, 128
Cicero, 159
Coke, 167
Coughlin, 181
Ferrer, 249
Hazlitt, 305
Hearst, 305, 306
Hobbes, 323
J. E. Hoover, 332
Ireland, 353
W. James, 360
Jefferson, 369
J. W. Johnson, 376
Kant, 383
Kingsley, 392
Lalor, 397
Lattimore, 401
Lehman, 406
Lincoln, 424, 425
Lippmann, 433
Magna Carta, 461
More, 505
Pope, 571
President's Commission, 573
Priestley, 573
Somervell, 646
United Nations, 700
Veblen, 709
G Washington, 725
Wilcox, 743

Rights of Man
Freneau, 260
H. George, 274
Herbert, 313
Ingersoll, 350
Kent, 387
Kropotkin, 395
Leo XIII, 414
Marx, 474
Paine, 543
Schweitzer, 622 623

Tertullian, 679
Tone, 691
United Nations, 700
W. Wilson, 750, 751
Right and Wrong
T. S. Eliot, 230
Garrison, 271
Heraclitus, 313
Hitler, 317
Hobbes, 321
Lincoln, 325
Machiavelli, 456
Manning, 465
Rob
Nearing, 520, 521
Wesley, 734
Rome, Roman, Romish
John Adams, 42, 45
S. Adams, 47
E. Allen, 52
Augustine, 71
Buckle, 125
Coleridge, 167
Colton, 168
Dante, 189
Dupin, 217
Gladstone, 278
Gregory VII, 290
T. H. Huxley, 344
Macaulay, 452
Machiavelli, 455
Manning, 464
Mill, 492
Milton, 498
Newman, 523
Paine, 544
T. Parker, 547
Savonarola, 616
Twain, 696
Vatican Council, 707
William the Silent, 747
W. Wilson, 751
Theodore Roosevelt
Frick, 264

V. Lindsay, 431
T. B. Reed, 580

Rule, Rulers, Ruling Class
M. J. Adler, 49
Brandeis, 111
Samuel Butler, 133
Debs, 196
Ellis, 231
Garrison, 271
Harlan, 300
Herron, 314
R. H. Jackson, 356
Lao-Tse, 398
Markham, 469
Mill, 490
Muller, 511
Snow, 644

Russia (see Soviet)
Biddle, 96
Churchill, 157
Marx, 475
Peter I, 558
Snow, 644
Steffens, 659
Truman, 693
Wright, 759

S

Sacco and Vanzetti
Broun, 116

Saint
Aquinas, 64
M. Arnold, 68
Bierce, 96
O. W. Holmes (Jr.), 330
Orwell, 537, 538

Salvation
Aquinas, 64
Augustine, 71
Boniface VIII, 105
Buck, 124

Scab
Debs, 197
London, 438

Schizophrenia
Bleuler, 101
Rank, 579

School, Schoolboy, Schoolroom
Cook, 175
Ferrer, 249
Garfield, 269
Grant, 288
H. Mann, 464
Mohammed, 499
Paine, 544
Pius XI, 565

Science, Scientists
Acton, 38
Amiel, 56
M. Arnold, 68
F. Bacon, 74, 75
Bagehot, 75
Blake, 100
Burbank, 126
Burroughs, 131
Samuel Butler, 133
Compton, 171
Comte, 171
C. Darwin, 191
J. Dewey, 204
Durant, 217
Einstein, 226, 227, 228
Emerson, 238
Erigena, 245
Freud, 263
Goethe, 283
Hazlitt, 305
Hobson, 323
E. W. Howe, 333
J. Huxley, 342, 343
T. H. Huxley, 344, 345
Ingersoll, 351
W. James, 360
Jefferson, 375
Keith, 385

Le Bon, 404
S. Lewis, 418
C. A. Lindbergh (Jr.), 429
Lysenko, 449
Mao Tse-tung, 466
Mencken, 486
Oppenheimer, 536
Pavlov, 553
B. A. Russell, 609
Sarton, 614
Adam Smith, 640
Spencer, 649
Spinoza, 652
Steinmetz, 661
Vatican Council, 707
Weltfish, 734
Whitehead, 738
Zangwill, 760

Scrap of Paper
Bethmann-Hollweg, 95

Scripture
Copernicus, 180
Erasmus, 244
Galileo, 265, 266
Lincoln, 428
Selden, 625
Vatican Council, 707
Williams, 747
Wolsey, 756

Sect
John Adams, 46
S. Adams, 47
Asoka, 69
Canon Laws, 139
Carroll, 146
Cobbett, 165
Garrison, 270
Girard, 277
Godwin, 280
Grant, 288
Jefferson, 363, 372
Macaulay, 452
Twain, 696
Voltaire, 715, 716

Security
Acton, 35, 37, 38
S. Anderson, 56
Eisenhower, 228
Keller, 386
Kennan, 387
Keynes, 389
Laski, 398
Lowell, 441
Markham, 468
W. C. Menninger, 489
Pasternak, 551

Sedition
F. Bacon, 73
Bunyan, 125
Cobb, 164, 165
U.S. Congress, 701

Segregation
U.S. Supreme Court, 702
E. Warren, 722

Self, Selfish
S. Anderson, 57
Einstein, 226
Kierkegaard, 391
D. H. Lawrence, 402
Stirner, 664
T. Wolfe, 755

Self-Government
Acton, 37
Nkrumah, 531

Self-Interest
Amiel, 55
Aristotle, 67
Bancroft, 82
Lincoln, 422
Mahan, 461
Marx, 476
Shaw, 629
G. Washington, 724

Self-Preservation
S. Adams, 47
Samuel Butler, 133

Emerson, 239
Jefferson, 370

Self-Reliance
Emerson, 238

Semantics
Chase, 152

Senate, Senators
Connally, 174
Evans, 247
John L. Lewis, 417
Rogers, 587
Truman, 694

Sermon on the Mount
John Adams, 44
Jefferson, 371

Sex
Anonymous, 59
Augustine, 71
Bergson, 93
Browne, 118
Carpenter 145
Ellis, 231 232
Freud, 262, 263
Hobson, 324
Ibsen, 346
D. H. Lawrence, 405
Malthus, 463
Marx, 476
Schopenhauer, 617
Schroeder, 620
Tertullian, 680
W. B. Wolfe, 755

Shakespeare
Santayana, 614
Wordsworth, 757

Shop, Shopkeeper
Disraeli, 208
Napoleon, 519
Adam Smith, 641

Silence
H. B. Adams, 41
Brandeis, 111

Kierkegaard, 391
Maurois, 481

Sin
Acton, 38
John Adams, 42
Angell, 58
Anonymous, 60
Augustine, 70, 71
Bryant, 123
Buck, 124
Bunyan, 125
Calvin, 138
S. Crane, 184
C. P. Curtis, 187
DuBois, 215
Freud, 261
Hume, 338
D. H. Lawrence, 402
Manu, 465
Newman, 524
Nietzsche, 527
O'Brien, 534
Shaw, 628, 629, 630
Spinoza, 652
Werfel, 734
O. Wilde, 745, 746
Wright, 758

Single Tax
H. George, 273
Tolstoy, 688

Skepticism
Coleridge, 167
Demosthenes, 201, 202
Emerson, 237
Gibbon, 276
T. H. Huxley, 345
Mill, 495
Nathan, 520
Nietzsche, 527
Santayana, 613
Schweitzer, 622

Slave, Slavery
Acton, 36, 37

John Adams, 43
S. Adams, 46
Alcott, 51
E. Allen, 52
Ambrose, 54
Aristotle, 66
Augustine, 70
Bakunin, 78, 79
Bebel, 86
Berenson, 91
John Brown, 117
Brownson, 120
Bryant, 122
Calhoun, 137
Cicero, 159
Confederate Constitution, 172
W. H. Davies, 194
Devereux, 203
Douglass, 214
Drummond, 215
Emerson, 237
Faulkner, 248
Fitzhugh, 251
Garrison, 270, 271
H. George, 273
Goethe, 283
Grant, 289
Hitler, 320
Ingersoll, 349
Jefferson, 362
Keller, 386
Lee, 404
Lenin, 410
Lincoln, 422, 427, 428
Lovejoy, 440
Lowell, 441, 442, 443
Machiavelli, 456
Lord Mansfield, 465
Markham, 468
Marx, 474
Masefield, 478
Methodist Episcopal Church, 489
Oastler, 534
Oppenheim, 533

T. Parker, 546
Pearse, 553
Rousseau, 599, 600, 601
Shelley, 633, 634
Sherman, 637
Spencer, 648
Stephens, 662
C. Sumner, 667
Taney, 673, 674
Tawney, 677
Thoreau, 684, 685
Tolstoy, 688, 689, 690
Vivekananda, 712
Wagner, 718
G. Washington, 726
D. Webster, 730
O. Wilde, 743

Slave Morality
Nietzsche, 527

Slogan
Conant, 172
Davenport, 193
Eastman, 218
Frankfurter, 256
Franklin, 258
Hitler, 317
Marx, 477
Nehru, 522
Nivelle, 531
Willkie, 748

Snobs
A. Huxley, 341
Thackeray, 680

Social (Forces), Social Justice, Order, Revolution, System
H. B. Adams, 41
A. Adler, 48, 49
Angell, 58
Aristotle, 67
Bakunin, 77
Bennett, 90
Berlin, 93
Brandeis, 110, 111, 112

Brennan, 113
Carpenter, 144
Compton, 171
Debs, 196
Eastman, 218
Fourier, 254
H. George, 274
Kent, 387
Lenin, 409
Lerner, 415, 416
Nathan, 520
Pius XI, 566
Reilly, 581
F. D. Roosevelt, 590
T. Roosevelt, 596
Rousseau, 600, 601
Sinclair, 639
E. H. Smith, 643
Society of Friends, 645
W. G. Sumner, 667
Tennyson, 678
Wells, 732, 733
Whitehead, 737, 738

**Social Democrat, Social Democrats, Social
    Democracy**
Lenin, 407
Mussolini, 513

Socialism
Acton, 37
Altgeld, 53
Anonymous, 62
Arcos, 66
Bakunin, 78
Bebel, 86
Bernstein, 95
Biddle, 96
Blum, 102
Brandeis, 110, 112
Carnegie, 143
H. S. Chamberlain, 150
Constantine, 175
Debs, 196
De Leon, 199
J. Dewey, 205

Eastman, 218
Engels, 240, 241
Fitzhugh, 251
H. George, 275
Gompers, 286
Gorky, 287
Haldane, 293
Hardie, 299
O. W. Holmes (Jr.), 330
Juarès, 362
Kautsky, 385
Khrushchev, 389, 390
Kropotkin, 394
Laski, 400
Lenin, 407, 408, 411, 412
Leo XIII, 414
V. Lindsay, 431
Lippmann, 432
Lloyd, 434
Lowell, 442
H. R. Luce, 445
Luxemburg, 448, 449
T. Mann, 464
Mao Tse-tung, 466
Marx, 472
W. Morris, 509, 510
Mussolini, 514, 518
Nehru, 521, 522
Niebuhr, 526
Nietzsche, 527, 528
Nkrumah, 531
Owsley, 540
Oxnam, 540
Parsons, 548
Pilsudski, 563
Pius XI, 565
Pius XII, 566
Republican Party, 581
Rocco, 586
F. D. Roosevelt, 590
T. Roosevelt, 598
Shaw, 629, 631, 632, 633
Silone, 639
Socialist Labor Party, 644

Sorel, 647, 648
Spencer, 650
Spengler, 651
Stalin, 655, 658
Steinmetz, 661
Tawney, 674, 675
Tito, 686
Veblen, 710
Vishinsky, 711
Webb, 727
Wells, 732, 733
Wilhelm II, 746
C. E. Wilson, 749

Society
 H. B. Adams, 40, 41
 John Adams, 42
 M. J. Adler, 50
 Aristotle, 67
 Bakunin, 78, 79
 Barlow, 82
 Baruch, 84
 H. W. Beecher, 87
 Burke, 126, 127, 129
 Carpenter, 146
 Cocteau, 166
 T. S. Eliot, 230
 Emerson, 237
 H. George, 273
 Godwin, 279
 Hand, 298
 F. Harrison, 302
 Haywood, 304
 Ibsen, 346
 Kingsley, 392
 La Rochefoucauld, 398
 Lenin, 407, 409, 410
 Lilienthal, 421
 Lincoln, 427
 Lindsey, 432
 McCarthy, 483
 Mill, 491, 494, 495
 Montesquieu, 502
 L. H. Morgan, 507
 Paine, 543

Spencer, 649
Thompson, 681
Turgot, 695
W. A. White, 735
Whitehead, 738
Williams, 748
E. Wilson, 749
Wordsworth, 757

Socrates
 Chekhov, 153
 Plutarch, 570

Soldier, Soldiers
 Cicero, 159
 Duffy, 216
 Eisenhower, 228
 Ford, 252
 O. W. Holmes (Jr.), 328
 Paine, 542
 U.S. Army, 701

Solitude
 Aristotle, 66
 Blackstone, 99
 Thomas Browne, 118
 Byron, 136
 De Quincey, 202
 Emerson, 239
 Maurois, 481
 Schopenhauer, 618

Soul
 Aristotle, 66
 Augustine, 70
 Dante, 189
 Edison, 219
 Faulkner 248
 Flaubert 251
 Malthus 463
 Markham, 469
 Marx, 476
 Masefield, 478
 Montaigne, 501
 J. P. Morgan, 506
 Paine, 542
 Renan 581

Socrates, 645
Voltaire, 713
Williams, 748

Sovereign, Sovereignty
Einstein, 222, 226
Laski, 400

Soviet (see Russia)
Gide, 276
Laski, 399
Luxemburg, 449
Steffens, 659
Tito, 686
Vishinsky, 711, 712

Spain
Bowers, 108
Hemingway, 311
Hitler, 319

Species
Burke, 130
de Maupertuis, 201
Lysenko, 449

Speech (see Free Speech)
Acton, 36
B. Adams, 39
John Adams, 43, 44
Altgeld, 53
F. Bacon, 72
H. W. Beecher, 87
Bismarck, 97
Brandeis, 111
Diogenes, 206

Spirit
Kierkegaard, 391
Napoleon, 518
Schweitzer, 621, 622, 623

Spoils
Acton, 35
Angell, 57
F. S. Fitzgerald, 251
Marcy, 467

Stalin
Trotsky, 693

Standard, Standards (Standard of Living)
H. B. Adams, 40
Bok, 103
N. Crane, 184
H. C. Hoover, 331
Meany, 484

Starvation
Bush, 132
O. Wilde, 745

State
Acton, 36, 37, 38
Aeschylus, 50
Angell, 58
Aristotle, 66, 67
Bakunin, 78, 79, 80
Banse, 82
Bellarmine, 89
Belloc, 89
Berlin, 93
Blake, 100
Bossuet, 108
Brandeis, 110, 11
Burke, 129
Coughlin, 18.
G. W. Curtis, 188
DeLeon, 200
Ellis, 231, 232
Emerson, 236, 238
Engels, 241, 242
Garrison, 270
Hegel, 307, 308
Hitler, 318
Hobson, 324
Ibsen, 347
Isocrates, 354
A. Jackson, 354
R. H. Jackson, 358
S. Johnson, 378
Kropotkin, 395
Laski, 399
Lassalle, 400
Lenin, 409, 410, 412
Leo XIII, 413, 415
Lilienthal, 421

Lippmann, 432
Louis XIV, 440
Machiavelli, 454, 456
J. Marshall, 470
Marx, 477
Mill, 494
Muller, 511
Mussolini, 514, 515, 516, 518
Napoleon, 518
Nietzsche, 528
Owen, 540
T. Parker, 547
Plato, 567, 568, 569
Rocco, 586
Ruskin, 603
Shaw, 628
Socrates, 645
Sorel, 647
Spinoza, 652
Sprading, 654
Stirner, 664, 665
Thoreau, 683, 684
Toynbee, 691
Treitscke, 692, 693
Vickers, 710
Vishinky, 711, 712
Wang-An-Shih, 721
D. Webster, 729
Whitman, 740
Zangwill, 761

Statesman
Clarke, 160
Coleridge, 168
Disraeli, 207
Emerson, 238
Yeats, 760

Statistics
H. B. Adams, 41
Bagehot, 76
Disraeli, 208

Status Quo
J. Dewey, 204
Emerson, 239

Hawkes, 303
Hobson, 323
B. A. Russell, 608
Schlesinger (Sr.), 616
Shahn, 628

Strike
T. S. Adams, 47
Bellamy, 88
Brandeis, 110
Broun, 116
Bryant, 122
Smedley Butler, 134
Coolidge, 177
Debs, 196
Franco, 256
Gompers, 286
Hillman, 316
Lincoln, 425, 428
London, 438
N.A.M., 520
Sorel, 647, 648

Struggle, Struggles
Croce, 185
Douglass, 214
Hugo, 336

Struggle for Existence
Archer, 65
C. Darwin, 192
Einstein, 222
Engels, 242
Freud, 260
H. George, 275
A. R. Wallace, 720

Stupidity
Adenauer, 48
Schiller, 616
O. Wilde, 745

Subversive
Guérard, 291
Hillman, 310
Hutchins, 339
Oxnam, 540

Success (Succeed)
Acton, 35
A. Adler, 49
Bellamy, 88
Einstein, 225, 226
Hitler, 317, 318
A. Huxley, 341
W. James, 358
Masefield, 479
C. Morley, 507
Nietzsche, 528
Pater, 552
Rousseau, 600
Thoreau, 682
B. T. Washington, 724

Sucker
P. T. Barnum, 83
Beaumarchais, 85

Suicide
H. B. Adams, 41
A. Adler, 49
Berlin, 94
E. Booth, 106
Emerson, 239
Franklin, 259
Mumford, 512
Nietzsche, 529

Sun
Copernicus, 181
Galileo, 265, 266

Superiority
A. Adler, 49
Aristotle, 67, 68
Confucius, 172, 173, **174**
T. Cooper, 180
Freud, 262
W. James, 361
Seneca, 626

Superman
Freud, 261
Nietzsche, 528, 529
Schweitzer, 623

Supernatural
E. Allen, 52
J. Dewey, 205
Hume, 338

Super-patriotism (see Patriotism)

Superstition
Acton, 35, 37
E. Allen, 52
F. Bacon, 73, 74
Buckle, 125
Burbank, 126
Burke, 126
Byron, 135
Carlile, 140
Cicero, 159
Coleridge, 167
P. Cooper, 180
Darwin, 192
Emerson, 233
H. George, 274
Gibbon, 276
E. Hubbard, 334
T. H. Huxley, 343
Ingersoll, 352
W. James, 361
Jefferson, 373
Joseph Lewis, 418
Luther, 446
Newman, 523
Oppenheim, 536
Paine, 542, 543
Pascal, 550
B. A. Russell, 606
Sarton, 614
Shaw, 628
Spinoza, 652
Stanton, 659
Sun Tzu, 668
Taylor, 678
Tolstoy, 690
Tyndall, 699
Voltaire, 713, 715, **717**

Supreme Court (see Court)
Byrnes, 135

A. Jackson, 354
R. Jackson, 357
A. Johnson, 376
John L. Lewis, 417
F. D. Roosevelt, 592

Surplus Value
Marx, 475

Survival, Survival of the Fittest
Bush, 132
Carnegie, 143
C. Darwin, 192
de Maupertuis, 201
T. H. Huxley, 344
Kropotkin, 394
Rockefeller (Sr.), 586
Sieyès, 638
Spencer, 650
A. R. Wallace, 720

Sword
Ingersoll, 353
Lytton, 450
Napoleon, 518
Virgil, 711
Wilhelm (Crown Prince), 747

Syndicalism
Cobb, 165
Sorel, 647

T

Taboo
Bell, 88
Carpenter, 146
W. O. Douglas, 212
Hobson, 324
Lindsey, 432

Taxes
Acton, 37
F. Bacon, 73
Berenson, 92
Hugo L. Black, 98
Blake, 101

Burke, 128
Cicero, 159
Coolidge, 176
Disraeli, 206
Erasmus, 245
Franklin, 258
Grant, 288
O. W. Holmes (Jr.), 329
Lytton, 449
J. Madison, 458
J. Marshall, 470
Marx, 472
Montesquieu, 502
J. P. Morgan, 506
Otis, 539
Plato, 568
Ricardo, 582
T. Roosevelt, 596
S. Smith, 644
Spencer, 649
Sutherland, 669
D. Webster, 728

Teach, Teachers
Castro, 148
Ingersoll, 352
Montessori, 504
E. Warren, 723

Temptation
Acton, 36
Jones, 380

Ten Commandments
John Adams, 44
Hitler, 320
T. B. Reed, 580
Truman, 695

Terror
Aesop, 50
Chesterton, 155
Hitler, 318
K. Liebknecht, 419
Robespierre, 584, 585
Trotsky, 693
Twain, 698

Theism, Theology
Bakunin, 78
Bradlaugh, 109
Burroughs, 131
Chesterton, 154
Comte, 171
C. Darwin, 193
E. Hubbard, 334
Lecky, 404
Mencken, 486
Voltaire, 716
Whitehead, 737

Theory
Bakunin, 77
Edison, 219

Thief
Anonymous, 61
Bunyan, 125
Wesley, 734

Things
Laski, 399
Socrates, 646
Thoreau, 685

Think, Thinker, Thinking
Cicero, 159
Descartes, 202
Edison, 219
Emerson, 234
Ford, 253
H. George, 275
Godwin, 279
Hobson, 324
Mencken, 486
Mill, 496
Pascal, 549
Pestalozzi, 557
Schweitzer, 621, 622
Virgil, 711
Wesley, 734
Wordsworth, 757

Thought
B. Adams, 39
H. B. Adams, 41

John Adams, 43
Amiel, 55
M. Arnold, 68
Berlin, 93
Burbank, 125
Coke, 166
Croce, 185
J. Dewey, 203, 204
Djilas, 208
Emerson, 233
Freud, 262
E. Hamilton, 297
Hand, 299
Hawkes, 303
Hazlitt, 305
Hutchins, 340
Ingersoll, 349, 351
Mao Tse-tung, 466
Paracelsus, 546
B. A. Russell, 605, 608
Sprading, 654
Van Buren, 705
Wotton, 758

Time
Brandeis, 112
C. Eliot, 229
Gladstone, 278
Hallam, 294
Hegel, 307
T. H. Huxley, 344
Lowell, 442
Machiavelli, 455
Seneca, 626
Voltaire, 714
Whittier, 742

Tobacco
Bogomoletz, 103
Caldwell, 137
James I, 358
Shaw, 632

Tolerance
Acton, 36, 38
S. Adams, 47
Heine, 309

Leo XIII, 413
Macaulay, 452
Mazzini, 482
Paine, 543
G. Washington, 725
Willkie, 748

Tools
Bergson, 92
Socialist Labor Party, 644

Totalitarian
Djilas, 209
W. O. Douglas, 214
Eastman, 218
Hand, 298
Hitler, 319
J. E. Hoover, 332
R. H. Jackson, 356
Meany, 484

Trade
B. Adams, 39
C. A. Beard, 85
Emerson, 238
Mill, 495
Thoreau, 682

Tradition
E. Allen, 52
Ballou, 81
Commager, 169
Galton, 266
Marx, 473
Milton, 497
J. Morley, 507, 509
Riesman, 583
Tolstoy, 690

Traitors (see Treason)
Galarza, 265
George III, 272
Ingersoll, 351
London, 438
Lowell, 442
F. D. Roosevelt, 595
Twain, 699

Transubstantiation
Byron, 136
Council of Trent, 182
Paine, 544

Treason (see Traitors)
Acton, 36
Benda, 90
Burke, 126, 128
Casement, 147
G. Eliot, 230
Harrington, 30
J. Madison, 459
T. Parker, 547
Robespierre, 584, 585
Steffens, 660
Willkie, 749

Treaties
Selassie, 625

Trinity
Athanasian Creed, 69
Ball, 80
Chworowsky, 157
Jefferson, 370, 373, 374
Maryland Assembly, 477
Paine, 542
Shaw, 629
Tolstoy, 689

Trojan Horse
Dimitrov, 206

Trouble, Time of
Toynbee, 691

True and False (see Truth, False)
Leonardo, 415
J. Morley, 507
Swedenborg, 669
Thoreau, 682

Truman Doctrine
Truman, 694

Trusts
Clark, 160
Cleveland, 164
Democratic Party, 201
Greeley, 289

Hardie, 299
Havemeyer, 302
G. W. Norris, 533
Republican Party, 581

Truth (see True and False)
Acton, 38
B. Adams, 39
H. B. Adams, 41
J. Donald Adams, 41, 42
John Adams, 46
A. Adler, 49
Agassiz, 50
E. Allen, 51, 52
Ammianus, 56
Anonymous, 59, 60, 63, 64
Aquinas, 64
Aristotle, 68
F. Bacon, 73, 75
R. Bacon, 75
Baha'u'llah, 76
Ballou, 81
Bancroft, 81
H. W. Beecher, 87
Bennett, 90
Bernays, 95
Blake, 100
D. Bliss, 102
Bohr, 103
Bok, 103
Bradlaugh, 109
Brandeis, 111
Brandes, 113
P. Brooks, 115
Broun, 116
John Mason Brown, 118
Browne, 118
Bruno, 121
Buckingham, 124
Buckle, 124
Burbank, 125, 126
R. Burns, 131
Bush, 132
Samuel Butler, 133

Calvin, 138
Camus, 138, 139
Carlyle, 141
Cavour, 149
Cervantes, 149
Chesterton, 155
Cicero, 159
Coleridge, 167
Colton, 168
Condorcet, 172
Confucius, 173, 174
T. Cooper, 180
Darrow, 191
Davenport, 193
E. Davis, 195
Debs, 197
Defoe, 198
J. Dewey, 204
W. O. Douglas, 213
Dryden, 215
Eddy, 218, 219
Einstein, 224, 226, 227
Eisner, 229
G. Eliot, 229
Ellenborough, 230
Emerson, 234, 235, 236, 238, 239
V. Fisher, 250
Franklin, 258
Frederick II, 259
Freud, 262
Frost, 264
T. Fuller, 265
Galileo, 265, 266
Galsworthy, 266
Gandhi, 267, 268
Garrison, 270
Godwin, 279, 280
Goethe, 283
Gracián, 287
Greeley, 289
Alexander Hamilton, 295
Hand, 299
Harvey, 302

Hawthorne, 303
Hazlitt, 304, 305
Heckscher, 307
Hegel, 308
Henry, 312
Heraclitus, 313
G. Herbert, 314
Hitler, 317, 318, 320
Hocking, 324
d'Holbach, 326
O. W. Holmes (Jr.), 329, 330
Howells, 333, 334
Humboldt, 337
T. H. Huxley, 343
Ibsen, 346, 347, 348
Ingersoll, 350, 352
W. James, 359, 360, 361
Jefferson, 362, 363, 366, 375
S. Johnson, 377, 379
Jones, 380
Jonson, 380
Keats, 385
Keith, 385
Koestler, 393
La Bruyère, 395
La Rochefoucauld, 398
Latimer, 401
D. H. Lawrence, 402
Lecky, 404
Leibnitz, 406
Lenin, 411
Leo XIII, 415
Leonardo, 415
Lincoln, 422, 424
C. A. Lindbergh (Sr.), 429
V. Lindsay, 431
Lindsey, 432
Lippmann, 433
Livy, 434
Locke, 435
London, 438
Lowell, 442, 444
Luther, 446, 448

MacLeish, 457
H. Mann, 464
T. Mann, 464
K. Mansfield, 465
Marcus Aurelius, 467
Masefield, 478, 479
Masters, 480
Matisse, 480
McKenney, 483
Melville, 485
Mencken, 486, 487
K. Menninger, 488
Menotti, 489
Mill, 492, 493, 494, 496
Milton, 497, 498
Montaigne, 501
More, 505
J. Morley, 508, 509
Morton, 511
Müller, 511
G. Murray, 512
Mussolini, 513, 514
Newman, 523, 524
Newton, 525
Nicholas of Cusa, 525
Nietzsche, 526, 529
F. Norris, 532
Oastler, 534
O'Neill, 535
Orozco, 537
Osler, 538
Pascal, 549, 550
Pasternak 550, 551
Peirce, 554
Penn, 555, 556
Phillips, 559, 560
Picasso, 562
Pius XI, 565
Plato, 567, 568
Ponsonby, 571
Pusey, 577
Reese, 580
Rolland, 588

Rousseau, 600
B. A. Russell, 607
Sarton, 614
Schopenhauer, 617, 618
Schweitzer, 620, 621, 622
Scripps, 624, 625
Seneca, 626, 627
Shaw, 629
John Smith, 643
Socrates, 645, 646
Sophocles, 647
Spencer, 649
Spinoza, 652
Stefansson, 659
Stekel, 661
A. E. Stevenson, 662, 663
R. L. Stevenson, 664
Story, 665
C. Sumner, 667
Swedenborg, 669
Swift, 670
Swinburne, 671
Swinton, 671
Tennyson, 678, 679
Thackeray, 680
Thoreau, 682, 684
Toller, 687, 688
Tolstoy, 689
Truman, 695
Twain, 697
M. Van Doren, 706
Voltaire, 713, 715, 716
H. A. Wallace, 720, 721
Wellington, 731
Whateley, 734
W. A. White, 735
Whitehead, 737
Whittier, 741, 742
O. Wilde, 745, 746
Williams, 747, 748
Woolf, 756
Wotton, 758
Wright, 758
Wycliffe, 759

Yeats, 760
B. Young, 760
Zola, 762, 763

Tyrant, Tyranny
John Adams, 45
Aesop, 50
Alfonso X, 51
Aristotle, 67, 68
Barère, 82
Barlow, 82
Bellamy, 89
Blackstone, 100
D. Brown, 117
Burke, 129
Byron, 135
Cicero, 158, 159
de Cleyre, 164
Colton, 168
Diogenes, 206
Disraeli, 207
Djilas, 208
Erskine, 246
Euripides, 246
Garrison, 271
Jefferson, 368
John of Salisbury, 376
A. Johnson, 376
Jones, 380
Kingsley, 391
Leggett, 406
Lincoln, 424
Macaulay, 453
Machiavelli, 456
Markham, 468
Paine, 542
Pym, 555, 556
Santayana, 613
Shelley, 633, 634, 635, 636
Spencer, 648
Voltaire, 715
Whitman, 739
William the Silent, 747
Wordsworth, 757
Wortman, 758

U

Un-American, Un-Americanism
Smedley Butler, 134
Commager, 169, 170
Cooke, 176
W. O. Douglas, 212
Meiklejohn, 485
T. Roosevelt, 597
W. Wilson, 751

Unbelief
Lippmann, 433
E. B. White, 734

Understand, Understanding
Anonymous, 64
Augustine, 71
F. Bacon, 74
Bush, 132
Hemingway, 310

Uniformity
Kennan, 387
G. W. Russell, 610

Union, Trade
T. S. Adams, 47
Bancroft, 81
H. W. Beecher, 87
Bellamy, 88
Brandeis, 110, 112
Broun, 116
Bryant, 122
Coughlin, 181
Darrow, 191
Debs, 197
DeLeon, 200
Democratic Party, 201
Eisenhower, 229
Engels, 240
Ford, 253
Gompers, 285
Greeley, 289
Kingsley, 392
Leggett, 405
Lenin 407

Leo XIII, 414
Phillips, 560, 561
Populist Party, 572
E. Roosevelt, 590
F. D. Roosevelt, 594
T. Roosevelt, 597
Adam Smith, 641
U.S. Congress, 702
U.S. Supreme Court, 703
Wright, 758, 759

Union (United States) (see America)
Franklin, 258
Garrison, 270, 271
A. Jackson, 354, 355
Jefferson, 364
Lincoln, 426
Stephens, 661
D. Webster, 729

Unitarian
Chworowsky, 157

United Nations
Hugo, 336
Hutchins, 339
Tennyson, 678
Warburg, 721
G. Washington, 727

United States (see America)
John Adams, 45
Balzac, 81
Grant, 288
Krushchev, 390
J. Marshall, 470, 471
Monroe, 500
O'Neill, 535
Paine, 544
Rhodes, 582
Shaw, 632
Siegfried, 638
Stalin, 658
Thompson, 681
Truman, 694
H. A. Wallace, 720
Whitman, 739

Unity
Acton, 38
M. Anderson, 56
Usury
F. Bacon, 73
Bakunin, 77
Blake, 101
Francis Xavier, 256
The Koran, 393
Utopia
Dostoyevski, 210
Gide, 277
More, 505
Sinclair, 639
Wells, 732

V

Value, Values
Mumford, 511, 512
Adam Smith, 641
Vatican
Barlow, 82
Garibaldi, 269
O. Wilde, 744
Vermont
Farley, 247
Whittier, 741
Vested Interests
Angell, 57
Samuel Butler, 133
Calhoun, 137
Coughlin, 181
Einstein, 221
H. George, 275
Hobson, 323
A. Jackson, 355
Keynes, 389
La Follette, 396
Laski, 399
C. B. Luce, 445
Tawney, 675
W. Wilson, 751

Vice (see Virtue and Vice)
Bolingbroke, 104
Browne, 119
Robert Burton, 132
Goldsmith, 283
Milton, 497
Molière, 499
Pope, 571
Walker, 719

Vice-President
John Adams, 43

Victor, Victory
Clausewitz, 160, 161
Emerson, 239
F. S. Fitzgerald, 251
Foch, 252
MacArthur, 450
Marx, 477
Montaigne, 501
Pyrrhus, 577
Rouget de Lisle, 599
G. W. Russell, 610
Sun Tzu, 668
W. Wilson, 751, 752

Violence
Debs, 196
Ferrer, 249
Freud, 262
Gandhi, 267
Emma Goldman, 283
Hitler, 318
C. E. Hughes, 335
Juarès, 362
Khrushchev, 389, 390
Mussolini, 514, 515
Nehru, 521
Peron, 557
Phillips, 560
Sorel, 647
Trotsky, 693

Virgin, Virginity
Council of Trent, 182

Jerome, 375, 376
Maryland Assembly, 477

Virtue
Addison, 48
Anonymous, 63
Aristotle, 66
F. Bacon, 73
Bennett, 90
Cicero, 158
Confucius, 173
Emerson, 235
Kant, 383
Lao-Tse, 398
Milton, 497, 498

Virtue and Vice
E. Allen, 52
Bolingbroke, 104

Voltaire
Bakunin, 77
Burke, 129
Casanova, 147
Chekhov, 153
Hugo, 336
Macaulay, 453
Tallentyre, 673

Vote
John Quincy Adams, 46
Mazzini, 482
T. B. Reed, 580
Reuther, 581
Root, 598
Thoreau, 683, 684
Twain, 699
Tweed, 699
Yeats, 760

Vox Populi
Alcuin, 51
Galton, 266
Gracián, 287
Alexander Hamilton, 295
Sherman, 637

W

Wage, Wages, Wage-Earners
T. S. Adams, 47
Anonymous, 62
Bellamy, 88
Brownson, 120
Carlyle, 142
Cleveland, 163, 164
Dana, 188
H. George, 273
Kingsley, 392
Leo XIII, 414
J. P. Morgan, 506
Phillips, 561
Pius XI, 565, 566
Powderly, 573
Ricardo, 582
U. S. Congress, 702

Wall Street
Smedley Butler, 134
Ickes, 348

Want, Wants
Horace, 333
Landor, 397
Millikan, 496
F. D. Roosevelt, 593
Smollett, 644
Tennyson, 678
H. A. Wallace, 720

War
Acton, 36, 37
B. Adams, 39
S. Adams, 47
Angell, 57, 58
Anonymous, 59, 62, 64
Aquinas, 64
Aristotle, 68
Augustine, 70
Banse, 82
K. Barth, 83
Baruch, 84
Bebel, 86
Bergson, 93

Bernard, 94
Bernhardi, 95
Biddle, 96
T. H. Bliss, 102
Born, 107
Bosquet, 107
Bowers, 108
Breen, 113
Burke, 130
Smedley Butler, 134, 135
Campbell, 138
Casey, 148
Channing, 151
Churchill, 157
Cicero, 158, 159
Clausewitz, 160, 161, 162
Clemenceau, 162
Coolidge, 177
Cousins, 182
D. Davis, 194
Debs, 196
Delbrueck, 199
Duffy, 216
Dunne, 217
Edison, 219
Einstein, 221, 223, 224, 226, 228
Eisenhower, 228, 229
T. S. Eliot, 230
Ellis, 231
Engels, 243
Erasmus, 244
J. A. Fisher, 250
Foch, 252
France, 255, 256
Franklin, 258
Freneau, 260
Freud, 262, 263
Garfield, 269
Gladstone, 278
Goebbels, 281
Gollancz, 285
von der Goltz, 285
Grant, 288, 289

Grey, 290
von Haeseler, 292
Halleck, 294
Alexander Hamilton, 295
Hearst, 305
Hemingway, 310, 311
Henry, 312
Heraclitus, 313
Herbert, 313
Hitler, 319, 321
Hobbes, 321
Hugo, 336
Inge, 349
W. James, 359, 361
Jaurès, 362
S. Johnson, 377
V. D. Jordan, 380
Kant, 383
Kropotkin, 394, 395
Laski, 400
Lee, 405
Lenin, 407, 408, 410, 411, **412**
Leo XIII, 415
Lie, 419
Lilburne, 420
C. A. Lindbergh (Jr.), 429
Lloyd George, 435
Longfellow, 439
Lowell, 443
Lucas, 444
Luxemburg, 448
MacArthur, 450
Machiavelli, 453, **456**
Madariaga, 458
Malinowski, 461, 462
Mao Tse-tung, 465, **466**
Marlowe, 469
G. Marshall, 470
Maupassant, 481
McKinley, 483
Mencken, 486
Milton, 498
Moltke, 499

Monroe, 500
Mussolini, 514, 517, **518**
Napoleon, 519
Nietzsche, 529
Nobel, 531
Norton, 533, 534
O'Casey, 534
Osborn, 538
Pascal, 549
Pearl, 553
Pershing, 557
Plato, 567, 568
Plutarch, 570
Ponsonby, 571
Pythagoras, 577
J. Reed, 579
Rhodes, 582
Richardson, 583
Rogers, 587
E. Roosevelt, 589
B. A. Russell, 605, **606**
Santayana, 613
Schweitzer, 623
Seneca, 626, 627
Service, 627
Sheen, 633
Shelley, 635, 636
Sherman, 637
Society of Friends, **645**
Sorel, 647
Spengler, 650
Stalin, 658
J. Sterling, 662
Strachey, 665
C. Sumner, 667
W. G. Sumner, 667
Sun Tzu, 668
Talleyrand, 673
Tawney, 676, 677
Tennyson, 678
Thomas, 681
Thucydides, 685
Tolstoy, 689

Treitschke, 692
Twain, 698
United Nations, **700**
Vickers, 710
Voltaire, 714, 716, 717
G. Washington, 725, 727
Wellington, 732
Wells, 732
Whittier, 741
O. Wilde, 745
Wilhelm II, 746
Wilhelm (Crown Prince), **747**
W. Wilson, 753
E. Young, 760
Zhukov, 762

War and Peace
Franklin, 258
Grant, 289
Longfellow, 439
G. C. Marshall, **470**
Y. Sterling, 662
Thompson, 681
Whittier, 741

Weak, Weakness
Anonymous, 62
Nietzsche, 527

Wealth
S. Adams, 47
Anonymous, 62
Aristotle, 67, 68
M. Arnold, 68
Bancroft, 81
Bellamy, 89
Bevan, 96
Book of Good Counsels, 105, 106
Brownson, 120
Burke, 128
Carnegie, 143, 144
Channing, 151
St. Chrysostom, 156
Cicero, 158
Cleveland, 163
Confucius, 173

Coolidge, 176
P. Cooper, 180
Coughlin, 181
Dante, 189
Dreiser, 215
Einstein, 227
Ely, 232
Erasmus, 245
Fabian Society, 247
Franklin, 259
Gandhi, 268
H. George, 272, 273, 274, 275
Godwin, 279
Goldsmith, 283
Hugo, 336
S. Johnson, 378
La Follette, 396
Lassalle, 400
Leggett, 405
Leo XIII, 414
Lieber, 419
Lloyd, 434
Locke, 437
Longfellow, 439
Lowell, 444
Lucretius, 445
MacArthur, 450
J. Madison, 460
J. P. Morgan, 506
Paine, 544
Phillips, 560
Populist Party, 572
Powderly, 573
Republican Party, 581
F. D. Roosevelt, 591
Shaw, 629
Shelley, 635, 636
Adam Smith, 641
Sprading, 655
W. G. Sumner, 667
Tawney, 675, 676
Thoreau, 682
Tilden, 685

W. K. Vanderbilt, 705
Veblen, 708, 709
Wagner, 718
D. Webster, 728
Wordsworth, 757

Welfare (see General Welfare)
Confucius, 174
Haywood, 304

Whore
Blake, 100
Defoe, 198

Will (see Free Will)
Amiel, 55
Bakunin, 78
Clausewitz, 161
Einstein, 221
Farrell, 248
Foch, 252
Hegel, 307, 308
Hugo, 336
Manning, 464
Rousseau, 599
B. A. Russell, 608
Schopenhauer, 617
Stalin, 657

Will to Power
Nietzsche, 526, 528, 529, 530

Wiretapping
Brandeis, 112
O. W. Holmes (Jr.), 330

Wisdom
Adenauer, 48
Anonymous, 63
Samuel Butler, 133
Einstein, 227
Griswold, 291
Heraclitus, 313
Hersey, 315
S. Johnson, 377
Santayana, 612

Witch, Witchcraft
E. Allen, 52

Blackstone, 99
Browne, 118
Bunyan, 125
W. C. Menninger, 489
Twain, 696, 697

Woman
Aristotle, 67
Carpenter, 144
Council of Elvira, 182
Emerson, 234
Freud, 263
Ibsen, 346
Ingersoll, 350, 351
The Koran, 393
D. H. Lawrence, 402
Luther, 447
Machiavelli, 454
Marx, 475
Nietsche, 527, 530
Reik, 580
Shaw, 631
Stanton, 659
Tertullian, 680
Walker, 719

Women's Rights
A. Adams, 39
Anonymous, 60
Anthony, 64
Carpenter, 144
Dunne, 217
M. Fuller, 265
Lincoln, 421
Pankhurst, 545
Parrington, 548
Schreiner, 618
Schwimmer, 623
Stanton, 659
Wollstonecraft, 755, 756
Woman's Rights Convention, 756

Word
J. Donald Adams, 41, 42
John Adams, 45

F. Bacon, 74
Burke, 129
Robert Burton, 132
Chase, 153
Conant, 172
Confucius, 172
Conrad, 175
Disraeli, 207
Hazlitt, 305
A. Herbert, 313
Hersey, 315
Hitler, 318
Hobbes, 322
O. W. Holmes (Jr.), 328
H. C. Hoover, 332
Hopkins, 332
Machiavelli, 456
Mussolini, 515
Nehru, 522
Santayana, 614
B. Smith, 642
Stalin, 658

Work, Workers, Workmen
M. J. Adler, 49
A.F.L., 54
Anonymous, 62
Bakunin, 77
Bancroft, 81
Ben-Gurion, 90
Brownson, 120
Bryant, 122
Capone, 140
Carlyle, 142, 143
Coolidge, 177
P. Cooper, 179
Darrow, 191
Davidson, 193, 194
Davies, 194
Debs, 197
De Valera, 203
W. O. Douglas, 212, 213
Edison, 219
Einstein, 225

Ford, 253
H. George, 274, 275
Gompers, 285
Haywood, 304
Howell, 333
Lassalle, 400
Leo XIII, 414, 415
Lincoln, 424, 428
Lowell, 442
Manning, 465
Marx, 472, 473, 474, 477
Mayo, 482
Melville, 485
Millikan, 496
G. Morris, 509
W. Morris, 509, 510
Mundelein, 512
Nearing, 520
Patterson, 552
Phillips, 560, 561
Reik, 580
Ruskin, 603
Sacco, 610
Service, 627
Shelley, 633
Adam Smith, 641
Tennyson, 678
O. Wilde, 743
T. Wolfe, 755

Working Class
Acton, 37
H. W. Beecher, 87
Engels, 240, 241
Geddes, 272
Gould, 287
Haywood, 304
Herron, 315
Herzl, 315
I. W. W., 348
Khrushchev, 390, 391
Lenin, 407
Marx, 475
Norris, 532

Reed, 579
Stalin, 655
Trotsky, 693
Wang-An-Shih, 721

World
H. B. Adams, 41
Alfronso X, 51
Archimedes, 65
Comte, 171
Copernicus, 180
T. S. Eliot, 230
Emerson, 239
Hutchins, 340
Mackinder, 457
Schopenhauer, 617
Thomas à Kempis, 680
Valéry, 705
Voltaire, 713, 714, 717
Wesley, 734

Worry
Mayo, 482

Worship
Amiel, 56
Coolidge, 176
Coughlin, 181
Dostoyevski, 210
Gibbon, 276

Writer, Writers, Writing
John Adams, 43, 44
S. Anderson, 56, 57
Beerbohm, 87
V. W. Brooks, 115
Camus, 139
Chekhov, 153
Farrell, 248
Hemingway, 311
S. Lewis, 418
Lippman, 433
Marx, 474
Reeve, 580

Rousseau, 600
Stalin, 658
Toller, 688
Voltaire, 715

Wrong
Acton, 36, 38
Altgeld, 53
H. George, 274
Luther, 448

X, Y, Z

Youth
Aristotle, 67
Erasmus, 245
Lawrence of Arabia, **403**
Melville, 485
Mussolini, 513
Tennyson, 678
Wagner, 717